Conversations

CONVERSATIONS
Readings for Writing
fourth edition

Jack Selzer
The Pennsylvania State University

ALLYN AND BACON

Boston   London   Toronto   Sydney   Tokyo   Singapore

Vice President: Eben W. Ludlow
Executive Marketing Manager: Lisa Kimball
Production Administrator: Rowena Dores
Editorial-Production Service: Omegatype Typography, Inc.
Composition and Prepress Buyer: Linda Cox
Manufacturing Buyer: Suzanne Lareau
Cover Administrator: Linda Knowles
Electronic Composition: Omegatype Typography, Inc.

Between the time Website information is gathered and published, some
sites may have closed. Also, the transcription of URLs can result in typo-
graphical errors. The publisher would appreciate notification where these
occur so that they may be corrected in subsequent editions.

Library of Congress Cataloging-in-Publication Data

Conversations : readings for writing / [compiled by] Jack Selzer. —
  4th ed.
    p.   cm.
    Includes bibliographical references and index.
    ISBN 0-205-29642-4 (alk. paper)
    1. College readers.   2. English language—Rhetoric Problems,
exercises, etc.   3. Report writing Problems, exercises, etc.
I. Selzer, Jack.
PE1417.C6545   2000
808'.0427—dc21   99–22374
                                                                    CIP

Printed in the United States of America

10 9 8 7 6 5 4 3 2 1   RRDV   04 03 02 01 00 99

Text credits appear on page 1069, which constitutes a continuation of this
copyright page.

For Molly and Maggie:
Still Their Book

Contents

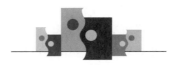

I. EDUCATION

sure-fire, "market-oriented" route to improved
education. Is it?

In all the uproar over "school choice," here's
another choice to consider: single-gender
schools.

Conditions at two Chicago-area schools illustrate
the inequalities that result from our system of
funding public education.

"Like most high schools, [Franklin High] just
rolls on, fettered by routines of long standing," so
teacher Horace Smith must compromise his principles.

"[T]he educational foundations of our society
are…being eroded by a rising tide of mediocrity
that threatens our very future.…"

A great English novelist describes and satirizes
the "progressive" education of his day (and
ours?).

"[T]hey mainly want to teach them not to question, not to challenge, not to imagine, but to be
obedient.…"

What's College For?   **81**

II. LANGUAGE

Affirmative Action

Sexual Harassment

IV.   FAMILY MATTERS

V.   CIVIL LIBERTIES AND CIVIL RIGHTS

Censorship I: Pornography   **570**

On Civil Disobedience   642

Should Abortion Be Legal?   700

VI.   CRIME AND PUNISHMENT

Contents

What Causes Crime?

VII.   SCIENCE AND SOCIETY

Should Research on Cloning
Be Permitted?   **919**

What Do You Make of the Internet?   **1018**

Rhetorical Contents

Comparison and Contrast

Analysis

Cause and Effect

Definition

Argument: Categorical Proposition ("X is in fact Y")

Argument: Refutation

Irony and Satire

Writing from Sources

Preface

Imagine that you enter a parlor. You come late. When you arrive, others have long preceded you, and they are engaged in a heated discussion, a discussion too heated for them to pause and tell you exactly what it is about. In fact, the discussion had already begun long before any of them got there, so that no one present is qualified to retrace for you all the steps that had gone before. You listen for a while, until you decide that you have caught the tenor of the argument; then you put in your oar. Someone answers; you answer him; another comes to your defense; another aligns himself against you, to either the embarrassment or gratification of your opponent, depending upon the quality of your ally's assistance.

This well-known passage from Kenneth Burke's *Philosophy of Literary Form* explains the basic metaphor and the orientation of this anthology of readings for first-year college composition courses. *Conversations* contains conversations: public discourse on contemporary issues that is calculated to engage students' interests, to encourage and empower their own contributions to contemporary civic discussions, and to represent a broad cross-section of the kinds of conversational styles and genres that are available to writers today.

What's Different about *Conversations?*

Conversations encourages student writing on important current civic issues. The premise of this reader is that writing is less a private act of making personal meaning out of thin air than it is a public and social act of making meaning within a specific rhetorical situation—a specific situation that guides and shapes the meaning-making activity. To put the matter more simply, writing emerges from other writing, other discourse. Though nearly every anthology claims to encourage student responses, those anthologies just as often actually intimidate students because they present only one or two authoritative voices on a given issue and because those voices are given little context outside the anthology; the student reads an essay by Quindlen or Baldwin or Woolf or some other eloquent writer and says to himself or herself, "Gee, that sure seems right to me. How could I disagree with such an expert?" By contrast, instead of one or two authoritative items on an issue or topic, this reader contains "conversations" on public issues or topics, conversations-with-contexts that will seem less intimidating and therefore invite student responses.

In fact, the book will encourage students to adopt a social and rhetorical model—a "conversation model"—for their own writing. Instead of seeing writing merely as private or as point-counterpoint debate, students should sense from *Conversations* that "people are talking about this issue—and I'd like to get in on the talk somewhere." The conversation metaphor does not mean that students should "write like they talk" (since conversational informality is not always appropriate in public discourse); rather, the metaphor simply implies that students should see writing as a response to other writing or to other forms of discourse, a response that students make after considering the implications and importance of what they have read and heard. Students should be encouraged to cooperate as well as to compete with other writers, to address subissues as well as the main chance, to seek consensus and new syntheses as often as victory.

Thus, *Conversations* is organized around focused, topical, contemporary public issues (e.g., censorship, what to do about public education, affirmative action, legalization of drugs, abortion, gun control), each within seven larger thematic groupings (education, language, race and gender, family matters, civil liberties and civil rights, crime and punishment, and science and society) that lend additional historical and conceptual perspective to those contemporary issues. *Intertextuality* would be the buzzword from contemporary critical theory: The book includes items that "talk to each other" both directly and indirectly. Some pieces speak directly and explicitly to each other (as in the case of the four-way discussion of single parenthood, or Milton Friedman's exchange with William Bennett about the legalization of drugs, or the e-mail discussion of electronic censorship). Some pieces refer only indirectly to others, as in the sections on education, gun control, and affirmative action. And still other items comment on selections in other sections of *Conversations:* for example, selections on education comment on those on language and race; the section on pornography is informed by the sections on gender and the causes of crime; the items on gay, lesbian, and bisexual rights are related to the section on AIDS and same-sex marriage. And so forth. There is certainly no reason why the selections in this anthology cannot be read individually as they are in other books, without reference to other selections, especially since the headnotes orient readers to each item. And there is certainly no reason why the selections could not be read in some other order than the order in which they are presented here. Nevertheless, *Conversations* does give students a particular incentive to write because it establishes contexts for writing.

The conversation model should make the book suitable to a range of writing courses. There is plenty of expository prose here: comparisons of all kinds; a careful analysis of the language of men and women by Deborah Tannen; overviews of the cloning issue and the meanings of "whiteness"; cool descriptions of schools and school choice, men and women, the internet, single parenthood, and a hanging; expositions of the reasons why women are excluded from science and why people commit crimes; etc.—lots of et cetera. The "modes of exposition" are illustrated by numerous selections, as the rhetorical table of contents makes clear. But *Conversations* will also accommodate courses with an argumentative edge, for this book includes a fair proportion of explicitly or implicitly argumentative writing and tends to encourage a broadly argumentative approach to all discourse. In short, the conversation metaphor implies an inclusive approach to prose, one that subsumes and includes exposition as well as argument, dialogue as well as dialectic. *Conversations* includes not only Jonathan Kozol's prescriptions for the high school classroom, but Theodore Sizer's descriptions as well; not only partisan arguments for and against gun control, but also a careful analysis of the issue by Leonard Kriegel; and not only passionate pro and con arguments on capital punishment, abortion, cloning, and same-sex marriage, but also dispassionate analyses of language issues, race and gender, the Internet, and more.

Consequently—and this is another notable feature of *Conversations*—this anthology includes a very broad range of genres and tries to represent as fully as possible the full spectrum of the "universe of discourse." True, essays are prominent in *Conversations*—familiar and formal essays, academic as well as nonacademic ones—because the essay is a common and important genre and because the form has important correspondences with other genres (e.g., the letter, the sermon, the report, the news story). But essays are not so prominent here as to exclude other genres. Students will find other ways of engaging in public discourse as well: through fiction, poetry, drama, letters of various kinds, Internet postings, public oratory, posters, congressional hearings and reports, cartoons, advertisements, journals, and more. The occasions for public discourse are many and various. Students and their teachers will find news stories and memoirs, literary narratives and studies of cultural artifacts, parodies and satires, letters to the editor and counterresponses, laws and proposed laws.

And they will hear a range of voices as well. *Conversations* assumes that students are ready, willing, and able to engage in civic, public discourse, but that does not preclude the possibility for personal inventiveness. Indeed, *Conversations* is committed to the proposition that there are many possible rhetorical stances, that there is no one "correct" way to address a reader. This anthology therefore exposes students to as many rhetorical choices as possible—from the studied erudition of John Simon to the semiformal, "objective" voice associated with the academy; from the conversational informality of E. B. White, Frederick Douglas, and Deborah Tannen to satiric invective by Judy Syfers Brady, David Horsey, and Lewis Grizzard; from the thrilling oratory of Sojourner Truth to the careful reasoning of Iris Young; from *Rolling Stone, Ms., Mother Jones,* and *The Village Voice* to *Esquire, The New Yorker,* and *The American Scholar;* from Jamaica Kincaid, Adrienne Rich, and Julia Alvarez to George Orwell, bell hooks, Richard Rodriguez, and Andrea Dworkin. Students will encounter mainstream texts and dissenting views, conventional rhetorical maneuvers and startlingly inventive ones. They will hear from famous professional writers and anonymous but eloquent fellow citizens; from public figures and fellow students (a dozen or so contributions by students are included); from women and men, gays and heterosexuals; from majority and minority voices. *Conversations* gives students a better chance to find their own voices because they've experienced a full range of possible voices in their reading.

"A rhetorician," says Kenneth Burke in his essay "Rhetoric—Old and New," "is like one voice in a dialogue. Put several such voices together, with each voicing its own special assertion, let them act upon one another in co-operative competition, and you get a dialectic that, properly developed, can lead to views transcending the limitations of each." Fostering that "co-operative competition" is the aim of *Conversations*.

Editorial Apparatus

Substantial editorial assistance has been provided to the users of *Conversations*. The book's Introduction orients students to social motives for writing and domesticates for them the metaphor of conversation. It also introduces students to the notion of critical or rhetorical reading, so that they might have a practical means of approaching every item in *Conversations*—and so that they might better understand how careful reading habits can reinforce effective writing habits. In addition, a headnote is provided for each selection so that students can orient themselves to the rhetoric of each piece. The headnotes provide background on the author (especially when prior knowledge about the author affects one's response to an item), on the topic of the selection (when the matter requires any explanation), and on the specific occasion for the piece (especially on when and where it was originally published). The assumption of most anthologies is that the original context of an essay or story— or whatever—doesn't matter much, or that the anthology itself comprises the context. *Conversations* assumes instead that careful reading must take into account the original circumstances that prompted a given piece of writing. Writing, after all, most often emerges from other writing, so situating each item by means of the headnotes is essential to the concept of *Conversations*. Finally, each of the seven major parts of the book includes an introductory overview of the particular issues under discussion in that part. In sum, the editorial apparatus ensures that the selections in *Conversations* can be used in any order that a teacher or student might wish.

Otherwise, the text of *Conversations* assumes that students are already quite capable readers. On the grounds that students and teachers can handle things on their own and can appropriate readings to their own ends, the book includes no questions after selections, no suggestions for writing assignments or class discussions, no exercises, and limited footnotes. Space that might have been devoted to those matters is given instead to additional selections so that teachers might have as many selections as possible from which to choose.

Instructor's Manual

Teachers who do want additional background on unfamiliar readings or specific suggestions for making the most of *Conversations* will find plenty of help in the detailed Instructor's Manual I compiled with Dominic Delli Carpini of York College of Pennsylvania. The manual contains further information on writers, overviews of the parts and discussions of each selection, some suggestions for further reading, and ideas for discussion and writing. It also offers pointers for teaching each "conversation"—for how particular selections can be used with other selections. Together, the editorial apparatus and the Instructor's Manual are designed to help *Conversations* engage the intelligence and passion of students and teachers, without getting in the way of either.

Acknowledgments

There may be only one name cited on the cover of *Conversations*, but this book too is the product of conversation—many conversations, in fact—with a number of people who collaborated in one way or another on its development and production. My greatest debt is to those who assisted me in finding appropriate selections. Andy Alexander, Chris Malone, and Anneliese Watt (Penn State), Rosa Eberly (now at the University of Texas), Dawn Keetley (now of the University of Wisconsin), and Jay Shuchter (Penn State) deserve special mention. But many others affected the outcome: Tom Miller and Tilly Warnock (University of Arizona); Umeeta Sadarangani (Parkland Community Col-

lege), Deborah Kirkman (University of Kentucky); Paul
Klemp (University of Wisconsin—Eau Claire); David Ran-
dall (Bloomsburg University); Tom Buckley and Linda Fer-
reira-Buckley (University of Texas); Tony O'Keeffe
(Bellarmine College); Debra Journet (University of Louis-
ville); Cynthia Miecznikowski Sheard (University of Ken-
tucky); and Jim Brasfield, Bob Burkholder, Deb Clarke,
Christopher Clausen, Bird Cupps, Mel DeYoung, Claudia
Limbert, Steve Mastrofski, Jeff Purvis, Blake Scott, and
Linda Selzer (all of Penn State). Several reviewers of previ-
ous editions of the book made excellent suggestions: Eu-
gene Antonio, Georgia Institute of Technology; Philip
Auslander, Georgia Institute of Technology; Margaret T.
Banocy-Payne, Tallahassee Community College; Stephen
Behrendt, University of Nebraska; John Bodnar, Prince
George's Community College; Vivian R. Brown, Laredo Jun-
ior College; Wyeth O. Burgess, Georgia Institute of Technol-
ogy; Christine Cetrulo, University of Kentucky; John
Cooper, University of Kentucky; Kitty Dean, Nassau Com-
munity College; John Dick, University of Texas at El Paso;
Jack Dodds, Harper College; Lester Faigley, University of
Texas at Austin; Robert Funk, Eastern Illinois University;
Ann George, Texas Christian University; Paula Gillespie,
Marquette University; JoEllen Hall, California State College,
Chico; Doug Hesse, Illinois State University; Dona Hickey,
University of Richmond; Missy James, Tallahassee Commu-
nity College; Keith Kroll, Kalamazoo Valley Community Col-
lege; Lia Kushnir, University of New Orleans; Robert
Lesman, Northern Virginia Community College; Gerald
Levin, University of Akron; Steve Lynn, University of South
Carolina–Columbia; Margaret Mahoney, Iowa State Univer-
sity; James May, Penn State University, Dubois; James C.
McDonald, University of Southwestern Louisiana; Robert
Miedel, La Salle University; George Otte, Baruch College,
CUNY; Gordon M. Pradl, New York University; David Rags-
dale, Kingwood College; Gerald Richman, Suffolk Univer-
sity; Patricia Roberts, University of North Carolina at
Greensboro; Joan Samuelson, Kingwood College; Sheila
Schwartz, Cleveland State University; Carol Senf, Georgia
Institute of Technology; Carolyn H. Smith, University of
Florida; Scott Stoddard, Nova University; Gloria Under-
wood, University of South Carolina–Columbia; Richard Vela,
Pembroke State University; Richard Zbaracki, Iowa State
University; Patsy Callaghan, Central Washington University;

Douglas Catron, Iowa State University; Rosa Eberly, University of Texas at Austin; Christy Friend, University of South Carolina, Columbia; Gregory Glau, Arizona State University; Ronald L. Pitcock, University of Kentucky; Richard Raymond, University of Arkansas at Little Rock; and Judith P. Schiffbauer, University of Kentucky. The fourth edition in particular profited from suggestions by Dominic Delli Carpini, York College of Pennsylvania; Virginia Chappell, Marquette University; Judith G. Gardner, The University of Texas at San Antonio; James Kastely, University of Houston; Pierre Laroche, Doña Ana Community College; Martha Marinara, University of Central Florida; Richard W. Moore, Delgado Community College; and Mary M. Salibrici, Syracuse University. Other colleagues across the country and at Penn State—particularly Don Bialostosky, Sharon Crowley, Rich Doyle, Nancy Lowe, Elaine Richardson, Marie Secor, Stuart Selber, and Jeff Walker—have stimulated my thinking on a daily basis. Janet Zepernick, Peggy Keating, Fiona Paton, and Suzanne Marcum worked diligently to secure permissions, and Todd Post, Anneliese Watt, Chris Malone, Andy Alexander, and Keith Waddle did research for some of the headnotes.

Thanks too to those on the production end of things. Kim Witherite Keller, Sam Gunderson, and especially Kathy Leitzell helped a great deal on earlier editions; they helped me out of a thousand small scrapes. Another thousand that I don't even know about were taken care of by Rowena Dores and Robert Howerton. Eben Ludlow has been an ideal editor: full of excellent suggestions, encouraging without ever being overbearing, supportive at every turn. His confidence in this project brought it into being and has sustained it now for a decade.

Introduction

Why Write?

Why do people write?

For many reasons, of course. Sometimes the impulse to write derives from a personal need. The motive to write can come from within. Everyone needs to sort out feelings at one time or another or to make some personal sense of the world and its parts, and a good way to do such sorting is by writing. If you keep a diary or journal, or if you've shared your most intimate feelings through correspondence with a trusted friend, or if you've written essays—or notes toward an essay—in order to explore possible explanations for things, then you know what it means to write for personal reasons. (A root meaning of the word *essay* is "to try out, to experiment.") People do need a means of expressing powerful feelings and personal insights, and writing seems to provide just the tranquility required for a gathering of thoughts.

Other times the world itself motivates a writer. We seem to have a need to note our observations about the world, especially if those observations are indeed noteworthy—if they seem special or unique in some way. Sometimes this process of "taking note" is relatively formalized, as when a scientist records observations in a log of some kind or when the president at the end of a day records significant details for future reference or when you keep score at a baseball game or when a reporter transcribes "just the facts" into a news article. But just as often it is something less formal—when you take notes for a course, for instance, or when I write something in my journal about the life and times of my two children. The drive "to hold the mirror up to nature," as Hamlet called it, to record our understanding about the way of the world, accounts for much of the prose we encounter and produce each day.

The motive to write can also derive from one's vocation. In other words, some people write because it's their life's work. They are professional writers—poets, news reporters, novelists, technical writers, screenwriters. And they are semiprofessional writers, people who don't think of themselves as writers but who indeed spend a large amount of their time writing—police officers, engineers, college professors, lawyers, physicians, corporate managers, teachers, and so forth. (You'd be surprised at how much time such people spend on the writing required by their jobs.) Professional writers and professionals who write sometimes put words onto paper for the reasons named in the previous paragraphs—to express personal feelings or ideas, or to record their impressions or interpretations of their workaday worlds. But they also often think in terms of a particular kind of writing—a genre—when they compose: Newspaper employees think of themselves as writing news stories or editorials; poets set out to write poems; engineers or police officers think of the reports they have to turn in; lawyers have to produce those legal briefs next week. Their sense of completing a particular genre can sometimes take precedence over other motives.

Of course all these motives to write are legitimate, and seldom do these motives exist in a pure state. It is probably better to think of motives to write, instead of *a* motive, and to think of primary and secondary motives, instead of a single, all-consuming aim. When John Milton wrote *Paradise Lost,* for instance, he was certainly out to record his assessment of the nature of things and to express his most personal thoughts—and to write an epic. When Henry David Thoreau wrote *Walden,* he certainly had personal motives—the book originated in his daily journals—but he wanted "to hold the mirror up to nature" as well. (The very title of *Walden* suggests that Thoreau was attempting to record his close observations of nature.)

But *Walden* and *Paradise Lost* are "public" documents, too—attempts to sway public opinion and public behavior. Thoreau advertised *Walden,* after all, as his attempt to "brag as lustily as Chanticleer [the rooster] in the morning, if only to wake my neighbor up." He wanted to awaken his fellow citizens to nature and to persuade them to renew their own lives after his own example and experience. Milton's stated purpose—"to justify the ways of God to man"—was just as social.

He wanted to change how people conceive of their relation to God and to detail his vision of the heroic life to be lived by every wayfaring Christian. Writing to persuade, to have an effect on the thinking of others, does not preclude writing to discover or writing to record or writing in a particular genre. Indeed, writing to persuade nearly always means writing *about something* in a *particular genre* for reasons that are *intensely personal*. But writing to persuade does mean writing something that has designs on the hearts or minds (or both) of particular readers. It is writing that is calculated to have an effect on a real reader. This goes for John Milton and Anna Quindlen, and it goes for you, too.

For though a writer may work in private, a writer is never really alone. A writer out "to wake people up" or "to justify the ways of God" to men and women is obviously anything but working privately, for the writer out to persuade is inherently social. But every other kind of writing is social as well. The engineer who writes a report on a project is out to influence the project's managers. A physician's report on a patient is used by other caregivers in the short run and long run to direct medical attention in a specific way. The lawyer's brief is meant to sway judges. The movie reviewer's account is designed to direct people to (or away from) the film. Even private writing is often quite public in fact. The letters in which you pour out your feelings get read by sympathetic and responsive friends. The essays you write to discover your version of the truth become written attempts to convert readers to that version. Even journal entries that no one but you will read are shaped to an extent by what society considers to be noteworthy and by what a different "you" will want to read a few years from now; and the very words you choose to use reflect a vocabulary you share with others and learn from others. Writing is a social act. It is a primary means for touching others, and reading what others have written is a primary way of being touched in turn. The words you read and write are surrounded and shaped by the words and attitudes and beliefs of the many people who share your society, your "social context." People may write to express themselves, or to complete a particular kind of writing, or to say something about their world—or some combination of these—but in some sense they do so in order to have an effect on someone else.

In fact, usually writing emerges quite specifically in response to other writing. When you write, your reasons for writing are nearly always related to the people around you and what they have said or written themselves. A friend expects a letter; a supervisor at work has asked for a report; a professor assigns a paper; a job is advertised that requires a written application; a story or an editorial is printed in a local paper or national magazine that arouses your ire; an encouraging teacher or a moving story inspires you to write a journal entry or your own story. That is why this book is titled *Conversations*. It assumes that your writing emerges from other writing or from other speech, and that other writing is likely to follow in response to your own. You want to stay in touch, answer a friend's questions, ask your own questions, and maybe gossip or otherwise entertain along the way, so you return a friend's letter; you expect a response in a week or two. You've listened to a controversy or witnessed some expression of confusion in one of your classes, so you write a paper to straighten things out; you anticipate an argument, a counterresponse (or assent and praise), in turn. You want the person who takes your job to have an easier time than you did, so you rewrite the directions on how to do it; you figure the next person will make further revisions next year. Your cousin asks you how you like your school, so you write to encourage her to join you there next year; you end by asking her to let you know if she needs more information. Writing is engaging in conversation. To get in on it, you have to know what others have said about the matter at hand, and you must be able to anticipate possible responses.

This collection of readings comprises "public conversations"—conversations on public issues that concern American society (in general and within your local community) as we contemplate a new century. Not every burning issue is represented here, of course; that would be impossible. But this book does include conversations—give-and-take discussions—on many matters that concern you and your community today. What do you want to get out of your years in college? What kind of experience should your college or university be providing? What changes ought to be made to improve U.S. secondary schools? Should English be our official or semiofficial national language? What does it (or should it) mean to be a woman or a man these days? Is affirmative action legitimate? Should we be doing something to strengthen the American family? Should pornography be banned or regulated? Should certain books be kept out of the curriculum? Should abortion remain legal? Should the ownership of handguns be restricted? What are the causes and cures of crime? Is capital punishment ever justified? Should drugs be legalized? Is mercy killing ever legitimate? How should we fight AIDS?

And so forth. This book assumes that you'll want to get in on some of those conversations, that you'll want to contribute to resolving some of those questions either nationally or within your own community.

For while there is plenty of discussion of these matters in the national media, there is plenty of local discussion as well. What you read here about the reform of secondary education or the control of the curriculum probably frames in many ways discussions of particular school matters in your local community. What you read here about race or censorship probably is relevant to what is happening someplace on your own campus. What you read here about gender issues will be relevant to your campus (do many women major in science or engineering at your school?), your community (does your town have adequate child-care facilities?), your job (how are women treated where you work?), even your own family (are family chores apportioned in stereotypical ways?). Sometimes you will want to be involved in a debate over The Larger Issue—for instance, should pornography be banned? Other times you'll want to take up more local concerns or subissues: Should X-rated films be shown on your campus? Does pornography demean women—or men? Is a particular item really pornographic? How might pornography be defined? Democracy can be seen as a sometimes messy but always spirited exchange of ideas on how we should conduct ourselves as a society and as individual communities. The readings here are designed to introduce you to public conversations going on in our democracy, and to encourage you to contribute in some way to those conversations yourself. Even if these particular issues do not always engage you personally, they should provide you with models of how to engage in public discussions when an issue does concern you.

There are plenty of ways to make such contributions. The contents to follow will introduce you to many different genres, many different kinds of writing. Essays are most prominent because the essay is a common genre and because the essay (or article) has important analogs with other forms, like the letter, the sermon, the report, or the editorial. But you will see other ways of engaging in public discourse as well—through fiction, poetry, speeches, plays, interviews, e-mail exchanges, cartoons, and advertisements, for instance. There are news stories and memoirs, reports and literacy narratives, personal letters and letters to the editor and counterresponses, parodies and satires, explanations and analyses and outright arguments. As you think about what to contribute to discussions going on around you, you'll need to think about how to contribute, too—in what form, in what manner.

Indeed, there are as many ways of addressing issues as reasons for doing so. Do you want to be formal, less formal, or downright intimate with your reader? Do you want to present yourself as something of an expert on the matter in question, or as someone on the same level as your readers? Do you want to speak dispassionately, or do you want to let your feelings show? Do you want to be explicit in stating your purpose, or less direct? Do you want to compose sentences that are careful and complex and qualified, or ones that are direct and emphatic? You'll see a broad range of tactics illustrated in the following pages, a broad range that will represent the possible ways of engaging in public discourse. You'll encounter mainstream, classic items—and dissenting views. You'll see conventional presentations and startlingly inventive ones. You'll see how famous professional writers earned their fame, and you'll hear from anonymous but just-as-eloquent fellow citizens and fellow students. You'll hear from women as well as men, from majority as well as minority voices. The idea is to give you a better chance of finding your voice in a given circumstance by exposing you to a full range of possible voices in your reading. The idea is to empower you to engage in civic discourse—now, today—on the issues that concern you and your community.

How to Read This Book—And an Example

As the previous section explains, an answer to the question "Why write?" ultimately depends on several factors: on the writer's personal needs and motives, on the state of the world or issues within our world, on a genre or form of writing that a writer may be drawn or compelled toward, and on a reader or a community of readers that the writer wants to influence. Many times all those factors, in combination, are involved in the decision to write.

All those factors, in combination, are also involved in decisions on *how* to write. Effective writers consider what they want to accomplish (aim), on what subject or issue, in what genre, for which particular readers. A writer's decisions on those matters compose what rhetoricians call a writer's "rhetorical stance"—what *you* decide to say to *someone* on a given *issue* in a particular *genre*. But the matter might be put more simply: Your decisions about how to write at a given time are colored by the *occasion* for that writing and your attitude toward that occasion. A football coach will prepare his team for a game by considering the opponent's strengths and weaknesses (audience), by thinking about his own aims (to win, of course, but also perhaps "to establish our running game" or "to get some experience for our younger players"), by assessing his own team's strengths, and so forth. Writers devise their own game plans as well, based on aim, issue, genre, and audience.

But what does all of that have to do with reading—with reading in general and reading this book in particular? When you read this book, try to distinguish between two kinds of reading that in practice usually go on together whenever you engage yourself with a particular document.

In the first kind of reading, think of yourself as part of each writer's intended audience—as someone who the writer actually hoped would read and respond to his or her message. In other words, in this first kind of reading, read as you normally read the things that are directed to you every day: as you would read a newspaper or an article in your favorite magazine or a personal letter from a friend. Read as if the writer has written just for you, and react accordingly. In most cases this will be quite easy to do, for most of the items in *Conversations* (e.g., the articles on abortion by Sallie Tisdale and Mike Royko, the exchange on pornography between John Irving and Andrea Dworkin) are directed to the public—people like you—and were written quite recently in magazines and newspapers that you read yourself. In some other cases you will feel more remote from an article because it was written some time ago (e.g., Clarence Darrow's address to the prisoners in Cook County Jail or Martin Luther King Jr.'s "Letter from Birmingham Jail") or because it is not on a topic that has interested you, but even then you can behave as a member of the writer's intended audience and react to the selection as if the piece were written directly to you.

In the second kind of reading—let's call it "critical reading" or "rhetorical reading"—you read a document not as the intended reader but as a student of it, as someone studying it to understand and appreciate its tactics. Since you are probably reading this book as part of a writing course, as a critical reader encountering the selections in *Conversations* you should remember your role as student and try to use the readings to advance your sophistication as a writer and an analyst of writing. Although you normally read as a writer's intended audience, when you read critically you try to get some distance on the experience; it's almost as if you are eavesdropping on what someone is saying to someone else, with the purpose of understanding better how it is said. When you read critically you not only react to the message, but you also appreciate *how* the writer is conveying that message to his or her intended audience, whether that intended audience includes you or not. For example, as a critical reader you try to consider how Sallie Tisdale's content, arrangement, and style advance her aims, or how Martin Luther King Jr. and Clarence Darrow adapted their presentations to the particular situations in which they found themselves. Again, let me emphasize that normally in the act of reading you read critically as well as for content, and the two activities aren't really separable. But for the sake of your progress in writing, here in this introduction to *Conversations* it is important to emphasize critical reading.

Critical readers—readers committed to understanding how prose works—must attend to the same matters that writers attend to: shaping an idea to an audience in a particular form for a specific purpose. When you read each item in this book, therefore, read with those matters in mind. Read the headnotes carefully, for the headnotes are designed to orient you to the original situation in which the writers found themselves: You'll hear about the writer's audience in the headnote, you'll learn more about the writer (especially when the writer is well-known enough that prior reputation affects the reading experience), and you'll learn anything else necessary to orient you to the original occasion of each selection. That way, you'll be in a position to read critically. When you do, consider the issue of course; consider what the writer has to offer on a given subject. But also consider the writer's purpose, the limitations (or opportunities) that a given genre exerts, and the way the item is adapted by the writer to specific readers' knowledge, attitudes, and needs. Consider how those matters affect *what* is said (what rhetoricians call "invention"—the art of discovering what information and arguments will affect readers), in what *order* it is said (or arrangement), and *how* it is said (style and tone). Reading, like writing, is a social and rhetorical activity. It involves not simply passively decoding a message but actively understanding the designs the message has for the reader and how it is calculated to achieve its effects.

Let me offer an extended example of critical reading. The first item in this book is E. B. White's short essay, "Education." What is its purpose? (If you haven't read "Education" yet, take five minutes to do so now; that way, you can more easily follow the rest of this introduction.) White wrote the essay half a cen-

tury ago, but you probably find it to be interesting still, in part
at least because it concerns a perennial question in our nation:
What should our schools be like? Is education better carried
out in large, fully equipped, but relatively impersonal settings,
or in smaller but intensely personal, teacher-dominated
schools? Which should count for more: the efficiencies of an
educational system that is "progressive" (the word comes
from paragraph two), or the personal traits of the individual
classroom teacher? The essay is a personal one, in that it is
the education of his son that White is "worried about"; yet it
is a public matter, too. After all, as the headnote indicates,
White published it in *The New Yorker*, a magazine with a readership wide and influential and far more national than its
name implies.

What is White's position on the issue? At first it might seem
that the author takes no side, that he simply wants to describe
objectively the two alternatives and to record his son's experiences in each circumstance. He gives equal time to each
school, he spends the same amount of space on concrete details about each, and he seems in firm control of his personal
biases ("I have always rather favored public schools").
Through his light and comic tone White implies that all will
be well for his son—and our children—in either circumstance, that the two schools each are to be neither favored nor
feared by us. "All one can say is that the situation is different"
(paragraph four), not better, in the two places.

Or is it? Many readers—myself among them—contend that
"Education" is less an objective, neutral appraisal than it is a
calculated argument that subtly favors the country school. To
such readers, White's objective pose is only that—a created
pose, an attempt to create a genial, sympathetic, and trustworthy speaker. By caring so obviously for his son (final paragraph), by confessing his biases, and by treating both schools
with distance and detachment and reliable detail, White creates what rhetoricians call "ethos"—that quality of a piece of
writing that persuades through the character of the speaker
or writer. By poking gentle humor at just about everything—
his son "the scholar"; his wife the prim graduate of Miss Winsor's private schools; himself "the victim of a young ceramist";
and, of course, both schools—White makes himself seem
enormously sympathetic and trustworthy: fair-minded and
unflappable, balanced and detached.

But is this reliable speaker arguing or describing? Those
who see the essay as an argument for the ways of the country
school can point to the emotional aspects of the essay—to its

pathos, in other words. The image of the one-room school-house, for instance, is imprinted in positive terms on the U.S. psyche, and White exploits that image for his argumen-tative purposes. The "scholar" walks miles through the snow to get his education; like the schoolhouse itself, he has the self-reliance and weather-resistance to care for himself and to fit into a class with children both younger and older; and he learns a practical curriculum—there is "no time at all for the esoteric"—"just as fast and as hard as he can." It is all Abra-ham Lincoln and *The Waltons,* isn't it? And the teacher who presides over the country school appeals to the reader's emo-tions as only The Ideal Mother can. This teacher-mother is not only "a guardian of their health, their clothes, their habits ... and their snowball engagements," but "she has been doing this sort of Augean task for twenty years, and is both kind and wise. She cooks for the children on the stove that heats the room, and she can cool their passions or warm their soup with equal competence."

No such individual Ideal Mother presides over the city school. Instead, that school is presided over by a staff of Edu-cational Professionals—a bus driver, half a dozen anonymous teachers, a nurse, an athletic instructor, dietitians. The school itself is institutional, regimented, professionalized. There the scholar is "worked on," "supervised," "pulled." Like the one-room schoolhouse, the regimented institution is ingrained in the national psyche. But in this case the emotional appeal is negative, for "The System" is something that Americans in-stinctively resist. True, the city school is no prison, and true, the scholar in this school learns "to read with a gratifying dis-cernment." But the accomplishments remain rather abstract. Faced with such an education, such a school, no wonder the students literally become ill. At least that is the implication of the end of paragraph three, where the account of the city school is concluded with an account of the networks of pro-fessional physicians that discuss diseases that never seem to appear in the country schools.

For these reasons many readers see "Education" as an ar-gument against the city school and an endorsement of the country one. They see the essay as a comparison with an aim like most comparison essays: to show a preference. The eval-uative aim is carried out by reference to specific criteria, namely that schools are better if they are less structured and if they make students want to attend (because motivated stu-dents learn better); a structured, supervised curriculum and facilities are inferior to a personalized, unstructured environment that makes students love school. Days at the country school pass "just like lightning"; to attend the country school the boy is willing literally to walk through snowdrifts, while to get to the city school he must be escorted to the bus stop—or be "pulled" there. The country school is full of "surprises" and "individual instruction," while the city school is full of supervision; there are no surprises in the "progressive" school. In a real sense, therefore, White persuades not only by the force of his personality or through emotional appeals but also through hard evidence, what rhetoricians call "logos." "Education" amounts to an argument by example wherein the single case—the boy scholar—stands for many such cases. This case study persuades like other case studies: by being presented as representative. White creates through his unnamed son, who is described as typical in every way, a representative example that stands for the education of Everychild. The particular details provided in the essay become not mere "concrete description" but hard evidence, good reasons, summoned to support White's implicit thesis. The logic of the piece seems to go something like this: "Country schools are a bit superior to city ones. They make up for what they lack in facilities with a more personal, less authoritarian atmosphere that children respond to."

E. B. White, then, wins his reader's assent by means of ethos, pathos, and logos. But the country-school approach is also reinforced by the essay's arrangement. Notice, for example, that the essay begins and ends with favorable accounts of the country school. In other words, the emphatic first and final positions of the essay are reserved for the virtues of country schools, while the account of the city school is buried in the unemphatic middle of the essay. The article could easily have begun with the second paragraph (wouldn't sentence two of paragraph two have made a successful opener?), but such a strategy would have promoted the value of the city school. By choosing to add the loving vignette of the Ideal Teacher in his opening paragraph, White disposes his readers to favor country schools from the very start. Notice too that the comparison of the two schools in the body of "Education" proceeds from city to country. Again, it didn't have to be so; White could have discussed the country school first, or he could have gone back and forth from city to country more often (adopting what some handbooks call an "alternating" method of comparison as opposed to the "divided" pattern that White actually did use). By choosing to deal first with the city school, all in one lump, and then to present the country school in another lump, White furthered his persuasive aim. After all, most "preference comparisons" move from the inferior item to the superior one. In other words, writers of comparisons usually move from "this one is good" to "but this other one is even better," rather than vice versa. So when White opts to deal first with the city schools, he subtly reinforces his persuasive end through very indirect means. White's arrangement serves his purpose in two ways, then: it permits him to end with the item he wishes to prefer; and it permits him to add an introductory paragraph that places his country school in that favorable spot as well.

Even the arrangement of details within White's individual paragraphs serves his goals. It appears that the central paragraphs (three, four, and five) are arranged chronologically, that details in those paragraphs are arranged according to the rhythm of the school day. But a closer examination shows that paragraph three closes on a note of sickness. That detail could have come earlier in the paragraph, but White places the negative detail in the emphatic final position. Similarly, the two paragraphs on the country school are manipulated for rhetorical ends. Why does White divide the account of the country school into two paragraphs? (After all, he dealt with the city school in one paragraph.) By doing so he is able to give special emphasis to the first sentence of one of his paragraphs, "There is no supervised play," highlighting thereby a key difference between the two schools.

A critical reading of "Education" must also consider expression, those sentence and word choices that are sometimes equated with the style of a particular essay or author. Like most rhetoricians, I personally resist the idea that "style is the person"—that style is something inherent in a writer, that it amounts to a sort of genetic code or set of fingerprints that are idiosyncratic to each person, that it is possible to speak generically of Anna Quindlen's style or Martin Luther King's style or E. B. White's style. It has always seemed to me more appropriate to think of style as characteristic of a particular *occasion* for writing, as something that is as appropriate to reader and subject and genre as it is to a particular author. Words and sentences are chosen in response to rhetorical and social circumstances, and those words and sentences change as the occasion changes. If it is possible to characterize E. B. White's style or Hemingway's style in general (and I'm not sure even of that), then it is so only with respect to certain kinds of writing that they did again and again and again. For when those writers found themselves writing outside *The New Yorker* (in White's case) or outside fiction (in Hemingway's), they did indeed adopt different stylistic choices. It is probably wiser to focus not on the apparent idiosyncrasies associated with a Quindlen or a King or a Hemingway or an E. B. White, but on the particular word and sentence choices at work in a particular rhetorical situation.

Take the case at hand. What stylistic choices are worthy of note in "Education"? How has White chosen particular sentence patterns and words in order to further the aims of his essay?

The sentences of White's essay are certainly appropriate for public discourse. There are roughly a thousand words and fifty sentences in "Education," so average sentence length comes to about twenty words. Many are shorter than twenty words, though (the shortest is five words), and only one forty-three-word sentence seems particularly long. The result is that this essay can probably be readily comprehended by most adults, without its sentences creating the impression of superficiality or childishness. (The sentences in White's book for children *Charlotte's Web,* by contrast, have an average length of about twelve words.)

Moreover, White's sentences are unpretentious. They move in conventional ways—from subjects and verbs to objects and modifiers. There are no sentence inversions (violations of the normal subject/verb/object order), few distracting interrupters (the parentheses and the "I suspect" in that one long sentence in paragraph two are exceptions), and few lengthy opening sentence modifiers that keep us too long from subjects and verbs. Not only that, the sentences are simple and unpretentious in another sense: White comparatively rarely uses subordinate (or modifying) clauses—clauses containing a subject and verb and beginning with *who* or *although* or *that* or *because* or the like. I count only two such modifying (or dependent) clauses in the first and third paragraphs, for instance, and just five in the second; if you don't think that is a low number, compare it to a six-hundred-word sample of your own prose. When White does add length to a sentence, he does it not by adding complex clauses that modify other clauses, but by adding independent clauses (ones that begin with *and* or *but*) and by adding phrases and modifiers in parallel series. Some examples? The children's teacher is a guardian "of their health, their clothes, their habits, their mothers, and their snowball engagements"; the boy "learned fast, kept well, and we were satisfied"; the bus "would sweep to a halt, open its mouth, suck the boy in, and spring away." And so forth. The *and*s make White's essay informal and conversational, never remote or scholarly or full of disclaimers and qualifiers.

White uses relatively simple sentence patterns in "Education," then, but his prose is still anything but simple. Some of his sentences are beautifully parallel: "she can cool their passions or warm their soup"; "she conceives their costumes, cleans up their noses, and shares their confidences"; "in a cinder court he played games supervised by an athletic instructor, and in a cafeteria he ate lunch worked out by a dietitian"; "when the snow is deep or the motor is dead"; "rose hips in fall, snowballs in winter." These precise, mirror-image parallel structures are known as isocolons to rhetoricians. White delights in them and in the artful informality they create. He uses parallel structures and relentless coordination—*and* after *and* after *and*—to make his prose accessible to a large audience of appreciative readers. And he uses those lists of specific items in parallel series to give his writing its remarkably concrete, remarkably vivid quality.

That brings us to White's word choices. They too contributed to White's purposes. Remember the sense of detachment and generosity in White's narrative voice, the ethos of involvement and detachment apparent in the speaker? In large measure that is the result of White's word choices. For instance, White has the ability to attach mock-heroic terminology to his descriptions so that he comes across as balanced and wise, as someone who doesn't take himself or his world too seriously. The boy is a "scholar" who "sallied forth" on a "journey" to school or to "make Indian weapons of a semi-deadly nature." The gentle hyperbole fits in well with the classical allusion inherent in the word "Augean" (one of Hercules' labors was to clean the Augean stables): there is a sophistication and worldly wisdom in the speaker's voice that qualifies him to speak on this subject. And remember the discussion of whether White's aim was purely descriptive or more argumentative in character? White's metaphors underscore his argumentative aim: the city school bus "was as punctual as death," a sort of macabre monster that "would sweep to a halt, open its mouth, suck the boy in, and spring away with an angry growl"; or it is "like a train picking up a bag of mail." At the country school, by contrast, the day passes "just like lightning." If the metaphors do not provide enough evidence of White's persuasive aim, consider the connotations of words—their emotional charges, that is—that are associated with the city school: *regimented, supervised, worked on, uniforms, fevers.* And then compare these with the connotation of some words White associates with the country school: *surprises, bungalow, weather-resistant, individual instruction, guardian,* and so forth. The diction and sentence choices made by White indeed do reinforce his argumentative purpose.

This analysis by no means exhausts the full measure of rhetorical sophistication that E. B. White brings to the composition of "Education." You may have noticed other tactics at work, or you may disagree with some of the generalizations presented here. But the purpose of this discussion is not to detail the rhetoric of White's "Education." It is merely to illustrate a method of critical reading that you might employ as you read the selections in this book and the public rhetoric that you encounter in your life each day. The point has been to encourage you to read not just for *what* is said—though this is crucial—but for *how* it is said as well. For reading is as "rhetorical" an activity as is writing. It depends on an appreciation of how writer, subject, and reader are all "negotiated" through a particular document.

If you read for "how" as well as "what," the distinction between the two may begin to shorten for you. Appreciation of the rhetoric of public discourse can make you more skeptical of the arguments presented to you and to other citizens. It can make you a reader less likely to be won over on slender grounds, more likely to remain the doubter than the easy victim or trusting soul who accepts all arguments at face value. Therefore, whether or not you decide to take part in any of the particular "conversations" captured in this book, your thinking can be stimulated by critical reading.

Not only that, you'll find yourself growing as a writer; if you read critically, you'll begin to adopt and adapt for your own purposes the best rhetorical maneuvers on display in this book and elsewhere. What is a particular writer's real aim? What evidence is used to win the assent of readers? How does a particular writer establish credibility? What kind of emotional and logical appeals are at work in a given circumstance? How does the arrangement of a presentation influence its reception? How can sentence style and word choices sustain a writer's aim? By asking and answering questions like these, you can gain confidence as reader and writer. By becoming better able to understand and appreciate the conversations going on around you, you'll learn to make more powerful and sophisticated contributions to the discussions that most engage you personally. Critical reading of the selections in this book can make you a better writer, a better citizen.

I.

EDUCATION

Introduction

Americans have always been passionate about issues related to education. Why? For one thing, education issues affect every American in a personal way. True, there is a strong anti-intellectual strain in our national culture; but it is also true that Americans pursue with a passion the ideal of "education for all" both as a means of self-improvement and as the source of the enlightened citizenry required by democratic institutions. For another thing, education issues are decided locally and immediately. The relatively decentralized nature of our educational "system" (U.S. education is hardly as monolithic as the term "system" implies) encourages continuing and passionate public discussion among citizens interested in shaping the policies and practices of local schools. (About 93 percent of the money spent on primary and secondary education in the United States in 1998 came from state and local governments. Incidentally, Americans spend more per capita on education than all but three other Western nations.)

Portions of three current discussions related to education are included in this part of *Conversations*. The first—"What to Do about the Schools"—concerns proposals for improving public education, particularly secondary education. In the past decade, particularly in response to the economic crises of the early 1980s and early 1990s, a number of committees and commissions launched well-publicized reform efforts aimed at everything from teacher education and school governance to classroom climate and the curriculum—at everything from competency testing and conduct codes to the size of schools and the wisdom of "tracking." Presidents Bush and Clinton also promoted reform efforts that they believed would invigorate U.S. education. Those calls for reform can be seen in the selections included here. Should schools be large, centralized, efficient, and comprehensive? Or should they be smaller and more personal—have all the advantages of small size? Is discipline a major problem in the schools, and (if so) how can it be improved? Or does an overemphasis on discipline make schools confining and constricting—places that value order and conformity over independence and freedom of inquiry? What about the curriculum—should it emphasize mastery of bodies of knowledge, "what every educated person needs to know"? Or instead should it emphasize learning skills—problem-solving ability, flexibility, independent thinking, and resourcefulness? Should the way schools are funded be reconsidered, to even out differences between the "haves" and the "have nots"? Or would that undermine a cornerstone of our educational tradition, local control? Should schools be "privatized"? Should citizens have more choice over which schools to attend? Could citizens through some sort of voucher system be given more choices over which school to attend? Or would that tend to widen the gap in educational opportunities now available to rich and poor? Does the concept of "charter schools," one that in a handful of states permits private companies or groups of teachers and parents or nonprofit organizations to operate schools—hold promise? And finally, what about the teachers? Should they be given better pay and more responsibility for what goes on in the classroom? Or should we continue to honor top-down administrative mechanisms for ensuring competency and consistency and currency?

The second set of readings addresses the question, "What Is College For?" No doubt on your own campus you have listened in on discussions of this topic in one form or another, and no doubt you have given your own educational goals considerable thought. In broad terms, the question can be posed this way: Is college an opportunity for personal growth and general intellectual development? Or is it a means to economic advancement? If college should foster both general education and professional specialization, then in what proportions should it do so? And through what means? Is college designed for the intellectual elite who are sophisticated enough to pursue truly advanced learning, or is it something that ought to be within the reach of most high school graduates? Does college offer a critical perspective on our institutions and habits? Or is it merely a way of socializing students into willing servants of the status quo?

That last question introduces the final group of readings, on the issue of literacy. After all, the matter of socialization relates to how people achieve literacy—how they develop their abilities to read and write in a given culture. The "literacy narratives" collected here typically record people's encounter with other cultures, for that is one of the conventions of this kind of writing; literacy narratives often dramatize a person's attempt to assimilate. Those who write literacy narratives usually mean to tell others about their struggle to accommodate the language structures and conventions associated with a culture that is "alien" in some way. Sometimes that encounter is presented in positive terms: the literacy narrative in that case records a story of positive transformation as the subject of the narrative attains new power and command by virtue of coming to grips with a new community and its language patterns. (That may be the subtext of Benjamin Franklin's literacy narrative, included in his famous *Autobiography.*) But other times the encounter can be less positive. The narrative can disclose the inability of a person to become integrated with a new community and can record the community's efforts to keep aliens outside. Still other literacy narratives can be ambiguous: as in the case of Eliza Doolittle, who becomes "a lady" in George Bernard Shaw's *Pygmalion* (and in the Broadway version of that play, *My Fair Lady*), but at a terrible cost to her own identity and autonomy, the protagonists of literacy narratives sometimes offer stories that are mixed in tone. Whatever the point of the story, literacy narratives nearly always give readers an opportunity to reflect on the profound power of language to shape lives (and in that sense, these narratives offer an ideal transition to the next section of *Conversations*, on Language). The narratives will also invite you to reflect on the record of your own growth as a language user, your own encounters through language with alien cultures of one kind or another, at a time when you are encountering a specific new "culture," that of your college or university. Did you grow from all those encounters? Were the transformations they brought about singularly powerful and useful? Or was something also lost in the transition from one kind of language use to another?

Some of these ideas related to education are developed further in Part Two of *Conversations*, which opens with a sort of literacy narrative, Richard Rodriguez's "Aria." Education issues also will develop in Part Three, in the section on Race and Gender, and in Part Five, which takes up issues of Civil Liberties and Civil Rights. But in this part of *Conversations*, the emphasis is on education in general and college education in particular. The readings you encounter should give you a better understanding of the issues that you and your classmates are grappling with right now. As you read, remember that the perennial nature of debates about education can be frustrating, especially to educational leaders. But the very relentlessness of the debates probably brings out the best feature of a democratic society: the freedom of citizens to shape policy through open and public exchange.

WHAT TO DO ABOUT THE SCHOOLS?

E. B. White
Education

E. B. White (1899–1985), who contributed regularly to The
New Yorker *and whose work has been collected into several
books, was perhaps America's most popular essayist. You may
also know him as the author of the children's classic* Charlotte's Web *(1952). First published in 1939 in* Harper's *and in
White's* One Man's Meat, *the following comparison of two educational philosophies remains relevant over half a century
later.*

I have an increasing admiration for the teacher in the   1
country school where we have a third-grade scholar in attendance. She not only undertakes to instruct her charges in all
the subjects of the first three grades, but she manages to function quietly and effectively as a guardian of their health, their
clothes, their habits, their mothers, and their snowball engagements. She has been doing this sort of Augean task for
twenty years, and is both kind and wise. She cooks for the
children on the stove that heats the room, and she can cool
their passions or warm their soup with equal competence.
She conceives their costumes, cleans up their messes, and
shares their confidences. My boy already regards his teacher
as his great friend, and I think tells her a great deal more than
he tells us.

The shift from city school to country school was something   2
we worried about quietly all last summer. I have always
rather favored public school over private school, if only because in public school you meet a greater variety of children.
This bias of mine, I suspect, is partly an attempt to justify my
own past (I never knew anything but public schools) and
partly an involuntary defense against getting kicked in the
shins by a young ceramist on his way to the kiln. My wife was
unacquainted with public schools, never having been exposed
(in her early life) to anything more public than the washroom

of Miss Winsor's. Regardless of our backgrounds, we both knew that the change in schools was something that concerned not us but the scholar himself. We hoped it would work out all right. In New York our son went to a medium-priced private institution with semi-progressive ideas of education, and modern plumbing. He learned fast, kept well, and we were satisfied. It was an electric, colorful, regimented existence with moments of pleasurable pause and giddy incident. The day the Christmas angel fainted and had to be carried out by one of the Wise Men was educational in the highest sense of the term. Our scholar gave imitations of it around the house for weeks afterward, and I doubt if it ever goes completely out of his mind.

3   His days were rich in formal experience. Wearing overalls and an old sweater (the accepted uniform of the private seminary), he sallied forth at morn accompanied by a nurse or a parent and walked (or was pulled) two blocks to a corner where the school bus made a flag stop. This flashy vehicle was as punctual as death: seeing us waiting at the cold curb, it would sweep to a halt, open its mouth, suck the boy in, and spring away with an angry growl. It was a good deal like a train picking up a bag of mail. At school the scholar was worked on for six or seven hours by half a dozen teachers and a nurse, and was revived on orange juice in mid-morning. In a cinder court he played games supervised by an athletic instructor, and in a cafeteria he ate lunch worked out by a dietitian. He soon learned to read with gratifying facility and discernment and to make Indian weapons of a semi-deadly nature. Whenever one of his classmates fell low of a fever the news was put on the wires and there were breathless phone calls to physicians, discussing periods of incubation and allied magic.

4   In the country all one can say is that the situation is different, and somehow more casual. Dressed in corduroys, sweatshirt, and short rubber boots, and carrying a tin dinner pail, our scholar departs at the crack of dawn for the village school, two and a half miles down the road, next to the cemetery. When the road is open and the car will start, he makes the journey by motor, courtesy of his old man. When the snow is deep or the motor is dead or both, he makes it on the hoof. In the afternoons he walks or hitches all or part of the way home in fair weather, gets transported in foul. The schoolhouse is a two-room frame building, bungalow type, shingles stained a burnt brown with weather-resistant stain. It has a chemical toilet in the basement and two teachers above the stairs. One

takes the first three grades, the other the fourth, fifth, and sixth. They have little or no time for individual instruction, and no time at all for the esoteric. They teach what they know themselves, just as fast and as hard as they can manage. The pupils sit still at their desks in class, and do their milling around outdoors during recess.

There is no supervised play. They play cops and robbers (only they call it "Jail") and throw things at one another— snowballs in winter, rose hips in fall. It seems to satisfy them. They also construct darts, pinwheels, and "pick-up-sticks" (jackstraws), and the school itself does a brisk trade in penny candy, which is for sale right in the classroom and which contains "surprises." The most highly prized surprise is a fake cigarette, made of cardboard, fiendishly lifelike.   5

The memory of how apprehensive we were at the beginning is still strong. The boy was nervous about the change too. The tension, on that first fair morning in September when we drove him to school, almost blew the windows out of the sedan. And when later we picked him up on the road, wandering along with his little blue lunch-pail, and got his laconic report "All right" in answer to our inquiry about how the day had gone, our relief was vast. Now, after almost a year of it, the only difference we can discover in the two school experiences is that in the country he sleeps better at night—and *that* probably is more the air than the education. When grilled on the subject of school-in-country vs. school-in-city, he replied that the chief difference is that the day seems to go so much quicker in the country. "Just like lightning," he reported.   6

Bruce Goldberg

A Liberal Argument for School Choice

The American Enterprise *published the following essay by Bruce Goldberg in the fall of 1996. (Goldberg's book,* Why Schools Fail, *appeared shortly after.)* The American Enterprise *is a product of the American Enterprise Institute for Public Policy, a staunchly conservative organization based in Washington, D.C., that is interested in influencing debate on public policy issues related to business, politics, and culture. The issue of* The American Enterprise *that contained this article contained several other essays related to education—on affirmative action in an Ivy League school, for example, and on the shortcomings of teachers' unions.*

1   Most critics of America's public schools attack from the right, in the name of Tradition and Authority. They complain that the schools are insufficiently rigorous in their methods, do not stress math and science, fail to inculcate "cultural literacy," emphasize individuality at the expense of discipline, and so on.

2   While I agree the public schools are failing, I disagree with the reasons these critics give. Nor do I share their criteria of educational success, which amount to little more than rising SAT scores. No, America's schools are failures *because* they systematically suppress children's interests, values, and idiosyncratic potentials. The denial of individuality—the idea that everyone must follow the same general plan—lies at the core of the schools' failure.

3   Still, whatever sort of changes one thinks would improve the schools, every would-be reformer must consider why the present system resists change when, even by its own standards, it is failing. On this issue, all varieties of reformers can agree: The school system resists change because it is a bureaucratic monopoly that displays the rigid, lethargic ineptitude of all such beasts. As David Boaz of the Cato Institute puts it, "The government schools have failed because they are socialist institutions. Like Soviet factories, they are technologically backward, overstaffed, inflexible, unresponsive to consumer demand, and operated for the convenience of top-level bureaucrats."

4   The same insight comes from an unlikely source, Albert Shanker, president of the American Federation of Teachers.

"It's time to admit," he writes, "that public education operates like a planned economy, a bureaucratic system in which everybody's role is spelled out in advance and there are few incentives for innovation and productivity. It's no surprise that our school system doesn't improve: It more resembles the communist economy than our own market economy."

Even within the educational establishment itself, calls for 5 change have been heard, but they have usually consisted of little more than educators exhorting each other to do better. "The public schools have to become committed to excellence," says Bill Honig, former California state superintendent of public instruction. "The quality of our schools must go up," says Ernest Boyer, president of the Carnegie Foundation for the Advancement of Teaching. Still, things remain essentially as they have always been. With so little incentive to improve, innovation is resisted at every level of the system. Even such a relatively simple change as the introduction of a new textbook is almost certain to encounter determined resistance. And the teachers' opposition is understandable: They have become accustomed to the old text, and they are not given any inducement to make the extra effort to learn the new one.

Indeed, there is little motivation for teachers to make any 6 extra effort, to improve their teaching skills, to learn new methods of instruction, to spend more time with a child who needs help. There is no reward for superior performance, period. Nor is there any penalty for incompetence. "The problem in the present regime," writes one observer, "is that performance remains virtually irrelevant to teacher security and advancement. Salary schedules," Milton Friedman points out, "tend to be uniform and determined far more by seniority, degrees received, and teaching certificates acquired than by merit." Some teachers, of course, are motivated by idealism, and they try harder for that reason. But they are a minority.

There are many other sources of inefficiency. To mention 7 just one, school districts are under constant pressure to spend all the money allocated to them. If they don't, it will go into the general fund or to another, less efficient district. And if a school district showed a surplus, "the excess funds might be subtracted from its allocation for the following year.... This common policy constitutes a strong deterrent against efficiency."

If history shows anything, it is that bureaucratic, monopo- 8 listic systems don't work. That is why the school system displays "all the energy and creativity of Soviet agriculture." The

first step toward improvement is to end the government monopoly in education and introduce competition into the field.
Ted Kolderie, director of the Hubert H. Humphrey Institute
of Public Affairs, points out that the basic question is not how
to improve the present educational system; it is how to create
a system that seeks improvement. For that, we must adopt a
proposal made by John Stuart Mill almost 150 years ago:

9   If the government would make up its mind to require for ev-
        ery child a good education, it might save itself the trouble of
        providing one. It might leave to parents to obtain the educa-
        tion where and how they pleased, and content itself with
        helping to pay the school fees of the poorer classes of chil-
        dren, and defraying the entire school expenses of those who
        have no one else to pay for them. An education established
        and controlled by the State should only exist, if it exists at all,
        as one among many competing experiments.

10   Changing to a competitive system would not be difficult.
        Numerous proposals already exist for funding a system of pa-
        rental choice. Perhaps the best known is economist Milton
        Friedman's voucher plan. Under that plan, parents of school-
        children would receive an educational voucher from the gov-
        ernment for an amount equal to the per-student expenditure
        on public schooling. The parents would then be free to use
        the voucher to pay for their child's education at a school of
        their choice, public or private. Many other funding possibili-
        ties are discussed in detail in Myron Lieberman's *Privatiza-
        tion and Educational Choice.*

11   A system of educational choice has many advantages. The
        most obvious is that instead of a stagnant, monopolistic re-
        gime that prevents others from trying to do better, a competi-
        tive environment exists that invites and encourages innovation.
        Another advantage is that it gives all parents an opportunity
        now open only to a few, namely the opportunity to select a
        school appropriate for their child. As Pete du Pont, former gov-
        ernor of Delaware and chairman of the Education Commis-
        sion of the States, explains,

12   My wife, Elise, and I have four children. They're all different,
        and they all had different educational needs. One is very
        bright and needed a rigorous academic environment. Another
        is dyslexic and needed a very special school. Another is scien-
        tifically inclined, the other more artistic; they needed schools
        that would suit them. Fortunately, Elise and I could afford to

choose the school best suited to each of our children. All parents should have that opportunity. One cannot treat all children the same way because every child is different.

The most important advantage of a competitive system is   13
the way it responds to the consumer: the family. As things stand now, parents who are dissatisfied with a school policy are virtually powerless. When they try to act on behalf of their children against a school policy, they are regarded as a nuisance. Suppose that a child, like one of Pete du Pont's children, is scientifically inclined. Because he is not artistically inclined, he doesn't like his art class. He's carving a head of Geronimo, but it doesn't look like anything. He can't get it to look like anything and he doesn't want to. He would just like to stop doing it and continue his investigation of paramecia, blood worms, frogs, fruit flies, rock formations, and constellations. Imagine that the parents come to school to request that the child be transferred to a different class where he would be more involved. Their chance of success is slim. The principal, or more likely some deputy, will say, "That's not a valid reason." And that will be the end of it. Maybe, if they are especially courageous, the parents will persist a bit longer: "But Edward doesn't like to whittle. Neither of us likes to whittle, for that matter. No one in our whole family is much of a whittler. Why should Edward have to do it? Forcing him to do something he finds so dull, day after day, does not seem to us to be a thoughtful way of dealing with a child." That too will have little effect. The school will say, "We don't give special treatment," or, "This is not a department store."

If a school in a competitive atmosphere were to respond   14
that way, the parents could take the child elsewhere. They would not have to accept such insensitive peremptory treatment. Because they would have options, the parents would be in a position to insist that Edward's character, interests, and needs be taken into account. They could decide that his being bored counted against the school. In the present system, the school counts it against Edward.

Under a scheme of competition, schools' own survival will   15
require them to be sensitive to parental concerns, with the result that greater attention will be given to the individuality of children. The school system will begin to recognize that different children have different needs.

Defenders of the present system challenge the idea of priva-   16
tizing schools on a number of grounds. The most frequent argument is that a system of competing schools, financed by the

government, would violate the constitutional principle of the separation of church and state. Since some parents would use the vouchers to send their children to parochial schools, it is argued, the government would be subsidizing religion. This objection does not have much weight. In the first place, there is no more reason for saying that the government would be subsidizing religion in this case than there is for saying it is subsidizing religion when it gives a welfare check to someone who uses part of the money to make a contribution to his church. The government would be subsidizing the education of children, some of whose parents might want that education to be in a sectarian institution.

17   In the second place, a school voucher system has long existed without being seen as a violation of the separation of church and state. At the end of World War II, under the G.I. Bill, returning veterans were given government money to pay for their college education, and it did not matter whether the recipient chose a church-related school, as many did. Indeed, the G.I. Bill is the model Friedman uses to explain his voucher plan.

18   Some critics have also objected that a choice system might eventually result in less freedom than at present because private schools that are now relatively free of government interference would, in the new system, find themselves facing more government regulation. Since the government would be involved in funding the system, this argument runs, it would have to establish criteria for what constitutes a school, which opens the possibility that all schools would have to adopt the same practices as the public ones.

19   The point is well taken. Any human institution can be corrupted. And so it might happen that competition would be introduced in name only. Not only might it happen, there will be pressure for it to happen. Government regulators tend to regulate as much as possible. But people will also see the connection between the degree of governmental control and the range of their choices. So some parents will be exerting a counterpressure to governmental attempts to impose uniformity. As they come to see the value of competition, more people will demand the same variety of choices in education that they are accustomed to in other areas of their lives.

20   Finally, the most fundamental objection to a choice system rests on the idea of parental choice itself. The schools, it is held, should not be responsive to parents. Parents shouldn't be able to tell a school what class a child should or shouldn't be in. Parents are not in a position to decide whether the

school's efforts are worthwhile. They are not experts. The education of a child is a matter for educational professionals. An English educator attacks parental choice head-on: "I'm not sure that parents know what is best educationally for their children. They know what's best for them to eat. They know the best environment they can provide at home. But we've been trained to ascertain the problems of children, to detect their weaknesses, to put right those things that need putting right, and we want to do this freely, with the cooperation of parents and not under undue strains."

The assertion that experts in educational science know   21
how to "put things right," or how to prevent a child's having "a lopsided mind," is supposed to convince us that parents should not be making educational decisions. In this view, parents are no more in a position to question the judgment of educators than they are to question the judgment of a brain surgeon.

Schooling, then, consists in the giving of psychosocial   22
treatment, in scientifically shaping the mind and character of a child. Parents are not simply sending their children to school to be taught. They are turning their children over to school to be constructed. As Horace Mann, the nineteenth-century "father" of the public school system, put it, "We who are engaged in the sacred cause of education are entitled to look upon all parents as having given hostages to our cause."

But educators' claims to scientific knowledge have no foun-   23
dation. There is no such thing as educational science, as the crumbled theories of earlier "experts" like Horace Mann and countless others caution us. Those who have wanted to control the lives of others have always claimed to know exactly what others need. They have always believed that their plans represent order and public-mindedness, as opposed to the chaos that would ensue without them. When Robert Owen defended imposing his way of thinking on the members of the (failed) utopian community of New Harmony, Indiana, he claimed that the issue was "whether the character of man shall continue to be formed under the guidance of the most inconsistent notions, the errors of which for centuries past have been manifest to every reflecting rational mind; or whether it shall be moulded under the direction of uniformly consistent principles, derived from the unvarying facts of the creation."

The authors of all such views are deluded in thinking that   24
their plans are "derived from the unvarying facts of the creation." "I have discovered what everyone needs," each one says. "My superior insight" or "my divine foresight" or "my

research in the field" has "enabled me to ascertain what human beings require if they are to become rational, enlightened, civilized, autonomous." Every one of those mind-
designing schemes, however, when looked at closely, has
turned out to have little to do with either science or order.
(The famed Horace Mann based his "science" of learning on
phrenology, the now-discredited pseudo-science of bumps on
the head.)

25   Schools have been imposing on children just the opposite
of what the professional educators claim. According to the
rhetoric of the public-school monopoly, today's schools follow
an ordered plan, constructed by experts, based on a scientific
understanding of mental development. But even the most casual look at what the school system actually offers shows
there is no ordered plan at all. "The public school curriculum," as critics David and Micki Colfax put it, consists of
"nothing more than a hodgepodge of materials and assumptions resulting from the historical interplay of educational
theories, political expedience, education fads and fashions,
pretensions to culture, demagoguery, and demography."

26   In truth, there is no "public school curriculum." Every
state, every county, every educational committee, has its own
idea of how to shape people and form their character. Every
educational theorist has his or her particular notion of what
constitutes indispensable human knowledge.

Even if educational theory were not riddled with ridiculous pretension, it would still be a mistake to try to impose a
blueprint for mental development on everyone. To do so is to
ignore the truth of Pete du Pont's observation that children all
have different needs. As John Stuart Mill wrote, "There is no
reason that all human existence should be constructed on
some one or some small number of patterns." "Human beings," he added, "are not like sheep; and even sheep are not
indistinguishably alike."

27   Horace Mann's central premise, writes his biographer
Jonathan Messerli, was that "all children everywhere were essentially the same." Therefore, "all could be taught, once the
correct techniques and goals were determined." He believed
that "a system of instruction which would work for some,
would work for all." In this way, today's public school system,
despite its lip service to diversity, is fundamentally at war
with individuality. And that is why it is failing.

David L. Kirp

What School Choice
Really Means

*David L. Kirp, a professor of public policy at the University of
California–Berkeley, has published over two dozen books on a
range of social issues, most of them related in one way or
another to education. He also writes regularly for a number of
magazines, including* The Atlantic Monthly, *where the following essay appeared in November 1992. The* Atlantic *is a
respected forum, mildly liberal in its outlook, that carries book
and movie reviews, original poetry and fiction, and commentary on current events and issues.*

On standard-issue maps of Manhattan, Ninety-sixth Street   1
on the Upper East Side is shown slightly thicker than the
lines representing neighboring streets, to signify that traffic
on it runs both east and west. There is no hint of a border on
these maps, no intimation that Ninety-sixth Street marks a division between two dramatically different worlds.

South of Ninety-sixth Street lie some of New York City's   2
most fashionable addresses. The continuing collapse of the
city's economy has touched even these streets, of course, and
now there are empty stores, unsellable condominiums. But
nannies still push strollers along Fifth Avenue and in Central
Park, and adolescents still stream forth from private schools.
Lawyers and investment bankers still look as if they had
stepped straight out of the display windows at Talbot's or
Brooks Brothers. Almost the only nonwhite faces to be seen
belong to the help.

To the north of Ninety-sixth Street lies East Harlem. On its   3
two hundred square blocks many of the brownstones are
empty, boarded up, covered with barbed wire and jagged bits
of glass to keep out the vagrants and drug addicts. Half of
East Harlem's population of 120,000 is Hispanic, and almost
all the rest is African-American. New arrivals come mostly
from dirt-poor Caribbean and Central American countries.
By all the standard social measures, East Harlem is among
the worst-off neighborhoods in the city.

Yet every school-day morning brings a remarkable sight, as   4
a thousand or so children from elsewhere in the city, many of
them from families that could easily afford private academies,
negotiate the buses and subways with practiced cool to join the

14,000 Hispanic and black children who attend East Harlem's elementary and junior high schools. These students come to East Harlem not because some official issued an integration order or redrew a school-district boundary but because their families have chosen to send them here. Remarkably, in some of the battered school buildings of this neighborhood, where these children attend classes with the children of the barrio, an exemplary education can be had. East Harlem's schools have, in fact, become famous, at least among educators, for their quality—relative to that of other inner-city schools, anyway— and the story of the transformation of these schools has by now acquired the status of an oft-told legend.

5   In 1970, when each of New York City's elementary and junior high schools was assigned to one of thirty-two community school districts, with powerful elected school boards that had the right to pick the local superintendent, East Harlem's schools, which make up District Four, were widely regarded as the city's worst. In 1974 the children scored thirty-second—dead last—on standardized reading tests. Absenteeism was chronic among teachers as well as students. Gangs had turned junior high corridors into battlegrounds, school bathrooms into drug bazaars. And yet scarcely a decade later this prototypical blackboard jungle had come to be hailed as something of a model for urban education. The most widely cited measure of its accomplishment is the reported improvement in reading achievement: by the mid-1980s East Harlem's scores had risen from the very worst citywide to a level approximating the citywide average.

6   Behind this change, East Harlem's boosters say, lies the simple but revolutionary fact that parents in East Harlem are now allowed to choose their children's schools—thereby introducing the salutary effects of competition into institutions dispirited by inertia, red tape, and the chaos of the surrounding community. These changes are not unique to East Harlem. Across the country, public school choice has been one of the most widely adopted reforms of the past decade, and enthusiasts for one or another version of school choice span the political spectrum. But what does make East Harlem special, and so worth paying attention to, is that it came first—and that New York has just decided to make a school-choice program citywide. In District Four choice has been sustained as a guiding philosophy for nearly two decades—a geological epoch in the faddish world of education policy. Moreover, the system of choice has been implemented in a city where the difficulties of making *anything* happen are well known, and in

a neighborhood characterized by deep social pathology. And it is undeniable that much of the education in East Harlem is better than what was available twenty years ago. But did choice make the difference? And how much difference has actually been made?

These are important questions, the answers to which have   7 implications for schools around the country—because even as legions of defenders hold up East Harlem as a national model, critics assail some of what has happened there as a triumph of public relations. Yes, they say, many East Harlem mini-schools may get a silk-stocking trade, and may offer instruction that is as good as in the better private schools, but just a few corridors away are classrooms with no middle-class students and all the familiar woes of inner-city education. And, they say, the way the system labeled "choice" works in practice makes such disparities inevitable.

The Revolution Begins

During the mid-1950s the novelist Dan Wakefield, then a   8 young reporter, lived in Spanish Harlem for six months and delivered a savage indictment of official neglect, especially in the public schools. "[The schools] have been of little help to the children of Spanish Harlem in escaping the realities of its streets, or…changing those realities to something like the promise of the posters that smile from the classrooms," Wakefield wrote in *Island in the City.* "The schools, in fact, have blocked out the possibilities of the world beyond even more profoundly than the tenement buildings around them." The situation only deteriorated in 1968, when black and radical white parents and teachers throughout the city fought the teachers' union and the education bureaucracy for greater local control over schools. They got it in 1970, after several bitter teachers' strikes, but the aftermath brought infighting of every kind among the board members of the thirty-two newly created school districts.

Things began to improve in District Four in 1973, when an   9 insurgent slate was elected to the school board. Robert Rodriguez, an East Harlem native who headed the slate and directed the East Harlem Neighborhood Manpower Service Center, was only twenty-one at the time. The new board chairman was committed to running a clean enterprise, in which educational priorities didn't get confused with personal agendas and board members didn't push pet programs or hand out patronage jobs to friends. Keeping fellow board members and local leaders from meddling in the details of personnel and programs didn't prove easy, however, and tensions ran so high that police officers were sometimes present at board meetings to assure order.

10   When Rodriguez came to power, the district superintendent was seen by many in the community as symbolizing the old, unresponsive regime. The superintendent was quickly forced out, and the board chose as his successor Anthony Alvarado, a charismatic thirty-year-old Puerto Rican from East Harlem. His fast-track career had taken him from Fordham University to half a dozen jobs in education, including running an experimental preschool and heading up a bilingual elementary school.

11   As the District Four superintendent, Alvarado brought in new black and Hispanic principals—a good idea in itself, and certainly also a way of fending off potential local critics. He also pushed an agenda that included alternative schools, bilingual schools (which now enroll 2,000 of the district's students), a district-wide reading program, and major infusions of federal and state dollars.

12   The alternative schools have gotten the most attention, yet they began almost accidentally. In 1974 Alvarado approached Deborah Meier, a longtime teacher on Manhattan's Upper West Side and a pedagogical reformer committed to bringing open classrooms to city schools, and asked if she would be interested in running her own elementary school. Meier jumped at the chance. In the school she had in mind, classrooms would have places to build things, quiet spaces for reading, and corners for painting. Teachers would move around, offering individual help. Classes would be small by city standards, and teachers would come to know their students well, because they would spend two years with the same children. The new school would depend for its survival on parents' willingness to accept the risks of an unfamiliar kind of education for their children, and also on teachers' willingness to surrender their lunch hours to students and their after-school hours to meetings that ran as long as in socialist heaven. The school had to start small, Meier argued, one grade at a time, with no set curriculum—"If the teacher cared a lot [about a topic] and the kids cared a lot, that was a good topic"—and no guaranteed results.

13   Although classes like this have been routine for half a century in the best progressive private academies, the school Meier and Alvarado proposed to create was a deviant institution in New York City public schools, where teachers typically

stood at the front of the classroom talking at rows of nodding heads and covering a prescribed curriculum. Central Park East, as Meier's elementary school was called, started out in the fall of 1974 on two floors of P.S. 171, a run-down elementary school with which it would be competing for students and resources. Many of the Puerto Rican parents living in the neighborhood, whose memories of their own education led them to equate quality with order, were suspicious of a white Jewish woman and her permissive ideas. Some community activists wanted a school rooted more in the language and struggles of the barrio than in the theories of John Dewey and Jean Piaget. But the school attracted students, and after a troubled first few years its reputation as a good place to learn began to spread. Soon there were more applicants than spaces, with many of the applications coming from outside East Harlem.

The same year that Central Park East opened its doors, two   14
other alternative schools opened, to serve grades five through nine: the East Harlem Performing Arts School and the BETA ("better education through alternatives") School, which took rejects from other schools, where they had made teachers' lives hell (the BETA School would close in 1990).

In 1976 Alvarado hired Seymour Fliegel, who had been a   15
teacher and administrator in Harlem for two decades, to oversee the existing alternative schools and help create many new ones. By 1982 two new primary schools, Central Park East II and River East, were launched to meet a rising demand for open classrooms. Though they began as spinoffs of Central Park East, and took students from a common pool of applicants, the new academies gradually developed their own identities. From the outset, places in these schools were much sought-after, and soon educators with other dreams appeared at Fliegel's doorstep. Alan Sofferman, who had taught fifth and sixth grades at P.S. 96, and who eventually became its assistant principal, imagined a School of Science and Humanities, as tradition-oriented as any parochial school. Students would wear uniforms, and silence would be observed as orderly ranks of pupils passed by one another in the corridors. Leonard Bernstein, a science teacher, designed the Isaac Newton School with the intention of exposing the brightest youngsters from the ghetto to state-of-the-art instruction in science and math. Beryl Epton, who had taught at the BETA School, wanted a chance to work with younger children who had troubled histories. She started the Children's Workshop, the smallest of East Harlem's alternative schools, a one-room

second-through-fourth-grade class for children who had been
or were likely to be held back because of behavioral problems. New schools opened almost every year, each one trying
to find its special niche. Their names reveal the range of aspirations: the Academy of Environmental Science, the Mari-
time School, the East Harlem Career Academy, the Talented
and Gifted School.

16   While every other district in the city was pleading poverty,
East Harlem usually found the money to do what it wanted.
For one thing, its administrators came to realize that because
the notion of choice pushed the right buttons at Ronald
Reagan's Department of Education, Washington after 1980
would be forthcoming with cash. At one point during the
1980s District Four received more federal money per student
than any other school district in the country. The Republicans
from Washington and the liberal Democrats from Spanish
Harlem have made strange bedfellows, and there are those
who say that the district was manipulated. Yet in the cutthroat world of New York City school politics, Washington's
support bought East Harlem a measure of protection.

17   District Four was also prepared to fend for itself. For years
it engaged heavily in the risky business of deficit financing,
and it outmaneuvered the dozing downtown bureaucrats.
The alternative schools, with their tiny staffs, could not live
with the seniority system that reigned in every other city district. So the principals (called directors) of the alternative
schools recruited teachers mainly by word of mouth, and
turned to Fliegel to slip the new teachers onto the payroll regardless of seniority.

18   The teachers' unions initially protested about all the rules
East Harlem was breaking. But they backed off when they
saw members volunteering to swap protections won through
collective bargaining for the rewards of professionalism. (Today the New York City teachers' contract specifies that with a
three-quarters-majority vote the teachers at any school can
waive rules about class size and teachers' schedules.)

19   "I could say, 'We had a long-range plan: we envisioned a
choice program ten years down the line,'" Fliegel says. "But
things don't work that way. It developed organically." Slowly,
if haphazardly, with a sizable dose of what Fliegel calls "creative noncompliance" with the rules, an alternative system
parallel to the regular schools emerged, with a handful of alternative elementary schools and a somewhat larger number
of junior highs—twenty-two alternative schools in all by
1982, offering a wide range of options. By then there were

enough options to enable every sixth-grade student in East
Harlem to have at least *some* choice, although competition
for places at the most popular schools was sufficiently intense
that the schools, not the parents ard students, ended up doing most of the picking. Still, by 1982 half of East Harlem's
junior high students were attending one of the alternative
schools, and by that year East Harlem had moved from
thirty-second to fifteenth in the city in reading scores. District
Four began getting national attention.

The Numbers Game

East Harlem officials focus on District Four's dramatically   20
improved test scores when trumpeting their success. In 1974,
they note only 15.3 percent of the district's students could
read at or above grade level; by 1988 the proportion had quadrupled, to 62.5 percent.

This fact is always seized on by those who would com-   21
mend the East Harlem experience to other school systems.
Yet those statistics, while technically correct, are somewhat
misleading, and a close look at them begins to reveal some
other realities of the East Harlem experience. The biggest improvements in reading scores occurred in 1975 (13 percentage points), when the choice program was just getting
started, and in 1986 (9.5 percentage points), when New York
City switched to a different test. In those two years reading
levels improved substantially all across the city.

Moreover, in 1988 the city was using a test whose norms—   22
the criteria for what should be expected by way of performance—had been set a decade earlier. But in the interim
there had been a marked increase in basic-skills levels, and so
the norms were out-of-date. It's as if a high-jump bar had remained at a certain height even as the jumpers had grown
taller. After new national norms were established, in 1989, the
proportion of youngsters performing at grade level dropped
to 42 percent in East Harlem (as against 48 percent citywide).
This doesn't mean that things weren't getting better in East
Harlem, but it does mean that the statistical gain is not as
fantastically large as is commonly claimed. Nor have matters
changed much since then. Last year 43 percent of students in
East Harlem (as compared with 49 percent of students citywide) were doing grade-level work.

Comparisons with other districts do show that from 1978,   23
when norms were previously established, to 1989 District

Four's reading scores rose by 14.2 percent, as compared with 2.3 percent for the city as a whole. That was the second-biggest improvement recorded in all of the city's districts. (The biggest improvement, 14.5 percent, occurred in Bedford-Stuyvesant, a Brooklyn district that is 98 percent black and Hispanic, whose school system combines choice at the junior high level with a strong emphasis on scholastic drills and testing.) Performance on the mathematics test has been far weaker. Since 1986, when the current citywide test for mathematics was adopted, District Four has fallen from twentieth to twenty-seventh place.

24   It is hard to know how much of the improvement in reading scores to attribute to choice. For one thing, much of the gain has been recorded in neighborhood elementary schools, where choice has not been as widely available as in the junior highs. For another, the district-wide data conceal variations as great as can be found among public schools anywhere in America. In 1991 at least 75 percent of the students at the most elite East Harlem schools, including the Talented and Gifted School (TAG) for elementary students and Manhattan East and Isaac Newton for junior high students, scored at or above grade level. At Central Park East Secondary School, with a more diverse student body, more than half of the junior high school students read at grade level. Until recently these schools received special funding from the federal magnet-schools program, and they have attracted most of the students who come from outside East Harlem. TAG, for example, is 40 percent white.

25   The question of who is attending which East Harlem schools goes to the heart of the system of choice. In its publicity brochures District Four describes its schools as "Schools That Dare to Compete," but the fact is that in many cases it is not the schools but the students that are competing—competing for the schools. A mother visiting New York Prep while I was there was eager to persuade its director at the time, Brian Spears, that her daughter, who was shyly tagging along, should be admitted.

26   "Why do you want to send your daughter here?" Spears asked.

27   "You've got computers and a good reading program," the mother said. "It's a safe school. I've got a younger daughter downstairs in the elementary school, and the principal there says it's good."

28   "There are two hundred and fifty applications for seventy places," Spears replied, and then added, "The fact that you've come down, shown an interest, that's very important."

Sometimes parents treat the selection process as casually 29
as if they were selecting a brand of cereal. Other parents—
ones considering elementary schools in particular—base
their decisions on factors like proximity and the safety of the
neighborhood, which are important but only indirectly related to the quality of the education their children will receive. And for the many youngsters who are characterized by
district officials as "at risk"—including children with young
mothers strung out on crack, children who have worn thin
the patience of their grandmothers, children living in group
homes or on the streets—there is no responsible adult to
make a choice.

Choice is a tool wielded less decisively by parents than by 30
the school directors, the most adept of whom, like Spears,
seek out students they think will succeed in their schools.
Five alternative junior highs recruit many of their best students from elementary schools located in the same building
that they themselves occupy. Until the past few years others
ran their own early-admissions programs, effectively picking
students before most parents had a chance to apply. It is
largely because of this hidden selection process—which
screens both for levels of skill and for traits of character—that
some very good schools have been created in East Harlem.

A hierarchy has emerged, reflecting the extent to which 31
schools can be selective. At the top are the so-called elite
schools, which the ablest East Harlem children and most of
the youngsters from outside neighborhoods attend. The
highly selective sixth-through-eighth-grade school Manhattan
East, which offers what it calls "a rigorous classical academic
program," attracts as many as eighty of its 215 students from
the world outside District Four; this integration would be less
likely to occur if the school had less say over who gets in from
the world *inside* District Four. The junior high school New
York Prep, in the middle of the academic pecking order but
with four applicants for every place, can also fill up with good
children and reject all likely troublemakers. At the bottom of
the heap are schools that virtually none of each year's 1,400
prospective seventh-graders in District Four would choose.
These get the hundreds of children who are left over after the
more successful schools have made their picks.

In theory, unsuccessful schools in a competitive system 32
would be shut down and replaced with more-popular alternatives. That can be hard to arrange, though, when one reason
that a school is unsuccessful is that it has been saddled with
the least-promising and most-disruptive students—a change

of name, director, and educational philosophy can accomplish only so much. It's also hard to arrange in the real world, where a teachers'-union contract guarantees job security and where many among the poor are possessive even of terrible schools, because these happen to be *their* schools. In nearly two decades only three alternative schools have been shut down in East Harlem. For all these reasons, a substantial proportion of elementary and junior high students wind up in schools that remain largely unaffected by the improvements in District Four.

An East Harlem Sampler

33   Diversity is just an abstraction until you walk into the East 109th Street building that a decade ago was a conventional junior high for 1,300 students. At that time it was a school with a reputation for student violence and dead-end teaching. Now the building houses four alternative elementary and junior high schools: the Harbor Performing Arts School, the Talented and Gifted School, the East Harlem Career Academy, and the Key School. Pedagogically these places are worlds apart, though they are separated physically by no more than a staircase or a fire door.

34   A visitor must sign in at a guard's desk before entering—a reminder that trouble is always possible from the crack dealers or the bullying high schoolers who hang around. When I visited the building, the guard was a young woman from the neighborhood, a recent high school graduate who returned to a book of word puzzles when no visitors were in sight. She carried no weapon and would have scared no one, but she offered at least the illusion of protection.

35   The Talented and Gifted School's name is no mere euphemism. Prospective TAG students take a battery of intelligence and psychological tests, and submit to interviews. The school rejects six children for every one it accepts. In one classroom I saw, pre-kindergartners age four were already beginning to write. A first-grade classroom was filled with stuffed dolls, likenesses of themselves that the children had crafted. "I'm Leslie," the writing on one doll proclaimed. "My puppy sleeps in my bed." "I'm Jenna," said the words on another. "I went to Florida." There was an "Artists' Touch" corner and an "Our Pets" corner. On the wall were cartoon figures demonstrating "angry," "afraid," and "frustrated." I asked the teacher's aide

whether "frustrated" wasn't too sophisticated a concept for these six-year-olds, but she assured me that they get it. One of the kids volunteered, "It's the feeling I have when I can't do what I want."

Two floors away, at the Harbor Performing Arts School,   36
with 210 seventh- through ninth-graders, a dance teacher led a dozen girls through a routine. The girls stood poised at the bar. "First position and stop and step back and step forward—don't use your arm, use your entire body...first position three, down on four...Please stop fidgeting. Don't give me third, Ebony—we're in fifth." A sign hanging in the room read, IF YOU'RE NOT WORKING ON YOURSELF, YOU'RE NOT WORKING, and intensity was sketched on the girls' straining faces. From down the hall came the sounds of a choir practicing a medley of songs. In a month the Harbor School's singers and dancers would begin rehearsing their major school production, a Broadway musical. The director at the time, Leslie Moore, told me that these classes build self-esteem. "If teenagers who are having trouble in math or English can succeed in singing or dancing," she said, "with all the discipline that that demands, they don't walk away defeated; they'll stay in school, maybe catch on to academic work. There's also some direct carry-over, since students in music or drama have to make sense of words."

Four hundred students apply for the seventy openings in   37
the seventh grade at Harbor. Some will go on to La Guardia High School of Music and Art and Performing Arts—in 1990 ten of the twelve who applied there were admitted—and more will attend prep schools or the city's selective high schools. A handful of alumni are celebrated, among them Amani A. W.-Murray, who has released a saxophone album to bravo reviews, and Carlos Guity, a boy from the slums of the southeast Bronx who became an acrobat with the Big Apple Circus.

A typical junior high teacher with 150 students to teach   38
over five periods can't be expected to remember all the students' names, let alone know very much about them. The intimate scale of some of the East Harlem junior high schools invites teachers to invest themselves, much like coaches, in their students' futures. On my initial visit to New York Prep, which occupies the fifth floor of an old elementary school, a boy whom I will call Jaime Morelia, home on vacation after his first term at a Connecticut prep school, came in to check up on his former teachers and see his friends. Jaime's natural ease made him seem more like a college freshman than a fifteen-year-old. He appeared to have made the transition

from Harlem to an elite private academy without difficulty. His grades were decent and his confidence was intact. "It's different there," he said. "The work isn't so easy. And it's quiet. I'm used to noise. But we had good preparation for it, and the school is small enough so you can become close to everybody."

39   Christina Giammalva, who until recently divided her time between teaching history at New York Prep and placing her students at prep schools, believed that Jaime would make it at prep school. Although there were students with stronger academic records and better test scores, Jaime was clear-headed, a survivor. When his father disappeared from the family picture, Jaime, then thirteen, became the man of the house. All during his time at New York Prep he had to juggle the heavy and sometimes conflicting demands of home and school.

40   In terms of overall reading scores, New York Prep isn't impressive: in 1991 only 35 percent of the students there were reading at or above grade level. But typically eight or nine of the seventy ninth-graders at New York Prep, many of whom have lived lives at least as hard as Jaime's, will go on to private schools. Student programs involving Scarsdale High and Princeton University, and field trips to places like Boston and Washington, D.C., show New York Prep's students something of the world beyond the ghetto. One or two afternoons after school every week, 120 of the 210 students spend nearly an hour getting to Columbia University, where they are tutored by law-school and business-school students. Those accepted by private schools take an intensive summer course to hone their academic skills and prepare them psychologically for what's ahead. Almost all will go on to college. Don't pay too much attention to the test scores, the teachers at New York Prep write in their recommendation letters, because we know this student. We won't hide the weaknesses, but we will tell you why they're manageable. In ordinary junior highs in inner cities this degree of involvement in the lives of students is largely unheard of.

41   The teachers' predictions cannot be infallible, of course, because few among us live perfectly mapped-out and predictable lives. Certainly not most fifteen-year-olds—they believe in their own immortality, and their eyes are on many prizes all at once.

42   We know how treacherous the passage from ghetto to private school can be from stories like that of Edmund Perry, whose journey from Harlem to Phillips Exeter Academy ended in robbery and death. Jaime's story is not so tragic, only shadowed and human. During his first year at prep school he

was caught cheating—in Spanish, of all subjects—and placed on probation. This past spring, at the end of his junior year, he used a teacher's telephone calling card to phone his mother and his friends in East Harlem. He was found out—how could it have been otherwise?—and expelled. Now he is enrolled in a New York City public high school.

What Jaime Morelia did was plainly wrong, and his moral compass was calibrated finely enough for him to know that. The deeper puzzle is why he behaved as he did. Christina Giammalva speculates that for Jaime the psychological distance may have been too great, the demands to conform to prep-school mores too imposing. Perhaps, Giammalva says, he made those phone calls to invite rejection, rather than be forced to do the rejecting.

Jaime's failure cannot be chalked up entirely to adolescent acting-out, because the school's insensitivity is pertinent too. When Jaime first got into trouble, his prep-school mentors never called his mother to enlist her support, and the first she heard of her son's expulsion was after the fact. Nor is the school's attitude unusual—and this makes the success stories even more special. Another graduate of New York Prep, a boy I'll call Jamail Robinson, was almost kept from returning to a private school where he had spent two years because his mother, a security guard raising two children, owed the school $1,000. School officials were ready to bounce Jamail without even talking to his mother; it took several anxious phone calls from Giammalva to get him reinstated. This past June, when Jamail graduated from a private school (one of half a dozen or so New York Prep alumni to do so), he was picked by both the faculty and the students as the senior who best embodied their school's ideals.

The Key School, which occupies the basement of the same building that houses the Talented and Gifted School and the Harbor School for the Performing Arts, is a school that reflects the underside of reform in East Harlem. None of the Key School's 120 seventh- through ninth-graders chose to be there. The places in this school are filled by youngsters who can't make it elsewhere, and enrollment at Key keeps climbing. Desperate administrators of other alternative schools plead with its director, Iris Novak, to take one more hard-to-handle adolescent, one more kid that nobody else wants. The last arrival had stolen $600 collected for a school dinner from a teacher's handbag at his old school. Since the BETA School closed, there are almost no other schools in the district for problem students. Those who can't make it here may be sent to special-education classes for the emotionally disabled, where about one East Harlem child in fifteen winds up.

46   The Key School is a dark place, out of sight, with none of the amenities of the more elite schools. Its ceilings vibrate whenever students from the Harbor School are playing basketball or practicing their ballet movements in the gym upstairs. Its name could be a metaphor for opening up new opportunities or, perhaps more fittingly, for locking a jail cell.

47   As I talked with Novak, students came and went, pleading for the key to the bathroom, a privilege granted at the absolute discretion of the director. It's an emergency, each of them insisted. A burly ninth-grader stormed in, demanding the return of his hat, which Novak had confiscated earlier in the day. "Gimme back my fuckin' hat," he screamed at Novak. "You think I'm a nice kid but I'm not. I'm mean." Novak wrote it all down, and then silenced the kid with a look and a rumbling voice that comes from having trained for the stage. "I'm not your mother or sister or girlfriend or grandmother. I'm the director of this school. I demand to be treated with respect. There will be no 'fuck, fuck' here. You are suspended." The day before, after one student had held up another at gunpoint on the sidewalk, security guards were called in; they put the suspect up against the wall and frisked him.

48   Only nine percent of the students at the Key School are reading at grade level. This isn't surprising, given the composition of the school. Even among East Harlem schools that are not designated as repositories for problem children, more than a few have only one youngster in five—if that—making the grade, and have experienced a decline in performance levels during the past decade. The worst of these schools was Music 13, which until June of 1990 (when it was shut down) coped with seventh- through ninth-graders.

49   "If you're interested in music, a strong academic background, and high standards," the brochure given to parents bravely announced, "Music 13 is the place to be." The name of Music 13 was intended to reveal its special focus, and there was an able music teacher, Luis Rosa, on the premises. But nobody really chose to attend Music 13, and by the end few at the school cared much about music anymore. The "13" in its name turned out to be more significant than the "Music."

50   The building that housed it was formerly Junior High School 13, and when two of Deborah Meier's schools were moved there in 1985, some neighborhood parents rebelled. *We want to keep our own school,* they insisted—even though the junior high had been such a misery that most parents had

stopped sending their children there years before. A number of teachers also wanted to stay on, and a grandfather clause in the union contract entitled them to do so. Some of the half dozen who remained—"the grandfathers"—epitomized much of what has gone wrong with many big-city schools. During my visit to the school one teacher read *The New York Times* while students chattered, another shouted desperately for order, and a third delivered a by-the-book lesson to a class of uninterested ninth-graders. Often the teachers didn't bother to show up, or else let the director know a day ahead of time that they felt "a sickness coming on." Music 13 had become a school in name but not intention, a place of last resort.

Students like an eighth-grader I'll call Kevin Jones were   51
stuck. "Kevin is intelligent and articulate, with a real talent for science and basketball," Ira Lyons, the third director Music 13 had had in five years, told me. "He has more brains than I do." Kevin first attended Isaac Newton, but was kicked out after being accused of smashing the headlights of the director's car. He has had fights with other students at Music 13. Family conferences came to nothing when the boy's elderly and deeply religious grandmother insisted that he was no trouble at home. "High-ability kickouts don't mesh with low-ability kids," Lyons said. "He belongs in a school that would challenge him." But no other school was interested.

Every urban school district has its Kevin Joneses, and they're   52
probably no worse off at a place like Music 13 than at some run-down junior high in the Bronx. That reality points to the expedient bargain that has in effect been struck in East Harlem among those who have worked for reform. The deal is essentially this: Through the mechanism called choice—a mechanism that gives some options to parents and students but at the same time is rigged to give even more options to school directors—we can greatly improve the situation for about a third of our students, offering them a far better education than they could otherwise have had in one of the most battered neighborhoods in America. Perhaps we can even offer something useful to another third of our students. But the bottom third will be virtually abandoned—as they would have been anyway.

School by School by School

Confronted with crumbling buildings and daily episodes of   53
violence, with splintered families and refractory bureaucrats—problems that elsewhere might in themselves suck up all the energy of school leaders—East Harlem has transformed a

number of its schools. Elsewhere, initiatives are frequently abandoned when their champions leave, but the alternative schools in East Harlem have survived the departure of Alvarado and Fliegel, the entrepreneurs who launched the plan. They have survived a procession of chancellors at 110 Livingston Street, most of whom have been cool to what the district is doing. They weathered a 1988 financial scandal that brought down Alvarado's successor, cast suspicion on Fliegel's successor as director of alternative schools (who was later exonerated), and for a while left East Harlem's schools in the hands of an acting superintendent who made no secret of her dislike for the alternative-schools program. Whether any further progress is possible in District Four—and whether other New York City districts will be able to proceed with plans for similar restructuring depends on the impact of the continuing fiscal crisis in the New York City schools.

54   East Harlem, with all its problems, has built a far better school system than I have seen in any comparable neighborhood. For all the hype about reading-test scores, what's more impressive is the students' generally clearer writing and focused thinking, their greater self-confidence and understanding, and their willingness and ability to enter the world beyond the ghetto in high school and afterward. Graduates from junior highs in East Harlem *are* making it out of the barrio. In the intensely competitive environment of New York City's elite high schools, sorting is nearly as rigid as it was under the old British eleven-plus exam system. The four examination schools—Bronx High School of Science, Stuyvesant High, La Guardia High School, and Brooklyn Technical High School—are among the very best high schools in the nation. Another handful, including Aviation High and East Harlem's Manhattan Center for Science and Mathematics, enroll the next tier of students. The nonselective schools get the leftovers. In the mid-1970s fewer than ten of East Harlem's junior high graduates were accepted by the examination high schools. By 1987 things had radically changed. East Harlem sent 139 youngsters, or ten percent of the district's graduating class that year, to those elite high schools—double the citywide average. An additional 13 percent enrolled at four other high schools that also screen their students—a rate four times as high as the city average. That same year at least thirty-six students from East Harlem received scholarships to private schools, including some of the best ones in the country.

55   Some of the students who travel to East Harlem from other parts of the city volunteered to me that for the first time

in their lives they are being treated with respect by teachers. Teachers reported that the smallness and autonomy of the alternative schools enable them to identify a distinctive voice in each of their children and to respond in kind. In the corridors and directors' offices where teachers congregate, the talk is mainly about what works in the classroom and what doesn't, not about Macy's sales and last night's Knicks game. Not all the schools are as innovative as those that Deborah Meier founded, for there are, after all, only a handful of such educators. But as the history of good urban parochial schools suggests, educational innovation isn't essential to success. What *is* essential is that the school take the time to shape an identity that seems right to those who inhabit the premises, and that this effort be sustained by teachers and administrators who have a measure of independence, a feeling of being driven, and a capacity to know each of their charges. If the idea of intimate enclaves in factory-like city schools is going to take hold, it must happen not by treating East Harlem as a model to be mechanically applied, and certainly not by taking literally the misleading metaphor of the schools as a marketplace. Instead, it must happen as an approach adapted to the particularities of place.

Schools like those in East Harlem are being asked to accomplish the impossible—to challenge the highly achieving and rescue those who otherwise would drop out, to ease racial separation and reduce inequity in schooling, and all the while to function as the cutting edge of educational innovation. In truth, there are no easy paths even to modest progress. What's needed can be as time-consuming and undramatic as meticulous planning, into-the-wee-hours sessions with anxious school-board members, months of meetings with teachers and school directors to give content to the dreams, and then endless reassurances to parents troubled by what is new and untried. And even then, as District Four shows, there may well remain a large portion of the student population for whom reform might just as well never have occurred. 56

It is essential to risk the mistakes that so often accompany newness and to resist overpromising. Each school will have to find its own way, because everywhere the talents and the possibilities are different, but out of the process something of real value can emerge. This much, at least, East Harlem has to teach the rest of America, as the nation quietly but unmistakably embarks on the great experiment of remaking its schools, one by one. 57

Susan Tarves
Another Kind of School Choice

Susan Tarves was a student in a first-year composition course at Penn State in 1998 when she wrote the following essay, which was intended as a contribution to a Philadelphia-area newspaper. A product of the (coed) Haverford, Pennsylvania, public schools, near Philadelphia, Tarves is currently undecided about an area of college study.

1   "School choice": everywhere you go these days, you hear about school choice. Usually the people who advocate (or oppose) school choice are referring to offering students a choice among public schools, or making it easier for parents to choose among public and private schools. But in fact there is also another school choice that is increasingly being discussed these days: the choice of a single-gender education. Recently many people have been advocating single-gender schools as a means of offering students a better educational experience; at the same time, others have been ridiculing single-gender schools as anachronistic. Do single-gender schools offer something special to their students? Is a gender-segregated environment the best option for your son or daughter? Let me outline the arguments for and against this educational philosophy so that you can make a more informed decision about the matter.

2   Just what is single-gender education? Actually, there are several forms of it, and different approaches to its implementation. Sometimes a coeducational school will offer certain courses to all students, separate students in those courses by gender, and structure the class and teaching method according to different learning styles depending on gender. The Walker School in Marietta, Georgia is an example of this approach. For her first two classes of the day, seventh grader Amanda Xiques does not encounter boys, reports Jeff Archer in *Education Weekly* (April 8, 1998). More commonly, however, an entire school consists of students of only one gender. Indeed, all-female and all-male institutions are widespread in this country. These schools are either private or parochial. Single-gender public elementary and high schools (but not colleges) are considered illegal in the United States because they constitute discrimination based on gender, explains Robert McGinnis

of the Family Research Council. Many all-male institutions, such as The Haverford School located outside of Philadelphia, have long and proud histories stretching back over a century. All female schools, including Villa Maria Academy in Malvern, Pennsylvania, have emerged more recently.

The Family Research Council offers several reasons why   3
single-gender schools offer a wise choice. Students of both genders enrolled in single-gender schools seem to enjoy higher academic performance: they interact more with faculty and exhibit increased verbal aggressiveness and higher intellectual self-esteem. Women at single-sex schools are more likely than their peers at coed institutions to pursue majors such as science, management, and economics. They also have more opportunities for leadership and aspire to higher academic degrees. Men at single-gender schools are more likely than their peers at coed schools to get good grades, participate in honors programs, graduate with honors, and pursue careers in business, law, or college teaching. Both men and women at single-sex schools are more likely than students at coed institutions to be satisfied with curricular variety, student and faculty relations, quality of instruction, and friendships with other students. According to research from the Harvard School of Education and the American Association of University Women (http://dsha.k12. wi.us/single.htm), in a coed classroom, teachers call on the boys four times more often than the girls; the teachers most often direct the "challenging questions" to the boys while the female students receive less difficult questions; the teachers are far more likely to praise and give positive reinforcement to the intellectual contributions of males in the classroom, while making note of the socialization skills of girls; and in general, teachers give more attention to boys than girls. It's little wonder, then, that many young women experience a decline in self-esteem as their voices become silenced.

Researchers confirm that by senior year, students at single-   4
gender schools excel beyond their peers from coed schools in the areas of reading, writing, and science. Overall graduates of women's high schools are more satisfied with their schools and the quality of the teaching, more open-minded about their roles and possibilities, and relieved of some of the social pressures of adolescence (http://dsha.k12.wi.us/single.htm). In her widely praised recent book *Reviving Ophelia: Saving the Selves of Adolescent Girls,* Dr. Mary Pipher explains the extent of gender discrimination in the typical classroom:

5　　In classes, boys are twice as likely to be seen as role models, five times as likely to receive teachers' attention and twelve times as likely to speak up in class. In textbooks, one-seventh of all illustrations of children are of girls. Teachers choose many more classroom activities that appeal to boys than to girls. Girls are exposed to almost three times as many boy-centered stories as girl-centered stories. Boys tend to be portrayed as clever, brave, creative and resourceful, while girls are depicted as kind, dependent and docile. Girls read six times as many biographies of males as of females. Boys are more likely to be praised for academics and intellectual work, while girls are more likely to be praised for their clothing, behaving properly and obeying rules. Boys are likely to be criticized for their behavior, while girls are criticized for intellectual inadequacy. (62)

6　　Proponents of single-gender schools, therefore, argue that separating girls and boys results in positive effects for both. Chris Mikles, the founder of a successful female-only math class, notes on the Contemporary Women's Issues Database that "Girls learn in different ways than boys, and, up until now, educators have failed to recognize that." "They [girls] are intellectually curious, serious about their studies, and achieve more," adds Robert Johnson (an English teacher in an all girl school) in *Failing at Fairness* by Myra and David Sadker. Many people support the belief that girls and boys respond differently to different learning styles. "Boys tend to compete in class, quickly raising their hands or even blurting out answers; girls more often work well in small groups with other students," reports Jeff Archer. By acknowledging these differences, single-gender schools benefit both boys and girls, many believe.

7　　Many people also agree that single-sex education is more comfortable for the students, especially during adolescence, typically an awkward time for teenagers who are beginning to gain interest in the opposite sex and striving to be accepted by their peers. "Sometimes you do feel more comfortable, more inclined to ask questions.... Your hand just seems to go up," says thirteen-year-old Amanda (reported by Archer). And it is not just girls who feel more comfortable. Boys at this age respond similarly to the girls. Sixth-grader Casey McDonagh says, "It's easier [in a single-sex environment] because we don't have to worry about being embarrassed in front of the girls," reports Ann O'Hanlon (in the January 24, 1998 *Washington Post*). By eliminating the element of possible embarrassment, girls and boys often find it easier to voice their opinion; therefore, they become more assertive and self-assured.

But not everyone feels so positive about single-gender edu-   8
cation. A report by The American Association for University Women, summarized by Beth Reinhard in the May/June 1998 issue of *Teacher Magazine,* contends that single-gender educa-tion is not necessarily better than coeducation. The group believes that it is "small classes and schools, a focused curric-ulum, and unbiased teaching are what matters," not gender segregation. In other words, the report indicates other factors besides gender segregation account for the high quality of many such schools. For example, teachers need to address the learning styles of individuals, not genders. Just because children are of the same gender, one cannot assume that they possess the same learning style; learning styles vary more among individuals than between genders.

Others contend that there is still far too little research to   9
justify a rush to single-gender education. James Bulter in an article entitled "Counterpoint" speaks for many others:

> Recently, some public schools have re-instituted single sex ed-   10
> ucation and this raises some serious questions. These schools
> use statistics from many studies to justify this decision. They
> claim that once girls reach the junior high and high school
> years, they let themselves be ignored in the fields of math and
> science in order not to show up the boys. If this is happening,
> then this is something we have to deal with but single sex edu-
> cation is not the answer.... If girls are being intimidated in the
> math and science fields then we need to change this. Some-
> body is obviously teaching girls this behavior so it should be
> able to be untaught. (www.ukiahilite.zapcom.net/pcpl.html)

In "Don't Separate the Girls from the Boys," Anne Fuentes (a   11
Prudential Fellow at Columbia Journalism School research-ing children's issues) agrees: "Single-sex education is worse than a cheap fix masked as educational reform. It's a strategy that depends on stereotyping both boys and girls. Boys learn that they are the problem. Girls learn that they are helpless victims who can't count on the system to create a safe learn-ing environment for all students."

Studies on the subject of single-gender schools are still pre-   12
liminary. Janice Weinman, executive director of American As-sociation of University Women, is "concerned that people are rushing it [single-gender education] without the research to

back it up," reports Archer. Critics of gender-segregated schools frequently charge that the students in those schools may be unprepared to interact with the opposite sex in college. "It was definitely an adjustment," Trish Henwood told me. (She is a freshman at Georgetown University who attended an all-girls high school outside of Philadelphia.) "I really wasn't quite sure how to act with guys in my classes. I hope it will just take a little time and I'll get used to it." Many feel that isolating the sexes is doing a social disservice to the students—that sheltering students from the real world makes little sense. When these students graduate from high school and enter college, they will suddenly be exposed to the opposite sex in classroom, work, and social environments. Often their ability to communicate with the opposite sex is weak in comparison with their peers who have been educated in a coed environment. "It's kind of frustrating; sometimes I feel like I'm the only one not used to having guys in my class," offers Trish Henwood. "Girls and boys are going to need to know how to deal with one another before they find themselves in a job situation," claims Bulter; "this would slow production and create higher degrees of stress." Students from gender-segregated schools may not only find themselves at a comparative disadvantage socially, but they may also find it difficult to relate to their peers of the opposite sex, simply because they have never had to do so in the past. A gender-sheltered environment, many feel, lacks the gender diversity needed to develop lifelong skills in students.

13   Is single-sex education the best choice for your child? Maybe. The argument between proponents and opponents may reflect the fact that research on the question is still preliminary and incomplete. It probably also reflects differences between what people value most about elementary and secondary education. In the end, a decision about which kind of school is best perhaps depends on the individual child.

Jonathan Kozol

A Tale of Two Schools: How Poor Children Are Lost to the World

The following article was published in the Los Angeles Times *in October 1991; it amounts to an excerpt from Kozol's polemical book* Savage Inequalities: Children in America's Schools, *published in the same year. In 1964, Kozol, a teacher at the time at an inner-city school in Boston, had described in* Death at an Early Age *the terrible conditions that he found in schools in poor neighborhoods.* Savage Inequalities *emerged from his visits twenty-five years later to similar schools in places like Camden, New Jersey; Bronx, New York; East St. Louis, Illinois; and Washington, D.C,—and from his conviction that the gap between schools for the rich and those for the poor in the United States has only been widening, not narrowing.*

New Trier's physical setting might well make the students 1
of Du Sable High School envious. The Chicago suburb school is, says a student, "a maple land of beauty and civility." While Du Sable is sited on one crowded Chicago city block, New Trier students have the use of 27 acres. While Du Sable's science students have to settle for makeshift equipment, New Trier's students have superior labs and up-to-date technology. One wing of the school, a physical-education center that includes three separate gyms, also contains a fencing room, a wrestling room and studios for dance instruction. In all, the school has seven gyms as well as an Olympic pool.

"This is a school with a lot of choices," says one student at 2
New Trier; and this hardly seems an overstatement if one studies the curriculum. Courses in music, art and drama are so varied and abundant that students can virtually major in these subjects in addition to their academic programs. The modern and classical language department offers Latin and six other foreign languages. In a senior literature class, students are reading Nietzsche, Darwin, Plato, Freud and Goethe.

Average class size is 24 children; classes for slower learners 3
hold 15.

The wealth of New Trier's geographical district provides 4
$340,000 worth of taxable property for each child; Chicago's property wealth affords only one-fifth this much. Nonetheless, *Town and Country,* which profiled the school, gives New Trier's parents credit for a "willingness to pay enough...in

taxes" to make this one of the state's best-funded schools. New Trier, according to the magazine, is "a striking example of what is possible when citizens want to achieve the best for their children." Families move here "seeking the best," and their children "make good use" of what they're given. Both statements may be true, but *Town and Country* flatters the privileged for having privilege but terms it aspiration.

5   "Competition is the lifeblood of New Trier," *Town and Country* writes. But there is one kind of competition that these children will not need to face. They will not compete against the children who attended Du Sable.

6   Conditions at Du Sable High School, which I visited in 1990, seem in certain ways to be improved. Improvement, however, is a relative term. Du Sable is better than it was three or four years ago. It is still a school that would be shunned—or, probably, shut down—if it were serving a white middle-class community. The building, a three-story Tudor structure, is in fairly good repair and, in this respect, contrasts with its immediate surroundings, which are almost indescribably despairing. The school, whose student population is 100% black, has no campus and no schoolyard, but there is at least a full-sized playing field and track. Overcrowding is not a problem. Much to the reverse, it is uncomfortably empty. Built in 1935 and holding some 4,500 students in past years, its student population is now fewer than 1,600. Of these students, according to data provided by the school, 646 are "chronic truants."

7   The graduation rate is 25%. Of those who get to senior year, only 17% are in a college-preparation program. Twenty percent are in the general curriculum, a stunning 63% in vocational classes.

8   A vivid sense of loss is felt by standing in the cafeteria in early spring, when students file in to choose their courses for the following year. "These are the ninth graders," says a supervising teacher; but, of the official freshman class of some 600 children, only 350 fill the room. An hour later the 11th graders come to choose their classes: I count at most 170 students.

9   The faculty includes some excellent teachers, but there are others, says the principal, who don't belong in education. "I can't do anything with them but I'm not allowed to fire them," he says.

10   In a 12th-grade English class, the students are learning to pronounce a list of words. The words are not derived from any context; they are simply written on a list. A tall boy strug-

gles to read "fastidious," "gregarious," "auspicious," "fatuous." When he struggles to pronounce "egregious," I ask him if he knows its meaning. It turns out that he has no idea. The teacher never asks the children to write the words or use them in a sentence. The lesson baffles me. It may be that these are words that will appear on a required test that states impose now in the name of "raising standards," but it all seems dreamlike and surreal.

After lunch, I talk with a group of students who are hoping   11
to go on to college but do not seem sure of what they'll need to do to make this possible. Only one out of five seniors in the group has filed an application, and it is already April. Pamela, the one who did apply, however, tells me she neglected to submit her grades and college-entrance test results and therefore has to start again. The courses she is taking seem to rule out application to a four-year college. She tells me she is taking Spanish, literature, physical education, Afro-American history and a class she terms "job strategy." When I ask her what this is, she says, "It teaches how to dress and be on time and figure your deductions." She's a bright, articulate student, and it seems quite sad that she has not had any of the richness of curriculum that would have been given to her at a high school like New Trier.

The children in the group seem not just lacking in impor-   12
tant, useful information that would help them to achieve their dreams, but, in a far more drastic sense, cut off and disconnected from the outside world. In talking of some recent news events, they speak of Moscow and Berlin, but all but Pamela are unaware that Moscow is the capital of the Soviet Union or that Berlin is in Germany. Several believe that Jesse Jackson is the mayor of New York City. Listening to their guesses and observing their confusion, I am thinking of the students at New Trier High. These children live in truly separate worlds. What do they have in common? Yet the kids before me seem so innocent and spiritually clean and also—most of all—so vulnerable. It's as if they have been stripped of all the armament— the reference points, the facts, the reasoning, the elemental weapons—that suburban children take for granted.

"It took an extraordinary combination of greed, racism,   13
political cowardice and public apathy," writes James D. Squires, the former editor of the Chicago Tribune, "to let the public schools in Chicago get so bad." He speaks of the schools as a costly result of "the political orphaning of the urban poor...daytime warehouses for inferior students...a bottomless pit."

14   The results of these conditions are observed in thousands
of low-income children in Chicago, who are virtually dis-
joined from the worldview, even from the basic reference
points, of the American experience. A 16-year-old girl who
has dropped out discusses her economic prospects with a TV
interviewer.

15   "How much money would you like to make in a year?" asks
the reporter.

16   "About $2,000," she replies.

17   The reporter looks bewildered by this answer. This teenage girl, he says, "has no clue that $2,000 a year isn't enough
to survive anywhere in America, not even in her world."

Theodore Sizer

Horace's Compromise

*Born in 1932 and now retired, Theodore Sizer formerly chaired
the education department at Brown University. His book*
Horace's Compromise: The Dilemma of the American High
School, *published in 1984, offers a program of reform for U.S.
high schools; the book describes the frustrations (and their
sources) of a fictional but representative English teacher,
Horace Smith, who is forced to compromise his best educational instincts in the face of a fragmented and fragmenting
high school system. In 1992, Sizer wrote* Horace's School,
*which proposes a series of solutions to Horace's problems and
those of his fictional Franklin High School. Sizer has pioneered
the Coalition of Essential Schools, which now has over 800
member schools. Following is the first chapter from* Horace's
School.*

1   Meet Horace Smith, fifty-nine, a veteran English teacher at
Franklin High. Among parents and graduates, he is widely
considered a star faculty member of this inner suburban high
school of 1350 pupils. Certainly he is respected by his colleagues; they find him the professional's professional, even to
a fault. While many of the faculty who are his age are already
considering retirement, thanks to the state's generous annuity
plan, Horace is not. He believes—perversely, he often thinks

—that Franklin High is not nearly what it could be. He wants
to stay on and make it better.

The good light in which the community sees the school is   2
not deserved, he feels. Franklin is a caring place, but the kids
worry Horace. Many are lively, well intentioned, and adept at
cranking out acceptable test scores, but they are without the
habits of serious thought, respectful skepticism, and curiosity
about much of what lies beyond their immediate lives. They
lack assurance, skill, and interest in confronting the stuff of
Franklin's curriculum and committing their God-given minds
to strenuous use.

Sure, they rack up lists of "extracurriculars" to dazzle uni-   3
versity admissions officers, but even when they show a dash
of substance, too many of them lack style, that gossamer
quality which separates the interesting person from the conventional one. They get top grades on the English Advanced
Placement exams, but never read a serious piece of fiction
outside or beyond school. They score high on the social studies tests, but later will vote for political candidates on impulse, if they vote at all.

The kids play a game with school, making deals with us,   4
striking bargains. What will be on the test, Mr. Smith? Will
this count in the grade, Mr. Smith? How many pages must
this be, Mr. Smith? When do we have to read this by, Mr.
Smith? If we do this, will you ease up on that? They all ought
to be ambassadors, Horace thinks, wheeler-dealers striking
bargains and making treaties. However, the treaties will be
ones to lessen work, lessen the pain of thinking anew, lessen
anything that may get into the way of having a happy time after school. Treaties to protect the Good Life. Horace snorts at
himself: What a cynic I am. Aren't we adults that way too, excessively so? What are all of us coming to?

Many of Horace's colleagues find his criticism harsh, but   5
he persists. We do not know the half of what these kids can
do, he contends. But, his friends retort, can one school turn
them around? The whole society is soft. The kids' culture is
defined by MTV and cravings created by national merchan-
dise. Even their parents do not want the school to change
much. Get Susie into a good college, they say. And if we do,
they love us. If we do not, they blame us. But *style*? Come on,
Horace.

Horace understands the familiar lament. And he knows   6
that Franklin hasn't many of the searing problems swamping
the nearby city schools. For kids in those schools, there's not
even a question of developing style; sheer survival is their

task. He also remembers the exceptional kids he taught who did have fresh, inquiring, informed minds, and thoughtful hearts too. Why can't we have more kids like those, he wonders. Schools can help shape them, or at the least encourage those happy tendencies. Why must schooling, and its typical products, be so mindless? It need not be so. And though the culture out there may be inattentive, the school—even Franklin High School—can do something about it.

7   That, Horace knows, is a presumption. Who are teachers to set standards? Who says that they have a corner on wisdom? Horace worries about this. The schools should reflect what the culture wants, and if the culture is careless, then the school can be careless.

8   But, then, what is the role of the teacher? Merely to be the agent of the culture? No, Horace says, we must try to be better than that. And, contrary to conventional wisdom, most parents are our allies. What they want, at heart, is more than a ticket for their offspring to a prestigious college. They want that, yes, but they want more; and it is by an alliance of aware and demanding teachers, parents, and adolescents that a better school can be molded, a thoughtful place to teach thoughtful young citizens.

9   A thoughtful place. Horace hesitates on this, because he knows from decades of experience that Franklin is, if nothing else, unexamined. Like most high schools, it just rolls on, fettered by routines of long standing. The result is a cacophony of jumbled practices, orchestrated only by a complex computer-driven schedule whose instrument is a bell system and whose ushers are assistant principals.

10   The faculty itself, he muses, is hardly thoughtful about its own situation. The status quo is never challenged. We have curriculum committees that talk only about revising the accepted subjects, never pondering what the curriculum could be. We have committees on schedule changes that never ask the basic questions about the uses of time. We "restructure" while assuming that all the existing building materials and architectural commitments—physical and intellectual—will remain as they are.

11   Horace knows that the status quo *is* the problem. It forces him to compromise in ways that cripple his teaching, his ability to create thoughtful students. Compromises are always necessary in the real world, Horace admits; and the issue, then, is which compromises will serve the students best. Only by examining the existing compromises, however painful that may be, and moving beyond them to better compromises, can

one form a more thoughtful school. And only in thoughtful schools can thoughtful students be hatched.

Horace's complaints are many and fundamental. It would be easier if the system were basically sound, but the lamentable truth is that it is not, and that the complex routines of schools are all related. Question one, and you question all. 12

Take Horace's student load. Officially it should be 120, five classes of twenty-four students each, the "contract ratio" for English teachers. This year it is 132. Horace's courses are popular, and he has difficulty saying no to eager kids, particularly those who have studied with him before. Horace knows that he should insist on a writing assignment from every one of those youngsters every day, or at least every other day, and that he should promptly read, comment on, and return these papers. But with 120? Impossible. Spending just five out-of-class minutes per week looking at the work of each student and, at least once a month, talking privately with the youngster would total ten hours—ten hours of enervating work, two hours every evening, Monday through Friday, week after week. And this in addition to all the rest he has to do outside those contact hours in class with the kids, not to mention his evening work at the family's liquor store to help meet the household bills. So, like most English teachers, he does not do the careful reading and criticizing he knows is so valuable for students. 13

Accordingly, Horace recognizes that he does not know many of his kids well enough to understand really how their minds work, how and why they make mistakes, what motivates them, what stars they seek to reach or whether each hankers after a star at all. Yes, most are acquaintances; they hail him in the hallways. But does he know them well enough to teach them powerfully, know the ways of their minds and moods? No, not even close. Horace compromises. He gets to know a few students well, usually those who interest him especially or who press themselves to his attention. The kids in the middle remain a genial blur. Indeed, Horace wryly admits most of them cherish their anonymity. If Mr. Smith really knows me, then he'd find out that.... 14

During the school day, the students come to Horace by "classes," ninth grade, tenth grade, and the rest. A student is in a particular class on the basis of her or his birthday. To be out of step, sixteen in the ninth grade or fourteen in the eleventh grade, is cause for comment, usually contemptuous. Dummy. Nerd. One of *those* kids. The assumption behind the system is that kids of the same age are essentially alike, more 15 or less teachable in the same ways and properly held to similar standards. Franklin High School splits each grade into three lumps, honors, college prep, and regular, as well as special needs. But the prevailing, and overwhelming, characterization of students is by grade level. Teachers ask, *What's your name? What grade are you in?* The answers provide the two critical labels. Because all the kids in each grade have experienced, it is presumed, the same number of hours of schooling, they should, save at the extremes, all know the same things.

16   Horace knows better. Young people grow intellectually, physically, and socially at different rates, often with mysterious spurts and stops along the way. Some kids excel at language and flounder in mathematics; the hotshot in one area is not necessarily great in another. Further, not all kids pay attention at school at any given moment, for benign or deplorable reasons. So by their high school years the youngster's potential and actual school performance often diverge: "ninth grade" is an administratively useful concept, but one that tells a teacher far less about a student's intellectual and emotional development than the grouping would suggest.

17   One copes, however, largely by not being careful, by deliberately not attending to the record and specialness and stage of growth and disposition of each youngster. They are all *ninth-graders.* Treat them the same—same curriculum, same textbook, same pedagogy, same tests, same standards, same everything.

18   It defies common sense, Horace knows. Age grading hurts some kids, swelling the heads of those who appear, for whatever obvious or mysterious reasons, to be "swift" and humiliating the "slow." Pigeonholing honors, regular, and special needs students sets up the self-fulfilling prophecies, *Oh no, Mr. Smith, I couldn't take AP English. I'm not an honors student....* Every year Horace sees the swift kid who plugs hard, with the confidence of being perceived as honors quality, and the slow youngster who ignores his talents, giving up, acting up, not caring, finding school a place of unrelieved and anticipated failure.

19   Franklin High School uses plenty of public relations talk about "taking each child individually," but the school's practices belie the boast. For example, there is virtually no attempt, Horace ruefully recalls, to get thorough information to a student's new teacher about the youngster's history in school. Students do have files someplace, Horace knows. Teachers don't read them, though, and are not encouraged to do so. In any event, there are too many to absorb. May as well

treat 'em all the same. Or accept someone else's judgment about how swift a kid is, and go with it. Expect more, or expect less. Compromise with your common sense: the kids are different, but we can't admit it, even to ourselves.

The curriculum does not help. Franklin High School has a   20
statement of goals, but it is as vague as it is hortatory and conventional. The goals connect only rhetorically with the formal Course of Study. The latter is laid out by course and grade and is usually cast as a list of ideas, classics to be read, facts, skills, procedures, and qualities of character to be admired, opportunities to stock one's mind. Simply, the curriculum, however artfully described, is a listing of what the *teachers* will do, what "things" the kids will be "exposed" to. The students remain invisible, lumped in their age-graded cohorts, ready to watch the teachers' parade of things.

Horace knows this is backward. What counts is what the   21
students do, as Horace has learned from the Theater Club plays he directs. The members know what the "target" is. Others find targets in some of the more imaginative Advanced Placement courses. But there are few such compelling ends in view in the core curriculum; the destinations are clearly cast in terms of what the students should be able to do. Except for aiming to help students pass the tests, the formal Course of Study Guide says little about what the material *means*. We teachers are "to cover" the Lake poets, and the students should then be able to answer questions about them. How the students are to *use* the experience is not addressed. This is as depressing as it is confusing, but Horace continues to compromise. We will all read *Hamlet* during the spring term, and there will be one test for all eleventh-graders. . . .

Franklin's "goal statement" talks of graduates able to   22
"function in society and the economy as useful citizens." Horace would put that as "making sense of the world." Either way, it assumes that Franklin alumni will see which issues are of consequence to themselves and others, will be competent to analyze these situations, to sort them out, and will be both able and disposed to do something about them. Some would say that this means that graduates should be interested in learning and practiced in teaching themselves, able to figure out their world and motivated to do something about it.

Fine, Horace thinks. But how is the school's curriculum or-   23
ganized? By subjects, most of which are poorly defined and each of which is planned in almost total isolation from the others. The stuff of these subjects is offered up to students in fifty-two-minute slivers of time, rapid fire.

24   Horace wonders whether this gives kids practice in making sense of the world. Even the teachers in the English Department can't agree on what their subject really is; the mathematics sequence has no planned connection with science courses; and the teachers of literature, art, music, and drama pay attention only to each art separately. Making sense is tough even for adults; despite its goal statement, Franklin gives students little practice in the craft. Indeed, the high school's presentation of the curriculum guarantees superficiality.

25   These realities sting Horace, but he goes along. He compromises. The faculty doesn't like to hear any sort of fundamental criticism. We're tired of being the butt of all the griping, they say. Furthermore, this list of subjects is what the colleges want. A likely story, Horace thinks. Do the colleges want kids schooled in intellectual chaos?

26   Give a little, get along, compromise. Yes, sometimes there is electricity in the classrooms, but not often enough. The kids compromise too, taking what is offered, observing that to which they are exposed, more or less cranking out the tests, and then forgetting most of it. Feeling good is important, not only about oneself but also about the school. Franklin Pride.

27   Horace remembers a devilish experiment that a visiting consultant recently suggested: give students a test they took twelve to fifteen months earlier, and see how they perform. What had they retained? Horace winces at the thought. Kids forget so much so quickly. It is better that school accentuate the immediate, the stuff of the last unit, rather than instill intellectual habits. Horace plays the game too. Last year's English is expected to be gone, and if we hold a student responsible for it, we are "unfair." And so we stress the immediate.

28   All this is agonizing for Horace. He resents his compromises, and derides himself for making them. Some respected colleagues share his frustration, but they know that an honest evaluation of the school's compromises will open a Pandora's box. Everything in the school affects everything else. That finely tuned complexity which is the daily schedule cannot withstand more than trivial adjustments, and more than trivial adjustments are needed to improve Franklin High. The ultimate frustration for Horace is that even if a corps of like-minded, risk-taking colleagues evolved an ambitious, sensible new plan for Franklin, they would not have the authority to act on it. The major elements of schooling are controlled outside the teachers' world. The state, or its contractor firms, writes the tests. The state mandates when each subject is to

be taught; it and the district control that key coinage of school, the time of teachers and students. Evaluations of school and teachers, the union contract, the departmental divisions, all run according to traditional formulas.

Horace knows that he has limited control over his own destiny. Others would have to affirm his intention to teach with better compromises, to organize his and the students' work along more sensible lines. Obviously, they don't trust us, Horace thinks. The folk higher up are sure they know better. We always have to ask permission. Teachers with hall passes not to the bathroom but to better schools, he snorts to himself. Of all Horace's feelings about his work, this is the most bitter.

David P. Gardner et al.
A Nation at Risk

In 1981, Secretary of Education T. H. Bell created the National Commission on Excellence in Education and directed it to report within eighteen months on the quality of education in U.S. schools. Sparked by a widespread public perception that "something is wrong" with our educational system, the Commission (chaired by David P. Gardner, president of the University of California, and comprising eighteen teachers, school administrators, university presidents, and distinguished public officials and business leaders) created a national stir with its final report, "A Nation at Risk," reprinted (with some small omissions) below. More than a decade later, the report continues to provide a context for discussions of educational reform in the United States.

Our Nation is at risk. Our once unchallenged preeminence in commerce, industry, science, and technological innovation is being overtaken by competitors throughout the world. This report is concerned with only one of the many causes and dimensions of the problem, but it is the one that undergirds American prosperity, security, and civility. We report to the American people that while we can take justifiable pride in what our schools and colleges have historically accomplished and contributed to the United States and the well-being of its people, the educational foundations of our society are presently being eroded by a rising tide of mediocrity that threatens our very future as a Nation and a people. What was unimaginable a generation ago has begun to occur—others are matching and surpassing our educational attainments.

2   If an unfriendly foreign power had attempted to impose on America the mediocre educational performance that exists today, we might well have viewed it as an act of war. As it stands, we have allowed this to happen to ourselves. We have even squandered the gains in student achievement made in the wake of the Sputnik challenge. Moreover, we have dismantled essential support systems which helped make those gains possible. We have, in effect, been committing an act of unthinking, unilateral educational disarmament.

3   Our society and its educational institutions seem to have lost sight of the basic purposes of schooling, and of the high expectations and disciplined effort needed to attain them. This report, the result of 18 months of study, seeks to generate reform of our educational system in fundamental ways and to renew the Nation's commitment to schools and colleges of high quality throughout the length and breadth of our land.

4   That we have compromised this commitment is, upon reflection, hardly surprising, given the multitude of often conflicting demands we have placed on our Nation's schools and colleges. They are routinely called on to provide solutions to personal, social, and political problems that the home and other institutions either will not or cannot resolve. We must understand that these demands on our schools and colleges often exact an educational cost as well as a financial one.

5   On the occasion of the Commission's first meeting, President Reagan noted the central importance of education in American life when he said: "Certainly there are few areas of American life as important to our society, to our people, and to our families as our schools and colleges." This report, therefore, is as much an open letter to the American people as it is a report to the Secretary of Education. We are confident that the American people, properly informed, will do what is right for their children and for the generations to come.

The Risk

6   History is not kind to idlers. The time is long past when America's destiny was assured simply by an abundance of

natural resources and inexhaustible human enthusiasm, and by our relative isolation from the malignant problems of older civilizations. The world is indeed one global village. We live among determined, well-educated, and strongly motivated competitors. We compete with them for international standing and markets, not only with products but also with the ideas of our laboratories and neighborhood workshops. America's position in the world may once have been reasonably secure with only a few exceptionally well-trained men and women. It is no longer.

The risk is not only that the Japanese make automobiles   7
more efficiently than Americans and have government subsidies for development and export. It is not just that the South Koreans recently built the world's most efficient steel mill, or that American machine tools, once the pride of the world, are being displaced by German products. It is also that these developments signify a redistribution of trained capability throughout the globe. Knowledge, learning, information, and skilled intelligence are the new raw materials of international commerce and are today spreading throughout the world as vigorously as miracle drugs, synthetic fertilizers, and blue jeans did earlier. If only to keep and improve on the slim competitive edge we still retain in world markets, we must dedicate ourselves to the reform of our educational system for the benefit of all—old and young alike, affluent and poor, majority and minority. Learning is the indispensable investment required for success in the "information age" we are entering.

Our concern, however, goes well beyond matters such as   8
industry and commerce. It also includes the intellectual, moral, and spiritual strengths of our people which knit together the very fabric of our society. The people of the United States need to know that individuals in our society who do not possess the levels of skill, literacy, and training essential to this new era will be effectively disenfranchised, not simply from the material rewards that accompany competent performance, but also from the chance to participate fully in our national life. A high level of shared education is essential to a free, democratic society and to the fostering of a common culture, especially in a country that prides itself on pluralism and individual freedom.

For our country to function, citizens must be able to reach   9
some common understandings on complex issues, often on short notice and on the basis of conflicting or incomplete evidence. Education helps form these common understandings, a point Thomas Jefferson made long ago in his justly famous dictum:

I know no safe depository of the ultimate powers of the society but the people themselves; and if we think them not enlightened enough to exercise their control with a wholesome discretion, the remedy is not to take it from them but to inform their discretion.

10   Part of what is at risk is the promise first made on this continent: All, regardless of race or class or economic status, are entitled to a fair chance and to the tools for developing their individual powers of mind and spirit to the utmost. This promise means that all children by virtue of their own efforts, competently guided, can hope to attain the mature and informed judgment needed to secure gainful employment and to manage their own lives, thereby serving not only their own interests but also the progress of society itself.

Indicators of the Risk

11   The educational dimensions of the risk before us have been amply documented in testimony received by the Commission. For example:

- International comparisons of student achievement, completed a decade ago, reveal that on 19 academic tests American students were never first or second and, in comparison with other industrialized nations, were last seven times.
- Some 23 million American adults are functionally illiterate by the simplest tests of everyday reading, writing, and comprehension.
- About 13 percent of all 17-year-olds in the United States can be considered functionally illiterate. Functional illiteracy among minority youth may run as high as 40 percent.
- Average achievement of high school students on most standardized tests is now lower than 26 years ago when Sputnik was launched.
- Over half the population of gifted students do not match their tested ability with comparable achievement in school.
- The College Board's Scholastic Aptitude Tests (SAT) demonstrate a virtually unbroken decline from 1963 to 1980. Average verbal scores fell over 50 points and

average mathematics scores dropped nearly 40 points.

- College Board achievement tests also reveal consistent declines in recent years in such subjects as physics and English.
- Both the number and proportion of students demonstrating superior achievement on the SATs (i.e., those with scores of 650 or higher) have also dramatically declined.
- There was a steady decline in science achievement scores of U.S. 17-year-olds as measured by national assessments of science in 1969, 1973, and 1977.
- Between 1975 and 1980, remedial mathematics courses in public 4-year colleges increased by 72 percent and now constitute one-quarter of all mathematics courses taught in those institutions.
- Average tested achievement of students graduating from college is also lower.
- Business and military leaders complain that they are required to spend millions of dollars on costly remedial education and training programs in such basic skills as reading, writing, spelling, and computation. The Department of the Navy, for example, reported to the Commission that one-quarter of its recent recruits cannot read at the ninth grade level, the minimum needed simply to understand written safety instructions. Without remedial work they cannot even begin, much less complete, the sophisticated training essential in much of the modern military.

These deficiencies come at a time when the demand for 12 highly skilled workers in new fields is accelerating rapidly. For example:

- Computers and computer-controlled equipment are penetrating every aspect of our lives—homes, factories, and offices.
- One estimate indicates that by the turn of the century millions of jobs will involve laser technology and robotics.
- Technology is radically transforming a host of other occupations. They include health care, medical science, energy production, food processing, construction, and the building, repair, and maintenance of

sophisticated scientific, educational, military, and industrial equipment.

13   Analysts examining these indicators of student performance and the demands for new skills have made some chilling observations. Educational researcher Paul Hurd concluded at the end of a thorough national survey of student achievement that within the context of the modern scientific revolution, "We are raising a new generation of Americans that is scientifically and technologically illiterate." In a similar vein, John Slaughter, a former Director of the National Science Foundation, warned of "a growing chasm between a small scientific and technological elite and a citizenry ill-informed, indeed uninformed, on issues with a science component."

14   But the problem does not stop there, nor do all observers see it the same way. Some worry that schools may emphasize such rudiments as reading and computation at the expense of other essential skills such as comprehension, analysis, solving problems, and drawing conclusions. Still others are concerned that an over-emphasis on technical and occupational skills will leave little time for studying the arts and humanities that so enrich daily life, help maintain civility, and develop a sense of community. Knowledge of the humanities, they maintain, must be harnessed to science and technology if the latter are to remain creative and humane, just as the humanities need to be informed by science and technology if they are to remain relevant to the human condition. Another analyst, Paul Copperman, has drawn a sobering conclusion. Until now, he has noted:

> Each generation of Americans has outstripped its parents in education, in literacy, and in economic attainment. For the first time in the history of our country, the educational skills of one generation will not surpass, will not equal, will not even approach, those of their parents.

15   It is important, of course, to recognize that *the average citizen* today is better educated and more knowledgeable than the average citizen of a generation ago—more literate, and exposed to more mathematics, literature, and science. The positive impact of this fact on the well-being of our country and the lives of our people cannot be overstated. Nevertheless, *the average graduate* of our schools and colleges today is not as well-educated as the average graduate of 25 or 35 years ago, when a much smaller proportion of our population com-

pleted high school and college. The negative impact of this
fact likewise cannot be overstated.

Hope and Frustration

Statistics and their interpretation by experts show only the   16
surface dimension of the difficulties we face. Beneath them
lies a tension between hope and frustration that characterizes
current attitudes about education at every level.

We have heard the voices of high school and college stu-   17
dents, school board members, and teachers; of leaders of industry, minority groups, and higher education; of parents and
State officials. We could hear the hope evident in their commitment to quality education and in their descriptions of
outstanding programs and schools. We could also hear the intensity of their frustration, a growing impatience with shoddiness in many walks of American life, and the complaint that
this shoddiness is too often reflected in our schools and colleges. Their frustration threatens to overwhelm their hope.

What lies behind this emerging national sense of frustra-   18
tion can be described as both a dimming of personal expectations and the fear of losing a shared vision for America.

On the personal level the student, the parent, and the car-   19
ing teacher all perceive that a basic promise is not being kept.
More and more young people emerge from high school ready
neither for college nor for work. This predicament becomes
more acute as the knowledge base continues its rapid expansion, the number of traditional jobs shrinks, and new jobs demand greater sophistication and preparation.

On a broader scale, we sense that this undertone of frustra-   20
tion has significant political implications, for it cuts across
ages, generations, races, and political and economic groups.
We have come to understand that the public will demand that
educational and political leaders act forcefully and effectively
on these issues. Indeed, such demands have already appeared
and could well become a unifying national preoccupation.
This unity, however, can be achieved only if we avoid the un-
productive tendency of some to search for scapegoats among
the victims, such as the beleaguered teachers.

On the positive side is the significant movement by politi-   21
cal and educational leaders to search for solutions—so far
centering largely on the nearly desperate need for increased
support for the teaching of mathematics and science. This
movement is but a start on what we believe is a larger and

more educationally encompassing need to improve teaching and learning in fields such as English, history, geography, economics, and foreign languages. We believe this movement must be broadened and directed toward reform and excellence throughout education.

Excellence in Education

22   We define "excellence" to mean several related things. At the level of the *individual learner,* it means performing on the boundary of individual ability in ways that test and push back personal limits, in school and in the workplace. Excellence characterizes a *school or college* that sets high expectations and goals for all learners, then tries in every way possible to help students reach them. Excellence characterizes a *society* that has adopted these policies, for it will then be prepared through the education and skill of its people to respond to the challenges of a rapidly changing world. Our Nation's people and its schools and colleges must be committed to achieving excellence in all these senses.

23   We do not believe that a public commitment to excellence and educational reform must be made at the expense of a strong public commitment to the equitable treatment of our diverse population. The twin goals of equity and high-quality schooling have profound and practical meaning for our economy and society, and we cannot permit one to yield to the other either in principle or in practice. To do so would deny young people their chance to learn and live according to their aspirations and abilities. It also would lead to a generalized accommodation to mediocrity in our society on the one hand or the creation of an undemocratic elitism on the other.

24   Our goal must be to develop the talents of all to their fullest. Attaining that goal requires that we expect and assist all students to work to the limits of their capabilities. We should expect schools to have genuinely high standards rather than minimum ones, and parents to support and encourage their children to make the most of their talents and abilities.

25   The search for solutions to our educational problems must also include a commitment to life-long learning. The task of rebuilding our system of learning is enormous and must be properly understood and taken seriously: Although a million and a half new workers enter the economy each year from our schools and colleges, the adults working today will still make up about 75 percent of the workforce in the year 2000.

These workers, and new entrants into the workforce, will need further education and retraining if they—and we as a Nation—are to thrive and prosper.

The Learning Society

In a world of ever-accelerating competition and change in   26
the conditions of the workplace, of ever-greater danger, and of ever-larger opportunities for those prepared to meet them, educational reform should focus on the goal of creating a Learning Society. At the heart of such a society is the commitment to a set of values and to a system of education that affords all members the opportunity to stretch their minds to full capacity, from early childhood through adulthood, learning more as the world itself changes. Such a society has as a basic foundation the idea that education is important not only because of what it contributes to one's career goals but also because of the value it adds to the general quality of one's life. Also at the heart of the Learning Society are educational opportunities extending far beyond the traditional institutions of learning, our schools and colleges. They extend into homes and workplaces; into libraries, art galleries, museums, and science centers; indeed, into every place where the individual can develop and mature in work and life. In our view, formal schooling in youth is the essential foundation for learning throughout one's life. But without life-long learning, one's skills will become rapidly dated.

In contrast to the ideal of the Learning Society, however, we   27
find that for too many people education means doing the minimum work necessary for the moment, then coasting through life on what may have been learned in its first quarter. But this should not surprise us because we tend to express our educational standards and expectations largely in terms of "minimum requirements." And where there should be a coherent continuum of learning, we have none, but instead an often incoherent, outdated patchwork quilt. Many individual, sometimes heroic, examples of schools and colleges of great merit do exist. Our findings and testimony confirm the vitality of a number of notable schools and programs, but their very distinction stands out against a vast mass shaped by tensions and pressures that inhibit systematic academic and vocational achievement for the majority of students. In some metropolitan areas basic literacy has become the goal rather than the starting point. In some colleges maintaining enrollments is of greater day-to-day concern than maintaining rigorous

academic standards. And the ideal of academic excellence as the primary goal of schooling seems to be fading across the board in American education.

28   Thus, we issue this call to all who care about America and its future: to parents and students; to teachers, administrators, and school board members; to colleges and industry; to union members and military leaders; to governors and State legislators; to the President; to members of Congress and other public officials; to members of learned and scientific societies; to the print and electronic media; to concerned citizens everywhere. America is at risk.

Recommendations

29   In light of the urgent need for improvement, both immediate and long term, this Commission has agreed on a set of recommendations that the American people can begin to act on now, that can be implemented over the next several years, and that promise lasting reform. The topics are familiar; there is little mystery about what we believe must be done. Many schools, districts, and States are already giving serious and constructive attention to these matters, even though their plans may differ from our recommendations in some details.

30   We wish to note that we refer to public, private, and parochial schools and colleges alike. All are valuable national resources. Examples of actions similar to those recommended below can be found in each of them.

31   We must emphasize that the variety of student aspirations, abilities, and preparation requires that appropriate content be available to satisfy diverse needs. Attention must be directed to both the nature of the content available and to the needs of particular learners. The most gifted students, for example, may need a curriculum enriched and accelerated beyond even the needs of other students of high ability. Similarly, educationally disadvantaged students may require special curriculum materials, smaller classes, or individual tutoring to help them master the material presented. Nevertheless, there remains a common expectation: We must demand the best effort and performance from all students, whether they are gifted or less able, affluent or disadvantaged, whether destined for college, the farm, or industry.

32   Our recommendations are based on the beliefs that everyone can learn, that everyone is born with an *urge* to learn which can be nurtured, that a solid high school education is within the reach of virtually all, and that life-long learning

will equip people with the skills required for new careers and for citizenship.

Recommendation A: Content. **We recommend** *that State* 33 *and local high school graduation requirements be strengthened and that,* at a minimum, all *students seeking a diploma be required to lay the foundations in the Five New Basics by taking the following curriculum during their 4 years of high school: (a) 4 years of English; (b) 3 years of mathematics; (c) 3 years of science; (d) 3 years of social studies; and (e) one-half year of computer science. For the college-bound, 2 years of foreign language in high school are strongly recommended in addition to those taken earlier.*

Recommendation B: Standards and Expectations. **We rec-** 34 **ommend** *that schools, colleges, and universities adopt more rigorous and measurable standards, and higher expectations, for academic performance and student conduct, and that 4-year colleges and universities raise their requirements for admission. This will help students do their best educationally with challenging materials in an environment that supports learning and authentic accomplishment.*

Recommendation C: Time. **We recommend** *significantly* 35 *more time be devoted to learning the New Basics. This will require more effective use of the existing school day, a longer school day, or a lengthened school year.*

Recommendation D: Teaching. **This recommendation** 36 *consists of seven parts. Each is intended to improve the preparation of teachers or to make teaching a more rewarding and respected profession. Each of the seven stands on its own and should not be considered solely as an implementing recommendation.*

1. Persons preparing to teach should be required to meet high educational standards, to demonstrate an aptitude for teaching, and to demonstrate competence in an academic discipline. Colleges and universities offering teacher preparation programs should be judged by how well their graduates meet these criteria.
2. Salaries for the teaching profession should be increased and should be professionally competitive, market-sensitive, and performance-based. Salary,

promotion, tenure, and retention decisions should be tied to an effective evaluation system that includes peer review so that superior teachers can be rewarded, average ones encouraged, and poor ones either improved or terminated.

3. School boards should adopt an 11-month contract for teachers. This would ensure time for curriculum and professional development, programs for students with special needs, and a more adequate level of teacher compensation.

4. School boards, administrators, and teachers should cooperate to develop career ladders for teachers that distinguish among the beginning instructor, the experienced teacher, and the master teacher.

5. Substantial nonschool personnel resources should be employed to help solve the immediate problem of the shortage of mathematics and science teachers. Qualified individuals including recent graduates with mathematics and science degrees, graduate students, and industrial and retired scientists could, with appropriate preparation, immediately begin teaching in these fields. A number of our leading science centers have the capacity to begin educating and retraining teachers immediately. Other areas of critical teacher need, such as English, must also be addressed.

6. Incentives, such as grants and loans, should be made available to attract outstanding students to the teaching profession, particularly in those areas of critical shortage.

7. Master teachers should be involved in designing teacher preparation programs and in supervising teachers during their probationary years.

America Can Do It

37   Despite the obstacles and difficulties that inhibit the pursuit of superior educational attainment, we are confident, with history as our guide, that we can meet our goal. The American educational system has responded to previous challenges with remarkable success. In the 19th century our land-grant colleges and universities provided the research and training that developed our Nation's natural resources and the rich agricultural bounty of the American farm. From the

late 1800s through mid-20th century, American schools provided the educated workforce needed to seal the success of the Industrial Revolution and to provide the margin of victory in two world wars. In the early part of this century and continuing to this very day, our schools have absorbed vast waves of immigrants and educated them and their children to productive citizenship. Similarly, the Nation's Black colleges have provided opportunity and undergraduate education to the vast majority of college-educated Black Americans.

More recently, our institutions of higher education have provided the scientists and skilled technicians who helped us transcend the boundaries of our planet. In the last 30 years, the schools have been a major vehicle for expanded social opportunity, and now graduate 75 percent of our young people from high school. Indeed, the proportion of Americans of college age enrolled in higher education is nearly twice that of Japan and far exceeds other nations such as France, West Germany, and the Soviet Union. Moreover, when international comparisons were last made a decade ago, the top 9 percent of American students compared favorably in achievement with their peers in other countries. 38

In addition, many large urban areas in recent years report that average student achievement in elementary schools is improving. More and more schools are also offering advanced placement programs and programs for gifted and talented students, and more and more students are enrolling in them. 39

We are the inheritors of a past that gives us every reason to believe that we will succeed. 40

A Final Word

This is not the first or only commission on education, and some of our findings are surely not new, but old business that now at last must be done. For no one can doubt that the United States is under challenge from many quarters. 41

Children born today can expect to graduate from high school in the year 2000. We dedicate our report not only to these children, but also to those now in school and others to come. We firmly believe that a movement of America's schools in the direction called for by our recommendations will prepare these children for far more effective lives in a far stronger America. 42

Our final word, perhaps better characterized as a plea, is that all segments of our population give attention to the 43 implementation of our recommendations. Our present plight did not appear overnight, and the responsibility for our current situation is widespread. Reform of our educational system will take time and unwavering commitment. It will require equally widespread, energetic, and dedicated action. For example, we call upon the National Academy of Sciences, National Academy of Engineering, Institute of Medicine, Science Service, National Science Foundation, Social Science Research Council, American Council of Learned Societies, National Endowment for the Humanities, National Endowment for the Arts, and other scholarly, scientific, and learned societies for their help in this effort. Help should come from students themselves; from parents, teachers, and school boards; from colleges and universities; from local, State, and Federal officials; from teachers' and administrators' organizations; from industrial and labor councils; and from other groups with interest in and responsibility for educational reform.

44   It is their America, and the America of all of us, that is at risk; it is to each of us that this imperative is addressed. It is by our willingness to take up the challenge, and our resolve to see it through, that America's place in the world will be either secured or forfeited. Americans have succeeded before and so we shall again.

Charles Dickens
What Is a Horse?

Was Charles Dickens (1812–1870) the greatest English novelist? This selection from the opening pages of Hard Times *(1854) illustrates Dickens's satiric edge; designed as a commentary on a "mechanical" system of education devised during the industrial revolution, it may also offer perspective on the schools of today.*

1   Thomas Gradgrind, sir. A man of realities. A man of fact and calculations. A man who proceeds upon the principle that two and two are four, and nothing over, and who is not to be talked into allowing for anything over. Thomas Gradgrind, sir—peremptorily Thomas—Thomas Gradgrind. With a rule and a pair of scales, and the multiplication table always in his

pocket, sir, ready to weigh and measure any parcel of human nature, and tell you exactly what it comes to. It is a mere question of figures, case of simple arithmetic. You might hope to get some other nonsensical belief into the head of George Gradgrind, or Augustus Gradgrind, or John Gradgrind, or Joseph Gradgrind (all suppositious, nonexistent persons), but into the head of Thomas Gradgrind—no sir!

In such terms Mr Gradgrind always mentally introduced 2 himself, whether to his private circle of acquaintance, or to the public in general. In such terms, no doubt, substituting the words 'boys and girls', for 'sir', Thomas Gradgrind now presented Thomas Gradgrind to the little pitchers before him, who were to be filled so full of facts.

Indeed, as he eagerly sparkled at them from the cellarage 3 before mentioned, he seemed a kind of cannon loaded to the muzzle with facts, and prepared to blow them clean out of the regions of the childhood at one discharge. He seemed a galvanizing apparatus, too, charged with a grim mechanical substitute for the tender young imaginations that were to be stormed away.

'Girl number twenty,' said Mr Gradgrind, squarely pointing 4 with his square forefinger, 'I don't know that girl. Who is that girl?'

'Sissy Jupe, sir,' explained number twenty, blushing, stand 5 ing up, and curtseying.

'Sissy is not a name,' said Mr Gradgrind. 'Don't call your 6 self Sissy. Call yourself Cecilia.'

'It's father as calls me Sissy, sir,' returned the young girl in 7 a trembling voice, and with another curtsey.

'Then he has no business to do it,' said Mr Gradgrind. 'Tell 8 him he mustn't. Cecilia Jupe. Let me see. What is your father?'

'He belongs to the horse-riding, if you please, sir.' 9

Mr Gradgrind frowned, and waved off the objectionable 10 calling with his hand.

'We don't want to know anything about that, here. You 11 mustn't tell us about that, here. Your father breaks horses, don't he?'

'If you please, sir, when they can get any to break, they do 12 break horses in the ring, sir.'

'You mustn't tell us about the ring, here. Very well, then. 13 Describe your father as a horsebreaker. He doctors sick horses, I dare say?'

'Oh yes, sir.' 14

'Very well, then. He is a veterinary surgeon, a farrier and 15 horsebreaker. Give me your definition of a horse.'

16   (Sissy Jupe thrown into the greatest alarm by this demand.)

17   'Girl number twenty unable to define a horse!' said Mr Gradgrind, for the general behoof of all the little pitchers. 'Girl number twenty possessed of no facts, in reference to one of the commonest of animals! Some boy's definition of a horse. Bitzer, yours.'

18   The square finger, moving here and there, lighted suddenly on Bitzer, perhaps because he chanced to sit in the same ray of sunlight which, darting in at one of the bare windows of the intensely whitewashed room, irradiated Sissy. For, the boys and girls sat on the face of the inclined plane in two compact bodies, divided up the centre by a narrow interval; and Sissy, being at the corner of a row on the sunny side, came in for the beginning of a sunbeam, of which Bitzer, being at the corner of a row on the other side, a few rows in advance, caught the end. But, whereas the girl was so dark-eyed and dark-haired, that she seemed to receive a deeper and more lustrous colour from the sun when it shone upon her, the boy was so light-eyed and light-haired that the self-same rays appeared to draw out of him what little colour he ever possessed. His cold eyes would hardly have been eyes, but for the short ends of lashes which, by bringing them into immediate contrast with something paler than themselves, expressed their form. His short-cropped hair might have been a mere continuation of the sandy freckles on his forehead and face. His skin was so unwholesomely deficient in the natural tinge, that he looked as though, if he were cut, he would bleed white.

19   'Bitzer,' said Thomas Gradgrind. 'Your definition of a horse.'

20   'Quadruped. Graminivorous. Forty teeth, namely twenty-four grinders, four eye-teeth, and twelve incisive. Sheds coat in the spring; in marshy countries, sheds hoofs, too. Hoofs hard, but requiring to be shod with iron. Age known by marks in mouth.' Thus (and much more) Bitzer.

21   'Now girl number twenty,' said Mr Gradgrind. 'You know what a horse is.'

Jerome Stern

What They Learn in School

Jerome Stern taught English at Florida State University for many years until his death in 1996. This "monologue" aired March 17, 1989, on National Public Radio's All Things Considered. *It was later reprinted in* Harper's *magazine.*

In the schools now, they want them to know all about marijuana, crack, heroin, and amphetamines,   1

Because then they won't be interested in marijuana, crack, heroin, and amphetamines,   2

But they don't want to tell them anything about sex because if the schools tell them about sex, then they will be interested in sex,   3

But if the schools don't tell them anything about sex,   4

Then they will have high morals and no one will get pregnant, and everything will be all right,   5

And they do want them to know a lot about computers so they will outcompete the Japanese,   6

But they don't want them to know anything about real science because then they will lose their faith and become secular humanists,   7

And they do want them to know all about this great land of ours so they will be patriotic,   8

But they don't want them to learn about the tragedy and pain in its real history because then they will be critical about this great land of ours and we will be passively taken over by a foreign power,   9

And they want them to learn how to think for themselves so they can get good jobs and be successful,   10

But they don't want them to have books that confront them with real ideas because that will confuse their values,   11

And they'd like them to be good parents,   12

But they can't teach them about families because that takes them back to how you get to be a family,   13

And they want to warn them about how not to get AIDS   14

But that would mean telling them how not to get AIDS,   15

And they'd like them to know the Constitution,   16

But they don't like some of those amendments except when they are invoked by the people they agree with,   17

And they'd like them to vote,   18

19   But they don't want them to discuss current events because
     it might be controversial and upset them and make them
     want to take drugs, which they already have told them all
     about,

20   And they want to teach them the importance of morality,

21   But they also want them to learn that Winning is not every-
     thing—it is the Only Thing,

22   And they want them to be well-read,

23   But they don't want them to read Chaucer or Shakespeare
     or Aristophanes or Mark Twain or Ernest Hemingway or
     John Steinbeck, because that will corrupt them,

24   And they don't want them to know anything about art
     because that will make them weird,

25   But they do want them to know about music so they can
     march in the band,

26   And they mainly want to teach them not to question, not to
     challenge, not to imagine, but to be obedient and behave
     well so that they can hold them forever as children to
     their bosoms as the second millennium lurches toward
     its panicky close.

WHAT'S COLLEGE FOR?

Alice Walker
Everyday Use

for your grandmama

Alice Walker (born 1944) is an essayist, poet, feminist, and activist, but she is best known for her Pulitzer Prize–winning third novel, The Color Purple *(1982). Asked why she writes, she once explained, "I'm really paying homage to people I love, the people who are thought to be dumb and backward but who were the ones who first taught me to see beauty." "Everyday Use" appeared in her acclaimed collection of stories,* In Love and Trouble, *published in 1973.*

I will wait for her in the yard that Maggie and I made so 1
clean and wavy yesterday afternoon. A yard like this is more
comfortable than most people know. It is not just a yard. It is
like an extended living room. When the hard clay is swept
clean as a floor and the fine sand around the edges lined with
tiny, irregular grooves anyone can come and sit and look up
into the elm tree and wait for the breezes that never come inside the house.

Maggie will be nervous until after her sister goes: she will 2
stand hopelessly in corners homely and ashamed of the burn
scars down her arms and legs, eyeing her sister with a mixture of envy and awe. She thinks her sister has held life always in the palm of one hand, that "no" is a word the world
never learned to say to her.

You've no doubt seen those TV shows where the child who 3
has "made it" is confronted, as a surprise, by her own mother
and father, tottering in weakly from backstage. (A pleasant
surprise, of course: What would they do if parent and child
came on the show only to curse out and insult each other?)
On TV mother and child embrace and smile into each other's

faces. Sometimes the mother and father weep, the child wraps them in her arms and leans across the table to tell how she would not have made it without their help. I have seen these programs.

4   Sometimes I dream a dream in which Dee and I are suddenly brought together on a TV program of this sort. Out of a dark and soft-seated limousine I am ushered into a bright room filled with many people. There I meet a smiling, gray, sporty man like Johnny Carson who shakes my hand and tells me what a fine girl I have. Then we are on the stage and Dee is embracing me with tears in her eyes. She pins on my dress a large orchid, even though she has told me once that she thinks orchids are tacky flowers.

5   In real life I am a large, big-boned woman with rough, man-working hands. In the winter I wear flannel nightgowns to bed and overalls during the day. I can kill and clean a hog as mercilessly as a man. My fat keeps me hot in zero weather. I can work outside all day, breaking ice to get water for washing; I can eat pork liver cooked over the open fire minutes after it comes steaming from the hog. One winter I knocked a bull calf straight in the brain between the eyes with a sledge hammer and had the meat hung up to chill before nightfall. But of course all this does not show on television. I am the way my daughter would want me to be: a hundred pounds lighter, my skin like an uncooked barley pancake. My hair glistens in the hot bright lights. Johnny Carson has much to do to keep up with my quick and witty tongue.

6   But that is a mistake. I know even before I wake up. Who ever knew a Johnson with a quick tongue? Who can even imagine me looking a strange white man in the eye? It seems to me I have talked to them always with one foot raised in flight, and my head turned in whichever way is farthest from them. Dee, though. She would always look anyone in the eye. Hesitation was no part of her nature.

7   "How do I look, Mama?" Maggie says, showing just enough of her thin body enveloped in pink skirt and red blouse for me to know she's there, almost hidden by the door.

8   "Come out into the yard," I say.

9   Have you ever seen a lame animal, perhaps a dog run over by some careless person rich enough to own a car, sidle up to someone who is ignorant enough to be kind to him? That is the way my Maggie walks. She has been like this, chin on chest, eyes on ground, feet in shuffle, ever since the fire that burned the other house to the ground.

Dee is lighter than Maggie, with nicer hair and a fuller fig-   10
ure. She's a woman now, though sometimes I forget. How long
ago was it that the other house burned? Ten, twelve years?
Sometimes I can still hear the flames and feel Maggie's arms
sticking to me, her hair smoking and her dress falling off her
in little black papery flakes. Her eyes seemed stretched open,
blazed open by the flames reflected in them. And Dee. I see her
standing off under the sweet gum tree she used to dig gum out
of: a look of concentration on her face as she watched the last
dingy gray board of the house fall in toward the red-hot brick
chimney. Why don't you do a dance around the ashes? I'd
wanted to ask her. She hated the house that much.

I used to think she hated Maggie, too. But that was before   11
we raised the money, the church and me, to send her to Au-
gusta to school. She used to read to us without pity; forcing
words, lies, other folks' habits, whole lives upon us two, sitting trapped and ignorant underneath her voice. She washed
us in a river of make-believe, burned us with a lot of knowledge we didn't necessarily need to know. Pressed us to her
with the serious way she read, to shove us away at just the
moment, like dimwits, we seemed about to understand.

Dee wanted nice things. A yellow organdy dress to wear to   12
her graduation from high school; black pumps to match a
green suit she'd made from an old suit somebody gave me.
She was determined to stare down any disaster in her efforts.
Her eyelids would not flicker for minutes at a time. Often I
fought off the temptation to shake her. At sixteen she had a
style of her own: and knew what style was.

I never had an education myself. After second grade the   13
school was closed down. Don't ask me why: in 1927 colored
asked fewer questions than they do now. Sometimes Maggie
reads to me. She stumbles along good-naturedly but can't see
well. She knows she is not bright. Like good looks and money,
quickness passed her by. She will marry John Thomas (who
has mossy teeth in an earnest face) and then I'll be free to sit
here and I guess just sing church songs to myself. Although I
never was a good singer. Never could carry a tune. I was always better at a man's job. I used to love to milk till I was
hooked in the side in '49. Cows are soothing and slow and
don't bother you, unless you try to milk them the wrong way.

I have deliberately turned my back on the house. It is three   14
rooms, just like the one that burned, except the roof is tin;
they don't make shingle roofs anymore. There are no real windows, just some holes cut in the sides, like the portholes in a

ship, but not round and not square, with rawhide holding the
shutters up on the outside. This house is in a pasture, too, like
the other one. No doubt when Dee sees it she will want to tear
it down. She wrote me once that no matter where we "choose"
to live, she will manage to come see us. But she will never
bring her friends. Maggie and I thought about this and Maggie
asked me, "Mama, when did Dee ever *have* any friends?"

15   She had a few. Furtive boys in pink shirts hanging about
on washday after school. Nervous girls who never laughed.
Impressed with her they worshiped the well-turned phrase,
the cute shape, the scalding humor that erupted like bubbles
in lye. She read to them.

16   When she was courting Jimmy T she didn't have much
time to pay to us, but turned all her faultfinding power on
him. He *flew* to marry a cheap gal from a family of ignorant
flashy people. She hardly had time to recompose herself.

17   When she comes I will meet—but there they are!

18   Maggie attempts to make a dash for the house, in her shuf-
fling way, but I stay her with my hand. "Come back here," I
say. And she stops and tries to dig a well in the sand with her
toe.

19   It is hard to see them clearly through the strong sun. But
even the first glimpse of leg out of the car tells me it is Dee.
Her feet were always neat-looking, as if God himself had
shaped them with a certain style. From the other side of the
car comes a short, stocky man. Hair is all over his head a foot
long and hanging from his chin like a kinky mule tail. I hear
Maggie suck in her breath. "Uhnnnh," is what it sounds like.
Like when you see the wriggling end of a snake just in front of
your foot on the road. "Uhnnnh."

20   Dee next. A dress down to the ground, in this hot weather.
A dress so loud it hurts my eyes. There are yellows and or-
anges enough to throw back the light of the sun. I feel my
whole face warming from the heat waves it throws out. Earrings gold, too, and hanging down to her shoulders. Bracelets
dangling and making noises when she moves her arm up to
shake the folds of the dress out of her armpits. The dress is
loose and flows, and as she walks closer, I like it. I hear Maggie go "Uhnnnh" again. It is her sister's hair. It stands straight
up like the wool on a sheep. It is black as night and around
the edges are two long pigtails that rope about like small liz-
ards disappearing behind the ears.

21   "Wa-su-zo-Tean-o!" she says, coming on in that gliding way
the dress makes her move. The short stocky fellow with the

hair to his navel is all grinning and he follows up with "Asala-malakim, my mother and sister!" He moves to hug Maggie but she falls back, right up against the back of my chair. I feel her trembling there and when I look up I see the perspiration falling off her chin.

"Don't get up," says Dee. Since I am stout it takes some- 22
thing of a push. You can see me trying to move a second or two before I make it. She turns, showing white heels through her sandals, and goes back to the car. Out she peeks next with a Polaroid. She stoops down quickly and lines up picture af-ter picture of me sitting there in front of the house with Mag-gie cowering behind me. She never takes a shot without making sure the house is included. When a cow comes nib-bling around the edge of the yard she snaps it and me and Maggie *and* the house. Then she puts the Polaroid in the back seat of the car, and comes up and kisses me on the forehead.

Meanwhile Asalamalakim is going through the motions 23
with Maggie's hand. Maggie's hand is as limp as a fish, and probably as cold, despite the sweat, and she keeps trying to pull it back. It looks like Asalamalakim wants to shake hands but wants to do it fancy. Or maybe he don't know how people shake hands. Anyhow, he soon gives up on Maggie.

"Well," I say. "Dee." 24

"No, Mama," she says. "Not 'Dee,' Wangero Leewanika 25
Kemanjo!"

"What happened to 'Dee'?" I wanted to know. 26

"She's dead." Wangero said. "I couldn't bear it any longer 27
being named after the people who oppress me."

"You know as well as me you was named after your aunt 28
Dicie," I said. Dicie is my sister. She named Dee. We called her "Big Dee" after Dee was born.

"But who was *she* named after?" asked Wangero. 29

"I guess after Grandma Dee," I said. 30

"And who was she named after?" asked Wangero. 31

"Her mother," I said, and saw Wangero was getting tired. 32
"That's about as far back as I can trace it," I said. Though, in fact, I probably could have carried it back beyond the Civil War through the branches.

"Well," said Asalamalakim, "there you are." 33

"Uhnnnh," I heard Maggie say. 34

"There I was not," I said, "before 'Dicie' cropped up in our 35
family, so why should I try to trace it that far back?"

He just stood there grinning, looking down on me like 36
somebody inspecting a Model A car. Every once in a while he and Wangero sent eye signals over my head.

37　　"How do you pronounce this name?" I asked.

38　　"You don't have to call me by it if you don't want to," said Wangero.

39　　"Why shouldn't I?" I asked. "If that's what you want us to call you, we'll call you."

40　　"I know it might sound awkward at first," said Wangero.

41　　"I'll get used to it," I said. "Ream it out again."

42　　Well, soon we got the name out of the way. Asalamalakim had a name twice as long and three times as hard. After I tripped over it two or three times he told me to just call him Hakim-a-barber. I wanted to ask him was he a barber, but I didn't really think he was, so I didn't ask.

43　　"You must belong to those beef-cattle peoples down the road," I said. They said "Asalamalakim" when they met you, too, but they didn't shake hands. Always too busy: feeding the cattle, fixing the fences, putting up salt-lick shelters, throwing down hay. When the white folks poisoned some of the herd the men stayed up all night with rifles in their hands. I walked a mile and a half just to see the sight.

44　　Hakim-a-barber said, "I accept some of their doctrines, but farming and raising cattle is not my style." (They didn't tell me, and I didn't ask, whether Wangero [Dee] had really gone and married him.)

45　　We sat down to eat and right away he said he didn't eat collards and pork was unclean. Wangero, though, went on through the chitlins and corn bread, the greens and everything else. She talked a blue streak over the sweet potatoes. Everything delighted her. Even the fact that we still used the benches her daddy made for the table when we couldn't afford to buy chairs.

46　　"Oh, Mama!" she cried. Then turned to Hakim-a-barber. "I never knew how lovely these benches are. You can feel the rump prints," she said, running her hands underneath her and along the bench. Then she gave a sigh and her hand closed over Grandma Dee's butter dish. "That's it!" she said. "I knew there was something I wanted to ask you if I could have." She jumped up from the table and went over in the corner where the churn stood, the milk in it clabber by now. She looked at the churn and looked at it.

47　　"This churn top is what I need," she said. "Didn't Uncle Buddy whittle it out of a tree you all used to have?"

48　　"Yes," I said.

49　　"Uh huh," she said happily. "And I want the dasher, too."

50　　"Uncle Buddy whittle that, too?" asked the barber.

51　　Dee (Wangero) looked up at me.

"Aunt Dee's first husband whittle the dash," said Maggie so   52
low you almost couldn't hear her. "His name was Henry, but
they called him Stash."

"Maggie's brain is like an elephant's," Wangero said, laugh-   53
ing. "I can use the churn top as a centerpiece for the alcove table," she said, sliding a plate over the churn, "and I'll think of
something artistic to do with the dasher."

When she finished wrapping the dasher the handle stuck   54
out. I took it for a moment in my hands. You didn't even have
to look close to see where hands pushing the dasher up and
down to make butter had left a kind of sink in the wood. In
fact, there were a lot of small sinks; you could see where
thumbs and fingers had sunk into the wood. It was beautiful
light yellow wood, from a tree that grew in the yard where Big
Dee and Stash had lived.

After dinner Dee (Wangero) went to the trunk at the foot of   55
my bed and started rifling through it. Maggie hung back in
the kitchen over the dishpan. Out came Wangero with two
quilts. They had been pieced by Grandma Dee and then Big
Dee and me had hung them on the quilt frames on the front
porch and quilted them. One was in the Lone Star pattern.
The other was Walk Around the Mountain. In both of them
were scraps of dresses Grandma Dee had worn fifty and more
years ago. Bits and pieces of Grandpa Jarrell's Paisley shirts.
And one teeny faded blue piece, about the size of a penny
matchbox, that was from Great Grandpa Ezra's uniform that
he wore in the Civil War.

"Mama," Wangero said sweet as a bird. "Can I have these   56
old quilts?"

I heard something fall in the kitchen, and a minute later   57
the kitchen door slammed.

"Why don't you take one or two of the others?" I asked.   58
"These old things was just done by me and Big Dee from
some tops your grandma pieced before she died."

"No," said Wangero. "I don't want those. They are stitched   59
around the borders by machine."

"That'll make them last better," I said.   60

"That's not the point," said Wangero. "These are all pieces   61
of dresses Grandma used to wear. She did all this stitching by
hand. Imagine!" She held the quilts securely in her arms,
stroking them.

"Some of the pieces, like those lavender ones, come from   62
old clothes her mother handed down to her," I said, moving up
to touch the quilts. Dee (Wangero) moved back just enough so
that I couldn't reach the quilts. They already belonged to her.

63   "Imagine!" she breathed again, clutching them closely to her bosom.

64   "The truth is," I said, "I promised to give them quilts to Maggie, for when she marries John Thomas."

65   She gasped like a bee had stung her.

66   "Maggie can't appreciate these quilts!" she said. "She'd probably be backward enough to put them to everyday use."

67   "I reckon she would," I said. "God knows I been saving 'em for long enough with nobody using 'em. I hope she will!" I didn't want to bring up how I had offered Dee (Wangero) a quilt when she went away to college. Then she had told me they were old-fashioned, out of style.

68   "But they're *priceless!*" she was saying now, furiously; for she has a temper. "Maggie would put them on the bed and in five years they'd be in rags. Less than that!"

69   "She can always make some more," I said. "Maggie knows how to quilt."

70   Dee (Wangero) looked at me with hatred. "You just will not understand. The point is these quilts, *these* quilts!"

71   "Well," I said, stumped. "What would *you* do with them?"

72   "Hang them," she said. As if that was the only thing you *could* do with quilts.

73   Maggie by now was standing in the door. I could almost hear the sound her feet made as they scraped over each other.

74   "She can have them, Mama," she said, like somebody used to never winning anything, or having anything reserved for her. "I can 'member Grandma Dee without the quilts."

75   I looked at her hard. She had filled her bottom lip with checkerberry snuff and it gave her face a kind of dopey, hang-dog look. It was Grandma Dee and Big Dee who taught her how to quilt herself. She stood there with her scarred hands hidden in the folds of her skirt. She looked at her sister with something like fear but she wasn't mad at her. This was Maggie's portion. This was the way she knew God to work.

76   When I looked at her like that something hit me in the top of my head and ran down to the soles of my feet. Just like when I'm in church and the spirit of God touches me and I get happy and shout. I did something I never had done before: hugged Maggie to me, then dragged her on into the room, snatched the quilts out of Miss Wangero's hands and dumped them into Maggie's lap. Maggie just sat there on my bed with her mouth open.

77   "Take one or two of the others," I said to Dee.

78   But she turned without a word and went out to Hakim-a-barber.

"You just don't understand," she said, as Maggie and I   79
came out to the car.

"What don't I understand?" I wanted to know.   80

"Your heritage," she said. And then she turned to Maggie,   81
kissed her, and said, "You ought to try to make something of
yourself, too, Maggie. It's really a new day for us. But from
the way you and Mama still live you'd never know it."

She put on some sunglasses that hid everything above the   82
tip of her nose and her chin.

Maggie smiled; maybe at the sunglasses. But a real smile,   83
not scared. After we watched the car dust settle I asked Maggie
to bring me a dip of snuff. And then the two of us sat there just
enjoying, until it was time to go in the house and go to bed.

bell hooks
Pedagogy and Political Commitment: A Comment

*bell hooks teaches at Oberlin College in Ohio. You will learn
more about her by reading the following essay, which is a chapter in her book* Talking Back: Thinking Feminist, Thinking
Black *(1989), one of her nine books on race, gender, politics,
and culture. (A second essay by bell hooks appears elsewhere in
this book, on page 239.)*

Education is a political issue for exploited and oppressed   1
people. The history of slavery in the United States shows that
black people regarded education—book learning, reading,
and writing—as a political necessity. Struggle to resist white
supremacy and racist attacks informed black attitudes toward education. Without the capacity to read and write, to
think critically and analytically, the liberated slave would remain forever bound, dependent on the will of the oppressor.
No aspect of black liberation struggle in the United States has
been as charged with revolutionary fervor as the effort to gain
access to education at all levels.

From slavery to the present, education has been revered in   2
black communities, yet it has also been suspect. Education
represented a means of radical resistance but it also led to

caste/class divisions between the educated and the uneducated, as it meant the learned black person could more easily adopt the values and attitudes of the oppressor. Education could help one assimilate. If one could not become the white oppressor, one could at least speak and think like him or her, and in some cases the educated black person assumed the role of mediator—explaining uneducated black folks to white folks.

3   Given this history, many black parents have encouraged children to acquire an education while simultaneously warning us about the danger of education. One very real danger, as many black parents traditionally perceived it, was that the learned black person might lose touch with the concrete reality of everyday black experience. Books and ideas were important but not important enough to become barriers between the individual and community participation. Education was considered to have the potential to alienate one from community and awareness of our collective circumstance as black people. In my family, it was constantly emphasized that too much book learning could lead to madness. Among everyday black folks, madness was deemed to be any loss of one's ability to communicate effectively with others, one's ability to cope with practical affairs.

4   These ambivalent attitudes toward education have made it difficult for black students to adapt and succeed in educational settings. Many of us have found that to succeed at the very education we had been encouraged to seek would be most easily accomplished if we separated ourselves from the experience of black folk, the underprivileged experience of the black underclass that was our grounding reality. This ambivalent stance toward education has had a tremendous impact on my psyche. Within the working-class black community where I grew up, I learned to be suspicious of education and suspicious of white folks. I went for my formative educational years to all-black schools. In those schools, I learned about the reality of white people but also about the reality of black people, about our history. We were taught in those schools to be proud of ourselves as black people and to work for the uplift of our race.

5   Experiencing as I did an educational environment structured to meet our needs as black people, we were deeply affected when those schools ceased to exist and we were compelled to attend white schools instead. At the white school, we were no longer people with a history, a culture. We did not exist as anything other than primitives and slaves. School was no longer the place where one learned how to use

education as a means to resist white-supremacist oppression. Small wonder that I spent my last few years of high school depressed about education, feeling as though we had suffered a grave loss, that the direction had shifted, the goals had changed. We were no longer taught by people who spoke our language, who understood our culture; we were taught by strangers. And further, we were dependent on those strangers for evaluation, for approval. We learned not to challenge their racism since they had power over us. Although we were told at home that we were not to openly challenge whites, we were also told not to learn to think like them.

Within this atmosphere of ambivalence toward education, 6 I, who had been dubbed smart, was uncertain about whether or not I wanted to go to college. School was an oppressive drag. Yet the fate of smart black women had already been decided; we would be schoolteachers. At the private, mostly white women's college where I spent my first year, I was an outsider. Determined to stay grounded in the reality of southern black culture, I kept myself aloof from the social practices of the white women with whom I lived and studied. They, in their turn, perceived me as hostile and alien. I, who had always been a member of a community, was now a loner. One of my white teachers suggested to me that the alienation I experienced was caused by being at a school that was not intellectually challenging, that I should go to Stanford where she had gone.

My undergraduate years at Stanford were difficult ones. 7 Not only did I feel myself alienated from the white people who were my peers and teachers, but I met black people who were different, who did not think the way I did about black culture or black life—who seemed in some ways as strange to me as white people. I had known black people from different classes in my hometown, but we still experienced much the same reality, shared similar world views. It was different at Stanford. I was in an environment where black people's class backgrounds and their values were radically different than my own.

To overcome my feelings of isolation, I bonded with work- 8 ers, with black women who labored as maids, as secretaries. With them I felt at home. During holiday break, I would stay in their homes. Yet being with them was not the same as being home. In their houses I was an honored guest, someone to be looked up to, because I was getting a college education. My undergraduate years at Stanford were spent struggling to find meaning and significance in education. I had to succeed. I

could not let my family or the race down. And so I graduated
in English. I had become an English major for the same reason that hundreds of students of all races become English
majors: I like to read. Yet I did not fully understand that the
study of literature in English departments would really mean
the study of works by white males.

9   It was disheartening for me and other non-white students
to face the extent to which education in the university was
not the site of openness and intellectual challenge we had
longed for. We hated the racism, the sexism, the domination.
I began to have grave doubts about the future. Why was I
working to be an academic if I did not see people in that environment who were opposing domination? Even those very
few concerned professors who endeavored to make courses
interesting, to create a learning atmosphere, rarely acknowledged destructive and oppressive aspects of authoritarian rule
in and outside the classroom. Whether one took courses from
professors with feminist politics or marxist politics, their presentations of self in the classroom never differed from the
norm. This was especially so with marxist professors. I asked
one of these professors, a white male, how he could expect students to take his politics seriously as a radical alternative to a
capitalist structure if we found marxist professors to be even
more oppressively authoritarian than other professors. Everyone seemed reluctant to talk about the fact that professors
who advocated radical politics rarely allowed their critique of
domination and oppression to influence teaching strategies.
The absence of any model of a professor who was combining a
radical politic opposing domination with practice of that politic in the classroom made me feel wary about my ability to do
differently. When I first began to teach, I tried not to emulate
my professors in any way. I devised different strategies and approaches that I felt were more in keeping with my politics.
Reading the work of Paulo Freire greatly influenced my sense
that much was possible in the classroom setting, that one did
not simply need to conform.

10   In the introduction to a conversation with Paulo Freire
published in *idac*, emphasis is placed on an educative process
that is not based on an authoritarian, dominating model
where knowledge is transferred from a powerful professor to
a powerless student. Education, it was suggested, could be a
space for the development of critical consciousness, where
there could be dialogue and mutual growth of both student
and professor:

If we accept education in this richer and more dynamic sense of acquiring a critical capacity and intervention in reality, we immediately know that there is no such thing as neutral education. All education has an intention, a goal, which can only be political. Either it mystifies reality by rendering it impenetrable and obscure—which leads people to a blind march through incomprehensible labyrinths—or it unmasks the economic and social structures which are determining the relationships of exploitation and oppression among persons, knocking down labyrinths and allowing people to walk their own road. So we find ourselves confronted with a clear option: to educate for liberation or to educate for domination.

In retrospect, it seems that my most radical professors were still educating for domination. And I wondered if this was so because we could not imagine how to educate for liberation in the corporate university. In Freire's case, he speaks as a white man of privilege who stands and acts in solidarity with oppressed and exploited groups, especially in their efforts to establish literacy programs that emphasize education for critical consciousness. In my case, as a black woman from a working-class background, I stand and act as a member of an oppressed, exploited group who has managed to acquire a degree of privilege. While I choose to educate for liberation, the site of my work has been within the walls of universities peopled largely by privileged white students and a few non-white students. Within those walls, I have tried to teach literature and Women's Studies courses in a way that does not reinforce structures of domination: imperialism, racism, sexism, and class exploitation.

I do not pretend that my approach is politically neutral, yet this disturbs students who have been led to believe that all education within the university should be "neutral." On the first day of classes, I talk about my approach, about the ways the class may be different from other classes as we work to create strategies of learning to meet our needs—and of course we must discover together what those needs are. Even though I explain that the class will be different, students do not always take it seriously. One central difference is that all students are expected to contribute to class discussion, if not spontaneously, then through the reading of paragraphs and short papers. In this way, every student makes a contribution, every student's voice is heard. Despite the fact that this may be stated

11

at the onset of class, written clearly on the syllabus, students will complain and whine about having to speak. It is only recently that I have begun to see much of the complaining as "change back" behavior. Students and teachers find it hard to shift their paradigms even though they have been longing for a different approach.

12   Struggling to educate for liberation in the corporate university is a process that I have found enormously stressful. Implementing new teaching strategies that aim to subvert the norm, to engage students fully, is really a difficult task. Unlike the oppressed or colonized, who may begin to feel as they engage in education for critical consciousness a newfound sense of power and identity that frees them from colonization of the mind, that liberates, privileged students are often downright unwilling to acknowledge that their minds have been colonized, that they have been learning how to be oppressors, how to dominate, or at least how to passively accept the domination of others. This past teaching year, a student confronted me (a black male student from a middle-class urban experience) in class with the question of what I expected from them (like his tone of voice was: did I have the right to expect anything). Seriously, he wanted to know what I wanted from them. I told him and the class that I thought the most important learning experience that could happen in our classroom was that students would learn to think critically and analytically, not just about the required books, but about the world they live in. Education for critical consciousness that encourages all students—privileged or non-privileged—who are seeking an entry into class privilege rather than providing a sense of freedom and release, invites critique of conventional expectations and desires. They may find such an experience terribly threatening. And even though they may approach the situation with great openness, it may still be difficult, and even painful.

13   This past semester, I taught a course on black women writers in which students were encouraged to think about the social context in which literature emerges, the impact of politics of domination—racism, sexism, class exploitation—on the writing. Students stated quite openly and honestly that reading the literature in the context of class discussion was making them feel pain. They complained that everything was changing for them, that they were seeing the world differently, and seeing things in that world that were painful to face. Never before had a group of students so openly talked about the way in which learning to see the world critically

was causing pain. I did not belittle their pain or try to rationalize it. Initially, I was uncertain about how to respond and just asked us all to think about it. Later, we discussed the way in which all their comments implied that to experience pain is bad, an indication that something is wrong. We talked about changing how we perceive pain, about our society's approach to pain, considering the possibility that this pain could be a constructive sign of growth. I shared with them my sense that the experience should not be viewed as static, that at another point the knowledge and new perspectives they had might lead to clarity and a greater sense of well-being.

Education for liberation can work in the university setting   14
but it does not lead students to feel they are enjoying class or necessarily feeling positive about me as a teacher. One aspect of radical pedagogy that has been difficult for me is learning to cope with not being seen positively by students. When one provides an experience of learning that is challenging, possibly threatening, it is not entertainment, or necessarily a fun experience, though it can be. If one primary function of such a pedagogy is to prepare students to live and act more fully in the world, then it is usually when they are in that context, outside the classroom, that they most feel and experience the value of what they have shared and learned. For me, this often means that most positive feedback I receive as a teacher comes after students have left the class and rarely during it.

Recently talking with a group of students and faculty at   15
Duke University, we focussed on the issue of exposure and vulnerability. One white male professor, who felt his politics to be radical, his teaching to be an education for liberation, his teaching strategies subversive, felt it was important that no one in the university's bureaucratic structure know what was happening in the classroom. Fear of exposure may lead teachers with radical visions to suppress insight, to follow set norms. Until I came to teach at Yale, no one outside my classes had paid much attention to what was going on inside them. At Yale, students talked a lot outside about my classes, about what happens in them. This was very difficult for me as I felt both exposed and constantly scrutinized. I was certainly subjected to much critical feedback both from students in my classes and faculty and students who heard about them. Their responses forced recognition of the way in which teaching that is overtly political, especially if it radically challenges the status quo, requires acknowledgement that to choose education as the practice of freedom is to take a political stance that may have serious consequences.

16   Despite negative feedback or pressures, the most rewarding aspect of such teaching is to influence the way students
mature and grow intellectually and spiritually. For those students who wish to try to learn in a new way but who have
fears, I try to reassure them that their involvement in different types of learning experiences need not threaten their security in other classes; it will not destroy the backing system
of education, so they need not panic. Of course, if all they can
do is panic, then that is a sign that the course is not for them.
My commitment to education as the practice of freedom is
strengthened by the large number of students who take my
courses and, by doing so, affirm their longing to learn in a
new way. Their testimony confirms that education as the
practice of liberation does take place in university settings,
that our lives are transformed there, that there we do meaningful radical political work.

Adrienne Rich

Claiming an Education

*"Claiming an Education" is the transcript of a talk first given
to new students at Douglass College, the Women's College of
Rutgers University, on September 6, 1977; later, it was included
in Adrienne Rich's book* On Lies, Secrets, and Silence. *Rich
(born 1929) is a noted teacher, essayist, and feminist who won
the National Book Award for poetry in 1974.*

1   For this convocation, I planned to separate my remarks
into two parts: some thoughts about you, the women students
here, and some thoughts about us who teach in a women's
college. But ultimately, those two parts are indivisible. If university education means anything beyond the processing of
human beings into expected roles, through credit hours, tests,
and grades (and I believe that in a women's college especially
it *might* mean much more), it implies an ethical and intellectual contract between teacher and student. This contract
must remain intuitive, dynamic, unwritten; but we must turn
to it again and again if learning is to be reclaimed from the
depersonalizing and cheapening pressures of the present-day
academic scene.

The first thing I want to say to you who are students is that   2
you cannot afford to think of being here to *receive* an education; you will do much better to think of yourselves as being
here to *claim* one. One of the dictionary definitions of the
verb "to claim" is: *to take as the rightful owner; to assert in the
face of possible contradiction.* "To receive" is *to come into possession of; to act as receptacle or container for; to accept as authoritative or true.* The difference is that between acting and
being acted-upon, and for women it can literally mean the
difference between life and death.

One of the devastating weaknesses of university learning, of   3
the store of knowledge and opinion that has been handed
down through academic training, has been its almost total
erasure of women's experience and thought from the curriculum, and its exclusion of women as members of the academic
community. Today, with increasing numbers of women students in nearly every branch of higher learning, we still see
very few women in the upper levels of faculty and administration in most institutions. Douglass College itself is a women's
college in a university administered overwhelmingly by men,
who in turn are answerable to the state legislature, again composed predominantly of men. But the most significant fact for
you is that what you learn here, the very texts you read, the
lectures you hear, the way your studies are divided into categories and fragmented one from the other—all this reflects, to
a very large degree, neither objective reality, nor an accurate
picture of the past, nor a group of rigorously tested observations about human behavior. What you can learn here (and I
mean not only at Douglass but any college in any university) is
how *men* have perceived and organized their experience, their
history, their ideas of social relationships, good and evil, sickness and health, etc. When you read or hear about "great issues," "major texts," "the mainstream of Western thought,"
you are hearing about what men, above all white men, in their
male subjectivity, have decided is important.

Black and other minority people have for some time recog-   4
nized that their racial and ethnic experience was not accounted for in the studies broadly labeled human; and that
even the sciences can be racist. For many reasons, it has been
more difficult for women to comprehend our exclusion, and
to realize that even the sciences can be sexist. For one thing,
it is only within the last hundred years that higher education
has grudgingly been opened up to women at all, even to
white, middle-class women. And many of us have found ourselves poring eagerly over books with titles like: *The Descent*

*of Man; Man and His Symbols; Irrational Man; The Phenome-
non of Man; The Future of Man; Man and the Machine; From
Man to Man; May Man Prevail?; Man, Science and Society;* or
One-Dimensional Man—books pretending to describe a "human" reality that does not include over one-half the human
species.

5   Less than a decade ago, with the rebirth of a feminist
movement in this country, women students and teachers in a
number of universities began to demand and set up women's
studies courses—to *claim* a woman-directed education. And,
despite the inevitable accusations of "unscholarly," "group
therapy," "faddism," etc., despite backlash and budget cuts,
women's studies are still growing, offering to more and more
women a new intellectual grasp on their lives, new understanding of our history, a fresh vision of the human experience, and also a critical basis for evaluating what they hear
and read in other courses, and in the society at large.

6   But my talk is not really about women's studies, much as I
believe in their scholarly, scientific, and human necessity.
While I think that any Douglass student has everything to
gain by investigating and enrolling in women's studies
courses, I want to suggest that there is a more essential experience that you owe yourself, one which courses in women's
studies can greatly enrich, but which finally depends on you,
in all your interactions with yourself and your world. This is
the experience of *taking responsibility toward yourself.* Our upbringing as women has so often told us that this should come
second to our relationships and responsibilities to other people. We have been offered ethical models of the self-denying
wife and mother; intellectual models of the brilliant but slap-
dash dilettante who never commits herself to anything the
whole way, or the intelligent woman who denies her intelligence in order to seem more "feminine," or who sits in passive silence ever when she disagrees inwardly with everything
that is being said around her.

7   Responsibility to yourself means refusing to let others do
your thinking, talking, and naming for you; it means learning
to respect and use your own brains and instincts; hence, grappling with hard work. It means that you do not treat your
body as a commodity with which to purchase superficial intimacy or economic security; for our bodies and minds are inseparable in this life, and when we allow our bodies to be
treated as objects, our minds are in mortal danger. It means
insisting that those to whom you give your friendship and
love are able to respect your mind. It means being able to say,

with Charlotte Brontë's *Jane Eyre:* "I have an inward treasure born with me, which can keep me alive if all the extraneous delights should be withheld or offered only at a price I cannot afford to give."

Responsibility to yourself means that you don't fall for shallow and easy solutions—predigested books and ideas, weekend encounters guaranteed to change your life, taking "gut" courses instead of ones you know will challenge you, bluffing at school and life instead of doing solid work, marrying early as an escape from real decisions, getting pregnant as an evasion of already existing problems. It means that you refuse to sell your talents and aspirations short, simply to avoid conflict and confrontation. And this, in turn, means resisting the forces in society which say that women should be nice, play safe, have low professional expectations, drown in love and forget about work, live through others, and stay in the places assigned to us. It means that we insist on a life of meaningful work, insist that work be as meaningful as love and friendship in our lives. It means, therefore, the courage to be "different"; not to be continuously available to others when we need time for ourselves and our work; to be able to demand of others— parents, friends, roommates, teachers, lovers, husbands, children—that they respect our sense of purpose and our integrity as persons. Women everywhere are finding the courage to do this, more and more, and we are finding that courage both in our study of women in the past who possessed it, and in each other as we look at other women for comradeship, community, and challenge. The difference between a life lived actively, and a life of passive drifting and dispersal of energies, is an immense difference. Once we begin to feel committed to our lives, responsible to ourselves, we can never again be satisfied with the old, passive way. 8

Now comes the second part of the contract. I believe that in a women's college you have the right to expect your faculty to take you seriously. The education of women has been a matter of debate for centuries, and old, negative attitudes about women's role, women's ability to think and take leadership, are still rife both in and outside the university. Many male professors (and I don't mean only at Douglass) still feel that teaching in a women's college is a second-rate career. Many tend to eroticize their women students—to treat them as sexual objects—instead of demanding the best of their minds. (At Yale a legal suit [*Alexander* v. *Yale*] has been brought against the university by a group of women students demanding a stated policy against sexual advances toward female students 9

by male professors.) Many teachers, both men and women,
trained in the male-centered tradition, are still handing the
ideas and texts of that tradition on to students without teaching them to criticize its antiwoman attitudes, its omission of
women as part of the species. Too often, all of us fail to teach
the most important thing, which is that clear thinking, active
discussion, and excellent writing are all necessary for intellectual freedom, and that these require *hard work*. Sometimes,
perhaps in discouragement with a culture which is both anti-
intellectual and antiwoman, we may resign ourselves to low
expectations for our students before we have given them half a
chance to become more thoughtful, expressive human beings.
We need to take to heart the words of Elizabeth Barrett
Browning, a poet, a thinking woman, and a feminist, who
wrote in 1845 of her impatience with studies which cultivate a
"passive recipiency" in the mind, and asserted that "women
want to be made to *think actively:* their apprehension is
quicker than that of men, but their defect lies for the most part
in the logical faculty and in the higher mental activities." Note
that she implies a defect which can be remedied by intellectual training, *not* an inborn lack of ability.

10   I have said that the contract on the student's part involves
that you demand to be taken seriously so that you can also go
on taking yourself seriously. This means seeking out criticism,
recognizing that the most affirming thing anyone can do for
you is demand that you push yourself further, show you the
range of what you *can* do. It means rejecting attitudes of "take-
it-easy," "why-be-so-serious," "why-worry-you'll-probably-get-
married-anyway." It means assuming your share of responsibility for what happens in the classroom, because that affects
the quality of your daily life here. It means that the student
sees herself engaged *with* her teachers in an active, ongoing
struggle for real education. But for her to do this, her teachers must be committed to the belief that women's minds and
experience are intrinsically valuable and indispensable to any
civilization worthy of the name; that there is no more exhila-
rating and intellectually fertile place in the academic world
today than a women's college—*if* both students and teachers
in large enough numbers are trying to fulfill this contract.
The contract is really a pledge of mutual seriousness about
women, about language, ideas, methods, and values. It is our
shared commitment toward a world in which the inborn potentialities of so many women's minds will no longer be
wasted, raveled-away, paralyzed, or denied.

Garry B. Trudeau
Doonesbury

Garry B. Trudeau (born 1948) is one of America's most influential (and controversial) political and social commentators. His vehicle is the comic strip "Doonesbury," which appears in more than 850 newspapers and whose audience may top 100 million readers.

DOONESBURY COPYRIGHT 1985 G. B. Trudeau. Reprinted with permission of Universal Press Syndicate. All rights reserved.

The ad for Hofstra University on this page appeared in several magazines and newspapers in 1989 and 1990; the ad for Yeshiva University on the next page appeared in the same places in 1997 and 1998. What does each ad imply about the purpose of a college education?

Determination and hard work, at any age, can lead to being the best. Hofstra University, just 50 years old, is already among the top ten percent of American colleges and universities in almost all academic criteria and resources.

Professionally accredited programs in such major areas as business, engineering, law, psychology and education.

A library with over 1.1 million volumes *on campus*—a collection larger than that of 95% of American universities.

Record enrollments with students from 31 states and 59 countries— with a student-faculty ratio of only 17 to 1.

The largest, most sophisticated non-commercial television facility in the East. A high technology undergraduate teaching resource with broadcast-quality production capability.

A ranking in *Barron's Guide to the Most Prestigious Colleges*—one of only 262 colleges and universities chosen from almost 4,000.

At Hofstra, determination, inspiration and hard work are qualities our faculty demands in itself and instills in our students.

These qualities are what it takes to be the best. In anything.

HOFSTRA UNIVERSITY
WE TEACH SUCCESS.

50th Anniversary
Hempstead, L.I. New York 11550

W. D. Snodgrass
The Examination

W. D. Snodgrass (born 1926), educated at Geneva College and the University of Iowa, teaches at the University of Delaware. His book of poetry Heart's Needle *won the Pulitzer Prize in 1960.*

1   Under the thick beams of that swirly smoking light,
    The black robes are clustering, huddled in together.
Hunching their shoulders, they spread short, broad sleeves
      like night-
    Black grackles' wings; then they reach bone-yellow

2   leathery fingers, each to each. And are prepared. Each turns
    His single eye—or since one can't discern their eyes,
That reflective single, moon-pale disc which burns
    Over each brow—to watch this uncouth shape that lies

3   Strapped to their table. One probes with his ragged nails
    The slate-sharp calf, explores the thigh and the lean thews
Of the groin. Others raise, red as piratic sails,
    His wing, stretching, trying the pectoral sinews.

4   One runs his finger down the whet of that cruel
    Golden beak, lifts back the horny lids from the eyes,
Peers down in one bright eye malign as a jewel,
    And steps back suddenly. "He is anaesthetized?"

5   "He is. He is. Yes. Yes." The tallest of them, bent
    Down by the head, rises: "This drug possesses powers
Sufficient to still all gods in this firmament.
    This is Garuda who was fierce. He's yours for hours.

6   "We shall continue, please." Now, once again, he bends
    To the skull, and its clamped tissues. Into the cran-
ial cavity, he plunges both of his hands
    Like obstetric forceps and lifts out the great brain,

7   Holds it aloft, then gives it to the next who stands
    Beside him. Each, in turn, accepts it, although loath,
Turns it this way, that way, feels it between his hands
    Like a wasp's nest or some sickening outsized growth.

They must decide what thoughts each part of it must think;   8
   They tap at, then listen beside, each suspect lobe;
Next, with a crow's quill dipped into India ink,
   Mark on its surface, as if on a map or globe,

Those dangerous areas which need to be excised.   9
   They rinse it, then apply antiseptics to it;
Now silver saws appear which, inch by inch, slice
   Through its ancient folds and ridges, like thick suet.

It's rinsed, dried, and daubed with thick salves. The smoky   10
    saws
   Are scrubbed, resterilized, and polished till they gleam.
The brain is repacked in its case. Pinched in their claws,
   Glimmering needles stitch it up, that leave no seam.

Meantime, one of them has set blinders to the eyes,   11
   Inserting light packing beneath each of the ears,
And calked the nostrils in. One, with thin twine, ties
   The genitals off. With long wood-handled shears,

Another chops pinions out of the scarlet wings.   12
   It's hoped that with disuse he will forget the sky
Or, at least, in time, learn, among other things,
   To fly no higher than his superiors fly.

Well; that's a beginning. The next time, they can split   13
   His tongue and teach him to talk correctly, can give
Him opinions on fine books and choose clothing fit
   For the integrated area where he'll live.

Their candidate may live to give them thanks one day.   14
   He will recover and may hope for such success.
He might return to join their ranks. Bowing away,
   They nod, whispering, "One of ours; one of ours. Yes. Yes."

John Searle
The Case for a Traditional Liberal Arts Education

John Searle, who has been a professor of philosophy at the University of California–Berkeley for many years, is best known for his advocacy of "speech-act theory," a theory of communication which has been both influential and roundly debated in philosophy, linguistics, and rhetoric since it appeared in Searle's Speech Acts: An Essay in the Philosophy of Language *in 1969. Searle has been controversial in other ways too, and the following essay is certainly polemical in many respects. "The Case for a Traditional Liberal Arts Education" was originally published, interestingly enough, in* The Journal of Blacks in Higher Education *(an academically oriented magazine specializing in articles that explore one or another aspect of the African American experience in higher education), in the fall of 1996. Perhaps anticipating that people might wonder why the essay appeared there, the editor's headnote to the article explained its placement in the journal by quoting Nobel prize winner Toni Morrison's statement that "the first gesture of contempt for working-class students is to trivialize and devalue their need for an interest in art, languages, and culture."*

1   There is supposed to be a major debate—or even a set of debates—going on at present concerning a crisis in the universities, specifically a crisis in the teaching of the humanities. This debate is supposed to be in large part about whether a certain traditional conception of liberal education should be replaced by something sometimes called "multiculturalism." These disputes have even reached the mass media, and several best-selling books are devoted to discussing them and related issues. Though the arguments are ostensibly about Western civilization itself, they are couched in a strange jargon that includes not only "multiculturalism" but also "the canon," "political correctness," "ethnicity," "affirmative action," and even more rebarbative expressions such as "hegemony," "empowerment," "poststructuralism," "deconstruction," and "patriarchalism."

2   Since I do not know of a neutral vocabulary, I will describe the debate as between the "defenders" and the "challengers"

of the tradition. I realize that there is a great deal of variety on each side and more than one debate going on, but I am going to try to expose some common core assumptions of each side, assumptions seldom stated explicitly but which form the unstated premises behind the enthymemes that each side tends to use. Let us start by stating naively the traditionalists' view of higher education and, equally naively, the most obvious of the challengers' objections to it. This will, I hope, enable us to get into the deeper features of the debate.

Here is the traditionalists' view: There is a certain tradition   3
in American higher education, especially in the teaching of the humanities. The idea behind this tradition is that there is a body of works of philosophy, literature, history, and art that goes from the Greeks right up to the present day, and though it is not a unified tradition, there are certain family resemblances among the leading works in it, and for want of a better name, we call it the Western intellectual tradition. It extends in philosophy from Socrates to Wittgenstein or, if you like, from the pre-Socratics to Quine, in literature from the Greek poets and playwrights right up to, for example, James Joyce and Ernest Hemingway. The idea is that if you are going to be an educated person in the United States, you must have some familiarity with some of the chief works in this tradition because it defines our particular culture. You do not know who you are, in a sense, unless you have some familiarity with these works, because America is a product of this tradition, and the United States Constitution in particular is a product of a certain philosophical element in this tradition, the European Enlightenment. And then, too, we think that many works in this tradition, some of those by Shakespeare and Plato, for example, are really so good that they are of *universal* human interest.

So much for the naive statement of the traditionalist view.   4
There is an objection put by the challengers, and the objection, to put it in its crudest form, is as follows: If you look closely at the reading lists of this "Great Tradition," you will discover that the books are almost all by white males from Europe and North America. There are vast areas of the earth and great civilizations whose achievements are totally unrepresented in this conception of "liberal education." Furthermore, within the population of the United States as it is presently constituted, there are lots of ethnic minorities, as well as the largest minority of all, women, whose special needs, interests, traditions, and achievements are underrepresented or in some cases not represented at all in this tradition.

5   What is the response of the traditionalists to this objection? At this point the debate already begins to get murky, because it is hard to find traditionalist authors who address the objection directly, so I am going to interject myself and present what I think the traditionalists should say, given their other assumptions. The traditionalist should just accept this objection as a valid criticism and amend the "canon" accordingly. If great works by Asian authors, for example, have been excluded from the "canon" of great works of literature, then by all means let us expand the so-called canon to include them. Closer to home, if great women writers have been excluded, often because they are women, then let us expand membership in the list to include them as well. According to the traditionalist theory, one of the advantages of higher education is that it enables us to see our own civilization and mode of sensibility as one possible form of life among others. And one of the virtues of the tradition is the enormous variety within it. In fact, there never was a "canon." There was a set of constantly revised judgments about which books deserve close study, which deserve to be regarded as "classics." So, based on the traditionalists' own conception, there should be no objection to enlarging the list to include classics from sources outside the Western tradition and from neglected elements within it.

6   As I have presented it, the challengers are making a commonsense objection, to which the traditionalists have a commonsense answer. So it looks as if we have an obvious solution to an interesting problem and can all go home. What is there left to argue about? But it is at this point that the debate becomes interesting. What I have discovered in reading books and articles about this debate is that the objection to the so-called canon—that it is unrepresentative, that it is too exclusive—cannot be met by opening membership to include works by previously excluded elements of the population, since some people would accept such reform as adequate, but many will not. Why not? In order to answer that question I am going to try to state the usually unstated presuppositions made by both the traditionalists and the challengers. I realize, to repeat, that there is a great deal of variety on both sides, but I believe that each side holds certain assumptions, and it is important to try to make them explicit. In the debates one sees, the fundamental issues often are not coming out into the open, and as a result the debaters are talking past each other, seldom making contact. One side accuses the other of

racism, imperialism, sexism, elitism, and of being hegemonic and patriarchal. The other side accuses the first of trying to destroy intellectual standards and of politicizing the university. So what is actually going on? What is in dispute?

Assumptions Behind the Tradition

I will try to state the assumptions behind the tradition as a set of propositions, confining myself to half a dozen for the sake of brevity. The first assumption is that the criteria for inclusion in the list of "the classics" is supposed to be a combination of intellectual merit and historical importance. Some authors, Shakespeare for example, are included because of the quality of their work; others, Marx for example, are included because they have been historically so influential. Some, Plato for instance, are both of high quality and historically influential.   7

A second assumption made by the traditionalists is that there are intersubjective standards of rationality, intelligence, truth, validity, and general intellectual merit. In our list of required readings we include Plato but not randomly selected comic strips, because we think there is an important distinction in quality between the two, and *we think we can justify the claim that there is a distinction*. The standards are not algorithmic. Making judgements of quality is not like measuring velocities, but it is not arbitrary either.   8

A third assumption behind the tradition is that one of the things we are to do is to enable our students to overcome the mediocrity, provincialism, or other limitations of whatever background from which they may have come. The idea is that your life is likely to be in large measure a product of a lot of historical accidents: the town you were born in, the community you grew up in, the sort of values you learned in high school. One of the aims of a liberal education is to liberate our students from the contingencies of their backgrounds. We invite the student into the membership of a much larger intellectual community. This third feature of the traditional educational theory, then, is what one might call an invitation to transcendence. The professor asks his or her students to read books that are designed to challenge any complacencies that the students may have brought to the university when they first arrived there.   9

A fourth assumption made by the traditionalists, which is related to the third, is that in the Western tradition, there is a   10

peculiar combination of what one might call extreme univer-
salism and extreme individualism. Again, this tends to be
tacit and is seldom made explicit. The idea is that the most
precious thing in the universe is the human individual, but
that the human individual is precious as part of the universal
human civilization. The idea is that one achieves one's maximum intellectual *individual* potential by coming to see oneself as part of a *universal* human species with a universal
human culture.

11   A fifth feature of this tacit theory behind educational traditionalism is that a primary function of liberal education is
criticism of oneself and one's community. According to this
conception, the unexamined life is not worth living, and the
examined life is life criticized. I do not know of any intellectual tradition that is as savagely self-critical as the Western
tradition. Its hero is Socrates, and of course we all know what
happened to him. "I would rather die by the present argument than live by any other," he said. This is the model we
hold up to our students: the lone individual, standing out
against the hypocrisy, stupidity, and dishonesty of the larger
community. And that tradition goes right through to the nineteenth and twentieth centuries, through Freud, Nietzsche,
Marx, and Bertrand Russell, to mention just a few. The tradition is that of the extremely critical intellectual commentator
attacking the pieties and inadequacies, the inconsistencies
and hypocrisies of the surrounding community.

12   I will mention a sixth and final feature. Objectivity and
truth are possible because there is an independently existing
reality to which our true utterances correspond. This view,
called realism, has often been challenged by various forms of
idealism and relativism within Western culture but it has remained the dominant metaphysical view in our culture. Our
natural science, for example, is based on it. A persistent topic
of debate is: How far does it extend? Is there, for example, an
independently existing set of moral values that we can discover, or are we, for example, just expressing our subjective
feelings and attitudes when we make moral judgments? I am
tempted to continue this list but I hope that what I have said
so far will give you a feel for the underlying assumptions of
the traditionalist theory of liberal education.

13   I am now going to try to do the same for the challengers,
but this is harder to do without distortion, simply because
there is more variety among the critics of the tradition than
there is in the tradition itself. Nonetheless, I am going to do
my best to try to state a widely held set of core assumptions

made by the challengers. Perhaps very few people, maybe no one, believe all of the assumptions I will try to make explicit, but they are those I have found commonly made in the debates. The first assumption made by the challengers is that the subgroup into which you were born—your ethnic, racial, class, and gender background—matters enormously; it is important for education. In the extreme version of this assumption, you are essentially defined by your ethnic, racial, class, and gender background. That is the most important thing in your life. The dean of an American state university told me, "The most important thing in my life is being a woman and advancing the cause of women." Any number of people think that the most important thing in their lives is their blackness or their Hispanic identity, et cetera. This is something new in American higher education. Of course, there have always been people who were defined or who preferred to be defined by their ethnic group or by other such affiliations, but it has not been part of the theory of what the university was trying to do that we should *encourage* self-definition by ethnicity, race, gender, or class. On the contrary, as I noted in my list of the traditionalist assumptions, we were trying to encourage students to rise above the accidents of such features. But to a sizable number of American academics, it has now become acceptable to think that the most important thing in one's life is precisely these features. Notice the contrast between the traditionalists and the challengers on this issue. For the traditionalists, what matters is the individual within the universal. For the challengers, the universal is an illusion, and the individual has an identity only as a member of some subgroup.

A second feature of this alternative view is the belief that, 14 to state it crudely, all cultures are equal. Not only are they morally equal, as human beings are morally equal, but all cultures are intellectually equal as well. According to this view, the idea that we have more to learn from the representatives of one race, gender, class, or ethnic group than we do from the representatives of others is simply racism and old-fashioned imperialism. It is simply a residue of Eurocentric imperialism to suppose, as the traditionalists have been supposing, that certain works of European white males are somehow superior to the products of other cultures, classes, genders, and ethnic groups. Belief in the superiority of the Western canon is a priori objectionable because all authors are essentially representatives of their culture, and all cultures are intellectually equal.

15   In this alternative view, a third feature is that when it
comes to selecting what you should read, representativeness
is obviously crucial. In a multiculturalist educational democracy, every culture must be represented. The difficulty with
the prevailing system is that most groups are underrepresented, and certain groups are not represented at all. The proposal of opening up doors just to let a few superstars in is no
good, because that still leaves you, in plain and simple terms,
with too many dead, white, European males. Even if you include every great woman novelist that you want to include—
every Jane Austen, George Eliot, and Virginia Woolf—you are
still going to have too many dead, white, European males on
your list. It is part of the elitism, the hegemonism, and the patriarchalism of the existing ideology that it tries to perpetuate
the same patterns of repression even while pretending to be
opening up. Worse yet, the lack of diversity in the curriculum
is matched by an equal lack of *diversity in the faculty*. It's no
use getting rid of the hegemony of *dead* white males in the
curriculum if the faculty that teaches the multicultural curriculum is still mostly *living* white males. Representativeness
is crucial not only in the curriculum but even more so in the
composition of the faculty.

16   I want to pause here to contrast these three assumptions of
the challengers with those of the traditionalists. The traditionalists think they are selecting both reading lists and faculty members on grounds of quality and not on grounds of
representation. They think they select Plato and Shakespeare,
for example, because they produced works of genius, not because they are specimens or representatives of some group.
The challengers think this is self-deception at best, oppression at worst. They think that since the canon consists mostly
of white European males, the authors must have been selected *because* they are white European males. And they think
that because most of the professors are white males, this fact
by itself is proof that there is something wrong with the composition of the faculty.

17   You can see the distinction between the challengers and
the traditionalists if you imagine a counterfactual situation.
Suppose it was discovered by an amazing piece of historical
research that the works commonly attributed to Plato and Aristotle were not written by Greek males but by two Chinese
women who were cast ashore on the coast of Attica when a
Chinese junk shipwrecked off the Pireaus in the late fifth century B.C. What difference would this make to our assessment
of the works of Plato and Aristotle? From the traditionalist

point of view, none whatever. It would be just an interesting historical fact. From the challengers' point of view, I think it would make a tremendous difference. Ms. Plato and Ms. Aristotle would now acquire a new authenticity as genuine representatives of a previously underrepresented minority, and the most appropriate faculty to teach their work would then be Chinese women. Implicit in the traditionalists' assumptions I stated is the view that the faculty member does not have to exemplify the texts he or she teaches. They assume that the works of Marx can be taught by someone who is not a Marxist, just as Aquinas can be taught by someone who is not a Catholic, and Plato by someone who is not a Platonist. But the challengers assume, for example, that women's studies should be taught by feminist women, Chicano studies by Chicanos committed to a certain set of values, and so on.

These three points, that you are defined by your culture, 18 that all cultures are created equal, and that representation is the criterion for selection both of the books to be read and the faculty to teach them, are related to a fourth assumption: The primary purpose of education in the humanities is political transformation. I have read any number of authors who claim this, and I have had arguments with several people, some of them in positions of authority in universities, who tell me that the purpose of education, in the humanities at least, is political transformation. For example, another dean at a big state university, herself a former Berkeley radical, has written that her academic life is just an extension of her political activities. In its most extreme version, the claim is not just that the purpose of education in the humanities *ought* to be political, but rather that all education always has been political and always will necessarily be political, so it might as well be beneficially political. The idea that the traditionalists with their "liberal education" are somehow teaching some politically neutral philosophical tradition is entirely a self-deceptive masquerade. According to this view, it is absurd to accuse the challengers of politicizing the university; it already is politicized. Education is political down to the ground. And, so the story goes, the difference between the challengers, as against the traditional approach, is that the traditional approach tries to disguise the fact that it is essentially engaged in the political indoctrination of generations of young people so that they will continue to accept a system of hegemonic, patriarchal imperialism. The challengers, on the other hand, think of themselves as accepting the inevitably political nature of the university, and they want to use it so that they and their students can be liberated into a genuine multicultural democracy. When they say that the purpose of the university is political, this is not some new proposal that they are making. They think of themselves as just facing up to the facts as they always have been.

19   Once you understand that the challengers regard the university as essentially political, then several puzzling features of the present debate become less puzzling. Why has radical politics migrated into academic departments of literature? In my intellectual childhood, there were plenty of radical activists about, but they tended to operate in a public political arena, or, to the extent they tended to be in universities at all, they were usually in departments of political science, sociology, and economics. Now, as far as I can tell, the leading intellectual centers of radical political activity in the United States are departments of English, French, and comparative literature. We are, for example, in the odd situation where America's two "leading Marxists" are both professors of English. How did this come about? What would Marx think if he knew that his main impact was on literary criticism? Well, part of the reason for the migration of radical politics into literature departments is that Marxism in particular and left-wing radicalism in general have been discredited as theories of politics, society, and historical change. If ever a philosophical theory was refuted by events, it was the Marxist theory of the inevitable collapse of the capitalist economies and their revolutionary overthrow by the working class, to be followed by the rise of a classless society. Instead, it is the Marxist economies that have collapsed and the Marxist governments that have been overthrown. So, having been refuted as theories of society, these views retreated into departments of literature, where to some extent they still flourish as tools of "interpretation."

20   There is a more important reason, however. During the 1960s a fairly sizable number of leftist intellectuals became convinced that the best arena of social change was culture, that high culture in general and university departments of literature in particular could become important weapons in the struggle to overcome racism, imperialism, et cetera. We are now witnessing some of the consequences of this migration. As someone—I think it was Irving Howe—remarked, it is characteristic of this generation of radicals that they don't want to take over the country, they want to take over the English department. But, I would add, they think taking over the

English department is the first step toward taking over the country.

So far, then, I have tried to isolate four presuppositions of   21
the challengers: that ethnicity is important; that cultures are intellectually equal; that representativeness is crucial in the curriculum and in faculty composition; and that an important function of the humanities is political and social change. Now let me identify a fifth: There are no such things as objective standards. As one pamphlet published by the American Council of Learned Societies put it, "As the most powerful modern philosophies and theories have been demonstrating, claims of disinterest, objectivity, and universality are not to be trusted, and themselves tend to reflect local historical conditions." According to the ACLS pamphlet, such claims usually involve some power grab on the part of the person who is claiming to be objective. This presupposition, that there are no objective or intersubjective standards to which one can appeal in making judgments of quality, is a natural underpinning of the first four. The idea that there might be some objective standards of what is good and what is bad, that you might be able to show that Shakespeare is better than Mickey Mouse, for example, threatens the concept that all cultures are equal and that representativeness must be the criterion for inclusion in the curriculum. The whole idea of objectivity, truth, rationality, intelligence, as they are traditionally construed, and distinctions of intellectual quality, are all seen as part of the same system of repressive devices.

This leads to the sixth presupposition, which is the hardest   22
of all to state, because it is an inchoate attitude rather than a precise thesis. Roughly speaking, it involves a marriage of left-wing politics with certain antirationalist strands derived from recent philosophy. The idea is that we should stop thinking there is an objective reality that exists independently of our representations of it; we should stop thinking that propositions are true when they correspond to that reality; and we should stop thinking of language as a set of devices for conveying meanings from speakers to hearers. In short, the sixth presupposition is a rejection of realism and truth in favor of some version of relativism, the idea that all of reality is ultimately textual. This is a remarkable guise for left-wing views to take, because until recently extreme left-wing views claimed to have a scientific basis. The current challengers are suspicious of science and equally suspicious of the whole apparatus

of rationality, objective truth, and metaphysical realism, which go along with the scientific attitude.

23   A seventh presupposition is this: Western civilization is historically oppressive. Domestically, its history is one of oppressing women, slaves, and serfs. Internationally, its history is one of colonialism and imperialism. It is no accident that the works in the Western tradition are by white males, because the tradition is dominated by a caste consisting of white males. In this tradition, white males are the group in power.

24   I have tried to make explicit some of the unstated assumptions of both sides, because I think that otherwise it is impossible to explain why the contestants don't seem to make any contact with each other. They seem to be talking about two different sets of issues. I believe that is because they proceed from different sets of assumptions and objectives. If I have succeeded here in articulating the two sets of assumptions, that should be enough. However, the philosopher in me insists on making a few comments about each side and stating a few assumptions of my own. I think the basic philosophical underpinnings of the challengers are weak. Let us start with the rejection of metaphysical realism. This view is derived from deconstructionist philosophers as well as from an interpretation of the works of Thomas Kuhn and Richard Rorty. The idea, roughly speaking, is that Kuhn is supposed to have shown that science does not give us an account of an independently existing reality. Rather, scientists are an irrational bunch who run from one paradigm to another, for reasons with no real connection to finding objective truths. What Kuhn did for science, Rorty supposedly also did for philosophy. Philosophers don't provide accounts that mirror how the world is, because the whole idea of language as mirroring or corresponding to reality is flawed from the beginning. (The works of Kuhn and Rorty, by the way, are more admired in academic departments of literature than they are in departments in the sciences and philosophy.) Whether or not this is the correct interpretation of the works of Kuhn, Rorty, and the deconstructionists, the effect of these works has been to introduce into various humanities departments versions of relativism, anti-objectivism, and skepticism about science and the correspondence theory of truth.

25   Because of the limitation of space, I am going to be rather swift in my refutation of this view. The only defense that one can give of metaphysical realism is a transcendental argument in one of Kant's many senses of that term. We assume

that something is the case and show how that metaphysical realism is a condition of possibility of its being the case. If both we and our adversaries share the assumption that something is the case and that which we assume presupposes realism, then the transcendental argument is a refutation of our adversaries' view. It seems to me obvious in this case that we as well as the antirealists assume we are communicating with each other in a public language. When the antirealists present us with an argument they claim to do so in a language that is publicly intelligible. But, I wish to argue, public intelligibility presupposes the existence of a publicly accessible world. Metaphysical realism is not a thesis; rather, it is the condition of the possibility of having theses which are publicly intelligible. Whenever we use a language that purports to have public objects of reference, we commit ourselves to realism. The commitment is not a specific theory as to *how* the world is, but rather that there is a way the world is. Thus, it is self-refuting for someone to claim in a public language that metaphysical realism is false, because a public language presupposes a public world, and that presupposition is metaphysical realism.

Though I will not develop it here, it seems that a similar argument applies to objective standards of rationality. Again, to put it very crudely, one can't make sense out of presenting a thesis, or having a belief, or defending a view without presupposing certain standards of rationality. The very notions of mental and linguistic representation already contain certain logical principles built into them. For those who think that I am exaggerating the extent to which the traditional values are challenged, I suggest they read the ACLS pamphlet from which I quoted earlier.   26

Another fallacious move made by the challengers is to infer,   27
from the fact that the university's educational efforts invariably have political consequences, that therefore the primary objective of the university and the primary criteria for assessing its success or failure should be political. The conclusion does not follow from the premise. Obviously, everything has political consequences, whether it's art, music, literature, sex, or gastronomy. For example, right now you could be campaigning for the next presidential election, and therefore this article has political consequences, because it prevents you from engaging in political activities in which you might otherwise be engaging. In this sense, *everything* is political. But from the fact that everything is political in this sense, it doesn't follow that our academic *objectives* are political, nor

does it follow that the criteria for assessing our successes and failures are political. The argument, in short, does not justify the current attempts to use the classroom and the curriculum as tools of political transformation.

28   A further fallacy concerns the notion of empowerment. The most general form of this fallacy is the supposition that power is a property of groups rather than of individuals and organizations. A moment's reflection will reveal that this is not true. Most positions of power in the United States are occupied by middle-aged white males, but it does not follow that power accrues to middle-aged white males as a group. Most white males, middle-aged or otherwise, are as powerless as anyone else. In these discussions, there is a fallacy that goes as follows: People assume because most people in positions of power are white males that therefore most white males are in a position of power. I hope the fallacy is obvious.

29   Finally, in my list of criticisms of the challengers, I want to point out that we should not be embarrassed by the fact that a disproportionately large percentage of the major cultural achievements in our society have been made by white males. This is an interesting historical fact that requires analysis and explanation. But it doesn't in any way discredit the works of, for example, Descartes or Shakespeare that they happen to have been white males, any more than it discredits the work of Newton and Darwin that they were both English. Representativeness as such is not the primary aim in the study of the humanities. Rather, representativeness comes in as a desirable goal when there is a question of articulating the different varieties of human experience. And our aim in seeking works that articulate this variety is always to find works of high quality. The problem with the predominance of white males is not that there is any doubt about the quality of the work, but that we have been excessively provincial, that great works in other cultures may have been neglected, and that, even within Western civilization, there have been groups, most notably women, whose works have been discriminated against.

30   My criticism of the traditionalists is somewhat different from my criticism of the challengers because I do not, as a matter of fact, find much that is objectionable in the assumptions behind the traditionalist philosophy of education. The difficulty is how those assumptions are being implemented in contemporary American universities.

31   There are many forms of decay and indeed corruption that have become entrenched in the actual practice of American

universities, especially where undergraduate education is concerned. The most obvious sign of decay is that we have simply lost enthusiasm for the traditional philosophy of a liberal education. As our disciplines have become more specialized, as we have lost faith in the ideal of an integrated undergraduate education, we simply provide the student with the familiar cafeteria of courses and hope things turn out for the best. The problem with the traditionalists' ideology is not that it is false but that it has run out of gas. It is somewhat hypocritical to defend a traditional liberal education with a well-rounded reading list that goes from Plato to James Joyce if one is unwilling actually to attempt to educate undergraduates in this tradition. I do not, frankly, think that the challengers have superior ideas. Rather, they have something which may be more important to influencing the way things are actually done. They have more energy and enthusiasm, not to say fanaticism and intolerance. In the long run, these may be more effective in changing universities than rigorous arguments can be.

LITERACY NARRATIVES: HOW DID YOU BECOME LITERATE?

Benjamin Franklin
From *The Autobiography of Benjamin Franklin*

If you have ever visited Philadelphia, you probably know quite a bit about Benjamin Franklin, for Franklin is literally that city's towering figure: his statue tops City Hall in the center of town. Franklin was one of those versatile and energetic polymaths that we associate with the American Revolution (Thomas Jefferson and George Washington were, of course, others): in the course of his long life, he was famous as an inventor, publisher, and statesman, and his pragmatic way of life stamped itself indelibly onto the American character.

Born in Boston in 1706, he arrived in Philadelphia as a teenager to make his fortune. Finding work as a printer, he rose quickly in his profession, took over a newspaper, published Poor Richard's Almanac *(a compendium of information and commonsense advice on every topic that made his name and fortune), and took an interest in civic affairs. After 1750, he was established enough to turn the rest of his life to science— his famous kite experiment related to electricity was conducted in 1752—and to politics. Franklin played a pivotal role in the establishment of the new United States by serving in the Second Continental Congress (which developed the Declaration of Independence), by securing support from France during the war with Britain, and by helping to resolve differences during the Constitutional Convention of 1787.*

Many of the details of Franklin's life are described in his memoir, The Autobiography, *which he began in 1771, abandoned for a time, and then completed just before he died in 1790. The following excerpts, parts of a "letter to his son" that grew into the larger* Autobiography, *concern how Franklin developed his rhetorical skill. (In the passage, the references to* Pilgrim's

Progress, *Bunyan's* Works, *Burton's* Historical Collections, *and so forth, all refer to well-known eighteenth-century books; the* Spectator *was an influential literary paper that was put out by Joseph Addison and Richard Steele from 1711–1712.)*

From a Child I was fond of Reading, and all the little　1 Money that came into my Hands was ever laid out in Books. Pleas'd with the Pilgrim's Progress, my first Collection was of John Bunyan's Works, in separate little Volumes. I afterwards sold them to enable me to buy R. Burton's Historical Collections; they were small Chapmen's Books and cheap, 40 or 50 in all. My Father's little Library consisted chiefly of Books in polemic Divinity, most of which I read, and have since often regretted, that at a time when I had such a Thirst for Knowledge, more proper Books had not fallen in my Way, since it was now resolv'd I should not be a Clergyman. Plutarch's Lives there was, in which I read abundantly, and I still think that time spent to great Advantage. There was also a Book of Defoe's, called an Essay on Projects, and another of Dr. Mather's, call'd Essays to do Good which perhaps gave me a Turn of Thinking that had an Influence on some of the principal future Events of my Life.

This Bookish Inclination at length determin'd my Father　2 to make me a Printer, tho' he had already one Son, (James) of that Profession. In 1717 my Brother James return'd from England with a Press and Letters to set up his Business in Boston. I lik'd it much better than that of my Father, but still had a Hankering for the Sea. To prevent the apprehended Effect of such an Inclination, my Father was impatient to have me bound to my Brother. I stood out some time, but at last was persuaded and signed the Indentures, when I was yet but 12 Years old. I was to serve as an Apprentice till I was 21 Years of Age, only I was to be allow'd Journeyman's Wages during the last Year. In a little time I made great Proficiency in the Business, and became a useful Hand to my Brother. I now had Access to better Books. An Acquaintance with the Apprentices of Booksellers, enabled me sometimes to borrow a small one, which I was careful to return soon and clean. Often I sat up in my Room reading the greatest Part of the Night, when the Book was borrow'd in the Evening and to be return'd early in the Morning lest it should be miss'd or wanted. And after some time an ingenious Tradesman Mr. Matthew Adams who had a pretty Collection of Books, and who frequented our Printing House,

took Notice of me, invited me to his Library, and very kindly
lent me such Books as I chose to read. I now took a Fancy to
Poetry, and made some little Pieces. My Brother, thinking it
might turn to account encourag'd me, and put me on composing two occasional Ballads. One was called the *Light
House Tragedy,* and contain'd an account of the drowning of
Capt. Worthilake with his Two Daughters; the other was a
Sailor Song on the Taking of *Teach* or Blackbeard the Pirate.
They were wretched Stuff, in the Grubstreet Ballad Stile,
and when they were printed he sent me about the Town to
sell them. The first sold wonderfully, the Event being recent,
having made a great Noise. This flatter'd my Vanity. But my
Father discourag'd me, by ridiculing my Performances, and
telling me Verse-makers were generally Beggars; so I es-
cap'd being a Poet, most probably a very bad one. But, as
Prose Writing has been of great Use to me in the Course of
my Life, and was a principal Means of my Advancement, I
shall tell you how in such a Situation I acquir'd what little
Ability I have in that Way.

3   There was another Bookish Lad in the Town, John Collins by Name, with whom I was intimately acquainted. We
sometimes disputed, and very fond we were of Argument,
and very desirous of confuting one another. Which disputa-
cious Turn, by the way, is apt to become a very bad Habit,
making People often extreamly disagreable in Company, by
the Contradiction that is necessary to bring it into Practice,
and thence, besides souring and spoiling the Conversation,
is productive of Disgusts and perhaps Enmities where you
may have occasion for Friendship. I had caught it by reading my Father's Books of Dispute about Religion. Persons of
good Sense, I have since observ'd, seldom fall into it, except
Lawyers, University Men, and Men of all Sorts that have
been bred at Edinborough. A Question was once some how
or other started between Collins and me, of the Propriety of
educating the Female Sex in Learning, and their Abilities
for Study. He was of Opinion that it was improper; and that
they were naturally unequal to it. I took the contrary Side,
perhaps a little for Dispute sake. He was naturally more eloquent, had a ready Plenty of Words, and sometimes as I
thought bore me down more by his Fluency than by the
Strength of his Reasons. As we parted without settling the
Point, and were not to see one another again for some time,
I sat down to put my Arguments in Writing, which I copied
and sent to him. He answer'd and I reply'd. Three or four

Letters of a Side had pass'd, when my Father happen'd to find my Papers, and read them. Without entring into the Discussion, he took occasion to talk to me about the Manner of my Writing, observ'd that tho' I had the Advantage of my Antagonist in correct Spelling and [punctuation] (which I ow'd to the Printing House) I fell far short in elegance of Expression, in Method and in Perspicuity, of which he convinc'd me by several Instances. I saw the Justice of his Remarks, and thence grew more attentive to the *Manner* in Writing, and determin'd to endeavour at Improvement.

About this time I met with an odd Volume of the Spectator. 4 It was the third. I had never before seen any of them. I bought it, read it over and over, and was much delighted with it. I thought the Writing excellent, and wish'd if possible to imitate it. With that View, I took some of the Papers, and making short Hints of the Sentiment in each Sentence, laid them by a few Days, and then without looking at the Book, try'd to compleat the Papers again, by expressing each hinted Sentiment at length and as fully as it had been express'd before, in any suitable Words, that should come to hand.

Then I compar'd my Spectator with the Original, dis- 5 cover'd some of my Faults and corrected them. But I found I wanted a Stock of Words or a Readiness in recollecting and using them, which I thought I should have acquir'd before that time, if I had gone on making Verses, since the continual Occasion for Words of the same Import but of different Length, to suit the Measure, or of different Sound for the Rhyme, would have laid me under a constant Necessity of searching for Variety, and also have tended to fix that Variety in my Mind, and make me Master of it. Therefore I took some of the Tales and turn'd them into Verse: And after a time, when I had pretty well forgotten the Prose, turn'd them back again. I also sometimes jumbled my Collections of Hints into Confusion, and after some Weeks, endeavour'd to reduce them into the best Order, before I began to form the full Sentences, and compleat the Paper. This was to teach me Method in the Arrangement of Thoughts. By comparing my work afterwards with the original, I discover'd many faults and amended them; but I sometimes had the Pleasure of Fancying that in certain Particulars of small Import, I had been lucky enough to improve the Method or the Language and this encourag'd me to think I might possibly in time come to be a tolerable English Writer, of which I was extreamly ambitious.

Frederick Douglass
From *The Narrative of the Life of Frederick Douglass*

*Frederick Douglass's rise from obscurity to prominence was
even more astounding than the rise of Benjamin Franklin.
Born a slave in 1818 under the name of Frederick Bailey—he
never knew his father and seldom saw his mother after he was
taken from her as a child—Douglass escaped to the North in
1839 and assumed a new identity. He quickly became active in
abolitionist circles and, after a decade of flight, was able to purchase his freedom. Later, he began his own newspaper,* The
North Star, *in Rochester, New York, as a vehicle for his beliefs
and causes. A prominent orator and essayist, during the Civil
War he urged President Lincoln to enlist African Americans in
the army, and after the war he continued to campaign for freedom, not only by advocating antilynching laws and better conditions for tenant farmers but also by supporting women's
suffrage.*

Douglass gives his own account of his early life in his Narrative of the Life of Frederick Douglass, *the most famous of
the hundreds of "slave narratives" (i.e., first-hand accounts of
slave life) that were published in the years before the Civil War.
(You may have read Toni Morrison's recent slave narrative,*
Beloved.*) When the book was published in 1845, it established
Douglass as a major voice in the antislavery movement and gave
rise to images of the self that would affect the way other Americans would forever think of themselves. The following passage
from Chapter 7 of the* Narrative *describes how Douglass began
to learn to read and write.*

1   I lived in Master Hugh's family about seven years. During
this time, I succeeded in learning to read and write. In accomplishing this, I was compelled to resort to various strat-
agems. I had no regular teacher. My mistress, who had
kindly commenced to instruct me, had, in compliance with
the advice and direction of her husband, not only ceased to
instruct, but had set her face against my being instructed by
any one else. It is due, however, to my mistress to say of her,
that she did not adopt this course of treatment immediately.
She at first lacked the depravity indispensable to shutting
me up in mental darkness. It was at least necessary for her

to have some training in the exercise of irresponsible power, to make her equal to the task of treating me as though I were a brute.

My mistress was, as I have said, a kind and tender-   2
hearted woman; and in the simplicity of her soul she commenced, when I first went to live with her, to treat me as she supposed one human being ought to treat another. In entering upon the duties of a slaveholder, she did not seem to perceive that I sustained to her the relation of a mere chattel, and that for her to treat me as a human being was not only wrong, but dangerously so. Slavery proved as injurious to her as it did to me. When I went there, she was a pious, warm, and tender-hearted woman. There was no sorrow or suffering for which she had not a tear. She had bread for the hungry, clothes for the naked, and comfort for every mourner that came within her reach. Slavery soon proved its ability to divest her of these heavenly qualities. Under its influence, the tender heart became stone, and the lamblike disposition gave way to one of tigerlike fierceness. The first step in her downward course was in her ceasing to instruct me. She now commenced to practise her husband's precepts. She finally became even more violent in her opposition than her husband himself. She was not satisfied with simply doing as well as he had commanded; she seemed anxious to do better. Nothing seemed to make her more angry than to see me with a newspaper. She seemed to think that here lay the *danger*. I have had her rush at me with a face made all up of fury, and snatch from me a newspaper, in a manner that fully revealed her apprehension. She was an apt woman; and a little experience soon demonstrated, to her satisfaction, that education and slavery were incompatible with each other.

From this time I was most narrowly watched. If I was in   3
a separate room any considerable length of time, I was sure to be suspected of having a book, and was at once called to give an account of myself. All this, however, was too late. The first step had been taken. Mistress, in teaching me the alphabet, had given me the *inch*, and no precaution could prevent me from taking the *ell*.

The plan which I adopted, and the one by which I was   4
most successful, was that of making friends of all the little white boys whom I met in the street. As many of these as I could, I converted into teachers. With their kindly aid, obtained at different times and in different places, I finally

succeeded in learning to read. When I was sent of errands, I always took my book with me, and by going one part of my errand quickly, I found time to get a lesson before my return. I used also to carry bread with me, enough of which was always in the house, and to which I was always welcome; for I was much better off in this regard than many of the poor white children in our neighborhood. This bread I used to bestow upon the hungry little urchins, who, in return, would give me that more valuable bread of knowledge. I am strongly tempted to give the names of two or three of those little boys, as a testimonial of the gratitude and affection I bear them; but prudence forbids;—not that it would injure me, but it might embarrass them; for it is almost an unpardonable offence to teach slaves to read in this Christian country. It is enough to say of the dear little fellows, that they lived on Philpot Street, very near Durgin and Bailey's ship-yard. I used to talk this matter of slavery over with them. I would sometimes say to them, I wished I could be as free as they would be when they got to be men. "You will be free as soon as you are twenty-one, *but I am a slave for life!* Have not I as good a right to be free as you have?" These words used to trouble them; they would express for me the liveliest sympathy, and console me with the hope that something would occur by which I might be free.

5   I was now about twelve years old, and the thought of being a *slave for life* began to bear heavily upon my heart. Just about this time, I got hold of a book entitled "The Columbian Orator." Every opportunity I got, I used to read this book. Among much of other interesting matter, I found in it a dialogue between a master and his slave. The slave was represented as having run away from his master three times. The dialogue represented the conversation which took place between them, when the slave was retaken the third time. In this dialogue, the whole argument in behalf of slavery was brought forward by the master, all of which was disposed of by the slave. The slave was made to say some very smart as well as impressive things in reply to his master—things which had the desired though unexpected effect; for the conversation resulted in the voluntary emancipation of the slave on the part of the master.

6   In the same book, I met with one of Sheridan's mighty speeches on and in behalf of Catholic emancipation. These were choice documents to me. I read them over and over again with unabated interest. They gave tongue to interest-

ing thoughts of my own soul, which had frequently flashed through my mind, and died away for want of utterance. The moral which I gained from the dialogue was the power of truth over the conscience of even a slaveholder. What I got from Sheridan was a bold denunciation of slavery, and a powerful vindication of human rights. The reading of these documents enabled me to utter my thoughts, and to meet the arguments brought forward to sustain slavery; but while they relieved me of one difficulty, they brought on another even more painful than the one of which I was relieved. The more I read, the more I was led to abhor and detest my enslavers. I could regard them in no other light than a band of successful robbers, who had left their homes, and gone to Africa, and stolen us from our homes, and in a strange land reduced us to slavery. I loathed them as being the meanest as well as the most wicked of men. As I read and contemplated the subject, behold! that very discontentment which Master Hugh had predicted would follow my learning to read had already come, to torment and sting my soul to unutterable anguish. As I writhed under it, I would at times feel that learning to read had been a curse rather than a blessing. It had given me a view of my wretched condition, without the remedy. It opened my eyes to the horrible pit, but to no ladder upon which to get out. In moments of agony, I envied my fellow-slaves for their stupidity. I have often wished myself a beast. I preferred the condition of the meanest reptile to my own. Any thing, no matter what, to get rid of thinking! It was this everlasting thinking of my condition that tormented me. There was no getting rid of it. It was pressed upon me by every object within sight or hearing, animate or inanimate. The silver trump of freedom had roused my soul to eternal wakefulness. Freedom now appeared, to disappear no more forever. It was heard in every sound, and seen in every thing. It was ever present to torment me with a sense of my wretched condition. I saw nothing without seeing it, I heard nothing without hearing it, and felt nothing without feeling it. It looked from every star, it smiled in every calm, breathed in every wind, and moved in every storm.

    I often found myself regretting my own existence, and 7 wishing myself dead; and but for the hope of being free, I have no doubt but that I should have killed myself, or done something for which I should have been killed. While in this state of mind, I was eager to hear any one speak of slavery. I was a ready listener. Every little while, I could hear something about the abolitionists. It was some time before I found what the word meant. It was always used in such connections as to make it an interesting word to me. If a slave ran away and succeeded in getting clear, or if a slave killed his master, set fire to a barn, or did any thing very wrong in the mind of a slaveholder, it was spoken of as the fruit of *abolition*. Hearing the word in this connection very often, I set about learning what it meant. The dictionary afforded me little or no help. I found it was "the act of abolishing;" but then I did not know what was to be abolished. Here I was perplexed. I did not dare to ask any one about its meaning, for I was satisfied that it was something they wanted me to know very little about. After a patient waiting, I got one of our city papers, containing an account of the number of petitions from the north, praying for the abolition of slavery in the District of Columbia, and of the slave trade between the States. From this time I understood the words *abolition* and *abolitionist,* and always drew near when that word was spoken, expecting to hear something of importance to myself and fellow-slaves. The light broke in upon me by degrees. I went one day down on the wharf of Mr. Waters; and seeing two Irishmen unloading a scow of stone, I went, unasked, and helped them. When we had finished, one of them came to me and asked me if I were a slave. I told him I was. He asked, "Are ye a slave for life?" I told him that I was. The good Irishman seemed to be deeply affected by the statement. He said to the other that it was a pity so fine a little fellow as myself should be a slave for life. He said it was a shame to hold me. They both advised me to run away to the north; that I should find friends there, and that I should be free. I pretended not to be interested in what they said, and treated them as if I did not understand them; for I feared they might be treacherous. White men have been known to encourage slaves to escape, and then, to get the reward, catch them and return them to their masters. I was afraid that these seemingly good men might use me so; but I nevertheless remembered their advice, and from that time I resolved to run away. I looked forward to a time at which it would be safe for me to escape. I was too young to think of doing so immediately; besides, I wished to learn how to write, as I might have an occasion to write my own pass. I consoled myself with the hope that I should one day find a good chance. Meanwhile, I would learn to write.

The idea as to how I might learn to write was suggested   8
to me by being in Durgin and Bailey's ship-yard, and frequently seeing the ship carpenters, after hewing, and getting
a piece of timber ready for use, write on the timber the
name of that part of the ship for which it was intended.
When a piece of timber was intended for the larboard side,
it would be marked thus—"L." When a piece was for the
starboard side, it would be marked thus—"S." A piece for
the larboard side forward, would be marked thus—"L. F."
When a piece was for starboard side forward, it would be
marked thus—"S. F." For larboard aft, it would be marked
thus—"L. A." For starboard aft, it would be marked thus—
"S. A." I soon learned the names of these letters, and for
what they were intended when placed upon a piece of timber in the ship-yard. I immediately commenced copying
them, and in a short time was able to make the four letters
named. After that, when I met with any boy who I knew
could write, I would tell him I could write as well as he. The
next word would be, "I don't believe you. Let me see you try
it." I would then make the letters which I had been so fortunate as to learn, and ask him to beat that. In this way I got a
good many lessons in writing, which it is quite possible I
should never have gotten in any other way. During this time,
my copy-book was the board fence, brick wall, and pavement; my pen and ink was a lump of chalk. With these, I
learned mainly how to write. I then commenced and continued copying the Italics in Webster's Spelling Book, until I
could make them all without looking on the book. By this
time, my little Master Thomas had gone to school, and
learned how to write, and had written over a number of
copy-books. These had been brought home, and shown to
some of our near neighbors, and then laid aside. My mistress used to go to class meeting at the Wilk Street meeting-
house every Monday afternoon, and leave me to take care of
the house. When left thus, I used to spend the time in writing in the spaces left in Master Thomas's copy-book, copying what he had written. I continued to do this until I could
write a hand similar to that of Master Thomas. Thus, after a
long, tedious effort for years, I finally succeeded in learning
how to write.

Julia Alvarez
My English

Julia Alvarez tells the story of her 1961 emigration from the Dominican Republic to the United States in the following memoir, which is one item in her 1998 collection of essays called Something to Declare. *Her experiences have also been told in several other books and in magazines such as* The American Scholar, Latina, *and the* Washington Post Magazine; *and they are reflected in her fiction as well, including* How the Garcia Girls Lost Their Accent *(1991). She teaches at Middlebury College in Vermont.*

1   Mami and Papi used to speak it when they had a secret they wanted to keep from us children. We lived then in the Dominican Republic, and the family as a whole spoke only Spanish at home, until my sisters and I started attending the Carol Morgan School, and we became a bilingual family. Spanish had its many tongues as well. There was the castellano of Padre Joaquín from Spain, whose lisp we all loved to imitate. Then the educated español my parents' families spoke, aunts and uncles who were always correcting us children, for we spent most of the day with the maids and so had picked up their "bad Spanish." Campesinas, they spoke a lilting, animated campuno, ss swallowed, endings chopped off, funny turns of phrases. This campuno was my true mother tongue, not the Spanish of Calderón de la Barca or Cervantes or even Neruda, but of Chucha and Iluminada and Gladys and Ursulina from Juncalito and Licey and Boca de Yuma and San Juan de la Maguana. Those women yakked as they cooked, they storytold, they gossiped, they sang—boleros, merengues, canciones, salves. Theirs were the voices that belonged to the rain and the wind and the teeny, teeny stars even a small child could blot out with her thumb.

2   Besides all these versions of Spanish, every once in a while another strange tongue emerged from my papi's mouth or my mami's lips. What I first recognized was not a language, but a tone of voice, serious, urgent, something important and top secret being said, some uncle in trouble, someone divorcing, someone dead. *Say it in English so the*

children won't understand. I would listen, straining to understand, thinking that this was not a different language but just another and harder version of Spanish. *Say it in English so the children won't understand.* From the beginning, English was the sound of worry and secrets, the sound of being left out.

I could make no sense of this "harder Spanish," and so I   3
tried by other means to find out what was going on. I knew my mother's face by heart. When the little lines on the corners of her eyes crinkled, she was amused. When her nostrils flared and she bit her lips, she was trying hard not to laugh. She held her head down, eyes glancing up, when she thought I was lying. Whenever she spoke that gibberish English, I translated the general content by watching the Spanish expressions on her face.

Soon, I began to learn more English, at the Carol Morgan   4
School. That is, when I had stopped gawking. The teacher and some of the American children had the strangest coloration: light hair, light eyes, light skin, as if Ursulina had soaked them in bleach too long, to' deteñío. I did have some blond cousins, but they had deeply tanned skin, and as they grew older, their hair darkened, so their earlier paleness seemed a phase of their acquiring normal color. Just as strange was the little girl in my reader who had a *cat* and a *dog*, that looked just like un gatito y un perrito. Her mami was *Mother* and her papi *Father.* Why have a whole new language for school and for books with a teacher who could speak it teaching you double the amount of words you really needed?

Butter, butter, butter, butter. All day, one English word that   5
had particularly struck me would go round and round in my mouth and weave through all the Spanish in my head until by the end of the day, the word did sound like just another Spanish word. And so I would say, "Mami, please pass la mantequilla." She would scowl and say in English, "I'm sorry, I don't understand. But would you be needing some butter on your bread?"

Why my parents didn't first educate us in our native lan-   6
guage by enrolling us in a Dominican school, I don't know. Part of it was that Mami's family had a tradition of sending the boys to the States to boarding school and college, and she had been one of the first girls to be allowed to join her brothers. At Abbot Academy, whose school song was our

lullaby as babies ("Although Columbus and Cabot never heard of Abbot, it's quite the place for you and me"), she had become quite Americanized. It was very important, she kept saying, that we learn our English. She always used the possessive pronoun: *your* English, an inheritance we had come into and must wisely use. Unfortunately, my English became all mixed up with our Spanish.

7   Mix-up, or what's now called Spanglish, was the language we spoke for several years. There wasn't a sentence that wasn't colonized by an English word. At school, a Spanish word would suddenly slide into my English like someone butting into line. Teacher, whose face I was learning to read as minutely as my mother's, would scowl but no smile played on her lips. Her pale skin made her strange countenance hard to read, so that I often misjudged how much I could get away with. Whenever I made a mistake, Teacher would shake her head slowly, "In English, YU-LEE-AH, there's no such word as *columpio*. Do you mean a *swing?*"

8   I would bow my head, humiliated by the smiles and snickers of the American children around me. I grew insecure about Spanish. My native tongue was not quite as good as English, as if words like *columpio* were illegal immigrants trying to cross a border into another language. But Teacher's discerning grammar-and-vocabulary-patrol ears could tell and send them back.

9   Soon, I was talking up an English storm. "Did you eat English parrot?" my grandfather asked one Sunday. I had just enlisted yet one more patient servant to listen to my rendition of "Peter Piper picked a peck of pickled peppers" at breakneck pace. "Huh?" I asked impolitely in English, putting him in his place. *Cat got your tongue? No big deal! So there! Take that! Holy Toledo!* (Our teacher's favorite "curse word.") *Go jump in the lake! Really dumb. Golly. Gosh.* Slang, clichés, sayings, hotshot language that our teacher called, ponderously, idiomatic expressions. Riddles, jokes, puns, conundrums. *What is yellow and goes click-click? Why did the chicken cross the road? See you later, alligator.* How wonderful to call someone an alligator and not be scolded for being disrespectful. In fact, they were supposed to say back, *In a while, crocodile.*

10   There was also a neat little trick I wanted to try on an English-speaking adult at home. I had learned it from Elizabeth, my smart-alecky friend in fourth grade, whom I alter-

nately worshiped and resented. I'd ask her a question that required an explanation, and she'd answer, "Because…" "Elizabeth, how come you didn't go to Isabel's birthday party?" "Because…" "Why didn't you put your name in your reader?" "Because…" I thought that such a cool way to get around having to come up with answers. So, I practiced saying it under my breath, planning for the day I could use it on an unsuspecting English-speaking adult.

One Sunday at our extended family dinner, my grandfather sat down at the children's table to chat with us. He was famous, in fact, for the way he could carry on adult conversations with his grandchildren. He often spoke to us in English so that we could practice speaking it outside the classroom. He was a Cornell man, a United Nations representative from our country. He gave speeches in English. Perfect English, my mother's phrase. That Sunday, he asked me a question. I can't even remember what it was because I wasn't really listening but lying in wait for my chance. "Because…," I answered him. Papito waited a second for the rest of my sentence and then gave me a thumbnail grammar lesson, "*Because* has to be followed by a clause." 11

"Why's that?" I asked, nonplussed. 12

"Because," he winked, "Just because." 13

A beginning wordsmith, I had so much left to learn; sometimes it was disheartening. Once Tío Gus, the family intellectual, put a speck of salt on my grandparents' big dining table during Sunday dinner. He said, "Imagine this whole table is the human brain. Then this teensy grain is all we ever use of our intelligence!" He enumerated geniuses who had perhaps used two grains, maybe three: Einstein, Michelangelo, da Vinci, Beethoven. We children believed him. It was the kind of impossible fact we thrived on, proving as it did that the world out there was not drastically different from the one we were making up in our heads. 14

Later, at home, Mami said that you had to take what her younger brother said "with a grain of salt." I thought she was still referring to Tío Gus's demonstration, and I tried to puzzle out what she was saying. Finally, I asked what she meant. "Taking what someone says with a grain of salt is an idiomatic expression in English," she explained. It was pure voodoo is what it was—what later I learned poetry could also do: a grain of salt could symbolize both the human 15 brain and a condiment for human nonsense. And it could be itself, too: a grain of salt to flavor a bland plate of American food.

16   When we arrived in New York, I was shocked. A country where everyone spoke English! These people must be smarter, I thought. Maids, waiters, taxi drivers, doormen, bums on the street, all spoke this difficult language. It took some time before I understood that Americans were not necessarily a smarter, superior race. It was as natural for them to learn their mother tongue as it was for a little Dominican baby to learn Spanish. It came with "mother's milk," my mother explained, and for a while I thought a mother tongue was a mother tongue because you got it from your mother's breast, along with proteins and vitamins.

17   Soon it wasn't so strange that everyone was speaking in English instead of Spanish. I learned not to hear it as English, but as sense. I no longer strained to understand, I understood. I relaxed in this second language. Only when someone with a heavy southern or British accent spoke in a movie, or at church when the priest droned his sermon— only then did I experience that little catch of anxiety. I worried that I would not be able to understand, that I wouldn't be able to "keep up" with the voice speaking in this acquired language. I would be like those people from the Bible we had studied in religion class, whom I imagined standing at the foot of an enormous tower that looked just like the skyscrapers around me. They had been punished for their pride by being made to speak different languages so that they didn't understand what anyone was saying.

18   But at the foot of those towering New York skyscrapers, I began to understand more and more—not less and less— English. In sixth grade, I had one of the first in a lucky line of great English teachers who began to nurture in me a love of language, a love that had been there since my childhood of listening closely to words. Sister Maria Generosa did not make our class interminably diagram sentences from a workbook or learn a catechism of grammar rules. Instead, she asked us to write little stories imagining we were snowflakes, birds, pianos, a stone in the pavement, a star in the sky. What would it feel like to be a flower with roots in the ground? If the clouds could talk, what would they say? She had an expressive, dreamy look that was accentuated by the wimple that framed her face.

Supposing, just supposing…My mind would take off,   19
soaring into possibilities, a flower with roots, a star in the
sky, a cloud full of sad, sad tears, a piano crying out each
time its back was tapped, music only to our ears.

Sister Maria stood at the chalkboard. Her chalk was al-   20
ways snapping in two because she wrote with such energy,
her whole habit shaking with the swing of her arm, her
hand tap-tap-tapping on the board. "Here's a simple sentence: 'The snow fell.'" Sister pointed with her chalk, her
eyebrows lifted, her wimple poked up. Sometimes I could
see wisps of gray hair that strayed from under her head-
dress. "But watch what happens if we put an adverb at the
beginning and a prepositional phrase at the end: 'Gently, the
snow fell on the bare hills.'"

I thought about the snow. I saw how it might fall on the   21
hills, tapping lightly on the bare branches of trees. Softly, it
would fall on the cold, bare fields. On toys children had left
out in the yard, and on cars and on little birds and on people
out late walking on the streets. Sister Maria filled the chalkboard with snowy print, on and on, handling and shaping
and moving the language, scribbling all over the board until
English, those verbal gadgets, those tricks and turns of
phrases, those little fixed units and counters, became a
charged, fluid mass that carried me in its great fluent waves,
rolling and moving onward, to deposit me on the shores of
my new homeland. I was no longer a foreigner with no
ground to stand on. I had landed in the English language.

Clint Swinson
Grandma

Clint Swinson wrote the following literacy narrative while he was enrolled in a first-year composition course at the University of Oklahoma. He has since graduated with a bachelor's degree in business administration (1998) and is pursuing a career within the high-end restaurant industry.

1   "Clint Robert, come over here and sit down at the table."

2   "But Grandma, I'm playing with my cars."

3   "You can play with them later, darling, I want to teach you something."

4   "OK, I'm coming."

5   That's just one of the many times that I went to learn something at my grandma's table. I was about three or four years old then, and I spent almost every day at my grandma's house. My mom worked, and since my grandma lived just across town she was the perfect babysitter. I spent many years going to my grandma's house; the years before I began school and many years after were spent at 2010 N. Broadway Street in Shawnee, Oklahoma. I spent much of my time playing cars, constructing tents both inside and outside the house, making crafts found in the latest *High-lights* magazine, or fighting with my little sister, Kim, who is three years younger than me. Grandma always found something for us to do. Sometimes we would help cook lunch, which was always ready by noon because my grandpa came home at that time. He was a postman. His route was in the neighborhood so he didn't have far to go. Lunch was spent listening to the KGFF, 1450 AM noontime report and the Paul Harvey News.

6   It was an age of innocence, a day that has passed—never to be seen again. It all seems to have changed. One doesn't see children begging to go to grandma's house. The kids of today seem grown up and caught up in worldly affairs, but I could have cared less what was going on around me. Just as long as I could go to my grandma's everything would be alright. If I could ride my tricycle under her gumball tree and jump and frolic in the leaves of fall; if I could make my grandma's couch into a boat and sail from country to country, then everything was great. That is what my grandma's

house is to me: a home full of memories, a home where I first learned to read and write.

My grandma was a teacher and a role model for me to 7 look up to. She taught her two sons right and wrong, and reading and writing. She passed her wisdom on to me both directly and indirectly. The direct ways are the ones I remember most. Pulling up a chair to her dining room table was a moment that sticks out most in my mind. She taught me to write my name. I remember trying to copy her handwriting, not quite knowing what those letters meant. It was new to me, and it took a while to learn. It was strange, looking at something I had written and being told it was my name but not being able to reason how to read it. I got to know how to pronounce a written word, even a word *I* had written. I learned a majority of the alphabet and practiced the "A,B,C" song all the time. In all the things I did, my grandma was there encouraging me and taking every ounce of patience she had to teach a three year old to write his name. This didn't take one day; it was a long process taking several months. Seasons passed but I caught on and learned to say my A,B,C's and to perfect the writing of my name. This was my first sense of accomplishment, and I owe this all to my Grandma Roella. Everything that I did from then on, I could write my name on. I could write my name on every drawing and picture in my numerous coloring books and all of the crafts I did.

Learning to write was something I did in the mornings at 8 Grandma's. In the afternoon I learned just as much if not more. After Grandma had done the dishes from lunch, it was time for Kim and me to have a nap. Of course with any nap there had to be a story read. Kim and I would get a blanket while Grandma got a book. Sometimes we picked the story, but it didn't matter, we all knew every one of them. Grandma would sit up in a big rocking-chair, and Kim and I would rest on her lap. She would begin to read, and Kim usually would fall off to sleep quickly, while I remained awake listening to the story. Grandma would read about the Bobsey Twins or the story of the five Chinese brothers. She read others like "Spot and Jane" and every other typical book that children are read, but I liked "The Five Chinese Brothers" the best. It was about a Chinese man that was unfairly sentenced to death by burning. The Chinese man asked if he could go home to bid farewell to his mother, and when he got home one of his other brothers went back in his place. This brother could not be burned, so they decided to drown him to fulfill the sentence. Again he asked if he could go home to bid his mother farewell, and another brother went back in his place. This brother could not drown, and this went on and on—one brother after the other—until they had stop trying to kill the Chinese man.

9   I remember this story so vividly because of the pictures of the brothers in the book. In some stories I remember the illustrations so clearly, but others didn't have pictures so it was up to my imagination to create them. Grandma always helped me and explained things that I didn't understand in the stories. She also stopped occasionally and asked me what a word was. If I didn't know, then she helped me sound it out. This was how I spent every afternoon. Of course I eventually fell off to sleep, but only after the end of the story, or when we had reached a good stopping point. In this way, Grandma helped me build a good foundation for reading in the future.

10   After I started school, I spent less time at Grandma's house, but by no means was my education through. When I walked into Grandma's house I continued to learn from her after school. She would ask me what I did and help me with problems I had. She also had her own questions for me. She asked me questions in order for me to fully understand the answers myself.

11   Kindergarten came easy because I had already perfected the alphabet. Grandma helped me through my first spelling test I encountered in the first grade. Later, in second grade, she was an influence on my penmanship when I had to learn to write in cursive. She also played a part in my being accepted to advanced reading in the third grade in that my vocabulary skills were enhanced by my grandmother. In fourth grade, my family moved to Tecumseh, which is about ten minutes away from Shawnee and my grandmother's house. Although I visited frequently on weekends, I no longer went to her house after school. But by then she had helped to equip me with the basics I needed for literacy in the future.

12   I acquired all the formal tools I needed to be a capable writer during the rest of my schooling. I had already learned basic grammar skills from my grandma that made writing short stories and essays simple. In the eighth grade a journal was introduced to me. The topic was whatever we wanted to write about; we did freewriting for fifteen min-

utes at a time. Creative, detailed, and sometimes humorous, these writings were mine

I never found these feelings again throughout high 13 school. Boring, stuffy, informative papers about trivial subjects were the context of my writings in high school. These writings never challenged me to achieve or express. Regurgitating facts from an article was what I became accomplished at in high school. Occasional poems were assigned to let me vent a few lines of originality. Being complacent about this, I forgot what it felt like to create sentences with words reflecting my own personality—words that could express my thoughts, my life, my atmosphere. Expression: isn't that the purpose of writing? I found myself very contained when writing in high school, having to stay within the guidelines. High school has left me with a bitter taste for writing, one that hasn't changed until now.

College has left for me a sweeter taste for writing. To 14 choose a topic of my very own, one that is mine again, not one that is hers or his, but mine, is refreshing. A work written in my own unique style is what I do best. My writing is the product of me alone now—or should I say me and the influence that has been with me from the beginning. From the first A in the alphabet to the last period on this page, my grandma Roella has been with me. In every aspect of literacy up to the present, I can't help but reflect upon that basic foundation laid by Grandma. That foundation is strong enough to support all that my imagination and creativity can build upon it.

While my sister Kim was going off to college, I learned 15 from a teacher far more qualified than any college professor. It was my grandma, and I owe the start of my literacy to her. From such a simple start, from writing the A,B,C's and my name, I have learned to produce many essays, short stories, reports, and poems. All have come from such a basic foundation that my grandma helped me build, the very foundation that I am still building on every day. She may not know it, but she has shaped my life in more ways than she can imagine.

Min-zhan Lu

From Silence to Words:
Writing as Struggle

Min-zhan Lu teaches a variety of courses related to composition, rhetoric, and literacy at Drake University in Iowa. She is active in professional organizations related to those areas, and in 1987, she published the following essay in College English, *which is produced by one of those organizations, the College Section of the National Council of Teachers of English, and which is read mostly by college English teachers. You will read more about Professor Lu's background when you read her narrative.*

1   My mother withdrew into silence two months before she died. A few nights before she fell silent, she told me she regretted the way she had raised me and my sisters. I knew she was referring to the way we had been brought up in the midst of two conflicting worlds—the world of home, dominated by the ideology of the Western humanistic tradition, and the world of a society dominated by Mao Tse-tung's Marxism. My mother had devoted her life to our education, an education she knew had made us suffer political persecution during the Cultural Revolution. I wanted to find a way to convince her that, in spite of the persecution, I had benefited from the education she had worked so hard to give me. But I was silent. My understanding of my education was so dominated by memories of confusion and frustration that I was unable to reflect on what I could have gained from it.

2   This paper is my attempt to fill up that silence with words, words I didn't have then, words that I have since come to by reflecting on my earlier experience as a student in China and on my recent experience as a composition teacher in the United States. For in spite of the frustration and confusion I experienced growing up caught between two conflicting worlds, the conflict ultimately helped me to grow as a reader and writer. Constantly having to switch back and forth between the discourse of home and that of school made me sensitive and self-conscious about the struggle I experienced every time I tried to read, write, or think in either discourse. Eventually, it led me to search for constructive uses for such struggle.

From early childhood, I had identified the differences be- 3
tween home and the outside world by the different languages I used in each. My parents had wanted my sister and
me to get the best education they could conceive of—
Cambridge. They had hired a live-in tutor, a Scot, to make
us bilingual. I learned to speak English with my parents, my
tutor, and my sisters. I was allowed to speak Shanghai dialect only with the servants. When I was four (the year after
the Communist revolution of 1949), my parents sent me to a
local private school where I learned to speak, read, and
write in a new language—Standard Chinese, the official
written language of New China.

In those days, I moved from home to school, from En- 4
glish to Standard Chinese to Shanghai dialect, with no apparent friction. I spoke each language with those who spoke
the language. All seemed quite "natural"—servants spoke
only Shanghai dialect because they were servants; teachers
spoke Standard Chinese because they were teachers; languages had different words because they were different languages. I thought of English as my family language,
comparable to the many strange dialects I didn't speak but
had often heard some of my classmates speak with their
families. While I was happy to have a special family language, until second grade I didn't feel that my family language was any different than some of my classmates' family
dialects.

My second grade homeroom teacher was a young gradu- 5
ate from a missionary school. When she found out I spoke
English, she began to practice her English on me. One day
she used English when asking me to run an errand for her.
As I turned to close the door behind me, I noticed the puzzled faces of my classmates. I had the same sensation I had
often experienced when some stranger in a crowd would
turn on hearing me speak English. I was more intensely
pleased on this occasion, however, because suddenly I felt
that my family language had been singled out from the family languages of my classmates. Since we were not allowed
to speak any dialect other than Standard Chinese in the
classroom, having my teacher speak English to me in class
made English an official language of the classroom. I began
to take pride in my ability to speak it.

This incident confirmed in my mind what my parents 6
had always told me about the importance of English to one's

life. Time and again, they had told me of how my paternal grandfather, who was well versed in classic Chinese, kept losing good-paying jobs because he couldn't speak English. My grandmother reminisced constantly about how she had slaved and saved to send my father to a first-rate missionary school. And we were made to understand that it was my father's fluent English that had opened the door to his success. Even though my family had always stressed the importance of English for my future, I used to complain bitterly about the extra English lessons we had to take after school. It was only after my homeroom teacher had "sanctified" English that I began to connect English with my education. I became a much more eager student in my tutorials.

7   What I learned from my tutorials seemed to enhance and reinforce what I was learning in my classroom. In those days each word had one meaning. One day I would be making a sentence at school: "The national flag of China is red." The next day I would recite at home, "My love is like a red, red rose." There seemed to be an agreement between the Chinese "red" and the English "red," and both corresponded to the patch of color printed next to the word. "Love" was my love for my mother at home and my love for my "motherland" at school: both "loves" meant how I felt about my mother. Having two loads of homework forced me to develop a quick memory for words and a sensitivity to form and style. What I learned in one language carried over to the other. I made sentences such as, "I saw a red, red rose among the green leaves," with both the English lyric and the classic Chinese lyric—red flower among green leaves—running through my mind, and I was praised by both teacher and tutor for being a good student.

8   Although my elementary schooling took place during the fifties, I was almost oblivious to the great political and social changes happening around me. Years later, I read in my history and political philosophy textbooks that the fifties were a time when "China was making a transition from a semi-feudal, semi-capitalist and semi-colonial country into a socialist country," a period in which "the Proletarians were breaking into the educational territory dominated by Bourgeois Intellectuals." While people all over the country were being officially classified into Proletarians, Petty-bourgeois, National-bourgeois, Poor-peasants, and Intellectuals, and were trying to adjust to their new social identities, my parents were allowed to continue the upper middle-class life

they had established before the 1949 Revolution because of my father's affiliation with British firms. I had always felt that my family was different from the families of my classmates, but I didn't perceive society's view of my family until the summer vacation before I entered high school.

First, my aunt was caught by her colleagues talking to her   9
husband over the phone in English. Because of it, she was criticized and almost labeled a Rightist. (This was the year of the Anti-Rightist movement, a movement in which the Intellectuals became the target of the "socialist class-struggle.") I had heard others telling my mother that she was foolish to teach us English when Russian had replaced English as the "official" foreign language. I had also learned at school that the American and British Imperialists were the arch-enemies of New China. Yet I had made no connection between the arch-enemies and the English our family spoke. What happened to my aunt forced the connection on me. I began to see my parents' choice of a family language as an anti-Revolutionary act and was alarmed that I had participated in such an act. From then on, I took care not to use English outside home and to conceal my knowledge of English from my new classmates.

Certain words began to play important roles in my new   10
life at the junior high. On the first day of school, we were handed forms to fill out with our parents' class, job, and income. Being one of the few people not employed by the government, my father had never been officially classified. Since he was a medical doctor, he told me to put him down as an Intellectual. My homeroom teacher called me into the office a couple of days afterward and told me that my father couldn't be an Intellectual if his income far exceeded that of a Capitalist. He also told me that since my father worked for Foreign Imperialists, my father should be classified as an Imperialist Lackey. The teacher looked nonplussed when I told him that my father couldn't be an Imperialist Lackey because he was a medical doctor. But I could tell from the way he took notes on my form that my father's job had put me in an unfavorable position in his eyes.

The Standard Chinese term "class" was not a new word   11
for me. Since first grade, I had been taught sentences such as, "The Working class are the masters of New China." I had always known that it was good to be a worker, but until then, I had never felt threatened for not being one. That fall, "class" began to take on a new meaning for me. I noticed a

group of Working-class students and teachers at school. I was made to understand that because of my class background, I was excluded from that group.

12   Another word that became important was "consciousness." One of the slogans posted in the school building read, "Turn our students into future Proletarians with socialist consciousness and education!" For several weeks we studied this slogan in our political philosophy course, a subject I had never had in elementary school. I still remember the definition of "socialist consciousness" that we were repeatedly tested on through the years: "Socialist consciousness is a person's political soul. It is the consciousness of the Proletarians represented by Marxist Mao Tse-tung thought. It takes expression in one's action, language, and lifestyle. It is the task of every Chinese student to grow up into a Proletarian with a socialist consciousness so that he can serve the people and the motherland." To make the abstract concept accessible to us, our teacher pointed out that the immediate task for students from Working-class families was to strengthen their socialist consciousnesses. For those of us who were from other class backgrounds, the task was to turn ourselves into Workers with socialist consciousnesses. The teacher never explained exactly how we were supposed to "turn" into Workers. Instead, we were given samples of the ritualistic annual plans we had to write at the beginning of each term. In these plans, we performed "self-criticism" on our consciousnesses and made vows to turn ourselves into Workers with socialist consciousnesses. The teacher's division between those who did and those who didn't have a socialist consciousness led me to reify the notion of "consciousness" into a thing one possesses. I equated this intangible "thing" with a concrete way of dressing, speaking, and writing. For instance, I never doubted that my political philosophy teacher had a socialist consciousness because she was from a steelworker's family (she announced this the first day of class) and was a Party member who wore grey cadre suits and talked like a philosophy textbook. I noticed other things about her. She had beautiful eyes and spoke Standard Chinese with such a pure accent that I thought she should be a film star. But I was embarrassed that I had noticed things that ought not to have been associated with her. I blamed my observation on my Bourgeois consciousness.

13   At the same time, the way reading and writing were taught through memorization and imitation also encour-

aged me to reduce concepts and ideas to simple definitions. In literature and political philosophy classes, we were taught a large number of quotations from Marx, Lenin, and Mao Tse-tung. Each concept that appeared in these quotations came with a definition. We were required to memorize the definitions of the words along with the quotations. Every time I memorized a definition, I felt I had learned a word: "The national red flag symbolizes the blood shed by Revolutionary ancestors for our socialist cause"; "New China rises like a red sun over the eastern horizon." As I memorized these sentences, I reduced their metaphors to dictionary meanings: "red" meant "Revolution" and "red sun" meant "New China" in the "language" of the Working class. I learned mechanically but eagerly. I soon became quite fluent in this new language.

As school began to define me as a political subject, my parents tried to build up my resistance to the "communist poisoning" by exposing me to the "great books"—novels by Charles Dickens, Nathaniel Hawthorne, Emily Brontë, Jane Austen, and writers from around the turn of the century. My parents implied that these writers represented how I, their child, should read and write. My parents replaced the word "Bourgeois" with the word "cultured." They reminded me that I was in school only to learn math and science. I needed to pass the other courses to stay in school, but I was not to let the "Red doctrines" corrupt my mind. Gone were the days when I could innocently write, "I saw the red, red rose among the green leaves," collapsing, as I did, English and Chinese cultural traditions. "Red" came to mean Revolution at school, "the Commies" at home, and adultery in *The Scarlet Letter*. Since I took these symbols and metaphors as meanings natural to people of the same class, I abandoned my earlier definitions of English and Standard Chinese as the language of home and the language of school. I now defined English as the language of the Bourgeois and Standard Chinese as the language of the Working class. I thought of the language of the Working class as someone else's language and the language of the Bourgeois as my language. But I also believed that, although the language of the Bourgeois was my real language. I could and would adopt the language of the Working class when I was at school. I began to put on and take off my Working class language in the same way I put on and took off my school clothes to avoid being criticized for wearing Bourgeois clothes.

15   In my literature classes, I learned the Working-class formula for reading. Each work in the textbook had a short
"Author's Biography": "XXX, born in 19– in the province of
XXX, is from a Worker's family. He joined the Revolution in
19–. He is a Revolutionary realist with a passionate love for
the Party and Chinese Revolution. His work expresses the
thought and emotions of the masses and sings praise to the
prosperous socialist construction on all fronts of China."
The teacher used the "Author's Biography" as a yardstick to
measure the texts. We were taught to locate details in the
texts that illustrated these summaries, such as words that
expressed Workers' thoughts and emotions or events that illustrated the Workers' lives.

16   I learned a formula for Working-class writing in the composition classes. We were given sample essays and told to
imitate them. The theme was always about how the collective taught the individual a lesson. I would write papers
about labor-learning experiences or school-cleaning days,
depending on the occasion of the collective activity closest
to the assignment. To make each paper look different, I
dressed it up with details about the date, the weather, the
environment, or the appearance of the Master-worker who
had taught me "the lesson." But as I became more and more
fluent in the generic voice of the Working-class Student, I
also became more and more self-conscious about the language we used at home.

17   For instance in senior high, we began to have English
classes ("to study English for the Revolution," as the slogan
on the cover of the textbook said), and I was given my first
Chinese-English dictionary. There I discovered the English
version of the term "class-struggle." (The Chinese characters for a school "class" and for a social "class" are different.) I had often used the English word "class" at home in
sentences such as, "So and so has class," but I had not connected this sense of "class" with "class-struggle." Once the
connection was made, I heard a second layer of meaning
every time someone at home said a person had "class." The
expression began to mean the person had the style and sophistication characteristic of the Bourgeoisie. The word lost
its innocence. I was uneasy about hearing that second layer
of meaning because I was sure my parents did not hear the
word that way. I felt that therefore I should not be hearing it
that way either. Hearing the second layer of meaning made
me wonder if I was losing my English.

My suspicion deepened when I noticed myself uncon-   18
sciously merging and switching between the "reading" of
home and the "reading" of school. Once I had to write a report on *The Revolutionary Family,* a book about an illiterate
woman's awakening and growth as a Revolutionary through
the deaths of her husband and all her children for the cause
of the Revolution. In one scene the woman deliberated over
whether she should encourage her youngest son to join the
Revolution. Her memory of her husband's death made her
afraid to encourage her son. Yet she also remembered her
earlier married life and the first time her husband tried to
explain the meaning of the Revolution to her. These memories made her feel she should encourage her son to continue
the cause his father had begun.

I was moved by this scene. "Moved" was a word my   19
mother and sisters used a lot when we discussed books. Our
favorite moments in novels were moments of what I would
now call internal conflict, moments which we said "moved"
us. I remember that we were "moved" by Jane Eyre when
she was torn between her sense of ethics, which compelled
her to leave the man she loved, and her impulse to stay with
the only man who had ever loved her. We were also moved
by Agnes in *David Copperfield* because of the way she restrained her love for David so that he could live happily with
the woman he loved. My standard method of doing a book
report was to model it on the review by the Publishing Bureau and to dress it up with detailed quotations from the
book. The review of *The Revolutionary Family* emphasized
the woman's Revolutionary spirit. I decided to use the scene
that had moved me to illustrate this point. I wrote the report
the night before it was due. When I had finished, I realized I
couldn't possibly hand it in. Instead of illustrating her Revolutionary spirit, I had dwelled on her internal conflict,
which could be seen as a moment of weak sentimentality
that I should never have emphasized in a Revolutionary her-
oine. I wrote another report, taking care to illustrate the
grandeur of her Revolutionary spirit by expanding on a quotation in which she decided that if the life of her son could
change the lives of millions of sons, she should not be-
grudge his life for the cause of Revolution. I handed in my
second version but kept the first in my desk.

I never showed it to anyone. I could never show it to peo-   20
ple outside my family, because it had deviated so much
from the reading enacted by the jacket review. Neither could

I show it to my mother or sisters, because I was ashamed to have been so moved by such a "Revolutionary" book. My parents would have been shocked to learn that I could like such a book in the same way they liked Dickens. Writing this book report increased my fear that I was losing the command over both the "language of home" and the "language of school" that I had worked so hard to gain. I tried to remind myself that, if I could still tell when my reading or writing sounded incorrect, then I had retained my command over both languages. Yet I could no longer be confident of my command over either language because I had discovered that when I was not careful—or even when I was—my reading and writing often surprised me with its impurity. To prevent such impurity, I became very suspicious of my thoughts when I read or wrote. I was always asking myself why I was using this word, how I was using it, always afraid that I wasn't reading or writing correctly. What confused me and frustrated me most was that I could not figure out why I was no longer able to read or write correctly without such painful deliberation.

21   I continued to read only because reading allowed me to keep my thoughts and confusion private. I hoped that somehow, if I watched myself carefully, I would figure out from the way I read whether I had really mastered the "languages." But writing became a dreadful chore. When I tried to keep a diary, I was so afraid that the voice of school might slip in that I could only list my daily activities. When I wrote for school, I worried that my Bourgeois sensibilities would betray me.

22   The more suspicious I became about the way I read and wrote, the more guilty I felt for losing the spontaneity with which I had learned to "use" these "languages." Writing the book report made me feel that my reading and writing in the "language" of either home or school could not be free of the interference of the other. But I was unable to acknowledge, grasp, or grapple with what I was experiencing, for both my parents and my teachers had suggested that, if I were a good student, such interference would and should not take place. I assumed that once I had "acquired" a discourse, I could simply switch it on and off every time I read and wrote as I would some electronic tool. Furthermore, I expected my reading and writings to come out in their correct forms whenever I switched the proper discourse on. I still regarded the discourse of home as natural and the dis-

course of school alien, but I never had doubted before that I could acquire both and switch them on and off according to the occasion.

When my experience in writing conflicted with what I   23
thought should happen when I used each discourse, I rejected my experience because it contradicted what my parents and teachers had taught me. I shied away from writing to avoid what I assumed I should not experience. But trying to avoid what should not happen did not keep it from recurring whenever I had to write. Eventually my confusion and frustration over these recurring experiences compelled me to search for an explanation: how and why had I failed to learn what my parents and teachers had worked so hard to teach me?

I now think of the internal scene for my reading and writ-   24
ing about *The Revolutionary Family* as a heated discussion between myself, the voices of home, and those of school. The review on the back of the book, the sample student papers I came across in my composition classes, my philosophy teacher—these I heard as voices of one group. My parents and my home readings were the voices of an opposing group. But the conversation between these opposing voices in the internal scene of my writing was not...polite and respectful.... Rather, these voices struggled to dominate the discussion, constantly incorporating, dismissing, or suppressing the arguments of each other, like the battles between the hegemonic and counter-hegemonic forces described in Raymond Williams' *Marxism and Literature....*

When I read *The Revolutionary Family* and wrote the first   25
version of my report, I began with a quotation from the review. The voices of both home and school answered, clamoring to be heard. I tried to listen to one group and turn a deaf ear to the other. Both persisted. I negotiated my way through these conflicting voices, now agreeing with one, now agreeing with the other. I formed a reading out of my interaction with both. Yet I was afraid to have done so because both home and school had implied that I should speak in unison with only one of these groups and stand away from the discussion rather than participate in it.

My teachers and parents had persistently called my atten-   26
tion to the intensity of the discussion taking place on the external social scene. The story of my grandfather's failure and my father's success had from my early childhood made me aware of the conflict between Western and traditional

Chinese cultures. My political education at school added another dimension to the conflict: the war of Marxist-Maoism
against them both. Yet when my parents and teachers called
my attention to the conflict, they stressed the anxiety of having to live through China's transformation from a semi-
feudal, semi-capitalist, and semi-colonial society to a socialist one. Acquiring the discourse of the dominant group was,
to them, a means of seeking alliance with that group and
thus of surviving the whirlpool of cultural currents around
them. As a result, they modeled their pedagogical practices
on this utilitarian view of language. Being the eager student,
I adopted this view of language as a tool for survival. It
came to dominate my understanding of the discussion on
the social and historical scene and to restrict my ability to
participate in that discussion.

27   To begin with, the metaphor of language as a tool for survival led me to be passive in my use of discourse, to be a by-
stander in the discussion. In Burke's "parlor," everyone is
involved in the discussion. As it goes on through history,
what we call "communal discourses"—arguments specific
to particular political, social, economic, ethnic, sexual, and
family groups—form, re-form and transform. To use a discourse in such a scene is to participate in the argument and
to contribute to the formation of the discourse. But when I
was growing up, I could not take on the burden of such an
active role in the discussion. For both home and school presented the existent conventions of the discourse each taught
me as absolute laws for my action. They turned verbal action into a tool, a set of conventions produced and shaped
prior to and outside of my own verbal acts. Because I saw
language as a tool, I separated the process of producing the
tool from the process of using it. The tool was made by
someone else and was then acquired and used by me. How
the others made it before I acquired it determined and guaranteed what it produced when I used it. I imagined that the
more experienced and powerful members of the community
were the ones responsible for making the tool. They were
the ones who participated in the discussion and fought with
opponents. When I used what they made, their labor and accomplishments would ensure the quality of my reading and
writing. By using it I could survive the heated discussion.
When my immediate experience in writing the book report
suggested that knowing the conventions of school did not

guarantee the form and content of my report, when it suggested that I had to write the report with the work and responsibility I had assigned to those who wrote book reviews in the Publishing Bureau, I thought I had lost the tool I had earlier acquired.

Another reason I could not take up an active role in the argument was that my parents and teachers contrived to provide a scene free of conflict for practicing my various languages. It was as if their experience had made them aware of the conflict between their discourse and other discourses and of the struggle involved in reproducing the conventions of any discourse on a scene where more than one discourse exists. They seemed convinced that such conflict and struggle would overwhelm someone still learning the discourse. Home and school each contrived a purified space where only one discourse was spoken and heard. In their choice of textbooks, in the way they spoke, and in the way they required me to speak, each jealously silenced any voice that threatened to break the unison of the scene. The homogeneity of home and of school implied that only one discourse could and should be relevant in each place. It led me to believe I should leave behind, turn a deaf ear to, or forget the discourse of the other when I crossed the boundary dividing them. I expected myself to set down one discourse whenever I took up another just as I would take off or put on a particular set of clothes for school or home.

Despite my parents' and teachers' attempts to keep home and school discrete, the internal conflict between the two discourses continued whenever I read or wrote. Although I tried to suppress the voice of one discourse in the name of the other, having to speak aloud in the voice I had just silenced each time I crossed the boundary kept both voices active in my mind. Every "I think..." from the voice of home or school brought forth a "However..." or a "But..." from the voice of the opponents. To identify with the voice of home or school, I had to negotiate through the conflicting voices of both by restating, taking back, qualifying my thoughts. I was unconsciously doing so when I did my book report. But I could not use the interaction comfortably and constructively. Both my parents and my teachers had implied that my job was to prevent that interaction from happening. My sense of having failed to accomplish what they had taught silenced me.

30   To use the interaction between the discourses of home
and school constructively, I would have to have seen reading
or writing as a process in which I worked my way toward a
stance through a dialectical process of identification and division. To identify with an ally, I would have to have grasped
the distance between where he or she stood and where I was
positioning myself. In taking a stance against an opponent,
I would have to have grasped where my stance identified
with the stance of my allies. Teetering along the "wavering
line of pressure and counter-pressure" from both allies and
opponents, I might have worked my way towards a stance
of my own (Burke, *A Rhetoric of Motives* 23). Moreover, I
would have to have understood that the voices in my mind,
like the participants in the parlor scene, were in constant
flux [see the epigraph in the Preface—editor]. As I came into
contact with new and different groups of people or read different books, voices entered and left. Each time I read or
wrote, the stance I negotiated out of these voices would always be at some distance from the stances I worked out in
my previous and my later readings or writings.

31   I could not conceive such a form of action for myself
because I saw reading and writing as an expression of an
established stance. In delineating the conventions of a discourse, my parents and teachers had synthesized the stance
they saw as typical for a representative member of the community. Burke calls this the stance of a "god" or the "proto-
type": Williams calls it the "official" or "possible" stance of
the community. Through the metaphor of the survival tool,
my parents and teachers had led me to assume I could automatically reproduce the official stance of the discourse I
used. Therefore, when I did my book report on *The Revolutionary Family*, I expected my knowledge of the official
stance set by the book review to ensure the actual stance of
my report. As it happened, I began by trying to take the official stance of the review. Other voices interrupted. I answered back. In the process, I worked out a stance
approximate but not identical to the official stance I began
with. Yet the experience of having to labor to realize my
knowledge of the official stance or to prevent myself from
wandering away from it frustrated and confused me. For
even though I had been actually reading and writing in a
Burkean scene, I was afraid to participate actively in the
discussion. I assumed it was my role to survive by staying
out of it.

Not long ago, my daughter told me that it bothered her to   32
hear her friend "talk wrong." Having come to the United
States from China with little English, my daughter has
become sensitive to the way English, as spoken by her
teachers, operates. As a result, she has amazed her teachers
with her success in picking up the language and in adapting
to life at school. Her concern to speak the English taught in
the classroom "correctly" makes her uncomfortable when
she hears people using "ain't" or double negatives, which
her teacher considers "improper." I see in her the me that
had eagerly learned and used the discourse of the Working
class at school. Yet while I was torn between the two conflicting worlds of school and home, she moves with seeming
ease from the conversations she hears over the dinner table
to her teacher's words in the classroom. My husband and I
are proud of the good work she does at school. We are glad
she is spared the kinds of conflict between home and school
I experienced at her age. Yet as we watch her becoming
more and more fluent in the language of the classroom, we
wonder if, by enabling her to "survive" school, her very fluency will silence her when the scene of her reading and
writing expands beyond that of the composition classroom.

For when I listen to my daughter, to students, and to   33
some composition teachers talking about the teaching and
learning of writing, I am often alarmed by the degree to
which the metaphor of a survival tool dominates their
understanding of language as it once dominated my own. I
am especially concerned with the way some composition
classes focus on turning the classroom into a monological
scene for the students' reading and writing. Most of our students live in a world similar to my daughter's, somewhere
between the purified world of the classroom and the complex world of my adolescence. When composition classes
encourage these students to ignore those voices that seem
irrelevant to the purified world of the classroom, most students are often able to do so without much struggle. Some
of them are so adept at doing it that the whole process has
for them become automatic.

However, beyond the classroom and beyond the limited   34
range of these students' immediate lives lies a much more
complex and dynamic social and historical scene. To help
these students become actors in such a scene, perhaps we
need to call their attention to voices that may seem irrelevant to the discourse we teach rather than encourage them

to shut them out. For example, we might intentionally complicate the classroom scene by bringing into it discourses that stand at varying distances from the one we teach. We might encourage students to explore ways of practicing the conventions of the discourse they are learning by negotiating through these conflicting voices. We could also encourage them to see themselves as responsible for forming or transforming as well as preserving the discourse they are learning.

35   As I think about what we might do to complicate the external and internal scenes of our students' writing, I hear my parents and teachers saying: "Not now. Keep them from the wrangle of the marketplace until they have acquired the discourse and are skilled at using it." And I answer: "Don't teach them to 'survive' the whirlpool of crosscurrents by avoiding it. Use the classroom to moderate the currents. Moderate the currents, but teach them from the beginning to struggle." When I think of the ways in which the teaching of reading and writing as classroom activities can frustrate the development of students, I am almost grateful for the overwhelming complexity of the circumstances in which I grew up. For it was this complexity that kept me from losing sight of the effort and choice involved in reading or writing with and through a discourse.

Chi-Fan Jennifer Ku

An Internal Divide

Chi-Fan Jennifer Ku wrote the following essay in 1997 for a first-year writing course at the University of Arizona. She won an award for her work on the sixteenth anniversary of her arrival in the United States.

During my senior year in high school, despite my being 1
an honors student, the registrar's office accidentally scheduled me for study hall, which I attended for a week until my
schedule could be changed. When the study hall teacher
was taking attendance, he called out my name, Chi-Fan Ku,
and told me that he wanted to see me afterwards. He sat me
down and asked slowly, pronouncing each word clearly, "Do
you understand English? Do you need a translator?" His
questions shocked me. I had lived in the United States for
15 years; I spoke English and Chinese fluently and understood the basics of Spanish. I was almost trilingual, yet I did
not know how to answer his questions.

"Yes sir, I understand English. I have been in the United 2
States since I was three years old." The study hall teacher
had no way of knowing that I had been a U.S. citizen for
over six years or that I had an English name and a legal
name, Jennifer and Chi-Fan, because very few Americans
could pronounce my birth name correctly. While the study
hall teacher probably wanted to help me, he simply assumed from my oriental name and my presence in study
hall that I did not understand enough English to take another class.

At my high school, the widely accepted, stereotypical im- 3
age was that all Chinese students were geniuses, the top students in the accelerated classes. The only exception was if a
Chinese student had recently arrived from another country.
Only then would you find a Chinese student in a non-
accelerated class or study hall. Such mistakes and misunderstandings result from conclusions based on a combination of physical features and preconceptions. While such
perceptions create misunderstandings between cultures,
they also create internal rifts within those who live as individuals straddling those cultures.

4   Due to economic conditions, cultural differences, and their unwillingness to assimilate into the American culture, the Chinese immigrants in the late 1800s endured hostile feelings from American citizens and the government. Many Americans wanted to deport all Chinese immigrants because they believed that the Chinese stole most of their jobs. Yet these Americans never stopped to think that the jobs the Chinese accepted were either jobs Americans refused or dangerous jobs that employers were unwilling to give to American workers. Why endanger American lives, when employers could exploit another group of people that few in the United States considered to be human beings? If they did not use the Chinese, then they would have exploited another group, such as the Japanese, the Mexicans, or the Irish.

5   The majority of Chinese immigrants did not want to stay in the United States. They only wanted to earn enough money to support their families in China. They were willing to risk their health, happiness, and lives for their family because to the Chinese, the family always comes first. If you succeed, the entire family succeeds. If you fail, the entire family is disgraced. This basic ideology is drilled into all Chinese at an early age. If the Americans had seen the terror, heartache, sacrifice, and shattered pride these hardworking Chinese immigrants faced each day, would they have demanded that the government pass the Chinese Exclusion Act? Would they have treated the Chinese like dogs? All the Americans saw were the golden complexion, the black hair, the queue hair style, the small almond-shaped eyes. To the Americans, the Chinese were simply automatons—people unwilling to assimilate, nothing like them.

6   Today, Chinese immigrants try to learn from their ancestors' mistakes. Some Chinese parents believe that only through assimilation can their children survive and succeed in the United States. They encourage their children to immerse themselves in the American culture; they believe this is the key to allowing their children to be successful in America. They believe assimilation will protect their children from racial bias and the suffering that previous Chinese immigrants have endured. "Learn to speak English without an accent," some parents tell their children. "Become educated about the American culture through music and fashion, accept the dominant religion, have only Americanized friends." Unfortunately, many American-born Chi-

nese, or ABCs, do not hear the one sentence that parents add to their long list of advice: "Do not forget who you are."

Some parents try to tell their children this indirectly by sending them to Chinese language schools. At such schools, Chinese teachers, who are usually other Chinese parents, try to teach us grammar, cultural traditions, and history. However, most Chinese students attend only to socialize with each other. Do they hear anything the teacher says? Do they understand that a proper Chinese student respects the teacher and listens attentively? Sometimes when I was in Chinese language school I wanted to slap my classmates and shake them. My heart screamed, "Have you drunk so much Coke and eaten so many Big Macs that you have forgotten who you are? How could you trade your Chinese heritage for a superficial image?" Most graduate from Chinese school without really knowing a word of Chinese. Sometimes being around them, I felt shame and disgrace; they did not know that their actions reflected upon all of us, just as the early Chinese immigrant represented his family and his nation.

Perhaps my feelings result from my fear that someday I may awaken from a deep sleep and realize that the American ghost that haunts me has stolen my Chinese spirit. In the Chinese culture, Chinese ghosts are dangerous, because they are cunning and can kill you by just looking at you. Only the confident, strong, and brave will be able to overcome and destroy such a terrifying being. The American ghost, according to many of my Chinese elders, is not dreadful and elusive like the Chinese ghost. Rather, the American ghost is just a term that some Chinese people use to describe Americans, because the first American missionaries that arrived in China had complexions that were considerably paler than those of the Chinese, so the Chinese believed they were ghosts. While my relatives do not fear them, I do. As Chinese American author Maxine Hong Kingston wrote in *The Woman Warrior: Memoirs of a Girlhood Among Ghosts*, "we were born among ghosts, were taught by ghosts, and were ourselves half ghosts." I am part American ghost. I cannot hide from it or deny its existence. But I must be careful; otherwise the American ghost will overcome and dominate me. Then my Chinese spirit would be forced to leave. Then I would forget who I am.

My American ghost has no manners; it appears suddenly, without an invitation. For example, when I visit my relatives in Taiwan, I do not know the proper titles I should use to address my elders. They laugh when they hear me speak because I do not speak correctly. They excuse me, however. "She is just an American," my relatives tell their friends. One of their friends once asked me if I knew who the American president was. When I responded, "Bill Clinton," she seemed surprised. "I thought that all Chinese children who grow up in America were stupid." Her words sliced through my heart. "I am not completely American!" I wanted to scream back at her. But such behavior would not have been proper. My aunts tell me my shorts need to be longer—they need to cover the knees and would be better if they reached mid-calf. My uncles point out that I am too fat. They suggest that I stop eating American food. My relatives and other Chinese people do not see the black haired, brown eyed, yellow complexioned Chinese girl. Instead, they tell me that I might as well dye my hair blond and wear blue contacts. My relatives and Chinese school teachers call me a banana—a person with a yellow complexion, who is completely white inside. Ironically, my classmates at Chinese school, who want to be the typical American, tell me that I am the stereotypical Chinese. They claim that I have the mentality of the traditional, nonconforming Chinese student—always serious, always studying.

10   I am American. I am not American. I am Chinese. I am not Chinese. How do I explain my situation to others if I am lost and confused? I cannot only accept my American background while ignoring my Chinese heritage. Nor can I live solely by feeding off my Chinese upbringing. I want to cry. I feel scared. I am alone. Yet I can find comfort in other sources, such as the works of some multicultural authors. Mexican American writer Gloria Anzaldúa recommends to those who live between cultures to "live *sin fronteras* / be a crossroads." We must find an existence that allows us to accept both cultures, yet not drown in either, a difficult task requiring all my concentration. Yet, when I find that place, I will not have any borders to prevent me from moving between both cultures—a place where my American ghost and Chinese spirit will coexist in harmony. One day I will succeed. One day I will smile because I will know who I am.

II.

LANGUAGE

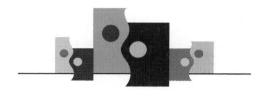

Introduction

People used to think of language as being ideologically neutral—as a sort of transparent window through which ideas are conveyed. Now many people agree that language is not transparent but colored by ideological and cultural biases. Far from being neutral, language is a product (as well as a producer) of culture. As such, it inevitably reflects (as well as shapes) that particular culture. The three issues explored in this part of *Conversations*—Should We Have a National Language?; Should There Be... A "Standard" English?; and Is English Sexist?—share the assumption that language is culture-bound, that social issues inevitably mingle with language issues.

The first section includes four items that are generally related to those in the previous section, items that include literacy narratives and that consider language against the backdrop of the ethnic diversity of the United States. (These readings also relate closely to the pieces in the section on defining race reprinted elsewhere in *Conversations*.) Should public policies enforce English as our national language and discourage the use of other tongues? For many years federal, state, and local governments, for instance, have supported the policy of giving students schoolwork in their native languages—English for most, but Spanish and Chinese and many other languages as well—so that students with limited proficiency in English would not fall behind in other subjects while they mastered English "as a second language." In 1974, Congress required schools to promote knowledge of students' native languages and cultures as well as to promote growth in English. But in the past decade the policy of bilingual education has come under fire. Some educators have contended that bilingual programs do not work well or that they are too expensive. Other critics, noting the importance of English as a unifying force in our society, contend that bilingual programs—because they interfere with students' mastery of English—prevent non-English-speaking citizens from assuming a central role in life in the United States. As a result, some citizens in over two dozen states have advocated, and in some cases even passed, laws designating English as "the official language" of the United States. They argue partly on the grounds of cost (bilingual education, bilingual ballots, bilingual forms and signs and menus all cost money), partly to promote a more unified nation, and partly to avoid the possibility that states in the Southwest might become Spanish-speaking "American Quebecs." (You probably remember that in 1995, the predominantly French-speaking Canadian province of Quebec nearly approved a resolution to secede from Canada.) Opponents contend that creating English as an official language would foster intolerance and bigotry, would compromise the civil rights of citizens who have not mastered English, and would undermine the richness of our nation's ethnic diversity.

The second section includes seven items that explore relationships between language and power, particularly about the ideology of standard American English. Is Black English a robust dialect that proceeds according to normal conventions of sound and structure? Or is it (especially in its written form) a substandard dialect that impedes communication and clouds thinking? Do Black English and other "nonstandard" dialects empower their users as fully as any other language, or do they undermine literacy, discourage the chances of their users for success in the main streams of American life, and keep their users politically and socially marginalized?

Power is also at the heart of feminist critiques of the English language. As the three selections and cartoon printed in this part on sexist language disclose, the English language can favor some groups at the expense of others—particularly men at the expense of women. To what extent does English, as the product of a culture dominated by males, demean and delimit women? To what extent does English perpetuate outworn cultural assumptions about women? In other words, to what extent is English itself sexist? And what can be done about it? Those are the questions taken up in this final section.

Most citizens in this country have been proud of the metaphor of the United States as a melting pot—a place where immigrants are assimilated into the fabric of American life and American language. Recently, another metaphor has been proposed: the United States as salad bowl, as a place where immigrant citizens become American but still retain their unique cultural flavor even as they contribute to the mix. Whatever the metaphor, language will continue to be an area where differences between individuals and their society are negotiated, where conflicts between "American society" and its diverse individuals are adjudicated. In other words, language itself will remain an issue.

SHOULD WE HAVE
A NATIONAL LANGUAGE?

Richard Rodriguez
Aria: A Memoir of a Bilingual Childhood

Richard Rodriguez, born in 1944 into a Spanish-speaking, Mexican American family, was educated at Stanford, Columbia, and Berkeley. Many of his eloquent essays—like the ones in his 1992 book Days of Obligation: An Argument with My Mexican Father—*mix memoir and argument, and many measure the gains and losses that result when English replaces Spanish that is spoken at home. This essay, first published in the magazine* The American Scholar *(1981), was incorporated into his acclaimed book* Hunger of Memory *(1982).*

1   I remember, to start with, that day in Sacramento, in a California now nearly thirty years past, when I first entered a classroom—able to understand about fifty stray English words. The third of four children, I had been preceded by my older brother and sister to a neighborhood Roman Catholic school. But neither of them had revealed very much about their classroom experiences. They left each morning and returned each afternoon, always together, speaking Spanish as they climbed the five steps to the porch. And their mysterious books, wrapped in brown shopping-bag paper, remained on the table next to the door, closed firmly behind them.

2   An accident of geography sent me to a school where all my classmates were white and many were the children of doctors and lawyers and business executives. On that first day of school, my classmates must certainly have been uneasy to find themselves apart from their families, in the first institution of their lives. But I was astonished. I was fated to be the "problem student" in class.

3   The nun said, in a friendly but oddly impersonal voice: "Boys and girls, this is Richard Rodriguez." (I heard her sound it out: *Rich-heard Road-ree-guess.*) It was the first time

I had heard anyone say my name in English. "Richard," the nun repeated more slowly, writing my name down in her book. Quickly I turned to see my mother's face dissolve in a watery blur behind the pebbled-glass door.

Now, many years later, I hear of something called "bilingual education"—a scheme proposed in the late 1960s by Hispanic-American social activists, later endorsed by a congressional vote. It is a program that seeks to permit non-English-speaking children (many from lower class homes) to use their "family language" as the language of school. Such, at least, is the aim its supporters announce. I hear them, and am forced to say no: It is not possible for a child, any child, ever to use his family's language in school. Not to understand this is to misunderstand the public uses of schooling and to trivialize the nature of intimate life.   4

Memory teaches me what I know of these matters. The boy reminds the adult. I was a bilingual child, but of a certain kind: "socially disadvantaged," the son of working-class parents, both Mexican immigrants.   5

In the early years of my boyhood, my parents coped very well in America. My father had steady work. My mother managed at home. They were nobody's victims. When we moved to a house many blocks from the Mexican-American section of town, they were not intimidated by those two or three neighbors who initially tried to make us unwelcome. ("Keep your brats away from my sidewalk!") But despite all they achieved, or perhaps because they had so much to achieve, they lacked any deep feeling of ease, of belonging in public. They regarded the people at work or in crowds as being very distant from us. Those were the others, *los gringos*. That term was interchangeable in their speech with another, even more telling: *los americanos*.   6

I grew up in a house where the only regular guests were my relations. On a certain day, enormous families of relatives would visit us, and there would be so many people that the noise and the bodies would spill out to the backyard and onto the front porch. Then for weeks no one would come. (If the doorbell rang, it was usually a salesman.) Our house stood apart—gaudy yellow in a row of white bungalows. We were the people with the noisy dog, the people who raised chickens. We were the foreigners on the block. A few neighbors would smile and wave at us. We waved back. But until I was seven years old, I did not know the name of the old couple living next door or the names of the kids living across the street.   7

8   In public, my father and mother spoke a hesitant, accented, and not always grammatical English. And then they
would have to strain, their bodies tense, to catch the sense of
what was rapidly said by *los gringos*. At home, they returned
to Spanish. The language of their Mexican past sounded in
counterpoint to the English spoken in public. The words
would come quickly, with ease. Conveyed through those
sounds was the pleasing, soothing, consoling reminder that
one was at home.

9   During those years when I was first learning to speak, my
mother and father addressed me only in Spanish; in Spanish
I learned to reply. By contrast, English (*inglés*) was the language I came to associate with gringos, rarely heard in the
house. I learned my first words of English overhearing my
parents speaking to strangers. At six years of age, I knew just
enough words for my mother to trust me on errands to stores
one block away—but no more.

10   I was then a listening child, careful to hear the very different sounds of Spanish and English. Wide-eyed with hearing,
I'd listen to sounds more than to words. First, there were English (gringo) sounds. So many words still were unknown to
me that when the butcher or the lady at the drugstore said
something, exotic polysyllabic sounds would bloom in the
midst of their sentences. Often the speech of people in public
seemed to me very loud, booming with confidence. The man
behind the counter would literally ask, "What can I do for
you?" But by being so firm and clear, the sound of his voice
said that he was a gringo; he belonged in public society. There
were also the high, nasal notes of middle-class American
speech—which I rarely am conscious of hearing today because I hear them so often, but could not stop hearing when I
was a boy. Crowds at Safeway or at bus stops were noisy with
the birdlike sounds of *los gringos*. I'd move away from them
all—all the chirping chatter above me.

11   My own sounds I was unable to hear, but I knew that I
spoke English poorly. My words could not extend to form
complete thoughts. And the words I did speak I didn't know
well enough to make distinct sounds. (Listeners would usually lower their heads to hear better what I was trying to
say.) But it was one thing for *me* to speak English with difficulty; it was more troubling to hear my parents speaking in
public: their high-whining vowels and guttural consonants;
their sentences that got stuck with "eh" and "ah" sounds; the
confused syntax; the hesitant rhythm of sounds so different
from the way gringos spoke. I'd notice, moreover, that my

parents' voices were softer than those of gringos we would meet.

I am tempted to say now that none of this mattered. (In 12 adulthood I am embarrassed by childhood fears.) And, in a way, it didn't matter very much that my parents could not speak English with ease. Their linguistic difficulties had no serious consequences. My mother and father made themselves understood at the county hospital clinic and at government offices. And yet, in another way, it mattered very much. It was unsettling to hear my parents struggle with English. Hearing them, I'd grow nervous, and my clutching trust in their protection and power would be weakened.

There were many times like the night at a brightly lit gaso- 13 line station (a blaring white memory) when I stood uneasily hearing my father talk to a teenage attendant. I do not recall what they were saying, but I cannot forget the sounds my father made as he spoke. At one point his words slid together to form one long word—sounds as confused as the threads of blue and green oil in the puddle next to my shoes. His voice rushed through what he had left to say. Toward the end, he reached falsetto notes, appealing to his listener's understanding. I looked away at the lights of passing automobiles. I tried not to hear any more. But I heard only too well the attendant's reply, his calm, easy tones. Shortly afterward, headed for home, I shivered when my father put his hand on my shoulder. The very first chance that I got, I evaded his grasp and ran on ahead into the dark, skipping with feigned boyish exuberance.

But then there was Spanish: *español*, the language rarely 14 heard away from the house; *español*, the language which seemed to me therefore a private language, my family's language. To hear its sounds was to feel myself specially recognized as one of the family, apart from *los otros*. A simple remark, an inconsequential comment could convey that assurance. My parents would say something to me and I would feel embraced by the sounds of their words. Those sounds said: *I am speaking with ease in Spanish. I am addressing you in words I never use with los gringos. I recognize you as someone special, close, like no one outside. You belong with us. In the family. Ricardo.*

At the age of six, well past the time when most middle-class 15 children no longer notice the difference between sounds uttered at home and words spoken in public, I had a different experience. I lived in a world compounded of sounds. I was a child longer than most. I lived in a magical world, surrounded by sounds both pleasing and fearful. I shared with my family a language enchantingly private—different from that used in the city around us.

16   Just opening or closing the screen door behind me was an important experience. I'd rarely leave home all alone or without feeling reluctance. Walking down the sidewalk, under the canopy of tall trees, I'd warily notice the (suddenly) silent neighborhood kids who stood warily watching me. Nervously, I'd arrive at the grocery store to hear there the sounds of the gringo, reminding me that in this so-big world I was a foreigner. But if leaving home was never routine, neither was coming back. Walking toward our house, climbing the steps from the sidewalk, in summer when the front door was open, I'd hear voices beyond the screen door talking in Spanish. For a second or two I'd stay, linger there listening. Smiling, I'd hear my mother call out, saying in Spanish, "Is that you, Richard?" Those were her words, but all the while her sounds would assure me: *You are home now. Come closer inside. With us.* "*Sí,*" I'd reply.

17   Once more inside the house, I would resume my place in the family. The sounds would grow harder to hear. Once more at home, I would grow less conscious of them. It required, however, no more than the blurt of the doorbell to alert me all over again to listen to sounds. The house would turn instantly quiet while my mother went to the door. I'd hear her hard English sounds. I'd wait to hear her voice turn to soft-sounding Spanish, which assured me, as surely as did the clicking tongue of the lock on the door, that the stranger was gone.

18   Plainly it is not healthy to hear such sounds often. It is not healthy to distinguish public from private sounds so easily. I remained cloistered by sounds, timid and shy in public, too dependent on the voices at home. And yet I was a very happy child when I was at home. I remember many nights when my father would come back from work, and I'd hear him call out to my mother in Spanish, sounding relieved. In Spanish, his voice would sound the light and free notes that he never could manage in English. Some nights I'd jump up just hearing his voice. My brother and I would come running into the room where he was with our mother. Our laughing (so deep was the pleasure!) became screaming. Like others who feel the pain of public alienation, we transformed the knowledge of our public separateness into a consoling reminder of our intimacy. Excited, our voices joined in a celebration of sounds. *We are speaking now the way we never speak out in public—we are together,* the sounds told me. Some nights no one seemed will-

ing to loosen the hold that sounds had on us. At dinner we invented new words that sounded Spanish, but made sense only to us. We pieced together new words by taking, say, an English verb and giving it Spanish endings. My mother's instructions at bedtime would be lacquered with mock-urgent tones. Or a word like *sí*, sounded in several notes, would convey added measures of feeling. Tongues lingered around the edges of words, especially fat vowels, and we happily sounded that military drum roll, the twirling roar of the Spanish *r*. Family language, my family's sounds: the voices of my parents and sisters and brother. Their voices insisting: *You belong here. We are family members. Related. Special to one another. Listen!* Voices singing and sighing, rising and straining, then surging, teeming with pleasure which burst syllables into fragments of laughter. At times it seemed there was steady quiet only when, from another room, the rustling whispers of my parents faded and I edged closer to sleep.

Supporters of bilingual education imply today that students   19
like me miss a great deal by not being taught in their family's language. What they seem not to recognize is that, as a socially disadvantaged child, I regarded Spanish as a private language. It was a ghetto language that deepened and strengthened my feeling of public separateness. What I needed to learn in school was that I had the right, and the obligation, to speak the public language. The odd truth is that my first-grade classmates could have become bilingual, in the conventional sense of the word, more easily than I. Had they been taught early (as upper middle-class children often are taught) a "second language" like Spanish or French, they could have regarded it simply as another public language. In my case, such bilingualism could not have been so quickly achieved. What I did not believe was that I could speak a single public language.

Without question, it would have pleased me to have heard   20
my teachers address me in Spanish when I entered the classroom. I would have felt much less afraid. I would have imagined that my instructors were somehow "related" to me; I would indeed have heard their Spanish as my family's language. I would have trusted them and responded with ease. But I would have delayed—postponed for how long?—having to learn the language of public society. I would have evaded— and for how long?—learning the great lesson of school: that I had a public identity.

Fortunately, my teachers were unsentimental about their   21
responsibility. What they understood was that I needed to speak public English. So their voices would search me out,

asking me questions. Each time I heard them I'd look up in surprise to see a nun's face frowning at me. I'd mumble, not really meaning to answer. The nun would persist. "Richard, stand up. Don't look at the floor. Speak up. Speak to the entire class, not just to me!" But I couldn't believe English could be my language to use. (In part, I did not want to believe it.) I continued to mumble. I resisted the teacher's demands. (Did I somehow suspect that once I learned this public language my family life would be changed?) Silent, waiting for the bell to sound, I remained dazed, diffident, afraid.

22   Because I wrongly imagined that English was intrinsically a public language and Spanish was intrinsically private, I easily noted the difference between classroom language and the language at home. At school, words were directed to a general audience of listeners. ("Boys and girls...") Words were meaningfully ordered. And the point was not self-expression alone, but to make oneself understood by many others. The teacher quizzed: "Boys and girls, why do we use that word in this sentence? Could we think of a better word to use there? Would the sentence change its meaning if the words were differently arranged? Isn't there a better way of saying much the same thing?" (I couldn't say. I wouldn't try to say.)

23   Three months passed. Five. A half year. Unsmiling, ever watchful, my teachers noted my silence. They began to connect my behavior with the slow progress my brother and sisters were making. Until, one Saturday morning, three nuns arrived at the house to talk to our parents. Stiffly they sat on the blue living-room sofa. From the doorway of another room, spying on the visitors, I noted the incongruity, the clash of two worlds, the faces and voices of school intruding upon the familiar setting of home. I overheard one voice gently wondering, "Do your children speak only Spanish at home, Mrs. Rodriguez?" While another voice added, "That Richard especially seems so timid and shy."

24   *That Rich-heard!*

25   With great tact, the visitors continued, "Is it possible for you and your husband to encourage your children to practice their English when they are home?" Of course my parents complied. What would they not do for their children's well-being? And how could they question the Church's authority which those women represented? In an instant they agreed to give up the language (the sounds) which had revealed and accentuated our family's closeness. The moment after the visitors left, the change was observed. "*Ahora,* speak to us only *en inglés,*" my father and mother told us.

At first, it seemed a kind of game. After dinner each night, the family gathered together to practice "our" English. It was still then *inglés*, a language foreign to us, so we felt drawn to it as strangers. Laughing, we would try to define words we could not pronounce. We played with strange English sounds, often overanglicizing our pronunciations. And we filled the smiling gaps of our sentences with familiar Spanish sounds. But that was cheating, somebody shouted, and everyone laughed.   26

In school, meanwhile, like my brother and sisters, I was required to attend a daily tutoring session. I needed a full year of this special work. I also needed my teachers to keep my attention from straying in class by calling out, *"Rich-heard"*—their English voices slowly loosening the ties to my other name, with its three notes, *Ri-car-do*. Most of all, I needed to hear my mother and father speak to me in a moment of seriousness in "broken"—suddenly heartbreaking—English. This scene was inevitable. One Saturday morning I entered the kitchen where my parents were talking, but I did not realize that they were talking in Spanish until, the moment they saw me, their voices changed and they began speaking English. The gringo sounds they uttered startled me. Pushed me away. In that moment of trivial misunderstanding and profound insight, I felt my throat twisted by unsounded grief. I simply turned and left the room. But I had no place to escape to where I could grieve in Spanish. My brother and sisters were speaking English in another part of the house.   27

Again and again in the days following, as I grew increasingly angry, I was obliged to hear my mother and father encouraging me: "Speak to us *en inglés*." Only then did I determine to learn classroom English. Thus, sometime afterward it happened: one day in school, I raised my hand to volunteer an answer to a question. I spoke out in a loud voice and I did not think it remarkable when the entire class understood. That day I moved very far from being the disadvantaged child I had been only days earlier. Taken hold at last was the belief, the calming assurance, that I *belonged* in public.   28

Shortly after, I stopped hearing the high, troubling sounds of *los gringos*. A more and more confident speaker of English, I didn't listen to how strangers sounded when they talked to me. With so many English-speaking people around me, I no longer heard American accents. Conversations quickened. Listening to persons whose voices sounded eccentrically pitched, I might note their sounds for a few seconds, but then I'd concentrate on what they were saying. Now when I heard   29 someone's tone of voice—angry or questioning or sarcastic or happy or sad—I didn't distinguish it from the words it expressed. Sound and word were thus tightly wedded. At the end of each day I was often bemused, and always relieved, to realize how "soundless," though crowded with words, my day in public had been. An eight-year-old boy, I finally came to accept what had been technically true since my birth: I was an American citizen.

30   But diminished by then was the special feeling of closeness at home. Gone was the desperate, urgent, intense feeling of being at home among those with whom I felt intimate. Our family remained a loving family, but one greatly changed. We were no longer so close, no longer bound tightly together by the knowledge of our separateness from *los gringos.* Neither my older brother nor my sisters rushed home after school any more. Nor did I. When I arrived home, often there would be neighborhood kids in the house. Or the house would be empty of sounds.

31   Following the dramatic Americanization of their children, even my parents grew more publicly confident—especially my mother. First she learned the names of all the people on the block. Then she decided we needed to have a telephone in our house. My father, for his part, continued to use the word gringo, but it was no longer charged with bitterness or distrust. Stripped of any emotional content, the word simply became a name for those Americans not of Hispanic descent. Hearing him, sometimes, I wasn't sure if he was pronouncing the Spanish word *gringo,* or saying gringo in English.

32   There was a new silence at home. As we children learned more and more English, we shared fewer and fewer words with our parents. Sentences needed to be spoken slowly when one of us addressed our mother or father. Often the parent wouldn't understand. The child would need to repeat himself. Still the parent misunderstood. The young voice, frustrated, would end up saying, "Never mind"—the subject was closed. Dinners would be noisy with the clinking of knives and forks against dishes. My mother would smile softly between her remarks; my father, at the other end of the table, would chew and chew his food while he stared over the heads of his children.

33   My mother! My father! After English became my primary language, I no longer knew what words to use in addressing my parents. The old Spanish words (those tender accents of sound) I had earlier used—*mamá* and *papá*—I couldn't use any more. They would have been all-too-painful reminders of

how much had changed in my life. On the other hand, the words I heard neighborhood kids call their parents seemed equally unsatisfactory. "Mother" and "father," "ma," "papa," "pa," "dad," "pop" (how I hated the all-American sound of that last word)—all these I felt were unsuitable terms of address for *my* parents. As a result, I never used them at home. Whenever I'd speak to my parents, I would try to get their attention by looking at them. In public conversations, I'd refer to them as my "parents" or my "mother" and "father."

My mother and father, for their part, responded differently, as their children spoke to them less. My mother grew restless, seemed troubled and anxious at the scarceness of words exchanged in the house. She would question me about my day when I came home from school. She smiled at my small talk. She pried at the edges of my sentences to get me to say something more. ("What...?") She'd join conversations she overheard, but her intrusions often stopped her children's talking. By contrast, my father seemed to grow reconciled to the new quiet. Though his English somewhat improved, he tended more and more to retire into silence. At dinner he spoke very little. One night his children and even his wife helplessly giggled at his garbled English pronunciation of the Catholic "Grace Before Meals." Thereafter he made his wife recite the prayer at the start of each meal, even on formal occasions when there were guests in the house. 34

Hers became the public voice of the family. On official business it was she, not my father, who would usually talk to strangers on the phone or in stores. We children grew so accustomed to his silence that years later we would routinely refer to his "shyness." (My mother often tried to explain: both of his parents died when he was eight. He was raised by an uncle who treated him as little more than a menial servant. He was never encouraged to speak. He grew up alone—a man of few words.) But I realized my father was not shy whenever I'd watch him speaking Spanish with relatives. Using Spanish, he was quickly effusive. Especially when talking with other men, his voice would spark, flicker, flare alive with varied sounds. In Spanish he expressed ideas and feelings he rarely revealed when speaking English. With firm Spanish sounds he conveyed a confidence and authority that English would never allow him. 35

The silence at home, however, was not simply the result of fewer words passing between parents and children. More profound for me was the silence created by inattention to sounds. At about the time I no longer bothered to listen with 36 care to the sounds of English in public, I grew careless about listening to the sounds made by the family when they spoke. Most of the time I would hear someone speaking at home and didn't distinguish his sounds from the words people uttered in public. I didn't even pay much attention to my parents' accented and ungrammatical speech—at least not at home. Only when I was with them in public would I become alert to their accents. But even then their sounds caused me less and less concern. For I was growing increasingly confident of my own public identity.

37   I would have been happier about my public success had I not recalled, sometimes, what it had been like earlier, when my family conveyed its intimacy through a set of conveniently private sounds. Sometimes in public, hearing a stranger, I'd hark back to my lost past. A Mexican farm worker approached me one day downtown. He wanted directions to some place. "*Hijito,*..." he said. And his voice stirred old longings. Another time I was standing beside my mother in the visiting room of a Carmelite convent, before the dense screen which rendered the nuns shadowy figures. I heard several of them speaking Spanish in their busy, singsong, overlapping voices, assuring my mother that yes, yes, we were remembered, all our family was remembered, in their prayers. Those voices echoed faraway family sounds. Another day a dark-faced old woman touched my shoulder lightly to steady herself as she boarded a bus. She murmured something to me I couldn't quite comprehend. Her Spanish voice came near, like the face of a never-before-seen relative in the instant before I was kissed. That voice, like so many of the Spanish voices I'd hear in public, recalled the golden age of my childhood.

38   Bilingual educators say today that children lose a degree of "individuality" by becoming assimilated into public society. (Bilingual schooling is a program popularized in the seventies, that decade when middle-class "ethnics" began to resist the process of assimilation—the "American melting pot.") But the bilingualists oversimplify when they scorn the value and necessity of assimilation. They do not seem to realize that a person is individualized in two ways. So they do not realize that, while one suffers a diminished sense of *private* individuality by being assimilated into public society, such assimilation makes possible the achievement of *public* individuality.

39   Simplistically again, the bilingualists insist that a student should be reminded of his difference from others in mass society, of his "heritage." But they equate mere separateness with

individuality. The fact is that only in private—with intimates—
is separateness from the crowd a prerequisite for individuality; an intimate "tells" me that I am unique, unlike all others,
apart from the crowd. In public, by contrast, full individuality
is achieved, paradoxically, by those who are able to consider
themselves members of the crowd. Thus it happened for me.
Only when I was able to think of myself as an American, no
longer an alien in gringo society, could I seek the rights and
opportunities necessary for full public individuality. The social and political advantages I enjoy as a man began on the
day I came to believe that my name is indeed *Rich-heard Road-
ree-guess.* It is true that my public society today is often impersonal; in fact, my public society is usually mass society. But
despite the anonymity of the crowd, and despite the fact that
the individuality I achieve in public is often tenuous—because
it depends on my being one in a crowd—I celebrate the day
I acquired my new name. Those middle-class ethnics who
scorn assimilation seem to me filled with decadent self-pity,
obsessed by the burden of public life. Dangerously, they romanticize public separateness and trivialize the dilemma of
those who are truly socially disadvantaged.

If I rehearse here the changes in my private life after my   40
Americanization, it is finally to emphasize a public gain. The
loss implies the gain. The house I returned to each afternoon
was quiet. Intimate sounds no longer greeted me at the door.
Inside there were other noises. The telephone rang. Neighborhood kids ran past the door of the bedroom where I was
reading my schoolbooks—covered with brown shopping-bag
paper. Once I learned the public language, it would never
again be easy for me to hear intimate family voices. More and
more of my day was spent hearing words, not sounds. But
that may only be a way of saying that on the day I raised my
hand in class and spoke loudly to an entire roomful of faces,
my childhood started to end.

Victor Villanueva Jr.

Whose Voice Is It Anyway? Rodriguez' Speech in Retrospect

Victor Villanueva Jr., on the faculty at Northern Arizona University until 1995, now teaches English at Washington State University. In 1993, he published the award-winning Bootstraps: From an American Academic of Color, *a personal and intellectual narrative of his own encounter with language issues in the United States in general and in the academy in particular. Villanueva also reveals a lot about himself in the following essay, which he wrote in 1987 for* English Journal, *a professional magazine directed to high school and elementary school English teachers.*

1   During the 1986 annual conference of the NCTE (National Council of Teachers of English) I attended a luncheon sponsored by the secondary section. Richard Rodriguez, author of *Hunger of Memory,* was the guest speaker. He spoke of how he came to be an articulate speaker of this standard dialect, and he spoke of the conclusions concerning language that his experiences had brought him to. He was impressive. I was taken by his quiet eloquence. His stage presence recalled Olivier's Hamlet. He spoke well. But for all his eloquence and his studied stage presence, I was nevertheless surprised by the audience's response, an enthusiastic, uncritical acceptance, marked by a long, loud standing ovation. I was surprised because he had blurred distinctions between language and culture, between his experiences and those more typical of the minority in America, between the history of the immigrant and that of the minority, in a way that I had thought would raise more than a few eyebrows. Yet all he raised was the audience to its feet.

2   In retrospect, I think I can understand the rave reception. The message he so softly delivered relieved us all of some anxiety. Classroom teachers' shoulders stoop under the weight of the paper load. They take 150 students through writing and grammar, spelling and punctuation. Within those same forty-five-minute spurts they also work on reading: drama, poetry, literature, the great issues in literature. After that, there's the writers' club or the school paper or the yearbook, coaching volleyball or producing the school play. And throughout it all, they are to remain sensitive to the language of the nonstand-

ard or non-English speaker. They are not really told how—
just "be sensitive," while parents, the media, sometimes it
seems the whole world, shake their fingers at them for not doing something about America's literacy problems. Richard
Rodriguez told the teachers to continue to be sensitive but to
forget about doing anything special. The old ways may be
painful, but they really are best. There is a kind of violence to
the melting pot, he said, but it is necessary. He said that this
linguistic assimilation is like alchemy, initially destructive
perhaps but magical, creating something new and greater
than what was. Do as you have always done. And the teachers
sighed.

Richard Rodriguez is the authority, after all: a bilingual   3
child of immigrant parents, a graduate of two of the nation's
more prestigious schools, Stanford and Berkeley, an English
teacher, the well-published author of numerous articles and a
well-received, well-anthologized book. He knows. And he says
that the teachers who insisted on a particular linguistic form
can be credited with his fame. But what is it, really, that has
made him famous? He is a fine writer; of that there can be no
doubt. But it is his message that has brought him fame, a
message that states that the minority is no different than any
other immigrant who came to this country not knowing its
culture or its language, leaving much of the old country behind to become part of this new one, and in becoming part of
America subtly changing what it means to be American. The
American who brought his beef and pudding from England
became the American of frankfurter, the bologna sandwich,
pizza. Typically American foods—like typical Americans—
partake of the world.

At the luncheon, Richard Rodriguez spoke of a TV ad for   4
Mexican-style Velveeta, "the blandest of American cheeses,"
he called it, now speckled with peppers. This cultural contrast, said Rodriguez, demonstrated how Mexico—no less
than England or Germany—is part of America.

But I think it shows how our times face a different kind of   5
assimilation. Let's put aside for the moment questions as to
why, if Mexicans really are being assimilated, they have taken
so much longer than other groups, especially since Mexicans
were already part of the West and Southwest when the West
and Southwest became part of America. Let's look, rather, at
the hyphen in Mexican-Velveeta. Who speaks of a German-
American sausage, for instance? It's a hot dog. Yet tacos remain ethnic, sold under a mock Spanish mission bell or a
sombrero. You will find refried beans under "ethnic foods" in

the supermarket, not among other canned beans, though items as foreign-sounding as sauerkraut are simply canned vegetables. Mexican foods, even when Americanized as the taco salad or Mexican-Velveeta, remain distinctly Mexican.[1]

6   And like the ethnic food, some ethnic minorities have not been assimilated in the way the Ellis Islanders were. The fires of the melting pot have cooled. No more soup. America's more a stew today. The difference is the difference between the immigrant and the minority, a difference having to do with how each, the immigrant and the minority, came to be Americans, the difference between choice and colonization. Those who emigrated from Europe chose to leave unacceptable conditions in search of better. Choice, I realize, is a tricky word in this context: religious persecution, debtor's prison, potato famine, fascism, foreign takeover, when compared with a chance at prosperity and self-determination, don't seem to make for much of a choice; yet most people apparently remained in their homelands despite the intolerable, while the immigrants did leave, and in leaving chose to sever ties with friends and families, created a distance between themselves and their histories, cultures, languages. There is something heroic in this. It's a heroism shared by the majority of Americans.

7   But choice hardly entered into most minorities' decisions to become American. Most of us recognize this when it comes to Blacks or American Indians. Slavery, forcible displacement, and genocide are fairly clear-cut. Yet the circumstances by which most minorities became Americans are no less clear-cut. The minority became an American almost by default, as part of the goods in big-time real estate deals or as some of the spoils of war. What is true for the Native American applies to the Alaska Native, the Pacific Islander (including the Asian), Mexican-Americans, Puerto Ricans. Puerto Rico was part of Christopher Columbus' great discovery, Arawaks and Boriquens among his "Indians," a real-estate coup for the Queen of Spain. Then one day in 1898, the Puerto Ricans who had for nearly four hundred years been

---

[1]Mexican food is not the only ethnic food on the market, of course. Asian and Mediterranean foods share the shelves. But this too is telling, since Asians alone had had restricted access to the US before the country ended its Open Door Immigration Policy. When the US closed its doors in 1924, it was to regulate the flow of less desirable "new immigrants"—the Eastern and Southern Europeans who remain "ethnic" to this day. See Oscar Handlin's *Race in American Life,* New York, Anchor, 1957.

made proud to be the offspring of Spain, so much so that their native Arawak and Boricua languages and ways were virtually gone, found themselves the property of the United States, property without the rights and privileges of citizenship until—conveniently—World War I. But citizenship notwithstanding, Puerto Rico remains essentially a colony today.[2]

One day in 1845 and in 1848 other descendants of Spain   8 who had all but lost their Indian identities found themselves Americans. These were the long-time residents and land-owners of the Republic of Texas and the California Republic: the area from Texas to New Mexico, Arizona, Utah, and California. Residents in the newly established US territories were given the option to relocate to Mexico or to remain on their native lands, with the understanding that should they remain they would be guaranteed American Constitutional rights. Those who stayed home saw their rights not very scrupulously guarded, falling victim over time to displacement, dislocation, and forced expatriation. There is something tragic in losing a long-established birthright, tragic but not heroic—especially not heroic to those whose ancestors had fled their homelands rather than acknowledge external rule.

The immigrant gave up much in the name of freedom—   9 and for the sake of dignity. For the Spanish-speaking minority in particular, the freedom to be American without once again relinquishing one's ancestry is also a matter of dignity.

This is not to say that Richard Rodriguez forfeited his dig-   10 nity in choosing not to be Ricardo. The Mexican's status includes not only the descendants of the West and Southwest, Spanish-speaking natives to America, but also immigrants and the descendants of immigrants. Richard Rodriguez is more the immigrant than the minority. His father, he told us, had left his native Mexico for Australia. He fell in love along the way, eventually settling with wife and family in Sacramento. America was not his father's first choice for a new home perhaps, but he did choose to leave his homeland in much the same way European immigrants had. The Rodriguezes no doubt felt the immigrants' hardships, the drive to assimilate, a drive compounded perhaps by the association in their and others' minds between them and the undocumented migrant worker or between them and the minority.

---

[2]Nor is it a simple matter of Puerto Rico's deciding whether it wants to remain a commonwealth, gaining statehood, or independence. The interests of US industry, of the US military, and the social and economic ramifications of Puerto Rico's widespread poverty complicate matters.

11   And it is this confusion of immigrant and minority in Richard Rodriguez with which we must contend. His message rings true to the immigrant heritage of his audience because it happens to be the immigrant's story. It is received as if it were a new story because it is confused with this story of the minority. The complexities of the minority are rendered simple—not easy, but easily understood.

12   Others tell the story of the minority. I think, for instance, of Piri Thomas and Tato Laviera, since theirs are stories of Puerto Ricans. My own parents had immigrated to New York from Puerto Rico, though not in the way of most. My mother, an American, a US citizen like all Puerto Ricans, fair-skinned and proud of her European descent, had been sold into servitude to a wealthy Chicago family. My father, recently discharged from the US Army, followed my mother, rescued his sweetheart, and together they fled to New York. I was born a year later, 1948.

13   My mother believed in the traditional idea of assimilation. She and my father would listen to the radio shows in English and try to read the American newspapers. They spoke to me in two languages from the start. The local parochial school's tuition was a dollar a month, so I was spared PS 168. Rodriguez tells of nuns coming to his home to suggest that the family speak English at home. For Rodriguez this was something of a turning point in his life; intimacy lost, participation in the public domain gained. A public language would dominate, the painful path to his assimilation, the path to his eventual success. A nun spoke to my parents, too, when I was in kindergarten. I spoke with an accent, they were told. They should speak to me in English. My mother could only laugh: my English was as it was *because* they spoke to me in English. The irony reinforced our intimacy while I continued to learn the "public language."

14   There is more to assimilating than learning the language. I earned my snacks at the Saturday matinee by reading the credits on the screen. I enjoyed parsing sentences, was good at it too. I was a Merriam-Webster spelling bee champ. I was an "A" student who nevertheless took a special Saturday course on how to do well on the standardized test that would gain me entry to the local Catholic high school. I landed in the public vo-tech high school, slotted for a trade. Jarapolk, whose parents had fled the Ukraine, made the good school; so did Marie Engels, the daughter of German immigrants. Lana Walker, a Black girl whose brains I envied, got as far as the alternate list. I don't recall any of the Black or Puerto Rican kids from my

class getting in. I never finished high school, despite my being a bright boy who knew the public language intimately.

I don't like thinking minorities were intentionally excluded   15 from the better school. I would prefer to think minorities didn't do as well because we were less conscious than the immigrants of the cultural distances we had to travel to be truly Americans. We were Americans, after all, not even seeing ourselves as separated by language by the time most of us got to the eighth grade. I spoke Spanglish at home, a hybrid English and Spanish common to New York Puerto Ricans; I spoke the Puerto Rican version of Black English in the streets, and as far as I knew, I spoke something close to the standard dialect in the classroom. We thought ourselves Americans, assimilated. We didn't know about cultural bias in standardized tests. I still don't do well on standardized tests.

A more pointed illustration of the difference between the   16 minority and the immigrant comes by way of a lesson from my father. I was around ten. We went uptown one day, apartment hunting. I don't recall how he chose the place. He asked about an apartment in his best English, the sounds of a Spanish speaker attempting his best English. No vacancies. My father thanked the man, then casually slipped into the customary small talk of the courteous exit. During the talk my father mentioned our coming from Spain. By the end of the chat a unit became available. Maybe my father's pleasing personality had gained us entry. More likely, Puerto Rican stereotypes had kept us out. The immigrant could enter where the minority could not. My father's English hadn't improved in the five minutes it had taken for the situation to change.

Today I sport a doctorate in English from a major university, study and teach rhetoric at another university, do research in and teach composition, continue to enjoy and teach English literature. I live in an all-American city in the heart of America. And I know I am not quite assimilated. In one weekend I was asked if I was Iranian one day and East Indian the next. "No," I said. "You have an accent," I was told. Yet tape recordings and passing comments throughout the years have told me that though there is a "back East" quality to my voice, there isn't much of New York to it anymore, never mind the Black English of my younger years or the Spanish of my youngest. My "accent" was in my not sounding midwestern, which does have a discernible, though not usually a pronounced, regional quality. And my "accent," I would guess, was in my "foreign" features (which pale alongside the brown skin of Richard Rodriguez).

18   Friends think I make too much of such incidents. Minority
hypersensitivity, they say. They desensitize me (and display
their liberal attitudes) with playful jabs at Puerto Ricans:
greasy hair jokes, knife-in-pocket jokes, spicy food jokes (and
Puerto Ricans don't even eat hot foods, unless we're eating
Mexican or East Indian foods). If language alone were the secret to assimilation, the rate of Puerto Rican and Mexican
success would be greater, I would think. So many Mexican-
Americans and Puerto Ricans remain in the barrios—even
those who are monolingual, who have never known Spanish.
If language alone were the secret, wouldn't the secret have
gotten out long before Richard Rodriguez recorded his memoirs? In fact, haven't we always worked with the assumption
that language learning—oral and written—is the key to parity,
even as parity continues to elude so many?

19   I'm not saying the assumption is wrong. I think teachers
are right to believe in the potential power of language. We
want our students to be empowered. That's why we read professional journals. That's why we try to accommodate the pronouncements of linguists. That's why we listen to the likes of
Richard Rodriguez. But he spoke more of the English
teacher's power than the empowerment of the student. "Listen to the sound of my voice," he said. He asked the audience
to forget his brown skin and listen to his voice, his "unac-
cented voice." "This is your voice," he told the teachers. Better
that we, teachers at all levels, give students the means to find
their own voices, voices that don't have to ask that we ignore
what we cannot ignore, voices that speak of their brown or
yellow or red or black skin with pride and without need for
bravado or hostility, voices that can recognize and exploit the
conventions we have agreed to as the standards of written
discourse—without necessarily accepting the ideology of
those for whom the standard dialect is the language of home
as well as commerce, for whom the standard dialect is as private as it is public, to use Rodriguez' terms.

20   Rodriguez said at the luncheon that he was not speaking
of pedagogy as much as of ideology. He was. It is an ideology
which grew out of the memoirs of an immigrant boy
confronting contrasts, a child accommodating his circumstances. He remembers a brown boy in a white middle-class
school and is forced to say no to bilingual education. His
classmates were the descendants of other immigrants, the
products of assimilation, leading him to accept the traditional American ideology of a multiculturalism that manifests as one new culture and language, a culture and

language which encompasses and transcends any one culture. I remember a brown boy among other brown boys and girls, blacks, and olives, and variations on white, and must agree with Richard that bilingualism in the classroom would have been impractical. But my classmates were in the process of assimilation—Polish, German, Ukrainian, and Irish children, the first of their families to enter American schools; my classmates were also Black and Puerto Rican. It seemed to this boy's eyes that the immigrants would move on but the minority would stay, that the colonized do not melt. Today I do not hear of the problems in educating new immigrants, but the problems of Black literacy continue to make the news. And I hear of an eighty per cent dropout rate among Puerto Ricans in Boston, of Mexicans in the Rio Grande Valley where the dropout rate exceeds seventy per cent, of places where English and the education system do not address the majority—Spanish speakers for whom menial labor has been the tradition and is apparently the future. I must ask how *not* bilingual education in such situations. One person's experiences must remain one person's, applicable to many others, perhaps, but not all others. Simple, monolithic, universal solutions simply can't work in a complex society.

When it comes to the nonstandard speaker, for instance, 21 we are torn between the findings of linguists and the demands of the marketplace. Our attempts at preparing students for the marketplace only succeed in alienating nonstandard speakers, we are told. Our attempts at accommodating their nonstandard dialects, we fear, only succeed in their being barred from the marketplace. So we go back to the basics. Or else we try to change their speech without alienating them, in the process perhaps sensing that our relativism might smack of condescension. Limiting the student's language to the playground and home still speaks of who's right and who's wrong, who holds the power. I would rather we left speaking dialects relatively alone (truly demonstrating a belief in the legitimacy of the nonstandard). The relationship between speaking and writing is complex, as the debate sparked by Thomas Farrell has made clear. My own research and studies, as well as my personal experiences, suggest that exposure to writing and reading affects speaking. My accent changes, it seems, with every book I read. We don't have to give voices to students. If we give them pen and paper and have them read the printed page aloud, no matter what their grade, they'll discover their own voices.

22   And if we let the printed page offer a variety of world
views, of ideologies, those voices should gather the power we
wish them to have. Booker T. Washington, Martin Luther
King, Jr., W. E. B. DuBois all wrote with eloquence. Each presents a different world view. Maxine Hong Kingston's "voice"
resounds differently from Frank Chin's. Ernesto Galarza saw
a different world than Richard Rodriguez. Rodriguez' is only
one view, one voice. Yet it's his voice which seems to resound
the loudest. Rodriguez himself provided the reason why this
is so. He said at the luncheon that the individual's story, the
biography or autobiography, has universal appeal because it
strikes at experiences we have in common. The immigrant's
story has the most in common with the majority.

23   Rodriguez implied that he didn't feel much kinship to minority writers. He said he felt a special bond with D. H.
Lawrence. It seems appropriate that Rodriguez, who writes
of his alienation from family in becoming part of the mainstream, would turn to Lawrence. Lawrence, too, was a
teacher turned writer. Lawrence, too, felt alienated from his
working-class background. It was Lawrence who argued, in
"Reflections on the Death of the Porcupine," that equality is
not achievable; Lawrence who co-opted, left the mastered to
join the masters. Is this what we want for our minority students? True, Lawrence's mastery of the English language cannot be gainsaid. I would be proud to have a Lawrence credit
me with his voice, would appreciate his accomplishment. But
I would rather share credit in a W. B. Yeats, Anglo and Irish,
assimilated but with a well-fed memory of his ancestry, master of the English language, its beauty, its traditions—and
voice of the colony.

Ron Unz and Gloria Matta Tuchman
The English Education for Children Initiative

California voters passed the following initiative (a reaction against bilingual education) on June 2, 1998; soon after, the law was challenged in the courts. Dubbed the "English for the Children Initiative" by its advocates, the resolution was designed to encourage immigrants to learn English as quickly as possible by means of "full immersion" into English instruction in the schools and to undermine the bilingual education measures that have prevailed in California schools for many years. Ron Unz, who grew up in a Yiddish-speaking household and who became wealthy after founding a Silicon Valley software firm, was defeated in a run for the California governorship in 1994; he then turned his attention to opposing bilingual education by chairing the English for the Children effort. Gloria Matta Tuchman has taught for many years at Taft Elementary School in Santa Ana, California, and was active in the initiative campaign.

The actual text of the English Education for Children Initiative follows.

SECTION 1. Chapter 3 (commencing with Section 300) is added to Part 1 of the Educational Code, to read: 1

CHAPTER 3. ENGLISH LANGUAGE EDUCATION FOR IMMIGRANT CHILDREN 2

ARTICLE 1. Findings and Declarations 3

300. The People of California find and declare as follows: 4

(a) WHEREAS the English language is the national public language of the United States of America and of the state of California, is spoken by the vast majority of California residents, and is also the leading world language for science, technology, and international business, thereby being the language of economic opportunity; and 5

(b) WHEREAS immigrant parents are eager to have their children acquire a good knowledge of English, thereby allowing them to fully participate in the American Dream of economic and social advancement; and 6

7   (c) WHEREAS the government and the public schools of California have a moral obligation and a constitutional duty to provide all of California's children, regardless of their ethnicity or national origins, with the skills necessary to become productive members of our society, and of these skills, literacy in the English language is among the most important; and

8   (d) WHEREAS the public schools of California currently do a poor job of educating immigrant children, wasting financial resources on costly experimental language programs whose failure over the past two decades is demonstrated by the current high drop-out rates and low English literacy levels of many immigrant children; and

9   (e) WHEREAS young immigrant children can easily acquire full fluency in a new language, such as English, if they are heavily exposed to that language in the classroom at an early age.

10   (f) THEREFORE it is resolved that: all children in California public schools shall be taught English as rapidly and effectively as possible.

11   ARTICLE 2. English Language Education

12   305. Subject to the exceptions provided in Article 3 (commencing with Section 310), all children in California public schools shall be taught English by being taught in English. In particular, this shall require that all children be placed in English language classrooms. Children who are English learners shall be educated through sheltered English immersion during a temporary transition period not normally intended to exceed one year. Local schools shall be permitted to place in the same classroom English learners of different ages but whose degree of English proficiency is similar. Local schools shall be encouraged to mix together in the same classroom English learners from different native-language groups but with the same degree of English fluency. Once English learners have acquired a good working knowledge of English, they shall be transferred to English language mainstream classrooms. As much as possible, current supplemental funding for English learners shall be maintained, subject to possible modification under Article 8 (commencing with Section 335) below.

13   306. The definitions of the terms used in this article and in Article 3 (commencing with Section 310) are as follows:

(a) "English learner" means a child who does not speak En-   14
glish or whose native language is not English and who is not
currently able to perform ordinary classroom work in English, also known as a Limited English Proficiency or LEP
child.

(b) "English language classroom" means a classroom in   15
which the language of instruction used by the teaching personnel is overwhelmingly the English language, and in which
such teaching personnel possess a good knowledge of the English language.

(c) "English language mainstream classroom" means a class-   16
room in which the students either are native English language speakers or already have acquired reasonable fluency
in English.

(d) "Sheltered English immersion" or "structured English im-   17
mersion" means an English language acquisition process for
young children in which nearly all classroom instruction is in
English but with the curriculum and presentation designed
for children who are learning the language.

(e) "Bilingual education/native language instruction" means a   18
language acquisition process for students in which much or
all instruction, textbooks, and teaching materials are in the
child's native language.

ARTICLE 3. Parental Exceptions   19

310. The requirements of Section 305 may be waived with the   20
prior written informed consent, to be provided annually, of
the child's parents or legal guardian under the circumstances
specified below and in Section 311. Such informed consent
shall require that said parents or legal guardian personally
visit the school to apply for the waiver and that they there be
provided a full description of the educational materials to be
used in the different educational program choices and all the
educational opportunities available to the child. Under such
parental waiver conditions, children may be transferred to
classes where they are taught English and other subjects
through bilingual education techniques or other generally
recognized educational methodologies permitted by law. Individual schools in which 20 students or more of a given
grade level receive a waiver shall be required to offer such a
class; otherwise, they must allow the students to transfer to a
public school in which such a class is offered.

21   311. The circumstances in which a parental exception waiver
     may be granted under Section 310 are as follows:

22   (a) Children who already know English: the child already pos-
     sesses good English language skills, as measured by standard-
     ized tests of English vocabulary comprehension, reading, and
     writing, in which the child scores at or above the state aver-
     age for his grade level or at or above the 5th grade average,
     whichever is lower; or

23   (b) Older children: the child is age 10 years or older, and it is
     the informed belief of the school principal and educational
     staff that an alternate course of educational study would be
     better suited to the child's rapid acquisition of basic English
     language skills; or

24   (c) Children with special needs: the child already has been
     placed for a period of not less than thirty days during that
     school year in an English language classroom and it is subse-
     quently the informed belief of the school principal and educa-
     tional staff that the child has such special physical,
     emotional, psychological, or educational needs that an alter-
     nate course of educational study would be better suited to the
     child's overall educational development. A written description
     of these special needs must be provided and any such deci-
     sion is to be made subject to the examination and approval of
     the local school superintendent, under guidelines established
     by and subject to the review of the local Board of Education
     and ultimately the State Board of Education. The existence of
     such special needs shall not compel issuance of a waiver, and
     the parents shall be fully informed of their right to refuse to
     agree to a waiver.

25   ARTICLE 4. Community-Based English Tutoring

26   315. In furtherance of its constitutional and legal require-
     ment to offer special language assistance to children coming
     from backgrounds of limited English proficiency, the state
     shall encourage family members and others to provide per-
     sonal English language tutoring to such children, and sup-
     port these efforts by raising the general level of English
     language knowledge in the community. Commencing with
     the fiscal year in which this initiative is enacted and for each
     of the nine fiscal years following thereafter, a sum of fifty mil-
     lion dollars ($50,000,000) per year is hereby appropriated
     from the General Fund for the purpose of providing addi-
     tional funding for free or subsidized programs of adult En-

glish language instruction to parents or other members of the community who pledge to provide personal English language tutoring to California school children with limited English proficiency.

316. Programs funded pursuant to this section shall be provided through schools or community organizations. Funding for these programs shall be administered by the Office of the Superintendent of Public Instruction, and shall be disbursed at the discretion of the local school boards, under reasonable guidelines established by, and subject to the review of, the State Board of Education. 27

ARTICLE 5. Legal Standing and Parental Enforcement 28

320. As detailed in Article 2 (commencing with Section 305) and Article 3 (commencing with Section 310), all California school children have the right to be provided with an English language public education. If a California school child has been denied the option of an English language instructional curriculum in public school, the child's parent or legal guardian shall have legal standing to sue for enforcement of the provisions of this statute, and if successful shall be awarded normal and customary attorney's fees and actual damages, but not punitive or consequential damages. Any school board member or other elected official or public school teacher or administrator who willfully and repeatedly refuses to implement the terms of this statute by providing such an English language educational option at an available public school to a California school child may be held personally liable for fees and actual damages by the child's parents or legal guardian. 29

ARTICLE 6. Severability 30

325. If any part or parts of this statute are found to be in conflict with federal law or the United States or the California State Constitution, the statute shall be implemented to the maximum extent that federal law, and the United States and the California State Constitution permit. Any provision held invalid shall be severed from the remaining portions of this statute. 31

ARTICLE 7. Operative Date 32

330. This initiative shall become operative for all school terms which begin more than sixty days following the date at which it becomes effective. 33

34   ARTICLE 8. Amendment.

35   335. The provisions of this act may be amended by a statute that becomes effective upon approval by the electorate or by a statute to further the act's purpose passed by a two-thirds vote of each house of the Legislature and signed by the Governor.

36   ARTICLE 9. Interpretation

37   340. Under circumstances in which portions of this statute are subject to conflicting interpretations, Section 300 shall be assumed to contain the governing intent of the statute.

The American Civil Liberties Union
Briefing Paper on "English Only"

The American Civil Liberties Union, famous for its defense of freedoms protected by the Constitution, has developed a reputation over many decades for taking up liberal causes and positions—sometimes very controversial ones. In 1997, the ACLU developed the following "Briefing Paper" and posted it on the World Wide Web. Note how it takes the form of a "Frequently Asked Questions" (or "FAQ") page—a common Internet genre.

Introduction

1   At the time of the nation's founding, it was commonplace to hear as many as 20 languages spoken in daily life, including Dutch, French, German and numerous Native American languages. Even the Articles of Confederation were printed in German, as well as English. During the 19th and early 20th centuries, the nation's linguistic diversity grew as successive waves of Europeans immigrated to these shores and U.S. territory expanded to include Puerto Rico, Hawaii and the Philippines.

2   Just as languages other than English have always been a part of our history and culture, debate over establishing a national language dates back to the country's beginnings. John

Adams proposed to the Continental Congress in 1780 that an official academy be created to "purify, develop, and dictate usage of" English. His proposal was rejected as undemocratic and a threat to individual liberty.

Nonetheless, restrictive language laws have been enacted periodically since the late 19th century, usually in response to new waves of immigration. These laws, in practice if not in intent, have punished immigrants for their foreignness and violated their rights.   3

In the early 1980s, again during a period of concern about new immigration, a movement arose that seeks the establishment of English as the nation's official language. The "English Only" movement promotes the enactment of legislation that restricts or prohibits the use of languages other than English by government agencies and, in some cases, by private businesses. The movement has met with some success, "English Only" laws having been passed in several states. And, for the first time in the nation's history, an English Language Amendment to the Constitution has been proposed.   4

The ACLU opposes "English Only" laws because they can abridge the rights of individuals who are not proficient in English, and because they perpetuate false stereotypes of immigrants and non-English speakers. We believe, further, that such laws are contrary to the spirit of tolerance and diversity embodied in our Constitution. An English Language Amendment to the Constitution would transform that document from being a charter of liberties and individual freedom into a charter of restrictions that limits, rather than protects, individual rights.   5

Here are the ACLU's answers to some questions frequently posed by the public about "English Only" issues.   6

Q: What is an "English Only" law?   7

A: "English Only" laws vary. Some state statutes simply declare English as the "official" language of the state. Other state and local edicts limit or bar government's provision of non-English language assistance and services. For example, some restrict bilingual education programs, prohibit multilingual ballots, or forbid non-English government services in general—including such services as courtroom translation or multilingual emergency police lines.   8

Q: Where have such laws been enacted?   9

A: Sixteen states have "English Only" laws, and many others are considering such laws. In some states, the laws were passed decades ago during upsurges of nativism, but most were passed   10 within the last few years. The "English Only" states are Arizona, Arkansas, California, Colorado, Florida, Georgia, Illinois, Indiana, Kentucky, Mississippi, Nebraska, North Carolina, North Dakota, South Carolina, Tennessee and Virginia.

11   **Q: What are the consequences of "English Only" laws?**

12   A: Some versions of the proposed English Language Amendment would void almost all state and federal laws that require the government to provide services in languages other than English. The services affected would include: health, education and social welfare services, job training, translation assistance to crime victims and witnesses in court and administrative proceedings; voting assistance and ballots, drivers' licensing exams, and AIDS-prevention education.

13   Passage of an "English Only" ordinance by Florida's Dade County in 1980, barring public funding of activities that involved the use of languages other than English, resulted in the cancellation of all multicultural events and bilingual services, ranging from directional signs in the public transit system to medical services at the county hospital.

14   Where basic human needs are met by bilingual or multilingual services, the consequences of their elimination could be dire. For example, the Washington Times reported in 1987 that a 911 emergency dispatcher was able to save the life of a Salvadoran woman's baby son, who had stopped breathing, by coaching the mother in Spanish over the telephone to administer mouth-to-mouth and cardio-pulmonary resuscitation until the paramedics arrived.

15   **Q: Do "English Only" laws affect only government services and programs?**

16   A: "English Only" laws apply primarily to government programs. However, such laws can also affect private businesses. For example, several Southern California cities have passed ordinances that forbid or restrict the use of foreign languages on private business signs.

17   Some "English Only" advocates have opposed a telephone company's use of multilingual operators and multilingual directories, Federal Communications Commission licensing of Spanish-language radio stations, and bilingual menus at fast food restaurants.

18   **Q: Who is affected by "English Only" laws?**

19   A: "English Only" campaigns target primarily Latinos and Asians, who make up the majority of recent immigrants. Most language minority residents are Spanish-speaking, a result of

the sharp rise in immigration from Latin America during the mid-1960s.

While the overwhelming majority of U.S. residents—96   20
percent—are fluent, approximately ten million residents are not fluent in English, according to the most recent census.

**Q: How do "English Only" laws deprive people of their   21
rights?**

A: The ACLU believes that "English Only" laws are incon-   22
sistent with the Equal Protection Clause of the Fourteenth Amendment. For example, laws that have the effect of elimi-nating courtroom translation severely jeopardize the ability of people on trial to follow and comprehend the proceedings. "English Only" laws interfere with the right to vote by ban-ning bilingual ballots, or with a child's right to education by restricting bilingual instruction. Such laws also interfere with the right of workers to be free of discrimination in work-places where employers have imposed "speak English only" rules.

In 1987, the ACLU adopted a national policy opposing "En-   23
glish Only" laws or laws that would "characterize English as the official language in the United States...to the extent that [they] would mandate or encourage the erosion" of the rights of language minority persons.

**Q: What kinds of language policies were adopted with
regard to past generations of immigrants?**   24

A: Our nation was tolerant of linguistic diversity up until   25
the late 1800s, when an influx of Eastern and Southern Euro-peans, as well as Asians, aroused nativist sentiments and prompted the enactment of restrictive language laws. A 1911 Federal Immigration Commission report falsely argued that the "old" Scandinavian and German immigrants had assimi-lated quickly, while the "new" Italian and Eastern European immigrants were inferior to their predecessors, less willing to learn English, and more prone to political subversion.

In order to "Americanize" the immigrants and exclude peo-   26
ple thought to be of the lower classes and undesirable, English literacy requirements were established for public employment, naturalization, immigration and suffrage. The New York State Constitution was amended to disfranchise over one million Yiddish-speaking citizens. The California Constitution was similarly amended to disfranchise the Chinese, who were seen as a threat to the "purity of the ballot box."

Ironically, during the same period, the government sought   27
to "Americanize" Native American Indian children by taking

them from their families and forcing them to attend English-language boarding schools, where they were punished for speaking their indigenous languages.

28   The intense anti-German sentiment that accompanied the outbreak of World War I prompted several states, where bilingual schools had been commonplace, to enact extreme language laws. For example, Nebraska passed a law in 1919 prohibiting the use of any other language than English through the eighth grade. The Supreme Court subsequently declared the law an unconstitutional violation of due process.

29   Today, as in the past, "English Only" laws in the U.S. are founded on false stereotypes of immigrant groups. Such laws do not simply disparage the immigrants' native languages but assault the rights of the people who speak the languages.

30   **Q: Why are bilingual ballots needed since citizenship is required to vote, English literacy is required for citizenship, and political campaigns are largely conducted in English?**

31   A: Naturalization for U.S. citizenship does not require English literacy for people over 50, and/or who have been in the U.S. for 20 years or more. Thus, there are many elderly immigrant citizens whose ability to read English is limited, and who cannot exercise their right to vote without bilingual ballots and other voter materials. Moreover, bilingual campaign materials and ballots foster a better informed electorate by increasing the information available to people who lack English proficiency.

32   **Q: Doesn't bilingual education slow immigrant children's learning of English, in contrast to the "sink or swim" method that was used in the past?**

33   A: The primary purpose of bilingual programs in elementary and secondary schools, which use both English and a child's native language to teach all subjects, is to develop proficiency in English and, thus, facilitate the child's transition to all-English instruction. Although debate about this approach continues, the latest studies show that bilingual education definitely enhances a child's ability to acquire the second language. Some studies even show that the more extensive the native language instruction, the better students perform all around, and that the bilingual method engenders a positive self-image and self-respect by validating the child's native language and culture.

The "sink or swim" experience of past immigrants left   34
more of them underwater than not. In 1911, the U.S. Immigration Service found that 77 percent of Italian, 60 percent of
Russian, and 51 percent of German immigrant children were
one or more grade levels behind in school compared to 28
percent of American-born white children. Moreover, those
immigrants who did manage to "swim" unaided in the past,
when agricultural and factory jobs were plentiful, might not
do so well in today's "high-tech" economy, with its more rigorous educational requirements.

**Q: But won't "English Only" laws speed up the assimi-   35
lation of today's immigrants into our society and prevent
their isolation?**

A: In fact, contrary to what "English Only" advocates as-   36
sume, the vast majority of today's Asian and Latino immigrants are acquiring English proficiency and assimilating as
fast as did earlier generations of Italian, Russian and German
immigrants. For example, research studies show that over 95
percent of first generation Mexican Americans are English
proficient, and that more than 50 percent of second generation Mexican Americans have lost their native tongue entirely.

In addition, census data reveals that nearly 90 percent of   37
Latinos five years old or older speak English in their households. And 98 percent of Latinos surveyed said they felt it is
"essential" that their children learn to read and write English
"perfectly." Unfortunately, not enough educational resources
are available for immigrants—over 40,000 are on the waiting
list for over-enrolled adult English classes in Los Angeles.
"English Only" laws do not increase resources to meet these
needs.

The best insurance against social isolation of those who   38
immigrate to our nation is acceptance—and celebration—of
the differences that exist within our ethnically diverse citizenry. The bond that unites our nation is not linguistic or ethnic homogeneity but a shared commitment to democracy,
liberty, and equality.

SHOULD THERE BE—OR CAN THERE BE—A "STANDARD" ENGLISH?

Barbara Mellix

From Outside, In

You will learn a lot about Barbara Mellix from reading the following essay, which was published in The Georgia Review *in the summer of 1987, just after Mellix completed her master's degree in creative writing at the University of Pittsburgh.* The Georgia Review *is a quarterly journal of arts and letters that includes scholarly articles, fiction, poetry, and book reviews.*

1 Two years ago, when I started writing this paper, trying to bring order out of chaos, my ten-year-old daughter was suffering from an acute attack of boredom. She drifted in and out of the room complaining that she had nothing to do, no one to "be with" because none of her friends were at home. Patiently I explained that I was working on something special and needed peace and quiet, and I suggested that she paint, read, or work with her computer. None of these interested her. Finally, she pulled up a chair to my desk and watched me, now and then heaving long, loud sighs. After two or three minutes (nine or ten sighs), I lost my patience. "Looka here, Allie," I said, "you too old for this kinda carryin' on. I done told you this is important. You wronger than dirt to be in here haggin' me like this and you know it. Now git on outta here and leave me off before I put my foot all the way down."

2 I was at home, alone with my family, and my daughter understood that this way of speaking was appropriate in that context. She knew, as a matter of fact, that it was almost inevitable; when I get angry at home, I speak some of my finest, most cherished black English. Had I been speaking to my daughter in this manner in certain other environments, she would have been shocked and probably worried that I had taken leave of my sense of propriety.

3 Like my children, I grew up speaking what I considered two distinctly different languages—black English and stan-

dard English (or as I thought of them then, the ordinary everyday speech of "country" coloreds and "proper" English) —and in the process of acquiring these languages, I developed an understanding of when, where, and how to use them. But unlike my children, I grew up in a world that was primarily black. My friends, neighbors, minister, teachers—almost everybody I associated with every day—were black. And we spoke to one another in our own special language: *That sho is a pretty dress you got on. If she don't soon leave me off I'm gon tell her head a mess. I was so mad I could'a pissed a blue nail. He all the time trying to low-rate somebody. Ain't that just about the nastiest thing you ever set ears on?*

Then there were the "others," the "proper" blacks, trans- 4 planted relatives and one-time friends who came home from the city for weddings, funerals, and vacations. And the whites. To these we spoke standard English. "Ain't?" my mother would yell at me when I used the term in the presence of "others." "You *know* better than that." And I would hang my head in shame and say the "proper" word.

I remember one summer sitting in my grandmother's 5 house in Greeleyville, South Carolina, when it was full of the chatter of city relatives who were home on vacation. My parents sat quietly, only now and then volunteering a comment or answering a question. My mother's face took on a strained expression when she spoke. I could see that she was being careful to say just the right words in just the right way. Her voice sounded thick, muffled. And when she finished speaking, she would lapse into silence, her proper smile on her face. My father was more articulate, more aggressive. He spoke quickly, his words sharp and clear. But he held his proud head higher, a signal that he, too, was uncomfortable. My sisters and brothers and I stared at our aunts, uncles, and cousins, speaking only when prompted. Even then, we hesitated, formed our sentences in our minds, then spoke softly, shyly.

My parents looked small and anxious during those occa- 6 sions, and I waited impatiently for leave-taking when we would mock our relatives the moment we were out of their hearing. "Reeely," we would say to one another, flexing our wrists and rolling our eyes, "how dooo you stan' this heat? Chile, it just too hy*ooo*-mid for words." Our relatives had made us feel "country," and this was our way of regaining pride in ourselves while getting a little revenge in the bargain. The words bubbled in our throats and rolled across our tongues, a balming.

7   As a child I felt this same doubleness in uptown Greeleyville where the whites lived. "Ain't that a pretty dress you're
wearing!" Toby, the town policeman, said to me one day when
I was fifteen. "Thank you very much," I replied, my voice
barely audible in my own ears. The words felt wrong in my
mouth, rigid, foreign. It was not that I had never spoken that
phrase before—it was common in black English, too—but I
was extremely conscious that this was an occasion for proper
English. I had taken out my English and put it on as I did my
church clothes, and I felt as if I were wearing my Sunday best
in the middle of the week. It did not matter that Toby had not
spoken grammatically correct English. He was white and
could speak as he wished. I had something to prove. Toby did
not.

8   Speaking standard English to whites was our way of demonstrating that we knew their language and could use it.
Speaking it to standard-English-speaking blacks was our way
of showing them that we, as well as they, could "put on airs."
But when we spoke standard English, we acknowledged (to
ourselves and to others—but primarily to ourselves) that our
customary way of speaking was inferior. We felt foolish,
embarrassed, somehow diminished because we were ashamed
to be our real selves. We were reserved, shy in the presence of
those who owned and/or spoke *the* language.

9   My parents never set aside time to drill us in standard
English. Their forms of instruction were less formal. When my
father was feeling particularly expansive, he would regale us
with tales of his exploits in the outside world. In almost flawless English, complete with dialogue and flavored with gestures and embellishment, he told us about his attempt to get a
haircut at a white barbershop; his refusal to acknowledge one
of the town merchants until the man addressed him as "Mis-
ter"; the time he refused to step off the sidewalk uptown to let
some whites pass; his airplane trip to New York City (to visit a
sick relative) during which the stewardesses and porters—
recognizing that he was a "gentleman"—addressed him as
"Sir." I did not realize then—nor, I think, did my father—that
he was teaching us, among other things, standard English and
the relationship between language and power.

10   My mother's approach was different. Often, when one of us
said, "I'm gon wash off my feet," she would say, "And what
will you walk on if you wash them off?" Everyone would
laugh at the victim of my mother's "proper" mood. But it was
different when one of us children was in a proper mood. "You
think you are so superior," I said to my oldest sister one day

when we were arguing and she was winning. "Superior!" my sister mocked. "You mean I'm acting 'biggidy'?" My sisters and brothers sniggered, then joined in teasing me. Finally, my mother said, "Leave your sister alone. There's nothing wrong with using proper English." There was a half-smile on her face. I had gotten "uppity," had "put on airs" for no good reason. I was at home, alone with the family, and I hadn't been prompted by one of my mother's proper moods. But there was also a proud light in my mother's eyes; her children were learning English very well.

Not until years later, as a college student, did I begin to understand our ambivalence toward English, our scorn of it, our need to master it, to own and be owned by it—an ambivalence that extended to the public school classroom. In our school, where there were no whites, my teacher taught standard English but used black English to do it. When my grammar-school teachers wanted us to write, for example, they usually said something like, "I want y'all to write five sentences that make a statement. Anybody git done before the rest can color." It was probably almost those exact words that led me to write these sentences in 1953 when I was in the second grade: 11

> The white clouds are pretty.
> There are only 15 people in our room.
> We will go to gym.
> We have a new poster.
> We may go out doors.

Second grade came after "Little First" and "Big First," so by then I knew the implied rules that accompanied all writing assignments. Writing was an occasion for proper English. I was not to write in the way we spoke to one another: The white clouds pretty; There ain't but fifteen people in our room; We going to gym; We got a new poster; We can go out in the yard. Rather I was to use the language of "other": clouds *are*, there *are*, we *will*, we *have*, we *may*.

My sentences were short, rigid, perfunctory, like the letters my mother wrote to relatives: 12

> Dear Papa,
>
> How are you? How is Mattie? Fine I hope. We are fine. We will come to see you Sunday. Cousin Ned will give us a ride.
> > Love,
> > Daughter

The language was not ours. It was something from outside us, something we used for special occasions.

13   But my coloring on the other side of that second-grade paper is different. I drew three hearts and a sun. The sun has a smiling face that radiates and envelopes everything it touches. And although the sun and the world are enclosed in a circle, the colors I used—red, blue, green, purple, orange, yellow, black—indicate that I was less restricted with drawing and coloring than I was with writing standard English. My valentines were not just red. My sun was not just a yellow ball in the sky.

14   By the time I reached the twelfth grade, speaking and writing standard English had taken on new importance. Each year, about half of the newly graduated seniors of our school moved to large cities—particularly in the North—to live with relatives and find work. Our English teacher constantly corrected our grammar: "Not 'ain't,' but 'isn't.' " We seldom wrote papers, and even those few were usually plot summaries of short stories. When our teacher returned the papers, she usually lectured on the importance of using standard English: "I *am;* you *are;* he, she, or it *is,*" she would say, writing on the chalkboard as she spoke. "How you gon git a job talking about 'I is,' or 'I isn't' or 'I ain't'?"

15   In Pittsburgh, where I moved after graduation, I watched my aunt and uncle—who had always spoken standard English when in Greeleyville—switch from black English to standard English to a mixture of the two, according to where they were or who they were with. At home and with certain close relatives, friends, and neighbors, they spoke black English. With those less close, they spoke a mixture. In public and with strangers, they generally spoke standard English.

16   In time, I learned to speak standard English with ease and to switch smoothly from black to standard or a mixture, and back again. But no matter where I was, no matter what the situation or occasion, I continued to write as I had in school:

Dear Mommie,

How are you? How is everybody else? Fine I hope. I am fine. So are Aunt and Uncle. Tell everyone I said hello. I will write again soon.
                Love,
                Barbara

At work, at a health insurance company, I learned to write letters to customers. I studied form letters and letters written by co-workers, memorizing the phrases and the ways in which they were used. I dictated:

> Thank you for your letter of January 5. We have made the changes in your coverage you requested. Your new premium will be $150 every three months. We are pleased to have been of service to you.

In a sense, I was proud of the letters I wrote for the company: they were proof of my ability to survive in the city, the outside world—an indication of my growing mastery of English. But they also indicated that writing was still mechanical for me, something that didn't require much thought.

Reading also became a more significant part of my life during those early years in Pittsburgh. I had always liked reading, but now I devoted more and more of my spare time to it. I read romances, mysteries, popular novels. Looking back, I realize that the books I liked best were simple, unambiguous: good versus bad and right versus wrong with right rewarded and wrong punished, mysteries unraveled and all set right in the end. It was how I remembered life in Greeleyville.   17

Of course I was romanticizing. Life in Greeleyville had not become very uncomplicated. Back there I had been—first as a child, then as a young woman with limited experience in the outside world—living in a relatively closed-in society. But there were implicit and explicit principles that guided our way of life and shaped our relationships with one another and the people outside—principles that a newcomer would find elusive and baffling. In Pittsburgh, I had matured, become more experienced. I had worked at three different jobs, associated with a wider range of people, married, had children. This new environment with different prescripts for living required that I speak standard English much of the time and slowly, imperceptibly, I had ceased seeing a sharp distinction between myself and "others." Reading romances and mysteries, characterized by dichotomy, was a way of shying away from change, from the person I was becoming.   18

But that other part of me—that part which took great pride in my ability to hold a job writing business letters—was increasingly drawn to the new developments in my life and the attending possibilities, opportunities for even greater change. If I could write letters for a nationally known business, could I not also do something better, more challenging, more important? Could I not, perhaps, go to college and become a school teacher? For years, afraid and a little embarrassed, I did no   19

more than imagine this different me, this possible me. But
sixteen years after coming north, when my youngest daughter
entered kindergarten, I found myself unable—or unwilling—
to resist the lure of possibility. I enrolled in my first college
course: Basic Writing, at the University of Pittsburgh.

20   For the first time in my life, I was required to write exten-
sively about myself. Using the most formal English at my
command, I wrote these sentences near the beginning of the
term:

> One of my duties as a homemaker is simply picking up after
> others. A day seldom passes that I don't search for a mislaid
> toy, book, or gym shoe, etc. I change the Ty-D-Bol, fight "ring
> around the collar," and keep our laundry smelling "April
> fresh." Occasionally, I settle arguments between my children
> and suggest things to do when they're bored. Taking tele-
> phone messages for my oldest daughter is my newest (and
> sometimes most aggravating) chore. Hanging the toilet
> paper roll is my most insignificant.

My concern was to use "appropriate" language, to sound as if
I belonged in a college classroom. But I felt separate from the
language—as if it did not and could not belong to me. I
couldn't think and feel genuinely in that language, couldn't
make it express what I thought and felt about being a housewife. A part of me resented, among other things, being judged
by such things as the appearance of my family's laundry and
toilet bowl, but in that language I could only imagine and
write about a conventional housewife.

21   For the most part, the remainder of the term was a period
of adjustment, a time of trying to find my bearings as a student in a college composition class, to learn to shut out my
black English whenever I composed, and to prevent it from
creeping into my formulations; a time for trying to grasp the
language of the classroom and reproduce it in my prose; for
trying to talk about myself in that language, reach others
through it. Each experience of writing was like standing naked
and revealing my imperfection, my "otherness." And each new
assignment was another chance to make myself over in language, reshape myself, make myself "better" in my rapidly
changing image of a student in a college composition class.

22   But writing became increasingly unmanageable as the
term progressed, and by the end of the semester, my sentences sounded like this:

> My excitement was soon dampened, however, by what
> seemed like a small voice in the back of my head saying that
> I should be careful with my long awaited opportunity. I felt
> frustrated and this seemed to make it difficult to concentrate.

There is a poverty of language in these sentences. By this
point, I knew that the clichéd language of my Housewife essay was unacceptable, and I generally recognized trite expressions. At the same time, I hadn't yet mastered the language of
the classroom, hadn't yet come to see it as belonging to me.
Most notable is the lifelessness of the prose, the apparent absence of a person behind the words. I wanted those sentences—and the rest of the essay—to convey the anguish of
yearning to, at once, become something more and yet remain
the same. I had the sensation of being split in two, part of me
going into a future the other part didn't believe possible. As
that person, the student writer at that moment, I was essentially mute. I could not—in the process of composing—use
the language of the old me, yet I couldn't imagine myself in
the language of "others."

I found this particularly discouraging because at mid-   23
semester I had been writing in a much different way. Note the
language of this introduction to an essay I had written then,
near the middle of the term:

> Pain is a constant companion to the people in "Footwork."
> Their jobs are physically damaging. Employers are insensi-
> tive to their feelings and in many cases add to their problems.
> The general public wounds them further by treating them
> with disgrace because of what they do for a living. Although
> the workers are as diverse as they are similar, there is a defi-
> nite link between them. They suffer a great deal of abuse.

The voice here is stronger, more confident, appropriating
terms like "physically damaging," "wounds them further," "insensitive," "diverse"—terms I couldn't have imagined using
when writing about my own experience—and shaping them
into sentences like, "Although the workers are as diverse as
they are similar, there is a definite link between them." And
there is the sense of a personality behind the prose, someone
who sympathizes with the workers: "The general public
wounds them further by treating them with disgrace because
of what they do for a living."

What caused these differences? I was, I believed, explain-   24
ing other people's thoughts and feelings, and I was free to

move about in the language of "others" so long as I was
speaking *of* others. I was unaware that I was transforming
into my best classroom language my own thoughts and feelings about people whose experiences and ways of speaking
were in many ways similar to mine.

25   The following year, unable to turn back or let go of what
had become something of an obsession with language (and
hoping to catch and hold the sense of control that had eluded
me in Basic Writing), I enrolled in a research writing course.
I spent most of the term learning how to prepare for and
write a research paper. I chose sex education as my subject
and spent hours in libraries, searching for information, reading, taking notes. Then (not without messiness and often-
demoralizing frustration) I organized my information into
categories, wrote a thesis statement, and composed my paper
—a series of paraphrases and quotations spaced between
carefully constructed transitions. The process and results felt
artificial, but as I would later come to realize I was passing
through a necessary stage. My sentences sounded like this:

> This reserve becomes understandable with examination of
> who the abusers are. In an overwhelming number of cases,
> they are people the victims know and trust. Family members,
> relatives, neighbors and close family friends commit seventy-
> five percent of all reported sex crimes against children, and
> parents, parent substitutes and relatives are the offenders in
> thirty to eighty percent of all reported cases. While assault by
> strangers does occur, it is less common, and is usually a sin-
> gle episode. But abuse by family members, relatives and
> acquaintances may continue for an extended period of time.
> In cases of incest, for example, children are abused repeat-
> edly for an average of eight years. In such cases, "the use of
> physical force is rarely necessary because of the child's trust-
> ing, dependent relationship with the offender. The child's
> cooperation is often facilitated by the adult's position of
> dominance, an offer of material goods, a threat of physical
> violence, or a misrepresentation of moral standards."

26   The completed paper gave me a sense of profound satisfaction, and I read it often after my professor returned it. I know
now that what I was pleased with was the language I used
and the professional voice it helped me maintain. "Use better
words," my teacher had snapped at me one day after reading
the notes I'd begun accumulating from my research, and

slowly I began taking on the language of my sources. In my next set of notes, I used the word "vacillating"; my professor applauded. And by the time I composed the final draft, I felt at ease with terms like "overwhelming number of cases," "single episode," and "reserve," and I shaped them into sentences similar to those of my "expert" sources.

If I were writing the paper today, I would of course do some   27
things differently. Rather than open with an anecdote—as my teacher suggested—I would begin simply with a quotation that caught my interest as I was researching my paper (and which I scribbled, without its source, in the margin of my notebook): "Truth does not do so much good in the world as the semblance of truth does evil." The quotation felt right because it captured what was for me the central idea of my essay—an idea that emerged gradually during the making of my paper—and expressed it in a way I would like to have said it. The anecdote, a hypothetical situation I invented to conform to the information in the paper, felt forced and insincere because it represented—to a great degree—my teacher's understanding of the essay, *her* idea of what in it was most significant. Improving upon my previous experiences with writing, I was beginning to think and feel in the language I used, to find my own voices in it, to sense that how one speaks influences how one means. But I was not yet secure enough, comfortable enough with the language to trust my intuition.

Now that I know that to seek knowledge, freedom, and   28
autonomy means always to be in the concentrated process of becoming—always to be venturing into new territory, feeling one's way at first, then getting one's balance, negotiating, accommodating, discovering one's self in ways that previously defined "others"—I sometimes get tired. And I ask myself why I keep on participating in this highbrow form of violence, this slamming against perplexity. But there is no real futility in the question, no hint of that part of the old me who stood outside standard English, hugging to herself a disabling mistrust of a language she thought could not represent a person with her history and experience. Rather, the question represents a person who feels the consequence of her education, the weight of her possibilities as a teacher and writer and human being, a voice in society. And I would not change that person, would not give back the good burden that accompanies my growing expertise, my increasing power to shape myself in language and share that self with "others."

"To speak," says Frantz Fanon, "means to be in a position   29
to use a certain syntax, to grasp the morphology of this or that

language, but it means above all to assume a culture, to support the weight of a civilization."* To write means to do the same, but in a more profound sense. However, Fanon also says that to achieve mastery means to "get" to a position of power, to "grasp," to "assume." This, I have learned—both as a student and subsequently as a teacher—can involve tremendous emotional and psychological conflict for those attempting to master academic discourse. Although as a beginning student writer I had a fairly good grasp of ordinary spoken English and was proficient at what Labov calls "code switching" (and what John Baugh in *Black Street Speech* terms "style shifting"), when I came face to face with the demands of academic writing, I grew increasingly self-conscious, constantly aware of my status as a black and a speaker of one of the many black English vernaculars, a traditional outsider. For the first time, I experienced my sense of doubleness as something menacing, a built-in enemy. Whenever I turned inward for salvation, the balm so available during my childhood, I found instead this new fragmentation which spoke to me in many voices. It was the voice of my desire to prosper, but at the same time it spoke of what I had relinquished and could not regain: a safe way of being, a state of powerlessness which exempted me from responsibility for who I was and might be. And it accused me of betrayal, of turning away from blackness. To recover balance, I had to take on the language of the academy, the language of "others." And to do that, I had to learn to imagine myself a part of the culture of that language, and therefore someone free to manage that language, to take liberties with it. Writing and rewriting, practicing, experimenting, I came to comprehend more fully the generative power of language. I discovered—with the help of some especially sensitive teachers—that through writing one can continually bring new selves into being, each with new responsibilities and difficulties, but also with new possibilities. Remarkable power, indeed. I write and continually give birth to myself.

Black Skin, White Masks (1952, rpt. New York: Grove Press, 1967), pp. 17–18.

Rachel L. Jones
What's Wrong with Black English

Rachel L. Jones contributed this essay to the "My Turn" column in Newsweek *in 1982, while she was a sophomore at Southern Illinois University. She currently writes for the* River Front Times, *a weekly newspaper in St. Louis, and contributes to National Public Radio.*

William Labov, a noted linguist, once said about the use of black English, "It is the goal of most black Americans to acquire full control of the standard language without giving up their own culture." He also suggested that there are certain advantages to having two ways to express one's feelings. I wonder if the good doctor might also consider the goals of those black Americans who have full control of standard English but who are every now and then troubled by that colorful grammar-to-the-winds patois that is black English. Case in point—me.   1

I'm a 21-year-old black born to a family that would probably be considered lower-middle class—which in my mind is a polite way of describing a condition only slightly better than poverty. Let's just say we rarely if ever did the winter-vacation thing in the Caribbean. I've often had to defend my humble beginnings to a most unlikely group of people for an even less likely reason. Because of the way I talk, some of my black peers look at me sideways and ask, "Why do you talk like you're white?"   2

The first time it happened to me I was nine years old. Cornered in the school bathroom by the class bully and her sidekick, I was offered the opportunity to swallow a few of my teeth unless I satisfactorily explained why I always got good grades, why I talked "proper" or "white." I had no ready answer for her, save the fact that my mother had from the time I was old enough to talk stressed the importance of reading and learning, or that L. Frank Baum and Ray Bradbury were my closest companions. I read all my older brothers' and sisters' literature textbooks more faithfully than they did, and even lightweights like the Bobbsey Twins and Trixie Belden were allowed into my bookish inner circle. I don't remember exactly what I told those girls, but I somehow talked my way out of a beating.   3

I was reminded once again of my "white pipes" problem while apartment hunting in Evanston, Illinois, last winter. I   4 doggedly made out lists of available places and called all around. I would immediately be invited over—and immediately turned down. The thinly concealed looks of shock when the front door opened clued me in, along with the flustered instances of "just getting off the phone with the girl who was ahead of you and she wants the rooms." When I finally found a place to live, my roommate stirred up old memories when she remarked a few months later, "You know, I was surprised when I first saw you. You sounded white over the phone." Tell me another one, sister.

5   I should've asked her a question I've wanted an answer to for years: how does one "talk white"? The silly side of me pictures a rabid white foam spewing forth when I speak. I don't use Valley Girl jargon, so that's not what's meant in my case. Actually, I've pretty much deduced what people mean when they say that to me, and the implications are really frightening.

6   It means that I'm articulate and well-versed. It means that I can talk as freely about John Steinbeck as I can about Rick James. It means that "ain't" and "he be" are not staples of my vocabulary and are only used around family and friends. (It is almost Jekyll and Hyde-ish the way I can slip out of academic abstractions into a long, lean, double-negative-filled dialogue, but I've come to terms with that aspect of my personality.) As a child, I found it hard to believe that's what people meant by "talking proper"; that would've meant that good grades and standard English were equated with white skin, and that went against everything I'd ever been taught. Running into the same type of mentality as an adult has confirmed the depressing reality that for many blacks, standard English is not only unfamiliar, it is socially unacceptable.

7   James Baldwin once defended black English by saying it had added "vitality to the language," and even went so far as to label it a language in its own right, saying, "Language [i.e., black English] is a political instrument" and a "vivid and crucial key to identity." But did Malcolm X urge blacks to take power in this country, "any way y'all can"? Did Martin Luther King Jr. say to blacks, "I has been to the mountaintop, and I done seed the Promised Land"? Toni Morrison, Alice Walker and James Baldwin did not achieve their eloquence, grace and stature by using only black English in their writing. Andrew Young, Tom Bradley and Barbara Jordan did not acquire political power by saying, "Y'all crazy if you ain't gon vote for me." They all have full command of standard English, and I don't think that knowledge takes away from their blackness or commitment to black people.

I know from experience that it's important for black peo- 8
ple, stripped of culture and heritage, to have something they
can point to and say, "This is ours, *we* can comprehend it, *we*
alone can speak it with a soulful flourish." I'd be lying if I said
that the rhythms of my people caught up in "some serious
rap" don't sound natural and right to me sometimes. But how
heartwarming is it for those same brothers when they hit the
pavement searching for employment? Studies have proven
that the use of ethnic dialects decreases power in the market-·
place. "I be" is acceptable on the corner, but not with the
boss.

Am I letting capitalistic, European-oriented thinking fog 9
the issue? Am I selling out blacks to an ideal of assimilating,
being as much like whites as possible? I have not formed a
personal political ideology, but I do know this: it hurts me to
hear black children use black English, knowing that they will
be at yet another disadvantage in an educational system
already full of stumbling blocks. It hurts me to sit in lecture
halls and hear fellow black students complain that the professor "be tripping dem out using big words dey can't understand." And what hurts most is to be stripped of my own
blackness simply because I know my way around the English
language.

I would have to disagree with Labov in one respect. My 10
goal is not so much to acquire full control of both standard
and black English, but to one day see more black people less
dependent on a dialect that excludes them from full participation in the world we live in. I don't think I talk white, I think I
talk right.

Geneva Smitherman

White English in Blackface, or Who Do I Be?

Geneva Smitherman is a professor of linguistics at Michigan State University. Her contention, printed here, that Black English is not slang but an English dialect that follows careful rules first appeared in The Black Scholar *in 1973.*

1   Ain nothin in a long time lit up the English teaching profession like the current hassle over Black English. One finds beaucoup sociolinguistic research studies and language projects for the "disadvantaged" on the scene in nearly every sizable black community in the country.[1] And educators from K-Grad. School bees debating whether: (1) blacks should learn and use only standard white English (hereafter referred to as WE); (2) blacks should command both dialects, i.e., be bidialectal (hereafter BD); (3) blacks should be allowed (??????) to use standard Black English (hereafter BE or BI). The appropriate choice having everything to do with American political reality, which is usually ignored, and nothing to do with the educational process, which is usually claimed. I say without qualification that we cannot talk about the Black Idiom apart from Black Culture and the Black Experience. Nor can we specify educational goals for blacks apart from considerations about the structure of (white) American society.

2   And we black folks is not gon take all that weight, for no one has empirically demonstrated that linguistic/stylistic features of BE impede educational progress in communication skills, or any other area of cognitive learning. Take reading. It's don been charged, but not actually verified, that BE interferes with mastery of reading skills.[2] Yet beyond pointing out

[1]For examples of such programs see *Non-Standard Dialect,* Board of Education of the City of New York (National Council of Teachers of English, 1968); San-Su C. Lin, *Pattern Practices in the Teaching of Standard English with a Non-Standard Dialect* (USOE Project 1339, 1965); Arno Jewett, Joseph Mersand, Doris Gunderson, *Improving English Skills of Culturally Different Youth in Large Cities* (U.S. Department of Health, Education and Welfare, 1964); *Language Programs for the Disadvantaged* (NCTE, 1965).

[2]See, for example, Joan Baratz and Roger Shuy, eds., *Teaching Black Children to Read* (Center for Applied Linguistics, 1969); A. L. Davis, ed., *On the Dialects of Children* (NCTE, 1968); Eldonna L. Evertts, ed., *Dimensions of Dialect* (NCTE, 1967).

the gap between the young brother/sistuh's phonological and syntactical patterns and those of the usually-middle-class-WE-speaking-teacher, this claim has not been validated. The distance between the two systems is, after all, short and is illuminated only by the fact that reading is taught *orally*. (Also get to the fact that preceding generations of BE-speaking folks learned to read, despite the many classrooms in which the teacher spoke a dialect different from that of their students.)

For example, a student who reads *den* for *then* probably   3
pronounces initial /th/ as /d/ in most words. Or the one who reads *doing* for *during* probably deletes intervocalic and final /r/ in most words. So it is not that such students can't read, they is simply employing the black phonological system. In the reading classrooms of today, what we bees needin is teachers with the proper attitudinal orientation who thus can distinguish actual reading problems from mere dialect differences. Or take the writing of an essay. The only percentage in writing a paper with WE spelling, punctuation, and usage is in maybe eliciting a positive *attitudinal* response from a prescriptivist middle-class-aspirant-teacher. Dig on the fact that sheer "correctness" does not a good writer make. And is it any point in dealing with the charge of BE speakers being "nonverbal" or "linguistically deficient" in oral communication skills—behind our many Raps who done disproved that in living, vibrant colors?[3]

What linguists and educators need to do at this juncture is   4
to take serious cognizance of the Oral Tradition in Black Culture. The uniqueness of this verbal style requires a language competence/performance model to fit the black scheme of things. Clearly BI speakers possess rich communication skills (i.e., are highly *competent* in using language), but as yet there bees no criteria (evaluative, testing, or other instrument of measurement), based on black communication patterns, wherein BI speakers can demonstrate they competence (i.e., *performance*). Hence brothers and sisters fail on language performance tests in English classrooms. Like, to amplify on what Nikki [Giovanni] said, that's why we always lose, not only cause we don't know the rules, but it ain't even our game.

[3]For the most racist and glaring of these charges, see Fred Hechinger, ed., *Pre-School Education Today* (Doubleday, 1966); for an excellent rebuttal, see William Labov, *Nonstandard English* (NCTE, 1970); for a complete overview of the controversy and issues involved as well as historical perspective and rebuttal to the non-verbal claim, see my "Black Idiom and White Institutions," *Negro American Literature Forum*, Fall 1971.

5   We can devise a performance model only after an analysis
of the components of BI. Now there do be linguists who supposedly done did this categorization and definition of BE.[4]
But the descriptions are generally confining, limited as they
are to discrete linguistic units. One finds simply ten to fifteen
patterns cited, as for example, the most frequently listed one,
the use of *be* as finite verb, contrasting with its deletion:
(a) *The coffee be cold* contrasts with (b) *The coffee cold,* the
former statement denoting a continuing state of affairs, the
latter applying to the present moment only. (Like if you the
cook, (a) probably get you fired, and (b) only get you talked
about.) In WE no comparable grammatical distinction exists
and *The coffee is cold* would be used to indicate both meanings. However, rarely does one find an investigation of the
total vitality of black expressive style, a style inextricable
from the Black Cultural Universe, for after all, BI connects
with Black Soul and niggers is more than deleted copulas.[5]

6   The Black Idiom should be viewed from two important
perspectives: linguistic and stylistic. The linguistic dimension
is comprised of the so-called nonstandard features of phonol-
ogy and syntax (patterns like *dis heah* and *The coffee be cold*),
and a lexicon generally equated with "slang" or hip talk. The
stylistic dimension has to do with *rapping, capping, jiving,*
etc., and with features such as cadence, rhythm, resonance,
gestures, and all those other elusive, difficult-to-objectify elements that make up what is considered a writer or speaker's
"style." While I am separating linguistic and stylistic features,
I have done so only for the purpose of simplifying the discussion since the BI speaker runs the full gamut of both dimensions in any given speech event.

7   I acknowledge from the bell that we's dealing with a dialect
structure which is a subsystem of the English language; thus
BE and WE may not appear fundamentally different. Yet,
though black folks speak English, it do seem to be an entirely
different lingo altogether. But wherein lies the uniqueness?

---

[4]The most thorough and scholarly of these, though a bit overly technical, is Walter Wolfram, *Detroit Negro Speech* (Center for Applied Linguistics, 1969).

[5]Kochman is one linguist who done gone this route; see for instance his
"Rapping in the Black Ghetto," *Trans-action* February 1969. However, he
makes some black folks mad because of what one of my students called his
"superfluity," and others shame cause of his exposure of our "bad" street
elements. Kochman's data: jam up with muthafuckas and pussy-copping
raps collected from Southside Chicago.

Essentially in language, as in other areas of Black Culture, we have the problem of isolating those elements indigenous to black folks from those cultural aspects shared with white folks. Anthropologist Johnnetta Cole suggests that Black Culture has three dimensions: (1) those elements shared with mainstream America; (2) those elements shared with all oppressed peoples; (3) those elements peculiar to the black condition in America.[6] Applying her concepts to language, I propose the accompanying schematic representation.

Referring to the first column, contemporary BE is simply   8
one of the many dialects of contemporary American English, and it is most likely the case that the linguistic patterns of BE differ from those of WE in surface structure only. There's no essential linguistic difference between *dis heah* and *this here*, and from a strictly linguistic point of view, *God don't never change* can be written *God doesn't ever change* (though definitely not from a socio-cultural/political perspective, as Baraka quite rightly notes).[7] Perhaps we could make a case for deep structure difference in the BE use of *be* as finite verb (refer to *The coffee be cold* example above), but we be hard pressed to find any other examples, and even in this case, we could posit that the copula exists in the deep structure, and is simply deleted by some low-level phonological deletion rule, dig: The coffee is cold... The coffee's cold... The coffee cold. My conclusion at this point is that despite the claims of some highly respected Creole linguists (with special propers to bad Sistuh Beryl Bailey),[8] the argument for deep structure differences between contemporary BE and WE syntax cannot pass the test of rigorous transformational analysis.

Referring to the second column, we note the psychologi-   9
cal tendency of oppressed people to adopt the modes of behavior and expression of their oppressors (also, during the African slave trade, the functional necessity of pidginized forms of European language). Not only does the conqueror force his victims into political subjugation, he also coerces them into adopting his language and doles out special rewards to those among the oppressed who best mimic his

[6]Johnnetta B. Cole, "Culture: Negro, Black and Nigger," *The Black Scholar*, June 1970.

[7]Imamu Baraka, "Expressive Language," *Home*, pp. 166–172.

[8]See her "Toward a New Perspective in Negro English Dialectology," *American Speech* (1965); and "Language and Communicative Styles of Afro-American Children in the United States," *Florida FL Reporter* 7 (Spring-Summer 1969).

FEATURES SHARED WITH MAINSTREAM AMERICA	FEATURES SHARED WITH ALL OPPRESSED PEOPLES	FEATURES UNIQUE TO BLACK AMERICANS
Linguistic	*Linguistic*	*Linguistic*
1. British/ American English lexicon 2. Most aspects of British/ American English phonology and syntax	1. Superimpositions of dominant culture's language on native language, yielding 2. Pidginized form of dominant culture's language, subject to becoming extinct, due to 3. Historical evolution, linguistic leveling out in direction of dominant culture's dialect	Unique meanings attributed to certain English lexical items *Stylistic* Unique communication patterns and rhetorical flourishes

language and cultural style. In the initial language contact stage, the victims attempt to assemble the new language into their native linguistic mold, producing a linguistic mixture that is termed *pidgin*. In the next stage, the pidgin may develop into a Creole, a highly systematic, widely used mode of communication among the oppressed, characterized by a substratum of patterns from the victim's language with an overlay of forms from the oppressor's language. As the oppressed people's identification with the victor's culture intensifies, the pidgin/Creole begins to lose its linguistic currency and naturally evolves in the direction of the victor's language. Reconstructing the linguistic history of BE, we theorize that it followed a similar pattern; due to the radically different condition of black oppression in America, the process of *de-creolization* is nearly complete and has been for perhaps over a hundred years.

10   The most important features of BI are, of course, those referred to in column three, for they point us toward the linguistic uniqueness and cultural significance of the Oral Tradition in the Black Experience. It should be clear that all along I been talkin about that Black Experience associated with the

grass-roots black folks, the masses, the sho-nuff niggers—in short, all those black folks who do not aspire to white middle-class American standards.

Within this tradition, language is used as a teaching/social- 11
izing force and as a means of establishing one's reputation via his verbal competence. Black talk is never meaningless cock-tail chit-chat but a functional dynamic that is simultaneously a mechanism for acculturation and information-passing and a vehicle for achieving group recognition. Black communica-tion is highly verbal and highly stylized; it is a performance before a black audience who become both observers and par-ticipants in the speech event. Whether it be through a slap-ping of hands ("giving five" or "giving skin"), Amen's, or Right on's, the audience influences the direction of a given rap and at the same time acknowledges or withholds its approval, depending on the linguistic skill and stylistic ingenuity of the speaker. I mean like a Brother is only as bad as his rap bees.

I. Toward a Black Language Model: Linguistic

While we concede that black people use the vocabulary of 12
the English language, certain words are always selected out of that lexicon and given a special black semantic slant. So though we rappin bout the same language, the reality refer-ents are different. As one linguist has suggested, the proper question is not what do words mean but what do the users of the words mean? These words may be associated with and more frequently used in black street culture but not necessar-ily. *Muthafucka* has social boundaries, but not *nigger*.

Referring to the lexicon of BI, then, the following general 13
principles obtain:

1. The words given the special black slant exist in a 14
dynamic state. The terms are discarded when they move into the white mainstream. (Example: One no longer speaks of a "hip" brother; now he is a "togetha" brother.) This was/is necessitated by our need to have a code that was/is undeci-pherable by foreigners (i.e., whites).

2. In BI, the concept of denotation vs. connotation does 15
not apply.

3. What does apply is shades of meaning along the conno- 16
tative spectrum. For example, depending on contextual envi-ronment, the word *bad* can mean extraordinary; beautiful; good; versatile; or a host of other terms of positive value. Dig

it; after watching a Sammy Davis performance, a BI speaker testified: "Sammy sho did some *bad* stuff," i.e., extraordinary stuff. Or upon observing a beautiful sister: "She sho is *bad*," i.e., beautiful, pretty, or good-looking. Or, noticing how a brother is dressed: "You sho got on some *bad* shit," i.e., *good* shit = attractively dressed.

17   Note that the above examples are all in the category of *approbation*. It is necessary to rap about *denigration* as well, since certain words in the black lexicon can frequently be used both ways. Consider the word *nigger*, for instance. "He's my main nigger" means my best friend (hence, approbation); "The nigger ain't shit," means he's probably lazy, trifling, scheming, wrong-doing, or a host of other *denigrating* terms, depending on the total context of the utterance.

18   4. Approbation and denigration relate to the semantic level; we can add two other possible functions of the same word on the grammatical level: *intensification* and *completion*. Slide back to *nigger* for a minute, and dig that often the word is void of real meaning and simply supplies the sentence with a subject. "Niggers was getting out of there left and right, then the niggers was running, and so the niggers said . . ." etc., etc., my main point being that a steady stream of overuse means neither denigration nor approbation. Some excellent illustrations of this function of the word are to be found in *Manchild in the Promised Land,* where you can observe the word used in larger contexts.

19   To give you a most vivid illustration, consider the use of what WE labels "obscenities." From the streets of Detroit: (a) "That's a bad *muthafucka*." Referring to a Cadillac Eldorado, obviously indicating approval. (b) "He's a no-good *muthafucka*." Referring to a person who has just "put some game" on the speaker, obviously indicating disapproval. (c) "You *muthafuckin* right I wasn't gon let him do that." Emphasizing how correct the listener's assessment is, obviously using the term as a grammatical intensifier, modifying "right." (d) "We wasn't doin nothing, just messing round and *shit*." Though a different "obscenity," the point is nonetheless illustrated, "shit" being used neutrally, as an expletive (filler) to complete the sentence pattern; semantically speaking, it is an empty word in this contextual environment.

20   Where I'm comin from is that the lexicon of BI, consisting of certain specially selected words, requires a unique scheme of analysis to account for the diverse range and multiplicity of

meanings attributed to these words. While there do be some dictionaries of Afro-American "slang," they fail to get at the important question: what are the psycho-cultural processes that guide our selection of certain words out of the thousands of possible words in the Anglo-Saxon vocabulary? Like, for instance, Kochman[9] has suggested that we value action in the black community, and so those words that have action implied in them, we take and give positive meanings to, such as *swing, game, hip, hustle,* etc.; whereas words of implied stasis are taken and given negative connotations, such as *lame, square, hung-up, stiffin and jivin,* etc. At any rate, what I've tried to lay here are some suggestions in this particular linguistic dimension; the definitive word on black lexicon is yet to be given.

I shall go on to discuss the stylistic dimension of black   21
communication patterns, where I have worked out a more definitive model.

II. Toward a Black Language Model: Stylistic

Black verbal style exists on a sacred-secular continuum, as   22
represented by the accompanying scheme. The model allows us to account for the many individual variations in black speech, which can all be located at some point along the continuum.

The sacred style is rural and Southern. It is the style of the   23
black preacher and that associated with the black church tradition. It tends to be more emotive and highly charged than the secular style. It is also older in time. However, though I've called it "sacred," it abounds in secularisms. Black church service tends to be highly informal, and it ain't nothin for a preacher to get up in the pulpit and, say, show off what he's wearing: "Y'all didn't notice the new suit I got on today, did y'all? Ain the Lord good to us...."

The secular style is urban and Northern, but since it probably had its beginnings in black folk tales and proverbs, its   24
roots are Southern and rural. This is the street culture; the style found in barbershops and on street corners in the black

---

[9]See Thomas Kochman, "The Kinetic Element in Black Idiom," paper read at the American Anthropological Association Convention, Seattle, Washington, 1968; also his *Rappin' and Stylin' Out: Communication in Urban Black America.*

SACRED	*SECULAR*
Political Rap Style	*Political Rap Style*
Examples: Jesse Jackson Martin Luther King	*Examples:* Malcom X Rap Brown
Political Literary Style	*Political Literary Style*
Examples: Barbara Ann Teer's National Black Theater Nikki Giovanni's "Truth Is on Its Way"	*Examples:* Don Lee Last Poets

ghettos of American cities. It tends to be more cool, more emotionally restrained than sacred style. It is newer and younger in time and only fully evolved as a distinct style with the massive wave of black migration to the cities.

25   Both sacred and secular styles share the following characteristics:

26   1. *Call and Response.*   This is basic black oral tradition. The speaker's solo voice alternates or is intermingled with the audience's response. In the sacred style, the minister is urged by the congregation's Amen's, That's right, Reverend's, or Preach Reverend's. One also hears occasional Take your time's when the preacher is initiating his sermon, the congregation desiring to savor every little bit of this good message they bout to hear. (In both sacred and secular political rap styles, the "Preach Reverend" is transposed to "Teach Brother.") In the secular style, the response can take the form of a back-and-forth banter between the speaker and various members of the audience. Or the audience might manifest its response in giving skin (fives) when a really down verbal point is scored. Other approval responses include laughter and phrases like "Oh, you mean, nigger," "Get back, nigger," "Git down, baby," etc.

27   2. *Rhythmic Pattern.*   I refer to cadence, tone, and musical quality. This is a pattern that is lyrical, sonorous, and generally emphasizing sound apart from sense. It is often established through repetition, either of certain sounds or words. The preacher will get a rhythm going, conveying his message through sound rather than depending on sheer semantic import. "I-I-I-I-I-Oh-I-I-Oh, yeah, Lord-I-I-heard the

voice of Jesus saying...." Even though the secular style is characterized by rapidity, as in the toasts (narrative tales of bad niggers and they exploits like Stag-O-Lee, or bad animals and they trickeration, like the Signifying Monkey), the speaker's voice tone still has that rhythmic, musical quality, just with a faster tempo.

3. *Spontaneity.* Generally, the speaker's performance is improvisational, with the rich interaction between speaker and audience dictating and/or directing the course and outcome of the speech event. Since the speaker does not prepare a formal document, his delivery is casual, nondeliberate, and uncontrived. He speaks in a lively, conversational tone, and with an ever-present quality of immediacy. All emphasis is on process, movement, and creativity of the moment. The preacher says "Y'all don wont to hear dat, so I'm gon leave it lone," and his audience shouts, "Naw, tell it Reverend, tell it!," and he does. Or, like, once Malcolm [X] mentioned the fact of his being in prison, and sensing the surprise of his audience, he took advantage of the opportunity to note that all black people were in prison: "That's what American means: prison."

4. *Concreteness.* The speaker's imagery and ideas center around the empirical world, the world of reality, and the contemporary Here and Now. Rarely does he drift off into esoteric abstractions; his metaphors and illustrations are commonplace and grounded in everyday experience. Perhaps because of his concreteness, there is a sense of identification with the event being described or narrated, as in the secular style where the toast-teller's identity merges with that of the protagonist of his tale, and he becomes Stag-O-Lee or Shine; or when the preacher assumes the voice of God or the personality of a Biblical character. Even the experience of being saved takes on a presentness and rootedness in everyday life: "I first met God in 1925...."

5. *Signifying.* This is a technique of talking about the entire audience or some member of the audience either to initiate verbal "war" or to make a point hit home. The interesting thang bout this rhetorical device is that the audience is not offended and realizes—naw, expects—the speaker to launch this offensive to achieve this desired effect. "Pimp, punk, prostitute, Ph.D.—all the P's—you still in slavery!" announces the Reverend Jesse Jackson. Malcolm puts down the nonviolent movement with: "In a revolution, you swinging, not singing." (Notice the characteristic rhythmic pattern in the above examples—the alliterative poetic effect of Jackson's statement and the rhyming device in Malcolm's.)

28

29

30

31   An analysis of black expressive style, such as presented
here, should facilitate the construction of a performance
instrument to measure the degree of command of the style of
any given BI speaker. Linguists and educators sincerely interested in black education might be about the difficult, complex
business of devising such a "test," rather than establishing
linguistic remediation programs to correct a nonexistent
remediation. Like in any other area of human activity, some
BI rappers are better than others, and today's most effective
black preachers, leaders, politicians, writers are those who
rap in the black expressive style, appropriating the ritual
framework of the Oral Tradition as vehicle for the conveyance
of they political ideologies. Which brings me back to what I
said from Jump Street. The real heart of this language controversy relates to/is the underlying political nature of the American educational system. Brother Frantz Fanon is highly
instructive at this point. From his "Negro and Language," in
Black Skin, White Masks:

> I ascribe a basic importance to the phenomenon of lan-
> guage.... To speak means...above all to assume a culture, to
> support the weight of a civilization.... Every dialect is a way
> of thinking.... And the fact that the newly returned [i.e.,
> from white schools] Negro adopts a language different from
> that of the group into which he was born is evidence of a dis-
> location, a separation....

In showing why the "Negro adopts such a position...with respect to European languages," Fanon continues:

> It is because he wants to emphasize the rupture that has now
> occurred. He is incarnating a new type of man that he
> imposes on his associates and his family. And so his old
> mother can no longer understand him when he talks to her
> about his *duds,* the family's *crummy joint,* the *dump*...all of
> it, of course, tricked out with the appropriate accent.
>   In every country of the world, there are climbers, "the
> ones who forget who they are," and in contrast to them, "the
> ones who remember where they came from." The Antilles
> Negro who goes home from France expresses himself in the
> dialect if he wants to make it plain that nothing has changed.

32   As black people go moving on up toward separation and
cultural nationalism, the question of the moment is not
which dialect, but which culture, not whose vocabulary but
whose values, not *I am* vs. *I be,* but WHO DO I BE?

John Simon
Why Good English Is Good for You

John Simon (born 1925) has reviewed theater and film for several magazines. An eloquent—and sometimes merciless—critic of the misuse of language, for many years he wrote a language column for Esquire. *Several of those columns were collected in* Paradigms Lost, *a book about the "decline of literacy." This essay is from that 1980 collection.*

What's good English to you that . . . you should grieve for it? What good is correct speech and writing, you may ask, in an age in which hardly anyone seems to know, and no one seems to care? Why shouldn't you just fling bloopers, bloopers riotously with the throng, and not stick out from the rest like a sore thumb by using the language correctly? Isn't grammar really a thing of the past, and isn't the new idea to communicate in *any* way as long as you can make yourself understood?

The usual, basic defense of good English (and here, again, let us not worry about nomenclature—for all I care, you may call it "Standard English," "correct American," or anything else) is that it helps communication, that it is perhaps even a *sine qua non* of mutual understanding. Although this is a crude truth of sorts, it strikes me as, in some ways, both more and less than the truth. Suppose you say, "Everyone in their right mind would cross on the green light" or "Hopefully, it won't rain tomorrow"; chances are very good that the person you say this to will understand you, even though you are committing obvious solecisms or creating needless ambiguities. Similarly, if you write in a letter, "The baby has finally ceased it's howling" (spelling *its* as *it's*), the recipient will be able to figure out what was meant. But "figuring out" is precisely what a listener or reader should not have to do. There is, of course, the fundamental matter of courtesy to the other person, but it goes beyond that: why waste time on unscrambling simple meaning when there are more complex questions that should receive our undivided attention? If the many cooks had to worry first about which out of a large number of pots had no leak in it, the broth, whether spoiled or not, would take forever to be ready.

It is, I repeat, only initially a matter of clarity. It is also a matter of concision. Space today is as limited as time. If you have only a thousand words in which to convey an important

message, it helps to know that "overcomplicated" is correct
and "overly complicated" is incorrect. Never mind the grammatical explanations; the two extra characters and one space
between words are reason enough. But what about the more
advanced forms of word-mongering that hold sway nowadays? Take redundancy, like the "hopes and aspirations" of
Jimmy Carter, quoted by Edwin Newman as having "a deeply
profound religious experience"; or elaborate jargon, as when
Charles G. Walcutt, a graduate professor of English at CUNY,
writes (again as quoted by Newman): "The colleges, trying to
remediate increasing numbers of...illiterates up to college
levels, are being high-schoolized"; or just obfuscatory verbiage of the pretentious sort, such as this fragment from a letter I received: "It is my impression that effective in*ter*personal
verbal communication depends on prior effective intra-
personal verbal communication." What this means is that if
you think clearly, you can speak and write clearly—except if
you are a "certified speech and language pathologist," like the
writer of the letter I quote. (By the way, she adds the letters
Ph.D. after her name, though she is not even from Germany,
where *Herr* and *Frau Doktor* are in common, not to say, vulgar, use.)

4   But except for her ghastly verbiage, our certified language
pathologist (whatever that means) is perfectly right: there is a
close connection between the ability to think and the ability
to use English correctly. After all, we think in words, we con-
ceptualize in words, we work out our problems inwardly with
words, and using them correctly is comparable to a craftsman's treating his tools with care, keeping his materials in
good shape. Would you trust a weaver who hangs her wet
laundry on her loom, or lets her cats bed down in her yarn?
The person who does not respect words and their proper relationships cannot have much respect for ideas—very possibly
cannot have ideas at all. My quarrel is not so much with
minor errors that we fall into from time to time even if we
know better as it is with basic sloppiness or ignorance or defiance of good English.

5   Training yourself to speak and write correctly—and I say
"training yourself" because nowadays, unfortunately, you
cannot depend on other people or on institutions to give you
the proper training, for reasons I shall discuss later—training
yourself, then, in language, means developing at the very least
two extremely useful faculties: your sense of discipline and
your memory. Discipline because language is with us always,
as nothing else is: it follows us much as, in the old morality
play, Good Deeds followed Everyman, all the way to the

grave; and, if the language is written, even beyond. Let me explain: if you can keep an orderly apartment, if you can see to it that your correspondence and bill-paying are attended to regularly, if your diet and wardrobe are maintained with the necessary care—good enough; you are a disciplined person.

But the preliminary discipline underlying all others is nev-   6
ertheless your speech: the words that come out of you almost as frequently and—if you are tidy—as regularly as your breath. I would go so far as to say that, immediately after your bodily functions, language is first, unless you happen to be an ascetic, an anchorite, or a stylite; but unless you are a sty*lite,* you had better be a sty*list.*

Most of us—almost all—must take in and give out lan-   7
guage as we do breath, and we had better consider the seriousness of language pollution as second only to air pollution. For the linguistically disciplined, to misuse or mispronounce a word is an unnecessary and unhealthy contribution to the surrounding smog. To have taught ourselves not to do this, or—being human and thus also imperfect—to do it as little as possible, means deriving from every speaking moment the satisfaction we get from a cap that snaps on to a container perfectly, an elevator that stops flush with the landing, a roulette ball that comes to rest exactly on the number on which we have placed our bet. It gives us the pleasure of hearing or seeing our words—because they are abiding by the rules—snapping, sliding, falling precisely into place, expressing with perfect lucidity and symmetry just what we wanted them to express. This is comparable to the satisfaction of the athlete or ballet dancer or pianist finding his body or legs or fingers doing his bidding with unimpeachable accuracy.

And if someone now says that "in George Eliot's lesser nov-   8
els, she is not completely in command" is perfectly comprehensible even if it is ungrammatical, the "she" having no antecedent in the nominative (*Eliot's* is a genitive), I say, "Comprehensible, perhaps, but lopsided," for the civilized and orderly mind does not feel comfortable with that "she"—does not hear that desired and satisfying click of correctness—unless the sentence is restructured as "George Eliot, in her lesser novels, is not..." or in some similar way. In fact, the fully literate ear can be thrown by this error in syntax; it may look for the antecedent of that "she" elsewhere than in the preceding possessive case. Be that as it may, playing without rules and winning—in this instance, managing to communicate without using good English—is no more satisfactory than winning in a sport or game by accident or by disregarding the rules: which is really cheating.

9   The second faculty good speech develops is, as I have mentioned before, our memory. Grammar and syntax are partly
logical—and to that extent they are also good exercisers and
developers of our logical faculty—but they are also partly
arbitrary, conventional, irrational. For example, the correct
"compared to" and "contrasted with" could, from the logical
point of view, just as well be "contrasted to" and "compared
with" ("compared with," of course, is correct, but in a different sense from the one that concerns us here, namely, the
antithesis of "contrasted with"). And, apropos *different*, logic
would have to strain desperately to explain the exclusive correctness of "different from," given the exclusive correctness of
"other than," which would seem to justify "different than,"
jarring though that is to the cultivated ear.

10   But there it is: some things are so because tradition, usage,
the best speakers and writers, the grammar books and dictionaries have made them so. There may even exist some hidden
historical explanation: something, perhaps, in the Sanskrit,
Greek, Latin, or other origins of a word or construction that
you and I may very easily never know. We can, however, memorize; and memorization can be a wonderfully useful thing—
surely the Greeks were right to consider Mnemosyne (memory) the mother of the Muses, for without her there would be
no art and no science. And what better place to practice one's
mnemonic skills than in the study of one's language?

11   There is something particularly useful about speaking correctly and precisely because language is always there as a
foundation—or, if you prefer a more fluid image, an under-
current—beneath what is going on. Now, it seems to me that
the great difficulty of life lies in the fact that we must almost
always do two things at a time. If, for example, we are walking and conversing, we must keep our mouths as well as feet
from stumbling. If we are driving while listening to music, we
must not allow the siren song of the cassette to prevent us
from watching the road and the speedometer (otherwise the
less endearing siren of the police car or the ambulance will
follow apace). Well, it is just this sort of bifurcation of attention that care for precise, clear expression fosters in us. By
learning early in life to pay attention to both what we are saying and to how we are saying it, we develop the much-needed
life skill of doing two things simultaneously.

12   Put another way, we foster our awareness of, and ability to
deal with, form and content. If there is any verity that modern
criticism has fought for, it is the recognition of that indissolu-
bility of content and form. Criticism won the battle, won it so

resoundingly that this oneness has become a contemporary commonplace. And shall the fact that form *is* content be a platitude in all the arts but go unrecognized in the art of self-expression, whether in conversation or correspondence, or whatever form of spoken or written utterance a human being resorts to? Accordingly, you are going to be judged, whether you like it or not, by the correctness of your thinking; there are some people to whose ear bad English is as offensive as gibberish, or as your picking your nose in public would be to their eyes and stomachs. The fact that people of linguistic sensibilities may be a dying breed does not mean that they are wholly extinct, and it is best not to take any unnecessary chances.

To be sure, if you are a member of a currently favored   13
minority, many of your linguistic failings may be forgiven you—whether rightly or wrongly is not my concern here. But if you cannot change your sex or color to the one that is getting preferential treatment—Bakke case or no Bakke case— you might as well learn good English and profit by it in your career, your social relations, perhaps even in your basic self-confidence. That, if you will, is the ultimate practical application of good English; but now let me tell you about the ultimate impractical one, which strikes me as being possibly even more important.

Somewhere in the prose writings of Charles Péguy, who   14
was a very fine poet and prose writer—and, what is perhaps even more remarkable, as good a human being as he was an artist—somewhere in those writings is a passage about the decline of pride in workmanship among French artisans, which, as you can deduce, set in even before World War I, wherein Péguy was killed. In the passage I refer to, Péguy bemoans the fact that cabinetmakers no longer finish the backs of furniture—the sides that go against the wall—in the same way as they do the exposed sides. What is not seen was just as important to the old artisans as what is seen—it was a moral issue with them. And so, I think, it ought to be with language. Even if no one else notices the niceties, the precision, the impeccable sense of grammar and syntax you deploy in your utterances, you yourself should be aware of them and take pride in them as in pieces of work well done.

Now, I realize that there are two possible reactions among   15
you to what I have said up to this point. Some of you will say to yourselves: what utter nonsense! Language is a flexible, changing, living organism that belongs to the people who speak it. It has always been changed according to the ways in

which people chose to speak it, and the dictionaries and books on grammar had to, and will have to, adjust themselves to the people and not the other way around. For isn't it the glory of language that it keeps throwing up new inventions as surf tosses out differently polished pebbles and bits of bottle glass onto the shore, and that in this inexhaustible variety, in this refusal to kowtow to dry-as-dust scholars, lies its vitality, its beauty?

16   Others among you, perhaps few in number, will say to yourselves: quite so, there is such a thing as Standard English, or purity of speech, or correctness of expression—something worth safeguarding and fostering; but how the devil is one to accomplish that under the prevailing conditions: in a democratic society full of minorities that have their own dialects or linguistic preferences, and in a world in which television, advertising, and other mass media manage daily to corrupt the language a little further? Let me try to answer the first group first, and then come back to the questions of the second.

17   Of course language is, and must be, a living organism to the extent that new inventions, discoveries, ideas enter the scene and clamor rightfully for designations. Political, social, and psychological changes may also affect our mode of expression, and new words or phrases may have to be found to reflect what we might call historical changes. It is also quite natural for slang terms to be invented, become popular, and, in some cases, remain permanently in the language. It is perhaps equally inevitable (though here we are on more speculative ground) for certain words to become obsolescent and obsolete, and drop out of the language. But does that mean that grammar and syntax have to keep changing, that pronunciations and meanings of words must shift, that more complex or elegant forms are obliged to yield to simpler or cruder ones that often are not fully synonymous with them and not capable of expressing certain fine distinctions? Should, for instance, "terrestrial" disappear entirely in favor of "earthly," or are there shades of meaning involved that need to remain available to us? Must we sacrifice "notwithstanding" because we have "in spite of" or "despite"? Need we forfeit "jettison" just because we have "throw overboard"? And what about "disinterested," which is becoming a synonym for "uninterested," even though that means something else, and though we have no other word for "disinterested"?

18   "Language has *always* changed," say these people, and they might with equal justice say that there has always been war

or sickness or insanity. But the truth is that some sicknesses that formerly killed millions have been eliminated, that some so-called insanity can today be treated, and that just because there have always been wars does not mean that someday a cure cannot be found even for that scourge. And if it cannot, it is only by striving to put an absolute end to war, by pretending that it can be licked, that we can at least partly control it. Without such assumptions and efforts, the evil would be so widespread that, given our current weaponry, we would no longer be here to worry about the future of language.

But we are here, and having evolved linguistically this far, 19 and having the means—books of grammar, dictionaries, education for all—to arrest unnecessary change, why not endeavor with might and mind to arrest it? Certain cataclysms cannot be prevented: earthquakes and droughts, for example, can scarcely, if at all, be controlled; but we can prevent floods, for which purpose we have invented dams. And dams are precisely what we can construct to prevent floods of ignorance from eroding our language, and, beyond that, to provide irrigation for areas that would otherwise remain linguistically arid.

For consider that what some people are pleased to call lin- 20 guistic evolution was almost always a matter of ignorance prevailing over knowledge. There is no valid reason, for example, for the word *nice* to have changed its meaning so many times—except ignorance of its exact definition. Had the change never occurred, or had it been stopped at any intermediate stage, we would have had just as good a word as we have now and saved some people a heap of confusion along the way. But if *nice* means what it does today—and it has two principal meanings, one of them, as in "nice distinction," alas, obsolescent—let us, for heaven's sake, keep it where it is, now that we have the means with which to hold it there.

If, for instance, we lose the accusative case *whom*—and we 21 are in great danger of losing it—our language will be the poorer for it. Obviously, "The man, whom I had never known, was a thief" means something other than "The man who I had never known was a thief." Now, you can object that it would be just as easy in the first instance to use some other construction; but what happens if *this* one is used incorrectly? Ambiguity and confusion. And why should we lose this useful distinction? Just because a million or ten million or a billion people less educated than we are cannot master the difference? Surely it behooves us to try to educate the ignorant up to our level rather than to stultify ourselves down to theirs.

Yes, you say, but suppose they refuse to or are unable to learn? In that case, I say, there is a doubly good reason for not going along with them. Ah, you reply, but they are the majority, and we must accept their way or, if the revolution is merely linguistic, lose our "credibility" (as the current parlance, rather confusingly, has it) or, if the revolution is political, lose our heads. Well, I consider a sufficient number of people to be educable enough to be capable of using *who* and *whom* correctly, and to derive satisfaction from this capability—a sufficient number, I mean, to enable us to preserve *whom*, and not to have to ask "for who the bell tolls."

22   The main problem with education, actually, is not those who need it and cannot get it, but those who should impart it and, for various reasons, do not. In short, the enemies of education are the educators themselves: miseducated, underpaid, overburdened, and intimidated teachers (frightened because, though the pen is supposed to be mightier than the sword, the switchblade is surely more powerful than the ferule), and professors who—because they are structural linguists, democratic respecters of alleged minority rights, or otherwise misguided folk—believe in the sacrosanct privilege of any culturally underprivileged minority or majority to dictate its ignorance to the rest of the world. For, I submit, an English improvised by slaves and other strangers to the culture—to whom my heart goes out in every human way—under dreadfully deprived conditions can nowise equal an English that the best literary and linguistic talents have, over the centuries, perceptively and painstakingly brought to a high level of excellence.

23   So my answer to the scoffers in this or any audience is, in simplest terms, the following: contrary to popular misconception, language does not belong to the people, or at least not in the sense in which *belong* is usually construed. For things can rightfully belong only to those who invent or earn them. But we do not know who invented language: is it the people who first made up the words for *father* and *mother*, for *I* and *thou*, for *hand* and *foot;* or is it the people who evolved the subtler shadings of language, its poetic variety and suggestiveness, but also its unambiguousness, its accurate and telling details? Those are two very different groups of people and two very different languages, and I, as you must have guessed by now, consider the latter group at least as important as the former. As for *earning* language, it has surely been earned by those who have striven to learn it properly, and here even economic

and social circumstances are but an imperfect excuse for bad usage; history is full of examples of people rising from humble origins to learn, against all kinds of odds, to speak and write correctly—even brilliantly.

Belong, then, should be construed in the sense that parks, national forests, monuments, and public utilities are said to belong to the people: available for properly respectful use but not for defacement and destruction. And all that we propose to teach is how to use and enjoy the gardens of language to their utmost aesthetic and salubrious potential. Still, I must now address myself to the group that, while agreeing with my aims, despairs of finding practical methods for their implementation.   24

True enough, after a certain age speakers not aware of Standard English or not exceptionally gifted will find it hard or impossible to change their ways. Nevertheless, if there were available funds for advanced methods in teaching; if teachers themselves were better trained and paid, and had smaller classes and more assistants; if, furthermore, college entrance requirements were heightened and the motivation of students accordingly strengthened; if there were no structural linguists and National Councils of Teachers of English filling instructors' heads with notions about "Students' Rights to Their Own Language" (they have every right to it as a *second* language, but none as a *first*); if teachers in all disciplines, including the sciences and social sciences, graded on English usage as well as on specific proficiencies; if aptitude tests for various jobs stressed good English more than they do; and, above all, if parents were better educated and more aware of the need to set a good example to their children, and to encourage them to learn correct usage, the situation could improve enormously.   25

Clearly, to expect all this to come to pass is utopian; some of it, however, is well within the realm of possibility. For example, even if parents do not speak very good English, many of them at least can manage an English that is good enough to correct a very young child's mistakes; in other words, most adults can speak a good enough four-year-old's idiom. They would thus start kids on the right path; the rest could be done by the schools.   26

But the problem is what to do in the most underprivileged homes: those of blacks, Hispanics, immigrants from various Asian and European countries. This is where day-care centers could come in. If the fathers and mothers could be gainfully   27 employed, their small children would be looked after by day-care centers where—is this asking too much?—good English could be inculcated in them. The difficulty, of course, is what to do about the discrepancy the little ones would note between the speech of the day-care people and that of their parents. Now, it seems to me that small children have a far greater ability to learn things, including languages, than some people give them credit for. Much of it is indeed rote learning, but, where languages are concerned, that is one of the basic learning methods even for adults. There is no reason for not teaching kids another language, to wit, Standard English, and turning this, if desirable, into a game: "At home you speak one way; here we have another language," at which point the instructor can make up names and explanations for Standard English that would appeal to pupils of that particular place, time, and background.

28   At this stage of the game, as well as later on in school, care should be exercised to avoid insulting the language spoken in the youngsters' homes. There must be ways to convey that both home and school languages have their validity and uses and that knowing both enables one to accomplish more in life. This would be hard to achieve if the children's parents were, say, militant blacks of the Geneva Smitherman sort, who execrate Standard English as a weapon of capitalist oppression against the poor of all races, colors, and religions. But, happily, there is evidence that most black, Hispanic, and other non-Standard English–speaking parents want their children to learn correct English so as to get ahead in the world.

29   Yet how do we defend ourselves against the charge that we are old fogeys who cannot emotionally adjust to the new directions an ever-living and changing language must inevitably take? Here I would want to redefine or, at any rate, clarify, what "living and changing" means, and also explain where we old fogeys stand. Misinformed attacks on Old Fogeydom, I have noticed, invariably represent us as people who shudder at a split infinitive and would sooner kill or be killed than tolerate a sentence that ends with a preposition. Actually, despite all my travels through Old Fogeydom, I have yet to meet one inhabitant who would not stick a preposition onto the tail of a sentence; as for splitting infinitives, most of us O.F.'s are perfectly willing to do that, too, but tactfully and sparingly, where it feels right. There is no earthly reason, for example "to dangerously live," when "to live dangerously"

sounds so much better; but it does seem right to say (and write) "What a delight to sweetly breathe in your sleeping lover's breath"; that sounds smoother, indeed sweeter, than "to breathe in sweetly" or "sweetly to breathe in." But infinitives begging to be split are relatively rare; a sensitive ear, a good eye for shades of meaning will alert you whenever the need to split arises; without that ear and eye, you had better stick to the rules.

About the sense in which language is, and must be, alive, let me speak while donning another of my several hats—actually it is not a hat but a cap, for there exists in Greenwich Village an inscription on a factory that reads "CRITIC CAPS." So with my drama critic's cap on, let me present you with an analogy. The world theater today is full of directors who wreak havoc on classic plays to demonstrate their own ingenuity, their superiority, as it were, to the author. These directors—aborted playwrights, for the most part—will stage productions of *Hamlet* in which the prince is a woman, a flaming homosexual, or a one-eyed hunchback.

Well, it seems to me that the same spirit prevails in our approach to linguistics, with every newfangled, ill-informed, know-nothing construction, definition, pronunciation enshrined by the joint efforts of structural linguists, permissive dictionaries, and allegedly democratic but actually demagogic educators. What really makes a production of, say, *Hamlet* different, and therefore alive, is that the director, while trying to get as faithfully as possible at Shakespeare's meanings, nevertheless ends up stressing things in the play that strike him most forcefully; and the same individuality in production design and performances (the Hamlet of Gielgud versus the Hamlet of Olivier, for instance—what a world of difference!) further differentiates one production from another, and bestows on each its particular vitality. So, too, language remains alive because each speaker (or writer) can and must *within the framework of accepted grammar, syntax, and pronunciation*, produce a style that is his very own, that is as personal as his posture, way of walking, mode of dress, and so on. It is such stylistic differences that make a person's—or a nation's—language flavorous, pungent, alive, and all this without having to play fast and loose with the existing rules.

But to have this, we need, among other things, good teachers and, beyond them, enlightened educators. I shudder when I read in the *Birmingham* (Alabama) *Post-Herald* on October 6, 1978, an account of a talk given to eight hundred English

30

31

32

teachers by Dr. Alan C. Purves, vice-president of the National Council of Teachers of English. Dr. Purves is quoted as saying things like "We are in a situation with respect to reading where . . . ," and culminating in the following truly horrifying sentence: "I am going to suggest that when we go back to the basics, I think what we should be dealing with is our charge to help students to be more proficient in producing meaningful language—language that says what it means." Notice all the deadwood, the tautology, the anacoluthon in the first part of that sentence; but notice especially the absurdity of the latter part, in which the dubious word "meaningful"—a poor relation of "significant"—is thought to require explaining to an audience of English teachers.

33   Given such leadership from the N.C.T.E., the time must be at hand when we shall hear—not just "Don't ask for who the bell rings" (*ask not* and *tolls* being, of course, archaic, elitist language), but also "It rings for you and I."

On Ebonics: A Discussion of Black English

In December 1996, the school board in Oakland, California, where 53 percent of the students are black, decided to recognize Black English (Ebonics) as a second language in the district and told its teachers to respect its use in the classroom. The board took steps to ensure that teachers would be able to understand Black English and able to translate Black English into standard English—and vice versa—when necessary.

The action of the school board inspired a nationwide debate about the wisdom, practicality, and fairness of incorporating Black English into the educational system. Magazine and newspaper editorial pages were filled with discussions about the issue. In the midst of the discussion, the leaders of the Internet group Interracial Voice *decided to encourage an Internet discussion of the matter. In the following months a great many people responded; here is a selection of some of the contributions that were made over the next sixteen months.*

Date: Mon, 30 Dec 1996
From: "Alton E. Paris" XXXXX@airmail.net
Organization: Quinn Chapel AME Church
Subject: Ebonics

How far have we fallen. Ebonics is just "bad" grammar. We 1
are afraid to say a person can be wrong. It is not disrespectful
to tell a child that he/she must learn to speak correct English.
The main purpose of school is to teach children to read,
write, speak, and calculate. Let me give you an example:

   In the late sixties I was stationed in France. One of my sons 2
reached kindergarten age and we were living in a small
French village near Metz, France. A friend suggested we send
him to French kindergarten. I had concerns because he could
not speak French. We went to see the school to see the principal, a priest, and expressed my concerns to him. His response
was, "That's OK. The French children do not speak French
either." Rodney learned French along with the little French
kids and was at their level in about six months. He was also
bi-lingual because we spoke English at home.

   Regards, Al Paris

From: n.hayes1@XXXXX.geis.com
Date: Mon, 6 Jan 97
Subject: Ebonics

The various registers of English should be given due respect. 3
For too long, white America has devalued Black English,
working to make it the symbol of stupidity. Nevertheless,
many Black linguistic patterns/words/phrases have come into
general use. They then are admitted (drum roll) into "Standard English" and Psychological destruction. People with African ancestry are generally aware of the scorn reserved for
Black English. Some blacks are negatively affected by this,
using Black English only when they are expressing negative
ideas and attitudes.

   Too many times in school, Black English is seen by teach- 4
ers as a fault to be corrected. I don't agree with the contention of some that black patterns of speech are genetically
determined. Some phrases are antique forms of English,
used during the 1700s, 1800s, that have since been dropped
by the white population. Many people are bilingual, trilingual

(especially abroad). Learning to differentiate between Standard English and Black English has been done by blacks for generations. The Oakland School District has publicly announced their respect for Black English; this is their revolutionary act.

Sincerely, Nancy Hayes

Date: Thu, 09 Jan 1997
From: Sharon Teuben-Rowe XXXXX@wam.umd.edu
Subject: Ebonics (BEV)—a linguist's view

5   The Oakland Unified Schools District and the general media haven't done an effective job of informing the public. The Oakland schools ARE NOT AND NEVER PLANNED TO TEACH EBONICS.

6   Once the school board passed its resolution regarding recognition, they would petition the Federal government for Bilingual Education funds for teacher training in linguistics and ESL and bilingual education teaching methodologies. This is about teacher education. OAKLAND IS NOT TEACHING EBONICS to anyone's children.

7   BEV has a regular grammar...a descriptive grammar... which utilizes tree diagrams and discusses morphological changes, syntax, semantics, and its lexicon among other linguistic science based features. Prescriptive grammar, the grammar rules we learn in school (subject-verb agreement, adjectives modifying nouns and the sins of splitting infinitives) are not the grammar rules referred to when BEV is said to have a grammar. Linguistic research focuses on descriptive grammar. School teachers teach prescriptive grammar...so OAKLAND TEACHERS ARE NOT TEACHING EBONICS since the corpus of research data on BEV is on its descriptive grammar.

8   BEV is a dialect of American English, not a slang, improper English, street English, gutter English, sign of stubbornness, poverty, ignorance, intellectual capacity, evil conspiracy, bad upbringing, parental neglect, teenage parenthood, hip-hop culture or any other uninformed pejorative. Dialects are communicative systems borne out of parent languages. They incorporate and systematically abbreviate forms, thus creating new ones. BEV uses an American English lexicon (words/vocabulary) and English and various West African descriptive grammar rules. It's not hokum, malevolent or goofy, it's linguistics. All modern languages began as dialects.

No one speaks BEV/Ebonics exclusively. Millions and mil-   9
lions of African Americans are bi-dialectal and engage in
code-switching. These speakers recognize the appropriateness of their communicative codes and act accordingly.

Examples of BEV are usually given in linguistic shorthand,   10
using the IPA (International Phonetic Alphabet) complete
with diacritics. Most so-called examples of BEV in the media
have been hideously erroneous...examples of contemporary
slang which is a separate linguistic feature.

Courtland Milloy's example works well.   11

/J^uwic^oj^Elo/ which ~sounds like Dju-weet-yo-jello?

There are several things going on here but a descriptive
grammar observation is the noun-consonant-noun pattern...
a morphological rule.

So, what do I think...after all that? Oakland was grossly   12
inarticulate in stating their intent and has published some
weakly written documents. A visit to their local linguist would
have helped. Nonetheless, this is not a silver bullet. Training
teachers is fine, but all children need to attend school regularly, have a place to study at home, have stability and consistency in the home which is conducive and supportive of their
academics and the children themselves must be motivated.
No amount of funding and teacher training will influence
these aspects of their lives.

Sharon

From: "Susanne Heine" XXXXX@mailbox.calypso.net
Subject: Ebonics: Or what are certain self-serving ignora-
muses trying to wreak?
Date: Fri, 13 Feb 1998

When I was a little girl in P.S. 116, Jamaica, Long Island, I   13
was mobbed for years by the other kids. "Long-haired yalla
bitch, always talkin white!"...and no, I didn't talk like them.
My mother, a woman from an educated creole (on her father's
side) South Carolina family didn't talk like them, either. Mom
and I read a lot, she often quoted poetry (everything from
James Weldon Johnson to Shakespeare), and she encouraged
me to write. Blessed with a rich lyric soprano voice (trained),
she often practised arias in the afternoon when we children
came home from school. She sang spirituals, Mozart, Bach,
art songs and airs while we did our homework. She loved language, and instilled in me the very same passion. In 1957,

when I took the SAT at age 16, I finished in the top 5% of the United States on the English section.

14   Since 1964, I have lived in Sweden. I have worked here, raised a family (2 children) with my ex, a German manufacturer, and I make a quite good living as a translator and editor of English, a highly sought-after commodity in the powerful cultural sphere that the European Union has become.

15   Last year when I read about the Ebonics nonsense in the international papers, I couldn't believe my eyes. It was as if I had been violently thrust back again into the schoolyard at P.S. 116: "Why you talkin white, bitch? Whussamatta wichtoo? You's uppity! C'mon, git huh yella butt!" But I couldn't react with the icy paralysed fear of the mobbed child any longer, all I could feel was a towering fury, the righteous rage, of an American once more watching her country's ideals betrayed. (Vietnam is a story all by itself; we needn't touch on it here.) Jefferson wrote of "life, liberty and the pursuit of happiness," and I believe that every American, regardless of color, is born to enjoy—at the very least—these entitlements.

16   My point is this: Are studies such as the Arts and Humanities, Physics, Mathematics, Economics, Linguistics, Psychology, Medicine, the Law etc., taught in Ebonics? Is there an extensive literature written in Ebonics? Have the laws, the Constitution, the history of the United States of America been translated into Ebonics for every black schoolchild to take part of and become enlightened by? Where are the universities that offer baccalaureates and doctorates to honor research that is performed in that language, using its references and sources? Which are the multinational companies crying out for expertise and trained professionals who have mastered Ebonics?

17   In fact, what is Ebonics at all, if not an atavistic manifestation of a slaveyard patois, which—if not for the intellectually, culturally and morally debilitating effects of a botched post-integration politics—would probably have weakened in importance of its own accord, made obsolescent by its own irrelevance? The Jewish and Italian kids I went to school with when I was eleven (the Russians had detonated an A-bomb, so the government snatched all us kids with IQs over 130 and sent us to special schools) all knew words (exotic), phrases (colorful) and expressions (usually downright rude) in their parents' languages, but that stuff was "inside" stuff; you didn't talk that way to your teachers, or to non-Jews and non-Italians. The patois stayed at home, because these kids were

preparing to switch tracks into the mainstream of American life, just as their parents willingly—and albeit with some pain—wanted them to do. Dominic, Murray, Sofia, Barbara, all of them were on the threshold of what their parents wanted for them. I was privileged to be among them and to catch the spark of their ambition. We weren't "ethnic," we were just damned smart.

In My Fair Lady, Higgins makes an observation on catching sight of Eliza: 18

Higgins:	Look at her, a prisoner of the gutter, Condemned by every syllable she utters— By right, she should be taken out and hung For the cold-blooded murder of the English tongue!
Eliza:	Aaoouww!
Higgins:	Chickens cackling in a barn, Just like this one—
Eliza:	Garn!
Higgins:	It's "Aaoouww" and "Garn!" that keep her in her place, Not her wretched clothes and dirty face...

That, of course, is the premise of Shaw's "Pygmalion." At a completely different level, it is also the key to the plight of the black underprivileged classes in America (and please, let's confine ourselves to class now; race is a tad too sticky and requires other parameters).

By 1981, I was tired of Europe in general and Sweden in 19 particular, so I went to live in California for a couple of years. Tuned into the old culture as only a former expatriate could be, I noticed how many new immigrants there were from all the Asian countries, as well as from Mexico, Latin America, the Middle East, the Horn of Africa and the Caribbean. As an American, I felt proud seeing how many of them had caught a foothold in society, were making a living, getting ahead and moving upwards. But at the same time, it galled me to see so many of my own people living as if they were still outsiders in their own country. At the checkout counter in the local supermarket in Hollywood, the clerks were mostly Asian, young kids whose names—judging from their name-tags—were "Scott" and "Kimberly" and "Sue-Ann," and who spoke clear, mainstream American. And I thought: If any one of these kids calls up looking for a new job somewhere, the person they get on the line will hear someone who speaks like he does himself, someone whose voice, intonation and vocabulary are in tune with what the customers want to hear, someone who in no way threatens him with some kind of cultural "otherness" that—sooner or later—will have to be dealt with. Out in the parking lot, the black kids were always hanging out, talking their slave patois (Oh God forgive me, I meant "Ebonics"!), too proud, and manifestly too ignorant, to take a job at a checkout counter, and looking at a future in which—hopefully!—Scott and Kimberly and Sue-Ann will be helping to pay their welfare checks.

20   Furthermore, I maintain that black people in America will never attain their rightful place in American society and business, will never be able to transcend the pain and backwardness of slavery or the intellectual squalor of the slave mentality, until they make the mainstream language their own. "In the Beginning was the Word, and the Word was God."

21   Calling the slaveyard patois that keeps black people in chains "Ebonics" is just another huckster's attempt to gold-plate slave shackles. I'll be damned if I'll buy it.

With all due respect, Susanne

From: "William Javier Nelson" XXXXX@aol.com
Subject: Ebonics—English as a second language
Date: Fri, 24 Apr 1998

Dear Susanne:

22   In addition to being a Ph.D. in Sociology, I am a licensed (state of Minnesota) E.S.L. instructor. What you said in your letter…is the basis for much of my philosophy when teaching English to Latinos.

23   I am also a Dominican and speak Spanish with a decided Dominican accent of the lower middle class (dropping the letter "s" from the ends of many words, etc.). When I am around other lower-middle class Dominicans of my ilk (mainly from the cities of Santo Domingo and Santiago, Dominican Republic) I can let my hair down and go to town. However, I still regularly do (and complete) the English language New York Times crossword (in ink).

Respectfully, William Javier Nelson

From: "Susanne Heine" XXXXX@mailbox.calypso.net
Subject: Re: Ebonics—English as a second language
Date: Fri, 25 Apr 1998

Dear William,

How nice hearing from you! And how encouraging it is to rea-   24
lise that there are people out there who have eyes to see and the
brains to fathom what I meant.... I feel that all of us, whatever
we want to call ourselves—black, brown, African-American,
mixed-race, mulatto or whatever—have been short-changed
by the way the US has progressed in the last 30 years or so.
We've lost sight of so many things that were important to an
older, and I dare say wiser, generation than ours. They were
wiser because anything they ever had, they had to earn, and
dearly too. There were no quick-fixes for them. They couldn't
turn millionaire overnight on the strength of some foul-
mouthed rap-jingle, or make heads turn on the street by getting themselves up like outlaws and giving society the finger.
Or fascinate the entire nation by giving the cops a run for
their money in a white Bronco...

As a fellow academic who works with language, you of   25
course understand how our use of it affects our destinies, and
I'm sure you know that this knowledge is not widespread
enough. I recognise what you mean when you say that, privately, you can "get down" with the folks who speak Spanish
the way you speak it: you feel idiomatically comfortable and
therefore in complete control socially. However, the fact that
this in no way threatens or is in conflict with your sense of
belonging in a public context, is a testimony to your sophistication, as well as to your complete grasp of the problem, such
as it is....

The point is this: the more we seek to disassociate ourselves   26
from America, the more justified she feels in turning her back
on us. We are probably the most genuine "Americans" of all;
there is not a race, not a national group, not a tribe that has
ever set foot on American soil that is not amply represented
among us. But how can we define ourselves as "Americans" if
we, of our own doing, abrogate our contract with what America has—in its finest moments—always believed itself to be?
Some people, black as well as white and for equally dubious
reasons, have been telling us for a long time that the one central and absolutely defining paradigm in our lives is our race.
Now the amazing thing is, WE HAVE ACCEPTED THAT! WE
HONESTLY BELIEVE THAT! We have made it part and parcel

of our identity, we have allowed that choice piece of nonsense to shape and pattern our lives, to influence our attitudes to ourselves as well as to the world at large, and we spend—if only subconsciously—every minute of our lives thinking about our colour as if it were a REAL factor in the world, like unemployment, or pollution or the price of butter, for God's sake! One thing that I have learnt in 34 years abroad is this: the colour of your skin has no more bearing on anything REAL than the colour of your eyes, or, for that matter, the colour of the tie you have on.

27   What does have meaning, on the other hand, is how you conduct yourself. How you act and move, how you relate to people physically as well as mentally. And most important, how you SPEAK. I'm sure that when you watch your students progress, you feel you are giving them a tool that they will be able to shape their world with, and William, you are so right.

28   Keep on believing!

All the best, Susanne

29   P.S. Yeah, I know what you mean. I still do the Times crossword in ink, though I can no longer boast of doing it in 15 minutes flat the way I could when I was twenty and living in New York. Boy, did that ever annoy my fellow commuters! Especially the chubby guy with his pencil and eraser!

bell hooks
Teaching New Worlds/
New Words

You can learn quite a bit about bell hooks from reading her well-known essays, which usually mix intensely personal elements with carefully considered conclusions. (For more on bell hooks and for another example of her prose, see her essay on college classrooms in Part I, Education, page 89.) This particular essay appeared in 1994 as a chapter of her book Teaching to Transgress: Education as the Practice of Freedom.

Like desire, language disrupts, refuses to be contained within boundaries. It speaks itself against our will, in words and thoughts that intrude, even violate the most private spaces of mind and body. It was in my first year of college that I read Adrienne Rich's poem, "The Burning of Paper Instead of Children." That poem, speaking against domination, against racism and class oppression, attempts to illustrate graphically that stopping the political persecution and torture of living beings is a more vital issue than censorship, than burning books. One line of this poem that moved and disturbed something within me: "This is the oppressor's language yet I need it to talk to you." I've never forgotten it. Perhaps I could not have forgotten it even if I tried to erase it from memory. Words impose themselves, take root in our memory against our will. The words of this poem begat a life in my memory that I could not abort or change. 1

When I find myself thinking about language now, these words are there, as if they were always waiting to challenge and assist me. I find myself silently speaking them over and over again with the intensity of a chant. They startle me, shaking me into an awareness of the link between languages and domination. Initially, I resist the idea of the "oppressor's language," certain that this construct has the potential to disempower those of us who are just learning to speak, who are just learning to claim language as a place where we make ourselves subject. *"This is the oppressor's language yet I need it to talk to you."* Adrienne Rich's words. Then, when I first read these words, and now, they make me think of standard English, of learning to speak against black vernacular, against the ruptured and broken speech of a dispossessed and displaced people. Standard English is not the speech of exile. It 2 is the language of conquest and domination; in the United States, it is the mask which hides the loss of so many tongues, all those sounds of diverse, native communities we will never hear, the speech of the Gullah, Yiddish, and so many other unremembered tongues.

3   Reflecting on Adrienne Rich's words, I know that it is not the English language that hurts me, but what the oppressors do with it, how they shape it to become a territory that limits and defines, how they make it a weapon that can shame, humiliate, colonize. Gloria Anzaldúa reminds us of this pain in *Borderlands/La Frontera* when she asserts, "So, if you want to really hurt me, talk badly about my language." We have so little knowledge of how displaced, enslaved, or free Africans who came or were brought against their will to the United States felt about the loss of language, about learning English. Only as a woman did I begin to think about these black people in relation to language, to think about their trauma as they were compelled to witness their language rendered meaningless with a colonizing European culture, where voices deemed foreign could not be spoken, were outlawed tongues, renegade speech. When I realize how long it has taken for white Americans to acknowledge diverse languages of Native Americans, to accept that the speech their ancestral colonizers declared was merely grunts and gibberish was indeed *language*, it is difficult not to hear in standard English always the sound of slaughter and conquest. I think now of the grief of displaced "homeless" Africans, forced to inhabit a world where they saw folks like themselves, inhabiting the same skin, the same condition, but who had no shared language to talk with one another, who needed "the oppressor's language." *"This is the oppressor's language yet I need it to talk to you."* When I imagine the terror of Africans on board slave ships, on auction blocks, inhabiting the unfamiliar architecture of plantations, I consider that this terror extended beyond fear of punishment, that it resided also in the anguish of hearing a language they could not comprehend. The very sound of English had to terrify. I think of black people meeting one another in a space away from the diverse cultures and languages that distinguished them from one another, compelled by circumstance to find ways to speak with one another in a "new world" where blackness or the darkness of one's skin and not language would become the space of bonding. How to remember, to reinvoke this terror. How to describe what it must have been like for Africans whose deepest bonds were historically forged in the place of shared

speech to be transported abruptly to a world where the very sound of one's mother tongue had no meaning.

I imagine them hearing spoken English as the oppressor's   4 language, yet I imagine them also realizing that this language would need to be possessed, taken, claimed as a space of resistance. I imagine that the moment they realized the oppressor's language, seized and spoken by the tongues of the colonized, could be a space of bonding was joyous. For in that recognition was the understanding that intimacy could be restored, that a culture of resistance could be formed that would make recovery from the trauma of enslavement possible. I imagine, then, Africans first hearing English as "the oppressor's language" and then re-hearing it as a potential site of resistance. Learning English, learning to speak the alien tongue, was one way enslaved Africans began to reclaim their personal power within a context of domination. Possessing a shared language, black folks could find again a way to make community, and a means to create the political solidarity necessary to resist.

Needing the oppressor's language to speak with one   5 another they nevertheless also reinvented, remade that language so that it would speak beyond the boundaries of conquest and domination. In the mouths of black Africans in the so-called "New World," English was altered, transformed, and became a different speech. Enslaved black people took broken bits of English and made of them a counter-language. They put together their words in such a way that the colonizer had to rethink the meaning of the English language. Though it has become common in contemporary culture to talk about the messages of resistance that emerged in the music created by slaves, particularly spirituals, less is said about the grammatical construction of sentences in these songs. Often, the English used in the song reflected the broken, ruptured world of the slave. When the slaves sang "nobody knows de trouble I see—" their use of the word "nobody" adds a richer meaning than if they had used the phrase "no one," for it was the slave's *body* that was the concrete site of suffering. And even as emancipated black people sang spirituals, they did not change the language, the sentence structure, of our ancestors. For in the incorrect usage of words, in the incorrect placement of words, was a spirit of rebellion that claimed language as a site of resistance. Using English in a way that ruptured standard usage and meaning, so that white folks could often not understand black speech, made English into more than the oppressor's language.

6   An unbroken connection exists between the broken English of the displaced, enslaved African and the diverse black
vernacular speech black folks use today. In both cases, the
rupture of standard English enabled and enables rebellion
and resistance. By transforming the oppressor's language,
making a culture of resistance, black people created an intimate speech that could say far more than was permissible
within the boundaries of standard English. The power of this
speech is not simply that it enables resistance to white supremacy, but that it also forges a space for alternative cultural
production and alternative epistemologies—different ways of
thinking and knowing that were crucial to creating a counter-
hegenomic worldview. It is absolutely essential that the revolutionary power of black vernacular speech not be lost in contemporary culture. That power resides in the capacity of
black vernacular to intervene on the boundaries and limitation of standard English.

7   In contemporary black popular culture, rap music has
become one of the spaces where black vernacular speech is
used in a manner that invites dominant mainstream culture
to listen—to hear—and, to some extent, be transformed.
However, one of the risks of this attempt at cultural translation is that it will trivialize black vernacular speech. When
young white kids imitate this speech in ways that suggest it is
the speech of those who are stupid or who are only interested
in entertaining or being funny, then the subversive power of
speech is undermined. In academic circles, both in the sphere
of teaching and that of writing, there has been little effort
made to utilize black vernacular—or, for that matter, any language other than standard English. When I asked an ethnically diverse group of students in a course I was teaching on
black women writers why we only hear standard English spoken in the classroom, they were momentarily rendered
speechless. Though many of them were individuals for whom
standard English was a second or third language, it had simply never occurred to them that it was possible to say something in another language, in another way. No wonder, then,
that we continue to think "This is the oppressor's language yet
I need it to talk to you."

8   I have realized that I was in danger of losing my relationship to black vernacular speech because I too rarely use it in
the predominantly white settings that I am most often in,
both professionally and socially. And so I have begun to work
at integrating into a variety of settings the particular Southern black vernacular speech I grew up hearing and speaking.

It has been hardest to integrate black vernacular in writing, particularly for academic journals. When I first began to incorporate black vernacular in critical essays, editors would send the work back to me in standard English. Using the vernacular means that translation into standard English may be needed if one wishes to reach a more inclusive audience. In the classroom setting, I encourage students to use their first language and translate it so they do not feel that seeking higher education will necessarily estrange them from that language and culture they know most intimately. Not surprisingly, when students in my Black Women Writers class began to speak using diverse language and speech, white students often complained. This seemed to be particularly the case with black vernacular. It was particularly disturbing to the white students because they could hear the words that were said but could not comprehend their meaning. Pedagogically, I encouraged them to think of the moment of not understanding what someone says as a space to learn. Such a space provides not only the opportunity to listen without "mastery," without owning or possessing speech through interpretation, but also the experience of hearing non-English words. These lessons seem particularly crucial in a multicultural society that remains white supremacist, that uses standard English as a weapon to silence and censor. June Jordan reminds us of this in *On Call* when she declares:

> I am talking about majority problems of language in a democratic state, problems of a currency that someone has stolen and hidden away and then homogenized into an official "English" language that can only express non-events involving nobody responsible, or lies. If we lived in a democratic state our language would have to hurtle, fly, curse, and sing, in all the common American names, all the undeniable and representative participating voices of everybody here. We would not tolerate the language of the powerful and, thereby, lose all respect for words, per se. We would make our language conform to the truth of our many selves and we would make our language lead us into the equality of power that a democratic state must represent.

That the students in the course on black women writers 9 were repressing all longing to speak in tongues other than standard English without seeing this repression as political was an indication of the way we act unconsciously, in complicity with a culture of domination.

10   Recent discussion of diversity and multiculturalism tend
to downplay or ignore the question of language. Critical feminist writings focused on issues of difference and voice have
made important theoretical interventions, calling for a recognition of the primacy of voices that are often silenced, censored, or marginalized. This call for the acknowledgement
and celebration of diverse voices, and consequently of diverse
language and speech, necessarily disrupts the primacy of
standard English. When advocates of feminism first spoke
about the desire for diverse participation in women's movement, there was no discussion of language. It was simply
assumed that standard English would remain the primary
vehicle for the transmission of feminist thought. Now that the
audience for feminist writing and speaking has become more
diverse, it is evident that we must change conventional ways
of thinking about language, creating spaces where diverse
voices can speak in words other than English or in broken,
vernacular speech. This means that at a lecture or even in a
written work there will be fragments of speech that may or
may not be accessible to every individual. Shifting how we
think about language and how we use it necessarily alters
how we know what we know. At a lecture where I might use
Southern black vernacular, the particular patois of my region,
or where I might use very abstract thought in conjuction with
plain speech, responding to a diverse audience, I suggest that
we do not necessarily need to hear and know what is stated in
its entirety, that we do not need to "master" or conquer the
narrative as a whole, that we may know in fragments. I suggest that we may learn from spaces of silence as well as
spaces of speech, that in the patient act of listening to another
tongue we may subvert that culture of capitalist frenzy and
consumption that demands all desire must be satisfied immediately, or we may disrupt that cultural imperialism that suggests one is worthy of being heard only if one speaks in
standard English.

11   Adrienne Rich concludes her poem with this statement:

    I am composing on the typewriter late at night, thinking of
    today. How well we all spoke. A language is a map of our fail-
    ures. Frederick Douglass wrote an English purer than Mil-
    ton's. People suffer highly in poverty. There are methods but
    we do not use them. Joan, who could not read, spoke some
    peasant form of French. Some of the sufferings are: it is hard
    to tell the truth; this is America; I cannot touch you now. In
    America we have only the present tense. I am in danger. You

are in danger. The burning of a book arouses no sensation in me. I know it hurts to burn. There are flames of napalm in Catonsville, Maryland. I know it hurts to burn. The typewriter is overheated, my mouth is burning, I cannot touch you and this is the oppressor's language.

To recognize that we touch one another in language seems   12
particularly difficult in a society that would have us believe that there is no dignity in the experience of passion, that to feel deeply is to be inferior, for within the dualism of Western metaphysical thought, ideas are always more important than language. To heal the splitting of mind and body, we marginalized and oppressed people attempt to recover ourselves and our experiences in language. We seek to make a place for the intimacy. Unable to find such a place in standard English, we create the ruptured, broken, unruly speech of the vernacular. When I need to say words that do more than simply mirror or address the dominant reality, I speak black vernacular. There, in that location, we make English do what we want it to do. We take the oppressor's language and turn it against itself. We make our words a counter-hegemonic speech, liberating ourselves in language.

Gary Larson grew up in Tacoma, Washington, and graduated from Washington State University. Though Larson no longer publishes new cartoons, "The Far Side" continues to be one of America's most popular (and offbeat) cartoons.

THE FAR SIDE   By GARY LARSON

"Ha! The idiots spelled 'surrender' with only one 'r'!"

IS ENGLISH SEXIST?

Beverly Gross

Bitch

Salmagundi, *a quarterly magazine of the humanities and social sciences that is produced at Skidmore College, carries poetry, fiction, critical essays, and social analyses on a variety of issues. In the summer of 1994, it published the following meditation on language by Beverly Gross, a professor of English at City University of New York.*

We were discussing Mary McCarthy's *The Group* in a 1
course called Women Writers and Literary Tradition. McCarthy's biographer Carol Gelderman, I told the class, had been
intrigued by how often critics called Mary McCarthy a bitch.
I read a few citations. "Her novels are crammed with cerebra-
tion and bitchiness" (John Aldridge). "Her approach to writing [is] reflective of the modern American bitch" (Paul
Schlueter). Why McCarthy? a student asked. Her unrelenting
standards, I ventured, her tough-minded critical estimates—
there was no self-censoring, appeasing Angel in the House of
Mary McCarthy's brain. Her combativeness (her marital battles with Edmund Wilson became the stuff of academic legend). Maybe there were other factors. But the discussion
opened up to the more inclusive issue of the word bitch itself.
What effect does that appellation have on women? What effect might it have had on McCarthy? No one ever called Edmund Wilson a bitch. Do we excuse, even pay respect when a
man is critical, combative, assertive? What is the male equivalent of the word bitch, I asked the class.

"Boss," said Sabrina Sims. 2

This was an evening class at a branch of the City University 3
of New York. Most of the students are older adults trying to fit
a college education into otherwise busy lives. Most of them
have fulltime jobs during the day. Sabrina Sims works on
Wall Street, is a single mother raising a ten year old daughter,
is black, and had to take an Incomplete in the course because
she underwent a kidney transplant in December.

4   Her answer gave us all a good laugh. I haven't been able to get it out of my mind. I've been thinking about bitch, watching how it is used by writers and in conversation, and have explored its lexical history. "A name of reproach for a woman" is how Doctor Johnson's Dictionary dealt with the word in the eighteenth century, as though anticipating the great adaptability of this particular execration, a class of words that tends toward early obsolescence. Not bitch, however, which has been around for a millennium, outlasting a succession of definitions. Its longevity is perhaps attributable to its satisfying misogyny. Its meaning matters less than its power to denounce and subjugate. Francis Grose in *A Classical Dictionary of the Vulgar Tongue* (1785) considered bitch "the most offensive appellation that can be given to an English woman, even more provoking than that of whore." He offered as evidence "a low London woman's reply on being called a bitch" in the late eighteenth century: "I may be a whore but can't be a bitch!" The meaning of bitch has changed over the centuries but it remains the word that comes immediately to the tongue, still "the most offensive appellation" the English language provides to hurl at a woman.

5   The *Oxford English Dictionary* records two main meanings for the noun bitch up through the nineteenth century:

1. The female of the dog

2. Applied opprobriously to a woman; strictly a lewd or sensual woman. Not now in decent use.

6   It was not until the twentieth century that bitch acquired its opprobrious application in realms irrespective of sensuality. The Supplement to the *OED* (1972) adds:

2a: "In mod. use, esp. a malicious or treacherous woman."

Every current desk dictionary supplies some such meaning:

A spiteful, ill-tempered woman [*World Book Dictionary*]

A malicious, unpleasant, selfish woman, esp. one who stops at nothing to reach her goal. [*Random House Dictionary*]

But malice and treachery only begin to tell the story. The informal questionnaire that I administered to my students and a number of acquaintances elicited ample demonstration of the slippery adaptability of bitch as it might be used these days:

a conceited person, a snob

a self-absorbed woman

a complainer

a competitive woman

a woman who is annoying, pushy, possibly underhanded (in short, a man in a woman's body)

someone rich, thin and free!

"A word used by men who are threatened by women" was 7 one astute response. Threat lurks everywhere: for women the threat is in being called a bitch. "Someone whiny, threatening, crabby, pestering" is what one woman offered as her definition. "Everything I try hard not to be," she added, "though it seeps through." I offer as a preliminary conclusion that bitch means to men whatever they find threatening in a woman and it means to women whatever they particularly dislike about themselves. In either case the word functions as a misogynistic club. I will add that the woman who defined bitch as everything she tries hard not to be when asked to free associate about the word came up immediately with "mother." That woman happens to be my sister. We share the same mother, who was often whiny and crabby, though I would never have applied the word bitch to her, but then again, I don't consider whiny, crabby and pestering to be prominent among my own numerous flaws.

Dictionaries of slang are informative sources, in touch as 8 they are with nascent language and the emotive coloration of words, especially words of abuse. A relatively restrained definition is offered by the only female lexicographer I consulted for whom bitch is "a nasty woman" or "a difficult task" (Anita Pearl, *Dictionary of Popular Slang*). The delineations of bitch by the male lexicographers abound with such cascading hostility that the compilers sometimes seem to be reveling in their task. For example, Howard Wentworth and Stuart Berg Flexner in *Dictionary of American Slang:*

A woman, usu., but not necessarily, a mean, selfish, malicious, deceiving, cruel, or promiscuous woman.

Eugene E. Landy's *The Underground Dictionary* (1971) offers:

1. Female who is mean, selfish, cruel, malicious, deceiving. a.k.a. cunt.

2. Female. See Female.

9   I looked up the entry for "Female" (Landy, by the way, provides no parallel entry for "Male"):

> beaver, bird, bitch, broad, bush, cat, chick, crack, cunt,
> douche, fish, fox, frail, garbage can, heffer, pussy, quail, ruca,
> scag, snatch, stallion, slave, sweet meat, tail, trick, tuna. See
> GIRLFRIEND; WIFE.

Richard A. Spear's *Slang and Euphemism* comments on the
derivative adjective:

> bitchy 1. pertaining to a mood wherein one complains inces-
> santly about anything. Although this applies to men or
> women, it is usually associated with women, especially when
> they are menstruating. Cf. DOG DAYS

10   Robert L. Chapman's definition in *Thesaurus of American
Slang* starts off like a feminist analysis:

> bitch. 1 n. A woman one dislikes or disapproves of.

Followed, however, by a sobering string of synonyms:
"broad, cunt, witch."

And then this most interesting note:

> Female equivalents of the contemptuous terms for men,
> listed in this book under "asshole," are relatively rare. Con-
> tempt for females, in slang, stresses their putative sexual pro-
> miscuity and weakness rather than their moral vileness and
> general odiousness. Some terms under "asshole," though,
> are increasingly used of women.

11   "See ball-buster." Chapman suggests under his second definition for bitch ("anything arduous or very disagreeable"). I
looked up "ball-buster":

> n. Someone who saps or destroys masculinity.
> ball-whacker
> bitch
> nut-cruncher.

Some*thing* has become some*one*. The ball-buster is not a   12
disagreeable thing but a disagreeable (disagreeing?) person.
A female person. "A woman one dislikes or disapproves of."
For someone so sensitive to the nuances of hostility and verbal putdown, Chapman certainly takes a circuitous route to
get to the underlying idea that no other dictionary even
touches: Bitch means ball-buster.

What one learns from the dictionaries: there is no classifi-   13
able thing as a bitch, only a label produced by the act of
name-calling. The person named is almost always a female.
The name-calling refers to alleged faults of ill-temper, selfish-
ness, malice, cruelty, spite, all of them faults in the realm of
interpersonal relating—women's faults: it is hard to think of a
put-down word encompassing these faults in a man. "Bas-
tard" and even "son of a bitch" have bigger fish to fry. And an
asshole is an asshole in and of himself. A bitch is a woman
who makes the name-caller feel uncomfortable. Presumably
that name-caller is a man whose ideas about how a woman
should behave toward him are being violated.

"Women," wrote Virginia Woolf, "have served all these cen-   14
turies as looking-glasses possessing the magic and delicious
power of reflecting the figure of man at twice its natural size."
The woman who withholds that mirror is a bitch. Bitchiness
is the perversion of womanly sweetness, compliance, pleas-
antness, ego-building. (Male ego-building, of course, though
that is a virtual tautology; women have egos but who builds
them?) If a woman is not building ego she is busting balls.

Ball-buster? The word is a nice synecdoche (like asshole)   15
with great powers of revelation. A ball-buster, one gathers, is
a demanding bitch who insists on overexertion from a man to
satisfy her sexual or material voraciousness. "The bitch is
probably his wife." But balls also bust when a disagreeable
woman undermines a guy's ego and "saps or destroys masculinity." The bitch could be his wife, but also his boss, Gloria
Steinem, the woman at the post office, the woman who
spurns his advances. The familiar Freudian delineation of the
male-female nexus depicts male sexuality as requiring the admiration, submission and subordination of the female. The
ultimate threat of (and to) the back-talking woman is male
impotence.

Bitch, the curse and concept, exists to insure male potency   16
and female submissiveness. Men have deployed it to defend
their power by attacking and neutralizing the upstart. "Bitch"
is admonitory, like "whore," like "dyke." Borrowing something

from both words, "bitch" is one of those verbal missiles with the power of shackling women's actions and impulses.

17   The metamorphosis of bitch from the context of sexuality (a carnal woman, a promiscuous woman) to temperament (an angry woman, a malicious woman) to power (a domineering woman, a competitive woman) is a touchstone to the changing position of women through this century. As women have become more liberated, individually and collectively, the word has taken on connotations of aggressive, hostile, selfish. In the old days a bitch was a harlot; nowadays she is likely to be a woman who won't put out. Female sensuality, even carnality, even infidelity, have been supplanted as what men primarily fear and despise in women. Judging by the contemporary colorations of the word bitch, what men primarily fear and despise in women is power.

18   Some anecdotes:
1) Barbara Bush's name-calling of Geraldine Ferraro during the 1984 presidential election: "I can't say it but it rhymes with 'rich.'"

19   How ladylike of the future First Lady to avoid uttering the unmentionable. The slur did its dirty work, particularly among those voters disturbed by the sudden elevation of a woman to such unprecedented political heights. In what possible sense did Barbara Bush mean that Geraldine Ferraro is a bitch? A loose woman? Hardly. A nasty woman? Not likely. A pushy woman? Almost certainly. The unspoken syllable was offered as a response to Ferraro's lofty ambitions, potential power, possibly her widespread support among feminists. Imagine a woman seeking to be vice-president instead of vice-husband.

20   The ascription of bitchery seems to have nothing to do with Ferraro's bearing and behavior. Certainly not the Ferraro who wrote about the event in her autobiography:

> Barbara Bush realized what a gaffe she had made...
>
> "I just want to apologize to you for what I said," she told me over the phone while I was in the middle of another debate rehearsal. "I certainly didn't mean anything by it."
>
> "Don't worry about it," I said to her. "We all say things at times we don't mean. It's all right."
>
> "Oh," she said breathlessly. "You're such a lady."

All I could think of when I hung up was: Thank God for
my convent school training.

2) Lady Ashley at the end of *The Sun Also Rises:* "It makes   21
one feel rather good, deciding not to be a bitch." The context
here is something like this: a bitch is a woman who ruins
young heroic bullfighters. A woman who is propelled by her
sexual drive, desires and vanity. The fascination of Brett Ashley is that she lives and loves like a man: her sexuality is unre-
pressed and she doesn't care much for monogamy. (Literary
critics until the 1960s commonly called her a nymphoma-
niac.) She turns her male admirers into women—Mike
becomes a self-destructive alcoholic, Robert a moony romantic, Pedro a sacrificial virgin, and Jake a frustrated eunuch.
At her entrance in the novel she is surrounded by an entou-
rage of twittering fairies. Lady Ashley is a bitch not because
she is nasty, bossy or ill-tempered (she has lovely manners
and a terrific personality). And perhaps not even because of
her freewheeling, strident sexuality. She is a bitch because
she overturns the male/female nexus. What could be a more
threatening infraction in a Hemingway novel?

2a) Speaking of Hemingway: After his falling out with Ger-   22
trude Stein who had made unflattering comments about his
writing in *The Autobiography of Alice B. Toklas,* Hemingway
dropped her off a copy of his newly published *Death in the
Afternoon* with the handwritten inscription, "A bitch is a
bitch is a bitch."
[Q.] Why was Gertrude Stein a bitch?
[A.] For no longer admiring Hemingway. A bitch is a
woman who criticizes.

3) "Ladies and gentlemen. I don't believe Mrs. Helmsley is   23
charged in the indictment with being a tough bitch" is how
her defense lawyer Gerald A. Feffer addressed the jury in
Leona Helmsley's trial for tax fraud and extortion. He
acknowledged that she was "sometimes rude and abrasive,"
and that she "may have overcompensated for being a
woman in a hard-edged men's business world." Recognizing
the difficulty of defending what the New York *Post* called
"the woman that everyone loves to hate," his tactic was to
preempt the prosecution by getting there first with "tough
bitch." He lost.

24   4) *Esquire* awarded a Dubious Achievement of 1990 to Victor Kiam, owner of the New England Patriots football team,
for saying "he could never have called Boston *Herald*
reporter Lisa Olson 'a classic bitch' because he doesn't use
the word classic." Some background on what had been one
of that year's most discussed controversies: Olson aroused
the ire of the Patriots for showing up in their locker room
with the male reporters after a game. Members of the Patriots, as *Esquire* states, surrounded her, "thrusting their genitals in her face and daring her to touch them."

25   Why is Lisa Olson a bitch? For invading the male domain
of sports reportage and the male territory of the locker room?
For telling the world, instead of swallowing her degradation,
pain and anger? The club owner's use of "bitch" seems meant
to conjure up the lurking idea of castrating female. Seen in
that light the Patriots' act of "thrusting their genitals in her
face" transforms an act of loutishness into a position of innocent vulnerability.

26   5) Bumper sticker observed on back of pickup truck:

> Impeach Jane Fonda, American Traitor Bitch

The bumper sticker seemed relatively new and fresh. I
observed it a full two decades after Jane Fonda's journey to
North Vietnam which is the event that surely inspired this
call to impeachment (from what? aerobics class?). Bitch
here is an expletive. It originates in and sustains anger. Calling Jane Fonda a "traitor" sounds a bit dated in the 1990s,
but adding "bitch" gives the accusation timelessness and
does the job of rekindling old indignation.

27   6) Claude Brown's account in *Manchild in the Promised
Land* of how he learned about women from a street-smart
older friend:

> Johnny was always telling us about bitches. To Johnny, every
> chick was a bitch. Even mothers were bitches. Of course
> there were some nice bitches, but they were still bitches. And
> a man had to be a dog in order to handle a bitch.
>   Johnny said once, "If a bitch ever tells you she's only got a
> penny to buy the baby some milk, take it. You take it, 'cause
> she's gon git some more. Bitches can always git some
> money." He really knew about bitches. Cats would say, "I saw

your sister today, and she is a fine bitch." Nobody was
offended by it. That's just the way things were. It was easy to
see all women as bitches.

Bitch in black male street parlance seems closer to its orig-   28
inal meaning of a female breeder—not a nasty woman and
not a powerful woman, but the biological bearer of litters.
The word is likely to be used in courting as well as in anger by
males seeking the sexual favor of a female, and a black female
addressed as bitch by an admirer is expected to feel not
insulted but honored by the attention. (Bitch signifies something different when black women use it competitively about
other black women.) But even as an endearment, from male
to female, there is no mistaking the lurking contempt.

A *Dictionary of Afro-American Slang* compiled by Clarence   29
Major (under the imprint of the leftist International Publishers) provides only that bitch in black parlance is "a mean,
flaunting homosexual," entirely omitting any reference to its
rampant use in black street language as the substitute word
for woman. A puzzling omission. Perhaps the word is so
taken for granted that its primary meaning is not even recognized as black vernacular.

Bitch, mama, motherfucker—how frequently motherhood   30
figures in street language. Mothers are the object of insults
when playing the dozens. The ubiquitous motherfucker simultaneously strikes out at one's immediate foe as well as the
sanctity of motherhood. Mama, which Clarence Major defines as "a pretty black girl," is an endearment that a man
might address to a sexy contemporary. "Hey mama" is tinged
with a certain sweetness. "Hey bitch" has more of an edge,
more likely to be addressed to a woman the man no longer
needs to sweet-talk. It is hard to think of white males coming
on by evoking motherhood or of white women going for it. A
white male addressing a woman as bitch is not likely to be expecting a sexual reward. She will be a bitch behind her back
and after the relationship is over or didn't happen.

The widespread use of bitch by black men talking to black   31
women, its currency in courting, and its routine acceptance by
women are suggestive of some powerful alienation in male-
female relations and in black self-identity. Although there may
be the possibility of ironic inversion, as in calling a loved one
nigger, a black man calling a loved one bitch is expressing contempt for the object of his desire with the gratuitous fillip of
associative contempt for the woman who gave him life. Bitch,
like motherfucker, bespeaks something threatening to the

male sense of himself, a furious counter to emasculation in a world where, as the young Claude Brown figured out, mothers have all the power. It is not hard to see that the problem of black men is much more with white racism than it is with black women. Whatever the cause, however, the language sure doesn't benefit the women. Here is still one more saddening instance of the victim finding someone even more hapless to take things out on. (Does this process explain why Clarence Major's only reference for bitch is to the "mean, flaunting homosexual"?)

32   7) "Do you enjoy playing that role of castrating bitch" is a question put to Madonna by an interviewer for *The Advocate.* Madonna's answer: "I enjoy expressing myself. . . ."

33   A response to another question about the public's reaction to her movie *Truth or Dare:* "They already think I'm a cunt bitch, they already think I'm Attila the Hun. They already compare me to Adolf Hitler and Saddam Hussein."

34   Bitch has lost its power to muzzle Madonna. Unlike other female celebrities who have cringed from accusations of bitchiness (Joan Rivers, Imelda Marcos, Margaret Thatcher, Nancy Reagan), Madonna has made her fortune by exploiting criticism. Her career has skyrocketed with the media's charges of obscenity and sacrilege; she seems to embrace the bitch label with the same eager opportunism.

35   "I enjoy expressing myself" is not merely the explanation for why Madonna gets called bitch; "I enjoy expressing myself" is the key to defusing the power of bitch to fetter and subdue. Madonna has appropriated the word and turned the intended insult to her advantage. This act of appropriation, I predict, will embolden others with what consequences and effects it is impossible to foresee.

Lewis Grizzard
Women Will Be Womyn

Lewis Grizzard (pronounced Griz-ZARD) was a columnist for the Atlanta Constitution, *where, until his death from heart disease in 1994 at the age of forty-seven, he regularly published a widely syndicated column that sometimes delighted and sometimes enraged his readers. A humorist and fiercely proud Southerner whose columns often mimicked redneck values, Grizzard took special pleasure in satirizing Northerners, feminists, and liberals. The following column appeared in 1991.*

The new-for-the-90s Webster's Collegiate Dictionary is out 1
and wouldn't you know it. There are now different ways to
spell certain words so as to accommodate the feminists.

There's even a new way to spell woman, according to the 2
new dictionary. It may now be spelled "womyn," so there's
no longer any need to use those awful three letters that spell
m-a-n.

There's more. HIStory. That's for guys. The new word is 3
HER-story, as in, "Joan Rivers was the worst morning television
show hostess in all of *herstory.*"

The report I read concerning the new dictionary did not, 4
however, tell of how certain other words, akin to the ones
above, can be altered in order to rid them of any sexist connotations.

I did some guessing, though. Here's some examples of 5
other changes:

- HERSTERECTOMY: Whoever heard of a man going through that type of operation?
- HERMALAYAS: Womyn should have a mountain range of their very own.
- HERSTERICAL: "Wanda was *hersterical* when she found out Bob had taken Bernice on a trip to the Hermalayas."
- HERMNS: Womyn sing in church, too.
- HERSY: "Bernice threw a *hersy* when she found out Wanda had found out about her trip to the Hermalayas with Bob."

You get my drift.   6

7   But let us take this a step further. Even if you spell woman "womyn," it still sounds the same. What womyn need in order to throw off the yoke of sexism when it comes to calling themselves something is an entirely new word.

8   Female doesn't work for obvious reasons. Changing that to fe-MULE would only encourage too many sexists to make remarks about the stereotypical tendency of a womyn to be stubborn.

9   I even thought it might work to turn women around backward. They would become "nemows," as in, "Boy, you should have seen the *nemows* in Ralph's last night."

10   But nemows still includes n-e-m, men spelled backward, a reminder of just how backward many of them still are despite all the efforts to teach them not to say, "You should have seen the chicks in Ralph's last night."

11   I did some thinking on this matter as well and came upon a few ideas of something new to call womyn.

- **GIRL PERSONS:** Too juvenile? You're right.
- **LADIES:** Some men name their dogs Lady, and there's that awful sexist joke that goes: "Who was that lady I saw you with last night?"
  "That was no lady. That was my wife."

12   Forget ladies.

- **ADNOFENAJS:** (Pronounced ad-NOFEN-ajuhs). That's Jane Fonda spelled backward, but it's a little cumbersome to say, "That adnofenaj should have been hanged for treason."
- **EELADNERBS:** (Pronounced eel-LADNER-buh). That's Brenda Lee spelled backward. I like Brenda Lee a lot more than Jane Fonda, but I guess most '90s womyn wouldn't.
- **CHICKS:** Just kidding.
- **RALPHETTES:** As in, "You shoulda seen the two Ralphettes we met last night at Ralph's."

13   Sorry, I just can't seem to get untracked here.

- **PLAINTIFFS:** That's got some possibilities. Like the guy said, "I've been divorced so many times, I just refer to all my ex-wives as Plaintiff."

I think that is probably as far as I should go here. The feminist hate mail will pour in for weeks as it is. 14

Oops! Did I say "mail"? 15

This cartoon appeared in The New Yorker, *famous for its very funny and rather sophisticated cartoons. Is the cartoon just for fun, or does it make a serious point?*

"You'll just love the way he handles."

Drawing by Bernard Schoenbaum; © 1991 The New Yorker Magazine, Inc.

Deborah Tannen
CrossTalk

Deborah Tannen, a professor of linguistics at Georgetown University in Washington, D.C., published You Just Don't Understand: Women and Men in Conversation *in 1990. An exploration of the complexities of communication between men and women, it became a national best-seller. The following selection from that book has been printed elsewhere as a self-contained piece.*

1   A woman who owns a bookstore needed to have a talk with the store manager. She had told him to help the bookkeeper with billing, he had agreed, and now, days later, he still hadn't done it. Thinking how much she disliked this part of her work, she sat down with the manager to clear things up. They traced the problem to a breakdown in communication.

2   She had said, "Sarah needs help with the bills. What do you think about helping her out?" He had responded, "OK," by which he meant, "OK, I'll think about whether or not I want to help her." During the next day, he thought about it and concluded that he'd rather not.

3   This wasn't just an ordinary communication breakdown that could happen between any two people. It was a particular sort of breakdown that tends to occur between women and men.

4   Most women avoid giving orders. More comfortable with decision-making by consensus, they tend to phrase requests as questions, to give others the feeling they have some say in the matter and are not being bossed around. But this doesn't mean they aren't making their wishes clear. Most women would have understood the bookstore owner's question, "What do you think about helping her out?" as assigning a task in a considerate way.

5   The manager, however, took the owner's words literally. She had asked him what he thought; she hadn't told him to *do* anything. So he felt within his rights when he took her at her word, thought about it and decided not to help Sarah.

6   Women in positions of authority are likely to regard such responses as insubordination: "He knows I am in charge, and he knows what I want; if he doesn't do it, he is resisting my authority."

There may be a kernel of truth in this view—most men are   7
inclined to resist authority if they can because being in a subordinate position makes them intensely uncomfortable. But
indirect requests that are transparent to women may be genuinely opaque to men. They assume that people in authority
will give orders if they really want something done.

These differences in management styles are one of many   8
manifestations of gender differences in how we talk to one
another. Women use language to create connection and rapport; men use it to negotiate their status in a hierarchical order. It isn't that women are unaware of status or that men
don't build rapport, but that *the genders tend to focus on different goals.*

The Source of Gender Differences

These differences stem from the way boys and girls learn   9
to use language while growing up. Girls tend to play indoors,
either in small groups or with one other girl. The center of a
girl's social life is her best friend, with whom she spends a
great deal of time sitting, talking and exchanging secrets. It is
the telling of secrets that makes them best friends. Boys tend
to play outdoors, in larger groups, usually in competitive
games. It's doing things together that makes them friends.

Anthropologist Marjorie Harness Goodwin compared boys   10
and girls at play in a black innercity neighborhood in Philadelphia. Her findings, which have been supported by researchers in other settings, show that the boys' groups are
hierarchical: high-status boys give orders, and low-status
boys have to follow them, so they end up being told what to
do. Girls' groups tend to be egalitarian: girls who appeared
"better" than others or gave orders were not countenanced
and in some cases were ostracized.

So while boys are learning to fear being "put down" and   11
pushed around, girls are learning to fear being "locked out."
Whereas high-status boys establish and reinforce their authority by giving orders and resisting doing what others want,
girls tend to make suggestions, which are likely to be taken up
by the group.

Cross-Gender Communication in the Workplace

The implications of these different conversational habits   12
and concerns in terms of office interactions are staggering.

Men are inclined to continue to jockey for position, trying to resist following orders as much as possible within the constraints of their jobs.

13   Women, on the other hand, are inclined to do what they sense their bosses want, whether or not they are ordered to. By the same token, women in positions of authority are inclined to phrase their requests as suggestions and to assume they will be respected because of their authority. These assumptions are likely to hold up as long as both parties are women, but they may well break down in cross-gender communication.

14   When a woman is in the position of authority, such as the bookstore owner, she may find her requests are systematically misunderstood by men. And when a woman is working for a male boss, she may find that her boss gives bald commands that seem unnecessarily imperious because most women would prefer to be asked rather than ordered. One woman who worked at an all-male radio station commented that the way the men she worked for told her what to do made her feel as if she should salute and say, "Yes, boss."

15   Many men complain that a woman who is indirect in making requests is manipulative: she's trying to get them to do what she wants without telling them to do it. Another common accusation is that she is insecure: she doesn't know what she wants. But if a woman gives direct orders, the same men might complain that she is aggressive, unfeminine or worse.

16   Women are in a double bind: *If we talk like women, we are not respected. If we talk like men, we are not liked.*

17   We have to walk a fine line, finding ways to be more direct without appearing bossy. The bookstore owner may never be comfortable by directly saying, "Help Sarah with the billing today," but she might find some compromise such as, "Sarah needs help with the billing. I'd appreciate it if you would make some time to help her out in the next day or two." This request is clear, while still reflecting women's preferences for giving reasons and options.

18   What if you're the subordinate and your boss is a man who's offending you daily by giving you orders? If you know him well enough, one potential solution is "metacommunication"—that is, talk about communication. Point out the differences between women and men, and discuss how you could accommodate to each other's styles. (You may want to give him a copy of this article or my book.)

19   But if you don't have the kind of relationship that makes metacommunication possible, you could casually, even jok-

ingly, suggest he give orders another way. Or just try to re-mind yourself it's a cross-cultural difference and try not to take his curtness personally.

How to Handle a Meeting

There are other aspects of women's styles that can work   20
against us in a work setting. Because women are most com-fortable using language to create rapport with someone they feel close to, and men are used to talking in a group where they have to prove themselves and display what they know, a formal meeting can be a natural for men and a hard nut to crack for women. Many women find it difficult to speak up at meetings; if they do, they may find their comments ignored, perhaps later to be resuscitated by a man who gets credit for the idea. Part of this is simply due to the expectation that men will have more important things to contribute.

But the way women and men tend to present themselves   21
can aggravate this inequity. At meetings, men are more likely to speak often, at length and in a declamatory manner. They may state their opinions as fact and leave it to others to chal-lenge them.

Women, on the other hand, are often worried about ap-   22
pearing to talk too much—a fear that is justified by research showing that when they talk equally, women are perceived as talking more than men. As a result, many women are hesitant to speak at a meeting and inclined to be succinct and tenta-tive when they do.

Developing Options

Working on changing your presentational style is one op-   23
tion; another is to make your opinions known in private con-versation with the key people before a meeting. And if you are the key person, it would be wise to talk personally to the women on your staff rather than assuming all participants have had a chance to express themselves at the meeting.

Many women's reticence about displaying their knowledge   24
at a meeting is related to their reluctance to boast. They find it more humble to keep quiet about their accomplishments and wait for someone else to notice them. But most men learn early on to display their accomplishments and skills. And women often find that no one bothers to ferret out their

25 achievements if they don't put them on display. Again, a
    woman risks criticism if she talks about her achievements,
    but this may be a risk she needs to take, to make sure she gets
    credit for her work.

26   I would never want to be heard as telling women to adopt
    men's styles across the board. For one thing, there are many
    situations in which women's styles are more successful. For
    example, the inclination to make decisions by consensus can
    be a boon to a woman in a managerial position. Many people,
    men as well as women, would rather feel they have influence
    in decision-making than be given orders.

27   Moreover, recommending that women adopt men's styles
    would be offensive, as well as impractical, because women
    are judged by the norms for women's behavior, and doing the
    same thing as men has a very different, often negative, effect.

A Starting Point

28   Simply knowing about gender differences in conversa-
    tional style provides a starting point for improving relations
    with the women and men who are above and below you in a
    hierarchy.

29   The key is *flexibility;* a way of talking that works beautifully
    with one person may be a disaster with another. If one way of
    talking isn't working, try another, rather than trying harder to
    do more of the same.

30   Once you know what the parameters are, you can become
    an observer of your own interactions, and a style-switcher
    when you choose.

III.

RACE AND GENDER

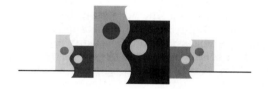

Introduction

One of the stunning social developments of the twentieth century has been the economic and political and cultural emergence of women and people of color. Beginning with the success of the women's suffrage movement early in the century and continuing through the civil rights movement and a series of legal and legislative victories in the past forty years, the women's movement and the movement for civil rights for nonwhite Americans have largely achieved the goal of political equality in the United States—at least on paper. But that has not closed discussion of women's concerns and of the means of combating racism, of course, because social, economic, and political parity between women and men and between African Americans and European Americans remains incomplete and because the specific terms of social and economic liberation have not yet been agreed on. In fact, discussion of racial issues and gender issues has intensified in the past decade as race and gender concerns continue to be negotiated through public discourse. This part of *Conversations* barely begins to capture the range of issues currently under debate, but it does present discussions of four general issues: How do you define race? How do you define gender? Should affirmative action policies continue? And how should we as a society address sexual harassment? (In addition, issues of race and gender are taken up elsewhere in this book, most notably—but not only—in Part II, Language, in Part IV, Family Matters, and the sections in Part V on pornography, civil disobedience, and abortion.)

In the midst of all the discussions related to race in the United States, it is inevitable that the question of the nature of race itself would be raised as an issue. Is race something that is biologically determined? If so, what features distinguish one race from another—skin color? The shape of one's eyes or nose? Or what? What happens to the concept of race when people of different "races" intermarry and have children? Is it reasonable to consider someone "black" if only one of that person's grandparents was African American, or does that merely perpetuate the outdated thinking of antimiscegenation laws? How and why do people think of themselves in one or another racial or ethnic category? Although people in the past assumed that racial designations corresponded to particular physical traits, now many argue that racial identities derive from social and historical forces, that those designations can vary over time—and that such designations are now being reconsidered in the United States. In this decade, since multicultural and multiethnic considerations have been pressed, since immigration from Latin America and Asia has created new citizens less easily categorized than in the past, since interracial marriage has become more common, and since some vestiges of segregation have become less virulent, it seems that racial categories are particularly being reconsidered. To many people, Americans have taken a too "binary" approach to race; while other nations (rightly or wrongly) often recognize gradations of color in their citizens, Americans often persist in thinking of race as an either-or proposition. While in one sense, Black–White antagonisms have persisted in the face of challenges to affirmative action and the continuation of social inequities in our society, in another sense those antagonisms seem somehow anachronistic as Americans shift their views of race in the face of a social interrogation of the concept of race itself. Consequently, the first section of this part considers definitions of race—especially the question of whether or not inherited notions of race benefit our national community.

The concept of race is not the only thing that is being redefined right now. Until very recently it was men who defined women, mostly in a misogynist (women-hating) tradition that is deeply seated in Western cultures. But the fact that women are now involved in defining gender roles has not effaced that tradition of misogyny, nor has it ended discussion of the nature of those roles. Just what form will the feminist revolution take? Just what is it that defines the essential natures of women and men? Beyond reproductive differences, are there inevitable distinctions between the sexes in terms of emotions, sexuality, physiology, morals, values, and so forth? Or are all such distinctions the result of social conditioning— social conditioning that might be altered? That is the basic issue under discussion in the second section of this part. A half dozen or so selections of various kinds describe, explain, dramatize, or argue for various positions on the question of the "essential natures" of women and men and the extent to which history and culture and environment determine those natures. The selections also illustrate the range of voices that can be summoned in support of a discussion of gender roles. While most of the selections address women's concerns directly, each one has direct and indirect implications for men as well. And as we enter a new century those implications must be faced each day.

Gender issues and race issues have been emphasized in a central document of the civil rights movement, the Civil

Rights Act of 1964, which attempted to eradicate discrimination from a range of public institutions in the United States. Part of Title VII of that act prohibited discrimination on the job because of race, color, religion, sex, or national origin:

> It shall be an unlawful employment practice for an employer... to fail or refuse to hire or to discharge any individual, or otherwise to discriminate against any individual with respect to his compensation, terms, conditions, or privileges of employment, because of such individual's race, color, religion, sex, or national origin.... It shall be an unlawful employment practice for any employer, labor organization, or joint labor-management committee controlling apprenticeship or other training or retraining, including on-the-job training programs, to discriminate against any individual because of his race, color, religion, sex, or national origin in admission to, or employment in, any program established to provide apprenticeship or other training.... If the court finds that the respondent has intentionally engaged in an unlawful employment practice... the court may enjoin the respondent from engaging in such unlawful employment practice, and order such affirmative action as may be appropriate.

Title VII thus initiated a period of "affirmative action" to redress past injustices and to establish for everyone the possibility of equal opportunity.

But just what should affirmative action mean? Should it be a means of ensuring that everyone has a chance to compete on equal terms for jobs and education? Or should it denote a more active process of ensuring equal results, especially for people who arrive at jobs and schools with disadvantages that arise from past inequality? For some people, affirmative action means the former; in the words of the late Hubert Humphrey, nothing in Title VII should "give any power to the [Civil Rights] Commission or any court to require hiring, firing, or promotion of employees in order to meet a racial quota." For others, however, affirmative action means action: active measures (at least in the short run) such as goals, timetables, guidelines, and quotas designed to promote balanced results.

Are such actions fair? Is affirmative action a legitimate, short-term measure for breaking up a rigid caste system and for ameliorating the long-term effects of Jim Crow laws, sexist traditions, and inequitable education policies? Or is it inherently unfair? Has the "short-term" expired by now? Can we now justify passing over someone or favoring someone else because of the group that person is born into? Is the goal of affirmative action the reduction of social injustice or proportional representation of all races and both sexes? Is affirmative action inefficient, in that it favors racial and gender factors over job performance? Or is it more efficient, in that it speeds the progress of women and minorities and therefore allows those people a chance, at last, to show their right stuff? Does affirmative action damage self-esteem or promote it? Should colleges and universities eliminate racial and gender preferences in admissions decisions? Finally, would affirmative action make better sense if it were administered on a class-wide basis instead of on the basis of race or gender? Those sensitive questions are discussed in the selections reprinted here on affirmative action.

This part of *Conversations* concludes with a set of readings that deals with the conditions women face at work. What happens—on the job and at home—when women enter professions and institutions traditionally dominated by men? How can women cope with unfriendly circumstances? Is it possible to keep unequal power relations at work from affecting personal relationships? In short: What about the question of sexual harassment at work—what is it, and what can be done about it? Should sexual harassment be defined broadly or very specifically? Are men as frequently as women the victims of harassment? Even before Anita Hill accused Supreme Court Justice Clarence Thomas of sexual harassment during Thomas's confirmation hearings in 1991, these questions were being discussed in our country; the readings in this section offer a range of answers, a range that will likely force you to rethink your own positions.

So where do you stand on these questions of race and gender? The selections in this part are designed to provoke further discussion, not to close it off. In fact, a premise of this part on race and gender is that by engaging in open, public discourse on these complex questions, writers can hasten the day when the effects of racial and sexual polarization—perhaps racial and sexual polarization itself—might be minimized and when codes of personal behavior might be more freely chosen, to the benefit of everyone.

DEFINING RACE

Sharon Begley
Three Is Not Enough

The following essay was published as a Newsweek *magazine story on February 13, 1995. Since the cover of* Newsweek *that day posed the question, "What Color Is Black?," this was one of several essays in the magazine that discussed one or another aspect of the issue of defining race: one considered biracial children and interracial marriage; another looked at affirmative action; still another was a historical analysis of definitions of race in the United States. Sharon Begley is a senior writer for* Newsweek, *where her work often appears.*

1   To most Americans race is as plain as the color of the nose on your face. Sure, some light-skinned blacks, in some neighborhoods, are taken for Italians, and some Turks are confused with Argentines. But even in the children of biracial couples, racial ancestry is writ large—in the hue of the skin and the shape of the lips, the size of the brow and the bridge of the nose. It is no harder to trace than it is to judge which basic colors in a box of Crayolas were combined to make tangerine or burnt umber. Even with racial mixing, the existence of primary races is as obvious as the existence of primary colors.

2   Or is it? C. Loring Brace has his own ideas about where race resides, and it isn't in skin color. If our eyes could perceive more than the superficial, we might find race in chromosome 11: there lies the gene for hemoglobin. If you divide humankind by which of two forms of the gene each person has, then equatorial Africans, Italians and Greeks fall into the "sickle-cell race"; Swedes and South Africa's Xhosas (Nelson Mandela's ethnic group) are in the healthy-hemoglobin race. Or do you prefer to group people by whether they have epicanthic eye folds, which produce the "Asian" eye? Then the !Kung San (Bushmen) belong with the Japanese and Chinese. Depending on which trait you choose to demarcate races, "you won't get anything that remotely tracks conventional

[race] categories," says anthropologist Alan Goodman, dean of natural science at Hampshire College.

The notion of race is under withering attack for political 3 and cultural reasons—not to mention practical ones like what to label the child of a Ghanaian and a Norwegian. But scientists got there first. Their doubts about the conventional racial categories—black, white, Asian—have nothing to do with a sappy "we are all the same" ideology. Just the reverse. "Human variation is very, very real," says Goodman. "But race, as a way of organizing [what we know about that variation], is incredibly simplified and bastardized." Worse, it does not come close to explaining the astounding diversity of humankind—not its origins, not its extent, not its meaning. "There is no organizing principle by which you could put 5 billion people into so few categories in a way that would tell you anything important about humankind's diversity," says Michigan's Brace, who will lay out the case against race at the annual meeting of the American Association for the Advancement of Science.

About 70 percent of cultural anthropologists, and half of 4 physical anthropologists, reject race as a biological category, according to a 1989 survey by Central Michigan University anthropologist Leonard Liebermnan and colleagues. The truths of science are not decided by majority vote, of course. Empirical evidence, woven into a theoretical whole, is what matters. The threads of the argument against the standard racial categories:

• **Genes:** In 1972, population biologist Richard Lewontin 5 of Harvard University laid out the genetic case against race. Analyzing 17 genetic markers in 168 populations such as Austrians, Thais and Apaches, he found that there is more genetic difference within one race than there is between that race and another. Only 6.3 percent of the genetic differences could be explained by the individuals' belonging to different races. That is, if you pick at random any two "blacks" walking along the street, and analyze their 23 pairs of chromosomes, you will probably find that their genes have less in common than do the genes of one of them with that of a random "white" person. Last year the Human Genome Diversity Project used 1990s genetics to extend Lewontin's analysis. Its conclusion: genetic variation from one individual to another of the same "race" swamps the average differences between racial groupings. The more we learn about humankind's genetic differences, says geneticist Luca Cavalli-Sforza of Stanford University, who chairs the committee that directs the biodiversity project, the more we see that they have almost nothing to do with what we call race.

6   • **Traits:** As sickle-cell "races" and epicanthic-fold "races" show, there are as many ways to group people as there are traits. That is because "racial" traits are what statisticians call non-concordant. Lack of concordance means that sorting people according to *these* traits produces different groupings than you get in sorting them by *those* (equally valid) traits. When biologist Jared Diamond of UCLA surveyed half a dozen traits for a recent issue of *Discover* magazine, he found that, depending on which traits you pick, you can form very surprising "races." Take the scooped-out shape of the back of the front teeth, a standard "Asian" trait. Native Americans and Swedes have these shovel-shaped incisors, too, and so would fall in the same race. Is biochemistry better? Norwegians, Arabians, north Indians and the Fulani of northern Nigeria, notes Diamond, fall into the "lactase race" (the lactase enzyme digests milk sugar). Everyone else—other Africans, Japanese, Native Americans—forms the "lactase-deprived race" (their ancestors did not drink milk from cows or goats and hence never evolved the lactase gene). How about blood types, the familiar A, B and O groups? Then Germans and New Guineans, populations that have the same percentages of each type, are in one race; Estonians and Japanese comprise a separate one for the same reason, notes anthropologist Jonathan Marks of Yale University. Depending on which traits are chosen, "we could place Swedes in the same race as either Xhosas, Fulani, the Ainu of Japan or Italians," writes Diamond.

7   • **Subjectivity:** If race is a valid biological concept, anyone in any culture should be able to look at any individual and say, Aha, you are a . . . It should not be the case, as French tennis star Yannick Noah said a few years ago, that "in Africa I am white, and in France I am black" (his mother is French and his father is from Cameroon). "While biological traits give the impression that race is a biological unit of nature," says anthropologist George Armelagos of Emory University, "it remains a cultural construct. The boundaries between races depend on the classifier's own cultural norms."

8   • **Evolution:** Scholars who believe in the biological validity of race argue that the groupings reflect human pre-history. That is, populations that evolved together, and separately from others, constitute a race. This school of thought holds that blacks should all be in one race because they are de-

scended from people who stayed on the continent where humanity began. Asians, epitomized by the Chinese, should be another race because they are the children of groups who walked north and east until they reached the Pacific. Whites of the pale, blond variety should be another because their ancestors filled Europe. Because of their appearance, these populations represent the extremes, the archetypes, of human diversity—the reds, blues and yellows from which you can make every other hue. "But if you use these archetypes as your groups you have classified only a very tiny proportion of the world's people, which is not very useful," says Marks, whose incisive new book "Human Biodiversity" deconstructs race. "Also, as people walked out of Africa, they were differentiating along the way. Equating 'extreme' with 'primordial' is not supported by history."

Often, shared traits are a sign of shared heritage—racial   9
heritage. "Shared traits are not random," says Alice Brues, an anthropologist at the University of Colorado. "Within a continent, you of course have a number of variants [on basic traits], but some are characteristic of the larger area, too. So it's natural to look for these major divisions. It simplifies your thinking." A wide distribution of traits, however, makes them suspect as evidence of a shared heritage. The dark skin of Somalis and Ghanaians, for instance, indicates that they evolved under the same selective force (a sunny climate). But that's all it shows. It does *not* show that they are any more closely related, in the sense of sharing more genes, than either is to Greeks. Calling Somalis and Ghanaians "black" therefore sheds no further light on their evolutionary history and implies—wrongly—that they are more closely related to each other than either is to someone of a different "race." Similarly, the long noses of North Africans and northern Europeans reveal that they evolved in dry or cold climates (the nose moistens air before the air reaches the lungs, and longer noses moisten more air). The tall, thin bodies of Kenya's Masai evolved to dissipate heat; Eskimos evolved short, squat bodies to retain it. Calling these peoples "different races" adds nothing to that understanding.

Where did the three standard racial divisions come from?   10
They entered the social, and scientific, consciousness during the Age of Exploration. Loring Brace doesn't think it's a coincidence that the standard races represent peoples who, as he puts it, "lived at the end of the Europeans' trade routes"—in Africa and China—in the days after Prince Henry the Navigator set sail. Before Europeans took to the seas, there was little

perception of races. If villagers began to look different to an
Englishman riding a horse from France to Italy and on to
Greece, the change was too subtle to inspire notions of races.
But if the English sailor left Lisbon Harbor and dropped anchor off the Kingdom of Niger, people looked so different he
felt compelled to invent a scheme to explain the world—and,
perhaps, distance himself from the Africans.

11   This habit of sorting the world's peoples into a small number of groups got its first scientific gloss from Swedish taxon-
omist Carolus Linnaeus. (Linnaeus is best known for his
system of classifying living things by genus and species—
Escherichia coli, Homo sapiens and the rest.) In 1758 he declared that humanity falls into four races: white (Europeans),
red (Native Americans), dark (Asians) and black (Africans).
Linnaeus said that Native Americans (who in the 1940s got
grouped with Asians) were ruled by custom. Africans were in-
dolent and negligent, and Europeans were inventive and gentle, said Linnaeus. Leave aside the racist undertones (not to
mention the oddity of ascribing gentleness to the group that
perpetrated the Crusades and Inquisition): that alone should
not undermine its validity. More worrisome is that the notion
and the specifics of race predate genetics, evolutionary biology and the science of human origins. With the revolutions in
those fields, how is it that the 18th-century scheme of race retains its powerful hold? Consider these arguments:

12   • **If I parachute into Nairobi, I know I'm not in Oslo:**
Colorado's Alice Brues uses this image to argue that denying
the reality of race flies in the face of common sense. But the
parachutists, if they were familiar with the great range of human diversity, could also tell that they were in Nairobi rather
than Abidjan—east Africans don't look much like west Africans. They could also tell they were in Istanbul rather than
Oslo, even though Turks and Norwegians are both called
Caucasian.

13   • **DOA, male, 5'11"...black:** When U.S. police call in a forensic anthropologist to identify the race of a skeleton, the scientist comes through 80 to 85 percent of the time. If race has
no biological validity, how can the sleuths get it right so often?
The forensic anthropologist could, with enough information
about bone structure and genetic markers, identify the region
from which the corpse came—south and west Africa, Southeast Asia and China, Northern and Western Europe. It just so
happens that the police would call corpses from the first two
countries black, from the middle two Asian, and the last pair
white. But lumping these six distinct populations into three

groups of two serves no biological purpose, only a social convention. The larger grouping may reflect how society views
humankind's diversity, but does not explain it.

• **African-Americans have more hypertension:** If race   14
is not real, how can researchers say that blacks have higher
rates of infant mortality, lower rates of osteoporosis and a
higher incidence of hypertension? Because a social construct
can have biological effects, says epidemiologist Robert Hahn
of the U.S. Centers for Disease Control and Prevention. Consider hypertension among African-Americans. Roughly 34
percent have high blood pressure, compared with about 16
percent of whites. But William Dressler finds the greatest
incidence of hypertension among blacks who are upwardly
mobile achievers. "That's probably because in mundane interactions, from the bank to the grocery store, they are treated in
ways that do not coincide with their self-image as respectable
achievers," says Dressler, an anthropologist at the University
of Alabama. "And the upwardly mobile are more likely to encounter discriminatory white culture." Lab studies show that
stressful situations—like being followed in grocery stores as if
you were a shoplifter—elevate blood pressure and lead to vas-
cular changes that cause hypertension. "In this case, race captures social factors such as the experience of discrimination,"
says sociologist David Williams of the University of Michigan.
Further evidence that hypertension has more to do with society than with biology: black Africans have among the lowest
rates of hypertension in the world.

If race is not a biological explanation of hypertension, can   15
it offer a biological explanation of something as complex as
intelligence? Psychologists are among the strongest proponents of retaining the three conventional racial categories. It
organizes and explains their data in the most parsimonious
way, as Charles Murray and Richard Herrnstein argue in "The
Bell Curve." But anthropologists say that such conclusions
are built on a foundation of sand. If nothing else, argues
Brace, every ethnic group evolved under conditions where intelligence was a requirement for survival. If there are intelligence "genes," they must be in all ethnic groups equally:
differences in intelligence must be a cultural and social
artifact.

Scientists who doubt the biological meaningfulness of race   16
are not nihilists. They just prefer another way of capturing,
and explaining, the great diversity of humankind. Even today
most of the world's peoples marry within their own group.

Intramarriage preserves features—fleshy lips, small ears, wide-set eyes—that arose by a chance genetic mutation long ago. Grouping people by geographic origins—better known as ethnicity—"is more correct both in a statistical sense and in understanding the history of human variation," says Hampshire's Goodman. Ethnicity also serves as a proxy for differences—from diet to a history of discrimination—that can have real biological and behavioral effects.

17   In a 1942 book, anthropologist Ashley Montagu called race "Man's Most Dangerous Myth." If it is, then our most ingenuous myth must be that we sort humankind into groups in order to understand the meaning and origin of humankind's diversity. That isn't the reason at all; a greater number of smaller groupings, like ethnicities, does a better job. The obsession with broad categories is so powerful as to seem a neurological imperative. Changing our thinking about race will require a revolution in thought as profound, and profoundly unsettling, as anything science has ever demanded. What these researchers are talking about is changing the way in which we see the world—and each other. But before that can happen, we must do more than understand the biologist's suspicions about race. We must ask science, also, why it is that we are so intent on sorting humanity into so few groups—us and Other—in the first place.

Karla Brundage
Passing

Karla Brundage, a graduate of Vassar College, teaches now in Hawaii. She offers more information about herself in the following essay, which was published in Multi-America, *a collection of several dozen essays exploring multiculturalism that was edited by the well-known writer and multiculturalist Ishmael Reed and published in 1997.*

1   It happens all the time...I am walking down the street and a complete stranger stops me, maybe even interrupting my conversation, and urgently asks, "What are you?"

Or I am minding my own business, living on my street, 2
when I notice that the Black woman who lives next door to
me, who has a child the same age as my child, blatantly ignores my "hellos" and my "we should have tea sometimes."
Then one day I find that we have a friend in common. From
this friend I learn the reason for her standoffishness. My
neighbor does not know I am Black, but I live with a very
Black man. She finds such a relationship repulsive. I make
her sick.

What about my other neighbor, a Black woman of forty- 3
plus with a grown child, who speaks only to my partner, and
won't even wave to me from the car?

Or what about my sister-in-law who warned me, serious 4
and superstitious, "Don't cut that hair, girl. You know your
man won't like it; you got good hair."

I can't forget my partner's teacher and spiritual leader, who 5
said offhand to him after meeting me, "Shit, man, you already
got yourself a white girl."

"White girl! White girl! How dare he," came my response. 6

My partner looked at me almost innocently and said, 7
"Karla, he didn't mean what you think he meant. What he
meant was…"

"Don't even try to explain. I know what he meant…" 8

"But…" 9

"I said, I know what he meant. I certainly don't need you to 10
try and explain it. End of conversation."

He was talking about passing. He was talking about all of 11
those instances I just listed. He was trying to explain my life
to me. Do I think I am white? Many people want to know. Do
I think I can pass as Black? I cannot give a definitive answer.
That is the problem. People are always trying to define me,
while at the same time limiting my answer. I have had people
ask me what I am, and then refuse to believe me. Others
never ask; they just hate me for not fitting into their little box.
Meanwhile, I have been teaching myself all my life to define
myself in uncertainties, in abstractions, in illusions. I am not
who you think I am. Even you, reader, may have a fixed opinion from generalizations that are easy to make. My vital statistics make stereotyping even easier.

I was born in Berkeley in 1967. My parents were flower 12
children. According to my father, they thought they could
save the world through love. The story is shaky. I think they
really got married for two totally different reasons. My
mother, who was born and raised in Tuskegee, Alabama, had
gone to all-white boarding schools much of her life. I don't

think she planned to marry white, but it happened. My father, who was from Pleasantville, New York, came from a dysfunctional alcoholic family. He was being educated at a liberal arts college, and he really felt that there was no better way to live out his newfound beliefs than by marrying this Black woman he met on a college exchange and with whom he fell head over heels in love. He believed—and still believes—that by having an interracial child, along with others in their generation they would be one step closer to ending racism.

13   So I was born with a cross to carry, so to speak. I say this because I have always known of my father's expectations as well as his bitterness that the sexual revolution did not save the world, and especially at the failure of his marriage, which could not overcome racism. But that's another story.

14   This is who I am and where I came from: conservative, middle class, educated, on both sides, Black and white. My parents were the rebels. They were married until I was three. During this time, my mother's first cousin, who was involved with SNCC, was killed for using a white bathroom. It is my opinion that my mother could never really love my father in the same way after that incident. After all, his family is very racist. I have some relatives who still refuse to meet me. After her cousin Sammy's death, my mother became involved with the Black Panthers, and my father became resentful that she could exclude him from her life when, in his mind, he had sacrificed his, having been disowned as a result of the marriage. So they moved to Hawaii to try to escape the racism that they had once been willing to fight. This is the beginning of my memory.

15   I lived with my mother. I had a happy childhood, most of which was spent outdoors, playing. However, although my mother is a professor in African American studies at the University of Hawaii, she could not provide for me what did not exist. I knew of racism, I knew I was Black, but I did not grow up knowing what it is to be Black. I had no Black culture or community. In Hawaii, there are many brown people. I was brown, so I fit right in. I basically grew up as a local girl. If people asked, I would tell them I was Black, but people rarely asked. In a weird way, I have been passing for something or another all my life.

16   I remember at seven and eight wishing to be Hawaiian. I wanted nothing more than to really be what people thought I was. I wanted to go to Kamehameha School, which is a school for people who have traceable Hawaiian blood in them. I can remember using my spare time, when I wasn't

swimming in the ocean or running relay races in our huge yard, trying to think up ways to get into that school. In the bathtub was one of my favorite places to dream. I would stand in front of the mirror wet and with a towel on, pretending it was native Hawaiian garb, and that I was really Hawaiian. I don't remember when I accepted the fact that it would not happen.

In seventh grade, my mother told me that we were going to move to the mainland for a couple of years. My fantasy changed, although not so abruptly. I remember now at age twelve lying in bed and praying to God: "God, please let California be fun. Let me have a boyfriend, and God, if there is any way, can you please take the time to look at my eyes? See God, they are brown. And God, my dad has blue eyes. I know that people in California have blue eyes and light skin. I mean, they are white. I don't have to be white, but maybe while I am there I will be a little lighter, and then I'll be tan, and if my eyes were blue...It would be perfect, not to mention my hair, which if it were just a little lighter. My dad has blond hair; if only I could just look more like my dad. I am not asking for much, just to look more like my dad than my mom. Please, God, just let me be more beautiful."

This is not a lie or even an exaggeration. I prayed this prayer all the way up until the night we left. Many years later when I read Toni Morrison's *The Bluest Eye*, I broke down crying from relief. My secret was out, and it wasn't just me. *The Bluest Eye* connected me to other Black women in a way I had never been able to connect, in that I am always told that, because of my near-white attributes, I somehow think I am better than others. That story is one of the truest tales I know.

So I moved, but not to California. Instead, I moved with my father to upstate New York; Hope, to be exact. I lived in Hope for one year. I hoped that no one would find out that I was black. I often wonder what it was that made me think I needed to pass in order to survive up there in the land where my father was raised and the KKK thrives. Was it my mother, who cried every day before I left, telling me that people are racist, especially when they see a brown girl with a white man? Or was it my father, who did not give me the strength to stand up for who I was. I remember telling him that I told my new friends I was Hawaiian, but I don't remember him giving me any helpful advice. I didn't even have to lie; it was easier than that. When they asked where I was from, I said, "Hawaii." And they said, "Oh, so you're Hawaiian, then." And I just smiled, my killer Hawaiian smile. All the people in Hope

17

18

19

were thrilled, because they had a real Hawaiian living in their town. My wish had come true.

20   The only problem was my mother. She ruined my plan. She called almost every other night from California, and cried. "Karla, don't deny me," she would say, "please, don't deny me. Don't lie about who you are." But I was thirteen, I had never been Black before, and I wanted to have friends. I was in a new place completely foreign to me. It was too hard. I chose to tell only one person who I really was. She was my best friend, her name was Squeaker. And Squeak she did. It wound up that eventually everybody found out that I was really Black. Some people resented that. Some were just bummed that I was not a "real" Hawaiian. But I really think that misleading them to think I was Hawaiian first softened the blow. I mean, I was already a cheerleader by the time the word got out. This was what I think was the beginning of a long series of events in which I learned how to objectify myself in order to survive. I was making myself more and more invisible, in order to escape the lasso of definition.

21   In ninth grade, I finally did move to Oakland, California. In Oakland, I was for the first time immersed in Black culture. And for the first time, I had a boyfriend who told me I was beautiful for who I was, a Black girl with a white father. Of course, this was my first love, and he was also mixed. What I did not know about was the deadly lines drawn between dark and light within the Black community itself. Since I did not know, I existed happily. Loving myself for perhaps the first time. I had Black and white friends. I declared myself a rebel from the traditional cliques of high school, the "stoners," who were white; the Chicanos; and the soul or disco lovers, who were Black. I declared myself a peacemaker between the three sides, neutral by virtue of my skin. After all, I looked more Chicano than anything. For a time it was my father's dream of racelessness come true.

22   When I finally went to college, passing became an issue again. Once again I found myself on a plane bound for upstate New York—Poughkeepsie, to be exact. Vassar College was like no place I had been before. Looking back on it, I see that I spent most of my college career in culture shock. I was not only adapting to race but to class differences. I entered Vassar with the same attitude that I had when I left Oakland. I was Black and white, and therefore part of both groups.

23   What I found at Vassar was that I could never be a part of the elite white world, and worse, the Blacks there resented me for even trying. I remember walking into the cafeteria on the

first day of school with my new roommate, who happened to be white. I walked past a table where all ten of the Black freshmen were eating dinner and said hello. They barely looked at me, and when I walked away I heard someone comment that I must think I am white. From the first day, I was never accepted by the African Americans at Vassar; it was a very small, very tight group. Those who were mixed were forced to choose sides, and most of us chose white. The animosity between lighter- and darker-skinned Blacks, especially women, was a part of Black culture that I did not yet understand. I did not get why they would hate me or why they would think I thought I was white.

I was so hurt. I figured if they did not like me, then I would   24
just hang out with the whites. This was a big mistake. During my entire college career, I was never invited to anyone's house for Thanksgiving, I was never asked to a ball. What I could not see was that with the whites, I was accepted as an object, an exotic. I existed on the periphery.

To lessen the pain, I drank excessively and found myself   25
sinking deeper and deeper into a hole of self-hatred. Yet I refused to see my rejection as racially motivated, until one night when I was at the school bar, drunk as usual. A man I had slept with grabbed me and locked me in a phone booth. While in the phone booth, we began to argue about what had happened between us. I accused him and many of his friends of using me. To this he replied, "Don't you see, Karla, it's your fault! You are beautiful, so beautiful and exotic, and don't you know what that does to men?"

That night I cut off all my hair. That night I also began to   26
see that I had been trying to be white most of the time I was at college, and that in reality, I did not know who I was. By the time I graduated, I was an alcoholic, and I knew that I had to go back to Oakland to be around Black people.

I don't know if I thought it would be better to be in the   27
Black community, but I knew that I was missing something. I have lived in Oakland for five years now, and one thing I have learned is that as a people, we as Blacks have been truly indoctrinated into racist ways. When I first arrived, I obtained a position as a teacher's aide at a home for emotionally disturbed teens, many of whom were Black. These youths had nothing to hide in their evaluations of me. I began to notice by their reactions to me the confusion we feel as a people about our skin. Most did not believe I was Black. I found myself in a position again where I felt forced to disguise my real identity. Instead of answering that I was part Black, mixed,

hapa, half, or mulatto—all terms that I had used my entire life—I found myself saying I was Black. I wanted so desperately to be accepted as Black, but still no one would believe me. Whenever I said, "Black," in response to the question, "What are you?", the person attacking me would say, "Black and what...?"

28   So, I began to denounce my whiteness. I was angry at my father for cursing me. I was angry at all white people for being racists and for promoting racism everywhere. Once again I looked for acceptance of my new identify in men. I chose Black men who were "revolutionary" in their beliefs, men who had forsaken the system completely. Over and over I found myself in the same predicament. I was not Black enough for them. Yet to this day almost all the men in that group are living with (off) white women. Naturally, I began to hate white women. All the anger I had felt at Vassar surfaced and I was able to bond with Black women for the first time, as well as justify my hypocrisy, until I began to realize that many Black women hated me, too, for the same reasons. They thought I was white.

29   This was my latest disillusion. It was really all too much for me. I opened my eyes and began to look at my life. Many of my friends are mixed. Not deliberately, but maybe out of some common pool of experience. I realized that it was not only hypocritical but impossible to hate my father, a part of myself. At the age of twenty-five, I finally realized that I am mixed. Not definable, not in any box, and probably not all that new a phenomenon. But certainly an enigma.

30   Still, people are constantly trying to define me—all people, white and Black. For a while I wanted to wear a sign around my neck that said, "I am Black." But slowly I began to realize, I am not just Black. I certainly am not white. I am mixed. What does it mean to be a mixed-race, Black/white woman in America in the nineties? Recently, my mother told me that we are actually one-eighth Cherokee. This is another part of me that I never even explored, let alone identified with. I am still trying to figure it all out, but I think right now it's about defining myself, taking that step to say, Hey, I am mixed. I am not going to pretend anymore. I am not going to go to Castlemont, a predominantly Black high school in East Oakland, and argue with teenagers about my race. I am not going to drive myself to the point of suicide trying to be white, either. I am just going to be me.

Linda Hogan

Linda Hogan, a Chickasaw, was born in Denver in 1947 and grew up in Oklahoma. A poet, novelist, essayist, and playwright, she now teaches creative writing at the University of Colorado. Hogan's work has won wide acclaim and many awards, including a Guggenheim Fellowship. Her poems often touch on environmental concerns, and she is active in the antinuclear movement. Her poem "The History of Red" comes from her 1993 collection The Book of Medicines, *and the one following it, "Heritage," appeared in* Red Clay, *a 1991 book of stories and poems.*

The History of Red

First   1
there was some other order of things
never spoken
but in dreams of darkest creation.

Then there was black earth,   2
lake, the face of light on water.
Then the thick forest all around
that light,
and then the human clay
whose blood we still carry
rose up in us
who remember caves with red bison
painted in their own blood,
after their kind.

A wildness   3
swam inside our mothers,
desire through closed eyes,
a new child
wearing the red, wet mask of birth,
delivered into this land
already wounded,
stolen and burned
beyond reckoning.

Red is this yielding land   4
turned inside out

by a country of hunters
with iron, flint and fire.
Red is the fear
that turns a knife back
against men, holds it at their throats,
and they cannot see the claw on the handle,
the animal hand
that haunts them
from some place inside their blood.

5   So that is hunting, birth,
and one kind of death.
Then there was medicine, the healing of wounds.
Red was the infinite fruit
of stolen bodies.
The doctors wanted to know
what invented disease
how wounds healed
from inside themselves
how life stands up in skin,
if not by magic.

6   They divined the red shadow of leeches
that swam in white bowls of water;
they believed stars
in the cup of sky,
They cut the wall of skin
to let
what was bad escape
but they were reading the story of fire
gone out
and that was a science.

7   As for the animal hand on death's knife,
knives have as many sides
as the red father of war
who signs his name
in the blood of other men.

8   And red was the soldier
who crawled
through a ditch
of human blood in order to live.
It was the canal of his deliverance.

It is his son who lives near me.   9
Red is the thunder in our ears
when we meet.
Love, like creation,
is some other order of things.

Red is the share of fire   10
I have stolen
from root, hoof, fallen fruit.
And this was hunger.

Red is the human house   11
I come back to at night
swimming inside the cave of skin
that remembers bison.
In that round nation
of blood
we are all burning,
red, inseparable fires
the living have crawled
and climbed through
in order to live
so nothing will be left
for death at the end.

This life in the fire, I love it,   12
I want it,
this life.

Heritage

From my mother, the antique mirror   1
where I watch my face take on her lines.
She left me the smell of baking bread
to warm fine hairs in my nostrils,
she left the large white breasts that weigh down
my body.

From my father I take his brown eyes,   2
the plague of locusts that leveled our crops,
they flew in formation like buzzards.

3   From my uncle the whittled wood
     that rattles like bones
     and is white
     and smells like all our old houses
     that are no longer there. He was the man
     who sang old chants to me, the words
     my father was told not to remember.

4   From my grandfather who never spoke
     I learned to fear silence.
     I learned to kill a snake
     when begging for rain.

5   And grandmother, blue-eyed woman
     whose skin was brown,
     she used snuff.
     When her coffee can full of black saliva
     spilled on me
     it was like the brown cloud of grasshoppers
     that leveled her fields.
     It was the brown stain
     that covered my white shirt.
     That sweet black liquid like the food
     she chewed up and spit into my father's mouth
     when he was an infant.

6   It was the brown earth of Oklahoma
     stained with oil.
     She said tobacco would purge your body of poisons.
     It has more medicine than stones and knives
     against your enemies.
     That tobacco is the dark night that covers me.

7   She said it is wise to eat the flesh of deer
     so you will be swift and travel over many miles.
     She told me how our tribe has always followed a stick
     that pointed west
     that pointed east.
     From my family I have learned the secrets
     of never having a home.

Demian Hess

But You Don't Look Chinese!

Demian Hess first published the following account of his expe-
riences in 1995 in the Journal of the Asian American Renaissance. *Since then the article has been reprinted on the Internet*
by the organization known as Interracial Voice, which pro-
motes understanding interracial issues.

I've never felt particularly "oppressed." Or outraged. Or an- 1
gry or upset or downtrodden or victimized. Well, maybe not
"never." But I've never carried a grudge about it. I've never
had an ax to grind. I've never felt I had a statement to make
about the RACISM in our SOCIETY or the OPPRESSION by
the DOMINANT CULTURE. Capital letters give me a headache, I guess. And I guess my friends would be surprised if I
did make a fuss.

"But, what have you got to complain about?" they say to 2
me. "You're not a minority." And when I point out to them
that, in fact, I am a minority: "Oh, well, yeah, your mom's
Chinese, but you're not. I mean, you don't look Chinese."

Yeah, I don't look Chinese. I've heard that before. 3

I remember this one time when I lived in Rhode Island. I 4
was taking the bus home from the beach when this old
woman got on board. The bus was half empty, but she chose
to sit down right next to me.

"You're Jewish, aren't you?" she said, just like that, right af- 5
ter she sat down. I stared at her for a second and then admitted that, yes, I was Jewish. I have no idea how she knew.
Maybe it was the nose. I had this tiny little bean-shaped nose
until I was about twelve, and then a huge mass exploded out
of my face. The family nose. The Jewish stigma.

"You can always tell," the old woman said, and patted my 6
knee. "It's so nice to have someone to talk to, I hardly ever see
anyone. My children, they never call, they never visit. It's so
hard when you're old. You'll see."

Then she stopped and squinted at me. "But you're not all 7
Jewish, are you?" she said. I shook my head and explained
that my mother was Chinese. "Oh," she said, and paused.
"Well, don't worry. It doesn't show."

She was right, it doesn't show. And I guess that I'm lucky it 8
doesn't show. But I wasn't born lucky. I was born looking Chinese and I grew up looking Chinese. When I was six, I had

straight black hair, this tiny little bean nose, almond-shaped eyes and yellow skin. I was very slight, not stocky-tending-to-fat like other kids. I seemed to speak differently, too, although I'm not sure whether that's actually a Chinese trait or not. Did it have something to do with the size and shape of my Asiatic larynx and nasal passages? I don't know, but to my ear I had a strange pitch to my voice, a sort of high, lilting, whistling quality that made me cringe to hear it on tape. I'm probably crazy to think there's anything Chinese about this part of myself.

9   Whether or not my voice was really different, my appearance certainly was, and none of the other kids in school ever let me forget it. When I was five, my folks had moved to a little farm in the Born Again Bible Belt of Minnesota. That's Hickesville, the Boonies, Red Neck City. Everyone was white. Germanic or Scandinavian, maybe a little English, but white. And Christian. My family wasn't any of those things. My parents were hippies, atheists, graduate students. And not white. Well, OK, so my father was white, but my mother definitely wasn't. The neighbors didn't know exactly what she was. Chinese? Indian? It didn't matter. She was brown. And so were her kids.

10   "Chin Chan, China man, get his meals from a garbage can." I heard that nearly every week from the other kids, as they danced around me during recess, making slanty eyes with their fingers. Actually, this came from the more enlightened bigots. The ones who had taken the time to study the issue and determine which racial category I belonged to and which slur was appropriate. Most didn't bother with such distinctions.

11   "You see this?" a student asked me one day, pointing to a small, green country on the globe. I peered at it. It was Nigeria. "See that? That says 'nigger.' That's where you're from, 'cause you're a nigger." Not only bigoted, but illiterate as well.

12   But the Chinese thing was only a phase, I grew out of it. One of those unpleasant things you need to get out of your system, like gawkiness, or acne, or a breaking voice. You know, growing pains. Sometime around the age of twelve, my nose exploded, my eyes grew round, my hair lightened and took on a bit of a wave. *Voilà,* instant white.

13   Well, not quite white. Maybe Mediterranean—anathema at one point in history as well, but pretty much accepted, nowadays, in polite society.

14   It seemed natural that I should turn white. My parents had never encouraged me to be Chinese. Well, I should say that

my mom never did. That was her job, right? To teach me to be
Chinese? My father was more than willing to spread his Jew-
ishness around. He wasn't religious himself, but he loved the
idea of being Jewish. The history, the culture, the jokes. "Oy,
the goyim," he'd say. "They got no chutzpah."

But my mom was silent about her heritage. It was the fam- 15
ily secret. Although she'd been raised in New York in China-
town speaking Chinese, she never uttered a word of it in the
house. She said she couldn't remember any. And she let us
kids bust up her family heirlooms, like the dowry swords
made from old coins that came from her grandparents' wedding. My sister and I smacked them together in sword fights,
the coins tinkling down around us like a metallic rainshower
with each thrust and parry.

The only hint of her past came from food. We ate a lot of 16
Chinese food. Stirfry for dinner. Soy sauce-braised carp, or
grouse, or pheasant, whenever we caught any. And chop-
sticks. But she cooked and served it up without comment,
whereas my father went through this big, Jewish routine
whenever he opened a box of matzo. "Bar-ruch a-ta Adonai
eh-lo-hei-nu," he'd intone, ripping off the cellophane.

After I started looking white, I never thought much about 17
being Chinese. It was out of sight, so I pretty much pushed it
out of mind. This lasted until I started applying to colleges. I
had to fill out all these forms and check boxes specifying
which race I was. All of the schools took pride in touting the
"diversity" of their students, so I immediately identified myself as Chinese American. I thought it was an advantage—a
unique feature that made me stand out from an anonymous
sea of applicants. I checked those boxes for "Asian/Pacific Islander" proudly. It was my most Chinese moment.

But when I got into school, being Chinese didn't seem like 18
a good idea after all. On the one hand, believe it or not, there
was guilt. Guilt for not looking Chinese. This came up right
away. During orientation week my freshman year, the minority students' center held a big get-together for its "community." I felt like I should go, having checked all those boxes on
my admissions forms. I felt sort of like I'd used the organization. Already the guilt was setting in.

As soon as I walked into the students' center, I knew I'd 19
gone to the wrong place. Just about everyone there looked really ethnic—African American, Asian, Native American, Latino. And there I was, this white-looking guy. A few other
students looked kind of white, too, but at least their name

tags made up for it: last names like "Chan" or "Lee" or "Wong." What's my last name? Jewish. Great.

20   I stood around feeling really out of place until this other student began talking to me. He was African American. "So what are you?" he asked me, right away. I was relieved to tell him my mom was Chinese, like I was explaining myself. "Oh, OK, yeah, you can sort of see it," he said, after eyeing me carefully. "But would you look at some of the guys here? I don't know what they're supposed to be." I left a little later and never went back.

21   It was just as well that I wasn't welcome at the minority center, because I found out that the other students on my freshman hall frowned on minorities. It wasn't a matter of racism. They weren't racist. Everyone on my hall welcomed diversity. Everyone went to rallies on the Green to protest the university's investment in South Africa. It was a question of style, of fitting in, of dressing like everyone else, being laid back, sociable, and cool. Foreign students, the ones straight from China and Korea, weren't bad because they were Chinese or Korean. African American students had every right to eat by themselves in the dining hall and have their own frats. But those students just weren't that cool. They didn't fit in with what was normal. You never saw that kind of behavior in the "Breakfast Club"—a film all the students on my hall tried to emulate. Well, OK, maybe you saw it in "Sixteen Candles"—from that weird, geeky, Chinese guy.

22   Don't misunderstand. I didn't pretend that I was white. I still admitted that I was half Chinese to everyone. But I avoided doing anything that would make me stand out and get labeled "Asian American." There were a few close calls all the same. I remember the worst incident.

23   The summer before my junior year I was working in Pennsylvania. Every now and then I had a long weekend and went up to Providence to hang out with a house full of friends. Quite often, I'd get there to find that all my friends had ditched me to take off for New York or Boston or Maine. So it would be me alone in the house with this Taiwanese student who was subletting a room. He didn't fit in too well. He had a bad hair cut and wore sneakers with black socks all the time. He spoke with an accent and studied engineering and economics. I talked to him a little, and we went to some movies. One time his mother came up from New York, and I took the two of them to the beach in my beat-up VW bug. She cooked us dinner later. She seemed really happy that her son had such a good American friend.

One thing that really drove me crazy was that this Chinese 24
guy was sleeping in a lawn chair because he hadn't realized
that his sublet would be unfurnished. I knew that an old
roommate had left her bed in the last apartment I'd lived in,
and I still had a key. It turns out that she had arranged to sell
the damn thing to the next people moving in, but I didn't care.
I hated her guts. So I went over there, got the bed, tied it
down to my Volkswagen, and drove it back to the Chinese
guy. He was really grateful.

I didn't see him much after I gave him the bed. I went back 25
down to Pennsylvania and didn't return to the start of school.
I ran into him halfway through the first semester in the dining hall. He was still wearing those awful clothes and was
with a big group of foreign students. He came up to me in the
middle of the dining room, grinning like an idiot. He was still
thanking me for the damn bed. He turned to the foreign students. "This is my friend," he said, really loudly. I smiled nervously, conscious of everyone watching and listening. "He's
Chinese, too," he exclaimed. The foreign students all gave me
an odd look—I couldn't read it. Surprise? Confusion? I
thought it was admiration. I went crimson from head to foot.
I didn't see him after that, although he gave me his phone
number in Providence, and New York.

Whenever I think about the incident, I still blush. I'm em- 26
barrassed by the way I acted, embarrassed for even thinking
they admired me because they couldn't tell I was Chinese. I
guess, even though I don't look Chinese, I can't escape it. It
keeps coming back in the way I worry and in the way I treat
other people. You know, sometimes the problem isn't what
others do to you, it's what you do to yourself.

On the whole, though, I feel pretty lucky that I don't have 27
to look Chinese and deal with all that other crap as well. I
know what the alternative would be. I only need to look at my
uncle. That's my mother's brother. He lives in the Northeast,
has a professional job, and drives a Porsche. He's always
rushing around, going to the club, the office, the gym. He got
married my last year in college and I went out for the wedding. I didn't know his wife, I'd only met her once: vague impression of blonde hair and blue eyes, the type my uncle
always goes for.

As soon as my uncle sees me, it starts. "God, you're lucky," 28
he says. "I wish I looked like you." My uncle, he's always going on about being Chinese, like it's the worst thing in the
world. I guess he's really just like me. He only wants to feel
sure of himself and to fit in. But in addition to the normal

human burden of insecurity is added the extra weight of being Chinese. This does not help his self image. It's not that
society is "oppressing" him or that he's being turned down for
jobs or that he's being snubbed at parties or anything really
important. It's just that he's not white, so he's not quite
"normal."

29   Whenever he goes to a bar, he's never that "guy standing
over there," or the "guy in the expensive suit," or the "guy
with the black hair," or the "good-looking guy" to any of the
women. He's always "that Asian guy." As in: "Yeah, look over
there at that Asian guy looking at you." It drives him crazy.

30   My uncle's telling me all this while we're whipping down
the highway in his Porsche. We're going to get something to
eat. We're heading for this Yuppie bar and restaurant he goes
to a lot when suddenly he hits the brakes.

31   "Shit," he says. "We can't go there, I'm not dressed. Whenever I go there I try to look really nice. Good suit, tie. I can't
go looking like this." So he screeches down the next exit and
heads the Porsche the other way.

32   "Maybe we'll go to Wong's, this Chinese place," he says to
me. "Yeah, that'd be good. It's open late, service is fast, it
doesn't matter how I'm dressed. Yeah, maybe Wong's'd be
good."

33   But then he hits the brakes again. No, no, no. Not Wong's.
Not tonight. He's getting married tomorrow (my God, why is
he getting married?), he can't deal with Wong's tonight. Can't
deal, I guess, with the Chinese ambiance. Can't deal with the
fact that he blends in there, that it looks like he belongs. Can't
deal with it because he doesn't want to belong. That's Chinese,
it's not white, it's just not normal.

34   So we're off at the next exit and heading back in the direction we were first going. Yeah, we'll go to the other place. It'll
be OK. We'll sit at the bar. You don't have to dress up at the
bar.

35   "You're lucky," he says to me. "Really lucky."

Ranier Spencer
Race and Mixed Race

*Ranier Spencer contributed the following article—which he
subtitles "a personal tour"—to a book entitled* As We Are Now:
Mixed Blood Essays on Race and Identity, *edited by William
S. Penn and published in 1997. Since the book was published
by the University of California Press, it certainly has an academic audience in mind, but the subject and presentation of
the book indicate that it sought a wide readership.*

*The truth is that there are no races; there is nothing in the
world that can do all we ask race to do for us.*
—Kwame Anthony Appiah
In My Father's House

The Dream

999 Afro-Americans arranged in a line—not by height or age—   1
*but chromatically, from darkest to lightest, lightest to darkest.
Colors blending slowly, imperceptibly, into one another. Not
just colors, but lips, noses, and types of hair too...light people
with thick lips and wide noses, dark people with thin noses and
straight hair. Enter a white person to take her place in line.
Does she go to the end? No, for she isn't the palest one there—
not by far. After much searching she finally finds one who
looks similar to herself, so much so that they could be sisters.
The only difference between them is that the black woman's
eyes are blue, while her own are brown. Meanwhile, the color
line has begun to curve in on itself—enveloping her, pushing
her up against her near-twin—until it finally engulfs itself as
well and simply dissolves....*

Race is our historical curse, our great confusion. Race is   2
what future generations will look back on with incredulity
and pity, just as present-day third-graders look back with
amazed disbelief on the cosmology of learned medieval Europeans: "How could they have been so stupid?" My personal
engagement with race and racial identity is a consequence of
my own lived experience as a so-called mixed-race person.
That experience has revolved around what we in this country

refer to as the One-Drop Rule, the idea that any trace of African ancestry—one drop of black blood, so to speak—is enough to make a person wholly and unalterably black. My personal journey has taken me from unconscious acceptance of the One-Drop Rule, to what I thought was considered agreement with it, to, finally, a critical rejection of the rule and the racial categories on which it is based.

3   Questioning a concept so embedded and so naturalized as race always involves the breaking up of foundations and the toppling of superstructures that appear unassailable. In my case it involved appraising and ultimately rejecting everything I'd thought previously about identity. However, this is not to say that I feel myself a tragic mulatto—an overused and exaggerated term—for there is a vast difference between wondering whether one is black or white and questioning whether anyone really is.[1] It is the transition between these two modes of thought, the transition from being trapped within the constraints of an entrenched system of thought to challenging that system and ultimately transcending it that is the essence of my personal racial journey.

News Flash

> Grouped by the sickle cell gene, Yemenites, Greeks, New Guineans, Thais, and Dinkas all belong in one race, Norwegians and several black African peoples in another. Grouped by lactase retention, northern and central Europeans, Arabians, and certain west Africans share the same race, while other African blacks, east Asians, American Indians, southern Europeans, and Australian Aborigines all make up another race. Grouped by finger print patterns....[2]

4   If there were a blood test that could determine definitively whether a person had any sub-Saharan African ancestors within the past 2,000 years, I doubt many white people would take it. Disruptions, disjunctions—it's so important that skeletons stay in their closets. Indeed, if there were a test to show the precise extent of European ancestry in individual Afro-Americans—just how much Irish and just how much English, for instance—I don't think many would really want to know, for it would be just the kind of interesting information that would complicate the very simple view most Americans have of race and identity.[3]

The scientific jury is in and has been for some time. Bio- 5
logical races don't exist, never have. Everyone is always already mixed. The Mediterranean slave trade of the ancient
world moved sub-Saharan Africans into North Africa and
Southern Europe, and moved Black Sea Europeans into
North and sub-Saharan Africa. The later trans-Atlantic slave
trade ensured contact between southern and northern Europeans, sub-Saharan West Africans, and the indigenous peoples of North and South America. Additionally, the still more
recent phenomenon of passing has served especially well as a
vehicle for the injection of African genetic material into unsuspecting white American families. Easily over a hundred
thousand blacks have passed into white society, easily.[4] Keeping in mind that a successful act of passing is one that goes
undetected, what white person can know that there is no African branch (or root) on her family tree? So many different
people today carry so many different genetic heritages that in
all likelihood when two white Americans mate they are transferring African genetic material without even being aware of
it. If only they knew...

Into the Mix: Beginnings

Mixed-race identity, or *mestizaje,* can be experienced in a vari- 6
ety of ways. It can be ignored, put in context, glorified,
denied, and, as with race, reified. *Mestizaje* has, for me,
always been just below the surface. As far back as I can
remember, I've known I was mixed. That was the word my
mother used—*mixed.* I don't remember my father talking
about it at all. His work at sea took him away much of the
year, so it's fair to say I grew up in a white household, albeit
an immigrant one, specifically a German one. Psychologists
and sociologists tell us that placing a child in this type of situation is a sure-fire recipe for identity confusion, but when I
was young you could have fooled me. I was simply who I was.
I knew I was unique the same way my friends all knew that
they were themselves unique. All this business of either con-
forming to rigid identity types or being labeled confused is a
pipe dream of psychologists desperately in search of a
theory...but more on that later.

Though it didn't start out that way, our neighborhood of 7
post–World War II attached houses in Queens, New York,
eventually became a black neighborhood, so nearly all my

friends outside of school were black. I don't recall this confusing me either, however; and in no sense was I torn by loyalties between my friends and home. In fact, I don't understand how such a loyalty dichotomy could even be possible. I was a little colored boy—*mixed*, if that level of precision was called for, and it usually wasn't. My nonblack school friends saw my mother from time to time, yet I was still a little colored boy to them. Racial issues certainly didn't complicate my life or cause me to hate who I was. Being called *yellow* by someone marginally darker than me was hardly a major psychological event. Indeed, when I was growing up in the early 1960s, having very dark skin color was what brought one the most insults and criticisms. From my own point of view, the two things I hated most about myself are still clear as a bell to me: (1) having an irredeemably strange name and (2) having a head that was flat in the back. These two things brought me more teasing than any child deserves. I'd gladly have traded anything for a normal head and a regular name.

8   As I recall, nearly all my friends had some aspect of identity that was in conflict with some imagined standard and therefore subject to teasing. Some were adopted, some were fostered; some were very poor, others were rather well-off; some were unhip, some had physical deformities, some were retarded mentally; some were ugly, some were gay, while some had seemingly nothing *wrong* with them and were teased precisely because of it.[5] I had an entire neighborhood of friends who treated me as well and as poorly as any other kid we knew. If one of them called me an Oreo or Frankenstein, I likely responded by insulting his mother, and then we'd probably go over to my house or his to play Monopoly, chess, Sorry, or slot cars.[6] Sticks and stones and all that.

Psychobabble and the Sociology of Reification

9   *That the Earth is flat is as easy to prove as driving a car. You never turn upside-down no matter how far you travel.*

10   Too few people know the difference between racism (which does exist) and race (which doesn't). The reality of the former implies nothing about the latter. Unfortunately, though, it is much safer and much less complicated to believe that racism somehow proves race, even though racism no more validates race than did medieval European belief in a flat Earth actually make the Earth flat. Racism acts to sup-

port and perpetuate racist systems of categorization and social evil, much like Christianity supported and perpetuated the arrogant notion that the Earth was the center of the Universe while in no sense proving that false claim. The same goes for calling race a social reality, and treating it as if it existed simply because so many people think it does. It might seem reasonable on the surface to suggest that we ought to consider race to be real if people's belief in it affects their lives and others', for I could then say that race is de facto real under such conditions. But this would be to confuse the pathology with its (nonexistent) object.

Take the case of witchcraft, for instance. There have been   11
sorry times in this world when people have believed so strongly in witches that in their paranoia they've put innocent persons to death. Yet the fervor of that belief is no reason to look back and agree with the unenlightened of those days that witches indeed existed among them. There is an important conceptual difference between recognizing that other people's mistaken belief in witchcraft may affect the way you express yourself publicly and acquiescing in the same belief merely because many other people do.[7] To accept the notion that other persons' beliefs can make race or witchcraft a reality is to believe that the Earth actually was flat during medieval times in Europe.

So the claim that race is a social reality is a mystification   12
that takes us nowhere. When sociologists tell us that race is a social reality (their caveats notwithstanding), they perpetuate the myth of race and thereby become part of the problem, helping to ensure that the unreal is reified and that the truth becomes heresy. The analogy with flat-Earth thinking is perfect.

Even before elementary school I had a clear conception of   13
the racial dynamics in my environment. My mother was white, my father was black, and my older brother and I were mixed. On another level I also knew that I was black and my brother was white. It was a fact of life, nothing at all confusing about it.[8] Nine years my senior, his looks, his hair texture, and the fact that the first seven years of his life were spent in Germany as a German all worked to channel his identity choices in certain directions, while my looks and my environment led me elsewhere. He never announced it (did he need to?), but there was no doubt he considered himself white. From his own phenotype to that of his various girlfriends to his musical tastes—and, I might add, his disparaging remarks about mine—it was both plain to see and utterly

sensible, especially to someone who grew up as part of it. And this was in no way an identity crisis, for *he* certainly wasn't confused, and he's never to my knowledge been taken to be black by anyone who didn't know his background. It would be silly to even call it passing, which is a psychological phenomenon more than a physical one anyway. So, who, if not the individual, decides mixed-race identity? Do we really want to leave it up to color-struck psychologists and professional organizations such as the National Association of Black Social Workers?[9] Those of us who consider it vitally important to dismantle the racial categories put in place by racists long ago are frustrated, especially when so-called black intellectuals uphold the same illogical, racist categories and presume to dictate *healthy* identity choices for people other than themselves.

14   Psychologists inform us, on the one hand, that there are races and that there are stages of racial development (analogous perhaps to the cosmological formation of flat planets?). They assure us of the importance of telling mixed-race children in no uncertain terms that they are black, so that they will develop positive racial identities. Otherwise such children will grow to be confused individuals, marginal people, Oreos. On the other hand, people who question black and white racial categories are said by many black psychologists to be classic examples of confused identity development. People who question the racial categories that fly in the face of their own personal histories and everyday experiences are *diagnosed* by the psychologist ideologues as paranoid, schizophrenic, and in denial of their true identities. Conveniently then, disagreement with such prescribed racial identity is proof of faulty psychological development.

15   But the simplistic notion of possessing a distinct racial identity is, like the pompous idea that the Sun revolves around the Earth, a farce. There is no identity; there are identities, various and fluid. Depending on the situation and my mood I can identify as an American, German-American, Afro-American, Afro-German, male, New Yorker, Texan, Georgian, antiracialist, antisexist, academic, human, straight-ahead jazz loving, baby boomer. I can deploy these identities separately or in combination with full consistency. No one of them necessarily defines me more than any other; all of them come into play to constitute my whole personality. Moreover, some of my identities will be with me for life, while others will fall away, as my child identity became a past identity at adulthood.

Yet, many psychologists persist in declaring that there are   16
such things as monoracial identities, that they are the primary category of personal identification, that they are crucial
to our psychological well-being, and that each mentally
healthy American has one and only one. I can't help wondering, though, why the uncritical acceptance of racial identity
(like the one-time dogmatic belief in geocentrism and flat-
Earth theory) is taken to be a sign of mature reasoning, while
the questioning of imposed racial categories marks one as
confused, which sounds ominously less like objective sociology or psychology than like the double-speak of religious dog-
matists excommunicating those members of the flock who
dare inconveniently to think for themselves. Consider the absurdity of the racial analysis: if the mixed-race person has difficulty identifying with the so-called black group, she is
confused, fractured, and therefore sick; if she is well-adjusted
and happy in identifying as neither black nor white but
mixed, she is diagnosed is being utterly sick since the test of
healthy identity for mixed-race persons is that they identify as
black. And all the while the prospect of American blacks—
with their centuries of European admixture—identifying as
black only is taken to be a sign of robust psychological development, as if the healthiest person is the one who never, ever
questions the identity imposed on her.

I prefer to see an unwillingness to accept racial categories   17
as the *beginning* of mature identity development. Far from being confused about who I am, I'm certain it's the psychologists who haven't a clue about their own identities, much less
about the identities of others. Simple reflection on the impossibility of racial categories turns the dogma of such identities
upside-down by asking questions no psychologist or sociologist can answer. What is a race? How many races are there?
Are any of them pure? Why can blacks be mixed but not
whites? Why is a single drop of blood enough to make a person
black but far from enough to make one a U.S. government-
recognized Indian? Aren't racial purity and mixed-race incompatible ideas? It is a curious phenomenon that Americans, black and white alike, are perfectly willing to accept the
so-called racial passer as white until the $\frac{1}{2}$, $\frac{1}{4}$, or $\frac{1}{256}$ of African
ancestry is uncovered. In what way, though, has the person
herself changed on the basis of that new knowledge? If what
we truly are concerned about are positive identities, then being positive about the various identities one *has* is the issue,
not being positive about whatever mythical racial identity a

racist society says one ought to have. And so I fantasize: a racist white politician suddenly discovers he is $\frac{1}{256}$ black, which makes him therefore, according his own rules, all and only black. I can always hope.

Mixture, Unmixture, Dissolution

18   I grew through childhood and into adulthood without incident. There were no stares that I noticed when walking with my mother, no insults from passing cars when my brother would occasionally fetch me home for dinner, no social ostracism of which I was aware when the entire family went out to eat.[10] The dreaded racial identity crisis predicted by today's psychologists missed me somehow.[11] No longer a little colored boy, I was a full-fledged Afro-American, a presumably well-adjusted black male who (like most Afro-Americans) happened to be mixed in some degree.[12] It wasn't until I was in my thirties, teaching philosophy at a small northeastern college, that *mestizaje* began to surface and affect me. Initially, it was just a feeling that logically it made no sense to categorize myself as black or half-black when I was clearly half-white as well. And if some rule said I couldn't be white, then surely I couldn't be black either. It seemed to me strange and inconsistent that racially mixed people could be black or mixed but not white. What was the secret?

19   At about this time my identity development received a boost from my being exposed to two theories that shared as a central theme the idea that race is real and that blacks are superior to whites. The first of these, Afrocentricity, in addition to agreeing with the racist notion of the One-Drop Rule, claimed also that the one drop takes you all the way back to Africa. According to Afrocentrism, American blacks are in a proper relation to themselves only when they have placed Africa at the center of their being. Simply put, Afrocentrism is said to be natural for blacks, and Eurocentrism for whites. Of course, both *centrisms* are erroneous. Europe is no more at the center of all things for white Americans than Africa is for Afro-Americans. Afrocentrism is a tit-for-tat response to Eurocentrism and as such is every bit as flawed and racist as the fractured theory it proposes to displace.

20   The Afrocentrists stated that the Afro-American had a circular pattern of thought, was community-oriented, antimaterial, and had non-exploitive relations with nature (unless, of

course, he suffered from confused racial-identity development); the white American was by nature individualistic, material, and had a linear thought pattern. I wondered, though,
what was supposed to be natural for mixed-race persons?[13]
Perhaps I had an oval thought pattern, or did it alternate between linear and circular depending on the day of the week?
Even more difficult to understand was how I was to be material and antimaterial both at the same time. Afrocentric writers did not offer much in the way of clarification, the
following analysis being a case in point:

> Africanity is a comprehensive theme shared by all types of
> Black families, a commonality tied to the African cultural
> heritage. The basis of that African cultural heritage is
> described as a oneness of being (everyone and everything is a
> part of the Supreme being) and the interconnectedness of all
> things.[14]

Given the crude, binary structuring of Afrocentric theory,   21
even the most basic of questions concerning the extensive
mixture of European and African genetic material in Afro-
Americans, and why this should result in Africanity but not
Eurocanity for Afro-American families are questions left
unaddressed, presumably because they would only complicate the ideology at work.

The other theory I came across, the Sun People/Ice People   22
hypothesis, said that the skin pigment melanin made blacks
friendly and cooperative; while a corresponding lack thereof
made whites hateful and evil by nature. The reason given had
to do with the ancestors of black Americans living peaceful,
communal lives under the friendly sun in Africa, while Europeans huddled barbarously in caves during the Ice Ages.
Molefi Asante writes that "it is again the strong inherent desire in European man growing out of the nomadic, hunting
context of Europe that makes him seek conquest of nature."[15]
According to this theory, which along with Afrocentrism enjoys a sad but understandable currency among those it is
meant to uplift, I was destined by nature at the very least to
be friendly and evil at the same time. As an American of European *and* African descent it was unclear what I was to do.

What these two simplistic, essentialist, and thoroughly rac-   23
ist theories did for me was to make me see that there were
some very deep and very serious inconsistencies involved in
accepting racial categories—inconsistencies that were brought

out especially by *mestizaje*. Slowly, what I'd taken for granted for more than three decades became a nagging philosophical problem. What was it about blackness that allowed it to be mixed with whiteness and yet stay black? And conversely, what was it about whiteness that caused it to be corrupted irretrievably by one drop of black blood, one black sperm, one black egg?

24   If there is such a thing as racial-identity development, then this is where mine began—with the first stirrings of skepticism toward the idea of race. For me, it was more than wanting to acknowledge both sides of my heritage, much more. Simply arguing that I was both black *and* white was not to the point, was not going far enough, for it was only an intermediate step on the path to rejecting race altogether. *Mestizaje* opened my eyes to the tyranny of the One-Drop Rule and forced me to question its meaning. I began to understand mixture that valued one component over the other for the racist hegemony it was. More than that, though, I found *mestizaje* capable of negating race altogether. *Mestizaje* is a contingent concept, its existence depending entirely on a prior notion of race. If you take race to be real, then either *mestizaje* is impossible or it is not. If *mestizaje* is impossible people are born either black or white only and not in-between. But it is precisely because American society recognizes some people to be born in-between that we have the One-Drop Rule.

25   We know that American society accepts the idea of *mestizaje* if by no other evidence than the mounds of laws and regulations generated in the past 370-odd years that govern the determination of racial identity in our society. We know because of words such as *mulatto, quadroon,* and *octoroon;* we know because of court cases; and we know because of blood quanta. We are all mixed—not just the visible mulattos—but everyone else as well. One does not walk down the streets of any town or city in this country and mistake the black inhabitants for West Africans. That has been impossible since the end of the African slave trade.

26   So, as long as people take race to be real, they also take *mestizaje* to be real; but this reality signals the impossibility of race, for race is nothing if not a rigid categorization. Race thought is safe thought, uncomplicated and familiar, while mestizaje is a disruptive, subversive threat to turn the whole universe upside down. Race, if you take it seriously, is pure stability and fixity. It depends on the words *white* and *black*

having concrete and unchanging meanings. Race cannot allow ambiguity, fluidity, or mixture, for it then ceases to refer to something pure, something distinct. The absolute strength of *mestizaje* is the power it has—by its even being able to be thought—of dissolving race and everything associated with it, ultimately dissolving even itself.

It was, finally, with more than a bit of shock and disappointment that I came to realize that all my life I had—by accepting that I was black and by accepting that I was mixed—bought fully into a doctrine of white supremacy, had accepted that whiteness was purity and perfection, had accepted that blackness was something much less. How else to explain acceptance of the One-Drop Rule? By accepting the idea that because one of my parents was black and one white I was therefore mixed or black but not white, I was endorsing the most subtle and pervasive form of white supremacy ever to exist. The perfect hegemony is the one you never notice.   27

No, I'm not white, and I don't want to be. Nor am I mixed   28
or black either, for the words are meaningless as predicates in the real world. Like the terms *unicorn* and *flat Earth* they describe fantasies, unrealities, wishes. My journey has taken me past constructions of race, past constructions of mixed-race, and into an understanding of human difference that does not include race as a meaningful category. Despite the psychologists' predictions, I survived my formative years as a mixed-race/black child in a so-called white household. I wasn't confused then about my identity when I thought I was mixed and when I thought I was black, but I was certainly wrong. Likewise, while the psychologists today may not be confused about who they think they are, they too are as wrong as they can be. Who is in denial of true identity? Is it the person who accepts and endorses a racist system of classification that has no scientific or logical reality, or the person who rejects the categorizations of others in favor of self-definition as a complex, genetically mixed, multi-identified human being? Who indeed?

Notes

1. It is a special difficulty of engaging the topic of race that one often must utilize terms that have no meaning, such as *black* and *white*, if only in order to demonstrate that they have no meaning. Throughout this essay, the words *black* and *white* should be read as if they were contained in quotation marks

and should be understood as if they read *so-called black* and *so-called white*. Nor is this inconsistent, or somehow an admission that race exists. That people indeed think they are white or black or Asian no more makes them so than thinking one stands on a flat Earth makes it so.

2. Jared Diamond, "Race without Color," *Discover*, November 1994, 84–88.

3. References to *America* and *Americans* are meant to be national, not continental, in character.

4. F. James Davis, in *Who Is Black?: One Nation's Definition* (University Park: Pennsylvania State University Press, 1991), calculates that "passing probably reached an all-time peak between 1880 and 1925" (56). Estimates of the number of black persons passing over into white society range from 2,000 per year to 12,000 per year during this time period. Even using only the lower rate, at least 90,000 blacks began passing as white during those forty-five years alone.

5. Lest the sarcasm slip by unnoticed, there is of course nothing wrong with any of these traits.

6. The Oreo reference would have been to being brown on the outside and white on the inside like the popular cookies, and the Frankenstein reference would have been to my head. Being teased about my head hurt me so much, while being called an Oreo didn't hurt at all. There is a difference that children can easily discern between insults and teasing that have some measure of truth to them and those that are just plain silly. Children are tougher than many psychologists are willing to give them credit for.

7. It's one thing to acknowledge that many people believe in a thing, whether race or witchcraft, but quite another to accept the thing as real on the basis of people's belief in it. The latter is what the social-reality concept entails.

8. I can only shake my head at all the psychologists and sociologists running around like Chicken Little, spreading alarms about imminent identity crises in the fragile lives of mixed-race and transracially adopted black children. It's a wonder any of us older ones survived at all without the benefit of these professionals' intervention.

9. The National Association of Black Social Workers is a premier evangelizer of racial religion. This organization has gone on record as opposing the adoption of black children by white parents on the grounds that such transracially adopted children would suffer racial identity crises, despite study after longitudinal study demonstrating precisely the opposite. The position of the National Association of Black Social Workers is that such children should remain institutionalized and in foster care rather than be adopted by willing white parents. The even more ominous side of this ideology is the group's asser-

tion that transracial adoptions are tantamount to cultural genocide, as if the children in question are some sort of renewable resource whose fleeting chance to have a loving adoptive family is less important than their sacrifice on the altar of pseudoscientific, pseudopsychological, and pseudosociological racial mythology.

10. This is not to say that no such incidents ever occurred. Whether or not such things happened, I never noticed any and therefore was not subjected to the inevitable identity crises promised by the psychologists.

11. It's interesting to note, too, that other predictions of dire consequences made by today's psychologists were not borne out by my generation. For instance, between kindergarten and the start of my Ph.D. program I had exactly one black teacher, yet, by all accounts, the lack of racial role models as teachers was of little, if any, consequence in my academic development. The same is true for my childhood contemporaries, many of whom are now successful doctors, lawyers, and entrepreneurs. There are good reasons for stamping out racial discrimination in teaching, but the role-model argument is a wrong-headed attempt at pseudopsychology. Why not make specific demands for light- and dark-skinned black teachers? Why not insist on visibly and invisibly mixed teachers as well? Why should *black* alone be enough of a predicate, as if all Afro-Americans are exactly the same?

12. Afro-Americans are always already mixed; they are Euro-Americans as much as they are Afro-Americans. But it's a curious thing that in the United States even those blacks who are recognized specifically as mixed-race lose their mixed status when they have children and simply become black parents. A child with two white and two black grandparents is mixed if the maternal and paternal grandparents are of the same race respectively, but black if they are not. In what sense is the one child mixed and the other black? In what sense is neither of them white? The One-Drop Rule acts continuously to erase mixture and to perpetuate the mythology of distinct races.

13. Putting aside again the fact that most, if not all, American blacks are part European anyway.

14. Terry Kershaw, "Toward a Black Studies Paradigm: An Assessment and Some Directions," *Journal of Black Studies* 22, no. 4 (June 1992): 482.

15. Molefi K. Asante, *Afrocentricity* (Trenton, N.J.: Africa World Press, 1988), 81.

Works Cited

Appiah, Anthony Kwame. *In My Father's House: Africa in the Philosophy of Culture.* Oxford: Oxford University Press, 1992.

Asante, Molefi K. *Afrocentricity.* Trenton, N.J.: Africa World Press, 1988.

Davis, F. James. *Who Is Black?: One Nation's Definition.* University Park: Pennsylvania State University Press, 1991.

Diamond, Jared. "Race without Color." *Discover,* November 1994, 82–89.

Kershaw, Terry. "Toward a Black Studies Paradigm: An Assessment and Some Directions." *Journal of Black Studies* 22, no. 4 (June 1992): 477–493.

David Roediger

White Looks: Hairy Apes, True Stories, and Limbaugh's Laughs

David Roediger teaches history at the University of Minnesota. He has published many articles on the subject of "whiteness," as well as two recent books, The Wages of Whiteness *and* Towards the Abolition of Whiteness. *In 1997, he contributed the following essay to* Whiteness: A Critical Reader, *a collection of essays edited by Mike Hill that is directed at an academic audience and that contributes generally to the field of cultural studies.*

1   The chauvinism and touchiness that begin this otherwise modest and even-tempered essay derive from my having grown up along that part of the Mississippi River that divides Missouri from Illinois. It is easy to be chauvinistic about that stretch of the river, the lone portion of the Mississippi to divide slavery from freedom. Along the river and its banks, from Hannibal to East St. Louis and from St. Louis to Cairo, great artists and great art have long been created. To an unrivaled extent, that art has challenged the lie of white supremacy, both implicitly in its celebration of black beauty and creativity and explicitly in its probing of the relationship between race and freedom. Geniuses such as Miles Davis, Chuck Berry, Scott Joplin, Katherine Dunham, Redd Foxx, Tina Turner, Quincy Troupe, Josephine Baker, Maya Angelou, Ntozake Shange, and Mark Twain have drawn on experiences

along the river to chart, move, explode, and ignore the color line. Even T. S. Eliot, the writer most eager to lose the region's accents, carried with him much of the river's race lore and popular culture.

As a setting for works of genius, the river separating Missouri from Illinois is equally impressive. Huck Finn learns the differences between slavery and freedom drifting down the river and discovers that it is not worthwhile to be white. Twain sets *Pudd'nhead Wilson,* with its fierce ridiculing of biological racism, in a town between St. Louis and Cairo. Sterling Brown's "Tornado Blues," with its wonderful meditations on race and tragedy, unfolds in St. Louis. Herman Melville's *The Confidence Man,* on one level a remarkable exploration of whiteness as a performance, unfolds on a steamboat bound from St. Louis south.[1]

The churlishness follows from the chauvinism. These days I seldom get through a month without hearing or reading— often the source is someone on the Left—that "whatever his politics," Rush Limbaugh is a "genius." His "genius" sometimes is said to lie in comedy, sometimes in understanding media, sometimes in knowing how to speak to the American people, and often in all three. I (always managing to smile cordially when such nonsense is trumpeted about William F. Buckley's "seriousness" and "intellect") rage when the adulation comes Limbaugh's way. The reason lies largely in Limbaugh's hometown of Cape Girardeau, Missouri, and in his roots in the local elite of that southern Missouri River city. He is my age, and because I grew up in cities north and south of the Cape, his type is familiar to me. It was this long-standing distaste for his class and his kind that made me bristle when Limbaugh was praised until I began watching his television show. Then I realized how thoroughly his "genius" rests on an unreflective and banal performance of whiteness, whose elements were as familiar to me as Limbaugh's sneer.

This chapter pairs the analysis of one piece of cultural work on race written partly by Twain with one written by Limbaugh. The juxtaposition underlines not only the differences between genius and banality but also the reality that banality can carry much more social power than genius can in regard to white consciousness. More broadly, this chapter uses material from Twain and Limbaugh, as well as from Eugene O'Neill, to call for a theorizing of racial formation that takes into account both what I call the "white look" and the imperialist gaze. My conclusion examines questions of method that emerge from the pairing of Twain's "white look"

2

3

4

with Limbaugh's and O'Neill's, suggesting how we might examine historically why certain white looks work and others do not.

"Looking It" at Them

5   Eugene O'Neill's fabulous 1922 play *The Hairy Ape* contains a striking line with great potential to challenge and enrich a materialist analysis of race. The play's drama hinges on the demise of Yank, a coal handler in the stokehold of an ocean-going ship. In the early scenes, Yank personifies all-American manhood, rejecting any and all hints that his work enslaves him, disdaining the hard scrubbing after shifts that other workers view as necessary to avoid acquiring the complexion of a "piebald nigger" and loudly enjoining others on the gang to ravage the "hungry," dark, and female furnace. But Yank's bravado cannot survive his obsession over a brief encounter with the steel heiress/social worker Mildred Douglas.

6   Preternaturally white and paler still in the presence of heat and "bored by her own anemia," Douglas goes below, convinced that she can find life, or at least diversion there. She finds Yank and faints at the combination of his dirt, his ferocity, his power, and his "gorilla face." Yank's mates explain to him that Douglas had to come to look at "'er slaves," to survey "the bloody animals below," to take in an exhibition of "bleedin' monkeys in a menagerie."[2]

7   Since Yank is the focus of her gaze and her terror, he is most susceptible to the fear of being seen as "a queerer kind of baboon than ever you'd find in darkest Africy." Lost in anxious reflection, Yank becomes both nonwhite and inhuman. Declaring himself the enemy of the "white-faced skinny tarts and de boobs that marry 'em," Yank wildly spirals downward. He comes to agree that he is a "hairy ape" and ends his life entering the gorilla cage at a New York City zoo. He wants to join the gorilla's "gang" who, instead, savages him. But the play's most revealing line reveals that Douglas probably never called Yank an ape. Instead, responding to Yank's panicked questioning about exactly what she said, the Irish character Paddy tellingly remarks, "She looked it at you if she didn't say the word itself."[3]

8   The idea that whiteness and nonwhiteness can be "looked at" others sits uneasily in a play saturated with references to the concrete realities of class, work, and power. To see these

structural matters as counterposed to the subjectivity of a
look is wrong, however. As the best of the substantial recent
scholarship on "imperialist gazes" has demonstrated, looks
both frame and capture relations of power. They at once express racism and privilege, valorizing tropes that grow out of
and alter how classes within the imperialist powers see both
the colonized and one another. Not merely the symptom of
imperial exploitation, the imperialist gaze is a shared social
activity of imperialist domination and consciousness. According to Mary Louise Pratt, for example, the gaze therefore can
be a perfect site to study the relation of domination.[4]

Indeed, in many ways, the recent writing on the imperialist   9
gaze and imperialist culture illuminates the process by which
O'Neill makes plausible the transition from native-born
American worker to ape. Douglas displays the desire to categorize and classify that is characteristic of imperialist gazers,
to "investigate everything" in London's slum as she has done
in New York. The commanding position of surveying from
above, which is typical of imperialist gazes, appears in Douglas's obsession with going below and, negatively, in her collapse when she looks at the workers from their level. Her
search for ersatz reciprocity with those she watches also typifies the ways in which imperialism "looks."

Most important, the coal handlers who insist that Yank   10
(and they) are looked at like zoo animals are right. The zoos,
world's fairs, and natural history museums gathered the
world's, but especially Africa's and Asia's, animals, and sometimes humans, classifying and displaying them, creating hierarchies and spectacles. As Donna Haraway observes, the
display of monkeys and apes offer opportunities to teach lessons of race and hierarchy. Indeed, Anne McClintock posits
"simian imperialism" as an important link between scientific
and popular racism.[5]

The idea that an American-born white worker could be   11
looked into nonwhiteness becomes far more plausible in light
of the history of New York City's Bronx Zoo, which in the
early twentieth century housed a human with its monkeys
and apes in the hugely publicized exhibition of him, an African, Ota Benga. When he was released after protests and his
own rebellion, his controllers attempted to transform Benga
into a factory worker. Cornelia Sears's penetrating work on
the display of "man-like apes" and "ape-like men" in proximity demonstrates that the animality of humans received emphasis alongside the humanity of the primates.

12   The Bronx Zoo's director, William Temple Hornaday, constructed in his writings a hierarchy of animals from large
brained to small brained, paralleling imperialist taxonomies.
Hornaday postulated that both Ota Benga and other big-
brained mammals were "workers" in his zoo. His remarkable
"The Wild Animal's Bill of Rights" held that "superior" animals had "no more inherent right to live a life of lazy and lux-
urious ease…than a man or woman has to live without
work." Real life almost outdistanced O'Neill's art in the case
of the Bronx Zoo. In 1924, a blue-eyed young Scottish American proposed that Hornaday confine him in the ape house, to
be displayed with the "Orangoutang and the Chimpanzee."[6]

13   But the imperialist gaze and imperialist culture take us
only so far in understanding Mildred Douglas's ability to
"look" Yank out of the ranks of white humanity. Rooted in the
heritage of slavery as much as in the expansion of empire and
in U.S. peculiarities as much as in global realities, Douglas's
ability to do in Yank rested as much on a "white look" as on
an imperialist gaze.[7] Yank is every inch an American, so
much so that at one point he can scarcely recall his own
name, having for so long identified with his nickname.

14   O'Neill's play unfolds amidst the early 1920s race baiting of
Southern and Eastern European immigrants, which culmi-
nated in the race-based immigration restriction legislation of
1924. References to Italian "ginees" (guineas) and "wops" dot
the text, alongside slurs on Irish American workers ("pad-
dies" and "micks") who earlier faced questions about their
whiteness. The references to workers as "slaves," though not
peculiar to the United States, carried particular resonances in
Yank's nation, the only one to begin industrializing with a
huge slave labor force.

15   Most broadly, the drama in *The Hairy Ape* turns critically
on a vicious parody of the blackface tradition of theatrical
performance—a tradition that in the United States focuses on
black–white issues rather than on imperialism.[8] Minstrelsy
and vaudeville blackface made comedy out of the ability of
white performers and their audiences to find fraternity based
on the ease with which blackening could be put on and taken
off. O'Neill fashioned tragedy out of a proletarian blackface in
which "rivulets of sooty sweat" could hardly be scrubbed out
and ultimately helped kill Yank.[9] The audience was disinvited
to participate in those happy white looks, at the stage and one
another, which made minstrelsy such a powerful glue in
white consciousness. Instead, Mildred Douglas's white look

was divisive—and sad, dead, and deadly. Mark Twain's take
on the white look is even more withering than O'Neill's, and
Rush Limbaugh's performance of the white look banally re-
prises the minstrel tradition. Taken together, these gazes go
far toward defining the problems and possibilities of understanding the white look.

Another Look

In 1874, the ex-Confederate soldier Mark Twain sent a pair of   16
sketches to William Dean Howells, editor of the prestigious
Atlantic Monthly. Twain, trying hard to escape being typed
merely as a regional humorist, had high hopes for one of the
two stories. The other he titled "A True Story" and made more
modest claims for it. Inviting Howells to pay for it "as lightly
as you choose," he explained that it was not his creation.
Rather, he had merely "set down" the story of an "old colored
woman," altering it only by choosing to "begin at the beginning." The ex-abolitionist Howells, cool to the story Twain
favored, settled enthusiastically on "True Story."[10] Thus came
a major breakthrough in Twain's career—and the publication
of one of his most enduring short stories—even though he
professed not to have written the story at all. Instead he
presented—as the subtitle put it, "Word for Word as I Heard
It"—a marvelous critique of white looking, an "autoethnogra-
phy" fashioned by an ex-slave.[11]

"True Story" begins with a paragraph of stage setting. The   17
narrator, with other whites, gazes down from a farmhouse
porch at Aunt Rachel, a "mighty" sixty-year-old black servant
sitting on the steps "respectfully below our level." Drawn
from Twain's residence in New York State, at the outset the
tale features "peal after peal" of laughter, rather than dialogue, from Aunt Rachel. Unlike James Fenimore Cooper,
who earlier in the century reacted to blacks laughing in New
York "in a way that seemed to set their very hearts rattling in
their ribs" with a combination of fascination and unease,
Twain's narration is utterly at ease.

Her work done, Rachel is "under fire" from the white fam-   18
ily, but the narrator sees her being "chafed without mercy
and...enjoying it." Her pleasure is natural, its being "no more
trouble for her to laugh than it is for a bird to sing." Rachel's
performance can be just what the narrator wants it to be. His
language echoes fantasies in which white men look down on

black women as sexual objects—Rachel would "sit with her face in her hands and shake with throes of enjoyment which she could no longer get breath enough to express"—but his gaze is apparently innocent. "Aunt Rachel," he asks, "how is it that you've lived sixty years and never had any trouble?"[12]

19   Then the story turns true. Rachel "stops quaking," is silent, and finally asks the narrator, "Misto C—, is you in 'arnest?" The narrator, "sobered," trusts in his white looks: "Why you *can't* have had any trouble. I've never heard you sigh, and never seen your eye when there wasn't a laugh in it." Facing the narrator directly, Rachel tells him about a life full of trouble, of slavery from the viewpoint of someone who has "been one of 'em my own se'f." Rising as she speaks, she soon "towers above" the white listeners. She describes the slave sales that tore her from her husband and seven children, describing how she was beaten for her tears during the sales and how she attempted to resist losing her "little Henry," her last child sold, by using her chains to beat those taking him. She spins out a wonderfully impossible tale of how, years later during the Civil War, fate and faith reunite her with Henry. Her closing words are withering examples of the "vigorous eloquence" with which Twain credited Mary Ann Cord, the former slave said to have related the story: "Oh, no, Misto C—, I haven't had no trouble. An' no joy." White looks saw nothing in this view.[13]

20   "True Story" explicitly turns on gazes, but it does not grow out of the dynamics of imperialism, rather, out of race and slavery. Twain explodes the logic of the white look but not that of the imperialist gaze. That he may have had private, career-connected reasons for doing so, that what he "heard" was not an untainted truth, and that Twain somehow ended up with the byline for a black woman's story all are of interest. But so too is the remarkable set of circumstances that made possible such a critique of whiteness.

21   The fact that such major literary figures as Howells and Twain, from the North and the semi-South, could validate this critique of the viewpoint of whiteness is remarkable. Two decades earlier, when Herman Melville made a parallel effort to equate whiteness and blindness in *Benito Cereno*, his marvellous novella about a slave revolt, the reception had been largely uncomprehending. But in 1874, a decade after slaves freed themselves and four years after they achieved full citizenship and suffrage, whites could not look at black subjects in anything like this fixed manner. The behavior of many sup-

posedly privileged and loyal ex–house slaves who, like Aunt Rachel, supported the Union Army during the war and moved away from the plantation after it, made into a reality the possibility that African Americans "are not what they seem."[14] For a time, the leading ex-abolitionist and the leading ex-Rebel cultural figures in the nation could agree that white looks are white lies and could write about an ex-slave's self-representation, a view that was also a searing commentary on whiteness.

Rush to Whiteness

Rush Limbaugh likewise hands over his medium to a black   22
speaker, but with a far different look and intent from Twain's. He regularly replays videos of excerpts of speeches by prominent African Americans. But Limbaugh chooses the replays for their bombast and grandiloquence for a point or two that he might later challenge, and especially for their stammers, mispronunciations, or grammatical shakiness. During the clip, Limbaugh appears in a small box in a lower corner of the screen as well as live before an overwhelmingly white studio audience. He wordlessly and continually comments on the speech and on the very idea of black expertise with a panoply of rolled eyes, raised brows, nods, snickers, and chortles. At the clip's end, the camera surveys the studio audience's satisfaction with Rush's performance and Rush's satisfaction with himself. In millions of homes, bars, college "Rush Clubs," and Limbaugh rooms of discount steakhouses, the chain is continued. White viewers can look at themselves, looking at the studio audience, looking at Rush, looking at Lani Guinier, or at Kweisi—Rush says Queasy—Mfume.

Deep connections between Limbaugh's white looks and the   23
history of imperialist gazes determined that Dr. Joycelyn Elders would be the favorite object of his split-screen attention. Indeed, so treasured were the former surgeon general's appearances that when she was removed from office, Limbaugh and his listeners were nearly inconsolable. That she was an African American woman with medical expertise made Elders an appropriate choice for ridicule. Her scientific jargon, her frequent slips, and the pseudoarmy uniform of her office played perfectly into the right-wing populist delight in deflating liberal intellectual pretensions that run though

much of Limbaugh's lampooning of what he calls "the Left," black or white.

24   But beyond all that, Limbaugh brought together through Elders familiar elements of the long history of the imperialist display of nonwhite female bodies. Like the promoters of the Hottentot Venus, like P. T. Barnum, and like *National Geographic,* he offered to the white male gaze the combination of sexual suggestion, images of black female bodies, and scientific expertise. The wonderful (for Limbaugh) twist in this instance was that the black woman provided the talk about sex and science on which Limbaugh could sit in judgment. Indeed, Elders's final undoing, which resulted from her open discussion of masturbation, put virtually the whole complex of images and actions surrounding the *National Geographic* into a house of mirrors.[15]

25   The dynamics of Limbaugh's clowning, leering gambit, however, differ enough from what we know about the workings of the imperialist gaze to suggest again the need to scrutinize and historicize the white look as a distinct subject. Limbaugh's look clashes dramatically with one much-emphasized attribute of the imperialist gaze—its production of the illusion of an absence of the European male viewer, an absence one critic characterized as the "real meaning of the Orientalist project." Limbaugh is not only present as he looks but is never more active on the show than when watching others speak. Moreover, Limbaugh does not occupy the vantage point of the imperial "master of all I survey." He is instead boxed in, dwarfed, low, and *still* in power. That power hinges in critical ways on a sense of reciprocity within the look, as theorists of the imperialist gaze would put it. But Rush-on-TV seeks none of the reciprocity with nonwhite subjects that Pratt so ably discusses in *Imperial Eyes.* He instead cultivates the reciprocity of white entertainer, white studio audience, and white viewers to endow his look with awful power. There is no risk for Limbaugh, as Homi Bhabha argues that there is for imperialist gazers, of the "threatened return of the look" by the nonwhite subject.[16]

26   This white reciprocity rests in large part on Limbaugh's ability to reprise the role of the straight man/interlocutor in countless blackface entertainments. He registers the initial interest and growing exasperation with the supposed crudities and excesses of black speech, appearance, and behavior. To be reminded of this resonance is apposite in that it evokes the white audience's ritualized watching of blackface comedi-

ans and of one another that by the 1830s had already made the production of white looks an important commodity on the minstrel stage.

Anne McClintock offers a wonderful argument, centered 27 mainly on the British Empire, that at imperialism's peak, the "commodity racism" attaching imperial conquest to advertised images of domestic products replaced scientific racism. But in the United States, minstrelsy, the massive commodification of black labor, and the more generalized connections of "whiteness" and "property" all made the commodity and consciousness of race connect far earlier and, especially through minstrelsy, influenced subsequent imperialist gazes. The most ubiquitous symbol of commodity racism in the United States, Aunt Jemima, was directly inspired by minstrel performance.[17] The hundreds of millions of white looks at her image on boxes helped allay the anxieties raised by the possibility that the Aunt Rachels were not what they looked to be. The hundreds of millions of white looks at a chortling Rush in boxes on the screen likewise reestablish control over the meaning and direction of laughter across the color line.

The Workings of Whiteness

Rush Limbaugh's white look has ratings. If his producers 28 wish, they can obtain figures on just how many viewers decide to tune out and go to sleep as he gapes and guffaws at tapes of "The Reh-vaarh-oond Jock-soon," as he pronounces it. They can find out how many are moved to stay tuned. Sophomoric and repetitive to the point of ritual, Limbaugh's antics are infinitely more popular than any of the brilliant critiques of whiteness—from slaves' folktales, to Twain, to Melville, to James Baldwin, and to Toni Morrison. This hard fact creates dilemmas in our theoretical and historical approaches to the understanding of white looks.

One temptation is to assume that because a minstrel- 29 derived white look like Limbaugh's still carries so much power, it represents the "white look"—singular and virtually transhistorical. This misstates the case, as do analyses that posit a singular imperialist gaze. However much one look might work better than others, white looks also come in multiple forms, carrying differing class and gender dynamics. The task is to investigate why some looks come to undergird a mass sense of whiteness and others do not. Mildred Douglas's "looking it" at Yank clearly qualifies as a white look and, like all white looks, centers on inclusion and exclusion. But however convincing O'Neill is in showing that a white look could work to make Yank nonwhite at a particular early 1920s juncture, its extreme identification of whiteness with great wealth made race too narrowly and purely a stand-in for class to compete with the populist, "y'all come" whiteness typified by Limbaugh's look. (Indeed, in many shows Limbaugh first delivers his populist performances of whiteness and then goes on to defend explicitly great differences of wealth as a positive good.)

30   In understanding why and how white looks work, it is necessary to emphasize that such looks are historical. As such, they draw on long patterns of seeing, such as those of the minstrel tradition, but they also change over time. The ability of "A True Story"'s white look to be shared by Twain, Howells, and at least some readers in the era of emancipation was clearly greater than it would have been in the period of reconsolidated white supremacy and diminishing opportunities for the black self-activity of the early twentieth century, for example. Even Limbaugh's look responds to its historical context in ways that make it far more than just minstrelsy plus electrification. For all its glee, it remains very much a post–black freedom movement look. Its utter silence—its boxed-in protection against any dialogue with the Other—fits snugly into a situation described by Michael Omi and Howard Winant, who argue that the recent rightward political motion on race has not been able to find easily an open racist voice. The capture of the moral high ground by the civil rights movement's rhetoric of equality has proved to be quite durable.[18] Even initiatives against racial equality have adopted the rhetoric of equal treatment and pressed white claims to status as victims, from the anti–affirmative action campaigns to Limbaugh's own recent protests that black folks can get away with saying *nigger* but whites cannot.

31   In this soil has grown among the white Right a feeling of being silenced. Limbaugh frequently describes his own "rightness" and "excellence" as resting on his saying what his listeners already believe. But he equally shares and embodies silent white looks. Limbaugh's jowls and blankness of expression perfectly suit him to be a put-upon white man at a time when many of his watchers see their whiteness as a weight rather than a privilege. But at the same time, silence itself has become far more freighted with meaning. Thus, when the

successful 1991 Mississippi gubernatorial candidate Kirk Fordice closed his dramatic antiwelfare campaign advertisement, it was with silence and a still photograph of a black woman and her baby. Fordice trusted that white viewers would fill in the gaps.[19] Limbaugh is seldom without words but is perhaps never more dangerous than when he is. The performance enables Limbaugh to walk the border between the unspoken and the (until recently) unspeakable. He both participates in the refurbishment of an openly racist discourse à la *The Bell Curve* and its mainstream press attention and retains the possibility of defending his performance not only as a joke and a neutral attack on liberals but also on the grounds that he didn't say a word.

But if this powerful, banal, silent onlooking fills new functions at the end of the twentieth century, it also should remind us of the need to consider the white look in the much longer run. From slave sales and whippings, to highly publicized and massively attended lynchings, to the world's fair displays of confined nonwhites, to Rush Limbaugh, white consciousness was formed not only out of terror but also out of the mutual, self-recognizing and changing witness of terror, out of white looks at the oppression of others and the privileges of one another.

32

Notes

1. Michael North, "The Dialect in/of Modernism: Pound and Eliot's Racial Masquerade," *American Literary History* 4 (Spring 1992): 56–76; Sterling Brown, *Southern Road* (Boston: Beacon Press, 1974), pp. 70–72; Carolyn Karcher, *Shadow over the Promised Land* (Baton Rouge: Louisiana State University Press, 1980), pp. 256–57.
2. Eugene O'Neill, *The Hairy Ape, Anna Christie, The First Man* (New York: Boni and Liveright, 1923), pp. 37–38, 19, 33, 39.
3. Ibid., pp. 44, 84, 42.
4. George Robertson, Melina Mash, Lisa Tickner, Jon Bird, Barry Curtis, and Tim Putnam, eds., *Travelers' Tales: Narratives of Home and Displacement* (London: Routledge, 1994); Linda Nochlin, "The Imaginary Orient," in her *The Politics of Vision* (London: Routledge, 1991); Homi Bhabha, "The Other Question: The Stereotype of Colonial Discourse," *Screen* 24 (1983): 16–36; Catherine Lutz and Jane L. Collins, *Reading National Geographic* (Chicago: University of Chicago Press, 1993); Mary Louise Pratt, *Imperial Eyes: Travel Writing and Transculturation* (London: Routledge, 1992).
5. O'Neill, *Hairy Ape*, p. 21; Donna Haraway, *Primate Visions: Gender, Race and Nature in the World of Modern Science* (New

York: Routledge, 1989); Anne McClintock, "Soft-Soaping Empire: Commodity Racism and Imperial Advertising," in Robertson et al., eds., *Travelers' Tales,* p. 139; Stephen Jay Gould, *The Mismeasure of Man* (New York: Norton, 1981), pp. 113–45.

6. Phillips Verner Bradford and Harvey Blume, *Ota: The Pygmy in the Zoo* (New York: St. Martin's Press, 1992), pp. 176, 227–28; Robert Rydell, *All the World's a Fair: Visions of Empire at American International Exhibitions* (Chicago: University of Chicago Press, 1984); Cornelia Sears, "Man-like Apes and Ape-like Men," paper delivered at the annual meeting of the Organization of American Historians, Washington, DC, 1995.

7. See bell hooks, "Representations of Whiteness," in her *Black Looks: Race and Representations* (London: Turnaround, 1992), pp. 165–78; Richard Dyer, "White," *Screen* 29 (1988): 44–65.

8. Eric Lott, *Love and Theft: Blackface Minstrelsy and the American Working Class* (New York: Oxford University Press, 1993); Alexander Saxton, "Blackface Minstrelsy and Jacksonian Ideology," *American Quarterly* 27 (1975):3–28.

9. O'Neill, *Hairy Ape,* pp. 30–31.

10. Shelley Fisher Fishkin, *Was Huck Black? Mark Twain and African-American Voices* (New York: Oxford University Press, 1993), pp. 96–99.

11. Pratt, *Imperial Eyes,* pp. 7–9.

12. Twain, "A True Story," in Charles Neider, ed., *The Complete Stories of Mark Twain* (Garden City, NY: Doubleday, 1957), pp. 94–95; James Fenimore Cooper, *Satanshoe* (Albany: State University of New York Press, 1990 [1845]), pp. 70, 69–86.

13. Twain, "True Story," pp. 95, 96, 98; Fishkin, *Was Huck Black?* pp. 8, 7–9, 31–33, 36–38, 99.

14. Karcher, *Shadow over the Promised Land,* pp. 2, 13; Robin D. G. Kelly, "'We Are Not What We Seem': Rethinking Black Working-Class Opposition in the Jim Crow South," *Journal of American History* 80 (June 1993): 75–112; Leon F. Litwack, *Been in the Storm So Long; The Aftermath of Slavery* (New York: Knopf, 1979), esp. pp. 105–7, 136–38, 155–57; Elsa Barkley Brown, "Negotiating and Transforming the Public Sphere, African American Political Life in the Transition from Slavery to Freedom," *Public Culture* 7 (1994): 107–46.

15. Coco Fusco, *English Is Broken Here* (New York: New Press, 1995), pp. 37–63; Lutz and Collins, *Reading National Geographic,* Bluford Adams, *Barnumizing Popular Culture* (forthcoming).

16. Giselda Pollock, "Territories of Desire," in Robertson et al., eds., *Travelers' Tales,* p. 77.

17. Anne McClintock, *Imperial Leather: Race, Gender and Sexual Conquest* (New York: Routledge, 1995), pp. 31–36, 207–31; Cheryl Harris, "Whiteness as Property," *Harvard Law Review* 106 (June 1993): 1707–91; Maurice Manring, "Aunt Jemima

    Explained: The Old South, the Absent Mistress, and the Slave
    in a Box" (master's thesis, University of Missouri, 1993).
18. Michael Omi and Howard Winant, *Racial Formation in the
    United States* (New York: Routledge, 1994), pp. 140–42.
19. See David R. Roediger, *Towards the Abolition of Whiteness*
    (London: Verso, 1994), pp. 6–8. See also Rachel DuPlessis,
    "'Hoo, Hoo, Hoo': Some Episodes in the Construction of Mod-
    ern Whiteness," *American Literature* 67 (December 1995): 671,
    for the acute observation that the "free white gaze upon blacks
    is part of the power of whiteness."

DEFINING GENDER

John Adams and Abigail Adams
Letters

Here are two letters and part of a third written by John Adams of Massachusetts, one of the Founding Fathers, and later the second president, of the United States, and his wife Abigail Adams (a formidable person as well) in the spring of 1776—while the nation was considering declaring its freedom from British rule. The first was sent by Abigail to John while he was in Philadelphia debating with his colleagues the merits of a declaration of independence: Note how Abigail uses the occasion to press her husband to "remember the ladies" in his discussions about freedom from tyranny. She was probably thinking not of suffrage—too radical an idea—but of fairer laws regarding inheritance, wifebeating, and so forth. The second is John's response to that letter. The third, John Adams's letter to James Sullivan (who had proposed that one's power at the ballot box should be proportional to one's financial worth), indicates that John Adams understood all too well the probable long-term implications of what was being written in the Declaration.

Letter from Abigail Adams to John Adams, March 31, 1776

1   I long to hear that you have declared an independancy—and by the way in the new Code of Laws which I suppose it will be necessary for you to make I desire you would Remember the Ladies, and be more generous and favourable to them than your ancestors. Do not put such unlimited power into the hands of the Husbands. Remember all Men would be tyrants if they could. If perticuliar care and attention is not paid to the Laidies we are determined to foment a Rebelion, and will not hold ourselves bound by any Laws in which we have no voice, or Representation.

That your Sex are Naturally Tyrannical is a Truth so thor- 2
oughly established as to admit of no dispute, but such of you
as wish to be happy willingly give up the harsh title of Master for the more tender and endearing one of Friend. Why
then, not put it out of the power of the vicious and the Lawless to use us with cruelty and indignity with impunity. Men
of Sense in all Ages abhor those customs which treat us only
as the vassals of your Sex. Regard us then as Beings placed
by providence under your protection and in immitation of
the Supreem Being make use of that power only for our
happiness.

Letter from John Adams to Abigail Adams, April 14, 1776

As to Declarations of Independency, be patient. Read our 3
Privateering Laws, and our Commercial Laws. What signifies
a Word.

As to your extraordinary Code of Laws, I cannot but laugh. 4
We have been told that our Struggle has loosened the bands
of Government every where. That Children and Apprentices
were disobedient—that schools and Colledges were grown
turbulent—that Indians slighted their Guardians and Negroes
grew insolent to their Masters. But your Letter was the first
Intimation that another Tribe more numerous and powerfull
than all the rest were grown discontented.—This is rather too
coarse a Compliment but you are so saucy, I wont blot it out.

Depend upon it, We know better than to repeal our Mascu- 5
line systems. Altho they are in full Force, you know they are
little more than Theory. We dare not exert our Power in its
full Latitude. We are obliged to go fair, and softly, and in Practice you know We are the subjects. We have only the Name of
Masters, and rather than give up this, which would com-
pleatly subject Us to the Despotism of the Peticoat, I hope
General Washington, and all our brave Heroes would fight. I
am sure every good Politician would plot, as long as he would
against Despotism, Empire, Monarchy, Aristocracy, Oligar-
chy, or Ochlocracy.—A fine Story indeed. I begin to think the
Ministry as deep as they are wicked. After stirring up Tories,
Landjobbers, Trimmers, Bigots, Canadians, Indians, Negroes,
Hanoverians, Hessians, Russians, Irish Roman Catholicks,
Scotch Renegadoes, at last they have stimulated the[m] to de-
mand new Priviledges and threaten to rebell.

Letter from John Adams to James Sullivan, May 26, 1776

6 ... The same reasoning which will induce you to admit all men who have no property, to vote, with those who have, for those laws which affect the person, will prove that you ought to admit women and children; for, generally speaking, women and children have as good judgments, and as independent minds, as those men who are wholly destitute of property; these last being to all intents and purposes as much dependent upon others, who will please to feed, clothe, and employ them, as women are upon their husbands, or children on their parents.

7 As to your idea of proportioning the votes of men, in money matters, to the property they hold, it is utterly impracticable. There is no possible way of ascertaining, at any one time, how much every man in a community is worth; and if there was, so fluctuating is trade and property, that this state of it would change in half an hour. . . .

8 Depend upon it, Sir, it is dangerous to open so fruitful a source of controversy and altercation as would be opened by attempting to alter the qualifications of voters; there will be no end of it. New claims will arise; women will demand a vote; lads from twelve to twenty-one will think their rights not enough attended to; and every man who has not a farthing, will demand an equal voice with any other, in all acts of state. It tends to confound all distinctions, and prostrate all ranks to one common level.

Sojourner Truth

Ain't I a Woman?

Sojourner Truth's story is fascinating and moving. Born in Ulster County, New York, into slavery around 1797 and given the name Isabella, she was sold three times before she turned twelve. Perhaps sexually abused by one of her owners, she fled to freedom in 1827, a year before slavery was outlawed in New York. In New York City she worked as a domestic and fell in with an evangelical preacher who encouraged her efforts to convert prostitutes. Though illiterate, she managed to negate the sale of her son Peter to the South when her former "owner" tried to accomplish the sale. In 1843, inspired by mystical visions, she took the name Sojourner Truth and set off alone and undeterred by her illiteracy to preach and sing about religion and the abolition of slavery. By 1850, huge crowds were coming to witness the oratory of the ex-slave with the resounding voice and message. During the Civil War she was presented to President Lincoln at the White House. After the war she spoke out for women's suffrage, but she never gave up her spiritual and racial themes—or her humor and exuberance. She continued to lecture until near her death in Battle Creek, Michigan, in 1883.

Sojourner Truth accepted neither the physical inferiority of women nor the idea that they should be placed on pedestals; nor did she subordinate women's rights to the pursuit of racial equality. At a women's rights convention in May 1851, Sojourner Truth rose extemporaneously to rebut speakers who had impugned the rights and capabilities of women. According to an eyewitness who recorded the scene in his diary, this is what she said:

Well, children, where there is so much racket there must 1
be something out of kilter. I think that 'twixt the negroes of
the South and the women at the North, all talking about
rights, the white men will be in a fix pretty soon. But what's
all this here talking about?

That man over there says that women need to be helped into 2
carriages, and lifted over ditches, and to have the best place everywhere. Nobody ever helps me into carriages, or over mud-puddles, or gives me any best place! And ain't I a woman? Look at me! Look at my arm! I have ploughed and planted, and gathered into barns, and no man could head me! And ain't I a

woman? I could work as much and eat as much as a man—
when I could get it—and bear the lash as well! And ain't I a
woman? I have borne thirteen children, and seen them most all
sold off to slavery, and when I cried out with my mother's grief,
none but Jesus heard me! And ain't I a woman?

3   Then they talk about this thing in the head; what's this they
call it? [Intellect, someone whispers.] That's it, honey. What's
that got to do with women's rights or negro's rights? If my cup
won't hold but a pint, and yours holds a quart, wouldn't you
be mean not to let me have my little half-measure full?

4   Then that little man in black there, he says women can't
have as much rights as men, 'cause Christ wasn't a woman!
Where did your Christ come from? Where did your Christ
come from? From God and a woman! Man had nothing to do
with Him.

5   If the first woman God ever made was strong enough to
turn the world upside down all alone, these women together
ought to be able to turn it back, and get it right side up again!
And now they is asking to do it, the men better let them.

6   Obliged to you for hearing on me, and now old Sojourner
ain't got nothing more to say.

Susan Glaspell

Trifles

*Susan Glaspell (1882–1948), an Iowan by birth and educa-
tion, moved east in 1911. A Pulitzer Prize–winning dramatist
and a prolific fiction writer, she cofounded the Provincetown
Playhouse on Cape Cod in 1915, which became a center for
experimental and innovative drama. In 1916, she wrote* Trifles,
*the one-act play reprinted here; then she adapted it a few
months later into the story "A Jury of Her Peers."*

Characters

GEORGE HENDERSON, *County Attorney*
HENRY PETERS, *Sheriff*
LEWIS HALE, *A Neighboring Farmer*
MRS. PETERS
MRS. HALE

SCENE

The kitchen in the now abandoned farmhouse of JOHN WRIGHT, *a*   1
gloomy kitchen, and left without having been put in order—
unwashed pans under the sink, a loaf of bread outside the
breadbox, a dish towel on the table—other signs of incompleted
work. At the rear the outer door opens and the SHERIFF *comes in*
followed by the COUNTY ATTORNEY *and* HALE. *The* SHERIFF *and* HALE
are men in middle life, the COUNTY ATTORNEY *is a young man; all*
are much bundled up and go at once to the stove. They are fol-
lowed by two women—the SHERIFF's *wife first; she is a slight wiry*
woman, a thin nervous face. MRS. HALE *is larger and would ordi-*
narily be called more comfortable looking, but she is disturbed
now and looks fearfully about as she enters. The women have
come in slowly, and stand close together near the door.

COUNTY ATTORNEY. [*Rubbing his hands.*] This feels good. Come   2
    up to the fire, ladies.

MRS. PETERS. [*After taking a step forward.*] I'm not—cold.   3

SHERIFF. [*Unbuttoning his overcoat and stepping away from the*   4
    stove as if to mark the beginning of official business.] Now,
    Mr. Hale, before we move things about, you explain to Mr.
    Henderson just what you saw when you came here yester-
    day morning.

COUNTY ATTORNEY. By the way, has anything been moved? Are   5
    things just as you left them yesterday?

SHERIFF. [*Looking about.*] It's just the same. When it dropped   6
    below zero last night I thought I'd better send Frank out
    this morning to make a fire for us—no use getting pneu-
    monia with a big case on, but I told him not to touch any-
    thing except the stove—and you know Frank.

COUNTY ATTORNEY. Somebody should have been left here   7
    yesterday.

SHERIFF. Oh—yesterday. When I had to send Frank to Morris   8
    Center for that man who went crazy—I want you to know I
    had my hands full yesterday. I knew you could get back
    from Omaha by today and as long as I went over every-
    thing here myself—

COUNTY ATTORNEY. Well, Mr. Hale, tell just what happened when   9
    you came here yesterday morning.

HALE. Harry and I had started to town with a load of potatoes.   10
    We came along the road from my place and as I got here I
    said, "I'm going to see if I can't get John Wright to go in
    with me on a party telephone." I spoke to Wright about it
    once before and he put me off, saying folks talked too
    much anyway, and all he asked was peace and quiet—I

guess you know about how much he talked himself; but I thought maybe if I went to the house and talked about it before his wife, though I said to Harry that I didn't know as what his wife wanted made much difference to John—

11   COUNTY ATTORNEY. Let's talk about that later, Mr. Hale. I do want to talk about that, but tell now just what happened when you got to the house.

12   HALE. I didn't hear or see anything; I knocked at the door, and still it was all quiet inside. I knew they must be up, it was past eight o'clock. So I knocked again, and I thought I heard somebody say, "Come in." I wasn't sure, I'm not sure yet, but I opened the door—this door [*Indicating the door by which the two women are still standing*] and there in that rocker—[*Pointing to it.*] sat Mrs. Wright. [*They all look at the rocker.*]

13   COUNTY ATTORNEY. What—was she doing?

14   HALE. She was rockin' back and forth. She had her apron in her hand and was kind of—pleating it.

15   COUNTY ATTORNEY. And how did she—look?

16   HALE. Well, she looked queer.

17   COUNTY ATTORNEY. How do you mean—queer?

18   HALE. Well, as if she didn't know what she was going to do next. And kind of done up.

19   COUNTY ATTORNEY. How did she seem to feel about your coming?

20   HALE. Why, I don't think she minded—one way or other. She didn't pay much attention. I said, "How do, Mrs. Wright, it's cold, ain't it?" And she said, "Is it?"—and went on kind of pleating at her apron. Well, I was surprised; she didn't ask me to come up to the stove, or to set down, but just sat there, not even looking at me, so I said, "I want to see John." And then she—laughed. I guess you would call it a laugh. I thought of Harry and the team outside, so I said a little sharp: "Can't I see John?" "No," she says, kind o' dull like. "Ain't he home?" says I. "Yes," says she, "he's home." "Then why can't I see him?" I asked her, out of patience. "'Cause he's dead," says she. *"Dead?"* says I. She just nod- ded her head, not getting a bit excited, but rockin' back and forth. "Why—where is he?" says I, not knowing what to say. She just pointed upstairs—like that [*Himself pointing to the room above.*] I got up, with the idea of going up there. I walked from there to here—then I says, "Why, what did he die of?" "He died of a rope round his neck," says she, and just went on pleatin' at her apron. Well, I went out and called Harry. I thought I might—need help. We went upstairs and there he was lyin'—

COUNTY ATTORNEY. I think I'd rather have you go into that   21
upstairs, where you can point it all out. Just go on now
with the rest of the story.

HALE. Well, my first thought was to get that rope off. It   22
looked . . . [*Stops, his face twitches*] . . . but Harry, he went up
to him, and he said, "No, he's dead all right, and we'd better not touch anything." So we went back down stairs.
She was still sitting that same way. "Has anybody been
notified?" I asked. "No," says she, unconcerned. "Who did
this, Mrs. Wright?" said Harry. He said it businesslike—
and she stopped pleatin' of her apron. "I don't know," she
says. "You don't *know*?" says Harry. "No," says she.
"Weren't you sleepin' in bed with him?" says Harry. "Yes,"
says she, "but I was on the inside." "Somebody slipped a
rope round his neck and strangled him and you didn't
wake up?" says Harry. "I didn't wake up," she said after
him. We must 'a looked as if we didn't see how that could
be, for after a minute she said, "I sleep sound." Harry was
going to ask her more questions but I said maybe we
ought to let her tell her story first to the coroner, or the
sheriff, so Harry went fast as he could to Rivers' place,
where there's a telephone.

COUNTY ATTORNEY. And what did Mrs. Wright do when she knew   23
that you had gone for the coroner?

HALE. She moved from that chair to this one over here [*Point-*   24
ing to a small chair in the corner.] and just sat there with
her hands held together and looking down. I got a feeling
that I ought to make some conversation, so I said I had
come in to see if John wanted to put in a telephone, and at
that she started to laugh, and then she stopped and looked
at me—scared. [*The* COUNTY ATTORNEY, *who has had his note-*
book out, makes a note.] I dunno, maybe it wasn't scared. I
wouldn't like to say it was. Soon Harry got back, and then
Dr. Lloyd came, and you, Mr. Peters, and so I guess that's
all I know that you don't.

COUNTY ATTORNEY. [*Looking around.*] I guess we'll go upstairs   25
first—and then out to the barn and around there. [*To the*
SHERIFF] You're convinced that there was nothing important
here—nothing that would point to any motive.

SHERIFF. Nothing here but kitchen things.   26
[*The* COUNTY ATTORNEY, *after again looking around the kitchen,*
opens the door of a cupboard closet. He gets up on a chair
and looks on a shelf. Pulls his hand away, sticky.]

COUNTY ATTORNEY. Here's a nice mess.   27
[*The women draw nearer.*]

28 MRS. PETERS. [*To the other woman.*] Oh, her fruit; it did freeze. [*To the* COUNTY ATTORNEY] She worried about that when it turned so cold. She said the fire'd go out and her jars would break.

29 SHERIFF. Well, can you beat the women! Held for murder and worryin' about her preserves.

30 COUNTY ATTORNEY. I guess before we're through she may have something more serious than preserves to worry about.

31 HALE. Well, women are used to worrying over trifles. [*The two women move a little closer together.*]

32 COUNTY ATTORNEY. [*With the gallantry of a young politician.*] And yet, for all their worries, what would we do without the ladies? [*The women do not unbend. He goes to the sink, takes a dipperful of water from the pail and pouring it into a basin, washes his hands. Starts to wipe them on the roller towel, turns it for a cleaner place.*] Dirty towels! [*Kicks his foot against the pans under the sink.*] Not much of a house-keeper, would you say, ladies?

33 MRS. HALE. [*Stiffly.*] There's a great deal of work to be done on a farm.

34 COUNTY ATTORNEY. To be sure. And yet [*With a little bow to her*] I know there are some Dickson county farmhouses which do not have such roller towels.
[*He gives it a pull to expose its full length again.*]

35 MRS. HALE. Those towels get dirty awful quick. Men's hands aren't always as clean as they might be.

36 COUNTY ATTORNEY. Ah, loyal to your sex, I see. But you and Mrs. Wright were neighbors. I suppose you were friends, too.

37 MRS. HALE. [*Shaking her head.*] I've not seen much of her of late years. I've not been in this house—it's more than a year.

38 COUNTY ATTORNEY. And why was that? You didn't like her?

39 MRS. HALE. I liked her all well enough. Farmers' wives have their hands full, Mr. Henderson. And then—

40 COUNTY ATTORNEY. Yes—?

41 MRS. HALE. [*Looking about.*] It never seemed a very cheerful place.

42 COUNTY ATTORNEY. No—it's not cheerful. I shouldn't say she had the homemaking instinct.

43 MRS. HALE. Well, I don't know as Wright had, either.

44 COUNTY ATTORNEY. You mean that they didn't get on very well?

45 MRS. HALE. No, I don't mean anything. But I don't think a place'd be any cheerfuller for John Wright's being in it.

46 COUNTY ATTORNEY. I'd like to talk more of that a little later. I want to get the lay of things upstairs now.
[*He goes to the left, where three steps lead to a stair door.*]

SHERIFF. I suppose anything Mrs. Peters does'll be all right. She 47
was to take in some clothes for her, you know, and a few little things. We left in such a hurry yesterday.

COUNTY ATTORNEY. Yes, but I would like to see what you take, 48
Mrs. Peters, and keep an eye out for anything that might be
of use to us.

MRS. PETERS. Yes, Mr. Henderson. 49
[*The women listen to the men's steps on the stairs, then look
about the kitchen.*]

MRS. HALE. I'd hate to have men coming into my kitchen, 50
snooping around and criticising.
[*She arranges the pans under sink which the* COUNTY ATTORNEY
had shoved out of place.]

MRS. PETERS. Of course it's no more than their duty. 51

MRS. HALE. Duty's all right, but I guess that deputy sheriff that 52
came out to make the fire might have got a little of this on.
[*Gives the roller towel a pull.*] Wish I'd thought of that
sooner. Seems mean to talk about her for not having things
slicked up when she had to come away in such a hurry.

MRS. PETERS. [*Who has gone to a small table in the left rear corner* 53
of the room, and lifted one end of a towel that covers a pan.]
She had bread set.
[*Stands still.*]

MRS. HALE. [*Eyes fixed on a loaf of bread beside the breadbox,* 54
*which is on a low shelf at the other side of the room. Moves
slowly toward it.*] She was going to put this in there. [*Picks
up loaf, then abruptly drops it. In a manner of returning to
familiar things.*] It's a shame about her fruit. I wonder if it's
all gone. [*Gets up on the chair and looks.*] I think there's
some here that's all right, Mrs. Peters. Yes—here; [*Holding
it toward the window.*] this is cherries too. [*Looking again.*]
I declare I believe that's the only one. [*Gets down, bottle in
her hand. Goes to the sink and wipes it off on the outside.*]
She'll feel awful bad after all her hard work in the hot
weather. I remember the afternoon I put up my cherries
last summer.
[*She puts the bottle on the big kitchen table, center of the
room. With a sigh, is about to sit down in the rocking-chair.
Before she is seated realizes what chair it is; with a slow look
at it, steps back. The chair which she has touched rocks back
and forth.*]

MRS. PETERS. Well, I must get those things from the front room 55
closet. [*She goes to the door at the right, but after looking
into the other room, steps back.*] You coming with me, Mrs.
Hale? You could help me carry them.

[*They go in the other room; reappear,* MRS. PETERS *carrying a dress and skirt,* MRS. HALE *following with a pair of shoes.*]

56   MRS. PETERS. My, it's cold in there.

[*She puts the clothes on the big table, and hurries to the stove.*]

57   MRS. HALE. [*Examining her skirt.*] Wright was close. I think maybe that's why she kept so much to herself. She didn't even belong to the Ladies Aid. I suppose she felt she couldn't do her part, and then you don't enjoy things when you feel shabby. She used to wear pretty clothes and be lively, when she was Minnie Foster, one of the town girls singing in the choir. But that—oh, that was thirty years ago. This all you was to take in?

58   MRS. PETERS. She said she wanted an apron. Funny thing to want, for there isn't much to get you dirty in jail, goodness knows. But I suppose just to make her feel more natural. She said they was in the top drawer in this cupboard. Yes, here. And then her little shawl that always hung behind the door. [*Opens stair door and looks.*] Yes, here it is.

[*Quickly shuts door leading upstairs.*]

59   MRS. HALE. [*Abruptly moving toward her.*] Mrs. Peters?

60   MRS. PETERS. Yes, Mrs. Hale?

61   MRS. HALE. Do you think she did it?

62   MRS. PETERS. [*In a frightened voice.*] Oh, I don't know.

63   MRS. HALE. Well, I don't think she did. Asking for an apron and her little shawl. Worrying about her fruit.

64   MRS. PETERS. [*Starts to speak, glances up, where footsteps are heard in the room above. In a low voice.*] Mr. Peters says it looks bad for her. Mr. Henderson is awful sarcastic in a speech and he'll make fun of her sayin' she didn't wake up.

65   MRS. HALE. Well, I guess John Wright didn't wake when they was slipping that rope under his neck.

66   MRS. PETERS. No, it's strange. It must have been done awful crafty and still. They say it was such a—funny way to kill a man, rigging it all up like that.

67   MRS. HALE. That's just what Mr. Hale said. There was a gun in the house. He says that's what he can't understand.

68   MRS. PETERS. Mr. Henderson said coming out that what was needed for the case was a motive; something to show anger, or—sudden feeling.

69   MRS. HALE. [*Who is standing by the table.*] Well, I don't see any signs of anger around here. [*She puts her hand on the dish towel which lies on the table, stands looking down at table, one half of which is clean, the other half messy.*] It's wiped to here. [*Makes a move as if to finish work, then turns and looks at loaf of bread outside the breadbox. Drops towel. In*

that voice of coming back to familiar things.] Wonder how
they are finding things upstairs. I hope she had it a little
more red-up up there. You know, it seems kind of *sneaking.*
Locking her up in town and then coming out here and trying to get her own house to turn against her!

MRS. PETERS. But Mrs. Hale, the law is the law.   70

MRS. HALE. I s'pose 'tis. [*Unbuttoning her coat.*] Better loosen up   71
your things, Mrs. Peters. You won't feel them when you go
out.

[MRS. PETERS *takes off her fur tippet, goes to hang it on hook at
back of room, stands looking at the under part of the small
corner table.*]

MRS. PETERS. She was piecing a quilt.   72

[*She brings the large sewing basket and they look at the
bright pieces.*]

MRS. HALE. It's log cabin pattern. Pretty, isn't it? I wonder if she   73
was goin' to quilt it or just knot it?

[*Footsteps have been heard coming down the stairs. The
SHERIFF enters followed by HALE and the COUNTY ATTORNEY.*]

SHERIFF. They wonder if she was going to quilt it or just knot it!   74

[*The men laugh; the women look abashed.*]

COUNTY ATTORNEY. [*Rubbing his hands over the stove.*] Frank's fire   75
didn't do much up there, did it? Well, let's go out to the
barn and get that cleared up.

[*The men go outside.*]

MRS. HALE. [*Resentfully.*] I don't know as there's anything so   76
strange, our takin' up our time with little things while
we're waiting for them to get the evidence. [*She sits down
at the big table smoothing out a block with decision.*] I don't
see as it's anything to laugh about.

MRS. PETERS. [*Apologetically.*] Of course they've got awful   77
important things on their minds.

[*Pulls up a chair and joins MRS. HALE at the table.*]

MRS. HALE. [*Examining another block.*] Mrs. Peters, look at this   78
one. Here, this is the one she was working on, and look at
the sewing! All the rest of it has been so nice and even. And
look at this! It's all over the place! Why, it looks as if she
didn't know what she was about!

[*After she has said this they look at each other, then start to
glance back at the door. After an instant MRS. HALE has pulled
at a knot and ripped the sewing.*]

MRS. PETERS. Oh, what are you doing, Mrs. Hale?   79

MRS. HALE. [*Mildly.*] Just pulling out a stitch or two that's not   80
sewed very good. [*Threading a needle.*] Bad sewing always
made me fidgety.

81 MRS. PETERS. [*Nervously.*] I don't think we ought to touch things.

82 MRS. HALE. I'll just finish up this end. [*Suddenly stopping and leaning forward.*] Mrs. Peters?

83 MRS. PETERS. Yes, Mrs. Hale?

84 MRS. HALE. What do you suppose she was so nervous about?

85 MRS. PETERS. Oh—I don't know. I don't know as she was nervous. I sometimes sew awful queer when I'm just tired. [MRS. HALE *starts to say something, looks at* MRS. PETERS, *then goes on sewing.*] Well, I must get these things wrapped up. They may be through sooner than we think. [*Putting apron and other things together.*] I wonder where I can find a piece of paper, and string.

86 MRS. HALE. In that cupboard, maybe.

87 MRS. PETERS. [*Looking in cupboard.*] Why, here's a birdcage. [*Holds it up.*] Did she have a bird, Mrs. Hale?

88 MRS. HALE. Why, I don't know whether she did or not—I've not been here for so long. There was a man around last year selling canaries cheap, but I don't know as she took one; maybe she did. She used to sing real pretty herself.

89 MRS. PETERS. [*Glancing around.*] Seems funny to think of a bird here. But she must have had one, or why would she have a cage? I wonder what happened to it.

90 MRS. HALE. I s'pose maybe the cat got it.

91 MRS. PETERS. No, she didn't have a cat. She's got that feeling some people have about cats—being afraid of them. My cat got in her room and she was real upset and asked me to take it out.

92 MRS. HALE. My sister Bessie was like that. Queer, ain't it?

93 MRS. PETERS. [*Examining the cage.*] Why, look at this door. It's broke. One hinge is pulled apart.

94 MRS. HALE. [*Looking too.*] Looks as if someone must have been rough with it.

95 MRS. PETERS. Why, yes.
    [*She brings the cage forward and puts it on the table.*]

96 MRS. HALE. I wish if they're going to find any evidence they'd be about it. I don't like this place.

97 MRS. PETERS. But I'm awful glad you came with me, Mrs. Hale. It would be lonesome for me sitting here alone.

98 MRS. HALE. It would, wouldn't it? [*Dropping her sewing.*] But I tell you what I do wish, Mrs. Peters. I wish I had come over sometimes when *she* was here. I—[*Looking around the room.*]—wish I had.

99 MRS. PETERS. But of course you were awful busy, Mrs. Hale—your house and your children.

MRS. HALE. I could've come. I stayed away because it weren't   100
cheerful—and that's why I ought to have come. I—I've never
liked this place. Maybe because it's down in a hollow and
you don't see the road. I dunno what it is but it's a lonesome
place and always was. I wish I had come over to see Minnie
Foster sometimes. I can see now—[*Shakes her head.*]

MRS. PETERS. Well, you mustn't reproach yourself, Mrs. Hale.   101
Somehow we just don't see how it is with other folks
until—something comes up.

MRS. HALE. Not having children makes less work—but it makes   102
a quiet house, and Wright out to work all day, and no company when he did come in. Did you know John Wright,
Mrs. Peters?

MRS. PETERS. Not to know him; I've seen him in town. They say   103
he was a good man.

MRS. HALE. Yes—good; he didn't drink, and kept his word as   104
well as most, I guess, and paid his debts. But he was a hard
man, Mrs. Peters. Just to pass the time of day with him—
[*Shivers.*] Like a raw wind that gets to the bone. [*Pauses,
her eye falling on the cage.*] I should think she would'a
wanted a bird. But what do you suppose went with it?

MRS. PETERS. I don't know, unless it got sick and died. [*She   105
reaches over and swings the broken door, swings it again.
Both women watch it.*]

MRS. HALE. You weren't raised round here, were you? [MRS.   106
PETERS *shakes her head.*] You didn't know—her?

MRS. PETERS. Not till they brought her yesterday.   107

MRS. HALE. She—come to think of it, she was kind of like a bird 108
herself—real sweet and pretty, but kind of timid and—fluttery. How—she—did—change. [*Silence; then as if struck by
a happy thought and relieved to get back to every day things.*]
Tell you what, Mrs. Peters, why don't you take the quilt in
with you? It might take up her mind.

MRS. PETERS. Why, I think that's a real nice idea, Mrs. Hale.   109
There couldn't possibly be any objection to it, could there?
Now, just what would I take? I wonder if her patches are in
here—and her things.

[*They look in the sewing basket.*]

MRS. HALE. Here's some red. I expect this has got sewing things 110
in it. [*Brings out a fancy box.*] What a pretty box. Looks like
something somebody would give you. Maybe her scissors
are in here. [*Opens box. Suddenly puts her hand to her
nose.*] Why—[MRS. PETERS *bends nearer, then turns her face
away.*] There's something wrapped up in this piece of silk.

MRS. PETERS. Why, this isn't her scissors.   111

112   MRS. HALE. [*Lifting the silk.*] Oh, Mrs. Peters—its—[MRS. PETERS
       bends closer.]
113   MRS. PETERS. It's the bird.
114   MRS. HALE. [*Jumping up.*] But, Mrs. Peters—look at it! Its neck!
       Look at its neck! It's all—other side *to.*
115   MRS. PETERS. Somebody—wrung—its—neck.
       [*Their eyes meet. A look of growing comprehension, of hor-
       ror. Steps are heard outside.* MRS. HALE *slips box under quilt
       pieces, and sinks into her chair. Enter* SHERIFF *and* COUNTY
       ATTORNEY. MRS. PETERS *rises.*]
116   COUNTY ATTORNEY. [*As one turning from serious things to little
       pleasantries.*] Well, ladies, have you decided whether she
       was going to quilt it or knot it?
117   MRS. PETERS. We think she was going to—knot it.
118   COUNTY ATTORNEY. Well, that's interesting, I'm sure. [*Seeing the
       birdcage.*] Has the bird flown?
119   MRS. HALE. [*Putting more quilt pieces over the box.*] We think
       the—cat got it.
120   COUNTY ATTORNEY. [*Preoccupied.*] Is there a cat?
       [MRS HALE *glances in a quick covert way at* MRS. PETERS.]
121   MRS. PETERS. Well, not *now.* They're superstitious, you know.
       They leave.
122   COUNTY ATTORNEY. [*To* SHERIFF PETERS, *continuing an interrupted
       conversation.*] No sign at all of anyone having come from
       the outside. Their own rope. Now let's go up again and go
       over it piece by piece. [*They start upstairs.*] It would have to
       have been someone who knew just the—[MRS. PETERS *sits
       down. The two women sit there not looking at one another,
       but as if peering into something and at the same time hold-
       ing back. When they talk now it is in the manner of feeling
       their way over strange ground, as if afraid of what they are
       saying, but as if they can not help saying it.*]
123   MRS. HALE. She liked the bird. She was going to bury it in that
       pretty box.
124   MRS. PETERS. [*In a whisper.*] When I was a girl—my kitten—there
       was a boy took a hatchet, and before my eyes—and before I
       could get there—[*Covers her face an instant.*] If they hadn't
       held me back I would have—[*Catches herself, looks upstairs
       where steps are heard, falters weakly.*]—hurt him.
125   MRS. HALE. [*With a slow look around her.*] I wonder how it
       would seem never to have had any children around.
       [*Pause.*] No, Wright wouldn't like the bird—a thing that
       sang. She used to sing. He killed that, too.
126   MRS. PETERS. [*Moving uneasily.*] We don't know who killed the
       bird.

MRS. HALE. I knew John Wright. 127

MRS. PETERS. It was an awful thing was done in this house that 128
night, Mrs. Hale. Killing a man while he slept, slipping a
rope around his neck that choked the life out of him.

MRS. HALE. His neck. Choked the life out of him. 129
[*Her hand goes out and rests on the birdcage.*]

MRS. PETERS. [*With rising voice.*] We don't know who killed him. 130
We don't *know.*

MRS. HALE. [*Her own feeling not interrupted.*] If there'd been 131
years and years of nothing, then a bird to sing to you, it
would be awful—still, after the bird was still.

MRS. PETERS. [*Something within her speaking.*] I know what still- 132
ness is. When we homesteaded in Dakota, and my first
baby died—after he was two years old, and me with no
other then—

MRS. HALE. [*Moving.*] How soon do you suppose they'll be 133
through, looking for the evidence?

MRS. PETERS. I know what stillness is. [*Pulling herself back.*] The 134
law has got to punish crime, Mrs. Hale.

MRS. HALE. [*Not as if answering that.*] I wish you'd seen Minnie 135
Foster when she wore a white dress with blue ribbons and
stood up there in the choir and sang. [*A look around the
room.*] Oh, I *wish* I'd come over here once in a while! That
was a crime! That was a crime! Who's going to punish
that?

MRS. PETERS. [*Looking upstairs.*] We mustn't—take on. 136

MRS. HALE. I might have known she needed help! I know how 137
things can be—for women. I tell you, it's queer, Mrs. Peters.
We live close together and we live far apart. We all go
through the same things—it's all just a different kind of the
same thing. [*Brushes her eyes; noticing the bottle of fruit,
reaches out for it.*] If I was you I wouldn't tell her her fruit
was gone. Tell her it *ain't.* Tell her it's all right. Take this in
to prove it to her. She—she may never know whether it was
broke or not.

MRS. PETERS. [*Takes the bottle, looks about for something to wrap 138
it in; takes petticoat from the clothes brought from the other
room, very nervously begins winding this around the bottle.
In a false voice.*] My, it's a good thing the men couldn't hear
us. Wouldn't they just laugh! Getting all stirred up over a
little thing like a—dead canary. As if that could have anything to do with—with—wouldn't they *laugh!*
[*The men are heard coming down stairs.*]

MRS. HALE. [*Under her breath.*] Maybe they would—maybe they 139
wouldn't.

140 COUNTY ATTORNEY. No, Peters, it's all perfectly clear except a reason for doing it. But you know juries when it comes to
women. If there was some definite thing. Something to
show—something to make a story about—a thing that
would connect up with this strange way of doing it—[*The
women's eyes meet for an instant. Enter* HALE *from outer door.*]

141 HALE. Well, I've got the team around. Pretty cold out there.

142 COUNTY ATTORNEY. I'm going to stay here a while by myself. [*To
the* SHERIFF.] You can send Frank out for me, can't you? I
want to go over everything. I'm not satisfied that we can't
do better.

143 SHERIFF. Do you want to see what Mrs. Peters is going to take
in? [*The* COUNTY ATTORNEY *goes to the table, picks up the apron,
laughs.*]

144 COUNTY ATTORNEY. Oh, I guess they're not very dangerous things
the ladies have picked out. [*Moves a few things about, disturbing the quilt pieces which cover the box. Steps back.*] No,
Mrs. Peters doesn't need supervising. For that matter, a
sheriff's wife is married to the law. Ever think of it that way,
Mrs. Peters?

145 MRS. PETERS. Not—just that way.

146 SHERIFF. [*Chuckling.*] Married to the law. [*Moves toward the
other room.*] I just want you to come in here a minute,
George. We ought to take a look at these windows.

147 COUNTY ATTORNEY. [*Scoffingly.*] Oh, windows!

148 SHERIFF. We'll be right out, Mr. Hale.

[HALE *goes outside. The* SHERIFF *follows the* COUNTY ATTORNEY
into the other room. Then MRS. HALE *rises, hands tight
together, looking intensely at* MRS. PETERS, *whose eyes make a
slow turn, finally meeting* MRS. HALE'S. *A moment* MRS. HALE
*holds her, then her own eyes point the way to where the box
is concealed. Suddenly* MRS. PETERS *throws back quilt pieces
and tries to put the box in the bag she is wearing. It is too big.
She opens box, starts to take bird out, cannot touch it, goes
to pieces, stands there helpless. Sound of a knob turning in
the other room.* MRS. HALE *snatches the box and puts it in the
pocket of her big coat. Enter* COUNTY ATTORNEY *and* SHERIFF.]

149 COUNTY ATTORNEY. [*Facetiously.*] Well, Henry, at least we found
out that she was not going to quilt it. She was going to—
what is it you call it, ladies?

150 MRS. HALE. [*Her hand against her pocket.*] We call it—knot it,
Mr. Henderson.

CURTAIN

Diane Wakoski
Belly Dancer

Diane Wakoski (born 1937) has spent much of her life in New York, though she was born in Whittier, California, and educated at Berkeley. She now teaches at Michigan State University. This poem is from Trilogy *(1966), one of several collections of her poetry.*

Can these movements which move themselves   1
be the substance of my attraction?
Where does this thin green silk come from that covers my
    body?
Surely any woman wearing such fabrics
would move her body just to feel them touching every part of
    her.

Yet most of the women frown, or look away, or laugh stiffly.   2
They are afraid of these materials and these movements in
    some way.
The psychologists would say they are afraid of themselves,
    somehow.
Perhaps awakening too much desire—
that their men could never satisfy?

So they keep themselves laced and buttoned and made up   3
in hopes that the framework will keep them stiff enough not
    to feel
the whole register.
In hopes that they will not have to experience that un-quench-
    able desire for rhythm and contact.

If a snake glided across this floor   4
most of them would faint or shrink away.
Yet that movement could be their own.
That smooth movement frightens them—
awakening ancestors and relatives to the tips of the arms and
    toes.

So my bare feet   5
and my thin green silks
my bells and finger cymbals
offend them—frighten their old-young bodies.

While the men simper and leer—
glad for the vicarious experience and exercise.
They do not realize how I scorn them:
or how I dance for their frightened,
unawakened, sweet
women.

Jamaica Kincaid

Girl

Born in St. Johns, on the Caribbean island of Antigua (the subject and setting of her 1988 book Small Place*), Jamaica Kincaid now lives with her family in Vermont. She is the author of a number of books of fiction, most of them derived from her own personal experiences, including* At the Bottom of the River *(1983), which contains the following chapter, titled "Girl." "Girl" also stands quite well on its own, however: Indeed, it first appeared on its own in the pages of* The New Yorker, *a monthly review of arts, letters, and public affairs that has a reputation for publishing outstanding writing and writers.*

1   Wash the white clothes on Monday and put them on the stone heap; wash the color clothes on Tuesday and put them on the clothesline to dry; don't walk barehead in the hot sun; cook pumpkin fritters in very hot sweet oil; soak your little clothes right after you take them off; when buying cotton to make yourself a nice blouse, be sure that it doesn't have gum on it, because that way it won't hold up well after a wash; soak salt fish overnight before you cook it; is it true that you sing benna in Sunday school?; always eat your food in such a way that it won't turn someone else's stomach; on Sundays try to walk like a lady and not like the slut you are so bent on becoming; don't sing benna in Sunday school; you mustn't speak to wharf-rat boys, not even to give directions; don't eat fruits on the street—flies will follow you; *but I don't sing benna on Sundays at all and never in Sunday school;* this is how to sew on a button; this is how to make a buttonhole for the button you have just sewed on; this is how to hem a dress

when you see the hem coming down and so to prevent yourself from looking like the slut I know you are so bent on becoming; this is how you iron your father's khaki shirt so that
it doesn't have a crease; this is how you iron your father's
khaki pants so that they don't have a crease; this is how you
grow okra—far from the house, because okra tree harbors red
ants; when you are growing dasheen, make sure it gets plenty
of water or else it makes your throat itch when you are eating
it; this is how you sweep a corner; this is how you sweep a
whole house; this is how you sweep a yard; this is how you
smile to someone you don't like too much; this how you smile
to someone you don't like at all; this is how you smile to
someone you like completely; this is how you set a table for
tea; this is how you set a table for dinner; this is how you set
a table for dinner with an important guest; this is how you set
a table for lunch; this is how you set a table for breakfast; this
is how to behave in the presence of men who don't know you
very well, and this way they won't recognize immediately the
slut I have warned you against becoming; be sure to wash every day, even if it is with your own spit; don't squat down to
play marbles—you are not a boy, you know; don't pick people's flowers—you might catch something; don't throw stones
at blackbirds, because it might not be a blackbird at all; this is
how to make a bread pudding; this is how to make doukona;
this is how to make pepper pot; this is how to make a good
medicine for a cold; this is how to make a good medicine to
throw away a child before it even becomes a child; this is how
to catch a fish; this is how to throw back a fish you don't like,
and that way something bad won't fall on you; this is how to
bully a man; this is how a man bullies you; this is how to love
a man, and if this doesn't work there are other ways, and if
they don't work don't feel too bad about giving up; this is how
to spit up in the air if you feel like it and this is how to move
quick so that it doesn't fall on you; this is how to make ends
meet; always squeeze bread to make sure it's fresh; *but what if
the baker won't let me feel the bread?;* you mean to say that after all you are really going to be the kind of woman who the
baker won't let near the bread?

Judy Syfers Brady
Why I Want a Wife

Judy Syfers Brady (born in 1937), active in support of women's causes, was educated at the University of Iowa. She now lives in San Francisco. This well-known essay appeared in the very first issue of Ms. *in 1972.*

1   I belong to that classification of people known as wives. I am A Wife. And, not altogether incidentally, I am a mother.

2   Not too long ago a male friend of mine appeared on the scene fresh from a recent divorce. He had one child, who is, of course, with his ex-wife. He is looking for another wife. As I thought about him while I was ironing one evening, it suddenly occurred to me that I, too, would like to have a wife. Why do I want a wife?

3   I would like to go back to school so that I can become economically independent, support myself, and, if need be, support those dependent upon me. I want a wife who will work and send me to school. And while I am going to school I want a wife to take care of my children. I want a wife to keep track of the children's doctor and dentist appointments. And to keep track of mine, too. I want a wife to make sure my children eat properly and are kept clean. I want a wife who will wash the children's clothes and keep them mended. I want a wife who is a good nurturant attendant to my children, who arranges for their schooling, makes sure that they have an adequate social life with their peers, takes them to the park, the zoo, etc. I want a wife who takes care of the children when they are sick, a wife who arranges to be around when the children need special care, because, of course I cannot miss classes at school. My wife must arrange to lose time at work and not lose the job. It may mean a small cut in my wife's income from time to time, but I guess I can tolerate that. Needless to say, my wife will arrange and pay for the care of the children while my wife is working.

4   I want a wife who will take care of *my* physical needs. I want a wife who will keep my house clean. A wife who will pick up after my children, a wife who will pick up after me. I want a wife who will keep my clothes clean, ironed, mended, replaced when need be, and who will see to it that my personal things are kept in their proper place so that I can find what I need the minute I need it. I want a wife who cooks the

meals, a wife who is a *good* cook. I want a wife who will plan the menus, do the necessary grocery shopping, prepare the meals, serve them pleasantly, and then do the cleaning up while I do my studying. I want a wife who will care for me when I am sick and sympathize with my pain and loss of time from school. I want a wife to go along when our family takes a vacation so that someone can continue to care for me and my children when I need a rest and a change of scene.

I want a wife who will not bother me with rambling complaints about a wife's duties. But I want a wife who will listen to me when I feel the need to explain a rather difficult point I have come across in my course of studies. I want a wife who will type my papers for me when I have written them.   5

I want a wife who will take care of the details of my social life. When my wife and I are invited out by my friends, I want a wife who will take care of the babysitting arrangements. When I meet people at school that I like and want to entertain, I want a wife who will have the house clean, will prepare a special meal, serve it to me and my friends, and not interrupt when I talk about things that interest me and my friends. I want a wife who will have arranged that the children are fed and ready for bed before my guests arrive so that the children do not bother us. I want a wife who takes care of the needs of my guests so that they feel comfortable, who makes sure that they have an ashtray, that they are passed the hors d'oeuvres, that they are offered a second helping of the food, that their wine glasses are replenished when necessary, that their coffee is served to them as they like it. And I want a wife who knows that sometimes I need a night out by myself.   6

I want a wife who is sensitive to my sexual needs, a wife who makes love passionately and eagerly when I feel like it, a wife who makes sure that I am satisfied. And, of course, I want a wife who will not demand sexual attention when I am not in the mood for it. I want a wife who assumes the complete responsibility for birth control, because I do not want more children. I want a wife who will remain sexually faithful to me so that I do not have to clutter up my intellectual life with jealousies. And I want a wife who understands that *my* sexual needs may entail more than strict adherence to monogamy. I must, after all, be able to relate to people as fully as possible.   7

If, by chance, I find another person more suitable as a wife than the wife I already have, I want the liberty to replace my present wife with another one. Naturally, I will expect a fresh, new life; my wife will take the children and be solely responsible for them so that I am left free.   8

9   When I am through with school and have a job, I want my
wife to quit working and remain at home so that my wife can
more fully and completely take care of a wife's duties.

10   My God, who *wouldn't* want a wife?

Kurt Fernsler
Why I Want a Husband

Kurt Fernsler (born in 1969) grew up in State College, Pennsyl-
vania, and graduated in 1992 from Penn State with a degree in
finance. He is now pursuing a career in law. The following
essay was written in 1988 for a class of fellow student writers,
all of whom had read Judy Syfers Brady's essay "Why I Want a
Wife."

1   I am not a husband. I am, however, a male, and have a father who is a husband. I am also fortunate enough to know a
great many men who are husbands and will probably become
a husband myself someday.

2   I recently read Judy Syfers' essay "Why I Want a Wife" and
decided a reply was in order. Though not the most qualified
author for such an undertaking, I felt it my duty to make an
effort. For I now realize that just as Judy Syfers wants a wife,
I want a husband.

3   I want a husband who brings home the bacon. I mean really rakes in the bucks. After all, I certainly can't have anything less than the best. My husband must be driven to
succeed; he must climb the corporate ladder quickly and efficiently. He must make every payroll and meet every deadline.
Anything less would be completely unacceptable.

4   And I want a husband who bears the burden of being the
wage earner without complaint. He must deal with the
stresses of his job without bringing his problems home from
the office so as not to upset me. I want a husband who deals
patiently and lovingly with screaming, fighting kids even after
a tough day. I want a husband who, for fairness sake, does the
dishes (even sometimes the wash) for me so that I can put my
feet up after dinner. And, I want a husband who will leave the

office during a busy day of work to check on a sick child while I'm out on the town shopping.

I want a husband who will gladly eat cold leftovers for a   5
week while I am relaxing with a friend in sunny California. My husband will have to sit through boring PTA meetings and ice-cream socials after a rough day at work. My husband must, of course, be courteous and kind to meddling gossiping friends. (After all, I am entitled to my friends, too.) I want a husband who listens patiently to my panic about the over-sudsing washing machine while he silently sweats about the thousands of dollars he just borrowed from the bank.

I want a husband who keeps the house and lawn looking   6
beautiful in his spare time. He must be willing to spend his Saturday afternoons weeding my garden, and he must give up that tee time with the guys when I decide the grass is a little too long. I want one who makes sure the car is fixed (engines are so complicated and dirty!) and takes care of all the "little" chores around the house—raking leaves in the fall, shoveling snow in the winter, painting the house in spring. And I want one who will take out the garbage. When he's done with these chores, he can take the kids to the zoo or the park or the ball-game because these are things a father should share with his children.

I want a husband who gladly pays for his wife's shopping   7
sprees without ever asking her where all the money goes. He will understand that women need to spend time with their friends. I want a husband who will watch the kids on vacation so his wife can shop and work on her tan. (He must accept the fact that after traveling so many miles, a shopping trip is the only way to wind down.)

And I want my husband to be completely receptive to my   8
sexual needs. He must completely understand when I have a "headache." He will be sensitive to my problems and respect my private life. I want a husband who understands that I must have my freedom. He will be ready to accept the possi-bility that I may need to "find myself" and may walk out at any time. He will understand, of course, that I will take half of everything we own. He would keep the kids, however, because I would need to start a brand new life for myself.

I want a husband who will do all these things for me for-   9
ever or until I decide we have enough money to retire, or until he has a heart attack and collapses in a heap. Yes, I want a husband.

How could anyone live without one?   10

Andrew Kimbrell
A Time for Men to Pull Together

A former concert pianist and music teacher, Andrew Kimbrell is now an attorney and lobbyist who lives and works in the Washington, D.C., area. Among other things, he sees himself as one spokesman for the so-called men's movement, an effort to liberate people from the notion that men must remain rational, unemotional, competitive, efficient breadwinners. He published the following essay in the May/June 1991 issue of the Utne Reader, *a magazine that bills itself as "the best of the alternative press" because it republishes articles on public affairs from other publications—somewhat in the tradition of* Reader's Digest, *except that* Reader's Digest *is quite traditional whereas* Utne Reader *articles reflect a more liberal and exploratory perspective. Since he wrote this essay, Kimbrell has published* The Masculine Mystique: The Politics of Masculinity *(1995).*

> *Our civilization is a dingy ungentlemanly*
> *business; it drops so much out of a man.*
> —Robert Louis Stevenson

1   Men are hurting—badly. Despite rumors to the contrary, men as a gender are being devastated physically and psychically by our socioeconomic system. As American society continues to empower a small percentage of men—and a smaller but increasing percentage of women—it is causing significant confusion and anguish for the majority of men.

2   In recent years, there have been many impressive analyses documenting the exploitation of women in our culture. Unfortunately, little attention has been given to the massive disruption and destruction that our economic and political institutions have wrought on men. In fact, far too often, men as a gender have been thought of as synonymous with the power elite.

3   But thinking on this subject is beginning to change. Over the last decade, men have begun to realize that we cannot properly relate to one another, or understand how some of us in turn exploit others, until we have begun to appreciate the extent and nature of our dispossessed predicament. In a variety of ways, men across the country are beginning to mourn their losses and seek solutions.

This new sense of loss among men comes from the deterio- 4
ration of men's traditional roles as protectors of family and
the earth (although not the sole protectors)—what psychologist Robert Mannis calls the *generative* potential of men. And
much of this mourning also focuses on how men's energy is
often channeled in the direction of destruction—both of the
earth and its inhabitants.

The mission of many men today—both those involved in 5
the men's movement and others outside it—is to find new
ways that allow men to celebrate their generative potential
and reverse the cycle of destruction that characterizes men's
collective behavior today. These calls to action are not abstract or hypothetical. The oppression of men, especially in
the last several decades, can be easily seen in a disturbing upward spiral of male self-destruction, addiction, hopelessness,
and homelessness.

While suicide rates for women have been stable over the last 6
20 years, among men—especially white male teenagers—they
have increased rapidly. Currently, male teenagers are five
times more likely to take their own lives than females. Overall, men are committing suicide at four times the rate of
women. America's young men are also being ravaged by alcohol and drug abuse. Men between the ages of 18 and 29 suffer
alcohol dependency at three times the rate of women of the
same age group. More than two-thirds of all alcoholics are
men, and 50 percent more men are regular users of illicit
drugs than women. Men account for more than 90 percent of
arrests for alcohol and drug abuse violations.

A sense of hopelessness among America's young men is not 7
surprising. Real wages for men under 25 have actually declined over the last 20 years, and 60 percent of all high school
dropouts are males. These statistics, added to the fact that
more than 400,000 farmers have lost their land in the last decade, account in part for the increasing rate of unemployment among men, and for the fact that more than 80 percent
of America's homeless are men.

The stress on men is taking its toll. Men's life expectancy is 8
10 percent shorter than women's, and the incidence of stress-
related illnesses such as heart disease and certain cancers remains inordinately high among men.

And the situation for minority men is even worse. One out 9
of four black men between the ages of 20 and 29 is either in
jail, on probation, or on parole—ten times the proportion for
black women in the same age range. More black men are in
jail than in college, and there are 40 percent more black

women than black men studying in our nation's colleges and universities. Homicide is the leading cause of death among black males ages 15 to 24. Black males have the lowest life expectancy of any segment of the American population. Statistics for Native American and Hispanic men are also grim.

10   Men are also a large part of the growing crisis in the American family. Studies report that parents today spend 40 percent less time with their children than did parents in 1965, and men are increasingly isolated from their families by the pressures of work and the circumstances of divorce. In a recent poll, 72 percent of employed male respondents agreed that they are "torn by conflict" between their jobs and the desire to be with their families. Yet the average divorced American man spends less than two days a month with his children. Well over half of black male children are raised without fathers. While the trauma of separation and divorce affects all members of a family, it is especially poignant for sons: Researchers generally agree that boys at all ages are hardest hit by divorce.

The Enclosure of Men

11   The current crisis for men, which goes far beyond statistics, is nothing new. We have faced a legacy of loss, especially since the start of the mechanical age. From the Enclosure Acts, which forced families off the land in Tudor England, to the ongoing destruction of indigenous communities throughout the Third World, the demands of the industrial era have forced men off the land, out of the family and community, and into the factory and office. The male as steward of family and soil, craftsman, woodsman, native hunter, and fisherman has all but vanished.

12   As men became the primary cog in industrial production, they lost touch with the earth and the parts of themselves that needed the earth to survive. Men by the millions—who long prided themselves on their husbandry of family, community, and land—were forced into a system whose ultimate goal was to turn one man against another in the competitive "jungle" of industrialized society. As the industrial revolution advanced, men lost not only their independence and dignity, but also the sense of personal creativity and responsibility associated with individual crafts and small-scale farming.

The factory wrenched the father from the home, and he   13
often became a virtual nonentity in the household. By separating a man's work from his family, industrial society
caused the permanent alienation of father from son. Even
when the modern father returns to the house, he is often too
tired and too irritable from the tensions and tedium of work
in the factory or corporation to pay close attention to his
children. As Robert Bly, in his best-selling book *Iron John*
(1990, Addison-Wesley), has pointed out, "When a father, absent during the day, returns home at six, his children receive
only his temperament, and not his teaching." The family, and
especially sons, lose the presence of the father, uncle, and
other male role models. It is difficult to calculate the full impact that this pattern of paternal absence has had on family
and society over the last several generations.

While the loss of fathers is now beginning to be discussed,   14
men have yet to fully come to terms with the terrible loss of
sons during the mechanized wars of this century. World War
I, World War II, Korea, and Vietnam were what the poet Robert Graves called "holocausts of young men." In the battle-
fields of this century, hundreds of millions of men were killed
or injured. In World Wars I and II—in which more than 100
million soldiers were casualties—most of the victims were
teenage boys, the average age being 18.5 years.

Given this obvious evidence of our exploitation, it is re-   15
markable that so few men have acknowledged the genocide
on their gender over the last century—much less turned
against those responsible for this vast victimization. Women
have increasingly identified their oppression in society; men
have not. Thankfully, some men are now working to create a
movement, or community, that focuses on awareness and understanding of men's loss and pain as well as the potential for
healing. Because men's oppression is deeply rooted in the political and economic institutions of modern society, it is critical that awareness of these issues must be followed by action:
Men today need a comprehensive political program that
points the way toward liberation. Instead of grieving over and
acting on our loss of independence and generativity, modern
men have often engaged in denial—a denial that is linked to
the existence of a "male mystique." This defective mythology
of the modern age has created a "new man." The male mystique recasts what anthropologists have identified as the
traditional male role throughout history—a man, whether
hunter-gatherer or farmer, who is steeped in a creative and

sustaining relationship with his extended family and the earth household. In the place of this long-enduring, rooted masculine role, the male mystique has fostered a new image of men: autonomous, efficient, intensely self-interested, and disconnected from community and the earth.

16   The male mystique was spawned in the early days of the modern age. It combines Francis Bacon's idea that "knowledge is power" and Adam Smith's view that the highest good is "the individual exerting himself to his own advantage." This power-oriented, individualistic ideology was further solidified by the concepts of the survival of the fittest and the ethic of efficiency. The ideal man was no longer the wise farmer, but rather the most successful man-eater in the Darwinian corporate jungle.

17   The most tragic aspect of all this for us is that as the male mystique created the modern power elite, it destroyed male friendship and bonding. The male mystique teaches that the successful man is competitive, uncaring, unloving. It celebrates the ethic of isolation—it turns men permanently against each other in the tooth and claw world of making a living. As the Ivan Boesky-type character in the movie *Wall Street* tells his young apprentice, "If you need a friend, get a dog."

18   The male mystique also destroys men's ties to the earth. It embodies the view of 17th century British philosopher John Locke that "[l]and that is left wholly to nature is called, as indeed it is, waste." A sustainable relationship with the earth is sacrificed to material progress and conspicuous consumption.

19   Ironically, men's own sense of loss has fed the male mystique. As men become more and more powerless in their own lives, they are given more and more media images of excessive, caricatured masculinity with which to identify. Men look to manufactured macho characters from the Wild West, working-class America, and modern war in the hope of gaining some sense of what it means to be a man. The primary symbols of the male mystique are almost never caring fathers, stewards of the land, or community organizers. Instead, over several decades these aggressively masculine figures have evolved from the Western independent man (John Wayne, Gary Cooper) to the blue-collar macho man (Sly Stallone and Robert DeNiro) and finally to a variety of military and police figures concluding with the violent revelry of *Robocop*.

20   Modern men are entranced by this simulated masculinity— they experience danger, independence, success, sexuality, ide-

alism, and adventure as voyeurs. Meanwhile, in real life most men lead powerless, subservient lives in the factory or office—frightened of losing their jobs, mortgaged to the gills, and still feeling responsible for supporting their families. Their lauded independence—as well as most of their basic rights—disappear the minute they report for work. The disparity between their real lives and the macho images of masculinity perpetrated by the media confuses and confounds many men. In his book *The Men from the Boys,* Ray Raphael asks, "But is it really that manly to wield a jackhammer, or spend one's life in the mines? Physical labor is often mindless, repetitive, and exhausting. . . . The workers must be subservient while on the job, and subservience is hard to reconcile with the masculine ideal of personal power."

Men can no longer afford to lose themselves in denial. We   21
need to experience grief and anger over our losses and not buy into the pseudo-male stereotypes propagated by the male mystique. We are not, after all, what we are told we are.

At the same time, while recognizing the pervasive victim-   22
ization of women, we must resist the view of some feminists that maleness itself, and not the current systems of social control and production, is primarily responsible for the exploitation of women. For men who are sensitive to feminist thinking, this view of masculinity creates a confusing and debilitating double bind: We view ourselves as oppressors yet experience victimization on the personal and social level. Instead of blaming maleness, we must challenge the defective mythology of the male mystique. Neither the male mystique nor the denigration of maleness offers hope for the future.

Fortunately, we may be on the verge of a historic shift in   23
male consciousness. Recently, there has been a rediscovery of masculinity as a primal creative and generative force equal to that of the recently recognized creative and nurturing power of the feminine. A number of thinkers and activists are urging men to substitute empathy for efficiency, stewardship for exploitation, generosity for the competitiveness of the marketplace.

At the forefront of this movement have been poet Robert   24
Bly and others working with him: psychologist James Hillman, drummer Michael Meade, Jungian scholar Robert Moore. Bly has called for the recognition and reaffirmation of the "wild" man. As part of Bly's crusade, thousands of men have come together to seek a regeneration of their sexuality and power, as they reject the cerebral, desiccated world of our competitive corporate culture. Another compelling analysis is

that of Jungian therapist Robert Mannis, who has called for a renewal of the ethic of "husbandry," a sense of masculine obligation involved with generating and maintaining a stable relationship to one's family and to the earth itself. And a growing number of men are mounting other challenges to the male mystique. But so far, the men's movement has remained primarily therapeutic. Little effort has been made to extend the energy of male self-discovery into a practical social and political agenda.

25   As many of us come to mourn the lost fathers and sons of the last decades and seek to re-establish our ties to each other and to the earth, we need to find ways to change the political, social, and economic structures that have created this crisis. A "wild man" weekend in the woods, or intense man-to-man discussions, can be key experiences in self-discovery and personal empowerment. But these personal experiences are not enough to reverse the victimization of men. As the men's movement gathers strength, it is critical that this increasing sense of personal liberation be channeled into political action. Without significant changes in our society there will only be continued hopelessness and frustration for men. Moreover, a coordinated movement pressing for the liberation of men could be a key factor in ensuring that the struggle for a sustainable future for humanity and the earth succeeds.

26   What follows is a brief political platform for men, a short manifesto with which we can begin the process of organizing men as a positive political force working for a better future. This is the next step for the men's movement.

Fathers and Children

27   Political efforts focusing on the family must reassert men's bonds with the family and reverse the "lost father" syndrome. While any long-term plan for men's liberation requires significant changes in the very structure of our work and economic institutions, a number of intermediate steps are possible: We need to take a leadership role in supporting parental leave legislation, which gives working parents the right to take time from work to care for children or other family members. And we need to target the Bush administration for vetoing this vital legislation. Also needed is pro-child tax relief such as greatly expanding the young child tax credit, which would provide income relief and tax breaks to

families at a point when children need the most parental care and when income may be the lowest.

We should also be in the forefront of the movement push- 28
ing for changes in the workplace including more flexible hours, part-time work, job sharing, and home-based employment. As economic analyst William R. Mattox Jr. notes, a simple step toward making home-based employment more viable would be to loosen restrictions on claiming home office expenses as a tax deduction for parents. Men must also work strenuously in the legal arena to promote more liberal visitation rights for non-custodial parents and to assert appropriateness of the father as a custodial parent. Non-traditional family structures should also be given more recognition in our society, with acknowledgment of men's important roles as stepfathers, foster fathers, uncles, brothers, and mentors. We must seek legislative ways to recognize many men's commitments that do not fit traditional definitions of family.

Ecology as Male Politics

A sustainable environment is not merely one issue among 29
others. It is the crux of all issues in our age, including men's politics. The ecological struggles of our time offer a unique forum in which men can express their renewed sense of the wild and their traditional roles as creators, defenders of the family, and careful stewards of the earth.

The alienation of men from their rootedness to the land has 30
deprived us all of what John Muir called the "heart of wilderness." As part of our efforts to re-experience the wild in ourselves, we should actively become involved in experiencing the wilderness first hand and organize support for the protection of nature and endangered species. Men should also become what Robert Bly has called "inner warriors" for the earth, involving themselves in non-violent civil disobedience to protect wilderness areas from further destruction.

An important aspect of the masculine ethic is defense of 31
family. Pesticides and other toxic pollutants that poison our food, homes, water, and air represent a real danger, especially to children. Men need to be adamant in their call for limitations on the use of chemicals.

Wendell Berry has pointed out that the ecological crisis is 32
also a crisis of agriculture. If men are to recapture a true sense of stewardship and husbandry and affirm the "seedbearing," creative capacity of the male, they must, to the extent possible,

become involved in sustainable agriculture and organic farming and gardening. We should also initiate and support legislation that sustains our farming communities.

Men in the Classrooms and Community

33   In many communities, especially inner cities, men are absent not only from homes but also from the schools. Men must support the current efforts by black men's groups around the country to implement male-only early-grade classes taught by men. These programs provide role models and a surrogate paternal presence for young black males. We should also commit ourselves to having a far greater male presence in all elementary school education. Recent studies have shown that male grade school students have a higher level of achievement when they are taught by male teachers. Part-time or full-time home schooling options can also be helpful in providing men a great opportunity to be teachers—not just temperaments—to their children.

34   We need to revive our concern for community. Community-based boys' clubs, scout troops, sports leagues, and big brother programs have achieved significant success in helping fatherless male children find self-esteem. Men's groups must work to strengthen these organizations.

Men's Minds, Men's Bodies, and Work

35   Men need to join together to fight threats to male health including suicide, drug and alcohol abuse, AIDS, and stress diseases. We should support active prevention and education efforts aimed at these deadly threats. Most importantly, men need to be leaders in initiating and supporting holistic and psychotherapeutic approaches that directly link many of these health threats to the coercive nature of the male mystique and the current economic system. Changes in diet, reduction of drug and alcohol use, less stressful work environments, greater nurturing of and caring for men by other men, and fighting racism, hopelessness, and homelessness are all important, interconnected aspects of any male health initiative.

Men without Hope or Homes

36   Men need to support measures that promote small business and entrepreneurship, which will allow more people to engage in crafts and human-scale, community-oriented

enterprises. Also important is a commitment to appropriate, human-scale technologies such as renewable energy sources. Industrial and other inappropriate technologies have led to men's dispossession, degradation—and increasingly to unemployment.

A related struggle is eliminating racism. No group of men 37 is more dispossessed than minority men. White men should support and network with African-American and other minority men's groups. Violence and discrimination against men because of their sexual preference should also be challenged.

Men, who represent more than four-fifths of the homeless, 38 can no longer ignore this increasing social tragedy. Men's councils should develop support groups for the homeless in their communities.

The Holocaust of Men

As the primary victims of mechanized war, men must op- 39 pose this continued slaughter. Men need to realize that the traditional male concepts of the noble warrior are undermined and caricatured in the technological nightmare of modern warfare. Men must together become prime movers in dismantling the military-industrial establishment and redistributing defense spending toward a sustainable environment and protection of family, school, and community.

Men's Action Network

No area of the men's political agenda will be realized until 40 men can establish a network of activists to create collective action. A first step might be to create a high-profile national coalition of the men's councils that are growing around the country. This coalition, which could be called the Men's Action Network (MAN), could call for a national conference to define a comprehensive platform of men's concerns and to provide the political muscle to implement those ideas.

A Man Could Stand Up

The current generation of men face a unique moment in 41 history. Though often still trapped by economic coercion and psychological co-optation, we are beginning to see that there is a profound choice ahead. Will we choose to remain subservient tools of social and environmental destruction or to fight for rediscovery of the male as a full partner and participant in family, community, and the earth? Will we remain mesmerized by the male mystique, or will we reclaim the true meaning of our masculinity?

42   There is a world to gain. The male mystique, in which many of today's men—especially the most politically powerful—are trapped, is threatening the family and the planet with irreversible destruction. A men's movement based on the recovery of masculinity could renew much of the world we have lost. By changing types of work and work hours, we could break our subordination to corporate managers and return much of our work and lives to the household. We could once again be teaching, nurturing presences to our children. By devoting ourselves to meaningful work with appropriate technology, we could recover independence in our work and our spirit. By caring for each other, we could recover the dignity of our gender and heal the wounds of addiction and self-destruction. By becoming husbands to the earth, we could protect the wild and recover our creative connections with the forces and rhythms of nature.

43   Ultimately we must help fashion a world without the daily frustration and sorrow of having to view each other as a collection of competitors instead of a community of friends. We must celebrate the essence and rituals of our masculinity. We can no longer passively submit to the destruction of the household, the demise of self-employment, the disintegration of family and community, and the desecration of our earth.

44   Shortly after the First World War, Ford Madox Ford, one of this century's greatest writers, depicted 20th century men as continually pinned down in their trenches, unable to stand up for fear of annihilation. As the century closes, men remain pinned down by an economic and political system that daily forces millions of us into meaningless work, powerless lives, and self-destruction. The time has come for men to stand up.

Ursula K. Le Guin
Limberlost

Ursula K. Le Guin (born 1929) is one of the most respected science fiction and fantasy writers in America: perhaps you have read her children's books or poetry or short fiction or one of her many novels—maybe The Left Hand of Darkness *(1969) or* The Dispossessed *(1974) or one of the pieces of her Earthsea Trilogy. A resident of Portland, Oregon, a conservationist, and a passionate devotee of the western United States, she has received a National Book Award and a host of other prizes for her work. In 1992, she contributed her story "Limberlost" to a book of readings called* Women Respond to the Men's Movement, *edited by Kay Leigh Hagan and containing contributions by many prominent feminists. In an afterword, Le Guin notes that although the story is presented as fiction, nothing except its title is invented: the events depicted actually took place in 1985. Le Guin had been invited to a conference on "The Great Mother" in order to read from her novel* Always Coming Home, *which celebrates a society where gender issues have been resolved, when she experienced something akin to the events fictionalized here.*

The poet revolved slowly counterclockwise in the small, dark, not very deep pool. The novelist sat on the alder log that dammed the creek to make the pool. Also on the log were the poet's clothes, except his underpants. Coming upstream to the swimming hole, they had passed a naked nut-brown maid, beached and frontal to the sun; but she was young and they were not; and the poet was not Californian. "You don't mind if I'm old-fashioned about modesty?" he had asked, disarmingly. The novelist, although a Californian, did not mind. The poet's massive body was impressive enough as it was. Age, slacking here and tightening there what had been all smooth evenness in youth, gave pathos and dignity to that strong beast turning in the dark water. Among roots and the dark shadows of the banks, the hands and arms shone white. The novelist's bare feet, though tanned, also gleamed pallid under the water, as she sat rather less than comfortably on the log, wondering whether she should have pulled off shirt and jeans and joined the poet in his pool. She had been at his conference less than an hour and did not know the rules. Did he want a companion, or a spectator? Did it matter? She splashed the water with her feet and deplored her inability to do, to know, what

1

she wanted herself—fifty-five years old and sitting in adolescent paralysis, a bump on a log. Should I swim? I don't want to. I want to. Should I? Which underpants am I wearing? This is like the first day of summer camp. I want to go home. I ought to swim. Ought I? Now?

2   The poet spared her further debate by hauling out on the far end of the log. He was shivering. The log was in sunlight, but the air was cool. Discovering that he would not soon get dry in wet boxer shorts, he did then remove them, but very modestly, back turned, sitting down again quickly. He spread his underpants out on the log to dry, and conversed with his guest.

3   An expansive gesture as he described the events of the first week of the conference swept his socks into the water. He caught one, but the current took the other out of reach. It sank slowly. He mourned; the novelist commiserated. He dismissed the sock.

4   "The Men have raised a Great Phallus farther up the river," he said, smiling. "It was their own idea. I'd show you, but it's off limits to the Women. A temenos. Very interesting, some of the ritual that has developed this week! I am hearing men talk—not sports scores and business, but talk—"

5   Impressed and interested, the novelist listened, trying to ignore a lesser fascination: the sock. It had reemerged, all the way across the sun-flecked water, under a muddy, rooty bank. It was now moving very slowly but apparently—yes—definitely clockwise in a circle that would bring it back toward the log. The novelist sought and found a broken branch and held it ready, idly teasing the water with it. Housewife, she thought, ashamed. Fixated on socks. Prose writer!

6   The poet, sensitive and alert even when talking of his concerns, observed, and asked what she was fishing for.

7   "Your sock is coming back," she said.

8   In a silence of complete fellow feeling, they both watched the stately progress of the floating sock coming round unhurried in the fullness of time, astronomically certain, till the current brought it within branch reach. It was lifted dripping on the forked end. In quiet triumph the novelist turned the branch to the poet, presenting the sock to its owner, who removed it from the branch and squeezed it thoughtfully.

9   Soon after this he dressed, and they returned downstream to the conference center and the scattered cabins under the redwoods.

10   The food was marvelous. Infinitely imaginatively vegetarian, eclectic but not hodgepodge: the chilis hot, the salads del-

icate, the curries fragrant. The kitchen staff who produced these wonders were unlike the other people at the conference, though in fact several of them were members of the conference working out their fees. When they came out front and listened to the lecture on the Hero, they disappeared into the others and she could not recognize them; but in the crowded, hot, flashing kitchen, each of them seemed almost formidably individual, laughing more than anyone else here, talking differently, moving with deft purpose, so that the onlooker felt superfluous and inferior, not because the cooks meant to impress or to exclude but only because, being busy with the work in hand, they were quite unconscious of doing so.

After dinner on the second day, in honey-colored evening 11 sunlight, crossing the broad wooden bridge across the creek between the main hall and her set of cabins, the novelist stopped and set her hands on the rough railing. I have been here before! I know this creek, this bridge, that trail going up into the trees—Such moments were a familiar accompaniment to tension and self-consciousness. She had felt them waiting to be asked to dance in dancing class at twelve, and at fifty in a hotel room in a city she had never seen before. Sometimes they justified themselves as a foresight remembered, bringing with them a queer double-exposure effect of that place where she had foreseen being in this place. But this time the experience was one of pure recognition, unexplainable but not uncanny, though solemnized by the extraordinary grandeur of the setting.

For the creek ran and the path led from fog-softened golden 12 light into a darkness under incredible trees. It was always dark under them, and silent, and bare, for their huge community admitted little on a smaller scale. In the open clearings weeds and brambles and birds and bugs made the usual lively mess and tangle; under the big trees the flash of a scrub jay's wing startled as it would in the austere reaches of a Romanesque church. To come under the trees was as definite a transition as entering a building, but a building the size of a county.

Yet in among those immense living trunks there were also 13 some black, buttressed objects that confused the sense of scale still further, for though squat, they were bigger than the cabins—much bigger. In bulk and girth, they were bigger than the trees. They were ruins. Tree ruins, the logged and burned-over stumps of the original forest. With effort, the novelist comprehended that the sequoias so majestically towering their taper bulk and gracile limbs all around here were second growth, not even a century old, mere saplings, shoots,

scions of the great presences that had grown here in a length
of silence now altogether and forever lost.

14   All the same, it was very quiet under the trees, and still qui-
eter at night. There were refinements of the absence of sound,
which the novelist had never before had the opportunity to
observe. The cabins of her group straggled along, one every
ten or twenty yards, unlighted, above the creek, which ran
shallow but almost soundless, as if obeying the authority of
the redwoods, their counsel of silence. There was no wind.
Fog would mosey in over the hills from the sea before dawn
to hush what was hushed already. Far away one small owl
called once. Later, one mosquito shrilled hopelessly for a moment at the screen.

15   The novelist lay in darkness on her narrow board bunk in
her sleeping bag listening to nothing and wondering if this
was the bag her daughter had been using when she got the flu
camping last summer and how long flu germs might live in
the dark, warm, moist medium of a zippered sleeping bag.
Her thoughts ran on such matters because she was acutely
uncomfortable. Sometimes she thought it was diarrhea,
sometimes a bladder infection, sometimes a coward spirit.
Whatever it was, would it force her yet again to leave the
germy warmth of the sleeping bag and take her flashlight and
try to find the evasive path up that ominous hiss to the all too
communal, doorless, wet-floored toilets, praying that nobody
would join her in her misery? Yes. No, maybe not. She heard
a screen door creak, a cabin or two downstream, and almost
immediately after, a soft, rushing noise: a man pissing off his
cabin porch onto the dark, soft, absorbent ground of redwood
leaf and twig and bark. O lucky Men, who need not crouch
and straddle! Her bladder twinged, remorseless. "I do not
have to go pee," she told herself, unconvinced. "I am not sick."
She listened to the terrific silence. Nothing lived. But there,
deep in the hollow darkness, a soft, lively sound: a little fart.
And, now that she was all ears, presently another fart, louder,
from a cabin on higher ground. The beans with chilis would
probably explain it. Or did it need explanation, did people like
cattle add nightly to the methane in the atmosphere, had
those who had slept in longhouses by this creek been accustomed to this soft concert? For it was pleasing, almost melo-
dious, this sparse pattern of a snore here—a long efflatus
there—a little sigh—against the black and utter stillness.

16   When she was nearly asleep, she heard voices far upstream, male voices, chanting, as if from the dawn of history.

Deep, primeval. The Men were performing the rituals of manhood. But the little farts in the night were nearer and dearer.

The Women sat in a circle on the sand, about thirty of   17
them. Nearby the shallow river widened to the sea. Soft, fog-paled sunshine of the north coast lay beautifully on low breakers and dunes. The Women passed an ornamented wooden wand from hand to hand; who held the wand, spoke; the others listened. It did not seem quite right to the novelist. A good thing, but not the right one. Men wanted wands, women did not, she thought. These women had dutifully accepted the wand, but left to themselves they might have preferred some handwork and sat talking round and about like a flock of sparrows. Sparrows are disorderly, don't take turns, don't shut up to listen to the one with the wand, peck and talk at the same time. The wind blew softly, the wand passed. A woman in her twenties who wore an emblem of carved wood and feathers on a chain round her neck read a manuscript poem in a trembling voice half lost in the distant sound of the breakers. "My arms are those wings," she read, her voice shaken by fear and passion till it broke. The wand passed. A blond, fine-boned woman in her forties spoke of the White Goddess, but the novelist had ceased to listen, nervously rehearsing what she would say, should she say it? should she not? The wand passed to her. "It seems to me, coming in from outside, into the middle of this, you know, just for a couple of days, but perhaps just because of that I can be useful, anyhow it seems to me that to some extent some of the women here are sort of looking for a, for something actually to sort of *do*. Instead of kind of talking mostly in a sort of derivative way," she said in a harsh, chirping voice like a sparrow's. Shaking, she passed the wand. After the circle broke up, several women told her with enthusiasm about the masked dancing last Wednesday night, when the Women had acted out the female archetype of their choice. "It got wild," one said cheerfully. Another woman told her that this leader of the Women had quarreled with that one and personalities were destroying harmony. Several of them started making a large dragon out of wet sand, and while doing so told her that this year was different from earlier years, before the Men and the Women were separated, and that the East Coast meetings were always more spiritual than the West Coast meetings, or vice versa. They all chattered till the Men came back from their part of the beach, some with faces marked splendidly with charcoal.

18   The fine-boned blond whom the novelist had not listened to rode beside her in the car going back inland, a long, rough road through the logged-out coast range. "I've been coming to this place all my life," she said with a laugh. "It was a summer camp. I started coming when I was ten. Oh, it was wonderful then! I still meet people who came to Limberlost."

19   "Limberlost!" said the novelist.

20   "It was Camp Limberlost," said the other woman, and laughed again, affectionately.

21   "But I went there," said the novelist. "I went to Camp Limberlost. You mean this is it? Where the conference is? But I was wondering, earlier this year, I realized I had no idea where it was, or how to find out. I didn't know where it was when I went there. It was in the redwoods, that's literally all I knew. We all got into a bus downtown, and talked for six hours, you know, and then we were there—you know how kids are, they don't *notice*—but it was a Girl Reserve camp then. The YW ran it. I had to join the Girl Reserves to come."

22   "The city took it over after the war," the other woman said, her eyes merry and knowing. "This really is it. This is Limberlost."

23   "But I don't remember it," the novelist said in distress.

24   "The conference is in the old Boys Camp. The Girls Camp was upstream about a mile. Maybe you never came down here."

25   Yes. The novelist remembered that Jan and Dorothy had cut Camp Fire one evening and sneaked out of camp and down the creek to Boys Camp. They had hidden across the creek behind stumps and shrubs in the twilight, they had hooted and bleated and meowed until the Boys began coming out of their cabins, and then a counselor had come out, and Jan and Dorothy had run away, and got back after dark, muddy and triumphant, madly giggling in the jammed cabin after Lights Out, reciting their adventure, counting coup....

26   But she had not gone with them. There was no way she could have remembered that bridge across the creek, the trail going up out of the evening light.

27   Still, how could she not have recognized the place as a whole—the forest, the cabins? Two weeks of three summers she had lived here, at twelve and thirteen and fourteen, and had she never noticed the silence? the size of the redwoods? the black, appalling, giant stumps?

28   It was forty years; the trees might have grown a good deal—and now as she thought it did seem that she and Jan had actually climbed one of the stumps one day, to sit and talk, cutting

Crafts, probably. But they hadn't thought anything about the stump but that it was climbable, a place to talk in privacy. No sense of what that huge wreck meant, except (like those who had cut the tree) to their own convenience; no notion of what it was in relation to anything else, or where it was, or where they were. They were here. Despairingly homesick the first night, thereafter settled in. At home in the world, as cheekily indifferent to cause and effect as sparrows, as ignorant of death and geography as the redwoods.

She had envied Jan and Dorothy their exploit, knowing   29
them to be a good deal braver than she was. They had agreed to take her back to Boys Camp with them, and hoot and meow, or just hide and watch, but they never got around to it. They all went to Camp Fire and sang lonesome cowboy songs instead. So she had never seen Boys Camp until she came here and sat on the log and watched the poet circle slowly in the pool, and what would she and Jan and Dorothy, fourteen, merciless, have thought of *that?* "Oh, Lord!" she said involuntarily.

The woman beside her in the car laughed, as if in sympathy.   30
"It's such a beautiful place," she said. "It's wonderful to be able to come back. What do you think of the conference?"

"I like the drumming," the novelist replied, after a pause,   31
with fervor. "The drumming is wonderful. I never did that before." Indeed she had found that she wanted to do nothing else. If only there weren't a lecture tonight and they could drum again after dinner, thirty or forty people each with a drum on or between their knees, the rhythm set and led by a couple of drummers who knew what they were doing and kept the easy yet complex beat and pattern going, going, going till there was nothing in consciousness but that and nothing else needed, no words at all.

The lecture was on the Wild Man. That night she woke up   32
in the pitch dark and went out without using her flashlight and pissed beside her cabin, almost noiselessly. She heard no local breaking of wind, but guessed that many of the cabins were still empty; the Men had all gone off upstream, off limits, after the lecture, and now she heard them not chanting but yelling and roaring, a wild noise, but so far away that it didn't make much of a dent on the silence here. Here at Limberlost.

In the low, cold mist of morning, the poet came from cabin   33
to cabin. The novelist heard him coming, chanting and making animal sounds, banging the screen doors of the cabins. He wore a dramatic animal mask, a gray, snarling, hairy snout. "Up! Up! Daybreak! The old wolf's at the door! The

wolf, the wolf!" he chanted entering a cabin in a predatory crouch. Sleepy voices protested laughingly. The novelist was already up and dressed and had performed t'ai chi. She had stayed inside the screened cabin instead of going out on its spacious porch, because she was self-conscious, because doing t'ai chi was just too damn much the kind of thing you did here and yet didn't fit at all with what they were doing here and anyhow she was going home today and would damn well do t'ai chi in the broom closet if that's where she felt like doing it.

34   The poet approached her cabin and paused. "Good morning!" he said politely and incongruously through his staring, hairy muzzle. "Good morning," said the novelist from behind her screens, feeling a surge of snobbish irritation at the silly poet parading his power to wake everybody up, but *she* was up already!—and at the same time yearning to be able to go out and pat the wolf, to call him brave, to play the game he wanted so much to play, or at least to offer him something better than a wet sock on a stick.

AFFIRMATIVE ACTION

Shelby Steele

A Negative Vote
on Affirmative Action

An English professor by trade, Shelby Steele (born 1946) is currently on leave from San Jose State University and serving as a Hoover Fellow at Stanford University. His essays, which frequently reflect on one or another aspect of race in the United States, especially on the causes of friction between African Americans and white Americans, have appeared in many respected magazines and newspapers, including The American Scholar, The Washington Post, *and* The New Republic. *He collected many of those essays, including the one reprinted here, in his 1990 book* The Content of Our Character: A New Vision of Race in America. *The article first appeared in* The New York Times Magazine *in 1990.*

In a few short years, when my two children will be applying to college, the affirmative-action policies by which most universities offer black students some form of preferential treatment will present me with a dilemma. I am a middle-class black, a college professor, far from wealthy, but also well removed from the kind of deprivation that would qualify my children for the label "disadvantaged." Both of them have endured racial insensitivity from whites. They have been called names, have suffered slights and have experienced first hand the peculiar malevolence that racism brings out of people. Yet they have never experienced racial discrimination, have never been stopped by their race on any path they have chosen to follow. Still, their society now tells them that if they will only designate themselves as black on their college applications, they will probably do better in the college lottery than if they conceal this fact. I think there is something of a Faustian bargain in this.

Of course many blacks and a considerable number of whites would say that I was sanctimoniously making affirmative action into a test of character. They would say that this small preference is the meagerest recompense for centuries of unrelieved oppression. And to these arguments other very obvious facts must be added. In America, many marginally competent or flatly incompetent whites are hired every day—some because their white skin suits the conscious or unconscious racial preference of their employers. The white children of alumni are often grandfathered into elite universities in what can only be seen as a residual benefit of historic white privilege. Worse, white incompetence is always an individual matter, but for blacks it is often confirmation of ugly stereotypes. Given that unfairness cuts both ways, doesn't it only balance the scales of history, doesn't this repair, in a small way, the systematic denial under which my children's grandfather lived out his days?

3   In theory, affirmative action certainly has all the moral symmetry that fairness requires. It is reformist and corrective, even repentent and redemptive. And I would never sneer at these good intentions. Born in the late 1940's in Chicago, I started my education (a charitable term, in this case) in a segregated school, and suffered all the indignities that come to blacks in a segregated society. My father, born in the South, made it only to the third grade before the white man's fields took permanent priority over his formal education. And though he educated himself into an advanced reader with an almost professorial authority, he could only drive a truck for a living, and never earned more than $90 a week in his entire life. So yes, it is crucial to my sense of citizenship, to my ability to identify with the spirit and the interests of America, to know that this country, however imperfectly, recognizes its past sins and wishes to correct them.

4   Yet good intentions can blind us to the effects they generate when implemented. In our society affirmative action is, among other things, a testament to white good will and to black power, and in the midst of these heavy investments its effects can be hard to see. But after 20 years of implementation I think that affirmative action has shown itself to be more bad than good and that blacks—whom I will focus on in this essay—now stand to lose more from it than they gain.

5   In talking with affirmative-action administrators and with blacks and whites in general, I found that supporters of affirmative action focus on its good intentions and detractors emphasize its negative effects. It was virtually impossible to find people outside either camp. The closest I came was a white male manager at a large computer company who said, "I

think it amounts to reverse discrimination, but I'll put up with a little of that for a little more diversity." But this only makes him a half-hearted supporter of affirmative action. I think many people who don't really like affirmative action support it to one degree or another anyway.

I believe they do this because of what happened to white 6
and black Americans in the crucible of the 1960's, when whites were confronted with their racial guilt and blacks tasted their first real power. In that stormy time white absolution and black power coalesced into virtual mandates for society. Affirmative action became a meeting ground for those mandates in the law. At first, this meant insuring equal opportunity. The 1964 civil-rights bill was passed on the understanding that equal opportunity would not mean racial preference. But in the late 60's and early 70's, affirmative action underwent a remarkable escalation of its mission from simple anti-discrimination enforcement to social engineering by means of quotas, goals, timetables, set-asides and other forms of preferential treatment.

Legally, this was achieved through a series of executive or- 7
ders and Equal Employment Opportunity Commission guidelines that allowed racial imbalances in the workplace to stand as proof of racial discrimination. Once it could be assumed that discrimination explained racial imbalances, it became easy to justify group remedies to presumed discrimination rather than the normal case-by-case redress.

Even though blacks had made great advances during the 8
60's without quotas, the white mandate to achieve a new racial innocence and the black mandate to gain power, which came to a head in the very late 60's, could no longer be satisfied by anything less than racial preferences. I don't think these mandates, in themselves, were wrong, because whites clearly needed to do better by blacks and blacks needed more real power in society. But as they came together in affirmative action, their effect was to distort our understanding of racial discrimination. By making black the color of preference, these mandates have reburdened society with the very marriage of color and preference (in reverse) that we set out to eradicate.

When affirmative action grew into social engineering, diver- 9
sity became a golden word. Diversity is a term that applies democratic principles to races and cultures rather than to citizens, despite the fact that there is nothing to indicate that real diversity is the same thing as proportionate representation. Too often the result of this, on campuses for example, has been a democracy of colors rather than of people, an artificial diver-

sity that gives the appearance of an educational parity between
black and white students that has not yet been achieved in reality. Here again, racial preferences allow society to leapfrog
over the difficult problem of developing blacks to parity with
whites and into a cosmetic diversity that covers the blemish of
disparity—a full six years after admission, only 26 to 28 percent of blacks graduate from college.

10   Racial representation is not the same thing as racial development. Representation can be manufactured; development
is always hard earned. But it is the music of innocence and
power that we hear in affirmative action that causes us to
cling to it and to its distracting emphasis on representation.
The fact is that after 20 years of racial preferences the gap between median incomes of black and white families is greater
than it was in the 1970's. None of this is to say that blacks
don't need policies that insure our right to equal opportunity,
but what we need more of is the development that will let us
take advantage of society's efforts to include us.

11   I think one of the most troubling effects of racial preferences for blacks is a kind of demoralization. Under affirmative
action, the quality that earns us preferential treatment is an
implied inferiority. However this inferiority is explained—and
it is easily enough explained by the myriad deprivations that
grew out of our oppression—it is still inferiority. There are explanations and then there is the fact. And the fact must be
borne by the individual as a condition apart from the explanation, apart even from the fact that others like himself also bear
this condition. In integrated situations in which blacks must
compete with whites who may be better prepared, these explanations may quickly wear thin and expose the individual to racial as well as personal self-doubt. (Of course whites also feel
doubt, but only personally, not racially.)

12   What this means in practical terms is that when blacks deliver themselves into integrated situations they encounter a
nasty little reflex in whites, a mindless, atavistic reflex that responds to the color black with negative stereotypes, such as intellectual ineptness. I think this reflex embarrasses most
whites today and thus it is usually quickly repressed. On an
equally atavistic level, the black will be aware of the reflex his
color triggers and will feel a stab of horror at seeing himself reflected in this way. He, too, will do a quick repression, but a
lifetime of such stabbings is what constitutes his inner realm
of racial doubt. Even when the black sees no implication of inferiority in racial preferences, he knows that whites do, so
that—consciously or unconsciously—the result is virtually the

same. The effect of preferential treatment—the lowering of normal standards to increase black representation—puts blacks at war with an expanded realm of debilitating doubt, so that the doubt itself becomes an unrecognized preoccupation that undermines their ability to perform, especially in integrated situations.

I believe another liability of affirmative action comes from the fact that it indirectly encourages blacks to exploit their own past victimization. Like implied inferiority, victimization is what justifies preference, so that to receive the benefits of preferential treatment one must, to some extent, become invested in the view of one's self as a victim. In this way, affirmative action nurtures a victim-focused identity in blacks and sends us the message that there is more power in our past suffering than in our present achievements.   13

When power itself grows out of suffering, blacks are encouraged to expand the boundaries of what qualifies as racial oppression, a situation that can lead us to paint our victimization in vivid colors even as we receive the benefits of preference. The same corporations and institutions that give us preference are also seen as our oppressors. At Stanford University, minority group students—who receive at least the same financial aid as whites with the same need—recently took over the president's office demanding, among other things, more financial aid.   14

But I think one of the worst prices that blacks pay for preference has to do with an illusion. I saw this illusion at work recently in the mother of a middle-class black student who was going off to his first semester of college: "They owe us this, so don't think for a minute that you don't belong there." This is the logic by which many blacks, and some whites, justify affirmative action—it is something "owed," a form of reparation. But this logic overlooks a much harder and less digestible reality, that it is impossible to repay blacks living today for the historic suffering of the race. If all blacks were given a million dollars tomorrow it would not amount to a dime on the dollar for three centuries of oppression, nor would it dissolve the residues of that oppression that we still carry today. The concept of historic reparation grows out of man's need to impose on the world a degree of justice that simply does not exist. Suffering can be endured and overcome, it cannot be repaid. To think otherwise is to prolong the suffering.   15

Several blacks I spoke with said they were still in favor of affirmative action because of the "subtle" discrimination blacks were subject to once they were on the job. One photo-   16

journalist said, "They have ways of ignoring you." A black female television producer said: "You can't file a lawsuit when
your boss doesn't invite you to the insider meetings without
ruining your career. So we still need affirmative action." Others mentioned the infamous "glass ceiling" through which
blacks can see the top positions of authority but never reach
them. But I don't think racial preferences are a protection
against this subtle discrimination; I think they contribute to it.

17   In any workplace, racial preferences will always create two-
tiered populations composed of preferreds and unpreferred.
In the case of blacks and whites, for instance, racial preferences imply that whites are superior just as they imply that
blacks are inferior. They not only reinforce America's oldest
racial myth but, for blacks, they have the effect of stigmatizing the already stigmatized.

18   I think that much of the "subtle" discrimination that blacks
talk about is often (not always) discrimination against the
stigma of questionable competence that affirmative action
marks blacks with. In this sense, preferences make scapegoats
of the very people they seek to help. And it may be that at a certain level employers impose a glass ceiling, but this may not be
against the race so much as against the race's reputation for
having advanced by color as much as by competence. This
ceiling is the point at which corporations shift the emphasis
from color to competency and stop playing the affirmative-
action game. Here preference backfires for blacks and becomes a taint that holds them back. Of course one could argue
that this taint, which is after all in the minds of whites, becomes nothing more than an excuse to discriminate against
blacks. And certainly the result is the same in either case—
blacks don't get past the glass ceiling. But this argument does
not get around the fact that racial preferences now taint this
color with a new theme of suspicion that makes blacks even
more vulnerable to discrimination. In this crucial yet gray area
of perceived competence, preferences make whites look better
than they are and blacks worse, while doing nothing whatever
to stop the very real discrimination that blacks may encounter.
I don't wish to justify the glass ceiling here, but only suggest the
very subtle ways that affirmative action revives rather than ex-
tinguishes the old rationalizations for racial discrimination.

19   I believe affirmative action is problematic in our society
because we have demanded that it create parity between the
races rather than insure equal opportunity. Preferential treatment does not teach skills, or educate, or instill motivation. It
only passes out entitlement, by color, a situation that in my

profession has created an unrealistically high demand for black professors. The social engineer's assumption is that this high demand will inspire more blacks to earn Ph.D's and join the profession. In fact, the number of blacks earning Ph.D's has declined in recent years. Ph.D's must be developed from preschool on. They require family and community support. They must acquire an entire system of values that enables them to work hard while delaying gratification.

It now seems clear that the Supreme Court, in a series of re-   20 cent decisions, is moving away from racial preferences. It has disallowed preferences except in instances of "identified discrimination," eroded the precedent that statistical racial imbalances are prima facie evidence of discrimination, and, in effect, granted white males the right to challenge consent decrees that use preference to achieve racial balances in the workplace. Referring to this and other Supreme Court decisions, one civil-rights leader said, "Night has fallen . . . as far as civil rights are concerned." But I am not so sure. The effect of these decisions is to protect the constitutional rights of everyone rather than to take rights away from blacks. Night has fallen on racial preferences, not on the fundamental rights of black Americans. The reason for this shift, I believe, is that the white mandate for absolution from past racial sins has weakened considerably in the 1980's. Whites are now less willing to endure unfairness to themselves in order to grant special entitlements to blacks, even when those entitlements are justified in the name of past suffering. Yet the black mandate for more power in society has remained unchanged. And I think part of the anxiety many blacks feel over these decisions has to do with the loss of black power that they may signal.

But the power we've lost by these decisions is really only   21 the power that grows out of our victimization. This is not a very substantial or reliable power, and it is important that we know this so we can focus more exclusively on the kind of development that will bring enduring power. There is talk now that Congress may pass new legislation to compensate for these new limits on affirmative action. If this happens, I hope the focus will be on development and antidiscrimination, rather than entitlement, on achieving racial parity rather than jerry-building racial diversity.

But if not preferences, what? The impulse to discriminate   22 *is* subtle and cannot be ferreted out unless its many guises are made clear to people. I think we need social policies that are committed to two goals: the educational and economic development of disadvantaged people regardless of race and the eradication from our society—through close monitoring and severe sanctions—of racial, ethnic or gender discrimination. Preferences will not get us to either of these goals, because they tend to benefit those who are not disadvantaged—middle-class white women and middle-class blacks—and attack one form of discrimination with another. Preferences are inexpensive and carry the glamour of good intentions—change the numbers and the good deed is done. To be against them is to be unkind. But I think the unkindest cut is to bestow on children like my own an undeserved advantage while neglecting the development of those disadvantaged children in the poorer sections of my city who will most likely never be in a position to benefit from a preference. Give my children fairness; give disadvantaged children a better shot at development—better elementary and secondary schools, job training, safer neighborhoods, better financial assistance for college and so on. A smaller percentage of black high school graduates go to college today than 15 years ago; more black males are in prison, jail or in some other way under the control of the criminal-justice system than in college. This despite racial preferences.

23   The mandates of black power and white absolution out of which preferences emerged were not wrong in themselves. What was wrong was that both races focused more on the goals of those mandates than on the means to the goals. Blacks can have no real power without taking responsibility for their own educational and economic development. Whites can have no racial innocence without earning it by eradicating discrimination and helping the disadvantaged to develop. Because we ignored the means, the goals have not been reached and the real work remains to be done.

Roger Wilkins

Racism Has Its Privileges

The Case for Affirmative Action

The Nation, a highly respected weekly magazine of current public affairs that is liberal in its orientation, published the following essay on March 27, 1995. Roger Wilkins, a member of the editorial board at The Nation, is also professor of history at George Mason University in northern Virginia.

The storm that has been gathering over affirmative action 1 for the past few years has burst. Two conservative California professors are leading a drive to place an initiative on the state ballot in 1996 that will ask Californians to vote affirmative action up or down. Since the state is beloved in political circles for its electoral votes, advance talk of the initiative has put the issue high on the national agenda. Three Republican presidential contenders—Bob Dole, Phil Gramm and Lamar Alexander—have already begun taking shots at various equal opportunity programs. Congressional review of the Clinton Administration's enforcement of these programs has begun. The President has started his own review, promising adherence to principles of nondiscrimination and full opportunity while asserting the need to prune those programs that are unfair or malfunctioning.

It is almost an article of political faith that one of the major 2 influences in last November's election was the backlash against affirmative action among "angry white men," who are convinced it has stacked the deck against them. Their attitudes are shaped and their anger heightened by unquestioned and virtually uncheckable anecdotes about victimized whites flooding the culture. For example, *Washington Post* columnist Richard Cohen recently began what purported to be a serious analysis and attack on affirmative action by recounting that he had once missed out on a job someplace because they "needed a woman."

Well, I have an anecdote too, and it, together with Cohen's, 3 offers some important insights about the debate that has flared recently around the issues of race, gender and justice. Some years ago, after watching me teach as a visiting professor for two semesters, members of the history department at George Mason University invited me to compete for a full

professorship and endowed chair. Mason, like other institutions in Virginia's higher education system, was under a court
order to desegregate. I went through the appropriate application and review process and, in due course, was appointed. A
few years later, not long after I had been honored as one of
the university's distinguished professors, I was shown an article by a white historian asserting that he had been a candidate for that chair but that at the last moment the job had
been whisked away and handed to an unqualified black. I
checked the story and discovered that this fellow had, in fact,
applied but had not even passed the first threshold. But his
"reverse discrimination" story is out there polluting the atmosphere in which this debate is taking place.

4   Affirmative action, as I understand it, was not designed to
punish anyone; it was, rather—as a result of a clear-eyed look
at how America actually works—an attempt to enlarge opportunity for *everybody*. As amply documented in the 1968
Kerner Commission report on racial disorders, when left to
their own devices, American institutions in such areas as college admissions, hiring decisions and loan approvals had
been making choices that discriminated against blacks. That
discrimination, which flowed from doing what came naturally, hurt more than blacks: It hurt the entire nation, as the
riots of the late 1960s demonstrated. Though the Kerner report focused on blacks, similar findings could have been
made about other minorities and women.

5   Affirmative action required institutions to develop plans
enabling them to go beyond business as usual and search for
qualified people in places where they did not ordinarily conduct their searches or their business. Affirmative action programs generally require some proof that there has been a
good-faith effort to follow the plan and numerical guidelines
against which to judge the sincerity and the success of the effort. The idea of affirmative action is *not* to force people into
positions for which they are unqualified but to encourage institutions to develop realistic criteria for the enterprise at
hand and then to find a reasonably diverse mix of people
qualified to be engaged in it. Without the requirements calling for plans, good-faith efforts and the setting of broad numerical goals, many institutions would do what they had
always done: assert that they had looked but "couldn't find
anyone qualified," and then go out and hire the white man
they wanted to hire in the first place.

6   Affirmative action has done wonderful things for the
United States by enlarging opportunity and developing and

utilizing a far broader array of the skills available in the American population than in the past. It has not outlived its usefulness. It was never designed to be a program to eliminate poverty. It has not always been used wisely, and some of its permutations do have to be reconsidered, refined or, in some cases, abandoned. It is not a quota program, and those cases where rigid numbers are used (except under a court or administrative order after a specific finding of discrimination) are a bastardization of an otherwise highly beneficial set of public policies.

President Clinton is right to review what is being done under present laws and to express a willingness to eliminate activities that either don't work or are unfair. Any program that has been in place for thirty years should be reviewed. Getting rid of what doesn't work is both good government and good politics. Gross abuses of affirmative action provide ammunition for its opponents and undercut the moral authority of the entire effort. But the President should retain—and strengthen where required—those programs necessary to enlarge social justice.   7

What makes the affirmative action issue so difficult is that it engages blacks and whites exactly at those points where they differ the most. There are some areas, such as rooting for the local football team, where their experiences and views are virtually identical. There are others—sometimes including work and school—where their experiences and views both overlap and diverge. And finally, there are areas such as affirmative action and inextricably related notions about the presence of racism in society where the divergences draw out almost all the points of difference between the races.   8

This Land Is My Land

Blacks and whites experience America very differently. Though we often inhabit the same space, we operate in very disparate psychic spheres.   9

Whites have an easy sense of ownership of the country; they feel they are entitled to receive all that is best in it. Many of them believe that their country—though it may have some faults—is superior to all others and that, as Americans, they are superior as well. Many of them think of this as a white country and some of them even experience it that way. They think of it as a land of opportunity—a good place with a lot of good people in it. Some suspect (others *know*) that the presence of blacks messes everything up.   10

11   To blacks there's nothing very easy about life in America, and any sense of ownership comes hard because we encounter so much resistance in making our way through the ordinary occurrences of life. And I'm not even talking here about overt acts of discrimination but simply about the way whites intrude on and disturb our psychic space without even thinking about it.

12   A telling example of this was given to me by a black college student in Oklahoma. He said whites give him looks that say: "What are *you* doing here?"

13   "When do they give you that look?" I asked.

14   "Every time I walk in a door," he replied.

15   When he said that, every black person in the room nodded, and smiled in a way that indicated recognition based on thousands of such moments in their own lives.

16   For most blacks, America is either a land of denied opportunity or one in which the opportunities are still grudgingly extended and extremely limited. For some—that one-third who are mired in poverty, many of them isolated in dangerous ghettos—America is a land of desperadoes and desperation. In places where whites see a lot of idealism, blacks see, at best, idealism mixed heavily with hypocrisy. Blacks accept America's greatness but are unable to ignore ugly warts that many whites seem to need not to see. I am reminded here of James Baldwin's searing observation from *The Fire Next Time:*

> The American Negro has the great advantage of having never believed that collection of myths to which white Americans cling: that their ancestors were all freedom-loving heroes, that they were born in the greatest country the world has ever seen, or that Americans are invincible in battle and wise in peace, that Americans have always dealt honorably with Mexicans and Indians and all other neighbors or inferiors, that American men are the world's most direct and virile, that American women are pure.

17   It goes without saying, then, that blacks and whites remember America differently. The past is hugely important since we argue a lot about who we are on the basis of who we think we have been, and we derive much of our sense of the future from how we think we've done in the past. In a nation in which few people know much history these are perilous arguments, because in such a vacuum, people tend to weave historical fables tailored to their political or psychic needs.

Blacks are still recovering the story of their role in Amer-   18
ica, which so many white historians simply ignored or told in
ways that made black people ashamed. But in a culture that
batters us, learning the real history is vital in helping blacks
feel fully human. It also helps us understand just how deeply
American we are, how richly we have given, how much has
been taken from us and how much has yet to be restored.
Supporters of affirmative action believe that broad and deep
damage has been done to American culture by racism and
sexism over the whole course of American history and that
they are still powerful forces today. We believe that minorities
and women are still disadvantaged in our highly competitive
society and that affirmative action is absolutely necessary to
level the playing field.

Not all white Americans oppose this view and not all black   19
Americans support it. There are a substantial number of
whites in this country who have been able to escape our racist
and sexist past and to enter fully into the quest for equal justice. There are other white Americans who are not racists but
who more or less passively accept the powerful suggestions
coming at them from all points in the culture that whites are
entitled to privilege and to freedom from competition with
blacks. And then there are racists who just don't like blacks or
who actively despise us. There are still others who may or
may not feel deep antipathy, but who know how to manipulate racism and white anxiety for their own ends. Virtually all
the people in the last category oppose affirmative action and
some of them make a practice of preying upon those in the
second category who are not paying attention or who, like the
Post's Richard Cohen, are simply confused.

The Politics of Denial

One of these political predators is Senate majority leader   20
Bob Dole. In his offhandedly lethal way, Dole delivered a
benediction of "let me now forgive us" on *Meet the Press* recently. After crediting affirmative action for the 62 percent of
the white male vote garnered by the Republicans, he remarked that slavery was "before we were born" and wondered whether future generations ought to have to continue
"paying a price" for those ancient wrongs.

Such a view holds that whatever racial problems we once   21
may have had have been solved over the course of the past
thirty years and that most of our current racial friction is

caused by racial and gender preferences that almost invariably work to displace some "qualified" white male. Words and
phrases like "punish" or "preference" or "reverse discrimination" or "quota" are dropped into the discourse to buttress
this view, as are those anecdotes about injustice to whites.
Proponents of affirmative action see these arguments as dis-
ingenuous but ingenious because they reduce serious and
complex social, political, economic, historical and psychological issues to bumper-sticker slogans designed to elicit Pavlov-
ian responses.

22   The fact is that the successful public relations assault on
affirmative action flows on a river of racism that is as broad,
powerful and American as the Mississippi. And, like the Mississippi, racism can be violent and deadly and is a permanent
feature of American life. But while nobody who is sane denies
the reality of the Mississippi, millions of Americans who are
deemed sane—some of whom are powerful and some even
thought wise—deny, wholly or in part, that racism exists.

23   It is critical to understand the workings of denial in this debate because it is used to obliterate the facts that created the
need for the remedy in the first place. One of the best examples of denial was provided recently by the nation's most
famous former history professor, House Speaker Newt Gingrich. According to *The Washington Post*, "Gingrich dismissed
the argument that the beneficiaries of affirmative action,
commonly African Americans, have been subjected to discrimination over a period of centuries. 'That is true of virtually every American,' Gingrich said, noting that the Irish were
discriminated against by the English, for example."

24   That is breathtaking stuff coming from somebody who
should know that blacks have been on this North American
continent for 375 years and that for 245 the country permitted slavery. Gingrich should also know that for the next hundred years we had legalized subordination of blacks, under a
suffocating blanket of condescension and frequently enforced
by nightriding terrorists. We've had only thirty years of something else.

25   That something else is a nation trying to lift its ideals out of
a thick, often impenetrable slough of racism. Racism is a hard
word for what over the centuries became second nature in
America—preferences across the board for white men and,
following in their wake, white women. Many of these men
seem to feel that it is un-American to ask them to share anything with blacks—particularly their work, their neighborhoods or "their" women. To protect these things—apparently

essential to their identity—they engage in all forms of denial. For a historian to assert that "virtually every American" shares the history I have just outlined comes very close to lying.

Denial of racism is much like the denials that accompany   26
addictions to alcohol, drugs or gambling. It is probably not stretching the analogy too much to suggest that many racist whites are so addicted to their unwarranted privileges and so threatened by the prospect of losing them that all kinds of defenses become acceptable, including insistent distortions of reality in the form of hypocrisy, lying or the most outrageous political demagogy.

"Those People" Don't Deserve Help

The demagogues have reverted to a new version of quite an   27
old trick. Before the 1950s, whites who were busy denying that the nation was unfair to blacks would simply assert that we didn't deserve equal treatment because we were *inferior*. These days it is not permissible in most public circles to say that blacks are inferior, but it is perfectly acceptable to target the *behavior* of blacks, specifically poor blacks. The argument then follows a fairly predictable line: The behavior of poor blacks requires a severe rethinking of national social policy, it is said. Advantaged blacks really don't need affirmative action anymore, and when they are the objects of such programs, some qualified white person (unqualified white people don't show up in these arguments) is (as Dole might put it) "punished." While it is possible that color-blind affirmative action programs benefiting all disadvantaged Americans are needed, those (i.e., blacks) whose behavior is so distressing must be punished by restricting welfare, shriveling the safety net and expanding the prison opportunity. All of that would presumably give us, in William Bennett's words, "what we want—a color-blind society," for which the white American psyche is presumably fully prepared.

There are at least three layers of unreality in these pre-   28
cepts. The first is that the United States is not now and probably never will be a color-blind society. It is the most color-conscious society on earth. Over the course of 375 years, whites have given blacks absolutely no reason to believe that they can behave in a color-blind manner. In many areas of our lives—particularly in employment, housing and education— affirmative action is required to counter deeply ingrained racist patterns of behavior.

29   Second, while I don't hold the view that all blacks who behave badly are blameless victims of a brutal system, I do believe that many poor blacks have, indeed, been brutalized by
our culture, and I know of *no* blacks, rich or poor, who haven't
been hurt in some measure by the racism in this country. The
current mood (and, in some cases like the Speaker's, the cultivated ignorance) completely ignores the fact that some blacks
never escaped the straight line of oppression that ran from slavery through the semislavery of sharecropping to the late mid-
century migration from Southern farms into isolated pockets
of urban poverty. Their families have always been excluded,
poor and without skills, and so they were utterly defenseless
when the enormous American economic dislocations that began in the mid-1970s slammed into their communities, followed closely by deadly waves of crack cocaine. One would
think that the double-digit unemployment suffered consistently over the past two decades by blacks who were *looking for
work* would be a permanent feature of the discussions about
race, responsibility, welfare and rights.

30   But a discussion of the huge numbers of black workers who
are becoming economically redundant would raise difficult
questions about the efficiency of the economy at a time when
millions of white men feel insecure. Any honest appraisal of
unemployment would reveal that millions of low-skilled white
men were being severely damaged by corporate and Federal
Reserve decisions; it might also refocus the anger of those
whites in the middle ranks whose careers have been shattered
by the corporate downsizing fad.

31   But people's attention is kept trained on the behavior of
some poor blacks by politicians and television news shows,
reinforcing the stereotypes of blacks as dangerous, as threats,
as unqualified. Frightened whites direct their rage at pushy
blacks rather than at the corporations that export manufacturing operations to low-wage countries, or at the Federal Reserve, which imposes interest rate hikes that slow down the
economy.

Who Benefits? We All Do

32   There is one final denial that blankets all the rest. It is that
only society's "victims"—blacks, other minorities and women
(who should, for God's sake, renounce their victimological
outlooks)—have been injured by white male supremacy.
Viewed in this light, affirmative action remedies are a kind of

zero-sum game in which only the "victims" benefit. But racist and sexist whites who are not able to accept the full humanity of other people are themselves badly damaged—morally stunted—people. The principal product of a racist and sexist society is damaged people and institutions—victims and victimizers alike. Journalism and education, two enterprises with which I am familiar, provide two good examples.

Journalistic institutions often view the nation through a   33
lens that bonds reality to support white privilege. A recent issue of *U.S. News & World Report* introduced a package of articles on these issues with a question on its cover: "Does affirmative action mean NO WHITE MEN NEED APPLY?" The words "No white men need apply" were printed in red against a white background and were at least four times larger than the other words in the question. Inside, the lead story was illustrated by a painting that carries out the cover theme, with a wan white man separated from the opportunity ladders eagerly being scaled by women and dark men. And the story yielded up the following sentence: "Affirmative action poses a conflict between two cherished American principles: the belief that all Americans deserve equal opportunities and the idea that hard work and merit, not race or religion or gender or birthright, should determine who prospers and who does not."

Whoever wrote that sentence was in the thrall of one of the   34
myths that Baldwin was talking about. The sentence suggests—as many people do when talking about affirmative action—that America is a meritocratic society. But what kind of meritocracy excludes women and blacks and other minorities from all meaningful competition? And even in the competition among white men, money, family and connections often count for much more than merit, test results (for whatever they're worth) and hard work.

The *U.S. News* story perpetuates and strengthens the view   35
that many of my white students absorb from their parents: that white men now have few chances in this society. The fact is that white men still control virtually everything in America except the wealth held by widows. According to the Urban Institute, 53 percent of black men aged 25-34 are either unemployed or earn too little to lift a family of four from poverty.

Educational institutions that don't teach accurately about   36
why America looks the way it does and why the distribution of winners and losers is as it is also injure our society. Here is another anecdote.

A warm, brilliant young white male student of mine came   37
in just before he was to graduate and said that my course in

race, law and culture, which he had just finished, had been the most valuable and the most disturbing he had ever taken. I asked how it had been disturbing.

38   "I learned that my two heroes are racists," he said.

39   "Who are your heroes and how are they racists?" I asked.

40   "My mom and dad," he said. "After thinking about what I was learning, I understood that they had spent all my life making me into the same kind of racists they were."

41   Affirmative action had brought me together with him when he was 22. Affirmative action puts people together in ways that make that kind of revelation possible. Nobody is a loser when that happens. The country gains.

42   And that, in the end, is the case for affirmative action. The arguments supporting it should be made on the basis of its broad contributions to the entire American community. It is insufficient to vilify white males and to skewer them as the whiners that journalism of the kind practiced by *U.S. News* invites us to do. These are people who, from the beginning of the Republic, have been taught that skin color is destiny and that whiteness is to be revered. Listen to Jefferson, writing in the year the Constitution was drafted:

> The first difference that strikes us is that of colour.... And is the difference of no importance? Is it not the foundation of a greater or less share of beauty in the two races? Are not the fine mixtures of red and white ... in the one, preferable to that eternal monotony, which reigns in the countenances, that immoveable veil of black which covers all the emotions of the other race? Add to these, flowing hair, a more elegant symmetry of form, their own judgment in favor of the whites, declared by their preference for them, as uniformly as is the preference of the Oran-ootan for the black women over those of his own species. The circumstance of superior beauty, is thought worthy attention in the propagation of our horses, dogs, and other domestic animals; why not in that of man?

In a society so conceived and so dedicated, it is understandable that white males would take their preferences as a matter of natural right and consider any alteration of that a primal offense. But a nation that operates in that way abandons its soul and its economic strength, and will remain mired in ugliness and moral squalor because so many people are excluded from the possibility of decent lives and from forming any sense of community with the rest of society.

Seen only as a corrective for ancient wrongs, affirmative   43
action may be dismissed by the likes of Gingrich, Gramm and
Dole, just as attempts to federalize decent treatment of the
freed slaves were dismissed after Reconstruction more than a
century ago. Then, striking down the Civil Rights Act of 1875,
Justice Joseph Bradley wrote of blacks that "there must be
some stage in the progress of his elevation when he takes the
rank of a mere citizen, and ceases to be the special favorite of
the laws, and when his rights, as a citizen or a man, are to be
protected in the ordinary modes by which other men's rights
are protected."

But white skin has made some citizens—particularly white   44
males—*the special favorites of the culture*. It may be that we
will need affirmative action until most white males are really
ready for a color-blind society—that is, when they are ready
to assume "the rank of a mere citizen." As a nation we took a
hard look at that special favoritism thirty years ago. Though
the centuries of cultural preference enjoyed by white males
still overwhelmingly skew power and wealth their way, we
have in fact achieved a more meritocratic society as a result
of affirmative action than we have ever previously enjoyed in
this country.

If we want to continue making things better in this society,   45
we'd better figure out ways to protect and defend affirmative
action against the confused, the frightened, the manipulators
and, yes, the liars in politics, journalism, education and wherever else they may be found. In the name of longstanding
American prejudice and myths and in the service of their own
narrow interests, power-lusts or blindness, they are truly vic-
timizing the rest of us, perverting the ideals they claim to stand
for and destroying the nation they pretend to serve.

Migdia Chinea-Varela
My Life as a "Twofer"

Migdia Chinea-Varela contributed this essay to Newsweek *on December 26, 1988.*

1   This Christmas I'll be celebrating my 10th anniversary as a card-carrying member of the film industry's Writers Guild. Ten brain-numbing years and a debilitating employment lull during the five-month-long writers' strike have taken their toll. Last week I'd awakened in what can only be described as profound financial melancholia and was taking inventory of my career alternatives when the phone rang. The caller was a friend at the Writers Guild of America, West. Great news, he said. Several production companies were starting "access" programs for minorities, women, the elderly and the disabled. They'd requested a sampler of scripts ASAP from which to fish out two, maybe *three* writers for free-lance assignments. It could even lead to staff jobs, he said.

2   My imagination flashes to a TV scene in which I grab the lifeline and submit my best script. I subsequently get chosen for a plum writing assignment that quickly turns into a staff position, where I do such a bang-up job that I become the show's producer and an Emmy award winner as well. In real life, however, I thank the guide rep for his good-faith efforts and tell him that my answer is no. Though I helped found and then chaired the Latino writer's committee, I don't want to send in my scripts.

3   Why? Why would anyone pass up such a sweet deal? Everyone knows how tough the film and television industry is. Yet contacts are everything, the insiders say. It helps if you have an agent with hot connections who believes in you and is willing to put in the time required to promote your career. It helps if you attended the "right" film school. It's a matter of timing. It's difficult for everyone. Yes, but consider this—if you're a member of a minority group, the equation should be multiplied by 10; and if you're a minority woman, then add 30 more points.

4   So what's my problem? Why not take advantage of every opportunity that comes my way? The answer is: I've been in this situation before and I don't like the way it makes me feel. There's something almost insulting about these well-meaning affirmative-action searches. In the past I'd always rationalized my participation partly because I needed the break and

even more because I needed the money. And as fate would have it, whenever a film- or TV-production company saw fit to round up minorities for a head count, I always came out on top. But the truth is that I've never felt good about it.

I've asked myself the obvious questions. Am I being picked 5 for my writing ability, or to fulfill a quota? Have I been selected because I'm a "twofer"—a female Hispanic—or because they were enthralled with my deftly drawn characters and strong, original story line? My writing career, it appears, has taken a particularly tortuous course. I've gone from being a dedicated writer to dedicated *minority* writer, which seems limiting for someone who was first inspired by Woody Allen.

Truth is, that even with the aid of special programs, job 6 assignments for writers who fit the "minority" category are inexplicably few and far between. The sad employment statistics reveal that ethnic minorities comprise less than 3 percent of our guild. Those who work do so less frequently and for a lot less money, yet the publicity harvested by the special programs creates the illusion of equal opportunity where very little exists. I don't want to seem overly gloomy. Nevertheless, my work's almost always seen on shows that have a minority star like "The Facts of Life," "What's Happening Now!" and "Punky Brewster."

Except for "The Cosby Show," minorities are not being 7 taken seriously enough to write about their real lives outside of the ghetto. Though few of us will admit to it—for fear of speaking out or being tagged as ungrateful—we're reminded of our status in not-so-subtle ways. I remember the time I was waiting for a story meeting where I wanted to pitch several ideas. As I chatted with the production secretary, an aspiring writer herself, I could hear laughter coming from inside the conference room. Finally, the executive in charge stepped outside, followed by five young men. Judging by the look of satisfaction on their faces, it had probably been a profitable session. The executive greeted me effusively by saying, as he turned to the rest of the group, "Meet M-I-G-D-I-A V-A-R-R-R-R-E-L-A. She's one of our minority writers." This comment drew a tight smile from my lips, as one and all present reacted with extravagant expressions of support. Somehow I knew right then and there that my project would be down for the count. KO'd with kindness.

Killer sharks: More recently, I was spilling my guts to a 8 friend with a recognizable name whose uncle was a famous writer. After sharing my woes and commiserating as fellow writers often do, we parted with that old cliché: "We're in the same boat." Suddenly it dawned on me that hell *no*, we're not even close. We're no doubt on the same ocean, but hardly in the same boat. From where I sit, my friend's being attended to on a luxury liner while I'm all alone paddling a canoe, surrounded by killer sharks and in the midst of a typhoon.

9   I'd like to think that after 10 years of paying my dues as a professional writer that I've earned the right to walk through the front door. After so many years, it's depressing to feel that I have to tag myself a minority as an incentive to those who may hire me. Why can't I get a job on my own merits? Am I destined to spend the rest of my writing career hooked up to these kinds of life-support systems?

10 I'm painfully aware that affirmative action, what little there is of it, may be the only way minorities are given a chance to compete. However, for me, it has become a stigma of sorts. In my view, there can be no affirmative action without segregation—nor any end to the segregation if our names must be kept on separate lists. I'd like to propose instead a simple scenario: a fair job market where employment is commensurate with ability regardless of gender, racial or ethnic background. I make a pitch, they like my story, I get the job. Why not?

Richard Kahlenberg
Class, Not Race

Richard Kahlenberg has completed a book on class-based affirmative action. On April 3, 1995, he contributed the following to The New Republic, *a politically middle-of-the-road publication on current affairs.*

1   In an act that reflected panic as much as cool reflection, Bill Clinton said recently that he is reviewing all federal affirmative action programs to see "whether there is some other way we can reach [our] objective without giving a preference by race or gender." As the country's mood swings violently against affirmative action, and as Republicans gear up to use the issue to bludgeon the Democratic coalition yet again in 1996, the whole project of legislating racial equality seems suddenly in doubt. The Democrats, terrified of the issue, are

now hoping it will just go away. It won't. But at every political impasse, there is a political opportunity. Bill Clinton now has a chance, as no other Democrat has had since 1968, to turn a glaring liability for his party into an advantage—without betraying basic Democratic principles.

There is, as Clinton said, a way "we can work this out." But 2 it isn't the "*Bakke* straddle," which says yes to affirmative action (race as a factor) but no to quotas. It isn't William Julius Wilson's call to "emphasize" race-neutral social programs, while downplaying affirmative action. The days of downplaying are gone; we can count on the Republicans for that. The way out—an idea Clinton hinted at—is to introduce the principle of race neutrality and the goal of aiding the disadvantaged into affirmative action preference programs themselves: to base preferences, in education, entry-level employment and public contracting, on class, not race.

Were Clinton to propose this move, the media would 3 charge him with lurching to the right. Jesse Jackson's presidential campaign would surely soon follow. But despite its association with conservatives such as Clarence Thomas, Antonin Scalia and Dinesh D'Souza, the idea of class-based affirmative action should in fact appeal to the left as well. After all, its message of addressing class unfairness and its political potential for building cross-racial coalitions are traditional liberal staples.

For many years, the left argued not only that class was im- 4 portant, but also that it was more important than race. This argument was practical, ideological and politic. An emphasis on class inequality meant Robert Kennedy riding in a motorcade through cheering white and black sections of racially torn Gary, Indiana, in 1968, with black Mayor Richard Hatcher on one side, and white working-class boxing hero Tony Zale on the other.

Ideologically, it was clear that with the passage of the Civil 5 Rights Act of 1964, class replaced caste as the central impediment to equal opportunity. Martin Luther King Jr. moved from the Montgomery Boycott to the Poor People's Campaign, which he described as "his last, greatest dream," and "something bigger than just a civil rights movement for Negroes." RFK told David Halberstam that "it was pointless to talk about the real problem in America being black and white, it was really rich and poor, which was a much more complex subject."

Finally, the left emphasized class because to confuse class 6 and race was seen not only as wrong but as dangerous. This notion was at the heart of the protest over Daniel Patrick Moynihan's 1965 report, *The Negro Family: The Case for National Action*, in which Moynihan depicted the rising rates of illegitimacy among poor blacks. While Moynihan's critics were wrong to silence discussion of illegitimacy among blacks, they rightly noted that the title of the report, which implicated all blacks, was misleading, and that fairly high rates of illegitimacy also were present among poor whites—a point which Moynihan readily endorses today. (In the wake of the second set of L.A. riots in 1992, Moynihan rose on the Senate floor to reaffirm that family structure "is not an issue of race but of class.... It is class behavior.")

7   The irony is that affirmative action based on race violates these three liberal insights. It provides the ultimate wedge to destroy Robert Kennedy's coalition. It says that despite civil rights protections, the wealthiest African American is more deserving of preference than the poorest white. It relentlessly focuses all attention on race.

8   In contrast, Lyndon Johnson's June 1965 address to Howard University, in which the concept of affirmative action was first unveiled, did not ignore class. In a speech drafted by Moynihan, Johnson spoke of the bifurcation of the black community, and, in his celebrated metaphor, said we needed to aid those "hobbled" in life's race by past discrimination. This suggested special help for disadvantaged blacks, not all blacks; for the young Clarence Thomas, but not for Clarence Thomas's son. Johnson balked at implementing the thematic language of his speech. His Executive Order 11246, calling for "affirmative action" among federal contractors, initially meant greater outreach and required hiring without respect to race. In fact, LBJ rescinded his Labor Department's proposal to provide for racial quotas in the construction industry in Philadelphia. It fell to Richard Nixon to implement the "Philadelphia Plan," in what Nixon's aides say was a conscious effort to drive a wedge between blacks and labor. (Once he placed racial preferences on the table, Nixon adroitly extricated himself, and by 1972 was campaigning against racial quotas.)

9   The ironies were compounded by the Supreme Court. In the 1974 case *DeFunis v. Odegaard*, in which a system of racial preferences in law school admissions was at issue, it was the Court's liberal giant, William O. Douglas, who argued that racial preferences were unconstitutional, and suggested instead that preferences be based on disadvantage. Four years later, in the *Bakke* case, the great proponent of affirmative action as a

means to achieve "diversity" was Nixon appointee Lewis F. Powell Jr. Somewhere along the line, the right wing embraced Douglas and Critical Race Theory embraced Powell.

Today, the left pushes racial preferences, even for the most advantaged minorities, in order to promote diversity and provide role models for disadvantaged blacks—an argument which, if it came from Ronald Reagan, the left would rightly dismiss as trickle-down social theory. Today, when William Julius Wilson argues the opposite of the Moynihan report— that the problems facing the black community are rooted more in class than race—it is Wilson who is excoriated by civil rights groups. The left can barely utter the word "class," instead resorting to euphemisms such as "income groups," "wage earners" and "people who play by the rules." 10

For all of this, the left has paid a tremendous price. On a political level, with a few notable exceptions, the history of the past twenty-five years is a history of white, working-class Robert Kennedy Democrats turning first into Wallace Democrats, then into Nixon and Reagan Democrats and ultimately into today's Angry White Males. Time and again, the white working class votes its race rather than its class, and Republicans win. The failure of the left to embrace class also helps turn poor blacks, for whom racial preferences are, in Stephen Carter's words, "stunningly irrelevant," toward Louis Farrakhan. 11

On the merits, the left has committed itself to a goal— equality of group results—which seems highly radical, when it is in fact rather unambitious. To the extent that affirmative action, at its ultimate moment of success, merely creates a self-perpetuating black elite along with a white one, its goal is modest—certainly more conservative than real equality of opportunity, which gives blacks and whites and other Americans of all economic strata a fair chance at success. 12

The priority given to race over class has inevitably exacerbated white racism. Today, both liberals and conservatives conflate race and class because it serves both of their purposes to do so. Every year, when SAT scores are released, the breakdown by race shows enormous gaps between blacks on the one hand and whites and Asians on the other. The NAACP cites these figures as evidence that we need to do more. Charles Murray cites the same statistics as evidence of intractable racial differences. We rarely see a breakdown of scores by class; which would show enormous gaps between rich and poor, gaps that would help explain the differences in scores by race. 13

14   On the legal front, it once made some strategic sense to emphasize race over class. But when states moved to the remedial phase—and began trying to address past discrimination—the racial focus became a liability. The strict scrutiny that struck down Jim Crow is now used, to varying degrees, to curtail racial preferences. Class, on the other hand, is not one of the suspect categories under the Fourteenth Amendment, which leaves class-based remedies much less assailable.

15   If class-based affirmative action is a theory that liberals should take seriously, how would it work in practice? In this magazine, Michael Kinsley has asked, "Does Clarence Thomas, the sharecropper's kid, get more or fewer preference points than the unemployed miner's son from Appalachia?" Most conservative proponents of class-based affirmative action have failed to explain their idea with any degree of specificity. Either they're insincere—offering the alternative only for tactical reasons—or they're stumped.

16   The former is more likely. While the questions of implementation are serious and difficult, they are not impossible to answer. At the university level, admissions committees deal every day with precisely the type of apples-and-oranges question that Kinsley poses. Should a law school admit an applicant with a 3.2 GPA from Yale or a 3.3 from Georgetown? How do you compare those two if one applicant worked for the Peace Corps but the other had slightly higher LSATs?

17   In fact, a number of universities already give preferences for disadvantaged students in addition to racial minorities. Since 1989 Berkeley has granted special consideration to applicants "from socioeconomically disadvantaged back-grounds...regardless of race or ethnicity." Temple University Law School has, since the 1970s, given preference to "applicants who have overcome exceptional and continuous economic deprivation." And at Hastings College of Law, 20 percent of the class is set aside for disadvantaged students through the Legal Equal Opportunity Program. Even the U.C.-Davis medical program challenged by Allan Bakke was limited to "disadvantaged" minorities, a system which Davis apparently did not find impossible to administer.

18   Similar class-based preference programs could be provided by public employers and federal contractors for high school graduates not pursuing college, on the theory that at that age their class-based handicaps hide their true potential and are not at all of their own making. In public contracting, government agencies could follow the model of New York

City's old class-based program, which provided preferences based not on the ethnicity or gender of the contractor, but to small firms located in New York City which did part of their business in depressed areas or employed economically disadvantaged workers.

The definition of class or disadvantage may vary according   19
to context, but if, for example, the government chose to require class-based affirmative action from universities receiving federal funds, it is possible to devise an enforceable set of objective standards for deprivation. If the aim of class-based affirmative action is to provide a system of genuine equality of opportunity, a leg up to promising students who have done well despite the odds, we have a wealth of sociological data to devise an obstacles test. While some might balk at the very idea of reducing disadvantage to a number, we currently reduce intellectual promise to numbers—SATs and GPAs— and adding a number for disadvantage into the calculus just makes deciding who gets ahead and who does not a little fairer.

There are three basic ways to proceed: with a simple, mod-   20
erate or complex definition. The simple method is to ask college applicants their family's income and measure disadvantage by that factor alone, on the theory that income is a good proxy for a whole host of economic disadvantages (such as bad schools or a difficult learning environment). This oversimplified approach is essentially the tack we've taken with respect to compensatory race-based affirmative action. For example, most affirmative action programs ask applicants to check a racial box and sweep all the ambiguities under the rug. Even though African Americans have, as justice Thurgood Marshall said in *Bakke,* suffered a history "different in kind, not just degree, from that of other ethnic groups," universities don't calibrate preferences based on comparative group disadvantage (and, in the Davis system challenged by Bakke, two-thirds of the preferences went to Mexican-Americans and Asians, not blacks). We also ignore the question of when an individual's family immigrated in order to determine whether the family was even theoretically subject to the official discrimination in this country on which preferences are predicated.

"Diversity" was supposed to solve all this by saying we don't   21
care about compensation, only viewpoint. But, again, if universities are genuinely seeking diversity of viewpoints, they should inquire whether a minority applicant really does have the "minority viewpoint" being sought. Derrick Bell's famous

statement—"the ends of diversity are not served by people who look black and think white"—is at once repellent and a relevant critique of the assumption that all minority members think alike. In theory, we need some assurance from the applicant that he or she will in fact interact with students of different backgrounds, lest the cosmetic diversity of the freshman yearbook be lost to the reality of ethnic theme houses.

22   The second way to proceed, the moderately complicated calculus of class, would look at what sociologists believe to be the Big Three determinants of life chances: parental income, education and occupation. Parents' education, which is highly correlated with a child's academic achievement, can be measured in number of years. And while ranking occupations might seem hopelessly complex, various attempts to do so objectively have yielded remarkably consistent results—from the Barr Scale of the early 1920s to Alba Edwards' Census rankings of the 1940s to the Duncan Scores of the 1960s.

23   The third alternative, the complex calculus of disadvantage, would count all the factors mentioned, but might also look at net worth, the quality of secondary education, neighborhood influences and family structure. An applicant's family wealth is readily available from financial aid forms, and provides a long-term view of relative disadvantage, to supplement the "snap-shot" picture that income provides. We also know that schooling opportunities are crucial to a student's life chances, even controlling for home environment. Some data suggest that a disadvantaged student at a middle-class school does better on average than a middle-class student at a school with high concentrations of poverty. Objective figures are available to measure secondary school quality—from per student expenditure, to the percentage of students receiving free or reduced-price lunches, to a school's median score on standardized achievement tests. Neighborhood influences, measured by the concentration of poverty within Census tracts or zip codes, could also be factored in, since numerous studies have found that living in a low-income community can adversely affect an individual's life chances above and beyond family income. Finally, everyone from Dan Quayle to Donna Shalala agrees that children growing up in single-parent homes have a tougher time. This factor could be taken into account as well.

24   The point is not that this list is the perfect one, but that it *is* possible to devise a series of fairly objective and verifiable factors that measure the degree to which a teenager's true potential has been hidden. (As it happens, the complex defini-

tion is the one that disproportionately benefits African Americans. Even among similar income groups, blacks are more likely than whites to live in concentrated poverty, go to bad schools and live in single-parent homes.) It's just not true that a system of class preferences is inherently harder to administer than a system based on race. Race only seems simpler because we have ignored the ambiguities. And racial preferences are just as easy to ridicule. To paraphrase Kinsley, does a new Indian immigrant get fewer or more points than a third-generation Latino whose mother is Anglo?

Who should benefit? Mickey Kaus, in "Class Is In," (Times   25
Review of Books, March 27) argued that class preferences should be reserved for the underclass. But the injuries of class extend beyond the poorest. The offspring of the working poor and the working class lack advantages, too, and indeed SAT scores correlate lockstep with income at every increment. Unless you believe in genetic inferiority, these statistics suggest unfairness is not confined to the underclass. As a practical matter, a teenager who emerges from the underclass has little chance of surviving at an elite college. At Berkeley, administrators found that using a definition of disadvantaged, under which neither parent attended a four-year college and the family could not afford to pay $1,000 in education expenses, failed to bring in enough students who were likely to pass.

Still, there are several serious objections to class-based   26
preferences that must be addressed.

1. *We're not ready to be color-blind because racial discrimina-*   27
tion continues to afflict our society. Ron Brown says affirmative action "continues to be needed not to redress grievances of the past, but the current discrimination that continues to exist." This is a relatively new theory, which conveniently elides the fact that preferences were supposed to be temporary. It also stands logic on its head. While racial discrimination undoubtedly still exists, the Civil Rights Act of 1964 meant to address prospective discrimination. Affirmative action—discrimination in itself—makes sense only to the extent that there is a current-day legacy of *past* discrimination which new prospective laws cannot reach back and remedy.

In the contexts of education and employment, the Civil   28
Rights Act already contains powerful tools to address intentional and unintentional discrimination. The Civil Rights Act of 1991 reaffirmed the need to address unintentional discrimination—by requiring employers to justify employment practices that are statistically more likely to hurt minorities—but it did so without crossing the line to required preferences.

This principle also applies to Title VI of the Civil Rights Act, so that if, for example, it can be shown that the SAT produces an unjustified disparate impact, a university can be barred from using it. In addition, "soft" forms of affirmative action, which require employers and universities to broaden the net and interview people from all races are good ways of ensuring positions are not filled by word of mouth, through wealthy white networks.

29   We have weaker tools to deal with discrimination in other areas of life—say, taxi drivers who refuse to pick up black businessmen—but how does a preference in education or employment remedy that wrong? By contrast, there is nothing illegal about bad schools, bad housing and grossly stunted opportunities for the poor. A class preference is perfectly appropriate.

30   2. *Class preferences will be just as stigmatizing as racial preferences.* Kinsley argues that "any debilitating self-doubt that exists because of affirmative action is not going to be mitigated by being told you got into Harvard because of your 'socioeconomic disadvantage' rather than your race."

31   But class preferences are different from racial preferences in at least two important respects. First, stigma—in one's own eyes and the eyes of others—is bound up with the question of whether an admissions criterion is accepted as legitimate. Students with good grades aren't seen as getting in "just because they're smart." And there appears to be a societal consensus—from Douglas to Scalia—that kids from poor backgrounds deserve a leg up. Such a consensus has never existed for class-blind racial preferences.

32   Second, there is no myth of inferiority in this country about the abilities of poor people comparable to that about African Americans. Now, if racial preferences are purely a matter of compensatory justice, then the question of whether preferences exacerbate white racism is not relevant. But today racial preferences are often justified by social utility (bringing different racial groups together helps dispel stereotypes) in which case the social consequences are highly relevant. The general argument made by proponents of racial preferences—that policies need to be grounded in social reality, not ahistorical theory—cuts in favor of the class category. Why? Precisely because there is no stubborn historical myth for it to reinforce.

33   Kaus makes a related argument when he says that class preferences "will still reward those who play the victim." But if objective criteria are used to define the disadvantaged,

there is no way to "play" the victim. Poor and working-class teenagers are the victims of class inequality not of their own making. Preferences, unlike, say, a welfare check, tell poor teenagers not that they are helpless victims, but that we think their long-run potential is great, and we're going to give them a chance—if they work their tails off—to prove themselves.

3. *Class preferences continue to treat people as members of*   34
groups as opposed to individuals. Yes. But so do university admissions policies that summarily reject students below a certain SAT level. It's hard to know what treating people as individuals means. (Perhaps if university admissions committees interviewed the teachers of each applicant back to kindergarten to get a better picture of their academic potential, we'd be treating them more as individuals.) The question is not whether we treat people as members of groups—that's inevitable—but whether the group is a relevant one. And in measuring disadvantage (and hidden potential) class is surely a much better proxy than race.

4. *Class-based affirmative action will not yield a diverse stu-*   35
dent body in elite colleges. Actually, there is reason to believe that class preferences will disproportionately benefit people of color in most contexts—since minorities are disproportionately poor. In the university context, however, class-based preferences were rejected during the 1970s in part because of fear that they would produce inadequate numbers of minority students. The problem is that when you control for income, African American students do worse than white and Asian students on the SAT—due in part to differences in culture and linguistic patterns, and in part to the way income alone as a measurement hides other class-based differences among ethnic groups.

The concern is a serious and complicated one. Briefly, there   36
are four responses. First, even Murray and Richard Herrnstein agree that the residual racial gap in scores has declined significantly in the past two decades, so the concern, though real, is not as great as it once was. Second, if we use the sophisticated definition of class discussed earlier—which reflects the relative disadvantage of blacks vis-à-vis whites of the same income level—the racial gap should close further. Third, we can improve racial diversity by getting rid of unjustified preferences—for alumni kids or students from underrepresented geographic regions—which disproportionately hurt people of color. Finally, if the goal is to provide genuine equal opportu-

nity, not equality of group result, and if we are satisfied that a meritocratic system which corrects for class inequality is the best possible approximation of that equality, then we have achieved our goal.

37   5. *Class-based affirmative action will cause as much resentment among those left out as race-based affirmative action.* Kinsley argues that the rejected applicant in the infamous Jesse Helms commercial from 1990 would feel just as angry for losing out on a class-based as a race-based preference, since both involve "making up for past injustice." The difference, of course, is that class preferences go to the actual victims of class injury, mooting the whole question of intergenerational justice. In the racial context, this was called "victim specificity." Even the Reagan administration was in favor of compensating actual victims of racial discrimination.

38   The larger point implicit in Kinsley's question is a more serious one: that any preference system, whether race- or class-based, is "still a form of zero-sum social engineering." Why should liberals push for class preferences at all? Why not just provide more funding for education, safer schools, better nutrition? The answer is that liberals should do these things; but we cannot hold our breath for it to happen. In 1993, when all the planets were aligned—a populist Democratic president, Democratic control of both Houses of Congress—they produced what *The New York Times* called "A BUDGET WORTHY OF MR. BUSH." Cheaper alternatives, such as preferences, must supplement more expensive strategies of social spending. Besides, to the extent that class preferences help change the focus of public discourse from race to class, they help reforge the coalition needed to sustain the social programs liberals want.

39   Class preferences could restore the successful formula on which the early civil rights movement rested: morally unassailable underpinnings and a relatively inexpensive agenda. It's crucial to remember that Martin Luther King Jr. called for special consideration based on class, not race. After laying out a forceful argument for the special debt owed to blacks, King rejected the call for a Negro Bill of Rights in favor of a Bill of Rights for the Disadvantaged. It was King's insight that there were nonracial ways to remedy racial wrongs, and that the injuries of class deserve attention along with the injuries of race.

40   None of this is to argue that King would have opposed affirmative action if the alternative were to do nothing. For

Jesse Helms to invoke King's color-blind rhetoric now that it is in the interests of white people to do so is the worst kind of hypocrisy. Some form of compensation is necessary, and I think affirmative action, though deeply flawed, is better than nothing.

But the opportunity to save affirmative action of any kind   41 may soon pass. If the Supreme Court continues to narrow the instances in which racial preferences are justified, if California voters put an end to affirmative action in their state and if Congress begins to roll back racial preferences in legislation which President Clinton finds hard to veto—or President Phil Gramm signs with gusto—conservatives will have less and less reason to bargain. Now is the time to call their bluff.

Ellen Willis
Race, Class, and the State

The following essay by Ellen Willis appeared in The Village Voice *in the middle of May 1995, a month or so after the previous essay by Richard Kahlenberg was published.* The Village Voice *is a weekly newspaper for New Yorkers that has a decidedly liberal and irreverent tone. It reports on current events (national and local) and very thoroughly covers contemporary culture—films, books, music, dance, and so forth. (Another essay by Willis is in the Family Matters part of* Conversations, *page 507. She is a journalism professor at New York University and author of* No More Nice Girls: Countercultural Essays *[1992].)*

"Class, Not Race" is the title of a recent *New Republic* arti-   1 cle by Richard Kahlenberg, which argues that affirmative action should be based on economic disadvantage. Those words could as easily be the bumper sticker for a larger political strategy long favored by liberals and populists distressed at the defection of working-class whites from the New Deal coalition. As Kahlenberg wistfully puts it, "An emphasis on class inequality meant Robert Kennedy riding in a motorcade through cheering white and black sections of racially torn

Gary, Indiana, in 1968, with black Mayor Richard Hatcher on one side, and white working-class boxing hero Tony Zale on the other."

2   I've never bought this formulation; to me it has always sounded suspiciously like "Economics Not Culture," a way of dismissing not only racial but sexual conflict. Anyway, I disagree with its basic assumption—I think the coalition was ultimately derailed less by race, per se, than by the "War on Poverty" approach to class politics, which pitted the poor against the working and lower-middle classes instead of focusing on their common interest in extending public services and universal social benefits financed by a progressive tax system. And now that Kahlenberg and other liberal commentators are applying this slogan to the affirmative action debate, it strikes me as a nice, progressive-sounding way to make an end run around a messy issue.

3   The original point of affirmative action, as I argued in an earlier column, was to tackle forms of reflexive, unconscious cultural discrimination against minorities and women that could not be attributed to individuals with provable intent. As an inherently modest strategy for integrating the middle class, it made sense only insofar as it reflected a social consensus that such forms of discrimination actually exist and are a serious problem. That consensus has now eroded to the point where even proponents of affirmative action justify it as reparations and "diversity"—i.e., representation—rather than as a remedy for ongoing discrimination. At the heart of anti–affirmative action resentment is the belief that blacks (the main target at the moment) are falsely blaming their condition on racism rather than on their own inferiority.

4   In the context of this history, "class not race" is something of a non sequitur. For one thing, while there is certainly cultural discrimination based on class, this is insult added to a more basic injury: unlike skin color or gender, class is inherently a vehicle of social stratification. And unlike racial minorities, Kahlenberg's proposed constituency, "the offspring of the working poor and the working class," are undoubtedly a majority of the population of their age group, and one that's growing all the time. To give working-class kids "genuine equal opportunity"—Kahlenberg's professed goal—would mean significantly curtailing the opportunities of the middle class and undermining the most basic function of the present educational system, which is to serve as a gatekeeper protecting middle- and upper-class privilege.

Needless to say, Kahlenberg has nothing this radical in   5
mind. Since actually doing away with class hierarchy is currently beyond the pale of serious political discussion, what
passes for debate about class in America generally boils down
to an argument between Darwinian meritocrats and advocates of mitigating class differences with social democratic
measures (including free or cheap higher education). And we
all know who's winning that argument these days. Under the
circumstances, Kahlenberg opts for Darwinian meritocracy
with a human face. "Why should liberals push for class preferences at all?" he asks. "Why not just provide more funding
for education, safer schools, better nutrition? The answer is
that liberals should do these things; but we cannot hold our
breath for it to happen." Instead, let's give "a leg up to promising students who have done well despite the odds."

Aside from his charming suggestion that the disadvantage   6
of coming from a single-parent home should be considered
when deciding who gets a leg up (don't single mothers have
enough problems without being accused of staying unmarried
so they can get their kids into Harvard?), Kahlenberg is probably right in thinking that working- and middle-class whites
will not resent this attempt to help Horatio Alger along in the
same way that they resent the competition of "unqualified"
blacks. But that's because giving a little help to the certifiably
deserving poor rocks no social boats; on the contrary it bol-
sters an increasingly shaky American myth (hard work will get
you anywhere, etc.), without raising any disturbing challenges
to received ideas of who deserves what. Tellingly, Kahlenberg
focuses entirely on education and doesn't consider how "class
preferences" might be applied to the workplace, though markers of class—dress, accent, cultural references, and so on—
figure prominently and prejudicially in hiring decisions.
Adapting affirmative action to confront such prejudices, far
from defusing the issue, would merely extend conflict about
multiculturalism into complicated new arenas.

I began working on this piece shortly before Oklahoma   7
City. After the bombing—which looks more and more like one
of those watershed events that give shape to a murky period
of history and reframe public debate—it occurred to me that
I was missing an important point about affirmative action,
probably because it was so obvious: the campaign against a.a.
is among other things a linchpin of the right's attack on federal authority. At present, the U.S. government remains the

chief source of whatever institutional power (as distinct from cultural influence) egalitarian social movements have managed to achieve since the New Deal. This fact has made the feds an unambiguous object of fear and loathing on the right; the welfare state has more or less replaced Communism as the catalyst of an alliance between restless post–Cold War capitalists and America's latest cultural antihero: the post–civil rights, post-Vietnam, postfeminist white guy out to prove life is a Michael Douglas movie. At the same time, the equation of social welfare with government is by no means unproblematic for the left.

8   The problem starts with the ongoing soul-search about why said white guys, most of whom are being royally screwed by said capitalists, nonetheless persist in seeing blacks/women/liberals/government as the enemy rather than the banks and the corporations. Liberal abdication on class issues is no doubt part of the answer, and so is the displacement of anger from rich and powerful targets to poor and vulnerable ones. But in my view, the most profound reason for this seeming contradiction is that economic motives are secondary to people's need for freedom and for satisfying sexual and emotional lives—and that when those needs are thwarted, enjoying power over others feels like a matter of psychic survival.

9   It follows from this perspective that opposing the right's assault on egalitarian social policies is hardly a simple matter of defending the welfare state. The state is, after all, an authoritarian institution. Its chief function is enforcing the existing social order; for the most part it serves the interests of other powerful institutions, from the corporation to the church. True, democratic ideology, various constitutional rights and liberties, and the electoral system make the American state and its agencies more vulnerable to public pressure than the corporation, the church, or any other "private" institution. Within limits, social movements have been able to influence and even participate in government, to correct private injustices and promote a vital public life. When such movements are powerful and potentially disruptive, the state will accommodate them because its ultimate imperative is maintaining social stability. But it's important to remember—and the left seems to have a hard time with this—that movements, not the state itself, are responsible for every hard-won egalitarian measure on the books.

10   Now that conservative movements are ascendant, the state is rapidly throwing off its social welfare baggage. Since the

right seems determined to wreck the entire existing infrastructure of public services and amenities, from support for
the poor and the aged to schools, hospitals, libraries, transit
systems, environmental protections—you name it—those of
us who oppose this destructive, indeed barbaric, impulse
have no choice, in the short run, but to defend government.
Yet without an alternative vision of how a genuinely free society might organize collective activity for the common good,
the left will always be caught in a contradiction: in a statist
system, social cooperation comes packaged with oppression,
which gives it a bad name.

Affirmative action reflects this dilemma. It was invented to   11
address the question "How can we placate minorities and
women in a way that will be as inexpensive and disturb the
social structure as little as possible?" The answer, in effect,
has been state-managed scarcity—giving "underrepresented
groups" a bit more of a shot at the decreasing number of decent jobs and at educational opportunities less and less likely
to lead to decent jobs. If the white guys feel had by this—well,
we're all being had. The issue is what to do about it other than
rush headlong toward fascism. Ignoring race (or sex, for that
matter) won't help.

Kurt Vonnegut Jr.
Harrison Bergeron

*After graduating from Cornell University, Kurt Vonnegut Jr.
(born in 1922 in Indianapolis) worked in journalism and public relations. Then he started publishing best-selling novels that
often feature imaginary (yet all too real) settings, a satiric edge,
and his characteristic narrative voice. Among them are* Cat's
Cradle, Slaughterhouse-Five, Breakfast of Champions, *and*
Jailbird. *"Harrison Bergeron" was published as part of his collection of stories titled* Welcome to the Monkey House *(1961).*

The year was 2081, and everybody was finally equal. They   1
weren't only equal before God and the law. They were equal
every which way. Nobody was smarter than anybody else. Nobody was better looking than anybody else. Nobody was

stronger or quicker than anybody else. All this equality was due to the 211th, 212th, and 213th Amendments to the Constitution, and to the unceasing vigilance of agents of the United States Handicapper General.

2   Some things about living still weren't quite right, though. April, for instance, still drove people crazy by not being springtime. And it was in that clammy month that the H-G men took George and Hazel Bergeron's fourteen-year-old son, Harrison, away.

3   It was tragic, all right, but George and Hazel couldn't think about it very hard. Hazel had a perfectly average intelligence, which meant she couldn't think about anything except in short bursts. And George, while his intelligence was way above normal, had a little mental handicap radio in his ear. He was required by law to wear it at all times. It was tuned to a government transmitter. Every twenty seconds or so, the transmitter would send out some sharp noise to keep people like George from taking unfair advantage of their brains.

4   George and Hazel were watching television. There were tears on Hazel's cheeks, but she'd forgotten for the moment what they were about.

5   On the television screen were ballerinas.

6   A buzzer sounded in George's head. His thoughts fled in panic, like bandits from a burglar alarm.

7   "That was a real pretty dance, that dance they just did," said Hazel.

8   "Huh?" said George.

9   "That dance—it was nice," said Hazel.

10   "Yup," said George. He tried to think a little about the ballerinas. They weren't really very good—no better than anybody else would have been, anyway. They were burdened with sashweights and bags of birdshot, and their faces were masked, so that no one, seeing a free and graceful gesture or a pretty face, would feel like something the cat drug in. George was toying with the vague notion that maybe dancers shouldn't be handicapped. But he didn't get very far with it before another noise in his ear radio scattered his thoughts.

11   George winced. So did two out of the eight ballerinas.

12   Hazel saw him wince. Having no mental handicap herself, she had to ask George what the latest sound had been.

13   "Sounded like somebody hitting a milk bottle with a ball peen hammer," said George.

14   "I'd think it would be real interesting, hearing all the different sounds," said Hazel, a little envious. "All the things they think up."

"Um," said George.   15
"Only, if I was Handicapper General, you know what I   16
would do?" said Hazel. Hazel, as a matter of fact, bore a
strong resemblance to the Handicapper General, a woman
named Diana Moon Glampers. "If I was Diana Moon
Glampers," said Hazel, "I'd have chimes on Sunday—just
chimes. Kind of in honor of religion."
"I could think, if it was just chimes," said George.   17
"Well—maybe make 'em real loud," said Hazel. "I think I'd   18
make a good Handicapper General."
"Good as anybody else," said George.   19
"Who knows better'n I do what normal is?" said Hazel.   20
"Right," said George. He began to think glimmeringly   21
about his abnormal son who was now in jail, about Harrison,
but a twenty-one-gun salute in his head stopped that.
"Boy!" said Hazel, "that was a doozy, wasn't it?"   22
It was such a doozy that George was white and trembling,   23
and tears stood on the rims of his red eyes. Two of the eight
ballerinas had collapsed to the studio floor, [and] were holding their temples.
"All of a sudden you look so tired," said Hazel. "Why don't   24
you stretch out on the sofa, so's you can rest your handicap
bag on the pillows, honeybunch." She was referring to the
forty-seven pounds of birdshot in a canvas bag, which was
padlocked around George's neck. "Go on and rest the bag for
a little while," she said. "I don't care if you're not equal to me
for a while."
George weighed the bag with his hands. "I don't mind it,"   25
he said. "I don't notice it any more. It's just a part of me."
"You been so tired lately—kind of wore out," said Hazel. "If   26
there was just some way we could make a little hole in the
bottom of the bag, and just take out a few of them lead balls.
Just a few."
"Two years in prison and two thousand dollars fine for ev-   27
ery ball I took out," said George. "I don't call that a bargain."
"If you could just take a few out when you came home   28
from work," said Hazel. "I mean—you don't compete with
anybody around here. You just set around."
"If I tried to get away with it," said George, "then other   29
people'd get away with it—and pretty soon we'd be right back
to the dark ages again, with everybody competing against everybody else. You wouldn't like that, would you?"
"I'd hate it," said Hazel.   30
"There you are," said George. "The minute people start   31
cheating on laws, what do you think happens to society?"

32   If Hazel hadn't been able to come up with an answer to this
question George couldn't have supplied one. A siren was going off in his head.

33   "Reckon it'd fall all apart," said Hazel.

34   "What would?" said George blankly.

35   "Society," said Hazel uncertainly. "Wasn't that what you
just said?"

36   "Who knows?" said George.

37   The television program was suddenly interrupted for a
news bulletin. It wasn't clear at first as to what the bulletin
was about, since the announcer, like all announcers, had a serious speech impediment. For about half a minute, and in a
state of high excitement, the announcer tried to say, "Ladies
and gentlemen—"

38   He finally gave up, handed the bulletin to a ballerina to
read.

39   "That's all right—" Hazel said of the announcer, "he tried.
That's the big thing. He tried to do the best he could with
what God gave him. He should get a nice raise for trying so
hard."

40   "Ladies and gentlemen—" said the ballerina, reading the
bulletin. She must have been extraordinarily beautiful, because the mask she wore was hideous. And it was easy to see
that she was the strongest and most graceful of all the dancers, for her handicap bags were as big as those worn by two-
hundred-pound men.

41   And she had to apologize at once for her voice, which was
a very unfair voice for a woman to use. Her voice was a warm,
luminous, timeless melody. "Excuse me—" she said, and she
began again, making her voice absolutely uncompetitive.

42   "Harrison Bergeron, age fourteen," she said in a grackle
squawk, "has just escaped from jail, where he was held on
suspicion of plotting to overthrow the government. He is a genius and an athlete, is under-handicapped, and should be regarded as extremely dangerous."

43   A police photograph of Harrison Bergeron was flashed on
the screen upside down, then sideways, upside down again,
then right side up. The picture showed the full length of Harrison against a background calibrated in feet and inches. He
was exactly seven feet tall.

44   The rest of Harrison's appearance was Halloween and hardware. Nobody had ever borne heavier handicaps. He had outgrown hindrances faster than the H-G men could think them
up. Instead of a little ear radio for a mental handicap, he wore

a tremendous pair of earphones, and spectacles with thick wavy lenses. The spectacles were intended to make him not only half blind, but to give him whanging headaches besides.

Scrap metal was hung all over him. Ordinarily, there was a certain symmetry, a military neatness to the handicaps issued to strong people, but Harrison looked like a walking junk-yard. In the race of life, Harrison carried three hundred pounds.

And to offset his good looks, the H-G men required that he wear at all times a red rubber ball for a nose, keep his eye-brows shaved off, and cover his even white teeth with black caps at snaggle-tooth random.

"If you see this boy," said the ballerina, "do not—I repeat, do not—try to reason with him."

There was the shriek of a door being torn from its hinges.

Screams and barking cries of consternation came from the television set. The photograph of Harrison Bergeron on the screen jumped again and again, as though dancing to the tune of an earthquake.

George Bergeron correctly identified the earthquake, and well he might have—for many was the time his own home had danced to the same crashing tune. "My God—" said George, "that must be Harrison!"

The realization was blasted from his mind instantly by the sound of an automobile collision in his head.

When George could open his eyes again, the photograph of Harrison was gone. A living, breathing Harrison filled the screen.

Clanking, clownish, and huge, Harrison stood in the center of the studio. The knob of the uprooted studio door was still in his hand. Ballerinas, technicians, musicians, and announc-ers cowered on their knees before him, expecting to die.

"I am the Emperor!" cried Harrison. "Do you hear? I am the Emperor! Everybody must do what I say at once!" He stamped his foot and the studio shook.

"Even as I stand here—" he bellowed, "crippled, hobbled, sickened—I am a greater ruler than any man who ever lived! Now watch me become what I *can* become!"

Harrison tore the straps of his handicap harness like wet tissue paper, tore straps guaranteed to support five thousand pounds.

Harrison's scrap-iron handicaps crashed to the floor.

Harrison thrust his thumbs under the bar of the padlock that secured his head harness. The bar snapped like celery.

Harrison smashed his headphones and spectacles against the wall.

59   He flung away his rubber-ball nose, revealed a man that would have awed Thor, the god of thunder.

60   "I shall now select my Empress!" he said, looking down on the cowering people. "Let the first woman who dares rise to her feet claim her mate and her throne!"

61   A moment passed, and then a ballerina arose, swaying like a willow.

62   Harrison plucked the mental handicap from her ear, snapped off her physical handicaps with marvelous delicacy. Last of all, he removed her mask.

63   She was blindingly beautiful.

64   "Now—" said Harrison, taking her hand, "shall we show the people the meaning of the word dance? Music!" he commanded.

65   The musicians scrambled back into their chairs, and Harrison stripped them of their handicaps, too. "Play your best," he told them, "and I'll make you barons and dukes and earls."

66   The music began. It was normal at first—cheap, silly, false. But Harrison snatched two musicians from their chairs, waved them like batons as he sang the music as he wanted it played. He slammed them back into their chairs.

67   The music began again and was much improved.

68   Harrison and his Empress merely listened to the music for a while—listened gravely, as though synchronizing their heartbeats with it.

69   They shifted their weights to their toes.

70   Harrison placed his big hands on the girl's tiny waist, letting her sense the weightlessness that would soon be hers.

71   And then, in an explosion of joy and grace, into the air they sprang!

72   Not only were the laws of the land abandoned, but the law of gravity and the laws of motion as well.

73   They reeled, whirled, swiveled, flounced, capered, gamboled, and spun.

74   They leaped like deer on the moon.

75   The studio ceiling was thirty feet high, but each leap brought the dancers nearer to it.

76   It became their obvious intention to kiss the ceiling.

77   They kissed it.

78   And then, neutralizing gravity with love and pure will, they remained suspended in air inches below the ceiling, and they kissed each other for a long, long time.

It was then that Diana Moon Glampers, the Handicapper   79
General, came into the studio with a double-barreled ten-
gauge shotgun. She fired twice, and the Emperor and the Empress were dead before they hit the floor.

Diana Moon Glampers loaded the gun again. She aimed it   80
at the musicians and told them they had ten seconds to get
their handicaps back on.

It was then that the Bergerons' television tube burned out.   81

Hazel turned to comment about the blackout to George.   82
But George had gone out into the kitchen for a can of beer.

George came back in with the beer, paused while a handi-   83
cap signal shook him up. And then he sat down again. "You
been crying?" he said to Hazel.

"Yup," she said.   84

"What about?" he said.   85

"I forget," she said. "Something real sad on television."   86

"What was it?" he said.   87

"It's all kind of mixed up in my mind," said Hazel.   88

"Forget sad things," said George.   89

"I always do," said Hazel.   90

"That's my girl," said George. He winced. There was the   91
sound of a riveting gun in his head.

"Gee—I could tell that one was a doozy," said Hazel.   92

"You can say that again," said George.   93

"Gee—" said Hazel, "I could tell that one was a doozy."   94

Tom Toles
Cut the Gordian Knot

You probably recognize Tom Toles's political cartoons from their distinctive style and sharp wit. The cartoons appear in many newspapers and magazines, including the conservative newsweekly U.S. News & World Report, *which carried the following cartoon in June 1995. What exactly is the object of this particular satire—or does it cut in several ways?*

SEXUAL HARASSMENT

Kati Marton
An All Too Common Story

Kati Marton, a writer and formerly a network correspondent, contributed the following commentary to Newsweek *on October 21, 1991, just after the Clarence Thomas/Anita Hill controversy over sexual harassment.*

Is there a woman in the American workplace for whom 1
Prof. Anita Hill's painful revelations regarding sexual harassment do not resonate? For me, her recollections revived an incident I had suppressed for more than a decade and a half. Unlike Professor Hill's experience, my memory of sexual harassment will not leave a deep imprint on the nation's psyche. Mine is but one woman's story. The professor and I are products of vastly different cultures and professions: she an Oklahoma farm girl; I, Budapest-born and -raised, a relative newcomer to this land. In common we had this: both of us were determined to succeed in highly competitive and conspicuously male-dominated professions: hers the law, mine the media. Yet, listening to her testimony, I was struck by how similarly she and I, different in almost every way, responded to sexual pressures in our professional lives. In the wake of Anita Hill's searing memories, I now see my own experience as part of a sad, pervasive pattern of sexual blackmail in offices across the land.

I was 25 years old at the time, the same age as Professor 2
Hill when she worked for Judge Clarence Thomas at the Equal Employment Opportunity Commission. I was only six months into my job as an on-air reporter for a network affiliate in Philadelphia. Like Professor Hill, I, too, lacked a résumé. I, too, loved my job. On the day in question, a station news executive and I traveled by train to New York so that I could receive a George Foster Peabody Award for my work on a documentary on the Philadelphia Orchestra's visit to China. I delivered an earnest and self-conscious acceptance speech

to the media heavyweights gathered in the gold-trimmed room. At one point, I momentarily lost my composure and my newly acquired American accent when I mentioned that only a few years before, I did not even speak English. But through it all I basked in the warm glow of my peers' approval. It should have been a proud day for a neophyte reporter. It did not turn out that way.

3   My executive escort, seemingly bristling with pride (it was the first time a local Philadelphia television reporter had won the coveted Peabody), invited me and a childhood friend from Budapest to the Russian Tea Room to toast the event. The hours passed in a happy haze. "Isn't it time we headed for the Metroliner back to Philadelphia?" I asked the executive around nightfall. Having said goodnight to my friend, we walked to the limousine my colleague had hired for the occasion. But the car did not follow the familiar route to Penn Station. Without a word of prompting, the limo pulled up in front of the Hilton hotel. Too astonished and too intimidated to muster anything like a firm protest, I found myself following the executive into the hotel elevator. "I only want to get to know you better," he explained. "To talk to you."

4   And talk I did, with the feverish urgency of a drowning person clinging to a life raft. I saw talk as my only escape from certain disaster, a compromise between humiliating the man to whom I owed my career and my own revulsion at the situation he had placed me in. So I talked about my childhood, embellishing and dramatizing, in the manner of a stand-up comic auditioning for the big time. By midnight I had run out of steam and stories so I prodded him to talk about his life, his troubles. It was the most exhausting tap dance of my life, but it was the only way I could think of to deflect this man from pursuing what I assumed to be his own objectives. There was no time to even wonder how in God's name he presumed this was where I wanted to spend the proudest night of my short career. What gave a man with whom I had exchanged one handshake—and that on the day I was hired—this right? He assumed that right. I, loving my job, thinking I got it only by a stroke of luck, became his accomplice by not walking out, by not even voicing outrage. I did not have the nerve.

5   At dawn, he finally drifted off to sleep and I made my bleary-eyed way to the train and to Philadelphia. Toward evening, as I faced the bright lights of the studio cameras, I saw him just arriving to work. He looked much more rested than I. By then all memories of the previous day's brief

moment of glory had been supplanted by other memories. Irrational feelings of guilt regarding my conduct began to nag at me. Had I given the wrong signals? He seemed such a nice, square sort of family man. And why had I not walked out on him? The minute a woman decides to stay and stay silent, in her own mind at least, she loses the moral edge. Like thousands of women in newsrooms, offices and factories, I had swapped the moral edge for job security. I did not think I had the luxury of choice in the matter.

I suppose the executive felt sure I would never talk about his abortive attempt at seduction. He was right. I never have, until now. Nor have I let myself take much pride in that hard-won Peabody Award, fearing that the other memories would rush in beside them. But hearing Professor Hill's taut recitation, accompanied by the belittling comments of certain members of the gentleman's club on Capitol Hill, forced me to mentally revisit that room in the Hilton. Professor Hill's dignity did not mask the lasting humiliation that is the inevitable residue of such moments.

There is more than personal catharsis at stake in owning up to this long-suppressed incident. I am writing this not only because the memory would not let go. I am writing because Professor Hill's voice moved me to do so. I wanted to say to the Senate panel, "Look, I know why she stayed on with the man who insulted her. So many of us have been there, not liked ourselves for it, but have stayed." And there is another impulse to my speaking out now. If men and women alike pronounce such degrading episodes unacceptable, perhaps our daughters might be spared similar choices in their professional lives. No one should have to purchase job security at so high a price.

Frederic Hayward

Sexual Harassment—From a Man's Perspective

*Frederic Hayward was executive director of Men's Rights, Inc.,
a not-for-profit corporation that raises awareness on men's
issues, when (in October 1990) he contributed the following
essay to* The Business Journal, *a publication that discusses
issues of general interest to businesspeople in the Sacramento,
California, area.*

1   The newcomer approaches a second man and snarls, "Hey,
pal, you got a problem?" "No." "Well, I don't like the way
you're lookin' at me." Typical macho behavior? Women are
above that sort of thing?

2   Not exactly. It is at the insistence of women that simply looking at a woman "the wrong way" is banned by government.

3   On the surface, Freedom of Vision seems like a more fundamental right even than Freedom of Speech. Yet, just as laws
against pornography can prohibit a man from looking at a naked woman, laws against sexual harassment can prohibit him
from looking at a clothed woman while imagining her naked.

4   If you stare at a man and he doesn't like it, you risk a
punch in the jaw. If you stare at a woman and she doesn't like
it, you risk a megabuck financial settlement and/or a ruined
career.

5   The problem is not, of course, that we make too much of
sexual harassment; rather, the problem is that our perspective
is biased by narrow, sexist, political interests.

6   A less-biased look at sexual harassment reveals, among
other things, a host of women and men who are victimized by
female abuse of sexual power. Ignore the immensity of that
power at your peril.

7   Before our gender consciousness was raised by feminism,
men had most of the political-economic power, while women
had most of the sexual power. The traditional male-female relationship was based on the exchange of these two power imbalances. The traditional male-female contract consisted of
the man tapping his source of power to give physical and financial security to the woman while she, in return, tapped
her sexual power to give him access to her body.

8   Recent events hint at the enormous sexual power that can
be unleashed. Gary Hart gambled and lost the presidency in

order to have sex with a woman. Jim Bakker gambled and lost a multimillion-dollar ministry in order to have sex with a woman. In the American embassy in Moscow, Sgt. Clayton Lonetree sacrificed our nation's security in order to have sex with a woman. If a man would trade away the highest office, the greatest prestige and the deepest loyalty in order to have sex with a woman, only the most dogmatic could deny that he would trade away a letter of recommendation.

Feminist protestations of women's powerlessness (hence,   9
innocence) notwithstanding, most of us personally know of women who have used and abused their sexual power. Questions arise: If I or a woman do not get into graduate school because a female competitor has more A's from sleeping with more professors (Ilene F. was the notorious but proud example from my own university) then what are we victims of? If I or a woman do not get a job because a female competitor displays more enticing cleavage, then what are we victims of? If I or a woman do not get a promotion because a female competitor has an affair with our boss, then what are we victims of?

We do not even have a name for it, let alone a law against it.   10
Any analysis of sexual office politics that ignores this component might be "politically correct," but is woefully inadequate.

Furthermore, the sexual harassment for which we do have   11
a name has a silent, twin brother.

In essence, sexual harassment means requiring a person to   12
carry out a traditional sex role as a subcondition for employment. Since a main component of the traditional female role is to provide sexual gratification, women usually find themselves caught in the well-publicized trap of providing sex as part of a job.

A main component of the traditional male role, on the   13
other hand, is to bear physical risk and undertake heavy labor. The twin brother of sexual harassment, then, entails the primary assumption of dangerous and beast-of-burden tasks as a condition for a man's employment.

A people-based definition of sexual harassment would prob-   14
ably include as many male as female victims. Not surprisingly, a frequent complaint of male security officers is that equally paid female co-workers are routinely given less than equally risky assignments. Male sales agents complain that they are forced into front-line duty when potentially violent customers appear. The federal Equal Employment Opportunity Commission and state agencies are singularly unresponsive to male "crybabies."

The bottom line is that men suffer a disproportionate   15
share of work-related accidents. The male-centered form of

sexual "harassment" kills. Indeed, *USA Today* reports that men, who comprise about half the work force, suffer 95 percent of at-work fatalities and 82 percent of at-work murders! (In a telling comment on the media's deflection of attention away from male victimization, however, the article was simply headlined: "732 women were murdered on the job.")

16   This is not to say, of course, that there are no male victims of the female-centered definition of sexual harassment, in which sexual favors become a condition of employment.

17   Since women are just as human as men, they are just as likely to abuse power. There are cases where men incur sexual pressure from female (and gay male) bosses.

18   But for men, sex has historically been a reward for money and power, while for women, sex has been a means to money and power. Again, the traditional contract acknowledged that women start with sexual power and need not trade for it.

19   The so-called shortage of eligible men, a common complaint in women's magazines, attests to the continuing expectation that a man is not "eligible" if he stands below the woman on the ladder of success. The reason a female vice president is less likely to sexually harass her male secretary, therefore, has nothing to do with her higher standard of behavior. It is simply that she is conditioned to prefer an affair with the president.

20   Even when the concern is limited to only-female victims of only-female defined sexual harassment, moreover, the male perspective needs to be included before effective solutions can be developed. Blaming one gender exclusively (men) is as politically popular as it is specious. Women do play a role in perpetrating the harassment ethic.

21   Not unusually, my own sexual harassment training was at the hands of a woman. When I was young, I did not believe the peers and movie characters who encouraged me to never take "no" for an answer. The person who finally convinced me was Jane B. She was mercifully blunt about why her initial romantic interest in me had dissipated into a platonic friendship. I was too much of a gentleman, she informed me. Before making decisions, I had naively asked for her input. Worst of all, when getting sexual, I had foolishly waited for permission. "Be a man!" was her closing advice.

22   I tested her sexual harassment encouragement on a succession of women and found that it worked. The consistent romantic failure that had been my reward for treating women with "respect" was replaced by consistent romantic success.

Popular wisdom has it backward: Sexist conditioning has   23
not left most women ill-prepared to say an assertive "no."
Rather, it has left most women ill-prepared to give assertive
"yesses." That is, most men already assume that if a woman
means "no," she says "no." But experience has taught us that
when a woman means "yes," we cannot count on hearing it
clearly.

Before men can unlearn harassing behavior, we need to ex-   24
perience female initiative. Until then, the game of romance
will continue to have men playing the actor/predator and
women playing the object/prey. Until then, men will never be
sure whether a particular "no" means "No, I'm not interested
at all," or "No, I'm not ready now, but I might be ready later,
so you better try again because that is the only way you will
find out," or "Yes, but I don't want you to lose respect for me
by sounding too easy."

To make matters worse, since women are comparatively   25
passive when it comes to initiating, men become conditioned
to responding to visual cues. Indeed, some women in my
workshops assert that giving visual cues is the female version
of initiating. The problem, however, is that men cannot always read the visual signals they receive.

If a woman dresses to kill, for example, hoping to arouse   26
the interest of those men she likes, non-targeted men receive
many of the same visual cues. More and more men are, in
fact, complaining that provocative dress constitutes sexual
harassment against them.

Furthermore, sexual harassment is not necessarily a physi-   27
cal attack; it can even be an unwanted glance. Yet, the only
purpose of showing cleavage is to have people admire it; can
we really place all the blame on the man for looking?

Recently, I accompanied an attorney on her way to inter-   28
view a potential client, a woman who felt she was unfairly
fired. The attorney explained that she did not yet know what
the actual complaint would be because she did not yet know
the gender of the boss. If the boss was male, he would be
charged with sexual harassment. In other words, his actual
conduct was irrelevant; if there is a conflict between a male
boss and a female employee, the charge is sexual harassment.
It's automatic.

Indeed, a personnel director at one of the nation's largest   29
computer firms expressed his dismay to me at how many
good male executives he has lost from accusations (and even
simple threats of accusations) of sexual harassment.

30   As homely Henry Kissinger remarked, power is the ultimate aphrodisiac. For every executive who chases his secretary around the desk, there is a secretary who dreams of
marrying an executive and not having to be a secretary any
more.

31   Given the bitterness that can attend a broken love affair
and the bitterness that can plague office politics, combining
the two can be a powerful motivation to reach for any available weapon. The same safeguards that protect an innocent
victim of sexual harassment are a potent arsenal in the hands
of a bitter colleague/ex-lover.

32   Statistics do not tell us, therefore, how prevalent the problem is. We know only that the problem is serious. We also
know that the problem will persist as long as we turn a deaf
ear and a blind eye to the male perspective.

Phyllis Doloff
Today's Woman:
Victim or Opportunist?

*Phyllis Doloff, a human resources professional and freelance
writer, lives in Westfield, New Jersey. In September 1998, she
contributed the following essay to* Across the Board, *a mass-
circulation magazine that appeals to people interested in
business-oriented topics. When the editors of the magazine
solicited responses to the essay, they were deluged. A selection
of those responses follows the essay.*

1   Way back in the Dark Ages, when I was a lissome 23-year-
old, a supervisor reached out and took a fulsome pinch of
my butt. Not once, but twice. The first time it happened, I
thought I was mistaken. A week later, he pinched me again.
Being a perceptive and insightful individual, I was pretty sure
that lightning and imaginary butt-pinchers don't strike twice.

2   It was the unenlightened '70s, and I was actually—albeit
briefly—flattered by the attention. (Remember, I was all of
23.) After a moment's deep reflection, I decided I was P.O.'d. I

wasn't emotionally damaged. I didn't lose my ability to concentrate or hold a job. I slept like a log. I never missed a meal. And since no one told me I should be horribly wounded, I wasn't. No one told me I was a victim, or hurt, or helpless. So I wasn't. My self-esteem was still quite intact. It didn't occur to me that I should be anything other than mildly annoyed at his impudence.

I wasn't alone in being unaware that I should be injured 3 beyond hope of repair. Other women have similar tales of being pinched or otherwise bothered, of being hassled for dates or sexual favors, of bosses or peers run amok with varying degrees of mild or serious affronts. They dealt with it in a variety of ways that ranged from ignoring the offender until he gave up, to laughter, to reasonable and dignified confrontation, to quitting their jobs and moving on.

I know of one legal secretary whose boss developed a pen- 4 chant for pinching her breasts. He did it once, and she called him on it. He said he'd been to the dentist, he'd had Novocain, and he wasn't responsible for his actions. When he did it a second time, she put down her legal pad and walked out the door. She phoned the firm's managing partner the next day and explained to him why she was quitting. She left, and moved on to bigger and better jobs. Today she shakes her head and laughs at the boss who was such a jerk.

Was she angry at having to leave her job? Yes, but she was 5 otherwise quite healthy and unscathed. It never occurred to her, or me, that we should die endless deaths over the embarrassing behavior of one obnoxious schmo. Or that we should require stupefying retribution to salve some unhealing Promethean wound. Or that the right pinch in the wrong place could be a winning lottery ticket.

I wonder now if I wasn't more wounded by those two 6 pinches than I knew. How have I carried on since the moment when that man grabbed my butt? Had that supervisor pinched the same tush 20 years later, I suppose I might have had to go to the media to exorcise his and my demons and to obtain closure.

In fact, more and more of the walking wounded are doing 7 just that. I've seen weepy women moistly recounting (or hinting at) intimate tales and details of humiliating and unforgivable crimes perpetrated against their psyches, their sleep patterns, and their careers. Mostly they're performing this private and personal ritual for a gaggle of reporters who are gasping with glee over their prurient scoop. How it restoreth the soul to appear on the front page of the tabloids or (better yet) on the evening news! Alternatively, many find the sins of others are best expiated in the penalty phase of a successful sexual-harassment suit. Fame and cash are still the best cures for what ails us.

8   Many years after the fateful pinch, I addressed a group of women about the issue of sexual harassment in the work-place. I was part of a panel that consisted of a psychologist, an attorney, and a union mediator. I represented the "corpo-rate human resources" perspective. The audience was 99.5 percent women, 100 percent of whom were rooting for a cracklin' good evening of advice on suing the pants off anyone who looked at them cross-eyed. They were hostile—not to the all-female panel, but to the possibility that someone might have the opportunity to offend them and get away without paying through the nose. The entire panel was in basic agree-ment—publicity and lawsuits are the last and worst resort. The goal in any such dispute is that the offended party come away with dignity restored and the offending party with a clear understanding of appropriate behavior. The audience was plainly disappointed.

9   So what happened between then and now? Are we really so fragile? We have come to believe that the daily slings and ar-rows of outrageous fortune—and personal interaction—are more than enough to render us completely helpless.

10   Well, not *completely* helpless. There *is* one way to restore shattered self-esteem. It takes only a good contingency law-yer, a lawsuit filed within the statute of limitations, and a large cash settlement. "It's not the money," the victim weeps to the TV camera. "But I *do* have my eye on that new Lexus coupe with the leather interior," is the subtext. After all, if it were *not* the money, the award would be donated to some le-gal fund to make it possible for other damaged souls to have their day in court. The motive, then, is personal satisfaction (known as "revenge" in a less enlightened age) and enough money to pay for the Lexus. Ah, retribution is divine.

11   Remember that supervisor who pinched me? I confronted him and told him never to touch me again. I suppose he was in his early 40s. (It was hard for me to tell. At the time every-one who was more than five years older than I looked to be about the same age—ancient.) He told me I must be mis-taken. But he never pinched me again. I never had an inter-view with Sally Jessy Raphael or an attorney to represent me. And my self-esteem is utterly whole and healthy. There's just one thing missing. The Lexus.

Responses to Phyllis Doloff:
Letters to the Editor of *Across the Board*

To the Editor:

The article glibly refers to "sexual harassment in the work-   12
place" yet does not define, or adhere to, the legal definition of
what constitutes sexual harassment. Of course, almost any
woman in her 40s and older (including this writer) can recount
incidents of unwanted and unprovoked misbehavior in the
workplace in the days when such was considered acceptable.
Many of us simply dealt with it and moved on. At the same time,
we fought for our rights and won certain protections.

In any situation, some women will handle a workplace   13
problem on their own. Some women will find it necessary
and prudent to work with their human-resources department
or through a union grievance procedure. Some women will
act as opportunists if they can, and unfortunately some will
exploit the media (and perhaps the justice system) and may
be awarded damages in excess of those actually sustained.
However, there are genuine victims in an unjust society. A few
of these people are vulnerable and will need help in dealing
with sexual harassment in the workplace. Needing help and
being helpless are not the same thing.

Doloff tells of a legal secretary who simply "put down her   14
legal pad and walked out the door." Try that in an inner city
with a high unemployment rate. Try filing for unemployment
benefits when you've voluntarily walked off a job. Try contact-
ing the New York State Division of Human Rights and see
how long the wait is to even make an appointment to fill out
the paperwork to file a sexual-harassment complaint. Try
checking the backlog of EEOC cases. Last but not least, try
finding an attorney to bring a civil lawsuit unless you've already gone through the proper channels to resolve the matter.
I would suggest that Doloff stop reading the tabloids and start
reading the *National Law Journal*.

—Betty Kranzdorf

To the Editor:

What a sad and pitiful state the "fairer sex" occupies these   15
30 years after the women's-liberation movement—damsels in
distress weeping and mud-slinging when Prince Charming
steps over the line or, sometimes, merely disappoints. Doloff
is much too gentle in chiding today's fragile victims. Far too
many women disgrace the term *woman* by rejecting the effort

required to earn the equality, self-respect, and personal power they claimed they wanted. It is tragic that they cling to ignoble legal powers rather than embracing life's challenges and difficulties.

—Judith Sherven

To the Editor:

16   A significant shift, one of perhaps evolutionary reach, is taking place between the genders. Women are entering and being accepted into public life in ways unparalleled in human history. Sexual-harassment laws are but one of the sentries at the dewline of that shift.

17   Granted, they have been abused. Hysteria—often ballooning into full-fledged paranoia—has nurtured a menacing environment, leading to an alienation between the genders that the laws were intended to prevent. That is heinous in some cases and costly in all. However, to trivialize the laws, as Doloff does, is dangerously shortsighted. By mocking what is emerging, she denies reality, is regressive, and contributes nothing in the long run.

18   Men and women must evolve new ways to view and live with one another. Sexual-harassment laws, being an imperfect and sometimes feeble guide, are more than merely restraints. They are the incipient voice of an emerging future we all must attend to, whether we like it or not.

—James Sniechowski

To the Editor:

19   If a woman experiences inappropriate attention from a man at work, she has several choices about how to interpret the man's actions, and how she can respond. She can shrug it off, thinking, "He's a jerk." She can confront him directly with her objection to his behavior; she can complain to her supervisor; she can file a grievance with HR; she can call an attorney; she can freak out, and go out on stress disability—or any combination of these actions. As women who claim to seek equal status in the world of work, we need to be very careful in the choices we make about seeking redress of perceived wrongs.

20   There is often a huge difference between the "intent" of a behavior and its impact. At least 80 percent of sexual harassment is unintentional. Most men think they are giving a woman a compliment when they tease, pat, pinch, ogle, or

make suggestive comments. If a woman simply points out the objectionable behavior to the man, he will usually stop it immediately. There is also a huge difference between how men and women view the same behavior. Studies show that if a man makes a suggestive comment to a woman, 75 percent of women report they would be offended. If a woman makes a suggestive comment to a man, 75 percent of men report that they would be flattered, and only 15 percent said they would be offended! This fact alone makes the probability of misunderstanding between the sexes very high.

That's not to say there are not legitimate instances of real   21
wrongdoing and harm inflicted that people need to be held accountable for. This is as true in cases of sexual harassment as it is for medical malpractice, defective products, etc. But we all need to pick and choose our battles more carefully. We also need to lighten up a bit and give each other some slack. Is there anyone among us who has not been guilty of inappropriate behavior at work? It is the nature of human beings in community that we hurt each other's feelings, misunderstand one another, disappoint each other.

Whenever any of us, male or female, unnecessarily adopts   22
the role of victim, we disempower ourselves and hinder the achievement of a workplace where men and women can work side by side in an atmosphere of trust, respect, openness, and honesty. To quote a fellow Angeleno, "Can't we all just get along?"

—Barbara Hately

IV.

FAMILY MATTERS

Introduction

During the 1996 presidential campaign, both Bob Dole and Bill Clinton promised to sustain vigorous efforts to protect the American family—one indication of just how broad concern about the family has become in the United States during the 1990s. That concern emerged again during the 1998 election campaign, as candidates from both major parties offered one after another solution to The Family Problem—whatever that may be. No doubt you have heard the general concerns mentioned again and again—concerns about the state of the family during a time of increasing divorce and out-of-wedlock births; concerns about child support that ought to be honored by absent spouses, but isn't; concerns about teenage crime, suicide, pregnancy, substance abuse, and truancy that seem to be associated with broken homes; concerns about the effectiveness of day care, education, and children's health; concerns about child abuse. Moreover, you have probably also heard discussions in the media about new family matters that have come about as a result of new social customs and developments in reproductive technology—about who should have custody of children in cases of divorce, about whether or not single-sex couples should share in the benefits and responsibilities of marriage, about controversial adoption cases of one kind or another. Consequently, this part of *Conversations* takes up several topics related to the family, most of which are related to each other in some way.

The first section offers several readings on broad questions about the current condition of the American family. Is the family indeed in trouble in our country? Does it require some sort of repair—or is our society simply experiencing understandable and temporary pains associated with a transition from the traditional, two-parent home to less monolithic, less misogynist, more varied, and ultimately healthier versions of the family? Are children in our society being routinely damaged by broken homes, absent fathers, and general neglect of the family, or are those problems the result of other social factors, mostly associated with poverty? Would tougher child support laws help to amend the family? Should we make it more difficult to divorce in our society? More difficult to reproduce outside marriage? More difficult to retain children born out of wedlock or living in abusive households? Do we need more stringent laws to discourage deadbeat fathers and mothers?

Those questions also lead to the next section, which takes up the specific issue of single parenthood. As you may know, during the past two decades the number of single-parent households in the United States has increased dramatically, as divorce and illegitimacy rates have increased. Since 1950, the number of children living in mother-only families has quadrupled, from about 5 million to about 20 million, and since 1970, the number of single parents has tripled, from about 4 million to about 12 million. Ten percent of all live births in the United States are to mothers under eighteen. In 1995, 30 percent of all U.S. children under eighteen lived with one parent (26 percent with the mother, 4 percent with the father), compared to 12 percent in 1970. As a result, Senator Daniel Patrick Moynihan (a Democrat) and former Vice President Dan Quayle (a Republican) have made well-publicized attempts to draw attention to the problem of single parenthood: Moynihan through congressional hearings and reports, Quayle through his much publicized charges that television's Murphy Brown was glamorizing unwed motherhood.

But is it a problem? Is single parenthood the cause of social ills? Or are single parents, especially if they work, the victim of difficult circumstances and unrealistic expectations, particularly if their spouses offer insufficient child support? And if single parenthood is a problem, what should be done about it? Can and should the federal government play a role in this matter at a time when many Americans are suspicious about the federal government's role in their lives? In 1995, Newt Gingrich introduced the Personal Responsibility Act, which would have eliminated welfare benefits for children born to unwed mothers under the age of eighteen and would have required mothers to establish paternity as a condition for receiving welfare: Is such an act a good idea? *Conversations* presents a spirited exchange among five women concerning all these questions.

This part of *Conversations* closes with a discussion of same-sex marriage at a time when many states are considering legislation that would permit it. Should such matches be sanctioned by our laws so that same-sex couples can enjoy the civic benefits associated with marriage—that is, health benefits tied to family membership, tax benefits, the right to adopt children, the right to inherit money, and so forth? Would recognizing same-sex partners as lawfully married somehow undermine the family? Or would it put unwelcome pressure on same-sex couples to conform to an institution that many people find ill-suited to same-sex couples?

If this introduction has focused more on questions than on answers, that is because the discussion of family matters in the United States is so problematic right now. The selections in this part will give you the opportunity to confront some of the most vexing questions in our culture—and an opportunity to have your own say during a time when people are particularly interested in reading about these questions.

CAN THE FAMILY BE SAVED?

Roger Rosenblatt

The Society That Pretends
to Love Children

Roger Rosenblatt (born 1940) is a writer and editor at Time
magazine; he is also a frequent contributor to the New York
Times Magazine, *a publication on current events that is
enclosed with every Sunday* Times. *The following essay
appeared in a special issue of the* New York Times Magazine
(October 8, 1995) on childhood in the United States.

Henry will not face me. We sit close together on small plas-   1
tic chairs in a classroom at P.S. 314, an elementary school in
the Sunset Park area of Brooklyn, where he works with small
children in a summer camp. Our knees, drawn high because
we are sitting on the low chairs, almost touch. Still, Henry an-
gles his body so that he shows me only his profile. If he turns
toward me briefly and catches my eye, he immediately turns
away again and gazes out the large schoolroom window at
kids on a stoop across the street.

His neighborhood, Sunset Park, consists of approximately   2
110,000 people, most of them poor, with a per capita income of
$11,115. A quarter of the residents have incomes below the
poverty line. They represent a variety of backgrounds—Puerto
Rican, African-American, Dominican, Mexican, Jordanian, Pa-
kistani, Chinese, Korean and Vietnamese. These groups are
the latest to populate Sunset Park. They follow the Irish, Finns,
Swedes, Norwegians, Poles and Italians of the late 19th century, and the Greeks, Russians and Jews of the early 20th. The
first area residents were the Dutch and the English, who established farms where the Canarsie Indians had lived.

A little over a mile wide and 2.6 miles long, the area lies be-   3
tween middle-class Bay Ridge to the south and gentrified
Park Slope to the north. The rectangle of the neighborhood

slopes down from the high ridge at Eighth Avenue to the east to Upper New York Bay, where the Statue of Liberty rises. At the top of the ridge is Sunset Park itself—an 18-acre public park with old trees and a W.P.A. swimming pool. On the grid of narrow streets and wide avenues between the ridge and the bay lie two- and three-story brownstones with attractive cornices; brick-and-masonry houses with little gardens in the front, where corn is sometimes grown, and many rows of drab no-color tenements. Henry lives in one of these. His home is near Third Avenue, which is close to the water, and is shadowed by the Gowanus Expressway, one of the highways built by Robert Moses to carry white people away from places like Sunset Park.

4   Henry is 16, tall for his age at about 6 foot 1. His skin is a dull dark brown; antiperspirant under his arms foams white against it. His hair is spun into curlicues. He rarely smiles, though when he does, he looks warm and welcoming—in contrast to his usual self-concealing blankness. He is sleepy this morning. He yawns frequently, and fully, his mouth wide open like a baby's.

5   "What else have you seen?" I ask him. He is talking about life on the streets.

6   "I saw a man throw a telephone out the window," he says. "It hit a baby in a carriage. It nearly killed her. So her father ran up the stairs, and he grabbed the man who threw the phone, and he cut him." He traces a line across his throat with his index finger. "He lived, but he's got this necklace now."

7   "Did you know the men involved?" I ask him.

8   "I knew the man who threw the phone," he says. "He's my mother's boyfriend."

9   "Why did he do that?"

10   "He was drunk, crazy." He shrugs to indicate that the behavior is normal for his mother's boyfriend.

11   "What did you do when the baby's father slit his throat?" I ask.

12   "I was happy," Henry says. "I laughed when he did it. I even testified against the boyfriend in court. My mother was mad. She's always mad at me." He gives me a glance, then turns his head to the side. "That was when things really blew up at home. So I went to the Center for Family Life and told Jennifer. She's been everything to me." He says this without emotion. "She makes me think about what I do."

13   "What about your mother?"

14   "She screams. Says I'm the Devil. Calls me stupid and retarded. She says I'm bad. I *am* bad." He holds his head down.

"I hang out. I write up—you know?—do graffiti. I fight, maybe less now, but I used to fight all the time. When I start fighting, it's like seek and destroy. You start with me and you're the enemy. Nobody else in sight. You my spotlight, my way out. You the exit door."

"The exit door from what?" He does not answer. "Are other grown-ups in your life good to you? Teachers?"   15

"Some are O.K.," he says. "I had a teacher tell me: 'I don't care if you come to class or not. I get paid anyway.'"   16

"Police?"   17

"When I got arrested for writing up, a woman cop told me she hopes they send me to jail."   18

"Ministers? Priests?" I ask.   19

He shakes his head. "I don't have religion."   20

"The Mayor? The Governor? The President?" I am speaking a foreign language. "Are there any grown-ups who help you?"   21

"Jennifer," he says softly. "People at the center."   22

I ask him: "Henry, do you think that your mother loves you?"   23

"She pretends to love me," he says.   24

The fact that Henry is poor and black, and that he lives in violent circumstances, makes him an unusually dramatic and sadly familiar example of the mistreatment of American children. But, for what he represents, he could be any child, anywhere in the country. I could have the wrong Henry. Henry is not a kid from Sunset Park, Brooklyn. He is a rich, white, 16-year-old senior at Groton, who has just cheated on his Greek exam because his father, a true-blue Yalie, yells at him constantly for being stupid and retarded and for not being good enough to get into Yale.   25

No, that isn't Henry, either. Henry is a 12-year-old girl from Corpus Christi, Tex., who is trying to get pregnant "to have love in my life." Or the boy whose father set him on fire to strike back at his wife in a custody case. Or those teen-agers who made a suicide pact in New Jersey. Henry is a 14-year-old girl from Aspen, Colo., who wears all that oversize clothing and who heads for the ladies' room immediately after meals. He is the toddler in Los Angeles whose grandmother punished him by holding a pillow over his head and squeezing him between a table and a sofa. His last words were "Me no breathe."   26

Here's Henry now. That's his key in the door. His folks are both at work and will be out till midnight. He has the house   27 to himself. He pours himself a Coors, calls his girlfriend to come over and plunks down in front of the TV to watch the Jenny Jones show bring him a picture of America.

28   Actually, the Henry of Sunset Park is a bit luckier than the tens of millions of American children, of all economic classes, races and regions, whom the country pretends to love. At least this Henry has an effective local social service agency— the Center for Family Life to which he has been referred— that is devoted to his well-being.

29   In 1993, according to several child interest groups like the Children's Defense Fund, an estimated three million children were reported to public social service agencies to be suffering from abuse or neglect. Some 1,300 of them died. Approximately half a million children are in foster care or similar substitute homes, an increase of 250,000 since 1986. About 14 million live in poverty. About 100,000 children are homeless. The welfare bill passed overwhelmingly by the Senate last month, ending guaranteed assistance to poor families, should add significantly to the number of children in need.

30   The American Humane Association reports that since 1988 American teen-age boys are more likely to die from gunshot wounds than from all natural causes combined. Studies of teen-age pregnancy in Seattle and Chicago show that two-thirds of teen-age mothers reported having been sexually abused. Figures on sexual abuse have been disputed as being too high, but even if the true figures are only half of those reported, they are still considerable.

31   While poor children, black and white, suffer a disproportionate share of ills, the increasing affliction of the American child occurs in rural regions as well as in the cities, and among the middle and upper classes, too. Responses to a survey of girls in grades 6 through 12 in mainly Midwestern states, in 111 communities with populations under 100,000, indicated that by grade nine, one in five girls had been sexually abused. By grade 10, the number was still one in five, but one in three girls had been abused physically, sexually or both. The survey defined physical abuse as an adult causing a scar, bruises, welts, bleeding or a broken bone and sexual abuse as a family member or "someone else" imposing sexual behavior on the child. In 1993, there were 19,466 incidents of child abuse reported to the Iowa Department of Human Services. The advocacy organization, Girls Inc. in Omaha, states that sexual abuse of girls reported in Nebraska (3 in a class of 25) is that of the national average. The abuse of boys is more rarely reported, so the numbers are probably comparable.

Statistics on poor families, like Henry's, are more available   32
than those on better-off families; welfare agencies rarely invade the homes of the rich. But the mistreatment of children
is also a middle-class problem. A random sampling of adolescents in Minnesota found that 6 percent of middle- or middle-
to-high-income families had at least one child in alcohol or
drug treatment programs by ages 14 to 17. Adolescents in an
additional 5 percent of families were using as much alcohol
and drugs as the kids who were in treatment.

Middle-class whites like to think that kids with guns are a   33
black or Latino inner-city menace exclusively. But William C.
Haynes, juvenile justice director of the Tennessee Commission
on Children and Youth, reports that groups of middle-class
white kids in Antioch had a gunfight armed with 9-millimeter
semiautomatic pistols. Richard Louv, the author of "Childhood's Future," notes that the shooting programs of the 4-H
Clubs drew at least 100,000 kids at the end of the 1980's, a
tenfold increase since the mid-1980's.

Two middle-class parents who work full time will, natu-   34
rally, spend less time with their children. In 1976, according
to the economist Sylvia Ann Hewlett, author of "When the
Bough Breaks," 11 percent of children under the age of 1 year
had mothers in the work force. By 1994, the number had
risen to 54.5 percent. Another economist, Victor Fuchs, contends that children have lost 10 to 12 hours a week of parental
time since 1960 because of the added number of hours that
both parents work. The Bureau of Labor Statistics reports
that the average work week was 43.3 hours in 1994, with professional people working an average of 43.8.

At an exhibit of children's artwork at Christie's in New York   35
City last year, paintings were displayed depicting "Images of
Mothers and Fathers." One, showing a man with his hands
held up in surrender and surrounded by clocks, carried the
caption: "This is my father." A ninth grader drew a picture of
her mother *as* a clock.

Neglect is a varied form of abuse and is difficult to pin   36
down. Martha Farrell Erickson of the Children, Youth and
Family Consortium at the University of Minnesota reports that
45 percent of child-abuse cases are officially cited as neglect,
but "it seems likely that the actual incidence is much higher."
Erickson also notes that many neglected children are infants:
"Given that neglect is often chronic rather than episodic, these
children may grow up thinking this is the way life is."

Violent and destructive behavior by middle-class and upper-   37
middle-class kids—generally considered to be a consequence

of neglect—is a daily news story. In the placid seaport town of Dartmouth, Mass., in 1993, three teen-agers burst into a high-school classroom, beat a freshman over the head with a base-ball bat and stabbed him to death. In Williamson County, Tenn., the richest county in the state, a boy driving the new car that his parents had just bought him shot and killed a horse in a field—for the fun of it. High-school kids go on destructive binges in Montana and Vermont. In 1989, ABC's television news program, "20/20," ran a piece on high-living teenagers in wealthy Pacific Palisades, Calif., who were lost to drugs and drink. Last year, the network news shows broadcast a video of middle-class teenagers in Florida on a rampage. They tore apart elegant homes, tortured a dog and cooked a goldfish in the microwave. The teenagers made the video themselves.

38   Divorce is not always a destructive event in a child's life, but it is more often so than the divorcing parents care to admit. Fully 40 percent of children living with their mothers do not see their fathers after the breakup. Of the 58 percent of divorced fathers ordered to pay child support, less than two-thirds actually pay in full. One father explained that he could not pay child support because he needed the money to board his two Doberman pinschers. Even when both parents maintain contact with the children, the children can pay penalties. The headmaster of one of New York's distinguished private schools tells of an afternoon when he was summoned to the school lobby, where two parents were shouting and fighting. Each had thought that the coming weekend was the one in which he or she was to take their child. When the headmaster arrived on the scene, the parents were yanking at the child's arms, stretching him between them.

39   If some wealthier parents are not looking out for their children, they are looking out for themselves. Many young couples simply do not have children, even if they are able to, because a child will cut into their income and their time for self-interested pursuits. Many who do have kids did not really want the responsibility of rearing a human being; they wanted another witty, charming, urbane adult in the house. So neglect was built into their vision of the child in the first place. And, of course, when the child turned out not to be the delightful companion the parents originally had in mind, they abandoned it to "independence."

40   In "Habits of the Heart," Robert Bellah points out that since 1965, Americans have been hooked on the therapeutic mentality. The social critic Christopher Lasch also concluded that therapy has replaced religion in American adult lives. A

guidance counselor in Alabama tells me that a reason many parents do not come home at night to their children is that they are taking therapy classes to help them be better parents.

The neglect and abuse of children is hardly new in American history. One may go back through the 350 years represented by the different inhabitants of Sunset Park alone, starting with the Puritans, and discover an unbroken pattern of beating children, psychologically tormenting children, imposing one or another form of miseducation on them, forcing them into labor, giving them too little freedom, or giving them too much. Every major intellectual influence on American children, from Locke to Spock, has wound up distorting their lives. In 1646, "stubborn child laws" were enacted (though never enforced) in Massachusetts, which provided the death penalty for a rebellious son. In the 1850's, the Rev. Samuel Arnold of Ossipee, N.H., nearly beat his adopted son to death because the boy failed to pronounce the words "utter" and "gutter" to the reverend's satisfaction. In 1985, a Sunset Park father, who wanted to show off how smart his 6-year-old son was, forced him to stand and read aloud from a book. When the boy mispronounced the word "bite" as "bit," his father slammed his fist on the kitchen table and made him read the book from the beginning.   41

The difference between past and present abuses is that today's children are not assaulted by one or two destructive forces. They are assaulted by everything, all at once. Individual parents may love their kids, but the society seems to wish the children disappeared. It is as if children are seen as interfering with life, rather than as contributing to it or perpetuating it. Modern living is too difficult, too much to handle or to bear. Children get in the way of one's pleasure or of one's survival. They compete for one's money, resources and affections. Worse, like Henry, they remind adults of their incapacity to love them.   42

"What is to be done?" I ask Mary Paul and Geraldine, the two Sisters of the Good Shepherd who founded the Center for Family Life 17 years ago. The center, which is a lay institution, addresses all sources of difficulty for children, works with the family members involved, and embraces every facet of life in the neighborhood. Besides counseling, it provides an employment agency, an emergency food program, advocacy and legal services, a theater program, a literacy program, summer camps like the one in which Henry works, day care for school-age children and a neighborhood foster-care program. The foster   43 families are selected within the community of the original family, so that the children do not lose touch with their homes.

44   "Better ask what is *not* to be done," Mary Paul says. "People do have positive goals in regard to children. But somehow these goals become subverted because, paradoxically, they become overcommitted to whatever they are doing. Life ceases to be an adaptation and an exchange with an outside environment. We become mere doers. We do and we do and we do, and we grow to be more narrowly focused and more narrowly driven. Soon we lose energy and we fail. It's the law of entropy."

45   "Does that happen in education?" I ask.

46   "Absolutely," she says. "A few years ago, schools in places like New York started out being attentive to the needs of children in a multicultural environment. Perfectly sensible, given all the new immigrant groups who were coming in. Then people became overcommitted to that one goal of multiculturalism. They forgot about what else was worthwhile in education. They thought that education was about self-esteem. They came up with the idea of teaching bilingualism, which serves no useful purpose at all for children trying to make it in American society. In Sunset Park, bilingualism is promoted solely to get patronage jobs for Spanish teachers."

47   "The reason we instituted neighborhood foster care," says Geraldine, "is that child welfare in this country—the Child Welfare Administration in particular—focuses only on the well-being of the child."

48   "The aim is to remove the child from the original family as far away as possible," Mary Paul says. "Often the taking of children is done abruptly. The C.W.A. will take a child from school because it's easier than confronting the mother. Sometimes children are removed in the middle of the night, with the police in attendance. They'll use even more coercive methods. I cannot stand the violence of it."

49   Geraldine breaks in. "This is why we began neighborhood foster care in Sunset Park. We've been doing this seven years now, and sometimes we succeed and sometimes not. But even the failures can be a partial success. A child whom we placed in foster care here has a mother who is seriously mentally ill. The woman will stand in the street and scream up at the windows of the little girl's foster parents' house. She will sit in the hallway and bang on the door with her fists all night. And she will not go for treatment. And still the little girl—because she has been allowed to remain close to her mother—sees the disease for what it is. She understands. It doesn't make the mother well but it helps the *girl*."

"Everyone suffers from tunnel vision," says Mary Paul. "We   50
are in an economic depression right now. All one reads is how
strapped city, state and Federal budgets are. Politicians win
points by coming up with ways to save the country money.
'We have to reduce the deficit. We have to reduce the national
debt.' For whose benefit should we rescue the economy? It is
always the children and the grandchildren. Yet how should
we save the economy?"

"Take money away from children," Geraldine offers, and   51
laughs.

"Exactly," says Mary Paul. "Take the money from the chil-   52
dren even though you are focusing on the children as the reason for rescuing the economy. By this logic, you will amass a
fortune as a legacy and, at the same time, kill off the legatees."

"When parents fail their children," says Geraldine, "it is al-   53
most always because of an excessive commitment to one or
another pursuit. Henry's mother yells at him and degrades
him because she thinks that's how to make him toe the mark.
And naturally, Henry is angry at her. He's in a constant rage.
And he takes out his rage in street fights."

"This is a poor neighborhood," says Mary Paul. "Money   54
drives much of people's behavior. The rage of parents who
have sacrificed so much and invested so much and then nothing works…they begin to see the child as a repudiation of
their capacity for giving."

"What happens when a parent assaults or kills a child?" I ask.   55

"You know," Mary Paul says, "the feeling that one has to   56
love a child can be overwhelming, especially for those—and
there are many—who do not. And then the child reminds you
every day of your inability to build a world for it. It calls forth
something that the parent cannot give.

"A Mexican mother in this neighborhood killed her child   57
by repeated beatings. It said in the papers that the family
'somehow made its way from Mexico to Sunset Park.' Somehow made its way! Can you imagine what commitment it
took to get from Mexico to here, what ambitions for a new life
they had? They wind up in a situation where all forms of love
and rationality are abandoned to that dream, which had at its
center the children, after all. And then one day the child becomes a noise. And the noise has to be stilled.

"We have to remind the child that it belongs to a commu-   58
nity. We have to do that for adults, too. Adults are yesterday's
children."

"A client of ours killed her daughter," says Geraldine. "The   59
girl was about 3½. She had diabetes and she was always

thirsty. So she would go to the refrigerator again and again for juice. The mother, who was unaware that the child had diabetes, was very poor. She had so little food. She told the girl not to keep going to the refrigerator, but the girl kept going anyway. So the mother hit her in the head, the child went into a coma and eventually died. The mother did not want to kill her little girl, of course. She was thinking about the juice."

60   Jennifer, the social worker who has been counseling Henry, says: "We spend so much time protecting ourselves from the realities because we can't bear to see what we are doing to our kids. How could we live with ourselves if we really knew what we are creating?"

61   She started working with Henry after the incident involving his mother's boyfriend. She had seen him around the center but had no idea of the trouble in his life until he approached her the day he testified against the boyfriend in court. His mother was shutting him out. "'I need to talk to you,' he told me." Then he burst into tears.

62   "The situation was terrible in the beginning. It is getting a bit better now. But with his mother at that time, my God! She did not speak to him for three whole months. The afternoon that Geraldine and I first went over to their house, the mother pulled a kitchen knife on Henry. He stood there helplessly, repeating, 'I don't want to hurt you.' And she kept screaming at him.

63   "Henry has a very tender heart. He is struggling with the question of whether it is possible to feel something without being hurt. Once he came to me and said. 'I saw something in the park today that almost made me tear. A mother and her daughter were sitting on a bench. The mother said, I love you. And the daughter said, I love *you*. I thought: Can people really be that way? And then I thought: Nah.'

64   "He is very gentle. He's wonderful with little kids in the summer camp. He would never harm a smaller child. But if an older person attacks or offends him, he is livid beyond control. He is so deeply hurt that the slightest thing sets him off. Fighting is a power issue for him. He tells me, 'When I'm in a fight, I think of my mother and it gives me the energy.'

65   "This graffiti business, this 'writing up.' I've said to him so many times: 'Please. Explain it to me. I want to understand.' Because he keeps getting arrested for these petty offenses, and they're building up to a point where a prosecutor will want to put him away. One time he was arrested for writing

up two days in a row. I get a call and I go down to the 68th Precinct, and there he is—no shoes on, handcuffed to the bench. The cop was awful. She said: 'I hope you go to jail because that's where you deserve to be.' So I wind up being on Henry's side, even though I want to confront him for doing the wrong thing.

"And the third day, there is Henry *again*, down at the station house, handcuffed to the bench. I said to him: 'Look. If you want to spend time with me, just say so. We'll go do something. You don't need to get arrested to get my attention.' He said, in that glum way of his, 'Very funny, Jennifer.' But on the way out, he leans down and tells me: 'You shouldn't help me. You should help someone else. It's past my time already.' He was 15." 66

Sitting with Henry in the P.S. 314 classroom, I ask him what he thinks about when he's alone. 67

"I think about the future, about getting out of here. I'd like to live somewhere else, upstate maybe. I wouldn't want to grow up and have a kid and live in this neighborhood. It's too dangerous. 68

"A man held a gun to my head one time, 'cause he wanted my fronts." Fronts are gold caps that kids wear on their teeth for show. I said, 'I won't take 'em off for you or anybody.'" 69

"Why not give him the fronts?" I ask. 70

"It's the way I am." 71

"Did you think he would shoot you?" He shrugs. "How would you treat a kid of your own?" 72

"I wouldn't hit him. I'd never hit him. If you hit a kid, he cries at first. Then he stops crying after a while and he doesn't care. You can hit him forever and it won't matter." 73

"Have people hit you?" He nods. "What for?" 74

"Writing up." 75

"Why do you keep doing it?" 76

"I don't know," he says. "I know it gets me into trouble, but I just can't stop." 77

"What do you write?" 78

"TM1," he says. "Everywhere I see some open space I write it. TM1. In the hallways, on the buildings, I just have to see it." 79

"What does TM1 mean?" 80

He looks me in the eye for the first time. "The Magnificent One," he says. 81

Joseph Shapiro and Joanne Schrof
Honor Thy Children

On February 27, 1995, U.S. News & World Report published the following "Special Report" on the family in America. Joseph Shapiro and Joanne Schrof are regular contributors to U.S. News, a weekly newsmagazine competing with Time and Newsweek that has a conservative editorial stance. (U.S. News staffers Mike Tharp and Dorian Friedman also contributed to the essay.)

1   Dad is destiny. More than virtually any other factor, a biological father's presence in the family will determine a child's success and happiness. Rich or poor, white or black, the children of divorce and those born outside marriage struggle through life at a measurable disadvantage, according to a growing chorus of social thinkers. And their voices are more urgent because an astonishing 38 percent of all kids now live without their biological fathers—up from just 17.5 percent in 1960. More than half of today's children will spend at least part of childhood without a father.

2   These new critics challenge the view that external forces like street crime, lousy schools and economic stress lie behind the crisis in families. The revised thinking is that it's the breakdown of families that feeds social ills. "Fatherlessness is the most destructive trend of our generation," argues David Blankenhorn, author of a provocative new book, *Fatherless America: Confronting Our Most Urgent Social Problem.*

3   The absence of fathers is linked to most social nightmares—from boys with guns to girls with babies. No welfare reform plan can cut poverty as thoroughly as a two-parent family. Some 46 percent of families with children headed by single mothers live below the poverty line, compared with 8 percent of those with two parents. Raising marriage rates will do far more to fight crime than building prisons or putting more cops on the streets. Studies show that only 43 percent of state prison inmates grew up with both parents and that a missing father is a better predictor of criminal activity than race or poverty. Growing up with both parents turns out to be a better antidote to teen pregnancy than handing out condoms. Sociologists Sara McLanahan and Gary Sandefur say in their recent book, *Growing Up With a Single Parent,* that young women who were reared in disrupted families are

twice as likely to become teen mothers. Social scientists have made similar links between a father's absence and his child's likelihood of being a dropout, jobless, a drug addict, a suicide victim, mentally ill and a target of child sexual abuse.

Bringing the issue into sharp focus are some brutal reali-   4
ties. Only 51 percent of kids still live with both biological parents. There were some 1.2 million divorces last year, about 53 percent of which involved minor children. In addition, 68 percent of black children and 30 percent of all kids are born outside of marriage. There are places in America where fathers—usually the best hope to socialize boys— are so rare that bedlam engulfs the community. Teachers, ministers, cops and other substitute authority figures fight losing battles in these places against gang members to present role models to preteen and teenage boys. The result is often an astonishing level of violence and incomprehensible incidents of brutality.

Americans know this and increasingly yearn for children   5
to have more protection. Fully 71 percent of those surveyed by U.S. News said it is "very important" for "every child to have his or her father living at home" and nearly 8 in 10 think both fathers and mothers should spend more time with their kids. Some 58 percent say it should be harder for couples with children to get a divorce. That's a position Vice President Al Gore wouldn't endorse. But in an interview with U.S. News, the administration's leading spokesman on the fatherhood issue laments the number of parents who won't "tough out" troubled marriages.

Most Americans reject the harshest solution advocated by   6
some conservatives: encouraging unwed mothers to put their children up for adoption by two-parent families. Seventy percent of those in the U.S. News survey said that when children are born to single mothers, it is "preferable for them to be raised by their mothers" than in a two-parent adoptive family.

It seems simple enough to say every child needs a father.   7
But must Daddy be a biological, married and in-residence paterfamilias, as Blankenhorn and his allies insist? These "new traditionalists" argue that the odds are overwhelming against a divorced dad or a father substitute. For proof, they argue that 18 million children should be entitled to $34 billion more in child support from noncustodial parents (about 90 percent of whom are fathers). Even the lucky child who sees his or her dad at least once a week—just 1 child in 6—often winds up with a "treat dad" for weekend movies, not a father to offer constant guidance and discipline.

8   It even turns out that the fairy tales contain germs of truth about stepparents. Youngsters in stepfamilies do no better, and often fare even worse, than children in homes headed by a single parent, according to several recent studies. Stepparents often bring needed income, but that advantage is offset by the emotional rivalries among parents and children in stepfamilies.

9   Finally, the new traditionalists dispute the idea that kids are worse off when stuck in their parents' lousy marriages. Divorce can increase an adult's happiness, but it is devastating to a child, says psychologist Judith Wallerstein, who has studied her child clients since 1971. One third report moderate or severe depression five years after a divorce. The hurt may remain hidden for years. They often grow up wary of love, marriage and family, and over a third have little or no ambition 10 years after their parents part. "Divorce is not just an episode in a child's life," notes Wallerstein. "It's like a natural disaster that really changes the whole trajectory of a child's life."

10   Blankenhorn, founder of the New York-based Institute for American Values, says action must be taken to slow family breakups. The "logic" of his argument, he says, may lead to steps like ending no-fault divorce and encouraging more single mothers to give up children for adoption. (Adoptive parents are the exception to his preference for biological ones.) He also urges that access to sperm banks be denied to unmarried women.

11   Blankenhorn and his allies are struggling against another group—call them fatherhood "reinventors"—who say it is wrongheaded to stigmatize absent fathers. Millions try to be good dads. And most children of divorce, despite the added risks, turn out fine. Besides, reinventors argue, high divorce rates result from irreversible cultural shifts that are best to accommodate rather than battle—like the economic independence of working women who no longer get stuck in abusive marriages. Reinventors say the solution is to build a network of support to help all fathers, including separated fathers or father figures, be involved in children's lives. Family-friendly workplaces, parenting classes and wider visitation rights are among the answers. Says Richard Louv, author of *FatherLove:* "We need all the fathers we can get."

12   These skirmishes show that fatherhood itself is in transition. Inside marriage, there is confusion as fathers are no longer a family's clear-cut breadwinner, the traditional role of a patriarch. Some blame "feminism," like the evangelical

Christian Promise Keepers, a burgeoning grass-roots movement that wants to bring a million men to Washington next year to proclaim their desire to be "godly" leaders of their families. Yet, others thank feminism for showing them a more satisfying model of parenting.

Unfortunately, even the most earnest attempts to strengthen fatherhood, whether they come from traditionalists or reinventors, seem destined for limited success. A close look at such efforts suggests just how hard it will be to find policies to decrease divorce or to make AWOL fathers less distant. 13

Can We Reconnect Fathers?

In Cleveland's Hough neighborhood, social worker Charles Ballard meets young men who have attended scores of funerals but few, if any, weddings. There are children, he says, who grow up not knowing the proper finger for wearing a wedding ring. But the 58-year-old Ballard—abandoned by his own father at age 3 and a father himself at 17—has overcome inner-city Cleveland's bleak economic and emotional landscape to teach poor fathers that the key to being a man is to be a good father. 14

Since 1982, Ballard's Institute for Responsible Fatherhood and Family Revitalization has worked to reconnect over 2,000 absent fathers with their children. Ballard does it through an intensive social-work approach—visiting the homes of his clients and referring them to parenting classes, drug abuse programs or GED courses. But Ballard's approach is also radical. He turns on its head the usual assumption that men cannot be responsible parents if they cannot find jobs. Convince young men first of the importance of being good fathers, Ballard argues, and they are then motivated to finish school and find work. Social workers have long known that teen mothers are most likely to complete school, get off drugs or find a job when they see it as a way of protecting their child. 15

Alonzo Warren proves the point. The unemployed 31-year-old father of six children by six different women was referred to Ballard when he went to the county seeking custody of his 9-year-old son, who was in the care of a relative. Although Warren's new job, cooking hamburgers at a nearby fast-food restaurant, pays just the minimum wage, his steady source of income puts him in a stronger position to persuade county social workers to allow him overnight visitations with his 16 son as well as to do more to support his other young children. "All the guys I know, even though we're not living with our kids, not a single day goes by when we don't worry about them," says Warren. "Even with our faults, they need us."

17   A study by Case Western Reserve University political science professors G. Regina Nixon and Anthony King shows that Ballard's one-on-one program, which lets fathers take the initiative in solving their own problems, gets some often astonishing results. Ninety-seven percent of the men began providing financial support for their children; 71 percent did not have any more children outside of marriage; only 12 percent had full-time work when they entered, but 62 percent found such work and 12 percent got part-time jobs. There was one glaring shortcoming: The program had less impact on marriage rates. Just 1 in 5 of the participants married. Although the study sample was small, the results persuaded the Ford Foundation to give Ballard a $400,000 grant to try to replicate his success in 14 other cities later this year.

18   Still, there are questions as to whether what works in Cleveland will work elsewhere. Ballard is a charismatic visionary whose day-to-day presence may be decisive. And other localities may balk at Ballard's insistence that his staffers neither drink nor smoke nor be homosexual.

19   Other experiments around the country show that it is not easy to match scarce jobs to unskilled workers. Parents' Fair Share, a multimillion-dollar federal demonstration program that began in nine cities in 1992, requires noncustodial fathers of children on welfare to attend employment training when they cannot afford to pay child support. Early results showed that, overall, only 22 percent of those referred to the program reported any employment. But peer support training sessions did appear to rekindle the fathers' desire to do right by their kids.

20   Other fathers similarly yearn for more of a role in their kids' lives. Many men, particularly those in fathers' rights groups, push for joint custody. Although these arrangements remain rare, 90 percent of fathers in them pay child support, which is about triple the national average. Men who feel they have a significant role in the lives of their sons and daughters spend more time with them and pay more child support. Still, three quarters of mothers oppose joint custody, which complicates their own parenting by giving ex-husbands decision-making power.

Should Divorce Be Harder?

It is still a mystery why divorce rates doubled in the decade   21
after the early 1960s. But Illinois State Rep. Bernard Peder-
sen blames the introduction of no-fault divorce laws that let
an unhappy spouse end a marriage unchallenged. So Peder-
sen, wed 45 years himself, proposed a law that would let marrying couples choose to put fault back in divorce. The effort
failed. So did attempts in states like Florida and Washington,
indicating that although it might cut the number of divorces,
Americans have no interest in returning to the days when
wives hired private detectives or even a surrogate blond to
catch philandering husbands.

Instead, most efforts have focused on teaching divorcing   22
parents to get along for the sake of the kids. In a soft voice, 8-
year-old Kaitlyn talks of her pain when her parents separated.
"I felt really sad because I thought it was something that happened to other people," she says, nervously swinging her legs,
which do not reach the hotel ballroom floor under her chair.
She is one of several children, ages 8 to 28, who tell their stories to groups of Maryland parents seeking divorce. Often the
soft sobbing of a parent is the only other sound in the room.

The sessions are a part of the most popular trend in family   23
courts today: parenting courses for divorcing adults. Not intended to stop divorce, the classes simply show parents how
to put their children's needs first. Connecticut and Utah require them for all divorcing adults, and more than 100 courts
elsewhere do the same. (One Chicago court, however, ruled it
unconstitutional to force unwilling parents to attend.) Studies show that parents come away more aware of divorce's impact on their youngsters, but there is no proof yet that fathers
increase the frequency of their visits or support payments.

And courses that typically last two to six hours can do little   24
to change a lifetime of problems, notes psychologist Sanford
Braver. "They do a good job of selling the idea that for the
sake of the children, it's important to get along," says the Arizona State University professor, who surveyed such programs. "But getting parents to put aside hurts and jealousies
and carry it off is another matter." Divorced dad Ed Cush-
man, 52, and his daughter Lora, 24, tell parents to "never give
up" trying to get along. Ed dropped by the pizza parlor where
Lora worked every week for a year until she would open up
to a reconciliation. Both agree their relationship is better
now than before the divorce. Still, father and daughter, who

participate in panels sponsored by the Children of Separation and Divorce Center in Columbia, Md., repaired their relationship only after years of counseling.

25   Edwin Smithers of Connecticut says a similar class improved his parenting, too. However, his wife and three daughters moved across country and now, Smithers says, it is his stepsons who benefit from his new skills. He thinks the same classes, earlier, might have saved his marriage. "Parent training should be required, the way we require driver's training before you get a driver's license," he says.

Can Marriage Be Taught?

26   "God hates divorce," says Michael McManus, citing Scripture (Malachi 2:16). Churches, says the author of *Marriage Savers*, can best take the lead in reversing the divorce rate. McManus has persuaded ministers in 28 cities to require engaged couples to undergo lengthy relationship counseling before marriage—three quarters of Americans marry in churches—and to train older couples to mentor the younger ones about how to resolve conflict. Amy and Jeff Olson took the marriage preparation course McManus runs at the Fourth Presbyterian Church in Bethesda, Md., and credit it with getting their marriage off to a firm start by resolving their differences over money management.

27   The Catholic Church has long practiced such premarital counseling. And it prohibits divorce. So it is not surprising that Massachusetts, the second-most-heavily-Catholic state, has the lowest divorce rate. McManus thinks the fact that some 75 Peoria, Ill., ministers adopted his idea has something to do with the fact that the number of divorces there fell from 1,210 in 1991 to 984 in 1994. But he notes that couples in Peoria often avoid such counseling by going to a minister who does not require it. Churches can also help long-married couples strengthen relationships. Yet the Marriage Encounter weekend retreats, which once attracted 100,000 couples a year, now get only 15,000. McManus attributes that to spouses' reluctance to probe trouble spots in their marriages.

28   Conservatives tend not to trust schools to teach family values. Largely unnoticed, however, is that high schools have become the new academies of parent training. Such classes are already a graduation requirement in at least eight states, including California, Delaware, Michigan, New Jersey, New York, Tennessee, Vermont and Virginia, notes Jan Bowers of

the Home Economics Education Association. And, another surprise, it is being taught in home economics classes. Home ec, now called family and consumer science, is not cooking and sewing anymore. Nor is it just for girls: Boys make up 42 percent of the students.

Two years ago, rural Anna, Ohio (population 1,164), made   29
parenting class a requirement for high school students. Although these boys may be many years from fatherhood, teacher Joanne Ansley notes that lessons in discipline or child development come in handy to the basketball star who coaches a youth team or the 16-year-old whose baby brother asks so many annoying questions.

Small-town Anna has its share of big-town problems. Town   30
ministers welcomed the parenting curriculum, in part, to stop early pregnancies. Students get a smack of reality when drawing up family budgets or visiting the nearby Wilson Memorial Hospital, to watch a film on childbirth. "A lot of people in Anna marry and have kids right out of high school, but the course helped me realize just how big of a responsibility fatherhood is," says Tony Albers, 17, who says he now plans to finish college and wait "at least until I'm 25" to start a family.

Blankenhorn, however, doubts that fatherhood can be   31
taught. It is a complicated, lifelong endeavor. "Parenting is not like plumbing or carpentering," he says. "It's not a set of techniques. It depends on a human identity." Some boys seem too young to take the lessons seriously and there is a good deal of adolescent horseplay on any given day in class. Moreover, precedents are not encouraging. Sex education was also intended to change behavior. But classroom lessons, no matter how well taught, are often forgotten in real-life situations, as is clear from rising teen pregnancy rates.

Can We Support Fatherhood?

Valente Jimenez knows plenty about machines. He is a me-   32
chanic who fixes air-conditioning units for the Los Angeles Department of Water and Power. After his wife gave birth, a company nurse instructed Jimenez how to work a device he didn't know much about: a breast pump. The company lent the electric breast pump, one of 90 it bought for its employees—80 percent of whom are men.

"Management sees this as an investment, as a good business   33
strategy," notes company work-family specialist Kimberlee Vandenakker. She cites reduced job turnover and absenteeism

since LADWP began its fathering program. Among other services to dads: LADWP lends beepers to expectant fathers working on power lines and other remote job sites; it sets up mentoring sessions with other fathers; it started a child-care center and offers unpaid paternity leave.

34   Most companies remain reluctant to offer such programs to mothers, much less to fathers. And men are even more reluctant to ask for father-friendly policies, says James Levine of the Families and Work Institute, who calls LADWP's program "the single best" for dads. Under the new federal family leave law, many working fathers are eligible for 12 weeks of unpaid parental leave, but it is the rare man who takes it. Moms usually prefer to be the one to take off, Levine says, because it is expected, they need to recover physically or breast-feed, or because their husbands bring home bigger paychecks.

35   At LADWP, most who take advantage of the fathers' policies come from white-collar jobs. Supervisors have more flexible schedules, and there is still the "macho" factor for some blue-collar workers. Jimenez's family was surprised when he agreed to care for his baby while his wife, Jeanne, took a four-day trip to visit family in Texas. Jimenez said the example of other fathers at work convinced him. "I come from a Hispanic family, and we didn't do that kind of stuff," he says. "But this program has opened my eyes."

36   Virtually all sides in the debate now agree that such changes in attitudes are the first and best hope for repairing fatherhood. The campaign to fight fatherlessness will be waged over a long period, much the same way campaigns worked to convince drivers that they should not drink or smokers that cigarettes ruin health. Government programs won't have nearly the impact as numberless one-on-one encounters over a lifetime between men and kids. Both the White House and House Republicans, for example, want to give parents a $500-per-child tax credit. While money helps, most family experts say there is no evidence that such policies directly influence decisions as personal as marriage and childbearing. Of course, there are partisan stakes in this fight. The *U.S. News* poll found that Americans trust Republicans more than Democrats—37 to 32 percent—to help make families stronger.

37   But most see the issue in transcendent terms. As Hillary Rodham Clinton told *U.S. News* last week: "It's difficult for fathers to put aside their own aspirations about their own lives," but one who can "put his child first . . . is giving a great

gift to a child." Real progress will come only when there is renewed conviction, as Blankenhorn argues, that "being a loving father and a good husband is the best part of being a
man."

Shere Hite
Bringing Democracy Home

In the spring of 1995, Ms. *magazine carried the following
excerpt from Shere Hite's book* The Hite Report on the Family:
Growing Up under Patriarchy *(1995), the product of her study
of several thousand families. Hite has made a reputation not
only on this report but also on her books* The Hite Report: A
Nationwide Study of Female Sexuality *(1976) and* The Hite
Report: A Study of Male Sexuality *(1981)—both controversial, widely discussed titles.*

Love and anger, love and obedience, love and power, love   1
and hate. These are all present in family relationships. It's easy
to say that they are inevitable, that stresses and strains are unavoidable, given "human nature." To some extent this is true,
but these stresses and strains are exaggerated by a tense and
difficult family system that is imposed upon our emotions and
our lives, structuring them to fit its own specified goals.

Is the family as we have known it for so long the only way   2
to create safe, loving, and caring environments for people?
The best way? To understand the family in Western tradition,
we must remember that much of what we see, say, and think
about it is based on the archetypal family that is so pervasive
in our society—Jesus, Mary, and Joseph. There is no daughter
icon. This is the "holy family" model that we are expected, in
one way or another, to live up to. But is this model really the
right one for people who believe in equality and justice? Does
it teach a good understanding of love and the way to make relationships work when we become adults?

One constantly hears that the family is in trouble, that it   3
doesn't work anymore, that we must find ways to help it. If
the family doesn't work, maybe there is something wrong

with its structure. People must have reasons for fleeing the nuclear family: human rights abuses and the battering of women are well documented in many governments' statistics.

4   The family is changing because only in recent decades has the process of democratization, which began in Western political life more than two centuries ago, reached private life. Although John Stuart Mill wrote in favor of women's rights in the egalitarian democratic theory he helped develop, the family and women's role in the world were left out of most discussions of democracy, left in the "sacred" religious domain. Women and nonproperty owners, as well as "minorities," did not have the vote when democracy first began. Men made a fatal mistake. The democracy they thought they could make work in the public sphere would not really work without democracy in private life.

5   Some people, of course, are alarmed by changes in the family. Reactionary fundamentalist groups have gone on the offensive to try to stop this process. Yet most people are happier with their personal lives today than people were 50 years ago. Women especially have more choices and freedom than they did in the past. There is a positive new diversity springing up in families and relationships today in Western society. This pluralism should be valued and encouraged: far from signaling a breakdown of society, it is a sign of a new, more open and tolerant society springing up, a new world being born out of the clutter of the old.

6   Democracy could work even better if we changed the aggressive personality that is being created by the patriarchal family system. Children brought up with choice about whether to accept their parents' power are more likely to be confident about believing in themselves and their own ideas, less docile or habituated to bending to power. Such a population would create and participate in public debate very differently. And there are many more advances we are on the threshold of achieving: naming and eliminating emotional violence, redefining love and friendship, progressing in the areas of children's rights and in men's questioning of their own lives.

7   My work salutes the gentler and more diverse families that seem to be arising. They are part of a system that does not keep its members in terror: fathers in terror lest they not be "manly" and able to support it all; mothers in terror lest they be beaten in their own bedrooms and ridiculed by their children; children in terror of being forced to do things against their will and having absolutely no recourse, no door open to them for exit.

What I am offering is a new interpretation of relationships 8
between parents and children, a new theory of the family. My
interpretation of the data from my questionnaires takes into
account not only the individual's unique experiences, as is
done in psychology, but also the cultural backdrop—the canvas of social "approval" or "disapproval" against which children's lives are lived. This interdisciplinary theory also takes
into account the historical ideology of the family; those who
took part in my research are living in a world where perception of "family" is filtered through the Christian model of the
"holy family" with its reproductive icons of Jesus, Mary, and
Joseph. But no matter how beautiful it appears (especially in
its promise of "true love"), this family model is an essentially
repressive one, teaching authoritarian psychological patterns,
meekness in women, and a belief in the unchanging rightness
of male power. In this hierarchical family, love and power are
inextricably linked, a pattern that has damaging effects not
only on all family members but on the politics of the wider
society. How can there be successful democracy in public life
if there is an authoritarian model in private life?

So used have we become to these symbols that we continue 9
to believe—no matter what statistics we see in the newspapers
about divorce, violence in the home, mental breakdown—that
the icons and the system they represent are right, fair, and
just. We assume without thinking that this model is the only
"natural" form of family, and that if there are problems it must
be the individual who is at fault, not the institution.

We need a new interpretation of what is going on. We may 10
be at one of the most important turning points of the Western
world, the creation of a new social base that will engender an
advanced and improved democratic political structure.

What Is the Family All About?

Creating new, more democratic families means taking a 11
clear and rational look at our institutions. We tend to forget
that the family was created in its current form in early patriarchy for political, not religious, reasons. The new political
order had to solve a specific problem: How could lineage or
inheritance flow through men (and not women as it had previously) if men do not bear children?

The modern patriarchal family was created so that each 12
man would "own" a woman who would reproduce for him.
He then had to control the sexuality of "his" woman, for how

else could he be sure that "his" child was really his? Restrictions were placed on women's lives and bodies by men; women's imprisonment in marriage was made a virtue, for example, through the later archetype of the self-sacrificing Mary, who was happy to be of service, never standing up for herself or her own rights. Mary, it is important to note, is a later version of a much earlier Creation Mother goddess. In her earlier form, she had many more aspects, more like the Indian goddess Kali than the "mother" whom the Christian patriarchal system devised.

13   Fortunately, the family is a human institution: humans made it and humans can change it. My research indicates that the extreme aggression we see in society is not a characteristic of biological "human nature" (as Freud concluded), nor a result of hormones. "Human nature" is a psychological structure that is carefully implanted in our minds—for life—as we learn the love and power equations of the family. Power and love are combined in the family structure: in order to receive love, most children have to humiliate themselves, over and over again, before power.

14   In our society, parents have the complete legal, economic, and social "right" to control children's lives. Parents' exclusive power over children creates obedience. Children are likely to take on authoritarian emotional, psychological, and sexual patterns, and to see power as one of the central categories of existence.

15   Love is at the heart—so to speak—of our belief in the importance of the family. The desire for love is what keeps us returning to the icons. Even when they don't seem to work in our lives, we try and try again. We are told that we will never find love if we don't participate in the family. We hear repeatedly that the only place we will ever be able to get security, true acceptance, and understanding is in the family; that we are only "half a family" or a "pretend family" if we create any other human group; that without being a member of the family we will be forever "left out," lonely, or useless. No one would want to deny the importance of love, or of lasting relationships with other people. But the violent, distorted definitions of love created by the patriarchal family make it difficult for love to last, and to be as profound as it could be.

16   How confusing it is for children, the idea of being loved! They are so often told by their parents, "Of course we love you, why do you even ask?" It is easy for children to believe that the emotion they feel when faced with a powerful person is "love"—or that the inscrutable ways of a person who is

sometimes caring and friendly, and other times punitive and angry, are loving. The problem then is that, since the parents are still the providers and "trainers" of the children, legally and economically the "owners" of the children, they exercise incredible power over the children—the very power of survival itself.

Children must feel gratitude, and so, in their minds, this 17 gratitude is mixed with love. How much of the love they feel is really supplication before the power of the parents? How will they define love later in life? Won't they be highly confused by passion (either emotional or physical) and what it means, unable to connect it with other feelings of liking and concern? Of course, long-term caring for others is something positive that can also be learned in families, but it can be learned in other kinds of families, not just the nuclear model.

Does "Love" Include Sex? The Body?

And what definition of love do children learn from the way 18 their parents relate physically? Isn't it strange to think of your parents having sex? Finding parents in any kind of physical embrace comes as a fascinating shock to most children: 83 percent of children in my research say their parents seem completely asexual.

It would be logical if children drew the conclusion that 19 "real love" is never sexual, or even physically affectionate. But isn't affection a great part of what love is? If parents don't hug and kiss each other, is the definition of adult "love" different? And if so, what is it? Why do parents feel that they shouldn't touch each other in front of the children? Because the children would be jealous? Because it would give the children sexual feelings and ideas? Or, do many parents really not want to touch each other? Children wonder, if the parents don't want to be affectionate, why exactly are they together? If they are only together "for the sake of the children," this puts an awfully big burden on the children to be "worth it" or to "make their parents happy," thus confusing the definitions of love even further.

Another way children learn that power and domination are 20 part of love is through observing the relationship of their parents. Gender tension and especially second-class treatment of the mother by the father is reported by the majority of people from two-parent families in this study. Girls in particular find this gender inequality mixed with "love" confusing, even psychologically violent and terrifying. Why? Because for girls it means coming to terms with what this power relationship will mean for them: Will they inherit this gender inequality? Can they avoid being considered lesser beings when they become women? How can they love a father who represents this system? Or a mother who lets herself participate in it?

Are Single-Parent Families Bad for Children?

21   There are very few carefully controlled studies of the effects of single-parent families on children. Today, much popular journalism assumes that the two-parent family is better for children. My data show that there are beneficial effects for the majority of children living in single-parent families. It is more positive for children not to grow up in an atmosphere poisoned by gender inequality.

22   Do girls who grow up with "only" their mother have a better relationship with her? According to my study, 49 percent of such girls felt that it was a positive experience; 20 percent did not like it; and the rest had mixed feelings. Mothers in one-parent families are more likely to feel freer to confide in daughters because no "disloyalty to the spouse" is implied. Daughters in such families are less likely to see the mother as a "wimp"—she is an independent person.

23   Boys who grow up with "only" their mother experience less pressure to demonstrate contempt for things "feminine" and for nonaggressive parts of themselves. In *The Hite Report on Men and Male Sexuality,* I was surprised to find that boys who grew up with their mother alone were much more likely to have good relationships with women in their adult lives: 80 percent of men from such families had formed strong, lasting ties with women (in marriage or long-term relationships), as opposed to only 40 percent from two-parent families. This does not mean that the two-parent family cannot be reformed so that it provides a peaceful environment for children—indeed this is part of the ongoing revolution in the family in which so many people today are engaged.

24   Single-parent families are mostly headed by mothers, yet there is an increasing number of single-father families. Many single fathers don't take much part in child care but instead hire female nannies or ask their mothers, sisters, or girlfriends to take care of the children. Men could change the style of families by taking more part domestically, and by

opening up emotionally and having closer contact with children. My research highlights men's traumatizing and enforced split from women at puberty....

Healing this is the single most important thing we as   25
a society could do to bridge the distance men feel from
"family."

Democracy of the Heart: A New Politics

If you listen to people talk about their families, it becomes   26
clear that we must give up on the outdated notion that the
only acceptable families are nuclear families. We should not
see the new society that has evolved over the last 40 years as a
disaster simply because it is not like the past.

The new diversity of families is part of a positive pluralism,   27
part of a fundamental transition in the organization of society that calls for open-minded brainstorming by all of us:
What do we believe "love" and "family" are? Can we accept
that the many people fleeing the nuclear family are doing so
for valid reasons? If reproduction is no longer the urgent priority that it was when societies were smaller, before industrialization took hold, then the revolt against the family is not
surprising. Perhaps it was even historically inevitable. It is
not that people don't want to build loving, family-style relationships, it is that they do not want to be forced to build
them within one rigid, hierarchical, heterosexist, reproductive framework. Diversity in family forms can bring joy and
enrichment to a society: new kinds of families can be the basis for a renaissance of spiritual dignity and creativity in political as well as personal life.

Continuing this process of bringing private life into an ethical and egalitarian frame of reference will give us the energy   28
and moral will to maintain democracy in the larger political
sphere. We can create a society with a new spirit and will—
but politics will have to be transformed. We can use the interactive frame of reference most often found today in friendships between women. Diversity in families can form the
basic infrastructure for a new and advanced type of political
democracy to be created, imagined, developed—a system that
suits the massive societies that communications technology
today has made into one "global village."

One cannot exaggerate the importance of the current debate: 29
there has been fascism in societies before; it could certainly

emerge again, alongside fascism in the family. If we believe in the democratic, humanist ideals of the last 200 years, we have the right, almost the duty, to make our family system a more just one; to follow our democratic ideals and make a new, more inclusive network of private life that will reflect not a preordained patriarchal structure, but our belief in justice and equality for all—women, men, and children. Let's continue the transformation, believe in ourselves, and go forward with love instead of fear. In our private lives and in our public world, let's hail the future and make history.

Stephanie Coontz

How Ignoring Historical and Societal Change Can Put Kids at Risk

Stephanie Coontz is a professional sociologist who teaches at Evergreen State College. In 1992, she published The Way We Never Were: American Families and the Nostalgia Trip, *a historical study of the American family that cut through many myths. In the wake of that book, she appeared on a number of talk shows—everything from* Oprah *to* Crossfire—*and began to work on a second book,* The Way We Really Are *(1997), which investigates current issues related to the family. The following is Chapter 8 of* The Way We Really Are. *(Notice that it contains references to Barbara Dafoe Whitehead and to Iris Marion Young, whose work is included in the next section of* Conversations.*)*

1   Even before recent economic setbacks, long-term historical processes had already undermined the ability of families to raise the next generation without outside assistance. Children used to be economic assets to a family, and the costs of raising them to an age where they could contribute to family subsistence were quite small. Industrialization gradually increased the expense of raising, educating, or training children and decreased their returns to the family, whether nuclear or extended. The cost of caring for all family dependencies rose

as it became more difficult to integrate caregiving with the locations and rhythms of modern workplaces.[1]

After the turn of the century, the abolition of child labor, positive though it was, further increased the costs of raising children. Marital desertion became a growing problem, since fathers were less likely to seek child custody or maintain contact once the economic benefits of children had fallen. At the same time, more and more elderly Americans were ending up in almshouses. States passed laws requiring adult children to support their parents and absent fathers to support their children but found them hard to enforce. Private charities were unable to come anywhere near meeting the needs of children or the elderly, and local institutions could no longer cope with the concentrations of poverty that occurred in urban areas.[2]

As early as the mid-nineteenth century, new public institutions, such as schools, had become essential supplements to family child rearing in all classes, and government had begun to recognize its responsibility to invest in programs to ensure safe and adequate supplies of food, clean air, water, housing, and sanitation facilities. In the early twentieth century, the federal government gradually took over many other functions that had formerly been provided by extended families and voluntary societies, establishing pensions, disability funds, insurance programs, and supplemental cash assistance for families. Government also performed a number of new functions, such as helping to protect family members from abuse. Some of the services government provided were inadequate, while others were unnecessarily intrusive. But I know of no serious historian who doesn't believe that children of all classes were better off as a result of government's expanded role.[3]

The growth of public schooling and government assistance programs for families reflected society's recognition that the rising cost of children made it essential for the task of raising and educating future workers to be shared by all members of society, not just dumped onto parents. The Federal government expanded the education system and instituted maternity and child nutrition programs in the early 1900s. During the 1930s, the Civilian Conservation Corps and the National Youth Administration were formed to meet what was agreed to be a societal, not just a parental, responsibility to find work for youths. In the 1940s, the government organized child care centers for women war-production workers. In the 1950s and 1960s, state and federal governments expanded their housing subsidies for families and began providing much more extensive higher education and job programs for young people.

Passing the Buck on Child Support

5   But in the economic and social climate that has prevailed
       since the mid-1970s, the long historical expansion of support
       systems for child raising has been reversed. Governments and
       corporations have transferred more and more of the costs of
       raising, educating, and training children back onto parents.
       As politicians and employers have demonstrated growing in-
       difference to the needs of the next generation, these attitudes
       have spread throughout society, with nonparents pushing the
       costs of the next generation onto parents and many parents
       engaging in their own cost-shifting behaviors.[4]

6   Spending on education, child and maternal health, and in-
       frastructure for the future generations has not kept up with
       needs for the past twenty years. Government has developed,
       economist Sylvia Hewlett observes, "a mindset...that is ex-
       traordinarily careless of children." As public policy analyst
       Iris Marion Young argues, "American society has been se-
       verely damaged by three decades of private and public disin-
       vestment in basic manufacturing, new and rehabilitated
       housing, bridges and rail lines, public education, adult re-
       training, and social services such as preventative health care
       and libraries." Yet parents are increasingly expected, on their
       own, "to fill these gaping holes in the American dream."[5]

7   The extent to which America has shifted the cost of raising
       children back onto parents can be seen in the extraordinary
       retreat from the expansion of public education—a child-
       centered reform in which the United States once led the
       world. A 1989 study by the Educational Writers Association
       found that a quarter of the country's school buildings were in-
       adequate, obsolete, or downright dangerous. A 1994 survey
       found that the conditions had continued to deteriorate, and
       the 1997 budget does not provide enough money to make a
       dent in the problem. Researchers report a direct correlation
       between poor physical conditions in schools and poor test
       scores.[6]

8   Teachers' salaries, expenditures per pupil, and other indi-
       cators of school quality (including the physical plant) signifi-
       cantly affect the employment prospects and wages of high
       school graduates. Yet unlike other nations, American schools
       are financed at the local rather than the federal level. If par-
       ents do not live in affluent communities with a high enough
       proportion of neighbors willing to vote for school bonds, they

have few ways of assuring a quality education other than to enroll their children in private schools. And voters, many of them parents who believe they already "did their bit" by raising their own children, are becoming less and less willing to subsidize schools for "other" people's kids. School bond failures are way up in comparison with earlier decades. At the same time, the property tax cuts of the 1970s and 1980s greatly decreased the resources available to schools.

Child advocate and educational researcher Jonathan Kozol reports that New York City spends half as much per student as surrounding suburbs. In 1992, the country's forty-seven largest urban school districts spent nearly *$900 less on each student* than did their suburban counterparts—even though the urban schools were far more likely to have students needing special services. There are also substantial variations *within* school districts. Poorer neighborhoods, which often contain more children, receive much lower public subsidies than affluent ones.[7]

International comparisons reveal that education is simply not a national priority in the United States the way it is in many countries. We have a piecemeal, incoherent system that fails to train teachers thoroughly, keep track of student progress in a consistent way, or ensure equality of access. Things are no better in the work world. Only 1 percent of the funding employers devote to training goes towards raising basic skills, those most needed by young entry-level workers. Both publicly and privately funded education is heavily skewed against the apprenticeship programs and vocational training needed by youngsters whose parents cannot afford to send them to college. Government spending on employment and training programs, in inflation-adjusted dollars, is today only one-third of what it was in 1980. At the same time, the cost of higher education has soared, while loans and scholarships have been cut back.[8]

Housing policies provide another example of government disinvestment in future generations. In the 1970s, government was financing about 400,000 new apartments a year. In 1996, Congress cut the number of new families who can expect rent subsidies or vouchers to zero.[9]

Economists and political scientists debate where this disinvestment in the next generation began and why it has spread so widely in the United States. Part of the problem is that the economic and political changes of the past few decades have increasingly put families with children at a disadvantage. The pressures of a fast-paced, winner-take-all economy handicap parents in comparison to nonparents, because parents have less time to produce income and more demands on them for redistribution than nonparents.

13   Under a system such as Social Security, furthermore, economist Nancy Folbre argues, nonparents can actually become "free riders" on parents. By now, most people realize that retirees get much more from Social Security than they actually put in. It is future workers, raised by parents at their personal expense, who create the Social Security funds on which all aging workers will later draw, even if they did not invest in rearing any of those future workers. Thus nonparents can benefit from other people's children without contributing to the costs of raising them.[10]

14   These trends have been exacerbated by what economist Robert Reich calls the "secession of the successful." Increasingly, affluent parents as well as nonparents have withdrawn funding from "public institutions shared by all and dedicated their savings to their own private services"—from exclusive schools and recreational facilities to private security for their walled-off neighborhoods. Government disinvestment widens the cycle, leaving middle-class families scrambling to buy privately what they can no longer count on receiving from public institutions, and needing to cut other expenses to make ends meet. In a tax system where voters have no say about whether expensive bombers get built, but plenty of chances to take out their frustrations in local school levies, children increasingly lose out in the contest for resources.[11]

15   In other words, long-term economic processes have gradually undermined Americans' consciousness of intergenerational obligations, while short-term economic setbacks have encouraged them to seize on quick-fix ways to keep more of their shrinking paychecks. Politicians have opportunistically encouraged people to rob the next generation. In confrontations over scarce resources or contested priorities, children, after all, are not an organized lobbying group.

16   The historical rise in the private costs of rearing children, combined with the recent public disinvestment in social capital, forms the background to what economist Joan Acker calls "a growing crisis of distribution" in modern industrial societies. In this crisis, it is not only children in single-parent families who have lost ground. There has been a decline in the economic and social resources available to children of *all* families except those in the top 20 percent of the income hierarchy.[12]

The Impact of Economic Inequality on Families

Cutbacks in social support systems, economic decline for   17
working families, growing poverty for the unemployed or
marginally employed, and highly visible affluence for the top
20 percent, along with the dazzling increase in consumer
goods and services, all combine to make family life more difficult and social solidarity more elusive for everyone. The
main countertrend to the job and wage setbacks in the United
States since the mid-1970s has been a tremendous expansion
of the consumer economy in fields that compete with family
life and social ties, providing youth of all classes with fleeting
and sometimes dangerous compensation for their exclusion
from meaningful participation in work, civic life, and public
space.

I spoke a year or so ago near Lakewood, California, a town   18
made famous by the Spur Posse, a group of high school athletes who developed a point system for sexual conquests. One
of the women at my talk had a son who attended the same
school as the Spur Posse youths, and she made a memorable
comment about the life that faces so many young people in
this city of middle-class homes but increasingly lower-class
jobs. "A lot of these kids," she said, "have way too little future,
but way too much *now*."[13]

For many families, of course, the *now* is already bleak, and   19
it is naive to think that parents can always protect their children from the impact of economic loss. Researchers find that
the risk of violent behavior is nearly six times higher among
people who are laid off from their jobs than among their employed counterparts, regardless of whether or not the individuals had a prior history of psychiatric disorder or alcohol
abuse. A study of 350 white families in rural Iowa found that
declining income, unstable work, or family debt in 1989 were
linked to significantly higher levels of aggression in middle-
school children two years later. These youths were more likely
to beat someone up, deface property, set fires, and use weapons against others than youths who had not experienced economic stress.[14]

One of the main ways that children are hurt by unemploy-   20
ment and income loss, in middle- and upper-income families
as well as low-income ones, is through the increase in stress
and depression that their parents experience. When parents
are distracted or irritated with each other because of financial

or job worries, they tend to be less supportive of their children. Too preoccupied to reinforce—or even notice—their children's considerate behavior, parents become overly sensitive to disruptive behavior because it adds to their feelings of stress. Their attempts to nip "bad" behavior in the bud increase hostile exchanges with their children. With their own emotional resources overtaxed, parents find it hard to summon the patience for negotiation, tact, and complex reasoning. Instead, they issue orders, followed by physical punishment when immediate obedience is not forthcoming. Parents may see children's resistance as yet another challenge to their authority and self-esteem, which are already threatened by economic setbacks having nothing to do with the kids.[15]

21   Often, parents are not aware that they have fallen into these patterns. When researchers ask parents who have been laid off about the effects on their families, few report problems. Some even tell researchers it's great to have the extra time with their kids. Children's accounts, however, almost invariably mention increased conflict and tension with parents. Observers' comparisons of interactions between employed and unemployed parents and their children suggests the kids' perceptions are more accurate than the parents'. Without other adult mentors or social support systems in the community, kids often bear the brunt of their parents' economic stress.[16]

22   Most of the effect of economic loss on children is channeled through changes in parenting practices, but economic insecurity also reduces kids' confidence in their parents and thereby increases their vulnerability to peer pressure. They become depressed and less motivated, and their lowered aspirations often have long-range consequences for their future.[17]

23   I got a vivid illustration of this a year or so ago when, after we had read studies of these family processes in class, one of my male students broke down crying. Embarrassed, he came to my office later and told me that he had transferred to the state college where I teach after two years at a community college and a year of full-time work. He had been raised to think he would go directly to a major university from high school. But his father had lost a well-paying job in the early 1980s, and by the time he found another, the family had gone through most of its savings.

24   My student told me how much he had resented his parents' inability to send him to the college of his choice. He had begun hanging out with a crowd that reinforced his growing contempt for his parents and their seemingly ineffectual re-

sponse to the family crisis. During his last two years of high school he had defied rules, frequently staying out all night, binging on alcohol, and letting his grades slip. There were shouting matches with his father, tearful recriminations from his mother.

Recently he and his parents had begun to mend their fences, but this was the first time, he said, he had really thought about how much pain his contempt had added to their lives. "I couldn't get past my father yelling at me and insulting me," he said. "I couldn't see how he must have been hurting. And when my mom cried, it just made me feel more like going out and getting stoned."   25

The effects of economic loss on children seem to be more pronounced for boys than for girls. In contrast to the cycles of anger and disrespect between sons and fathers triggered by economic hardship, mothers in deprived families often gain regard for their daughters' opinions, allowing them to participate more in family decisions. There are also gender differences in the ways that economic loss affects parenting. Both fathers and mothers are likely to respond to economic stress with inconsistent and harsh parenting, but men are more likely to explode at their children.[18]   26

When marital conflict is part of the equation, things get even worse. Fathers tend to react to children in an increasingly hostile, arbitrary manner, while children tend "to question the father's authority and form coalitions with the mother against the father." A strong marital relationship can temper these reactions, but economic loss has been found to produce dramatic declines in marital quality and supportiveness. Furthermore, whereas support from husbands lessens the impact of economic hardship on women's parenting practices, support from wives does not always have the same effect on fathers. Even with highly supportive wives, men under economic stress are far more likely to be explosive, inconsistent parents.[19]   27

Individuals with exceptionally good interpersonal skills can and do survive economic stress without such severe reactions, but those from less than ideal backgrounds, who in better conditions often overcome their personal weaknesses, may find the gains they have made over the years wiped away. For example, the Iowa study found that parents who had grown up in troubled families had fewer people skills and less self-confidence as adults. They were therefore "less capable of eliciting social support from others" to help them "withstand   28 the psychological onslaught of economic disadvantage." As the social safety net has unraveled, such individuals and their children increasingly fall by the wayside.[20]

The Effects of Poverty on Families and Children

29   Here's what Robert Rector of the Heritage Foundation has to say about the relationship between economic trends and family issues: "Is poverty harmful for children? I think not. Your bank account does not indicate the type of home you have."[21]

30   Do Rector and his counterparts have any idea of the terrible binds faced by unemployed or impoverished Americans, or of the havoc that poverty wreaks on families? I think not. Consider the fact that the number of underweight infants seen at hospitals rises sharply in the three months after the coldest snap of winter, in what Dr. Deborah Frank calls the "heat-or-eat" choice that many families have to make.[22]

31   Actually, the size of people's bank accounts has a lot to do with what type of home they can provide, which in turn has a tremendous impact on children's health and well-being. For example, poor children are especially likely to live in older homes where drinking water still flows through lead pipes and where there hasn't been a new paint job since 1978—the last year lead-based paint was used. It's estimated that 64 million homes contain lead-based paint. More than 1.7 million American children suffer from lead poisoning, the Environmental Protection Agency reported in 1996.[23]

32   Children who have been exposed to lead are seven times less likely to graduate from high school, six times more likely to have a reading disability, and six times more likely to engage in violence than other children, regardless of their family background. A four-year study of more than 800 boys in Pittsburgh, released February 7, 1996, showed that boys with higher lead levels were more likely than other boys to engage in antisocial acts, regardless of their parents' marital status or intelligence, and aside from any differences in income, medical problems, race, or ethnicity. Another study that followed 987 African-American children from birth to age 22 found that a history of lead poisoning was "the strongest predictor of disciplinary problems in junior high school boys and the third strongest predictor of both juvenile and adult offenses."[24]

33   Rector also claims that "the biggest dietary problem of people living in poverty is obesity, not hunger." Many poor adults

are obese, since empty calories cost less than fruits or fish, but for kids, this is simply false. Children in poverty are not more overweight than other children, but they are two to three times more likely to suffer from stunted growth. Columnist George Will says of the urban poor, "theirs is a poverty of inner resources." Yes, indeed—like nutrients. In 1992, an estimated 12 million American children had diets whose nutrient levels were significantly below the recommended allowances established by the National Academy of Sciences. Iron deficiency anemia affects nearly a quarter of America's impoverished children, and this condition is associated with long-term intellectual impairment. An article in the *American Journal of Epidemiology* concludes that "differences in nutritional status between poor and nonpoor children remain large even when controls for other characteristics associated with poverty, such as low maternal educational attainment, single-parent family structure, young maternal age, low maternal academic ability, and minority racial identification, are included."[25]

34   Poverty exerts direct effects on children's health and mental functioning even in the most solid families, with completely devoted and competent parents. But poverty, like job and income loss in general, also strains marital relationships and parent–child interactions. With nowhere to turn, increasingly cut off from social support or hope for help from public agencies, desperate parents sometimes behave in desperate ways.

35   Contrary to much of the discussion in the family values camp, most of the parenting problems in impoverished families have to do with harsh, punitive discipline rather than permissiveness. But poverty can distract parents from effective follow-through on discipline. A study of children raised during the Great Depression of the 1930s found that poverty interfered with parental control over youths, making delinquency more likely "regardless of children's initial temperament, the parents' own tendencies toward crime or deviance or mental instability, marital status and other factors." It's interesting to note that the two peaks in murder rates in the twentieth century occurred in 1933 and 1993. Yet whereas researchers easily recognize the social roots of violence in the Great Depression, many persist in denying the social and economic causes of today's troubled family and neighborhood relationships.[26]

36   Exceptionally competent parents, of course, can protect their children from many risks. Considering how many children from deprived backgrounds manage to get through school, avoid criminal involvement, and find jobs, it's clear

that there are some very competent and caring parents in poverty-stricken communities. Indeed, when you look at the effort it takes in such communities to keep children fed and physically safe, not to mention finding them warm clothes to wear and a quiet place to study, you have to admire the heroism that so many parents show. But if we made heroism a requirement for raising children, how many of us would have been issued the children with which we've been blessed? And even heroes can lose a child to lead poisoning, asthma, violence, or the bad breaks that occur so much more often in impoverished neighborhoods than in affluent communities.[27]

37   Impoverished families in urban areas are especially vulnerable today because changes in the nature and location of jobs over the past two decades mean that urban poverty has come to play an unprecedented role in society. Once urban poverty was a harsh but temporary way of forcing rural migrants to accept the demands and rhythms of industrial work in the city, as well as providing a cheap labor pool to hold down wages. Today, however, it permanently channels people out of the labor market—and, increasingly, out of any claim to common humanity with those who venture into the city to eat, shop, or work downtown and then retreat to their suburban homes at night.[28]

38   The proportion of poor people who live in areas where at least 40 percent of the other residents are also poor has more than doubled since the mid-1970s. And the chance of escaping poverty has declined. "In the 1970s, 37 out of 100 people who were poor moved out of poverty within a year; by the 1980s that figure was only 23 out of 100."[29]

39   The length of time spent in poverty has a powerful impact on children's well-being. Simple annual comparisons of income levels do not adequately measure the degree of disadvantage experienced by children who live for years at a time in areas of concentrated poverty. Persistent poverty during the first five years of life, for example, leaves children with an IQ deficit of more than nine points, regardless of family structure, race, ethnic group, or maternal education. Several studies have shown that the corrosive effect of chronic poverty outweighs the impact of individual life events and family histories on people's depression levels and coping skills.[30]

40   It is no wonder, then, that the odds of extreme behavioral problems are more than twice as high for poor children as for nonpoor ones. The most careful studies suggest that poverty, economic insecurity, and the effects of neglected neighborhoods pose stronger risks to children than growing up in

single-parent families, and are better predictors of low educational achievement or serious difficulties with the law. A child's chance of experiencing a poor home environment goes up in association with a number of different factors, including single parenthood, large numbers of siblings, and low maternal education, but the largest effects are almost invariably found to be family and neighborhood poverty rather than family structure.[31]

Poor children are twice as likely to drop out of high school   41
as other children. Mothers in one-parent families that are poor are no more likely to be abusive than mothers in two-parent families that are poor, but poor mothers—single or married—are significantly more likely to be abusive than mothers with incomes above the poverty line. For men, single fatherhood by itself does have an independent effect on abuse rates, but poverty has a stronger impact. Poor single fathers are three times as likely as nonpoor single fathers to abuse their children, and four times as likely as nonpoor fathers in a two-parent family.[32]

Poverty, Family Form, and Crime: What Sociological Studies Can and Cannot Tell Us

You've undoubtedly heard studies quoted that contradict   42
the findings presented here, especially when it comes to explaining antisocial behavior. Many researchers claim that even after controlling for income, single parenthood is the major cause of crime and violence. Barbara Dafoe Whitehead of the Institute for American Values, who wrote the "Dan Quayle Was Right" article in 1993, is often cited on this point. According to Whitehead, "more than 70 percent of all juveniles in state reform institutions come from fatherless homes." Mayors, police, and social workers, she claims, "consistently point to family breakup as the most important source of rising rates of crime." In the eight months after Whitehead's article appeared, I almost never gave a lecture without being drawn aside at the end by a single mother, often with the article in hand and the quote circled, asking me fearfully if I thought that her situation would really cause her child to end up in trouble with the law. Whitehead had clearly reached a mass audience and touched a raw nerve.[33]

But the studies are not nearly so unanimous as Whitehead   43
suggests. According to a 1993 report of the National Academy

of Sciences, for example, "personal and neighborhood income are the strongest predictors of violent crime." A recent summary of research on gangs, issued by the U.S. Department of Justice, concluded that single-parent families do not on their own predict gang membership. Martin Sanchez Janowski spent ten years hanging out with gangs to write an ethnographic account of their activities. He found that there were "as many gang members from homes where the nuclear family was intact as there were from families where the father was absent" and "as many members who claim close relationships with their families as those who denied them." Of course, many gangs are concentrated in neighborhoods that have high rates of single-parent families, so they will have a higher than average number of kids from one-parent families, but not necessarily disproportionate for their community.[34]

44   Cause and effect in human behavior are seldom simple. If single parenthood "caused" crime and violence, then Sweden and Denmark ought to have higher rates than the United States, instead of rates that are dramatically lower. Indeed, research in other countries does not find the same association between single-parent families and adolescent risk-taking behaviors that so much American research notes, which suggests that something more complicated is going on.[35]

45   Even in American studies, there is good reason to doubt how powerful the reported "associations" really are. Researchers who say they have "controlled" for other variables often overlook the dynamics of class. Controlling for income, for example, does not take into account the broader patterns of a person's life. College students frequently have very low incomes, but their social status and future prospects are generally greater than someone who pulls down a higher wage working at a low-skill, dead-end job. An African-American family with the same income as a white family is likely to have less than half as many total assets. Nor are all poverty incomes alike. The deeper and more long-lasting poverty is, the worse its effects. Yet many studies do not distinguish between current income and long-term economic status.[36]

46   A few years ago, there was a short-lived fad for public officials or reporters to try living on a welfare mother's budget or a poverty-level income for a month. The conclusion was usually: "It's very hard, but it can be done." Every time I glanced at such a magazine article or heard a news story about such an experiment on the radio, I knew I could expect a visit from an African-American friend of mine who had spent her first

twenty-two years in a housing project in the San Francisco Bay Area. As the only professor she had access to, it was my job to brew the coffee and let her vent.

"Did they have their teeth unstraightened or their grammar undone, so everyone would know they were bottom of the barrel?" she would demand. "Did they first wear their car down to its last legs so that a tire or part would be sure to go and they'd have to choose between paying the rent and making it to a job interview? Did they throw out all the staples in their kitchen before they started cooking on a food-stamp allotment? Did they let their kids get mugged a couple of times and then, just to teach them that life is hard, make sure that they also got shoved up against a nearby building by the cops every few days?"

My friend's outbursts were sometimes emotionally draining for us both, but they certainly reinforced in me a healthy skepticism about what you can and can't capture in a study of the separate "factors" affecting youthful behavior. Most statistics also do not control for bias in police and court records or reports of outside observers. When researchers have asked young people themselves how much delinquency they engage in, "family structure was unrelated to the seriousness of the offense." But school officials, juvenile authorities, and police are more likely to record behaviors committed by children from single-parent families and more likely to take measures against those kids.[37]   47

Youths from single-parent families are certainly overrepresented among the prison population. Part of the reason is that the majority of people in prison come from impoverished, desperate neighborhoods where there are high proportions of single-parent families that generally are a result, not a cause, of the community's problems. Another part of the story is legal bias. "When a white middle-class youth is arrested for a non-violent offense," writes former Judge Lois Forer, "the juvenile court usually 'adjusts' the offense. The boy has no record. In the inner city, youths are routinely adjudicated delinquent. Later this record counts heavily against them." Public defenders consistently tell me that they have a much slimmer chance of getting a youngster off with probation if the child has one parent than if he has two, regardless of the nature of the crime committed.[38]   48

Criminologist William Chambliss has spent several years,   49
along with his students, riding with the Rapid Deployment Unit of the Washington, D.C., Metropolitan Police. He points out that "the intensive surveillance of black neighborhoods"

leads to arrest and sentencing disparities that actually help *create* the single-parent families that "pro-family" spokespeople tell us are the source of crime.[39]

50   To deny that one-parent families are the cause of crime and violence is not to say there aren't some potentially dangerous interactions that occur between family structure, economic stress, parenting behaviors, and child outcomes. This is especially true in neighborhoods whose men have been marginalized by economic change. But crime and violence generally result only from the interaction and mutual reinforcement of *several* different factors, not from family factors alone.

51   One study found that on its own a high concentration of poverty in a neighborhood is not always linked to predelinquent childhood behaviors. Nor is a high level of residential turnover. But if the two factors exist together they do produce significant antisocial behavior. Similarly, "economic deprivation combined with a lack of social support creates an especially dangerous situation for children." The more risk factors at play, the more likely children are to get into trouble. One study found that more than half of adolescent delinquents "grew up with five or more separate risk factors."[40]

52   Children in inner-city African-American communities, for example, have risk factors piled on top of each other. Chronic joblessness, extreme segregation, economic and political abandonment of the cities, and the resultant discouragement, researcher Philip Bowman argues, have made the transition from adolescence to adulthood an acute challenge for impoverished African Americans.[41]

53   Columnist George Will has a simple formula to explain their problems: "What is called the race crisis is a class problem arising from dysfunctional families and destructive behaviors." He's got it partly right. Many family forms and behaviors that are commonly attributed to race are in fact responses to class position. But race and racism help explain why African Americans and Latinos are concentrated in the industries and regions where economic setbacks have been the most devastating, and why minorities have accumulated so few assets over the years, leaving them especially vulnerable to unemployment and income loss. And the evidence suggests that the rest of Will's statement is almost exactly backward. America's class problem is a major *cause* of dysfunctional families and destructive behaviors, especially among impoverished racial groups on whom government and society have turned their backs.[42]

In many inner-city communities, long-term poverty com- 54
bines with lack of social support, dilapidated schools, over-
crowded classrooms, and the sense that the rest of society
doesn't care to create chronic despair in children, punctuated
by bouts of rage. Herb Schreier, chief of psychiatry at Children's Hospital in Oakland, California, described to me how
some of the kids in an African-American and Asian high
school went on a rampage after the fire that swept through
Berkeley and Oakland in 1991. When the teachers talked with
the students later, it turned out that they were infuriated by
the outpouring of public sympathy and aid that victims of the
fire had received. How could they have reacted so disgrace-
fully to such a heartwarming response? Almost exactly two
years earlier the Cypress Expressway had collapsed in the
great Bay Area earthquake. The rubble was still sitting in
their neighborhood, and this devastated community had received no such aid and sympathy. "No one cares about *us*,"
the kids said. "No one ever does anything about us."

No wonder such youths become alienated. They have 55
watched their parents get fired after diligently trudging off to
a menial job for twenty years. They have seen building after
building on their block abandoned. And when some kids have
the perfectly normal response of throwing stones at a vacant
building, the broken windows and boards stay unrepaired. Everything in their environment is ugly except for the images on
TV. And don't think they don't notice: One of the first proposals the notorious Bloods and Crips gangs made to the city of
L.A. after the riots in 1992 was that the city place flowerboxes
on their street corners. It hasn't happened yet. Meanwhile,
mired in poverty but surrounded by images of affluence, is it
any wonder that young people look for some other way to get
a piece of the American dream?[43]

Joe Marshall, cofounder of the Omega Boys Club, works 56
with youth in an impoverished San Francisco neighborhood
very similar to that in which he grew up. He remarks that
there are not more hard-core "bad guys" today, but there are
fewer alternatives to throwing in your lot with them. In his
youth, he recalls, poverty was widespread, but at least there
were jobs that gave young people work experience, spending
money, and a sense of dignity. Even with high unemployment
rates and low wages, the hope that these jobs provided kept
most people working or looking for work. Kids who fell for
the lure of easy money or the street life used to see it as a bad
choice they had made. "Don't turn out like me," they would
tell younger boys. "Run on home now." Today, with fewer and

fewer alternatives almost every year, the "bad guys" play a different role.[44]

57   Not every social ill in America, of course, is caused by economic deprivation. Conservatives are quite right to say that poverty alone does not explain the alienation and fragmentation so prevalent today, or the terrible turmoil in so many families. But the shattering of older social expectations, along with the evolution of rich and poor into two separate universes, explains much of it. And the abandonment of the social safety net explains even more. As Jerome Skolnick put it in his 1994 presidential address to the American Society of Criminology, "Unemployment is a risk factor for crime. Patterned unemployment through time, and across racial and ethnic divisions, is a cause." Especially, criminologist Gilbert Geiss points out, when unemployment and poverty rub shoulders with "a society of affluence, in which your self-esteem is tied to failure to achieve that affluence."[45]

58   It is time to abandon denial, self-righteousness, and scapegoating and to deal directly with the moral issues raised by these economic changes and by the last few decades of disinvestment in the younger generation. The question that gets lost in the debate over marital stability, parental responsibility, and personal character is whether we as a nation are willing to foster long-term commitments in economic and social life, whether we as a people have the character to defer immediate gratification in order to invest in the future of our communities. At heart, this is not a family crisis but a social crisis.

59   The worst effect of today's family values crusade is that by blaming our problems on the breakdown of the traditional family it fails to recognize the strengths of today's diverse families—strengths we can mobilize to help *solve* our social problems. We need to reject the false notion that there is one perfect family form that automatically protects its members from outside forces, while other family forms or values automatically put them at risk. *All* families are at risk when they're left to face new challenges on their own. All families have the potential to rise above their weaknesses when they get support and encouragement from others.

60   When you read life histories of children from impoverished neighborhoods, the first point that strikes you is the stunning number of obstacles they face, the hundreds of tiny curves where it's possible to fall off a path much narrower and higher than any that more privileged children have to tread. But the second point is how eager most parents are to do right by their children.

Similarly, when I talk with families undergoing major   61
changes in their marital roles, family norms, or work relations, I am constantly amazed by their resilience and creativity. What they need is social and moral support to meet their
challenges and hone their strengths. What they don't need is
to be subjected to a family values exam on which they are
graded on the basis of some standardized form that was codified a century ago.

Notes

1. Nancy Folbre, *Who Pays for the Kids? Gender and the Struc-
   tures of Constraint* (New York: Routledge, 1994), pp. 112–119;
   James Coleman, "The Rational Reconstruction of Society,"
   American Sociological Review 58 (1993), p. 12.
2. John Coatsworth, "Presidential Address," *American Historical
   Review* 101 (1996), p. 9; P. Lindsay Chase-Landsdale and
   Maris A. Vinovskis, "Whose Responsibility? An Historical
   Analysis of the Changing Roles of Mothers, Fathers, and Soci-
   ety," in P. Lindsay Chase-Lansdale and J. Brooks-Gunn, eds.,
   Escape from Poverty: What Makes a Difference for Children?
   (New York: Cambridge University Press, 1995); Linda Gordon,
   *Heroes of Their Own Lives: The Politics and History of Family
   Violence, Boston 1880–1960* (New York: Viking, 1988), p. 42.
3. Michael Katz, *Improving Poor People: The Welfare State, the
   "Underclass," and Urban Schools as History* (Princeton, N.J.:
   Princeton University Press, 1995); Gordon, *Heroes of Their
   Own Lives,* p. 42; Brian Gratton and Frances Rotundo, "Indus-
   trialization, the Family Economy, and the Economic Status of
   the American Elderly," *Social Science History* 15 (1991),
   p. 356; Walter Trattner, *From Poor Law to Welfare State: A History of Social Welfare in America* (New York: Free Press, 1984);
   Seth Koven and Sonya Michel, eds., *Mothers of a New World:
   Maternalist Politics and the Origins of Welfare States* (New
   York: Routledge, 1993); Gwendolyn Mink, *The Wages of Moth-
   erhood: Inequality in the Welfare State, 1917–1942* (Ithaca, N.Y.:
   Cornell University Press, 1995); Julius B. Richmond, "The
   Hull House Era: Vintage Years for Children," *American Jour-
   nal of Orthopsychiatry* 65 (1995).
4. Judith Bruce, Cynthia Lloyd, and Ann Leonard, with Patrice
   Engle and Niev Duffy, *Families in Focus: New Perspectives on
   Mothers, Fathers, and Children* (New York: The Population
   Council, 1995), p. 14; Geoffrey Holtz, *Welcome to the Jungle:
   The Why Behind "Generation X"* (New York: St. Martin's Press,
   1995), p. 50; Mike Males, *The Scapegoat Generation: America's
   War on Adolescents* (Monroe, Me.: Common Courage Press,
   1996), p. 10; Sylvia Hewlett, *When the Bough Breaks: The Costs*

of Neglecting Our Children (New York: Basic Books, 1991), p. 211; Lynn Curtis, *The State of Families* (Milwaukee, Wisc.: Family Service America, 1995), p. 25; *Welfare Myths: Fact or Fiction? Exploring the Truth About Welfare* (New York: Center on Social Welfare Policy and Law, 1996), p. 36; Steven Rendall, Jim Naurekas, and Jeff Cohen, *The Way Things Aren't: Rush Limbaugh's Reign of Error* (New York: The New Press, 1995), p. 25.

5. Hewlett, *When the Bough Breaks*, p. 211; Iris Marion Young, "Reply to Jean Elshtain and Margaret Steinfels," *Dissent* (Spring 1994), p. 272; Joan Smith, "Transforming Households: Working-Class Women and Economic Crisis," *Social Problems* 34 (1987), p. 436.

6. *Olympian*, December 13, 1989, p. A8; Betsy Wagner and Stephen Hedges, "Education in Decay," *U.S. News & World Report*, September 12, 1994, p. 79; Joseph Altonji and Thomas Dunn, "Using Siblings to Estimate the Effect of School Quality on Wages," *Center for Urban Affairs and Policy Research Working Paper 96–10* (Evanston, Ill.: Northwestern University, 1996); Shazia Rufiullah Miller and James Rosenbaum, "The Missing Link: Social Infrastructure and Employers' Use of Information," *Center for Urban Affairs and Policy Research Working Paper 96–15* (Evanston, Ill.: Northwestern University, 1996).

7. Jonathan Kozol, *Savage Inequalities: Children in America's Schools* (New York: Crown, 1991), p. 237; "Hard Data," *Washington Post Weekly Edition*, September 28–October 4, 1992, p. 37.

8. David Whitman, "The Forgotten Half," *U.S. News & World Report*, June 26, 1989; Randy Abelda, Nancy Folbre, and the Center for Popular Economies, *The War Against the Poor: A Defense Manual* (New York: The New Press, 1996), p. 68; Peter Applebome, "U.S. Gets 'Average' Grade in Math and Science Studies," *New York Times*, November 21, 1996.

9. Jason De Parle, "Slamming the Door," *New York Times*, October 20, 1996, p. 52.

10. Folbre, *Who Pays for the Kids?* pp. 112–119, 208–210.

11. Bruce et al., *Families in Focus*, p. 14; Folbre, *Who Pays for the Kids?;* Holly Sklar, *Chaos or Community? Seeking Solutions, Not Scapegoats for Bad Economics* (Boston: South End Press, 1995), p. 145.

12. Folbre, *Who Pays for the Kids?;* Pamela Smock, "Gender and the Short-Run Economic Consequences of Marital Disruption," *Social Forces* 73 (1994), p. 259; Joan Acker, "Class, Gender, and the Relations of Distribution," *Signs* 13 (1988), p. 496.

13. For an insightful analysis of the class, cultural, and sexual tensions behind the Spur Posse story, see Joan Didion, "Trouble in Lakewood," *The New Yorker*, July 26, 1993.

14. Vonnie McCloyd, "The Impact of Economic Hardship on Black Families and Children: Psychological Distress, Parenting, and Socioemotional Development," *Child Development* 61 (1990), pp. 324–325; Richard Gelles, "Though a Sociological Lens: Social Structure and Family Violence," in Richard Gelles and Donileen Loseke, eds., *Current Controversies on Family Violence* (Newbury Park, Calif.: Sage, 1993), p. 33; Ralph Catalano et al., "Using ECA Data to Examine the Effect of Job Layoffs on Violent Behavior," *Hospital and Community Psychiatry* 44 (1993), pp. 874, 878; Rand D. Conger, Xiaojia Ge, Glen H. Elder, Jr., Frederick O. Lorenz, and Ronald L. Simons, "Economic Stress, Coercive Family Process, and Developmental Problems of Adolescents," *Child Development* 65 (1994).

15. Robert Solow, *Wasting America's Future* (Boston: Beacon Press, 1994), pp. 30–32; Gene H. Brody, Zolinda Stoneman, and Douglas Flor, "Linking Family Process and Academic Competence among Rural African American Youths," *Journal of Marriage and the Family* 57 (1995), p. 567; Ralph Catalano, "The Health Effects of Economic Insecurity," *American Journal of Public Health* 81 (1991), p. 1149; Conger et al., "Economic Stress, Coercive Family Process"; McLoyd, "Impact of Economic Hardship," pp. 330–331; P. Lindsay Chase-Lansdale and Jeanne Brooks-Gunn, "Introduction," in Chase-Lansdale and Brooks-Gunn, eds., *Escape from Poverty*, p. 3; Gerald Patterson, John Reid, and Thomas Dishion, *Antisocial Boys* (Eugene, Ore.: Castalia, 1992); Craig Mason, Ana Mari Cauce, Nancy Gonzales, Yumi Hiraga, and Kwai Grove, "An Ecological Model of Externalizing Behaviors in African-American Adolescents: No Family Is an Island," *Journal of Research on Adolescence* 4, no. 4 (1994), p. 651; Rand D. Conger and Glen H. Elder, Jr., in collaboration with Frederick O. Lorenz, Ronald L. Simons, and Les B. Whitbeck, *Families in Troubled Times: Adapting to Change in Rural America* (New York: Aldine de Gruyter, 1994), pp. 219–220.

16. McLoyd, "Impact of Economic Hardship," p. 324; Vonnie McLoyd and Constance Flanagan, eds., *Economic Stress: Effects on Family Life and Child Development* (San Francisco: Jossey-Bass, 1991).

17. Conger and Elder et al., *Families in Troubled Times*, p. 261; Constance Flanagan, "Families and Schools in Hard Times," and Rainier Silberstien, Sabine Walper, and Helfried Albrecht, "Family Income Loss and Economic Hardship: Antecedents of Adolescents' Problem Behavior," in McLoyd and Flanagan, eds., *Economic Stress*.

18. Flanagan, "Families and Schools in Hard Times," p. 19; McLoyd, "Impact of Economic Hardship," p. 319; Jeffrey K. Liker and Glen H. Elder, Jr., "Economic Hardship and Marital Relations in the 1930s," *American Sociological Review* 48 (June 1983), p. 356.

19. McLoyd, "Impact of Economic Hardship," pp. 330, 336; Ann Crouter and Beth Manke, "The Changing American Workplace: Implications for Individuals and Families," *Family Relations* 43 (1994), p. 119; Liker and Elder, "Economic Hardship and Marital Relations in the 1930s," p. 343; Conger and Elder et al., *Families in Troubled Times*, p. 219–221.

20. Conger and Elder et al., *Families in Troubled Times*, p. 259.

21. Rector quoted in *Washington Post National Weekly Edition*, September 11–17, 1995, p. 8.

22. Perri Klass, "Tackling Problems We Thought We Solved," *New York Times Magazine*, December 13, 1992, p. 62; Robert A. Hahn, Elaine Eaker, Nancy D. Barker, Steven M. Teutsch, Waldemar Sosniak, and Nancy Krieger, "Poverty and Death in the United States—1973 and 1991," *Epidemiology* 6 (1995), p. 490. My thanks to Carole Oshinsky of the New York-based National Center for Children in Poverty for supplying additional references and fact sheets.

23. "Tough Lead-Paint Rule Issued," *Olympian*, March 7, 1996, p. A4; Geoffrey Cowley, "Children in Peril," *Newsweek Special Issue*, Summer 1991, p. 20; James Sargent, Mary Jean Brown, Jean Freeman, Adrian Bailey, David Goodman, and Daniel H. Freeman, Jr., "Childhood Lead Poisoning in Massachusetts Communities: Its Association with Sociodemographic and Housing Characteristics," *American Journal of Public Health* 85 (1995), p. 531; Jane Brody, "Aggressiveness and Delinquency in Boys Is Linked to Lead in Bones," *New York Times*, February 7, 1996, p. B6.

24. Harold Hodgkinson, "Reform Versus Reality," *Phi Delta Kappan*, September, 1991, p. 14; Herbert Needleman, "Childhood Exposure to Lead: A Common Cause of School Failure," *Phi Delta Kappan*, September 1992, p. 36; Brody, "Aggressiveness Linked to Lead."

25. Rector quoted in Albeda and Folbre, *The War Against the Poor*, p. 34. See also Solow, *Wasting America's Future*, p. 15; J. Larry Brown and Ernesto Pollitt, "Malnutrition, Poverty and Intellectual Development," *Scientific American*, February 1996, p. 38; Rendall, Naurekas, and Cohen, *The Way Things Aren't*, p. 22; Jane E. Miller and Sanders Korenman, "Poverty and Children's Nutritional Status in the United States," *American Journal of Epidemiology* 140 (1994), p. 233. Estimates of the prevalence of hunger are currently being revised, with researchers beginning to talk about "food insecurity" rather than hunger and malnutrition alone. The Food Security Study, directed by Dr. John T. Cook, should be available in 1997. For further information, contact the Center on Hunger, Poverty and Nutrition Policy, Tufts University, Medford, Massachusetts 02155. The George Will quote appeared in Will, "Soft Voice in a Deadly Crisis," *Washington Post*, June 19, 1994.

26. Solow, *Wasting America's Future*, pp. 29–36, 88; Mason et al., "An Ecological Model of Externalizing Behaviors in African-American Adolescents"; Robert Sampson and John Laub, "Urban Poverty and the Family Context of Delinquency: A New Look at Structure and Process in a Classic Study," *Child Development* 65 (1994); Males, *The Scapegoat Generation*, p. 109.

27. Katherine Brown Rosier and William A. Corsaro, "Competent Parents, Complex Lives: Managing Parenthood in Poverty," *Journal of Contemporary Ethnography* 22 (1993); Patricia Garrett, Nicholas Ng'andu, and John Ferron, "Poverty Experiences of Young Children and the Quality of Their Home Environments," *Child Development* 65 (1994); Bonnie Leadbeater and Sandra Bishop, "Predictors of Behavior Problems in Preschool Children of Inner-City Afro-American and Puerto Rican Adolescent Mothers," *Child Development* 65 (1994).

28. Michael Katz, ed., *The "Underclass" Debate: Views from History* (Princeton, N.J.: Princeton University Press, 1993); Douglas Massey and Nancy Denton, *American Apartheid: Segregation and the Making of the Underclass* (Cambridge, Mass.: Harvard University Press, 1993).

29. Katz, *The "Underclass" Debate;* James Gabarino and Kathleen Kolstelny, "Neighborhood and Community Influences on Parenting," in Tom Luster and Lynn Okagaki, eds., *Parenting: An Ecological Perspective* (Hillsdale, N.J.: Lawrence Erlbaum, 1993), p. 205.

30. Jane McLeod and Michael Shanahan, "Poverty, Parenting, and Children's Mental Health," *American Sociological Review* 58 (1993), p. 351; Spencer Rich, "Study: Poverty in First 5 Years Lowers Kids' IQs," *Morning News Tribune*, March 28, 1993; Greg J. Duncan et al., "Economic Deprivation and Early-Childhood Development," *Child Development* 65 (1994), pp. 296–318; McLoyd "Impact of Economic Hardship," p. 318; Gabarino and Kostelny, "Neighborhood and Community Influences on Parenting," p. 205.

31. Solow, *Wasting America's Future*, pp. 82, 90; Greg J. Duncan, Jeanne Brooks-Gunn, and Pamela Kato Klebanov, "Economic Deprivation and Early Childhood Development," *Child Development* 65 (1994), p. 296; Pamela Kato Klebanov, Jeanne Brooks-Gunn, and Greg J. Duncan, "Does Neighborhood and Family Poverty Affect Mothers' Parenting, Mental Health, and Social Support?" *Journal of Marriage and the Family* 56 (May 1994), p. 441; Sanders Korenman, Jane Miller, and John Sjaastad, "Long-Term Poverty and Child Development in the United States: Results from the NLSY" (National Longitudinal Study of Youth), *Children and Youth Services Review* 17 (1995); Carolyn Smith and Marvin Krohn, "Delinquency and Family Life Among Male Adolescents," *Journal of Youth and Adolescence* 24 (1995).

32. Albeda and Folbre, *War against the Poor*, p. 27; James Garbar-
    ino, "The Meaning of Poverty in the World of Children," *Amer-
    ican Behavioral Scientist* 35 (1992), p. 228; Solow, *Wasting
    America's Future*, p. 82.

33. Barbara Dafoe Whitehead, "Dan Quayle Was Right," *Atlantic
    Monthly*, April 1993, p. 77.

34. Solow, *Wasting America's Future*, pp. 82–91; Irving Spergel et
    al., *Gang Suppression and Intervention: Problem and Response*
    (Washington, D.C.: U.S. Department of Justice, 1994), p. 4;
    Martin Sanchez Jankowski, *Islands in the Street: Gangs and
    American Urban Society* (Berkeley: University of California,
    1991), p. 39. For an insight into the socioeconomic and cul-
    tural context of gangs, see the disturbing memoir of gang life
    by Luis Rodriguez, *Always Running: La Vida Loca: Gang Days
    in L.A.* (New York: Simon and Schuster, 1993). Rodriguez
    came from a two-parent family that tried continually to escape
    the poverty of L.A.'s barrios and to provide an education for
    their kids. What turned Rodriguez around was not his family
    life but the sense of pride and social solidarity he began to feel
    when he was exposed to the Chicano power movement.

35. Marvin Free, Jr., "Clarifying the Relationship Between the
    Broken Home and Juvenile Delinquency: A Critique of the
    Current Literature," *Deviant Behavior: An Interdisciplinary
    Journal* 12 (1991), p. 130.

36. Melvin Oliver and Thomas Shapiro, *Black Wealth/White
    Wealth: A New Perspective on Racial Inequality* (New York: Rout-
    ledge, 1995), p. 119; Korenman, Miller, and Sjaastad, "Long-
    Term Poverty," pp. 147–148; Greg Duncan, Wei-Jun Yeung, and
    Jeanne Brooks-Gunn, *Does Childhood Poverty Affect the Life
    Chances of Children?* Working Paper 96–2, Center for Urban
    Affairs and Policy Research, Northwestern University, April
    24, 1996; Solow, *Wasting America's Future*, p. 91; Jeanne
    Brooks-Gunn, "Strategies for Altering the Outcomes of Poor
    Children and Their Families," in Chase-Lansdale and Brooks-
    Gunn, eds., *Escape from Poverty*, pp. 88–89.

37. Free, "Clarifying the Relationship Between the Broken Home
    and Juvenile Delinquency," pp. 144, 158.

38. Free, "Clarifying the Relationship Between the Broken Home
    and Juvenile Delinquency," p. 158; Sklar, *Chaos or Commu-
    nity?* pp. 128–129.

39. Sklar, *Chaos or Community?* p. 128; William Chambliss, "Po-
    licing the Ghetto Underclass: The Politics of Law and Law En-
    forcement," *Social Problems* 41 (1994).

40. Karole Kumpfer, *Strengthening America's Families: Promising
    Parenting Strategies for Delinquency Prevention* (Washington,
    D.C.: Office of Juvenile Justice and Delinquency Prevention,
    1993), p. 9; Solow, *Wasting America's Future*, pp. 53–55; Rob-
    ert Angel and Jacqueline Angel, *Painful Inheritance: Health*

and the New Generation of Fatherless Families (Madison: University of Wisconsin Press, 1993), pp. 22, xix; Patricia Hashima and Paul Amato, "Poverty, Social Support, and Parental Behavior," *Child Development* 65 (1994), p. 400.

41. Sam Roberts, *Who We Are: A Portrait of America Based on the Latest U.S. Census* (New York: Times Books, 1995), p. 181; Reynolds Farley and Walter Allen, *The Color Line and the Quality of Life in America* (New York: Russell Sage, 1987); Maxine Baca Zinn, "Minority Families in Crisis: The Public Discussion" (Memphis, Tenn.: Center for Research on Women, 1985); "Still Far from the Dream: Recent Developments in Black Income, Employment and Poverty," Washington, D.C.: Center on Budget and Policy Priorities, October 1988; Phillip Bowman, "The Adolescent-to-Adult Transition: Discouragement Among Jobless Black Youth," in McLoyd and Flanagan, eds., *Economic Stress.*

42. George Will, "Powell's Candidacy in Question," *Olympian,* April 16, 1995, p. A9; John Mirowsky and Catherine E. Ross, *Social Causes of Psychological Distress* (New York: Aldine de Gruyter, 1989), p. 17.

43. To see the odds such children and their families face, even when they try their best, watch the documentary *Hoop Dreams,* or read Alex Kotlowitz, *There Are No Children Here: The Story of Two Boys Growing Up in the Other America* (New York: Doubleday, 1991).

44. For more on Marshall's work, see his book, *Street Soldier: One Man's Struggle to Save a Generation—One Life at a Time* (New York: Delacorte, 1996).

45. Jerome Skolnick, "What Not to Do About Crime," *Criminology* 33 (1995), p. 2; Geiss quoted in Mike Males and Faye Docuyanan, "Crack-down on Kids," *The Progressive,* February 1996, p. 24.

IS SINGLE PARENTHOOD A PROBLEM?

Barbara Dafoe Whitehead
Dan Quayle Was Right

The Atlantic Monthly, a respected left-of-center magazine of current affairs and opinion, received more letters in response to the following excerpted essay by Barbara Dafoe Whitehead than it has ever received in response to an article. When it was published in April 1993, its title was alluding to former Vice President Dan Quayle's controversial opposition to the family arrangements of TV character Murphy Brown. Whitehead, a native of Wisconsin (born 1944) and a research associate at the Institute for American Values, a nonpartisan, New York City organization devoted to issues of the family, in part defends a position that she expressed in an earlier article in the Washington Post, *which helped motivate the vice president to make family issues central to the 1992 presidential campaign.*

1   Divorce and out-of-wedlock childbirth are transforming the lives of American children. In the postwar generation more than 80 percent of children grew up in a family with two biological parents who were married to each other. By 1980 only 50 percent could expect to spend their entire childhood in an intact family. If current trends continue, less than half of all children born today will live continuously with their own mother and father throughout childhood. Most American children will spend several years in a single-mother family. Some will eventually live in stepparent families, but because stepfamilies are more likely to break up than intact (by which I mean two-biological-parent) families, an increasing number of children will experience family breakup two or even three times during childhood.

2   According to a growing body of social-scientific evidence, children in families disrupted by divorce and out-of-wedlock birth do worse than children in intact families on several measures of well-being. Children in single-parent families are six times as likely to be poor. They are also likely to stay poor

longer. Twenty-two percent of children in one-parent families will experience poverty during childhood for seven years or more, as compared with only two percent of children in two-parent families. A 1988 survey by the National Center for Health Statistics found that children in single-parent families are two to three times as likely as children in two-parent families to have emotional and behavioral problems. They are also more likely to drop out of high school, to get pregnant as teenagers, to abuse drugs, and to be in trouble with the law. Compared with children in intact families, children from disrupted families are at a much higher risk for physical or sexual abuse.

Contrary to popular belief, many children do not "bounce back" after divorce or remarriage. Difficulties that are associated with family breakup often persist into adulthood. Children who grow up in single-parent or stepparent families are less successful as adults, particularly in the two domains of life—love and work—that are most essential to happiness. Needless to say, not all children experience such negative effects. However, research shows that many children from disrupted families have a harder time achieving intimacy in a relationship, forming a stable marriage, or even holding a steady job.

Despite this growing body of evidence, it is nearly impossible to discuss changes in family structure without provoking angry protest. Many people see the discussion as no more than an attack on struggling single mothers and their children: Why blame single mothers when they are doing the very best they can? After all, the decision to end a marriage or a relationship is wrenching, and few parents are indifferent to the painful burden this decision imposes on their children. Many take the perilous step toward single parenthood as a last resort, after their best efforts to hold a marriage together have failed. Consequently, it can seem particularly cruel and unfeeling to remind parents of the hardships their children might suffer as a result of family breakup. Other people believe that the dramatic changes in family structure, though regrettable, are impossible to reverse. Family breakup is an inevitable feature of American life, and anyone who thinks otherwise is indulging in nostalgia or trying to turn back the clock. Since these new family forms are here to stay, the reasoning goes, we must accord respect to single parents, not criticize them. Typical is the view expressed by a Brooklyn woman in a recent letter to *The New York Times:* "Let's stop moralizing or blaming single parents

and unwed mothers, and give them the respect they have
earned and the support they deserve."

5   Such views are not to be dismissed. Indeed, they help to explain why family structure is such an explosive issue for Americans. The debate about it is not simply about the social-
scientific evidence, although that is surely an important part
of the discussion. It is also a debate over deeply held and often
conflicting values. How do we begin to reconcile our long-
standing belief in equality and diversity with an impressive
body of evidence that suggests that not all family structures
produce equal outcomes for children? How can we square traditional notions of public support for dependent women and
children with a belief in women's right to pursue autonomy
and independence in childbearing and child-rearing? How do
we uphold the freedom of adults to pursue individual happiness in their private relationships and at the same time respond to the needs of children for stability, security, and
permanence in their family lives? What do we do when the interests of adults and children conflict? These are the difficult
issues at stake in the debate over family structure.

6   In the past these issues have turned out to be too difficult
and too politically risky for debate. In the mid-1960s Daniel
Patrick Moynihan, then an assistant secretary of labor, was
denounced as a racist for calling attention to the relationship
between the prevalence of black single-mother families and
the lower socioeconomic standing of black children. For
nearly twenty years the policy and research communities
backed away from the entire issue. In 1980 the Carter Administration convened a historic White House Conference on
Families, designed to address the growing problems of children and families in America. The result was a prolonged,
publicly subsidized quarrel over the definition of "family." No
President since has tried to hold a national family conference.
Last year, at a time when the rate of out-of-wedlock births
had reached a historic high, Vice President Dan Quayle was
ridiculed for criticizing Murphy Brown. In short, every time
the issue of family structure has been raised, the response has
been first controversy, then retreat, and finally silence.

7   Yet it is also risky to ignore the issue of changing family
structure. In recent years the problems associated with family
disruption have grown. Overall child well-being has declined,
despite a decrease in the number of children per family, an increase in the educational level of parents, and historically
high levels of public spending. After dropping in the 1960s
and 1970s, the proportion of children in poverty has in-

creased dramatically, from 15 percent in 1970 to 20 percent in 1990, while the percentage of adult Americans in poverty has remained roughly constant. The teen suicide rate has more than tripled. Juvenile crime has increased and become more violent. School performance has continued to decline. There are no signs that these trends are about to reverse themselves.

If we fail to come to terms with the relationship between   8
family structure and declining child well-being, then it will be increasingly difficult to improve children's life prospects, no matter how many new programs the federal government funds. Nor will we be able to make progress in bettering school performance or reducing crime or improving the quality of the nation's future work force—all domestic problems closely connected to family breakup. Worse, we may contribute to the problem by pursuing policies that actually increase family instability and breakup.

From Death to Divorce

Across time and across cultures, family disruption has   9
been regarded as an event that threatens a child's well-being and even survival. This view is rooted in a fundamental biological fact: unlike the young of almost any other species, the human child is born in an abjectly helpless and immature state. Years of nurture and protection are needed before the child can achieve physical independence. Similarly, it takes years of interaction with at least one but ideally two or more adults for a child to develop into a socially competent adult. Children raised in virtual isolation from human beings, though physically intact, display few recognizably human behaviors. The social arrangement that has proved most successful in ensuring the physical survival and promoting the social development of the child is the family unit of the biological mother and father. Consequently, any event that permanently denies a child the presence and protection of a parent jeopardizes the life of the child.

The classic form of family disruption is the death of a parent. Throughout history this has been one of the risks of   10
childhood. Mothers frequently died in childbirth, and it was not unusual for both parents to die before the child was grown. As recently as the early decades of this century children commonly suffered the death of at least one parent. Almost a quarter of the children born in this country in 1900 lost one parent by the time they were fifteen years old. Many

of these children lived with their widowed parent, often in a household with other close relatives. Others grew up in orphanages and foster homes.

11   The meaning of parental death, as it has been transmitted over time and faithfully recorded in world literature and lore, is unambiguous and essentially unchanging. It is universally regarded as an untimely and tragic event. Death permanently severs the parent-child bond, disrupting forever one of the child's earliest and deepest human attachments. It also deprives a child of the presence and protection of an adult who has a biological stake in, as well as an emotional commitment to, the child's survival and well-being. In short, the death of a parent is the most extreme and severe loss a child can suffer.

12   Because a child is so vulnerable in a parent's absence, there has been a common cultural response to the death of a parent: an outpouring of support from family, friends, and strangers alike. The surviving parent and child are united in their grief as well as their loss. Relatives and friends share in the loss and provide valuable emotional and financial assistance to the bereaved family. Other members of the community show sympathy for the child, and public assistance is available for those who need it. This cultural understanding of parental death has formed the basis for a tradition of public support to widows and their children. Indeed, as recently as the beginning of this century widows were the only mothers eligible for pensions in many states, and today widows with children receive more generous welfare benefits from Survivors Insurance than do other single mothers with children who depend on Aid to Families With Dependent Children.

13   It has taken thousands upon thousands of years to reduce the threat of parental death. Not until the middle of the twentieth century did parental death cease to be a commonplace event for children in the United States. By then advances in medicine had dramatically reduced mortality rates for men and women.

14   At the same time, other forms of family disruption—separation, divorce, out-of-wedlock birth—were held in check by powerful religious, social, and legal sanctions. Divorce was widely regarded both as a deviant behavior, especially threatening to mothers and children, and as a personal lapse: "Divorce is the public acknowledgment of failure," a 1940s sociology textbook noted. Out-of-wedlock birth was stigmatized, and stigmatization is a powerful means of regulating behavior, as any smoker or overeater will testify. Sanctions against nonmarital childbirth discouraged behavior that hurt

children and exacted compensatory behavior that helped them. Shotgun marriages and adoption, two common responses to nonmarital birth, carried a strong message about the risks of premarital sex and created an intact family for the child.

Consequently, children did not have to worry much about losing a parent through divorce or never having had one because of nonmarital birth. After a surge in divorces following the Second World War, the rate leveled off. Only 11 percent of children born in the 1950s would by the time they turned eighteen see their parents separate or divorce. Out-of-wedlock childbirth barely figured as a cause of family disruption. In the 1950s and early 1960s, five percent of the nation's births were out of wedlock. Blacks were more likely than whites to bear children outside marriage, but the majority of black children born in the twenty years after the Second World War were born to married couples. The rate of family disruption reached a historic low point during those years.

A new standard of family security and stability was established in postwar America. For the first time in history the vast majority of the nation's children could expect to live with married biological parents throughout childhood. Children might still suffer other forms of adversity—poverty, racial discrimination, lack of educational opportunity—but only a few would be deprived of the nurture and protection of a mother and a father. No longer did children have to be haunted by the classic fears vividly dramatized in folklore and fable—that their parents would die, that they would have to live with a stepparent and stepsiblings, or that they would be abandoned. These were the years when the nation confidently boarded up orphanages and closed foundling hospitals, certain that such institutions would never again be needed. In movie theaters across the country parents and children could watch the drama of parental separation and death in the great Disney classics, secure in the knowledge that such nightmare visions as the death of Bambi's mother and the wrenching separation of Dumbo from his mother were only make-believe.

In the 1960s the rate of family disruption suddenly began to rise. After inching up over the course of a century, the divorce rate soared. Throughout the 1950s and early 1960s the divorce rate held steady at fewer than ten divorces a year per 1,000 married couples. Then, beginning in about 1965, the rate increased sharply, peaking at twenty-three divorces per 1,000 marriages by 1979. (In 1974 divorce passed death as the leading cause of family breakup.) The rate has leveled off at about twenty-one divorces per 1,000 marriages—the figure for 1991. The out-of-wedlock birth rate also jumped. It went from five percent in 1960 to 27 percent in 1990. In 1990 close to 57 percent of births among black mothers were nonmarital, and about 17 percent among white mothers. Altogether, about one out of every four women who had a child in 1990 was not married. With rates of divorce and nonmarital birth so high, family disruption is at its peak. Never before have so many children experienced family breakup caused by events other than death. Each year a million children go through divorce or separation and almost as many more are born out of wedlock.

18   Half of all marriages now end in divorce. Following divorce, many people enter new relationships. Some begin living together. Nearly half of all cohabiting couples have children in the household. Fifteen percent have new children together. Many cohabiting couples eventually get married. However, both cohabiting and remarried couples are more likely to break up than couples in first marriages. Even social scientists find it hard to keep pace with the complexity and velocity of such patterns. In the revised edition (1992) of his book *Marriage, Divorce, Remarriage*, the sociologist Andrew Cherlin ruefully comments: "If there were a truth-in-labeling law for books, the title of this edition should be something long and unwieldy like *Cohabitation, Marriage, Divorce, More Cohabitation, and Probably Remarriage.*"

19   Under such conditions growing up can be a turbulent experience. In many single-parent families children must come to terms with the parent's love life and romantic partners. Some children live with cohabiting couples, either their own unmarried parents or a biological parent and a live-in partner. Some children born to cohabiting parents see their parents break up. Others see their parents marry, but 56 percent of them (as compared with 31 percent of the children born to married parents) later see their parents' marriages fall apart. All told, about three quarters of children born to cohabiting couples will live in a single-parent home at least briefly. One of every four children growing up in the 1990s will eventually enter a stepfamily. According to one survey, nearly half of all children in stepparent families will see their parents divorce again by the time they reach their late teens. Since 80 percent of divorced fathers remarry, things get even more complicated when the romantic or marital history of the noncustodial parent, usually the father, is taken into account. Consequently, as it affects a significant number of children,

family disruption is best understood not as a single event but as a string of disruptive events: separation, divorce, life in a single-parent family, life with a parent and live-in lover, the remarriage of one or both parents, life in one stepparent family combined with visits to another stepparent family; the breakup of one or both stepparent families. And so on. This is one reason why public schools have a hard time knowing whom to call in an emergency.

Given its dramatic impact on children's lives, one might reasonably expect that this historic level of family disruption would be viewed with alarm, even regarded as a national crisis. Yet this has not been the case. In recent years some people have argued that these trends pose a serious threat to children and to the nation as a whole, but they are dismissed as declinists, pessimists, or nostalgists, unwilling or unable to accept the new facts of life. The dominant view is that the changes in family structure are, on balance, positive.

A Shift in the Social Metric

There are several reasons why this is so, but the fundamental reason is that at some point in the 1970s Americans changed their minds about the meaning of these disruptive behaviors. What had once been regarded as hostile to children's best interests was now considered essential to adults' happiness. In the 1950s most Americans believed that parents should stay in an unhappy marriage for the sake of the children. The assumption was that a divorce would damage the children, and the prospect of such damage gave divorce its meaning. By the mid-1970s a majority of Americans rejected that view. Popular advice literature reflected the shift. A book on divorce published in the mid-1940s tersely asserted: "Children are entitled to the affection and *association* of two parents, not one." Thirty years later another popular divorce book proclaimed just the opposite: "A two-parent home is not the only emotional structure within which a child can be happy and healthy.... The parents who take care of themselves will be best able to take care of their children." At about the same time, the long-standing taboo against out-of-wedlock childbirth also collapsed. By the mid-1970s three fourths of Americans said that it was not morally wrong for a woman to have a child outside marriage.

Once the social metric shifts from child well-being to adult well-being, it is hard to see divorce and nonmarital birth in

anything but a positive light. However distressing and difficult they may be, both of these behaviors can hold out the
promise of greater adult choice, freedom, and happiness. For
unhappy spouses, divorce offers a way to escape a troubled or
even abusive relationship and make a fresh start. For single
parents, remarriage is a second try at marital happiness as
well as a chance for relief from the stress, loneliness, and economic hardship of raising a child alone. For some unmarried
women, nonmarital birth is a way to beat the biological clock,
avoid marrying the wrong man, and experience the pleasures
of motherhood. Moreover, divorce and out-of-wedlock birth
involve a measure of agency and choice; they are man- and
woman-made events. To be sure, not everyone exercises choice
in divorce or nonmarital birth. Men leave wives for younger
women, teenage girls get pregnant accidentally—yet even
these unhappy events reflect the expansion of the boundaries
of freedom and choice.

23   This cultural shift helps explain what otherwise would be
inexplicable: the failure to see the rise in family disruption as
a severe and troubling national problem. It explains why
there is virtually no widespread public sentiment for restig-
matizing either of these classically disruptive behaviors and
no sense—no public consensus—that they can or should be
avoided in the future. . . .

Dinosaurs Divorce

24   It is true that many adults benefit from divorce or remarriage. According to one study, nearly 80 percent of divorced
women and 50 percent of divorced men say they are better off
out of the marriage. Half of divorced adults in the same study
report greater happiness. A competent self-help book called
Divorce and New Beginnings notes the advantages of single
parenthood: single parents can "develop their own interests,
fulfill their own needs, choose their own friends and engage
in social activities of their choice. Money, even if limited, can
be spent as they see fit." Apparently, some women appreciate
the opportunity to have children out of wedlock. "The real
world, however, does not always allow women who are dedicated to their careers to devote the time and energy it takes to
find—or be found by—the perfect husband and father wannabe," one woman said in a letter to *The Washington Post*. A
mother and chiropractor from Avon, Connecticut, explained
her unwed maternity to an interviewer this way: "It is selfish,
but this was something I needed to do for me."

There is very little in contemporary popular culture to con- 25 tradict this optimistic view. But in a few small places another perspective may be found. Several racks down from its divorce cards, Hallmark offers a line of cards for children—To Kids With Love. These cards come six to a pack. Each card in the pack has a slightly different message. According to the package, the "thinking of you" messages will let a special kid "know how much you care." Though Hallmark doesn't quite say so, it's clear these cards are aimed at divorced parents. "I'm sorry I'm not always there when you need me but I hope you know I'm always just a phone call away." Another card reads: "Even though your dad and I don't live together anymore, I know he's still a very special part of your life. And as much as I miss you when you're not with me, I'm still happy that you two can spend time together."

Hallmark's messages are grounded in a substantial body of 26 well-funded market research. Therefore it is worth reflecting on the divergence in sentiment between the divorce cards for adults and the divorce cards for kids. For grown-ups, divorce heralds new beginnings (A HOT NEW SINGLE). For children, divorce brings separation and loss ("I'm sorry I'm not always there when you need me").

An even more telling glimpse into the meaning of family 27 disruption can be found in the growing children's literature on family dissolution. Take, for example, the popular children's book *Dinosaurs Divorce: A Guide for Changing Families* (1986), by Laurene Krasny Brown and Marc Brown. This is a picture book, written for very young children. The book begins with a short glossary of "divorce words" and encourages children to "see if you can find them" in the story. The words include "family counselor," "separation agreement," "alimony," and "child custody." The book is illustrated with cartoonish drawings of green dinosaur parents who fight, drink too much, and break up. One panel shows the father dinosaur, suitcase in hand, getting into a yellow car.

The dinosaur children are offered simple, straightforward 28 advice on what to do about the divorce. *On custody decisions:* "When parents can't agree, lawyers and judges decide. Try to be honest if they ask you questions; it will help them make better decisions." *On selling the house:* "If you move, you may have to say good-bye to friends and familiar places. But soon your new home will feel like the place you really belong." *On the economic impact of divorce:* "Living with one parent almost always means there will be less money. Be prepared to give up some things." *On holidays:* "Divorce may mean twice as much celebrating at holiday times, but you may feel pulled apart." *On parents' new lovers:* "You may sometimes feel jealous and want your parent to yourself. Be polite to your parents' new friends, even if you don't like them at first." *On parents' remarriage:* "Not everyone loves his or her stepparents, but showing them respect is important."

29   These cards and books point to an uncomfortable and generally unacknowledged fact: what contributes to a parent's happiness may detract from a child's happiness. All too often the adult quest for freedom, independence, and choice in family relationships conflicts with a child's developmental needs for stability, constancy, harmony, and permanence in family life. In short, family disruption creates a deep division between parents' interests and the interests of children.

30   One of the worst consequences of these divided interests is a withdrawal of parental investment in children's well-being. As the Stanford economist Victor Fuchs has pointed out, the main source of social investment in children is private. The investment comes from the children's parents. But parents in disrupted families have less time, attention, and money to devote to their children. The single most important source of disinvestment has been the widespread withdrawal of financial support and involvement by fathers. Maternal investment, too, has declined, as women try to raise families on their own and work outside the home. Moreover, both mothers and fathers commonly respond to family breakup by investing more heavily in themselves and in their own personal and romantic lives.

31   Sometimes the tables are completely turned. Children are called upon to invest in the emotional well-being of their parents. Indeed, this seems to be the larger message of many of the children's books on divorce and remarriage. *Dinosaurs Divorce* asks children to be sympathetic, understanding, respectful, and polite to confused, unhappy parents. The sacrifice comes from the children: "Be prepared to give up some things." In the world of divorcing dinosaurs, the children rather than the grown-ups are the exemplars of patience, restraint, and good sense.

Three Seventies Assumptions

32   As it first took shape in the 1970s, the optimistic view of family change rested on three bold new assumptions. At that time, because the emergence of the changes in family life was so recent, there was little hard evidence to confirm or dispute

these assumptions. But this was an expansive moment in American life.

The first assumption was an economic one: that a woman   33
could now afford to be a mother without also being a wife. There were ample grounds for believing this. Women's workforce participation had been gradually increasing in the postwar period, and by the beginning of the 1970s women were a strong presence in the workplace. What's more, even though there was still a substantial wage gap between men and women, women had made considerable progress in a relatively short time toward better-paying jobs and greater employment opportunities. More women than ever before could aspire to serious careers as business executives, doctors, lawyers, airline pilots, and politicians. This circumstance, combined with the increased availability of child care, meant that women could take on the responsibilities of a breadwinner, perhaps even a sole breadwinner. This was particularly true for middle-class women. According to a highly regarded 1977 study by the Carnegie Council on Children, "The greater availability of jobs for women means that more middle-class children today survive their parents' divorce without a catastrophic plunge into poverty."

Feminists, who had long argued that the path to greater   34
equality for women lay in the world of work outside the home, endorsed this assumption. In fact, for many, economic independence was a stepping-stone toward freedom from both men and marriage. As women began to earn their own money, they were less dependent on men or marriage, and marriage diminished in importance. In Gloria Steinem's memorable words, "A woman without a man is like a fish without a bicycle."

This assumption also gained momentum as the meaning of   35
work changed for women. Increasingly, work had an expressive as well as an economic dimension: being a working mother not only gave you an income but also made you more interesting and fulfilled than a stay-at-home mother. Consequently, the optimistic economic scenario was driven by a cultural imperative. Women would achieve financial independence because, culturally as well as economically, it was the right thing to do.

The second assumption was that family disruption would   36
not cause lasting harm to children and could actually enrich their lives. *Creative Divorce: A New Opportunity for Personal Growth*, a popular book of the seventies, spoke confidently to this point: "Children can survive any family crisis without

permanent damage—and grow as human beings in the process. . . ." Moreover, single-parent and stepparent families created a more extensive kinship network than the nuclear family. This network would envelop children in a web of warm and supportive relationships. "Belonging to a stepfamily means there are more people in your life," a children's book published in 1982 notes. "More sisters and brothers, including the step ones. More people you think of as grandparents and aunts and uncles. More cousins. More neighbors and friends. . . . Getting to know and like so many people (and having them like you) is one of the best parts of what being in a stepfamily. . . is all about."

37   The third assumption was that the new diversity in family structure would make America a better place. Just as the nation has been strengthened by the diversity of its ethnic and racial groups, so it would be strengthened by diverse family forms. The emergence of these brave new families was but the latest chapter in the saga of American pluralism.

38   Another version of the diversity argument stated that the real problem was not family disruption itself but the stigma still attached to these emergent family forms. This lingering stigma placed children at psychological risk, making them feel ashamed or different; as the ranks of single-parent and stepparent families grew, children would feel normal and good about themselves.

39   These assumptions continue to be appealing, because they accord with strongly held American beliefs in social progress. Americans see progress in the expansion of individual opportunities for choice, freedom, and self-expression. Moreover, Americans identify progress with growing tolerance of diversity. Over the past half century, the pollster Daniel Yankelovich writes, the United States has steadily grown more openminded and accepting of groups that were previously perceived as alien, untrustworthy, or unsuitable for public leadership or social esteem. One such group is the burgeoning number of single-parent and stepparent families.

The Education of Sara McLanahan

40   In 1981 Sara McLanahan, now a sociologist at Princeton University's Woodrow Wilson School, read a three-part series by Ken Auletta in *The New Yorker*. Later published as a book titled *The Underclass*, the series presented a vivid portrait of the drug addicts, welfare mothers, and school dropouts who

took part in an education-and-training program in New York City. Many were the children of single mothers, and it was Auletta's clear implication that single-mother families were contributing to the growth of an underclass. McLanahan was taken aback by this notion. "It struck me as strange that he would be viewing single mothers at that level of pathology."

"I'd gone to graduate school in the days when the politically 41 correct argument was that single-parent families were just another alternative family form, and it was fine," McLanahan explains, as she recalls the state of social-scientific thinking in the 1970s. Several empirical studies that were then current supported an optimistic view of family change. (They used tiny samples, however, and did not track the well-being of children over time.)

One, *All Our Kin,* by Carol Stack, was required reading for 42 thousands of university students. It said that single mothers had strengths that had gone undetected and unappreciated by earlier researchers. The single-mother family, it suggested, is an economically resourceful and socially embedded institution. In the late 1970s McLanahan wrote a similar study that looked at a small sample of white single mothers and how they coped. "So I was very much of that tradition."

By the early 1980s, however, nearly two decades had 43 passed since the changes in family life had begun. During the intervening years a fuller body of empirical research had emerged: studies that used large samples, or followed families through time, or did both. Moreover, several of the studies offered a child's-eye view of family disruption. The National Survey on Children, conducted by the psychologist Nicholas Zill, had set out in 1976 to track a large sample of children aged seven to eleven. It also interviewed the children's parents and teachers. It surveyed its subjects again in 1981 and 1987. By the time of its third round of interviews the eleven-year-olds of 1976 were the twenty-two-year-olds of 1987. The California Children of Divorce Study, directed by Judith Wallerstein, a clinical psychologist, had also been going on for a decade. E. Mavis Hetherington, of the University of Virginia, was conducting a similar study of children from both intact and divorced families. For the first time it was possible to test the optimistic view against a large and longitudinal body of evidence.

It was to this body of evidence that Sara McLanahan 44 turned. When she did, she found little to support the optimistic view of single motherhood. On the contrary. When she published her findings with Irwin Garfinkel in a 1986 book,

Single Mothers and Their Children, her portrait of single motherhood proved to be as troubling in its own way as Auletta's.

45   One of the leading assumptions of the time was that single
motherhood was economically viable. Even if single mothers
did face economic trials, they wouldn't face them for long, it
was argued, because they wouldn't remain single for long:
single motherhood would be a brief phase of three to five
years, followed by marriage. Single mothers would be economically resilient: if they experienced setbacks, they would
recover quickly. It was also said that single mothers would be
supported by informal networks of family, friends, neighbors,
and other single mothers. As McLanahan shows in her study,
the evidence demolishes all these claims.

46   For the vast majority of single mothers, the economic spectrum turns out to be narrow, running between precarious and
desperate. Half the single mothers in the United States live
below the poverty line. (Currently, one out of ten married
couples with children is poor.) Many others live on the edge
of poverty. Even single mothers who are far from poor are
likely to experience persistent economic insecurity. Divorce
almost always brings a decline in the standard of living for
the mother and children.

47   Moreover, the poverty experienced by single mothers is no
more brief than it is mild. A significant number of all single
mothers never marry or remarry. Those who do, do so only after spending roughly six years, on average, as single parents.
For black mothers the duration is much longer. Only 33 percent of African-American mothers had remarried within ten
years of separation. Consequently, single motherhood is
hardly a fleeting event for the mother, and it is likely to occupy a third of the child's childhood. Even the notion that single mothers are knit together in economically supportive
networks is not borne out by the evidence. On the contrary,
single parenthood forces many women to be on the move, in
search of cheaper housing and better jobs. This need-driven
restless mobility makes it more difficult for them to sustain
supportive ties to family and friends, let alone other single
mothers.

48   Single-mother families are vulnerable not just to poverty
but to a particularly debilitating form of poverty: welfare dependency. The dependency takes two forms: First, single
mothers, particularly unwed mothers, stay on welfare longer
than other welfare recipients. Of those never-married mothers who receive welfare benefits, almost 40 percent remain on
the rolls for ten years or longer. Second, welfare dependency

tends to be passed on from one generation to the next. McLanahan says, "Evidence on intergenerational poverty indicates that, indeed, offspring from [single-mother] families are far more likely to be poor and to form mother-only families than are offspring who live with two parents most of their pre-adult life." Nor is the intergenerational impact of single motherhood limited to African-Americans, as many people seem to believe. Among white families, daughters of single parents are 53 percent more likely to marry as teenagers, 111 percent more likely to have children as teenagers, 164 percent more likely to have a premarital birth, and 92 percent more likely to dissolve their own marriages. All these intergenerational consequences of single motherhood increase the likelihood of chronic welfare dependency.

McLanahan cites three reasons why single-mother families   49
are so vulnerable economically. For one thing, their earnings are low. Second, unless the mothers are widowed, they don't receive public subsidies large enough to lift them out of poverty. And finally, they do not get much support from family members—especially the fathers of their children. In 1982 single white mothers received an average of $1,246 in alimony and child support, black mothers an average of $322. Such payments accounted for about 10 percent of the income of single white mothers and for about 3.5 percent of the income of single black mothers. These amounts were dramatically smaller than the income of the father in a two-parent family and also smaller than the income from a second earner in a two-parent family. Roughly 60 percent of single white mothers and 80 percent of single black mothers received no support at all.

Until the mid-1980s, when stricter standards were put in   50
place, child-support awards were only about half to two-thirds what the current guidelines require. Accordingly, there is often a big difference in the living standards of divorced fathers and of divorced mothers with children. After divorce the average annual income of mothers and children is $13,500 for whites and $9,000 for nonwhites, as compared with $25,000 for white nonresident fathers and $13,600 for nonwhite nonresident fathers. Moreover, since child-support awards account for a smaller portion of the income of a high-earning father, the drop in living standards can be especially sharp for mothers who were married to upper-level managers and professionals.

Unwed mothers are unlikely to be awarded any child sup-   51
port at all, partly because the paternity of their children may

not have been established. According to one recent study, only 20 percent of unmarried mothers receive child support.

52   Even if single mothers escape poverty, economic uncertainty remains a condition of life. Divorce brings a reduction in income and standard of living for the vast majority of single mothers. One study, for example, found that income for mothers and children declines on average about 30 percent, while fathers experience a 10 to 15 percent increase in income in the year following a separation. Things get even more difficult when fathers fail to meet their child-support obligations. As a result, many divorced mothers experience a wearing uncertainty about the family budget: whether the check will come in or not; whether new sneakers can be bought this month or not; whether the electric bill will be paid on time or not. Uncertainty about money triggers other kinds of uncertainty. Mothers and children often have to move to cheaper housing after a divorce. One study shows that about 38 percent of divorced mothers and their children move during the first year after a divorce. Even several years later the rate of moves for single mothers is about a third higher than the rate for two-parent families. It is also common for a mother to change her job or increase her working hours or both following a divorce. Even the composition of the household is likely to change, with other adults, such as boyfriends or babysitters, moving in and out.

53   All this uncertainty can be devastating to children. Anyone who knows children knows that they are deeply conservative creatures. They like things to stay the same. So pronounced is this tendency that certain children have been known to request the same peanut-butter-and-jelly sandwich for lunch for years on end. Children are particularly set in their ways when it comes to family, friends, neighborhoods, and schools. Yet when a family breaks up, all these things may change. The novelist Pat Conroy has observed that "each divorce is the death of a small civilization." No one feels this more acutely than children.

54   Sara McLanahan's investigation and others like it have helped to establish a broad consensus on the economic impact of family disruption on children. Most social scientists now agree that single motherhood is an important and growing cause of poverty, and that children suffer as a result. (They continue to argue, however, about the relationship between family structure and such economic factors as income inequality, the loss of jobs in the inner city, and the growth of

low-wage jobs.) By the mid-1980s, however, it was clear that the problem of family disruption was not confined to the urban underclass, nor was its sole impact economic. Divorce and out-of-wedlock childbirth were affecting middle- and upper-class children, and these more privileged children were suffering negative consequences as well. It appeared that the problems associated with family breakup were far deeper and far more widespread than anyone had previously imagined.

The Missing Father

Judith Wallerstein is one of the pioneers in research on the   55
long-term psychological impact of family disruption on children. The California Children of Divorce Study, which she directs, remains the most enduring study of the long-term effects of divorce on children and their parents. Moreover, it represents the best-known effort to look at the impact of divorce on middle-class children. The California children entered the study without pathological family histories. Before divorce they lived in stable, protected homes. And although some of the children did experience economic insecurity as the result of divorce, they were generally free from the most severe forms of poverty associated with family breakup. Thus the study and the resulting book (which Wallerstein wrote with Sandra Blakeslee), *Second Chances: Men, Women, and Children a Decade After Divorce* (1989), provide new insight into the consequences of divorce which are not associated with extreme forms of economic or emotional deprivation.

When, in 1971, Wallerstein and her colleagues set out to   56
conduct clinical interviews with 131 children from the San Francisco area, they thought they were embarking on a short-term study. Most experts believed that divorce was like a bad cold. There was a phase of acute discomfort, and then a short recovery phase. According to the conventional wisdom, kids would be back on their feet in no time at all. Yet when Wallerstein met these children for a second interview more than a year later, she was amazed to discover that there had been no miraculous recovery. In fact, the children seemed to be doing worse.

The news that children did not "get over" divorce was not   57
particularly welcome at the time. Wallerstein recalls, "We got angry letters from therapists, parents, and lawyers saying we were undoubtedly wrong. They said children are really much

better off being released from an unhappy marriage. Divorce, they said, is a liberating experience." One of the main results of the California study was to overturn this optimistic view. In Wallerstein's cautionary words, "Divorce is deceptive. Legally it is a single event, but psychologically it is a chain—sometimes a never-ending chain—of events, relocations, and radically shifting relationships strung through time, a process that forever changes the lives of the people involved."

58   Five years after divorce more than a third of the children experienced moderate or severe depression. At ten years a significant number of the now young men and women appeared to be troubled, drifting, and underachieving. At fifteen years many of the thirtyish adults were struggling to establish strong love relationships of their own. In short, far from recovering from their parents' divorce, a significant percentage of these grownups were still suffering from its effects. In fact, according to Wallerstein, the long-term effects of divorce emerge at a time when young adults are trying to make their own decisions about love, marriage, and family. Not all children in the study suffered negative consequences. But Wallerstein's research presents a sobering picture of divorce. "The child of divorce faces many additional psychological burdens in addition to the normative tasks of growing up," she says.

59   Divorce not only makes it more difficult for young adults to establish new relationships. It also weakens the oldest primary relationship: that between parent and child. According to Wallerstein, "Parent-child relationships are permanently altered by divorce in ways that our society has not anticipated." Not only do children experience a loss of parental attention at the onset of divorce, but they soon find that at every stage of their development their parents are not available in the same way they once were. "In a reasonably happy intact family," Wallerstein observes, "the child gravitates first to one parent and then to the other, using skills and attributes from each in climbing the developmental ladder." In a divorced family, children find it "harder to find the needed parent at needed times." This may help explain why very young children suffer the most as the result of family disruption. Their opportunities to engage in this kind of ongoing process are the most truncated and compromised.

60   The father-child bond is severely, often irreparably, damaged in disrupted families. In a situation without historical precedent, an astonishing and disheartening number of American fathers are failing to provide financial support to their children. Often, more than the father's support check is miss-

ing. Increasingly, children are bereft of any contact with their fathers. According to the National Survey of Children, in disrupted families only one child in six, on average, saw his or her father as often as once a week in the past year. Close to half did not see their father at all in the past year. As time goes on, contact becomes even more infrequent. Ten years after a marriage breaks up, more than two thirds of children report not having seen their father for a year. Not surprisingly, when asked to name the "adults you look up to and admire," only 20 percent of children in single-parent families named their father, as compared with 52 percent of children in two-parent families. A favorite complaint among Baby Boom Americans is that their fathers were emotionally remote guys who worked hard, came home at night to eat supper, and didn't have much to say to or do with the kids. But the current generation has a far worse father problem: many of their fathers are vanishing entirely.

61 Even for fathers who maintain regular contact, the pattern of father-child relationships changes. The sociologists Andrew Cherlin and Frank Furstenberg, who have studied broken families, write that the fathers behave more like other relatives than like parents. Rather than helping with homework or carrying out a project with their children, nonresidential fathers are likely to take the kids shopping, to the movies, or out to dinner. Instead of providing steady advice and guidance, divorced fathers become "treat" dads.

62 Apparently—and paradoxically—it is the visiting relationship itself, rather than the frequency of visits, that is the real source of the problem. According to Wallerstein, the few children in the California study who reported visiting with their fathers once or twice a week over a ten-year period still felt rejected. The need to schedule a special time to be with the child, the repeated leave-takings, and the lack of connection to the child's regular, daily schedule leaves many fathers adrift, frustrated, and confused. Wallerstein calls the visiting father a parent without portfolio.

63 The deterioration in father-child bonds is most severe among children who experience divorce at an early age, according to a recent study. Nearly three quarters of the respondents, now young men and women, report having poor relationships with their fathers. Close to half have received psychological help, nearly a third have dropped out of high school, and about a quarter report having experienced high levels of problem behavior or emotional distress by the time they became young adults.

Long-Term Effects

64   Since most children live with their mothers after divorce, one might expect that the mother-child bond would remain unaltered and might even be strengthened. Yet research shows that the mother-child bond is also weakened as the result of divorce. Only half of the children who were close to their mothers before a divorce remained equally close after the divorce. Boys, particularly, had difficulties with their mothers. Moreover, mother-child relationships deteriorated over time. Whereas teenagers in disrupted families were no more likely than teenagers in intact families to report poor relationships with their mothers, 30 percent of young adults from disrupted families have poor relationships with their mothers, as compared with 16 percent of young adults from intact families. Mother-daughter relationships often deteriorate as the daughter reaches young adulthood. The only group in society that derives any benefit from these weakened parent-child ties is the therapeutic community. Young adults from disrupted families are nearly twice as likely as those from intact families to receive psychological help.

65   Some social scientists have criticized Judith Wallerstein's research because her study is based on a small clinical sample and does not include a control group of children from intact families. However, other studies generally support and strengthen her findings. Nicholas Zill has found similar long-term effects on children of divorce, reporting that "effects of marital discord and family disruption are visible twelve to twenty-two years later in poor relationships with parents, high levels of problem behavior, and an increased likelihood of dropping out of high school and receiving psychological help." Moreover, Zill's research also found signs of distress in young women who seemed relatively well adjusted in middle childhood and adolescence. Girls in single-parent families are also at much greater risk for precocious sexuality, teenage marriage, teenage pregnancy, nonmarital birth, and divorce than are girls in two-parent families.

66   Zill's research shows that family disruption strongly affects school achievement as well. Children in disrupted families are nearly twice as likely as those in intact families to drop out of high school; among children who do drop out, those from disrupted families are less likely eventually to earn a diploma or a GED. Boys are at greater risk for dropping out than girls, and are also more likely to exhibit aggressive, acting-out behaviors. Other research confirms these findings. According to a study

by the National Association of Elementary School Principals, 33 percent of two-parent elementary school students are ranked as high achievers, as compared with 17 percent of single-parent students. The children in single-parent families are also more likely to be truant or late or to have disciplinary action taken against them. Even after controlling for race, income, and religion, scholars find significant differences in educational attainment between children who grow up in intact families and children who do not. In his 1992 study *America's Smallest School: The Family,* Paul Barton shows that the proportion of two-parent families varies widely from state to state and is related to variations in academic achievement. North Dakota, for example, scores highest on the math-proficiency test and second highest on the two-parent-family scale. The District of Columbia is second lowest on the math test and lowest in the nation on the two-parent-family scale.

Zill notes that "while coming from a disrupted family significantly increases a young adult's risks of experiencing social, emotional or academic difficulties, it does not foreordain such difficulties. The majority of young people from disrupted families have successfully completed high school, do *not* currently display high levels of emotional distress or problem behavior, and enjoy reasonable relationships with their mothers." Nevertheless, a majority of these young adults do show maladjustment in their relationships with their fathers.   67

These findings underscore the importance of both a mother and a father in fostering the emotional well-being of children. Obviously, not all children in two-parent families are free from emotional turmoil, but few are burdened with the troubles that accompany family breakup. Moreover, as the sociologist Amitai Etzioni explains in a new book, *The Spirit of Community,* two parents in an intact family make up what might be called a mutually supportive education coalition. When both parents are present, they can play different, even contradictory, roles. One parent may goad the child to achieve, while the other may encourage the child to take time out to daydream or toss a football around. One may emphasize taking intellectual risks, while the other may insist on following the teacher's guidelines. At the same time, the parents regularly exchange information about the child's school problems and achievements, and have a sense of the overall educational mission. However, Etzioni writes,   68

> The sequence of divorce followed by a succession of boy or girlfriends, a second marriage, and frequently another divorce

and another turnover of partners often means a repeatedly disrupted educational coalition. Each change in participants involves a change in the educational agenda for the child. Each new partner cannot be expected to pick up the previous one's educational post and program.... As a result, changes in parenting partners mean, at best, a deep disruption in a child's education, though of course several disruptions cut deeper into the effectiveness of the educational coalition than just one....

Poverty, Crime, Education

69   Family disruption would be a serious problem even if it affected only individual children and families. But its impact is far broader. Indeed, it is not an exaggeration to characterize it as a central cause of many of our most vexing social problems. Consider three problems that most Americans believe rank among the nation's pressing concerns: poverty, crime, and declining school performance.

70   More than half of the increase in child poverty in the 1980s is attributable to changes in family structure, according to David Eggebeen and Daniel Lichter, of Pennsylvania State University. In fact, if family structure in the United States had remained relatively constant since 1960, the rate of child poverty would be a third lower than it is today. This does not bode well for the future. With more than half of today's children likely to live in single-parent families, poverty and associated welfare costs threaten to become even heavier burdens on the nation.

71   Crime in American cities has increased dramatically and grown more violent over recent decades. Much of this can be attributed to the rise in disrupted families. Nationally, more than 70 percent of all juveniles in state reform institutions come from fatherless homes. A number of scholarly studies find that even after the groups of subjects are controlled for income, boys from single-mother homes are significantly more likely than others to commit crimes and to wind up in the juvenile justice, court, and penitentiary systems. One such study summarizes the relationship between crime and one-parent families in this way: "The relationship is so strong that controlling for family configuration erases the relationship between race and crime and between low income and crime. This conclusion shows up time and again in the literature." The nation's mayors, as well as police officers, social

workers, probation officers, and court officials, consistently
point to family breakup as the most important source of rising rates of crime.

Terrible as poverty and crime are, they tend to be concen-   72
trated in inner cities and isolated from the everyday experience
of many Americans. The same cannot be said of the problem
of declining school performance. Nowhere has the impact of
family breakup been more profound or widespread than in the
nation's public schools. There is a strong consensus that the
schools are failing in their historic mission to prepare every
American child to be a good worker and a good citizen. And
nearly everyone agrees that the schools must undergo dramatic reform in order to reach that goal. In pursuit of that
goal, moreover, we have suffered no shortage of bright ideas or
pilot projects or bold experiments in school reform. But there
is little evidence that measures such as curricular reform,
school-based management, and school choice will address, let
alone solve, the biggest problem schools face: the rising number of children who come from disrupted families.

The great educational tragedy of our time is that many   73
American children are failing in school not because they are
intellectually or physically impaired but because they are
emotionally incapacitated. In schools across the nation principals report a dramatic rise in the aggressive, acting-out behavior characteristic of children, especially boys, who are
living in single-parent families. The discipline problems in today's suburban schools—assaults on teachers, unprovoked
attacks on other students, screaming outbursts in class—outstrip the problems that were evident in the toughest city
schools a generation ago. Moreover, teachers find many children emotionally distracted, so upset and preoccupied by the
explosive drama of their own family lives that they are unable
to concentrate on such mundane matters as multiplication
tables.

In response, many schools have turned to therapeutic re-   74
mediation. A growing proportion of many school budgets is
devoted to counseling and other psychological services. The
curriculum is becoming more therapeutic: children are taking courses in self-esteem, conflict resolution, and aggression
management. Parental advisory groups are conscientiously
debating alternative approaches to traditional school discipline, ranging from teacher training in mediation to the introduction of metal detectors and security guards in the schools.
Schools are increasingly becoming emergency rooms of the
emotions, devoted not only to developing minds but also to

repairing hearts. As a result, the mission of the school, along with the culture of the classroom, is slowly changing. What we are seeing, largely as a result of the new burdens of family disruption, is the psychologization of American education.

75   Taken together, the research presents a powerful challenge to the prevailing view of family change as social progress. Not a single one of the assumptions underlying that view can be sustained against the empirical evidence. Single-parent families are not able to do well economically on a mother's income. In fact, most teeter on the economic brink, and many fall into poverty and welfare dependency. Growing up in a disrupted family does not enrich a child's life or expand the number of adults committed to the child's well-being. In fact, disrupted families threaten the psychological well-being of children and diminish the investment of adult time and money in them. Family diversity in the form of increasing numbers of single-parent and stepparent families does not strengthen the social fabric. It dramatically weakens and undermines society, placing new burdens on schools, courts, prisons, and the welfare system. These new families are not an improvement on the nuclear family, nor are they even just as good, whether you look at outcomes for children or outcomes for society as a whole. In short, far from representing social progress, family change represents a stunning example of social regress.

The Two-Parent Advantage

76   All this evidence gives rise to an obvious conclusion: growing up in an intact two-parent family is an important source of advantage for American children. Though far from perfect as a social institution, the intact family offers children greater security and better outcomes than its fast-growing alternatives: single-parent and stepparent families. Not only does the intact family protect the child from poverty and economic insecurity; it also provides greater noneconomic investments of parental time, attention, and emotional support over the entire life course. This does not mean that all two-parent families are better for children than all single-parent families. But in the face of the evidence it becomes increasingly difficult to sustain the proposition that all family structures produce equally good outcomes for children.

77   Curiously, many in the research community are hesitant to say that two-parent families generally promote better out-

comes for children than single-parent families. Some argue that we need finer measures of the extent of the family-structure effect. As one scholar has noted, it is possible, by disaggregating the data in certain ways, to make family structure "go away" as an independent variable. Other researchers point to studies that show that children suffer psychological effects as a result of family conflict preceding family breakup. Consequently, they reason, it is the conflict rather than the structure of the family that is responsible for many of the problems associated with family disruption. Others, including Judith Wallerstein, caution against treating children in divorced families and children in intact families as separate populations, because doing so tends to exaggerate the differences between the two groups. "We have to take this family by family," Wallerstein says.

Some of the caution among researchers can also be attributed to ideological pressures. Privately, social scientists worry that their research may serve ideological causes that they themselves do not support, or that their work may be misinterpreted as an attempt to "tell people what to do." Some are fearful that they will be attacked by feminist colleagues, or, more generally, that their comments will be regarded as an effort to turn back the clock to the 1950s—a goal that has almost no constituency in the academy. Even more fundamental, it has become risky for anyone—scholar, politician, religious leader—to make normative statements today. This reflects not only the persistent drive toward "value neutrality" in the professions but also a deep confusion about the purposes of public discourse. The dominant view appears to be that social criticism, like criticism of individuals, is psychologically damaging. The worst thing you can do is to make people feel guilty or bad about themselves. [78]

When one sets aside these constraints, however, the case against the two-parent family is remarkably weak. It is true that disaggregating data can make family structure less significant as a factor, just as disaggregating Hurricane Andrew into wind, rain, and tides can make it disappear as a meteorological phenomenon. Nonetheless, research opinion as well as common sense suggests that the effects of changes in family structure are great enough to cause concern. Nicholas Zill argues that many of the risk factors for children are doubled or more than doubled as the result of family disruption. "In epidemiological terms," he writes, "the doubling of a hazard is a substantial increase.... the increase in risk that dietary cholesterol poses for cardiovascular disease, for example, is [79] far less than double, yet millions of Americans have altered their diets because of the perceived hazard."

80   The argument that family conflict, rather than the breakup of parents, is the cause of children's psychological distress is persuasive on its face. Children who grow up in high-conflict families, whether the families stay together or eventually split up, are undoubtedly at great psychological risk. And surely no one would dispute that there must be societal measures available, including divorce, to remove children from families where they are in danger. Yet only a minority of divorces grow out of pathological situations; much more common are divorces in families unscarred by physical assault. Moreover, an equally compelling hypothesis is that family breakup generates its own conflict. Certainly, many families exhibit more conflictual and even violent behavior as a consequence of divorce than they did before divorce.

81   Finally, it is important to note that clinical insights are different from sociological findings. Clinicians work with individual families, who cannot and should not be defined by statistical aggregates. Appropriate to a clinical approach, moreover, is a focus on the internal dynamics of family functioning and on the immense variability in human behavior. Nevertheless, there is enough empirical evidence to justify sociological statements about the causes of declining child well-being and to demonstrate that despite the plasticity of human response, there are some useful rules of thumb to guide our thinking about and policies affecting the family.

82   For example, Sara McLanahan says, three structural constants are commonly associated with intact families, even intact families who would not win any "Family of the Year" awards. The first is economic. In intact families, children share in the income of two adults. Indeed, as a number of analysts have pointed out, the two-parent family is becoming more rather than less necessary, because more and more families need two incomes to sustain a middle-class standard of living.

83   McLanahan believes that most intact families also provide a stable authority structure. Family breakup commonly upsets the established boundaries of authority in a family. Children are often required to make decisions or accept responsibilities once considered the province of parents. Moreover, children, even very young children, are often expected to behave like mature adults, so that the grown-ups in the family can be free to deal with the emotional fallout of the failed relationship. In some instances family disruption

creates a complete vacuum in authority; everyone invents his or her own rules. With lines of authority disrupted or absent, children find it much more difficult to engage in the normal kinds of testing behavior, the trial and error, the failing and succeeding, that define the developmental pathway toward character and competence. McLanahan says, "Children need to be the ones to challenge the rules. The parents need to set the boundaries and let the kids push the boundaries. The children shouldn't have to walk the straight and narrow at all times."

Finally, McLanahan holds that children in intact families 84 benefit from stability in what she neutrally terms "household personnel." Family disruption frequently brings new adults into the family, including stepparents, live-in boyfriends or girlfriends, and casual sexual partners. Like stepfathers, boyfriends can present a real threat to children's, particularly to daughters', security and well-being. But physical or sexual abuse represents only the most extreme such threat. Even the very best of boyfriends can disrupt and undermine a child's sense of peace and security, McLanahan says. "It's not as though you're going from an unhappy marriage to peacefulness. There can be a constant changing until the mother finds a suitable partner."

McLanahan's argument helps explain why children of wid- 85 ows tend to do better than children of divorced or unmarried mothers. Widows differ from other single mothers in all three respects. They are economically more secure, because they receive more public assistance through Survivors Insurance, and possibly private insurance or other kinds of support from family members. Thus widows are less likely to leave the neighborhood in search of a new or better job and a cheaper house or apartment. Moreover, the death of a father is not likely to disrupt the authority structure radically. When a father dies, he is no longer physically present, but his death does not dethrone him as an authority figure in the child's life. On the contrary, his authority may be magnified through death. The mother can draw on the powerful memory of the departed father as a way of intensifying her parental authority: "Your father would have wanted it this way." Finally, since widows tend to be older than divorced mothers, their love life may be less distracting.

Regarding the two-parent family, the sociologist David 86 Popenoe, who has devoted much of his career to the study of families, both in the United States and in Scandinavia, makes this straightforward assertion:

Social science research is almost never conclusive. There are always methodological difficulties and stones left unturned. Yet in three decades of work as a social scientist, I know of few other bodies of data in which the weight of evidence is so decisively on one side of the issue: on the whole, for children, two-parent families are preferable to single-parent and step-families.

The Regime Effect

87   The rise in family disruption is not unique to American society. It is evident in virtually all advanced nations, including Japan, where it is also shaped by the growing participation of women in the work force. Yet the United States has made divorce easier and quicker than in any other Western nation with the sole exception of Sweden—and the trend toward solo motherhood has also been more pronounced in America. (Sweden has an equally high rate of out-of-wedlock birth, but the majority of such births are to cohabiting couples, a long-established pattern in Swedish society.) More to the point, nowhere has family breakup been greeted by a more triumphant rhetoric of renewal than in America.

88   What is striking about this rhetoric is how deeply it reflects classic themes in American public life. It draws its language and imagery from the nation's founding myth. It depicts family breakup as a drama of revolution and rebirth. The nuclear family represents the corrupt past, an institution guilty of the abuse of power and the suppression of individual freedom. Breaking up the family is like breaking away from Old World tyranny. Liberated from the bonds of the family, the individual can achieve independence and experience a new beginning, a fresh start, a new birth of freedom. In short, family breakup recapitulates the American experience.

89   This rhetoric is an example of what the University of Maryland political philosopher William Galston has called the "regime effect." The founding of the United States set in motion a new political order based to an unprecedented degree on individual rights, personal choice, and egalitarian relationships. Since then these values have spread beyond their original domain of political relationships to define social relationships as well. During the past twenty-five years these values have had a particularly profound impact on the family.

90   Increasingly, political principles of individual rights and choice shape our understanding of family commitment and

solidarity. Family relationships are viewed not as permanent or binding but as voluntary and easily terminable. Moreover, under the sway of the regime effect the family loses its central importance as an institution in the civil society, accomplishing certain social goals such as raising children and caring for its members, and becomes a means to achieving greater individual happiness—a lifestyle choice. Thus, Galston says, what is happening to the American family reflects the "unfolding logic of authoritative, deeply American moral-political principles."

One benefit of the regime effect is to create greater equality 91 in adult family relationships. Husbands and wives, mothers and fathers, enjoy relationships far more egalitarian than past relationships were, and most Americans prefer it that way. But the political principles of the regime effect can threaten another kind of family relationship—that between parent and child. Owing to their biological and developmental immaturity, children are needy dependents. They are not able to express their choices according to limited, easily terminable, voluntary agreements. They are not able to act as negotiators in family decisions, even those that most affect their own interests. As one writer has put it, "a newborn does not make a good 'partner.'" Correspondingly, the parental role is antithetical to the spirit of the regime. Parental investment in children involves a diminished investment in self, a willing deference to the needs and claims of the dependent child. Perhaps more than any other family relationship, the parent-child relationship—shaped as it is by patterns of dependency and deference—can be undermined and weakened by the principles of the regime.

More than a century and a half ago Alexis de Tocqueville 92 made the striking observation that an individualistic society depends on a communitarian institution like the family for its continued existence. The family cannot be constituted like the liberal state, nor can it be governed entirely by that state's principles. Yet the family serves as the seedbed for the virtues required by a liberal state. The family is responsible for teaching lessons of independence, self-restraint, responsibility, and right conduct, which are essential to a free, democratic society. If the family fails in these tasks, then the entire experiment in democratic self-rule is jeopardized.

To take one example: independence is basic to successful 93 functioning in American life. We assume that most people in America will be able to work, care for themselves and their families, think for themselves, and inculcate the same traits of independence and initiative in their children. We depend on families to teach people to do these things. The erosion of the two-parent family undermines the capacity of families to impart this knowledge; children of long-term welfare-dependent single parents are far more likely than others to be dependent themselves. Similarly, the children in disrupted families have a harder time forging bonds of trust with others and giving and getting help across the generations. This, too, may lead to greater dependency on the resources of the state.

94   Over the past two and a half decades Americans have been conducting what is tantamount to a vast natural experiment in family life. Many would argue that this experiment was necessary, worthwhile, and long overdue. The results of the experiment are coming in, and they are clear. Adults have benefited from the changes in family life in important ways, but the same cannot be said for children. Indeed, this is the first generation in the nation's history to do worse psychologically, socially, and economically than its parents. Most poignantly, in survey after survey the children of broken families confess deep longings for an intact family.

95   Nonetheless, as Galston is quick to point out, the regime effect is not an irresistible undertow that will carry away the family. It is more like a swift current, against which it is possible to swim. People learn; societies can change, particularly when it becomes apparent that certain behaviors damage the social ecology, threaten the public order, and impose new burdens on core institutions. Whether Americans will act to overcome the legacy of family disruption is a crucial but as yet unanswered question.

Ellen Willis
Why I'm Not "Pro-Family"

Ellen Willis, author of No More Nice Girls: Countercultural
Essays *(1992), teaches journalism at NYU. The article published here originally appeared in* Glamour *(October 1994), a
national magazine devoted to fashions, cultural matters,
careers, nutrition, and civic issues interesting to women.
(Another essay by Willis appears in the section of* Conversations *on affirmative action, page 395.)*

In 1992, "Family Values" bombed in Houston. Right-wing- 1
ers at the Republican convention, sneering at career women
and single mothers, turned voters off. Now the Democrats are
in power—yet ironically, the family issue has reemerged,
more strongly than ever. Last year New York's influential
Democratic senator, Daniel Patrick Moynihan, suggested that
in relaxing the stigma against unmarried childbearing, we
had laid the groundwork for the burgeoning crime rate. Then
The Atlantic published a cover story provocatively titled: "Dan
Quayle Was Right." Its author, social historian Barbara Dafoe
Whitehead, invoked recent research to argue that high rates
of divorce and single parenthood hurt children and underlie
"many of our most vexing social problems."

The article hit a nerve. It provoked an outpouring of mail, 2
was condensed for *Reader's Digest* and won an award from the
National Women's Political Caucus. Commentators both conservative and liberal praised it in newspapers across the country. Together, Moynihan's and Whitehead's salvos launched a
national obsession with "the decline of the family." President
Clinton joined the bandwagon: "For 30 years," he declared in
his State of the Union message, "family life in America has
been breaking down."

The new advocates of the family seem more sympathetic to 3
women than their right-wing precursors. They know women
are in the workforce to stay; they are careful to talk about
the time pressures faced by "parents"—not "mothers"—with
jobs, and they put an unaccustomed emphasis on men's family obligations, such as contributing their fair share of child
support. Some advocate liberal reforms ranging from anti-
poverty programs to federally funded child care to abortion
rights, arguing that such measures are pro-family because

they help existing families. (A recent Planned Parenthood fund-raising letter proclaims, "Pro-choice is pro-family.")

4   I'm all for reforms that make it easier to give children the care they need, and I'm certainly in favor of men's equal participation in childrearing. My quarrel is with the underlying terms of the discussion, especially the assumption that anyone who cares about children must be "pro-family." I grew up in the fifties, in a family with two committed parents—the kind of home the pro-familists idealize. I had security; I had love. Yet like many of my peers, especially women, I saw conventional family life as far from ideal and had no desire to replicate it. It wasn't only that I didn't want to be a housewife like my mother; I felt that family life promoted self-abnegation and social conformity while stifling eroticism and spontaneity. I thought the nuclear family structure was isolating, and that within it, combining childrearing with other work would be exhausting, even if both parents shared the load—impressions I can now confirm from experience.

5   To me the alternative that made the most sense was not single parenthood—we needed *more* parents, not fewer, to share the daily responsibilities of childrearing and homemaking. In the seventies, a number of people I knew were bringing up children in communal households, and I imagined someday doing the same. But by the time my companion and I had a child ten years ago, those experiments and the counterculture that supported them were long gone.

6   From my perspective, the new champions of the family are much like the old. They never consider whether the current instability of families might signal that an age-old institution is failing to meet modern needs and ought to be reexamined. The idea that there could be other possible structures for domestic life and childrearing has been excluded from the conversation—so much so that cranks like me who persist in broaching the subject are used to getting the sort of tactful and embarrassed reaction accorded, say, people who claim to have been kidnapped by aliens. And the assumption that marriage is the self-evident solution to single parents' problems leads to impatience and hostility toward anyone who can't or won't get with the nuclear-family program.

7   Consider the hottest topic on the pro-family agenda: the prevalence of unwed motherhood in poor black communities. For Moynihan and other welfare reformers, the central cause of inner-city poverty and crime is not urban economic collapse, unemployment or racism, but fatherless households. Which means the solution is to bring back the stigma of "ille-

gitimacy" and restrict or eliminate welfare for single mothers. Clinton has proposed requiring welfare recipients to leave the rolls after two years and look for work, with temporary government jobs as a backup (where the permanent jobs are supposed to come from, in an economy where massive layoffs and corporate shrinkage are the order of the day, is not explained).

As the reformers profess their concern for poor children (while proposing to make them even poorer), the work ethic (as jobs for the unskilled get even scarcer) and the overburdened taxpayer, it's easy to miss their underlying message— that women have gotten out of hand. They may pay lip service to the idea that men too should be held responsible for the babies they father. But in practice there is no way to force poor, unemployed men to support their children or to stigmatize men as well as women for having babies out of wedlock. This is, after all, still a culture that regards pregnancy as the woman's problem and childrearing as the woman's job. And so, predictably, women are the chief targets of the reformers' punitive policies and rhetoric. It's women who will lose benefits; women who stand accused of deliberately having babies as a meal ticket; women who are (as usual) charged with the social failures of their sons. Given the paucity of decently paying jobs available to poor women or the men they're likely to be involved with, demanding that they not have children unless they have jobs or husbands to support them is tantamount to demanding that they not have children at all. (Note the logic: Motherhood is honorable work if supported by a man but parasitic self-indulgence if supported by the public.) Put that demand together with laws restricting abortion for poor women and teenagers, and the clear suggestion is that they shouldn't have sex either.

While this brand of misogyny is specifically aimed at poor black women, it would be a mistake to think the rest of us are off the hook. For one thing (as Whitehead and other pro-familists are quick to remind us), it's all too easy in this age of high divorce and unemployment rates for a woman who imagined herself securely middle-class to unexpectedly become an impoverished single mother. Anyway, there is a thin line between fear and loathing of welfare mothers and moral distaste for unmarried mothers per se. Secretary of Health and Human Services Donna Shalala, a feminist and one of the more liberal members of the Clinton cabinet, has said, "I don't like to put this in moral terms, but I do believe that having children out of wedlock is just wrong." The language the welfare reformers use—the vocabulary of *stigma* and

8

9

illegitimacy—unnervingly recalls the repressive moral climate of my own teenage years.

10   I can't listen to harangues about illegitimacy without getting posttraumatic flashbacks. Let's be clear about what the old stigma meant: a vicious double standard of sexual morality for men and women; the hobbling of female sexuality with shame, guilt and inhibition; panic over dislodged diaphragms and late periods; couples trapped into marriages one or both never wanted; pregnant girls barred from school and hidden in homes for unwed mothers; enormous pressure on women to get married early and not be too picky about it.

11   Is it silly to worry that in the post–*Roe* v. *Wade*, post-Pill nineties some version of fifties morality could reassert itself? I don't think so. Activists with a moral cause can be very persuasive. Who would have imagined a few years ago that there would be a public debate about restricting cigarettes as an addictive drug? Abortion may still be legal, but its opponents have done a good job of bringing back its stigma (ironically, this is one reason a lot of pregnant teenagers decide to give birth).

12   Many pro-familists, above all those who call themselves communitarians, are openly nostalgic for a sterner moral order. They argue that we have become a society too focused on rights instead of duties, on personal freedom and happiness instead of sacrifice for the common good. If the welfare reformers appeal to people's self-righteousness, the communitarians tap an equally potent emotion—guilt. In our concern for our own fulfillment, they argue, we are doing irreparable harm to our children.

13   Whitehead's *Atlantic* article cites psychologist Judith Wallerstein and other researchers to support her contention that while adults have benefited from the freedom to divorce and procreate outside marriage, children have suffered. Children in single-parent families, Whitehead warns, are not only at great risk of being poor but are more likely to have emotional and behavioral problems, drop out of school, abuse drugs. She calls on Americans to recognize that our experiment with greater freedom has failed and to "act to overcome the legacy of family disruption."

14   I don't doubt that the fragility of today's family life is hard on kids. It doesn't take a social scientist to figure out that a lone parent is more vulnerable than two to a host of pressures, or that children whose familial world has just collapsed need support that their parents, depleted by the struggle to

get their own lives in order, may not be able to give. But Whitehead's response, and that of communitarians generally, amounts to lecturing parents to pull up their socks, stop being selfish, and do their duty. This moralistic approach does not further a discussion of what to do when adults' need for satisfying relationships conflicts with children's need for stability. It merely stops the conversation.

Women, of course, are particularly susceptible to guilt 15 mongering: If children are being neglected, if marriages are failing, whose fault can it be but ours? And come on now, who is that "parent" whose career is really interfering with family life? (Hint: It's the one who gets paid less.) While the children Judith Wallerstein interviewed were clearly miserable about their parents' breakups, she made it eq ally clear that the parents weren't self-indulgent monsters, only people who could no longer stand the emotional deadness of their lives. Are we prepared to say that it's too bad, but their lives simply don't matter?

This is the message I get from David Blankenhorn, coeditor 16 of a pro-family anthology and newsletter, who exhorts us to "analyze the family *primarily* through the eyes of children" (my emphasis). I think this idea is profoundly wrongheaded. Certainly we need to take children seriously, which means empathizing with their relatively powerless perspective and never unthinkingly shifting our burdens to their weaker backs. On the other hand, children are more narcissistic than most adults ever dream of being—if my daughter had her way, I'd never leave the house. They too have to learn that other people's needs and feelings must be taken into account.

Besides, children are the next generation's adults. There's 17 something tragic about the idea that parents should sacrifice their own happiness for the sake of children who will grow up to sacrifice in turn (in my generation, that prospect inspired pop lyrics like, "Hope I die before I get old"). Instead of preaching sacrifice, we should be asking what it is about our social structure that puts adults and children at such terrible odds, and how we might change this. Faced with a shortage of food, would we decide parents have to starve so their kids can eat—or try to figure out how to increase food production?

Intelligent social policy on family issues has to start with a 18 deeper understanding of why marriage and the two-parent family are in trouble: not because people are more selfish than they used to be but because of basic—and basically desirable—changes in our culture. For most of history, marriage has not been primarily a moral or an emotional commitment but an economic and social contract. Men supported women and children and had unquestioned authority as head of the household. Women took care of home, children, and men's personal and sexual needs. Now that undemocratic contract, on which an entire social order rested, is all but dead. Jobs and government benefits, along with liberalized sexual mores, allow women and their children to survive (if often meagerly) outside marriage; as a result, women expect more of marriage and are less willing to put up with unsatisfying or unequal relationships. For men, on the other hand, traditional incentives to marry and stay married have eroded.

19   What's left when the old contract is gone is the desire for love, sexual passion, intimate companionship. But those desires are notoriously inadequate as a basis for domestic stability. Human emotions are unpredictable. People change. And in the absence of the social compulsion exerted by that contract, moral platitudes about sacrifice count for little. Nor is it possible to bring back the compulsion without restoring inequality as well. Restrict divorce? Men who want out will still abandon their families as they did in the past; it's women with young children and less earning power who are likely to be trapped. Punish single parenthood? Women will bear the brunt.

20   The dogmatic insistence that only the two-parent family can properly provide for children is a self-fulfilling prophecy. As even some pro-familists recognize, the larger society must begin to play an active part in meeting the economic and social needs the family once fulfilled. This means, first of all, making a collective commitment to the adequate support of every child. Beyond that, it means opening our minds to the possibility of new forms of community, in which children have close ties with a *number* of adults and therefore a stable home base that does not totally depend either on one vulnerable parent or on one couple's emotional and sexual bond.

21   Of course, no social structure can guarantee permanence: In earlier eras, families were regularly broken up by death, war and abandonment. Yet a group that forms for the specific purpose of cooperative child-rearing might actually inspire more long-term loyalty than marriage, which is supposed to provide emotional and sexual fulfillment but often does not. The practical support and help parents would gain from such an arrangement—together with the greater freedom to pursue their own personal lives—would be a strong incentive for staying in it, and the inevitable conflicts and incompatibilities

among the group members would be easier to tolerate than the intense deprivation of an unhappy marriage.

It's time, in other words, to think about what has so long   22 been unthinkable, to replace reflexive dismissiveness with questions. What, for instance, can we learn from the kibbutz—how might some of its principles be adapted to Americans' very different circumstances? What worked and didn't work about the communal experiments of the sixties and seventies? What about more recent projects, like groups of old people moving in together to avoid going to nursing homes? Or the "co-housing" movement of people who are buying land in the suburbs or city apartment buildings and dividing the space between private dwellings and communal facilities such as dining rooms and child-care centers?

I'm not suggesting that there's anything like an immediate   23 practical solution to our present family crisis. What we can do, though, is stop insisting on false solutions that scapegoat women and oversimplify the issues. Perhaps then a real discussion—worthy of Americans' inventiveness and enduring attraction to frontiers—will have a chance to begin.

Iris Marion Young

Making Single Motherhood Normal

Iris Marion Young, a philosopher by trade and a leading feminist who now teaches at the University of Pittsburgh, has written Throwing Like a Girl and Other Essays in Feminist Philosophy and Social Theory *(1990) and* Justice and the Politics of Difference *(1990). She contributed the following essay in the winter of 1994 to* Dissent, *a very liberal bimonthly journal of public affairs. A few months later her essay was answered in* Dissent *by Jean Bethke Elshtain, a prominent political scientist from Vanderbilt who has a particular interest in family issues. Margaret O'Brien Steinfels, the editor of* Commonweal *magazine (a liberal publication on public affairs loosely associated with Catholicism—and another place where Elshtain also places some of her work), also responded in the same issue of* Dissent *to Young's essay, right after Elshtain's piece. Iris Young then responded to both Elshtain and Steinfels. Their entire exchange is reprinted here.*

1   When Dan Quayle denounced Murphy Brown for having a baby without a husband in May 1992, most liberals and leftists recognized it for the ploy it was: a Republican attempt to win an election by an irrational appeal to "tradition" and "order." To their credit, American voters did not take the bait. The Clinton campaign successfully turned the family values rhetoric against the GOP by pointing to George Bush's veto of the Family and Medical Leave Act and by linking family well-being to economic prosperity.

2   Nonetheless, family values rhetoric has survived the election. Particularly disturbing is the fact that the refrain has been joined by people who, by most measures, should be called liberals, but who can accept only the two-parent heterosexual family. Communitarians are leading the liberal chorus denouncing divorce and single motherhood. In *The Spirit of Community*, Amitai Etzioni calls for social measures to privilege two-parent families and encourage parents to take care of young children at home. Etzioni is joined by political theorist William Galston—currently White House adviser on domestic policy—in supporting policies that will make divorce more difficult. Jean Bethke Elshtain is another example of a social liberal—that is, someone who believes in state regulation of business, redistributive economic policies, religious toleration and broad principles of free speech—who argues that not all kinds of families should be considered equal from the point of view of social policy or moral education. William Julius Wilson, another academic who has been close to Democratic party policy makers, considers out-of-wedlock birth to be a symptom of social pathology and promotes marriage as one solution to problems of urban black poverty.

3   Although those using family values rhetoric rarely mention gays and lesbians, this celebration of stable marriage is hardly good news for gay and lesbian efforts to win legitimacy for their lives and relationships. But I am concerned here with the implications of family values rhetoric for another despised and discriminated-against group: single mothers. Celebrating marriage brings a renewed stigmatization of these women, and makes them scapegoats for social ills of which they are often the most serious victims. The only anti-

dote to this injustice is for public policy to regard single mothers as normal, and to give them the social supports they need to overcome disadvantage.

Most people have forgotten another explicit aim of Dan 4 Quayle's appeal to family values: to "explain" the disorders in Los Angeles in May 1992. Unmarried women with children lie at the source of the "lawless social anarchy" that sends youths into the streets with torches and guns. Their "welfare ethos" impedes individual efforts to move ahead in society.

Liberal family values rhetoric also finds the "breakdown" 5 of "the family" to be a primary cause of all our social ills. "It is not an exaggeration," says Barbara Dafoe Whitehead in the *Atlantic* (April 1993) "to characterize [family disruption] as a central cause of many of our most vexing social problems, including poverty, crime, and declining school performance." Etzioni lays our worst social problems at the door of self-indulgent divorced or never-married parents. "Gang warfare in the streets, massive drug abuse, a poorly committed workforce, and a strong sense of entitlement and a weak sense of responsibility are, to a large extent, the product of poor parenting." Similarly, Galston attributed fearsome social consequences to divorce and single parenthood. "The consequences of family failure affect society at large. We all pay for systems of welfare, criminal justice, and incarceration, as well as for physical and mental disability; we are all made poorer by the inability or unwillingness of young adults to become contributing members of society; we all suffer if our society is unsafe and divided."

Reductionism in the physical sciences has faced such dev- 6 astating criticism that few serious physicists would endorse a theory that traced a one-way causal relationship between the behavior of a particular sort of atom and, say, an earthquake. Real-world physical phenomena are understood to have many mutually conditioning forces. Yet here we have otherwise subtle and intelligent people putting forward the most absurd social reductionism. In this simplistic model of society, the family is the most basic unit, the first cause that is itself uncaused. Through that magical process called socialization, families cause the attitudes, dispositions, and capacities of individual children who in turn as adults cause political and economic institutions to work or not work.

The great and dangerous fallacy in this imagery, of course, 7 is its implicit assumption that non-familial social processes do not cause family conditions. How do single-mother families

"cause" poverty, for example? Any sensible look at some of
these families shows us that poverty is a cause of their difficulties and failures. Doesn't it make sense to trace some of the
conflicts that motivate divorce to the structure of work or to
the lack of work? And what about all the causal influences on
families and children over which parents have very little
control—peer groups, dilapidated and understaffed schools,
consumer culture, television and movie imagery, lack of investment in neighborhoods, cutbacks in public services? Families unprotected by wide networks of supportive institutions
and economic resources are bound to suffer. Ignoring the
myriad social conditions that affect families only enables the
government and the public to escape responsibility for investing in the ghettos, building new houses and schools, and creating the millions of decent jobs that we need to restore
millions of people to dignity.

8   Family-values reductionism scapegoats parents, and especially single parents, and proposes a low-cost answer to
crime, poverty, and unemployment: get married and stay
married.

9   Whitehead, Galston, Etzioni, and others claim that there is
enough impressive evidence that divorce harms children emotionally to justify policies that discourage parents from divorcing. A closer look at the data, however, yields a much more
ambiguous picture. One meta-analysis of ninety-two studies of
the effects of divorce on American children, for example, finds
statistically insignificant differences between children of divorced parents and children from intact families in various
measures of well-being. Many studies of children of divorce
fail to compare them to children from "intact" families, or fail
to rule out predivorce conditions as causes. A ten-year longitudinal study released in Australia last June found that conflict between parents—whether divorced or not—is a frequent
cause of emotional distress in children. This stress is mitigated, however, if the child has a close supportive relationship with at least one of the parents. Results also suggest that
Australia's stronger welfare state and less adversarial divorce
process may partly account for differences with U.S. findings.

10   Thus the evidence that divorce produces lasting damage to
children is ambiguous at best, and I do not see how the ambiguities can be definitively resolved one way or the other. Complex and multiple social causation makes it naive to think we
can conclusively test for a clear causal relationship between
divorce and children's well-being. Without such certainty,
however, it is wrong to suggest that the liberty of adults in

their personal lives should be restricted. Galston and Etzioni endorse proposals that would impose a waiting period between the time a couple applied for divorce and the beginning of divorce proceedings. Divorce today already often drags on in prolonged acrimony. Children would likely benefit more from making it easier and less adversarial.

Although many Americans agree with me about divorce,   11
they also agree with Quayle, Wilson, Galston, and others that single motherhood is undesirable for children, a deviant social condition that policy ought to try to correct. Etzioni claims that children of single parents receive less parental supervision and support than do children in two-parent families. It is certainly plausible that parenting is easier and more effective if two or more adults discuss the children's needs and provide different kinds of interactions for them. It does not follow, however, that the second adult must be a live-in husband. Some studies have found that the addition of any adult to a single-mother household, whether a relative, lover, or friend, tends to offset the tendency of single parents to relinquish decision making too early. Stephanie Coontz suggests that fine-tuned research on single-parent families would probably find that they are better for children in some respects and worse in others. For example, although adults in single-parent families spend less time supervising homework, single parents are less likely to pressure their children into social conformity and more likely to praise good grades.

Much less controversial is the claim that children in single-   12
parent families are more often poor than those in two-parent families. One should be careful not to correlate poverty with single-parenthood, however; according to Coontz, a greater part of the increase in family poverty since 1979 has occurred in families with both spouses present, with only 38 percent concentrated in single-parent families. As many as 50 percent of single-parent families are likely to be poor, which is a shocking fact, but intact two-parent families are also increasingly likely to be poor, especially if the parents are in their twenties or younger.

It is harder to raise children alone than with at least one   13
other adult, and the stresses of doing so can take their toll on children. I do not question that children in families that depend primarily on a woman's wage-earning ability are often disadvantaged. I do question the conclusion that getting single mothers married is the answer to childhood disadvantage.

14   Conservatives have always stated a preference for two-parent families. Having liberals join this chorus is disturbing because it makes such preference much more mainstream, thus legitimizing discrimination against single mothers. Single mothers commonly experience credit and employment discrimination. Discrimination against single mothers in renting apartments was legal until 1988, and continues to be routine in most cities. In a study of housing fairness in Pittsburgh in which I participated, most people questioned said that rental housing discrimination is normal in the area. Single mothers and their children also face biases in schools.

15   There is no hope that discrimination of this sort will ever end unless public discourse and government policy recognize that female-headed families are a viable, normal, and permanent family form, rather than something broken and deviant that policy should eradicate. Around one-third of families in the United States are headed by a woman alone; this proportion is about the same world-wide. The single-mother family is not going to fade away. Many women raise children alone because their husbands left them or because lack of access to contraception and abortion forced them to bear unwanted children. But many women are single mothers by choice. Women increasingly initiate divorces, and many single mothers report being happier after divorce and uninterested in remarriage, even when they are poorer.

16   Women who give birth out of wedlock, moreover, often have chosen to do so. Discussion of the "problem" of "illegitimate" births commonly assumes the image of the irresponsible and uneducated teenager (of color) as the unwed mother. When citing statistics about rising rates of out-of-wedlock birth, journalists and scholars rarely break them down by the mother's age, occupation, and so on. Although the majority of these births continue to be to young mothers, a rising proportion are to mid-life women with steady jobs who choose to have children. Women persist in such choices despite the fact that they are stigmatized and sometimes punished for them.

17   In a world where it can be argued that there are already too many people, it may sometimes be wrong for people to have babies. The planned birth of a third child in a stable two-parent family may be morally questionable from this point of view. But principles of equality and reproductive freedom must hold that there is nothing *more* wrong with a woman in her thirties with a stable job and income having a baby than with a similar married couple.

If teen pregnancy is a social problem, this is not because 18
the mothers are unmarried, but because they are young. They
are inexperienced in the ways of the world and lack the skills
necessary to get a job to support their children; once they become parents, their opportunities to develop those skills usually decrease. But these remain problems even when the
women marry the young men with whom they have conceived children. Young inexperienced men today are just as ill
prepared for parenting and just as unlikely to find decent
jobs.

Although many young unmarried women who bear chil- 19
dren do so because they are effectively denied access to abortions, many of these mothers want their babies. Today the
prospects for meaningful work and a decent income appear
dim to many youth, and especially to poor youth. Having a
baby can give a young woman's life meaning, earn her respectful attention, make her feel grown up, and give her an
excuse to exit the "wild" teenager scene that has begun to
make her uncomfortable. Constructing an education and employment system that took girls as seriously as boys, that
trained girls and boys for meaningful and available work
would be a far more effective antidote to teen birth than rep-
rimanding, stigmatizing, and punishing these girls.

Just as we should examine the assumption that something 20
is wrong with a mid-life woman having a child without a husband, so we ought to ask a more radical question: just what *in
principle* is *more* wrong in a young woman's bearing a child
without a husband than in an older woman's doing so? When
making their reproductive decisions, everyone ought to ask
whether there are too many people in the world. Beyond that,
I submit that we should affirm an unmarried young woman's
right to bear a child as much as any other person's right.

There is reason to think that much of the world, including 21
the United States, has plural childbearing cultures. Recently I
heard a radio interview with an eighteen-year-old African
American woman in Washington, D.C. who had recently
given birth to her second child. She affirmed wanting both
children, and said that she planned to have no more. She lives
in a subsidized apartment and participates in a job training
program as a condition for receiving AFDC. She resisted the
interviewer's suggestion that there was something morally
wrong or at least unfortunate with her choices and her life.
She does not like being poor, and does not like having uncertain child care arrangements when she is away from her children. But she believes that in ten years, with hard work,

social support, and good luck, she will have a community college degree and a decent job doing something she likes, as does her mother, now thirty-four.

22   There is nothing in principle wrong with such a pattern of having children first and getting education and job training later. Indeed, millions of white professional women currently in their fifties followed a similar pattern. Most of them, of course, were supported by husbands, and not state subsidy, when they stayed home to take care of their young children. Our racism, sexism, and classism are only thinly concealed when we praise stay-at-home mothers who are married, white, and middle class, and propose a limit of two years on welfare to unmarried, mostly non-white, and poor women who do the same thing. From a moral point of view, is there an important difference between the two kinds of dependence? If there is any serious commitment to equality in the United States, it must include an equal respect for people's reproductive choices. In order for children to have equal opportunities, moreover, equal respect for parents, and especially mothers, requires state policies that give greater support to some than others.

23   If we assume that there is nothing morally wrong with single-mother families, but that they are often disadvantaged by lack of child care and by economic discrimination and social stigma, then what follows for public policy? Some of the answers to this question are obvious, some not so obvious, but in the current climate promoting a stingy and punitive welfare state, all bear discussion. I will close by sketching a few proposals.

24   1. *There is nothing in principle any more wrong with a teenage woman's choice to have a child than with anyone else's.* Still, there is something wrong with a society that gives her few alternatives to a mothering vocation and little opportunity for meaningful job training. If we want to reduce the number of teenage women who want to have babies, then education and employment policies have to take girls and women much more seriously.

25   2. *Whether poor mothers are single because they are divorced or because they never married, it is wrong for a society to allow mothers to raise children in poverty and then tell them that it's their fault when their children have deprived lives.* Only if the economy offered women decent-paying jobs, moreover, would forcing welfare women to get jobs lift them out of poverty. Of course, with good job opportunities most of them

would not need to be forced off welfare. But job training and employment programs for girls and women must be based on the assumption that a large proportion of them will support children alone. Needless to say, there is a need for massive increases in state support for child care if these women are to hold jobs. Public policy should, however, also acknowledge that taking care of children at home is work, and then support this work with unstigmatized subsidy where necessary to give children a decent life.

3. *The programs of schools, colleges, and vocational and*   26
professional training institutions ought to accommodate a plu-
rality of women's life plans, combining childbearing and child-
rearing with other activities. They should not assume that there is a single appropriate time to bear and rear children. No woman should be disadvantaged in her education and employment opportunities because she has children at age fifteen, twenty-five, thirty-five, or forty-five (for the most part, education and job structures are currently such that each of these ages is the "wrong time").

4. *Public policy should take positive steps to dispel the*   27
assumption that the two-parent heterosexual nuclear family is
normal and all other family forms deviant. For example, the state should assist single-parent support systems, such as the "mothers' houses" in some European countries that provide spaces for shared child minding and cooking while at the same time preserving family privacy.

5. *Some people might object that my call for recognizing sin-*   28
gle motherhood as normal lets men off the hook when it comes
to children. Too many men are running out on pregnant women and on the mothers of their children with whom they have lived. They are free to seek adventure, sleep around, or start new families, while single mothers languish in poverty with their children. This objection voices a very important concern, but there are ways to address it other than forcing men to get or stay married to the mothers of their children.

First, the state should force men who are not poor them-   29
selves to pay child support for children they have recognized as theirs. I see nothing wrong with attaching paychecks and bank accounts to promote this end. But the objection above requires more than child support. Relating to children is a good thing in itself. Citizens who love and are committed to some particular children are more apt than others to think of the world in the long term, and to see it from the perspective of the more vulnerable people. Assuming that around one-third of households will continue to be headed by women

alone, men should be encouraged to involve themselves in close relationships with children, not necessarily their biological offspring.

30   6. *More broadly, the American public must cease assuming that support and care for children are the responsibility of their parents alone, and that parents who require social support have somehow failed.* Most parents require social support, some more than others. According to Coontz, for a good part of American history this fact was assumed. I am not invoking a Platonic vision of communal childrearing; children need particular significant others. But non-parents ought to take substantial economic and social responsibility for the welfare of children.

31   After health care, Clinton's next big reform effort is likely to be aimed at welfare. Condemning single mothers will legitimate harsh welfare reforms that will make the lives of some of them harder. The left should press instead for the sorts of principles and policies that treat single mothers as equal citizens.

Jean Bethke Elshtain
Single Motherhood
A Response to Iris Young

1   What I found most surprising in Iris Young's analysis ("Making Single Motherhood Normal," Winter 1994) is the radical disconnection between her policy proposals and the constraints and possibilities of our current situation. She calls for "massive increases in state support for child care" when state budgets are strapped, cutbacks are being ordered across the board, and new initiatives in health care will gobble up whatever additional revenues are available. (Presumably she supports universal health care and favors moves in that direction.) She calls for "public policy" to dispel any notion of "normality" in family structure. But, surely, we have already conducted that experiment and it has failed. It has failed for the very people it was designed to help—single mothers and

their children. I will offer up evidence on this score—evidence Young systematically overlooks.

She calls for states to "force men" to "pay child support for   2
children they have recognized as theirs." She claims men shouldn't be let off the hook where their responsibilities are concerned. But her formulation continues to put the onus for child-rearing and child "recognition," if you will, on women. In fact, startlingly, her argument is a call for a return to a particularly rigid form of "separate spheres," something I thought feminists had a strong stake in criticizing and reforming. Once again we are in a world of "women and children only," where a woman can do it all by herself, thank you. A man could easily bypass Young's requirement by refusing to recognize a child as "his." Who is to compel this recognition if the institutional framework within which it has taken place historically—the two-parent family—has been entirely dismantled as a "norm" or "ideal" of any sort? There are no "fathers" or "daddies" in Young's universe with direct, daily responsibility for child care and family sustenance, something not reducible to a paycheck. Still, Young would "encourage" men to "involve themselves in close relationships with children, not necessarily their biological offspring." How? Why? What institutional forms will nurture and sustain such relationships? Are we to see forlorn bands of disconnected men roaming neighborhoods, knocking on doors, and asking if there is a baby inside they can "bond" with for a few hours? Young's rhetorical demolition of what she takes to be onerous tradition combined with her wholly abstract, vague pleas for connection and responsibility shows us again that politics of denunciation and sentimentalism that undermined much of 1960s radicalism. (I know: I was there.)

Let's enter the real world. For Young misses altogether   3
what is at stake in the travail of the present moment. She reverts to the claim that "poverty" is the cause of all other troubles. This is curious because Young thrashes reductionism before rapidly moving to her own reductionist formula, namely, that any "sensible look" at the plight of poor families reveals that "poverty" is the cause of, well, being poor. Here she reproduces the very "one-way" causal claims she attacked just a few sentences earlier. The problem, of course, is that matters are far more complex than this. The mountain of evidence now available from reputable scholars tells us that cultural changes—alterations in norms and values—are not mere epiphenomenal foam on the causal sea but are themselves vectors of economic trouble. We know that poverty is

associated with single parents. This means mothers, often very young mothers (those "babies having babies" Jesse Jackson talks about) in a father-absent situation. We also know, from the National Commission on Children, the Center for the Study of Social Policy, the U.S. Department of Health and Human Services, and dozens of other reliable sources that children growing up in single-parent households are at greater risk on every index of well-being (crime, violence, substance abuse, mental illness, dropping out of school, and so on).

4   But mark this: there is no compelling evidence that a decline in government spending accounts for the past several decades' burgeoning litany of risks to children. Economists Victor Fuchs and Diane Reklis have shown that the well-being of children worsened in a period when "purchases of goods and services for children by government rose very rapidly, as did real household income per child, and the poverty rate of children plummeted. Thus, we must seek explanations for the rising problems of that period in the cultural realm." The period to which Fuchs and Reklis refer is the 1960–1970 decade. If you continue to track direct government expenditures per child up to the present moment you find no compelling correlation between government support and child well-being per se. Indeed, we are spending more for children today in the public sphere than ever before. The sad truth is that our public investment in children is being outstripped by "private disinvestment," in other words, the breakup of the two-parent home. If you control for all other factors, *including* economic status, you learn that father absence is the single most important risk factor for children, whether one is talking about poor health or poverty or behavioral problems (the latter being a euphemistic way of gesturing toward drug addiction, being the victim or perpetrator of violence, adolescent out-of-wedlock birth, and so on). Do we change all of this by making a one-parent family suddenly "normal"? That won't stop children from suffering. That won't help a child find security and trust and safety. Of course, we should do our best for all children. But that means doing our best to create situations that do best for children, not continuing to try to patch things up when we *know*, because the evidence is in, that some familial arrangements are better for children than others.

5   The *Kids Count Data Book*, published by the liberal Center for the Study of Social Policy, one of the most widely accepted scholarly sources in this area, offers up annual "Profiles of Child Well-Being." The most recent profile included the fol-

lowing startling information. Researchers looked at two groups and compared them: couples who completed high school, married, and waited until age twenty to have their first child against couples who did none of the above—they neither married nor finished school, and in which the girl gave birth before age twenty. In the first group, the number of children who fell below the poverty line was 8 percent. In the second group, the number of children who fell below the poverty line was a startling 79 percent. What this suggests is that marriage, somewhat delayed child-bearing, and high school completion—cultural and educational factors—fuel economic outcomes. It is high time we set aside economic reductionism of the sort Young oddly endorses and looked to the dissolution of the fabric of families and communities, a tragedy entangled with the repudiation of those "norms" for male and female responsibility for children that Young finds oppressive because they "stigmatize" single mothers. The stigma attached to single motherhood has virtually disappeared, if we trust the survey data, but the problems associated with the children of single parents do not go away so readily.

If we are to see investment "in the ghettos," the building of   6 new houses and schools, the creation of "millions of decent jobs," no less, we need people capable of holding jobs; we need secure social institutions; we need children who are compelled by parents to stay in school; we need all the things Young blithely ignores. The most successful organizing for change over the past fifty years has come from poor and working-class communities who form broad-based coalitions to work for housing, jobs, schools, in the most devastated urban areas—from Brownsville to San Antonio. I have in mind, for example, the activities of the Industrial Areas Foundation. If Young wants to see revitalization of communities in action she should check out the work of the East Brooklyn Congregations (EBC) and their Nehemiah Homes project or Baltimoreans United in Leadership Development (BUILD), a group that has made significant strides in school reform in the inner city. There are dozens and dozens of such examples. The organizing base is families and churches—the remnants of intact institutions—for you cannot make lasting, meaningful change of any kind outside institutions.

Civic philosophy dies when academics, in the name of rad-   7 icalism, in the name, heaven help us, of that democratic socialism for which this journal has traditionally stood, endorse values that erode the only possible bases for creating and sustaining community institutions over time—calling for more individualism (hence Young's celebration of an individual woman's "choice" to have a baby whether she is thirteen years old or fifty, as if that choice and not any consideration of the child's well-being were the only value at stake); more vast government projects, hence more clientage; normlessness as a norm; and on and on. It is depressing to see these old nostrums refurbished as radical or reformist when they could scarcely be more conformist—to the naively anti-institutionalist, hyper-individualist tendencies of our time, with a heavy dollop of "separate spheres with a feminist face" thrown in for good measure.

Margaret O'Brien Steinfels
Rights and Responsibilities
A Response to Iris Young

1   Fully achieved, Iris Young's proposals would be a disaster for women and children, probably for men too, and certainly for liberal and left politics.

2   She is wrong on three points, at least: single mothers are *not* despised; liberals don't view single mothers as the sole source of our social ills; liberalism has *not* abandoned its heritage by rallying to the two-parent family.

3   If only *Time* magazine had made Marla Maples—an unwed mother—the woman of the year, we would fully realize that a mother's unwedded state is no bar to celebrity or social lionizing—and a kiss on the cheek from (former) Mayor David Dinkins. The press and television treat single motherhood as a variant of the American family. I suspect that teachers, principals, social workers, acquaintances, and neighbors don't ask and don't care. That changes when the individual choice of single motherhood becomes a collective responsibility. It is women who have children that they can't support or get fathers to support that exercise tax-paying Americans, at least some of whom are single-mother families themselves! Plain and simple, the problem is not single mothers but single mothers who depend on the rest of us to support them and their children.

The Reagan administration and accompanying pundits   4
convinced the American electorate that the welfare system
now functions as a dowry system for adolescent girls, who,
becoming pregnant, are launched into motherhood and
adulthood with food stamps, child support, housing allowances, and Medicaid long before they are ready to be good
mothers. And it doesn't end there, the critics go on: rather
than supporting people in need until they can get back on
their feet, the system is failing children and undermining
young men's sense of responsibility for their children. Conservatives think that welfare is hurting poor people. Among others, a lot of poor people agree with them.

This analysis has penetrated the thinking of Democrats   5
and other liberals. Some speak of job training, of community
service in return for welfare. Some speak of two-year limits;
others of withholding aid for infants born when a woman is
already on welfare; all stand behind that once unthinkable
policy of dunning delinquent dads for court-ordered child
support. Even Wisconsin, with its tradition of progressive
politics, is bailing out of the federal welfare system in order to
limit and control in its own expenditures.

Should these be counted traitors to the liberal cause?   6

Those old enough to remember will recall that liberals cre-   7
ated the welfare system to keep families together, to help tide
over those in temporary trouble, and to help widows maintain a household. Aid to Families with Dependent Children
(AFDC) and other welfare measures were never meant to support teenage moms or help their boyfriends elude the responsibilities of fatherhood; nor were they intended to make up
for missing child-support payments. The system has been
adapted to meet these needs on the assumption that women
with children often have no other recourse. Often they do not.
When, however, the system itself seems to encourage unwed
motherhood or male abandonment and to contribute to family breakdown, reasonable people ask their politicians why.
To their credit some liberals are reconsidering the merits of
the two-parent family. Were two-parent families to come back
into vogue, our social ills would not disappear. But there is
reason to expect that children would have saner, more secure,
and—boys especially—more disciplined upbringings. These
would be a good in themselves.

Iris Young wants us to assume that "there is nothing mor-   8
ally wrong with single-mother families." What does she
mean? Women of any age, educational attainment, income

level, or marital status should be able to bear and raise a child. I agree. At least I agree that no one else—the state, the father, the woman's relatives—has a right to force a woman to get an abortion if she is pregnant. Or force her to use contraception. Or, barring abusive or seriously neglectful behavior, take her child from her. In that sense the mother-child relationship is sacrosanct; the right to conceive and bear a child is basic.

9   But not every exercise of a "right" adds up to a moral good. Nations have a right to protect their sovereignty; not every act in pursuit of that right is moral. Individuals in our society have a right to free speech; not every sentence uttered in exercising that right constitutes a moral good. The analogy applies to childbearing decisions: it may be a right, but that does not make it a moral good. Single motherhood—though not wrong in and of itself—can undermine the well-being of others.

10   First, there is the child and his or her need for care, comfort, and stability—constant attention as an infant and consistent attention as a child and adolescent. Even with two (or more) adults, this is an arduous undertaking spanning more than two decades. Can single-mother families really meet this responsibility? Many do; many others do not.

11   Then, consider alternative child-care support systems. There is the woman's own family, which may be her surest recourse. But what if this, too, is a single-mother family? or siblings need attention? or husband and wife both work? A single mother's need may be great, but families have limits. Other child-caring facilities—day-care centers, schools, camps—are available, but they may be overwhelmed with the needs of materially and emotionally deprived children. Young believes more money and more personnel are the answer. But can a single mother (or father) act on the assumption that they are? And from where do these additional and abundant new resources come?

12   This brings us to the question of the common good and the implicit social contract on which it rests. Young refers to the "state" and the "welfare state" as if these were entities capable of delivering goods and services at will. The United States is a democracy that eventually comes to reflect—if only imperfectly—the views of its citizens. Underlying at least some of the critical views of welfare—which Young thinks stingy—is a sense of quid pro quo: Social responsibility ought to encourage individual responsibility, not undermine or replace it. Is that unreasonable? The reservoirs of social responsibility that Young wants to draw upon will be swiftly depleted in a society

whose citizens, women and men alike, do not habitually feel and exercise responsibility for themselves and their families.

Our social experiment in single motherhood over the last twenty-five years is failing great numbers of women and children while corroding the bonds that tie men to familial responsibilities. In the name of reform, we should not take from them the admittedly meager resources provided by the current system. But neither can opinion makers, academics, or intellectual elites, feminist and otherwise, go on arguing that this situation is normal, and will be made even "more normal" by increased welfare payments and better support systems.   13

The communitarians have a slogan that we might all take to heart: strong rights entail strong responsibilities—that goes for the right to bear and raise children.   14

Iris Marion Young

Response to Elshtain and Steinfels

Jean Elshtain and Margaret Steinfels and I agree at least on one thing: too many children are poor, badly educated, at risk of being un- or underemployed, becoming substance dependent, criminal, or dead. What we disagree on are the solutions to these problems. Indeed, for all their strong language, I find neither offering any action. Calls for "secure institutions," restoring the "fabric of families," and living up to "strong responsibilities" are empty exhortations unless we specify just who should take responsibility to do what. The form of the rhetoric, moreover, leaves the impression that it's "they" and not "we" who have shirked responsibilities. This vague rhetoric seems to function as an excuse not only for doing nothing, but for not even thinking about what to do.   1

Elshtain and Steinfels both claim that "we" have undertaken a "social experiment" in single motherhood that has "failed." What odd phrasing! Who are "we" who designed such a cruel "experiment"? But, of course, no one designed the patchwork of plural family living arrangements in the United States today. In some respects, it has always been with   2 us. There is no question, however, that the last two decades have seen more divorce and less marriage, though the rate of teenage pregnancy has not in fact increased.

3   What do Elshtain and Steinfels propose that we do about the lives of children? We should, in the words of Elshtain, "create situations that do best for children," that is, promote intact two-parent families. But how shall we do that? It is hard to believe that Elshtain and Steinfels would forbid divorce. Perhaps they favor making divorce more difficult, as some recommend, with a waiting period. This assumes that couples now rush into divorce without thinking, which is for the most part not so. Since divorce in the United States is already painful and costly, especially when there are children, making divorce more difficult is not likely to reduce appreciably the number of divorces.

4   And what shall we do about women who give birth without being married? Again, Elshtain and Steinfels would not force abortions, and I suspect that they would not force men to marry and live with the women they have impregnated. Would they recommend punishing women who give birth out of wedlock as a deterrent to others, or punishing fathers who do not marry them? This alternative is frighteningly close to the minds of some people in the current debate, but it doesn't sound like Elshtain or Steinfels. Perhaps the carrot is a better idea: cash awards and medals for couples who get and stay married.

5   The most that Elshtain's and Steinfels's calls for restoration of family values and responsibilities can mean practically is that public discussion promote the idea that intact two-parent families are better than other families; churches, schools, community groups, perhaps occasional television ad campaigns should send out this message. If such a society-wide educational campaign were implemented, it might indeed have some measurable impact on marriage and divorce rates, but I submit not very much. Thus I find Elshtain and Steinfels recommending virtually no social action to improve the lives of children.

6   Their insistence that although women have a "right" to parent alone, their family lives are less valuable, moreover, is an affront to the worth and dignity of women who have tried marriage and found it wanting, are out on their own with their children, and are not interested in a new husband. Is a liberal society really to condemn these women, and if it does can it claim it is respecting them as equal citizens?

With the communitarian refrain, "strong rights entail 7 strong responsibilities," Steinfels suggests that it's about time the parents of those children did something, instead of sitting around waiting for handouts from the state. Elshtain, too, suggests a kind of quid pro quo: if we are to see investment in dilapidated neighborhoods, building of new schools and houses, we need secure social institutions and children who are compelled by their parents to stay in school. Once parents get off their duffs and build these institutions and discipline their children, then maybe we can talk about social support.

Are Elshtain and Steinfels really suggesting that single 8 mothers (not all of whom are poor) or poor people (not all of whom are in families with one parent) are, as a group, more irresponsible than other people? When middle-class, married couples refuse to support the local school system through a tax increase, complain about the quality of the schools, and enroll their kids in private school, are they behaving responsibly? When bank executives refuse to make loans to home-owners and businesses in poor neighborhoods and invest instead in risky tourism ventures on the other side of the country, are they behaving responsibly? I submit that irresponsibility is randomly distributed across race, class, gender, and family form, and I agree that there is far too much of it. But I also submit that most people most of the time are trying to meet their responsibilities to their families, friends, and coworkers. Less often, perhaps, do people think about and meet their responsibilities to distant strangers, but here responsibility increases with social privilege. We live in a time of a "responsibility deficit," some say, but I don't know the measure of responsibility levels. If the measure for single mothers is the income level of their children and the state of the schools, health clinics, and parks in the neighborhoods where they live, then this is a most unforgivable example of blaming the victims.

I completely agree with Elshtain that a vigorous and just 9 society depends on the active participation of citizens in civic institutions of their own making, either not connected or only loosely connected to the state—neighborhood cleanup crews, parent councils in schools, volunteer social services, community arts and culture centers, cooperatives, political advocacy organizations. Despite communitarian complaints, I find no evidence that this sort of volunteer community organizing and service provision has waned in the United States in the last two decades. The heroic activities of organizations like the Industrial Areas Foundation or the Cabrini Green Tenants

Association, which Elshtain applauds, are very often led by single mothers. Other such volunteer civic activities are led by the "forlorn bands of disconnected men" Elshtain imagines "roaming neighborhoods." Many men run athletic and cultural programs for children, or volunteer in tutoring centers, drug-prevention, and skills-building workshops. Despite what I regard as a healthy level of civic activity in the United States among people of both genders and all races and classes, there is certainly need for more. Public expenditures on street lighting and better transportation, along with private corporate decisions to reduce working hours without reducing pay, might enable more people to engage in more self-defined civic activities to improve their lives and their neighborhoods.

10   It is Elshtain and Steinfels who have their heads in the sand if they think that "private disinvestment" in the two-parent family has destroyed our schools and taken jobs away from the neighborhoods. American society has been severely damaged by three decades of private and public disinvestment in basic manufacturing, new and rehabilitated housing, bridges and rail lines, public education, adult retraining, and social services such as preventive health care and libraries. Volunteers can only barely begin to fill these gaping holes in the American dream.

11   Elshtain and Steinfels write as though I have called for more of the same tired old welfare policies in order to respond to the stresses of single motherhood and the economic disadvantage many children suffer. But my policy principles call for social *investment* (this word that Elshtain seems to find so hyperbolic), not draining handouts. Private industry should bear as much responsibility for this investment, moreover, as government does. Elshtain suggests that a condition for the creation of decent jobs is that children be motivated to stay in school. Only a little reflection should suggest that precisely the reverse is true. She accuses me of resuscitating a separate spheres ideology that would keep women at home caring for children, yet scoffs at my call for the massive increases in state support for child care that would enable more mothers—and fathers—to work outside the home and volunteer, knowing that their children were cared for. Steinfels suggests that parents cannot assume that more money and personnel will make quality child care more available and affordable. I do not understand why we cannot assume that it would help a great deal.

Neither Elshtain nor Steinfels mentions the single most   12
important cause of the economic disadvantage in which children of many single mothers live: low wages for women's
work. Coupled with the scarcity or expense of child care, low
wages make it rational for many women to stay on welfare.
Millions of single mothers nevertheless take jobs that enable
them and their children only barely to escape poverty, if that.
We do not have to accept as given the sex segregation of
women's work that helps keep those wages low. It is simple
sexism to decide that the only way to pull the children of single mothers out of poverty is to get them live-in fathers; it is
also an unrealistic expectation, since male unemployment
rates have been steadily rising in the last decade, and male
wage rates have been falling. Public and private programs
should be devoted to training women for higher wage jobs and
raising the wages of traditionally female jobs. This is not a
wasteful handout; it is justice.

Decent schools, housing, infrastructure, decent jobs for all   13
able to work, wage equalization, and affordable child care
can come about only through significant levels of public
spending combined with both coerced and voluntary efforts
of private capital. Elshtain and Steinfels throw up their hands
at the absurdity of such a statement in these days "when state
budgets are strapped, cutbacks are being ordered across the
board." Are these facts of nature? If caring progressives treat
them as such, then we are certainly doomed. Americans must
engage in a serious and prolonged discussion of public and
private spending and taxation, with the aim of shifting resources from waste and quick profits to investment in people
and neighborhoods.

Topping the agenda for such discussion must be the fat pub-   14
lic larder where we still see very little in the way of cutbacks:
military spending. According to the Center for Defense Information, Clinton's 1994 budget contains $340 billion in military
spending, only $10 billion lower than Bush's 1993 budget.
Compare this to $54 billion for education and social services,
or $11 billion for community and regional development. In his
State of the Union Address, Clinton vowed not to cut another
dime from military spending. Surely this is madness. I
wouldn't say that we should leave ourselves defenseless, or
even unable to fight one imperialist war at a time; let's just take
half of that $340 billion over the next five years and rechannel
it into job-creating schools, day-care centers, new houses and
apartments, steel, clean trains, parks, libraries, bridges and
roads, and, yes, community organizing clearinghouses.

SHOULD SAME-SEX COUPLES BE PERMITTED TO MARRY?

Evan Wolfson
Why We Should Fight for the Freedom to Marry

Evan Wolfson is an attorney and the director of the Marriage Project for Lambda Legal Defense and Education Fund in New York City. He is an expert on the legal issues raised by same-sex marriage. In 1996, he wrote the following essay for the Journal of Gay, Lesbian, and Bisexual Identity. *The essay was paired in a "Point-Counterpoint" section with the next essay in* Conversations, *by Victoria Brownworth.*

1   Imagine if tomorrow, by act of law, lesbians and gay men were denied the right to raise children together in a protected relationship[1] or to have their committed relationships recognized and given benefits such as annuities, pension plans, Social Security, and Medicare.[2] Or if by act of law, same-sex couples who had lived together for the longest time were not allowed joint filing of tax returns, joint insurance policies for home, auto, and health, or access during dissolution or divorce to protections such as community property and child support.[3]

2   Imagine how you would feel if you and your partner were told that, because of that act of law, you had to choose between love and country because your same-sex relationship was not respected for immigration and residency.[4] Or that the act of law meant that your partner's death left you without rights of inheritance, protection against eviction from the home you had shared, exemption from oppressive taxation, or even bereavement leave.[5] Imagine that the act of law stamped you as unqualified to make decisions about your partner's health or medical treatment, or even her or his funeral arrangements.[6] Or that the act of law branded you as

permanent sexual outlaws, unequal citizens, and even not fully human—because of the gender of the person you love.[7]

In fact, that act of law has already happened; it's called "same-sex couples can't get married." All this unequal treatment and more is already there, because in all 50 states, lesbians and gay men are denied the basic human right, the constitutional freedom, to marry.[8]

Because literally hundreds of important legal, economic, practical, and social benefits and protections flow directly from marriage,[9] the exclusion from this central social institution wreaks real harm on real-life same-sex couples every day. From lesbian mothers denied custody of their children or the right to adopt their partners' children (case after case), to gay men literally separated at the Immigration and Naturalization office because they could not find a country that would allow them to live together (case after case), to gay people out in the cold when a relationship ended, or unable to get an order of protection against domestic violence when the relationship went sour—the denial of marriage rights has been a stone wall against which we have run up again and again.

Today the movement and its allies face critical choices. Do we work not just to *win* the freedom to marry (which we are likely to do), but to *keep* it (against the coming backlash)? Or do we fail to organize, fail to do the necessary political organizing and coalition-building, fail to get out front and frame the debate in our way—and thus miss a vital opportunity to engage the public and educate the world about our family relationships? Will we get so caught up in our own intracommunity discussions about "redefining the family," or our own all-or-nothing rhetoric, that we are once again caught unprepared for the actual legal, political, and cultural battles soon to be unfolding in every state, this time around the galvanizing question of whether gay people should be able to keep the freedom to marry we hopefully will win in Hawaii?

Lambda's landmark case in Hawaii, *Baehr v. Lewin*,[10] seems headed toward victory. The battle over marriage rights and lesbian and gay relationships is heading toward unprecedented national dimensions, front-page headlines, courts, and legislatures in every state. Will we pull together and prepare, or will we miss the boat?

Although no discrimination is exactly the same, and there is no reason to get into an argument over some "hierarchy of oppression,"[11] there are many analogies to be drawn from this nation's previous experience in excluding people from the institution of marriage. For example, Stephanie Smith of the

National Center for Lesbian Right/Lesbians of Color Project has spoken eloquently of the parallels between the "different-sex restriction" still in force against gay and lesbian people's choice of a marital partner and the "same-race restriction" that less than 30 years ago prevented interracial couples from marrying.[12]

8   Consider this law imposing a "same-race restriction" on marriage struck down (only twenty-seven years ago!) by the U.S. Supreme Court in *Loving v. Virginia:*[13] "All marriages between a white person and a colored person shall be absolutely *void* without any decree of divorce or other legal process." Notice how closely it resembles the equally offensive and unconstitutional bill imposing a "different-sex restriction" on marriage, recently proposed in South Dakota: "Any marriage between persons of the same gender is null and *void* from the beginning."[14]

9   In *Loving,* a black woman and a white man were criminally convicted for violating Virginia's miscegenation law, which imposed a "same-race restriction" on marriage. Exiling (!) the Lovings from their home state for 25 years and declaring their marriage "void," the trial judge stated,

> Almighty God created the races white, black, yellow, malay, and red, and he placed them on separate continents.... The fact that he separated the races shows that he did not intend for the races to mix.[15]

The Supreme Court struck down this "same-race restriction" on marital choice as a "measure...designed to maintain White Supremacy." In much the same way, the "different-sex restriction" deprives gay and lesbian people of a basic human right and brands us as inferior, second-class citizens, thus justifying and reinforcing stereotypes and prejudice as well as other discrimination.

10   People today forget how the language now being used against same-sex couples' equal marriage rights not so long ago was used against interracial couples—denying people's equal human dignity and freedom to share in the rights and responsibilities of marriage. Today, you even hear some *gay* and *lesbian* people saying that the fact that marriage is today denied to same-sex couples shows that it is intrinsically heterosexual, ignoring the fact that marriage (like other social institutions we are part of or seek to make our own choices whether or not to be part of) has changed throughout history to meet the needs and values of real people.[16]

Now imagine if the Lovings had been told that instead of   11
challenging this discrimination and fighting for their right to
marry, they should instead devote their limited resources
solely to unhooking benefits and protections from marriage.
Or if the lawyers working on their case from the ACLU and
the Japanese-American Citizens League (both of which have
endorsed Lambda's Marriage Resolution calling for equal
marriage rights for gay people)[17] had said that we should not
work on ending the ban on interracial marriage until we
achieve universal health care.

Would anyone say that people in love should accept discrim-   12
ination based on their race or religion until other injustices are
rectified? Or would we say that *both* the discrimination and
the other injustices should be combatted and those like the
Lovings are right to challenge their exclusion from a central
social institution? Would we counsel the Lovings to accept
unequal treatment, or even "separate-but-equal"? And if we
wouldn't, why should people facing discrimination based on
their gender or sexual orientation, or the gender or sexual orientation of the person they love most, have to accept it either?

History is upon us. For many, perhaps most, gay and non-   13
gay people, marriage is important in its own right. Regardless, marriage is now also a vehicle, a forum, a venue for the
titanic battles at hand. And each of us, every organization,
must decide: Am I going to be a part of this battle, are we
fighting to win, or am I going to sit this one out or focus elsewhere? Unquestionably, there is much work and many issues
that are important. Yet saying "Let's not work for this" is in effect saying "You should not have this," for as Martin Luther
King, Jr., instructs, "It is a historical fact that privileged
groups seldom give up their privileges voluntarily.... Freedom
is never voluntarily given by the oppressor; it must be demanded by the oppressed."[18]

I believe that the cultural, political, and legal battles about   14
to erupt over our freedom to marry require us to seize the
challenge and opportunity by beginning to prepare NOW.
What is that opportunity, and what must we do?

The coming (and inevitable) battles over marriage will give   15
us the opportunity to educate the nation about the reality and
diversity of lesbian and gay lives and family relationships. We
can tell true and compelling stories about who we are; what
our needs are as couples, as parents, as partners, as people;
and how the denial of the right to marry harms us. We can
tell of the lesbians and gay men of color in our communities,
the economically disadvantaged, the religiously oriented, the

parents, the long-term partners "in sickness and in health," the functional families, the rural and domestic—all injured in tangible and intangible ways by being denied their freedom to define their own family and make their own choice about marriage.

16   This fight and the stakes cut across race, gender, and class lines.[19] For decades, the radical right has been campaigning against, and mischaracterizing, our desire and need for equal marriage rights;[20] it is time that we, too, started talking about it, framing the discussion accurately and compellingly.

17   What can people do? To me it boils down to the nitty-gritty work of social change: engaging people through education and asking for their support. We must give a wake-up call and a heads-up to ourselves and our allies, and create a climate of receptivity among others. To that end, Lambda and other groups have created the Marriage Resolution:

> Because marriage is a basic human right and an individual personal choice, RESOLVED, the State should not interfere with same-gender couples who choose to marry and share fully and equally in the rights, responsibilities, and commitment of civil marriage.

The Marriage Resolution is a vehicle for (a) promoting the necessary discussion and consideration of our equal marriage rights among gay and nongay people (and organizations), (b) collecting signatories to build and demonstrate a growing coalition (Lambda to be a central repository, with list to be shared), and (c) giving people a tool and a task in building that coalition and approaching others.

18   By asking any organization you belong to or feel comfortable approaching to consider and adopt the Resolution, you are moving people and helping forge a coalition that can snowball. With the Marriage Resolution and materials from Lambda, everyone can become a one-person wave of activism toward friends, families, allies, and organizations. We can firm up our supporters, while softening up the initially hostile or uninformed, but *reachable* mass of most Americans.

19   Nor is it just nongay people who need education about lesbian and gay families. Many gay people do not know that we are denied the right to marry; many gay people do not realize how denial directly deprives us of a litany of benefits and protections, rights and responsibilities. And many people do not understand just how false a choice it is to be presented with

the question, "Should we work for marriage, or for domestic partnership?"[21]

First, there is nothing antithetical about believing that gay   20
people should be able to exercise the equal right to marry
and, at the same time, believing that other family forms—
including perhaps, but not limited to, domestic partnership—
are valuable and should be treated fairly. We know this
because at Lambda, we litigated and won benefits for gay and
nongay unmarried partners of city employees in New York[22]
and continue to press other "domestic partnership" cases.

Some say that if gay men and lesbians were allowed to   21
marry, "the entire domestic-partnership movement would dry
up tomorrow."[23] Of course, either this is untrue or it is a revealing insight into the lesbian and gay community's relative
support for marriage vis-à-vis domestic partnership, once
given a meaningful option (as we will have been, when the
Hawaii Supreme Court hands down its final ruling). If the assertion were true, would the proper course for the movement
be to foist domestic partnership on those who would prefer a
choice regarding marriage? Is losing marriage as an option
(after we win it in Hawaii or elsewhere) an acceptable price to
pay for fueling the domestic partnership "movement"?

Of course, we need not assume the assertion to be true.   22
Clearly there are many of us committed to meeting the needs
of all families and individuals without sole regard to marriage. But I do not believe lesbians and gay men who wish to
marry should be denied that freedom, that equality, that
choice, simply because of who they are or whom they love.

Second, although the recent trend toward adopting domes-   23
tic partnership ordinances and policies locality by locality,
and increasing efforts to equalize access to employment benefits company by company, are welcome and important innovations, we should keep one thing clear: domestic partnership
is not marriage. Allowing lesbians and gay men access only to
domestic partnerships, while reserving marriage for different-
sex couples, is a form of second-class citizenship, and perpetuates discrimination.

And, despite the hard work and best intentions of many ac-   24
tivists,[24] it is indeed second-class. For one thing, "domestic
partnership" has become kind of a shorthand phrase for a variety of different means of winning some slice of benefits and/
or recognition for unmarried couples; it means different things
to different people, ranging from voluntary company policies
on benefits, to civic registries, to a hypothesized flexible family

form. Domestic partnership does not *exist* as a unitary "thing" or national institution, unlike marriage, which is recognized across state lines and at every level of society. Moreover, not only is domestic partnership unequal to marriage in the sense that "separate but equal is inherently unequal," but under the domestic partnership ordinances and policies adopted so far, the benefits on their own terms are not equal to those provided to married partners.

25   For example, many of the ordinances require domestic partners to undertake the responsibilities and legal obligations that accompany marriage, but do not in exchange give domestic partners even most of the benefits of marriage. Nor do they provide equal recognition. The ordinances, because local, do not—and could not—assure domestic partners the full range of benefits extended married partners at the state level; even were a state to adopt statewide domestic partnership, it would be unable to deliver *federal* and out-of-state benefits and protections. The ordinances do not—and most likely, under federal law, could not—mandate that private employers treat domestic partners the same as married partners; even the 30 or so cities and the 2 states[25] that have the best domestic partnership programs at most provide health benefits only to *government* employees. The ordinances do not—and are not permitted to—provide domestic partners parental protections and benefits that are provided to married partners.

26   Arguably, the greatest success of the "domestic partnership" "movement" has been persuading many private universities and companies *voluntarily* to give their gay and lesbian employees (and it is *almost always* restricted to gay and lesbian) some of the benefits given their married employees.[26] When challenged in court, whether in Colorado[27] or California,[28] Massachusetts,[29] Minnesota,[30] Wisconsin,[31] or more recently, Georgia,[32] domestic partnership has almost always lost.

27   At the same time, ironically, under most, if not all of these laws, the criteria for establishing a domestic partnership are far more onerous than those imposed on a couple seeking to marry. Thus, on the one hand, domestic partnership fails to resonate with the emotional and declarative (and often religious) power most people feel inheres in marriage. On the other hand, domestic partnership fails to "redefine the family" or "equalize access" to benefits, because it is hampered by legal obstacles and by the need to define it as a status so as to, once again, exclude people not in a sufficiently committed, interdependent, or caretaking relationship. Why is it some-

how correct to fight for domestic partnership or accept it as a step toward something else, while incorrect to make the same calculus with regard to (the far more resonant, potent, and benefit-laden institution of) marriage?

The domestic partnership approach is a healthy step   28
toward eliminating marital status discrimination and arbitrariness in the recognition of valuable family relationships. Recognizing "domestic partnerships" or adopting policies equalizing access to benefits is likely to be one of the best steps available to a locality, private institution, company, or university—as distinguished from a state. Such steps help demonstrate the marital nature, the spousal equivalence, of gay and lesbian relationships, while at the same time showing the absence of any legitimate, let alone compelling, State interest in disparate treatment or segregated status. But, ultimately, domestic partnership alone is not enough. As feminist columnist Anna Quindlen put it in coming out for equal marriage rights,

> there is no secular reason that we should take a patchwork approach of corporate, governmental, and legal steps to guarantee what can be done simply, economically, conclusively, and inclusively with the words, "I do."[33]

Our demand as gay and lesbian people for equal choices   29
and recognition with regard to our family relationships does not undermine our demand as conscientious citizens to decouple benefits from arbitrary criteria of any kind. But, equally, our desire to achieve a more just, contextual allocation of benefits should not require us to accept an inferior status with regard to marriage or other choices. The couples in Hawaii—Ninia and Genora, Pat and Joe—are just as entitled as anyone to decide for themselves how to define their families and live their lives.

A few marriage critics express a concern that winning the   30
right to marry may somehow "delegitimiz[e] some of us in the eyes of other gays and lesbians in the name of legitimizing all of us in the eyes of heterosexuals."[34] This will be true only if "we" let it be true. As Professor Ruthann Robson, no supporter of equal marriage rights, frankly concedes, "legalized lesbian marriage would not invent the good lesbian/deviant lesbian dichotomy."[35] It is our job as activists not to conflate rhetoric with reality, not to confuse tactics with objectives, and not to rely on one vehicle or voice to achieve the full social change we want. We must see opportunities in

challenges, while always tactically advancing so as to, at least, *lose* forward.

31   In my view, it is telling that the one state in the country where there is any serious discussion about legislative adoption of a "comprehensive" statewide domestic partnership law is Hawaii. And it's no coincidence that that discussion, and that serious possibility, has opened up only in response to the likely victory in our case and the coalition-building, education, and organizing that have accompanied our fight over marriage rights.

32   The battles over equal marriage rights *are* coming. They will be fought, not just in Hawaii, but in every state and in Washington, D.C. Every lesbian and gay issue and community will be affected by those battles; every issue and community stands to benefit or be harmed, depending in part on how we seize the opportunity and begin preparing now. There will be victories and setbacks; we must persevere through both over the long haul. We must use the battleline of marriage as a powerful opportunity to advance on many fronts, and to tell the truth about who we are and how we love.

33   In three states, we have seen the backlash against equality begin before we have even "lashed," before we have even won the equal right to marry. In Utah, South Dakota, and Alaska, radical-right legislators introduced antimarriage legislation aimed preemptively at thwarting recognition of marriages we someday may lawfully celebrate in Hawaii or elsewhere.[36] The results of these opening skirmishes are revealing. In Utah, by cheating, the bill passed through the legislature and became law.[37] In Alaska, it is too soon to predict.

34   But in South Dakota, thanks to the hard work of local activists together with NGLTF and Lambda, we won.[38] In round 1, the legislature rejected the assault on our equal right to marry and see those marriages recognized throughout the nation, just as other lawful marriages are. This victory came even before we had a chance to organize, prepare, build a coalition, ask for support, and frame the discussion. It offers us hope: we *can* win.

35   We have not yet begun to fight. It is time to demand full, full, full equality, and to tell the truth about who we are and what we want for ourselves and our loved ones. Although no one victory (be it marriage, antidiscrimination laws, or the right to adopt) is the end of our fight, you cannot be for "equality" while acquiescing in the denial of so fundamental a freedom as the *equal* right to choose whether and whom to marry. We may never all agree on marriage or any other sin-

gle issue or vehicle. But we at Lambda and the many others who are joining us in this effort believe that the coming battles around marriage will affect far more than just ("just"!) the freedom to marry. What we need for now is less "point/counterpoint" and more ways for all of us, and our allies, to pull together.

Gay and lesbian people want the right to choose whether 36 and whom to marry for the same mix of personal, economic, and practical reasons that nongay people do. As Lambda's landmark case in Hawaii progresses toward a much-hoped-for and anticipated victory, we must educate ourselves and others about the importance of, and need for, equal marriage rights for lesbians and gay men. Anticipating and seizing the opportunities that the marriage battles will engender, we must get to work—now.

Notes

1. See, e.g. *Matter of Dana,* No. 93-0747 (nonbiological mother not permitted to adopt partner's child without cutoff of parental rights because they are not married).

2. See, e.g., *Bagley v. California Federal Bank,* No. CV 93-7027MRP (unmarried gay couple not permitted to have employee loan discount available to married nongay couple).

3. See, e.g., Anne Stroock, "Gay Divorces Complicated by Lack of Laws," *San Francisco Chronicle,* May 14, 1990, A4 (denial of parental rights to nonbiological parent, one of the consequences wrought by the denial of marriage rights to same-sex partners); Kirk Johnson, "Gay Divorce: Few Markers in This Realm," *N.Y. Times,* Aug. 12, 1994, A20 ("Because gay people cannot be legally married in the United States, there is, for starters, no access to divorce court.").

4. E.g., *Sullivan v. INS,* 772 E2d 609 (noncitizen partner in long-term gay couple denied right to remain with his partner in United States because not married); see also Kimberly Griffin, "To Have and to Hold: Gay Marriage, the Next Frontier," *Windy City Times,* June 2, 1994, 1, 46 (stories of binational couples facing prospect of separation because unable to marry and remain together legally).

5. E.g., *Brinkin v. Southern Pac. Transp. Co.,* 572 ESupp. 236 (death of partner after 11 years together does not qualify employee for bereavement leave).

6. E.g., *Guardianship of Sharon Kowalski,* 382 N.W.2d 861 (Minn. 1986), *reversed,* 478 N.W.2d 790 (Minn In re...1991).

7. See, generally, Evan Wolfson and Robert S. Mower, "When the Police Are in Our Bedroom, Shouldn't the Courts Go in After Them? An Update on the Fight Against 'Sodomy' Laws," 21 *Fordham Urb. I., J.* 997 (1994).

8. See *Baehr v. Lewin,* 852 P.2d 44, 59 (1993; Hawaii Supreme Court describes the "encyclopedic" "multiplicity of rights and benefits that are contingent upon [marital] status"); see also *Van Dyck v. Van Dyck,* 425 S.E.2d 853 (Ga. 1993).

9. See Richard D. Mohr, "The Case for Gay Marriage," 9 *Notre Dame J. Law, Ethics Pub. Pol.* 215, 227–228 (1995); Craig A. Bowman and Blake M. Cornish, "A More Perfect Union: A Legal and Social Analysis of Domestic Partnership Ordinances," 92 *Colum. L. Rev.* 1164, 1167–1168 (1992).

10. 852 P.2d 44, 75 (Haw. 1993). For a discussion of this epochal case and its implications, see, e.g., Evan Wolfson, "Crossing the Threshold: Equal Marriage Rights for Lesbians and Gay Men, and the Intra-Community Critique," 21 *N.Y.U. Rev. L. Soc. Change 567,* 572–581 (1994) (hereinafter: "Crossing the Threshold").

11. Henry Louis Gates, Jr., "Blacklash," *The New Yorker,* May 11, 1993, 42–43 ("trying to establish a pecking order of oppression is generally a waste of time").

12. Michelangelo Signorile, "Wedding Bell Blues," *Out Magazine,* May 1995, 26 (quoting Smith's remarks to the 1995 Black Gay & Lesbian Leadership Forum Summit in Los Angeles, at which she described how her own parents had to leave their home state of Missouri to find a state that would marry them).

13. 388 U.S. 1 (1967) (striking down Virginia's same-race restriction on an individual's choice of marital partner).

14. H.B. 1184, "An Act to prohibit a marriage between persons of the same gender" (1995). Saying that either an interracial or a same-sex couple's marriage is "void" means more than that a court may choose not to recognize such a marriage; it means that "by definition," it is not a marriage.

15. 388 U.S., 3; see "Crossing the Threshold" at 575–576.

16. "Crossing the Threshold," 588–591.

17. "Crossing the Threshold," 82, discusses the Marriage Resolution. A list of signatories is available through Lambda Legal Defense & Education Fund, 666 Broadway, New York, NY 10012, which organizations may also contact to sign on. On the JACL's endorsement of equal marriage rights, see Gerard Lim, "JACL Formally Adopts Same-Sex Marriage," *AsianWeek,* Aug. 12, 1994, 7.

18. Martin Luther King, Jr., *Why We Can't Wait,* 80. In a similar vein, the Jewish scholar, Rabbi Hillel, instructed, "If I am not for myself, who will be?" We must demand our full equality, specifically including the freedom to marry; our opponents will certainly be mentioning marriage.

19. "People had never really thought of gay marriage as a 'people of color' issue. [But following presentations at the Black Lesbian & Gay Leadership Forum Summit, e]veryone started talking about talking to their ministers, their parents, their

neighbors. They began seeing that this is not about class and privilege and a bunch of rich people flying off to Hawaii. It's about defining what a family is to each of us." "Wedding Bell Blues," 26.

20. "Crossing the Threshold," 595–596.

21. The following discussion of "domestic partnership" is drawn from a fuller treatment in "Crossing the Threshold," 604–608; see also the discussion of the stakes and limitations in domestic partnership in Bowman & Cornish, *passim.*

22. See *Gay Teachers Ass'n v. Bd. of Educ.* No. 43069/88 on file with Lambda.

23. See Chris Bull, "Till Death Do Us Part," *The Advocate,* Nov. 30, 1993, 40, 46 (quoting activist).

24. I include myself in this, for I have litigated "domestic partnership" cases and have urged it as a strategy for winning recognition and benefits for more families, facilitating people's ability to define their families and see their needs addressed fairly. But it is not a substitute for the freedom to marry, nor need we present it as such.

25. Vermont and New York provide access to certain benefits to unmarried state workers and their partners.

26. See, e.g., David Jefferson, "Gay Employees Win Benefits for Partners at More Corporations," *Wall St. Journal,* Mar. 18, 1994, p. A1, col. 1. To get a periodic reporting of the latest companies and jurisdictions providing some benefits and/or recognition to unmarried couples, see *Lesbian & Gay Law Ass'n, Lesbian/Gay Law Notes* ed. Arthur S. Leonard.

27. *Ross v. Denver Dep't of Health & Hospitals,* 883 P.2d 516 (Colo. Ct. App. 1994).

28. *Hinman v. Dep't of Personnel Administration,* 213 Cal. Rptr 410, 419–20.

29. *Huff v. Chapel Hill. Chauncy Hall,* No. 93-BEM-1041 (Sept. 14, 1994).

30. *Lilly v. City of Minneapolis,* 527 NW2d 107, *rev. denied,* Mar. 31, 1995.

31. *Phillips v. Wisc. Personnel Commission,* 482 NW2d 121 (Wis. Ct. App. 1992).

32. *City of Atlanta v. McKinney,* 1995 WL 116312 (Ga. S. Ct. Mar. 14, 1995).

33. Anna Quindlen, "Evan's Two Moms," *N.Y. Times,* Feb. 5, 1992, A23 (supporting gay people's freedom to marry).

34. Steven K. Homer, Note, "Against Marriage," 29 *Harv. C.R.-C.L. L. Rev.* 505, 528 (1994).

35. Ruthann Robson, *Lesbian (Out)law,* 128 n.12 (citing Joan Nestle, *A Restricted Country,* at 123, 1987).

36. See David W. Dunlap. "Some States Trying to Stop Gay Marriages Before They Start," *N.Y. Times,* Mar. 15, 1995, p. A18, col. 1.

37. See "Recognition of Marriages," H.B. 366, Gen. Sess. (1995); "Utah Won't Accept Same-Sex Marriages," *N.Y. Times,* Mar. 3, 1995, p. B&, col.4; Peter Freiberg, "Gays Win in South Dakota, Lose in Utah," *Wash. Blade,* Mar. 3, 1993, p. 1, col. 1.
38. Freiberg.

Victoria Brownworth

Tying the Knot or the Hangman's Noose: The Case against Same-Sex Marriage

Victoria Brownworth, a columnist for the Philadelphia Inquirer, *has written at least eight books on various topics related to social reform. In 1996, she contributed the following essay to the* Journal of Gay, Lesbian, and Bisexual Identity. *The essay was paired in a "Point-Counterpoint" section with the previous essay in* Conversations, *by Evan Wolfson.*

1   It was a steamy Sunday in June. Rain teemed around us as we drove up the windy little road to the fieldstone church. We were late; the ceremony had already begun.

2   The heterosexual wedding my partner and I were attending was that of two of her closest friends, an editor ("Teresa") and an artist ("Tim"), both devout Catholics. The bride was, indisputably, a virgin on her wedding day (despite an 8-year courtship). And regardless of the terrible weather and the soggy demeanor of the majority of the guests, the ceremony was beautiful: a sung Mass, additional vows, a rather stiff but heartfelt commentary by the priest about the sanctity and difficulty inherent in "real" marriage, "real" commitment. There was a very moving moment when the bridegroom's voice broke as he repeated his vows to his soon-to-be wife. Like most of the women in the church, I cried. It was perhaps the most emotional wedding I have ever attended. It was certainly—Charles and Diana aside—the most memorable.

3   This wedding took place several years ago. Our friends now have a young daughter and a house in the suburbs. She remains on the fast track at her publishing house, regardless

of baby, house and husband. He is struggling a bit, juggling house-husbandry with artistic career. They are still in love, still committed, still the epitome of the 30-something upper-middle-class married couple.

I have attended many weddings in my life. I was married   4
myself at 17 on a beautiful sunny October day in a ceremony nearly identical to that of Tim and Teresa. But no wedding has ever affected me, with the possible exception of my own, in the way Tim and Teresa's did. For weeks, even months, after the ceremony, I felt a deep and powerful yearning to have what Teresa and Tim had, to replicate their experience and the emotions it stirred in myself and others at their wedding.

Those feelings were generated by the accoutrements of the   5
ceremony itself as well as by the response to it by others. It may have been what the priest said about the marriage contract. It may have been the catch in Tim's voice as he pledged himself to the woman he had been in love with since they met in college. It may have been the simple lyrical folk songs and hymns sung between aspects of the Mass. Or it may have been that I finally understood something about marriage that I had never understood before that afternoon.

My partner and I were the only lesbians in attendance that   6
day. And in that resoundingly heterosexual company, celebrating the quintessential heterosexual act, I have never felt more queer, more separate, more outside the realm of heterosexual society.

It was nothing anyone did. My partner and I "fit in" com-   7
fortably with the other guests, many of whom we knew well. And yet there was the most dramatic sense of isolation that accompanied that wedding, for me. It stayed with me for weeks, and as I write this, the feelings are nearly as compelling as they were 4 years ago.

Despite its beauty and seeming honesty, this wedding crys-   8
tallized my sense that marriage is—no matter how beautiful the ceremony and no matter how devoted the love between the couple entering into it—a contract, first and foremost, an agreement to abide by a set of rules that are predicated on property and ownership, on class distinctions (for centuries only the monied and classed could afford marriage), on material possessions ("with all my worldly goods, I thee endow"—especially the wife's dowry.). Marriage is as much about separation (as in keeping the basic separation between the sexes) as it is about cleaving, or two people becoming one.

The wife is "given away" by her father to her husband. The   9
wife changes her name (even today, in over 85% of marriages)

from that of her father to that of her husband. Marriage is a contract that says two individuals will now be subsumed into one couple, "until death do us part." But from the outset, it is one member of the partnership who is subsumed by the contract itself, one member who is "given away," one member who is expected to be virginal, pure, unsullied (not previously owned), one member who loses her name, her personhood, her separateness from this contract on her life.

10   I remember with great clarity the first time I received a piece of mail addressed to "Mrs. John Doe" and realized that person was supposed to be me, and that I was expected to be not only pleased that I was the "Mrs.," the literal attachment to my husband's name, but proud that I had achieved this social status—a status in which I was no longer myself, but an extension of whomever my husband was.

11   At Teresa and Tim's wedding, this sense of status achieved was inherent in everything from the sermonette the priest gave, to the kinds of wedding gifts received, to the place where the reception itself was held. And when it was time, single women pushed and shoved to catch the bouquet—in the hope that they would be the next to move into the valued place of "wife."

12   I have been to many queer weddings in the last decade. Almost all of those have been lesbian couples. Some have been very traditional, such as the marriage of a close friend and her partner by a rabbi, under the *chupah,* or the ceremony of another couple, both dressed in wedding gowns with veils and trains, in a garden, by a gay minister. Others have been slightly less formal, with "vows" exchanged without benefit of clergy. These ceremonies were also lovely, three-handkerchief events, full of sentiment and promise. And they have all had the same trappings of straight weddings, including lots of flowers, lots of presents, lots of free-flowing champagne, and lots of bad music.

13   But unlike our friends Tim and Teresa, none of these queer couples is still together—despite the wedding gifts, despite having children together, despite buying houses, despite entering into the appearance of a marriage contract.

14   The queer promarriage lobby would say that my friends are anomalous—that it is more likely for a lesbian marriage to last than that of a straight couple. Maybe. Statistically, fully half of all straight marriages dissolve into divorce, despite the glitter and expense, the promises and contracts of the wedding day itself. However, I believe that the reason for that is that marriage is an unnatural state predicated on the domi-

nance of one partner over another. I also think that's why lesbian marriages—or at least those of my friends—don't last.
There's less tolerance for that domination between two
women than there is between a man and a woman.

And John Boswell's wonderful treatise on the early days of   15
queer marriage aside, marriage in the last six centuries has
been and continues to be about ownership: It is about the
buying, selling and trading of a commodity—women—and by
extension, children and property. Marriage has only *rarely*
been about the uniting of two people in love; most often it has
been about the uniting of two families over property.

In the United States, women were not allowed to own   16
property in their own name until this century. Married
women were not allowed to own property, maintain custody
of children, get a divorce, or have any legal autonomy from
their husbands prior to this century.

But marriage has not generally become less repressive in   17
this century. The links between marriage and property (the
women *as* property) remain. In most countries, a woman cannot have an abortion without her husband's consent. Spousal
consent has also been incorporated into abortion control laws
in several U.S. states and territories (though this is under appeal). In India and Pakistan today, this minute, women are frequently burned alive because their dowries were deemed
insufficient by their in-laws. If the old bride is burned up, a
new bride—and a new dowry—can be gotten for the husband.

In nearly every Muslim country and a majority of African   18
nations, and in European countries to which these people
emigrate, girls and women are genitally mutilated; their clitorises and labia are sheared off with knives, razors, sharp
stones, and what remains is sewn together, with only a tiny
hole left for menstrual flow to escape. This process is to make
them sexually "pure." If a girl is not rendered sexually pure,
she is not marriageable, and if she is not marriageable, she
and her family are disgraced.

On their wedding night, the husband slices his wife's labia   19
open and has sex with her. Some women bleed to death. Others are permanently maimed. Others go crazy from the pain
and horror of it all. Still others die later in childbirth because
of the scarring. Millions of women and girls are mutilated in
this way every year. While I was living in London in 1989, two
young Somali girls died from this procedure several miles
from where I lived.

In the United States, American men "buy" brides from   20
other countries—most frequently South Asia, Polynesia, and

Russia. These women are eager to escape the poverty and re-pression of their own countries, and the men who barter for them are eager for women who are more "traditional" wives—that is, women who will efface themselves, who will cook, clean, perform sexually, and have babies with no ques-tions asked and no hope of egalitarianism as part of the mar-riage bond. In early March, one of these men shot his pregnant wife, a Filipino, to death in a Seattle courtroom as she tried to have their marriage annulled on the basis of his abuse of her. The man also killed the woman representing the wife and the wife's sister.

21   Yet in spite of the truly horrific history of marriage in this country and around the world, marriage has become a top priority for the lesbian and gay civil rights movement. What I hear frequently from other queers is how important it is for us to be able to be married, that the status of marriage offers its participants material and social benefits that cannot be ac-crued or accessed except through marriage and the social contract that is at its foundation.

22   Nearly everyone who supports the "ideal" of same-sex mar-riage also believes strongly that lesbians and gay men should be able to serve openly in the military. And for the last 5 years, these two issues have been the primary focus of the entire les-bian and gay civil rights movement, superseding even con-cerns over the AIDS epidemic.

23   I find this link between marriage and the military both in-triguing and repellent. It is, to my mind, similar to the links in the alleged "prolife" movement, where the vast majority of those who call themselves prolife are both antiabortion and pro-death penalty: paradox as paradigm.

24   As lesbians and gay men, we are fundamentally outside the heterosexual culture and society. We are *not* simply separated by our sexual partners, and those queers who say the only dif-ference between us and straights is whom we fuck are peril-ously ignorant. We have our own queer culture and society, just like people of color have their society separate from white European culture, or Jews have a society predicated on a history completely separate from Christians'. Just as there is something more than the difference between Hanukkah and Christmas separating Jew from Christians, there is more than two penises or two clitorises separating queers from straights.

25   That is why the choice of marriage and the military as the fundamental "issues" of queer liberation seems so ultimately perverse, because these two institutions (marriage and the

military), both of which are predicated on the most repressive, oppressive, and dangerous aspects of society, are inherently heterosexual. They are grounded in the inequities of
heterosexuality. They are inherently *anti*-queer. And what's
more, they don't even work for straight society.

I recently saw a group wedding of gay men and lesbians on   26
an episode of the Chicago talk show "Jerry Springer." There
was a lot of discussion about the appropriateness of queer
marriages; there were objections from straight relatives of the
queer betrothed; and there was the glitzy wedding on national television (albeit, in my viewing area, at 4 A.M.).

What disturbed me most about this program (since I am   27
also disturbed that anyone would want to get married on a
talk show in the first place) was the fact that none of the
queers could really explain *why* they wanted to get married.
None of them cited the generally accepted party line on this:
shared health benefits, tax benefits, maternity and bereavement policies. All of them said, because that's what straight
people do when they are in love and *want to show everyone
they love each other.*

How much of marriage is predicated on this idea of "show-   28
ing" and "disclosing" your romantic passion to the world in
return for the contract that gives social approbation? At Teresa and Tim's wedding, approval was thicker in the air than
humidity on that rainy June afternoon. They were *doing the
right thing,* and they were doing it in "the sight of God and of
His company." They were signing a contract with the community to "be fruitful and multiply." But most importantly, and
perhaps most obviously, they were entering into a contract to
continue the tradition of heterosexuality.

That is a contract that should be anathema to any queer,   29
because this contractual agreement doesn't just exclude
queers, it presumes they either don't or shouldn't exist—that
the world is fundamentally a straight place, and that we have
no business being in it—that we are true anomolies, freaks of
nature (or nurture, depending on whom you listen to). Marriage is the proof of this, say most straights. In fact, marriage,
and the whole Judeo-Christian concept of it, was an essential
element of Supreme Court Justice Byron White's ruling
against constitutional protection for lesbians and gay men in
the pivotal 1986 *Bowers v. Hardwick* case, which upheld Georgia's antisodomy law.

Marriage is about the elevation of the heterosexual couple to   30
the highest social status. And that glorification of the heterosexual couple is everywhere in our national consciousness,

from our literature and culture to our mass media and advertising. Marriage is the pinnacle of heterosexual achievement, and true success for men and women cannot be achieved without it. It is a contract with society and with the state.

31   And in America, marriage devolves from the fundamentally upper-class invention of European marriage culture. For centuries the lower socioeconomic classes could not afford the luxury of marriage and the dowries and property negotiations that were at its root; today they eschew it. According to U.S. Census figures, few of the poor are married; and fewer African Americans, whose cultural heritage in America—including slavery—disallowed marriage for generations, are married than whites. For generations in the United States, the married state has been associated with class: "poor white trash" don't get married; they just "shack up" together. Women of lower socioeconomic classes were/are considered fair sexual game for men of higher class status, but ultimately these women are considered unmarriageable because of their class status. The same is true for women of color *vis-à-vis* white men. The links between social and class status (as well as material wealth) and marriage are inescapable; the institution of the dowry—still very much alive throughout the world—exists because the woman is not enough of a package for the groom on her own. She is of secondary class status simply by virtue of being a woman and therefore the dowry must sweeten the deal so she can be passed from father to husband.

32   With its complicated and often horrific history, what makes marriage so appealing to lesbians and gay men? Why should we want to follow this bloody and repressive path? And how do we hope to achieve the real goal of marriage as it has been established for centuries—which is to maintain and nurture the culture of heterosexuality? Isn't our struggle to be "allowed" to marry predicated on a desire to be assimilated into straight society, to gain approbation of that society, and to accrue the social, material, class, and other gratuities that are accessible only to those members of society who follow the normative (i.e., heterosexual) pattern? And do we really believe that marriage—which fails for over half the heterosexuals who enter into it—*is* the normative pattern? Is marriage, which continues to decimate and restrict the lives of women all around the globe, the highest level of achievement lesbians and gay men can aspire to in our quest for civil rights and legal and political equality (social equality outside our own community being not realistically attainable)?

As a frequent guest on television and radio talk shows, I   33
am usually asked if I am "the girl" in my lesbian relationship
because my hair is long, I wear skirts and makeup, and have
what is presumed by heterosexual society to be a feminine appearance. I just as frequently instruct my audiences that feminine and masculine characteristics are subject to cultural
whim; if my partner wears pants and I wear skirts, it does not
mean that she is the "man" and I am the "woman."

Marriage is not, irrespective of alterations in vows, a rela-   34
tionship built on equality or even love. And the testament to
this fact lies in the fact that marriage is more a contract with
the state than it is with the individual betrothed. And that is
why we need to look at our drive to gain acceptance for same-
sex marriages. This is *not* an appropriate goal for our movement any more than promoting the idea that lesbians and gay
men should be slave owners would be appropriate. Just because straight people and heterosexual society do something
does not mean we should strive to do it too. Just because heterosexual couples like Teresa and Tim derive social approval
for their "achievement" of marriage doesn't mean that same
approbation can ever accrue to same-sex marriages.

Nor does the addition of same-sex couples to the marriage   35
"concept" alter the basic oppressive nature of that concept.
Lesbian and gay male couples who enter into marriage cannot change the fundamental structure of marriage because
that structure is about maintaining social control over
women, it is about denying the existence of nonheterosexu-
als, it is about defining divisions of paid and unpaid labor
within the society (male labor is paid, female labor is unpaid), it is about maintaining class inequities, it is about ownership of children.

Not only can we not fit into that social construct, we   36
shouldn't want to. Our entire lesbian and gay civil rights
movement is *supposed* to be about inclusivity, equality, egalitarianism. The marriage contract—legal marriage based on
the social contract with the state—is the antithesis of what
our movement is based on.

Striving for the benefits of domestic partnerships arrange-   37
ments, which are inclusive, rather than exclusive, and making
statements of personal romantic commitment (whether for
life or for the moment) remain the only truly acceptable avenues for lesbians and gay men to travel down in their quest
for civil rights. These would offer us the things we want: the
benefits the state can offer us for being couples—health, tax,

and other benefits that go with societal recognition of the established couple.

38   Rather than striving toward the socially unreachable and politically unacceptable goal of same-sex marriage, we should be working at abolishing marriage altogether—at least in its current form. As members of one of the most oppressed cultures on the planet, we should be mindful of the history of oppression inextricably connected to marriage. And we should also be mindful of the importance of our cultural individuality. We should not allow the isolation and yearning we might feel within the heterosexual society (or at a wedding) to consume us and alter our political course.

39   Heterosexuals want to keep the marriage contract for themselves. Lesbians and gay men should acknowledge that this is best for us all. Queers can do better than borrowing from the worst elements of straight culture when our own is so rich and full of real, not institutionalized, promise.

Anna Quindlen
Evan's Two Moms

Anna Quindlen (born 1955) for a number of years wrote a widely praised, syndicated column for the New York Times *and many other newspapers. She won a Pulitzer Prize for commentary in 1992. Her work has been collected in several books, including* Thinking Out Loud: On the Personal, the Political, the Public, and the Private *(1993). The following essay (which is referenced by Evan Wolfson's article beginning on page 534) comes from that collection.*

1   Evan has two moms. This is no big thing. Evan has always had two moms—in his school file, on his emergency forms, with his friends. "Ooooh, Evan, you're lucky," they sometimes say. "You have two moms." It sounds like a sitcom, but until last week it was emotional truth without legal bulwark. That was when a judge in New York approved the adoption of a six-year-old boy by his biological mother's lesbian partner. Evan. Evan's mom. Evan's other mom. A kid, a psychologist, a pediatrician. A family.

The matter of Evan's two moms is one in a series of events 2
over the last year that lead to certain conclusions. A Minnesota appeals court granted guardianship of a woman left a
quadriplegic in a car accident to her lesbian lover, the culmi-
nation of a seven-year battle in which the injured woman's
parents did everything possible to negate the partnership between the two. A lawyer in Georgia had her job offer withdrawn after the state attorney general found out that she and
her lesbian lover were planning a marriage ceremony; she's
brought suit. The computer company Lotus announced that
the gay partners of employees would be eligible for the same
benefits as spouses.

Add to these public events the private struggles, the cou- 3
ples who go from lawyer to lawyer to approximate legal protections their straight counterparts take for granted, the AIDS
survivors who find themselves shut out of their partners' dying days by biological family members and shut out of their
apartments by leases with a single name on the dotted line,
and one solution is obvious.

Gay marriage is a radical notion for straight people and a 4
conservative notion for gay ones. After years of being sledge-
hammered by society, some gay men and lesbian women are
deeply suspicious of participating in an institution that seems
to have "straight world" written all over it.

But the rads of twenty years ago, straight and gay alike, 5
have other things on their minds today. Family is one, and the
linchpin of family has commonly been a loving commitment
between two adults. When same-sex couples set out to make
that commitment, they discover that they are at a disadvantage: No joint tax returns. No health insurance coverage for
an uninsured partner. No survivor's benefits from Social Security. None of the automatic rights, privileges, and responsibilities society attaches to a marriage contract. In Madison,
Wisconsin, a couple who applied at the Y with their kids for a
family membership were turned down because both were
women. It's one of those small things that can make you feel
small.

Some took marriage statutes that refer to "two persons" at 6
their word and applied for a license. The results were court
decisions that quoted the Bible and embraced circular argument: marriage is by definition the union of a man and a
woman because that is how we've defined it.

No religion should be forced to marry anyone in violation 7
of its tenets, although ironically it is now only in religious ceremonies that gay people can marry, performed by clergy who

find the blessing of two who love each other no sin. But there is no secular reason that we should take a patchwork approach of corporate, governmental, and legal steps to guarantee what can be done simply, economically, conclusively, and inclusively with the words "I do."

8   "Fran and I chose to get married for the same reasons that any two people do," said the lawyer who was fired in Georgia. "We fell in love; we wanted to spend our lives together." Pretty simple.

9   Consider the case of *Loving* v. *Virginia,* aptly named. At the time, sixteen states had laws that barred interracial marriage, relying on natural law, that amorphous grab bag for justifying prejudice. Sounding a little like God throwing Adam and Eve out of paradise, the trial judge suspended the one-year sentence of Richard Loving, who was white, and his wife, Mildred, who was black, provided they got out of the State of Virginia.

10   In 1967 the Supreme Court found such laws to be unconstitutional. Only twenty-five years ago and it was a crime for a black woman to marry a white man. Perhaps twenty-five years from now we will find it just as incredible that two people of the same sex were not entitled to legally commit themselves to each other. Love and commitment are rare enough; it seems absurd to thwart them in any guise.

Barbara Findlen
Is Marriage the Answer?

Barbara Findlen is the executive editor of Ms. *magazine, the famous feminist publication that carried the following article in the May/June 1995 issue.*

1   In December 1990, Ninia Baehr and Genora Dancel applied for a marriage license at their local health department office in Honolulu. When the license was denied because they are both women, they—along with two other same-sex couples who applied for marriage licenses on the same day—sued the state of Hawaii on the grounds of discrimination. The three couples—two lesbian and one gay male—were well

prepared: before applying for the licenses, they'd already determined that they might have a shot at changing Hawaii's marriage laws.

And indeed, by May 1993, the Hawaii Supreme Court ruled   2
that prohibiting members of the same sex from marrying constitutes sex discrimination and is therefore a violation of the state constitution, which includes an equal rights amendment. The supreme court then proceeded to send the case back to a lower court, ordering the state to show a "compelling interest" in maintaining the discrimination. Remarkably, most observers believe that, barring a change in the makeup of the court or some other extreme circumstance, the couples will triumph when the case is finally decided sometime within the next 18 months.

The case is significant, not just for the future of gay mar-   3
riage, but also for the fate of domestic partnership agreements, which give benefits such as health insurance coverage to unmarried couples. Some activists are wondering, for example, what will become of the dozens of domestic partnership policies that have sprung up over the last decade, many of which also benefit unmarried heterosexual couples. If gay marriage were to become legal, entities that currently offer these policies might decide that since anyone can marry, benefits should be offered only to spouses. Domestic partnership policies would therefore be seen as unnecessary. Many of those who favor domestic partnership policies over marriage espouse the arguably radical notion that *no* rights or benefits should be based on marriage. Other critics would even prefer to see marriage, with its patriarchal trappings, abolished altogether.

While some people might view lesbian and gay marriage as   4
a radical development because it would at last put homosexual relationships on a par with heterosexual ones, domestic partnership advocates view it as conservative because it upholds the basic primacy of marriage as the foundation of the family and marginalizes people who are outside that unit. Notes Paula L. Ettelbrick, a legislative counsel at New York's Empire State Pride Agenda: "The marriage campaign has moved our community to a more conservative, middle-of-the-road political perspective. It has taken people out of the broader, social justice view of family."

But there are different agendas among those who advocate   5
domestic partnership, acknowledges Matt Coles, the director of the ACLU Lesbian and Gay Rights Project and coauthor of one of the first domestic partnership policies ever proposed

in the U.S. (for the city of San Francisco in 1980). Some view domestic partnership as a straightforward equal-pay-for-equal-work issue: employment benefits that are offered to employees' legal spouses should be offered to partners of unmarried employees. For others, it's a way station en route to lesbian and gay marriage. Still others see it as a way to begin to fundamentally redefine the legal meaning of "family," thus undermining the power of the patriarchal nuclear family.

6   Melinda Paras, executive director of the National Gay and Lesbian Task Force (NGLTF), is aiming for the latter. "Part of our struggle," she says, "is to fight for a broader definition of families. Domestic partners shouldn't have to be gay or lesbian. They shouldn't have to be having sex. They can be two adults sharing a home and sharing commitment, responsible to each other."

7   Currently, about 35 municipalities and scores of private companies, educational institutions, and nonprofit organizations offer some kind of policy that bestows benefits on unmarried cohabiting couples—gay *and* straight. There are two kinds of domestic partnership policies—those offered by the private sector, which generally do not provide benefits to unmarried heterosexuals, and municipal policies created by city governments, which cover both same-sex and opposite-sex partners. A typical municipal policy might well define domestic partners in terms similar to those of Paras. In Madison, Wisconsin, for example, they can be any two unrelated adults "in a relationship of mutual support, caring, and commitment." In Seattle, the partners must "have a close and personal relationship" and share "basic living expenses." In many cities, more straight couples than gay couples register as domestic partners. Municipalities establish a registry, and city employees who file are usually given a certificate that validates their domestic partnership and often provides access to spousal equivalent benefits (health insurance, bereavement leave, and other benefits granted to married employees). People who don't work for the city may also receive a certificate. Though organizations in the private sector, such as auto clubs or health clubs, may honor this municipal certificate as a basis for providing benefits, it's strictly optional, and the benefits offered by the city to nonemployees are limited—perhaps access to family memberships at a museum or a gym, or the right to hospital or jail visitation.

8   Private sector policies tend to be much narrower than municipal policies. Most apply only to same-sex partners. The ma-

jor benefit is usually health insurance, and some policies even stop short of that, offering only bereavement or family care leave, use of recreational facilities, access to married faculty or student housing—benefits that cost the institution little.

The rationale behind most private sector plans is: lesbian and gay employees can't marry, so as a matter of workplace equity, they should have access to benefits they would have if they could marry. Nancy Polikoff, a law professor whose work has focused on lesbian and gay families, cites the policy at her own institution, American University, which applies only to same-sex domestic partners. "What happens when there's gay and lesbian marriage?" she says. "That's the end of domestic partnership benefits. We will be told, 'Get married.' What does that say about the notion that we can choose not to get married?"   9

What about a corporation like Levi Strauss & Co., which offers benefits to unmarried heterosexual partners? It's hard to predict whether policies like that will disappear, but it seems likely that the possibility of same-sex marriage would remove a lot of the impetus behind the domestic partnership movement. Although the policies often benefit straight people, the initiative has mostly come from lesbians and gay men, who don't have access to marriage rights.   10

"My big fear," says Ettelbrick, "is that if gay people were allowed to marry tomorrow, I know that we would lose a substantial part of our community that is working on domestic partner benefits. The point is that neither straight people nor gay people should have to get married in order to have some very basic protections for the families that they've chosen. I don't think we have a unified sense of social reform anymore. We have a piece-by-piece approach—we'll make change where we can. We no longer have bigger picture items on our agendas."   11

Domestic partnership, like many other issues that now concern this country, is curiously tied to health care. The word "benefit," after all, is often synonymous with health insurance. And why, many ask, is health insurance coverage tied to marital, couple, or employment status? "If universal health care were available, no one would be forced to say, 'I want to be able to get married to take advantage of my partner's health insurance benefits,'" says Polikoff. "What we ought to do is let every employee designate a person to receive co-benefits. That person could be your sexual partner, best friend, aunt, or sister. Why are we making people's sexual partners more important than   12

others with whom they share their lives? This kind of arrangement would be my way station to uncoupling all of these benefits from marriage and creating a world in which the things
that are now considered components of marriage become social entitlements or can be designated by individuals."

13   Adds Robin Kane, NGLTF's communications director: "We
could wait for universal health care coverage to be enacted by
Congress. We could wait for the Hawaii marriage ruling to
come down and then for every state to battle out whether or
not they'll recognize it. But in the meantime, there are people
who are actually getting health insurance for their partners
through domestic partner benefits."

14   But domestic partnership policies don't hold a candle to
the entitlements that come with marriage. It is already possible to approximate some of the rights granted automatically
to married people—inheritance can be addressed through
wills, the right to make health care decisions through durable
powers of attorney. Compare these with the rights that come
with a marriage license and cannot be exercised by unmarried couples, no matter where they live or what agreements
they have made: the right to joint parenting, through birth or
adoption; the right to file joint income tax returns; legal immigration and residency for partners from other countries;
benefits such as annuities, pensions, and Social Security for
surviving spouses; wrongful death benefits for surviving partners; immunity from having to testify in court against a
spouse.

15   Jane, a health club manager, and Beth, a teacher in suburban New York (not their real names), know the consequences
of not having those rights. Five years ago, Jane gave birth to a
daughter conceived via insemination by an anonymous donor. When a married couple have a baby in this way, the husband is automatically declared the father. Beth's application
to legally adopt their daughter was denied on the grounds
that the couple, who have been together for 18 years, were
not married. "I'm considered her mother by our community,
day care, school, and families," says Beth, "but I have no legal
rights as her mother."

16   Whether or not lesbians and gay men should fight for the
right to marry has been a subject of debate in the gay community for years. In 1989, the lesbian and gay magazine *Outlook*
published opposing articles, "Since When Is Marriage a Path
to Liberation?" by Paula Ettelbrick, and "Why Gay People
Should Seek the Right To Marry," by Thomas B. Stoddard.

Both authors are lawyers who were working for the Lambda Legal Defense and Education Fund at the time. "Marriage runs contrary to two of the primary goals of the lesbian and gay movement: the affirmation of gay identity and culture, and the validation of many forms of relationships," argued Ettelbrick. Answered Stoddard: "The issue is not the desirability of marriage, but rather the desirability of the right to marry."

Even Beth and Jane aren't sure they would exercise that   17
right. "It's for heterosexuals," says Jane. "Our union doesn't need that ceremony. We would only do it for legal protection."

Feminists have long criticized the institution of marriage   18
as a place of oppression, danger, and drudgery for women. Nineteenth-century feminists protested that a woman's legal identity literally disappeared upon marriage. Even in 1969, a New York City organization called the Feminists declared: "All the discriminatory practices against women are patterned and rationalized by this slavery-like practice. We can't destroy the inequities between men and women until we destroy marriage." These days the uneasiness is due to marriage's power as the singular definer of family, a reinforcer of sex roles, and an institution of heterosexual privilege. Karen Lindsey has been thinking about different forms of family for more than 15 years. Her 1981 book, *Friends as Family*, begins, "The traditional family isn't working," and goes on to explore workplace families, "honorary kin," and chosen families. "In my ideal world, there would be no such thing as marriage," she says today. "What there would be is individuals choosing to live together on whatever terms meet their needs, and then appropriate legal connections to address those needs."

"People say that there are all these goodies that go with be-   19
ing married and why shouldn't gay people get to have them," agrees Polikoff. "My vision is one in which the goodies are not tied to marriage."

As feminists, Ninia Baehr and Genora Dancel, two of the   20
Hawaii plaintiffs, are well aware of these arguments. But for them, the decision to marry was an emotional, not a political, one. Baehr, who was the codirector of the women's center at the University of Hawaii when the suit was filed, says: "If I had sat down and planned my career as a feminist years ago, I would never have said, 'The most important thing I can do is legalize marriage for lesbian and gay people.' But the reality is that when I met Genora, I thought, 'My God, she's the one that I've been dreaming about.' I wanted to get married. I

wanted to be able to say at the end of my life that I had loved someone really well for a long time."

21   Hawaii state legislators meanwhile are doing whatever they can to keep Baehr and Dancel and the other two couples from legally tying the knot. Alarmed at the prospect of their state being the first to allow gay marriage, they passed a law last year that explicitly defines marriage as being between a man and a woman. However, this legislation will presumably be subject to the same "compelling interest" requirement as the previous policy, so it's unlikely that the law will change the outcome of the case. A few legislators have proposed amending the state constitution to exclude same-sex marriage—the one sure way around the state supreme court—but these proposals have failed.

22   Although the Hawaii court ruling would apply only to marriages performed in that state, the decision could spark legal chaos all over the country. Lesbian and gay couples will likely flock to Hawaii to marry, then return to their home states and try to file joint tax returns, sign up for spousal health insurance coverage, or adopt children together. Currently every state recognizes marriages performed in other states. Couples who are denied recognition of their legal same-sex marriages granted in Hawaii will have grounds to sue their home states.

23   "There will be litigation in many states for years to come," says Evan Wolfson, cocounsel for the three Hawaii couples and director of the Lambda Legal Defense and Education Fund's Marriage Project. The dozens of expected cases could implicate even the federal government, which relies on the states to determine who is married for purposes of taxes, Social Security benefits, immigration, and other matters. And though all marriage laws are state laws, the question potentially could be settled by the U.S. Supreme Court. If that happened, lawyers for the couples would likely base their arguments on the provision of the U.S. Constitution that requires states to give "full faith and credit" to the lawful marriages of other states.

24   And these other states are keeping an anxious eye on Hawaii. The state legislature of Utah has passed legislation that would refuse recognition of any same-sex marriage performed in another state. South Dakota also tried, but failed, to pass such a law.

25   The ACLU's Matt Coles thinks one significant result of the pending Hawaii ruling will be a proliferation of domestic partnership protections for lesbians and gay men as states

try—by offering spousal equivalent benefits—to avoid the need to recognize gay marriage.

NGLTF's Paras says: "I think we will end up with marriage 26 and domestic partnership as simultaneously existing legal constructs. Marriage will be a huge battle that will mostly be lost for a long time. In the meantime, domestic partnership practices are expanding and will become a much larger body of law and policy. By the time equality finally gets won universally, we'll be in a whole other place about the definition of family, and gay marriage may become almost irrelevant."

V.

CIVIL LIBERTIES AND CIVIL RIGHTS

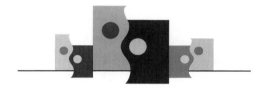

Introduction

A basic premise of *Conversations* is that writing typically emerges from other writing. As a demonstration of that premise, consider the very large body of writing that has emerged from some very basic texts in our political history. Consider, for instance, the words of the First Amendment to the Constitution:

> Congress shall make no law respecting an establishment of religion, or prohibiting the free exercise thereof; or abridging the freedom of speech, or of the press; or the right of the people peaceably to assemble, and to petition the Government for a redress of grievances.

Or consider section one of the Fourteenth Amendment, ratified in 1868:

> All persons born or naturalized in the United States, and subject to the jurisdiction thereof, are citizens of the United States and of the State wherein they reside. No State shall make or enforce any law which shall abridge the privileges or immunities of citizens of the United States; nor shall any State deprive any person of life, liberty, or property, without due process of law; nor deny to any person within its jurisdiction the equal protection of the laws.

Or this fragment from the Declaration of Independence:

> We hold these Truths to be self-evident, that all Men are created equal, that they are endowed by their Creator with certain inalienable Rights, that among these are Life, Liberty, and the Pursuit of Happiness. That to secure these rights, Governments are instituted among Men. . . .

The readings in Part V explore some of the implications of these seminal passages.

Two sets of readings on the issue of censorship are included: one (on pornography) that picks up gender and language concerns from Part II; and another (the case of possible restrictions on electronic communications) that looks forward to Internet issues that are discussed in Part VII of this book.

Is pornography harmful? Should it be censored or restricted? Speaking for the affirmative, many women (as well as men) contend that pornography does indeed have harmful effects, that pornography provides a dangerous "theory" on how to treat women and rape or other forms of misogyny, the "practice." But other people see pornography as neutral in its effects or contend that the First Amendment protects all varieties of speech and writing from censorship. Did the framers of the Constitution intend to protect free speech and a free press in an absolute sense (as Hugo Black and William Douglas argued in a 1957 Supreme Court decision)? Or were the framers speaking only of political speech and writing (as the seven other Supreme Court justices agreed in that same 1957 case)? Is it indeed constitutional to restrict pornography? (After all, we do restrict libel, and we ban cigarette ads on TV and ads aimed at minors, on the grounds of their harmful effects and apolitical content.) And just what is pornography, anyway? Can it be defined in a way that makes restrictions practical, or would such definitions and restrictions undermine artistic and political freedom? The issue of pornography makes for strange bedfellows; it is an issue about which liberals and conservatives disagree among themselves, and it is an issue that has divided feminists. In fact, the argument among feminists is represented in this section by Susan Brownmiller and Andrea Dworkin, who find themselves arguing with Nadine Strossen.

Liberals and conservatives also break ranks over whether or not it would be wise to censor the Internet. Is the Internet being used to purvey pornography? Is pornography on the Internet readily available to children? Should hate speech on the Internet be a prosecutable offense, or is it speech protected by the First Amendment? If we restrict pornography and other forms of communication on the Internet, will that lead to further restrictions on a medium for communication that is apparently open and accessible now? This section of *Conversations* considers these questions by offering an exchange among many Internetters themselves, conducted mostly on the Internet, concerning the wisdom of laws that would censor pornography available through the computer.

The conflict between the individual and society, so apparent in discussions of censorship, is central to culture in the United States because we value both the dignity of the private individual and the importance of public institutions sanctioned through the democratic process. Faced with the dilemma of paying taxes to support a popular war, which he disagreed with, Henry David Thoreau proposed civil disobedience—a private act of personal conscience against "the tyranny of the majority." Later in history, Mahatma Gandhi and Martin Luther King Jr. refined civil disobedience into an effective tactic for achieving public justice and political equality. Were they right to do so? What is civil disobedience anyway? Is it a legitimate political tool or an invitation to anarchy that would destroy the principle of democratic rule? What should people do when "higher laws" put them in conflict with majority rule? What else can a democratic society do except be ruled by a majority? Can such a majority be a "tyranny," or is it the resistance to legitimate, democratic authority that is arrogant and tyrannical? Could civil disobedience even exist in a truly tyrannical society, one without a free press and trial by jury, one in which political minorities disappear in the middle of the night? The selections in this civil disobedience section articulate and debate the question of the legitimacy of civil disobedience, and they also offer a critical context for understanding a central document of civil disobedience and the U.S. civil rights movement: King's "Letter from Birmingham Jail."

Civil disobedience has been a common tactic since the mid-1950s, especially in connection with campaigns to expand the civil rights of African Americans and women. Civil disobedience has also been employed at times by pro-life groups eager to see the practice of abortion restricted in the United States; that is only one indication that the recognition of the right to abortion is inspiring probably the most heated discussion now taking place in our society. Since the Supreme Court in the *Roe* v. *Wade* decision of 1973 legalized abortions performed in the first three months of a pregnancy, a pitched battle has been fought between those absolutely committed to upholding the Supreme Court position and those just as absolutely committed to overturning it. One camp, which sees the developing fetus as only a potential human being, is protective of women's right to privacy and personal freedom; the other camp, which sees the fetus as a human being with the rights of a human being, supports various restrictions on the right to abortion, if not an outright reversal of *Roe* v. *Wade*. In both camps, many people are convinced that only one side or the other can prevail in the abortion debate—that "victory" without substantial compromise can be achieved through the ballot box, rallies, and Supreme Court appointments. Those who seek absolute victory on either side are often so committed to their positions that they are unwilling to participate in reasoned discussions. They often produce more heat than light on the subject.

But other people are convinced that a resolution of the issue of abortion is not just possible but essential. Some pro-choice advocates understand abortion as a morally cloudy act and recognize that the Supreme Court has already placed some restrictions on abortion (i.e., abortion is restricted to the first months of pregnancy). On the other side, many pro-life advocates are confronting the apparent fact that our Constitution permits abortion, whether they like it or not, and are pursuing efforts to persuade people to avoid abortion not because it is illegal but because better contraceptive choices are usually available, if people would only seek them out. Members of both camps, in short, are seeking continuing discussion, reasoned exchange, and mutual respect; and they tend to hold out a hope for negotiated consensus on the matter—incremental progress toward national agreement. When does a fetus become a person? What circumstances justify abortion? Are there ways of reducing abortions and at the same time protecting women's right to privacy (e.g., through improved methods of contraception)? Are any additional restrictions on abortions (*Roe* v. *Wade* restricts abortions to the first three months of pregnancy) sensible? Can those restrictions protect the rights of everyone involved, even as those rights are also somewhat compromised? These matters are confronted in the readings in the section on abortion.

Five other readings follow on another matter of civil rights. In the past decade, members of another minority group—homosexuals—have clamored for additional civil rights, often quite publicly through marches and protests and other highly publicized tactics marshaled by organizations such as Act Up and Queer Nation. Should homosexuals be permitted to serve openly in the military? Should they be protected by fair housing and fair employment practices? Should gay couples be permitted to claim the rights enjoyed by married couples, such as the right to adopt children or share health benefits? Does the AIDS epidemic have implications for civil rights in this country? Those last two questions are taken up in greater detail in the section on same-sex marriage in Part IV, Family Matters, and in the section on combating AIDS in Part VII, Science and Society (for AIDS is an issue that is certainly not limited to the gay community).

No doubt questions like the ones posed in the paragraphs above are being discussed on every campus in the United States this year.

CENSORSHIP I: PORNOGRAPHY

President's Commission on
Obscenity and Pornography

Majority Report

In 1967, Congress by law established an eighteen-member spe-
cial commission (appointed by President Nixon) to study the
impact of obscenity and pornography on American life. After
gathering testimony, reviewing research, and conferring at
length, the commission in 1970 recommended against legisla-
tion that would restrain pornography. A minority of the mem-
bers of the commission, feeling differently, submitted their own
dissenting report. Excerpts from both follow.

1   Discussions of obscenity and pornography in the past have
often been devoid of fact. Popular rhetoric has often contained a variety of estimates of the size of the "smut" industry
and assertions regarding the consequences of the existence of
these materials and exposure to them. Many of these statements, however, have had little anchoring in objective evidence. Within the limits of its time and resources, the
Commission has sought, through staff and contract research,
to broaden the factual basis for future continued discussion.
The Commission is aware that not all issues of concern have
been completely researched nor all questions answered. It
also recognizes that the interpretations of a set of "facts" in
arriving at policy implications may differ even among men of
good will. Nevertheless, the Commission is convinced that on
most issues regarding obscenity and pornography the discussion can be informed by important and often new facts. It
presents its Report, hopeful that it will contribute to this discussion at a new level. . . .

2   Exposure to erotic stimuli appears to have little or no effect
on already established attitudinal commitments regarding
either sexuality or sexual morality. A series of four studies
employing a large array of indicators found practically no significant differences in such attitudes before and after single

or repeated exposures to erotica. One study did find that after exposure persons became more tolerant in reference to other persons' sexual activities although their own sexual standards did not change. One study reported that some persons' attitudes toward premarital intercourse became more liberal after exposure, while other persons' attitudes became more conservative, but another study found no changes in this regard. The overall picture is almost completely a tableau of no significant change. . . .

Statistical studies of the relationship between availability   3
of erotic materials and the rates of sex crimes in Denmark indicate that the increased availability of explicit sexual materials has been accompanied by a decrease in the incidence of sexual crime. Analysis of police records of the same types of sex crimes in Copenhagen during the past 12 years revealed that a dramatic decrease in reported sex crimes occurred during this period and that the decrease coincided with changes in Danish law which permitted wider availability of explicit sexual materials. Other research showed that the decrease in reported sexual offenses cannot be attributed to concurrent changes in the social and legal definitions of sex crimes or in public attitudes toward reporting such crimes to the police, or in police reporting procedures.

Statistical studies of the relationship between the availabil-   4
ity of erotic material and the rates of sex crimes in the United States presents a more complex picture. During the period in which there has been a marked increase in the availability of erotic materials, some specific rates of arrest for sex crimes have increased (e.g., forcible rape) and others have declined (e.g., overall juvenile rates). For juveniles, the overall rate of arrests for sex crimes decreased even though arrests for nonsexual crimes increased by more than 100%. For adults, arrests for sex offenses increased slightly more than did arrests for nonsex offenses. The conclusion is that, for America, the relationship between the availability of erotica and changes in sex crime rates neither proves nor disproves the possibility that availability of erotica leads to crime, but the massive overall increases in sex crimes that have been alleged do not seem to have occurred. . . .

I. Non-Legislative Recommendation

The Commission believes that much of the "problem"   5
regarding materials which depict explicit sexual activity

stems from the inability or reluctance of people in our society to be open and direct in dealing with sexual matters....

6   The Commission believes that accurate, appropriate sex information provided openly and directly through legitimate channels and from reliable sources in healthy contexts can compete successfully with potentially distorted, warped, inaccurate, and unreliable information about clandestine, illegitimate sources; and it believes that the attitudes and orientations toward sex produced by the open communication of appropriate sex information from reliable sources through legitimate channels will be normal and healthy, providing a solid foundation for the basic institutions of our society.

7   The Commission, therefore,...*recommends that a massive sex education effort be launched....* The Commission feels that such a sex education program would provide a powerful positive approach to the problems of obscenity and pornography. By providing accurate and reliable sex information through legitimate sources, it would reduce interest in and dependence upon clandestine and less legitimate sources. By providing healthy attitudes and orientations toward sexual relationships, it would provide better protection for the individual against distorted and warped ideas he may encounter regarding sex. By providing greater ease in talking about sexual matters in appropriate contexts, the shock and offensiveness of encounters with sex would be reduced....

II. Legislative Recommendation

8   *The Commission recommends that federal, state, and local legislation prohibiting the sale, exhibition, or distribution of sexual materials to consenting adults should be repealed....*

Our conclusion is based upon the following considerations:

9   1. Extensive empirical investigation, both by the Commission and by others, provides no evidence that exposure to or use of explicit sexual materials plays a significant role in causation of social or individual harms such as crime, delinquency, sexual or nonsexual deviancy or severe emotional disturbances.... Empirical investigation thus supports the opinion of a substantial majority of persons professionally engaged in the treatment of deviancy, delinquency and antisocial behavior, that exposure to sexually explicit materials has no harmful causal role in these areas. Studies show that a

number of factors, such as disorganized family relationships and unfavorable peer influences, are intimately related to harmful sexual behavior or adverse character development. Exposure to sexually explicit materials, however, cannot be counted as among these determinative factors.

2. On the positive side, explicit sexual materials are sought   10
as a source of entertainment and information by substantial numbers of American adults. At times, these materials also appear to serve to increase and facilitate constructive communication about sexual matters within marriage. The most frequent purchaser of explicit sexual materials is a college-educated, married male, in his thirties or forties, who is of above average socio-economic status. Even where materials are legally available to them, young adults and older adolescents do not constitute an important portion of the purchasers of such materials.

3. Society's attempts to legislate for adults in the area of   11
obscenity have not been successful. Present laws prohibiting the consensual sale or distribution of explicit sexual materials to adults are extremely unsatisfactory in their practical application. The Constitution permits material to be deemed "obscene" for adults only if, as a whole, it appeals to the "prurient" interest of the average person, is "patently offensive" in light of "community standards," and lacks "redeeming social value." These vague and highly subjective aesthetic, psychological and moral tests do not provide meaningful guidance for law enforcement officials, juries or courts. As a result, law is inconsistently and sometimes erroneously applied and the distinctions made by courts between prohibited and permissible materials often appear indefensible. Errors in the application of the law and uncertainty about its scope also cause interference with the communication of constitutionally protected materials.

4. Public opinion in America does not support the imposi-   12
tion of legal prohibitions upon the right of adults to read or see explicit sexual materials. While a minority of Americans favors such prohibitions, a majority of the American people presently are of the view that adults should be legally able to read or see explicit sexual materials if they wish to do so.

5. The lack of consensus among Americans concerning   13
whether explicit sexual materials should be available to adults in our society, and the significant number of adults who wish to have access to such materials, pose serious problems regarding the enforcement of legal prohibitions upon adults, even aside from the vagueness and subjectivity of

present law. Consistent enforcement of even the clearest prohibitions upon consensual adult exposure to explicit sexual
materials would require the expenditure of considerable law
enforcement resources. In the absence of a persuasive demonstration of damage flowing from consensual exposure to
such materials, there seems no justification for thus adding to
the overwhelming tasks already placed upon the law enforcement system. Inconsistent enforcement of prohibitions, on
the other hand, invites discriminatory action based upon considerations not directly relevant to the policy of the law. The
latter alternative also breeds public disrespect for the legal
process.

14 6. The foregoing considerations take on an added significance because of the fact that adult obscenity laws deal in the
realm of speech and communication. Americans deeply value
the right of each individual to determine for himself what
books he wishes to read and what pictures or films he wishes
to see. Our traditions of free speech and press also value and
protect the right of writers, publishers, and booksellers to
serve the diverse interests of the public. The spirit and letter
of our Constitution tell us that government should not seek to
interfere with these rights unless a clear threat of harm
makes that course imperative. Moreover, the possibility of the
misuse of general obscenity statutes prohibiting distributions
of books and films to adults constitutes a continuing threat to
the free communication of ideas among Americans—one of
the most important foundations of our liberties.

15 7. In reaching its recommendation that government
should not seek to prohibit consensual distributions of sexual
materials to adults, the Commission discussed several arguments which are often advanced in support of such legislation. The Commission carefully considered the view that
adult legislation should be retained in order to aid in the protection of young persons from exposure to explicit sexual
materials. We do not believe that the objective of protecting
youth may justifiably be achieved at the expense of denying
adults materials of their choice. It seems to us wholly inappropriate to adjust the level of adult communication to that
considered suitable for children. Indeed, the Supreme Court
has unanimously held that adult legislation premised on this
basis is a clearly unconstitutional interference with liberty. . . .

16 8. The Commission has also taken cognizance of the concern of many people that the lawful distribution of explicit
sexual materials to adults may have a deleterious effect upon
the individual morality of American citizens and upon the

moral climate in America as a whole. This concern appears to flow from a belief that exposure to explicit materials may cause moral confusion which, in turn, may induce antisocial or criminal behavior. As noted above, the Commission has found no evidence to support such a contention. Nor is there evidence that exposure to explicit sexual materials adversely affects character or moral attitudes regarding sex and sexual conduct....

President's Commission on Obscenity and Pornography

Minority Report

Overview

The Commission's majority report is a Magna Carta for the pornographer.... The fundamental "finding" on which the entire report is based is: that "empirical research" has come up with "no reliable evidence to indicate that exposure to explicit sexual materials plays a significant role in the causation of delinquent or criminal behavior among youth or adults." The inference from this statement, i.e., pornography is harmless, is not only insupportable on the slanted evidence presented; it is preposterous. How isolate one factor and say it causes or does not cause criminal behavior? How determine that one book or one film caused one man to commit rape or murder? A man's entire life goes into one criminal act. No one factor can be said to have caused that act. 1

The Commission has deliberately and carefully avoided coming to grips with the basic underlying issue. The government interest in regulating pornography has always related primarily to the prevention of moral corruption and *not* to prevention of overt criminal acts and conduct, or the protection of persons from being shocked and/or offended. The basic question is whether and to what extent society may establish and maintain certain moral standards. If it is conceded that society has a legitimate concern in maintaining 2 moral standards, it follows logically that government has a legitimate interest in at least attempting to protect such standards against any source which threatens them....

3   Sex education, recommended so strongly by the majority, is the panacea for those who advocate license in media. The report suggests sex education, with a plaint for the dearth of instructors and materials. It notes that three schools have used "hard-core pornography" in training potential instructors. The report does not answer the question that comes to mind immediately: Will these instructors not bring the hard-core pornography into the grammar schools? Many other questions are left unanswered: How assure that the instructor's moral or ethical code (or lack of same) will not be communicated to children? Shouldn't parents, not children, be the recipients of sex education courses?

4   Children cannot grow in love if they are trained with pornography. Pornography is loveless; it degrades the human being, reduces him to the level of animal. And if this Commission majority's recommendations are heeded, there will be a glut of pornography for teachers and children.

5   In contrast to the Commission report's amazing statement that public opinion in America does not support the imposition of legal prohibitions upon the consensual distribution of pornography to adults, we find, as a result of public hearings conducted by two of the undersigned in eight cities throughout the country, that the majority of the American people favor tighter controls. Twenty-six out of twenty-seven witnesses at the hearing in New York City expressed concern and asked for remedial measures. Witnesses were a cross section of the community, ranging from members of the judiciary to members of women's clubs. This pattern was repeated in the cities of New Orleans, Indianapolis, Chicago, Salt Lake City, San Francisco, Washington, D.C., and Buffalo.... Additionally, law enforcement officers testifying at the Hill-Link hearings were unanimous in declaring that the problem of obscenity and pornography is a serious one.... We point also to the results of a Gallup poll, published in the summer of 1969. Eighty-five out of every 100 adults interviewed said they favored stricter state and local laws dealing with pornography sent through the mails, and 76 of every 100 wanted stricter laws on the sort of magazines and newspapers available on newsstands....

6   Some have argued that because sex crimes have apparently declined in Denmark while the volume of pornography has increased, we need not be concerned about the potential

effect in our country of this kind of material (because, essentially, of Denmark's benign experience). However two considerations must be noted. First we are a different culture with a greater commitment to the Judeo-Christian tradition; and secondly, we are actually only a year or so behind Denmark in the distribution and sale of pornography. Hardcore written pornography can be purchased anywhere in the U.S. now. Hardcore still pictures and movies can now be purchased over the counter in some cities. Anything can be purchased through the mails. And in a few cities people can attend hardcore pornographic movies. About the only thing we don't have, which Denmark has, are live sex shows. What is most relevant are sex crime statistics in this country, not Denmark . . . :

> *Reported Rapes (verified)*
> Up 116% 1960–69 (absolute increase)
> Up   93% 1960–69 (controlled for Pop. Growth)

> *Rape Arrests*
> Up 56.6% all ages 1960–69
> Up 85.9% males under 18 1960–69

However, it should be stated that conclusively proving causal relationships among social science type variables is extremely difficult if not impossible. Among adults whose life histories have included much exposure to pornography it is nearly impossible to disentangle the literally hundreds of causal threads or chains that contributed to their later adjustment or maladjustment. Because of the extreme complexity of the problem and the uniqueness of the human experience it is doubtful that we will ever have absolutely convincing scientific proof that pornography is or isn't harmful. And the issue isn't restricted to, "Does pornography cause or contribute to sex crimes?" The issue has to do with how pornography affects or influences the individual in his total relationship to members of the same as well as opposite sex, children and adults, with all of its ramifications.

Susan Brownmiller

Let's Put Pornography
Back in the Closet

*Susan Brownmiller is a journalist, novelist, women's rights
activist, and a founder of Women against Pornography. Her
book* Against Our Will: Men, Women, and Rape, *published in
1975, articulates a position on pornography that has been
developed by later feminists. The following essay originally
appeared in* Newsday, *a Long Island newspaper, in 1979 and a
year later in* Take Back the Night, *a collection of essays against
pornography.*

1   Free speech is one of the great foundations on which our
democracy rests. I am old enough to remember the Hollywood Ten, the screenwriters who went to jail in the late 1940s
because they refused to testify before a congressional committee about their political affiliations. They tried to use the
First Amendment as a defense, but they went to jail because
in those days there were few civil liberties lawyers around
who cared to champion the First Amendment right to free
speech, when the speech concerned the Communist Party.

2   The Hollywood Ten were correct in claiming the First
Amendment. Its high purpose is the protection of unpopular
ideas and political dissent. In the dark, cold days of the 1950s,
few civil libertarians were willing to declare themselves First
Amendment absolutists. But in the brighter, though frantic,
days of the 1960s, the principle of protecting unpopular political speech was gradually strengthened.

3   It is fair to say now that the battle has largely been won.
Even the American Nazi Party has found itself the beneficiary
of the dedicated, tireless work of the American Civil Liberties
Union. But—and please notice the quotation marks coming
up—"To equate the free and robust exchange of ideas and
political debate with commercial exploitation of obscene
material demeans the grand conception of the First Amendment and its high purposes in the historic struggle for freedom. It is a misuse of the great guarantees of free speech and
free press."

4   I didn't say that, although I wish I had, for I think the words
are thrilling. Chief Justice Warren Burger said it in 1973, in the
United States Supreme Court's majority opinion in *Miller* v.
California. During the same decades that the right to political

free speech was being strengthened in the courts, the nation's obscenity laws also were undergoing extensive revision.

It's amazing to recall that in 1934 the question of whether   5
James Joyce's *Ulysses* should be banned as pornographic actually went before the Court. The battle to protect *Ulysses* as a work of literature with redeeming social value was won. In later decades, Henry Miller's *Tropic* books, *Lady Chatterley's Lover* and the *Memoirs of Fanny Hill* also were adjudged not obscene. These decisions have been important to me. As the author of *Against Our Will*, a study of the history of rape that does contain explicit sexual material, I shudder to think how my book would have fared if James Joyce, D. H. Lawrence and Henry Miller hadn't gone before me.

I am not a fan of *Chatterley* or the *Tropic* books, I should   6
quickly mention. They are not to my literary taste, nor do I think they represent female sexuality with any degree of accuracy. But I would hardly suggest that we ban them. Such a suggestion wouldn't get very far anyway. The battle to protect these books is ancient history. Time does march on, quite methodically. What, then, is unlawfully obscene, and what does the First Amendment have to do with it?

In the Miller case of 1973 (not Henry Miller, by the way, but   7
a porn distributor who sent unsolicited stuff through the mails), the Court came up with new guidelines that it hoped would strengthen obscenity laws by giving more power to the states. What it did in actuality was throw everything into confusion. It set up a three-part test by which materials can be adjudged obscene. The materials are obscene if they depict patently offensive, hard-core sexual conduct; lack serious scientific, literary, artistic or political value; and appeal to the prurient interest of an average person—as measured by contemporary community standards.

"Patently offensive," "prurient interest" and "hard-core"   8
are indeed words to conjure with. "Contemporary community standards" are what we're trying to redefine. The feminist objection to pornography is not based on prurience, which the dictionary defines as lustful, itching desire. We are not opposed to sex and desire, with or without the itch, and we certainly believe that explicit sexual material has its place in literature, art, science and education. Here we part company rather swiftly with old-line conservatives who don't want sex education in the high schools, for example.

No, the feminist objection to pornography is based on our   9
belief that pornography represents hatred of women, that pornography's intent is to humiliate, degrade and dehumanize

the female body for the purpose of erotic stimulation and pleasure. We are unalterably opposed to the presentation of the female body being stripped, bound, raped, tortured, mutilated and murdered in the name of commercial entertainment and free speech.

10 These images, which are standard pornographic fare, have nothing to do with the hallowed right of political dissent. They have everything to do with the creation of a cultural climate in which a rapist feels he is merely giving in to a normal urge and a woman is encouraged to believe that sexual masochism is healthy, liberated fun. Justice Potter Stewart once said about hard-core pornography, "You know it when you see it," and that certainly used to be true. In the good old days, pornography looked awful. It was cheap and sleazy, and there was no mistaking it for art.

11 Nowadays, since the porn industry has become a multimillion dollar business, visual technology has been employed in its service. Pornographic movies are skillfully filmed and edited, pornographic still shots using the newest tenets of good design artfully grace the covers of *Hustler, Penthouse* and *Playboy,* and the public—and the courts—are sadly confused.

12 The Supreme Court neglected to define "hard-core" in the Miller decision. This was a mistake. If "hard-core" refers only to explicit sexual intercourse, then that isn't good enough. When women or children or men—no matter how artfully— are shown tortured or terrorized in the service of sex, that's obscene. And "patently offensive," I would hope, to our "contemporary community standards."

13 Justice William O. Douglas wrote in his dissent to the Miller case that no one is "compelled to look." This is hardly true. To buy a paper at the corner newsstand is to subject oneself to a forcible immersion in pornography, to be demeaned by an array of dehumanized, chopped-up parts of the female anatomy, packaged like cuts of meat at the supermarket. I happen to like my body and I work hard at the gym to keep it in good shape, but I am embarrassed for my body and for the bodies of all women when I see the fragmented parts of us so frivolously, and so flagrantly, displayed.

14 Some constitutional theorists (Justice Douglas was one) have maintained that any obscenity law is a serious abridgement of free speech. Others (and Justice Earl Warren was one) have maintained that the First Amendment was never intended to protect obscenity. We live quite compatibly with a host of free-speech abridgements. There are restraints against false and misleading advertising or statements—shouting

"fire" without cause in a crowded movie theater, etc.—that do not threaten, but strengthen, our societal values. Restrictions on the public display of pornography belong in this category.

The distinction between permission to publish and permission to display publicly is an essential one and one which I think consonant with First Amendment principles. Justice Burger's words which I quoted above support this without question. We are not saying "Smash the presses" or "Ban the bad ones," but simply "Get the stuff out of our sight." Let the legislatures decide—using realistic and humane contemporary community standards—what can be displayed and what cannot. The courts, after all, will be the final arbiters.

John Irving

Pornography and the New Puritans

If you saw the film The World According to Garp, *you have had some experience with the work of John Irving (born 1942), for he is the author of the novel on which the film was based as well as six other novels. He contributed the following essay to the* New York Times Book Review *in March 1992. Notice that a response to the article, also printed in the* Times Book Review, *is reprinted right after it.*

These are censorial times. I refer to the pornography victims' compensation bill, now under consideration by the Senate Judiciary Committee—that same bunch of wise men who dispatched such clearheaded, objective jurisprudence in the Clarence Thomas hearings. I can't wait to see what they're going to do with this maladroit proposal. The bill would encourage victims of sexual crimes to bring civil suits against publishers and distributors of material that is "obscene or constitutes child pornography"—*if* they can prove that the material was "a substantial cause of the offense," *and if* the publisher or distributor should have "foreseen" that such material created an "unreasonable risk of such a crime." If this bill passes, it will be the first piece of legislation to give credence to the unproven theory that sexually explicit material actually *causes* sexual crimes.

2   At the risk of sounding old-fashioned, I'm still pretty sure that rape and child molestation predate erotic books and pornographic magazines and X-rated videocassettes. I also remember the report of the two-year, $2 million President's Commission on Obscenity and Pornography (1970), which concluded there was "no reliable evidence...that exposure to explicit sexual material plays a significant role in the causation of delinquent or criminal sexual behavior." In 1986, not satisfied with that conclusion, the Meese commission on pornography and the Surgeon General's conference on pornography also failed to establish such a link. Now, here they go again.

3   This time, it's Republican Senators Mitch McConnell of Kentucky, Charles Grassley of Iowa and Strom Thurmond of South Carolina; I can't help wondering if they read much. Their charmless bill is a grave mistake for several reasons; for starters, it's morally reprehensible to shift the responsibility for any sexual crime onto a third party—namely, *away* from the actual perpetrator.

4   And then, of course, there's the matter of the bill running counter to the spirit of the First Amendment of the United States Constitution; this bill is a piece of back-door censorship, plain and simple. Moreover, since the laws on obscenity differ from state to state, and no elucidation of the meaning of obscenity is presented in the bill, how are the publishers or distributors to know in advance if their material is actionable or not? It is my understanding, therefore, that the true intent of the bill is to make the actual creators of this material think very conservatively—that is, when their imaginations turn to sex and violence.

5   I recall that I received a lot of unfriendly mail in connection with a somewhat explicit scene in my novel *The World According to Garp*, wherein a selfish young man loses part of his anatomy while enjoying oral sex in a car. (I suppose I've always had a fear of rear-end collisions.) But thinking back about that particular hate mail, I don't recall a single letter from a young woman saying that she intended to rush out and *do* this to someone; and in the 14 years since that novel's publication, in more than 35 foreign languages, no one who actually *has done* this to someone has written to thank me for giving her the idea. Boy, am I lucky!

6   In a brilliant article on the Op-Ed page of *The New York Times*, Teller, of those marvelous magicians Penn & Teller,

had this to say about the pornography victims' compensation bill: "The advocates of this bill seem to think that if we stop showing rape in movies people will stop committing it in real life. Anthropologists call this 'magical thinking.' It's the same impulse that makes people stick pins in voodoo dolls, hoping to cripple an enemy. It feels logical, but it does not work." (For those of you who've seen these two magicians and are wondering which is Penn and which is Teller, Teller is the one who never talks. He *writes* very well, however.) "It's a death knell for creativity, too," Teller writes. "Start punishing make-believe, and those gifted with imagination will stop sharing it." He adds, "We will enter an intellectual era even more insipid than the one we live in."

Now *there's* a scary idea! I remember when the film version 7 of Günter Grass's novel *The Tin Drum* was banned in Canada. I always assumed it was the eel scene that offended the censors, but I don't know. In those days, a little naked sex—in the conventional position—was permissible, but unpleasant suggestiveness with eels was clearly going too far. But now, in the light of this proposed pornography victims' compensation bill, is there any evidence to suggest that there have been *fewer* hellish incidents of women being force-fed eels in Canada than in those countries where the film was available? Somehow, I doubt it. I know that they're out there—those guys who want to force-feed eels to women—but I suspect they're going to do what they're going to do, unaided by books or films. The point is: let's do something about *them*, instead of trying to control what they read or see.

It dismays me how some of my feminist friends are hot to 8 ban pornography. I'm sorry that they have such short memories. It wasn't very long ago when a book as innocent and valuable as *Our Bodies, Ourselves* was being banned by school boards and public libraries across the country. The idea of this good book was that women should have access to detailed information about their bodies and their health, yet the so-called feminist ideology behind the book was thought to be subversive; indeed, it was (at that time) deplored. But many writers and writers' organizations (like PEN) wrote letters to those school boards and those public libraries. I can't speak to the overall effectiveness of these letters in regard to reinstating the book, but I'm aware that some of the letters worked; I wrote several of those letters. Now here are some of my old friends, telling me that attitudes toward rape and child molestation can be changed only if we remove the offensive *ideas*. Once again, it's ideology that's being banned. And although the movement to ban pornography is especially self-righteous, it looks like blacklisting to me.

9   Fascism has enjoyed many name changes, but it usually amounts to banning something you dislike and can't control. Take abortion, for example. I think groups should have to apply for names; if the Right to Life people had asked me, I'd have told them to find a more fitting label for themselves. It's morally inconsistent to manifest such concern for the poor fetus in a society that shows absolutely no pity for the poor child after it's born.

10   I'm also not so sure that these so-called Right to Lifers are as fired up about those fetuses as they say. I suspect what really makes them sore is the idea of women having sex and somehow not having to *pay* for it—pay in the sense of suffering all the way through an unwanted pregnancy. I believe this is part of the loathing for promiscuity that has always fueled those Americans who feel that a life of common decency is slipping from their controlling grasp. This notion is reflected in the unrealistic hope of those wishful thinkers who tell us that sexual abstinence is an alternative to wearing a condom. But I say how about *carrying* a condom, just in case you're moved to *not* abstain?

11   No one is coercing women into having abortions, but the Right to Lifers want to coerce women into having babies; that's why the pro-choice people are well named. It's unfortunate, however, that a few of my pro-choice friends think that the pornography victims' compensation bill is a good idea. I guess that they're really not entirely pro-choice. They want the choice to reproduce or not, but they *don't* want too broad a choice of things to read and see; they know what *they* want to read and see, and they expect other people to be content with what they want. This sounds like a Right to Life idea to me.

12   Most feminist groups, despite their vital advocacy of full enforcement of laws against violence to women and children, seem opposed to Senate Bill 1521. As of this writing, both the National Organization for Women in New York State and in California have written to the Senate Judiciary Committee in opposition to the bill, although the Los Angeles chapter of NOW states that it has "no position." I admit it is perverse of me even to imagine what Tammy Bruce thinks about the pornography victims' compensation bill; I hope Ms. Bruce is not such a loose cannon as she appears, but she has me worried. Ms. Bruce is president of L.A. NOW, and she has lately distinguished herself with two counts of knee-jerk overreaction. Most recently, she found the Academy of Motion Picture Arts

and Sciences to be guilty of an "obvious exhibition of sexism" in not nominating Barbra Streisand for an Oscar for best director. Well, maybe. Ms. Streisand's other talents have not been entirely overlooked; I meekly submit that the academy might have found *The Prince of Tides* lacking in directorial merit—it wouldn't be the first I've heard of such criticism. (Ms. Bruce says the L.A. chapter received "unrelenting calls" from NOW members who were riled up at the perceived sexism.)

Most readers will remember Tammy Bruce for jumping all 13
over that nasty novel by Bret Easton Ellis. To refresh our memories: Simon & Schuster decided at the 11th hour not to publish *American Psycho* after concluding that its grisly content was in "questionable taste." Now please don't get excited and think I'm going to call that censorship; that was merely a breach of contract. And besides, Simon & Schuster has a right to its own opinion of what questionable taste is. *People* magazine tells us that Judith Regan, a vice president and senior editor at Simon & Schuster, recently had a book idea, which she pitched to Madonna. "My idea was for her to write a book of her sexual fantasies, her thoughts, the meanderings of her erotic mind," Ms. Regan said. The pity is, Madonna hasn't delivered. And according to Mitchell Fink, author of the Insider column for *People,* "Warner Books confirmed it is talking about a book—no word on what kind—with Madonna." I don't know Madonna, but maybe she thought the Simon & Schuster book idea was in questionable taste. Simon & Schuster, clearly, subscribes to more than one opinion of what questionable taste *is.*

But only two days after Mr. Ellis's book was dropped by 14
Simon & Schuster, Sonny Mehta, president of Alfred A. Knopf and Vintage Books, bought *American Psycho,* which was published in March 1991. Prior to the novel's publication, Ms. Bruce called for a boycott of all Knopf and Vintage titles—except for books by feminist authors, naturally—until *American Psycho* was withdrawn from publication (it wasn't), or until the end of 1991. To the charge of censorship, Ms. Bruce declared that she was *not* engaged in it; she sure fooled me.

But Ms. Bruce wasn't alone in declaring what *wasn't* cen- 15
sorship, nor was she alone in her passion; she not only condemned Mr. Ellis's novel—she condemned its availability. And not only the book itself *but its availability* were severely taken to task in the very pages in which I now write. In December 1990—three months *before American Psycho* was published, and at the urging of *The Book Review*—Roger Rosenblatt settled Mr. Ellis's moral hash in a piece of writing prissy enough

to please Jesse Helms. According to Mr. Rosenblatt, Jesse Helms has never engaged in censorship, either. For those of us who remain improperly educated in regard to what censorship actually *is*, Mr. Rosenblatt offers a blanket definition. "Censorship is when a government burns your manuscript, smashes your presses and throws you in jail," he says.

16   Well, as much as I may identify with Mr. Rosenblatt's literary taste, I'm of the opinion that there are a few forms of censorship more subtle than that, and Mr. Rosenblatt has engaged in one of them. If you slam a book when it's published, that's called book reviewing, but if you write about a book three months in advance of its publication and your conclusion is "don't buy it," your intentions are more censorial than critical.

17   And it *is* censorship when the writer of such perceived trash is not held *as* accountable as the book's publisher; the pressure that was brought to bear on Mr. Mehta was totally censorial. *The Book Review* is at its most righteous in abusing Mr. Mehta, who is described as "clearly as hungry for a killing as Patrick Bateman." (For those of you who don't know Mr. Ellis's book, Patrick Bateman is the main character and a serial killer.) Even as reliable a fellow as the editorial director of *Publisher's Weekly*, John F. Baker, described *American Psycho* as a book that "does transcend the boundaries of what is acceptable in mainstream publishing."

18   It's the very idea of making or keeping publishing "acceptable" that gives *me* the shivers, because that's the same idea that lurks behind the pornography victims' compensation bill—making the *publisher* (not the perpetrator of the crime or the writer of the pornography) responsible for what's "acceptable." If you want to bash Bret Easton Ellis for what he's written, go ahead and bash him. But when you presume to tell Sonny Mehta, or any other publisher, what he can or can't—or should or shouldn't—*publish*, that's when you've stepped into dangerous territory. In fact, that's when you're knee-deep in blacklisting, and you ought to know better—all of you.

19   Mr. Rosenblatt himself actually says, "No one argues that a publishing house hasn't the right to print what it wants. We fight for that right. But not everything is a right. At some point, someone in authority somewhere has to look at Mr. Ellis's rat and call the exterminator." Now this is interesting, and perhaps worse than telling Sonny Mehta what he should

or shouldn't publish—because that's exactly what Mr. Rosenblatt *is* doing while he's *saying* that he isn't.

Do we remember that tangent of the McCarran-Walter Act   20
of 1952, that finally defunct business about ideological exclusion? That was when we kept someone from coming into our country because we perceived that the person had *ideas* that were in conflict with the "acceptable" ideas of our country. Under this act of exclusion, writers as distinguished as Graham Greene and Gabriel Garcia Márquez were kept out of the United States. Well, when we attack what a publisher has the right to publish, we are simply applying the old ideological exclusion act at home. Of all people, those of us in the idea business should know better than that.

As for the pornography victims' compensation bill, the vote   21
in the Senate Judiciary Committee will be close. As of this writing, seven senators have publicly indicated their support of the bill; they need only one more vote to pass the bill out of committee. Friends at PEN tell me that the committee has received a lot of letters from women saying that support of the bill would in some way "make up for" the committee's mishandling of the Clarence Thomas hearings. Some women are putting the decision to support Justice Thomas alongside the decision to find William Kennedy Smith innocent of rape; these women think that a really strong antipornography bill will make up for what they perceive to be the miscarriage of justice in both cases.

The logic of this thinking is more than a little staggering.   22
What would these women think if lots of men were to write the committee and say that because Mike Tyson has been found guilty of rape, what we need is *more* pornography to make up for what's happened to Iron Mike? This would make a lot of sense, wouldn't it?

I conclude that these are not only censorial times; these are   23
stupid times. However, there is some hope that opposition to Senate Bill 1521 is mounting. The committee met on March 12 but the members didn't vote on the bill. Discussion was brief, yet encouraging. Colorado Senator Hank Brown told his colleagues that there are serious problems with the legislation; he should be congratulated for his courageous decision to oppose the other Republicans on the committee, but he should also be encouraged not to accept any compromise proposal. Ohio Senator Howard Metzenbaum suggested that imposing third-party liability on producers and distributors of books, magazines, movies and recordings raises the question

of whether the bill shouldn't be amended to cover the firearms and liquor industries as well.

24   It remains to be seen if the committee members will resist the temptation to *fix* the troubled bill. I hope they will understand that the bill cannot be fixed because it is based on an erroneous premise—namely, that publishers or distributors should be held liable for the acts of criminals. But what is important for us to recognize, even if this lame bill is amended out of existence or flat-out defeated, is that *new* antipornography legislation will be proposed.

25   Do we remember Nancy Reagan's advice to would-be drug users? ("Just say no.") As applied to drug use, Mrs. Reagan's advice is feeble in the extreme. But writers and other members of the literary community *should* just say no to censorship in any and every form. Of course, it will always be the most grotesque example of child pornography that will be waved in front of our eyes by the Good Taste Police. If we're opposed to censorship, they will say, are we in favor of filth like this?

26   No; we are not in favor of child pornography if we say no to censorship. If we disapprove of reinstating public hangings, that doesn't mean that we want all the murderers to be set free. No writer or publisher or *reader* should accept censorship in any form; fundamental to our freedom of expression is that each of us has a right to decide what is obscene and what isn't.

27   But lest you think I'm being paranoid about the iniquities and viciousness of our times, I'd like you to read a description of Puritan times. It was written in 1837—more than 150 years ago—and it describes a scene in a Puritan community in Massachusetts that you must imagine taking place more than 350 years ago. This is from a short story by Nathaniel Hawthorne called "Endicott and the Red Cross," which itself was written more than 10 years before Hawthorne wrote *The Scarlet Letter*. This little story contains the germ of the idea for that famous novel about a woman condemned by Puritan justice to wear the letter A on her breast. But Hawthorne, obviously, had been thinking about the iniquities and viciousness of early New England morality for many years.

28   Please remember, as you read what Nathaniel Hawthorne thought of the Puritans, that the Puritans are not dead and gone. We have many new Puritans in our country today; they are as dangerous to freedom of expression as the old Puritans ever were. An especially sad thing is, a few of these new Puritans are formerly liberal-thinking feminists.

"In close vicinity to the sacred edifice [the meeting-house]   29
appeared that important engine of Puritanic authority, the
whipping-post—with the soil around it well trodden by the
feet of evil doers, who had there been disciplined. At one corner of the meeting-house was the pillory, and at the other the
stocks; . . . the head of an Episcopalian and suspected Catholic
was grotesquely incased in the former machine; while a fel-
low-criminal, who had boisterously quaffed a health to the
king, was confined by the legs in the latter. Side by side, on the
meeting-house steps, stood a male and a female figure. The
man was a tall, lean, haggard personification of fanaticism,
bearing on his breast this label,—A WANTON GOSPELLER,—
which betokened that he had dared to give interpretations of
Holy Writ unsanctioned by the infallible judgment of the civil
and religious rulers. His aspect showed no lack of zeal . . . even
at the stake. The woman wore a cleft stick on her tongue, in
appropriate retribution for having wagged that unruly member against the elders of the church; and her countenance and
gestures gave much cause to apprehend that, the moment the
stick should be removed, a repetition of the offence would
demand new ingenuity in chastising it.

"The above-mentioned individuals had been sentenced to   30
undergo their various modes of ignominy, for the space of
one hour at noonday. But among the crowd were several
whose punishment would be life-long; some, whose ears had
been cropped, like those of puppy dogs; others, whose cheeks
had been branded with the initials of their misdemeanors;
one, with his nostrils slit and seared; and another, with a hal-
ter about his neck, which he was forbidden ever to take off, or
to conceal beneath his garments. Methinks he must have
been grievously tempted to affix the other end of the rope to
some convenient beam or bough. There was likewise a young
woman, with no mean share of beauty, whose doom was to
wear the letter A on the breast of her gown, in the eyes of all
the world and her own children. And even her own children
knew what that initial signified. Sporting with her infamy, the
lost and desperate creature had embroidered the fatal token
in scarlet cloth, with golden thread and the nicest art of nee-
dlework; so that the capital A might have been thought to
mean Admirable, or anything rather than Adulteress.

"Let not the reader argue, from any of these evidences of   31
iniquity, that the times of the Puritans were more vicious than
our own."

In my old-fashioned opinion, Mr. Hawthorne sure got that   32
right.

Andrea Dworkin
Reply to John Irving

As she notes in the following reply, Andrea Dworkin (born 1947) has written (with University of Michigan law professor Catherine MacKinnon) antipornography ordinances for Minneapolis, Indianapolis, and other cities. (The ordinances later were overturned by the courts.) A successful and controversial essayist and fiction writer, she has also written Pornography: Men Possessing Women *(1988) and* Pornography and Civil Rights *(1988), both of which argue in favor of the kinds of laws that she advocates.*

To the Editor:

1   As a woman determined to destroy the pornography industry, a writer of 10 published books and someone who reads, perhaps I should be the one to tell John Irving ("Pornography and the New Puritans," March 29) who the new Puritan is. The old Puritans wouldn't like her very much; but then, neither does Mr. Irving.

2   I am 45 years old now. When I was a teen-ager, I baby-sat. In any middle-class home one could always find the dirty books—on the highest shelf, climbing toward God, usually behind a parched potted plant. The books themselves were usually "Ulysses," "Tropic of Cancer" or "Lady Chatterley's Lover." They always had as a preface or afterword the text of an obscenity decision in which the book was exonerated and art extolled. Or a lawyer would stand in for the court to tell us that through his mighty efforts law had finally vindicated a persecuted genius.

3   Even at 15 and 16, I noticed something strange about the special intersection of art, law and sex under the obscenity rubric: some men punished other men for producing or publishing writing that caused arousal in (presumably) still other men. Although Mrs. Grundy got the blame, women didn't make these laws or enforce them or sit on juries to deliberate guilt or innocence. This was a fight among men—but about what?

4   Meanwhile, my life as a woman in prefeminist times went on. This means that I thought I was a human being with rights. But before I was much over 18, I had been sexually assaulted three times. Did I report these assaults (patriarchy's first question, because surely the girl must be lying)?

When I was 9, I told my parents. To protect me, for better 5
or worse, they did not call the police.

The second time, beaten as well as raped, I told no one. I 6
was working for a peace group, and I heard jokes about rape
day in and day out. What do you tell the draft board when
they ask you if you would kill a Nazi who was going to rape
your sister? "I'd tell my sister to have a good time" was the
answer of choice.

The third time, I was 18, a freshman in college, and I had 7
been arrested for taking part in a sit-in outside the United
Nations to protest the Vietnam War. It was February of 1965.
This time, my experience was reported in *The New York Times,*
newspapers all around the world and on television: girl in
prison—New York's notorious Women's House of Detention—
says she was brutalized by two prison doctors. Forced entry
with a speculum—for 15 days I had vaginal bleeding, a vagina
so bruised and ripped that my stone-cold family doctor burst
into tears when he examined me.

I came out of the Women's House of Detention mute. 8
Speech depends on believing you can make yourself understood: a community of people will recognize the experience
in the words you use and they will care. You also have to be
able to understand what happened to you enough to convey
it to others. I lost speech. I was hurt past what I had words
for. I lived out on the streets for several days, not having a
bed of my own, still bleeding; and finally spoke because
Grace Paley convinced me that she would understand and
care. Then I spoke a lot. A grand jury investigated. Colum-
nists indicted the prison. But neither of the prison doctors
was charged with sexual assault or sexual battery. In fact, no
one ever mentioned sexual assault. The grand jury concluded
that the prison was fine. In despair, I left the country—to be a
writer, my human dream.

A year later I came back. I have since discovered that what 9
happened to me is common: homeless, poor, still sexually
traumatized, I learned to trade sex for money. I spent a lot of
years out on the street, living hand to mouth, these New York
streets and other streets in other hard cities. I thought I was a
real tough woman, and I was: tough-calloused; tough-numb;
tough-desperate; tough-scared; tough-hungry; tough-beaten
by men often; tough-done it every which way including up.
All of my colleagues who fight pornography with me know
about this. I know about the lives of women in pornography
because I lived the life. So have many feminists who fight
pornography. Freedom looks different when you are the one

it is being practiced on. It's his, not yours. Speech is different, too. Those sexy expletives are the hate words he uses on you while he is using you. Your speech is an inchoate protest never voiced.

10   In my work, fiction and nonfiction, I've tried to voice the protest against a power that is dead weight on you, fist and penis organized to keep you quiet. I would do virtually anything to get women out of prostitution and pornography, which is mass-produced, technologized prostitution. With pornography, a woman can still be sold after the beatings, the rapes, the pain, the humiliation have killed her. I write for her, on behalf of her. I know her. I have come close to being her.

11   I read a lot of books. None of them ever told me the truth about what happens to women until feminists started writing and publishing in this wave, over these last 22 years. Over and over, male writers consider prostituted women "speech"— their speech, their right. Without this exploitation, published for profit, the male writer feels censored. The woman lynched naked on a tree, or restrained with ropes and a ball gag in her mouth, has what? Freedom of what?

12   I lost my ability to speak—became mute—a second time in my life. I've written about being a battered wife: I was beaten and tortured over a period of a few years. Amnesty International never showed up. Toward the end, I lost all speech. Words were useless to the likes of me. I had run away and asked for help—from friends, neighbors, the police—and had been turned away many times. My words didn't seem to mean anything, or it was O.K. to torture me.

13   Taken once by my husband to a doctor when hurt, I risked asking for help. The doctor said he could write me a prescription for Valium or have me committed. The neighbors heard the screaming, but no one did anything. So what are words? I have always been good with them, but never good enough to be believed or helped. No, there were no shelters then.

14   But I am talking about speech: it isn't easy for me. I come to speech from under a man, tortured and tormented. What he did to me took away everything; he was the owner of everything. He hurt all the words out of me, and no one would listen anyway. I come to speech from under the brutalities of thousands of men. For me, the violence of marriage was worse than the violence of prostitution; but this is no choice. Men act out pornography. They have acted it out on me. Women's lives become pornography. Mine did. And so for 20 years now I have been looking for the words to say what I know.

But maybe liberal men—so open-minded and intellectually   15
curious—can't find the books that would teach them about
women's real lives. Maybe, while John Irving and PEN are
defending *Hustler*, snuff films and *Deep Throat*, the direct
product of the coercion of Linda Marchiano, political dissi-
dents like myself are anathema—especially to the free-speech
fetishists—not because the publishing industry punishes
prudes but because dissenters who mean it, who stand
against male power over women, are pariahs.

Maybe Mr. Irving and others do not know that in the world   16
of women, pornography is the real geography of how men use
us and torment us and hate us.

With Catharine A. MacKinnon, I drafted the first civil law   17
against pornography. It held pornographers accountable for
what they do: they traffic women (contravening the United
Nations Universal Declaration of Human Rights and the Convention on the Elimination of All Forms of Discrimination
Against Women); they eroticize inequality in a way that materially promotes rape, battery, maiming and bondage; they
make a product that they know dehumanizes, degrades and
exploits women; they hurt women to make the pornography,
and then consumers use the pornography in assaults both
verbal and physical.

Mr. Irving refers to a scene in *The World According to Garp*   18
in which a woman bites off a man's penis in a car when the
car is accidentally rammed from behind. This, he says, did
not cause women to bite off men's penises in cars. I have written (in my novels, *Ice and Fire* and *Mercy,* and in the story
"The New Woman's Broken Heart") about a woman raped by
two men sequentially, the first aggressor routed by the second
one, to whom the woman, near dead, submits; he bites
viciously and repeatedly into her genitals. When I wrote it,
someone had already done it—to me. Mr. Irving uses his
imagination for violent farce. My imagination can barely
grasp my real life. The violence, as Mr. Irving must know, goes
from men to women.

Women write to me because of our shared experiences. In   19
my books they find their lives—until now beyond the reach of
language. A letter to me dated March 11 says in part: "The
abuse was quite sadistic—it involved bestiality, torture, the
making of pornography. Sometimes, when I think about my
life, I'm not sure why I'm alive, but I'm always sure about why
I do what I do, the feminist theory and the antipornography
activism." Another letter, dated March 13, says: "It was only
when I was almost [raped] to pieces that I broke down and

learned to hate.... I have never stopped resenting the loss of innocence that occurred the day I learned to hate."

20   Male liberals seem to think we fight pornography to protect sexual innocence, but we have none to protect. The innocence we want is the innocence that lets us love. People need dignity to love.

21   Mr. Irving quoted Hawthorne's condemnation of Puritan orthodoxy in the short story "Endicott and the Red Cross"—a graphic description of public punishments of women: bondage, branding, maiming, lynching. Today pornographers do these things to women, and the public square is a big place— every newsstand and video store. A photograph shields rape and torture for profit. In defending pornography as if it were speech, liberals defend the new slavers. The only fiction in pornography is the smile on the woman's face.

Nadine Strossen

The Perils of Pornophobia

Nadine Strossen's essay on pornography appeared in The Humanist *in the spring of 1995. Strossen, a member of the faculty at New York Law School, is president of the American Civil Liberties Union, an organization famous for defending the constitutional rights of U.S. citizens. Her essay was adapted from her 1995 book* Defending Pornography: Free Speech, Sex, and the Fight for Women's Rights.

1   In 1992, in response to a complaint, officials at Pennsylvania State University unceremoniously removed Francisco de Goya's masterpiece, *The Nude Maja*, from a classroom wall. The complaint had not been lodged by Jesse Helms or some irate member of the Christian Coalition. Instead, the complainant was a feminist English professor who protested that the eighteenth-century painting of a recumbent nude woman made her and her female students "uncomfortable."

2   This was not an isolated incident. At the University of Arizona at Tucson, feminist students physically attacked a graduate student's exhibit of photographic self-portraits. Why?

The artist had photographed *herself* in her *underwear.* And at the University of Michigan Law School feminist students who had organized a conference on "Prostitution: From Academia to Activism" removed a feminist-curated art exhibition held in conjunction with the conference. Their reason? Conference speakers had complained that a composite videotape containing interviews of working prostitutes was "pornographic" and therefore unacceptable.

What is wrong with this picture? Where have they come 3
from—these feminists who behave like religious conservatives, who censor works of art because they deal with sexual themes? Have not feminists long known that censorship is a dangerous weapon which, if permitted, would inevitably be turned against them? Certainly that was the irrefutable lesson of the early women's rights movement, when Margaret Sanger, Mary Ware Dennett, and other activists were arrested, charged with "obscenity" and prosecuted for distributing educational pamphlets about sex and birth control. Theirs was a struggle for freedom of sexual expression and full gender equality, which they understood to be mutually reinforcing.

Theirs was also a lesson well understood by the second 4
wave of feminism in the 1970s, when writers such as Germaine Greer, Betty Friedan, and Betty Dodson boldly asserted that women had the right to be free from discrimination not only in the workplace and in the classroom but in the bedroom as well. Freedom from limiting, conventional stereotypes concerning female sexuality was an essential aspect of what we then called "women's liberation." Women should not be seen as victims in their sexual relations with men but as equally assertive partners, just as capable of experiencing sexual pleasure.

But it is a lesson that, alas, many feminists have now 5
forgotten. Today, an increasingly influential feminist pro-censorship movement threatens to impair the very women's rights movement it professes to serve. Led by law professor Catharine MacKinnon and writer Andrea Dworkin, this faction of the feminist movement maintains that sexually oriented *expression*—not sex-segregated labor markets, sexist concepts of marriage and family, or pent-up rage—is the preeminent cause of discrimination and violence against women. Their solution is seemingly simple: suppress all "pornography."

Censorship, however, is never a simple matter. First, the 6
offense must be described. And how does one define something so infinitely variable, so deeply personal, so uniquely

individualized as the image, the word, and the fantasy that cause sexual arousal? For decades, the U.S. Supreme Court has engaged in a Sisyphean struggle to craft a definition of *obscenity* that the lower courts can apply with some fairness and consistency. Their dilemma was best summed up in former Justice Potter Stewart's now famous statement: "I shall not today attempt further to define [obscenity]; and perhaps I could never succeed in intelligibly doing so. But I know it when I see it."

7   The censorious feminists are not so modest as Justice Stewart. They have fashioned an elaborate definition of *pornography* that encompasses vastly more material than does the currently recognized law of *obscenity*. As set out in their model law (which has been considered in more than a dozen jurisdictions in the United States and overseas, and which has been substantially adopted in Canada), pornography is "the sexually explicit subordination of women through pictures and/or words." The model law lists eight different criteria that attempt to illustrate their concept of "subordination," such as depictions in which "women are presented in postures or positions of sexual submission, servility, or display" or "women are presented in scenarios of degradation, humiliation, injury, torture . . . in a context that makes these conditions sexual." This linguistic driftnet can ensnare anything from religious imagery and documentary footage about the mass rapes in the Balkans to self-help books about women's health. Indeed, the Boston Women's Health Book Collective, publisher of the now-classic book on women's health and sexuality, *Our Bodies, Ourselves,* actively campaigned against the MacKinnon-Dworkin model law when it was proposed in Cambridge, Massachusetts, in 1985, recognizing that the book's explicit text and pictures could be targeted as pornographic under the law.

8   Although the "MacDworkinite" approach to pornography has an intuitive appeal to many feminists, it is *itself* based on subordinating and demeaning stereotypes about women. Central to the pornophobic feminists—and to many traditional conservatives and right-wing fundamentalists, as well—is the notion that *sex* is inherently degrading to women (although not to men). Not just sexual expression but sex itself—even consensual, nonviolent sex—is an evil from which women, like children, must be protected.

9   MacKinnon puts it this way: "Compare victims' reports of rape with women's reports of sex. They look a lot alike. . . . The major distinction between intercourse (normal) and rape

(abnormal) is that the normal happens so often that one cannot get anyone to see anything wrong with it." And from Dworkin: "Intercourse remains a means or the means of physiologically making a woman inferior." Given society's pervasive sexism, she believes, women cannot freely consent to sexual relations with men; those who do consent are, in Dworkin's words, "collaborators...experiencing pleasure in their own inferiority."

These ideas are hardly radical. Rather, they are a reincarnation of disempowering puritanical, Victorian notions that feminists have long tried to consign to the dustbin of history: woman as sexual victim; man as voracious satyr. The Mac-Dworkinite approach to sexual expression is a throwback to the archaic stereotypes that formed the basis for nineteenth-century laws which prohibited "vulgar" or sexually suggestive language from being used in the presence of women and girls. 10

In those days, women were barred from practicing law and serving as jurors lest they be exposed to such language. Such "protective" laws have historically functioned to bar women from full legal equality. Paternalism always leads to exclusion, discrimination, and the loss of freedom and autonomy. And in its most extreme form, it leads to purdah, in which women are completely shrouded from public view. 11

The pro-censorship feminists are not fighting alone. Although they try to distance themselves from such traditional "family-values" conservatives as Jesse Helms, Phyllis Schlafly, and Donald Wildmon, who are less interested in protecting women than in preserving male dominance a common hatred of sexual expression and fondness for censorship unite the two camps. For example, the Indianapolis City Council adopted the MacKinnon-Dworkin model law in 1984 thanks to the hard work of former council member Beulah Coughenour, a leader of the Indiana Stop ERA movement. (Federal courts later declared the law unconstitutional.) And when Phyllis Schlafly's Eagle Forum and Beverly LaHaye's Concerned Women for America launched their "Enough Is Enough" anti-pornography campaign, they trumpeted the words of Andrea Dworkin in promotional materials. 12

This mutually reinforcing relationship does a serious disservice to the fight for women's equality. It lends credibility to and strengthens the right wing and its anti-feminist, anti-choice, homophobic agenda. This is particularly damaging in light of the growing influence of the religious right in the Republican Party and the recent Republican sweep of both 13

Congress and many state governments. If anyone doubts that the newly empowered GOP intends to forge ahead with anti-woman agendas, they need only read the party's "Contract with America" which, among other things, reintroduces the recently repealed "gag rule" forbidding government-funded family-planning clinics from even discussing abortion with their patients.

14   The pro-censorship feminists base their efforts on the largely unexamined assumption that ridding society of pornography would reduce sexism and violence against women. If there were any evidence that this were true, anti-censorship feminists—myself included—would be compelled at least to reexamine our opposition to censorship. But there is no such evidence to be found.

15   A causal connection between exposure to pornography and the commission of sexual violence has never been established. The National Research Council's Panel on Understanding and Preventing Violence concluded in a 1993 survey of laboratory studies that "demonstrated empirical links between pornography and sex crimes in general are weak or absent." Even according to another research literature survey that former U.S. Surgeon General C. Everett Koop conducted at the behest of the staunchly anti-pornography Meese Commission, only two reliable generalizations could be made about the impact of "degrading" sexual material on its viewers: it caused them to think that a variety of sexual practices was more common than they had previously believed, and to more accurately estimate the prevalence of varied sexual practices.

16   Correlational studies are similarly unsupportive of the procensorship cause. There are no consistent correlations between the availability of pornography in various communities, states, and countries and their rates of sexual offenses. If anything, studies suggest an inverse relationship: a greater availability of sexually explicit material seems to correlate not with higher rates of sexual violence but, rather, with higher indices of gender equality. For example, Singapore, with its tight restrictions on pornography, has experienced a much greater increase in rape rates than has Sweden, with its liberalized obscenity laws.

17   There *is* mounting evidence, however, that MacDworkinite-type laws will be used against the very people they are supposed to protect—namely, women. In 1992, for example, the Canadian Supreme Court incorporated the MacKinnon-Dworkin concept of pornography into Canadian obscenity law. Since that ruling, in *Butler* v. *The Queen*—which MacKin-

non enthusiastically hailed as "a stunning victory for women"—well over half of all feminist bookstores in Canada have had materials confiscated or detained by customs. According to the *Feminist Bookstore News*, a Canadian publication, "The *Butler* decision has been used . . . only to seize lesbian, gay, and feminist material."

Ironically but predictably, one of the victims of Canada's 18 new law is Andrea Dworkin herself. Two of her books, *Pornography: Men Possessing Women* and *Women Hating*, were seized, customs officials said, because they "illegally eroticized pain and bondage." Like the MacKinnon-Dworkin model law, the *Butler* decision makes no exceptions for material that is part of a feminist critique of pornography or other feminist presentation. And this inevitably overbroad sweep is precisely why censorship is antithetical to the fight for women's rights.

The pornophobia that grips MacKinnon, Dworkin, and 19 their followers has had further counterproductive impacts on the fight for women's rights. Censorship factionalism within the feminist movement has led to an enormously wasteful diversion of energy from the real cause of and solutions to the ongoing problems of discrimination and violence against women. Moreover, the "porn-made-me-do-it" defense, whereby convicted rapists cite MacKinnon and Dworkin in seeking to reduce their sentences, actually impedes the aggressive enforcement of criminal laws against sexual violence.

A return to the basic principles of women's liberation 20 would put the feminist movement back on course. We women are entitled to freedom of expression—to read, think, speak, sing, write, paint, dance, dream, photograph, film, and fantasize as we wish. We are also entitled to our dignity, autonomy, and equality. Fortunately, we can—and will—have both.

Maria Soto
Is It Pornography?

Maria Soto is a student at the University of Kentucky, where she wrote the following essay in a first-year writing course. Born in Panama, raised in Nicaragua, and a resident for a time in Brazil, she speaks a number of languages fluently; but English is of course not her first language. Just after this essay was completed, Calvin Klein responded to public pressure and removed the ads that Soto discusses.

1   During September of 1995 a major controversy arose about the printed ads of Calvin Klein that were exposed, publicly, on buses in New York City, as well as in advertisements in various magazines. Many people considered the ads to be child pornography because the pictures in the ads showed adolescents (apparently minors) in very seductive poses; those people felt that the ads shouldn't be on the streets or in any kind of magazine. However, before censoring something as pornographic, we have to determine if it is really pornographic or simply a use of sensuality to sell a product. In order to be able to make any judgment of that, we need first to determine what child pornography is. By reading and by discussing with other people what constitutes child pornography, I have concluded that child pornography is any material that focuses on the sexuality of a child, that has the intention to be pornographic, and that humiliates those who view the material. Calvin Klein ads may be in poor taste, but they are not child pornography because they don't contain the elements of child pornography.

2   The first part of the definition states that child pornography is any material that focuses on the sexuality of a child, that is, material which drives the attention of the viewer to the sexual organs of the child and shows sexual activities. For example, a picture that shows a ten-year-old girl nude, and in which the camera takes a close-up of her sexual organs, can be defined as child pornography because it focuses on the sexual organs of the girl. On the other hand, a work of art in which a girl is nude but which drives the attention of the viewer not to her sexuality but to something else, is not child pornography. Edvuard Munch's "Puberty" for instance, portrays nudity, but it emphasizes the girl's suffering, so it is not pornography. Although no one can deny that the models in CK ads are posed in sensual positions, no sexual activity is

portrayed, and no sexual organ is shown. A young girl in one of the ads, for instance, is pushing her jeans down as if to take them off, she is looking at the viewer in a challenging way, and her tiny T-shirt is barely covering her stomach; but while the picture is sexually suggestive, it does not depict sexual acts or focus on sexual organs. In another ad, a girl dressed in the same sort of tiny T-shirt is lying sideways on a bench, her jeans pulled down on her hips and an inch or two of her stomach showing. The picture could suggest the idea that she is not an innocent girl, and it undoubtedly focuses on her sensuality; but it doesn't amount to child pornography because it does not focus on her sexual organs or portray any sexual activity. Moreover, to me the girl looks like one of those teenagers that you see every day, walking on the street, wearing her jeans on her hips, and showing off her underwear. What is shown in the CK ads is not far away from the way many teens dress nowadays. Of course, sensuality is explicit in the ads and not on the streets, but judging something as pornographic because it is sensual is not legitimate.

Another important part of the definition of child pornography is the intention of the material. A pornographic item has as its main objective the provocation of sexual arousal; pornography provokes sexual desire. A picture of a ten-year-old girl who is bare and who is opening her legs in front of the camera is certainly material for a hard-core pornographic magazine because the purpose of the picture is to arouse other people sexually. Determining the intention to be pornographic is of course difficult at times because not all material that focuses on the sexuality of a child is intended for pornographic purposes. To use an obvious example, many medical reports contain pictures that emphasize the sexual organs of children, but the intention of those pictures is educational. Nevertheless, for something sexually explicit to be considered pornographic, it must have the intention of arousing sexual desire. Otherwise, it could be considered a scientific or an artistic work.   3

Calvin Klein ads are not meant to be pornographic; they are meant to sell products. In order to sell their products, the CK ads try to identify the models in the ads with adolescents because adolescents are beginning to use their sexuality to attract their peers. The models in the ads look very sensual, as if they can seduce anyone, so that insecure adolescents will think that "maybe if I wear Calvin Klein jeans, I'll be as seductive as that girl and maybe some boy will finally look at me." Adolescents identify with the models and therefore buy CK   4 jeans: it's that simple. And it works. As Alan Millstein, editor of the Fashion Network report, said in a recent issue of *Time*, CK jeans are "flying out of the stores" as a result of the ads. You can see the phenomenon yourself the next time you go to a mall and see a group of teenagers all looking alike: with the same jeans, the same hairstyle, the same shoes. And it's not just any kind of jeans; they have to be produced by Guess? or Calvin Klein. In short, for better or for worse, the sensuality used in CK ads is just the expression of the patterns of behavior and beliefs of many American adolescents. The ads are intended to sell jeans—it's that simple.

5   Finally, in cases of child pornography, humiliation is typically present; pornography degrades and exploits a person. Although pornography includes humiliation, not all humiliating material is pornographic. For example, imagine a picture of a prostitute working on the streets; the picture is humiliating because it shows the exploitation of human beings, but it is not pornographic because it does not focus on the sexuality of the prostitute and because its intention is not pornographic. On the other hand, a young boy or girl in a porno movie is being exploited because, undoubtedly, the movie is showing a relationship of unequal power between a weak child and a strong adult who can manipulate the actions of the child.

6   In Calvin Klein ads, no humiliation is present because they are not being degraded or exploited. The pictures do not imply a relationship of power and submission between the person who took the picture and the persons depicted. Instead, as Calvin Klein himself affirmed in a statement published in the *New York Times* on August 28, the ads intend to show "the strength of character and independence" of the young people photographed. In other words, the ads try to demonstrate that adolescents can take care of themselves and make the right decisions (even, apparently, in the case of buying jeans). The ads I looked at while preparing this essay showed teenagers with confident faces and self-assured poses.

7   In spite of Calvin Klein's personal defense, many people persist in believing that the ads are instances of child pornography because young models are being posed seductively and suggestively; the ads seem to be sexualizing children. However, sexuality and sensuality are things natural to adolescence, not things unnatural. Whether people like it or not, it is normal and natural for a teenager to explore his or her sensuality. I'm not saying that showing the sexual parts of a teenager with the intention to arouse someone is not pornographic; it is. Nor am I saying that showing a picture of an eight-year-old in a sensual

way is natural. It isn't. But the Calvin Klein ads are showing adolescents who really are using sensuality as a way to attract their peers, and, more important, the ads are intended to be commercial, not pornographic.

The only serious mistake that I can see in the ads is that   8
they address a topic that is still taboo in our society, one that we continue to avoid confronting because it's easier to cheat ourselves into believing that adolescents are far away from being sexually active. Why is our society afraid to confront the sexuality of adolescents?

Will these ads cause adolescents to be more sexually   9
active? I doubt it. It seems to me that the ads, more than playing with the sensuality of the models, are dealing with the social value of teenagers in our society. Although the main question around the Calvin Klein ads was whether or not they were pornographic, to me what needs to get the attention of the community is the social mores that the ads reflect. The ads seem to me to show us our adolescents—how they use things to attract people—things like cars, hairstyles, and clothing. It appears that we must have things in order to live and to be respected; we must have things in order to seem attractive or interesting human beings. Calvin Klein ads show how empty our culture is, how we value superficial things and attitudes. In that sense, the ads are discouraging indeed; frustrating indeed.

But they aren't pornographic.   10

CENSORSHIP II:
SHOULD ELECTRONIC
NETWORKS BE RESTRICTED?

Philip Elmer-Dewitt
Cyberporn

The following was a Time *magazine cover story on July 3, 1995. Philip Elmer-Dewitt is affiliated with* Time *and writes frequently about computers for the magazine. He also appeared on an ABC-TV* Nightline *segment with Ted Koppel concerning "cyberporn." After you read his article, be sure to read responses to it that appeared just after its publication on several Internet "chats"; some of them are reprinted here in* Conversations *just after Elmer-Dewitt's essay. And be aware that two people referenced in Elmer-Dewitt's essay (Andrea Dworkin and Nadine Strossen) are included in the previous section of* Conversations. *Incidentally, the law referred to in the article—the "Exon bill"— was passed in 1995 but was later declared unconstitutional. A subsequent piece of legislation, the federal Child Online Protection Act (1997), was struck down by the courts in 1999.*

1   Sex is everywhere these days—in books, magazines, films, television, music videos and bus-stop perfume ads. It is printed on dial-a-porn business cards and slipped under windshield wipers. It is acted out by balloon-breasted models and actors with unflagging erections, then rented for $4 a night at the corner video store. Most Americans have become so inured to the open display of eroticism—and the arguments for why it enjoys special status under the First Amendment—that they hardly notice it's there.

2   Something about the combination of sex and computers, however, seems to make otherwise worldly-wise adults a little crazy. How else to explain the uproar surrounding the discovery by a U.S. Senator—Nebraska Democrat James Exon—that pornographic pictures can be downloaded from the Internet and displayed on a home computer? This, as any

computer-savvy undergrad can testify, is old news. Yet suddenly the press is on alert, parents and teachers are up in arms, and lawmakers in Washington are rushing to ban the smut from cyberspace with new legislation—sometimes with little regard to either its effectiveness or its constitutionality.

If you think things are crazy now, though, wait until the politicians get hold of a report coming out this week. A research team at Carnegie Mellon University in Pittsburgh, Pennsylvania, has conducted an exhaustive study of online porn—what's available, who is downloading it, what turns them on—and the findings (to be published in the *Georgetown Law Journal*) are sure to pour fuel on an already explosive debate.   3

The study, titled *Marketing Pornography on the Information Superhighway*, is significant not only for what it tells us about what's happening on the computer networks but also for what it tells us about ourselves. Pornography's appeal is surprisingly elusive. It plays as much on fear, anxiety, curiosity and taboo as on genuine eroticism. The Carnegie Mellon study, drawing on elaborate computer records of online activity, was able to measure for the first time what people actually download, rather than what they say they want to see. "We now know what the consumers of computer pornography really look at in the privacy of their own homes," says Marty Rimm, the study's principal investigator. "And we're finding a fundamental shift in the kinds of images they demand."   4

What the Carnegie Mellon researchers discovered was: 5

There's an awful lot of porn online. In an 18-month study, the team surveyed 917,410 sexually explicit pictures, descriptions, short stories and film clips. On those Usenet newsgroups where digitized images are stored, 83.5% of the pictures were pornographic.   6

It is immensely popular. Trading in sexually explicit imagery, according to the report, is now "one of the largest (if not the largest) recreational applications of users of computer networks." At one U.S. university, 13 of the 40 most frequently visited newsgroups had names like *alt.sex.stories, rec.arts.erotica* and *alt.sex.bondage.*   7

It is a big moneymaker. The great majority (71%) of the sexual images on the newsgroups surveyed originate from adult-oriented computer bulletin-board systems (**BBS**) whose operators are trying to lure customers to their private collections of X-rated material. There are thousands of these BBS   8 services, which charge fees (typically $10 to $30 a month) and take credit cards; the five largest have annual revenues in excess of $1 million.

9   *It is ubiquitous.* Using data obtained with permission from BBS operators, the Carnegie Mellon team identified (but did not publish the names of) individual consumers in more than 2,000 cities in all 50 states and 40 countries, territories and provinces around the world—including some countries like China, where possession of pornography can be a capital offense.

10   *It is a guy thing.* According to the BBS operators, 98.9% of the consumers of online porn are men. And there is some evidence that many of the remaining 1.1% are women paid to hang out on the "chat" rooms and bulletin boards to make the patrons feel more comfortable.

11   *It is not just naked women.* Perhaps because hard-core sex pictures are so widely available elsewhere, the adult BBS market seems to be driven largely by a demand for images that can't be found in the average magazine rack: pedophilia (nude photos of children), hebephilia (youths) and what the researchers call paraphilia—a grab bag of "deviant" material that includes images of bondage, sadomasochism, urination, defecation, and sex acts with a barnyard full of animals.

12   The appearance of material like this on a public network accessible to men, women and children around the world raises issues too important to ignore—or to oversimplify. Parents have legitimate concerns about what their kids are being exposed to and, conversely, what those children might miss if their access to the Internet were cut off. Lawmakers must balance public safety with their obligation to preserve essential civil liberties. Men and women have to come to terms with what draws them to such images. And computer programmers have to come up with more enlightened ways to give users control over a network that is, by design, largely out of control.

13   The Internet, of course, is more than a place to find pictures of people having sex with dogs. It's a vast marketplace of ideas and information of all sorts—on politics, religion, science and technology. If the fast-growing World Wide Web fulfills its early promise, the network could be a powerful engine of economic growth in the 21st century. And as the Carnegie Mellon study is careful to point out, pornographic image files, despite their evident popularity, represent only about 3% of all the messages on the Usenet newsgroups, while the Usenet itself represents only 11.5% of the traffic on the Internet.

As shocking and, indeed, legally obscene as some of the on-   14
line porn may be, the researchers found nothing that can't be
found in specialty magazines or adult bookstores. Most of the
material offered by the private BBS services, in fact, is simply
scanned from existing print publications.

But pornography is different on the computer networks.   15
You can obtain it in the privacy of your home—without having
to walk into a seedy bookstore or movie house. You can download only those things that turn you on, rather than buy an entire magazine or video. You can explore different aspects of
your sexuality without exposing yourself to communicable
diseases or public ridicule. (Unless, of course, someone gets
hold of the computer files tracking your online activities, as
happened earlier this year to a couple dozen crimson-faced
Harvard students.)

The great fear of parents and teachers, of course, is not that   16
college students will find this stuff but that it will fall into the
hands of those much younger—including some, perhaps, who
are not emotionally prepared to make sense of what they see.

Ten-year-old Anders Urmacher, a student at the Dalton   17
School in New York City who likes to hang out with other kids
in the Treehouse chat room on America Online, got E-mail
from a stranger that contained a mysterious file with instructions for how to download it. He followed the instructions,
and then he called his mom. When Linda Mann-Urmacher
opened the file, the computer screen filled with 10 thumbnail-
size pictures showing couples engaged in various acts of sodomy, heterosexual intercourse and lesbian sex. "I was not aware
that this stuff was online," says a shocked Mann-Urmacher.
"Children should not be subjected to these images."

This is the flip side of Vice President Al Gore's vision of an   18
information superhighway linking every school and library in
the land. When the kids are plugged in, will they be exposed
to the seamiest sides of human sexuality? Will they fall prey
to child molesters hanging out in electronic chat rooms?

It's precisely these fears that have stopped Bonnie Fell of   19
Skokie, Illinois, from signing up for the Internet access her
three boys say they desperately need. "They could get bombarded with X-rated porn, and I wouldn't have any idea," she
says. Mary Veed, a mother of three from nearby Hinsdale,
makes a point of trying to keep up with her computer-literate
12-year-old, but sometimes has to settle for monitoring his
phone bill. "Once they get to be a certain age, boys don't always tell Mom what they do," she says.

"We face a unique, disturbing and urgent circumstance,   20
because it is children who are the computer experts in our

nation's families," said Republican Senator Dan Coats of Indiana during the debate over the controversial anti-cyberporn bill he co-sponsored with Senator Exon.

21   According to at least one of those experts—16-year-old David Slifka of Manhattan—the danger of being bombarded with unwanted pictures is greatly exaggerated. "If you don't want them you won't get them," says the veteran Internet surfer. Private adult BBSs require proof of age (usually a driver's license) and are off-limits to minors, and kids have to master some fairly daunting computer science before they can turn so-called binary files on the Usenet into high-resolution color pictures. "The chances of randomly coming across them are unbelievably slim," says Slifka.

22   While groups like the Family Research Council insist that online child molesters represent a clear and present danger, there is no evidence that it is any greater than the thousand other threats children face every day. Ernie Allen, executive director of the National Center for Missing and Exploited Children, acknowledges that there have been 10 or 12 "fairly high-profile cases" in the past year of children being seduced or lured online into situations where they are victimized. Kids who are not online are also at risk, however; more than 800,000 children are reported missing every year in the U.S.

23   Yet it is in the name of the children and their parents that lawmakers are racing to fight cyberporn. The first blow was struck by Senators Exon and Coats, who earlier this year introduced revisions to an existing law called the Communications Decency Act. The idea was to extend regulations written to govern the dial-a-porn industry into the computer networks. The bill proposed to outlaw obscene material and impose fines of up to $100,000 and prison terms of up to two years on anyone who knowingly makes "indecent" material available to children under 18.

24   The measure had problems from the start. In its original version it would have made online-service providers criminally liable for any obscene communications that passed through their systems—a provision that, given the way the networks operate, would have put the entire Internet at risk. Exon and Coats revised the bill but left in place the language about using "indecent" words online. "It's a frontal assault on the First Amendment," says Harvard law professor Laurence Tribe. Even veteran prosecutors ridicule it. "It won't pass scrutiny even in misdemeanor court," says one.

25   The Exon bill had been written off for dead only a few weeks ago. Republican Senator Larry Pressler of South Dakota,

chairman of the Commerce committee, which has jurisdiction over the larger telecommunications-reform act to which it is attached, told T̄ıme that he intended to move to table it.

That was before Exon showed up in the Senate with his 26 "blue book." Exon had asked a friend to download some of the rawer images available online. "I knew it was bad," he says. "But then when I got on there, it made *Playboy* and *Hustler* look like Sunday-school stuff." He had the images printed out, stuffed them in a blue folder and invited his colleagues to stop by his desk on the Senate floor to view them. At the end of the debate—which was carried live on C-SPAN—few Senators wanted to cast a nationally televised vote that might later be characterized as sanctioning pornography. The bill passed 84 to 16.

Civil libertarians were outraged. Mike Godwin, staff coun- 27 sel for the Electronic Frontier Foundation, complained that the indecency portion of the bill would transform the vast library of the Internet into a children's reading room, where only subjects suitable for kids could be discussed. "It's government censorship," said Marc Rotenberg of the Electronic Privacy Information Center. "The First Amendment shouldn't end where the Internet begins."

The key issue, according to legal scholars, is whether the In- 28 ternet is a print medium (like a newspaper), which enjoys strong protection against government interference, or a broadcast medium (like television), which may be subject to all sorts of government control. Perhaps the most significant import of the Exon bill, according to EFF's Godwin, is that it would place the computer networks under the jurisdiction of the Federal Communications Commission, which enforces, among other rules, the injunction against using the famous seven dirty words on the radio. In a T̄ıme/cnn poll of 1,000 Americans conducted last week by Yankelovich Partners, respondents were sharply split on the issue: 42% were for FCC-like control over sexual content on the computer networks; 48% were against it.

By week's end the balance between protecting speech and 29 curbing pornography seemed to be tipping back toward the libertarians. In a move that surprised conservative support- ers, House Speaker Newt Gingrich denounced the Exon amendment. "It is clearly a violation of free speech, and it's a violation of the right of adults to communicate with each other," he told a caller on a cable-TV show. It was a key defec- tion, because Gingrich will preside over the computer- decency debate when it moves to the House in July. Mean- while, two U.S. Representatives, Republican Christopher Cox

of California and Democrat Ron Wyden of Oregon, were putting together an anti-Exon amendment that would bar federal
regulation of the Internet and help parents find ways to block
material they found objectionable.

30   Coincidentally, in the closely watched case of a University of
Michigan student who published a violent sex fantasy on the
Internet and was charged with transmitting a threat to injure
or kidnap across state lines, a federal judge in Detroit last week
dismissed the charges. The judge ruled that while Jake Baker's
story might be deeply offensive, it was not a crime.

31   How the Carnegie Mellon report will affect the delicate political balance on the cyberporn debate is anybody's guess.
Conservatives thumbing through it for rhetorical ammunition will find plenty. Appendix B lists the most frequently
downloaded files from a popular adult BBS, providing both
the download count and the two-line descriptions posted by
the board's operator. Suffice it to say that they all end in ex-
clamation points, many include such phrases as "nailed to a
table!" and none can be printed in TIME.

32   How accurately these images reflect America's sexual interests, however, is a matter of some dispute. University of Chicago sociologist Edward Laumann, whose 1994 *Sex in America*
survey painted a far more humdrum picture of America's sex
life, says the Carnegie Mellon study may have captured what
he calls the "gaper phenomenon." "There is a curiosity for
things that are extraordinary and way out," he says. "It's like
driving by a horrible accident. No one wants to be in it, but
we all slow down to watch."

33   Other sociologists point out that the difference between
the Chicago and Carnegie Mellon reports may be more apparent than real. Those 1 million or 2 million people who download pictures from the Internet represent a self-selected
group with an interest in erotica. The *Sex in America* respondents, by contrast, were a few thousand people selected to
represent a cross section of all America.

34   Still, the new research is a gold mine for psychologists, social scientists, computer marketers and anybody with an interest in human sexual behavior. Every time computer users
logged on to one of these bulletin boards, they left a digital
trail of their transactions, allowing the pornographers to com-
pile data bases about their buying habits and sexual tastes.
The more sophisticated operators were able to adjust their inventory and their descriptions to match consumer demand.

35   Nobody did this more effectively than Robert Thomas,
owner of the Amateur Action BBS in Milpitas, California, and a

kind of modern-day Marquis de Sade, according to the Carnegie Mellon report. He is currently serving time in an obscenity case that may be headed for the Supreme Court.

Thomas, whose BBS is the online-porn market leader, discovered that he could boost sales by trimming soft- and hardcore images from his data base while frontloading his files with pictures of sex acts with animals (852) and nude prepubescent children (more than 5,000), his two most popular categories of porn. He also used copywriting tricks to better serve his customers' fantasies. For example, he described more than 1,200 of his pictures as depicting sex scenes between family members (father and daughter, mother and son), even though there was no evidence that any of the participants were actually related. These "incest" images were among his biggest sellers, accounting for 10% of downloads.

The words that worked were sometimes quite revealing. Straightforward oral sex, for example, generally got a lukewarm response. But when Thomas described the same images using words like choke or choking, consumer demand doubled.

Such findings may cheer antipornography activists; as feminist writer Andrea Dworkin puts it, "the whole purpose of pornography is to hurt women." Catharine MacKinnon, a professor of law at the University of Michigan, goes further. Women are doubly violated by pornography, she writes in *Vindication and Resistance,* one of three essays in the forthcoming *Georgetown Law Journal* that offer differing views on the Carnegie Mellon report. They are violated when it is made and exposed to further violence again and again every time it is consumed. "The question pornography poses in cyberspace," she writes, "is the same one it poses everywhere else: whether anything will be done about it."

But not everyone agrees with Dworkin and MacKinnon, by any means; even some feminists think there is a place in life—and the Internet—for erotica. In her new book, *Defending Pornography,* Nadine Strossen argues that censoring sexual expression would do women more harm than good, undermining their equality, their autonomy and their freedom.

The Justice Department, for its part, has not asked for new antiporn legislation. Distributing obscene material across state lines is already illegal under federal law, and child pornography in particular is vigorously prosecuted. Some 40 people in 14 states were arrested two years ago in Operation Longarm for exchanging kiddie porn online. And one of the leading characters in the Carnegie Mellon study—a former

Rand McNally executive named Robert Copella, who left book publishing to make his fortune selling pedophilia on the networks—was extradited from Tijuana, and is now awaiting sentencing in a New Jersey jail.

41 For technical reasons, it is extremely difficult to stamp out anything on the Internet—particularly images stored on the Usenet newsgroups. As Internet pioneer John Gilmore famously put it, "The Net interprets censorship as damage and routes around it." There are border issues as well. Other countries on the Internet—France, for instance—are probably no more interested in having their messages screened by U.S. censors than Americans would be in having theirs screened by, say, the government of Saudi Arabia.

42 Historians say it should come as no surprise that the Internet—the most democratic of media—would lead to new calls for censorship. The history of pornography and efforts to suppress it are inextricably bound up with the rise of new media and the emergence of democracy. According to Walter Kendrick, author of *The Secret Museum: Pornography in Modern Culture,* the modern concept of pornography was invented in the 19th century by European gentlemen whose main concern was to keep obscene material away from women and the lower classes. Things got out of hand with the spread of literacy and education, which made pornography available to anybody who could read. Now, on the computer networks, anybody with a computer and a modem can not only consume pornography but distribute it as well. On the Internet anybody can be Bob Guccione.

43 That might not be a bad idea, says Carlin Meyer, a professor at New York Law School whose *Georgetown* essay takes a far less apocalyptic view than MacKinnon's. She argues that if you don't like the images of sex the pornographers offer, the appropriate response is not to suppress them but to overwhelm them with healthier, more realistic ones. Sex on the Internet, she maintains, might actually be good for young people. "[Cyberspace] is a safe space in which to explore the forbidden and the taboo," she writes. "It offers the possibility for genuine, unembarrassed conversations about *accurate* as well as fantasy images of sex."

44 That sounds easier than it probably is. Pornography is powerful stuff, and as long as there is demand for it, there will always be a supply. Better software tools may help check the worst abuses, but there will never be a switch that will cut it off entirely—not without destroying the unbridled expres-

sion that is the source of the Internet's (and democracy's) greatest strength. The hard truth, says John Perry Barlow, co-founder of the EFF and father of three young daughters, is that the burden ultimately falls where it always has: on the parents. "If you don't want your children fixating on filth," he says, "better step up to the tough task of raising them to find it as distasteful as you do yourself."

The Aftermath of "Cyberporn"

Responses on the Internet

What follows is a sampling of the responses to Philip Elmer-Dewitt's article "Cyberporn." They appeared on Internet chat-lines just after his Time *essay hit the newsstands in the final days of June 1995. While some names have been edited out, otherwise the responses are printed here as they originally appeared.*

From: Jwarren@well.com
Date: June 29, 1995

If you liked NIGHTLINE's 6/27 Obscenity, You'll *Love*   1
TIME's Cover Story
Never one to be left behind in a sex feeding frenzy, last week's "July 3" issue of Time has an *amazingly* unbalanced sex cover story—complete with carefully posed wide-eyed child on the cover. To the outrage of many of us, its chief propagandist is Philip Elmer-DeWitt, whom many of us had believed until now was net-literate and a responsible reporter.

But this is a hatchet job—complete with biased, inflammatory reporting based on unrefereed, secret student "research" that is already being called seriously flawed in other periodicals such as the Washington Post. (It's the same inflammatory drivel foisted on a naive audience by Ted Koppel's staff.)

I keep thinking about the last century when various local politicos were frightened into passing ordinances requiring a bell-ringer to walk fifty paces ahead of any of those scary, terrifying gas buggies.

And I can't help but wonder, more and more . . . is this just a sex feeding frenzy by irresponsible, byline-seeking pack hacks and circulation-pumping editors and TV show producers—or is someone feeding them this trash, and encouraging their wildly biased, wildly inaccurate-by-omission National Inquirer look-alike "reports"?

After all, what better way to stampede a systematically misinformed public into supporting censorship and suppression?

—jim

From: XXXX@XXXX.army.mil
Date: Fri, 30 Jun 95 9:38:48 EDT

2   Last night I found a set of FAQs that explained the pictures area on the newsgroups. From the explanation that they presented, it ain't easy to get pictures back, in fact it is a major pain in one's butt! Either todays kids are vastly more patient and resourceful than I was in my youth, and/or they have too much free time on their hands. Oh well, times change.

Date: Wed, 28 Jun 1995 22:57:10–0700
From: XXXX@XXXX.com
Subject: Indecent, Vile, Filthy

3   I am having the same experience as you, cruising the net for sex, not finding much. It takes lots of time.

A search with Yahoo gave me some titillating newsgroups, some recently posted pornographic fantasies in alt.sex.stories. I got an 800 number to phone, and reached a live woman in Dominican Republic. There are discussions about porn movies, and porn stars on the net, but they have been removed, with reference to fear of Exon. I found an interesting questionnaire for Bay Area Swingers which was really quite tastefully done . . .

But not much true filth. This file won't do too much harm.

Date: Tue, 4 Jul 1995 12:34:42–0400
From: "Brock N. Meeks" <brock@well.com>
CyberWire Dispatch // Copyright © 1995 //

4   Jacking in from the "Point-Five Percent Solution" Port:
Washington, DC—Time magazine's credibility is hemorrhaging.

The magazine's recent "Cyberporn" cover story has ignited a fire storm of criticism owing to its overblown coverage of a statistically inconsequential study, written by a university undergraduate.

Time's story is being assailed as "reckless," "shoddy work," and an outright "fraud" by academics and civil liberties groups.

Martin Rimm, who as an electrical engineering major at Carnegie Mellon University took 18 months to complete the study, says 90% of the criticism "is junk."

The writer of the Time story, Philip Elmer-Dewitt, characterized the attacks as "a lot of rhetoric from a professional lobbyist and a professor who called it reckless and criminal before she had read" the study.

Besides the pejoratives used to question how academically rigorous the Rimm study is, Time's critics also are chaffing at the veil of secrecy that has surrounded the study.

Time, the Georgetown Law Review (where the study was formally published, despite the fact that it only deals with points of law inside of footnotes) and ABC's Nightline, in a kind of media collusion, refused to let anyone outside those organizations do an independent review of the study before publication. Each cited secrecy and a prior arrangement with Rimm as the reason.

At least a week before publication, Time magazine was alerted to several potential problems in the study's methodology. "I raised what I thought were several red flags," said Donna Hoffman, an associate professor of management in the Owen School at Vanderbilt University, and one of the most respected researchers on Net access issues. "Those concerns were apparently ignored," she said.

Further, at least two legal experts, Mike Goodwin of the Electronic Frontier Foundation and Danny Weitzner of the Center for Democracy and Technology, were refused access to the study, despite being asked by Rimm to review the report's legal footnotes. Both declined to provide any legal analysis, issuing warnings that such analysis was impossible without seeing the footnotes in context.

Time magazine, aware of all this, ran its story without noting any of the criticism.

The 00.5 Percent Solution

One of the most egregious spin elements that Time used on the story was hyping Rimm's claim that 83.5% of all images on Usenet are "pornographic."

That 83.5% figure has already been seized upon by some members of Congress looking to bludgeon the First Amendment by placing unconstitutional constraints on Internet content. This figure is likely to become a rallying cry of the First Amendment impaired; it has already been trumpeted in at least one Senate floor speech.

Small problem: That figure—and the study which ejaculated its results to a select media group under the cloak of secrecy—is severely flawed, according to several academics and civil liberties groups that have since obtained and analyzed a copy.

By Rimm's own admission, the 83.5% figure is derived from a seven-day time slice of the postings to only 17 of some 32 Usenet groups that typically carry image files. Usenet is comprised of thousands of newsgroups, the vast majority of which are text based.

Further, Rimm's own figures show that his so-called "pornographic" images comprise merely ONE-HALF OF ONE PERCENT (00.5%) of all Internet traffic.

Time reporter Philip Elmer-DeWitt did report this fact. Sort of.

But readers of the Time story have to wade nearly 1,000 words into the story before stumbling across this passage:

> "As the Carnegie Mellon study is careful to point out, pornographic image files...represent only about 3 percent of all the messages on the Usenet newsgroups, while the Usenet itself represents only 11.5 percent of the traffic on the Internet."

Elmer-DeWitt would later claim during an online discussion on the WELL that he didn't finish the math, citing the .5% figure, because readers tend to get lost when more than two figures are cranked into a paragraph. (See, Time takes care of you!)

Cooking the Books

To juice the coverage, Time also cited that the study had "surveyed 917,410 sexually explicit pictures, descriptions, short stories and film clips."

These files, however, were dredged up from adult BBS systems; NOT from Internet newsgroups, a point that is not entirely clear when reading the article.

The 917K figure is further misleading because even Rimm admits in his paper that he winnowed out so many files that his analysis is based on merely 294,114 files. And that STILL doesn't tell the whole story.

"Naked Bitch with Mardi Gras Beads"

To analyze such a huge number of files, by visually verifying that something called "Naked Bitch with Mardi Gras Beads" is actually a woman and not a hoaxed picture of a female dog (as was actually the case), would have taken years. Instead, Rimm's analysis is based overwhelmingly on file *descriptions* only; not actual viewing, using an artificial intelligence program.

Yet a reader of Time's cover story gets none of this analysis.

Walking Back the Cat

How did a major magazine like Time get roped into reporting as "exhaustive," such an apparently flawed document? It was likely a combination of several factors, including errors in judgment, fatigue, and the need to scoop the competition on a hot button issue of the day.

The intelligence community often debriefs its operations through an exercise called "walking back the cat." During this exercise, the major players are gathered and the mission is examined in detail.

While not all the information surrounding the events that led up to the Time cover story are known, let's walk back the cat on what we do know.

Early 1994:   Rimm assembles his "research team" to begin trolling some 68 adult BBSs. His team is instructed to try and obtain as much as possible data on the BBS customers through a kind of "social engineering."

Cyberwire Dispatch interviewed 15 major adult BBS operators to ask about their participation with Rimm. None of them remember ever having spoken to Rimm or a member of his "research team" about the study.

Dispatch asked Rimm; "Did your team go undercover, as it were, when getting permission from these [BBS operators] to use their information?" He replied only: "Discreet, ain't we?"

When asked how he was able to obtain detailed customer profiles from usually skeptical operators of adult BBSs he says: "If you were a pornographer, and you don't have fancy computers or Ph.D. statisticians to assist you, wouldn't you be just a wee bit curious to see how you could adjust your inventories to better serve your clientele? Wouldn't you want to know that maybe you should decrease the number of oral sex images and increase the number of bondage images? Wouldn't you want someone to analyze your logfiles to better serve the tastes of each of your customers?"

October 1994: Eight months before the "exclusive first look" that Time touts about its story on Rimm's findings, "people involved in the study were pitching it to the media," reports Michael C. Berch, editor of *INFOBAHN* magazine, in a posting to the alt.internet.media-coverage newsgroup.

Berch said he took a flyer on the story because he had "other coverage of Internet erotica" in the works.

Rimm says he has no knowledge of the exclusive offered to *INFOBAHN* or any other publication before shopping it to Time.

During this time, Rimm also shops a draft of his study to the CMU administration, according to a Time magazine report last year. Shocked at the findings, the school scurries to implement a full-scale censorship of alt.sex groups from the schools Usenet feed.

November 1994: All hell breaks loose. Word gets out that Carnegie Mellon University has decided to make public its policy to censor all alt.sex newsgroups from flowing into its computers.

The ensuing turmoil surrounding the CMU decision draws media attention and Time is there.

Time reporter Elmer-DeWitt hooks up with Rimm and, using sparse stats drawn from the Rimm paper, he writes in their November 21, 1994, issue a story headlined "Censoring Cyberspace."

In the story he refers to Rimm as only a "research associate." Elmer-DeWitt's story says the CMU administration acted on a draft of Rimm's study "about to be released." In actuality, the study doesn't see the light of day until some seven months later and only then under a secrecy agreement between Rimm and Time and the Georgetown Law Review.

Elmer-DeWitt writes in that November article that Rimm has, "put together a picture collection that rivaled Bob Guccione's (917,410 in all)."

In reality, Rimm had few, if any, actual images. The 917K figure then, as now, refers only to descriptions of images. And when the data was finally washed, only some 214K of those image *descriptions* were valid.

Fast Forward to March 1995:   Rimm finally finds a place to publish: the Georgetown Law Review. But he cuts a deal first: No one—absolutely no one—outside of the law review's immediate staff is allowed to read the full study.

David G. Post, a visiting associate professor of law at the Georgetown University Law Center, is approached "to help several of the student editors with questions that they had arising out of the study," he writes in a "Preliminary Discussion of Methodological Peculiarities in the Rimm Study of Pornography on the 'Information Superhighway,'" distributed after the Time article runs.

But when Post, who says he has "research interests in this area," asks to be shown a copy of the study before advising the students, he too is rebuffed. "[T]hey were unable to do so because of a secrecy arrangement they had made with Mr. Rimm," he writes in his preliminary discussion.

Post also writes: "One would have, perhaps, more confidence in the results of the Rimm study had it been subjected to more vigorous peer review."

However, law review journals, unlike rigorous scientific journals, are not routinely peer reviewed.

But this study and its purported results were anything but "routine." The potential magnitude of the study—which was not lost on Rimm; he'd already seen the white-bread Administration at CMU rush to trample the First Amendment after reading an early draft—should have been enough for the Georgetown Law Review, not to mention the editors at Time, to *demand* outside review and Rimm be damned.

Professor Hoffman readily acknowledges that law reviews aren't subject to peer reviews. (Note: Maybe this is why the majority of lawyers can't write their way past a moderately bright 14-year-old.) However, she says quite bluntly and correctly: "A study like this belongs in a peer-reviewed journal if it's going to be used to impact public policies and stimulate public debate on an important societal issue."

June 1995:   Mike Godwin, online counsel for the Electronic Frontier Foundation and attorney Daniel Weitzner, deputy director of the Center for Democracy and Technology, are, at separate times, asked by Rimm to review the legal footnotes for accuracy.

Godwin and Weitzner say the task is impossible without seeing the full report. They are denied that request.

Weitzner fires off several critical concerns he has about the footnotes anyway, noting that any kind of real analysis is impossible.

Rimm later "thanks" Weitzner for his "participation," even though Weitzner clearly had denied the review request.

June 8–18, 1995: A copy of the study arrives at Time magazine where it sits idle. Elmer-DeWitt is up to his journalistic elbows trying to edit a major Time cover story on Estrogen. The story is complex and riding herd on it stresses Elmer-DeWitt.

The good news: Word filters down to him that his promotion, which has "been in the works for some time," he says, will be official in a couple of weeks, about the time of his vacation and right after he puts another major cover story to bed: the flash point "Cyberporn" story.

Four Time correspondents are assigned to the story to help with the research.

Time passes quickly. Rimm's story, like a forest fire, begins to create its own atmosphere, that rarefied air of "The Exclusive." In the unrelenting, brutalizing competition of the newsweeklies, the scoop is the ace in the hole.

The Time editors were convinced the Rimm study was their Ace. Somebody should have told them it was dealt from the bottom of the deck.

So now Elmer-DeWitt begins pushing for his story, citing its exclusive nature. But Elmer-DeWitt is negotiating the story's placement based on character flaw: He was already sold on the story, having used it back in November during the CMU censorship dust up. The story held up then, it should hold up on the cover. Besides, if it was good enough for the Georgetown Law Review, it was good enough for Time.

And Elmer-DeWitt plays the law review card, readily admitting: "If [Georgetown] hadn't accepted [Rimm's study] for publication, we wouldn't have done our story."

At this point, Elmer-DeWitt has too much invested in the story. Somehow he ignores the lingering doubts and presses forward with the writing. Later, on the WELL he will admit to be personally "pulling for" the validity of Rimm's study.

Meanwhile, one of his reporters, Hannah Bloch, is picking up some bad vibes from Professor Hoffman.

Hoffman and her husband/research partner Tom Novak have tagged-teamed some of the Net's trickiest usage based problems, developing some of the first quantitative models for accurate WEB "traffic accounting." And even from reading the abstract of Rimm's study, Hoffman smells sloppy research. "This is a nice example of bad research," she says.

After the Bloch-Hoffman telephone tag review finally ends, Hoffman says she still feels like Bloch "didn't get it." Hoffman e-mails Elmer-DeWitt directly with her concerns.

When Hoffman asks Elmer-DeWitt to see a copy of the study, he balks, citing the secrecy arrangement with Rimm. Hoffman lays out her concerns about Rimm's methodology and e-mails them to Elmer-DeWitt. Among those concerns, Hoffman notes that a study of such reported significance should have been subject to some kind of peer review.

But Elmer-DeWitt blows off Hoffman's concerns, not because of flawed logic or some perceived hidden agenda. Nope, Elmer-DeWitt decides to dismiss Hoffman out of hand when he discovers—quite suddenly—that law review journals are rarely peer reviewed. This somehow significantly lowers the credibility factor of Hoffman's concerns in Elmer-Dewitt's mind and, for whatever reason, he ignores them.

The concerns are never raised. Not in editorial meetings. Not in the text of the story. Nowhere. A Time reader is led to believe that the study was rigorous and without fault.

In truth, the story had been criticized on several levels and by several different people. The connection? None, save for their concern about sloppy research.

So Elmer-DeWitt presses on. Don't let facts stand in the way... he has a story to write; a vacation to get ready for. This is his baby, and he's under the gun to deliver.

June 19–23: With barely a chance to breathe after the work on Time's Estrogen cover story, as well as several other stories, Elmer-DeWitt wades into the reports from his other correspondents.

He fields editorial questions from higher up. There are still gaping, mawing [*sic*] holes in the story. By the end of the day Monday, the 19th, he knows he has to start writing come Tuesday morning. This is crunch time. There is no more slack in the schedule. Artwork has been commissioned. The cover slot secured. His vacation is looking better all the time...

Meanwhile, Time's public relations arm is cranking into high gear. They know they have a hot cover coming up. They want to get the most mileage out of it that they can. Where do they turn? Television.

They consult with Rimm. He's pitched the idea of giving the story to 20/20's Barbara Walters. Rejected. Too lightweight. Larry King Live is suggested. Good talk hype, high visibility, but not a serious enough venue.

Rejected. *Conan* and the *Late Show* were never considered.

Finally, the Time spin doctors decide on Ted Koppel and Nightline. "We thought Koppel would do a more balanced job," Elmer-DeWitt said.

Time calls ABC. "It's an exclusive and it's yours if you want it." Nobody mentions the fact that ABC was the third choice...

Another secrecy deal is cut. Nightline can't give the study to anyone else either. The article hits the stands on the 26th, but by that time Elmer-DeWitt will be vacationing. The ABC producers decide to tape him Friday, the 23rd.

Thursday hits and Elmer-DeWitt meets the 6 P.M. deadline. Researchers comb the story. Top editors read it, too. "Needs some work," they say and Elmer-DeWitt cranks up the computer to satisfy his bosses. The issue is put to bed.

Friday, June 23rd—It's Darkest Before the Dawn: At 22-hundred hours, 43 minutes, The Computer Underground Digest's Jim Thomas uploads to the WELL, under a new topic residing inside the "media" conference, an urgent message being sent through Cyberspace by Voters Telecom Watch.

The VTW alert puts the Net on notice: Time is ready to publish on Monday a study of porn on the Net. The VTW alert acts like an early warning flare: "The catch is that no one even knows if the study's methods are valid, because no one is being allowed to read it due to an exclusive deal between Time and the institution that funded the study."

Saturday, June 24th—Bad Moon Rising: Early in the morning, Hoffman logs on to the WELL and jolts the media conference, calling the Rimm study "reckless research" and noting how difficult it is to discuss porn on the Net without throwing fuel on the fire.

Elmer-DeWitt follows some five hours later with his own assessment of Hoffman's opening salvo. He says that Hoffman is right about fueling the fire. But he drops a bomb of his own: He wonders aloud how Hoffman can call the study reckless when she's never even read it.

However, he conveniently forgets to tell other WELL members that he denied several requests—Hoffman's among them—from people to see the full study before they commented on the record. He also fails to mention that it was a secret agreement with Rimm that made any independent review of the study impossible.

This early exchange, in a topic called merely "Newsweeklies," set the stage for what would become a romp into "way new" journalism of the first degree.

Over the course of the next eight days, this topic on the WELL would ignite a grassroots investigative team held together with no particular agenda other than seeing all the facts about the Time story vetted.

Steven Levy, a writer for *Newsweek*, weighs in. He's also written something about Porn and the Net for his publication that will run on Monday. The Rimm study gets a single, dubious paragraph.

Levy would have missed the Rimm reference altogether, but Georgetown law professor David Post tips him to the fact that Time is running the story.

Levy scrambles himself to get a copy of the study. He gets shut out. The law review won't give him a copy, citing the secrecy arrangement with Rimm.

Levy tries to find out what Rimm or the Law Review are getting in return for all their secrecy. Each tells Levy to talk to the other. He gets no answer.

In the WELL conference he voices his concern about such secrecy arrangements, wondering if it was trade off for assurances that the story would get a cover.

What Levy doesn't know is that in the coming days, the mere mention of Rimm's study in his story causes the blood pressure to rise within the Time top editorial staff. Gone was their "exclusive," or so they thought, despite the fact that Levy had virtually no detailed knowledge of the Rimm paper. Elmer-Dewitt will be made to answer for "the leak," when Time does a postmortem on the story.

Elmer-DeWitt barks back at Levy, defending the secret agreement with Rimm. He says he's "much more comfortable" with that arrangement than with same that *Newsweek* has made with top business executives. He drops Levy a compliment, calling him "one of the best," and then backhands him: "It's not my fault he works for the magazine that secured exclusive rights to Hitler's 'diaries.'"

He later takes back the remark about the Hitler diaries, admitting it was "a low blow," explaining he found it a bit ironic for Newsweek to be claiming the high moral ground.

A critical mass begins to form. WELLites begin to limber up, taking free shots at Time and Elmer-DeWitt . . . and all before anyone has seen the story.

EFF's Godwin weighs in, the voice of reason: "Let's hold off criticizing Time until we see what the story looks like." And yet, in the coming days, it will be Godwin that rises up as judge, jury, and executioner of Elmer-DeWitt and Time.

The fun has just begun and Elmer-DeWitt is about to step into a virtual home only the Menendez brothers could love.

June 25, 7:36 P.M.—The Feeding Begins: "The Time article is available on America Online right now," is the single line message posted to Newsweeklies on the WELL.

A feeding frenzy is about to take place and over the course of the next several days the WELL topic will resemble a great roiling, shark infested pool. Time and Elmer-Dewitt are the chum.

The events that shake out over the next few days, while localized on the WELL, are significant. First, the article's principal author has his virtual "home base" on the WELL. Second, the WELL becomes the focal point of the most intensive and extensive critiques of the Rimm study, a factor that proves invaluable, considering that Rimm was successful in bypassing this traditional academic gauntlet.

The early reviews of the Time story are horrendous. Someone suggests that the phrase "Rimm Job" will be used to identify overhyped undergraduate studies that masquerade as major newsmagazine cover stories.

Monday June 26, O-Dark-Thirty: Elmer-DeWitt logs in and posts a comment at 2:38 A.M. That prompts John Seabrook of the New Yorker magazine to query nearly 3 hours later: "You're up early. Trouble sleeping?"

At 2:39 P.M. Godwin's life for the next eight days is defined by this posting: "Philip's story is an utter disaster, and it will damage the debate about this issue because we will have to spend lots of time correcting misunderstandings that are directly attributable to the story."

Godwin proceeds to take huge, vicious chunks from the underbelly of the Time article by attacking its least defensible position: The infamous 83.5% figure.

Godwin will continue to feast at the table of Time for days to come, at times posting several devastating comments in a row. He is a machine. He admits to "obsessing" on the issue, but "I'm obsessing over what is the truth," he tells Dispatch about midnight.

He is on the edge of a day too far gone to care about, at the brink of the next too dark to foretell.

He has been unrelenting in his strategic dismantling of Elmer-DeWitt and the Rimm paper. Even his voice sounds tired. But all this takes its toll: Elmer-DeWitt had been a friend. "I feel like something has died," he will say later. And to a large extent, something has.

The packaging of the story gets hammered as well. The shock artwork, which includes a damn near pornographic image in its own right—what can only be described as a man fucking a computer terminal—is outrageously sensationalistic. Elmer-DeWitt even admits at one point that he agrees with views that the art is "over the top."

9:30 Monday Evening . . . : By now Elmer-DeWitt and Time are bloody if not bowed. A crack in Time's story begins to surface.

Elmer-Dewitt admits it himself, acknowledging that he should have had a "graph" in the story that referenced the advance criticism of the study that he knew about. "That was probably a screw up," he writes on the WELL. He says he "couldn't risk" giving anyone, such as Hoffman, an advance copy of the study for fear it would "leak."

Tuesday June 27th—The Plot Moistens: Virtually bleeding from a thousand cuts, Elmer-DeWitt acknowledges that the pressure got to him while writing the story. In fact, he says that if he and his team had had more time and "more presence of mind," they would have called in an "outside expert" to review the study.

But "presence of mind" was apparently lacking. Elmer-DeWitt admits that he had to go from editing one cover story to writing the next with only the weekend to rejuvenate. "Such is the life at a newsmagazine these days," he writes.

CuD's Jim Thomas surfs into a WEB site that is supposed to carry the Rimm study. What Thomas finds instead is a brief description of the study, a pointer to the law review article and a phone number were you can buy it—not download it.

And then he points out a curious note contained on the page: "Current plans for pages include the Introductory text from this article and the conspiracies which have reached the ears of the researchers." But there's no other explanation.

Nightline runs its exclusive-by-arrangement segment. Elmer-DeWitt has already been taped the previous Friday. Godwin goes head to head with Ralph Reed of the Christian Coalition.

Godwin becomes an instant hero: He jumps first into the discussion and is able to play the "family values" card before Reed. But Reed is tossing out facts and figures as if he has somehow been given an advance copy of the so-secret study.

When Rimm is asked if Reed had some kind of advance peek at the study, Rimm says: "Ralphy never saw the fucking study."

Wednesday, June 28th: Hoffman appears back on the WELL after a two day absence. She is shocked: In the media topic alone there have been 250 new posts.

Hoffman announces that she and her husband/partner, having finally obtained a copy of the study, are beginning a systematic critique of the Rimm report.

Six days later the Hoffman/Novak report is complete, all 9,000 words of it. It turns out to be devastating.

Professor David Post, from the Georgetown University Law center, cruises onto the Net with his own detailed critique of the Rimm study. Post deconstructs Rimm's report in the same manner as the Hoffman/Novak paper.

Thursday, June 29th: Hoffman discovers that the cryptic WEB page message alluding to "conspiracies" is aimed at her. On the WEB site, it seems Hoffman is being singled out for being a bit too vocal.

Hoffman fires off a nasty note to Rimm's faculty advisors at CMU. They answer quickly, apologizing for "conspiracy" language that "has no place in academic discourse," according to Marvin Sirbu, one of Rimm's advisors.

Rimm answers Hoffman, too. He apologizes for the WEB page, saying that the person who put it up had done so "accidentally."

The WEB page goes back to "normal."

Friday, June 30–Monday, July 3rd: There is not a minute's rest for Elmer-Dewitt. He is continuously hounded whenever he goes online. All this is very tiring for Elmer-DeWitt. Finally, after a long protracted battle on the WELL, Elmer-DeWitt seems to be inching nearer defeat, at least on certain points.

David Kline, a freelance writer and contributor to Wired magazine, logs in and writes that Elmer-DeWitt didn't conduct what he calls "journalistic due diligence" by investigating the study thoroughly and by not mentioning that other experts raised several doubts.

Kline's message has rung the brass bell.

The next time Elmer-DeWitt logs in, he cites Kline's message saying: "I think he's put his finger on precisely where I screwed up."

And yet, the story won't die. Going into Monday night (July 3), Rimm himself was preparing a detailed assault on the Hoffman/Novak critique.

I asked for an advance copy... Rimm said it was secret until he was ready to announce it.

Why am I not surprised?

Meeks (whew... finally) out...

July 10, 1995

An Open Letter to Phil Elmer-DeWitt and TIME's Responsible Editors (& T. Koppel)

Hi Phil—

It was sad and frustrating to see—and vigorously participate in—the net's flames that poured over you after you honchoed the cyberporn "report." I know you, and I know you are much, much better than that illustrates. 5

You and Time earned the flaming that you got, because you and your editors were the ones with the power to impact public and political opinion, and thus the responsibility to do it *very* carefully. Even under the insane pressure of a weekly deadline in the cutthroat newsweekly racket.

What's done's done. I'm writing about the immediate future—hopefully in time to make a difference. I know you and Time are planning a follow-up—which may be no more than the usual wee-tiny, "Oopps, we made a few little errors," quiblette, buried in some obscure corner of a week's prose.

I urge you: Please—don't do it that way. Such an approach—the press's usual approach to admitting errors—is simply not acceptable. Be assured that it will simply provoke another round of equally earned net-wide flames.

YOU, PHIL, AND TIME *CAN* RECEIVE WELL-EARNED APPLAUSE:

1. Do a second major article on cyberporn and its much more important issue, cybercensorship by government as opposed as to censorship via the delete button.

2. Bluntly, fully and in detail, rip apart the Rimm study with the same zeal that you or Time would put into a secret,

unrefereed procigarette tobacco study by an undergraduate student—if it had received the cover-story prominence and immediately been quoted on the floor of Congress.

3. Bluntly report and criticize your and Time's failings.

4. But most of all, present the other side of the censorship case—including emphasis on the alternatives that net-illiterate, now frightened, justifiably concerned parents, teachers and librarians can use to protect their children from doing what kids have always done ... going where they're told not to go.

5. And have your p.r. department promote *this*, too, to Ted Koppel. Although Nightline's set-up piece was appalling, Ted himself—operating from unfortunate personal ignorance—*tried* to do an even-handed job of drawing out some of the issues ... to the extent that he understood them. I am convinced that he will do a better job, with better research beforehand, if he takes the time to cover cybercensorship excused by the minority of *global* cyberporn that exists.

Soon, more and more print journalists will be doing their work online. The clear and present danger is that, by the time they and their publishers arrive online, the government will have established a long string of precedents for government-imposed content control.

Phil, over and over, we have seen that the net and the public have a great capacity for forgiveness—when national leaders have screwed up and promptly, bluntly and without excuses admitted it. Janet Reno after Waco is an example.

If you or your barricaded editors try to gloss this over, or give excuses, or whine forthwith, "We were imperfect, but ..." scenarios, you will guarantee extensive, continuing, *earned* criticism.

If you—yourselves—rip the hell out of your own story, and present the other side as provocatively as you presented the Rimmtrash, (1) you will be doing a MUCH-needed service to the nation and the political process, and (2) you and Time will *earn* praise for correcting a mistake in an equally prominent, *responsible* manner.

Please Phil ... do it. You are good enough and honorable enough to do so.

> Your friend (believe it or not),
> —jim
> Jim Warren, GovAccess list-owner/editor
> (jwarren@well.com)
> Advocate & columnist, MicroTimes,
> Government Technology, BoardWatch, etc.
> 345 Swett Rd., Woodside CA 94062

Date: Fri, 7 Jul 1995 05:36:33 -0700
From: John Brueck <jbrueck@svpal.org>

Reading your articles [by Brock Meeks] on Time Warner   6
and Nightline on Internet "porn," it occurs to me that it is
interesting that Time in particular is raising this issue about
an area that essentially is controllable by choice or by
parents.

What really offends me and others is the trash on daytime
talk shows and the gangsta rap on MTV.

The prime producer of gangsta rap is Time Warner. Are
they trying to divert attention from there [sic] own far less
controllable enterprise to the detriment of the internet?

        Just a Paranoid Opinion

From: XXXXX.XXXX@compuserve.com
Date: 16 Jun 95 17:41:20 EDT

As a criminal defense lawyer generally concerned with the   7
"mundane" areas of homicide, drugs, and assorted sex crimes,
and aware of the hysteria in certain quarters re. "netcrime,"
the only benefit I see from the various proposed laws this forum so vigorously posts is that my business will increase,
unfortunately at the expense of law-abiding and tax-paying
citizens who pose no danger to anybody, child or otherwise.

I truly hope that some reasonable minds recognize this for
the nonissue that it is and focus on real issues not so susceptible to pithy soundbites, i.e., the budget!

Cynic that I am, I have a horrible feeling that net regulation will become the Prohibition of the 90s. I hope that I am
wrong.

Date: Sun, 9 Jul 1995 11:51:19 -0400
From: farber@central.cis.upenn.edu (David Farber)

"Rimm, Martin (1995), 'The Pornographer's Handbook;   8
How to Exploit Women, Dupe Men, & Make Lots of Money,'
Carnegie, March (ISBN 0962547654)."

This seems real. Maybe there is a serious ethics issue that
CMU and the ACM should face up to.

From: dave@xxxxxx.com
Date: Tue, 4 Jul 1995 12:22:34 -0500

9   You talk about someone orchestrating (?) a media indictment of porn. However, I think it's a lot simpler than that. Remember the years of articles about the epidemic of strangers
abducting kids? Notice how that story suddenly went away.

It's because, after years of hysteria, a reporter checked with
the FBI and found that nationwide they had (it was 7 or 70)
outstanding cases of children abducted by strangers. That
was it. And once the facts were out—it died down. Now it's
missing (custody disputes) and exploited (my parents made
me do chores) children.

You have the same thing here. Look at Newsweek which
had a reasonably balanced series of articles. Why? I think it's
because their reporters [Steven Levy] are pretty net-wise
[very much so!] and so, when told to do a subscription-build-
ing piece, they were limited by their knowledge of the net [not
so—Elmer-Dewitt is quite knowledgeable of the net; just got
caught between eager-to-pander editors and questionable "research," without enough time to perform the due diligence
that was needed—jim].

While other magazines, with reporters who know nothing
about the subject, are therefore free to make more outlandish
claims—without violating their ethics. (News ethics say you
can't lie, but that ignorance is fine.)

Forwarded-by: xxxxxx@CS.Berkeley.EDU

10   The Cato Institute has released a study "New Age Com-
stockery: Exon vs. the Internet" by Robert Corn-Revere, dated
June 28, 1995, which goes into the history of decency laws in
the U.S.

It seems that we had our first version of these with the
"Comstock law" of 1873, which was designed to keep people
from sending improper stuff through the postal service (snail-
mail). See, this guy Comstock noticed that people were sending pictures of Sally-next-door to the soldiers on the front.
This was bad and had to be stopped.

According to the study,

As is often the case, invention became the mother of repression. Congress reacted quickly to the postmaster's report,

passing a law in 1865 making it a crime to send any "obscene book, pamphlet, picture, print, or other publication of vulgar and indecent character" through the U.S. mail.

That law was strengthened several years later at the insistence of Anthony Comstock, a former dry goods clerk who exerted broad influence as secretary of the New York Society for the Suppression of Vice. Under the popularly named "Comstock law," which prohibited use of the mails to send any "obscene, lewd, or lascivious book, pamphlet, picture, paper, print, or other publication of an indecent character," thousands of authors were jailed and literally tons of literature destroyed.

The full study is at http://www.cato.org/main/pa232.html.

Date: 06 Jul 95 08:27:59 EDT
From: xxxxx.2044@compuserve.com>

...the Comstock analogy is narrowly based on a U.S. 11 Postal Service metaphor, which captures very little of what goes on online.

We should also avoid aggrandizing this Exon amendment into all kinds of things it isn't. For instance, it is far from representative of "cybercensorship." That is a multidimensional subject growing daily, as more and more regulators and businesses gain their sea legs online. It's not just about porn, but everything else people would like to see controlled in their dispersion through the Net.

By the way, as hysteria over the Exon amendment grows, it's important to remember that a federal adult materials law can do some pretty cool things for online services, if properly drafted. First, it can extend the "safe harbor" treatment currently given to phone sex services to online services, meaning that if you do what the statute says, you know you'll stay out of trouble. Second, it can unify the law on a national level, so system operators don't have to tear their hair out wondering what the standards for adult materials are in each state where their users are located.

The broadest view of censorship online issues I have seen is still "Technologies of Freedom," by Ithiel de sola Pool. It lays out the historical structure of differential First Amendment protection in the major media in the U.S., pointing out how entirely different regulatory regimes arose in the different media, for various reasons. As "cyberspace" develops, it will have its own characteristic forms of regulation, taking its place alongside other media like newspapers, television, telephone and the postal system as a uniquely regulated kind of speech medium.

Date: Tue, 04 Jul 1995 12:34:49 GMT
From: xxxxxxdad@crecon.demon.co.uk>

12　　As some of you will know, I'm dead set against the Exon Bill (so who isn't) and dead set against censorshit (so who in their right mind isn't). I've spoken out (online) against Net Nanny (based on its prerelease publicity including the press release its company placed on the Net). However, having had a chance to see it at a computer expo here in Birmingham UK last week, I offer the following comments:

Net Nanny is coming to the UK all set for Windows and DOS. I played with it a bit. The way it works is totally configurable by the parent or the system administrator or whatever. The in-charge person loads the program into a hidden directory on the hard drive and through whatever process (not worth describing, very easy) enters a "dictionary" of prohibited words. Anytime any of the words in the "dictionary" show up the program in which it shows (either having been typed from the keyboard or brought in via modem or in any way written to the screen), that specific program closes. And once closed it cannot be reopened until the machine is rebooted.

However, the in-charge person can get back into the program (apparently, the demoing sales person wasn't clear on it) and can do various other functions, because the key to the program lives on a floppy disk that the in-charge person keeps possession of. Logs of activity can be brought up and printed out, showing what words were accessed, how many times, in what programs, etc.

In other words, it is the only type of censorship I approve of, if censorship there has to be, i.e., the parent or teacher censoring what the child has access to rather than some government bureaucrat or anonymous corporate flak.

It arrives in the UK in two weeks in both DOS and Windows Versions.

If only they'd stop the scare mongering, sensationalist sales tactics.

Bruce

Date: Thu, 29 Jun 1995 07:21:40 +0000
From: xxxxxx@dircon.co.uk

I agree with you wholeheartedly that Exon's bill is ridicu- 13
lous and unconstitutional, but I don't think there's any question about the easy availability of things on the net that a lot of
parents wouldn't want their children to see. Such things as the
alt.sex and the alt.binaries.pictures hierarchies spring to mind.

My personal opinion is that if my kid has the technical fi-
nesse to download and decode said binaries, more power to
him/her, but I can understand that a lot of parents don't. The
answer is, of course, more parental supervision and com-
puter-savvy-ness, but it weakens our argument against Exon
to say, "Oh no, there isn't easily accessible stuff that anyone
would think pornographic..."

Date: Fri, 07 Jul 1995 11:18:41 -0500 (CDT)
From: hoffman@colette.ogsm.vanderbilt.edu
(Donna Hoffman)

Note that his advisor Sirbu doesn't put his name on the "re- 14
buttal." I've heard that the CS department wanted to issue a
statement saying it had nothing to do with it but that the department head refused, worrying it would look bad.

I've also heard that one of the advisors hasn't even seen the
article and hasn't been involved with the project for over 6
months.

One of the "contributors" wrote a scathing critique (Sigel),
and another who was acknowledged not only never saw the
study but refused to make comments.

I've also heard the social science faculty are upset that the
EE faculty won't just stand up and say this thing is a fraud
and unethical.

But the CMU ADMINISTRATION is sending out press releases congratulating themselves for being on the cover of
Time and Nightline, so there you have it.

Meanwhile, the Net community manages to stay informed about the debate, with posts as they occur, at http://www2000.ogsm.vanderbilt.edu/cyberporn.debate.cgi

Date: Thu, 13 Jul 1995 13:34:56 -0700
From: "Brock N. Meeks" <brock@well.com>
Subject: CWD—Porn-O-Plenty

15   Warning: This article contains sexually graphic language, funded in part by grants from Carnegie Mellon University. No, I'm not joking.

CyberWire Dispatch // Copyright © 1995 ///

Jacking in from the "Mr. Toad's Wild Ride" Port:

Washington, DC—If I were drunk or stoned or Hunter Thompson or a combination of any of those, maybe this past week would make sense.

But there is no empty Jack Daniels bottle on the floor, there is no drug residue dusting the desktop, and unless that wino on the street corner I can see from my office window, the one harassing the hooker, is Thompson—and you just never know—then I'm left all alone with a virtual Marty Rimm staring back at me from my Mac in the form of E-mail, inside a folder called "Rimm Job."

You know Marty. He's the current media lightning rod. Time magazine recently ran a cover story—"Cyberporn"—based on work he did while an undergraduate at Carnegie Mellon University. Marty's taken a lot of heat for that work... he's about to take a lot more, owing to a little moonlighting publishing venture he had going while conducting the study.

This story should write itself, but it doesn't. I've had phone calls, E-mail, and more phone calls. Each of them adds another small piece to the "Marty and Brock Show" to which I've been an unwitting dupe in for the past week. A fairly simple puzzle a week ago, it has now become a 10,000 piece jigsaw of the Milky Way.

Marty calls me "friend" for some reason and asks me questions via E-mail like "why do I like you, Brock?" Well, how the hell do I know?

And things just keep getting more and more bizarre. It's like I've stepped into some kind of karmic black hole where a lot of good shit happens, but you can't tell anyone about it. At least not right away, because first you're bound to figure out "What It All Means."

But I can't. Maybe I'll never figure it out. Which means this is an ugly story, which means I have to write it ugly or it doesn't get written. So here goes and god help us all . . .

The same Marty that wrote the study on which Time magazine hung its June 26th "Cyberporn" cover story is the same Marty that wrote a dicey little paperback called the "Pornographer's Handbook: How to Exploit Women, Dupe Men and Make Lots of Money."

Somehow, somewhere, someone named "John Russel Davis" gets a hold of this porn handbook and begins to upload excerpts from it to the Internet.

It's 6:27 A.M. on July 11th and the only message I get from Marty is a one-liner: "Who is John Russel Davis?" I have no clue. This is the last I hear from Marty all day. He has gone into hiding, suddenly retreating from our E-mail tug-of-war.

The Marty has "gone dark."

Routine checks of E-mail reveal nothing. At 11:26 P.M. the "RimmSat" lights up. The Marty is back online.

He fires off this message to me: "Look, I'm pissed off about what Carolyn is spreading around certain Usenet newsgroups after I broke up with her. Someone named John Russel Davis from AOL appears to be helping her. If you don't know what newsgroups they are, I certainly am not going to be the one to tell you, but let's just say it's where bbs sysops hangout. Maybe then you'll know why I am so silent."

For those playing without a scorecard, "Carolyn" is "Carolyn Speranza" as in the person listed in "Books in Print" as the illustrator for Marty's "how to" porn marketing manual. She also happens to be listed as an advisor for his academic paper.

But Marty's outburst is a mystery to me. Having been wrapped in a regular reporting gig as Washington Bureau Chief for Interactive Week, I haven't been trolling the Usenet. When I tell him this, he gets insulting: "Brock, I thought you were more clever than this. If you were a bbs sysop, and you just got onto the Usenet for the first time . . . where would you go? But I've said too much, and I don't know what is the lesser of two evils: not to tell you (and hope it goes away), or you will eventually find out later anyway and be pissed off and nobody looks good."

The red flag has been waved and I call in the troops, posting a cryptic message on the WELL asking for assistance in tracking down messages from "John Russel Davis." Aaron Dickey, who toils away in the stock listings department for the Associated Press, takes up the challenge and delivers—in spades.

Into my mailbox flow excerpts of Marty's "how to" manual. Here is a sample of his turgid prose, taken from the Usenet posting, from a chapter on Anal Sex: "When searching for the best anal sex images, you must take especial care to always portray the woman as smiling, as deriving pleasure from being penetrated by a fat penis into her most tender crevice. The male, before ejaculation, is remarkably attuned to the slightest discrepancy; he is as much focused on her lips as on her anus. The slightest indication of pain can make some men limp."

The early returns on the excerpts are that they are a hoax. People castigate the anonymous "Davis" for having tried to foist such a laughable scam on the Net.

But Marty knows different and when I ask if these postings are authentic, he writes: "The excerpts circulating around the Usenet were stolen from my marketing book, Brock. You are the only one I am telling."

This would be the same "marketing book" that in another of these same Usenet excerpts says: "I spent two full years as a researcher at Carnegie Mellon University, where I received four grants to study adult materials on the Internet, Usenet, World Wide Web, and Adult BBS from around the world. Despite countless deprivations and temptations, I have examined this topic with great diligence, having obtained nearly one million descriptions of adult images which were downloaded by consumers more than eight million times. I developed linguistic parsing software to sort these images into 63 different classifications from oral to anal, from lesbian to bondage, from watersports to bestiality."

If that was your jaw hitting the floor, imagine what's happening at Carnegie Mellon about now.

Marty, at first, seemed unruffled by all this. When I asked him what kind of "damage control" he might be formulating to respond to the news of his little self-publishing venture, which, by the way, is listed as having the "Carnegie" imprint and which happens to have the same address in Pittsburgh as someone named "Martin Rimm," Marty replied: "What attention? I don't see it. This is just an oddity. Do you have reason to suspect otherwise?"

But by the night of July 13th, at virtually the 11th hour, he tries to cut a deal with me. He notes that people monitoring the Usenet groups think the excerpts "are a fraud." He says the only ones that know they are real are me and him (forgetting, I suppose, about Carolyn and "Davis"). He says he could essentially upload to the Net a kind of confession, "claiming authorship and you lose your scoop." In return for not blowing my scoop, he wants me to send him an advance copy of this article so he can review it.

He says I'm "close" on some things, but that I have missed "too much" of the story. We could work together, he promises. We could establish a "working relationship," something we obviously don't have now because my earlier article on this whole wretched debacle was "pathetically inaccurate," he claims.

If I comply with his deal, I would then know all, he says: "You will really understand what I did and did not do. If you want."

In case you're wondering, Marty is reading this for the first time along with the rest of you. He has never seen a word of it, other than his own E-mail messages reproduced here.

Not eight hours after he wanted to cut a deal, to "negotiate from the edge," as John Schwartz of the Washington Post characterizes such desperate ploys, he sends a message July 13 (Thursday) that is frantic and elusive: "The thing is about to blow, probably by Friday at noon. I am not happy about this. I don't like it. I don't want it. But I consider you the lesser of two evils. I am going away in about a half hour and will probably return next week."

I have no idea what "the thing" is. I have no idea what the "lesser of two evils" is.

Hell, right now, I'm not even sure he's telling me the truth.

Indeed, throughout this investigation, he has led me back and forth, playing games, trickling out information like some damn chinese water torture.

Mike Godwin, staff counsel for the Electronic Frontier Foundation, who has made the discrediting of the Time "Cyberporn" cover story and Marty's study something of a personal Jihad, sums up Marty like this: "The more you research Rimm, the more a portrait emerges of someone wily, subtle, glib, manipulative. Even when he tells you he's being totally honest, totally frank, you have this lurking feeling that below the surface he's calculating the precise effect his choice of words—both his admissions and his omissions—will have on you."

Godwin is dead bang on.

An old college classmate of Marty's, Bret Pettichord, surfaced during this whole affair. He and Marty went to the New College in Sarasota, Fla., in 1984. They were philosophy majors. It was a small school, Petticort says, so "everyone knew everyone." Marty was a loner. But Marty had a peculiar quirk: He studied tapes of the Rev. Jerry Falwell. "Not for the message," Petticort said, "Marty didn't buy into that." Instead, Marty was "fascinated by how Falwell was able to sway people with his rhetoric...and he studied that." But as far as Petticort knows, Marty never practiced it while in college. They drifted apart, meeting briefly around 1986. When the "Marty as Media Lightning Rod" emerged, Petticort got back in touch. Marty's response: "I'm busy now."

Before the Great Usenet Excerpt incident, Marty was already pacing back and forth across my computer screen.

When the listing of his porn book from "Books in Print" hit the Net, it was like someone had lit Marty's fuse.

When I asked him to explain the book, he answered with two questions: "[T]ell me (1) whether you actually have a copy of the "Porn Handbook," and (2) where you got it."

I answered that I had sources in "low places" and that I didn't appreciate having to "bargain" with him for information. His book "wasn't hard to track down," I told him.

His secret now blown, he goes ballistic: "It looks like that *bitch* got a copy too," he wrote, complete with asterisks, referring to Vanderbilt Professor Donna Hoffman, one of his earliest critics. "To say I'm pissed is an understatement," he wrote in E-mail. "They all agreed not to photocopy it—I'm going to nail them for copyright violation." The "they" he refers to there are the adult BBS operators.

I know, throughout this story you have to keep telling yourself: I am not in the Twilight Zone...I am *not* in the Twilight Zone. But I swear, I'm not making any of this up.

How did Marty pull this off? Adult BBS operators aren't known for their openness and trusting attitudes, in general. When I asked Marty how he was able to do what had taken me years to do—develop sources inside this network of adult BBS operators—he said: "[Y]ou didn't have powerful software which you could use to convince them that you indeed had something to offer. What took you years I could do in anywhere from five minutes to two months. You'll have to figure the rest out."

That software, of course, was the same software he mentions so prominently in his academic study, the one published by the Georgetown Law Journal, the one that starts out telling how pornographers have started to use "sophisticated software" to help them become better marketers.

Are you catching the trend here? It's the ultimate media hack. He's working both sides of the fence. On one hand, Marty is helping the porn operators better market their wares, enabling them to place the stuff more strategically on-line. And then he writes a study with which he reels in an "exclusive" Time magazine "Cyberporn" cover story decrying the fact that, oh-my-gawd, there's an ever increasing amount of porn online, due in part to better marketing tactics by adult BBS operators.

I tell Marty that I think it's "brilliant" that he was able to work the "acquisition of data" from BBS operators so that he could use it for his "how to" porn marketing manual and also crank it into his academic study.

His reply: "If I do say so myself."

It was so brilliant, in fact, that it almost backfired on him on the day the Time magazine story ran. You see, the BBS operators *didn't know* Marty was collecting their data for an academic study; they thought it was going to be used only by Marty, who would in turn, help them better market their porn.

Now, Marty didn't tell me that, directly, he made a game of it, making me ask questions and pose them to him in the form of a theory. So, when I ran the above theory by him, the one where he dupes the BBS operators and uses the data for both his porn book and the study, he wrote: "I'm somewhat impressed that you picked this up. Yes, I got about a dozen surprised calls this week [when the Time cover story ran] from sysops, but the academic study and BBS marketing manual were kept entirely separate . . . so they (the porn BBS operators) took no offense."

But the academic community has . . . except Carnegie Mellon University. To CMU Marty is the new "Media Darling."

Meanwhile, charges of unethical research practices are being launched and brought to the attention of the CMU administration.

Jim Thomas, a professor of sociology/criminal justice at Northern Illinois University, wrote a blistering attack challenging the ethics underlying Marty's study. Thomas's writing is brutal, written in the cold measured prose of an academic: "The most serious and explicit ethical violation is the deceptive nature in which Carnegie Mellon collected the data. Virtually every principle of informed consent was breached, because there is sufficient evidence to conclude that the research team gathered data deceptively, perhaps even fraudulently."

Marty's senior advisor, CMU professor Marvin Sirbu, is no-where to be found. He has refused to answer questions E-mailed to him about whether he knew Marty was using uni-versity funds to gather data for a "how to" porn marketing book at the same time he was using the data for his academic study.

When Marty is asked whether Sirbu knew of his actions, he writes only: "Ask him."

Apparently Marty did run his methodology past George Duncan, a professor of statistics at the Heinz School at CMU. Marty says Duncan is a "privacy expert." However, Marty doesn't list Duncan among the many so-called advisors for his study. "In hindsight, I guess I should have listed him," he told me during our only phone interview.

When Duncan is asked about Marty's methodology he says he sees nothing wrong. When I ask him if he knows the data Marty was collecting was being used for the "Pornographer's Handbook" he says, "that's totally implausible." When I tell him that Marty has confirmed it and that I know for sure he used the data to help write the porn book, Duncan still says, "Well, that's just ridiculous."

What's not ridiculous is the fallout and the "collateral dam-age" as the military likes to say, in which they really mean "the number of innocent civilians that are murdered by a bomb meant only for a strategic target."

First there is the reputation of Time magazine. This can be summed up in one word: Toast. They will have to scramble big time to recover from having been spun by Marty "Mr. Porn Handbook" Rimm.

Then there is CMU. Your call here is as good as mine. The university, even as this article is grinding to a close, still refers to Marty's study as "the CMU study." They'll have to dodge a few bullets on this one now.

And then there is the Net itself. It will likely take some time to heal the damage here, too. Of course there is pornography on the Net, but it's not nearly as pervasive as recent events have made it out to be. And what's more encouraging, is that there is "real research," ironically enough, from Carnegie Mellon itself, that indicates that sexually oriented material, while available on the Net, isn't really that big a drawing point.

As CMU professor Sara Kiesler, one of the principles of a study called "HomeNet" says: "What's important is to look at how people use the Net and what they are actually looking at, as opposed to looking at what is actually on the Net itself."

Her study is finding that very few people access sexually oriented material, even when they know its readily available, she said. And when they do access it, it's mostly out of curiosity. She says, "There's not a high percentage of repeat access."

That should be the word that gets out; not the by now well-debunked "83.5% of the Usenet is porn" figure that sadly (thank you Time magazine) is becoming the sound bite of the Religious Right and certain dense senators.

As for Marty? Well, he's been accepted by MIT's Technology and Policy Program, where he'll go for his masters. I'm sure he'll do just fine . . . after all, he does have this little publishing venture to help him cover expenses.

Meeks out . . .

ON CIVIL DISOBEDIENCE

Henry David Thoreau
Civil Disobedience

*Henry David Thoreau (1817–1862) is best known for his clas-
sic* Walden *(1854), an autobiographical, satiric, spiritual, scientific, and naturalistic "self-help book" based on his two years'
stay at Walden Pond, near Boston. A friend of Ralph Waldo
Emerson and other transcendentalists, Thoreau expressed his
idealism in a number of concrete ways, for example, in his
opposition to slavery and the Mexican War. His refusal to pay
taxes to support the Mexican War inspired his essay "Civil Disobedience" (1849). First delivered as a lecture in 1848, "Civil
Disobedience" influenced the thinking of Mahatma Gandhi
and Martin Luther King Jr.*

1   I heartily accept the motto,—"That government is best
which governs least"; and I should like to see it acted up to
more rapidly and systematically. Carried out, it finally
amounts to this, which also I believe,—"That government is
best which governs not at all"; and when men are prepared
for it, that will be the kind of government which they will
have. Government is at best but an expedient; but most governments are usually, and all governments are sometimes, in-
expedient. The objections which have been brought against a
standing army, and they are many and weighty, and deserve
to prevail, may also at last be brought against a standing government. The standing army is only an arm of the standing
government. The government itself, which is only the mode
which the people have chosen to execute their will, is equally
liable to be abused and perverted before the people can act
through it. Witness the present Mexican war, the work of
comparatively a few individuals using the standing government as their tool; for, in the outset, the people would not
have consented to this measure.

2   This American government—what is it but a tradition,
though a recent one, endeavoring to transmit itself unim-

642

paired to posterity, but each instant losing some of its integrity? It has not the vitality and force of a single living man; for a single man can bend it to his will. It is a sort of wooden gun to the people themselves. But it is not the less necessary for this; for the people must have some complicated machinery or other, and hear its din, to satisfy that idea of government which they have. Governments show thus how successfully men can be imposed on, even impose on themselves, for their own advantage. It is excellent, we must all allow. Yet this government never of itself furthered any enterprise, but by the alacrity with which it got out of its way. *It* does not keep the country free. *It* does not settle the West. *It* does not educate. The character inherent in the American people has done all that has been accomplished; and it would have done somewhat more, if the government had not sometimes got in its way. For government is an expedient by which men would fain succeed in letting one another alone; and, as has been said, when it is most expedient, the governed are most let alone by it. Trade and commerce, if they were not made of India-rubber, would never manage to bounce over the obstacles which legislators are continually putting in their way; and, if one were to judge these men wholly by the effects of their actions and not partly by their intentions, they would deserve to be classed and punished with those mischievous persons who put obstructions on the railroads.

But, to speak practically and as a citizen, unlike those who   3 call themselves no-government men, I ask for, not at once no government, but *at once* a better government. Let every man make known what kind of government would command his respect, and that will be one step toward obtaining it.

After all, the practical reason why, when the power is once   4 in the hands of people, a majority are permitted, and for a long period continue, to rule is not because they are most likely to be in the right, nor because this seems fairest to the minority, but because they are physically the strongest. But a government in which the majority rule in all cases cannot be based on justice, even as far as men understand it. Can there not be a government in which majorities do not virtually decide right and wrong, but conscience?—in which majorities decide only those questions to which the rule of expediency is applicable? Must the citizen ever for a moment, or in the least degree, resign his conscience to the legislator? Why has every man a conscience, then? I think that we should be men first, and subjects afterward. It is not desirable to cultivate a respect for the law, so much as for the right. The only obligation

which I have a right to assume is to do at any time what I
think right. It is truly enough said, that a corporation has no
conscience; but a corporation of conscientious men is a corporation *with* a conscience. Law never made men a whit
more just; and, by means of their respect for it, even the well-
disposed are daily made the agents of injustice. A common
and natural result of an undue respect for law is, that you
may see a file of soldiers, colonel, captain, corporal, privates,
powder-monkeys, and all, marching in admirable order over
hill and dale to the wars, against their will, ay, against their
common sense and consciences, which makes it very steep
marching indeed, and produces a palpitation of the heart.
They have no doubt that it is a damnable business in which
they are concerned; they are all peaceably inclined. Now,
what are they? Men at all? or small movable forts and magazines, at the service of some unscrupulous man in power?
Visit the Navy-Yard, and behold a marine, such a man as an
American government can make, or such as it can make a
man with its black arts,—a mere shadow and reminiscence of
humanity, a man laid out alive and standing, and already, as
one may say, buried under arms with funeral accompani-
ments, though it may be,—

"Not a drum was heard, not a funeral note,
    As his corse to the rampart we hurried;
Not a soldier discharged his farewell shot
    O'er the grave where our hero we buried."[1]

5   The mass of men serve the state thus, not as men mainly,
but as machines, with their bodies. They are the standing
army, and the militia, jailers, constables, posse comitatus, etc.
In most cases there is no free exercise whatever of the judgment or of the moral sense; but they put themselves on a level
with wood and earth and stones; and wooden men can perhaps be manufactured that will serve the purpose as well.
Such command no more respect than men of straw or a lump
of dirt. They have the same sort of worth only as horses and
dogs. Yet such as these even are commonly esteemed good
citizens. Others—as most legislators, politicians, lawyers,
ministers, and office-holders—serve the state chiefly with
their heads; and, as they rarely make any moral distinctions,
they are as likely to serve the Devil, without *intending* it, as

[1]From "Burial of St. John Moore at Corunna" by Charles Wolfe (1817).

God. A very few, as heroes, patriots, martyrs, reformers in the great sense, and *men*, serve the state with their consciences also, and so necessarily resist it for the most part; and they are commonly treated as enemies by it. A wise man will only be useful as a man, and will not submit to be "clay," and "stop a hole to keep the wind away," but leave that office to his dust at least:—

"I am too high-born to be propertied,
To be a secondary at control,
Or useful serving-man and instrument
To any sovereign state throughout the world."[2]

He who gives himself entirely to his fellow-men appears to 6
them useless and selfish; but he who gives himself partially to
them is pronounced a benefactor and philanthropist.

How does it become a man to behave toward this Ameri- 7
can government to-day? I answer, that he cannot without disgrace be associated with it. I cannot for an instant recognize
that political organization as *my* government which is the
slave's government also.

All men recognize the right of revolution; that is, the right 8
to refuse allegiance to, and to resist, the government, when its
tyranny or its inefficiency are great and unendurable. But almost all say that such is not the case now. But such was the
case, they think, in the Revolution of '75. If one were to tell
me that this was a bad government because it taxed certain
foreign commodities brought to its ports, it is most probable
that I should not make an ado about it, for I can do without
them. All machines have their friction; and possibly this does
enough good to counterbalance the evil. At any rate, it is a
great evil to make a stir about it. But when the friction comes
to have its machine, and oppression and robbery are organized, I say, let us not have such a machine any longer. In
other words, when a sixth of the population of a nation which
has undertaken to be the refuge of liberty are slaves, and a
whole country is unjustly overrun and conquered by a foreign
army, and subjected to military law, I think that it is not too
soon for honest men to rebel and revolutionize. What makes
this duty the more urgent is the fact that the country so overrun is not our own, but ours is the invading army.

[2]The line before the quotation is from *Hamlet* V. i. 236–37; the quotation
is from Shakespeare's *King John* V. ii. 79–82.

9   Paley,[3] a common authority with many on moral questions, in his chapter on the "Duty of Submission to Civil Government," resolves all civil obligation into expediency; and he
proceeds to say, "that so long as the interest of the whole society requires it, that is, so long as the established government
cannot be resisted or changed without public inconveniency,
it is the will of God that the established government be
obeyed, and no longer.... This principle being admitted, the
justice of every particular case of resistance is reduced to a
computation of the quantity of the danger and grievance on
the one side, and of the probability and expense of redressing
it on the other." Of this, he says, every man shall judge for
himself. But Paley appears never to have contemplated those
cases to which the rule of expediency does not apply, in which
a people, as well as an individual, must do justice, cost what it
may. If I have unjustly wrested a plank from a drowning man,
I must restore it to him though I drown myself. This, according to Paley, would be inconvenient. But he that would save
his life, in such a case, shall lose it. This people must cease to
hold slaves, and to make war on Mexico, though it cost them
their existence as a people.

10   In their practice, nations agree with Paley; but does any
one think that Massachusetts does exactly what is right at the
present crisis?

"A drab of state, a cloth-o'-silver slut,
To have her train borne up, and her soul trail in the dirt."

Practically speaking the opponents to a reform in Massachusetts are not a hundred thousand politicians at the South, but
a hundred thousand merchants and farmers here, who are
more interested in commerce and agriculture than they are in
humanity, and are not prepared to do justice to the slave and
to Mexico, *cost what it may.* I quarrel not with far-off foes, but
with those who, near at home, coöperate with, and do the
bidding of, those far away, and without whom the latter
would be harmless. We are accustomed to say, that the mass
of men are unprepared; but improvement is slow, because the
few are not materially wiser or better than the many. It is not
so important that many should be as good as you, as that
there be some absolute goodness somewhere; for that will
leaven the whole lump. There are thousands who are *in opin-*

---

[3]William Paley (1743–1805), English theologian.

ion opposed to slavery and to the war, who yet in effect do nothing to put an end to them; who, esteeming themselves children of Washington and Franklin, sit down with their hands in their pockets, and say that they know not what to do, and do nothing; who even postpone the question of freedom to the question of free-trade, and quietly read the prices-current along with the latest advices from Mexico, after dinner, and, it may be, fall asleep over them both. What is the price-current of an honest man and patriot to-day? They hesitate, and they regret, and sometimes they petition; but they do nothing in earnest and with effect. They will wait, well disposed, for others to remedy the evil, that they may no longer have it to regret. At most, they give only a cheap vote, and a feeble countenance and Godspeed, to the right, as it goes by them. There are nine hundred and ninety-nine patrons of virtue to one virtuous man. But it is easier to deal with the real possessor of a thing than with the temporary guardian of it.

All voting is a sort of gaming, like checkers or backgammon, with a slight moral tinge to it, a playing with right and wrong, with moral questions; and betting naturally accompanies it. The character of the voters is not staked. I cast my vote, perchance, as I think right; but I am not vitally concerned that that right should prevail. I am willing to leave it to the majority. Its obligation, therefore, never exceeds that of expediency. Even voting *for the right* is *doing* nothing for it. It is only expressing to men feebly your desire that it should prevail. A wise man will not leave the right to the mercy of chance, nor wish it to prevail through the power of the majority. There is but little virtue in the action of masses of men. When the majority shall at length vote for the abolition of slavery, it will be because they are indifferent to slavery, or because there is but little slavery left to be abolished by their vote. *They* will then be the only slaves. Only *his* vote can hasten the abolition of slavery who asserts his own freedom by his vote.

I hear of a convention to be held at Baltimore, or elsewhere, for the selection of a candidate for the Presidency, made up chiefly of editors, and men who are politicians by profession; but I think, what is it to any independent, intelligent, and respectable man what decision they may come to? Shall we not have the advantage of his wisdom and honesty, nevertheless? Can we not count upon some independent votes? Are there not many individuals in the country who do not attend conventions? But no: I find that the respectable man, so called, has immediately drifted from his position,

11

12

and despairs of his country, when his country has more reason to despair of him. He forthwith adopts one of the candidates thus selected as the only *available* one, thus proving that
he is himself *available* for any purposes of the demagogue.
His vote is of no more worth than that of any unprincipled
foreigner or hireling native, who may have been bought. O for
a man who is a *man*, and, as my neighbor says, has a bone in
his back which you cannot pass your hand through! Our statistics are at fault: the population has been returned too large.
How many *men* are there to a square thousand miles in this
country? Hardly one. Does not America offer any inducement
for men to settle here? The American has dwindled into an
Odd Fellow,—one who may be known by the development of
his organ of gregariousness, and a manifest lack of intellect
and cheerful self-reliance; whose first and chief concern, on
coming into the world, is to see that the Almshouses are in
good repair; and, before yet he has lawfully donned the virile
garb, to collect a fund for the support of the widows and or-
phans that may be; who, in short, ventures to live only by the
aid of the Mutual Insurance company, which has promised to
bury him decently.

13   It is not a man's duty, as a matter of course, to devote himself to the eradication of any, even the most enormous wrong;
he may still properly have other concerns to engage him; but it
is his duty, at least, to wash his hands of it, and, if he gives it no
thought longer, not to give it practically his support. If I devote
myself to other pursuits and contemplations, I must first see,
at least, that I do not pursue them sitting upon another man's
shoulders. I must get off him first, that he may pursue his
contemplations too. See what gross inconsistency is tolerated. I have heard some of my townsmen say, "I should like to
have them order me out to help put down an insurrection of
the slaves, or to march to Mexico;—see if I would go"; and yet
these very men have each, directly by their allegiance, and so
indirectly, at least, by their money, furnished a substitute.
The soldier is applauded who refuses to serve in an unjust
war by those who do not refuse to sustain the unjust government which makes the war; is applauded by those whose own
act and authority he disregards and sets at naught; as if the
state were penitent to that degree that it hired one to scourge
it while it sinned, but not to that degree that it left off sinning
for a moment. Thus, under the name of Order and Civil Government, we are all made at last to pay homage to and support our own meanness. After the first blush of sin comes its
indifference; and from immoral it becomes, as it were, *un-*

moral, and not quite unnecessary to that life which we have made.

The broadest and most prevalent error requires the most   14
disinterested virtue to sustain it. The slight reproach to which
the virtue of patriotism is commonly liable, the noble are
most likely to incur. Those who, while they disapprove of the
character and measures of a government, yield to it their allegiance and support are undoubtedly its most conscientious
supporters, and so frequently the most serious obstacles to
reform. Some are petitioning the state to dissolve the Union,
to disregard the requisitions of the President. Why do they
not dissolve it themselves,—the union between themselves
and the state,—and refuse to pay their quota into its treasury?
Do not they stand in the same relation to the state that the
state does to the Union? And have not the same reasons prevented the state from resisting the Union which have prevented them from resisting the state?

How can a man be satisfied to entertain an opinion merely,   15
and enjoy *it?* Is there any enjoyment in it, if his opinion is
that he is aggrieved? If you are cheated out of a single dollar
by your neighbor, you do not rest satisfied with knowing that
you are cheated, or with saying that you are cheated, or even
with petitioning him to pay you your due; but you take effectual steps at once to obtain the full amount, and see that you
are never cheated again. Action from principle, the perception and the performance of right, changes things and relations; it is essentially revolutionary, and does not consist
wholly with anything which was. It not only divides states
and churches, it divides families; ay, it divides the *individual,*
separating the diabolical in him from the divine.

Unjust laws exist: shall we be content to obey them, or   16
shall we endeavor to amend them, and obey them until we
have succeeded, or shall we transgress them at once? Men
generally, under such a government as this, think that they
ought to wait until they have persuaded the majority to alter
them. They think that, if they should resist, the remedy would
be worse than the evil. But it is the fault of the government itself that the remedy *is* worse than the evil. *It* makes it worse.
Why is it not more apt to anticipate and provide for reform?
Why does it not cherish its wise minority? Why does it cry
and resist before it is hurt? Why does it not encourage its citizens to be on the alert to point out its faults, and *do* better
than it would have them? Why does it always crucify Christ,
and excommunicate Copernicus and Luther, and pronounce
Washington and Franklin rebels?

17   One would think, that a deliberate and practical denial of its authority was the only offense never contemplated by government; else, why has it not assigned its definite, its suitable and proportionate penalty? If a man who has no property refuses but once to earn nine shillings for the state, he is put in prison for a period unlimited by any law that I know, and determined only by the discretion of those who place him there; but if he should steal ninety times nine shillings from the state, he is soon permitted to go at large again.

18   If the injustice is part of the necessary friction of the machine of government, let it go, let it go; perchance it will wear smooth,—certainly the machine will wear out. If the injustice has a spring, or a pulley, or a rope, or a crank, exclusively for itself, then perhaps you may consider whether the remedy will not be worse than the evil; but if it is of such a nature that it requires you to be the agent of injustice to another, then, I say, break the law. Let your life be a counter friction to stop the machine. What I have to do is to see, at any rate, that I do not lend myself to the wrong which I condemn.

19   As for adopting the ways which the state has provided for remedying the evil, I know not of such ways. They take too much time, and a man's life will be gone. I have other affairs to attend to. I came into this world, not chiefly to make this a good place to live in, but to live in it, be it good or bad. A man has not everything to do, but something; and because he cannot do *everything*, it is not necessary that he should do *something* wrong. It is not my business to be petitioning the Governor or the Legislature any more than it is theirs to petition me; and if they should not hear my petition, what should I do then? But in this case the state has provided no way; its very Constitution is the evil. This may seem to be harsh and stubborn and unconciliatory; but it is to treat with the utmost kindness and consideration the only spirit that can appreciate or deserves it. So is all change for the better, like birth and death, which convulse the body.

20   I do not hesitate to say, that those who call themselves Abolitionists should at once effectually withdraw their support, both in person and property, from the government of Massachusetts, and not wait till they constitute a majority of one, before they suffer the right to prevail through them. I think that it is enough if they have God on their side, without waiting for that other one. Moreover, any man more right than his neighbors constitutes a majority of one already.

21   I meet this American government, or its representative, the state government, directly, and face to face, once a year—no

more—in the person of its tax-gatherer; this is the only mode in which a man situated as I am necessarily meets it; and it then says distinctly, Recognize me; and the simplest, the most effectual, and, in the present posture of affairs, the indispensablest mode of treating with it on this head, of expressing your little satisfaction with and love for it, is to deny it then. My civil neighbor, the tax-gatherer, is the very man I have to deal with,—for it is, after all, with men and not with parchment that I quarrel,—and he has voluntarily chosen to be an agent of the government. How shall he ever know well what he is and does as an officer of the government, or as a man, until he is obliged to consider whether he shall treat me, his neighbor, for whom he has respect, as a neighbor and well-disposed man, or as a maniac and disturber of the peace, and see if he can get over this obstruction to his neighborliness without a ruder and more impetuous thought or speech corresponding with his action. I know this well, that if one thousand, if one hundred, if ten men whom I could name,—if ten *honest* men only,—ay, if *one* HONEST man, in this State of Massachusetts, *ceasing to hold slaves*, were actually to withdraw from this copartnership, and be locked up in the county jail therefor, it would be the abolition of slavery in America. For it matters not how small the beginning may seem to be; what is once well done is done forever. But we love better to talk about it: that we say is our mission. Reform keeps many scores of newspapers in its service, but not one man. If my esteemed neighbor, the State's ambassador, who will devote his days to the settlement of the question of human rights in the Council Chamber, instead of being threatened with the prisons of Carolina, were to sit down the prisoner of Massachusetts, that State which is so anxious to foist the sin of slavery upon her sister,—though at present she can discover only an act of inhospitality to be the ground of a quarrel with her,— the Legislature would not wholly waive the subject the following winter.

Under a government which imprisons any unjustly, the   22
true place for a just man is also a prison. The proper place today, the only place which Massachusetts has provided for her freer and less desponding spirits, is in her prisons, to be put out and locked out of the State by her own act, as they have already put themselves out by their principles. It is there that the fugitive slave, and the Mexican prisoner on parole, and the Indian come to plead the wrongs of his race should find them; on that separate, but more free and honorable ground, where the State places those who are not *with* her, but *against*

her,—the only house in a slave State in which a free man can
abide with honor. If any think that their influence would be
lost there, and their voices no longer afflict the ear of the
State, that they would not be as an enemy within its walls,
they do not know by how much truth is stronger than error,
nor how much more eloquently and effectively he can combat
injustice who has experienced a little in his own person. Cast
your whole vote, not a strip of paper merely, but your whole
influence. A minority is powerless while it conforms to the
majority; it is not even a minority then; but it is irresistible
when it clogs by its whole weight. If the alternative is to keep
all just men in prison, or give up war and slavery, the State
will not hesitate which to choose. If a thousand men were not
to pay their tax-bills this year, that would not be a violent and
bloody measure, as it would be to pay them, and enable the
State to commit violence and shed innocent blood. This is, in
fact, the definition of a peaceable revolution, if any such is
possible. If the tax-gatherer, or any other public officer, asks
me, as one has done, "But what shall I do?" my answer is, "If
you really wish to do anything, resign your office." When the
subject has refused allegiance, and the officer has resigned
his office, then the revolution is accomplished. But even suppose blood should flow. Is there not a sort of blood shed when
the conscience is wounded? Through this wound a man's real
manhood and immortality flow out, and he bleeds to an everlasting death. I see this blood flowing now.

23   I have contemplated the imprisonment of the offender,
rather than the seizure of his goods,—though both will serve
the same purpose,—because they who assert the purest right,
and consequently are most dangerous to a corrupt State, commonly have not spent much time in accumulating property. To
such the State renders comparatively small service, and a
slight tax is wont to appear exorbitant, particularly if they are
obliged to earn it by special labor with their hands. If there
were one who lived wholly without the use of money, the State
itself would hesitate to demand it of him. But the rich man—
not to make any invidious comparison—is always sold to the
institution which makes him rich. Absolutely speaking, the
more money, the less virtue; for money comes between a man
and his objects, and obtains them for him; and it was certainly
no great virtue to obtain it. It puts to rest many questions
which he would otherwise be taxed to answer; while the only
new question which it puts is the hard but superfluous one,
how to spend it. Thus his moral ground is taken from under
his feet. The opportunities of living are diminished in propor-

tion as what are called the "means" are increased. The best thing a man can do for his culture when he is rich is to endeavor to carry out those schemes which he entertained when he was poor. Christ answered the Herodians according to their condition. "Show me the tribute-money," said he;—and one took a penny out of his pocket;—if you use money which has the image of Caesar on it, and which he has made current and valuable, that is, *if you are men of the State,* and gladly enjoy the advantages of Caesar's government, then pay him back some of his own when he demands it. "Render therefore to Caesar that which is Caesar's, and to God those things which are God's,"—leaving them no wiser than before as to which was which; for they did not wish to know.

When I converse with the freest of my neighbors, I perceive that, whatever they may say about the magnitude and seriousness of the question, and their regard for the public tranquillity, the long and the short of the matter is, that they cannot spare the protection of the existing government, and they dread the consequences to their property and families of disobedience to it. For my own part, I should not like to think that I ever rely on the protection of the State. But, if I deny the authority of the State when it presents its tax-bill, it will soon take and waste all my property, and so harass me and my children without end. This is hard. This makes it impossible for a man to live honestly, and at the same time comfortably, in outward respects. It will not be worth the while to accumulate property; that would be sure to go again. You must hire or squat somewhere, and raise but a small crop, and eat that soon. You must live within yourself, and depend upon yourself always tucked up and ready for a start, and not have many affairs. A man may grow rich in Turkey even, if he will be in all respects a good subject of the Turkish government. Confucius said: "If a state is governed by the principles of reason, poverty and misery are subjects of shame; if a state is not governed by the principles of reason, riches and honors are the subjects of shame." No: until I want the protection of Massachusetts to be extended to me in some distant Southern port, where my liberty is endangered, or until I am bent solely on building up an estate at home by peaceful enterprise, I can afford to refuse allegiance to Massachusetts, and her right to my property and life. It costs me less in every sense to incur the penalty of disobedience to the State than it would to obey. I should feel as if I were worth less in that case.

Some years ago, the State met me in behalf of the Church, and commanded me to pay a certain sum toward the support of a clergyman whose preaching my father attended, but never I myself. "Pay," it said, "or be locked up in the jail." I declined to pay. But, unfortunately, another man saw fit to pay it. I did not see why the schoolmaster should be taxed to support the priest, and not the priest the schoolmaster; for I was not the State's schoolmaster, but I supported myself by voluntary subscription. I did not see why the lyceum should not present its tax-bill, and have the State to back its demand, as well as the Church. However, at the request of the selectmen, I condescended to make some such statement as this in writing:—"Know all men by these presents, that I, Henry Thoreau, do not wish to be regarded as a member of any incorporated society which I have not joined." This I gave to the town clerk; and he has it. The State, having thus learned that I did not wish to be regarded as a member of that church, has never made a like demand on me since; though it said that it must adhere to its original presumption that time. If I had known how to name them, I should then have signed off in detail from all the societies which I never signed on to; but I did not know where to find a complete list.

26   I have paid no poll-tax[4] for six years. I was put into jail once on this account, for one night; and, as I stood considering the walls of solid stone, two or three feet thick, the door of wood and iron, a foot thick, and the iron grating which strained the light, I could not help being struck with the foolishness of that institution which treated me as if I were mere flesh and blood and bones, to be locked up. I wondered that it should have concluded at length that this was the best use it could put me to, and had never thought to avail itself of my services in some way. I saw that, if there was a wall of stone between me and my townsmen, there was still a more difficult one to climb or break through before they could get to be as free as I was. I did not for a moment feel confined, and the walls seemed a great waste of stone and mortar. I felt as if I alone of all my townsmen had paid my tax. They plainly did not know how to treat me, but behaved like persons who are underbred. In every threat and in every compliment there was a blunder; for they thought that my chief desire was to stand the other side of that stone wall. I could not but smile to see how industriously they locked the door on my meditations, which followed them out again without let or hin-

---

[4]Tax assessed against a person (not property); payment was frequently prerequisite for voting.

drance, and *they* were really all that was dangerous. As they could not reach me, they had resolved to punish my body; just as boys, if they cannot come at some person against whom they have a spite, will abuse his dog. I saw that the State was half-witted, that it was timid as a lone woman with her silver spoons, and that it did not know its friends from its foes, and I lost all my remaining respect for it, and pitied it.

Thus the State never intentionally confronts a man's sense, intellectual or moral, but only his body, his senses. It is not armed with superior wit or honesty, but with superior physical strength. I was not born to be forced. I will breathe after my own fashion. Let us see who is the strongest. What force has a multitude? They only can force me who obey a higher law than I. They force me to become like themselves. I do not hear of *men* being *forced* to live this way or that by masses of men. What sort of life were that to live? When I meet a government which says to me, "Your money or your life," why should I be in haste to give it my money? It may be in a great strait, and not know what to do: I cannot help that. It must help itself; do as I do. It is not worth the while to snivel about it. I am not responsible for the successful working of the machinery of society. I am not the son of the engineer. I perceive that, when an acorn and a chestnut fall side by side, the one does not remain inert to make way for the other, but both obey their own laws, and spring and grow and flourish as best they can, till one, perchance, overshadows and destroys the other. If a plant cannot live according to its nature, it dies; and so a man. 27

The night in prison was novel and interesting enough. The prisoners in their shirt-sleeves were enjoying a chat and the evening air in the doorway, when I entered. But the jailer said, "Come, boys, it is time to lock up;" and so they dispersed, and I heard the sound of their steps returning into the hollow apartments. My room-mate was introduced to me by the jailer as "a first-rate fellow and a clever man." When the door was locked, he showed me where to hang my hat, and how he managed matters there. The rooms were whitewashed once a month; and this one, at least, was the whitest, most simply furnished, and probably the neatest apartment in the town. He naturally wanted to know where I came from, and what brought me there; and, when I had told him, I asked him in my turn how he came there, presuming him to be an honest man, of course; and, as the world goes, I believe he was. "Why," said he, "they accuse me of burning a barn; but I never did it." As near as I could discover, he had probably 28 gone to bed in a barn when drunk, and smoked his pipe there; and so a barn was burnt. He had the reputation of being a clever man, had been there some three months waiting for his trial to come on, and would have to wait as much longer; but he was quite domesticated and contented, since he got his board for nothing, and thought that he was well treated.

29   He occupied one window, and I the other; and I saw that if one stayed there long, his principal business would be to look out the window. I had soon read all the tracts that were left there, and examined where former prisoners had broken out, and where a grate had been sawed off, and heard the history of the various occupants of that room; for I found that even here there was a history and a gossip which never circulated beyond the walls of the jail. Probably this is the only house in the town where verses are composed, which are afterward printed in a circular form, but not published. I was shown quite a long list of verses which were composed by some young men who had been detected in an attempt to escape, who avenged themselves by singing them.

30   I pumped my fellow-prisoner as dry as I could, for fear I should never see him again; but at length he showed me which was my bed, and left me to blow out the lamp.

31   It was like traveling into a far country, such as I had never expected to behold, to lie there for one night. It seemed to me that I never had heard the town-clock strike before, nor the evening sounds of the village; for we slept with the windows open, which were inside the grating. It was to see my native village in the light of the Middle Ages, and our Concord was turned into a Rhine stream, and visions of knights and castles passed before me. They were the voices of old burghers that I heard in the streets. I was an involuntary spectator and audi-tor of whatever was done and said in the kitchen of the adja-cent village-inn,—a wholly new and rare experience to me. It was a closer view of my native town. I was fairly inside of it. I never had seen its institutions before. This is one of its pecu-liar institutions; for it is a shire town. I began to comprehend what its inhabitants were about.

32   In the morning, our breakfasts were put through the hole in the door, in small oblong-square tin pans, made to fit, and holding a pint of chocolate, with brown bread, and an iron spoon. When they called for the vessels again, I was green enough to return what bread I had left; but my comrade seized it, and said that I should lay that up for lunch or din-ner. Soon after he was let out to work at haying in a neighbor-ing field, whither he went every day, and would not be back

till noon; so he bade me good-day, saying that he doubted if he should see me again.

When I came out of prison—for some one interfered, and paid that tax,—I did not perceive that great changes had taken place on the common, such as he observed who went in a youth and emerged a tottering and gray-headed man; and yet a change had to my eyes come over the scene,—the town, and State, and country,—greater than any that mere time could effect. I saw yet more distinctly the State in which I lived. I saw to what extent the people among whom I lived could be trusted as good neighbors and friends; that their friendship was for summer weather only; that they did not greatly propose to do right; that they were a distinct race from me by their prejudices and superstitions, as the China-men and Malays are; that in their sacrifices to humanity they ran no risks, not even to their property; that after all they were not so noble but they treated the thief as he had treated them, and hoped, by a certain outward observance and a few prayers, and by walking in a particular straight though use-less path from time to time, to save their souls. This may be to judge my neighbors harshly; for I believe that many of them are not aware that they have such an institution as the jail in their village. 33

It was formerly the custom in our village, when a poor debtor came out of jail, for his acquaintances to salute him, looking through their fingers, which were crossed to repre-sent the grating of a jail window, "How do ye do?" My neigh-bors did not thus salute me, but first looked at me, and then at one another, as if I had returned from a long journey. I was put into jail as I was going to the shoemaker's to get a shoe which was mended. When I was let out the next morning, I proceeded to finish my errand, and, having put on my mended shoe, joined a huckleberry party, who were impatient to put themselves under my conduct; and in half an hour,— for the horse was soon tackled,—was in the midst of a huckle-berry field, on one of our highest hills, two miles off, and then the State was nowhere to be seen. 34

This is the whole history of "My Prisons." 35

Mahatma Gandhi
Letter to Lord Irwin

*Mahatma Gandhi (*Mahatma *means "of great soul") was born in India in 1869, studied law in London, and in 1893 went to South Africa, where he opposed discriminatory legislation against Indians, was exposed to the writing of Henry David Thoreau, and carried on a famous correspondence with the Russian novelist Leo Tolstoy concerning civil disobedience. In 1914, he returned to India, and about 1920 began a lifetime of committed support for India's independence from England— notably through the practice and encouragement of nonviolent resistance (*satyagraha). *After a decade of sporadic civil disobedience and periodic imprisonments, Gandhi in 1930 prepared a Declaration of Independence for India and soon after led a remarkable (and famous) 200-mile march to the sea to collect salt in symbolic defiance of the English government's monopoly on that product; by the end of the year, more than 100,000 people were jailed in the campaign. India of course did finally achieve independence, in 1947. The following year, while trying to calm tensions between Hindus and Moslems, Gandhi was assassinated.*

The following letter was sent by Gandhi to the British viceroy in India, Lord Irwin, in March 1930, just ten days before the salt march was to begin. It was sent from Satyagraha Ashram, a community established to practice Gandhi's method of nonviolent resistance.

Satyagraha Ashram, Sabarmati,
March 2, 1930

Dear Friend,

1   Before embarking on civil disobedience and taking the risk I have dreaded to take all these years, I would fain approach you and find a way out.

2   My personal faith is absolutely clear. I cannot intentionally hurt anything that lives, much less fellow human beings, even though they may do the greatest wrong to me and mine. Whilst, therefore, I hold the British rule to be a curse, I do not intend harm to a single Englishman or to any legitimate interest he may have in India.

3   I must not be misunderstood. Though I hold the British rule in India to be a curse, I do not, therefore, consider Englishmen in general to be worse than any other people on

earth. I have the privilege of claiming many Englishmen as dearest friends. Indeed much that I have learnt of the evil of British rule is due to the writings of frank and courageous Englishmen who have not hesitated to tell the unpalatable truth about that rule.

And why do I regard the British rule as a curse?   4

It has impoverished the dumb millions by a system of pro-   5 gressive exploitation and by a ruinously expensive military and civil administration which the country can never afford.

It has reduced us politically to serfdom. It has sapped the   6 foundations of our culture. And, by the policy of cruel disarmament, it has degraded us spiritually. Lacking the inward strength, we have been reduced, by all but universal disarmament, to a state bordering on cowardly helplessness.

In common with many of my countrymen, I had hugged the   7 fond hope that the proposed Round Table Conference might furnish a solution. But, when you said plainly that you could not give any assurance that you or the British Cabinet would pledge yourselves to support a scheme of full Dominion Status, the Round Table Conference could not possibly furnish the solution for which vocal India is consciously, and the dumb millions are unconsciously, thirsting.

It seems as clear as daylight that responsible British states-   8 men do not contemplate any alteration in British policy that might adversely affect Britain's commerce with India or require an impartial and close scrutiny of Britain's transactions with India. If nothing is done to end the process of exploitation India must be bled with an ever increasing speed. The Finance Member regards as a settled fact the 1/6 ratio which by a stroke of the pen drains India of a few crores.[1] And when a serious attempt is being made through a civil form of direct action, to unsettle this fact, among many others, even you cannot help appealing to the wealthy landed classes to help you to crush that attempt in the name of an order that grinds India to atoms.

Unless those who work in the name of the nation under-   9 stand and keep before all concerned the motive that lies behind the craving for independence, there is every danger of independence coming to us so changed as to be of no value to those toiling voiceless millions for whom it is sought and for whom it is worth taking. It is for that reason that I have been

---

[1] In Indian currency, a crore is equivalent to ten million rupees.

recently telling the public what independence should really mean.

10   Let me put before you some of the salient points.

11   The terrific pressure of land revenue, which furnishes a large part of the total, must undergo considerable modification in an independent India. Even the much vaunted permanent settlement benefits the few rich zamindars,[2] not the ryots.[3] The ryot has remained as helpless as ever. He is a mere tenant at will. Not only, then, has the land revenue to be considerably reduced, but the whole revenue system has to be so revised as to make the ryot's good its primary concern. But the British system seems to be designed to crush the very life out of him. Even the salt he must use to live is so taxed as to make the burden fall heaviest on him, if only because of the heartless impartiality of its incidence. The tax shows itself still more burdensome on the poor man when it is remembered that salt is the one thing he must eat more than the rich man both individually and collectively.

12   The iniquities sampled above are maintained in order to carry on a foreign administration, demonstrably the most expensive in the world. Take your own salary. It is over Rs. 21,000 per month, besides many other indirect additions. The British Prime Minister gets £5,000 per year, i.e., over Rs. 5,400 per month at the present rate of exchange. You are getting over Rs. 700 per day against India's average income of less than annas 2 per day. The Prime Minister gets Rs. 180 per day against Great Britain's average income of nearly Rs. 2 per day. Thus you are getting much over five thousand times India's average income. The British Prime Minister is getting only ninety times Britain's average income. On bended knees I ask you to ponder over this phenomenon. I have taken a personal illustration to drive home a painful truth. I have too great a regard for you as a man to wish to hurt your feelings. I know that you do not need the salary you get. Probably the whole of your salary goes for charity. But a system that provides for such an arrangement deserves to be summarily scrapped.

13   If India is to live as a nation, if the slow death by starvation of her people is to stop, some remedy must be found for immediate relief. The proposed Conference is certainly not the remedy. It is not a matter of carrying conviction by argument.

---

[2] A zamindar is a landowner.
[3] A ryot is a tenant farmer.

The matter resolves itself into one of matching forces. Conviction or no conviction, Great Britain would defend her Indian commerce and interests by all the forces at her command. India must consequently evolve force enough to free herself from that embrace of death.

It is common cause that, however disorganized and, for   14
the time being, insignificant it may be, the party of violence is gaining ground and making itself felt. Its end is the same as mine. But I am convinced that it cannot bring the desired relief to the dumb millions. And the conviction is growing deeper and deeper in me that nothing but unadulterated non-violence can check the organized violence of the British Government. Many think that non-violence is not an active force. My experience, limited though it undoubtedly is, shows that non-violence can be an intensely active force. It is my purpose to set in motion that force as well against the organized violent force of the British rule as [against] the unorganized violent force of the growing party of violence. To sit still would be to give rein to both the forces above mentioned. Having an unquestioning and immovable faith in the efficacy of non-violence as I know it, it would be sinful on my part to wait any longer.

This non-violence will be expressed through civil disobedi-   15
ence, for the moment confined to the inmates of the Satyagraha Ashram, but ultimately designed to cover all those who choose to join the movement with its obvious limitations.

I know that in embarking on non-violence I shall be run-   16
ning what might fairly be termed a mad risk. But the victories of truth have never been won without risks, often of the gravest character. Conversion of a nation that has consciously or unconsciously preyed upon another, far more numerous, far more ancient and no less cultured than itself, is worth any amount of risk.

I have deliberately used the word "conversion." For my am-   17
bition is no less than to convert the British people through non-violence, and thus make them see the wrong they have done to India. I do not seek to harm your people. I want to serve them even as I want to serve my own. I believe that I have always served them. I served them up to 1919 blindly. But when my eyes were opened and I conceived non-cooperation, the object still was to serve them. I employed the same weapon that I have in all humility successfully used against the dearest members of my family. If I have equal love for your people with mine it will not long remain hidden. It will be acknowledged by them even as the members of my family

acknowledged it after they had tried me for several years. If
the people join me as I expect they will, the sufferings they
will undergo, unless the British nation sooner retraces its
steps, will be enough to melt the stoniest hearts.

18   The plan through civil disobedience will be to combat such
evils as I have sampled out. If we want to sever the British
connection it is because of such evils. When they are removed
the path becomes easy. Then the way to friendly negotiation
will be open. If the British commerce with India is purified of
greed, you will have no difficulty in recognizing our independence. I respectfully invite you then to pave the way for immediate removal of those evils, and thus open a way for a real
conference between equals, interested only in promoting the
common good of mankind through voluntary fellowship and
in arranging terms of mutual help and commerce equally
suited to both. You have unnecessarily laid stress upon the
communal problems that unhappily affect this land. Important though they undoubtedly are for the consideration of any
scheme of government, they have little bearing on the greater
problems which are above communities and which affect
them all equally. But if you cannot see your way to deal with
these evils and my letter makes no appeal to your heart,
on the 11th day of this month, I shall proceed with such
co-workers of the Ashram as I can take, to disregard the
provisions of the salt laws. I regard this tax to be the most in-
iquitous of all from the poor man's standpoint. As the independence movement is essentially for the poorest in the land
the beginning will be made with this evil. The wonder is that
we have submitted to the cruel monopoly for so long. It is, I
know, open to you to frustrate my design by arresting me. I
hope that there will be tens of thousands ready, in a disciplined manner, to take up the work after me, and, in the act of
disobeying the Salt Act to lay themselves open to the penalties
of a law that should never have disfigured the Statute-book.

19   I have no desire to cause you unnecessary embarrassment,
or any at all, so far as I can help. If you think that there is any
substance in my letter, and if you will care to discuss matters
with me, and if to that end you would like me to postpone
publication of this letter, I shall gladly refrain on receipt of a
telegram to that effect soon after this reaches you. You will,
however, do me the favour not to deflect me from my course
unless you can see your way to conform to the substance of
this letter.

20   This letter is not in any way intended as a threat but is a
simple and sacred duty peremptory on a civil resister. There-

fore I am having it specially delivered by a young English friend who believes in the Indian cause and is a full believer in non-violence and whom Providence seems to have sent to me, as it were, for the very purpose.

> I remain,
> Your sincere friend,
> M. K. Gandhi

Martin Luther King Jr.
Love, Law, and Civil Disobedience

Born in Atlanta and educated at Morehouse College, Crozer Theological Seminary (near Philadelphia), and Boston University, Martin Luther King Jr. (1929–1968) was the most visible leader of the civil rights movement of the 1960s. An ordained minister with a doctorate in theology from Boston University, he worked especially in the South and through nonviolent means to overturn segregation statutes, to increase the number of African American voters, and to support other civil rights initiatives. Reverend King won the Nobel Peace Prize in 1964. When he was assassinated in 1968, all America mourned. The following item is a transcript of a speech that Dr. King delivered in 1961 to the annual meeting of the Fellowship of the Concerned in Atlanta. After you read the address, note how several passages reappeared later (in a somewhat different form) in his "Letter from Birmingham Jail," page 676.

Members of the Fellowship of the Concerned, of the Southern Regional Council, I need not pause to say how very delighted I am to be here today, and to have the opportunity of being a little part of this very significant gathering. I certainly want to express my personal appreciation to Mrs. Tilly and the members of the Committee, for giving me this opportunity. I would also like to express just a personal word of thanks and appreciation for your vital witness in this period of transition which we are facing in our Southland, and in the nation, and I am sure that as a result of this genuine concern, and your significant work in communities all across the South, we have a better South today and I am sure will have a better South tomorrow with your continued endeavor. And I do want to express my personal gratitude and appreciation to you of the Fellowship of the Concerned for your significant work and for your forthright witness.

2   Now, I have been asked to talk about the philosophy behind the student movement. There can be no gainsaying of the fact that we confront a crisis in race relations in the United States. This crisis has been precipitated on the one hand by the determined resistance of reactionary forces in the South to the Supreme Court's decision in 1954 outlawing segregation in the public schools. And we know that at times this resistance has risen to ominous proportions. At times we find the legislative halls of the South ringing loud with such words as interposition and nullification. And all of these forces have developed into massive resistance. But we must also say that the crisis has been precipitated on the other hand by the determination of hundreds and thousands and millions of Negro people to achieve freedom and human dignity. If the Negro stayed in his place and accepted discrimination and segregation, there would be no crisis. But the Negro has a new sense of dignity, a new self respect, and new determination. He has re-evaluated his own intrinsic worth. Now this new sense of dignity on the part of the Negro grows out of the same longing for freedom and human dignity on the part of the oppressed people all over the world; for we see it in Africa, we see it in Asia, and we see it all over the world. Now we must say that this struggle for freedom will not come to an automatic halt, for history reveals to us that once oppressed people rise up against that oppression, there is no stopping point short of full freedom. On the other hand, history reveals to us that those who oppose the movement for freedom are those who are in privileged positions who very seldom give up their privileges without strong resistance. And they very seldom do it voluntarily. So the sense of struggle will continue. The question is how will the struggle be waged.

3   Now there are three ways that oppressed people have generally dealt with their oppression. One way is the method of acquiescence, the method of surrender; that is, the individuals will somehow adjust themselves to oppression, they adjust themselves to discrimination or to segregation or colonialism or what have you. The other method that has been used in history is that of rising up against the oppressor with corrod-

ing hatred and physical violence. Now of course we know about this method in western civilization, because in a sense it has been the hallmark of its grandeur, and the inseparable twin of western materialism. But there is a weakness in this method because it ends up creating many more social problems than it solves. And I am convinced that if the Negro succumbs to the temptation of using violence in his struggle for freedom and justice, unborn generations will be the recipients of a long and desolate night of bitterness. And our chief legacy to the future will be an endless reign of meaningless chaos.

But there is another way, namely the way of non-violent resistance. This method was popularized in our generation by a little man from India, whose name was Mohandas K. Gandhi. He used this method in a magnificent way to free his people from the economic exploitation and the political domination inflicted upon them by a foreign power. 4

This has been the method used by the student movement in the South and all over the United States. And naturally whenever I talk about the student movement I cannot be totally objective. I have to be somewhat subjective because of my great admiration for what the students have done. For in a real sense they have taken our deep groans and passionate yearnings for freedom, and filtered them in their own tender souls, and fashioned them into a creative protest which is an epic known all over our nation. As a result of their disciplined, non-violent, yet courageous struggle, they have been able to do wonders in the South, and in our nation. But this movement does have an underlying philosophy, it has certain ideas that are attached to it, it has certain philosophical precepts. These are the things that I would like to discuss for the few moments left. 5

I would say that the first point or the first principle in the movement is the idea that means must be as pure as the end. This movement is based on the philosophy that ends and means must cohere. Now this has been one of the long struggles in history, the whole idea of means and ends. Great philosophers have grappled with it, and sometimes they have emerged with the idea, from Machiavelli on down, that the end justifies the means. There is a great system of thought in our world today, known as Communism. And I think that with all of the weaknesses and tragedies of Communism, we find its greatest tragedy right here, that it goes under the philosophy that the end justifies the means that are used in the process. So we can read or we can hear the Lenins say that 6 lying, deceit, or violence, that many of these things justify the ends of the classless society.

7   This is where the student movement and the non-violent movement that is taking place in our nation would break with Communism and any other system that would argue that the end justifies the means. For in the long run, we must see that the end represents the means in process and the ideal in the making. In other words, we cannot believe, or we cannot go with the idea that the end justifies the means because the end is pre-existent in the means. So the idea of non-violent resistance, the philosophy of non-violent resistance, is the philosophy which says that the means must be as pure as the end, that in the long run of history, immoral destructive means cannot bring about moral and constructive ends.

8   There is another thing about this philosophy, this method of non-violence which is followed by the student movement. It says that those who adhere to or follow this philosophy must follow a consistent principle of non-injury. They must consistently refuse to inflict injury upon another. Sometimes you will read the literature of the student movement and see that, as they are getting ready for the sit-in or stand-in, they will read something like this, "if you are hit do not hit back, if you are cursed do not curse back." This is the whole idea, that the individual who is engaged in a non-violent struggle must never inflict injury upon another. Now this has an external aspect and it has an internal one. From the external point of view it means that the individuals involved must avoid external physical violence. So they don't have guns, they don't retaliate with physical violence. If they are hit in the process, they avoid external physical violence at every point. But it also means that they avoid internal violence of spirit. This is why the love ethic stands so high in the student movement. We have a great deal of talk about love and non-violence in this whole thrust.

9   Now when the students talk about love, certainly they are not talking about emotional bosh, they are not talking about merely a sentimental outpouring; they're talking something much deeper, and I always have to stop and try to define the meaning of love in this context. The Greek language comes to our aid in trying to deal with this. There are three words in the Greek language for love; one is the word Eros. This is a beautiful type of love, it is an aesthetic love. Plato talks about it a great deal in his dialogue, the yearning of the soul for the realm of the divine. It has come to us to be a sort of romantic love, and so in a sense we have read about it and experienced

it. We've read about it in all the beauties of literature. I guess in a sense Edgar Allan Poe was talking about Eros when he talked about his beautiful Annabelle Lee, with the love surrounded by the halo of eternity. In a sense Shakespeare was talking about Eros when he said "Love is not love which alters when alteration finds, or bends with the remover to remove; O, no! it is an ever fixed mark that looks on tempest and is never shaken, it is the star to every wandering bark." (You know, I remember that because I used to quote it to this little lady when we were courting; that's Eros.) The Greek language talks about Philia which was another level of love. It is an intimate affection between personal friends, it is a reciprocal love. On this level you love because you are loved. It is friendship.

Then the Greek language comes out with another word   10
which is called the Agape. Agape is more than romantic love, agape is more than friendship. Agape is understanding, creative, redemptive, good will to all men. It is an overflowing love which seeks nothing in return. Theologians would say that it is the love of God operating in the human heart. So that when one rises to love on this level, he loves men not because he likes them, not because their ways appeal to him, but he loves every man because God loves him. And he rises to the point of loving the person who does an evil deed while hating the deed that the person does. I think this is what Jesus meant when he said "love your enemies." I'm very happy that he didn't say like your enemies, because it is pretty difficult to like some people. Like is sentimental, and it is pretty difficult to like someone bombing your home; it is pretty difficult to like somebody threatening your children; it is difficult to like congressmen who spend all of their time trying to defeat civil rights. But Jesus says love them, and love is greater than like. Love is understanding, redemptive, creative, good will for all men. And it is this idea, it is this whole ethic of love which is the idea standing at the basis of the student movement.

There is something else: that one seeks to defeat the unjust   11
system, rather than individuals who are caught in that system. And that one goes on believing that somehow this is the important thing, to get rid of the evil system and not the individual who happens to be misguided, who happens to be misled, who was taught wrong. The thing to do is to get rid of the system and thereby create a moral balance within society.

Another thing that stands at the center of this movement is   12
another idea: that suffering can be a most creative and powerful social force. Suffering has certain moral attributes involved,

but it can be a powerful and creative social force. Now, it is very interesting at this point to notice that both violence and non-violence agree that suffering can be a very powerful social force. But there is this difference: violence says that suffering can be a powerful social force by inflicting the suffering on somebody else; so this is what we do in war, this is what we do in the whole violent thrust of the violent movement. It believes that you achieve some end by inflicting suffering on another. The non-violent say that suffering becomes a powerful social force when you willingly accept that violence on yourself, so that self-suffering stands at the center of the non-violent movement and the individuals involved are able to suffer in a creative manner, feeling that unearned suffering is redemptive, and that suffering may serve to transform the social situation.

13   Another thing in this movement is the idea that there is within human nature an amazing potential for goodness. There is within human nature something that can respond to goodness. I know somebody's liable to say that this is an unrealistic movement if it goes on believing that all people are good. Well, I didn't say that. I think the students are realistic enough to believe that there is a strange dichotomy of disturbing dualism within human nature. Many of the great philosophers and thinkers through the ages have seen this. It caused Ovid the Latin poet to say, "I see and approve the better things of life, but the evil things I do." It caused even St. Augustine to say "Lord, make me pure, but not yet." So that that is in human nature. Plato centuries ago said that the human personality is like a charioteer with two headstrong horses, each wanting to go in different directions, so that within our own individual lives we see this conflict and certainly when we come to the collective life of man, we see a strange badness. But in spite of this there is something in human nature that can respond to goodness. So that man is neither innately good nor is he innately bad; he has potentialities for both. So in this sense, Carlyle was right when he said that "there are depths in man which go down to the lowest hell, and heights which reach the highest heaven, for are not both heaven and hell made out of him, everlasting miracle and mystery that he is?" Man has the capacity to be good, man has the capacity to be evil.

14   And so the non-violent resister never lets this idea go, that there is something within human nature that can respond to goodness. So that a Jesus of Nazareth or a Mohandas Gandhi can appeal to human beings and appeal to that element of

goodness within them, and a Hitler can appeal to the element of evil within them. But we must never forget that there is something within human nature that can respond to goodness, that man is not totally depraved, to put it in theological terms, the image of God is never totally gone. And so the individuals who believe in this movement and who believe in non-violence and our struggle in the South, somehow believe that even the worst segregationist can become an integrationist. Now sometimes it is hard to believe that this is what this movement says, and it believes it firmly, that there is something within human nature that can be changed, and this stands at the top of the whole philosophy of the student movement and the philosophy of non-violence.

It says something else. It says that it is as much a moral obligation to refuse to cooperate with evil as it is to cooperate with good. Non-cooperation with evil is as much a moral obligation as the cooperation with good. So that the student movement is willing to stand up courageously on the idea of civil disobedience. Now I think this is the part of the student movement that is probably misunderstood more than anything else. And it is a difficult aspect, because on the one hand the students would say, and I would say, and all the people who believe in civil rights would say, obey the Supreme Court's decision of 1954 and at the same time, we would disobey certain laws that exist on the statutes of the South today.   15

This brings in the whole question of how can you be logically consistent when you advocate obeying some laws and disobeying other laws. Well, I think one would have to see the whole meaning of this movement at this point by seeing that the students recognize that there are two types of laws. There are just laws and there are unjust laws. And they would be the first to say obey the just laws, they would be the first to say that men and women have a moral obligation to obey just and right laws. And they would go on to say that we must see that there are unjust laws. Now the question comes into being, what is the difference, and who determines the difference, what is the difference between a just and an unjust law?   16

Well, a just law is a law that squares with a moral law. It is a law that squares with that which is right, so that any law that uplifts human personality is a just law. Whereas that law which is out of harmony with the moral is a law which does not square with the moral law of the universe. It does not square with the law of God, so for that reason it is unjust and any law that degrades the human personality is an unjust law.   17

18   Well, somebody says that that does not mean anything to
me: first, I don't believe in these abstract things called moral
laws and I'm not too religious, so I don't believe in the law of
God: you have to get a little more concrete, and more practical. What do you mean when you say that a law is unjust, and
a law is just? Well, I would go on to say in more concrete
terms that an unjust law is a code that the majority inflicts on
the minority that is not binding on itself. So that this becomes difference made legal. Another thing that we can say is
that an unjust law is a code which the majority inflicts on the
minority, which that minority had no part in enacting or creating, because that minority had no right to vote in many instances, so that the legislative bodies that made these laws
were not democratically elected. Who could ever say that the
legislative body of Mississippi was democratically elected, or
the legislative body of Alabama was democratically elected,
or the legislative body even of Georgia has been democratically elected, when there are people in Terrell County and in
other counties because of the color of their skin who cannot
vote? They confront reprisals and threats and all of that; so
that an unjust law is a law that individuals did not have a part
in creating or enacting because they were denied the right to
vote.

19   Now by the same token a just law would be just the opposite. A just law becomes sameness made legal. It is a code that
the majority, who happen to believe in that code, compel the
minority, who don't believe in it, to follow, because they are
willing to follow it themselves, so it is sameness made legal.
Therefore the individuals who stand up on the basis of civil
disobedience realize that they are following something that
says that there are just laws and there are unjust laws. Now,
they are not anarchists. They believe that there are laws
which must be followed; they do not seek to defy the law, they
do not seek to evade the law. For many individuals who would
call themselves segregationists and who would hold on to segregation at any cost seek to defy the law, they seek to evade
the law, and their process can lead on into anarchy. They seek
in the final analysis to follow a way of uncivil disobedience,
not civil disobedience. And I submit that the individual who
disobeys the law, whose conscience tells him it is unjust and
who is willing to accept the penalty by staying in jail until
that law is altered, is expressing at the moment the very highest respect for law.

20   This is what the students have followed in their movement.
Of course there is nothing new about this; they feel that they

are in good company and rightly so. We go back and read the *Apology* and the *Crito*, and you see Socrates practicing civil disobedience. And to a degree academic freedom is a reality today because Socrates practiced civil disobedience. The early Christians practiced civil disobedience in a superb manner, to a point where they were willing to be thrown to the lions. They were willing to face all kinds of suffering in order to stand up for what they knew was right even though they knew it was against the laws of the Roman Empire.

We could come up to our own day and we see it in many   21 instances. We must never forget that everything that Hitler did in Germany was "legal." It was illegal to aid and comfort a Jew, in the days of Hitler's Germany. But I believe that if I had the same attitude then as I have now I would publicly aid and comfort my Jewish brothers in Germany if Hitler were alive today calling this an illegal process. If I lived in South Africa today in the midst of the white supremacy law in South Africa, I would join Chief Luthuli and others in saying break these unjust laws. And even let us come up to America. Our nation in a sense came into being through a massive act of civil disobedience, for the Boston Tea Party was nothing but a massive act of civil disobedience. Those who stood up against the slave laws, the abolitionists, by and large practiced civil disobedience. So I think these students are in good company, and they feel that by practicing civil disobedience they are in line with men and women through the ages who have stood up for something that is morally right.

Now there are one or two other things that I want to say   22 about this student movement, moving out of the philosophy of non-violence, something about what it is a revolt against. On the one hand it is a revolt against the negative peace that has encompassed the South for many years. I remember when I was in Montgomery, Ala., one of the white citizens came to me one day and said—and I think he was very sincere about this—that in Montgomery for all of these years we have been such a peaceful community, we have had so much harmony in race relations and then you people have started this movement and boycott, and it has done so much to disturb race relations, and we just don't love the Negro like we used to love them, because you have destroyed the harmony and the peace that we once had in race relations. And I said to him, in the best way I could say and I tried to say it in non-violent terms, we have never had peace in Montgomery, Ala., we have never had peace in the South. We have had a negative peace, which is merely the absence of tension; we've had a negative peace in which the Negro patiently accepted his situation and his plight, but we've never had true peace, we've never had positive peace, and what we're seeking now is to develop this positive peace. For we must come to see that peace is not merely the absence of some negative force, it is the presence of a positive force. True peace is not merely the absence of tension, but it is the presence of justice and brotherhood. I think this is what Jesus meant when he said, I come not to bring peace but a sword. Now Jesus didn't mean he came to start war, to bring a physical sword, and he didn't mean, I come not to bring positive peace. But I think what Jesus was saying in substance was this, that I come not to bring an old negative peace, which makes for stagnant passivity and deadening complacency, I come to bring something different, and whenever I come, a conflict is precipitated, between the old and the new, whenever I come a struggle takes place between justice and injustice, between the forces of light and the forces of darkness. I come not to bring a negative peace, but a positive peace, which is brotherhood, which is justice, which is the Kingdom of God.

23   And I think this is what we are seeking to do today, and this movement is a revolt against a negative peace and a struggle to bring into being a positive peace, which makes for true brotherhood, true integration, true person-to-person relationships. This movement is also revolt against what is often called tokenism. Here again many people do not understand this; they feel that in this struggle the Negro will be satisfied with tokens of integration, just a few students and a few schools here and there and a few doors open here and there. But this isn't the meaning of the movement and I think that honesty impels me to admit it everywhere I have an opportunity, that the Negro's aim is to bring about complete integration in American life. And he has come to see that token integration is little more than token democracy, which ends up with many new evasive schemes and it ends up with new discrimination, covered up with such niceties of complexity. It is very interesting to discover that the movement has thrived in many communities that had token integration. So this reveals that the movement is based on a principle that integration must become real and complete, not just token integration.

24   It is also a revolt against what I often call the myth of time. We hear this quite often, that only time can solve this problem. That if we will only be patient, and only pray—which we must do, we must be patient and we must pray—but there are

those who say just do these things and wait for time, and time will solve this problem. Well, the people who argue this do not themselves realize that time is neutral, that it can be used constructively or destructively. At points the people of ill will, the segregationists, have used time much more effectively than the people of good will. So individuals in the struggle must come to realize that it is necessary to aid time, that without this kind of aid, time itself will become an ally of the insurgent and primitive forces of social stagnation. Therefore, this movement is a revolt against the myth of time.

There is a final thing that I would like to say to you, this 25 movement is a movement based on faith in the future. It is a movement based on a philosophy, the possibility of the future bringing into being something real and meaningful. It is a movement based on hope. I think this is very important. The students have developed a theme song for their movement, maybe you've heard it. It goes something like this, "we shall overcome, deep in my heart, I do believe, we shall overcome," and then they go on to say another verse, "we are not afraid, we are not afraid today, deep in my heart I do believe, we shall overcome." So it is out of this deep faith in the future that they are able to move out and adjourn the councils of despair, and to bring new light in the dark chambers of pessimism. I can remember the times that we've been together. I remember that night in Montgomery, Ala., when we had stayed up all night, discussing the Freedom Rides, and that morning came to see that it was necessary to go on with the Freedom Rides, that we would not in all good conscience call an end to the Freedom Rides at that point. And I remember the first group got ready to leave, to take a bus for Jackson, Miss.; we all joined hands and started singing together. "We shall overcome, we shall overcome." And something within me said, now how is it that these students can sing this, they are going down to Mississippi, they are going to face hostile and jeering mobs, and yet they could sing, "We shall overcome." They may even face physical death, and yet they could sing, "We shall overcome." Most of them realized that they would be thrown into jail, and yet they could sing. "We shall overcome, we are not afraid." Then something caused me to see at that moment the real meaning of the movement. That students had faith in the future. That the movement was based on hope, that this movement had something within it that says somehow even though the arc of the moral universe is long, it bends toward justice. And I think this should be a challenge to all others who are struggling to transform the dangling discords of our Southland into a beautiful symphony of brotherhood. There is something in this student movement which says to us, that we shall overcome. Before the victory is won some may have to get scarred up, but we shall overcome. Before the victory of brotherhood is achieved, some will maybe face physical death, but we shall overcome. Before the victory is won, some will lose jobs, some will be called Communists, and reds, merely because they believe in brotherhood, some will be dismissed as dangerous rabblerousers and agitators merely because they're standing up for what is right, but we shall overcome. That is the basis of this movement, and as I like to say, there is something in this universe that justifies Carlyle in saying no lie can live forever. We shall overcome because there is something in this universe which justifies William Cullen Bryant in saying truth crushed to earth shall rise again. We shall overcome because there is something in this universe that justifies James Russell Lowell in saying, truth forever on the scaffold, wrong forever on the throne. Yet that scaffold sways the future, and behind the dim unknown standeth God within the shadows, keeping watch above His own. With this faith in the future, with this determined struggle, we will be able to emerge from the bleak and desolate midnight of man's inhumanity to man, into the bright and glittering daybreak of freedom and justice. Thank you.

On April 12, 1963, in order to have himself arrested on a symbolic day (Good Friday), Reverend Martin Luther King Jr. disobeyed a court injunction forbidding demonstrations in Birmingham, Alabama. That same day, eight leading white Birmingham clergymen (Christian and Jewish) published a letter in the Birmingham News *calling for the end of protests and exhorting protesters to work through the courts for the redress of their grievances. On the morning after his arrest, while held in solitary confinement, King began his response to these clergymen—his famous "Letter from Birmingham Jail." Begun in the margins of newspapers and on scraps of paper and finished by the following Tuesday, the letter was widely distributed and later became a central chapter in King's* Why We Can't Wait *(1964).*

Public Statement by Eight Alabama Clergymen

April 12, 1963

We the undersigned clergymen are among those who, in January, issued "An Appeal for Law and Order and Common Sense," in dealing with racial problems in Alabama. We expressed understanding that honest convictions in racial matters could properly be pursued in the courts, but urged that decisions of those courts should in the meantime be peacefully obeyed. 1

Since that time there had been some evidence of increased forbearance and a willingness to face facts. Responsible citizens have undertaken to work on various problems which cause racial friction and unrest. In Birmingham, recent public events had given indication that we all have opportunity for a new constructive and realistic approach to racial problems. 2

However, we are now confronted by a series of demonstrations by some of our Negro citizens, directed and led in part by outsiders. We recognize the natural impatience of people who feel that their hopes are slow in being realized. But we are convinced that these demonstrations are unwise and untimely. 3

We agree rather with certain local Negro leadership which has called for honest and open negotiation of racial issues in our area. And we believe this kind of facing of issues can best be accomplished by citizens of our own metropolitan area, white and Negro, meeting with their knowledge and experience of the local situation. All of us need to face that responsibility and find proper channels for its accomplishment. 4

Just as we formerly pointed out that "hatred and violence have no sanction in our religious and political traditions," we also point out that such actions as incite to hatred and violence, however technically peaceful those actions may be, have not contributed to the resolution of our local problems. We do not believe that these days of new hope are days when extreme measures are justified in Birmingham. 5

We commend the community as a whole, and the local news media and law enforcement officials in particular, on the calm manner in which these demonstrations have been handled. We urge the public to continue to show restraint should the demonstrations continue, and the law enforcement 6 officials to remain calm and continue to protect our city from violence.

7   We further strongly urge our own Negro community to withdraw support from these demonstrations, and to unite locally in working peacefully for a better Birmingham. When rights are consistently denied, a cause should be pressed in the courts and in negotiations among local leaders, and not in the streets. We appeal to both our white and Negro citizenry to observe the principles of law and order and common sense. Signed by:

> C. C. J. Carpenter, D.D., LL.D.,
> *Bishop of Alabama*
> Joseph A. Durick, D.D.,
> *Auxiliary Bishop, Diocese of Mobile, Birmingham*
> *Rabbi* Milton L. Grafman,
> *Temple Emanu-El, Birmingham, Alabama*
> *Bishop* Paul Hardin,
> *Bishop of the Alabama-West Florida Conference*
> *of the Methodist Church*
> *Bishop* Nolan B. Harmon,
> *Bishop of the North Alabama Conference*
> *of the Methodist Church*
> George M. Murray, D.D., LL.D.,
> *Bishop Coadjutor, Episcopal Diocese of Alabama*
> Edward V. Ramage,
> *Moderator, Synod of the Alabama Presbyterian*
> *Church in the United States*
> Earl Stallings,
> *Pastor, First Baptist Church, Birmingham, Alabama*

Martin Luther King Jr.
Letter from Birmingham Jail

April 16, 1963

My Dear Fellow Clergymen:

1   While confined here in the Birmingham city jail, I came across your recent statement calling my present activities "unwise and untimely." Seldom do I pause to answer criti-

cism of my work and ideas. If I sought to answer all the criticisms that cross my desk, my secretaries would have little time for anything other than such correspondence in the course of the day, and I would have no time for constructive work. But since I feel that you are men of genuine good will and that your criticisms are sincerely set forth, I want to try to answer your statement in what I hope will be patient and reasonable terms.

I think I should indicate why I am here in Birmingham, 2 since you have been influenced by the view which argues against "outsiders coming in." I have the honor of serving as president of the Southern Christian Leadership Conference, an organization operating in every southern state, with headquarters in Atlanta, Georgia. We have some eighty-five affiliated organizations across the South, and one of them is the Alabama Christian Movement for Human Rights. Frequently we share staff, educational and financial resources with our affiliates. Several months ago the affiliate here in Birmingham asked us to be on call to engage in a nonviolent direct-action program if such were deemed necessary. We readily consented, and when the hour came we lived up to our promise. So I, along with several members of my staff, am here because I was invited here. I am here because I have organizational ties here.

But more basically, I am in Birmingham because injustice 3 is here. Just as the prophets of the eighth century B.C. left their villages and carried their "thus saith the Lord" far beyond the boundaries of their home towns, and just as the Apostle Paul left his village of Tarsus and carried the gospel of Jesus Christ to the far corners of the Greco-Roman world, so am I compelled to carry the gospel of freedom beyond my own home town. Like Paul, I must constantly respond to the Macedonian call for aid.

Moreover, I am cognizant of the interrelatedness of all 4 communities and states. I cannot sit idly by in Atlanta and not be concerned about what happens in Birmingham. Injustice anywhere is a threat to justice everywhere. We are caught in an inescapable network of mutuality, tied in a single garment of destiny. Whatever affects one directly, affects all indirectly. Never again can we afford to live with the narrow, provincial "outside agitator" idea. Anyone who lives inside the United States can never be considered an outsider anywhere within its bounds.

You deplore the demonstrations taking place in Birming- 5 ham. But your statement, I am sorry to say, fails to express a similar concern for the conditions that brought about the demonstrations. I am sure that none of you would want to rest content with the superficial kind of social analysis that deals merely with effects and does not grapple with underlying causes. It is unfortunate that demonstrations are taking place in Birmingham, but it is even more unfortunate that the city's white power structure left the Negro community with no alternative.

6   In any nonviolent campaign there are four basic steps: collection of the facts to determine whether injustices exist; negotiation; self-purification; and direct action. We have gone through all these steps in Birmingham. There can be no gainsaying the fact that racial injustice engulfs this community. Birmingham is probably the most thoroughly segregated city in the United States. Its ugly record of brutality is widely known. Negroes have experienced grossly unjust treatment in the courts. There have been more unsolved bombings of Negro homes and churches in Birmingham than in any other city in the nation. These are the hard, brutal facts of the case. On the basis of these conditions, Negro leaders sought to negotiate with the city fathers. But the latter consistently refused to engage in good-faith negotiation.

7   Then, last September, came the opportunity to talk with leaders of Birmingham's economic community. In the course of the negotiations, certain promises were made by the merchants—for example, to remove the stores' humiliating racial signs. On the basis of these promises, the Reverend Fred Shuttlesworth and the leaders of the Alabama Christian Movement for Human Rights agreed to a moratorium on all demonstrations. As the weeks and months went by, we realized that we were the victims of a broken promise. A few signs, briefly removed, returned; the others remained.

8   As in so many past experiences, our hopes had been blasted, and the shadow of deep disappointment settled upon us. We had no alternative except to prepare for direct action, whereby we would present our very bodies as a means of laying our case before the conscience of the local and the national community. Mindful of the difficulties involved, we decided to undertake a process of self-purification. We began a series of workshops on nonviolence, and we repeatedly asked ourselves: "Are you able to accept blows without retaliating?" "Are you able to endure the ordeal of jail?" We decided to schedule our direct-action program for the Easter season, realizing that except for Christmas, this is the main shopping period of the year. Knowing that a strong economic-

withdrawal program would be the by-product of direct action, we felt that this would be the best time to bring pressure to bear on the merchants for the needed change.

Then it occurred to us that Birmingham's mayoral election was coming up in March, and we speedily decided to postpone action until after election day. When we discovered that the Commissioner of Public Safety, Eugene "Bull" Connor, had piled up enough votes to be in the run-off, we decided again to postpone action until the day after the run-off so that the demonstrations could not be used to cloud the issues. Like many others, we waited to see Mr. Connor defeated, and to this end we endured postponement after postponement. Having aided in this community need, we felt that our direct action program could be delayed no longer. 9

You may well ask: "Why direct action? Why sit-ins, marches and so forth? Isn't negotiation a better path?" You are quite right in calling for negotiation. Indeed, this is the very purpose of direct action. Nonviolent direct action seeks to create such a crisis and foster such a tension that a community which has constantly refused to negotiate is forced to confront the issue. It seeks so to dramatize the issue that it can no longer be ignored. My citing the creation of tension as part of the work of the nonviolent-resister may sound rather shocking. But I must confess that I am not afraid of the word "tension." I have earnestly opposed violent tension, but there is a type of constructive, nonviolent tension which is necessary for growth. Just as Socrates felt that it was necessary to create a tension in the mind so that individuals could rise from the bondage of myths and half-truths to the unfettered realm of creative analysis and objective appraisal, so must we see the need for nonviolent gadflies to create the kind of tension in society that will help men rise from the dark depths of prejudice and racism to the majestic heights of understanding and brotherhood. 10

The purpose of our direct-action program is to create a situation so crisis-packed that it will inevitably open the door to negotiation. I therefore concur with you in your call for negotiation. Too long has our beloved Southland been bogged down in a tragic effort to live in monologue rather than dialogue. 11

One of the basic points in your statement is that the action that I and my associates have taken in Birmingham is untimely. Some have asked: "Why didn't you give the new city administration time to act?" The only answer that I can give to this query is that the new Birmingham administration must be prodded about as much as the outgoing one, before it 12 will act. We are sadly mistaken if we feel that the election of Albert Boutwell as mayor will bring the millennium to Birmingham. While Mr. Boutwell is a much more gentle person than Mr. Connor, they are both segregationists, dedicated to maintenance of the status quo. I have hope that Mr. Boutwell will be reasonable enough to see the futility of massive resistance to desegregation. But he will not see this without pressure from devotees of civil rights. My friends, I must say to you that we have not made a single gain in civil rights without determined legal and nonviolent pressure. Lamentably, it is an historical fact that privileged groups seldom give up their privileges voluntarily. Individuals may see the moral light and voluntarily give up their unjust posture; but, as Reinhold Niebuhr has reminded us, groups tend to be more immoral than individuals.

13   We know through painful experience that freedom is never voluntarily given by the oppressor; it must be demanded by the oppressed. Frankly, I have yet to engage in a direct-action campaign that was "well timed" in the view of those who have not suffered unduly from the disease of segregation. For years now I have heard the word "Wait!" It rings in the ear of every Negro with piercing familiarity. This "Wait" has almost always meant "Never." We must come to see, with one of our distinguished jurists, that "justice too long delayed is justice denied."

14   We have waited for more than 340 years for our constitutional and God-given rights. The nations of Asia and Africa are moving with jetlike speed toward gaining political independence, but we still creep at horse-and-buggy pace toward gaining a cup of coffee at a lunch counter. Perhaps it is easy for those who have never felt the stinging darts of segregation to say, "Wait." But when you have seen vicious mobs lynch your mothers and fathers at will and drown your sisters and brothers at whim; when you have seen hate-filled policemen curse, kick and even kill your black brothers and sisters; when you see the vast majority of your twenty million Negro brothers smothering in an airtight cage of poverty in the midst of an affluent society; when you suddenly find your tongue twisted and your speech stammering as you seek to explain to your six-year-old daughter why she can't go to the public amusement park that has just been advertised on television, and see tears welling up in her eyes when she is told that Funtown is closed to colored children, and see ominous clouds of inferiority beginning to form in her little mental sky, and see her beginning to distort her personality by developing

an unconscious bitterness toward white people; when you
have to concoct an answer for a five-year-old son who is asking: "Daddy, why do white people treat colored people so
mean?"; when you take a cross-country drive and find it necessary to sleep night after night in the uncomfortable corners
of your automobile because no motel will accept you; when
you are humiliated day in and day out by nagging signs reading "white" and "colored"; when your first name becomes
"nigger," your middle name becomes "boy" (however old you
are) and your last name becomes "John," and your wife and
mother are never given the respected title "Mrs."; when you
are harried by day and haunted by night by the fact that you
are a Negro, living constantly at tiptoe stance, never quite
knowing what to expect next, and are plagued with inner fears
and outer resentments; when you are forever fighting a degen-
erating sense of "nobodiness"—then you will understand why
we find it difficult to wait. There comes a time when the cup
of endurance runs over, and men are no longer willing to be
plunged into the abyss of despair. I hope, sirs, you can understand our legitimate and unavoidable impatience.

You express a great deal of anxiety over our willingness to   15
break laws. This is certainly a legitimate concern. Since we so
diligently urge people to obey the Supreme Court's decision
of 1954 outlawing segregation in the public schools, at first
glance it may seem rather paradoxical for us consciously to
break laws. One may well ask: "How can you advocate breaking some laws and obeying others?" The answer lies in the
fact that there are two types of laws: just and unjust. I would
be the first to advocate obeying just laws. One has not only a
legal but a moral responsibility to obey just laws. Conversely,
one has a moral responsibility to disobey unjust laws. I would
agree with St. Augustine that "an unjust law is no law at all."

Now, what is the difference between the two? How does   16
one determine whether a law is just or unjust? A just law is a
man-made code that squares with the moral law or the law of
God. An unjust law is a code that is out of harmony with the
moral law. To put it in the terms of St. Thomas Aquinas: An
unjust law is a human law that is not rooted in eternal law
and natural law. Any law that uplifts human personality is
just. Any law that degrades human personality is unjust. All
segregation statutes are unjust because segregation distorts
the soul and damages the personality. It gives the segregator a
false sense of superiority and the segregated a false sense of
inferiority. Segregation, to use the terminology of the Jewish
philosopher Martin Buber, substitutes an "I–it" relationship

for an "I–thou" relationship and ends up relegating persons to the status of things. Hence segregation is not only politically, economically and sociologically unsound, it is morally wrong and sinful. Paul Tillich has said that sin is separation. Is not segregation an existential expression of man's tragic separation, his awful estrangement, his terrible sinfulness? Thus it is that I can urge men to obey the 1954 decision of the Supreme Court, for it is morally right; and I can urge them to disobey segregation ordinances, for they are morally wrong.

17   Let us consider a more concrete example of just and unjust laws. An unjust law is a code that a numerical or power majority group compels a minority group to obey but does not make binding on itself. This is *difference* made legal. By the same token, a just law is a code that a majority compels a minority to follow and that it is willing to follow itself. This is *sameness* made legal.

18   Let me give another explanation. A law is unjust if it is inflicted on a minority that, as a result of being denied the right to vote, had no part in enacting or devising the law. Who can say that the legislature of Alabama which set up that state's segregation laws was democratically elected? Throughout Alabama all sorts of devious methods are used to prevent Negroes from becoming registered voters, and there are some counties in which, even though Negroes constitute a majority of the population, not a single Negro is registered. Can any law enacted under such circumstances be considered democratically structured?

19   Sometimes a law is just on its face and unjust in its application. For instance, I have been arrested on a charge of parading without a permit. Now, there is nothing wrong in having an ordinance which requires a permit for a parade. But such an ordinance becomes unjust when it is used to maintain segregation and to deny citizens the First-Amendment privilege of peaceful assembly and protest.

20   I hope you are able to see the distinction I am trying to point out. In no sense do I advocate evading or defying the law, as would the rabid segregationist. That would lead to anarchy. One who breaks an unjust law must do so openly, lovingly, and with a willingness to accept the penalty. I submit that an individual who breaks a law that conscience tells him is unjust, and who willingly accepts the penalty of imprisonment in order to arouse the conscience of the community over its injustice, is in reality expressing the highest respect for law.

21   Of course, there is nothing new about this kind of civil disobedience. It was evidenced sublimely in the refusal of

Shadrach, Meshach and Abednego to obey the laws of Neb-
uchadnezzar, on the ground that a higher moral law was at
stake. It was practiced superbly by the early Christians, who
were willing to face hungry lions and the excruciating pain of
chopping blocks rather than submit to certain unjust laws of
the Roman Empire. To a degree, academic freedom is a reality today because Socrates practiced civil disobedience. In
our own nation, the Boston Tea Party represented a massive
act of civil disobedience.

We should never forget that everything Adolf Hitler did in   22
Germany was "legal" and everything the Hungarian freedom
fighters did in Hungary was "illegal." It was "illegal" to aid
and comfort a Jew in Hitler's Germany. Even so, I am sure
that, had I lived in Germany at the time, I would have aided
and comforted my Jewish brothers. If today I lived in a Communist country where certain principles dear to the Christian
faith are suppressed, I would openly advocate disobeying that
country's antireligious laws.

I must make two honest confessions to you, my Christian   23
and Jewish brothers. First, I must confess that over the past
few years I have been gravely disappointed with the white
moderate. I have almost reached the regrettable conclusion
that the Negro's great stumbling block in his stride toward
freedom is not the White Citizen's Counciler or the Ku Klux
Klanner, but the white moderate, who is more devoted to "order" than to justice; who prefers a negative peace which is the
absence of tension to a positive peace which is the presence of
justice; who constantly says: "I agree with you in the goal you
seek, but I cannot agree with your methods of direct action";
who paternalistically believes he can set the timetable for another man's freedom; who lives by a mythical concept of time
and who constantly advises the Negro to wait for a "more convenient season." Shallow understanding from people of good
will is more frustrating than absolute misunderstanding from
people of ill will. Lukewarm acceptance is much more bewil-
dering than outright rejection.

I had hoped that the white moderate would understand   24
that law and order exist for the purpose of establishing justice
and that when they fail in this purpose they become the dangerously structured dams that block the flow of social
progress. I had hoped that the white moderate would understand that the present tension in the South is a necessary
phase of the transition from an obnoxious negative peace, in
which the Negro passively accepted his unjust plight, to a
substantive and positive peace, in which all men will respect

the dignity and worth of human personality. Actually, we who engage in nonviolent direct action are not the creators of tension. We merely bring to the surface the hidden tension that is already alive. We bring it out in the open, where it can be seen and dealt with. Like a boil that can never be cured so long as it is covered up but must be opened with all its ugliness to the natural medicines of air and light, injustice must be exposed, with all the tension its exposure creates, to the light of human conscience and the air of national opinion before it can be cured.

25   In your statement you assert that our actions, even though peaceful, must be condemned because they precipitate violence. But is this a logical assertion? Isn't this like condemning a robbed man because his possession of money precipitated the evil act of robbery? Isn't this like condemning Socrates because his unswerving commitment to truth and his philosophical inquiries precipitated the act by the misguided populace in which they made him drink hemlock? Isn't this like condemning Jesus because his unique God-consciousness and never-ceasing devotion to God's will precipitated the evil act of crucifixion? We must come to see that, as the federal courts have consistently affirmed, it is wrong to urge an individual to cease his efforts to gain his basic constitutional rights because the quest may precipitate violence. Society must protect the robbed and punish the robber.

26   I had also hoped that the white moderate would reject the myth concerning time in relation to the struggle for freedom. I have just received a letter from a white brother in Texas. He writes: "All Christians know that the colored people will receive equal rights eventually, but it is possible that you are in too great a religious hurry. It has taken Christianity almost two thousand years to accomplish what it has. The teachings of Christ take time to come to earth." Such an attitude stems from a tragic misconception of time, from the strangely irrational notion that there is something in the very flow of time that will inevitably cure all ills. Actually, time itself is neutral; it can be used either destructively or constructively. More and more I feel that the people of ill will have used time much more effectively than have the people of good will. We will have to repent in this generation not merely for the hateful words and actions of the bad people but for the appalling silence of the good people. Human progress never rolls in on wheels of inevitability; it comes through the tireless efforts of men willing to be co-workers with God, and without this hard work, time itself becomes an ally of the forces of social stag-

nation. We must use time creatively, in the knowledge that time is always ripe to do right. Now is the time to make real the promise of democracy and transform our pending national elegy into a creative psalm of brotherhood. Now is the time to lift our national policy from the quicksand of racial injustice to the solid rock of human dignity.

You speak of our activity in Birmingham as extreme. At 27 first I was rather disappointed that fellow clergymen would see my nonviolent efforts as those of an extremist. I began thinking about the fact that I stand in the middle of two opposing forces in the Negro community. One is a force of complacency, made up in part of Negroes who, as a result of long years of oppression, are so drained of self-respect and a sense of "somebodiness" that they have adjusted to segregation; and in part of a few middle-class Negroes who, because of a degree of academic and economic security and because in some ways they profit by segregation, have become insensitive to the problems of the masses. The other force is one of bitterness and hatred, and it comes perilously close to advocating violence. It is expressed in the various black nationalist groups that are springing up across the nation, the largest and best-known being Elijah Muhammad's Muslim movement. Nourished by the Negro's frustration over the continued existence of racial discrimination, this movement is made up of people who have lost faith in America, who have absolutely repudiated Christianity, and who have concluded that the white man is an incorrigible "devil."

I have tried to stand between these two forces, saying that 28 we need emulate neither the "do-nothingism" of the complacent nor the hatred and despair of the black nationalist. For there is the more excellent way of love and nonviolent protest. I am grateful to God that, through the influence of the Negro church, the way of nonviolence became an integral part of our struggle.

If this philosophy had not emerged, by now many streets 29 of the South would, I am convinced, be flowing with blood. And I am further convinced that if our white brothers dismiss as "rabble-rousers" and "outside agitators" those of us who employ nonviolent direct action, and if they refuse to support our nonviolent efforts, millions of Negroes will, out of frustration and despair, seek solace and security in black-nationalist ideologies—a development that would inevitably lead to a frightening racial nightmare.

Oppressed people cannot remain oppressed forever. The 30 yearning for freedom eventually manifests itself, and that is what has happened to the American Negro. Something within has reminded him of his birthright of freedom, and something without has reminded him that it can be gained. Consciously or unconsciously, he has been caught up by the *Zeitgeist*, and with his black brothers of Africa and his brown and yellow brothers of Asia, South America and the Caribbean, the United States Negro is moving with a sense of great urgency toward the promised land of racial justice. If one recognizes this vital urge that has engulfed the Negro community, one should readily understand why public demonstrations are taking place. The Negro has many pent-up resentments and latent frustrations, and he must release them. So let him march; let him make prayer pilgrimages to the city hall; let him go on freedom rides—and try to understand why he must do so. If his repressed emotions are not released in nonviolent ways, they will seek expression through violence; this is not a threat but a fact of history. So I have not said to my people: "Get rid of your discontent." Rather, I have tried to say that this normal and healthy discontent can be channeled into the creative outlet of nonviolent direct action. And now this approach is being termed extremist.

31   But though I was initially disappointed at being categorized as an extremist, as I continued to think about the matter I gradually gained a measure of satisfaction from the label. Was not Jesus an extremist for love: "Love your enemies, bless them that curse you, do good to them that hate you, and pray for them which despitefully use you, and persecute you." Was not Amos an extremist for justice: "Let justice roll down like waters and righteousness like an ever-flowing stream." Was not Paul an extremist for the Christian gospel: "I bear in my body the marks of the Lord Jesus." Was not Martin Luther an extremist: "Here I stand; I cannot do otherwise, so help me God." And John Bunyan: "I will stay in jail to the end of my days before I make a butchery of my conscience." And Abraham Lincoln: "This nation cannot survive half slave and half free." And Thomas Jefferson: "We hold these truths to be self-evident, that all men are created equal..." So the question is not whether we will be extremists, but what kind of extremists we will be. Will we be extremists for hate or for love? Will we be extremists for the preservation of injustice or for the extension of justice? In that dramatic scene on Calvary's hill three men were crucified. We must never forget that all three were crucified for the same crime—the crime of extremism. Two were extremists for immorality, and thus fell below their environment. The other, Jesus Christ, was an extremist for

love, truth and goodness, and thereby rose above his environment. Perhaps the South, the nation and the world are in dire need of creative extremists.

I had hoped that the white moderate would see this need. Perhaps I was too optimistic; perhaps I expected too much. I suppose I should have realized that few members of the oppressor race can understand the deep groans and passionate yearnings of the oppressed race, and still fewer have the vision to see that injustice must be rooted out by strong, persistent and determined action. I am thankful, however, that some of our white brothers in the South have grasped the meaning of this social revolution and committed themselves to it. They are still all too few in quantity, but they are big in quality. Some—such as Ralph McGill, Lillian Smith, Harry Golden, James McBride Dabbs, Ann Braden and Sarah Patton Boyle—have written about our struggle in eloquent and prophetic terms. Others have marched with us down nameless streets of the South. They have languished in filthy, roach-infested jails, suffering the abuse and brutality of policemen who view them as "dirty nigger-lovers." Unlike so many of their moderate brothers and sisters, they have recognized the urgency of the moment and sensed the need for powerful "action" antidotes to combat the disease of segregation. [32]

Let me take note of my other major disappointment. I have been so greatly disappointed with the white church and its leadership. Of course, there are some notable exceptions. I am not unmindful of the fact that each of you has taken some significant stands on this issue. I commend you, Reverend Stallings, for your Christian stand on this past Sunday, in welcoming Negroes to your worship service on a nonsegregated basis. I commend the Catholic leaders of this state for integrating Spring Hill College several years ago. [33]

But despite these notable exceptions, I must honestly reiterate that I have been disappointed with the church. I do not say this as one of those negative critics who can always find something wrong with the church. I say this as a minister of the gospel, who loves the church; who was nurtured in its bosom; who has been sustained by its spiritual blessings and who will remain true to it as long as the cord of life shall lengthen. [34]

When I was suddenly catapulted into the leadership of the bus protest in Montgomery, Alabama, a few years ago, I felt we would be supported by the white church. I felt that the white ministers, priests and rabbis of the South would be among our strongest allies. Instead, some have been outright [35] opponents, refusing to understand the freedom movement and misrepresenting its leaders; all too many others have been more cautious than courageous and have remained silent behind the anesthetizing security of stained-glass windows.

36   In spite of my shattered dreams, I came to Birmingham with the hope that the white religious leadership of this community would see the justice of our cause and, with deep moral concern, would serve as the channel through which our just grievances could reach the power structure. I had hoped that each of you would understand. But again I have been disappointed.

37   I have heard numerous southern religious leaders admonish their worshipers to comply with a desegregation decision because it is the law, but I have longed to hear white ministers declare: "Follow this decree because integration is morally right and because the Negro is your brother." In the midst of blatant injustices inflicted upon the Negro, I have watched white churchmen stand on the sideline and mouth pious irrelevancies and sanctimonious trivialities. In the midst of a mighty struggle to rid our nation of racial and economic injustice, I have heard many ministers say: "Those are social issues, with which the gospel has no real concern." And I have watched many churches commit themselves to a completely otherworldly religion which makes a strange, un-Biblical distortion between body and soul, between the sacred and the secular.

38   I have traveled the length and breadth of Alabama, Mississippi and all the other southern states. On sweltering summer days and crisp autumn mornings I have looked at the South's beautiful churches with their lofty spires pointing heavenward. I have beheld the impressive outlines of her massive religious-education buildings. Over and over I have found myself asking: "What kind of people worship here? Who is their God? Where were their voices when the lips of Governor Barnett dripped with words of interposition and nullification? Where were they when Governor Wallace gave a clarion call for defiance and hatred? Where were their voices of support when bruised and weary Negro men and women decided to rise from the dark dungeons of complacency to the bright hills of creative protest?"

39   Yes, these questions are still in my mind. In deep disappointment I have wept over the laxity of the church. But be assured that my tears have been tears of love. There can be no deep disappointment where there is not deep love. Yes, I love the church. How could I do otherwise? I am in the rather

unique position of being the son, the grandson and the great-grandson of preachers. Yes, I see the church as the body of Christ. But, oh! How we have blemished and scarred that body through social neglect and through fear of being non-conformists.

There was a time when the church was very powerful—in 40 the time when the early Christians rejoiced at being deemed worthy to suffer for what they believed. In those days the church was not merely a thermometer that recorded the ideas and principles of popular opinion; it was a thermostat that transformed the mores of society. Whenever the early Christians entered a town, the people in power became disturbed and immediately sought to convict the Christians for being "disturbers of the peace" and "outside agitators." But the Christians pressed on, in the conviction that they were "a colony of heaven," called to obey God rather than man. Small in number, they were big in commitment. They were too God-intoxicated to be "astronomically intimidated." By their effort and example they brought an end to such ancient evils as infanticide and gladiatorial contests.

Things are different now. So often the contemporary church 41 is a weak, ineffectual voice with an uncertain sound. So often it is an arch-defender of the status quo. Far from being disturbed by the presence of the church, the power structure of the average community is consoled by the church's silent—and often even vocal—sanction of things as they are.

But the judgment of God is upon the church as never be- 42 fore. If today's church does not recapture the sacrificial spirit of the early church, it will lose its authenticity, forfeit the loyalty of millions, and be dismissed as an irrelevant social club with no meaning for the twentieth century. Every day I meet young people whose disappointment with the church has turned into outright disgust.

Perhaps I have once again been too optimistic. Is orga- 43 nized religion too inextricably bound to the status quo to save our nation and the world? Perhaps I must turn my faith to the inner spiritual church, the church within the church, as the true *ekklesia* and the hope of the world. But again I am thankful to God that some noble souls from the ranks of organized religion have broken loose from the paralyzing chains of conformity and joined us as active partners in the struggle for freedom. They have left their secure congregations and walked the streets of Albany, Georgia, with us. They have gone down the highways of the South on tortuous rides for freedom. Yes, they have gone to jail with us. Some have been dismissed from their churches, have lost the support of their bishops and fellow ministers. But they have acted in the faith that right defeated is stronger than evil triumphant. Their witness has been the spiritual salt that has preserved the true meaning of the gospel in these troubled times. They have carved a tunnel of hope through the dark mountain of disappointment.

44   I hope the church as a whole will meet the challenge of this decisive hour. But even if the church does not come to the aid of justice, I have no despair about the future. I have no fear about the outcome of our struggle in Birmingham, even if our motives are at present misunderstood. We will reach the goal of freedom in Birmingham and all over the nation, because the goal of America is freedom. Abused and scorned though we may be, our destiny is tied up with America's destiny. Before the pilgrims landed at Plymouth, we were here. Before the pen of Jefferson etched the majestic words of the Declaration of Independence across the pages of history, we were here. For more than two centuries our forebears labored in this country without wages; they made cotton king; they built the homes of their masters while suffering gross injustice and shameful humiliation—and yet out of a bottomless vitality they continued to thrive and develop. If the inexpressible cruelties of slavery could not stop us, the opposition we now face will surely fail. We will win our freedom because the sacred heritage of our nation and the eternal will of God are embodied in our echoing demands.

45   Before closing I feel impelled to mention one other point in your statement that has troubled me profoundly. You warmly commended the Birmingham police force for keeping "order" and "preventing violence." I doubt that you would have so warmly commended the police force if you had seen its dogs sinking their teeth into unarmed, nonviolent Negroes. I doubt that you would so quickly commend the policemen if you were to observe their ugly and inhumane treatment of Negroes here in the city jail; if you were to watch them push and curse old Negro women and young Negro girls; if you were to see them slap and kick old Negro men and young boys; if you were to observe them, as they did on two occasions, refuse to give us food because we wanted to sing our grace together. I cannot join you in your praise of the Birmingham Police Department.

46   It is true that the police have exercised a degree of discipline in handling the demonstrators. In this sense they have conducted themselves rather "nonviolently" in public. But for

what purpose? To preserve the evil system of segregation. Over the past few years I have consistently preached that nonviolence demands that the means we use must be as pure as the ends we seek. I have tried to make clear that it is wrong to use immoral means to attain moral ends. But now I must affirm that it is just as wrong, or perhaps even more so, to use moral means to preserve immoral ends. Perhaps Mr. Connor and his policemen have been rather nonviolent in public, as was Chief Pritchett in Albany, Georgia, but they have used the moral means of nonviolence to maintain the immoral end of racial injustice. As T. S. Eliot has said: "The last temptation is the greatest treason: To do the right deed for the wrong reason."

I wish you had commended the Negro sit-inners and demonstrators of Birmingham for their sublime courage, their willingness to suffer and their amazing discipline in the midst of great provocation. One day the South will recognize its real heroes. They will be the James Merediths, with the noble sense of purpose that enables them to face jeering and hostile mobs, and with the agonizing loneliness that characterizes the life of the pioneer. They will be old, oppressed, battered Negro women, symbolized in a seventy-two-year-old woman in Montgomery, Alabama, who rose up with a sense of dignity and with her people decided not to ride segregated buses, and who responded with ungrammatical profundity to one who inquired about her weariness: "My feets is tired, but my soul is at rest." They will be the young high school and college students, the young ministers of the gospel and a host of their elders, courageously and nonviolently sitting in at lunch counters and willingly going to jail for conscience sake. One day the South will know that when these disinherited children of God sat down at lunch counters, they were in reality standing up for what is best in the American dream and for the most sacred values in our Judaeo-Christian heritage, thereby bringing our nation back to those great wells of democracy which were dug deep by the founding fathers in their formulation of the Constitution and the Declaration of Independence. 47

Never before have I written so long a letter. I'm afraid it is much too long to take your precious time. I can assure you that it would have been much shorter if I had been writing from a comfortable desk, but what else can one do when he is alone in a narrow jail cell, other than write long letters, think long thoughts and pray long prayers? 48

49   If I have said anything in this letter that overstates the truth and indicates an unreasonable impatience, I beg you to forgive me. If I have said anything that understates the truth and indicates my having a patience that allows me to settle for anything less than brotherhood, I beg God to forgive me.

50   I hope this letter finds you strong in the faith. I also hope that circumstances will soon make it possible for me to meet each of you, not as an integrationist or a civil-rights leader but as a fellow clergyman and a Christian brother. Let us all hope that the dark clouds of racial prejudice will soon pass away and the deep fog of misunderstanding will be lifted from our fear-drenched communities, and in some not too distant tomorrow the radiant stars of love and brotherhood will shine over our great nation with all their scintillating beauty.

> Yours for the cause of Peace and Brotherhood,
> Martin Luther King Jr.

Lewis H. Van Dusen Jr.

Civil Disobedience: Destroyer of Democracy

Lewis H. Van Dusen Jr. (born 1910) has practiced law in Philadelphia since 1935. Decorated for valor during World War II, he also served with the State Department during his distinguished career. He has written many essays for professional journals; the following one appeared in 1969 in the American Bar Association Journal.

1   As Charles E. Wyzanski, Chief Judge of the United States District Court in Boston, wrote in the February 1968, *Atlantic:* "Disobedience is a long step from dissent. Civil disobedience involves a deliberate and punishable breach of legal duty." Protesters might prefer a different definition. They would rather say that civil disobedience is the peaceful resistance of conscience.

2   The philosophy of civil disobedience was not developed in our American democracy, but in the very first democracy of

Athens. It was expressed by the poet Sophocles and the philosopher Socrates. In Sophocles' tragedy, Antigone chose to obey her conscience and violate the state edict against providing burial for her brother, who had been decreed a traitor. When the dictator Creon found out that Antigone had buried her fallen brother, he confronted her and reminded her that there was a mandatory death penalty for this deliberate disobedience of the state law. Antigone nobly replied, "Nor did I think your orders were so strong that you, a mortal man, could overrun the gods' unwritten and unfailing laws."

Conscience motivated Antigone. She was not testing the 3 validity of the law in the hope that eventually she would be sustained. Appealing to the judgment of the community, she explained her action to the chorus. She was not secret and surreptitious—the interment of her brother was open and public. She was not violent; she did not trespass on another citizen's rights. And finally, she accepted without resistance the death sentence—the penalty for violation. By voluntarily accepting the law's sanctions, she was not a revolutionary denying the authority of the state. Antigone's behavior exemplifies the classic case of civil disobedience.

Socrates believed that reason could dictate a conscientious 4 disobedience of state law, but he also believed that he had to accept the legal sanctions of the state. In Plato's *Crito*, Socrates from his hanging basket accepted the death penalty for his teaching of religion to youths contrary to state laws.

The sage of Walden, Henry David Thoreau, took this philos- 5 ophy of nonviolence and developed it into a strategy for solving society's injustices. First enunciating it in protest against the Mexican War, he then turned it to use against slavery. For refusing to pay taxes that would help pay the enforcers of the fugitive slave law, he went to prison. In Thoreau's words, "If the alternative is to keep all just men in prison or to give up slavery, the state will not hesitate which to choose."

Sixty years later, Gandhi took Thoreau's civil disobedience 6 as his strategy to wrest Indian independence from England. The famous salt march against a British imperial tax is his best-known example of protest.

But the conscientious law breaking of Socrates, Gandhi, 7 and Thoreau is to be distinguished from the conscientious law testing of Martin Luther King, Jr., who was not a civil disobedient. The civil disobedient withholds taxes or violates state laws knowing he is legally wrong, but believing he is morally right. While he wrapped himself in the mantle of Gandhi and Thoreau, Dr. King led his followers in violation of state laws he believed were contrary to the Federal Constitution. But since Supreme Court decisions in the end generally upheld his many actions, he should not be considered a true civil disobedient.

8   The civil disobedience of Antigone is like that of the pacifist who withholds paying the percentage of his taxes that goes to the Defense Department, or the Quaker who travels against State Department regulations to Hanoi to distribute medical supplies, or the Vietnam war protester who tears up his draft card. This civil disobedient has been nonviolent in his defiance of the law; he has been unfurtive in his violation; he has been submissive to the penalties of the law. He has neither evaded the law nor interfered with another's rights. He has been neither a rioter nor a revolutionary. The thrust of his cause has not been the might of coercion but the martyrdom of conscience.

Was the Boston Tea Party Civil Disobedience?

9   Those who justify violence and radical action as being in the tradition of our Revolution show a misunderstanding of the philosophy of democracy.

10   James Farmer, former head of the Congress of Racial Equality, in defense of the mass action confrontation method, has told of a famous organized demonstration that took place in opposition to political and economic discrimination. The protestors beat back and scattered the law enforcers and then proceeded to loot and destroy private property. Mr. Farmer then said he was talking about the Boston Tea Party and implied that violence as a method for redress of grievances was an American tradition and a legacy of our revolutionary heritage. While it is true that there is no more sacred document than our Declaration of Independence, Jefferson's "inherent right of rebellion" was predicated on the tyrannical denial of democratic means. If there is no popular assembly to provide an adjustment of ills, and if there is no court system to dispose of injustices, then there is, indeed, a right to rebel.

11   The seventeenth century's John Locke, the philosophical father of the Declaration of Independence, wrote in his *Second Treatise on Civil Government:* "Wherever law ends, tyranny begins...and the people are absolved from any further obedience. Governments are dissolved from within when the legislative [chamber] is altered. When the government

[becomes]...arbitrary disposers of lives, liberties and fortunes of the people, such revolutions happen...."

But there are some sophisticated proponents of the revolutionary redress of grievances who say that the test of the need for radical action is not the unavailability of democratic institutions but the ineffectuality of those institutions to remove blatant social inequalities. If social injustice exists, they say, concerted disobedience is required against the constituted government, whether it be totalitarian or democratic in structure.   12

Of course, only the most bigoted chauvinist would claim that America is without some glaring faults. But there has never been a utopian society on earth and there never will be unless human nature is remade. Since inequities will mar even the best-framed democracies, the injustice rationale would allow a free right of civil resistance to be available always as a shortcut alternative to the democratic way of petition, debate and assembly. The lesson of history is that civil insurgency spawns far more injustices than it removes. The Jeffersons, Washingtons, and Adamses resisted tyranny with the aim of promoting the procedures of democracy. They would never have resisted a democratic government with the risk of promoting the techniques of tyranny.   13

Legitimate Pressures and Illegitimate Results

There are many civil rights leaders who show impatience with the process of democracy. They rely on the sit-ins, boycott or mass picketing to gain speedier solutions to the problems that face every citizen. But we must realize that the legitimate pressures that won concessions in the past can easily escalate into the illegitimate power plays that might extort demands in the future. The victories of these civil rights leaders must not shake our confidence in the democratic procedures, as the pressures of demonstration are desirable only if they take place within the limits allowed by law. Civil rights gains should continue to be won by the persuasion of Congress and other legislative bodies and by the decision of courts. Any illegal entreaty for the rights of some can be an injury to the rights of others, for mass demonstrations often trigger violence.   14

Those who advocate taking the law into their own hands should reflect that when they are disobeying what they consider to be an immoral law, they are deciding on a possibly   15

immoral course. Their answer is that the process for democratic relief is too slow, that only mass confrontation can
bring immediate action, and that any injuries are the inevitable cost of the pursuit of justice. Their answer is, simply put,
that the end justifies the means. It is this justification of any
form of demonstration as a form of dissent that threatens to
destroy a society built on the rule of law.

16   Our Bill of Rights guarantees wide opportunities to use
mass meetings, public parades, and organized demonstrations to stimulate sentiment, to dramatize issues, and to
cause change. The Washington freedom march of 1963 was
such a call for action. But the rights of free expression cannot
be mere force cloaked in the garb of free speech. As the courts
have decreed in labor cases, free assembly does not mean
mass picketing or sit-down strikes. These rights are subject to
limitations of time and place so as to secure the rights of
others. When militant students storm a college president's
office to achieve demands, when certain groups plan rush-
hour car stalling to protest discrimination in employment,
these are not dissent, but a denial of rights to others. Neither is
it the lawful use of mass protest, but rather the unlawful use
of mob power.

17   Justice Black, one of the foremost advocates and defenders
of the right of protest and dissent, has said:

> ...Experience demonstrates that it is not a far step from
> what to many seems to be the earnest, honest, patriotic,
> kind-spirited multitude of today, to the fanatical, threaten-
> ing, lawless mob of tomorrow. And the crowds that press in
> the streets for noble goals today can be supplanted tomorrow
> by street mobs pressuring the courts for precisely opposite
> ends.[1]

18   Society must censure those demonstrators who would trespass on the public peace, as it must condemn those rioters
whose pillage would destroy the public peace. But more
ambivalent is society's posture toward the civil disobedient.
Unlike the rioter, the true civil disobedient commits no
violence. Unlike the mob demonstrator, he commits no
trespass on others' rights. The civil disobedient, while deliberately violating a law, shows an oblique respect for the law by

---

[1]In *Cox v. Louisiana,* 379 U.S. 536, 575, 584 (1965).

voluntarily submitting to its sanctions. He neither resists arrest nor evades punishment. Thus, he breaches the law but not the peace.

But civil disobedience, whatever the ethical rationaliza-   19
tion, is still an assault on our democratic society, an affront to our legal order and an attack on our constitutional government. To indulge civil disobedience is to invite anarchy, and the permissive arbitrariness of anarchy is hardly less tolerable than the repressive arbitrariness of tyranny. Too often the license of liberty is followed by the loss of liberty, because into the desert of anarchy comes the man on horseback, a Mussolini or a Hitler.

Violations of Law Subvert Democracy

Law violations, even for ends recognized as laudable, are   20
not only assaults on the rule of law, but subversions of the democratic process. The disobedient act of conscience does not ennoble democracy; it erodes it.

First, it courts violence, and even the most careful and lim-   21
ited use of nonviolent acts of disobedience may help sow the dragon-teeth of civil riot. Civil disobedience is the progenitor of disorder, and disorder is the sire of violence.

Second, the concept of civil disobedience does not invite   22
principles of general applicability. If the children of light are morally privileged to resist particular laws on grounds of conscience, so are the children of darkness. Former Deputy Attorney General Burke Marshall said: "If the decision to break the law really turned on individual conscience, it is hard to see in law how [the civil rights leader] is better off than former Governor Ross Barnett of Mississippi who also believed deeply in his cause and was willing to go to jail."[2]

Third, even the most noble act of civil disobedience as-   23
saults the rule of law. Although limited as to method, motive and objective, it has the effect of inducing others to engage in different forms of law breaking characterized by methods unsanctioned and condemned by classic theories of law violation. Unfortunately, the most patent lesson of civil disobedience is not so much nonviolence of action as defiance of authority.

[2]"The Protest movement and the Law," *Virginia Legal Review* 51 (1965), 785.

24   Finally, the greatest danger in condoning civil disobedience as a permissible strategy for hastening change is that it
undermines our democratic processes. To adopt the techniques of civil disobedience is to assume that representative
government does not work. To resist the decisions of courts
and the laws of elected assemblies is to say that democracy
has failed.

25   There is no man who is above the law, and there is no man
who has a right to break the law. Civil disobedience is not
above the law, but against the law. When the civil disobedient
disobeys one law, he invariably subverts all law. When the
civil disobedient says that he is above the law, he is saying
that democracy is beneath him. His disobedience shows a
distrust for the democratic system. He is merely saying that
since democracy does not work, why should he help make it
work. Thoreau expressed well the civil disobedient's disdain
for democracy:

> As for adopting the ways which the state has provided for
> remedying the evil, I know not of such ways. They take too
> much time and a man's life will be gone. I have other affairs
> to attend to. I came into this world not chiefly to make this a
> good place to live in, but to live in it, be it good or bad.[3]

26   Thoreau's position is not only morally irresponsible but politically reprehensible. When citizens in a democracy are
called on to make a profession of faith, the civil disobedients
offer only a confession of failure. Tragically, when civil disobedients for lack of faith abstain from democratic involvement, they help attain their own gloomy prediction. They
help create the social and political basis for their own despair.
By foreseeing failure, they help forge it. If citizens rely on an-
tidemocratic means of protest, they will help bring about the
undemocratic result of an authoritarian or anarchic state.

27   How far demonstrations properly can be employed to produce political and social change is a pressing question, particularly in view of the provocations accompanying the National
Democratic Convention in Chicago last August and the reaction of the police to them. A line must be drawn by the judiciary between the demands of those who seek absolute order,
which can lead only to a dictatorship, and those who seek absolute freedom, which can lead only to anarchy. The line,

---

[3]Thoreau, "Civil Disobedience" (see page 637).

wherever it is drawn by our courts, should be respected on the college campus, on the streets, and elsewhere.

Undue provocation will inevitably result in overreaction, human emotions being what they are. Violence will follow. This cycle undermines the very democracy it is designed to preserve. The lesson of the past is that democracies will fall if violence, including the intentional provocations that will lead to violence, replaces democratic procedures, as in Athens, Rome, and the Weimar Republic. This lesson must be constantly explained by the legal profession. 28

We should heed the words of William James: 29

> Democracy is still upon its trial. The civic genius of our people is its only bulwark and . . . neither battleships nor public libraries nor great newspapers nor booming stocks: neither mechanical invention nor political adroitness, nor churches nor universities nor civil service examinations can save us from degeneration if the inner mystery be lost.
>
> That mystery, at once the secret and the glory of our English-speaking race, consists of nothing but two habits. . . . [O]ne of them is the habit of trained and disciplined good temper towards the opposite party when it fairly wins its innings. The other is that of fierce and merciless resentment toward every man or set of men who break the public peace.[4]

[4]James, *Pragmatism* (1907), pp. 127–28.

SHOULD ABORTION BE LEGAL?

Gwendolyn Brooks
The Mother

Gwendolyn Brooks (born 1917) is one of the most important American poets of this century. In her many books of poetry she often concentrates on the struggle of the individual against difficult circumstances, as in the following poem. "The Mother" first appeared in Brooks's first book, A Street in Bronzeville *(1945), which takes the reader on a trip through the various facets of an African American community; most recently it was reprinted in her 1991 book* Blacks. *Brooks currently lives in Chicago.*

1 Abortions will not let you forget.
You remember the children you got that you did not get,
The damp small pulps with a little or with no hair,
The singers and workers that never handled the air.
You will never neglect or beat
Them, or silence or buy with a sweet.
You will never wind up the sucking-thumb
Or scuttle off ghosts that come.
You will never leave them, controlling your luscious sigh,
Return for a snack of them, with gobbling mother-eye.

2 I have heard in the voices of the wind the voices of my dim
    killed children.
I have contracted. I have eased
My dim dears at the breasts they could never suck.
I have said, Sweets, if I sinned, if I seized
Your luck
And your lives from your unfinished reach,
If I stole your births and your names,
Your straight baby tears and your games,
Your stilted or lovely loves, your tumults, your marriages,
    aches, and your deaths,
If I poisoned the beginnings of your breaths,
Believe that even in my deliberateness I was not deliberate.

Though why should I whine,   3
Whine that the crime was other than mine?—
Since anyhow you are dead.
Or rather, or instead,
You were never made.
But that too, I am afraid,
Is faulty: oh, what shall I say, how is the truth to be said?
You were born, you had body, you died.
It is just that you never giggled or planned or cried.

Believe me, I loved you all.   4
Believe me, I knew you, though faintly, and I loved, I loved
    you
All.

Sallie Tisdale
We Do Abortions Here

*A registered nurse and writer, Tisdale (born 1957) has pub-
lished two books about the nursing profession,* The Sorcerer's
Apprentice: Medical Miracles and Other Disasters *(1986) and*
Harvest Moon: Portrait of a Nursing Home *(1987), as well as*
Lot's Wife: Salt and the Human Condition *(1988). (She has
also published a book on the issue of pornography,* Talk Dirty
to Me, *and she writes frequently for* Tricycle, *a Zen Buddhist
publication.) In the following essay, published in 1987 in*
Harper's *magazine (a prestigious forum for discussions of
American culture and politics), Tisdale describes her experiences as a nurse in an abortion clinic. Does her essay take a
position on the abortion question?*

We do abortions here; that is all we do. There are weary,   1
grim moments when I think I cannot bear another basin of
bloody remains, utter another kind phrase of reassurance. So
I leave the procedure room in the back and reach for a new
chart. Soon I am talking to an eighteen-year-old woman pregnant for the fourth time. I push up her sleeve to check her
blood pressure and find row upon row of needle marks, neat
and parallel and discolored. She has been so hungry for her

drug for so long that she has taken to using the loose skin of her upper arms; her elbows are already a permanent ruin of bruises. She is surprised to find herself nearly four months pregnant. I suspect she is often surprised, in a mild way, by the blows she is dealt. I prepare myself for another basin, another brief and chafing loss.

2   "How can you stand it?" Even the clients ask. They see the machine, the strange instruments, the blood, the final stroke that wipes away the promise of pregnancy. Sometimes I see that too: I watch a woman's swollen abdomen sink to softness in a few stuttering moments and my own belly flip-flops with sorrow. But all it takes for me to catch my breath is another interview, one more story that sounds so much like the last one. There is a numbing sameness lurking in this job: the same questions, the same answers, even the same trembling tone in the voices. The worst is the sameness of human failure, of inadequacy in the face of each day's dull demands.

3   In describing this work, I find it difficult to explain how much I enjoy it most of the time. We laugh a lot here, as friends and as professional peers. It's nice to be with women all day. I like the sudden, transient bonds I forge with some clients: moments when I am in my strength, remembering weakness, and a woman in weakness reaches out for my strength. What I offer is not power, but solidness, offered almost eagerly. Certain clients waken in me every tender urge I have—others make me wince and bite my tongue. Both challenge me to find a balance. It is a sweet brutality we practice here, a stark and loving dispassion.

4   I look at abortion as if I am standing on a cliff with a telescope, gazing at some great vista. I can sweep the horizon with both eyes, survey the scene in all its distance and size. Or I can put my eye to the lens and focus on the small details, suddenly so close. In abortion the absolute must always be tempered by the contextual, because both are real, both valid, both hard. How can we do this? How can we refuse? Each abortion is a measure of our failure to protect, to nourish our own. Each basin I empty is a promise—but a promise broken a long time ago.

5   I grew up on the great promise of birth control. Like many women my age, I took the pill as soon as I was sexually active. To risk pregnancy when it was so easy to avoid seemed stupid, and my contraceptive success, as it were, was part of the promise of social enlightenment. But birth control fails, far more frequently than laboratory trials predict. Many of our clients take the pill; its failure to protect them is a shocking

realization. We have clients who have been sterilized, whose husbands have had vasectomies; each one is a statistical misfit, fine print come to life. The anger and shame of these women I hold in one hand, and the basin in the other. The distance between the two, the length I pace and try to measure, is the size of an abortion.

The procedure is disarmingly simple. Women are sur- 6 prised, as though the mystery of conception, a dark and hidden genesis, requires an elaborate finale. In the first trimester of pregnancy, it's a mere few minutes of vacuuming, a neat tidying up. I give a woman a small yellow Valium, and when it has begun to relax her, I lead her into the back, into bareness, the stirrups. The doctor reaches in her, opening the narrow tunnel to the uterus with a succession of slim, smooth bars of steel. He inserts a plastic tube and hooks it to a hose on the machine. The woman is framed against white paper that crackles as she moves, the light bright in her eyes. Then the machine rumbles low and loud in the small windowless room; the doctor moves the tube back and forth with an efficient rhythm, and the long tail of it fills with blood that spurts and stumbles along into a jar. He is usually finished in a few minutes. They are long minutes for the woman; her uterus frequently reacts to its abrupt emptying with a powerful, unceasing cramp, which cuts off the blood vessels and enfolds the irritated, bleeding tissue.

I am learning to recognize the shadows that cross the faces 7 of the women I hold. While the doctor works between her spread legs, the paper drape hiding his intent expression, I stand beside the table. I hold the woman's hands in mine, resting them just below her ribs. I watch her eyes, finger her necklace, stroke her hair. I ask about her job, her family; in a haze she answers me; we chatter, faces close, eyes meeting and sliding apart.

I watch the shadows that creep up unnoticed and suddenly 8 darken her face as she screws up her features and pushes a tear out each side to slide down her cheeks. I have learned to anticipate the quiver of chin, the rapid intake of breath, and the surprising sobs that rise soon after the machine starts to drum. I know this is when the cramp deepens, and the tears are partly the tears that follow pain—the sharp, childish crying when one bumps one's head on a cabinet door. But a well of woe seems to open beneath many women when they hear that thumping sound. The anticipation of the moment has finally come to fruit; the moment has arrived when the loss is no longer an imagined one. It has come true.

9   I am struck with the sameness and I am struck every day by the variety here—how this commonplace dilemma can so display the differences of women. A twenty-one-year-old woman, unemployed, uneducated, without family, in the fifth month of her fifth pregnancy. A forty-two-year-old mother of teenagers, shocked by her condition, refusing to tell her husband. A twenty-three-year-old mother of two having her seventh abortion, and many women in their thirties having their first. Some are stoic, some hysterical, a few giggle uncontrollably, many cry.

10   I talk to a sixteen-year-old uneducated girl who was raped. She has gonorrhea. She describes blinding headaches, attacks of breathlessness, nausea. "Sometimes I feel like two different people," she tells me with a calm smile, "and I talk to myself."

11   I pull out my plastic models. She listens patiently for a time, and then holds her hands wide in front of her stomach.

12   "When's the baby going to go up into my stomach?" she asks.

13   I blink. "What do you mean?"

14   "Well," she says, still smiling, "when women get so big, isn't the baby in your stomach? Doesn't it hatch out of an egg there?"

15   My first question in an interview is always the same. As I walk down the hall with the woman, as we get settled in chairs and I glance through her files, I am trying to gauge her, to get a sense of the words, and the tone, I should use. With some I joke, with others I chat, sometimes fall into a brisk, business-line patter. But I ask every woman, "Are you sure you want to have an abortion?" Most nod with grim knowing smiles. "Oh, yes," they sigh. Some seek forgiveness, offer excuses. Occasionally a woman will flinch and say, "Please don't use that word."

16   Later I describe the procedure to come, using care with my language. I don't say "pain" any more than I would say "baby." So many are afraid to ask how much it will hurt. "My sister told me—" I hear. "A friend of mine said—" and the dire expectations unravel. I prick the index finger of a woman for a drop of blood to test, and as the tiny lancet approaches the skin she averts her eyes, holding her trembling hand out to me and jumping at my touch.

17   It is when I am holding a plastic uterus in one hand, a suction tube in the other, moving them together in imitation of the scrubbing to come, that women ask the most secret question. I am speaking in a matter-of-fact voice about "the tissue" and "the contents" when the woman suddenly catches my eye

and asks, "How big is the baby now?" These words suggest a
quiet need for a definition of the boundaries being drawn. It
isn't so odd, after all, that she feels relief when I describe the
growing bud's bulbous shape, its miniature nature. Again I
gauge, and sometimes lie a little, weaseling around its infan-
tile features until its clinging power slackens.

But when I look in the basin, among the curdlike blood   18
clots, I see an elfin thorax, attenuated, its pencilline ribs all in
parallel rows with tiny knobs of spine rounding upwards. The
translucent arm and hand swim beside.

A sleepy-eyed girl, just fourteen, watched me with a slight   19
and goofy smile all through her abortion. "Does it have little
feet and little fingers and all?" she'd asked earlier. When the
suction was over she sat up woozily at the end of the table
and murmured, "Can I see it?" I shook my head firmly.

"It's not allowed," I told her sternly, because I knew she   20
didn't really want to see what was left. She accepted this
statement of authority, and a shadow of confused relief
crossed her plain, pale face.

Privately, even grudgingly, my colleagues might admit the   21
power of abortion to provoke emotion. But they seem to prefer
the broad view and disdain the telescope. Abortion is a matter
of choice, privacy, control. Its uncertainty lies in specific cases:
retarded women and girls too young to give consent for surgery, women who are ill or hostile or psychotic. Such common
dilemmas are met with both compassion and impatience; they
slow things down. We are too busy to chew over ethics. One
person might discuss certain concerns, behind closed doors, or
describe a particularly disturbing dream. But generally there is
to be no ambivalence.

Every day I take calls from women who are annoyed that   22
we cannot see them, cannot do their abortion today, this
morning, now. They argue the price, demand that we stay after hours to accommodate their job or class schedule. Abortion is so routine that one expects it to be like a manicure:
quick, cheap, and painless.

Still, I've cultivated a certain disregard. It isn't negligence,   23
but I don't always pay attention. I couldn't be here if I tried to
judge each case on its merits; after all, we do over a hundred
abortions a week. At some point each individual in this line of
work draws a boundary and adheres to it. For one physician
the boundary is a particular week of gestation; for another, it
is a certain number of repeated abortions. But these boundaries can be fluid too: one physician overruled his own limit

to abort a mature but severely malformed fetus. For me, the limit is allowing my clients to carry their own burden, shoulder the responsibility themselves. I shoulder the burden of trying not to judge them.

24   This city has several "crisis pregnancy centers" advertised in the Yellow Pages. They are small offices staffed by volunteers, and they offer free pregnancy testing, glossy photos of dead fetuses, and movies. I had a client recently whose mother is active in the antiabortion movement. The young woman went to the local crisis center and was told that the doctor would make her touch the dismembered baby, that the pain would be the most horrible she could imagine, and that she might, after an abortion, never be able to have children. All lies. They called her at home and at work, over and over and over, but she had been wise enough to give a false name. She came to us a fugitive. We who do abortions are marked, by some, as impure. It's dirty work.

25   When a delivery man comes to the sliding glass window by the reception desk and tilts a box toward me, I hesitate. I read the packing slip, assess the shape and weight of the box in the light of its supposed contents. We request familiar faces. The doors are carefully locked; I have learned to half glance around at bags and boxes, looking for a telltale sign. I register with security when I arrive, and I am careful not to bang a door. We are a little on edge here.

26   Concern about size and shape seem to be natural, and so is the relief that follows. We make the powerful assumption that the fetus is different from us, and even when we admit the similarities, it is too simplistic to be seduced by form alone. But the form is enormously potent—humanoid, powerless, palm-sized, and pure, it evokes an almost fierce tenderness when viewed simply as what it appears to be. But appearance, and even potential, aren't enough. The fetus, in becoming itself, can ruin others: its utter dependence has a sinister side. When I am struck in the moment by the contents in the basin, I am careful to remember the context, to note the tearful teenager and the woman sighing with something more than relief. One kind of question, though, I find considerably trickier.

27   "Can you tell what it is?" I am asked, and this means gender. This question is asked by couples, not women alone. Always couples would abort a girl and keep a boy. I have been asked about twins, and even if I could tell what race the father was.

28   An eighteen-year-old woman with three daughters brought her husband to the interview. He glared first at me, then at his

wife, as he sank lower and lower in the chair, picking his teeth with a toothpick. He interrupted a conversation with his wife to ask if I could tell whether the baby would be a boy or a girl. I told him I could not.

"Good," he replied in a slow and strangely malevolent   29 voice, "'cause if it was a boy I'd wring her neck."

In a literal sense, abortion exists because we are able to ask   30 such questions, able to assign a value to the fetus which can shift with changing circumstances. If the human bond to a child were as primitive and unflinchingly narrow as that of other animals, there would be no abortion. There would be no abortion because there would be nothing more important than caring for the young and perpetuating the species, no reason for sex but to make babies. I sense this sometimes, this wordless organic duty, when I do ultrasounds.

We do ultrasound, a sound-wave test that paints a faint,   31 gray picture of the fetus, whenever we're uncertain of gestation. Age is measured by the width of the skull and confirmed by the length of the femur or thighbone; we speak of a pregnancy as being a certain "femur length" in weeks. The usual concern is whether a pregnancy is within the legal limit for an abortion. Women this far along have bellies which swell out round and tight like trim muscles. When they lie flat, the mound rises softly above the hips, pressing the umbilicus upward.

It takes practice to read an ultrasound picture, which is   32 grainy and etched as though in strokes of charcoal. But suddenly a rapid rhythmic motion appears—the beating heart. Nearby is a soft oval, scratched with lines—the skull. The leg is harder to find, and then suddenly the fetus moves, bobbing in the surf. The skull turns away, an arm slides across the screen, the torso rolls. I know the weight of a baby's head on my shoulder, the whisper of lips on ears, the delicate curve of a fragile spine in my hand. I know how heavy and correct a newborn cradled feels. The creature I watch in secret requires nothing from me but to be left alone, and that is precisely what won't be done.

These inadvertently made beings are caught in a twisting   33 web of motive and desire. They are at least inconvenient, sometimes quite literally dangerous in the womb, but most often they fall somewhere in between—consequences never quite believed in come to roost. Their virtue rises and falls outside their own nature: they become only what we make them. A fetus created by accident is the most absolute kind of surprise. Whether the blame lies in a failed IUD, a slipped condom, or a false impression of safety, that fetus is a thing whose creation has been actively worked against. Its existence is an error. I think this is why so few women, even late in pregnancy, will consider giving a baby up for adoption. To do so means making the fetus real—imagining it as something whole and outside oneself. The decision to terminate a pregnancy is sometimes so difficult and confounding that it creates an enormous demand for immediate action. The decision is rejection; the pregnancy has become something to be rid of, a condition to be ended. It is a burden, a weight, a thing separate.

34   Women have abortions because they are too old, and too young, too poor, and too rich, too stupid, and too smart. I see women who berate themselves with violent emotions for their first and only abortion, and others who return three times, five times, hauling two or three children, who cannot remember to take a pill or where they put the diaphragm. We talk glibly about choice. But the choice for what? I see all the broken promises in lives lived like a series of impromptu obstacles. There are the sweet, light promises of love and intimacy, the glittering promise of education and progress, the warm promise of safe families, long years of innocence and community. And there is the promise of freedom: freedom from failure, from faithlessness. Freedom from biology. The early feminist defense of abortion asked many questions, but the one I remember is this: is biology destiny? And the answer is yes, sometimes it is. Women who have the fewest choices of all exercise their right to abortion the most.

35   Oh, the ignorance. I take a woman to the back room and ask her to undress; a few minutes later I return and find her positioned discreetly behind a drape, still wearing underpants. "Do I have to take these off too?" she asks, a little shocked. Some swear they have not had sex. Many do not know what a uterus is, how sperm and egg meet, how sex makes babies. Some late seekers do not believe themselves pregnant; they believe themselves *impregnable*. I was chastised when I began this job for referring to some clients as girls: it is a feminist heresy. They come so young, snapping gum, sockless and sneakered, and their shakily applied eyeliner smears when they cry. I call them girls with maternal benignity. I cannot imagine them as mothers.

36   The doctor seats himself between the woman's thighs and reaches into the dilated opening of a five-month pregnant uterus. Quickly he grabs and crushes the fetus in several

places, and the room is filled with a low clatter and snap of forceps, the click of the tanaculum,[1] and a pulling, sucking sound. The paper crinkles as the drugged and sleepy woman shifts, the nurse's low, honey-brown voice explains each step in delicate words.

I have fetus dreams, we all do here: dreams of abortions one after the other; of buckets of blood splashed on the walls; trees full of crawling fetuses. I dreamed that two men grabbed me and began to drag me away: "Let's do an abortion," they said with a sickening leer, and I began to scream, plunged into a vision of sucking, scraping pain, of being spread and torn by impartial instruments that do only what they are bidden. I woke from this dream barely able to breathe and thought of kitchen tables and coat hangers, knitting needles striped with blood, and women all alone clutching a pillow in their teeth to keep the screams from piercing the apartment-house walls. Abortion is the narrowest edge between kindness and cruelty. Done as well as it can be, it is still violence—merciful violence, like putting a suffering animal to death.

Maggie, one of the nurses, received a call at midnight not long ago. It was a woman in her twentieth week of pregnancy; the necessarily gradual process of cervical dilation begun the day before had stimulated labor, as it sometimes does. Maggie and one of the doctors met the woman at the office in the night. Maggie helped her onto the table, and as she lay down the fetus was delivered into Maggie's hands. When Maggie told me about it the next day, she cupped her hands into a small bowl—"It was just like a little kitten," she said softly, wonderingly. "Everything was still attached."

At the end of the day I clean out the suction jars, pouring blood into the sink, splashing the sides with flecks of tissue. From the sink rises a rich and humid smell, hot, earthy, and moldering; it is the smell of something recently alive beginning to decay. I take care of the plastic tub on the floor, filled with pieces too big to be trusted to the trash. The law defines the contents of the bucket I hold protectively against my chest as "tissue." Some would say my complicity in filling that bucket gives me no right to call it anything else. I slip the tissue gently into a bag and place it in the freezer, to be burned at another time. Abortion requires of me an entirely new set of assumptions. It requires a willingness to live with conflict,

37

38

39

---

[1]A type of sharp forceps used on bleeding arteries.

fearlessness, and grief. As I close the freezer door, I imagine a
world where this won't be necessary, and then return to the
world where it is.

Mary Meehan

A Pro-Life View from the Left

*Mary Meehan has written many articles on various topics for
respected newspapers and periodicals such as* The Nation, The
Washington Monthly, *and* The Washington Post. *In 1980, she
contributed the following article to* The Progressive, *a monthly
magazine that, true to its name, takes a liberal stance toward
current public issues.*

1   The abortion issue, more than most, illustrates the occasional tendency of the Left to become so enthusiastic over
what is called a "reform" that it forgets to think the issue
through. It is ironic that so many on the Left have done on
abortion what conservatives and Cold War liberals did on
Vietnam: They marched off in the wrong direction, to fight
the wrong war, against the wrong people.

2   Some of us who went through the anti-war struggles of the
1960s and early 1970s are now active in the right-to-life
movement. We do not enjoy opposing our old friends on the
abortion issue, but we feel that we have no choice. We are
moved by what pro-life feminists call the "consistency
thing"—the belief that respect for human life demands opposition to abortion, capital punishment, euthanasia, and war.
We don't think we have either the luxury or the right to
choose some types of killing and say that they are all right,
while others are not. A human life is a human life; and if
equality means anything, it means that society may not value
some human lives over others.

3   Until the last decade, people on the Left and Right generally agreed on one rule: We all protected the young. This was
not merely agreement on an ethical question: It was also an
expression of instinct, so deep and ancient that it scarcely required explanation.

Protection of the young included protection of the unborn, 4
for abortion was forbidden by state laws throughout the
United States. Those laws reflected an ethical consensus, not
based solely on religious tradition but also on scientific evidence that human life begins at conception. The prohibition
of abortion in the ancient Hippocratic Oath is well known.
Less familiar to many is the Oath of Geneva, formulated by
the World Medical Association in 1948, which included these
words: "I will maintain the utmost respect for human life from
the time of conception." A Declaration of the Rights of the
Child, adopted by the United Nations General Assembly in
1959, declared that "the child, by reason of his physical and
mental immaturity, needs special safeguards and care, including appropriate legal protection, before as well as after birth."

It is not my purpose to explain why courts and parliaments 5
in many nations rejected this tradition over the past few decades, though I suspect their action was largely a surrender to
technical achievement—if such inventions as suction aspira-
tors can be called technical achievements. But it is important
to ask why the Left in the United States generally accepted legalized abortion.

One factor was the popular civil-libertarian rationale for 6
freedom of choice in abortion. Many feminists presented it as
a right of women to control their own bodies. When the objection was raised that abortion ruins *another person's* body,
they respond that a) it is not a body, just a "blob of proto-
plasm" (thereby displaying ignorance of biology); or b) it is not
really a "person" until it is born. When it was suggested that
this is a wholly arbitrary decision, unsupported by any biological evidence, they said, "Well, that's your point of view. This is
a matter of individual conscience, and in a pluralistic society
people must be free to follow their consciences."

Unfortunately, many liberals and radicals accepted this 7
view without further question. Perhaps many did not know
that an eight-week-old fetus has a fully human form. They did
not ask whether American slaveholders before the Civil War
were right in viewing blacks as less than human and as private property; or whether the Nazis were correct in viewing
mental patients, Jews, and Gypsies as less than human and
therefore subject to the final solution.

Class issues provided another rationale. In the late 1960s, 8
liberals were troubled by evidence that rich women could
obtain abortions regardless of the law, by going to careful
society doctors or to countries where abortion was legal.

Why, they asked, should poor women be barred from something the wealthy could have? One might turn this argument on its head by asking why rich children should be denied protection that poor children have.

9 But pro-life activists did not want abortion to be a class issue one way or the other; they wanted to end abortion everywhere, for all classes. And many people who had experienced poverty did not think providing legal abortion was any favor to poor women. Thus, in 1972, when a Presidential commission on population growth recommended legalized abortion, partly to remove discrimination against poor women, several commission members dissented.

10 One was Graciela Olivarez, a Chicana who was active in civil rights and anti-poverty work. Olivarez, who later was named to head the Federal Government's Community Services Administration, had known poverty in her youth in the Southwest. With a touch of bitterness, she said in her dissent, "The poor cry out for justice and equality and we respond with legalized abortion." Olivarez noted that blacks and Chicanos had often been unwanted by white society. She added, "I believe that in a society that permits the life of even one individual (born or unborn) to be dependent on whether that life is 'wanted' or not, all its citizens stand in danger." Later she told the press, "We do not have equal opportunities. Abortion is a cruel way out."

11 Many liberals were also persuaded by a church/state argument that followed roughly this line: "Opposition to abortion is a religious viewpoint, particularly a Catholic viewpoint. The Catholics have no business imposing their religious views on the rest of us." It is true that opposition to abortion is a religious position for many people. Orthodox Jews, Mormons, and many of the fundamentalist Protestant groups also oppose abortion. (So did the mainstream Protestant churches until recent years.) But many people are against abortion for reasons that are independent of religious authority or belief. Many would still be against abortion if they lost their faith; others are opposed to it after they *have* lost their faith, or if they never had any faith. Only if their non-religious grounds for opposition can be proven baseless could legal prohibition of abortion fairly be called an establishment of religion. The pro-abortion forces concentrate heavily on religious arguments against abortion and generally ignore the secular arguments—possibly because they cannot answer them.

12 Still another, more emotional reason is that so many conservatives oppose abortion. Many liberals have difficulty ac-

cepting the idea that Jesse Helms can be right about *anything*.
I do not quite understand this attitude. Just by the law of av-
erages, he has to be right about something, sometime. Standing at the March for Life rally at the U.S. Capitol last year, and
hearing Senator Helms say that "We reject the philosophy
that life should be only for the planned, the perfect, or the
privileged," I thought he was making a good civil-rights
statement.

If much of the leadership of the pro-life movement is right-   13
wing, that is due largely to the default of the Left. We "little
people" who marched against the war and now march against
abortion would like to see leaders of the Left speaking out on
behalf of the unborn. But we see only a few, such as Dick Gregory, Mark Hatfield, Jesse Jackson, Richard Neuhaus, Mary
Rose Oakar. Most of the others either avoid the issue or support abortion. We are dismayed by their inconsistency. And
we are not impressed by arguments that we should work and
vote for them because they are good on such issues as food
stamps and medical care.

Although many liberals and radicals accepted legalized   14
abortion, there are signs of uneasiness about it. Tell someone
who supports it that you have many problems with the issue,
and she is likely to say, quickly, "Oh, I don't think I could ever
have one myself, but...." or "I'm really not pro-*abortion*; I'm
pro-*choice*" or "I'm *personally* opposed to it, but...."

Why are they personally opposed to it if there is nothing   15
wrong with it?

Perhaps such uneasiness is a sign that many on the Left   16
are ready to take another look at the abortion issue. In the
hope of contributing toward a new perspective, I offer the following points:

First, it is out of character for the Left to neglect the weak   17
and helpless. The traditional mark of the Left has been its
protection of the underdog, the weak, and the poor. The unborn child is the most helpless form of humanity, even more
in need of protection than the poor tenant farmer or the mental patient or the boat people on the high seas. The basic instinct of the Left is to aid those who cannot aid themselves—
and that instinct is absolutely sound. It is what keeps the human proposition going.

Second, the right to life underlies and sustains every other   18
right we have. It is, as Thomas Jefferson and his friends said,
self-evident. Logically, as well as in our Declaration of Independence, it comes before the right to liberty and the right to
property. The right to exist, to be free from assault by others,

is the basis of equality. Without it, the other rights are meaningless, and life becomes a sort of warfare in which force decides everything. There is no equality, because one person's convenience takes precedence over another's life, provided only that the first person has more power. If we do not protect this right for everyone, it is not guaranteed for everyone, because anyone can become weak and vulnerable to assault.

19   *Third,* abortion is a civil-rights issue. Dick Gregory and many other blacks view abortion as a type of genocide. Confirmation of this comes in the experience of pro-life activists who find open bigotry when they speak with white voters about public funding of abortion. Many white voters believe abortion is a solution for the welfare problem and a way to slow the growth of the black population. I worked two years ago for a liberal, pro-life candidate who was appalled by the number of anti-black comments he found when discussing the issue. And Representative Robert Dornan of California, a conservative pro-life leader, once told his colleagues in the House, "I have heard many rock-ribbed Republicans brag about how fiscally conservative they are and then tell me that I was an idiot on the abortion issue." When he asked why, said Dornan, they whispered, "Because we have to hold them down, we have to stop the population growth." Dornan elaborated: "To them, population growth means blacks, Puerto Ricans, or other Latins," or anyone who "should not be having more than a polite one or two 'burdens on society.'"

20   *Fourth,* abortion exploits women. Many women are pressured by spouses, lovers, or parents into having abortions they do not want. Sometimes the coercion is subtle, as when a husband complains of financial problems. Sometimes it is open and crude, as when a boyfriend threatens to end the affair unless the woman has an abortion, or when parents order a minor child to have an abortion. Pro-life activists who do "clinic counseling" (standing outside abortion clinics, trying to speak to each woman who enters, urging her to have the child) report that many women who enter clinics alone are willing to talk and to listen. Some change their minds and decide against abortion. But a woman who is accompanied by someone else often does not have the chance to talk, because the husband or boyfriend or parent is so hostile to the pro-life worker.

21   Juli Loesch, a feminist/pacifist writer, notes that feminists want to have men participate more in the care of children, but abortion allows a man to shift total responsibility to the woman: "He can *buy* his way out of accountability by making

'The Offer' for 'The Procedure.'" She adds that the man's sexual role "then implies—exactly nothing: no relationship. How quickly a 'woman's right to choose' comes to serve a 'man's right to use.'" And Daphne de Jong, a New Zealand feminist, says, "If women must submit to abortion to preserve their lifestyle or career, their economic or social status, they are pandering to a system devised and run by men for male convenience." She adds, "Of all the things which are done to women to fit them into a society dominated by men, abortion is the most violent invasion of their physical and psychic integrity. It is a deeper and more destructive assault than rape. . . ."

Loesch, de Jong, Olivarez, and other pro-life feminists believe men should bear a much greater share of the burdens of child-rearing than they do at present. And de Jong makes a radical point when she says, "Accepting short-term solutions like abortion only delays the implementation of real reforms like decent maternity and paternity leaves, job protection, high-quality child care, community responsibility for dependent people of all ages, and recognition of the economic contribution of childminders." Olivarez and others have also called for the development of safer and more effective contraceptives for both men and women. In her 1972 dissent, Olivarez noted with irony that "medical science has developed four different ways for killing a fetus, but has not yet developed a safe-for-all-to-use contraceptive."

Fifth, abortion is an escape from an obligation that is owed to another. Doris Gordon, Coordinator of Libertarians for Life, puts it this way: "Unborn children don't cause women to become pregnant but parents cause their children to be in the womb, and as a result, they need parental care. As a general principle, if we are the cause of another's need for care, as when we cause an accident, we acquire an obligation to that person as a result. . . . We have no right to kill in order to terminate any obligation."

Sixth, abortion brutalizes those who perform it, undergo it, pay for it, profit from it, and allow it to happen. Too many of us look the other way because we do not want to think about abortion. A part of reality is blocked out because one does not want to see broken bodies coming home, or going to an incinerator, in those awful plastic bags. People deny their own humanity when they refuse to identify with, or even acknowledge, the pain of others.

With some it is worse: They are making money from the misery of others, from exploited women and dead children.

Doctors, businessmen, and clinic directors are making a great
deal of money from abortion. Jobs and high incomes depend
on abortion; it's part of the gross national product. The parallels of this with the military-industrial complex should be obvious to anyone who was involved in the anti-war movement.
26   And the "slippery slope" argument is right: People really do
go from accepting abortion to accepting euthanasia and accepting "triage" for the world hunger problem and accepting
"lifeboat ethics" as a general guide to human behavior. We
slip down the slope, back to the jungle.
27   To save the smallest children, and to save its own conscience, the Left should speak out against abortion.

Sally Quinn

Our Choices, Ourselves

Sally Quinn (born 1941), a novelist, a writer for The Washington Post *since 1969, and a well-known and respected Washington "insider," contributed the following article to the* Post *in
April 1992.*

1   When I was in college, a classmate told a group of us about
a friend who had gotten pregnant and had been too scared to
tell anyone. Now she was almost eight months along and
showing. She had found someone to perform an abortion for
her (illegal, of course; this was 1963) and was agonizing over
what to do. She should definitely have the abortion, we all
agreed. There was really no other choice.
2   When I think now how sanguine we all were about our position on aborting an 8-month-old, presumably normal, fetus
it makes me shudder. A fetus, we figured, was just that—a
fetus—until it came out of the mother's body; and up until
that time, even at nine months, it was okay to abort it.
3   Thinking about that also makes me realize how far we've
come in terms of our awareness of the complexity of the abortion issue. And thinking about it on a day like today, when
tens of thousands of abortion rights advocates hold their

March for Women's Lives here, makes me realize how far we have to go.

For me, today's protest, sponsored by the National Organization for Women and other groups, is a reminder that the biggest problem with the abortion issue today is the nearly absolute polarization of both sides. Like a marriage on the rocks, the two sides have hardened their positions. The sad thing is that most American women fall somewhere in between but are driven by politics to adopt rigid views.

Part of the problem is the labels. Those who are against abortion call themselves "pro-life" and refer to their opponents as "pro-abortion." On the other side are the abortion-rights advocates who refer to those who oppose abortion as "antiabortion" and "anti-choice."

The "label war" is out of balance. I can't understand how people who oppose abortion rights managed to wrest away the "pro-life" label. In the same way that conservatives managed to appropriate the American flag, the position of caring about human life has been virtually surrendered. But I am for abortion rights, and I am as much—if not more— prolife as anyone. And I won't give that away.

The polarization gets intense because the antiabortion people start with the position that abortion is murder. It's that simple, they say. From the moment of conception, from the second that the egg is fertilized by the sperm, it becomes a human life. Period.

Of course, no one then acts as if the fetus is a human life. The IRS does not let us count the fetus as a dependent. No one to my knowledge has ever suggested that a fetus ought to be baptized. And so on.

The fact is that most women are extremely conflicted about the idea of abortion, particularly late-term abortions; even a National Abortion Rights League spokeswoman will say, as she did late last week, "We don't love abortion." Anyone who has been pregnant can tell you that after you have felt that quickening in your womb, after a fetus has kicked in your belly, the very idea of abortion becomes painfully difficult.

Yet every woman who has amniocentesis or a chorionic villus sampling (a similar, but earlier test) does it because she at least entertains the possibility of having an abortion if something is wrong with the fetus. One reason so many women opt for the CVS (despite the greater risk of miscarriage) is that they can't bear the idea of a late abortion. An amnio cannot give you results until the fetus is almost five months old. At five months, an abortion is, in effect, the delivery of a dead baby. You don't need the label "pro-life" to know that.

11   The single worst month of my life was the month between the time I had the amnio and the time I got the results. All the time, my child was kicking in my stomach. He was a part of me by then. I had invested so much in him that the idea of losing him was unthinkable.

12   All the choices were unthinkable. Modern-day tests like amnios and sonograms can tell you many abnormalities that could show up. They range in severity from anencephaly (being born without a brain, like the child in Florida last week), to Marfan syndrome, a connective tissue disorder that Abraham Lincoln may have had. Down syndrome is a major reason for an amnio, especially in older women. Spina bifida is revealed by a blood test. Both have varying degrees of severity.

13   As I lay in my bed each night, I was haunted by the idea of my child having any one of hundreds of possible defects. What would I do if.... If the diagnosed deformity were severe, the decision was obvious to me. In the case of less crippling defects, the decision would be heartwrenchingly confusing. None was easy.

14   Heart defects don't show up on the amnio, and my son was born with a heart defect. Most heart defects are easily repaired and the children go on to lead normal lives. Today, the defect is detectable by sonogram and women can choose to abort. Knowing what joy our son has brought to us, that would be unthinkable. And unbearable.

15   I had a friend whose amnio revealed that her baby would be born with severe defects. She decided to abort. She's never been the same since. And she never had another child.

16   The antiabortion people, meanwhile, have painted supporters of abortion rights as murderers, a bunch of sex-crazed women who don't want to suffer the consequences of their actions and don't give a damn about human life. But that is, of course, a fantasy. The reality is that favoring abortion rights is not the same as favoring abortion. It means you are concerned about privacy. It means you don't want someone else to impose his or her views—personal, political or religious—on you. According to the latest *Washington Post* survey, 57 percent of American women favor abortion rights—a figure that has been fairly consistent over the years.

17   At least half of my friends have had abortions at some time in their lives, and I'll bet that is not an unusual statistic for most American women of my age. It has always been scary

and sad. People are always surprised at how difficult emotionally it can be. And this is when it is safe and legal; there are about 1.6 million abortions performed each year in the United States.

In the days when abortion was unsafe and illegal (and the annual death rate was in the thousands), several of my mother's friends died from botched abortions. Some of these were already mothers—some with several children. I had friends who couldn't have children after badly botched abortions. I had a beautiful and brilliant friend in college who was afraid of an illegal abortion. She went to a home for unwed mothers and gave her baby up for adoption. She has been in and out of mental institutions ever since.   18

Even a few years ago, it was thought that only bad girls and actresses got pregnant out of wedlock. And not so long ago, I would have had an abortion if I'd gotten pregnant before marriage. There were times when I thought I was pregnant. The fear was indescribable. Even after abortion was legal, the fear was indescribable.   19

Though I believe in choice, it is perfectly understandable to me that some people do not believe that abortion is ever justified. Many Catholics hold this view. I have a Catholic friend who told me that they would not choose to have amniocentesis if his wife got pregnant because "I don't know whether or not I would have the strength to make the right decision if something turned out wrong."   20

Such people may even believe that abortion is akin to murder. But they're not prepared to accuse others whose opinions differ of committing murder.   21

Of course this "pro-life" position is not consistent. If it is murder, and it's premeditated, shouldn't the punishment be the same as for any murder conviction? And for those "pro-life" people in favor of the death penalty, shouldn't any mother who willingly aborts a child be put to death? Hanged by the neck until dead, fried in the chair, given an injection? And that goes for the doctor who performs the abortion, and anyone who aids it.   22

It's either murder or it ain't. You can't have it both ways.   23

Particularly specious are those who say abortion is murder but it's okay in the case of rape or incest.   24

Excuse me? The innocent "child" is murdered because it had the unfortunate luck of being conceived illegally? Does the manner of conception make the child any less human? By this reasoning, a 5-year-old who is discovered to have been conceived in incest could be put to death.   25

26   There are many reasons why someone may choose to abort. Rape or incest, birth defects, poverty, illness, a mother either too young or too old.

27   But there are other more subtle reasons too. If a mother feels unprepared, emotionally or psychologically or physically, whose decision should it be? Who, after all, will live with the consequences?

28   Often that decision to abort is nothing less than a pro-life decision. Anyone who has walked through a neo-natal ward in a hospital and seen the half-pound "babies" with dark glasses on and tubes coming out every pore, crack babies, AIDS babies, abandoned babies and babies who will grow up to be retarded or profoundly emotionally disturbed, can't help wondering about the quality of life these children will have.

29   It seems to me that those who are pro-choice may know what lies in store for these children—and care more about life than many of those who call themselves "pro-life."

30   If the abortion question had not so polarized America, the two "sides" might be better able to talk about such questions. But I get the impression that many antiabortion or "pro-life" advocates, for all their talk of "ethics" and "morality," have little concern for what happens to the babies after they are born. The mere fact of life is their only concern. But who will shoulder the financial and emotional burdens of these "lives"? Once it's a "life" they lose interest.

31   Meanwhile, a question haunts all of us who are in favor of abortion rights: When does life begin, anyway?

32   Under the *Roe* v. *Wade* ruling, a woman has virtually unrestricted access to abortion in the first trimester, may be subject to specific regulations in the second trimester and can be barred (except when it affects maternal health) in the third. This Solomon-like decision seems a proper way to look at it. On the one hand, I don't want anyone telling me what to do with my body; on the other, I have difficulty with the concept of aborting a 9-month-old fetus. I'm not ready to call it murder, but I have grave doubts.

33   But I don't like to admit any hesitancy or doubt. I fear being pounced on by those who will take my lack of conviction—my unwillingness to dig my heels in—as agreement with antiabortion advocates.

34   A 9-month-old fetus can certainly live independently. So, in some cases, can a 7-month-old fetus. Is it all right to kill the fetus inside the mother's body? I think not.

Catherine Stern aborted her 7-month-old fetus when she 35
learned it had no arms and legs and was possibly brain-dam-
aged. Would I have done that? Yes, devastating as it would
have been. But the consequences of not doing it would have
been worse.

In the future, science may allow us to know far more about 36
a fetus—from her IQ and height to the color of its hair. But
what if the fetus is projected to have an IQ of 80? Or if it were
homely? Would I allow an abortion if it were up to me? What
about choosing to abort if it's the "wrong" sex—already commonplace in some Third World countries, where female babies are devalued? I find these notions reprehensible, yet I'm
unwilling to say where I would draw the line.

Meanwhile, some people are using abortion as a form of 37
birth control. I know a woman who brags that she's had eight
abortions rather than use contraceptives, which she derides
as "inconvenient." How do I feel about this? The way most
people do, regardless of where they stand on today's march:
Disgusted. Am I prepared to tell her that she can't have more
abortions? The answer is no.

That is how things have become polarized: Some antiabor- 38
tionists have poisoned the well to the point where they have
even made contraception and sex education controversial.
And by taking the position that abortion is murder, they have
forced those of us who believe in abortion rights to take an
equally hard-line position, no matter how bothered we are by
some of the results.

The fact is that you can't reduce this argument to simple 39
choices, and you can't avoid it by simple rules. There are a lot
of issues that women on both sides of the abortion issue
would agree on if they simply were able to admit their honest
doubts, but politics has made it even more divisive.

The First Amendment permits anyone to carry fetuses 40
around in bottles and say, "Is this what you want?" But the
black-and-white nature of the resulting argument destroys
any possibility of commonality of beliefs, or feelings, or emotions or interests.

If most women had the choice, they would acknowledge 41
that one group should not have the power to determine the
lives of another. And ultimately that has to be the way it is. Ultimately, the debate is not about murder, or even choice, but
the most intimate kind of privacy.

If I got pregnant today, would I have an abortion? I know 42
the answer to that, and it's nobody's business but mine. And
that's the point.

Mike Royko
A Pox on Both Your Houses

Royko (1922–1997), a syndicated columnist associated with the Chicago Tribune—*and with Chicago in general, since he worked as a reporter for several Chicago newspapers for many years—wrote the following commentary in July 1992, a few days after the Supreme Court upheld both* Roe v. Wade *and most parts of a controversial Pennsylvania law requiring women desiring an abortion to wait 24 hours, to receive written material on the medical procedure, and, if they are minors, to inform their parents. Mike Royko won a Pulitzer Prize for social commentary.*

1   "Why are all those women so mad?" asked Slats Grobnik, gesturing at the TV set. "The old man stop for a few after work?"

2   No, it is far more serious than that. They are an anti-abortion group, furious because the Supreme Court has upheld the right of women to get abortions.

3   The TV switched to another angry group of women.

4   "Now what's this bunch mad about? They're yelling louder than the others."

5   They are a pro-abortion group, and they are furious because the Supreme Court has upheld a few restrictions.

6   "Like what?"

7   A 24-hour waiting period. Parental consent for teen-agers. And women being told what their options are, such as adoption, and what kind of medical and financial help is available if she has the baby.

8   "Wait a minute, I don't get it."

9   Get what?

10   "I can see how the anti-abortion crowd would be mad because abortions are still legal, right?"

11   That's what the court said.

12   "Then if they're legal, what's the other side got to beef about?"

13   They don't like any kind of restrictions. They feel it is a threat to their control over their own bodies.

14   "Waiting 24 hours? Nowadays, you got to wait 24 hours for everything. It takes longer than that to get a tooth drilled or your car tuned up. So what's the big rush? And what's wrong

with telling some girl about financial help or that there are
people who want to adopt kids?"

They believe that is not society's business to intrude on   15
their right to control their own bodies.

"Hey, when the draft board told me I was gonna go fight in   16
Korea, that was messing with my right to control my body,
because I guarantee you, I didn't want my body being shot up
by no Chinese commies. So I wind up putting in two years
with society, by way of the government, telling my body
where it's going to go and what it's going to do. If I want to
stick a needle in my arm and shoot up with dope, that's illegal. Even though that arm is part of my body right?"

Correct.   17

"See, that's what bothers me about this abortion fight.   18
These people don't always make sense."

Which side?   19

"Both sides. They're not always, what'ya call it, consis-   20
tent?"

In what way?   21

"Well, the one side says they are pro-life. Now, does that   22
mean that they're against frying someone in the electric
chair?"

I would doubt that.   23

"That's what I thought, because I know a few of the pro-life   24
ladies and they want to hang 'em high. And were they against
us dropping bombs and killing women and children in Iraq
because we wanted to put this rich emir back on his throne in
Kuwait?"

I would guess that they were part of the mainstream of   25
public opinion that delighted in the triumphs of our heroic
video war.

"That's what I think. So when they say they're pro-life, it all   26
depends on what life, right?"

Yes, the unborn.   27

"And don't get me wrong. I don't have any trouble with   28
that. Especially when I read that there's been 26 million abortions in the last 19 years. You know what that works out to on
my pocket calculator?"

Lots.   29

"Yeah, more than 26,000 a week. About 3,700 a day. About   30
156 an hour. Almost three a minute. Think about it. Every 20
or 30 seconds, there's an abortion. Are there really that many
people whose lives are gonna be ruined if they have a kid? I'm
supposed to believe that it's a disaster if they gotta wait 24
hours? Or if someone talks to them about adoption?"

31   But it is a question of choice, which is why they call themselves pro-choice.

32   "They don't sound like they're in favor of a choice if they're
in a flap because they don't want some young girl to wait 24
hours or to listen to what somebody's got to say about her options. Another thing—how do they feel about frying John
Gacy, that serial killer who buried his victims under his
house?"

33   What does he have to do with it?

34   "Well, I noticed something. Some women I know who are
in favor of abortion are against the death penalty, and that
don't make sense to me. How can you be in favor of killing
some harmless little thing in a woman's tummy but you get
all weepy when they pull the switch on some ax murderer? I
don't see how you can be for one and not the other."

35   Well, maybe they believe that the decision as to whether
John Gacy is executed should be made by his mother.

36   "Yeah, I guess that makes sense, kind of a pro-choice
thing."

37   Right. So, where do you stand?

38   "On what?"

39   Abortion. Are you for it or against it?

40   "Forget it. If I say I'm against, then they'll say I'm in favor
of killing women, right?"

41   It wouldn't surprise me.

42   "And if I'm for it, they'll say I'm a baby-killer, right?"

43   Almost a certainty.

44   "So you're not gonna corner me. There's one thing I'm sure
of, though. We got to check on the diets of American women."

45   What do their diets have to do with it?

46   "If there's been 26 million abortions over the last 19 years,
they should try eating more brain foods."

Jim McCloskey and Mike Luckovich
Editorial Cartoons on Abortion

Nearly every American is shocked whenever a physician or other health-care worker is injured or murdered by anti-abortion fanatics. Late in 1993, the murder of a Florida physician motivated the following two editorial cartoons. The first, by Jim McCloskey of the Creators Syndicate, Incorporated, appeared in a number of newspapers; the second, by Mike Luckovich, appeared in the Atlanta Constitution. *The two illustrate how differing assumptions can lead to differing responses to the same incident.*

GAY, LESBIAN, AND BISEXUAL RIGHTS

Michael Cunningham

Taking the Census of Queer Nation

Michael Cunningham is a member of the gay rights group Act Up. *A writer of fiction and nonfiction, he contributed the following essay to* Mother Jones *in the summer of 1992.* Mother Jones, *published bimonthly, is a liberal, irreverent magazine of commentary on current affairs. (Some of the names of people in this essay—the ones identified by first name only—have been changed.)*

1   Tim and I were walking home late from St. Vincent's Hospital in New York City, where we'd been sitting with what remained of a friend named John. We went every night, although John had been unconscious for nearly a week. We hoped that if we held his hand and spoke to him something might still register. Doctors suspect that hearing is the last sense to go. You should talk to the dying.

2   As Tim and I walked home through the streets of the West Village, we talked about John's funeral. "Definitely something glamorous," Tim said. "He'd hate anything morbid."

3   I agreed. When he was healthy, John had dyed his hair platinum. He'd worn baggy shorts and purple high tops. Lamentation wasn't his style.

4   On the corner where we parted, I looked closely at Tim's face. He was deeply pale, putty-colored, and his eyes looked unnaturally large in his skull. He had AIDS too. He was still working full-time and keeping two hospital vigils.

5   "What are you eating?" I asked. "You look like you've lost weight."

6   He waved my question away. "I'm eating all the right things," he said. "I'm taking perfect care of myself. Give it a rest, Mom."

We said good-night, and he turned down Fourth Street, a 7
scrawny, determined figure in oversized hoop earrings. I
watched him for a moment, thinking about the workings of
ordinary courage.

I'd just made it home and into bed when the phone rang. It 8
was Tim.

"Hi," he said. "Guess where I'm calling from? St. Vincent's." 9

"Shit," I said. "Did John die right after we left?" 10

"No, it's not John," he said. His voice carried a thin, slightly 11
blurred tone of good cheer, as if he'd been drugged. "It's me. I
got beaten up. About five minutes after I left you. By three
guys."

I went to get him with another friend of his, an English 12
journalist named Karen. Tim was woozy and slightly manic
from painkillers, and his fair hair was swathed in bandages.
Karen asked him if he'd gotten a good look at the men who
beat him.

"You know, I don't exactly remember them," he said in a 13
chipper voice. "I know they were yelling 'faggot' at me. And I
think I yelled back. Something like, 'You got it, sweethearts—
who wants to be first?' Then I was in the emergency room, being stitched up. Poof. There one minute, here the next."

Karen and I got him back to his apartment and put him to 14
bed. We sat with him until he fell asleep. Karen whispered,
"He looks about fifteen, doesn't he?" He did look preternaturally young and wan, his blue-veined eyelids translucent, the
bandage white around his head. He was a cheerful, domestically inclined boy from Indiana. He adored his friends, had a
cat named Aretha, and always fell asleep before it was time to
go out to the clubs. Someone had hit his frail, compromised
body with a two-by-four. Someone, somewhere in the city, was
congratulating himself at that moment. Someone was laughing and popping a beer.

To calm myself I laid my hand, gently, on Tim's scrawny 15
chest. I felt the steady effort of his breathing. After a moment,
Karen put her hand on top of mine. "This makes me crazy," I
said to her. "This makes me want to hurt people." I was furious at myself for failing to watch out for Tim. And I was angry
at Tim. Why did he have to talk back to those morons?

Karen shook her head disapprovingly, and I was suddenly, 16
fiercely angry at her as well. Because she and her girlfriend
are staunchly opposed to violence in any form. Because she
refuses to have anything to do with activist groups like ACT
UP (the AIDS Coalition to Unleash Power) or Queer Nation,
the radical gay-rights organization spawned by ACT UP to

strike back at all the people who'd beat up an innocent gay
kid like Tim. Because several weeks earlier, as we passed a series of posters announcing the homosexuality of some very
big—and very closeted—Hollywood stars, she hissed: "The
fascists who force other people to come out are doing us
more harm than good."

17   If you're straight, it may be hard to understand the need for
an obstreperous, in-your-face organization like Queer Nation.
It may be hard to imagine the intricate combination of rage
and terror that constitutes the gay zeitgeist of 1992. There's a
virus ticking its way through the arteries of people we love.
That would be enough to make us crazy, right there. But what's
driven some of us around the bend is the fact that, even as our
friends keep dying, the hatred of homosexuals flourishes.

18   Gay-bashing is up all over the country. Homophobia is
thriving like mosquitoes in August, and it comes as often as
not in relatively subtle, nonviolent packages. Take Magic
Johnson, for instance. Shortly after announcing he was HIV-
positive, he inspired wild applause on the Arsenio Hall show
when he said, "I'm nowhere near homosexual." People
cheered. If you're a person of color, try to imagine a celebrity
telling an appreciative audience, "I thank God I'm white!" If
you're Jewish, imagine the same audience clapping and whistling when a celebrity announces, "No way am I a Jew."

19   If you're gay and you're not angry, you're just not paying attention.

20   I myself belong to ACT UP. I've helped engineer an on-
screen takeover of the *MacNeil/Lehrer Newshour* (you'd be
surprised at how easy it is to get into a television studio). I've
chained myself to the White House gates. I've committed
these and other acts of civil disobedience in the company of
people I consider heroes. I confess up front to deep affection
and respect for Queer Nation, which was launched just over
two years ago by a band of ACT UP members from New York
City who wanted to concentrate on gay issues outside the
realm of AIDS.

21   Queer Nation is a peculiar mix of outrage and wackiness—
you could call it the illegitimate child of Huey Newton and
Lucy Ricardo. Male and female members go en masse to
straight bars and hockey games, where they kiss their lovers
passionately. They stage impromptu fashion shows in suburban shopping malls, featuring men in tutus and women in
Harley-Davidson gear.

22   The name itself started as a joke of sorts. "Queer Nation"
was a temporary moniker, offered in jest. Once the founding

members got used to it, though, they didn't mind the idea of throwing a word like "queer" back in the faces of those who'd been spitting it at them for decades. They decided they could repossess the insult; they could cauterize it by taking it on themselves. Besides, the word emphasizes difference. Members aren't trying to say to the straight world, "Accept us, because we're just like you." That was the old tactic, which is now known disparagingly as assimilationism. Queer Nation's official tag line is "We're here. We're queer. Get used to it."

By the time it was a year old, Queer Nation existed in over   23
sixty cities, from New York and San Francisco to Indianapolis and Shreveport. Now, just past its second anniversary, no one's quite sure how many chapters there are. The rise has been swift but chaotic, and established chapters have burned out nearly as quickly as new ones have appeared. Since I started writing this article, the Eugene and Houston chapters have taken off while the San Francisco chapter has dissolved.

Like ACT UP, Queer Nation is ferociously democratic and   24
decentralized. Its founders were determined not to emulate what they called the "hierarchical, patriarchal" pecking order by which most groups—from the Young Republicans to the Crips and the Bloods—are run. At every chapter, anyone who shows up at a meeting is instantaneously a full member. Some chapters are run by consensus; some simply function as a forum for people who want to recruit others for demonstrations. The prevailing aim—you could call it an obsession—is to exclude no one.

It would be easy to play up Queer Nation's kind intentions   25
and zany antics. But members can also be loudly confrontational. They've irritated a lot of people, including other lesbians and gay men. Gay opposition is wildly various, but I can offer a quintessential scenario. Say your parents are visiting from Michigan, and you've finally decided to come out to them. You're a relatively ordinary citizen with a nine-to-five job. In a quiet restaurant, over coffee, you say it: "Listen, I guess you may have suspected this. I don't want to keep secrets from you anymore. I'm gay." Your mother cries and tells you she loves you anyway. She says it with a certain forced conviction, which doesn't quite ring true. Your father is murderously silent. This is the hardest thing you've ever done. As you leave the restaurant, your mother is sniffling and your father is glacial. You're searching for something else to say, some way to make them understand that you haven't suddenly transformed yourself into an alien. As you struggle for

the right words, you walk out of the restaurant into a band of men and women carrying Queer Power signs. They're blowing whistles. Some wear nose rings and combat boots. Two of the men have on dresses, and one sports a Nancy Sinatra wig. As they pass, somebody slaps a Day-Glo sticker on your father's seersucker jacket. The sticker says Go Girl.

26   Opposition to Queer Nation's tactics doesn't end with questions of style or demeanor. Last September, gay riots exploded in Los Angeles and San Francisco after California governor Pete Wilson vetoed AB 101, a bill that would have outlawed job discrimination on the basis of sexual orientation. After his veto, Queer Nationals and other gay activists hurled police barricades through windows. They set fires in the streets. And some of them threatened to expose gay members of Wilson's staff, further igniting the ongoing debate about outing, tactics, and propriety.

27   Gay activists face a fundamental question familiar to feminists and civil-rights leaders, among others. Do we play by the rules, court public sympathy, and push steadily but politely for recognition? Or do we make ourselves so unpleasant that yielding to our demands finally becomes easier than ignoring us? I myself favor the noisier alternatives. I believe the AIDS epidemic has taught us that nobody will listen unless we scream. But still, I'm plagued by doubts. At ACT UP meetings, when members talk about planning a new action that will "show our anger," I find myself asking, What exactly do we expect people to do with our anger once we've shown it to them? As I set out to visit Queer Nation chapters around the country, that question was on my mind. And on my first stop, in Atlanta, Georgia, a woman named Cheryl Summerville was pondering it too.

28   Cheryl Summerville may have been the best-behaved lesbian in the world. She lived outside Atlanta with her lover, Sandra Riley, in a house the two women helped build themselves. She and Riley were raising Summerville's son from a long-dissolved marriage and were thinking of having a child of their own. Summerville had a decent job as a cook at the local Cracker Barrel, one of a chain of country-style restaurants.

29   But in February of 1991, the associate manager of the restaurant, Marilee Gonzalez, called Summerville into her office. Gonzalez, who had been friendly with Summerville, told her in a nervous but formal tone that Cracker Barrel had decided to reexamine its policy about gay and lesbian employees. She asked, "Are you a lesbian?"

Summerville answered: "Marilee, you know I am. You go- 30
ing to fire me for that?"

That day, Summerville received a pink slip on the orders of 31
Cracker Barrel district manager Jody Waller. The restaurant's
general manager filed a separation notice with the Georgia
Department of Labor, on which he wrote: "This employee is
being terminated due to violation of company policy. The employee is gay."

Waller was complying with a memo sent to the managers 32
of all outlets by Cracker Barrel's main office in Lebanon, Tennessee. The memo said, in part: "It is inconsistent with our
concept and values, and is perceived to be inconsistent with
those of our customer base, to continue to employ individuals
in our operating units whose sexual preferences fail to demonstrate normal heterosexual values which have been the
foundation of families in our society."

In all, eighteen lesbians and gay men were fired from 33
Cracker Barrel's outlets. Some managers called the employees they suspected into their offices and formally asked if they
were homosexual. Others just convened staff meetings and
announced that certain employees were being terminated in
accordance with company policy.

Summerville simply didn't get it at first. In every respect 34
but one, she'd always been a model of conventional good behavior. She'd received a "personal achievement award," given
by Cracker Barrel to outstanding staff members, and was up
for another. She'd helped build a house with her own hands,
adored her parents and son, earned a living through hard
work. Her single transgression was to love another woman
and, even in that, she'd been modest and forthright. She
hadn't concealed her love for Sandra Riley, nor had she
flaunted it. Now she was out of work, for failing to display
normal values.

At first, Summerville assumed she could take Cracker Bar- 35
rel to court. But only a few states and about sixty cities and
counties have barred discrimination on the basis of sexual
preference in both public and private employment. Atlanta
isn't among them. When Summerville learned she had no legal recourse, she called ACT UP for help, but was told that it
worked only on issues relating directly to AIDS. She was referred to the Atlanta chapter of Queer Nation.

Summerville was not a political person. She wasn't tor- 36
tured by ideals or abstractions—she just wanted to live an uncomplicated life. The idea of speaking to a group that called
itself Queer Nation gave her a kind of vertigo. "It took me a

week to get up the nerve," she says. She and Sandra Riley made a dry run in their car past the Five Points Community Center, where the group's next meeting was to take place. The center looked ordinary enough. But still.

37   On the night of the meeting, she and Riley were so nervous they arrived twenty minutes early. As the members started drifting in, Summerville was surprised to find that they looked like everybody else. "I didn't expect just normal-looking people," she says. "I thought we were in the wrong place. They were wearing just jeans and T-shirts. One of 'em came in in a suit, and I sure as hell didn't expect that."

38   Despite this, Summerville and Riley stood out, even among the conservatively dressed men. They are ample women, and they dress along suburban lines. Sandra Riley favors ruffles. She carries a pocketbook. "To start with, they ignored us," Summerville recalls. "They probably thought we'd stumbled into the wrong place or something."

39   But after the meeting was called to order, the first item of business was the firings at Cracker Barrel. "Somebody asked, 'What are we going to do about this?'" Summerville remembers. "And I said: 'Hey it was me. I'm one of 'em.'" Everyone turned to look at the short, stocky woman in a sweatshirt and jeans. "I want to know what we can do about it," she said.

40   The first demonstration against Cracker Barrel was held in a rainstorm. Thirty-plus people marched in front of the restaurant with signs, urging customers to stay away until the chain reversed its policy. It was, generally, a humiliating experience. "It was just kind of nasty," Summerville says. "It was pouring, and a few of us slipped in the mud. People laughed at us."

41   Before the picket lines started, members had been rebuffed when they tried to meet with the Cracker Barrel management to present their complaints. Soon after, the central office sent a memo to all Cracker Barrel outlets, claiming that its "recent position on the employment of homosexuals in a limited number of stores may have been a well-intentioned over-reaction to the perceived values of our customers and their comfort levels with these individuals."

42   If the firings themselves didn't qualify as national news, Cracker Barrel's subsequent change of heart apparently did. The controversy was reported in *The New York Times*, the *Wall Street Journal*, and the *Atlanta Journal & Constitution*, which also ran an editorial excoriating Cracker Barrel and asking how any discrimination could have possibly been "well-intentioned."

While it withdrew its chainwide policy about the discharge   43
of homosexuals, Cracker Barrel turned down Queer Nation's
demand that individual outlets be specifically forbidden from
practicing sexual discrimination in hiring. It also refused to
rehire the fired employees, and balked at Queer Nation's request for a written apology.

In March of last year, Queer Nation started staging sit-ins   44
aimed at cutting Cracker Barrel's profits. The idea was simple: members filled as many tables as possible, ordered the
bare minimum, and sat there for two or three hours. When
they ordered their coffees or Cokes, the protesters at each table gave their waitress a five-dollar tip wrapped in a note that
said: "We realize that you are not the source of the discriminatory policy of Cracker Barrel. We in no way want to penal-
ize you or make your life more difficult. On the contrary, we
want to assure that YOU are not the next victim of renegade
bigotry at Cracker Barrel."

Every few weeks, Queer Nation hit a different Cracker Barrel   45
outlet, always on Sunday, after church. Last June, I went to the
ninth Cracker Barrel sit-in with Lynn Cothren, a thin blond
man wearing madras shorts and love beads. Cothren, a founding member of Queer Nation/Atlanta, is something of an anomaly. In an organization that eschews the very idea of leaders, he
boldly proclaimed himself chair of the Atlanta chapter. The
demonstrations against Cracker Barrel were largely his idea.

Nearly 120 people had gathered in a parking lot next to the   46
Cracker Barrel in Union City, about ten miles outside Atlanta.
They were a living monument to the notion that, aside from
some fundamental appetites, human beings have very little in
common. There were women in plaid flannel shirts, and
women with rouge and pink lipstick. There were middle-aged
men in sweat suits, bodybuilders, and reedy, acne-scarred
boys who still carried the mortified auras of their adolescent
torments.

Everyone was nervous. Most of the protesters had picketed   47
or participated in sit-ins before, but none had ever been arrested for civil disobedience. Although the towers and spires
of Atlanta were visible on the horizon, Union City was a conservative town. No one was sure what would happen or how
any of us would be treated when taken to jail.

Cheryl Summerville and Sandra Riley stood close together,   48
holding hands in the parking lot. Neither had slept the night
before. Riley, a large woman with long hair and a lovely, innocent face, looked as if she might cry at any moment. But
when Summerville told her that she thought she should

change her mind, Riley said: "What am I going to do while you're in jail? Sit outside worrying about you? No thanks." To be arrested, Riley wore heels and a blue flowered dress. She carried a white pocketbook.

49   After we all assembled, we filed into the restaurant. To reach the dining room we passed through a gift shop that sold penny candy, stars-and-stripes decals, and plaster cherry pies with lattice crusts. The restaurant proper featured turn-of-the-century memorabilia screwed to its walls—farm implements and brown photographs of families. Hard shadowless light caromed off its acoustic ceiling.

50   I sat at a table with a fiftyish woman named Marty. She'd come with her gay son and his lover and a young lesbian named Elizabeth, who'd been cut off by her family. Marty introduced her as "my adopted daughter." When I asked Marty how she felt about her son being gay, she drawled, "I've known he was gay since he was in the fourth grade, so I've had plenty of time to get used to it." When I asked if she'd rather he was straight, she said, "Well, he's a hell of a lot happier than one of his brothers, who's married with two kids."

51   A cheerful waitress brought us menus, and we told her we were just having coffee. We gave her her five-dollar tip up front, wrapped in the note explaining what we were doing there. She smiled graciously, and pocketed the tip and the note without reading it. Slowly the restaurant filled with protesters. I drifted through, asking the few remaining nonmembers for reactions. A beige-faced woman in a biscuit-colored jumpsuit said: "I don't carry on about my sexuality in public. I don't know why you all have to carry on about yours." At another table, a man with a beard said: "Cracker Barrel was right to fire those people. What with AIDS and all, I don't want 'em touching food my kids are gonna eat."

52   Most of the waitresses didn't appear to mind. Some even seemed to be having a good time. An older woman swept through the room periodically, filling coffee cups, and when she got to us she said to Marty: "Honey, I'm cuttin' you off. You're starting to shake the whole table."

53   I went to Cothren's table and asked him what, exactly, he thought this protest was accomplishing. He looked at me as if he couldn't believe I would ask such a question. "We're putting direct pressure on them," he said. "We're cutting into their business."

54   "But so far," I said, "you've gotten only one minor concession. Obviously, their fundamental attitude hasn't changed. None of the people who were fired have their jobs back."

"We're going to win," Cothren answered in an impatient 55
tone, as if I simply didn't understand the righteousness of
Queer Nation's cause or the immensity of his will.

An hour passed before Jody Waller, the district manager, ap- 56
peared with two cops and began working his way through the
restaurant, table by table. Waller was a trim man with glasses
and a receding hairline, wearing a tie and a navy blazer. At
each table he announced: "I'm asking you to leave now. If you
don't leave, you'll be arrested. Do you understand?"

Eighteen people chose to stay and be arrested. The rest of us 57
went to the jail house to wait until they were released. We
marched in an orderly circle before the jail, which was located
in a town that seemed to consist only of the jail, a post office,
and several unprosperous-looking antique stores. We carried
signs that said There's Bigotry in My Biscuit and Cracker Barrel
Serves Hate. We displayed the signs to ourselves and to an occasional passing car. In two hours, not a single person walked
by on the street.

At the end of two hours, several demonstrators were re- 58
leased. We gathered around them expectantly, and they told
us they'd been treated with surprising respect. A court date
had been set for mid-August, when a judge would rule on
Cracker Barrel's trespassing charge. Summerville and Riley
stood close together, talking happily to their friends. Riley's
white shoes were unsmudged.

We started back to our cars, planning to meet at a bar in 59
Atlanta for a celebratory beer. But as we were dispersing, a
battered pickup truck roared toward us from down the street.
As it screamed past, a gang of shirtless teenage boys yelled,
"Faggots." They all wore their hair below their shoulders, a
minor cosmetic freedom won by others before they were
born. They turned around and passed us a second time, still
hollering insults.

They left a chill in the air. Any one of them could have been 60
Jody Waller's wild son, testing his limits before he grew up
and got his own job managing a Cracker Barrel. Cothren
didn't hesitate. He turned and marched back into the jail—a
skinny, wrathful twenty-eight-year-old man in Bermuda
shorts—to demand that his pot-bellied jailers track down the
boys and arrest them for verbal assault.

As I traveled around the country visiting other chapters of 61
Queer Nation, I kept thinking, God, these people are young. If
furious exuberance is the organization's most salient feature,
youth is a close second. I've just turned thirty-nine, and in my

travels I met only a handful of women and men my age or older. More often, I found myself among people who could literally have been my sons or daughters. The media liaison from the now-defunct San Francisco chapter tried to reassure me that the group's reputation for youth was exaggerated, saying proudly, "Some of us are in our late twenties and even our early thirties."

62   Youth, with its energy and its bottomless outrage, may account for that fact that Queer Nation demonstrations are sometimes ignited by events that seem less than urgent. When the residents of Gay Court, in a suburban community east of San Francisco, petitioned to change the name of their street to High Eagle Road, a band of protesters from Queer Nation showed up with banners and bullhorns. In New York City, I went with about twenty activists to stage a "kiss-in" in a straight bar, where the patrons frankly couldn't have cared less. Looking for drama, I asked a straight-looking guy in a crewneck sweater what he thought about all this. "All *what?*" he asked.

63   "Those people over there," I said. "The ones who are kissing. The ones with the stickers that say 'Queer.'"

64   He looked calmly at a pair of tattooed men who were kissing passionately among a bevy of big-haired secretaries sipping margaritas. He shrugged. "Guess it means they're queer," he replied.

65   Youth, combined with Queer Nation's adamantly non-hierarchical structure, may also partially account for the fact that the group is often disorganized nearly to the point of incoherence. In preparing to write this article, I made dozens of calls across the country and learned repeatedly that the person whose name I'd been given had left town for a few months, or moved away entirely, or fought with other members and quit. Members conceive passionate devotions and then burn out. They leave Queer Nation over philosophical differences, or because their grades are suffering, or because they've fallen in love with other members who don't return their affections.

66   When I called a contact person in Shreveport, Louisiana, his mother answered the phone and told me, cordially, that her son had gone to live with his lover. When I reached him at his lover's house, he said that Queer Nation/Shreveport consisted entirely of himself and another man occasionally distributing literature on safer sex.

67   I had planned to attend a demonstration being held by Queer Nation of Lincoln, Nebraska. Together with Queer

Nation/Iowa City, members were going to Iowa State University in Ames, where a heterosexual supremacist group—consisting of about a dozen people committed to fighting the very concept of gay rights—was campaigning for formal recognition by the university. Queer Nation was going to parade in front of the group leader's house, kissing and holding hands. I was looking forward to the demonstration. I'd made plane reservations. But when I called about some last-minute details, I learned that the action had been called off because a main organizer had set fire to another member's house.

I did go to Salt Lake City, because I'd heard Queer Nation   68
was thriving there and because the woman I'd first contacted continued to answer her phone over a period of several months. Still, I arrived too late. By the time my plane landed, the group was in disarray. A splinter group had formed. Members were writing vicious lampoons of one another in the chapter's newsletter.

I admit it. I was beginning to feel a certain despair.   69

I also visited Queer Nation/San Francisco, which several   70
months after I left degenerated into internecine battles and then disbanded entirely. In January of 1991, it was among the largest chapters in the country, attracting as many as four hundred to its weekly meetings. It carried out one of Queer Nation's most notorious protests, when bands of Queer Nationals did everything possible to disrupt the filming of *Basic Instinct*, a thriller about murderous lesbians and bisexual women.

By autumn, its numbers had dropped to the low twenties.   71
Last December, the few remaining members agreed to dissolve the group. Some members there even call Queer Nation/San Francisco a "fad that fizzled out." Others say that it was done in by racism and sexism among the members themselves.

Tensions had flourished from the beginning. Soon after the   72
San Francisco chapter was established, bands of women and people of color started LABIA (Lesbians and Bi-Women in Action) and United Colors. These organizations-within-the-organization were called "focus groups" and were meant to concentrate on issues that might escape the attention of the larger body.

As ever-increasing numbers packed themselves into   73
the dour ochre-and-brown auditorium of San Francisco's Women's Building, members of LABIA and United Colors consistently felt that certain white men dominated. At one meeting last winter, several members came to the floor and asked the group at large to contribute a hundred dollars to a

march. They were turned down—no big deal. But after the meeting, a group of white male members started arguing about the march with a group of women. The argument grew so heated that the women left, with the men following them down the street, still shouting their opinions. The men's raucous voices brought faces to apartment windows; a passerby asked the women if they needed help.

74   Later, the men claimed they'd only been carrying on an impassioned discourse. The women said they'd been terrorized. This was one of a number of incidents in which some of the white men told one version of a story and the women or people of color told another. Several months later, when a band of men from Queer Nation plastered stickers on the home of a lesbian city supervisor, LABIA pulled out altogether, claiming that the male "terrorism" could no longer be countenanced.

75   Christine Carraher, one of the founding members of the bisexual focus group UBIQUITOUS, explains: "There's a wide gulf between a lot of lesbians and gay men. Sometimes I think it's worse than the one that exists between straight men and women."

76   "Some of these guys believe feminists are doing to men what Big Nurse did to the warders in *One Flew Over the Cuckoo's Nest*," said a male member of the group.

77   As these tensions built, a big, noisy, politically savvy New Yorker named Mitchell Halberstadt started showing up at meetings and shouting other members out of the room. Halberstadt is a classic New York activist, all bombast and aggression. When he arrived in San Francisco, he brought his swagger to a group that employed two "vibes watchers" at every meeting to make sure no one felt intimidated, and permitted members to stop the meeting and discuss their grievances every time they felt personally insulted. But now, if women or people of color stopped a meeting to complain of a racist or sexist remark, they were often shouted down by Halberstadt and several other men. Because there was no formalized code of behavior for the meetings, and no decision could be made without consensus, the abusive tirades had to be tolerated. More and more people left.

78   At a meeting in early November, there was another confrontation. When one of the few female members started to walk out of the room, Halberstadt barred the door, screaming, "How dare you try to leave!" Frank Herron, a physically imposing man, told Halberstadt he was out of line and that he would do anything to stop him from threatening the others.

And so the group that had pledged itself to banding together against homophobia was about to begin slugging it out over racism and sexism.

In an attempt to recover some sense of equilibrium, the 79 members who stayed on—down to about twenty-five—held a special session in late November to discuss ways in which the general meetings could be better managed. At the session, John Woods of United Colors and a white member named Allen Carson proposed that the group agree to a ban on all sexist and racist language, although they did not offer a specific list of forbidden terms. Halberstadt blocked the proposal and later claimed: "My politics are antiauthoritarian. [This is] a power grab by wannabe bureaucrats."

Soon after that session, the handful of remaining members 80 called a "hiatus" until March, at which time they would regroup and see what, if anything, they could get to rise from the ashes.

When I accepted the assignment to write about Queer 81 Nation a year ago, I was full of zeal. I confess to ending my story in a state of confusion. I had expected to write a story about heroism, and I did, in fact, meet heroic people everywhere I went. I'd prefer to write only about their strength and solidarity. I don't like reporting about the squabbles, the naiveté, the self-destructive tendencies. I likewise don't quite know what to make of the fact that, of the chapters I visited, the only one that's holding together effectively—the group in Atlanta—is the only one with an old-fashioned leader. (Cheryl Summerville is now the chapter's cochair.) It's also the only one embroiled in a battle with a clear-cut villain, which may help account for its strength. Fighting homophobia, sexism, and racism, is, for most of us, a little like battling crabgrass. It's everywhere, so intricately stitched into the lawn that you can't quite tell where to begin.

My misgivings about Queer Nation stem mainly from its 82 tendency toward self-destruction, and this criticism is shared by other lesbians and gay men. Becky Moorman, publisher of *The Bridge*, a lesbian and gay magazine based in Utah, says: "The [lesbian and gay] community's really divided about what Queer Nation is doing. Their protests aren't focused. They need to decide who they're speaking to and what they're trying to say." Anthony Christiansen, an openly gay Ph.D. candidate in Columbia University's clinical-psychology program, adds: "Queer Nation focuses so much on our difference [from heterosexuals], they lose track of our connectedness. There are millions of complex situations out there—being gay isn't as cut-and-dried as they'd like to make out."

83   That may be the heart of the problem. We are probably the most diverse of all persecuted groups. A Martian field biologist sent to earth to capture two homosexual specimens could easily bring back a twenty-three-year-old white guy with an MBA from Yale and a sixty-five-year-old black lesbian separatist from Detroit. Queer Nation, fostered by people who've been unfairly excluded, is determined to be utterly inclusive. That's turning out to mean equal voice not only for women and men of all colors but also for the foolish, the prejudiced, and the outright deluded.

84   Perhaps Queer Nation is simply an early, flawed step toward a new kind of lesbian and gay militancy. Frank Herron of San Francisco insists that the city's chapter hasn't been a failure: "It's spawned a dozen groups doing different things. We've drawn a lot of people into activism." Herron sees the future of gay activism as a welter of small groups modeled on revolutionary cells. "Twelve people can reach a decision more easily than five hundred can," he says. "If these twelve need help, they work with another group of twelve. I don't know if we'll ever have a cohesive national gay activist organization."

85   Meanwhile, it's difficult not to feel panicky, because, as we argue over structure and focus, as we bicker among ourselves, our people are being attacked in increasing numbers. Since I was in Atlanta, Cheryl Summerville and Sandra Riley have become more famous and, simultaneously, more widely despised. After Summerville appeared on the Oprah Winfrey show in January, her sixteen-year-old son was so tormented by his classmates that she and Riley chose to move him to another school. There have been hate letters and threats. Riley has closed her sewing and alterations business so that she can be home when the boy gets back from school.

86   And as we struggle to set a coherent agenda, our people continue to die. My friend Tim, for one, died while I was working on this story. It was sudden, if that term can be applied to someone who'd had AIDS for almost three years. He was comparatively well and then he caught pneumonia and then he died. His parents, who hadn't spoken to him in years, didn't want his ashes. Karen is keeping them in a box in her apartment until we decide what to do with them. Another friend has taken Aretha, Tim's cat.

87   Just before Tim died, I found myself sitting with Karen at his bedside. He was unconscious, breathing noisily and steadily on a respirator. As Karen and I sat watching him, I

told her I was struggling to write an article about Queer Nation. She shrugged dismissively. "A bunch of thugs," she said.

"Right," I said. "That's right. And you've got a better idea,   88
haven't you?" My voice was loud enough to surprise me.

"Honey, calm down," she said with a nervous smile.   89

"You've got a much better solution," I said. "It's very effec-   90
tive to be discreet in public and send a little money to the Gay
Men's Health Crisis and write features about the ten best
espresso bars in lower Manhattan. Thank you for your contribution."

A nurse put her head through the curtains and asked if ev-   91
erything was all right. We told her not to worry, to get on with
her other business.

"You don't need to scream at me," Karen said quietly after   92
the nurse had gone.

"I know," I said.   93

"I'm not the one you're really angry at."   94

"I know. Let's not talk about it, okay?"   95

Of course, she was right. But I couldn't calm myself. Later, 96
after Tim died, I was able to see how stupid I'd been. How
quickly I'd self-destructed. Karen had been there for me to
scream at, and, even more important, she understood what I
was screaming about. A man like Jody Waller, standing
smugly with two cops behind him, doesn't get the point.
There's no outward evidence that he suspects he's doing anything wrong.

Karen and I will never be friends. Now that Tim is gone,   97
there's no reason for us to know each other. But during Tim's
last days, she and I managed to act like compatriots. We had
to. There was a funeral to plan, and, if we didn't do it, nobody
would.

It's hard to know what to do sometimes. I wish I felt more   98
certain about how to proceed. I wish I'd walked Tim home
that night after we left St. Vincent's. I keep thinking I could
have protected him.

Bruce Bawer

Notes on Stonewall

*Bruce Bawer (born 1956 in New York City) is a professional
writer with a background in literary studies. In addition to several books on one or another literary matter (his most recent is*
Prophets and Professors*), he has published a book of poems
and a volume of film criticism. Bawer's 1993 book* A Place at
the Table: The Gay Individual in American Society *was for
several months the number-one best-seller in gay bookstores. A
former director of the National Book Critics Circle, Bawer
reviews books frequently for the* New York Times Book Review
and the Washington Post Book World *and has also published
essays and reviews in* The American Scholar, The Nation, The
Hudson Review, Newsweek, *and* The Advocate. *"Notes on
Stonewall" appeared in* The New Republic, *a respected magazine on public affairs that once had a liberal slant but now
occupies a middle position editorially.*

1   Twenty five years ago, in the early morning hours of June
28, 1969, several patrons at the Stonewall bar in Greenwich
Village, many of them flamboyant drag queens and prostitutes, refused to go quietly when police carried out a routine
raid on the place. Their refusal escalated into five days of rioting by hundreds of people. Though it wasn't the first time
anyone had contested the right of the state to punish citizens
just for being gay, that rioting marked a pivotal moment because news of it spread in every direction and sparked the
imaginations of countless gay men and lesbians around the
world. It made them examine, and reject, the silence, shame
and reflexive compliance with prejudice to which most of
them had simply never conceived a realistic alternative.

2   There is something wondrous about Stonewall, and it is
this: that a mere handful of late-night bar patrons, many of
them confused, lonely individuals living at the margins of society, started something that made a lot of lesbians and gay
men do some very serious thinking of a sort they had never
quite done before—thinking that led to action and to a movement. It was the beginning of a revolution in attitudes toward
homosexuality. How odd it is to think that those changes
could all be traced back to a drunken riot at a Greenwich Village bar on a June night in 1969. But they can. And that's why
Stonewall deserves to be commemorated.

Today, however, Stonewall is not only commemorated but   3
mythologized. Many gay men and lesbians routinely speak of
it as if it was a sacred event that lies beyond the reach of objective discourse. They talk as if there was no gay rights activism at all before Stonewall, or else they mock pre-Stonewall
activists as Uncle Toms. They recite the name "Stonewall" itself with the same reverence that American politicians reserve
for the names of Washington and Lincoln. And indeed the
word is perfectly suited to the myth, conjuring as it does an
image of a huge, solid barrier separating the dark ages prior
to the day that Judy Garland died from the out-loud-and-
proud present. Every year, on what has long since become an
all-purpose gay holiday—a combination of Independence Day,
May Day, Mardi Gras and, since the advent of HIV, Memorial
Day as well—millions ritualistically revisit the raucous, defiant marginality of Stonewall in marches around the world.
This year in New York, on the twenty-fifth anniversary, the
ritual will reach a climax. For many, Stonewall has already
become a Platonic model of gay activism—and, indeed, a
touchstone of gay identity.

A few weeks ago, in a sermon about an entirely different   4
subject, the rector of the Episcopal church I belong to in
New York used the phrase "the politics of nostalgia." The
phrase has stuck in my mind, for it seems to me that both
sides of the gay rights struggle are trapped in what may well
be characterized as a politics of nostalgia. Many of those
who resist acceptance of homosexuality and reject equal
rights for gay men and lesbians know on some level that they
are wrong, but they cling to old thinking because a change,
however just, seems to them a drastic departure from the
comfortable world of "don't ask, don't tell." Some gay people,
likewise, cling to what might be called the Stonewall sensibility, reacting defensively and violently, as if to some horrendous blasphemy or betrayal, even to the hint that perhaps the
time has come to move in some way beyond that sensibility.
Such people often declare proudly that they have been "in
the trenches" for twenty-five years, which is to say that in a
way they have been reliving Stonewall every day since June
1969.

Yet every day *can't* be Stonewall—or shouldn't. And in fact   5
the time *has* come to move beyond the Stonewall sensibility.
For, thanks largely to developments that can trace their inspiration to that barroom raid, some things *have* changed since
1969. Levels of tolerance have risen; gay rights laws have been
passed; in the last quarter-century, and especially recently, gay

Americans have come out of the closet in increasing numbers. As a result, it has become clear to more and more heterosexuals that gay America is as diverse as straight America—that many of the people who were at the Stonewall bar on that night twenty-five years ago represent an anachronistic politics that largely has ceased to have salience for gay America today. To say this is not to condemn people who consider themselves members of that fringe or to read them out of the gay community. It is simply to say that for gay America to continue to be defined largely by its fringe is a lie, and that this lie, like all lies about homosexuality, needs to be countered vigorously. The Stonewall sensibility—like the Stonewall myth—has to be abandoned.

6   On May 6 *The New York Times* described the arguments among gay leaders about the planning of Stonewall 25, the forthcoming New York event that will culminate in a march on the United Nations. Some of these leaders worried that Stonewall 25 wouldn't focus enough on the fact that many of the Stonewall heroes were transvestite and transsexual hustlers. One woman wanted, in her words, to "radicalize" Stonewall 25. "Stonewall," she told the *Times*, "was a rebellion of transgender people, and this event has the potential to reduce our whole culture to an Ikea ad."

7   It is strange to read the words of those who speak, on the one hand, as if Stonewall, in and of itself, achieved something once and for all time that gay Americans are now free to celebrate, and, on the other, as if the kind of growing acceptance that is represented by the depiction of a middle-class gay couple in a furniture commercial on network T.V. is bad news, a threat to a Stonewall-born concept of gay identity as forever marginal. It would almost seem as if those leaders don't realize that Stonewall was only part of a long, complex process that is still proceeding, and that the best way to honor it is to build upon it by directing that process as wisely and responsibly as we can.

8   In the May 3 issue of the gay magazine *The Advocate*, activist Torie Osborn wrote that thirty-nine gay leaders, whom she described as "our community's best and brightest," had gathered recently to discuss the state of the movement and "retool [it] to match the changing times." The group, she wrote, "had a collective 750 years of experience in gay rights or other political work." But even as she wrote of seeking "common ground" and "common vision" among the gay leaders, Osborn reaffirmed the linking of gay rights to "other progressive movements with which many of us identify."

In other words, she embraced the standard post-Stonewall   9
practice of indiscriminately linking the movement for gay
equal rights with any left-wing cause to which any gay leader
might happen to have a personal allegiance. That practice
dates back to 1969, when radical activists, gay and straight,
were quick to use the gay rights movement as a way to prosecute their own unrelated revolutionary agendas. Such linkages have been a disaster for the gay rights movement; not
only do they falsely imply that most gay people sympathize
with those so-called progressive movements, but they also
serve to reinforce the idea of homosexuality itself as a "progressive" phenomenon, as something that is essentially political in nature. Osborn wrote further that she and the other gay
leaders at the summit "talked about separating strategic
thinking into two discrete areas: our short-term political
fights and the long-term cultural war against systematic
homophobia." And she added that "we have virtually no helpful objective data or clear strategy on the long-term war,
which grapples with deep-seated sexphobia as well as hetero-
sexism." Her conclusion (my emphasis): "*We need to start
working on this problem.*"

With all due respect to Osborn and her fellow gay leaders,   10
it seems to me more than a bit astonishing that in spite of
their collective 750 years of experience, at least some of them
only now have begun to realize that homosexuals should be
giving thought to something other than short-term political
conflicts. At the same time, those leaders still can't quite understand the long-term challenge as anything other than, in
Osborn's words, a "war." Nor can they see that achieving real
and lasting equality is a matter not of changing right-wingers
into left-wingers, or of emancipating Americans from "sexphobia," but of liberating people from their discomfort with
homosexuality, their automatic tendency to think of homosexuals in terms of sex and their often bizarre notions of who
gay people are, what gay people value and how gay people
live.

Perhaps, at the threshold of the second generation of the   11
post-Stonewall gay rights movement, it behooves us to recall
that, as I've noted, there *was* at least some species of gay activism prior to Stonewall. Years before those patrons at the
Stonewall bar hurled garbage, beer bottles, feces and four-
letter words at the policemen who had come to arrest them, a
few small groups of men in business suits and women in
dresses staged sober, orderly marches at which they carried
signs that announced their own homosexuality and that re-

spectfully demanded an end to anti-homosexual prejudice. Those people were even more radical than the rioters at Stonewall, and—dare I say it?—perhaps even more brave, given how few they were, how premeditated their protests and how much some of them had to lose by publicly identifying themselves as gay. They were heroes, too; they won a few legal battles and they might have won more. Sure, Stonewall was, without question, an important step—indeed, the biggest single step the gay rights movement has taken. But that's all it was: a step, the first big one in a long, difficult journey. It was a reaction to intolerance, and it set us on the road to tolerance. The next road leads to acceptance—acceptance not only of gay people by straight people, but an easier acceptance by young gay people of their own sexuality. It's a different road—and, in a way, a harder one.

12   First-generation post-Stonewall gay activists saw themselves as street combatants in a political war. Second generation activists would better see themselves as participants in an educational program of which the expressly political work is only a part. Getting America to accept homosexuality will first be a matter of education. The job is not to shout at straight Americans, "We're here, we're queer, get used to it." The job is to do the hard, painstaking work of *getting* straight Americans used to it. This isn't dramatic work; nor is it work that provides a quick emotional release. Rather, it requires discipline, commitment, responsibility.

13   In some sense, of course, most straight Americans *are* used to the idea of people being gay. The first generation of the post-Stonewall gay rights movement has accomplished that. At the same time, it has brought us to a place where many straight Americans are sick and tired of the very word "gay." They've heard it a million times, yet they don't understand it nearly well enough. They still feel uncomfortable, confused, threatened. They feel that the private lives of homosexuals have been pushed "in their faces," but they don't really *know* about those private lives.

14   And why should they be expected to? Yes, at Gay Pride Day marches, some gay men and lesbians, like the Stonewall rioters, have exposed America to images of raw sexuality—images that variously amuse, titillate, shock and offend while revealing nothing important about who most of those people really are. Why, then, do some people do such things? Perhaps because they've been conditioned to think that on that gay high holy day, the definitively gay thing to do is to be as

defiant as those heroes twenty-five years ago. Perhaps they do it because they can more easily grasp the concept of enjoying one day per year of delicious anarchy than of devoting 365 days per year to a somewhat more disciplined and strategically sensible demonstration designed to advance the causes of respect, dignity and equality.

And perhaps they do it because, frankly, it is relatively easy   15
to do. Just as standing up at a White House press conference and yelling at the president can take less courage than coming out to your parents or neighbors or employers, so taking off your pants or your bra for a Gay Pride Day march in the company of hundreds of thousands of known allies can be easier than taking down your defenses for a frank conversation with a group of colleagues at an office lunch about how it was to grow up gay. For an insecure gay man or lesbian, moreover, explaining can feel awfully close to apologizing, and can open one up to charges of collaboration with the enemy by those who join the author Paul Monette in seeing America as the "Christian Reich" and themselves as members of the queer equivalent of the French resistance.

As a friend said to me recently, building acceptance of ho-   16
mosexuals is like teaching a language. When gays speak about themselves, they are speaking one language; when most straight people speak about gays, they are speaking another. Most heterosexuals look at gay lives the way I look at a page of German. I may be able to pick out a few familiar words, but I feel awkward when I use them, and if I try to put together a sentence I'm likely to find myself saying something I don't mean at all, perhaps even something offensive or hurtful. There's only one way to get past that feeling of confusion: tireless, meticulous dedication to study. You can't learn a foreign language overnight, and you can't teach it by screaming it at people. You teach it word by word, until, bit by bit, they feel comfortable speaking it and can find their way around the country where it's spoken. That's the job of the second generation of post-Stonewall gay activism: to teach those who don't accept us the language of who gay people are and where gay people live. Indeed, to the extent that professional homophobes have stalled progress in the movement toward legal and social parity for gay men and lesbians, it is not because those homophobes are so crafty, and certainly not because they are right. It is because they have spoken to straight America in its own language and addressed its concerns, whereas gay Americans, more often than not, out of an understandable fear and defensive self-righteousness, haven't.

17   Some reviewers in the gay press read the title of my book,
A Place at the Table: The Gay Individual in American Society, as
a sign that I, personally, long to sit at a dinner table with people like Pat Buchanan and Jerry Falwell—that this book is my
attempt to indicate to them that I'm a nice, well-mannered
gay man and that I, along with the other nice, well-mannered
gay men, should be allowed at the table while the "bad," ill-
mannered gays are excluded. Some other gay press reviewers
have understood that I don't mean that at all, and that I feel
everyone should be welcome at the American table, but they
have angrily rejected the idea: "Why," one critic wrote,
"should *I* want to sit at that table?" A writer for the gay magazine *Out* dismissed the book in one line: "Bruce Bawer has
written a book about the gay individual in American society
entitled *A Place at the Table.* Some will prefer take-out."

18   What these reactions signify to me is a powerful tendency
among some homosexuals to recoil reflexively from the vision
of an America where gays live as full and open members of
society, with all the rights, responsibilities and opportunities
of heterosexuals. Many gay people, indeed, have a deep, unar-
ticulated fear of that metaphorical place at the table. This is
understandable: gay people, as a rule, are so used to minimizing their exposure to homophobia, by living either in the
closet or on the margins of society, that for someone—even a
fellow gay person—to come along and invoke an image of gay
America sitting openly at a table with straight America can
seem, to them, like a hostile act. This sense of threat—this devotion to the margin—may help explain the gay-activist ran-
cor toward the movie *Philadelphia.* But most gay men and
lesbians were happy to see a movie that showed homosexuality as part of the mainstream, just as most are pleased by the
new tendency to depict gay life, in everything from Ikea ads
to movies like *Four Weddings and a Funeral* in a matter-of-fact
way, as an integrated part of society.

19   Am I attacking radicalism? No. I'm saying that the word
"radical" must be defined anew by each generation. In the
late twentieth century, when radicalism has often been
viewed as a fashion choice, it's easy to lose sight of what real
radicalism is. It's not a matter of striking a defiant pose and
maintaining that pose over a period of years; it's not a matter
of signing on to a certain philosophy or program and adher-
ing to it inflexibly for the rest of your life. And it's not always
a matter of manning barricades or crouching in trenches. It's
a matter of honest inquiry, of waking up every morning and
looking at the social circumstances in which you find yourself

and having the vision to perceive what needs to be done and the courage to follow up on that vision, wherever it may take you. It's a matter of going to the *root* of the problem, wherever that root may lie.

And going to the root of this particular problem means go-   20
ing to the root of prejudice. It means probing the ignorance and fear that are responsible for the success of anti-gay crusaders. It means seriously addressing those opponents' arguments against gay rights, in which they combine a defense of morality and "family values" with attacks on homosexuality as anti-God, anti-American and anti-family. Too often, the first generation of the post-Stonewall gay movement has responded to such rhetoric by actually saying and doing things that have only reinforced the homophobes' characterization of homosexuality. The second generation of the movement would do well to respond not by attacking the American values and ridiculing the religious faith that these people claim as a basis for their prejudice, but by making it clear just how brutal, how un-American and how anti-religious their arguments and their prejudice are.

And there are a *lot* of untruths out there to overcome. More   21
and more people understand that homosexuals are no more likely to be child molesters than heterosexuals are, but there remains on the part of many people a lingering discomfort about such notions, and anti-gay crusaders exploit that discomfort with ambiguous, dishonest rhetoric suggesting that homosexuals are (to quote a recent statement published in *The Wall Street Journal* by a group of religious figures calling itself the Ramsey Colloquium) a threat to the "vulnerabilities of the young." That's a lie. But how can homosexuals help heterosexuals understand it's a lie so long as some gay political leaders, in the best Stonewall tradition, feel more comfortable condemning the Log Cabin Republicans than they do condemning the North American Man-Boy Love Association?

Likewise, more and more people understand that homo-   22
sexuals' lives are no more about sex than their lives are, but there are many who still *don't* understand that, and the anti-gay crusaders exploit their ignorance by saying (again in the words of the Ramsey Colloquium) that gay people "define" themselves by their "desires alone," that they seek "liberation from constraint," from obligations to the larger society and especially to the young, and from all human dignity. *That's* a lie. But how can gays help straights understand it's a lie so long as a few marchers on Gay Pride Day feel the best way to

represent all gay men and lesbians is to walk down the avenue in their underwear?

23   Anti-gay propagandists shrewdly exploit the fact that we live in times when there's ample reason for concern about children. American children today grow up in an often uncivil and crime-ridden society, and with a pop culture that is at best value-neutral and at worst aggressive and ugly. Altogether too many of those kids grow up inured to the sight of beggars sleeping on the sidewalk, of condoms and hypodermic needles in the gutter, of pornographic magazines on display at street-corner kiosks. Anti-gay propagandists routinely link homosexuality to these phenomena, seeing homosexual orientation, and gay people's openness about it, and gay people's desire for equal rights and equal respect, as yet more signs of the decline of morals, of the family, of social cohesion and stability and of civilization generally.

24   One of Stonewall's legacies is that gay leaders have too often accepted this characterization of the conflict and see any attempt to correct it as "sex-negative." The second generation of post-Stonewall gay activism has to make it clear that that's not the way the sides break down at all, and that when it comes to children, the real interests of parents and of gay people (many of whom are themselves parents, of course) are not unalterably opposed, but are, in fact, perfectly congruent. Gay adults care about children, too; and they know from experience something that straight parents can only strive to understand—namely, what it's like to grow up gay.

25   Homosexuals, of course, are *not* a threat to the family; among the things that threaten the family are parents' profound ignorance about homosexuality and their reluctance to face the truth about it. In the second generation of the post-Stonewall gay rights movement, gay adults must view it as an obligation to ensure that parents understand that truth—and understand, too, that according equal rights to homosexuals and equal recognition to same-sex relationships (and creating an atmosphere in which gay men and lesbians can live openly without fear of losing their jobs or homes or lives) would not threaten the institution of the family but would actually strengthen millions of American families.

26   It is ironic that, to a large extent, what perpetuates Stonewall-style antagonism between gay and straight are not our differences, really, but traits that we all share as human beings. We all, for instance, fear the unknown. To most straight people, homosexuality is an immense unknown; to gay people, a society that would regard sexual orientation

indifferently and grant homosexuals real equality is also an immense unknown. But it is also our humanity that makes most of us long to know and live with the truth, even in the wake of a lifetime of lies. The greatest tribute we can pay to the memory of Stonewall is to work in our own homes and workplaces to dismantle, lie by lie, the wall of lies that has divided the families of America for too long.

John Berresford
Rights and Responsibilities, Not Freebies and Frolics

John Berresford does most of his writing as part of his job as an antitrust lawyer for the Federal Communications Commission in Washington, but he did find time to contribute the following article to The Washington Post *in June 1995. The* Post *is a politically moderate newspaper with a national as well as local readership, rather like* The New York Times.

I am gay and have been in the gay rights movement since I came out in 1981. I am also a conservative, a libertarian.   1

Sad to say, the gay rights movement has always been seen as being on the political left, as one more whining interest group claiming entitlement to all sorts of special treatment from the government. Or we are seen as having a simply fabulous time cavorting at Gay Pride parades and throwing condoms at Catholic services. Whether as crybabies or as Dionysian celebrants, we always appear outside the mainstream.   2

I cringe at both images. Most gay men and women do not go around demanding government favors or living a hedonistic "gay lifestyle." But just enough of us act out these images, or tolerate them, that they become real in the public mind. Middle America feels uncomfortable about this, at the very least. Our right-wing enemies love it, because it gives them someone to hate and someone to use as a foil for attracting mainstream support to their own causes. By accepting, and in   3 some cases cultivating, these images, we lose friends and help our enemies.

4   As a conservative, I wish such images would evaporate. If there was ever a time when they made sense, on grounds of either truthfulness or usefulness, it ended when the Republicans took control of Congress. The waiting line for government benefits now leads nowhere, and public frolics now gain nothing but disapproval.

5   What can government give gays? Merely the form, not the substance, of what we need and want. What we are really after is not merely legal rights but acceptance into the mainstream of American life—and acceptance is granted or withheld by the mainstream majority at its pleasure. If we want to be accepted, we must be welcomed. Lord knows it's easier to change the votes of a few legislators than the hearts and minds of millions of our fellow citizens. But politicians are weathervanes, they are not the wind.

6   So we should end some of our present practices:

7   We should loudly reject all "compensatory" agendas: hiring quotas, affirmative action and group reparations—all of which I've heard advocated for "when we get our rights." The people who benefit most from such programs are the bureaucrats who administer them and the members of the "victim" groups with the best political connections.

8   We should stop pressing for "domestic partners" legislation. It creates a special class of rights for a small class of people. The real beneficiaries would be the lawyers who would litigate the differences and similarities between domestic partnership and marriage.

9   We should not hate Jesse Helms, Pat Robertson and their allies. Leave the hating to them. They will eventually destroy themselves, as Joe McCarthy and other haters did.

10   We should stop feeling sorry for ourselves. We may be victims, but frankly no one cares. This country's wellsprings of liberal guilt began running dry about 20 years ago, and by now they are flat empty.

11   Finally, we should stop seeing AIDS as anybody else's problem. The sad fact is that every gay man who got AIDS by sex got it from another gay man, and by doing something he chose to do. People with AIDS deserve sympathy, but it is the sympathy one extends to a chain smoker who comes down with lung cancer. It is not the same kind of sympathy one feels for someone who was struck by lightning or run down by a drunk driver.

But that's enough on the negative side. What positive ac- 12
tions can we take?

For starters, each of us should come out whenever it is rea- 13
sonably safe. The best way to explode the myths about us is
for each of us to become known as just another human being
with the same needs, goals and drives as other human beings—except in a single respect that poses no threat to anyone else.

Our legislative goal should be for civil rights legislation 14
with disclaimers of any quotas, guidelines, reparations or
government-imposed and group-based remedies. It should
emphasize private lawsuits for damages rather than enforcement of a bureaucracy.

In the legislatures, we should also lobby for the right to 15
marry. Domestic-partners legislation makes us an officially
sanctioned class of oddities and freaks. By seeking marriage,
we demonstrate our wish to be part of the great American
middle-class way of life.

Among ourselves, we must be willing to talk about morals, 16
to impose them on ourselves and to do so conspicuously. As
long as our primary image is one of gleeful promiscuity—an
image promoted not only by our enemies but also by our own
magazines and our own bars—we will be ostracized. Until we
start imposing honesty, fidelity and emotion on our lives—in
other words, until we are willing to talk about moral standards—we will make little real progress in social acceptance.

In a curious way, AIDS itself may be helping us find social 17
acceptance. This terrible disease has brought to a screeching
halt—at least in my generation of gay men—the manic booz-
ing, drugging, and screwing of the '70s and '80s. It has forced
us to attend more to friendships, stability and the consequences of our action. It has opened us to human suffering;
one friend told me that caring for someone with AIDS was the
first unselfish thing he had done in his adult life. AIDS has
enabled us to show, to ourselves and to the mainstream, that
we too are capable of great suffering, compassion, work and
sacrifice. By our work with each other, we have shown mainstream society what we have to offer it, and how much it loses
and wastes by excluding us.

The common theme of all this is simply facing the facts, 18
working to bring out the best in ourselves and offering something admirable to the mainstream. All these views put me in
odd company politically. But if you had to agree about everything with everyone else in an organization before you could

join it, we'd have 260 million political parties in this country. Conservatives are the people I happen to agree with most of the time. At least they are attempting to deal with the moral issues of our time (such as welfare dependency and violence) on a moral plane, and not as something for which the only remedy is another government program and more spending.

19   After I come out to them, I find that most conservatives are perfectly tolerant (and not as cloyingly condescending as my liberal straight friends). The Helmses and Robertsons are in the minority. And it eventually dawns on the conservatives that if they want to keep the support of gays like me, they had better keep at least a distance between themselves and the haters.

20   Finally, moving in conservative circles permits me to ask my conservative friends where this country would be without those great gays—Whittaker Chambers, J. Edgar Hoover, Walt Whitman and Cardinal Spellman. It's a polite way to remind them that we have been in their midst and doing good deeds from the beginning.

21   My liberal friends tend to employ three styles of attack on my views. The first is ad hominem: How can you talk about morality when we all know that once you did this or that randy deed? My answer is that (a) the fact that your first response is to attack the messenger (me) shows that you can't repel the message; and (b) I had my adolescence like everyone else, and it's over.

22   My liberal friends' second attack is some variation on "Do you mean that you're against all attempts to right the wrongs that have been done to us?" My answer is that I am as much in favor of basic civil rights for gays as they are. Where we differ is in the need for group-based remedies and in perceiving ourselves as victims whose main recourse should be coercion by the government.

23   The third attack from my liberal friends is usually some form of "Well, you have a good point, but...." At that, I know I've made some progress.

24   I have a feeling there are many more conservative gays than there seem to be. The time is ripe for us to leave the plantation of liberal government and start acting like what we are—a group of adults who want to live lives as normal and as healthy as everyone else in the mainstream. If we do, I think we will be on the path to my dream—an America in which being gay is no more remarkable than being left-handed.

Yale Kamisar

Drugs, AIDS, and the Threat to Privacy

Yale Kamisar is a prominent member of the faculty at the University of Michigan Law School. The author of Constitutional Law: Cases, Comments, Questions *and many other publications in academic law, he contributed the following analysis to* The New York Times Magazine, *a Sunday supplement to* The New York Times, *on September 13, 1987.*

"Time works changes, brings into existence new conditions   1
and purposes," wrote Supreme Court Justice Joseph McKenna
in 1910. "Therefore, a principle to be vital must be capable of
wider application than the mischief which gave it birth. . . . [In
interpreting] a constitution . . . our contemplation cannot be
only of what has been but of what may be."

Few legal developments better illustrate these words   2
than the history of the Fourth Amendment, which protects
"the right of the people to be secure in their persons,
homes, papers, and effects, against unreasonable searches
and seizures."

The wording is succinct and majestic. But it is also vague   3
and general. Whether and how to apply the Fourth Amendment to new conditions has generated great controversy—
none of it greater than the current debate over mass drug testing and mandatory AIDS testing.

The two so-called plagues of the 1980's—what government   4
officials have called the "national epidemic" of illicit drug use
and the "global epidemic" of acquired immune deficiency
syndrome—have put enormous pressure on the Fourth
Amendment. Proposals that would require certain groups to
submit to random urinalysis tests for drugs, or to blood tests
for the AIDS virus, directly threaten the concept of "individualized suspicion" that lies at the heart of the amendment. In
brief, this notion holds that the government should not be
able to interfere with someone's liberty, or invade his privacy,
unless officials can demonstrate that they have "probable
cause" to believe that particular person is committing, or has
committed, a crime. The amendment forbids the Government
to issue search warrants unless officials can satisfy the "probable cause" requirement.

5   The concept of individualized suspicion would seem to be incompatible—to put it mildly—with random drug tests or "routine" blood tests for the AIDS virus. At the moment, drug testing is being challenged in the courts; the directive for "routine" AIDS testing is likely to challenged in the future. Some day, I venture to say, Americans may look back on the legal rulings about drug and AIDS testing as the most dramatic illustrations in history of how to apply the Fourth Amendment to new conditions—or as the the most striking examples of the failure to do so.

6   Until recently, the best example of the struggle to adapt the Fourth Amendment to new developments was the Supreme Court's consideration of wiretapping and electronic eavesdropping. In the first wiretapping case to reach the Court, in 1928, Chief Justice William Howard Taft, writing for a 5–4 majority, concluded that, so long as electronic surveillance did not involve a physical entry into a person's home or office, it fell outside the Fourth Amendment. Conversations, he reasoned, were not "things" to be "seized" within the meaning of the amendment.

7   But as more and more sophisticated means of electronic snooping emerged, it became increasingly clear that this "property-trespass" theory of the Fourth Amendment could not survive. In 1967, the Warren Court finally rejected it, noting that the Fourth Amendment "protects people, not places," and thus applies whenever the Government violates a person's "justifiable" expectation of privacy.

8   So the Court finally deemed tapping and bugging "searches." It didn't necessarily follow, however, that all such searches were inherently intrusive as to be *unreasonable*. Today, law enforcement authorities may still conduct "electronic surveillance"—but only after having convinced a judge that they have satisfied the "individualized suspicion" requirement.

9   In the case of drug and mandatory AIDS testing, however, the constitutional problems are much less clear-cut.

10   Last year, President Reagan signed an executive order calling for widespread mandatory drug testing of some Federal employees, and a growing number of state and local agencies have followed suit. Last spring, the President announced that the Federal Government would begin mandatory AIDS testing of selected groups—would-be immigrants, illegal aliens seeking amnesty and Federal prisoners—who do not enjoy the usual Fourth Amendment protections. The President

also called upon the states to provide what he called "routine" testing (which, according to some officials, seems to be a softer way of saying mandatory testing) for inmates in state and local prisons, patients at venereal disease clinics and drug-abuse centers, and couples applying for marriage licenses.

The battle over drug testing is already being waged in the state and Federal appellate courts and should reach the Supreme Court soon. Its outcome is bound to have an important bearing on AIDS testing. 11

Almost every court that has addressed the issue has rejected the Government's argument that because urinalysis does not involve a physical invasion, or even a touching, of the body, it does not constitute a search (an argument that might well have prevailed in the Taft Court). Instead, the courts have ruled that urinalysis falls under the Fourth Amendment because a person has a reasonable expectation of privacy with respect to personal information contained in his body fluids. Moreover, a urine test is often conducted under the close surveillance of a government representative—an embarrassing, if not humiliating, experience. 12

Many questions have been raised about the effectiveness of mass drug testing, and still more about that of mandatory AIDS testing. But even if the courts agree that mandatory testing is effective, effectiveness alone is still not sufficient justification to initiate a search. As one Federal court recently noted: "There is no doubt about it—searches and seizures can yield a wealth of information useful to the searcher. (That is why King George III's men so frequently searched the colonists.) That potential, however, does not make [a government search] a constitutionally reasonable one." 13

Sol Wachtler, Chief Judge of the New York State Court of Appeals, made this point last June, in the course of striking down a New York school district's requirement that all probationary teachers submit to urinalysis: "By restricting the government to reasonable searches, the State and Federal Constitutions recognize that there comes a point at which searches intended to serve the public interest, however effective, may themselves undermine the public's interest in maintaining the privacy, dignity and security of its members." 14

May the Government require those seeking public employment to submit to a drug test? No, answer civil-liberties lawyers, quickly invoking the doctrine of "unconstitutional conditions," which says the Government may not condition employment on the surrender of constitutional rights. 15

16   Often this is the right answer, but not always. Under
certain circumstances, the Government may deprive public
employees of some of the rights they would have as
citizens—not on the simplistic theory that one is obliged
to accept employment on the Government's terms, but on the
ground that sometimes a citizen's full enjoyment of his constitutional rights may be demonstrably incompatible with the
mission of the particular public agency employing him.

17   In April, for example, a Federal Court of Appeals in New
Orleans sustained a program requiring all Customs Service
employees seeking transfers to certain jobs to submit to urine
testing. The court underscored "the strong governmental interest in employing individuals for key positions in drug enforcement who themselves are not drug users."

18   On the other hand, a similar case last March, an intermediate New Jersey court, basing its decision exclusively on its
State Constitution, reached the opposite conclusion. As this
court saw it, a Newark police directive mandating that all
members of the narcotics bureau submit to periodic drug tests
authorized searches without individualized suspicion, despite
the fact that the record "did not indicate that drug use within
the narcotic bureau...is extensive." The court maintained
that objective indications of drug use—such as absenteeism,
chronic lateness, general deterioration of work habits—along
with confidential information would be adequate to identify
officers who might be using drugs.

19   The main targets of governmental drug testing so far have
been public employees, but proposed AIDS testing is likely to
be far more widespread. In view of the Fourth Amendment's
notion of individualized suspicion, how could the Government require all hospital patients or all marriage license
applicants to submit to AIDS tests? After all, no court would
ever approve a "dragnet" or "blanket" search of all people living in a high-crime neighborhood simply because such an
operation would turn up evidence of criminal conduct on the
part of some residents—as undoubtedly it would. (The
requirement that marriage license applicants be tested for
syphilis, still in force in many states, has apparently never
been tested on Fourth Amendment grounds. The procedure's
wide acceptance is likely to influence the courts when they
address the AIDS question.)

20   But there are potential precedents. Although the Supreme
Court has not specifically addressed these questions, in recent
years lower Federal courts have consistently upheld what

might be called "dragnet searches" of passengers at airport departure gates, and "blanket" metal-detector searches at the doors of courthouses and other government buildings.

In effect, the courts have carved out an exception to the traditional Fourth Amendment constraints that would allow what have been variously described as "regulatory searches," "administrative searches," or "inspections." (The original precedent involved granting government inspectors the power to examine residential and commercial buildings for possible violations of health, safety and sanitation standards.) The essence of this exception is that searches not conducted as part of a typical police investigation to secure criminal evidence but as part of a "general regulatory scheme"—one applying standardized procedures to minimize the potential for arbitrariness—need not be based on individualized suspicion. 21

The handiness of the administrative search concept has gladdened the hearts of many government lawyers. But it has alarmed other observers, including me. Today, potential administrative searches are buzzing around the Fourth Amendment like a swarm of bees. With drug and AIDS testing, the drone may soon be deafening. 22

As Wayne LaFave, a professor of law at the University of Illinois at Urbana and author of the leading treatise on search and seizure, points out: "Unless the administrative search is limited to truly extraordinary situation where rigorous application of typical Fourth Amendment standards would be *intolerable*, the amendment will largely disappear. The need to detect drug users is important, but hardly more so than the need to search for narcotics dealers, kidnappers and murderers. Yet we have never demanded 100 percent enforcement of the criminal law. Instead, we are committed to a philosophy of tolerating a certain level of undetected crime as preferable to an oppressive state." 23

Judge Benjamin Cardozo once observed that "the great tides and currents which engulf the rest of men do not turn aside in their course and pass judges by." The rulings upholding airport and courthouse searches—which were a response to the dramatic increase in airplane hijackings and the bombings of government buildings—illustrate Judge Cardozo's point. The danger today is that judges will be unduly influenced by the contemporary tides and currents—by rising fears of illicit-drug and AIDS "epidemics." 24

25   Someday, the Supreme Court may rule that concerns about
physical safety are sufficiently compelling to justify random
drug testing of prison guards or other law-enforcement officers, or perhaps even other public employees who perform
dangerous tasks. But that is a long way from saying that
schoolteachers, or public employees generally, no matter
what the nature of their jobs, must submit to random drug
testing. Or that large groups of people must undergo "routine" AIDS testing.

26   However great the threat posed by illicit drug use and the
AIDS virus, the "individualized suspicion" concept must remain the heart of the Fourth Amendment. I believe we should
greet claims of "national interest," "emergency," or "necessity" with considerable skepticism. Slogans like these can
be—and have been—a free people's most effective tranquilizers. As we mark the Constitution's 200th anniversary, we
would do well to remember that.

Dan Chaon
Transformations

*Dan Chaon lives in Cleveland, Ohio, and teaches at Cleveland
State University. He has published a number of short stories;
the one reprinted here appeared in 1991 in* Story, *a prestigious
quarterly that prints only short fiction.*

1   The first time I saw my brother Corky in women's clothes,
I was eleven and he was fourteen. He came out of my parents'
bedroom in my mother's good dress, the one with bird of paradise flowers patterned on it, and her high heels and lipstick.
I thought he was kidding. He chased after me, talking in a
Southern accent, and I ran off laughing. Corky was always
pretending to be someone else, dressing up in clothes he'd
bought at the Catholic rummage house or found in the
garage, imitating the mannerisms of his math teacher, or
Uncle Evan, who drove semi trucks and stuttered, or some

disc jockey on the radio. I didn't realize then, not for years and years actually, that he was gay and all.

He is still your brother, my father told me when he showed 2 me the picture. This was the second time I'd seen Corky in women's clothes. In the photo, he was wearing a big red wig, a blue-jean skirt, pumps, and a blouse with fringe. He looked like a country singer. My father asked me: "Do you know who this is?" All I said was, Yes, and, It figures.

My father shook his head at me. He liked to pretend that he 3 didn't care what Corky was, just so long as he was happy. That was the official line. But I'd seen the kind of cloudy distance that came into his eyes when he talked to Corky on the phone. I'd noticed him, once, studying an old Polaroid of the three of us, pheasant hunting, examining it as if looking for clues. I'd seen his expression when one of his buddies from the electrician's union asked: "So how's that boy of yours doing back East?" My father shifted from foot to foot. "Oh, fine, fine," he said quickly, and looked down.

But he looked me sternly in the eyes. "He is still your 4 brother," he said. He folded his thick hands, staring glumly at the glossy black-and-white photo.

"My sister, you mean," I said. 5

He frowned. "You're getting pretty smart-mouthed," he 6 said. He laid the photo on the kitchen table between us, like some important document I was supposed to sign. "He does this as entertainment," my father said. The words "CABARET BERLINER, New York," were printed on the bottom of the picture.

"I'll bet," I said. 7

My brother worked at a bar in New York City. We'd known 8 that. We also knew he was gay. He'd told my parents over the phone after he'd been away a year. I wasn't sure how they reacted at first, though they seemed calm by the time they got around to telling me. Corky had come to a decision, my father said, and my mother nodded grimly. For a long time afterward, my father wouldn't refer to it at all except as "your brother's decision," though he also pointed out to me that the words "fag" and "queer" were worse than swearing as far as he was concerned.

Corky was going to college in New York at the time, but he 9 dropped out shortly after to audition for plays and work in bars at night. He hadn't been home since he told them. Instead, he sent clippings, pictures, lists of productions he was trying out for. "One thing about Corky," my father pointed out to me as he looked through the packets Corky sent. "At least he knows what he wants, and he's not afraid to go after it."

10   It was my senior year in high school, and my father thought I had no ambition. Maybe that was true. In any case, I wasn't like Corky had been when he was in high school. His senior year, there was always something about him taped to the refrigerator—a certificate of merit, or a clipping from the local paper about a scholarship he'd won. He pinned the acceptance letters from colleges in neat rows on a bulletin board in our room, as if they were rare butterflies.

11   That was why I was surprised when he called to say he was taking some time off to attend my high school graduation. I went to the Catholic school as Corky had, but there was no chance of me ending up valedictorian like him. For a while maybe people wondered whether I'd be a teacher's pet like Corky, and they even sometimes called me by his name. But it didn't take them long to find out that I wasn't going to leave any brilliant reputation in my wake. My father always said that I didn't "apply myself" like Corky did. Out of ninety-six seniors I was ranked forty-ninth. I would just be a vague, doughy face in the middle of the third row. There was no great cause for celebration. I hadn't found a job or a college to attend in the fall. But at least my parents had a son who could give them grandchildren, they could appreciate that. And as for that fat, mustached drama teacher, Sister Vincent, who continually remembered Corky's beautiful singing voice and his performance in *South Pacific*, well, I wished she could see his new song and dance at Cabaret Berliner.

12   Corky came home two days before graduation. My mother and father and I went to pick him up at Stapleton Airport in Denver. The whole way there, I worried. I couldn't help but imagine Corky appearing to us in a feather boa and an evening gown or something, trotting down the ramp to meet us with a big lipstick grin. I told myself I was being low-minded and ugly, but that image of him kept popping into my mind. My face felt hot.

13   Meanwhile, my parents acted like everything was wonderful. The full moon reflected off the early May snow that still lay on the fields, and my father kept howling like a wolf. It seemed to amuse my mother, because she chuckled every time he did it, and laughed aloud when he grabbed her around the waist and growled.

I was sitting in the back seat, watching the car drift toward 14
the center of the road while they horsed around. "I hope we
wreck," I said.

The three of us stood there in the waiting area, watching 15
the planes land. We didn't recognize Corky when he approached us, but at least he was wearing normal clothes. He'd
dyed his hair bright red—it was shoulder-length, tied in a ponytail. When he was close enough, I noticed the little crease
in his earlobe that meant it was pierced, but he didn't have an
earring. He hugged my mother, kissing her lightly. Then he
turned and kissed my father. My father always kissed us on
the lips, and wasn't even afraid to do it in public. He puckered
up like a cartoon character, and it would've been funny if he
wasn't so earnest about it. Here he was, this big, middle-aged
construction worker, smacking lips with his son. He didn't
even hesitate knowing Corky was gay, though I looked around
to see if people were staring.

When my brother turned to me, I stuck out my hand. I 16
didn't want him kissing on me. "So," he said, and squeezed
my palm, hard. "The graduate!"

I shrugged. "Yeah, well," I said. "I'm just glad it's over." 17

He kept holding my hand till I pulled back a little. He 18
grinned. "Congratulations," he said.

"Congratulations to you, too," I said, though I didn't know 19
why.

As we drove back to Mineral, I watched my brother suspi- 20
ciously. Ever since we were little he'd always been the center
of things, and I doubted that he'd come all that way just to
congratulate me. I kept expecting him to take over at any
minute. I remembered how, when we were young, we had a
place behind the house, an old shed we'd furnished with lawn
chairs and cinder blocks and such. This became the plantation from *Gone with the Wind*—Corky was Rhett and Scarlett,
I was the slaves; or a rocket—Corky was the captain and the
alien invaders, I was the crew that got killed. Once, when I
was eleven and he was fifteen, and he was going to play the
lead in *South Pacific*, he got me all excited about trying out
for the part of his little Polynesian son. He gave me the music
and then made fun of me, standing by the bedroom door and
warbling like an old chicken.

Maybe, I thought, Corky had changed. It had been a long 21
time since I'd really spoken to him. It had been several years
since I'd seen him, and I seldom felt like talking to him on the
phone. Even when my father *did* put me on the line, I couldn't

think of what to say. "What's new," Corky would ask, and I'd shrug: "Nothing." Maybe he'd become a totally different person, and I hadn't known.

22 But I couldn't tell. He was so motionless as we drove that he hardly seemed real. He just stared, like some stone idol, out toward the passing telephone poles and fields and the grasshopper oil wells nodding against the moonlit sky. His hands remained in his lap, except once, when he suddenly touched his hair with his fingertips as if adjusting a hat. When my parents asked him a question he leaned forward, smiling politely. "What? What did you say?"

23 It was late, nearly one in the morning, when we got home. Corky went to the bedroom to unpack—our old room, my room now—and when I came in he was already stretched out on the upper bunk. It used to be that I slept in the bottom and he slept in the top, but since he'd left I'd been using the lower bunk to store papers and laundry and stuff. He looked down at me and smiled.

24 "That's my bed," I told him.

25 He sat up and his bare feet dangled over the edge, swinging lightly. He was wearing silky-looking pajamas. We'd always just slept in our underwear, and I imagined that this was what he wore when he lay down next to another man. "That's rich," he said. "You know, all these years I wanted that bottom bunk. I suppose you always wanted the top."

26 "I didn't care one way or another," I said. I began to take handfuls of dirty laundry from the bottom bunk and put them on the floor. "You can sleep there if you want."

27 He nodded and lay back. "It's been a long time since I've heard any news from you."

28 "Yeah, well," I said. "My life isn't that exciting."

29 "You've really changed the room around," he said. He gestured to a poster of a model in a white bikini who was holding a six-pack of beer. "She's sexy," he said.

30 "Yeah," I said. "I guess."

31 He looked from the poster to me, his lips puckered out a little. "So," he said at last. "Do you have a girlfriend, Todd?"

32 "Yes," I said. "Sort of." I didn't. I had friends that were girls, and one of them I took to most of the dances. But I wasn't like some of the guys in school, who'd been going steady with one girl since eighth grade. All the girls I liked had either paired off or weren't interested. The furtive gropes and kisses after dances hadn't amounted to much. I was afraid that even if I got a girl to do more, I'd be clumsy, and I couldn't stand the

thought of her laughing, maybe telling her friends. "You know," I told Corky. "I date around and stuff."

"Good for you," he said. He pulled his feet up onto the bed the way a fish would flip its tail. Then he laughed. I could feel my ears warming.   33

"What's so funny?" I said.   34

"Nothing," he said. "Just the way you said it." He deepened   35
his voice to a macho swagger. "'I date around and stuff.'" He laughed again. "You used to be such a little high-voiced thing."

"Hm," I said. He leaned back and I turned off the light. I   36
moved over near the closet, where it was darkest, so I could undress without him seeing me. The hangers made wind-chime sounds as I brushed them.

"It's so weird, being home," he said. His voice floated from   37
the top bunk as I took off my shirt. I decided to sleep in my jeans. I didn't have any pajamas. "You can't believe how strange it is."

"Well, nothing has changed," I said. I groped across the   38
dim room to my bed. I could see the lump where he was lying, a shadow bending toward me.

"No," he said, "no." And then, slowly: "So did you see the pic-   39
ture I sent?" The house was still. I could hear water whispering through the pipes in the walls; I could hear him breathing.

"I saw it." I tried to make my voice noncommittal. I sighed   40
deeply, like I was already almost asleep.

He didn't say anything for a long time, and I thought he   41
might have drifted off. When he spoke out of the dark, finally, his voice sounded odd, twittery, not like him, and it made my neck prickle. "Sometimes," he said, "I'm glad I sent it and other times not." I didn't say anything. "Todd?" he whispered.

I waited. I recalled the way we used to lie in our bunks   42
when we were little and tell each other jokes and make up songs. I remembered how I would go to sleep to the sound of his murmuring, crooning. "What," I whispered back finally.

"How did Mom and Dad react?"   43

"How should I know?" I mumbled. "They don't tell me   44
anything."

"What did they say?"   45

"What did you expect them to say?"   46

"I don't know," he said. "It's hard to explain."   47

But I didn't want him to explain. I didn't want to keep pic-   48
turing him in that outfit, swishing and singing, maybe kissing a member of his audience, leaving a bright wing of lipstick on his forehead. "They didn't say much of anything," I told him. "They don't care what you do in your personal life."

49   "Do you?"
50   "Why should I?" I whispered. I rolled over, pretending to be
asleep.

51   When I woke, my brother was already up. I could hear him
talking in the kitchen, and the sound of eggs cracking on a
skillet. I went to the bathroom to shower and when I came
back to dress, I couldn't help but notice Corky's suitcase. It
was expensive-looking, dark strips of leather bound around
brick-red cloth. Through the walls I could hear the vague
whisper of conversation and I bent down, running my hands
along the sides, finding the zipper.
52   Most of the things had been taken out. He'd put them in
dresser drawers my mother had cleared out for him. But
there was a compartment along one side, and when I opened
it, I found what I figured I'd find. It gave me a fluttery feeling
in my stomach: a skirt, a flowered blouse, pantyhose, a box of
make-up with the colors arranged chromatically. Beneath
that were more photos—Corky gripping a fireman's pole, his
leg sliding along it, his eyes looking seductively away; being
lifted by a group of men in tuxedos, his head flung back, his
arms open wide, jeweled necklaces in his clenched fists.
There were two clippings of advertisements for Cabaret Berliner: a drawing of a man's hairy leg with a high heel on his
foot, and underneath, in small letters, the words: Corky Pe-
tersen with Sister Mary Josephine—After Tea Dance Party.
Another had a photo of Corky in his cowgirl outfit. I wondered if he was planning to show us a sample of his act. I
closed the suitcase quickly.
53   They didn't look up when I came into the kitchen. They
were sitting at the table, eating toast and scrambled eggs.
Corky was telling my father that New York City was in a state
of collapse and had been ever since Reagan took office. He
said the homeless filled the streets, that a bag lady had died
on his doorstep. My father kept nodding very seriously,
frowning, "Mm-hmm," as if he were talking to a grownup. He
never spoke to me that way. Then Corky began to tell about
the semis that parked outside his apartment at night, and
how his whole place filled up with diesel fumes. He was
afraid to light a cigarette. In the middle of this, he looked up
and saw me standing there. "Well, hello, Sleeping Beauty," he
said, and cocked his hand on his hip.
54   I glared at him. "Mornin'," I said in my deepest voice. I slid
into the chair at the far end of the table.
55   "You hungry, punkin?" my mother asked brightly.

I looked sternly at her. I wanted to tell them that my name   56
was Todd, not Sleeping Beauty or pumpkin. But all I said
was, No. Then I looked at Corky. "So how come you live in
New York if you don't like it?"

Corky shrugged. "Frankly," he said, "there's no other place   57
I could stand." Then he leaned toward my father and lowered
his voice. "I'll tell you what's really scary," he said. "This
AIDS thing. Out here, I'm sure no one realizes, but it's really
terrifying."

My father blushed and we were all silent. "Well," my father   58
said, and cleared his throat. "I hope you're being careful." He
picked at his eggs.

"Careful?" Corky said. He gave a short laugh. "I can't even   59
tell you. The other night I was out with this guy." He stopped.
All of us were sitting stiffly, and my father had a pinched look
on his face. He touched his eyelids, as if to clear away the image of Corky and this man, this lover.

"Well, anyway," Corky said. "He didn't even want to kiss.   60
He goes: 'I don't know you well enough yet.'" He took a bite of
toast, nervously, then looked over at me and winked. I kept
my face expressionless. He winked again. "So, Todd." He said
my name as if it were some ridiculously cheerful exclama-
tion, like "gee whiz," or "wowee," the kind of thing he used to
say with mocking relish when he was in high school. "Tomorrow's the big day!" he said. "Graduation. Commencement.
The beginning of a new life."

"Right," I said. I didn't like to think about it that way. I   61
couldn't imagine myself working a regular job forty hours a
week, or leaving home for college or the service; it seemed
amazing to me that Corky lived alone, and paid his own bills,
got up in the morning without my mother waking him.

"Yes, Toddy," my mother said quickly. "We haven't seen you   62
in your cap and gown."

"Yeah, and you're not going to either," I said.   63

"What's the matter," my father said. I could see how it was   64
going to go. They'd do anything to escape more information
about Corky's sex life. "Are you ashamed of your cap and
gown?"

"I just don't want to put it on, that's all," I said. "What's the   65
big deal?"

"Oh, come on, Todd," my brother said. He grinned. I shook   66
my head at all of them. It figured—even with all of them looking at me, the focus was still on Corky underneath.

"I feel like a dancing dog," I said. I pushed away from the   67
table.

68   When I went into my bedroom, I just stood there for a minute, staring at Corky's suitcase, then to the window. The morning was warm and clear. Outside, the grass was a sickly yellow-green in the patches that appeared where the snow had drawn back. It made me think of a horror movie I'd seen where the smooth, pale skin of a dead woman peeled away to reveal a monster's face. At last, I went to the closet and took the box out. The cap and gown were still wrapped in plastic, and I tore it away roughly. I slid the gown over my head, the silky cloth slick against my bare arms, my neck. I fit the cap over my hair, and it fit snugly. It made me think of a wig. The tassel dangled in front of my nose.

69   When I came into the kitchen my brother began to hum a jazzy "Pomp and Circumstance," snapping his fingers. The gown billowed around me, the cap tilted against my line of vision, and I shambled forward, trying to imagine how Clint Eastwood would walk in a cap and gown.

70   "You look real nice," my father nodded.

71   "Stand up straight," my mother said.

72   It would have been nice to say that I was going out that night with a group of friends to some party out on somebody's farm where everyone was singing and carrying on around a keg an older brother had bought. Some of my classmates were doing that, but not *my* friends. Jeanine's grandparents were coming in from California that night, Craig's family was taking him out to dinner, Lisa and Jeff, both of them too straight for their own good, were going to a special Mass or wake or whatever it was for graduating seniors. I remember Corky and the other seniors who were in plays had a formal dinner for themselves. They'd sent out calligraphied invitations, and dressed up in coats and ties. At the party, they'd put parts of Corky's valedictorian speech to the music of *My Fair Lady*. He'd come home late, singing in a Cockney accent at the top of his lungs.

73   And what did I do? I sat around. Corky was busy providing the entertainment. As I sat after breakfast and read a horror book, my brother helped with the dishes and told my mother about Jacek, a Yugoslavian man he'd dated, a man who made independent films and had done a video for a rock group. Actually, Corky didn't say they'd dated. That was only to be guessed from the careful description he'd given. My mother drew various dishes out of the soapy water, nodding as if she didn't quite understand what it all meant.

After lunch, we went for a drive. Corky seemed excited. He   74
wanted to drive by Rattlesnake Knob, he said, and take pictures to show his friends in New York. I pictured him joking
about it at some cocktail party, showing his photos to a group
of lithe, smirking gay men, as they stood before the huge picture window of some penthouse, surrounding Corky, looking
at the pictures and then to the city lights that blurred to daz-
zles, to the Statue of Liberty with the moon hanging over her
head. "How quaint," they'd murmur.

The four of us squeezed into the cab of the pickup, with   75
Corky and me in the middle. We drove out toward the hills,
and when we passed the rock house, Corky made us stop.

The house stood in the middle of a field. It had been built   76
by pioneers and the sod roof had long since collapsed. The
rest of it had been built of pumice rock they'd gathered from
the hills, and from the smattering of trees they'd found by the
creek and cut down. It was still recognizable as a house, there
was still the frame of the doors and windows, though the
wood was mostly rotten and even the stone walls were crumbling. My father used to take us out here when we were little,
and tell us about pioneers. Corky wanted to take a picture.

He got out of the truck and strode purposefully through   77
the ditch to the fence. We followed after. He stretched the
lines of barbed wire apart so he could squeeze through, then
paused on the other side and looked closely at the wire. "Hey,
Dad," he said, as we came to the edge of the fence. "Look at
the strands of this wire. It's really intricate. Is that rare?"

My father bent over to look with Corky, so their foreheads   78
nearly touched, so they looked like mirror images of one another, leaning over, hands on their knees. "No," my father
said. "No, not rare. Just old." He sighed, straightening up. It
used to be that, wherever we went, my father would be pointing things out, explaining things. As we'd drive up into the
hills, my father would tell us how the trickle of creek we'd
passed a mile back had made them; over millions of years a
valley was created with hills on either side. I remember imagining the gray hills with their jagged lace of pumice cliffs, rising up on either side, pushing slowly out of the flat prairie
like mushrooms. He taught us trivia that seemed amazing
then—how to tell a rattlesnake from a bullsnake; types of
barbed wire. Maybe he was remembering the same thing, because he just stood there, touching his fingers to his eyelids,
as Corky clicked his camera at the rusty barbed wire.

"So," my brother said to me as we walked across the pas-   79
ture to the rock house. "Am I going to get to meet one of these

girlfriends of yours? Is one of them going to stop by the house
tomorrow?"

80   "I don't know," I said. My parents looked at me. They didn't
say anything, but it still made me feel like a failure. They
knew I didn't have a girlfriend. Even in the one thing I had
over Corky I was a flop. Corky stopped in front of the rock
house, which was surrounded by tall dry weeds, and put his
hands on his hips. He looked over his shoulder at me, and I
sighed. My parents glanced at me, and I stared down at the
sod. "They're not really girlfriends," I said. "They're just
friend friends."

81   When I looked up, my eyes met Corky's. I couldn't tell what
he was thinking. "Hey," he said. "Why don't you all stand in
front of the place? That'll make a nice shot."

82   We arranged ourselves—my father stood behind my
mother and me and pulled us close to him so he could hide
his pot belly. He and Corky were the tall ones in the family,
and I'd inherited my mother's shortness. We pressed together.
"Smile," Corky called, and stepped back. I set my lips into one
of those smiles I knew was crooked and silly, but I couldn't
stop it. "That's great," Corky said. He aimed the camera at us.
"It's one of those pictures you'll keep forever, you know?" We
separated from our cluster. Corky took another picture.

83   As we walked back to the car, Corky put his arm around my
shoulders. I stiffened, but I didn't shrug him off. "I think just
plain friends are the best kind," he said.

84   "Yeah, right," I said. He tilted his head as if a cool breeze
were blowing.

85   "I sing this song in my show called 'We're Only Friends.' It's
really great. I've got this sort of Dietrich look, and the tune is
a 30s German thing, you know." He began to sing softly, his
voice raspy, deep, but strikingly like a woman's. His voice carried, wafting in the open air.

86   I didn't know what he was trying to prove. Maybe he was
trying to get us used to the idea. Maybe he was just needling
my parents. Maybe he was showing off. Whatever he thought,
the Subject kept coming into our conversations. He had given
a man my mother's recipe for fried chicken. He used "Blue
Moon," my father's favorite song, as the closing number for
his show. He kept at it, through dinner, after, as we were
watching TV, tossing little bits out for our consideration. My
father had gotten a glazed look, as if he could hear someone
far away calling his name. My mother looked more and more
bewildered.

As for me, I found myself thinking about the clothes I'd   87
seen in his suitcase. I wondered if and when he was planning
to put them on.

When he came into the bedroom late that night I was lying   88
on the bottom bunk, reading my book. "Corky," I said. He was
bent down, searching through his suitcase. "Do you—" I
cleared my throat. I watched him collect a toothbrush and
dental floss from his bag. "I mean you normally wear normal
clothes, don't you?"

He looked up at me, not smiling. "I only dress for my act, if   89
that's what you mean."

I nodded. I took a deep breath. "How come you packed   90
women's clothes?"

His eyes narrowed. I remembered how he used to have his   91
secret drawers, a scrapbook full of old clippings and things,
the way he'd come in and found me looking through it. "Keep
out of my stuff, you pig!" he'd shouted, and started punching
me.

"What do you mean?" he said softly. He was looking me   92
up and down, appraising me, and I watched him set the
items in his hand back into the bag. He unzipped the compartment and pulled out the make-up kit, the photos. "This
stuff?" he said fiercely. For a minute, I shrank back, as if he
were my older brother again and I'd ruined another game.
He stared at me, and then suddenly shook his head. "Todd,"
he said, as if remembering some other brother that wasn't
me. "I thought maybe someone might have wanted to see my
show." He shook his head. "People pay money to see it." He
put the blouse to his face. "Here," he said, and threw it at
me, hitting the book I was still holding in my hand. "Smell
it."

It must have been the look on my face that made him   93
laugh. I held it and sniffed the air. I had dark thoughts about
what I was supposed to smell.

"Old Spice," he said. "For the manly man." It was my fa-   94
ther's brand. "It's a joke," he said. He picked out the bunch of
pictures and clippings and walked over to the bunks with
them. He put them on top of the blouse. "If you want to look
at this stuff, you can," he said. "I'm going to brush my teeth."

Before he got to the door, he turned. "What did you think?"   95
he said. "I came home for the sole purpose of ruining your
graduation by running around in drag?"

I looked down at the pictures of him. "Why *did* you come   96
home?" I said.

He put his back to me. "Because I was stupid," he said.   97

98   At my graduation party, my relatives drank and gave me
money. Commencement was as long and dull as the past four
years of high school had been. In her speech, the valedictorian
kept referring to the future as a train, and I imagined myself
standing on the railroad tracks, watching it bear down on me.

99   The party made it even worse. There I was, in the middle of
the living room, holding a paper plate—melting ice cream, a
slice of chocolate cake—dabbing the frosting from the base of
the little wax graduate that had been in the center of the cake,
that my mother had insisted I take as a memento. After the
first time, when my uncle Evan had come up to me and
handed me an envelope, and asked me what my plans were,
and I tried to tell him I had a lot of options I was considering,
I gave up. The next time, when my aunt Susan handed me a
card and asked me the same question, I just shrugged.

100   Which of them had futures that were so wonderful? I
watched my great-aunt Birdie, already drunk even before
noon. She'd been married twice and now was living with
some man in Denver. Or my cousin David, who'd just gone
bankrupt. Or Grandpa Mitch, who a few months before had a
heart attack, who had to crawl from the bedroom, down the
hall to the phone. "Oh, he looks so thin, so pale," they whispered behind his back. "He shouldn't be in that old house
alone." Soon, he'd be in a rest home. My parents sat on the
couch near my grandfather, looking nervously at Corky. It
was sickening. They'd spent the better part of their lives raising us, and look what that got them.

101   Corky was across the room, sitting on a folding chair with
his legs crossed. He was right on the edge of the kitchen; people had to walk past him to get to the food and the beer. I
watched my relatives move slowly by, their eyes fixed on him.
They asked him how life was treating him in the Big Apple,
and tightened their smiles.

102   I stirred my ice cream and cake together. Even I couldn't
help staring at him. Aunt Birdie came weaving up to me, fid-
dling with the tab on her beer. A napkin was stuck to her shoe,
dragging behind her as she sidled up to me. "Congratulations,
precious," she said, and pushed her lips to my forehead, leaning against me for support. "What's in your future?" she
asked, and pushed a crumpled bill into my jacket pocket. I
shook my head. "Nothing." Corky had lit another cigarette
and was saying: "That sounds an awful lot like a play I auditioned for." Aunt Birdie kissed me on the eyelid, and I slid
away from her grasp. I decided I needed to go outside for a
while.

It was cold. I leaned against the side of the house and   103
bunched my jacket together at the neck, staring out past the
yard to the driveway, which was crowded with my relative's
vehicles. I breathed slowly. For a minute I'd imagined I might
spin out of control. I might have broken free of Aunt Birdie,
lisping and sashaying, cooing: "My new play I auditioned for.
Oh, how wonderful I am." I might have told everyone, in a
loud voice, what hypocrites my parents were: "We're so proud
of our Corky! How nice it is to have a son who's so glamorous
and successful."

Corky came out a few moments later. He exhaled smoke as   104
he poked his head out the door. "Todd," he said. "You're missing your party." He kept his body inside the house, so it
looked like his head was disembodied, moving along the
doorframe. He bent so he could look at me upside down. It
was an old game from childhood. We used to practice miming
around the edges of the doors, so from the other side it looked
like we were floating, or being lifted by an invisible force.
"Todd," he said, in a Donald Duck voice. "Why so glum,
Todd?" His head vanished then, like a puppet yanked from a
stage. He came out of the house, and stood beside me.

In the house, someone had turned on music, my father's   105
Patsy Cline tape. It drifted mournfully in the stillness, wisping
through the walls.

I sighed. "Did you ever," I said at last, "wonder what was   106
going to happen to you?"

There was a flicker in his eyes, as if he'd forgotten something important. His smile wavered. "No," he said.

I considered this. Probably, he'd always known. "Well," I   107
said. "What do you think will happen to me, then? Because I
wonder. I wonder a lot."

He stared at me for a long time, and then put another ciga-   108
rette to his lips. "You'll probably be miserable," he said. "Like
everybody else." Our eyes met, and then we both looked
down. His words hung there, with both of us considering
them—as if he'd dropped a bowl at my feet, and we were both
looking at the shards of broken glass. In the house, I could
hear my father laughing.

"Thanks a lot," I said stiffly. "Sorry I asked."   109

He shrugged, and pulled a folded bill out of his pocket. He   110
pushed it into my hand. "Maybe I will go squeeze into that
dress," he whispered.

"Don't," I said through my teeth. I looked at the piece of pa-   111
per in my hand. A hundred-dollar bill. "I can't take this," I
said. "That's too much."

112   He lifted his eyebrows, and I watched him put it back in his pocket. His hand slid out of his pocket holding a nickel, which he flipped toward me. I fumbled, caught it. "There," he said.

113   "Very funny," I said. He dragged deeply on his cigarette.

114   We stared at each other. "Go ahead," my brother whispered. Smoke curled around his face as he breathed, and he pushed his hands through his dyed hair, loosening his ponytail. "I know you're dying to. Say 'faggot.' Say 'cocksucker.'" He smirked at me. But then as I watched, it seemed that some awful transformation was coming over his face. It was trembling and contorting like there was something beneath it trying to escape. For a second I imagined that he must be seeing something terrifying, a dark shape lunging at us, and I turned quickly. But there was only the empty yard.

115   "Say it," he whispered. "Say it."

VI.

CRIME AND
PUNISHMENT

Introduction

You've heard all the statistics.

According to the Department of Justice, a violent crime occurs somewhere in the United States every twenty seconds. A murder occurs every half hour (about 23,000 in 1995). Someone is raped every six minutes. Over fifteen million arrests were made in 1995, over a million of them for drug abuse violations. Many more Americans are in prison, per capita, than citizens in any other "developed" nation. The point is this: Crime has become an inescapable fact of life in the United States. And what to do about it has become a perennial issue, as the selections in this part demonstrate.

The first set of readings, a sort of transition from the previous part on civil liberties and civil rights, discusses the question of gun control. Should the ownership and possession of firearms be restricted? An absolute "no" is the answer of those who wish to protect citizens' right to bear arms. They cite for support the Second Amendment to our Constitution: "A well regulated militia being necessary to the security of a free state, the right of the people to keep and bear arms shall not be infringed." On the other hand, a number of people (some of them included in this book) contend that the right to purchase and keep guns is not absolute, that we already restrict in certain reasonable ways "the right to bear arms" (e.g., you can't own rocket launchers or a tank; you can't own guns if you're a minor or a convicted felon or mentally incompetent). Faced with certain abuses—shocking assassinations; 25,000 shooting deaths each year—proponents of gun control simply argue for additional reasonable restrictions, particularly on the handguns that are so available in our society and so commonly employed in the conduct of violent crime. Just what is it about Americans and guns, anyway? Why do they figure so prominently in our society? Can anything be done about it? Should anything be done about it? Do guns cause crime, or are people responsible?

That brings up the question posed by the second set of readings in this part of *Conversations:* What is the source of crime, anyway? Is crime simply a manifestation of our human fallibility, our human sinfulness, that Americans are simply unwilling to face up to? Or do economic circumstances cause crime? Are most people driven to crime, desperate to meet their daily needs or determined to strike out against a system that keeps them attached permanently to an underclass? Is crime a blow against "the system"? Then again, if economic circumstances cause crime, why were crime rates lower during the Great Depression than during the economic boom years of the 1960s or 1980s? Or does crime have a broader social explanation? Is it an outgrowth of our society's rootlessness, or our fragmented families, or impersonal "value-free" schools? Is crime an inevitable by-product of a national identity that prizes nonconformity and anti-authoritarianism? (Think of Bonnie and Clyde, and Thelma and Louise.) Or is crime glorified and perpetuated by the media—by violent movies and newspaper sensationalism and television shows? (In this connection, you may wish to read or reread earlier sections in this book on the effects of television and pornography.) Finally, two contributions to this part ask if some people are simply programmed to commit crime by their genetic disposition, their lack of intelligence, or their gender. Such arguments were dismissed after World War II because they had been promulgated by fascists responsible for horrible crimes against humanity, but in the past decade they have been put forward again by people who ask why men commit more crimes than women do and whether there is indeed a genetic predisposition to criminal behavior.

The third group of readings debate the justice and wisdom of capital punishment. From the mid-1960s to 1977 no executions were carried out in the United States as the nation debated the abuses in the application of capital punishment and the wisdom of carrying out such punishment at all; indeed, capital punishment has been outlawed in a great many nations and condemned by the Roman Catholic Church. But in 1976, the Supreme Court by a 5–4 vote decided that capital punishment is constitutional under certain circumstances. Executions inevitably followed, and so the debate about capital punishment has been renewed: Is capital punishment an expression of justice, "an eye for an eye"? Is it a useful deterrent to other would-be murderers? Or does it feed one of our basest instincts—for revenge? Is the death penalty cruel and unusual punishment? Is it unfairly applied to minority criminals, especially for crimes against majority members? If so, is this an argument for abolition, or for improving our system of justice?

Part VI concludes with a discussion of whether illegal drugs should be regulated or made legal. In the face of persistent and debilitating drug use, some have proposed legalization—not because they see drugs as less than a menace, but because they trust in other measures than law to fight it. Those who would legalize drugs propose that we approach drug abuse as an economic and medical problem rather than as a legal one. Legalizers (or "decriminalizers") wish to minimize the effects of illegal drugs by eliminating black market profits; legalization would drive down drug prices, the argument goes, and therefore reduce secondary crime motivated by the need to finance the drug habit. Legalizers would regulate drugs and tax drug producers, as liquor is regulated and taxed; the revenues could be used for education and drug prevention campaigns, and for treatment of drug addicts. Those who would legalize drugs argue by analogy to the prohibition of alcohol in the 1920s, a prohibition that made average citizens into criminals, made gangsters and rumrunners into millionaires, and reduced respect for law throughout the land. But those against legalization also point to Prohibition—to the end of Prohibition in 1930, when alcohol use skyrocketed. They argue that legalizing drugs would result in an inevitable spread in the use of cocaine and heroin, and an inevitable increase in cocaine babies, child abuse, wrecked automobiles and airplanes, and wrecked lives. And they contend that it is against the American grain to legalize immoral acts, no matter how often the acts are being committed.

In any case, what to do about drugs—and what to do about crime and criminals in general—will continue to engage our national attention.

SHOULD GUNS BE REGULATED?

Leonard Kriegel
A Loaded Question: What Is It About Americans and Guns?

Leonard Kriegel (born 1933), a writer of fiction and essays, contributed the following piece to Harper's *magazine, a publication featuring contributions on U.S. politics and culture, in mid-1992. The article itself will tell you more about him.*

I have fired a gun only once in my life, hardly experience   1
enough to qualify one as an expert on firearms. As limited as
my exposure to guns has been, however, my failure to
broaden that experience had nothing at all to do with moral
disapproval or with the kind of righteous indignation that
views an eight-year-old boy playing cops and robbers with a
cap pistol as a preview of the life of a serial killer. None of us
can speak with surety about alternative lives, but had circumstances been different I suspect I not only would have hunted
but very probably would have enjoyed it. I might even have
gone in for target shooting, a "sport" increasingly popular in
New York City, where I live (like bowling, it is practiced in-
door in alleys). To be truthful, I have my doubts that target
shooting would really have appealed to me. But in a country
in which grown men feel passionately about a game as visibly
ludicrous as golf, anything is possible.

The single shot I fired didn't leave me with a traumatic ha-   2
tred of or distaste for guns. Quite the opposite. I liked not
only the sense of incipient skill firing that shot gave me but
also the knowledge that a true marksman, like a good hitter
in baseball, had to practice—and practice with a real gun.
Boys on the cusp of adolescence are not usually disciplined,
but they do pay attention to the demands of skill. Because I
immediately recognized how difficult it would be for me to

practice marksmanship, I was brought face to face with the fact that my career as a hunter was over even before it had started.

3   Like my aborted prospects as a major league ballplayer, my short but happy life as a hunter could be laid at the metaphorical feet of the polio virus which left me crippled at the age of eleven. Yet the one thing that continues to amaze me as I look back to that gray February afternoon when I discovered the temptation of being a shooter and hunter is that I did not shoot one or the other of the two most visible targets—myself or my friend Jackie, the boy who owned the .22.

4   Each of us managed to fire one shot that afternoon. And when we returned to the ward in which we lived along with twenty other crippled boys between the ages of nine and thirteen, we regaled our peers with a story unashamedly embellished in the telling. As the afternoon chill faded and the narrow winter light in which we had hunted drifted toward darkness, Jackie managed to hide the .22 from ward nurses and doctors on the prowl. What neither of us attempted to hide from the other boys was our brief baptism in the world of guns.

5   Like me, Jackie was a Bronx boy, as ignorant about guns as I was. Both of us had been taken down with polio in the summer of '44. We had each lost the use of our legs. We were currently in wheelchairs. And we had each already spent a year and a half in the aptly named New York State Reconstruction Home, a state hospital for long-term physical rehabilitation. Neither of us had ever fired anything more lethal than a Daisy air rifle, popularly known as a BB gun—and even that, in my case at least, had been fired under adult supervision. But Jackie and I were also American claimants, our imaginations molded as much by Hollywood westerns as by New York streets. At twelve, I was a true Jeffersonian who looked upon the ownership of a six-shooter as every American's "natural" right.

6   To this day I don't know how Jackie got hold of that .22. He refused to tell me. And I still don't know how he got rid of it after our wheelchair hunt in the woods. For months afterward I would try to get him to promise that he and I would go hunting again, but, as if our afternoon hunt had enabled him to come to terms with his own illusions about the future (something that would take me many more years), Jackie simply shook his head and said, "That's over." I begged, wheedled, cajoled, threatened. Jackie remained

obdurate. A single shot for a single hunt. It would have to be sufficient.

I never did find out whether or not I hit the raccoon. On 7 the ride back to the ward, Jackie claimed I had. After he fired his shot, he dropped from his wheelchair and slid backward on his rump to the abandoned water pipe off the side of the dirt road into which the raccoon had leaped at the slashing crack of the .22. His hand came down on something red—a bloodstain, he excitedly suggested, as he lifted himself into his wheelchair and we turned to push ourselves back to the ward. It looked like a rust stain to me, but I didn't protest. I was quite willing to take whatever credit I could. That was around an hour after the two of us, fresh from lunch, had pushed our wheelchairs across the hospital grounds, turning west at the old road that cut through the woods and led to another state home, this one ministering to the retarded. The .22, which lay on Jackie's lap, had bounced and jostled as we maneuvered our wheelchairs across that rutted road in search of an animal—any animal would do— to shoot. The early February sky hung above us like a charcoal drawing, striations of gray slate shadings feeding our nervous expectation.

It was Jackie who first spotted the raccoon. Excited, he 8 handed the .22 to me, a gesture spurred, I then thought, by friendship. Now I wonder whether his generosity wasn't simply self-protection. Until that moment, the .22 lying across Jackie's dead legs had been an abstraction, as much an imitation gun as the "weapons" boys in New York City constructed out of the wood frames and wood slats of fruit and vegetable crates, nails, and rubber bands—cutting up pieces of discarded linoleum and stiff cardboard to use as ammunition. I remember the feel of the .22 across my own lifeless legs, the weight of it surprisingly light, as I stared at the raccoon who eyed us curiously from in front of the broken pipe. Then I picked up the gun, aimed, and squeezed the trigger, startled not so much by the noise nor by the slight pull, but by the fact that I had actually fired at something. The sound of the shot was crisp and clean. I felt as if I had done something significant.

Jackie took the gun from me. "Okay," he said eagerly. "My 9 turn now." The raccoon was nowhere in sight, but he aimed in the direction of the water pipe into which it had disappeared and squeezed the trigger. I heard the crack again, a freedom of music now, perhaps because we two boys had

suddenly been bound to each other and had escaped, for this
single winter afternoon moment, the necessary but mundane courage which dominates the everyday lives of crippled
children. "Okay," I heard him cry out happily, "we're god-
damn killers now."

10   A formidable enough hail and farewell to shooting. And
certainly better than being shot at. God knows what happened to that raccoon. Probably nothing; but for me, firing
that single shot was both the beginning and the end of my life
as a marksman. The raccoon may have been wounded, as
Jackie claimed. Perhaps it had crawled away, bleeding, to die
somewhere in the woods. I doubt it. And I certainly hope I
didn't hit it, although in February 1946, six months before I
returned to the city and to life among the "normals," I would
have taken its death as a symbolic triumph. For that was a
time I needed any triumph I could find, no matter how minor.
Back then it seemed natural to begin an uncertain future with
a kill—even if one sensed, as I did, that my career as a hunter
was already over. The future was hinting at certain demands
it would make. And I was just beginning to bend into myself,
to protect my inner man from being crushed by the knowledge of all I would never be able to do. Hunting would be just
another deferred dream.

11   But guns were not a dream. Guns were real, definitive,
stamped on the imagination of their functional beauty. A gun
was not a phallic symbol; a gun didn't offer me revenge on polio; a gun would not bring to life dead legs or endow deferred
dreams with substance. I am as willing as the next man to
quarantine reality within psychology. But if a rose is no more
than a rose, then tell me why a gun can't simply be a gun?
Guns are not monuments to fear and aspiration any more
than flowers are.

12   I was already fascinated by the way guns looked. I was
even more fascinated by what they did and by what made
people use them. Like any other twelve-year-old boy, I was absorbed by talk about guns. Six months after the end of the
Second World War, boys in our ward were still engrossed by
the way talking about guns entangled us in the dense under-
brush of the national psyche. And no one in that ward was
more immersed in weaponry than I. On the verge of adolescence, forced to seek and find adventure in my own imagination, I was captivated by guns.

It was a fascination that would never altogether die. A few   13
weeks ago I found myself nostalgically drifting through the
arms and armor galleries of the Metropolitan Museum of Art.
Years ago I had often taken my young sons there. A good part
of my pleasure now derived from memories pinned to the
leisurely innocence of those earlier visits. As I wandered
among those rich cabinets displaying ornate pistols and rifles
whose carved wood stocks were embossed with gold and silver and ivory and brass, I was struck by how incredibly lovely
many of these weapons were. It was almost impossible to
conceive of them as serving the function they had been designed to serve. These were not machines designed to kill and
maim. Created with an eye to beauty, their sense of decora-
tive purpose was as singular as a well-designed eighteenth-
century silver drinking cup. These guns in their solid display
cases evoked a sense of the disciplined craftsmanship to
which a man might dedicate his life.

Flintlocks, wheel locks, a magnificent pair of ivory pistols   14
owned by Catherine the Great—all of them as beckoning to
the touch of fingers, had they not been securely locked behind glass doors, as one of those small nineteenth-century
engraved cameos that seem to force time itself to surrender
its pleasures. I gazed longingly at a seventeenth-century
wheel lock carbine, coveting it the way I might covet a drinking cup by Cellini or a small bronze horse and rider by Bologna. Its beautifully carved wooden stock had been inlaid
with ivory, brass, silver, and mother-of-pearl, its pride of arti-
sanship embossed with the name of its creator, Caspar Spät.
I smiled with pleasure. Then I wandered through the galleries until I found myself in front of a case displaying eighteenth-century American flintlock rifles, all expressing the
democratic spirit one finds in Louis Sullivan's buildings or
Whitman's poetry or New York City playgrounds built by the
WPA during the Great Depression. Their polished woods
were balanced by ornately carved stag-antler powder horns,
which hung like Christmas decorations beneath them. To the
right was another display case devoted to long-barreled Colt
revolvers; beyond that, a splendidly engraved 1894 Winches-
ter rifle and a series of Smith & Wesson revolvers, all of them
decorated by Tiffany.

And yet they were weapons, designed ultimately to do what   15
weapons have always done—destroy. Only in those childlike
posters of the 1970s did flower stems grow out of the barrel of

a gun. People who shoot, like people who cook, understandably choose the best tools available. And if it is easier to hit a target with an Uzi than a homemade zip gun, chances are those who want to hit the target will feel few qualms about choosing the Uzi.

16   Nonetheless, these galleries are a remarkable testimony to the functional beauty of guns. Nor am I the only person who has been touched by their beauty. The problem is to define where the killing ceases and the beauty begins. At what point does a young boy's sense of adventure transform itself into the terror of blood and destruction and pain and death? I remember my sons' excitement when they toured these splendid galleries with me. (Yes, doctor, I did permit them to enjoy guns. And neither became a serial killer.) These weapons helped bring us together, bound father and sons, just as going to baseball games or viewing old Chaplin movies had.

17   Geography may not be the sole father of morality, but one would have to be remarkably naive to ignore its claims altogether. As I write this, I can see on the table in front of me a newspaper headlining the most recent killings inflicted on New York City's anarchic populace. Firearms now rule street and schoolyard, even as the rhetoric of politicians demanding strict gun control escalates—along with the body count.

18   And yet I recognize that one man's fear and suffering is another man's freedom and pleasure. Here is the true morality of geography. Like it or not, we see the world against a landscape of accommodation. Guns may be displayed behind glass cases in that magnificent museum, but in the splendid park in which that museum has been set down like a crowning jewel, guns have been known to create not art but terror. Functional beauty, it turns out, does not alter purpose.

19   I have a friend who has lived his entire life in small towns in Maine. My friend is both a hunter and a connoisseur of guns. City streets and guns may be a volatile mix, but the Maine woods and guns apparently aren't. Rifles and pistols hang on my friend's living room wall like old family portraits. They are lived with as comfortably as a family heirloom. My friend speaks knowingly of their shape, describes each weapon lovingly, as if it possessed its own substance. He is both literate and civilized, but he would never deny that these guns are more than a possession to him. They are an altar before which he bends the knee, a right of ownership he considers inviolable, even sacrosanct. And yet my friend is not a violent man.

I, too, am not a violent man. But I am a New Yorker. And   20
like most people who live in this city, I make certain assumptions about the value of the very indignities one faces by
choosing to live here. If I didn't, I probably couldn't remain in
New York. For with all of the problems it forces one to face,
the moral geography of New York also breeds a determination not to give in to the daily indignities the city imposes.

During the summer of 1977, I lived within a different   21
moral geography. I was teaching a graduate seminar on Manhood and American Culture at the University of New Mexico
in Albuquerque, tracing the evolution of the American man
from Ben Franklin's sturdy, middle-class acolyte to the rug-
ged John Wayne of *Stagecoach*. Enchanted by the New Mexico landscape, I would frequently drive off to explore the
small towns and brilliant canyons in whose silences ghosts
still lingered. One day a friend volunteered to drive with me
into the Manzano Mountains. I had announced my desire
to look at the ruins of a seventeenth-century mission fort
at Gran Quivira, while he wanted me to meet a man who had,
by himself, built a house in those haunting, lovely mountains.

Tension between Anglos and Hispanics was strong in New   22
Mexico in the summer of 1977. Even a stranger could feel a
palpable, almost physical, struggle for political and cultural
hegemony. Coming from a New York in which the growing
separation of black and white was already threatening to
transform everyday life into a racial battlefield, I did not feel
particularly intimidated by this. Instead of black and white,
New Mexico's ethnic and racial warfare would be between
Anglo, Hispanic, and Indian. Mountainair, where we were to
visit my friend's friend, was considered an Anglo town. Chilili,
some miles up the road, was Hispanic.

My friend's friend had built his house on the outskirts of   23
Mountainair, with a magnificent view of ponderosa pine. He
was a man in his early sixties and had come to New Mexico
from Virginia soon after World War II to take a job as a technical writer in a nuclear research laboratory in Albuquerque.
Before the war he had done graduate work in literature at the
University of Virginia, but the demands of fatherhood had decided him against finishing his doctorate. Like so many
Americans before him, he had taken wife and young children
to start over in the West.

In the warmth and generosity of his hospitality, however,   24
he remained a true Southerner. As we sat and talked and
laughed in a huge sun-drenched living room that opened onto

that magnificent view of the mountains and pines and long
New Mexico sky, I could not help but feel that here was the
very best of this nation—a man secure in himself, a man of
liberal sympathies and a broad understanding of human behavior and a love of children and grandchildren and wife, a
man who spoke perceptively of Jane Austen's novels and
spoke sadly of the savage threat of drugs (his oldest son, a veteran of the war in Vietnam, was living with him, along with
wife and three-year-old daughter, trying to purge the heroin
addiction that threatened to wreck his life).

25   I remember him happily holding forth on Jane Austen's
Persuasion when his body suddenly seemed to freeze in mid-
sentence. I could hear a motor in the distance. Without another word, he turned and crossed the room. Twin double-
barreled shotguns hung on the wall above the fireplace. He
took one, his right hand scooping shells from a canvas bag
hanging from a thong looped around a horseshoe nail banged
shoulder-high into the wall. His son, the ex-Marine, grabbed
the other gun and scooped shells from the same bag. Through
the glassed-in cathedral living room leading to the porch, I
watched the two of them stand side by side, shotguns pointed
at a pickup truck already out of range. "Those bastards!" I
heard my host snarl.

26   "We'll get 'em yet, Pop," his son said. "I swear it."

27   After we left to drive on to the ruins of Gran Quivira, I
asked the friend who had accompanied me to explain what
had happened. "A pickup truck from Chilili. Hispanics driving up the mountain to cut trees. It's illegal. But they do it
anyway."

28   "Do the trees belong to your friend?"

29   "Not his trees. Not his mountain." Then he shrugged.

30   "But it's his gun."

31   I angrily cast my eyes at the man and find myself staring
into the twin barrels of a shotgun loosely held but pointed
directly at me. It is that same summer in Albuquerque, three
weeks later, and I am sitting in the driver's seat of my car, my
ten-year-old son, Bruce, directly behind me. Alongside him is
the eleven-year-old daughter of the man who had invited me
to teach at the University of New Mexico. I have just backed
my car away from a gasoline pump to allow another car to
move out of the garage into the road. As the other car came
out of the gas station, the man with the shotgun adroitly cut

me off and maneuvered his rust-pocked yellow pickup ahead of me in line before I could get back to the gas pump.

My first reaction is irritation with my car, as if the steel and chrome were sentient and responsible. It is the same ugly gold 1971 Buick in which, five summers earlier, I had driven through a Spanish landscape remarkably similar to the New Mexico in which I now find myself. Bruce had been with me then, too, along with his older brother and mother. But it is not the Buick that attracts men with guns. Nor is it that mythical violence of American life in which European intellectuals believe so fervently. In Spain we had been stopped at a roadblock, a sandbagged machine gun aimed by one of Franco's troops perusing traffic like a farmer counting chickens in a henhouse. The soldiers had asked for passports, scowled at the children, examined the Buick as if it were an armored tank, inspecting glove compartment and trunk and wedging their hands into the spaces between seat and back. At the hotel restaurant at which we stopped for lunch twenty minutes later, we learned that two *guardia civil* had been ambushed and killed by Basque guerrillas. During Franco's last years, such acts grew more and more frequent. Spain was filled with guns and soldiers. One was always aware of the presence of soldiers patrolling the vacation beaches of the Costa del Sol—and particularly aware of their guns. 32

As I am aware of the shotgun now. And as I am growing aware of that same enraged sense of humiliation and helplessness that seized me as those Spanish soldiers examined car and sons and wife, their guns casually pointed at all I loved most in the world, these other lives that made my life significantly mine. "Guns don't kill, people do!" Offer that mind-deadening cliché to a man at a roadblock watching the faces of soldiers for whom the power of a gun is simply that it permits them to feel contempt for those without guns. Tell that to a man sitting in a car with two young children, contemplating doing what he knows he cannot do because the gun is in another man's hands. Both in Spain and in this New Mexico that Spain had planted in the New World like a genetic acorn breeding prerogatives of power, guns endowed men with a way to settle all questions of responsibility. 33

The man with the shotgun says nothing. He simply holds the weapon in his beefy hand, its muzzle casually pointed in my direction. I toy with the notion of getting out of the car and confronting him. I am angry, enraged. I don't want to 34 give in to his rude power. Only my son and my colleague's daughter are in the back of the car. Defensively, I turn to look at them. My colleague's daughter is wide-eyed and frightened. Bruce is equally frightened, but his eyes are on me. I am his father and he expects me to do something, to say something, to alter the balance of expectation and reality. Our car was on line for gas first. To a ten-year-old, justice is a simple arithmetic.

35   To that ten-year-old's father it is not necessarily more complex. I could tell myself that it was insane to tell a man pointing a shotgun at me and these two children that he has broken the rules. Chances are he wouldn't have fired, would probably have responded with a shrug of the shoulders no more threatening than a confession of ignorance.

36   Obviously, none of this mattered. My growing sense of humiliation and rage had nothing to do with having to wait an extra minute or two while the station attendant filled the tank of the pickup. I was in no particular rush. I was simply returning home from a day-long excursion to a state park, where my son and his new friend had crawled through caves and climbed rocks splashed by a warm spring. But I was facing a man with a shotgun, a man who understood that people with guns define options for themselves.

37   The man with the gun decides whether or not to shoot, just as he chooses where to point his gun. It is not political power that stems from the barrel of a gun, as Maoists used to proclaim so ritualistically. It is individual power, the ability to impose one's presence on the world, simply because guns always do what language only sometimes does: Guns command! Guns command attention, guns command discipline, guns command fear.

38   And guns bestow rights and prerogatives, even to those who have read Jane Austen and engaged the world in their own comedy of manners. There is a conditional nature to all rights. And there are obligations that should not be shunted aside. Guns are many things, some symbolic, some all too real. But in real life they are always personal and rarely playful. They measure not capacity but the obligation the bearer of the gun has to believe that power belongs not to the gun but to him. And yet were I to tell this to my friend in Maine—that sophisticated, literate, humane man—I suspect he would turn to me and say, "That's right. There's always got to be somebody's finger on the trigger."

A confession, then: I may be as fascinated by guns as my 39
gun-owning and gun-loving friend in Maine, but were it up to
me, I would rid America of its guns. I would be less verbally
self-righteous about gun control than I was in the past, for I
think I have begun to understand those who, like my friend in
Maine, have arguments of their own in defense of guns. They
are formidable arguments. Their fear matches mine, and I
assume that their anguish over the safety of their children is
also equal to mine. I, too, know the statistics. I can repeat, as
easily as he can, that in Switzerland, where an armed citizenry is the norm, the homicide rate is far lower than in
many countries that carefully control the distribution of guns
to their populace. Laws are simply words on paper—unless
they embody what a population wants.

There is no logic with which I can convince my gun-owning 40
friend in Maine. But there are images I wish I could get him to
focus on. Like me, he is a writer. Only I write about cities, and
my friend writes about the Maine woods. He is knowledgeable
about animals and rocks and trees and silence, and I am knowledgeable about stubs of grass growing between cracks in a concrete sidewalk and the pitch and pull of conflicting voices
demanding recognition. I wish I could explain to him the precise configuration of that double-barreled shotgun pointing at
me and those two children. Maybe then I could convince him
that truth is not merely a matter of geography. Yes, guns don't
kill and people do—but in the America he and I share, those
people usually kill with guns.

Four years after that incident at the gas station, I was sit- 41
ting with Bruce in a brasserie in Paris. It was a sunny July afternoon and we were eating lunch at a small outside table, the
walls of the magisterial Invalides beckoning to us from across
the street. Bruce was fourteen, and fifteen minutes earlier he
had returned from his first trip alone on the Paris Metro.
Suddenly a man approached, eyes menacing and bloodshot.
He was short and thick, his body seemingly caked by the mus-
cularity of a beaten-down club fighter or an unemployed ste-
vedore. He stared at us, eyes filled with the rage of the insane.
Then he flexed his muscles as if he were on exhibit as a circus
strong man, cried out something—a sound I remember as a
cross between gargling and choking—and disappeared just as
suddenly down the street.

The incident still haunts me. The French, I suspect, are as 42
violent as they like to claim we Americans are. But in Paris it

is difficult for a man filled with rage and craziness to get hold
of a gun. Not impossible, mind you, just difficult. Somewhere
along the line, the French have learned not that guns don't kill
and people do but that people with guns can kill. And they
know what we have yet to acknowledge—that when the Fu-
ries dance in the head it's best to keep the weapons in display
cases in the museum. For that, at least, I wish my friend in
Maine could learn to be grateful. As I was, eating lunch with
my son in Paris.

Roy Innis

Gun Control Sprouts
from Racist Soil

*Roy Innis was born in the Virgin Islands in 1934. As a youth he
moved with his family to New York City, and he has continued
to make his home there. He contributed the following article to*
The Wall Street Journal *in November 1991 while he was serving as the national chairman of the Congress of Racial Equality.*

1   What irony. Most black leaders (as distinct from rank-and-
file blacks) are supporters, at least in public, of the gun
control—really, prohibition—movement. Do they realize that
America's gun-control movement sprouted from the soil of
Roger B. Taney, the racist chief justice who wrote the infamous *Dred Scott* decision of 1857?

2   In the early part of the 19th century, Dred Scott, a black
slave, had been taken by his owner from Missouri, a slave
state, to Illinois, a free state. From there he was taken into the
Wisconsin territory, free territory above the 36° 30' latitude of
the Missouri Compromise. After living in free territory for a
while, he returned with his owner to Missouri.

3   When his owner died in 1846, Scott sued in the state courts
of Missouri for his freedom, on the ground that he had lived in
free territory. He won his case, but it was reversed in the Missouri Supreme Court. Scott appealed to the federal courts,
since the person he was actually suing, John Sanford, the exec-
utor of the estate that owned Scott, lived in New York.

It was in that setting that Chief Justice Taney made his in- 4
famous rulings:

1. That black people, whether free or slave, were not citizens of the U.S.; therefore, they had no standing in
   court.
2. Scott was denied freedom.
3. The Missouri Compromise was ruled unconstitutional.

Well known to most students of race relations is the former 5
attorney general and secretary of the Treasury's pre-civil war
dictum that black people "being of an inferior order" had "no
right which any white man was bound to respect." Much less
known are his equally racist pronouncements denying black
people, whether slave or free, specific constitutional protections enjoyed by whites.

In *Dred Scott* Chief Justice Taney, writing for the court's 6
majority, stated that if blacks were "entitled to the privileges
and immunities of citizens, . . . it would give persons of the negro race, who were recognized as citizens in any one state of
the union, the right . . . to keep and carry arms wherever they
went. And all of this would be done in the face of the subject
race of the same color, both free and slaves, and inevitably
producing discontent and insubordination among them, and
endangering the peace and safety of the state. . . ."

Although much of Justice Taney's overly racist legal rea- 7
soning was repudiated by events that followed—such as the
Civil War and Reconstruction—the subliminal effects were
felt throughout that era. In the post-Reconstruction period,
when the pendulum swung back to overt racism, Justice
Taney's philosophy resurfaced. It was during this period that
racial paranoia about black men with guns intensified. It was
potent enough to cause the infringement on the Second
Amendment to the Constitution's "right . . . to keep and bear
arms."

Under natural law, a freeman's right to obtain and main- 8
tain the implements of self-defense has always been sacred.
This right was restricted or prohibited for serfs, peasants and
slaves. Gun control was never an issue in America until after
the Civil War when black slaves were freed.

It was this change in the status of the black man, from 9
slave to freeman, that caused racist elements in the country
(North and South) to agitate for restrictions on guns—ignoring long established customs and understanding of the Second Amendment. The specter of a black man with rights of a

freeman, bearing arms, was too much for the early heirs of
Roger Taney to bear.

10   The 14th and 15th Amendments to the Constitution, along
with the various Reconstruction civil rights acts, prevented
gun prohibitionists from making laws that were explicitly
racist and that would overtly deny black people the right to
bear arms. The end of Reconstruction signaled the return of
Taneyism—overtly among the masses and covertly on the Supreme Court. Gun-control legislation of the late 19th and
early 20th centuries, enacted at the state and local levels, was
implicitly racist in conception. And in operation, those laws
invidiously targeted blacks.

11   With the influx of large numbers of Irish, Italian and Jewish immigrants into the country, gun laws now also targeted
whites from the underprivileged classes of immigrants. Eventually these oppressive gun laws were extended to affect all
but a privileged few. Throughout the history of New York
state's Sullivan law, enacted at the start of the 20th century,
mainly the rich and powerful have had easy access to licenses
to carry handguns. Some of the notables who have received
that privilege include Eleanor Roosevelt, John Lindsay,
Donald Trump, Arthur Sulzberger, Joan Rivers and disk
jockey Howard Stern.

12   Of the 27,000 handgun carry permits in New York City,
fewer than 2% are issued to blacks—who live and work in
high-crime areas and really are in need of protection.

13   And what of the origins of the National Rifle Association,
which is wrongly viewed as a racist organization by the black
supporters of gun prohibition? It was inspired and organized
by Union Army officers after the Civil War.

Elizabeth Swazey
Women and Handguns

*Elizabeth Swazey, an attorney, a certified firearms instructor,
and the director of the National Rifle Association's group on
women's issues, has been writing a column every other month
for* American Rifleman *magazine (a publication of the NRA
that is devoted to articles of various kinds on various kinds of
firearms and related issues). The following such column
appeared in 1992.*

James Michael Barnes failed to appear in court on March   1
8, 1991. He was dead.

According to New Jersey *Courier-Post* staff reporters Alan   2
Guenther and Renee Winkler, by February 1990 the relationship between Amy Gardiner and James Michael Barnes had
broken off. On February 9, he appeared on Gardiner's doorstep to return some of her things. Instead, he raped her. He
even photographed the event. Barnes pled guilty to assault
and was sentenced to two years probation. He also was ordered to stay away from Gardiner and her relatives.

He didn't. According to court documents, Barnes broke   3
into Gardiner's home, stole from her, left a hot iron on her
carpet and smeared her walls and furniture with feces.

During this period, Barnes was charged with robbing and   4
intimidating another ex-girlfriend. Bail was set at $50,000
cash. Barnes stayed in jail until January 17. On that date,
prosecutors sought to have his opportunity for bail revoked
on grounds he was a threat to Gardiner. But the judge actually *reduced* Barnes' bail to $25,000. Barnes posted the 10%
required and was free that afternoon.

Free to look for Amy Gardiner.   5

But in the meantime, Gardiner had done three things. She   6
had filed harassment charges against Barnes; she had
changed her address; and she had purchased a shotgun. Two
weeks later at 9:30 in the evening, Gardiner's doorbell rang.
She was alone and didn't answer the door. Soon the telephone
rang. When she answered, the caller hung up. Sensing danger, Gardiner went to the bedroom to get the shotgun. Barnes,
armed with a revolver and a disturbed mind, kicked in the
front door and stormed into the bedroom, threatening to kill
her. Gardiner fired once. Barnes died. The terror was over.
But at what cost?

7   Taking the life of another human being, *no matter how justified,* carries a heavy burden. Why New Jersey Superior Court Judge Joseph F. Green, Jr., allowed Barnes to buy temporary freedom for $2,500 is beyond me. Is that the price he places on a woman's suffering, on the white-hot fear she felt that night, alone, with a madman trying to kill her?

8   Amy Gardiner could be any of us, *You, Your wife, daughter or friend.* According to the Dept. of Justice, three of four American women will face crime in their lifetimes. And, as has been held in another case, "...a government and its agents are under no general duty to provide public services, such as police protection, to any particular individual citizen...." *Warren v. District of Columbia,* 444 A.2d 1 (D.C.App.181).

9   Or, put another way, "[T]here is no constitutional right to be protected by the state against being murdered by criminals or madmen." *Bowers v. DeVito,* 686 F.2d 616, at 618 (7th Cir. 1982).

10   Amy Gardiner faced a criminal madman. Thankfully, the innocent life prevailed. And while it is human nature to avoid thinking about unpleasant topics, we must recognize that *any one of us* could be violently attacked. Until our criminal justice system becomes a victims' justice system—and NRA is helping turn the tide through our *CrimeStrike* program—violent criminals like James Michael Barnes will continue to be routinely set free. We need to decide, in advance, how to respond if you, I or a loved one is threatened.

11   Owning a gun, and whether to use it in lawful self-defense, are *deeply personal choices* that each individual must make. For those who decide in favor of gun ownership, NRA can help. We offer introductory Personal Protection Seminars for women across the country, and the intensive Personal Protection Program to men and women nationwide through a network of certified instructors. Information about both is available by simply calling (800) 368-5714 or (202) 828-6224.

12   Handgun Control, Inc. (HCI) doesn't want women to have this choice. The group's Chairman Emeritus Pete Shields advises women faced with criminal attack to "give them what they want." But what James Michael Barnes wanted was for Amy Gardiner *to be dead.*

13   Sometimes HCI softens its message by expressing "concern" that if a woman tried to use a gun in self-defense, it would be taken away and used against her. Why doesn't HCI Chair Sarah Brady ever say this about men? Amy Gardiner faced an armed attacker and prevailed. And the most recent

National Crime Survey by the Bureau of Justice Statistics found that in *less than 1%* of cases did criminals manage to turn guns against their owners.

HCI says one of its principal political goals this year is to conduct a "public information campaign" about "the extremist nature of the gun lobby and alert women . . . that they've been targeted as a new market. . . ." 14

So the lines are drawn: NRA says defend your right to defend yourself. HCI says give criminals what they want. Now who's extreme? 15

National Rifle Association
Don't Edit the Bill of Rights

*The ad printed on these two pages, developed and paid for by
the National Rifle Association Institute for Legislative Action,
appeared in* USA Today *and many other newspapers in December
1991—on the 200th anniversary of the ratification of the
Bill of Rights.*

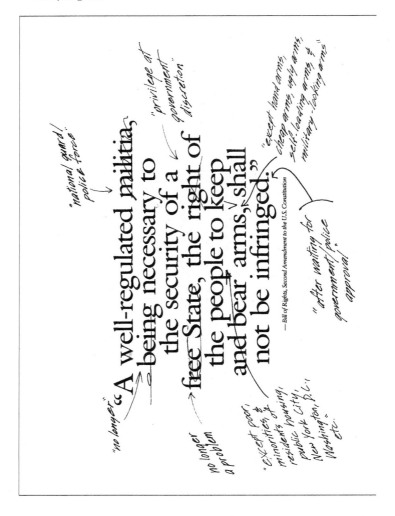

Before anyone edits the Bill of Rights, the authors would like to have a word with you:

"No free man shall ever be debarred the use of arms."

THOMAS JEFFERSON

"Arms in the hands of citizens may be used at individual discretion...in private self-defense."

JOHN ADAMS

"[The Constitution preserves] the advantage of being armed which Americans possess over the people of almost every other nation...[where] the governments are afraid to trust the people with arms."

JAMES MADISON

"...arms discourage and keep the invader and plunderer in awe, and preserve order in the world as well as property.... Horrid mischief would ensue were [the law-abiding] deprived of the use of them."

THOMAS PAINE

"Laws that forbid the carrying of arms...disarm only those who are neither inclined nor determined to commit crimes.... Such laws make things worse for the assaulted and better for the assailants; they serve rather to encourage than to prevent homicides, for an unarmed man may be attacked with greater confidence than an armed man."

THOMAS JEFFERSON, quoting Cesare Beccaria

"A militia, when properly formed, are in fact the people themselves...and include all men capable of bearing arms.... To preserve liberty it is essential that the whole body of the people always possess arms and be taught alike...how to use them."

RICHARD HENRY LEE

"The Constitution shall never be construed to prevent the people of the United States who are peaceable citizens from keeping their own arms."

SAMUEL ADAMS

"I ask, sir, what is the militia? It is the whole people.... To disarm the people is the best and most effectual way to enslave them..."

GEORGE MASON

A message in celebration of the 200th Anniversary of the Ratification of the Bill of Rights, December 15, 1791. Paid for by the National Rifle Association Institute for Legislative Action. For more information call 202-828-6310.

Paul Lawton
Constitutional Law and the Second Amendment

Paul Lawton was a student at the University of Texas at Austin when he wrote the following essay for a writing course there. He's pursuing a career in journalism.

In the end more than they wanted freedom, they wanted security. When the Athenians finally wanted not to give to society but for society to give to them, when the freedom they wished for was freedom from responsibility, then Athens ceased to be free.

—Edward Gibbon (1737–1794)

1   In 1994 Congress passed an outright ban on nineteen different types of assault weapons under the Schumer amendment to the Clinton Crime Bill. Representative John Dingell (D–MI) remarked when the bill passed that the ban was "obnoxious, offensive and contrary to the rights of all Americans." This, however, did not stop the representative from voting for the Crime Bill, in which the ban was contained. His reasoning was that he considered the remainder of the bill to be "smart and tough" (*Washington Times*, 8/26/94). While the representative seemed to have "voted his conscience" on the bill, one wonders if this ban circumvented the Second Amendment to satisfy the American public's need for safer streets.

2   The push against the assault weapons was extremely popular last year, and lawmakers were quick to jump on the bandwagon against weapons that are designed to "kill humans." Many argued that the weapons had no useful purpose for hunting and that the weapons were also impractical for defending the homestead. But even so, the federal government is supposed to amend the Constitution before they do something that is strictly prohibited by its own guidelines. For instance, to circumvent the First Amendment's right to burn the American flag, the bill would need, under Article Five of the Constitution, a two-thirds approval in both houses. The bill would then need to be approved by three-fourths of the state legislatures before burning the flag could not be considered protected speech under the First Amendment.

There is nothing inherently wrong or evil with this amend-   3
ment process. Indeed, Chief Justice John Marshall wrote in
the nineteenth century that the Constitution was "intended to
endure for ages to come, and, consequently, to be adapted to
the various crises of human affairs." Marshall presented the
very modern idea that the Constitution is meant to be
amended to fit the various needs of future generations. Thus,
many people gripped with fear from violent crime in America
would probably express a wish to ban weapons whose sole
purpose is the taking of human life.

However, many groups including the para-militaries which   4
have recently been labeled as promoters of hate, have es-
poused the view that assault weapons are covered under the
Second Amendment and cannot, without amendment, be legally banned by the federal government. The pro-gun control
movement has argued quite the opposite, that the Second
Amendment does not guarantee, in fact, an individual right
and only refers to a state militia's right to bear arms.

In order to understand what the pro-gun control move-   5
ment believes about the Second Amendment's application to
individual rights, it is important to look at the actual text of
the amendment:

> A well-regulated Militia, being necessary for the security of a
> free State, the right of the people to keep and bear Arms,
> shall not be infringed.

One can clearly see the confusion that the word "Militia"   6
brings into the meaning of the amendment. Thus, the Pro-
Gun Control Movement, along with the American Bar Association, the ACLU, and texts such as Tribe's *American Constitutional Law*, have enunciated that the Second Amendment only
applies to state militias and makes no reference to an individual right.

From this interpretation, it has been assumed that, since   7
the right to bear arms is not an individual right, the extent to
which citizens may keep weapons can be limited by the federal government. To many so-called experts, the federal government was thus within its legal limits to ban assault
weapons. However, by taking a close look at the actual language of the Second Amendment and the legal precedent set
by the Supreme Court of the United States, it becomes obvious that the 102nd Congress passed a law that was entirely
unconstitutional and the very antithesis of what the past and
current interpretation of the amendment should allow.

8   The language of the Second Amendment can most clearly be linked to the generation of the idea that only the militia has the right to "keep and bear arms." However, Roy Copperud, a leading legal expert who is impartial to the gun control debate, was recently interviewed on the possible interpretations of the amendment. Copperud concluded that the structure of the sentence indicates that existence of the right to keep arms is assumed and that "the thrust of the sentence is that the right shall be preserved inviolate for the sake of ensuring a militia." He also concluded that the language of the amendment, although still acceptable in modern times, could be rewritten as, "Since a well-regulated militia is necessary to the security of a free state, the right of the people to keep and bear arms shall not be abridged" (Schulman, Second Amendment Foundation). This clearly shows that the meaning of the sentence is that all citizens need weapons to protect the state and that the federal government should realize this fact and not interfere with the natural right of the people to protect themselves and their society.

9   The intent and belief in an armed populace is clearly present in the Founding Father's rhetoric. Thomas Jefferson wrote that "the strongest reason for the people to retain the right to keep and bear arms is, as a last resort, to protect themselves against tyranny in government." This Lockonian philosophy that man has a natural justified right for self-protection was present in many of the leaders of the time and reflects itself in the language of the Bill of Rights and consequently the Second Amendment.

10   This clearly shows that the language of the amendment does not coincide with the contemporary interpretation of the amendment. However, this is not the *coup de grace* of the pro-gun control argument. Rather it presents only half a case in a constitutional interpretation. The second half of the case is the Supreme Court's judicial precedent on the Second Amendment.

11   Judicial precedent is important because the Court is not able to go back in time and ask the original framers what they meant and how far the federal government can go before it is infringing on the rights of the people. Thus, the Court looks at its own past decisions to help decide if a law is in fact unconstitutional. Unfortunately for the pro-gun control movement, the judicial precedent of the Court does not indicate a strong agreement with the assault weapon ban of 1994.

12   Perhaps the first case the court talked about concerning the right to bear arms is the 1856 *Scott* v. *Sandford* case, most

commonly referred to as the Dred Scott decision. Though the final decision was remarkably barbaric, the rhetoric used by the judges to defend their decision shows an opinion of the court that affirms the belief that the right to arms is a natural right of free men. In the opinion, the judges ruled that one of the criteria for Scott to be free would be the right of free speech and the right "to keep and carry arms wherever...[he] went" (LEXIS, 60 U.S. 393).

The next case, which dealt specifically with the Second   13
Amendment, was *United States v. Cruikshank* in 1876 where the court recognized that the right to keep and bear arms "is not a right granted by the Constitution... [but n]either is it in any manner dependent upon that instrument for its existence" (LEXIS).

But perhaps the most stunning indictment against the As-   14
sault Weapons Ban comes from *United States v. Miller* in 1939. Here the court devised a test to discern if a weapon is applicable under the Second Amendment clause. The weapon in question was a sawed-off shotgun and the court ruled that:

> In the absence of any evidence tending to show that possession or use of a "shotgun having a barrel of less than eighteen inches in length" at this time has some reasonable relationship to the preservation or efficiency of a well-regulated militia, we cannot say that the Second Amendment guarantees the right to keep and bear such an instrument. Certainly it is not within judicial note that this weapon is any part of the ordinary military equipment or that its use could contribute to the common defense.

Thus, the court ruled that the weapon must be of military use   15
to be protected under the Second Amendment, which clearly destroys the pro-gun opinion that assault weapons can be banned because they are neither hunting nor self-protection firearms. Here the Court ruled the opposite to be true. Only weapons used for military purpose are protected (153 U.S. 535).

The Court also issued an opinion in Miller that the militia   16
mentioned in the Second Amendment consists of "all males physically capable of acting in concert for the common defense." They further elaborated on the duties of this civilian militia by saying that "when called for service these men...[are] expected to appear bearing arms supplied by themselves and of the kind in common use at the time" (307

U.S. 174). More precisely, contrary to Miller, the Court declared that the people mentioned in the Second Amendment included all citizens of the United States and not just young males. The 1990 *United States* v. *Verdugo-Urquirdez* decision further clarified that the Second Amendment applies to all citizens and legal aliens in the United States (110 S. Ct. 3039).

17　　　　Thus, the court decisions render a view of the Second Amendment that cannot possibly allow for the prohibition of any weapon that might be used for war. Since the Bill of Rights is the final say on whether the government has overstepped its boundaries, it becomes clear that the 1994 U.S. Congress overstepped its boundaries into the rights of its rulers. It seems incomprehensible that this bill would pass when a scant fourteen years ago the Subcommittee on the Constitution of the Committee on the Judiciary remarked that "The conclusion is thus inescapable that the history, concept, and wording of the Second Amendment to the Constitution of the United States, as well as its interpretation by every major commentator and court in the first half-century after its ratification, indicates that what is protected is an individual right of a private citizen to own and carry firearms in a peaceful manner." This careless disregard for both the limitations and rules of the Constitution certainly should make the federal government suspect to the American people. For in the end, the rights guaranteed in the amendments are the only protection against a tyrannical government the people have. Any attempt to erode these liberties should be inquired about to the fullest extent. Any attempt to circumvent this process should be considered inexcusable.

Robert Goldwin
Gun Control Is Constitutional

Goldwin is a scholar affiliated with the American Enterprise Institute, a conservative research institute. He contributed the following to The Wall Street Journal, *the conservative business-news daily, in December 1991. The letters published after it and responding to it appeared a few weeks later in the same newspaper.*

Congress has been dismayingly inconsistent in its voting on gun-control legislation this year, first passing the Brady Bill, then moving in the opposite direction by defeating a provision to ban certain assault weapons and ammunition. But in one respect members of Congress are consistent: they demand respect for our "constitutional right to own a gun." They cite the Constitution's Second Amendment and argue it prohibits effective national regulation of the private ownership of guns.

But there are strong grounds for arguing that the Second Amendment is no barrier to gun-control legislation. In my opinion, it even provides a solid constitutional basis for effective national legislation to regulate guns and gun owners.

The best clues to the meaning of the key words and phrases are in debates in the First Congress of the United States. The Members of that Congress were the authors of the Second Amendment. A constitutional amendment calling for the prohibition of standing armies in time of peace was proposed by six state ratifying conventions. Virginia's version, later copied by New York and North Carolina, brought together three elements in one article—affirmation of a right to bear arms, reliance on state militia, and opposition to a standing army.

"That the people have a right to keep and bear arms; that a well regulated militia, composed of the body of the people trained to arms, is the proper, natural, and safe defense of a free state; that standing armies, in times of peace, are dangerous to liberty, and therefore ought to be avoided. . . ."

The purpose was to limit the power of the new Congress to establish a standing army, and instead to rely on state militias under the command of governors. The Constitution was ratified without adopting any of the scores of proposed amendments. But in several states ratification came only with solemn pledges that amendments would follow.

6   Soon after the First Congress met, James Madison, elected
as a congressman from Virginia on the basis of such a pledge,
proposed a number of amendments resembling yet different
from articles proposed by states. These eventually became the
Bill of Rights. In the version of the arms amendment he presented, Madison dropped mention of a standing army and
added a conscientious objector clause.

7   "The right of the people to keep and bear arms shall not be
infringed, a well armed and well regulated militia being the
best security of a free country, but no person religiously scrupulous of bearing arms shall be compelled to render military
service in person."

8   In this version, "bearing arms" must mean "to render military service," or why else would there have to be an exemption for religious reasons? What right must not be infringed?
The right of the people to serve in the militia.

9   This militia amendment was referred to a congressional
committee and came out of committee in this form:

10   "A well regulated militia, composed of the body of the people, being the best security of a free state, the right of the
people to keep and bear arms shall not be infringed; but no
person religiously scrupulous shall be compelled to bear
arms."

11   Two significant changes had been made: first, the phrase
"to render military service in person" was replaced by the
phrase, "to bear arms," again indicating that they are two
ways to say the same thing; second, an explanation was added
that the "militia" is "composed of the body of the people."

12   The House then debated this new version in committee of
the whole and, surprisingly, considering the subsequent history of the provision, never once did any member mention
the private uses of arms, for self-protection, or hunting, or
any other personal purpose. The debate focused exclusively
on the conscientious objector provision. Eventually the committee's version was narrowly approved. The Senate in turn
gave it its final form: briefer, unfortunately more elliptical,
and with the exemption for conscientious objectors deleted:

13   "A well-regulated militia, being necessary to the security of
a free state, the right of the people to keep and bear arms,
shall not be infringed."

14   Certain explanations were lost or buried in this legislative
process: that the right to bear arms meant the right to serve in
the militia; that just about everybody was included in the militia; and that the amendment as a whole sought to minimize
if not eliminate reliance on a standing army by emphasizing

the role of the state militia, which would require that everyone be ready to be called to serve.

But what about the private right "to keep and bear arms," 15 to own a gun for self-defense and hunting? Isn't that clearly protected by the amendment? Didn't just about everyone own a gun in 1791? Wouldn't that "right" go without saying? Yes, of course, it would go without saying, especially then when there were no organized police forces and when hunting was essential to the food supply.

But such facts tell us almost nothing relevant to our ques- 16 tion. Almost everyone also owned a dog for the same purposes. The Constitution nevertheless says nothing about the undeniable right to own a dog. There are uncountable numbers of rights not enumerated in the Constitution. These rights are neither denied nor disparaged by not being raised to the explicit constitutional level. All of them are constitutionally subject to regulation.

The right to bear arms protected in the Second Amend- 17 ment has to do directly with "a well-regulated militia." More evidence of the connection can be found in the Militia Act of 1792.

"Every free able-bodied white male citizen" (it was 1792, 18 after all) was required by the act to "enroll" in the militia for training and active service in case of need. When reporting for service, every militiaman was required to provide a prescribed rifle or musket, and ammunition.

Here we see the link of the private and public aspects of 19 bearing arms. The expectation was that every man would have his own firearms. But the aspect that was raised to the level of constitutional concern was the public interest in those arms.

What does this mean for the question of gun control to- 20 day? Well, for example, it means that Congress has the constitutional power to enact a Militia Act of 1992, to require every person who owns a gun or aspires to own one to "enroll" in the militia. In plain 1990s English, if you want to own a gun, sign up with the National Guard.

Requiring every gun owner to register with the National 21 Guard (as we require 18-year-olds to register with the Selective Service) would provide the information about gunowners sought by the Brady and Staggers bills, and much more. Standards could be set for purchase or ownership of guns, and penalties could be established.

Restoring a 200-year-old understanding of the Constitution 22 may be difficult, but there isn't time to dawdle. Americans now own more than 200 million guns, and opinion polls show Americans want gun control. Why not avail ourselves of the Second Amendment remedy? Call in the militia, which is, after all, "composed of the body of the people."

Responses to Robert Goldwin: Letters to the Editor of the *Wall Street Journal*

1   In his "Gun Control Is Constitutional" the American Enterprise Institute's Robert A. Goldwin's principal concern, it seems, is to deny that the right to keep and bear arms precludes the power to regulate gun ownership and use. Few would disagree. Even activities protected by the First Amendment may be regulated when they threaten the rights of others.

2   But Mr. Goldwin also writes that "The right to bear arms protected in the Second Amendment has to do directly with 'a well regulated militia'"; thus, arguably, he continues, "if you want to own a gun, sign up with the National Guard." Clearly, this goes well beyond regulating to protect the rights of others. This would condition the "right" to keep and bear arms on joining the National Guard.

3   Mr. Goldwin's mistake stems from his having confused a necessary with a sufficient condition. The Second Amendment, in its language and its history, makes plain that the need for a well-regulated militia is a *sufficient* condition for the right to keep and bear arms. Yet Mr. Goldwin treats it as a *necessary* condition, which enables him to conclude that Congress could deny an individual the right to own a gun if he did not join the National Guard.

4   Mr. Goodwin makes this mistake, in turn, because he has misread Madison's original version of the Second Amendment, which exempted conscientious objectors from military service. Thus he says that "In this version, 'bearing arms' must mean 'to render military service,' or why else would there have to be an exemption for religious reasons? What right must not be infringed? The right of the people to serve in the militia."

Plainly, any conscientious objector provision would arise 5
not from a *right* but from a *duty* to serve in the militia. Yet Mr.
Goldwin believes the amendment means, as he later says,
"that the right to bear arms meant the right to serve in the militia." Thus does he reduce the first of these rights to the second, when clearly it is much broader.

Roger Pilon
Senior Fellow and Director
Center for Constitutional Studies
CATO Institute

The militia is not the National Guard but rather the people 1
of the original states. In Ohio, we have an Ohio militia that is
not a part of the National Guard. The fear of standing armies
and the control these armed men gave a central government
was foremost in the Framers' minds when writing the Bill of
Rights. Thomas Jefferson moved to prevent this type of power
in a few people's hands by the Second Amendment. He stated,
"No free man shall ever be debarred the use of arms."
    The addition in the early drafts of a conscientious-objector 2
clause was added for the preservation of religious freedoms,
which the Colonists had not had in England. It is unfortunate
today's "scholars" seem to spend their time picking apart history and the great thoughts of the visionary men who formed
this country.
    In my personal celebration of this 200-year-old document, 3
I have pledged the following: I will give up my freedom of
speech when they cut out my tongue; I will give up my right
to worship when they have slain my God and myself; I will assemble with the people of my choice even when they are im-
prisoned, and I will give up my rifle when they pry my cold
dead fingers from around it.

Samuel R. Bush III

Let those who want guns join the National Guard, says Mr. 1
Goldwin. Ah, the sanctimonious arrogance of it. What gives
Mr. Goldwin the right to deny mine when I abide by the laws?
    He stresses the differences between the world of 1791 and 2
today to suit his prejudice. He studiously ignores other major
differences between 1791 and today.

3   In 1791, punishment was swifter and surer. Plea bargaining was not epidemic; judges did not provide revolving doors on prisons. There was no army of drug dealers and junkies preying on the public. If anything, the reasons for citizens to own weapons for self-defense are more compelling today than they were in 1791.

4   Let Mr. Goldwin show us how he would make us safer in our homes and we might understand his wish to strip away our only sure defense.

Carl Roessler

1   Mr. Goldwin suggests gun control via enlistment in the National Guard. Swell idea. Updating the right to bear arms from 1791 to 1991, when I report for service, I'll bring, as required, a few items consistent with the current infantryman's inventory: a Barett Light .50 semiautomatic sniper rifle, so I can reach out and touch people half a mile away; a Squad Automatic Weapon firing 5.56mm rounds at the rate of a whole lot per second out of 30-round clips or hundred-round belts; a 40mm grenade launcher...but you get the idea. Then, as a thoroughly modern, well-regulated militiaman, I'll take my weapons home, just as did Morgan's riflemen, and the musket bearers of Lexington and Concord, and the Colonial light artillerists.

Andrew L. Isaac

Daniel Polsby

The False Promise
of Gun Control

The following essay appeared in March 1994 in The Atlantic
Monthly, *a venerable, mildly left-of-center monthly magazine
that carries book and movie reviews, original poetry and fiction, and commentary on current events and issues. Daniel
Polsby (born 1945) has been a full-time professor of law at
Northwestern University for over two decades. He teaches
courses in criminal law and regularly writes on constitutional,
criminal, and family law for academic publications.*

During the 1960s and 1970s the robbery rate in the United   1
States increased sixfold, and the murder rate doubled; the rate
of handgun ownership nearly doubled in that period as well.
Handguns and criminal violence grew together apace, and
national opinion leaders did not fail to remark on the
coincidence.

It has become a bipartisan article of faith that more hand-   2
guns cause more violence. Such was the unequivocal conclusion of the National Commission on the Causes and Prevention
of Violence in 1969, and such is now the editorial opinion of
virtually every influential newspaper and magazine, from *The
Washington Post* to *The Economist* to the *Chicago Tribune*.
Members of the House and Senate who have not dared to confront the gun lobby concede the connection privately. Even if
the National Rifle Association can produce blizzards of angry
calls and letters to the Capitol virtually overnight, House members one by one have been going public, often after some new
firearms atrocity at a fast-food restaurant or the like. And last
November they passed the Brady bill.

Alas, however well accepted, the conventional wisdom   3
about guns and violence is mistaken. Guns don't increase national rates of crime and violence—but the continued proliferation of gun-control laws almost certainly does. Current
rates of crime and violence are a bit below the peaks of the
late 1970s, but because of a slight oncoming bulge in the risk
population of males aged fifteen to thirty-four, the crime rate
will soon worsen. The rising generation of criminals will have
no more difficulty than their elders did in obtaining the tools
of their trade. Growing violence will lead to calls for laws still

more severe. Each fresh round of legislation will be followed by renewed frustration.

4   Gun-control laws don't work. What is worse, they act perversely. While legitimate users of firearms encounter intense regulation, scrutiny, and bureaucratic control, illicit markets easily adapt to whatever difficulties a free society throws in their way. Also, efforts to curtail the supply of firearms inflict collateral damage on freedom and privacy interests that have long been considered central to American public life. Thanks to the seemingly never-ending war on drugs and long experience attempting to suppress prostitution and pornography, we know a great deal about how illicit markets function and how costly to the public attempts to control them can be. It is essential that we make use of this experience in coming to grips with gun control.

5   The thousands of gun-control laws in the United States are of two general types. The older kind sought to regulate how, where, and by whom firearms could be carried. More recent laws have sought to make it more costly to buy, sell, or use firearms (or certain classes of firearms, such as assault rifles, Saturday-night specials, and so on) by imposing fees, special taxes, or surtaxes on them. The Brady bill is of both types: it has a background-check provision, and its five-day waiting period amounts to a "time tax" on acquiring handguns. All such laws can be called scarcity-inducing, because they seek to raise the cost of buying firearms, as figured in terms of money, time, nuisance, or stigmatization.

6   Despite the mounting number of scarcity-inducing laws, no one is very satisfied with them. Hobbyists want to get rid of them, and gun-control proponents don't think they go nearly far enough. Everyone seems to agree that gun-control laws have some effect on the distribution of firearms. But it has not been the dramatic and measurable effect their proponents desired.

7   Opponents of gun control have traditionally wrapped their arguments in the Second Amendment to the Constitution. Indeed, most modern scholarship affirms that so far as the drafters of the Bill of Rights were concerned, the right to bear arms was to be enjoyed by everyone, not just a militia, and that one of the principal justifications for an armed populace was to secure the tranquillity and good order of the community. But most people are not dedicated antiquitarians, and would not be impressed by the argument "I admit that my behavior is very dangerous to public safety, but the Second Amendment says I have a right to do it anyway." That would

be a case for repealing the Second Amendment, not respecting it.

Fighting the Demand Curve

Everyone knows that possessing a handgun makes it easier 8
to intimidate, wound, or kill someone. But the implication of
this point for social policy has not been so well understood. It
is easy to count the bodies of those who have been killed or
wounded with guns, but not easy to count the people who
have avoided harm because they had access to weapons.
Think about uniformed police officers, who carry handguns
in plain view not in order to kill people but simply to daunt
potential attackers. And it works. Criminals generally do not
single out police officers for opportunistic attack. Though officers can expect to draw their guns from time to time, few
even in big-city departments will actually fire a shot (except
in target practice) in the course of a year. This observation
points to an important truth: people who are armed make
comparatively unattractive victims. A criminal might not
know if any one civilian is armed, but if it becomes known
that a large number of civilians do carry weapons, criminals
will become warier.

Which weapons laws are the right kinds can be decided 9
only after considering two related questions. First, what is the
connection between civilian possession of firearms and social
violence? Second, how can we expect gun-control laws to alter people's behavior? Most recent scholarship raises serious
questions about the "weapons increase violence" hypothesis.
The second question is emphasized here, because it is routinely overlooked and often mocked when noticed; yet it is crucial. Rational gun control requires understanding not only the
relationship between weapons and violence but also the relationship between laws and people's behavior. Some things are
very hard to accomplish with laws. The purpose of a law and
its likely effects are not always the same thing. Many statutes
are notorious for the way in which their unintended effects
have swamped their intended ones.

In order to predict who will comply with gun-control laws, 10
we should remember that guns are economic goods that are
traded in markets. Consumers' interest in them varies. For religious, moral, aesthetic, or practical reasons, some people
would refuse to buy firearms at any price. Other people willingly pay very high prices for them.

11   Handguns, so often the subject of gun-control laws, are desirable for one purpose—to allow a person tactically to dominate a hostile transaction with another person. The value of a weapon to a given person is a function of two factors: how much he or she wants to dominate a confrontation if one occurs, and how likely it is that he or she will actually be in a situation calling for a gun.

12   Dominating a transaction simply means getting what one wants without being hurt. Where people differ is in how likely it is that they will be involved in a situation in which a gun will be valuable. Someone who *intends* to engage in a transaction involving a gun—a criminal, for example—is obviously in the best possible position to predict that likelihood. Criminals should therefore be willing to pay more for a weapon than most other people would. Professors, politicians, and newspaper editors are, as a group, at very low risk of being involved in such transactions, and they thus systematically underrate the value of defensive handguns. (Correlative, perhaps, is their uncritical readiness to accept studies that debunk the utility of firearms for self-defense.) The class of people we wish to deprive of guns, then, is the very class with the most inelastic demand for them—criminals—whereas the people most likely to comply with gun-control laws don't value guns in the first place.

Do Guns Drive Up Crime Rates?

13   Which premise is true—that guns increase crime or that the fear of crime causes people to obtain guns? Most of the country's major newspapers apparently take this problem to have been solved by an article published by Arthur Kellermann and several associates in the October 7, 1993, *New England Journal of Medicine*. Kellermann is an emergency-room physician who has published a number of influential papers that he believes discredit the thesis that private ownership of firearms is a useful means of self-protection. (An indication of his wide influence is that within two months the study received almost 100 mentions in publications and broadcast transcripts indexed in the Nexis data base.) For this study Kellermann and his associates identified fifteen behavioral and fifteen environmental variables that applied to a 388-member set of homicide victims, found a "matching" control group of 388 non–homicide victims, and then ascertained how the two groups differed in gun ownership. In in-

terviews Kellermann made clear his belief that owning a handgun markedly increases a person's risk of being murdered.

But the study does not prove that point at all. Indeed, as   14
Kellermann explicitly conceded in the text of the article, the causal arrow may very well point in the other direction: the threat of being killed may make people more likely to arm themselves. Many people at risk of being killed, especially people involved in the drug trade or other illegal ventures, might well rationally buy a gun as a precaution, and be willing to pay a price driven up by gun-control laws. Crime, after all, is a dangerous business. Peter Reuter and Mark Kleiman, drug-policy researchers, calculated in 1987 that the average crack dealer's risk of being killed was far greater than his risk of being sent to prison. (Their data cannot, however, support the implication that ownership of a firearm causes or exacerbates the risk of being killed.)

Defending the validity of his work, Kellermann has empha-   15
sized that the link between lung cancer and smoking was initially established by studies methodologically no different from his. Gary Kleck, a criminology professor at Florida State University, has pointed out the flaw in this comparison. No one ever thought that lung cancer causes smoking, so when the association between the two was established the direction of the causal arrow was not in doubt. Kleck wrote that it is as though Kellermann, trying to discover how diabetics differ from other people, found that they are much more likely to possess insulin than nondiabetics, and concluded that insulin is a risk factor for diabetes.

The New York Times, the *Los Angeles Times, The Washington*   16
Post, The Boston Globe, and the *Chicago Tribune* all gave prominent coverage to Kellermann's study as soon as it appeared, but none saw fit to discuss the study's limitations. A few, in order to introduce a hint of balance, mentioned that the NRA, or some member of its staff, disagreed with the study. But readers had no way of knowing that Kellermann himself had registered a disclaimer in his text. "It is possible," he conceded, "that reverse causation accounted for some of the association we observed between gun ownership and homicide." Indeed, the point is stronger than that: "reverse causation" may account for *most* of the association between gun ownership and homicide. Kellermann's data simply do not allow one to draw any conclusion.

If firearms increased violence and crime, then rates of   17
spousal homicide would have skyrocketed, because the stock

of privately owned handguns has increased rapidly since the mid-1960s. But according to an authoritative study of spousal homicide in the *American Journal of Public Health,* by James Mercy and Linda Saltzman, rates of spousal homicide in the years 1976 to 1985 fell. If firearms increased violence and crime, the crime rate should have increased throughout the 1980s, while the national stock of privately owned handguns increased by more than a million units in every year of the decade. It did not. Nor should the rates of violence and crime in Switzerland, New Zealand, and Israel be as low as they are, since the number of firearms per civilian household is comparable to that in the United States. Conversely, gun-controlled Mexico and South Africa should be islands of peace instead of having murder rates more than twice as high as those here. The determinants of crime and law-abidingness are, of course, complex matters, which are not fully understood and certainly not explicable in terms of a country's laws. But gun-control enthusiasts, who have made capital out of the low murder rate in England, which is largely disarmed, simply ignore the counterexamples that don't fit their theory.

18   If firearms increased violence and crime, Florida's murder rate should not have been falling since the introduction, seven years ago, of a law that makes it easier for ordinary citizens to get permits to carry concealed handguns. Yet the murder rate has remained the same or fallen every year since the law was enacted, and it is now lower than the national murder rate (which has been rising). As of last November 183,561 permits had been issued, and only seventeen of the permits had been revoked because the holder was involved in a firearms offense. It would be precipitate to claim that the new law has "caused" the murder rate to subside. Yet here is a situation that doesn't fit the hypothesis that weapons increase violence.

19   If firearms increased violence and crime, programs of induced scarcity would suppress violence and crime. But— another anomaly—they don't. Why not? A theorem, which we could call the futility theorem, explains why gun-control laws must either be ineffectual or in the long term actually provoke more violence and crime. Any theorem depends on both observable fact and assumption. An assumption that can be made with confidence is that the higher the number of victims a criminal assumes to be armed, the higher will be the risk—the price—of assaulting them. By definition, gun-control laws should make weapons scarcer and thus more expensive. By our prior reasoning about demand among vari-

ous types of consumers, after the laws are enacted criminals should be better armed, compared with noncriminals, than they were before. Of course, plenty of noncriminals will remain armed. But even if many noncriminals will pay as high a price as criminals will to obtain firearms, a larger number will not.

Criminals will thus still take the same gamble they already   20
take in assaulting a victim who might or might not be armed. But they may appreciate that the laws have given them a freer field, and that crime still pays—pays even better, in fact, than before. What will happen to the rate of violence? Only a relatively few gun-mediated transactions—currently, five percent of armed robberies committed with firearms—result in someone's actually being shot (the statistics are not broken down into encounters between armed assailants and unarmed victims, and encounters in which both parties are armed). It seems reasonable to fear that if the number of such transactions were to increase because criminals thought they faced fewer deterrents, there would be a corresponding increase in shootings. Conversely, if gun-mediated transactions declined— if criminals initiated fewer of them because they feared encountering an armed victim or an armed good Samaritan— the number of shootings would go down. The magnitude of · these effects is, admittedly, uncertain. Yet it is hard to doubt the general tendency of a change in the law that imposes legal burdens on buying guns. The futility theorem suggests that gun-control laws, if effective at all, would unfavorably affect the rate of violent crime.

The futility theorem provides a lens through which to see   21
much of the debate. It is undeniable that gun-control laws work—to an extent. Consider, for example, California's background-check law, which in the past two years has prevented about 12,000 people with a criminal record or a history of mental illness or drug abuse from buying handguns. In the same period Illinois's background-check law prevented the delivery of firearms to more than 2,000 people. Surely some of these people simply turned to an illegal market, but just as surely not all of them did. The laws of large numbers allow us to say that among the foiled thousands, some potential killers were prevented from getting a gun. We do not know whether the number is large or small but it is implausible to think it is zero. And, as gun-control proponents are inclined to say, "If only one life is saved . . ."

The hypothesis that firearms increase violence does pre-   22
dict that if we can slow down the diffusion of guns, there will

be less violence; one life, or more, *will* be saved. But the futility theorem asks that we look not simply at the gross number
of bad actors prevented from getting guns but at the effect the
law has on *all* the people who want to buy a gun. Suppose we
succeed in piling tax burdens on the acquisition of firearms.
We can safely assume that a number of people who might use
guns to kill will be sufficiently discouraged not to buy them.
But we cannot assume this about people who feel that they
must have guns in order to survive financially and physically.
A few lives might indeed be saved. But the overall rate of violent crime might not go down at all. And if guns are owned
predominantly by people who have good reason to think they
will use them, the rate might even go up.

23   Are there empirical studies that can serve to help us choose
between the futility theorem and the hypothesis that guns
increase violence? Unfortunately, no: the best studies of the
effects of gun-control laws are quite inconclusive. Our statistical tools are too weak to allow us to identify an effect clearly
enough to persuade an open-minded skeptic. But it is precisely when we are dealing with undetectable statistical effects that we have to be certain we are using the best models
available of human behavior.

Sealing the Border

24   Handguns are not legally for sale in the city of Chicago,
and have not been since April of 1982. Rifles, shotguns, and
ammunition are available, but only to people who possess an
Illinois Firearm Owner's Identification card. It takes up to a
month to get this card, which involves a background check.
Even if one has a FOID card there is a waiting period for the delivery of a gun. In few places in America is it as difficult to get
a firearm legally as in the city of Chicago.

25   Yet there are hundreds of thousands of unregistered guns
in the city, and new ones arriving all the time. It is not difficult to get handguns—even legally. Chicago residents with
FOID cards merely go to gun shops in the suburbs. Trying to establish a city as an island of prohibition in a sea of legal firearms seems an impossible project.

26   Is a state large enough to be an effective island, then? Suppose Illinois adopted Chicago's handgun ban. Same problem
again. Some people could just get guns elsewhere: Indiana actually borders the city, and Wisconsin is only forty miles
away. Though federal law prohibits the sale of handguns in

one state to residents of another, thousands of Chicagoans with summer homes in other states could buy handguns there. And, of course, a black market would serve the needs of other customers.

When would the island be large enough to sustain a   27 weapons-free environment? In the United States people and cargoes move across state lines without supervision or hindrance. Local shortages of goods are always transient, no matter whether the shortage is induced by natural disasters, prohibitory laws, or something else.

Even if many states outlawed sales of handguns, then, they   28 would continue to be available, albeit at a somewhat higher price, reflecting the increased legal risk of selling them. Mindful of the way markets work to undermine their efforts, gun-control proponents press for federal regulation of firearms, because they believe that only Congress wields the authority to frustrate the interstate movement of firearms.

Why, though, would one think that federal policing of ille-   29 gal firearms would be better than local policing? The logic of that argument is far from clear. Cities, after all, are comparatively small places. Washington, D.C., for example, has an area of less than 45,000 acres. Yet local officers have had little luck repressing the illegal firearms trade there. Why should federal officers do any better watching the United States' 12,000 miles of coastline and millions of square miles of interior? Criminals should be able to frustrate federal police forces just as well as they can local ones. Ten years of increasingly stringent federal efforts to abate cocaine trafficking, for example, have not succeeded in raising the street price of the drug.

Consider the most drastic proposal currently in play, that   30 of Senator John Chafee, of Rhode Island, who would ban the manufacture, sale, and home possession of handguns within the United States. This proposal goes far beyond even the Chicago law, because existing weapons would have to be surrendered. Handguns would become contraband, and selling counterfeit, stolen, and contraband goods is big business in the United States. The objective of law enforcement is to raise the costs of engaging in crime and so force criminals to take expensive precautions against becoming entangled with the legal system. Crimes of a given type will, in theory, decline as soon as the direct and indirect costs of engaging in them rise to the point at which criminals seek more profitable opportunities in other (not necessarily legal) lines of work.

In firearms regulation, translating theory into practice will   31 continue to be difficult, at least if the objective is to lessen the practical availability of firearms to people who might abuse them. On the demand side, for defending oneself against predation there is no substitute for a firearm. Criminals, at least, can switch to varieties of law-breaking in which a gun confers little or no advantage (burglary, smash-and-grab), but people who are afraid of confrontations with criminals, whether rationally or (as an accountant might reckon it) irrationally, will be very highly motivated to acquire firearms. Long after the marijuana and cocaine wars of this century have been forgotten, people's demand for personal security and for the tools they believe provide it will remain strong.

32   On the supply side, firearms transactions can be consummated behind closed doors. Firearms buyers, unlike those who use drugs, pornography, or prostitution, need not recurrently expose themselves to legal jeopardy. One trip to the marketplace is enough to arm oneself for life. This could justify a consumer's taking even greater precautions to avoid apprehension, which would translate into even steeper enforcement costs for the police.

33   Don Kates Jr., a San Francisco lawyer and a much-published student of this problem, has pointed out that during the wars in Southeast and Southwest Asia local artisans were able to produce, from scratch, serviceable pot-metal counterfeits of AK-47 infantry rifles and similar weapons in makeshift backyard foundries. Although inferior weapons cannot discharge thousands of rounds without misfiring, they are more than deadly enough for light to medium service, especially by criminals and people defending themselves and their property, who ordinarily use firearms by threatening with them, not by firing them. And the skills necessary to make them are certainly as widespread in America as in the villages of Pakistan or Vietnam. Effective policing of such a cottage industry is unthinkable. Indeed, as Charles Chandler has pointed out, crude but effective firearms have been manufactured in prisons—highly supervised environments, compared with the outside world.

34   Seeing that local firearms restrictions are easily defeated, gun-control proponents have latched onto national controls as a way of finally making gun control something more than a gesture. But the same forces that have defeated local regulation will defeat further national regulation. Imposing higher costs on weapons ownership will, of course, slow down the weapons trade to some extent. But planning to slow it down in such a way as to drive down crime and violence, or to prevent motivated purchasers from finding ample supplies of

guns and ammunition, is an escape from reality. And like many another such, it entails a morning after.

Administering Prohibition

Assume for the sake of argument that to a reasonable de-   35
gree of criminological certainty, guns are every bit the public-
health hazard they are said to be. It follows, and many journalists and a few public officials have already said, that we
ought to treat guns the same way we do smallpox viruses or
other critical vectors of morbidity and mortality—namely, isolate them from potential hosts and destroy them as speedily as
possible. Clearly, firearms have at least one characteristic that
distinguishes them from smallpox viruses: nobody wants to
keep smallpox viruses in the nightstand drawer. Amazingly
enough, gun-control literature seems never to have explored
the problem of getting weapons away from people who very
much want to keep them in the nightstand drawer.

Our existing gun-control laws are not uniformly permis-   36
sive and, indeed, in certain places are tough even by international standards. Advocacy groups seldom stress the
considerable differences among American jurisdictions, and
media reports regularly assert that firearms are readily available to anybody anywhere in the country. This is not the case.
For example, handgun restrictions in Chicago and the District of Columbia are much less flexible than the ones in the
United Kingdom. Several hundred thousand British subjects
may legally buy and possess sidearms, and anyone who joins
a target-shooting club is eligible to do so. But in Chicago and
the District of Columbia, excepting peace officers and the
like, only grandfathered registrants may legally possess handguns. Of course, tens or hundreds of thousands of people in
both those cities—nobody can be sure how many—do in fact
possess them illegally.

Although there is, undoubtedly, illegal handgun ownership   37
in the United Kingdom, especially in Northern Ireland (where
considerations of personal security and public safety are decidedly unlike those elsewhere in the British Isles), it is probable that Americans and Britons differ in their disposition to
obey gun-control laws: there is reputed to be a marked national disparity in compliance behavior. This difference, if it
exists, may have something to do with the comparatively
marginal value of firearms to British consumers. Even before
it had strict firearms regulation, Britain had very low rates of

crimes involving guns; British criminals, unlike their American counterparts, prefer burglary (a crime of stealth) to robbery (a crime of intimidation).

38   Unless people are prepared to surrender their guns voluntarily, how can the U.S. government confiscate an appreciable fraction of our country's nearly 200 million privately owned firearms? We know that it is possible to set up weapons-free zones in certain locations—commercial airports and many courthouses and, lately, some troubled big-city high schools and housing projects. The sacrifices of privacy and convenience, and the costs of paying guards, have been thought worth the (perceived) gain in security. No doubt it would be possible, though it would probably not be easy, to make weapons-free zones of shopping centers, department stores, movie theaters, ball parks. But it is not obvious how one would cordon off the whole of an open society.

39   Voluntary programs have been ineffectual. From time to time community-action groups or police departments have sponsored "turn in your gun" days, which are nearly always disappointing. Sometimes the government offers to buy guns at some price. This approach has been endorsed by Senator Chafee and the *Los Angeles Times*. Jonathan Alter, of *Newsweek*, has suggested a variation on this theme: youngsters could exchange their guns for a handshake with Michael Jordan or some other sports hero. If the price offered exceeds that at which a gun can be bought on the street, one can expect to see plans of this kind yield some sort of harvest—as indeed they have. But it is implausible that these schemes will actually result in a less-dangerous population. Government programs to buy up surplus cheese cause more cheese to be produced without affecting the availability of cheese to people who want to buy it. So it is with guns.

40   One could extend the concept of intermittent roadblocks of the sort approved by the Supreme Court for discouraging drunk driving. Metal detectors could be positioned on every street corner, or ambulatory metal-detector squads could check people randomly, or hidden magnetometers could be installed around towns, to detect concealed weapons. As for firearms kept in homes (about half of American households), warrantless searches might be rationalized on the well-established theory that probable cause is not required when authorities are trying to correct dangers to public safety rather than searching for evidence of a crime.

41   In a recent "town hall" meeting in California, President Bill Clinton used the word "sweeps," which he did not define, to

describe how he would confiscate firearms if it were up to him. During the past few years the Chicago Housing Authority chairman, Vincent Lane, has ordered "sweeps" of several gang-ridden public-housing projects, meaning warrantless searches of people's homes by uniformed police officers looking for contraband. Lane's ostensible premise was that possession of firearms by tenants constituted a lease violation that, as a conscientious landlord, he was obliged to do something about. The same logic could justify any administrative search. City health inspectors in Chicago were recently authorized to conduct warrantless searches for lead hazards in residential paint. Why not lead hazards in residential closets and nightstands? Someone has probably already thought of it.

Ignoring the Ultimate Sources of Crime and Violence

42   The American experience with prohibition has been that black marketeers—often professional criminals—move in to profit when legal markets are closed down or disturbed. In order to combat them, new laws and law-enforcement techniques are developed, which are circumvented almost as soon as they are put in place. New and yet more stringent laws are enacted, and greater sacrifices of civil liberties and privacy demanded and submitted to. But in this case the problem, crime and violence, will not go away, because guns and ammunition (which, of course, won't go away either) do not cause it. One cannot expect people to quit seeking new weapons as long as the tactical advantages of weapons are seen to outweigh the costs imposed by prohibition. Nor can one expect large numbers of people to surrender firearms they already own. The only way to make people give up their guns is to create a world in which guns are perceived as having little value. This world will come into being when criminals choose not to use guns because the penalties for being caught with them are too great, and when ordinary citizens don't think they need firearms because they aren't afraid of criminals anymore.

43   Neither of these eventualities seems very likely without substantial departures in law-enforcement policy. Politicians' nostrums—increasing the punishment for crime, slapping a few more death-penalty provisions into the code—are taken seriously by few students of the crime problem. The existing

penalties for predatory crimes are quite severe enough. The problem is that they are rarely meted out in the real world. The penalties formally published by the code are in practice steeply discounted, and criminals recognize that the judicial and penal systems cannot function without bargaining in the vast majority of cases.

44   This problem is not obviously one that legislation could solve. Constitutional ideas about due process of law make the imposition of punishments extraordinarily expensive and difficult. Like the tax laws, the criminal laws are basically voluntary affairs. Our system isn't geared to a world of wholesale disobedience. Recalibrating the system simply by increasing its overall harshness would probably offend and then shock the public long before any of its benefits were felt.

45   To illustrate, consider the prospect of getting serious about carrying out the death penalty. In recent years executions have been running at one or two dozen a year. As the late Supreme Court Justice Potter Stewart observed, those selected to die constitute a "capriciously selected random handful" taken from a much larger number of men and women who, just as deserving of death, receive prison sentences. It is not easy to be exact about that much larger number. But as an educated guess, taking into account only the most serious murders—the ones that were either premeditated or committed in the course of a dangerous felony—there are perhaps 5,000 prisoners a year who could plausibly be executed in the United States: say, 100,000 executions in the next twenty years. It is hard to think that the death penalty, if imposed on this scale, would not noticeably change the behavior of potential criminals. But what else in national life or citizens' character would have to change in order to make that many executions acceptable? Since 1930 executions in the United States have never exceeded 200 a year. At any such modest rate of imposition, rational criminals should consider the prospect of receiving the death penalty effectively nil. On the best current evidence, indeed, they do. Documentation of the deterrent effect of the death penalty, as compared with that of long prison sentences, has been notoriously hard to produce.

46   The problem is not simply that criminals pay little attention to the punishments in the books. Nor is it even that they also know that for the majority of crimes, their chances of being arrested are small. The most important reason for criminal behavior is this: the income that offenders can earn in the world of crime, as compared with the world of work, all too often makes crime appear to be the better choice.

Thus the crime bill that Bill Clinton introduced last year,   47
which provides for more prisons and police officers, should
be of only very limited help. More prisons means that fewer
violent offenders will have to be released early in order to
make space for new arrivals; perhaps fewer plea bargains will
have to be struck—all to the good. Yet a moment's reflection
should make clear that one more criminal locked up does not
necessarily mean one less criminal on the street. The situation
is very like one that conservationists and hunters have always
understood. Populations of game animals readily recover
from hunting seasons but not from loss of habitat. Mean
streets, when there are few legitimate entry-level opportunities for young men, are a criminal habitat so to speak, in the
social ecology of modern American cities. Cull however much
one will, the habitat will be reoccupied promptly after its previous occupant is sent away. So social science has found.

Similarly, whereas increasing the number of police officers   48
cannot hurt, and may well increase people's subjective feelings of security, there is little evidence to suggest that doing
so will diminish the rate of crime. Police forces are basically
reactive institutions. At any realistically sustainable level of
staffing they must remain so. Suppose 100,000 officers were
added to police rosters nationwide, as proposed in the current crime bill. This would amount to an overall personnel increase of about 18 percent, which would be parceled out
according to the iron laws of democratic politics—distributed
throughout states and congressional districts—rather than
being sent to the areas that most need relief. Such an increase, though unprecedented in magnitude, is far short of
what would be needed to pacify some of our country's worst
urban precincts.

There is a challenge here that is quite beyond being met   49
with tough talk. Most public officials can see the mismatch
between their tax base and the social entropies they are being
asked to repair. There simply isn't enough money; existing
public resources, as they are now employed, cannot possibly
solve the crime problem. But mayors and senators and police
chiefs must not say so out loud: too-disquieting implications
would follow. For if the authorities are incapable of restoring
public safety and personal security under the existing ground
rules, then obviously the ground rules must change, to give
private initiative greater scope. Self-help is the last refuge of
nonscoundrels.

Communities must, in short, organize more effectively to   50
protect themselves against predators. No doubt this means

encouraging properly qualified private citizens to possess and carry firearms legally. It is not morally tenable—nor, for that matter, is it even practical—to insist that police officers, few of whom are at a risk remotely as great as are the residents of many city neighborhoods, retain a monopoly on legal firearms. It is needless to fear giving honest men and women the training and equipment to make it possible for them to take back their own streets.

51   Over the long run, however, there is no substitute for addressing the root causes of crime—bad education and lack of job opportunities and the disintegration of families. Root causes are much out of fashion nowadays as explanations of criminal behavior, but fashionable or not, they are fundamental. *The root cause of crime is that for certain people, predation is a rational occupational choice.* Conventional crime-control measures, which by stiffening punishments or raising the probability of arrest aim to make crime pay less, cannot consistently affect the behavior of people who believe that their alternatives to crime will pay virtually nothing. Young men who did not learn basic literacy and numeracy skills before dropping out of their wretched public schools may not have been worth hiring at the minimum wage set by George Bush, let alone at the higher, indexed minimum wage that has recently been under discussion by the Clinton Administration. Most independent studies of the effects of raising minimum wages show a similar pattern of excluding the most vulnerable. This displacement, in turn, makes young men free, in the nihilistic, nothing-to-lose sense, to dedicate their lives to crime. Their legitimate opportunities, always precarious in a society where race and class still matter, often diminish to the point of being for all intents and purposes absent.

52   Unfortunately, many progressive policies work out in the same way as increases in the minimum wage—as taxes on employment. One example is the Administration's pending proposal to make employer-paid health insurance mandatory and universal. Whatever the undoubted benefits of the plan, a payroll tax is needed to make it work. Another example: in recent years the use of the "wrongful discharge" tort and other legal innovations has swept through the courts of more than half the states, bringing to an end the era of "employment at will," when employees (other than civil servants) without formal contracts—more than three quarters of the work force—could be fired for good reason, bad reason, or no reason at all. Most commentators celebrated the loss of the at-will rule. How

could one object to a new legal tenet that prohibited only arbitrary and oppressive behavior by employers?

But the costs of the rule are not negligible, only hidden. At-will employment meant that companies could get out of the relationship as easily as employees could. In a world where dismissals are expensive rather than cheap, and involve lawyers and the threat of lawsuits, rational employers must become more fastidious about whom they hire. By raising the costs of ending the relationship, one automatically raises the threshold of entry. The burdens of the rule fall unequally. Worst hit are entry-level applicants who have little or no employment history to show that they would be worth their pay. 53

Many other tax or regulatory schemes, in the words of Professor Walter Williams, of George Mason University, amount to sawing off the bottom rungs of the ladder of economic opportunity. By suppressing job creation and further diminishing legal employment opportunities for young men on the margin of the work force, such schemes amount to an indirect but unequivocal subsidy to crime. 54

The solution to the problem of crime lies in improving the chances of young men. Easier said than done, to be sure. No one has yet proposed a convincing program for checking all the dislocating forces that government assistance can set in motion. One relatively straightforward change would be reform of the educational system. Nothing guarantees prudent behavior like a sense of the future, and with average skills in reading, writing, and math, young people can realistically look forward to constructive employment and the straight life that steady work makes possible. 55

But firearms are nowhere near the root of the problem of violence. As long as people come in unlike sizes, shapes, ages, and temperaments, as long as they diverge in their taste for risk and their willingness and capacity to prey on other people or to defend themselves from predation, and above all as long as some people have little or nothing to lose by spending their lives in crime, dispositions to violence will persist. 56

This is what makes the case for the right to bear arms, not the Second Amendment. It is foolish to let anything ride on hopes for effective gun control. As long as crime pays as well as it does, we will have plenty of it, and honest folk must choose between being victims and defending themselves. 57

WHAT CAUSES CRIME?

Clarence Darrow

Address to the Prisoners in the Cook County Jail

Clarence Darrow (1857–1928) was the most famous U.S. law-yer of the early twentieth century. An eloquent speaker from Youngstown, Ohio, who practiced mostly in Chicago, Darrow defended Eugene V. Debs and other controversial labor leaders, Nathan Leopold and Richard Loeb (two notorious murderers), and John Scopes in the famous Monkey Trial of 1925. The fol-lowing is a transcript of a speech that Darrow delivered to pris-oners in Chicago in 1902.

1   If I looked at jails and crimes and prisoners in the way the ordinary person does, I should not speak on this subject to you. The reason I talk to you on the question of crime, its cause and cure, is that I really do not in the least believe in crime. There is no such thing as a crime as the word is gener-ally understood. I do not believe there is any sort of distinc-tion between the real moral conditions of the people in and out of jail. One is just as good as the other. The people here can no more help being here than the people outside can avoid being outside. I do not believe that people are in jail be-cause they deserve to be. They are in jail simply because they cannot avoid it on account of circumstances which are en-tirely beyond their control and for which they are in no way responsible.

2   I suppose a great many people on the outside would say I was doing you harm if they should hear what I say to you this afternoon, but you cannot be hurt a great deal anyway, so it will not matter. Good people outside would say that I was re-ally teaching you things that were calculated to injure society, but it's worth while now and then to hear something different from what you ordinarily get from preachers and the like. These will tell you that you should be good and then you will

get rich and be happy. Of course we know that people do not get rich by being good, and that is the reason why so many of you people try to get rich some other way, only you do not understand how to do it quite as well as the fellow outside.

There are people who think that everything in this world is an accident. But really there is no such thing as an accident. A great many folks admit that many of the people in jail ought to be there, and many who are outside ought to be in. I think none of them ought to be here. There ought to be no jails; and if it were not for the fact that people on the outside are so grasping and heartless in their dealings with the people on the inside, there would be no such institution as jails.

I do not want you to believe that I think all you people here are angels. I do not think that. You are people of all kinds, all of you doing the best you can—and that is evidently not very well. You are people of all kinds and conditions and under all circumstances. In one sense everybody is equally good and equally bad. We all do the best we can under the circumstances. But as to the exact things for which you are sent here, some of you are guilty and did the particular act because you needed the money. Some of you did it because you are in the habit of doing it, and some of you because you are born to it, and it comes to be as natural as it does, for instance, for me to be good.

Most of you probably have nothing against me, and most of you would treat me the same way as any other person would, probably better than some of the people on the outside would treat me, because you think I believe in you and they know I do not believe in them. While you would not have the least thing against me in the world, you might pick my pockets. I do not think all of you would, but I think some of you would. You would not have anything against me, but that's your profession, a few of you. Some of the rest of you, if my doors were unlocked, might come in if you saw anything you wanted—not out of any malice to me, but because that is your trade. There is no doubt there are quite a number of people in this jail who would pick my pockets. And still I know this—that when I get outside pretty nearly everybody picks my pocket. There may be some of you who would hold up a man on the street, if you did not happen to have something else to do, and needed the money; but when I want to light my house or my office the gas company holds me up. They charge me one dollar for something that is worth twenty-five cents. Still all these people are good people; they are pillars of society and support the churches, and they are respectable.

6   When I ride on the streetcars I am held up—I pay five cents
for a ride that is worth two and a half cents, simply because a
body of men have bribed the city council and the legislature,
so that all the rest of us have to pay tribute to them.

7   If I do not want to fall into the clutches of the gas trust and
choose to burn oil instead of gas, then good Mr. Rockefeller
holds me up, and he uses a certain portion of his money to
build universities and support churches which are engaged in
telling us how to be good.

8   Some of you are here for obtaining property under false
pretenses—yet I pick up a great Sunday paper and read the
advertisements of a merchant prince—"Shirtwaists for 39
cents, marked down from $3.00."

9   When I read the advertisements in the paper I see they are
all lies. When I want to get out and find a place to stand anywhere on the face of the earth, I find that it has all been taken
up long ago before I came here, and before you came here,
and somebody says, "Get off, swim into the lake, fly into the
air; go anywhere, but get off." That is because these people
have the police and they have the jails and the judges and the
lawyers and the soldiers and all the rest of them to take care
of the earth and drive everybody off that comes in their way.

10   A great many people will tell you that all this is true, but
that it does not excuse you. These facts do not excuse some fellow who reaches into my pocket and takes out a five-dollar bill.
The fact that the gas company bribes the members of the legislature from year to year, and fixes the law, so that all you people are compelled to be "fleeced" whenever you deal with
them; the fact that the streetcar companies and the gas companies have control of the streets; and the fact that the landlords
own all the earth—this, they say, has nothing to do with you.

11   Let us see whether there is any connection between the
crimes of the respectable classes and your presence in the jail.
Many of you people are in jail because you have really committed burglary; many of you, because you have stolen something. In the meaning of the law, you have taken some other
person's property. Some of you have entered a store and carried off a pair of shoes because you did not have the price.
Possibly some of you have committed murder. I cannot tell
what all of you did. There are a great many people here who
have done some of these things who really do not know themselves why they did them. I think I know why you did them—
every one of you; you did these things because you were
bound to do them. It looked to you at the time as if you had a
chance to do them or not, as you saw fit; but still, after all,

you had no choice. There may be people here who had some money in their pockets and who still went out and got some more money in a way society forbids. Now, you may not yourselves see exactly why it was you did this thing, but if you look at the question deeply enough and carefully enough you will see that there were circumstances that drove you to do exactly the thing which you did. You could not help it any more than we outside can help taking the positions that we take. The reformers who tell you to be good and you will be happy, and the people on the outside who have property to protect— they think that the only way to do it is by building jails and locking you up in cells on weekdays and praying for you Sundays.

I think that all of this has nothing whatever to do with right conduct. I think it is very easily seen what has to do with right conduct. Some so-called criminals—and I will use this word because it is handy, it means nothing to me—I speak of the criminals who get caught as distinguished from the criminals who catch them—some of these so-called criminals are in jail for their first offenses, but nine tenths of you are in jail because you did not have a good lawyer and, of course, you did not have a good lawyer because you did not have enough money to pay a good lawyer. There is no very great danger of a rich man going to jail. 12

Some of you may be here for the first time. If we would open the doors and let you out, and leave the laws as they are today, some of you would be back tomorrow. This is about as good a place as you can get anyway. There are many people here who are so in the habit of coming that they would not know where else to go. There are people who are born with the tendency to break into jail every chance they get, and they cannot avoid it. You cannot figure out your life and see why it was, but still there is a reason for it; and if we were all wise and knew all the facts, we could figure it out. 13

In the first place, there are a good many more people who go to jail in the wintertime than in the summer. Why is this? Is it because people are more wicked in winter? No, it is because the coal trust begins to get in its grip in the winter. A few gentlemen take possession of the coal, and unless the people will pay seven or eight dollars a ton for something that is worth three dollars, they will have to freeze. Then there is nothing to do but to break into jail, and so there are many more in jail in the winter than in summer. It costs more for gas in the winter because the nights are longer, and people go to jail to save gas bills. The jails are electric-lighted. You may 14 not know it, but these economic laws are working all the time, whether we know it or do not know it.

15   There are more people who go to jail in hard times than in good times—few people, comparatively, go to jail except when they are hard up. They go to jail because they have no other place to go. They may not know why, but it is true all the same. People are not more wicked in hard times. That is not the reason. The fact is true all over the world that in hard times more people go to jail than in good times, and in winter more people go to jail than in summer. Of course it is pretty hard times for people who go to jail at any time. The people who go to jail are almost always poor people—people who have no other place to live, first and last. When times are hard, then you find large numbers of people who go to jail who would not otherwise be in jail.

16   Long ago, Mr. Buckle, who was a great philosopher and historian, collected facts, and he showed that the number of people who are arrested increased just as the price of food increased. When they put up the price of gas ten cents a thousand, I do not know who will go to jail, but I do know that a certain number of people will go. When the meat combine raises the price of beef, I do not know who is going to jail, but I know that a large number of people are bound to go. Whenever the Standard Oil Company raises the price of oil, I know that a certain number of girls who are seamstresses, and who work night after night long hours for somebody else, will be compelled to go out on the streets and ply another trade, and I know that Mr. Rockefeller and his associates are responsible and not the poor girls in the jails.

17   First and last, people are sent to jail because they are poor. Sometimes, as I say, you may not need money at the particular time, but you wish to have thrifty forehanded habits, and do not always wait until you are in absolute want. Some of you people are perhaps plying the trade, the profession, which is called burglary. No man in his right senses will go into a strange house in the dead of night and prowl around with a dark lantern through unfamiliar rooms and take chances of his life, if he has plenty of the good things of the world in his own home. You would not take any such chances as that. If a man had clothes in his clothespress and beefsteak in his pantry and money in the bank, he would not navigate around nights in houses where he knows nothing about the premises whatever. It always requires experience and education for this profession, and people who fit themselves for it are no more to blame than I am for being a lawyer. A man

would not hold up another man on the street if he had plenty of money in his own pocket. He might do it if he had one dollar or two dollars, but he wouldn't if he had as much money as Mr. Rockefeller has. Mr. Rockefeller has a great deal better hold-up game than that.

The more that is taken from the poor by the rich, who have   18
the chance to take it, the more poor people there are who are compelled to resort to these means for a livelihood. They may not understand it, they may not think so at once, but after all they are driven into that line of employment.

There is a bill before the legislature of this state to punish   19
kidnaping children with death. We have wise members of the legislature. They know the gas trust when they see it and they always see it—they can furnish light enough to be seen; and this legislature thinks it is going to stop kidnaping children by making a law punishing kidnapers of children with death. I don't believe in kidnaping children, but the legislature is all wrong. Kidnaping children is not a crime, it is a profession. It has been developed with the times. It has been developed with our modern industrial conditions. There are many ways of making money—many new ways that our ancestors knew nothing about. Our ancestors knew nothing about a billion-dollar trust; and here comes some poor fellow who has no other trade and he discovers the profession of kidnaping children.

This crime is born, not because people are bad; people   20
don't kidnap other people's children because they want the children or because they are devilish, but because they see a chance to get some money out of it. You cannot cure this crime by passing a law punishing by death kidnapers of children. There is one way to cure it. There is one way to cure all these offenses, and that is to give the people a chance to live. There is no other way, and there never was any other way since the world began; and the world is so blind and stupid that it will not see. If every man and woman and child in the world had a chance to make a decent, fair, honest living, there would be no jails and no lawyers and no courts. There might be some persons here or there with some peculiar formation of their brain, like Rockefeller, who would do these things simply to be doing them; but they would be very, very few, and those should be sent to a hospital and treated, and not sent to jail; and they would entirely disappear in the second generation, or at least in the third generation.

I am not talking pure theory. I will just give you two or   21
three illustrations.

22   The English people once punished criminals by sending them away. They would load them on a ship and export them to Australia. England was owned by lords and nobles and rich people. They owned the whole earth over there, and the other people had to stay in the streets. They could not get a decent living. They used to take their criminals and send them to Australia—I mean the class of criminals who got caught. When these criminals got over there, and nobody else had come, they had the whole continent to run over, and so they could raise sheep and furnish their own meat, which is easier than stealing it. These criminals then became decent, respectable people because they had a chance to live. They did not commit any crimes. They were just like the English people who sent them there, only better. And in the second generation the descendants of those criminals were as good and respectable a class of people as there were on the face of the earth, and then they began building churches and jails themselves.

23   A portion of this country was settled in the same way, landing prisoners down on the southern coast; but when they got here and had a whole continent to run over and plenty of chances to make a living, they became respectable citizens, making their own living just like any other citizen in the world. But finally the descendants of the English aristocracy who sent the people over to Australia found out they were getting rich, and so they went over to get possession of the earth as they always do, and they organized land syndicates and got control of the land and ores, and then they had just as many criminals in Australia as they did in England. It was not because the world had grown bad; it was because the earth had been taken away from the people.

24   Some of you people have lived in the country. It's prettier than it is here. And if you have ever lived on a farm you understand that if you put a lot of cattle in a field, when the pasture is short they will jump over the fence; but put them in a good field where there is plenty of pasture, and they will be law-abiding cattle to the end of time. The human animal is just like the rest of the animals, only a little more so. The same thing that governs in the one governs in the other.

25   Everybody makes his living along the lines of least resistance. A wise man who comes into a country early sees a great undeveloped land. For instance, our rich men twenty-five years ago saw that Chicago was small and knew a lot of people would come here and settle, and they readily saw that if they had all the land around here it would be worth a good deal, so they grabbed the land. You cannot be a landlord be-

cause somebody has got it all. You must find some other calling. In England and Ireland and Scotland less than five per
cent own all the land there is, and the people are bound 'to
stay there on any kind of terms the landlords give. They must
live the best they can, so they develop all these various professions—burglary, picking pockets, and the like.

Again, people find all sorts of ways of getting rich. These   26
are diseases like everything else. You look at people getting
rich, organizing trusts and making a million dollars, and
somebody gets the disease and he starts out. He catches it just
as a man catches the mumps or the measles; he is not to
blame, it is in the air. You will find men speculating beyond
their means, because the mania of money-getting is taking
possession of them. It is simply a disease—nothing more,
nothing less. You cannot avoid catching it; but the fellows
who have control of the earth have the advantage of you. See
what the law is: when these men get control of things, they
make the laws. They do not make the laws to protect anybody; courts are not instruments of justice. When your case
gets into court it will make little difference whether you are
guilty or innocent, but it's better if you have a smart lawyer.
And you cannot have a smart lawyer unless you have money.
First and last it's a question of money. Those men who own
the earth make the laws to protect what they have. They fix
up a sort of fence or pen around what they have, and they fix
the law so the fellow on the outside cannot get in. The laws
are really organized for the protection of the men who rule
the world. They were never organized or enforced to do justice. We have no system for doing justice, not the slightest in
the world.

Let me illustrate: Take the poorest person in this room. If   27
the community had provided a system of doing justice, the
poorest person in this room would have as good a lawyer as
the richest, would he not? When you went into court you
would have just as long a trial and just as fair a trial as the
richest person in Chicago. Your case would not be tried in fifteen or twenty minutes, whereas it would take fifteen days to
get through with a rich man's case.

Then if you were rich and were beaten, your case would be   28
taken to the Appellate Court. A poor man cannot take his case
to the Appellate Court; he has not the price. And then to the
Supreme Court. And if he were beaten there he might perhaps go to the United States Supreme Court. And he might
die of old age before he got into jail. If you are poor, it's a
quick job. You are almost known to be guilty, else you would

not be there. Why should anyone be in the criminal court if he were not guilty? He would not be there if he could be anywhere else. The officials have no time to look after all these cases. The people who are on the outside, who are running banks and building churches and making jails, they have no time to examine 600 or 700 prisoners each year to see whether they are guilty or innocent. If the courts were organized to promote justice the people would elect somebody to defend all these criminals, somebody as smart as the prosecutor—and give him as many detectives and as many assistants to help, and pay as much money to defend you as to prosecute you. We have a very able man for state's attorney, and he has many assistants, detectives, and policemen without end, and judges to hear the cases—everything handy.

29   Most all of our criminal code consists in offenses against property. People are sent to jail because they have committed a crime against property. It is of very little consequence whether one hundred people more or less go to jail who ought not to go—you must protect property, because in this world property is of more importance than anything else.

30   How is it done? These people who have property fix it so they can protect what they have. When somebody commits a crime it does not follow that he has done something that is morally wrong. The man on the outside who has committed no crime may have done something. For instance: to take all the coal in the United States and raise the price two dollars or three dollars when there is no need of it, and thus kill thousands of babies and send thousands of people to the poorhouse and tens of thousands to jail, as is done every year in the United States—this is a greater crime than all the people in our jails ever committed; but the law does not punish it. Why? Because the fellows who control the earth make the laws. If you and I had the making of the laws, the first thing we would do would be to punish the fellow who gets control of the earth. Nature put this coal in the ground for me as well as for them and nature made the prairies up here to raise wheat for me as well as for them, and then the great railroad companies came along and fenced it up.

31   Most all of the crimes for which we are punished are property crimes. There are a few personal crimes, like murder— but they are very few. The crimes committed are mostly those against property. If this punishment is right the criminals must have a lot of property. How much money is there in this crowd? And yet you are all here for crimes against property. The people up and down the Lake Shore have not committed

crime; still they have so much property they don't know what to do with it. It is perfectly plain why these people have not committed crimes against property; they make the laws and therefore do not need to break them. And in order for you to get some property you are obliged to break the rules of the game. I don't know but what some of you may have had a very nice chance to get rich by carrying a hod for one dollar a day, twelve hours. Instead of taking that nice, easy profession, you are a burglar. If you had been given a chance to be a banker you would rather follow that. Some of you may have had a chance to work as a switchman on a railroad where you know, according to statistics, that you cannot live and keep all your limbs more than seven years, and you can get fifty dollars or seventy-five dollars a month for taking your lives in your hands; and instead of taking that lucrative position you chose to be a sneak thief, or something like that. Some of you made that sort of choice. I don't know which I would take if I was reduced to this choice. I have an easier choice.

I will guarantee to take from this jail, or any jail in the 32 world, five hundred men who have been the worst criminals and law-breakers who ever got into jail, and I will go down to our lowest streets and take five hundred of the most abandoned prostitutes, and go out somewhere where there is plenty of land, and will give them a chance to make a living, and they will be as good people as the average in the community.

There is one remedy for the sort of condition we see here. 33 The world never finds it out, or when it does find it out it does not enforce it. You may pass a law punishing every person with death for burglary, and it will make no difference. Men will commit it just the same. In England there was a time when one hundred different offenses were punishable with death, and it made no difference. The English people strangely found out that so fast as they repealed the severe penalties and so fast as they did away with punishing men by death, crime decreased instead of increased; that the smaller the penalty the fewer the crimes.

Hanging men in our county jails does not prevent murder. 34 It makes murderers.

And this has been the history of the world. It's easy to see 35 how to do away with what we call crime. It is not so easy to do it. I will tell you how to do it. It can be done by giving the people a chance to live—by destroying special privileges. So long as big criminals can get the coal fields, so long as the big criminals have control of the city council and get the public streets for streetcars and gas rights—this is bound to send thousands of poor people to jail. So long as men are allowed to monopolize all the earth, and compel others to live on such terms as these men see fit to make, then you are bound to get into jail.

36   The only way in the world to abolish crime and criminals is to abolish the big ones and the little ones together. Make fair conditions of life. Give men a chance to live. Abolish the right of private ownership of land, abolish monopoly, make the world partners in production, partners in the good things of life. Nobody would steal if he could get something of his own some easier way. Nobody will commit burglary when he has a house full. No girl will go out on the streets when she has a comfortable place at home. The man who owns a sweatshop or a department store may not be to blame himself for the condition of his girls, but when he pays them five dollars, three dollars, and two dollars a week, I wonder where he thinks they will get the rest of their money to live. The only way to cure these conditions is by equality. There should be no jails. They do not accomplish what they pretend to accomplish. If you would wipe them out there would be no more criminals than now. They terrorize nobody. They are a blot upon any civilization, and a jail is an evidence of the lack of charity of the people on the outside who make the jails and fill them with the victims of their greed.

Richard J. Herrnstein and James Q. Wilson
Are Criminals Made or Born?

Richard J. Herrnstein was a professor of psychology at Harvard before he passed away in 1994. His colleague James Wilson, a professor of government at Harvard who is now retired, also specializes in criminology. Together they published the book Crime and Human Nature *(1985); the following essay was adapted from that book and published in* The New York Times Magazine *in 1985.*

1   A revolution in our understanding of crime is quietly overthrowing some established doctrines. Until recently, criminologists looked for the causes of crime almost entirely in the

offenders' social circumstances. There seemed to be no short-age of circumstances to blame: weakened, chaotic or broken families, ineffective schools, antisocial gangs, racism, pov-erty, unemployment. Criminologists took seriously, more so than many other students of social behavior, the famous dic-tum of the French sociologist Emile Durkheim: Social facts must have social explanations. The sociological theory of crime had the unquestioned support of prominent editorial-ists, commentators, politicians and most thoughtful people.

Today, many learned journals and scholarly works draw a different picture. Sociological factors have not been aban-doned, but increasingly it is becoming clear to many scholars that crime is the outcome of an interaction between social factors and certain biological factors, particularly for the of-fenders who, by repeated crimes, have made public places dangerous. The idea is still controversial, but increasingly, to the old question "Are criminals born or made?" the answer seems to be: both. The causes of crime lie in a combination of predisposing biological traits channeled by social circum-stance into criminal behavior. The traits alone do not inevita-bly lead to crime; the circumstances do not make criminals of everyone; but together they create a population responsible for a large fraction of America's problem of crime in the streets.

Evidence that criminal behavior has deeper roots than so-cial circumstances has always been right at hand, but social science has, until recent years, overlooked its implications. As far as the records show, crime everywhere and throughout history is disproportionately a young man's pursuit. Whether men are 20 or more times as likely to be arrested as women, as is the case in Malawi or Brunei, or only four to six times as likely, as in the United States or France, the sex difference in crime statistics is universal. Similarly, 18-year-olds may sometimes be four times as likely to be criminal as 40-year-olds, while at other times only twice as likely. In the United States, more than half of all arrests for serious property crimes are of 20-year-olds or younger. Nowhere have older persons been as criminal as younger ones.

It is easy to imagine purely social explanations for the ef-fects of age and sex on crime. Boys in many societies are trained by their parents and the society itself to play more roughly and aggressively than girls. Boys are expected to fight back, not to cry, and to play to win. Likewise, boys in many cultures are denied adult responsibilities, kept in a state of prolonged dependence and confined too long in schools that many of them find unrewarding. For a long time, these factors were thought to be the whole story.

5   Ultimately, however, the very universality of the age and sex differences in crime have alerted some social scientists to the implausibility of a theory that does not look beyond the accidents of particular societies. If cultures as different as Japan's and Sweden's, England's and Mexico's, have sex and age differences in crime, then perhaps we should have suspected from the start that there was something more fundamental going on than parents happening to decide to raise their boys and girls differently. What is it about boys, girls and their parents, in societies of all sorts, that leads them to emphasize, rather than overcome, sex differences? Moreover, even if we believed that every society has arbitrarily decided to inculcate aggressiveness in males, there would still be the greater criminality among *young* males to explain. After all, in some cultures, young boys are not denied adult responsibilities but are kept out of school, put to work tilling the land and made to accept obligations to the society.

6   But it is no longer necessary to approach questions about the sources of criminal behavior merely with argument and supposition. There is evidence. Much crime, it is agreed, has an aggressive component, and Eleanor Emmons Maccoby, a professor of psychology at Stanford University, and Carol Nagy Jacklin, a psychologist now at the University of Southern California, after reviewing the evidence on sex differences in aggression, concluded that it has a foundation that is at least in part biological. Only that conclusion can be drawn, they said, from data that show that the average man is more aggressive than the average woman in all known societies, that the sex difference is present in infancy well before evidence of sex-role socialization by adults, that similar sex differences turn up in many of our biological relatives—monkeys and apes. Human aggression has been directly tied to sex hormones, particularly male sex hormones, in experiments on athletes engaging in competitive sports and on prisoners known for violent or domineering behavior. No single line of evidence is decisive and each can be challenged, but all together they convinced Drs. Maccoby and Jacklin, as well as most specialists on the biology of sex differences, that the sexual conventions that assign males the aggressive roles have biological roots.

7   That is also the conclusion of most researchers about the developmental forces that make adolescence and young adulthood a time of risk for criminal and other nonconven-

tional behavior. This is when powerful new drives awaken, leading to frustrations that foster behavior unchecked by the internalized prohibitions of adulthood. The result is usually just youthful rowdiness, but, in a minority of cases, it passes over the line into crime.

The most compelling evidence of biological factors for criminality comes from two studies—one of twins, the other of adopted boys. Since the 1920's it has been understood that twins may develop from a single fertilized egg, resulting in identical genetic endowments—identical twins—or from a pair of separately fertilized eggs that have about half their genes in common—fraternal twins. A standard procedure for estimating how important genes are to a trait is to compare the similarity between identical twins with that between fraternal twins. When identical twins are clearly more similar in a trait than fraternal twins, the trait probably has high heritability. 8

There have been about a dozen studies of criminality using twins. More than 1,500 pairs of twins have been studied in the United States, the Scandinavian countries, Japan, West Germany, Britain and elsewhere, and the result is qualitatively the same everywhere. Identical twins are more likely to have similar criminal records than fraternal twins. For example, the late Karl O. Christiansen, a Danish criminologist, using the Danish Twin Register, searched police, court and prison records for entries regarding twins born in a certain region of Denmark between 1881 and 1910. When an identical twin had a criminal record, Christiansen found, his or her co-twin was more than twice as likely to have one also than when a fraternal twin had a criminal record. 9

In the United States, a similar result has recently been reported by David Rowe, a psychologist at the University of Oklahoma, using questionnaires instead of official records to measure criminality. Twins in high school in almost all the school districts of Ohio received questionnaires by mail, with a promise of confidentiality as well as a small payment if the questionnaires were filled out and returned. The twins were asked about their activities, including their delinquent behavior, about their friends, and about their co-twins. The identical twins were more similar in delinquency than the fraternal twins. In addition, the twins who shared more activities with each other were no more likely to be similar in delinquency than those who shared fewer activities. 10

No single method of inquiry should be regarded as conclusive. But essentially the same results are found in studies of 11 adopted children. The idea behind such studies is to find a sample of children adopted early in life, cases in which the criminal histories of both adopting and biological parents are known. Then, as the children grow up, researchers can discover how predictive of their criminality are the family histories of their adopting and biological parents. Recent studies show that the biological family history contributes substantially to the adoptees' likelihood of breaking the law.

12   For example, Sarnoff Mednick, a psychologist at the University of Southern California, and his associates in the United States and Denmark have followed a sample of several thousand boys adopted in Denmark between 1927 and 1947. Boys with criminal biological parents and noncriminal adopting parents were more likely to have criminal records than those with noncriminal biological parents and criminal adopting parents. The more criminal convictions a boy's natural parents had, the greater the risk of criminality for boys being raised by adopting parents who had no records. The risk was unrelated to whether the boy or his adopting parents knew about the natural parents' criminal records, whether the natural parents committed their crimes before or after the boy was given up for adoption, or whether the boy was adopted immediately after birth or a year or two later. The results of this study have been confirmed in Swedish and American samples of adopted children.

13   Because of studies like these, many sociologists and criminologists now accept the existence of genetic factors contributing to criminality. When there is disagreement, it is about how large the genetic contribution to crime is and about how the criminality of biological parents is transmitted to their children.

14   Both the twin and adoption studies show that genetic contributions are not alone responsible for crime—there is, for example, some increase in criminality among boys if their adopted fathers are criminal even when their biological parents are not, and not every co-twin of a criminal identical twin becomes criminal himself. Although it appears, on average, to be substantial, the precise size of the genetic contribution to crime is probably unknowable, particularly since the measures of criminality itself are now so crude.

15   We have a bit more to go on with respect to the link that transmits a predisposition toward crime from parents to children. No one believes there are "crime genes," but there are two major attributes that have, to some degree, a heritable

base and that appear to influence criminal behavior. These are intelligence and temperament. Hundreds of studies have found that the more genes people share, the more likely they are to resemble each other intellectually and temperamentally.

Starting with studies in the 1930's, the average offender in 16 broad samples has consistently scored 91 to 93 on I.Q. tests for which the general population's average is 100. The typical offender does worse on the verbal items of intelligence tests than on the nonverbal items but is usually below average on both.

Criminologists have long known about the correlation 17 between criminal behavior and I.Q., but many of them have discounted it for various reasons. Some have suggested that the correlation can be explained away by the association between low socioeconomic status and crime, on the one hand, and that between low I.Q. and low socioeconomic status, on the other. These criminologists say it is low socioeconomic status, rather than low I.Q., that fosters crime. Others have questioned whether I.Q. tests really measure intelligence for the populations that are at greater risk for breaking the law. The low scores of offenders, the argument goes, betray a culturally deprived background or alienation from our society's values rather than low intelligence. Finally, it is often noted that the offenders in some studies have been caught for their crimes. Perhaps the ones who got away have higher I.Q.s.

But these objections have proved to be less telling than 18 they once seemed to be. There are, for example, many poor law-abiding people living in deprived environments, and one of their more salient characteristics is that they have higher I.Q. scores than those in the same environment who break the law.

Then, too, it is a common misconception that I.Q. tests are 19 invalid for people from disadvantaged backgrounds. If what is implied by this criticism is that scores predict academic potential or job performance differently for different groups, then the criticism is wrong. A comprehensive recent survey sponsored by the National Academy of Sciences concluded that "tests predict about as well for one group as for another." And that some highly intelligent criminals may well be good at eluding capture is fully consistent with the belief that offenders, in general, have lower scores than nonoffenders.

If I.Q. and criminality are linked, what may explain the 20 link? There are several possibilities. One is that low scores on I.Q. tests signify greater difficulty in grasping the likely consequences of action or in learning the meaning and significance of moral codes. Another is that low scores, especially on the verbal component of the tests, mean trouble in school, which leads to frustration, thence to resentment, anger and delinquency. Still another is that persons who are not as skillful as others in expressing themselves verbally may find it more rewarding to express themselves in ways in which they will do better, such as physical threat or force.

21   For some repeat offenders, the predisposition to criminality may be more a matter of temperament than intelligence. Impulsiveness, insensitivity to social mores, a lack of deep and enduring emotional attachments to others and an appetite for danger are among the temperamental characteristics of high-rate offenders. Temperament is, to a degree, heritable, though not as much so as intelligence. All parents know that their children, shortly after birth, begin to exhibit certain characteristic ways of behaving—they are placid or fussy, shy or bold. Some of the traits endure, among them aggressiveness and hyperactivity, although they change in form as the child develops. As the child grows up, these traits, among others, may gradually unfold into a disposition toward unconventional, defiant or antisocial behavior.

22   Lee Robins, a sociologist at Washington University School of Medicine in St. Louis, reconstructed 30 years of the lives of more than 500 children who were patients in the 1920's at a child guidance clinic in St. Louis. She was interested in the early precursors of chronic sociopathy, a condition of antisocial personality that often includes criminal behavior as one of its symptoms. Adult sociopaths in her sample who did not suffer from psychosis, mental retardation or addiction, were, without exception, antisocial before they were 18. More than half of the male sociopaths had serious symptoms before they were 11. The main childhood precursors were truancy, poor school performance, theft, running away, recklessness, slovenliness, impulsiveness and guiltlessness. The more symptoms in childhood, the greater the risk of sociopathy in adulthood.

23   Other studies confirm and extend Dr. Robins's conclusions. For example, two psychologists, John J. Conger of the University of Colorado and Wilbur Miller of Drake University in Des Moines, searching back over the histories of a sample of delinquent boys in Denver, found that "by the end of the third grade, future delinquents were already seen by their teachers as more poorly adapted than their classmates. They appeared

to have less regard for the rights and feelings of their peers; less awareness of the need to accept responsibility for their obligations, both as individuals and as members of a group, and poorer attitudes toward authority."

Traits that foreshadow serious, recurrent criminal behav- 24 ior have been traced all the way back to behavior patterns such as hyperactivity and unusual fussiness, and neurological signs such as atypical brain waves or reflexes. In at least a minority of cases, these are detectable in the first few years of life. Some of the characteristics are sex-linked. There is evidence that newborn females are more likely than newborn males to smile, to cling to their mothers, to be receptive to touching and talking, to be sensitive to certain stimuli, such as being touched by a cloth, and to have less upper-body strength. Mothers certainly treat girls and boys differently, but the differences are not simply a matter of the mother's choice—female babies are more responsive than male babies to precisely the kind of treatment that is regarded as "feminine." When adults are asked to play with infants, they play with them in ways they think are appropriate to the infants' sexes. But there is also some evidence that when the sex of the infant is concealed, the behavior of the adults is influenced by the conduct of the child.

Premature infants or those born with low birth weights 25 have a special problem. These children are vulnerable to any adverse circumstances in their environment—including child abuse—that may foster crime. Although nurturing parents can compensate for adversity, cold or inconsistent parents may exacerbate it. Prematurity and low birth weight may result from poor prenatal care, a bad diet or excessive use of alcohol or drugs. Whether the care is due to poverty, ignorance or anything else, here we see criminality arising from biological, though not necessarily genetic, factors. It is now known that these babies are more likely than normal babies to be the victims of child abuse.

We do not mean to blame child abuse on the victim by say- 26 ing that premature and low-birth-weight infants are more difficult to care for and thus place a great strain on the parents. But unless parents are emotionally prepared for the task of caring for such children, they may vent their frustration at the infant's unresponsiveness by hitting or neglecting it. Whatever it is in parent and child that leads to prematurity or low birth weight is compounded by the subsequent interaction between them. Similarly, children with low I.Q.s may have difficulty in understanding rules, but if their parents also have poor verbal skills, they may have difficulty in communicating rules, and so each party to the conflict exacerbates the defects of the other.

27   The statement that biology plays a role in explaining human behavior, especially criminal behavior, sometimes elicits a powerful political or ideological reaction. Fearful that what is being proposed is a crude biological determinism, some critics deny the evidence while others wish the evidence to be confined to scientific journals. Scientists who have merely proposed studying the possible effects of chromosomal abnormalities on behavior have been ruthlessly attacked by other scientists, as have those who have made public the voluminous data showing the heritability of intelligence and temperament.

28   Some people worry that any claim that biological factors influence criminality is tantamount to saying that the higher crime rate of black compared to white Americans has a genetic basis. But no responsible work in the field leads to any such conclusion. The data show that of all the reasons people vary in their crime rates, race is far less important than age, sex, intelligence and the other individual factors that vary within races. Any study of the causes of crime must therefore first consider the individual factors. Differences among races may have many explanations, most of them having nothing to do with biology.

29   The intense reaction to the study of biological factors in crime, we believe, is utterly misguided. In fact, these discoveries, far from implying that "criminals are born" and should be locked up forever, suggest new and imaginative ways of reducing criminality by benign treatment. The opportunity we have is precisely analogous to that which we had when the biological bases of other disorders were established. Mental as well as physical illness—alcoholism, learning disabilities of various sorts, and perhaps even susceptibilies to drug addiction—now seem to have genetic components. In each case, new understanding energized the search for treatment and gave it new direction. Now we know that many forms of depression can be successfully treated with drugs; in time we may learn the same of Alzheimer's disease. Alcoholics are helped when they understand that some persons, because of their predisposition toward addiction to alcohol, should probably never consume it at all. A chemical treatment of the predisposition is a realistic possibility. Certain types of slow

learners can already be helped by special programs. In time, others will be also.

Crime, admittedly, may be a more difficult program. So   30 many different acts are criminal that it is only with considerable poetic license that we can speak of "criminality" at all. The bank teller who embezzles $500 to pay off a gambling debt is not engaging in the same behavior as a person who takes $500 from a liquor store at the point of a gun or one who causes $500 worth of damage by drunkenly driving his car into a parked vehicle. Moreover, crime, unlike alcoholism or dyslexia, exposes a person to the formal condemnation of society and the possibility of imprisonment. We naturally and rightly worry about treating all "criminals" alike, or stigmatizing persons whom we think might become criminal by placing them in special programs designed to prevent criminality.

But these problems are not insurmountable barriers to   31 better ways of thinking about crime prevention. Though criminals are of all sorts, we know that a very small fraction of all young males commit so large a fraction of serious street crime that we can properly blame these chronic offenders for most such crime. We also know that chronic offenders typically begin their misconduct at an early age. Early family and preschool programs may be far better repositories for the crime-prevention dollar than rehabilitation programs aimed—usually futilely—at the 19- or 20-year-old veteran offender. Prevention programs risk stigmatizing children, but this may be less of a risk than is neglect. If stigma were a problem to be avoided at all costs, we would have to dismantle most special-needs education programs.

Having said all this, we must acknowledge that there is at   32 present little hard evidence that we know how to inhibit the development of delinquent tendencies in children. There are some leads, such as family training programs of the sort pioneered at the Oregon Social Learning Center, where parents are taught how to use small rewards and penalties to alter the behavior of misbehaving children. There is also evidence from David Weikart and Lawrence Schweinhart of the High/Scope Educational Research Foundation at Ypsilanti, Mich., that preschool education programs akin to Project Head Start may reduce later delinquency. There is nothing yet to build a national policy on, but there are ideas worth exploring by carefully repeating and refining these pioneering experimental efforts.

33   Above all, there is a case for redirecting research into the causes of crime in ways that take into account the interaction of biological and social factors. Some scholars, such as the criminologist Marvin E. Wolfgang and his colleagues at the University of Pennsylvania, are already exploring these issues by analyzing social and biological information from large groups as they age from infancy to adulthood and linking the data to criminal behavior. But much more needs to be done.

34   It took years of patiently following the life histories of many men and women to establish the linkages between smoking or diet and disease; it will also take years to unravel the complex and subtle ways in which intelligence, temperament, hormonal levels and other traits combine with family circumstances and later experiences in school and elsewhere to produce human character.

Dorothy Nelkin and M. Susan Lindee
Elvis' DNA: The Gene as a Cultural Icon

Dorothy Nelkin teaches sociology and law at New York University, and M. Susan Lindee is a historian of science at the University of Pennsylvania. The following article, adapted from their book The DNA Mystique: The Gene as a Cultural Icon *(1995), was published in* The Humanist *in the spring of 1995. The article has been edited slightly; omissions are indicated with ellipses.*

1   In popular culture, Elvis Presley has become a genetic construct, driven by his genes to his unlikely destiny. In the 1985 biography *Elvis and Gladys*, for example, Elaine Dundy attributed Presley's success to the genetic characteristics of his mother's multiethnic family. "Genetically speaking," she wrote, "what produced Elvis was quite a mixture." To his "French Norman blood was added Scots-Irish blood," as well as "the Indian strain supplying the mystery and the Jewish strain supplying spectacular showmanship." All this combined with his "circumstances, social conditioning, and reli-

gious upbringing... [produced] the enigma that was Elvis."
Dundy traced Elvis' musical talents to his father (who "had a
very good voice") as well as his mother (who had "the instincts of a performer"). His parents provided a musical environment, Dundy noted, but "even without it, one wonders if
Elvis, with his biological musical equipment, would not still
have become a virtuoso."

Another Elvis biographer, Albert Goldman, focused on his   2
subject's "bad" genes, describing him in *Elvis* as "the victim of
a fatal hereditary disposition." Using language reminiscent of
the stories of the Jukes and Kallikaks, the degenerate families
of the early eugenics movement, Goldman attributed Elvis'
character to ancestors who constituted "a distinctive breed of
southern yeomanry" commonly known as hillbillies. A genealogy research organization, Goldman said, had traced Presley's lineage back nine generations to a nineteenth-century
"coward, deserter, and bigamist." In Goldman's narrative, this
genetic heritage explained Elvis' downfall: his addiction to
drugs and alcohol, his emotional disorders, and his premature
death were all in his genes. His fate was a readout of his DNA.

The idea that "good" and "bad" character traits (and desti-   3
nies) are the consequence of "good" and "bad" genes appears
in a wide range of popular sources. In these works, the gene is
described in moral terms and seems to dictate the actions of
criminals, celebrities, political leaders, and literary and scientific figures. Films present stories of "tainted blood" and "born
achievers," of success and failure, of kindness and cruelty, all
written in the genes. The most complicated human traits are
also blamed on DNA. Media stories (for example, Alan Wex-
ler's article in the August 13, 1993, *Newsday*) feature various
jokes about Republican genes, MBA genes, lawyer genes, and
public-interest genes. Human behaviors linked to DNA in
these accounts range from the trivial—a preference for flashy
belt buckles—to the tragic—a desire to murder children.

Such popular constructions of behavior draw on the   4
increasing public legitimacy of the scientific field of behavioral genetics. Behavioral geneticists have been able to
demonstrate that some relatively complicated behaviors—
certainly in experimental animals and possibly in human
beings—are genetically determined. Studies of animals reveal
the genetic bases of survival instincts, mating rituals, and certain aspects of learning and memory. Border collies herd
sheep in a unique characteristic way whether they have been
trained or not, even if they have never seen sheep before.
Some behaviors associated with particular hormones have

been indirectly linked to genes: both aggressive and nurturing behaviors—in mice—can be manipulated with adjustments of hormone levels. Though such research highlights the biological events involved in some behaviors, it does not support the popular idea that genes determine human personality traits or such complex phenomena as success, failure, political leanings, or criminality.

5　　Nonetheless, the claims that genes control human behaviors have received significant support from some behavioral geneticists who have positioned themselves as public scientists. Among the most cited and widely promoted scientists in this field is University of Minnesota psychologist Thomas Bouchard. Bouchard, a student of Arthur Jensen, has studied identical twins reared apart in order to determine the relationship between genetics and IQ, personality, and behavior. Bouchard's work has attracted significant popular attention since he began promoting his findings in 1982, but it has been controversial in the scientific community. Identical twins growing up in different families have long been seen as "natural experiments" in human genetics, even by the eugenicists of the 1920s. Bouchard, like others before him, has concluded that all similarities in identical twins reared apart are caused by their shared genes. But Bouchard's research subjects were self-selected (he advertised to find them) and interested in being twinlike. Some of them had also been reared together for several years before they were adopted into different families, therefore sharing at least an early environment. In addition, in any population a certain number of similarities will appear by chance. The fact that two people enjoy the same soft drink—in a culture in which soft drinks are widely consumed—is not evidence that they share a gene for the consumption of that soft drink.

6　　For years Bouchard had problems getting his papers accepted for publication in scientific journals. Convinced of his work's importance, however, he submitted his findings to the press before they were peer-reviewed, or even when they had been rejected by scientific publications. The media responded with extraordinary interest, attracted to the drama in "the eerie world of re-united twins" and the potential for controversy over the sensitive issue of genes and IQ. *U.S. News and World Report* reported on the twin studies by describing the character traits that are "bred in our bones." Quirks such as wearing flashy belt buckles, liking particular television programs, or drinking coffee cold and problems such as addiction or eating disorders were all described as originating in the genes. The "Donahue Show" began a program on the twin studies with films on animal behavior, suggesting that, like animals, we "get a push before the womb." *Time* magazine criticized the political liberals who explained crime and poverty as byproducts of destructive environments. An article in *Science Writer* magazine argued that the twin studies were "one more proof that parenting has its limits." And the *Boston Globe* announced that "geneticists now have ascendancy in the nature-nurture debate."

In October 1990, *Science* became the first major professional journal to publish Bouchard's work. There followed a media blitz. The *Philadelphia Inquirer* headlined its front-page story "Personality mostly a matter of genes" and welcomed the "landmark" study that proved that personality is put in place at the "instant" of conception. Even religiosity and church attendance, the article said, were determined by genes. Magazine articles touted Bouchard's research as part of the swelling tide of evidence for the importance of genes. 7

Since 1983, when behavioral genetics first appeared as a category in the *Reader's Guide to Periodical Literature*, hundreds of articles about the relationship between genetics and behavior have appeared in magazines, newspapers, and fictional accounts, often presented as the cutting edge of current science. Included among the traits attributed to heredity have been mental illness, aggression, homosexuality, exhibition, dyslexia, addiction, job and educational success, arson, tendency to tease, propensity for risk-taking, timidity, social potency, tendency to giggle or to use hurtful words, traditionalism, and zest for life. 8

Many of the stories of good and bad traits address a common and troubling contradiction. Why do some individuals, despite extremely difficult childhoods, become productive, even celebrated members of society, while other children, granted every opportunity and advantage, turn out badly? What accounts for the frequent disparity between achievement and hard work? Genetics appears to provide an explanation. Individuals succeed or fail not so much because of their efforts, their will, or their social circumstances but because they are genetically programmed for that fate. 9

Evil in the Genes

The existence of evil has posed problems for philosophers and theologians for much of human history. Religious systems 10 have personified evil as a supernatural being; folklore has located it in natural disaster, mythical beasts, or the "evil eye." Evil can be seen as the cosmic consequence of fate (the bad "luck of the draw") or the result of voluntary human action or moral failure. The agents invoked to explain the presence of evil are commonly powerful, abstract, and invisible—demons, gods, witches, a marked soul, and, today, the biochemistry of the brain. Environmental contingencies, similarly powerful and abstract—such as patterns of authority discussed by Stanley Milgram in "Behavioral Studies of Obedience" (*Journal of Abnormal and Social Psychology*) or social reinforcements advanced by B. F. Skinner in *Beyond Freedom and Dignity*—have also been seen as the sources of evil. But the belief that the "devil made me do it" does not significantly differ in its consequences from the belief that "my genes made me do it." Both seek to explain behavior that threatens the social contract; both locate control over human fate in powerful abstract entities capable of dictating human action in ways that mitigate moral responsibility and alleviate personal blame.

11   The response to research on the so-called criminal chromosome suggests the appeal of this view. In 1965 the British cytogeneticist Patricia Jacobs found that a disproportionate number of men in an Edinburgh correctional institution, instead of being XY (normal) males, were XYY males. Jacobs suggested that the extra Y chromosome "predisposes its carriers to unusually aggressive behavior." Other researchers later questioned whether XYY males were more aggressive, suggesting instead that they suffered from diminished intellectual functioning that made it more likely that they would be incarcerated. And the original estimate of the rate of XYY males occurring in the population in general was later revised upward, so that the difference in the prison population and the general population appeared to be less great than it had once seemed.

12   But the "criminal chromosome" had a remarkable popular life, first attracting the attention of the press in April 1968 when it was invoked to explain one of the most gruesome crimes of the decade. A *New York Times* reporter wrote that Richard Speck, then awaiting sentencing in the murder, one night, of nine student nurses, planned to appeal his case on the grounds that he was XYY. This story—which was incorrect (Speck was an XY male)—provoked a public debate about the causes of criminal behavior. *Newsweek* asked if criminals were "Born bad?" ("Can a man be born a criminal?") *Time*

headlined a story "Chromosomes and crime." By the early 1970s, at least two films had featured an XYY male criminal, and a series of crime novels had made their focus an XYY hero who struggled with his compulsion to commit crimes.

References to the criminal chromosome continued to 13 shape popular views of violence. In 1986, the *New York Times* asked, "Should such persons [XYY males] be held responsible for their crimes, or treated as victims of conditions for which they are not responsible, on a par with the criminally insane?" And in 1992, a PBS series on "The Mind" introduced a segment on violence: "Recent research suggests that even the acts of a serial killer may have a biological or genetic basis." Similarly, in February 1993 Phil Donahue advised his listeners on "how to tell if your child is a serial killer." His guest, a psychiatrist, described a patient who had been raised in a "Norman Rockwell" setting but then, driven by his extra Y chromosome, killed 11 women.

News reporters and talk-show hosts refer to "bad seeds," 14 "criminal genes,"and "alcohol genes." CBS talk-show host Oprah Winfrey found it meaningful to ask a guest whether her twin sister's "being bad" was "in her blood." In the movie *JFK*, one character tells another, "You're as crazy as your mama—goes to show it's in the genes." To *New York Times Magazine* writer Deborah Franklin, evil is "embedded in the coils of chromosomes that our parents pass to us at conception." And Camille Paglia described her theory of nature in *Sex, Art, and American Culture* as following Sade rather than Rousseau:

> Aggression and violence are primarily not learned but instinctual, nature's promptings, bursts of primitive energy from the animal realm that man has never left. . . . Dionysus, trivialized by Sixties polemicists, is not pleasure but pleasure-pain, the gross continuum of nature, the subordination of all living things to biological necessity.

Genetic or biological explanations of "bad" behavior are 15 sufficiently prevalent to serve as a common source of irony. A 1991 segment of the comic strip "Calvin and Hobbes" featured Calvin's perplexed father asking his son: "You've been hitting rocks in the house? What on earth would make you do something like that?" Calvin replied: "Poor genetic material." In another strip that same year, Calvin described a vicious "snow snake": "I suppose if I had two Y chromosomes I'd feel hostile, too!" And a barroom cartoon by Nick Downes (reprinted in the April 24, 1992, issue of *Science*) portrayed "Dead-Eye Dan, known far and wide for his fast gun, mean temper, and extra Y chromosome."

16   Bad genes have also become a facetious metaphor to describe national aggression. James O. Jackson's *Time* article, "The New Germany Flexes Its Muscles," described the nation as "a child of doubtful lineage adopted as an infant into a loving family; the child has been good, obedient, and industrious, but friends and neighbors are worried that evil genes may still lurk beneath a well-mannered surface." Christopher Lehmann-Haupt, in his *New York Times* article "Studying Soccer Violence by the Civilized British," blamed the violence on the "genetic drive to wage war against the outlander."

17   Some individuals, so the media imply, are "born to kill" and will do so despite environmental advantages. In December 1991, a 14-year-old high school boy was arrested for the murder of a schoolmate. The *New York Times* account of this event interpreted it as a key piece of evidence in "the debate over whether children misbehave because they had bad childhoods or because they are just bad seeds." The boy's parents had provided a good home environment, the reporter asserted; they had "taken the children to church almost every Sunday, and sacrificed to send them to a Catholic grammar school." Yet their son had been arrested for murder. This troubling inconsistency between the child's apparently decent background and his violent behavior called for explanation. The reporter resolved the mystery through the explanatory power of inheritance; the moral of the story was clearly stated in its headline: "Raising Children Right Isn't Always Enough." The implication? There are, indeed, "bad seeds.". . .

18   This same theme appeared in the news reports of a debate over the body and blood of Westley Allan Dodd, a serial killer of children who was hanged in January 1993. Dodd insisted that he could not be cured and that if he had the opportunity he would kill again and "enjoy it." His ordinary childhood offered no convincing explanation for his monstrous behavior. He had not been an abused child. After Dodd's execution, scientists attempted to obtain pieces of his brain and vials of his blood to determine whether his behavior could be attributed to neurological abnormalities or "gene oddities." Such stories arise from a conflict between childhood experience and adult behavior; when the two seem to conflict, biological predisposition seems to provide a plausible and appealing resolution.

19   Research that links criminal behavior to biological forces fuels the hope that genetic information will make possible the

prediction, and therefore the control, of deviant behavior. Certain scientists encourage such expectations. In a 1992 *Science* editorial, "Elephants, Monstrosities, and the Law," the journal's editor, biologist Daniel Koshland, told stories about acts of violence: "An elephant goes berserk at the circus, an elderly pillar of the community is discovered to be a child molester, a man admits to killing many young boys...a disgruntled employee shoots seven co-workers." Each crime, wrote Koshland, had a common origin—an abnormality of the brain....

Even when scientists emphasize the complexity of biological and environmental conditions that could lead to violence, media accounts highlight the importance of genetics. The press coverage of the National Research Council's 1992 report, *Understanding and Preventing Violence*, is a case in point. The report said that violence arises from the "interactions among individuals' psychosocial development, neurological and hormonal differences, and social processes." It stressed the uncertain implications of research when it came to genetic influence on anti-social behavior: "These studies suggest at most a weak role for genetic processes in influencing potentials for violent behavior. The correlations and concordances of behavior in two of the three studies are consistent with a positive genetic effect, but are statistically insignificant." While not ruling out genetic processes, the NRC suggested: "If genetic predispositions to violence are discovered, they are likely to involve many genes and substantial environmental interaction rather than any simple genetic marker." 20

Only 14 of the 464 pages of the NRC report actually dealt with the biological perspectives on violence, and less than two pages were about genetics. Nevertheless, Fox Butterfield's article on the report in the November 13, 1992, *New York Times* was headlined: "Study Cites Role of Biological and Genetic Factors in Violence." Genes appear far more newsworthy than social or economic circumstances as a source of anti-social behavior. While genetic theories of violence have been controversial, denounced as politically and racially motivated, some journalists have dismissed critiques as "politically correct." In an April 19, 1993, article in *Time*, Anastasia Toufexis, looking for the causes of "the savagery that is sweeping America," suggested that society's ills cannot fully be responsible, that violence may be caused by "errant genes." "Science could help shed light on the roots of violence and offer new solutions for society," she added, "but not if the research is suppressed." 21

22   Biological theories also appeal as explanations of group violence and war. A 1991 textbook, *Social Psychology*, uses "genetic similarity theory" to explain "the tendency to dislike
members of groups other than our own." Discrimination
against those who are different, say authors R. A. Baron and
D. Byrne, is part of inherited human tendencies to defend
those possessing similar genes. Extending this idea to explain
war, Michael Ghiglieri, in a November 1987 *Discover* article,
described a study of chimps and speculated whether war runs
in our genes like baldness or diabetes." Such explanations extend the popular theories of the late 1960s and early 1970s,
when a spate of books appeared explaining human behavior
to a lay audience in evolutionary terms. These included Robert Ardrey's *The Territorial Imperative* (1966), Konrad Lorenz's
On Aggression (1966), Desmond Morris' *The Naked Ape*
(1967), and Lionel Tiger and Robin Fox's *The Imperial Animal*
(1970). Promoting a biological model of organized human aggression, these authors explained it as a productive and necessary social activity. The books were fashionable, attracting
a wide readership and extensive media coverage. Reviewing
the response to aggression research, Temple University
psychologist Jeffrey Goldstein found that the media systematically covered studies that offer evidence of genetic explanations of violence but were less interested in research on the
influence of social and economic conditions.

23   Some biologists and social scientists have criticized research on the genetic predisposition to organized aggression
for concealing inadequate methodologies behind quantitative
data and for minimizing the influence of social, political, and
economic factors on aggressive behavior. In May 1986, Jeffrey
Goldstein helped assemble a group of these critics to discuss
biological theories about the origin of warfare. Meeting in
Spain, they produced the Seville Statement on Violence,
which strongly repudiated the idea that war is biologically
necessary or genetically controlled. "It is scientifically incorrect to say that war is caused by 'instinct' or any single
motivation . . . scientifically incorrect to say that humans have
a 'violent brain' . . . scientifically incorrect to say that in the
course of human evolution there has been a selection for aggressive behavior more than for other kinds of behavior." The
statement concluded that "biology does not condemn humanity to war. The same species who invented war is capable of
inventing peace."

24   This brief but unambiguous text was signed by twenty
well-known scholars from around the world and endorsed by

the American Psychological Association, the American Anthropological Association, the International Society for Research on Aggression, and Psychologists for Social Responsibility. Yet despite considerable efforts to publicize the statement, it attracted little media attention. A journalist responding to the efforts to disseminate the Seville material expressed the prevailing attitude: "Call me when you find the gene for war."

The interest in "bad genes"—the genes for deviance—   25 reflects a tendency to medicalize social problems. This is especially evident in scientific and social speculation about the nature and etiology of addiction. Definitions of alcoholism have shifted over time from sin to sickness, from moral transgression to medical disease, depending on prevailing social, political, and moral agendas. Debates over the etiology of alcoholism go back to ancient Rome, but the modern conception of alcoholism as a disease is usually attributed to the nineteenth-century theories of Benjamin Rush (1745–1813). Early leaders of the American temperance movement, likewise, defined alcoholism as a disease, but when the movement began to advocate outright prohibition, alcoholism was redefined, along with syphilis and opiate addiction, as a "vice"—a manifestation of immoral behavior. A moral concept of voluntary addiction replaced the model of disease, and the politics of prohibition in the 1920s turned alcoholism into a problem more legal than medical. At the same time, eugenicists were compiling family studies supposedly demonstrating its inherited nature.

In 1935, E. M. Jellinek, reviewing the biological literature on   26 alcoholism for a major Carnegie Foundation report, formulated a medical model that explained alcoholism in terms of the interaction of alcohol with an individual's physical and psychological characteristics and his or her social circumstances. This analysis, later republished by Jellinek as *The Disease Concept of Alcoholism*, focused attention on what made people susceptible. The same year, Alcoholics Anonymous was founded on the doctrine that alcoholism was a compelling biological drive that could be cured only by total abstinence and moral rectitude. AA's position contributed to the revival of the medical model, promoting the idea that alcoholics had "predisposing characteristics" that distinguished them from others. This view has persisted, in its contemporary form focusing on the genetic basis of alcoholism.

Common observation shows that alcoholism runs in fami-   27 lies. As in the case of violence, however, this in itself does not reveal the cause. Many traits run in families—poverty, for example, or poor manners—without being a consequence of heredity. The prevalence of alcoholism in certain families could reflect role models, the availability of alcohol, or the reaction to abuse. Nevertheless, a common perception was expressed by George Nobbe in his 1989 *Omni* article, "Alcoholic Genes": "Addicted to the bottle? It may be in your genes." The gene for alcoholism became a theme of the Oprah Winfrey and Phil Donahue shows. Shifra Diamond's August 1990 *Mademoiselle* article, "Drinking Habits May Be in the Family," asked: "Do you have a gene that makes you a designated drinker?" and suggested that "even if you have exceptional self-discipline, you could still be at high risk." And Nancy Reagan's famous anti-drug slogan, "Just Say No," provoked a 1991 *Christian Science Monitor* editorial about the "genes-impelled compulsion" to take drugs.

28   In the 1990 article "Scientists Pinpoint Brain Irregularities in Drug Addicts," *New York Times* reporter Daniel Goleman presented several cases to dramatize the genetic basis of alcoholism. A 26-year-old executive had been the class clown as a child and president of his high school class. Always extroverted and outgoing, he partied a lot and, as he matured, started taking drugs in order to stay high. Addiction appealed because of his "natural bent." Another young man had been anxious as a child until he discovered that alcohol made him relax. His father was an alcoholic, so he had easy access to liquor; Goleman, however, quoted sources that explained his addiction in terms of biological vulnerability.

29   Goleman's stories suggested one reason for the appeal of genetic explanations: they implied that biological markers will make it possible to identify those at risk of addiction. He quoted a scientist who optimistically claimed that genetic engineering will eventually eliminate the gene and therefore the problems of addiction. In effect, like genetic explanations of violence, identifying an "alcoholism gene" offers the hope that addiction can be controlled—not through the uncertain route of social reform but through biological manipulation. . . .

30   To explain addictive behavior in absolute genetic or biological terms is to extract it from the social setting that defines and interprets behavior. There are no criminal genes or alcohol genes, only genes for the proteins that influence hormonal and physiological processes. And only the most general outline of social behavior can be genetically coded. Even behaviors known to be genetically inscribed, such as the

human ability to learn spoken language, do not appear if the environment does not promote them. Children do not learn to speak unless they hear spoken language, even though the ability to speak is genetic, a biological trait of the human species. In the case of alcoholism, for example, any biological or genetic predisposition that may exist can only become a full-blown pattern of behavior in an environment in which alcohol is readily available and socially approved. As this suggests, there are many interests at stake in the etiology of addiction, for causal explanations for addiction imply moral judgments about the responsibility and blame.

If defined as a sin, alcoholism represents an individual's   31
flaunting of social norms; if defined as a social problem, it represents a failure of the community environment; if defined as intrinsic to the product consumed, it represents the need for alcohol regulation. But if defined as a genetically determined trait, neither society nor the alcohol industry appears responsible. And if behavior is completely determined— either by genetics or environment—even the addicted individual cannot really be blamed. . . .

The appropriation of DNA—the good or bad gene—to ex-   32
plain individual differences recasts common beliefs about the importance of heredity in powerful scientific terms. Science becomes a way to empower prevailing beliefs, justifying existing social categories and expectations as based on natural forces. The great, the famous, the rich and successful are what they are because of their genes. So, too, the deviant and the dysfunctional are genetically fated. Opportunity is less important than predisposition. Some are destined for success; others for problems or, at least, a lesser fate. The star— or the criminal—is not made but born.

This is a particularly striking theme in American society,   33
where the very foundation of the democratic experiment was the belief in the improvability—indeed, the perfectibility—of all human beings. Belief in genetic destiny implies there are natural limits constraining the possibilities for both individuals and for social groups. Humankind is not perfectible, because the species' flaws and failings are inscribed in an unchangeable text—the DNA—that will persist in creating murderers, addicts, the insane, and the incompetent, even under the most ideal social circumstances. In popular stories, children raised in ideal homes become murderers and children raised in difficult home situations become well-adjusted high achievers. The moral? No possible social system, no ideal nurturing plan can prevent the violent acts that seem to

threaten the social fabric of contemporary American life. Only biological controls, it seems, can solve such problems.

34   The idea of genetic predisposition encourages a passive attitude toward social injustice, an apathy about continuing social problems, and a reason to preserve the status quo. Genetic explanations, however, are malleable. They can be appropriated to justify prevailing stereotypes and maintain current social arrangements, but they can also be used to promote group identity or to celebrate human differences. The diverse social, political, and moral dimensions of such explanations become more transparent as they appear with growing frequency in stories and debates about the social meaning of sex, race, and sexual orientation.

Alison Bass

Why Aren't There More Women Murderers?

Bass was a staff writer for The Boston Globe *newspaper, where this article appeared in 1992.*

1   Accused serial killer Aileen Wuornos, who was recently sentenced to death in Florida, is the exception that doesn't prove the rule.

2   The rule is that women, unlike men, don't kill strangers or even casual acquaintances, except in very rare cases of self-defense. When women do kill—and they do so at astonishingly lower rates than men, who commit 85 percent of all homicides—the vast majority kill family members, usually men who have battered them for years.

3   As many as 90 percent of the women in jail today for murdering men have been battered by those men. A much smaller number—about 3 in 100,000—kill their children as a result of a postpartum psychosis that has gone untreated.

4   There is also a smattering of women with a history of mental disorders who kill in a psychotic rage. And then there is the rare woman who kills family members for money; according to historical accounts, Lizzie Borden was one.

Fewer than 3 percent of serial killers are female, according   6
to FBI statistics. No one knows why this disparity exists, although many researchers believe that differences in brain
chemistry may be the primary reason why men are so much
more violent than women.

Usually, female multiple killers are caretakers—most often   7
nurses—who rationalize their crimes as mercy killings. Nurse
Genene Jones, for example, was suspected of killing as many
as 16 children in a Texas hospital with a lethal drug in an attempt to prove to administrators that the hospital needed a
pediatric intensive care unit; she was convicted of killing one
infant and sentenced to 99 years in prison.

Another multiple killer, Velma Barfield, who was electro-   8
cuted in North Carolina in 1984 (the first woman to be executed in 26 years), admitted killing four family members after
years of sexual and physical abuse.

But Aileen Wuornos, who authorities say killed seven men,   9
is the first woman in FBI annals accused in a multiple killing
of strangers, a series of murders that spanned several years.
In many respects, Wuornos, a bisexual prostitute whose alleged victims had picked her up for sex, fits the profile of a
male killer.

"She has the characteristics we see with our male killers,"   10
said John Douglas, unit chief of behavioral sciences for the
FBI at Quantico, Va. "Like many of our male killers, she
comes from a very dysfunctional background where she was
abused, physically and sexually. But usually women from that
kind of background internalize the abuse and their feelings.
While the men turn to aggression, the women turn to alcohol,
drugs, prostitution and suicide."

Women who have been badly abused as children also tend   11
to get involved with violent men who abuse them and their
children, perpetuating the cycle of violence into the next generation. One 1991 study by New York University researchers
found that 21 females who had been incarcerated for criminal behavior as teenagers did not—as many of their male
counterparts did—commit violent crimes as adults: instead
the majority became enmeshed in violent relationships,
abused or neglected their children, and lost custody of them
as a result.

Other research indicates that women who have been sexu-   12
ally abused as children—unlike men similarly abused—do
not commit sexual crimes.

"Women don't have sexual deviations—they don't make ob-   13
scene phone calls, they don't flash, they don't have paraphilias

[addictions to bizarre practices, such as having sex with a corpse]," says Ann Burgess, professor of psychiatric nursing at the University of Pennsylvania and an authority on sexual homicide. "It is rare for a woman to murder more than one person, and they never commit sexual crimes."

14   The big question is why.

15   While there is no definitive data on the subject, Burgess and other forensic experts believe there are sharp differences between men and women's brain chemistry, and that those differences are accentuated by cultural differences in the way males and females are raised.

16   "It must be a combination of things, but we know it can't be culture alone," says Angela Browne, a social psychologist at the University of Massachusetts Medical Center and a specialist on women who kill. "You can change environments across cultures, and across almost all cultures men are far more prone to homicide than women. Men are also more prone to socially sanctioned actions that lead to death, like civil strife and war."

17   "It makes sense to conclude that physiological rather than simply societal influences are at play," agrees Dr. Dorothy Otnow Lewis, professor of psychiatry at New York University and an authority on violence.

18   In detailed research, Lewis has found that men who have been horribly abused as children and suffer from a constellation of psychiatric and neurological disorders are much more likely than others to become extremely violent. But as Lewis notes, it takes the Y chromosome, i.e., maleness, to complete the picture.

19   Lewis and others believe male hormones such as testosterone and androgen play a key role in making men much more aggressive than women. But merely having a high level of testosterone does not make someone violent; many men with high levels are simply more competitive. They channel their hormonal drives into constructive pursuits.

20   It seems equally clear that culture plays a role.

21   "Men are brought up to fight and to defend themselves, and they are reinforced for engaging in those behaviors," says Robert Prentky, a forensic psychologist at New England Forensic Associates in Arlington and an authority on sexual violence. "When they are challenged by a bully at school, their fathers will teach them how to fight with their fists. But how many times do parents teach girls to defend themselves?"

22   Girls are taught to nurture and care for others; some psychologists believe females may be biochemically "wired" to

be more giving and nurturing. For whatever reason, women respond to conflict in ways very different than men do.

"Women may be emotionally abusive and damaging,   23
rather than physically abusive," says Browne, author of a book called *When Battered Women Kill.* "Even though women could theoretically equalize their lesser strength with a gun, they still don't perpetrate violence in very large numbers."

The statistics show that most women do not become vio-   24
lent unless they are in fear of their own lives or their children's. In research on battered women who kill their male partners, Browne found the majority of women were responding to threats against their children. And the rest had reason to believe that, after battering them for years, the men in their lives planned to kill them.

Browne also found that the rate of women who kill their   25
partners has fallen 25 percent since the mid-70s, when many shelters for battered women were opened and police started adopting tougher policies on domestic violence. There has been no comparable decrease in the rates of men who kill their female partners. (Of all the male-female partner killings in the United States, 61 percent of the victims were women.)

Research also shows that a small percentage of women kill   26
when their biochemistry goes haywire, as the result of drugs, alcohol, mental disease or pregnancy. The few female mass murderers had long histories of untreated severe mental disorders, such as paranoid schizophrenia and manic mood swings. Among them was Sylvia Seegrist, who in 1985 shot three people during a psychotic rampage at a Philadelphia area mall.

Perhaps the most preventable cause of lethal violence is   27
postpartum psychosis, which afflicts about one woman in 1,000. Fully 3 percent of women with this disorder kill their infants, according to Susan Hickman, a San Diego psychotherapist and specialist in postpartum psychiatric disorders.

"Women with postpartum psychiatric illnesses often expe-   28
rience sleep and appetite disturbances, and in the most extreme cases they hallucinate, hear voices and imagine things," she said. "Often there is some kind of delusional construct involving the infant; for example, a delusion about the baby's being the devil. These delusions often take a religious tone."

Hickman and others believe this psychosis is biochemical in   29
nature. During pregnancy, the placenta takes over some of the body's hormone production, and in most cases after delivery

the pituitary gland, which regulates hormones, kicks back in. But in a few cases, Hickman speculates, the pituitary fails to kick back in and the woman's hormones become unbalanced, causing postpartum depression or psychosis.

30   "There is a neuroleptic medication that will control the symptoms very rapidly," Hickman says. "A woman can continue to nurse her baby and be restored to her normal functioning with the medication. And over time her body chemistry will level itself out and she should have no recurrence of symptoms, unless she has another pregnancy."

31   Aileen Wuornos, of course, was not pregnant. Nor, apparently, was she suffering from a serious mental disorder that clouded her judgment about right and wrong.

32   She had, however, experienced a brutal childhood. Her father was convicted of molesting a seven-year-old girl and implicated in the murder of another. When Wuornos was six months old, her mother handed her over to her grandparents, who physically abused her. Her grandfather also sexually abused her. At 13, she became pregnant after being raped by a stranger, according to psychiatrist Susan C. Vaughan of Columbia/New York State Psychiatric Institute, who has written about the case.

33   Thrown out of her grandparents' home when she became pregnant, Wuornos stayed in a home for unwed mothers until her baby was born and given up for adoption. After that, she lived on her own—in a neighbor's junked car or in a woods nearby—and turned to prostitution, drinking and drugs. She roamed the Midwest for years, supporting herself as a prostitute, and when she was 21, she tried to kill herself by shooting herself in the stomach, Vaughan wrote in the winter 1991 issue of the *American Academy of Psychoanalysis Forum*.

34   In the early 1980s, Wuornos was convicted of robbery. Florida police believe the murders did not begin until 1988, when Wuornos was living with another woman and supporting her through prostitution. After police caught up with her in January 1991, she admitted to killing two men who had picked her up for sex. She said she shot them repeatedly after they refused to pay her.

35   "Her motive may have been displaced rage motive—she just wanted to kill these men for revenge," Prentky speculates. "Other women may have her fantasies, but they don't act on it."

Earl Ofari Hutchinson

The Criminalization
of Black Men

Earl Ofari Hutchinson is a TV commentator and the author of
The Assassination of the Black Male Image. *He published the*
following piece in 1997 in a book called MultiAmerica: Essays
on Cultural Wars and the Cultural Peace *that was edited by*
the well-known writer Ishmael Reed.

The sun broke through the gray morning clouds as I jogged   1
along the streets near my home. When I stopped at an intersection to wait for the light to change, I caught the eye of a
driver, a young white woman. She looked nervous and frightened. In a quick move, she snapped down the lock on her car
door and sped off before the light changed.

This was not the first time I was the object of suspicion by   2
fearful whites. I have been followed by security guards and
clerks in stores. Women have clutched their purses when I approached. Cabdrivers have refused to pick me up. I've been
stopped and questioned by police even though I wore a suit
and tie and drove a late model car. Many black males tell the
same tales. In fact, they've become so routine that they simply
chalk them up to white America's deep fear of black males.

But there's more. A few months after the jogging incident,   3
I was sitting in my car in the parking lot of an office building
waiting for a business acquaintance to arrive. A young black
man approached the car. He was neatly dressed. My first impulse was to lock the door and roll up the window. It turned
out that he was only trying to locate another office building
on the same street.

As he walked away, I thought of the woman who locked her   4
door when she saw me. Her fear of black men had become
my fear. The image of black criminality has been shoved so
deep into America's collective psyche that no one is immune
from fear. This includes many blacks.

In a way I can understand why. Crime is an intensely per-   5
sonal and emotional issue for those victimized. The trauma is
deep and the memories cause perpetual pain for the victims
and their families. It stirs the deepest human fears and vulnerabilities. But when racial and sexual stereotypes are
mixed in, personal fear becomes public hysteria.

6   A study on reader perception of crime reported in the *Chicago Tribune* found that in several crime-related stories the paper mentioned that the suspect was a white male under age twenty-five. Many readers still identified the suspect as a black male under age twenty-five.

7   This was more than a case of warped perceptions of crime. Tal Mendleberg, a Princeton political scientist, analyzed the hidden racial content of political ads used in the 1988 presidential election. She zeroed in on the campaign ad used by George Bush on escaped black convict Willie Horton. The ad charged that Horton raped a Maryland woman while on furlough from prison in Massachusetts. Bush claimed that the ad was intended only to paint his opponent, Massachusetts Democrat Michael S. Dukakis, as soft on crime. Democrats charged that the ad pandered to racism. Bush denied it.

8   Mendleberg showed a group of participants campaign footage that included part of the Horton ad. She asked if they felt more threatened by crime, or perceived another message. The other message was race. The ad hardened the participants' attitude toward criminals. But it also hardened them to all blacks. Mendleberg concluded that they "decided they really didn't want more spending to aid blacks."

9   There is one exception: Americans are willing to spend more to lock them up. Crime has taken a tortured path to become America's number one fear. In February 1993, crime ranked nearly dead last on the list of issues that most troubled Americans; only 4 percent called it the major problem. Less than a year later, 19 percent said it was the number one problem facing America.

10   What happened? In California, the Assembly Commission on the Status of the African-American Male noted that four out of ten males entering California prisons are black. Less than half of lower-income black males under age twenty-one live in two-parent households. Black males with a high school education are twice as likely as white males to be unemployed. The national figures mirrored California's numbers.

11   President Clinton sensed the public fear and quickly moved to dislodge the Bush administration's $30 billion Federal Omnibus Crime Bill, which was bottled up in Congress for the three previous years. Congress procrastinated for a few months while engaging in the usual partisan political sparring. But the murder of twelve-year-old Polly Klass in California, shootings in Denver area fast-food restaurants, the attack on U.S. Olympic skater Nancy Kerrigan, and the murder of six and wounding of twenty commuters on a Long

Island commuter train by an unemployed black handyman, Colin Ferguson, all in 1993, did it.

With the exception of Ferguson, these highly publicized 12 crimes were committed by white men. Yet much of the public still saw crime with a young black male face. It was only a matter of time before the crime bill became law. A handful of critics, mostly civil libertarians and black leaders, warned that the provisions were too costly, racially discriminatory, and veered dangerously close to constitutional violations. They were brushed aside. Clinton and Congress congratulated each other when the bill passed in August 1994.

Crime was the hottest ticket item in America. States 13 rushed to pass three-strikes and two-strikes legislation, hired more police and prosecutors, and stiffened sentences. The Department of Justice poured several million dollars into the development of *Star Wars*–type high-tech gadgetry: "smart" guns, anti-high-chase microwave devices, super-sticky foams, remote-control spikes, night-vision goggles, highway satellite systems, and remote-controlled robots.

The crime mania nearly doubled America's prison popu- 14 lation, from 900,000 in 1987 to 1.4 million in 1994. The prison-industrial complex replaced the nearly defunct military-industrial complex as America's largest growth industry. In California, there would be plenty of new prison cells. State taxpayers would pay $21 billion over the next thirty years to build twenty-five new prisons. While they would pay $1.8 billion to run their eight campuses of the University of California system, they would spend $5 billion to run their prisons. Construction companies, contractors, architectural firms, and lobbyists would make billions. Wall Street would rake in a neat $35 million from the sale of California's $5.6 billion in lease revenue bonds the legislature floated without taxpayer approval.

What did this buy? The Rand Corporation claimed the 15 money would reduce felonies by only 8 percent. The vast majority who would fill the new jail cells wouldn't be violent felons. They would be poor blacks and Latinos, who'd committed mostly property or drug-related crimes. Rand didn't state that if California taxpayers spent a fraction of the three-strikes budget on drug counseling, vocational job and skills training, and education and violence reduction programs, many of those people would not be in those cells.

The criminalization of black men perpetuated the danger- 16 ous cycle of arrest and incarceration. The cycle has trapped thousands. In 1992, one out of four young black men were in jail, or prison, on parole, or probation. Nearly half of America's 1 million prisoners were black. The topheavy number of black men in jail reinforced the public view that they committed most of the major violent crime in America.

17   They didn't. In 1992:

- White males committed 54% of violent crimes in America.
- White males were 70% of the juveniles arrested nationally for criminal offenses.
- White males were 80% of America's drug users and abusers.
- White males committed 60% of the urban hate crimes.
- White males committed the majority of serial and mass murders.

18   This last point deserves special comment. I wondered why much of the media, the public, and sociologists weren't as obsessed with the serial murders committed mostly by white males as they were with black crime. I did a computer scan of four hundred academic journals between 1992 and 1994; there were 1,691 research articles published on crime. Forty identifiable research articles dealt specifically with black crime. Two identifiable research articles dealt with serial/ mass murders. The one detailed article on serial murders was published in a small journal, *the Omega-Journal of Death and Dying.* The authors admitted that there was a "poverty of rigorous research in the area." It may stay that way.

19   I also closely monitored the press reports on the prison murder of mass murderer Jeffrey Dahmer in November 1994. The media spin was sympathy and compassion for Dahmer. His mother tearfully made the talk show rounds. In the *Los Angeles Times* account, Dahmer's prosecutor, psychologist, defense attorney, and relatives were quoted. They recast him as a tragic figure.

20   The prosecutor thundered that "this is not justice." The psychiatrist called him "pleasant, polite, free of prejudice and gentle." There was a brief quote from an attorney representing the family of one of his victims. There was only passing reference to the fact that fourteen out of seventeen of his known victims were black men; the other three were Hispanic or Asian. Ironically, Dahmer had no sympathy for himself. His mother told an interviewer that "he felt that he deserved anything he gets."

Suburban whites may have nightmares about being at-   21
tacked by blacks, but their waking reality is that their attacker
will be white. In 1990, 70 percent of violent crimes against
whites were committed by other whites. However, many
white offenders don't wind up behind bars. Their increasing
absence from the prisons has become noticeable. A District of
Columbia judge was curious to see what the jails were like
that he sent defendants to. After he visited several, he was
struck by the fact that most of those inside were black. He
knew from his experience on the bench that many whites
were charged with crimes. He wondered what happened to
them.

There was a clue: 78 percent of the 580 white middle-class   22
males convicted of defrauding savings and loans (and taxpayers) of nearly $8 billion went to prison during the early 1990s.
Most didn't stay very long. Only 4 percent were sentenced to
ten years or more. The average sentence was 36.4 months.
The median time served was two years. A car thief spent 38
months in prison; a burglar, 55.6 months. In California, only
one in four S&L fraud suspects was prosecuted. In Texas, one
in seven was prosecuted. For those with the money, personal
and family connections, and political clout to avoid prison,
crime did indeed pay.

Despite the fears of many white and non-whites, few Amer-   23
icans really know how dangerous their streets are. *Newsweek*
in 1994 still punched the murder panic button hard. It
warned that murder was epidemic and the nation's streets
had become free-fire zones. There were gruesome photos of
mostly young black and Hispanic male victims. But a cursory
glance at *Newsweek*'s numbers showed that Americans were
actually at less risk of becoming murder victims in 1990 (9.5
per 100,000) than in 1980 (10.2 per 100,000). In fact, Americans actually stood a better chance of being murdered during
the 1920s Prohibition era than in 1994.

The richer, older, and whiter a person, the less chance they   24
have of being a crime victim. Older white women are the least
victimized of any group in America. Those who earn more
than $50,000 are two to three times less likely to be crime vic-
tims than the general population. For whites aged fifty to
sixty-four, the victim rate dropped 35 percent. Whites are
marginally at greater risk of being robbed by blacks. It has
less to do with their color than their numbers and location.
There are seven times more whites than blacks in America.
Most of them aren't robbed in their homes or neighborhoods
but rather on urban streets.

25 The arrest totals are further inflated by police saturation of black neighborhoods, gang sweeps, drug raids, and racially tainted "zero-tolerance" stop and search policies. Compton, a California city with a black and Latino majority, went one better. In 1993, it criminalized every youth in the city. The police department's database contained the names of 10,435 gang members in the city. It was a curious figure. The 1990 Census counted only 8,558 males aged fifteen to twenty-five in the city. There were three possible explanations: the database was faulty; the information was inputted incorrectly; or as one observer quipped, maybe there were gang members such as Crips moonlighting as Bloods, and vice versa.

26 During the past decade, drug-related arrests account for the sharp rise in America's jail and prison population. Some police officials publicly admit that these arrests are a tragic game of numbers that police and politicians play to calm a jittery public. Project housing dwellers can't hire pricey attorneys or make bail. They are easy to try, convict, or pressure into a plea bargain. A typical conspiracy investigation against white suburbanite drug dealers could last six months or more and in the end net fewer than six arrests. The white suburbanites could make bail and hire private counsel: They are not easy to try, convict, or pressure into a plea bargain. This wouldn't play well to the public; judges and prosecutors know this.

27 Former Reagan drug czar William Bennett laid it on the cost-effective line: "It's easier and less expensive to arrest black drug users and dealers than whites." The price is higher than he thinks. Bennett, much of the press, and lawmakers operate under the assumption that crack cocaine trafficking and abuse are solely black crimes. Congress responded to that public perception by making the minimum sentence longer for crack during the mid-1980s.

28 It's true that blacks are disproportionately more involved in crack dealing and are arrested more often. But many whites are also deeply involved in the crack trade and those arrested do have more serious criminal histories than blacks. Yet black crack traffickers still receive on average longer sentences than white crack traffickers.

29 If blacks did commit most of the violent crime in America, most whites still wouldn't be at risk. According to official figures, blacks commit nearly half the murders and robberies: 94 percent of their victims are other blacks. Blacks are mostly a menace not to society but to themselves.

30 The perception that they are a menace to whites has been magnified by the TV networks, which have spent the past

twenty years honing tabloid-style reporting techniques. During the 1970s, the men who ran the ABC affiliates in Philadelphia and New York decided to rev up the ratings. They created *Action News.*

The concept was simple: Find crime, crime, and more   31
crime. News teams roamed city streets looking for police car chases, crashes, gang shootouts, and drug busts. Most importantly, the city streets were in black neighborhoods. It was bloody. It was exploitive. It was racist. It was a smash success. The public loved it. Network profits jumped and their ratings soared. *Action News,* which began as a lead-in to the regular newscast, soon became *the* news. Local affiliates in every city copied it.

By 1990, 68 percent of Americans were hooked on the   32
Action News nightly broadcast. The networks spun off legions of hybrid clones. These shows simulated live-action crime chases and busts. *Top Cops, Cops,* and *America's Most Wanted* often depicted whites as heroes and blacks as villains. This convinced even more Americans that violence-prone, drugged-out black men put their lives at great risk.

They didn't. But many Americans still exaggerate black   33
crime even when the crimes are committed by others. In 1992 in Los Angeles, TV reporters stretched credulity to the limits during the civil disturbances. For three days the black and increasingly Latino inner city was judged by white, middle-class reporters, men and women. They lived far from the area, and in many cases needed maps to find the streets. They relentlessly tailored their reports to depict the violence as the handiwork of black rioters. Racism, poverty, alienation, and the indifference of the city's political power structure were barely mentioned.

The reporters couldn't ignore the abominable verdict in the   34
state trial of the four LAPD officers who beat Rodney King. But they made no serious effort to analyze the criminal justice system, explain why the jury contained no blacks, or discuss the racism that motivated the jurors' decision. There was one passing reference in the *L.A. Times* to the negative remarks of white jurors about King's physical prowess and alleged aggressive actions.

One juror even made a borderline racially derogatory re-   35
mark about him, and hinted that he got what he deserved. Hardly anyone second-guessed the inept and ineffectual prosecution strategy that practically tossed the case to the defense.

Instead, reporters stumbled over each other to stick micro-   36
phones and cameras in the face and mouth of any black they

could find on the streets. They framed questions to get sensational sound bites, and badgered their respondents to say something inflammatory. The networks repeatedly played the tape of the young blacks beating white truck driver Reginald Denny, further inflaming fear and anger in the white suburbs. The media's message to sympathetic whites was that the Denny beating canceled out the moral outrage over the King beating.

37   Reporters, news anchors, and in-studio talking heads gleefully milked the black-white conflict angle for all it was worth. But TV was an open mirror. Viewers could plainly see many of those doing the looting and burning were nonblacks. The streets at times looked like a microcosm of the United Nations.

38   A Rand Corporation study of the racial breakdown of 5,000 riot-related cases processed through Los Angeles municipal courts tallied these arrest totals: Latinos, 2,852; blacks 2,037; Anglos 601; and others, 147. Young men aged eighteen to thirty-four made up the highest percentage of those arrested (30 percent). They were young men of all categories, not exclusively black.

39   The number of whites arrested was nearly one third of the total black arrests. A Rand criminologist was puzzled by the fixation of the press on black rioters when the majority of those rioting weren't black. "This was clearly not a black riot. It was a minority riot." The report appeared as a news item in the back pages of the *L.A. Times;* the rest of the press ignored it. The media misrepresented the civil disturbances as a "black riot," and the effect was easy to equate: Blacks + violence = public fear.

40   America is a victim of its own warped reality. Many whites and some blacks in their rush to construct a national security state have swallowed their own myths about black crime and violence. They believe that young blacks kill because they enjoy violence, steal because they are part of a subculture of poverty, and join gangs and deal drugs because they have low self-esteem and aspirations.

41   The truth is much different. Crime and violence can't be separated from the ills of American society. Victims and victimizers come in all colors, classes, and genders. As long as many Americans are convinced that crime comes only with a young black male face, justice will always come in the form of a police nightstick and a prison cell.

CAPITAL PUNISHMENT

George Orwell

A Hanging

*Born Eric Arthur Blair in India in 1903, educated in England,
and a member of the Imperial Police in Burma for five years,
George Orwell was England's most prominent political writer
in the decade before his death in 1950. A socialist but no communist, he wrote numerous books of fiction and nonfiction,
but he is best remembered for* Animal Farm *(1945) and* 1984
(1948)—novels that contributed to our culture terms such as
doublespeak *and* Big Brother. *His fictional description of "A
Hanging" appeared in* Shooting an Elephant and Other
Essays *(1950); it was first published in 1931.*

It was in Burma, a sodden morning of the rains. A sickly   1
light, like yellow tinfoil, was slanting over the high walls into
the jail yard. We were waiting outside the condemned cells, a
row of sheds fronted with double bars, like small animal
cages. Each cell measured about ten feet by ten and was quite
bare within except for a plank bed and a pot for drinking
water. In some of them brown, silent men were squatting at
the inner bars, with their blankets draped round them. These
were the condemned men, due to be hanged within the next
week or two.

One prisoner had been brought out of his cell. He was a   2
Hindu, a puny wisp of a man, with a shaven head and vague
liquid eyes. He had a thick, sprouting mustache, absurdly too
big for his body, rather like the mustache of a comic man on
the films. Six tall Indian warders were guarding him and getting him ready for the gallows. Two of them stood by with
rifles and fixed bayonets, while the others handcuffed him,
passed a chain through his handcuffs and fixed it to their
belts, and lashed his arms tight to his sides. They crowded
very close about him, with their hands always on him in a
careful, caressing grip, as though all the while feeling him to
make sure he was there. It was like men handling a fish which

871

is still alive and may jump back into the water. But he stood quite unresisting, yielding his arms limply to the ropes, as though he hardly noticed what was happening.

3   Eight o'clock struck and a bugle call, desolately thin in the wet air, floated from the distant barracks. The superintendent of the jail, who was standing apart from the rest of us, moodily prodding the gravel with his stick, raised his head at the sound. He was an army doctor, with a gray toothbrush mustache and a gruff voice. "For God's sake, hurry up, Francis," he said irritably. "The man ought to have been dead by this time. Aren't you ready yet?"

4   Francis, the head jailer, a fat Dravidian in a white drill suit and gold spectacles, waved his black hand. "Yes sir, yes sir," he bubbled. "All iss satisfactorily prepared. The hangman iss waiting. We shall proceed."

5   "Well, quick march, then. The prisoners can't get their breakfast till this job's over."

6   We set out for the gallows. Two warders marched on either side of the prisoner, with their rifles at the slope; two others marched close against him, gripping him by arm and shoulder, as though at once pushing and supporting him. The rest of us, magistrates and the like, followed behind. Suddenly, when we had gone ten yards, the procession stopped short without any order or warning. A dreadful thing had happened—a dog, come goodness knows whence, had appeared in the yard. It came bounding among us with a loud volley of barks and leapt round us wagging its whole body, wild with glee at finding so many human beings together. It was a large woolly dog, half Airedale, half pariah. For a moment it pranced around us, and then, before anyone could stop it, it had made a dash for the prisoner, and jumping up tried to lick his face. Everybody stood aghast, too taken aback even to grab the dog.

7   "Who let that bloody brute in here?" said the superintendent angrily. "Catch it, someone!"

8   A warder detached from the escort charged clumsily after the dog, but it danced and gamboled just out of his reach, taking everything as part of the game. A young Eurasian jailer picked up a handful of gravel and tried to stone the dog away, but it dodged the stones and came after us again. Its yaps echoed from the jail walls. The prisoner, in the grasp of the two warders, looked on incuriously, as though this was another formality of the hanging. It was several minutes before someone managed to catch the dog. Then we put my handkerchief through its collar and moved off once more, with the dog still straining and whimpering.

It was about forty yards to the gallows. I watched the bare   9
brown back of the prisoner marching in front of me. He
walked clumsily with his bound arms, but quite steadily, with
that bobbing gait of the Indian who never straightens his
knees. At each step his muscles slid neatly into place, the lock
of hair on his scalp danced up and down, his feet printed
themselves on the wet gravel. And once, in spite of the men
who gripped him by each shoulder, he stepped lightly aside to
avoid a puddle on the path.

It is curious; but till that moment I had never realized what   10
it means to destroy a healthy, conscious man. When I saw the
prisoner step aside to avoid the puddle, I saw the mystery, the
unspeakable wrongness, of cutting a life short when it is in full
tide. This man was not dying, he was alive just as we are alive.
All the organs of his body were working—bowels digesting
food, skin renewing itself, nails growing, tissues forming—all
toiling away in solemn foolery. His nails would still be growing when he stood on the drop, when he was falling through
the air with a tenth-of-a-second to live. His eyes saw the yellow gravel and the gray walls, and his brain still remembered,
foresaw, reasoned—even about puddles. He and we were a
party of men walking together, seeing, hearing, feeling,
understanding the same world; and in two minutes, with a
sudden snap, one of us would be gone—one mind less, one
world less.

The gallows stood in a small yard, separate from the main   11
grounds of the prison, and overgrown with tall prickly weeds.
It was a brick erection like three sides of a shed, with plank-
ing on top, and above that two beams and a crossbar with the
rope dangling. The hangman, a gray-haired convict in the
white uniform of the prison, was waiting beside his machine.
He greeted us with a servile crouch as we entered. At a word
from Francis the two warders, gripping the prisoner more
closely than ever, half led, half pushed him to the gallows and
helped him clumsily up the ladder. Then the hangman
climbed up and fixed the rope round the prisoner's neck.

We stood waiting, five yards away. The warders had   12
formed in a rough circle round the gallows. And then, when
the noose was fixed, the prisoner began crying out to his god.
It was a high, reiterated cry of "Ram! Ram! Ram! Ram!" not
urgent and fearful like a prayer or cry for help, but steady,
rhythmical, almost like the tolling of a bell. The dog answered
the sound with a whine. The hangman, still standing on the
gallows, produced a small cotton bag like a flour bag and
drew it down over the prisoner's face. But the sound, muffled

by the cloth, still persisted, over and over again: "Ram! Ram! Ram! Ram! Ram!"

13   The hangman climbed down and stood ready, holding the lever. Minutes seemed to pass. The steady, muffled crying from the prisoner went on and on, "Ram! Ram! Ram!" never faltering for an instant. The superintendent, his head on his chest, was slowly poking the ground with his stick; perhaps he was counting the cries, allowing the prisoner a fixed number—fifty, perhaps, or a hundred. Everyone had changed color. The Indians had gone gray like bad coffee, and one or two of the bayonets were wavering. We looked at the lashed, hooded man on the drop, and listened to his cries—each cry another second of life; the same thought was in all our minds; oh, kill him quickly, get it over, stop that abominable noise!

14   Suddenly the superintendent made up his mind. Throwing up his head he made a swift motion with his stick. "Chalo!" he shouted almost fiercely.

15   There was a clanking noise, and then dead silence. The prisoner had vanished, and the rope was twisting on itself. I let go of the dog, and it galloped immediately to the back of the gallows; but when it got there it stopped short, barked, and then retreated into a corner of the yard, where it stood among the weeds, looking timorously out at us. We went round the gallows to inspect the prisoner's body. He was dangling with his toes pointed straight downwards, very slowly revolving, as dead as a stone.

16   The superintendent reached out with his stick and poked the bare brown body; it oscillated slightly. "*He's* all right," said the superintendent. He backed out from under the gallows, and blew out a deep breath. The moody look had gone out of his face quite suddenly. He glanced at his wristwatch. "Eight minutes past eight. Well, that's all for this morning, thank God."

17   The warders unfixed bayonets and marched away. The dog, sobered and conscious of having misbehaved itself, slipped after them. We walked out of the gallows yard, past the condemned cells with their waiting prisoners, into the big central yard of the prison. The convicts, under the command of warders armed with lathis, were already receiving their breakfast. They squatted in long rows, each man holding a tin pannikin, while two warders with buckets marched around ladling out rice; it seemed quite a homely, jolly scene, after the hanging. An enormous relief had come upon us now that the job was done. One felt an impulse to sing, to break into a run, to snigger. All at once everyone began chattering gaily.

The Eurasian boy walking beside me nodded towards the 18 way we had come, with a knowing smile: "Do you know sir, our friend (he meant the dead man) when he heard his appeal had been dismissed, he pissed on the floor of his cell. From fright. Kindly take one of my cigarettes, sir. Do you not admire my new silver case, sir? From the boxwallah, two rupees eight annas. Classy European style."

Several people laughed—at what, nobody seemed certain. 19

Francis was walking by the superintendent, talking garru- 20 lously: "Well, sir, all has passed off with the utmost satisfacto- riness. It was all finished—flick! Like that. It iss not always so—oah, no! I have known cases where the doctor was obliged to go beneath the gallows and pull the prisoner's legs to ensure decease. Most disagreeable!"

"Wriggling about, eh? That's bad," said the superintendent. 21

"Ach, sir, it iss worse when they become refractory! One 22 man, I recall, clung to the bars of hiss cage when we went to take him out. You will scarcely credit, sir, that it took six warders to dislodge him, three pulling at each leg. We rea- soned with him, 'My dear fellow,' we said, 'think of all the pain and trouble you are causing to us!' But no, he would not listen! Ach, he was very troublesome!"

I found that I was laughing quite loudly. Everyone was 23 laughing. Even the superintendent grinned in a tolerant way. "You'd better all come out and have a drink," he said quite genially. "I've got a bottle of whiskey in the car. We could do with it."

We went through the big double gates of the prison into 24 the road. "Pulling at his legs!" exclaimed a Burmese magis- trate suddenly, and burst into a loud chuckling. We all began laughing again. At that moment Francis' anecdote seemed extraordinarily funny. We all had a drink together, native and European alike, quite amicably. The dead man was a hundred yards away.

Edward I. Koch
Death and Justice

Outspoken and controversial, Edward I. Koch (born 1924) served as the Democratic mayor of New York City from 1978 to 1989. He has always been eager to engage in public debate on controversial issues in his three books, in his hundreds of speeches, and in his published articles. In 1985, he contributed the following essay to The New Republic, *an influential public affairs magazine generally considered middle-of-the-road in its outlook.*

1   Last December a man named Robert Lee Willie, who had been convicted of raping and murdering an 18-year-old woman, was executed in the Louisiana state prison. In a statement issued several minutes before his death, Mr. Willie said: "Killing people is wrong.... It makes no difference whether it's citizens, countries, or governments. Killing is wrong." Two weeks later in South Carolina, an admitted killer named Joseph Carl Shaw was put to death for murdering two teenagers. In an appeal to the governor for clemency, Mr. Shaw wrote: "Killing is wrong when I did it. Killing is wrong when you do it. I hope you have the courage and moral strength to stop the killing."

2   It is a curiosity of modern life that we find ourselves being lectured on morality by cold-blooded killers. Mr. Willie previously had been convicted of aggravated rape, aggravated kidnapping, and the murders of a Louisiana deputy and a man from Missouri. Mr. Shaw committed another murder a week before the two for which he was executed, and admitted mutilating the body of the 14-year-old girl he killed. I can't help wondering what prompted these murderers to speak out against killing as they entered the death-house door. Did their newfound reverence for life stem from the realization that they were about to lose their own?

3   Life is indeed precious, and I believe the death penalty helps to affirm this fact. Had the death penalty been a real possibility in the minds of these murderers, they might well have stayed their hand. They might have shown moral awareness before their victims died, and not after. Consider the tragic death of Rosa Velez, who happened to be home when a man named Luis Vera burglarized her apartment in Brook-

lyn. "Yeah, I shot her," Vera admitted. "She knew me, and I knew I wouldn't go to the chair."

During my 22 years in public service, I have heard the pros **4** and cons of capital punishment expressed with special intensity. As a district leader, councilman, congressman, and mayor, I have represented constituencies generally thought of as liberal. Because I support the death penalty for heinous crimes of murder, I have sometimes been the subject of emotional and outraged attacks by voters who find my position reprehensible or worse. I have listened to their ideas. I have weighed their objections carefully. I still support the death penalty. The reasons I maintain my position can be best understood by examining the arguments most frequently heard in opposition.

1. *The death penalty is "barbaric."* Sometimes opponents of **5** capital punishment horrify with tales of lingering death on the gallows, of faulty electric chairs, or of agony in the gas chamber. Partly in response to such protests, several states such as North Carolina and Texas switched to execution by lethal injection. The condemned person is put to death painlessly, without ropes, voltage, bullets, or gas. Did this answer the objections of death penalty opponents? Of course not. On June 22, 1984, *The New York Times* published an editorial that sarcastically attacked the new "hygienic" method of death by injection, and stated that "execution can never be made humane through science." So it's not the method that really troubles opponents. It's the death itself they consider barbaric.

Admittedly, capital punishment is not a pleasant topic. **6** However, one does not have to like the death penalty in order to support it any more than one must like radical surgery, radiation, or chemotherapy in order to find necessary these attempts at curing cancer. Ultimately we may learn how to cure cancer with a simple pill. Unfortunately, that day has not yet arrived. Today we are faced with the choice of letting the cancer spread or trying to cure it with the methods available, methods that one day will almost certainly be considered barbaric. But to give up and do nothing would be far more barbaric and would certainly delay the discovery of an eventual cure. The analogy between cancer and murder is imperfect, because murder is not the "disease" we are trying to cure. The disease is injustice. We may not like the death penalty, but it must be available to punish crimes of cold-blooded murder, cases in which any other form of punishment would be inadequate and, therefore, unjust. If we create a society in which injustice is not tolerated, incidents of murder—the most flagrant form of injustice—will diminish.

7   2. *No other major democracy uses the death penalty.* No other major democracy—in fact, few other countries of any description—are plagued by a murder rate such as that in the United States. Fewer and fewer Americans can remember the days when unlocked doors were the norm and murder was a rare and terrible offense. In America the murder rate climbed 122 percent between 1963 and 1980. During that same period, the murder rate in New York City increased by almost 400 percent, and the statistics are even worse in many other cities. A study at M.I.T. showed that based on 1970 homicide rates a person who lived in a large American city ran a greater risk of being murdered than an American soldier in World War II ran of being killed in combat. It is not surprising that the laws of each country differ according to differing conditions and traditions. If other countries had our murder problem, the cry for capital punishment would be just as loud as it is here. And I daresay that any other major democracy where 75 percent of the people supported the death penalty would soon enact it into law.

8   3. *An innocent person might be executed by mistake.* Consider the work of Adam Bedau, one of the most implacable foes of capital punishment in this country. According to Mr. Bedau, it is "false sentimentality to argue that the death penalty should be abolished because of the abstract possibility that an innocent person might be executed." He cites a study of the 7,000 executions in this country from 1893 to 1971, and concludes that the record fails to show that such cases occur. The main point, however, is this. If government functioned only when the possibility of error didn't exist, government wouldn't function at all. Human life deserves special protection, and one of the best ways to guarantee that protection is to assure that convicted murderers do not kill again. Only the death penalty can accomplish this end. In a recent case in New Jersey, a man named Richard Biegenwald was freed from prison after serving 18 years for murder; since his release he has been convicted of committing four murders. A prisoner named Lemuel Smith, who, while serving four life sentences for murder (plus two life sentences for kidnapping and robbery) in New York's Green Haven Prison, lured a woman corrections officer into the chaplain's office and strangled her. He then mutilated and dismembered her body. An additional life sentence for Smith is meaningless. Because

New York has no death penalty statute, Smith has effectively been given a license to kill.

But the problem of multiple murder is not confined to the 9 nation's penitentiaries. In 1981, 91 police officers were killed in the line of duty in this country. Seven percent of those arrested in the cases that have been solved had a previous arrest for murder. In New York City in 1976 and 1977, 85 persons arrested for homicide had a previous arrest for murder. Six of these individuals had two previous arrests for murder, and one had four previous murder arrests. During those two years the New York police were arresting for murder persons with a previous arrest for murder on the average of one every 8.5 days. This is not surprising when we learn that in 1975, for example, the median time served in Massachusetts for homicide was less than two-and-a-half years. In 1976 a study sponsored by the Twentieth Century Fund found that the average time served in the United States for first-degree murder is ten years. The median time served may be considerably lower.

4. *Capital punishment cheapens the value of human life.* On 10 the contrary, it can be easily demonstrated that the death penalty strengthens the value of human life. If the penalty for rape were lowered, clearly it would signal a lessened regard for the victims' suffering, humiliation, and personal integrity. It would cheapen their horrible experience, and expose them to an increased danger of recurrence. When we lower the penalty for murder, it signals a lessened regard for the value of the victim's life. Some critics of capital punishment, such as columnist Jimmy Breslin, have suggested that a life sentence is actually a harsher penalty for murder than death. This is sophistic nonsense. A few killers may decide not to appeal a death sentence, but the overwhelming majority make every effort to stay alive. It is by exacting the highest penalty for the taking of human life that we affirm the highest value of human life.

5. *The death penalty is applied in a discriminatory manner.* 11 This factor no longer seems to be the problem it once was. The appeals process for a condemned prisoner is lengthy and painstaking. Every effort is made to see that the verdict and sentence were fairly arrived at. However, assertions of discrimination are not an argument for ending the death penalty but for extending it. It is not justice to exclude everyone from the penalty of the law if a few are found to be so favored. Justice requires that the law be applied equally to all.

12   6. *Thou Shalt Not Kill.* The Bible is our greatest source of
moral inspiration. Opponents of the death penalty frequently
cite the sixth of the Ten Commandments in an attempt to
prove that capital punishment is divinely proscribed. In the
original Hebrew, however, the Sixth Commandment reads,
"Thou Shalt Not Commit Murder," and the Torah specifies
capital punishment for a variety of offenses. The biblical
viewpoint has been upheld by philosophers throughout history. The greatest thinkers of the 19th century—Kant, Locke,
Hobbes, Rousseau, Montesquieu, and Mill—agreed that natural law properly authorizes the sovereign to take life in
order to vindicate justice. Only Jeremy Bentham was ambivalent. Washington, Jefferson, and Franklin endorsed it. Abra-
ham Lincoln authorized executions for deserters in wartime.
Alexis de Tocqueville, who expressed profound respect for
American institutions, believed that the death penalty was
indispensable to the support of social order. The United
States Constitution, widely admired as one of the seminal
achievements in the history of humanity, condemns cruel
and inhuman punishment, but does not condemn capital
punishment.

13   7. *The death penalty is state-sanctioned murder.* This is the
defense with which Messrs. Willie and Shaw hoped to soften
the resolve of those who sentenced them to death. By saying
in effect, "You're no better than I am," the murderer seeks to
bring his accusers down to his own level. It is also a popular
argument among opponents of capital punishment, but a
transparently false one. Simply put, the state has rights that
the private individual does not. In a democracy, those rights
are given to the state by the electorate. The execution of a
lawfully condemned killer is no more an act of murder than is
legal imprisonment an act of kidnapping. If an individual
forces a neighbor to pay him money under threat of punishment, it's called extortion. If the state does it, it's called taxation. Rights and responsibilities surrendered by the individual
are what give the state its power to govern. This contract is
the foundation of civilization itself.

14   Everyone wants his or her rights, and will defend them
jealously. Not everyone, however, wants responsibilities, especially the painful responsibilities that come with law enforcement. Twenty-one years ago a woman named Kitty Genovese
was assaulted and murdered on a street in New York. Dozens
of neighbors heard her cries for help but did nothing to assist
her. They didn't even call the police. In such a climate the
criminal understandably grows bolder. In the presence of

moral cowardice, he lectures us on our supposed failings and
tries to equate his crimes with our quest for justice.

The death of anyone—even a convicted killer—diminishes   15
us all. But we are diminished even more by a justice system
that fails to function. It is an illusion to let ourselves believe
that doing away with capital punishment removes the murderer's deed from our conscience. The rights of society are
paramount. When we protect guilty lives, we give up innocent
lives in exchange. When opponents of capital punishment say
to the state: "I will not let you kill in my name," they are also
saying to murderers: "You can kill in your *own* name as long
as I have an excuse for not getting involved."

It is hard to imagine anything worse than being murdered   16
while neighbors do nothing. But something worse exists.
When those same neighbors shrink back from justly punishing the murderer, the victim dies twice.

Jacob Weisberg
This Is Your Death

The following account appeared in The New Republic *in July
1991.* The New Republic *is a weekly magazine of opinion
about various public issues; it is considered to be middle-of-
the-road in its general slant on things. In what way is Weisberg's article a contribution to the national discussion on the
death penalty? Is Weisberg's own position on the death penalty
apparent here?*

Thanks to the decision of a California district judge last   1
week, the American public has been spared the spectacle of
criminals being executed on television. But the lawsuit, filed
by KQED, the public television station in San Francisco, still
served a useful function. It reminded people not only that the
United States remains the only advanced democracy that exe-
cutes criminals, but that it is the only country in the world
with a grotesque array of execution techniques worth televising. A century ago Americans knew full well what it meant for
the state to hang someone from the end of a rope. Today,

thanks to the century-long search for a more "humane" method, we know little about the range of practices that would be featured on the execution channel.

2   Of the five means of execution still extant in the United States, the oldest is hanging, which was nearly universal before 1900. The gallows was last used in Kansas in 1965 and remains an option in Delaware, Montana, and Washington State. If a hanging were ever televised, viewers would see the blindfolded prisoner standing on a trap door with a rope fastened around his neck, the knot under his left ear. So long as he is hooded, it is impossible to know for how long after the trap door opens the victim suffers, or at what point he loses consciousness. But according to Harold Hillman, a British physiologist who has studied executions, the dangling person feels cervical pain, and probably suffers from an acute headache as well, a result of the rope closing off the veins of the neck.

3   In the opinion of Dr. Cornelius Rosse, the chairman of the Department of Anatomy at the University of Washington School of Medicine, the belief that fracture of the spinal cord causes instantaneous death is wrong in all but a small fraction of cases. The actual cause of death is strangulation or suffocation. In medical terms, the weight of the prisoner's body causes tearing of the cervical muscles, skin, and blood vessels. The upper cervical vertebrae are dislocated, and the spinal cord is separated from the brain, which causes death.

4   Clinton Duffy, the warden at San Quentin from 1942 to 1954, who participated in sixty hangings, described his first thus:

> The man hit bottom and I observed that he was fighting by pulling on the straps, wheezing, whistling, trying to get air, that blood was oozing through the black cap. I observed also that he urinated, defecated, and droppings fell on the floor, and the stench was terrible. I also saw witnesses pass out and have to be carried from the witness room. Some of them threw up.

It took ten minutes for the condemned man to die. When he was taken down and the cap removed, "big hunks of flesh were torn off" the side of his face where the noose had been, "his eyes were popped," and his tongue was "swollen and hanging from his mouth." His face had also turned purple. The annals of Walla Walla State Penitentiary in Washington, which was seeking to hire an executioner in 1988 when

Charles Campbell obtained a stay of execution, are filled with horror stories: prisoners partially decapitated by overlong drops, or pleading with hangmen to take them up and drop them again.

Almost as rare as hanging—but still around—is the firing squad. Gary Gilmore, who was shot in Utah in 1977, was the last to die by this method, which remains an option only there and in Idaho. Gilmore was bound to a chair with leather straps across his waist and head, and in front of an oval-shaped canvas wall. A black hood was pulled over his head. A doctor then located his heart with a stethoscope and pinned a circular white cloth target over it. Five shooters armed with .30-caliber rifles loaded with single rounds (one of them blank to spare the conscience of the executioners) stood in an enclosure twenty feet away. Each man aimed his rifle through a slot in the canvas and fired. 5

Though shooting through the head at close range causes nearly instantaneous death, a prisoner subjected to a firing squad dies as a result of blood loss caused by rupture of the heart or a large blood vessel, or tearing of the lungs. The person shot loses consciousness when shock causes a fall in the support of blood to the brain. If the shooters miss, by accident or intention, the prisoner bleeds to death slowly, as Elisio J. Mares did in Utah in 1951. It took Gilmore two minutes to die. 6

It was to mitigate the barbarism of these primitive methods that New York introduced the electric chair in 1890 as a humane alternative. Eighty-three people have been electrocuted since the Supreme Court reinstated capital punishment in 1976, making the method the most common one now in use. It is probably the most gruesome to watch. After being led into the death chamber, the prisoner is strapped to the chair with belts that cross his chest, groin, legs, and arms. Two copper electrodes are then attached: one to his leg, a patch of which will have been shaved bare to reduce resistance to electricity, and another to his shaved head. The electrodes are either soaked in brine or treated with gel (Electro-Creme) to increase conductivity and reduce burning. The prisoner will also be wearing a diaper. 7

The executioner gives a first jolt of between 500 and 2,000 volts, which lasts for thirty seconds. Smoke usually comes out of the prisoner's leg and head. A doctor then examines him. If he's not dead, another jolt is applied. A third and fourth are given if needed to finish the job. It took five jolts to kill Ethel Rosenberg. In the grisly description of Justice Brennan: 8

...the prisoner's eyeballs sometimes pop out and rest on [his] cheeks. The prisoner often defecates, urinates, and vomits blood and drool. The body turns bright red as its temperature rises, and the prisoner's flesh swells and his skin stretches to the point of breaking. Sometimes the prisoner catches on fire, particularly if [he] perspires excessively. Witnesses hear a loud and sustained sound like bacon frying, and the sickly sweet smell of burning flesh permeates the chamber.

An electrocuted corpse is hot enough to blister if touched. Thus autopsy must be delayed while internal organs cool. According to Robert H. Kirschner, the deputy chief medical examiner of Cook County, Illinois, "The brain appears cooked in most cases."

9   There is some debate about what the electrocuted prisoner experiences before he dies, but most doctors I spoke to believe that he feels himself being burned to death and suffocating, since the shock causes respiratory paralysis as well as cardiac arrest. According to Hillman, "It must feel very similar to the medieval trial by ordeal of being dropped in boiling oil." Because the energy of the shock paralyzes the prisoner's muscles, he cannot cry out. "My mouth tasted like cold peanut butter. I felt a burning in my head and my left leg, and I jumped against the straps," Willie Francis, a 17-year-old who survived an attempted execution in 1946, is reported to have said. Francis was successfully executed a year later.

10   Though all methods of execution can be botched, electrocutions go wrong frequently and dramatically, in part because the equipment is old and hard to repair. At least five have gone awry since 1983. If the electrical current is too weak, the prisoner roasts to death slowly. An instance of this was the May 4, 1990, killing of Jesse Joseph Tafero in Florida. According to witnesses, when the executioner flipped the switch, flames and smoke came out of Tafero's head, which was covered by a mask and cap. Twelve-inch blue and orange flames sprouted from both sides of the mask. The power was stopped, and Tafero took several deep breaths. The superintendent ordered the executioner to halt the current, then try it again. And again.

11   The affidavits presented for an internal inquiry into what went wrong describe the bureaucratization of the death penalty brilliantly. In the words of one of the officials:

... while working in the Death Chamber, proceeding with the execution as scheduled, I received an indication from Mr. Barton to close my electric breaker. I then told the executioner to close his electric breaker. When the executioner completed the circuit, I noticed unusual fire and smoke coming from the inmate's headpiece. After several seconds, I received an indication to open the electrical breaker to stop the electrical flow. At this time, I noticed the body move as if to be gasping for air. After several seconds, I received the indication to close the breaker the second time, which I did. Again, I noticed the unusual fire and smoke coming from the headpiece. After several seconds, I received the third indication to close the breaker, and again, the fire and smoke came from the headpiece...

And so on. Apparently a synthetic sponge, soaked in brine, had been substituted for the natural one applied to Tafero's head. This reduced the flow of electricity to as little as one hundred volts, and ended up torturing the prisoner to death. According to the state prison medical director, Frank Kligo, who attended, it was "less than aesthetically attractive."

Advanced technology does not always make the death penalty less painful to undergo or more pleasant to watch. The gas chamber, which was invented by an army medical corps officer after World War I, was first introduced as a humane alternative to the electric chair in 1924 in Nevada. The original idea, which proved impracticable, was to surprise the prisoner by gassing him in his cell without prior warning. Seven states, including California, still use the gas chamber. The most recent fatality was Leo Edwards, a 36-year-old who was killed in Jackson County, Mississippi, in 1989. 12

Had KQED won its suit, millions of viewers would have joined a dozen live witnesses in seeing Robert Alton Harris, who murdered two teenage boys in San Diego in 1978, led into a green, octagonal room in the basement of San Quentin Penitentiary. Inside the chamber are two identical metal chairs with perforated seats, marked "A" and "B." The twin chairs were last used in a double execution in 1962. If Harris's execution goes ahead this year or next, two orderlies will fasten him into chair A, attaching straps across his upper and lower legs, arms, groin, and chest. They will also affix a long stethoscope to Harris's chest so that a doctor on the outside can pronounce death. 13

14   Beneath the chair is a bowl filled with sulfuric acid mixed
with distilled water, with a pound of sodium cyanide pellets
suspended in a gauze bag just above. After the door is sealed,
and when the warden gives the signal, an executioner in a
separate room flicks a lever that releases the cyanide into the
liquid. This causes a chemical reaction that releases hydrogen
cyanide gas, which rises through the holes in the chair. Like
most death row prisoners, Harris is likely to have been
reduced to a state of passive acquiescence by his years on
death row, and will probably follow the advice of the warden
to breathe deeply as soon as he smells rotten eggs. As long as
he holds his breath nothing will happen. But as soon as he
inhales, according to the testimony of Duffy, the former warden, Harris will lose consciousness in a few seconds. "At first
there is evidence of extreme horror, pain, and strangling. The
eyes pop. The skin turns purple and the victim begins to
drool. It is a horrible sight," he testified.

15   In medical terms, victims of cyanide gas die from hypoxia,
which means the cut-off of oxygen to the brain. The initial
result of this is spasms, as in an epileptic seizure. Because of
the straps, however, involuntary body movements are
restrained. Seconds after he first inhales, Harris will feel himself unable to breathe, but will not lose consciousness immediately. "The person is unquestionably experiencing pain and
extreme anxiety," according to Dr. Richard Traystman of Johns
Hopkins. "The pain begins immediately and is felt in the arms,
shoulders, back, and chest. The sensation is similar to the pain
felt by a person during a heart attack, where essentially the
heart is being deprived of oxygen." Traystman adds: "We
would not use asphyxiation, by cyanide gas or by any other
substance, in our laboratory to kill animals that have been
used in experiments."

16   Harris will stop wriggling after ten or twelve minutes, and
the doctor will pronounce him dead. An exhaust fan then
sucks the poison air out of the chamber. Next the corpse is
sprayed with ammonia, which neutralizes traces of the cyanide that may remain. After about half an hour, orderlies enter
the chamber, wearing gas masks and rubber gloves. Their
training manual advises them to ruffle the victim's hair to
release any trapped cyanide gas before removing him.

17   Thanks to these grotesqueries, states are increasingly turning to lethal injection. This method was imagined for decades
(by Ronald Reagan, among others, when he was governor of
California in 1973), but was technically invented in 1977 by

Dr. Stanley Deutsch, who at the time chaired the Anesthesiology Department at Oklahoma University Medical School. In response to a call by an Oklahoma state senator for a cheaper alternative to repairing the state's derelict electric chair, Deutsch described a way to administer drugs through an intravenous drip so as to cause death rapidly and without pain. "Having been anesthetized on several occasions with ultra short-acting barbiturates and having administered these drugs for approximately 20 years, I can assure you that this is a rapid, pleasant way of producing unconsciousness," Deutsch wrote to state senator Bill Dawson in February 1977. The method was promptly adopted in Oklahoma, and is now either the exclusive method or an option in half of the thirty-six states with death penalty laws. It is becoming the method of choice around the country because it is easier on both the witnesses and the prisoner.

A recent injectee was Lawrence Lee Buxton, who was killed 18 in Huntsville, Texas, on February 26. Buxton was strapped to a hospital gurney, built with an extension panel for his left arm. Technicians stuck a catheter needle into Buxton's arm. Long tubes connected the needle through a hole in a cement block wall to several intravenous drips. The first, which was started immediately, dispensed harmless saline solution. Then, at the warden's signal, a curtain went up, which permitted the witnesses—reporters and friends of the soon-to-be deceased—to view the scene. Unlike some prisoners, Buxton did not have a long wait before the warden received a call from the governor's office, giving the final go-ahead.

According to Lawrence Egbert, an anesthesiologist at the 19 University of Texas in Dallas who has campaigned against lethal injection as a perversion of medical practice, the first drug administered was sodium thiopental, a common barbiturate used as an anesthetic, which puts patients quickly to sleep. A normal dose for a long operation is 1,000 milligrams; Buxton got twice that. As soon as he lost consciousness, the executioner administered pavulon, another common muscle relaxant used in heart surgery. The dose was 100 milligrams, ten times the usual, which stops the prisoner's breathing. This would have killed him in about ten minutes; to speed the process, an equal dose of potassium chloride was subsequently administered. This is another drug commonly used in bypass surgery that relaxes the heart and stops it pumping. It works in about ten seconds. All witnesses heard was the prisoner take a deep breath, then a gurgling noise as his tongue dropped back in his mouth. Watt Espy, who has compiled a list of 17,718 executions in America, from the early period of drownings, burnings, sawings-in-half, pressings-to-death, and even the crucifixions of two mutinous Continental Army soldiers, compares lethal injection to the way a devoted owner treats "a faithful dog he's loved and cherished."

20   The only physical pain, if the killing is done correctly, "is the pain of the initial prick of the needle," according to Traystman. There are, however, some potential hitches. Since doctors are precluded by medical ethics from participating in executions, except to pronounce death, the injections are often performed by incompetent or inexperienced technicians. If a death worker injects the drugs into muscle instead of a vein, or if the needle becomes clogged, extreme pain can result. This is what happened when James Autry was killed in 1984 in Texas. *Newsweek* reported that he "took at least ten minutes to die and throughout much of that time was conscious, moving about, and complaining of pain." Many prisoners have damaged veins from injecting drugs intravenously, and technicians sometimes struggle to find a serviceable one. When Texas executed Stephen Morin, a former heroin addict, orderlies prodded his arms with catheters for forty-one minutes. Being strapped to a table for a lengthy period while waiting to die is a form of psychological torture arguably worse than most physical kinds. This is demonstrated by the fact that mock executions, which cause no physical pain, are a common method of torture around the world. The agony comes not from the prospect of pain, but from the expectation of death.

21   Televised executions would mark the reversal of the process described in Louis P. Masur's *Rites of Execution* and Robert Johnson's *Death Work,* whereby executions have been removed further and further from the community that compels them. Through the eighteenth century, executions were atavistic spectacles performed in full public view. In the nineteenth they were moved inside the prison yard and witnessed by only a few. In the twentieth century, executions moved deep inside the bowels of prisons, where they were performed ever more quickly and quietly to attract minimal notice. American death penalty opponents in the 1800s supported the abolition of public executions as a way-station to ending all executions. They thought that eliminating the grossest manifestations of public barbarism would inevitably lead to the end of capital punishment as an institution. The reform had

the opposite effect, however. Invisible executions shocked the sensibilities of fewer people, and dampened the momentum of the reform movement.

Those abolitionists who now support televising executions   22
have absorbed this historical lesson. They want to bring back the equivalent of public executions in order to shock the public into opposing all executions. They hope to accomplish with pictures what Arthur Koestler did with words in his 1955 tract *Reflections on Hanging*, the publication of which led to the abolition of the rope in Great Britain in 1969.

But advances in the art of killing may have deprived them   23
of that tactic. The prospect of televised executions is likely to accelerate the trend away from grisly methods and toward ever more hermetic ways of dispatching wrongdoers. Had the KQED suit been successful, Henry Schwarzschild, a retired ACLU death penalty expert, speculates that California would have responded by quickly joining the national trend toward lethal injection.

Michael Kroll of the Death Penalty Information Center   24
objects to televising executions for exactly this reason. He argues that a video camera would capture only a "very antiseptic moment at the end of a very septic process." With the advent of death by the needle, execution itself is becoming so denatured and mechanistic as to be unshocking even to most live witnesses. This throws death penalty opponents back upon a less vivid, but more compelling case: that it is punishing people with death, not the manner in which they are killed, that is the true issue here; that capital punishment is to be opposed not simply because it is cruel, but because it is wrong.

Doug Marlette

Doug Marlette, who won the Pulitzer Prize for editorial car-
tooning, draws for New York Newsday, *and his sometimes*
controversial work is regularly reprinted in Newsweek, The
Washington Post, *and elsewhere. Eleven collections of his*
work have been published, including In Your Face: A Cartoonist at Work *(1991), where the following cartoon appeared. The*
cartoon was first published on Good Friday, as you might
guess from the content, while Marlette worked for The Charlotte *[North Carolina]* Observer.

SHOULD DRUGS BE LEGALIZED?

Kurt Schmoke

A War for the Surgeon General, Not the Attorney General

One of the most outspoken advocates of legalizing drugs has been Kurt Schmoke (born 1949), who served as mayor of Baltimore beginning in 1987. Previously, as Assistant U.S. Attorney and as State's Attorney for Baltimore, Schmoke was a highly visible prosecutor of drug cases. The following argument appeared in New Perspectives Quarterly, *a public affairs forum, in the summer of 1989. It was adapted from his testimony before a congressional committee on September 29, 1988.*

In the last ten years, the US has become absolutely awash in   1
illegal drugs. Tougher laws, greater efforts at interdiction, and
stronger rhetoric at all levels of government and from both political parties have not and will not be able to stop the flow.
That is why we must begin to consider what heretofore has
been beyond the realm of consideration: decriminalization.

Addiction Is a Disease

The violence brought about by the black market in drugs is   2
attributable in large part to the fact that we have chosen to
make criminals out of millions of people who have a disease. In
the words of the American Medical Association, "It is clear that
addiction is not simply the product of a failure of individual
will-power.... It is properly viewed as a disease, and one that
physicians can help many individuals control and overcome."

The nature of addiction is very important to the argument   3
in favor of decriminalization. The sad truth is that heroin and
morphine addiction is, for most users, a lifetime affliction
that is impervious to any punishment that the criminal-
justice system could reasonably mete out.

4   Given the nature of addiction—whether to narcotics or cocaine—and the very large number of Americans using drugs
(the National Institute on Drug Abuse estimates that one in
six working Americans has a substance abuse problem), laws
restricting their possession and sale have had predictable
consequences—most of them bad.

Crimes Committed by Addicts

5   Addicts commit crimes in order to pay for their drug habits. According to the Justice Department, 90 percent of those
who voluntarily seek treatment are turned away. In other
words, on any given day, nine out of every ten addicts have no
legal way to satisfy their addiction. And, failing to secure
help, an untreated addict will commit a crime every other day
to maintain his habit.

6   Whether one relies on studies, or on simple observation, it
is indisputable that drug users are committing vast amounts
of crime. Baltimore, the city with which I am most familiar, is
no exception. According to James A. Inciardi, of the Division
of Criminal Justice at the University of Delaware, a 1983
study of addicts in Baltimore showed that "... there were high
rates of criminality among heroin users during those periods
that they were addicted and markedly lower rates during
times of nonaddiction." The study also showed that addicts
committed crimes on a persistent day-to-day basis and over a
long period of time. And the trends are getting worse. Thus,
while the total number of arrests in Baltimore remained
almost unchanged between 1983 and 1987, there was an approximately 40 percent increase in the number of drug-
related arrests.

7   On the other hand, statistics recently compiled by the
Maryland Drug and Alcohol Abuse Administration indicate
that crime rates go down among addicts when treatment is
available. Thus, for example, of the 6,910 Baltimore residents
admitted to drug-abuse treatment in fiscal 1987, 4,386 or 63
percent had been arrested one or more times in the 24-month
period prior to admission to treatment, whereas of the 6,698
Baltimore residents who were discharged from drug treatment in fiscal 1987, 6,152 or 91.8 percent were not arrested
during the time of their treatment. These statistics tend to
support the view that one way to greatly reduce drug-related
crime is to assure addicts legal access to methadone or other
drugs.

Overload of the Criminal-Justice System

We cannot prosecute our way out of the drug problem. 8
There are several reasons for this, but the most basic reason
is that the criminal-justice system cannot—without sacrific-
ing our civil liberties—handle the sheer volume of drug-related cases.

Nationwide last year, over 750,000 people were arrested for 9
violating drug laws. Most of these arrests were for possession.
In Baltimore, there were 13,037 drug-related arrests in 1987.
Between January 1, 1988 and July 1, 1988, there were 7,981
drug-related arrests. Those numbers are large, but they
hardly reflect the annual total number of drug violations
committed in Baltimore. Should we, therefore, try to arrest
still more? Yes—as long as the laws are on the books. But as a
practical matter, we don't have any place to put the drug offenders we are now arresting. The population in the Baltimore City Jail is currently 2,900 inmates, even though its
inmate capacity is only 2,700. This shortage of prison space
has led to severe overcrowding, and Baltimore is now under
court order to reduce its jail population.

Will more prisons help? Not in any significant way. We 10
simply cannot build enough of them to hold all of America's
drug offenders—which number in the millions. And even if
we could, the cost would far exceed what American taxpayers
would be willing to pay.

Decriminalization is the single most effective step we could 11
take to reduce prison overcrowding. And with less crowded
prisons, there will be less pressure on prosecutors to plea bargain and far greater chance that non-drug criminals will go to
jail—and stay in jail.

The unvarnished truth is that in our effort to prosecute and 12
imprison our way out of the drug war, we have allowed the
drug lords to put us exactly where they want us: wasting enormous resources—both in money and in personnel—attacking
the fringes of the problem (the drug users and small-time
pushers), while the heart of the problem—the traffickers and
their profits—goes unsolved.

Failed Supply-Side Policies

Not only can we not prosecute our way out of our. 13
drug morass, we cannot interdict our way out of it either.
Lately, there have been calls for stepped-up border patrols,

increased use of the military and greater pressure on foreign governments.

14   Assuming these measures would reduce the supply of illegal drugs, that reduction would not alleviate the chaos in our cities. According to statistics recently cited by the American Medical Association, Latin American countries produced between 162,000 and 211,400 metric tons of cocaine in 1987. That is five times the amount needed to supply the US market. Moreover, we are probably only interdicting 10 to 15 percent of the cocaine entering this country. Thus, even if we quadrupled the amount of cocaine we interdict, the world supply of cocaine would still far outstrip US demand.

15   If the drug laws in the US simply didn't achieve their intent, perhaps there would be insufficient reason to get rid of them. But these laws are doing more than not working—they are violating Hippocrates' famous admonition: First, do no harm.

16   The legal prohibition of narcotics, cocaine and marijuana demonstrably increases the price of those drugs. For example, an importer can purchase a kilogram of heroin for $10,000. By the time that kilogram passes through the hands of several middlemen, its street value can reach $1,000,000. Such profits can't help but attract major criminal entrepreneurs willing to take any risk to keep their product coming to the American market.

Victimization of Children

17   Perhaps the most tragic victims of our drug laws are children. Many, for example, have been killed as innocent bystanders in gun battles among traffickers. Furthermore, while it is true that drug prohibition probably does keep some children from experimenting with drugs, almost any child who wants drugs can get them. Keeping drugs outlawed has not kept them out of children's hands.

18   Recent statistics in both Maryland and Baltimore prove the point: In a 1986–87 survey of Maryland adolescents, 13 percent of eighth graders, 18.5 percent of tenth graders and 22.3 percent of twelfth graders report that they are currently using drugs. In Baltimore, the percentages are 16.6, 16.5 and 20.3, respectively. It should be noted that these numbers exclude alcohol and tobacco, and that current use means at least once a month. It should also be noted that these numbers show a decrease from earlier surveys in 1982 and 1984.

Nevertheless, the fact remains that drugs are being widely used by students. Moreover, these numbers do not include the many young people who have left school or who failed to report their drug use.

A related problem is that many children, especially those living in the inner city, are frequently barraged with the message that selling drugs is an easy road to riches. In Baltimore, as in many other cities, small children are acting as lookouts and runners for drug pushers, just as they did for bootleggers during Prohibition. Decriminalization and the destruction of the black market would end this most invidious form of child labor. [19]

As for education, decriminalization will not end the *Just Say No* and similar education campaigns. On the contrary, more money will be available for such programs. Decriminalization will, however, end the competing message of "easy money" that the drug dealers use to entice children. Furthermore, decriminalization will free up valuable criminal-justice resources that can be used to find, prosecute and punish those who sell drugs to children. [20]

This said, if there has been one problem with the current drug-reform debate, it has been the tendency to focus on narrow problems and narrow solutions. That is, we talk about the number of people arrested, the number of tons of drugs entering our ports, the number of available treatment centers, and so on, but there is a bigger picture out there. We, as a nation, have not done nearly enough to battle the social and economic problems that make drug abuse an easy escape for the despairing, and drug trafficking an easy answer to a lack of education and joblessness. [21]

Adolescents who take drugs are making a not-so-subtle statement about their confidence in the future. Children without hope are children who will take drugs. We need to give these children more than simple slogans. We need to give them a brighter tomorrow, a sense of purpose, a chance at economic opportunity. It is on that battlefield that the real war against drugs must be fought. [22]

Spread of AIDS

The 1980s have brought another major public health problem that is being made still worse because of our drug laws: AIDS. Contaminated intravenous drug needles are now the principal means of transmission for the HIV infection. The us- [23]

ers of drug needles infect not only those with whom they share needles, but also their sex partners and their unborn children.

24   One way to effectively slow this means of transmission would be to allow addicts to exchange their dirty needles for clean ones. However, in a political climate where all illicit drug use is condemned, and where possession of a syringe can be a criminal offense, few jurisdictions have been willing to initiate a needle exchange program. This is a graphic example, along with our failure to give illegal drugs to cancer patients with intractable pain, of our blind pursuit of an irrational policy.

The Mixed Message of Tobacco and Alcohol

25   The case for the decriminalization of drugs becomes even stronger when illegal drugs are looked at in the context of legal drugs.

26   It is estimated that over 350,000 people will die this year from tobacco-related diseases. Last year the number was equally large. And it will be again next year. Why do millions of people continue to engage in an activity which has been proven to cause cancer and heart disease? The answer is that smoking is more than just a bad habit. It is an addiction. In 1988, Surgeon General C. Everett Koop called nicotine as addictive as heroin and cocaine. And yet, with the exception of taxes and labeling, cigarettes are sold without restriction.

27   By every standard we apply to illicit drugs, tobacco should be a controlled substance. But it is not, and for good reason. Given that millions of people continue to smoke—many of whom would quit if they could—making cigarettes illegal would be an open invitation to a new black market.

28   The certain occurrence of a costly and dangerous illegal tobacco trade (if tobacco were outlawed) is well understood by Congress, the Bush Administration and the criminal-justice community. No rationally thinking person would want to bring such a catastrophe down upon the US—even if it would prevent some people from smoking.

29   Like tobacco, alcohol is a drug that kills thousands of Americans every year. It plays a part in more than half of all automobile fatalities and is also frequently involved in suicides, non-automobile accidents, domestic disputes and crimes of violence. Millions of Americans are alcoholic, and alcohol costs the nation billions of dollars in health care and lost productivity. So why not ban alcohol? Because, as al-

most every American knows, we already tried that. Prohibition turned out to be one of the worst social experiments this country has ever undertaken.

I will not review the sorry history of Prohibition except to   30
make two important points. The first is that in repealing Prohibition, we made significant mistakes that should not be repeated in the event that drug use is decriminalized. Specifically, when alcohol was again made legal in 1934, we made no significant effort to educate people as to its dangers. There were no (and still are no) *Just Say No* campaigns against alcohol. We allowed alcohol to be advertised and have associated it with happiness, success and social acceptability. We have also been far too lenient with drunk drivers.

The second point is that, notwithstanding claims to the   31
contrary by critics of decriminalization, there are marked parallels between the era of Prohibition and our current policy of making drugs illegal, and important lessons to be learned from our attempts to ban the use and sale of alcohol.

During Prohibition, the government tried to keep alcohol   32
out of the hands of millions of people who refused to give it up. As a result, our cities were overrun by criminal syndicates enriching themselves with the profits of bootleg liquor and terrorizing anyone who got in their way. We then looked to the criminal-justice system to solve the crime problems that Prohibition created. But the criminal-justice system—outmanned, outgunned and often corrupted by enormous black market profits—was incapable of stopping the massive crime wave that Prohibition brought, just as it was incapable of stopping people from drinking.

As a person now publicly identified with the movement to   33
reform our drug laws through the use of some form of decriminalization, I consider it very important to say that I am not soft on either drug use or drug dealers. I am a soldier in the war against drugs. As Maryland's State Attorney, I spent years prosecuting and jailing drug traffickers, and had one of the highest rates of incarceration for drug convictions in the country. And if I were still State's Attorney, I would be enforcing the law as vigorously as ever. My experience as a prosecutor did not in any way alter my passionate dislike for drug dealers, it simply convinced me that the present system doesn't work and cannot be made to work.

During the Revolutionary War, the British insisted on   34
wearing red coats and marching in formation. They looked very pretty. They also lost. A good general does not pursue a strategy in the face of overwhelming evidence of failure.

Instead, a good general changes from a losing strategy to one that exploits his enemy's weakness, while exposing his own troops to only as much danger as is required to win. The drug war can be beaten and the public health of the US can be improved if we are willing to substitute common sense for rhetoric, myth and blind persistence, and to put the war in the hands of the Surgeon General, not the Attorney General.

William Bennett
Should Drugs Be Legalized?

Prominent Republican leader William Bennett (born 1943) studied and played football (and the guitar for a rock group) at Williams College. Later he earned a doctorate in philosophy at the University of Texas and a law degree at Harvard, and taught at the University of Southern Mississippi, Boston University, and the University of Wisconsin. He joined the Reagan administration as chair of the National Endowment for the Humanities in 1981 and became Secretary of Education in 1985; in 1988, he was appointed as the nation's "drug czar"—in charge of waging President Bush's "war on drugs." He published the following argument in 1990 in Reader's Digest. *Note, too, the exchange between Bennett and Milton Friedman that is reprinted after this selection.*

1   Since I took command of the war on drugs, I have learned from former Secretary of State George Schultz that our concept of fighting drugs is "flawed." The only thing to do, he says, is to "make it possible for addicts to buy drugs at some regulated place." Conservative commentator William F. Buckley, Jr., suggests I should be "fatalistic" about the flood of cocaine from South America and simply "let it in." Syndicated columnist Mike Royko contends it would be easier to sweep junkies out of the gutters "than to fight a hopeless war" against the narcotics that send them there. Labeling our efforts "bankrupt," federal judge Robert W. Sweet opts for legalization, saying, "If our society can learn to stop using butter, it should be able to cut down on cocaine."

2   Flawed, fatalistic, hopeless, bankrupt! I never realized surrender was so fashionable until I assumed this post.

Though most Americans are overwhelmingly determined 3
to go toe-to-toe with the foreign drug lords and neighborhood
pushers, a small minority believe that enforcing drug laws
imposes greater costs on society than do drugs themselves.
Like addicts seeking immediate euphoria, the legalizers want
peace at any price, even though it means the inevitable proliferation of a practice that degrades, impoverishes and kills.

I am acutely aware of the burdens drug enforcement 4
places upon us. It consumes economic resources we would
like to use elsewhere. It is sometimes frustrating, thankless
and often dangerous. But the consequences of *not* enforcing
drug laws would be far more costly. Those consequences involve the intrinsically destructive nature of drugs and the toll
they exact from our society in hundreds of thousands of lost
and broken lives . . . human potential never realized . . . time
stolen from families and jobs . . . precious spiritual and economic resources squandered.

That is precisely why virtually every civilized society has 5
found it necessary to exert some form of control over mind-
altering substances and why this war is so important. Americans feel up to their hips in drugs now. They would be up to
their necks under legalization.

Even limited experiments in drug legalization have shown 6
that when drugs are more widely available, addiction sky-
rockets. In 1975 Italy liberalized its drug law and now has one
of the highest heroin-related death rates in Western Europe.
In Alaska, where marijuana was decriminalized in 1975, the
easy atmosphere has increased usage of the drug, particularly
among children. Nor does it stop there. Some Alaskan school-
children now tout "coca puffs," marijuana cigarettes laced
with cocaine.

Many legalizers concede that drug legalization might in- 7
crease use, but they shrug off the matter. "It may well be that
there would be more addicts, and I would regret that result,"
says Nobel laureate economist Milton Friedman. The late
Harvard Medical School psychiatry professor Norman Zin-
berg, a longtime proponent of "responsible" drug use, admitted that "use of now illicit drugs would certainly increase.
Also, casualties probably would increase."

In fact, Dr. Herbert D. Kleber of Yale University, my deputy 8
in charge of demand reduction, predicts legalization might
cause "a five-to-sixfold increase" in cocaine use. But legalizers regard this as a necessary price for the "benefits" of legalization. What benefits?

9   1. *Legalization will take the profit out of drugs.* The result supposedly will be the end of criminal drug pushers and the big foreign drug wholesalers, who will turn to other enterprises because nobody will need to make furtive and dangerous trips to his local pusher.

10   But what, exactly, would the brave new world of legalized drugs look like? Buckley stresses that "adults get to buy the stuff at carefully regulated stores." (Would you want one in *your* neighborhood?) Others, like Friedman, suggest we sell the drugs at "ordinary retail outlets."

11   Former City University of New York sociologist Georgette Bennett assures us that "brand-name competition will be prohibited" and that strict quality control and proper labeling will be overseen by the Food and Drug Administration. In a touching egalitarian note, she adds that "free drugs will be provided at government clinics" for addicts too poor to buy them.

12   Almost all the legalizers point out that the price of drugs will fall, even though the drugs will be heavily taxed. Buckley, for example, argues that somehow federal drugstores will keep the price "low enough to discourage a black market but high enough to accumulate a surplus to be used for drug education."

13   Supposedly, drug sales will generate huge amounts of revenue, which will then be used to tell the public not to use drugs and to treat those who don't listen.

14   In reality, this tax would only allow government to *share* the drug profits now garnered by criminals. Legalizers would have to tax drugs heavily in order to pay for drug education and treatment programs. Criminals could undercut the official price and still make huge profits. What alternative would the government have? Cut the price until it was within the lunch-money budget of the average sixth-grade student?

15   2. *Legalization will eliminate the black market.* Wrong. And not just because the regulated prices could be undercut. Many legalizers admit that drugs such as crack or PCP are simply too dangerous to allow the shelter of the law. Thus criminals will provide what the government will not. "As long as drugs that people very much want remain illegal, a black market will exist," says legalization advocate David Boaz of the libertarian Cato Institute.

16   Look at crack. In powdered form, cocaine was an expensive indulgence. But street chemists found that a better and far less expensive—and far more dangerous—high could be achieved by mixing cocaine with baking soda and heating it.

Crack was born, and "cheap" coke invaded low-income communities with furious speed.

An ounce of powdered cocaine might sell on the street for $1200. That same ounce can produce 370 vials of crack at $10 each. Ten bucks seems like a cheap hit, but crack's intense ten- to 15-minute high is followed by an unbearable depression. The user wants more crack, thus starting a rapid and costly descent into addiction.   17

If government drugstores do not stock crack, addicts will find it in the clandestine market or simply bake it themselves from their legally purchased cocaine.   18

Currently crack is being laced with insecticides and animal tranquilizers to heighten its effect. Emergency rooms are now warned to expect victims of "sandwiches" and "moon rocks," life-threatening smokable mixtures of heroin and crack. Unless the government is prepared to sell these deadly variations of dangerous drugs, it will perpetuate a criminal black market by default.   19

And what about children and teen-agers? They would obviously be barred from drug purchases, just as they are prohibited from buying beer and liquor. But pushers will continue to cater to these young customers with the old, favorite come-ons—a couple of free fixes to get them hooked. And what good will anti-drug education be when these youngsters observe their older brothers and sisters, parents and friends lighting up and shooting up with government permission?   20

Legalization will give us the worst of both worlds: millions of *new* drug users *and* a thriving criminal black market.   21

3. *Legalization will dramatically reduce crime.* "It is the high price of drugs that leads addicts to robbery, murder and other crimes," says Ira Glasser, executive director of the American Civil Liberties Union. A study by the Cato Institute concludes: "Most, if not all, 'drug-related murders' are the result of drug prohibition."   22

But researchers tell us that many drug-related felonies are committed by people involved in crime *before* they started taking drugs. The drugs, so routinely available in criminal circles, make the criminals more violent and unpredictable.   23

Certainly there are some kill-for-a-fix crimes, but does any rational person believe that a cut-rate price for drugs at a government outlet will stop such psychopathic behavior? The fact is that under the influence of drugs, normal people do not act normally, and abnormal people behave in chilling and horrible ways. DEA agents told me about a teen-age addict in   24

Manhattan who was smoking crack when he sexually abused and caused permanent internal injuries to his one-month-old daughter.

25   Children are among the most frequent victims of violent, drug-related crimes that have nothing to do with the cost of acquiring the drugs. In Philadelphia in 1987 more than half the child-abuse fatalities involved at least one parent who was a heavy drug user. Seventy-three percent of the child-abuse deaths in New York City in 1987 involved parental drug use.

26   In my travels to the ramparts of the drug war, I have seen nothing to support the legalizers' argument that lower drug prices would reduce crime. Virtually everywhere I have gone, police and DEA agents have told me that crime rates are highest where crack is cheapest.

27   4. *Drug use should be legal since users only harm themselves.* Those who believe this should stand beside the medical examiner as he counts the 36 bullet wounds in the shattered corpse of a three-year-old who happened to get in the way of his mother's drug-crazed boyfriend. They should visit the babies abandoned by cocaine-addicted mothers— infants who already carry the ravages of addiction in their own tiny bodies. They should console the devastated relatives of the nun who worked in a homeless shelter and was stabbed to death by a crack addict enraged that she would not stake him to a fix.

28   Do drug addicts only harm themselves? Here is a former cocaine addict describing the compulsion that quickly draws even the most "responsible" user into irresponsible behavior: "Everything is about getting high, and any means necessary to get there becomes rational. If it means stealing something from somebody close to you, lying to your family, borrowing money from people you know you can't pay back, writing checks you know you can't cover, you do all those things— things that are totally against everything you have ever believed in."

29   Society pays for this behavior, and not just in bigger insurance premiums, losses from accidents and poor job performance. We pay in the loss of a priceless social currency as families are destroyed, trust between friends is betrayed and promising careers are never fulfilled. I cannot imagine sanctioning behavior that would increase that toll.

30   I find no merit in the legalizers' case. The simple fact is that drug use is wrong. And the moral argument, in the end, is the most compelling argument. A citizen in a drug-induced haze, whether on his back-yard deck or on a mattress in a

ghetto crack house, is not what the founding fathers meant by the "pursuit of happiness." Despite the legalizers' argument that drug use is a matter of "personal freedom," our nation's notion of liberty is rooted in the ideal of a self-reliant citizenry. Helpless wrecks in treatment centers, men chained by their noses to cocaine—these people are slaves.

Imagine if, in the darkest days of 1940, Winston Churchill had rallied the West by saying, "This war looks hopeless, and besides, it will cost too much. Hitler can't be *that* bad. Let's surrender and see what happens." That is essentially what we hear from the legalizers. 31

This war *can* be won. I am heartened by indications that education and public revulsion are having an effect on drug use. The National Institute on Drug Abuse's latest survey of current users shows a 37-percent *decrease* in drug consumption since 1985. Cocaine is down 50 percent; marijuana use among young people is at its lowest rate since 1972. In my travels I've been encouraged by signs that Americans are fighting back. 32

I am under no illusion that such developments, however hopeful, mean the war is over. We need to involve more citizens in the fight, increase pressure on drug criminals and build on antidrug programs that have proved to work. This will not be easy. But the moral and social costs of surrender are simply too great to contemplate. 33

Milton Friedman
Prohibition and Drugs

When he was on the faculty of the University of Chicago, Milton Friedman won the Nobel Prize for his "monetarist" school of economics, one that stresses stable growth in the supply of money and credit in an economy. A conservative who influenced the policies of Ronald Reagan and George Bush, he enjoys writing about a range of public issues. Recently a senior research fellow at the Hoover Institute at Stanford University and now retired, he wrote the two following essays on the legalization of drugs—one for Newsweek *(1972) and one for* The Wall Street Journal *(1989).*

The Wall Street Journal *article, which contains a reference
in paragraph five to the* Newsweek *essay, is an "open letter" to
William Bennett, the nation's "drug czar" (i.e., director of the
Office of National Drug Policy) under former President Bush.
Bennett is the author of the previous essay in this section as
well as the response to Milton Friedman that is reprinted after
Friedman's two essays. Friedman's own counter-response fol-
lows that, on page 911.*

1   "The reign of tears is over. The slums will soon be only a
memory. We will turn our prisons into factories and our jails
into storehouses and corncribs. Men will walk upright now,
women will smile, and the children will laugh. Hell will be
forever for rent."

2   That is how Billy Sunday, the noted evangelist and leading
crusader against Demon Rum, greeted the onset of Prohibition in early 1920. We know now how tragically his hopes
were doomed. New prisons and jails had to be built to house
the criminals spawned by converting the drinking of spirits
into a crime against the state. Prohibition undermined respect for the law, corrupted the minions of the law, created a
decadent moral climate—but did not stop the consumption of
alcohol.

3   Despite this tragic object lesson, we seem bent on repeating precisely the same mistake in the handling of drugs.

Ethics and Expediency

4   On ethical grounds, do we have the right to use the machinery of government to prevent an individual from becoming an
alcoholic or a drug addict? For children, almost everyone
would answer at least a qualified yes. But for responsible
adults, I, for one, would answer no. Reason with the potential
addict, yes. Tell him the consequences, yes. Pray for and with
him, yes. But I believe that we have no right to use force, directly or indirectly, to prevent a fellow man from committing
suicide, let alone from drinking alcohol or taking drugs.

5   I readily grant that the ethical issue is difficult and that
men of goodwill may well disagree. Fortunately, we need not
resolve the ethical issue to agree on policy. *Prohibition is an
attempted cure that makes matters worse—for both the addict
and the rest of us.* Hence, even if you regard present policy toward drugs as ethically justified, considerations of expediency make that policy most unwise.

Consider first the addict. Legalizing drugs might increase   6
the number of addicts, but it is not clear that it would. Forbidden fruit is attractive, particularly to the young. More important, many drug addicts are deliberately made by pushers,
who give likely prospects their first few doses free. It pays the
pusher to do so because, once hooked, the addict is a captive
customer. If drugs were legally available, any possible profit
from such inhumane activity would disappear, since the addict could buy from the cheapest source.

Whatever happens to the number of addicts, the individual   7
addict would clearly be far better off if drugs were legal. Today, drugs are both incredibly expensive and highly uncertain
in quality. Addicts are driven to associate with criminals to
get the drugs, become criminals themselves to finance the
habit, and risk constant danger of death and disease.

Consider next the rest of us. Here the situation is crystal-   8
clear. The harm to us from the addiction of others arises almost wholly from the fact that drugs are illegal. A recent
committee of the American Bar Association estimated that
addicts commit one-third to one-half of all street crime
in the U.S. Legalize drugs, and street crime would drop dramatically.

Moreover, addicts and pushers are not the only ones cor-   9
rupted. Immense sums are at stake. It is inevitable that some
relatively low-paid police and other government officials—
and some high-paid ones as well—will succumb to the temptation to pick up easy money.

Law and Order

Legalizing drugs would simultaneously reduce the amount   10
of crime and raise the quality of law enforcement. Can you
conceive of any other measure that would accomplish so
much to promote law and order?

But, you may say, must we accept defeat? Why not simply   11
end the drug traffic? That is where experience under Prohibition is most relevant. We cannot end the drug traffic. We may
be able to cut off opium from Turkey—but there are innumerable other places where the opium poppy grows. With French
cooperation, we may be able to make Marseilles an unhealthy
place to manufacture heroin—but there are innumerable
other places where the simple manufacturing operations involved can be carried out. So long as large sums of money are
involved—and they are bound to be if drugs are illegal—it is

literally hopeless to expect to end the traffic or even to reduce
seriously its scope.

12   In drugs, as in other areas, persuasion and example are
likely to be far more effective than the use of force to shape
others in our image.

Milton Friedman

An Open Letter to Bill Bennett

Dear Bill:

1   In Oliver Cromwell's eloquent words, "I beseech you, in the
bowels of Christ, think it possible you may be mistaken"
about the course you and President Bush urge us to adopt to
fight drugs. The path you propose of more police, more jails,
use of the military in foreign countries, harsh penalties for
drug users, and a whole panoply of repressive measures can
only make a bad situation worse. The drug war cannot be
won by those tactics without undermining the human liberty
and individual freedom that you and I cherish.

2   You are not mistaken in believing that drugs are a scourge
that is devastating our society. You are not mistaken in believing that drugs are tearing asunder our social fabric, ruining
the lives of many young people, and imposing heavy costs on
some of the most disadvantaged among us. You are not mistaken in believing that the majority of the public share your
concerns. In short, you are not mistaken in the end you seek
to achieve.

3   Your mistake is failing to recognize that the very measures
you favor are a major source of the evils you deplore. Of
course the problem is demand, but it is not only demand, it is
demand that must operate through repressed and illegal
channels. Illegality creates obscene profits that finance the
murderous tactics of the drug lords; illegality leads to the corruption of law enforcement officials; illegality monopolizes
the efforts of honest law forces so that they are starved for
resources to fight the simpler crimes of robbery, theft and
assault.

4   Drugs are a tragedy for addicts. But criminalizing their use
converts that tragedy into a disaster for society, for users and

non-users alike. Our experience with the prohibition of drugs is a replay of our experience with the prohibition of alcoholic beverages.

I append excerpts from a column that I wrote in 1972 on "Prohibition and Drugs." The major problem then was heroin from Marseilles; today, it is cocaine from Latin America. Today, also, the problem is far more serious than it was 17 years ago: more addicts, more innocent victims; more drug pushers, more law enforcement officials; more money spent to enforce prohibition, more money spent to circumvent prohibition.

Had drugs been decriminalized 17 years ago, "crack" would never have been invented (it was invented because the high cost of illegal drugs made it profitable to provide a cheaper version) and there would today be far fewer addicts. The lives of thousands, perhaps hundreds of thousands of innocent victims would have been saved, and not only in the U.S. The ghettos of our major cities would not be drug-and-crime-infested no-man's lands. Fewer people would be in jails, and fewer jails would have been built.

Colombia, Bolivia and Peru would not be suffering from narco-terror, and we would not be distorting our foreign policy because of narco-terror. Hell would not, in the words with which Billy Sunday welcomed Prohibition, "be forever for rent," but it would be a lot emptier.

Decriminalizing drugs is even more urgent now than in 1972, but we must recognize that the harm done in the interim cannot be wiped out, certainly not immediately. Postponing decriminalization will only make matters worse, and make the problem appear even more intractable.

Alcohol and tobacco cause many more deaths in users than do drugs. Decriminalization would not prevent us from treating drugs as we now treat alcohol and tobacco: prohibiting sales of drugs to minors, outlawing the advertising of drugs and similar measures. Such measures could be enforced, while outright prohibition cannot be. Moreover, if even a small fraction of the money we now spend on trying to enforce drug prohibition were devoted to treatment and rehabilitation, in an atmosphere of compassion not punishment, the reduction in drug usage and in the harm done to the users could be dramatic.

This plea comes from the bottom of my heart. Every friend of freedom, and I know you are one, must be as revolted as I am by the prospect of turning the United States into an armed camp, by the vision of jails filled with casual drug users and of an army of enforcers empowered to invade the liberty of citizens on slight evidence. A country in which shooting down unidentified planes "on suspicion" can be seriously considered as a drug-war tactic is not the kind of United States that either you or I want to hand on to future generations.

William Bennett

A Response to Milton Friedman

Dear Milton:

1   There was little, if anything, new in your open letter to me calling for the legalization of drugs (*The Wall Street Journal,* Sept. 7). As your 1972 article made clear, the legalization argument is an old and familiar one, which has recently been revived by a small number of journalists and academics who insist that the only solution to the drug problem is no solution at all. What surprises me is that you would continue to advocate so unrealistic a proposal without pausing to consider seriously its consequences.

2   If the argument for drug legalization has one virtue it is its sheer simplicity. Eliminate laws against drugs, and street crime will disappear. Take the profit out of the black market through decriminalization and regulation, and poor neighborhoods will no longer be victimized by drug dealers. Cut back on drug enforcement, and use the money to wage a public health campaign against drugs, as we do with tobacco and alcohol.

Counting Costs

3   The basic premise of all these propositions is that using our nation's laws to fight drugs is too costly. To be sure, our attempts to reduce drug use do carry with them enormous costs. But the question that must be asked—and which is totally ignored by the legalization advocates—is, what are the costs of *not* enforcing laws against drugs?

In my judgment, and in the judgment of virtually every seri- 4
ous scholar in this field, the potential costs of legalizing drugs
would be so large as to make it a public policy disaster.

Of course, no one, including you, can say with certainty 5
what would happen in the U.S. if drugs were suddenly to become a readily purchased product. We do know, however,
that wherever drugs have been cheaper and more easily obtained, drug use—and addiction—has skyrocketed. In opium
and cocaine producing countries, addiction is rampant
among the peasants involved in drug production.

Professor James Q. Wilson tells us that during the years in 6
which heroin could be legally prescribed by doctors in Britain, the number of addicts increased forty-fold. And after the
repeal of Prohibition—an analogy favored but misunderstood
by legalization advocates—consumption of alcohol soared by
350%.

Could we afford such dramatic increases in drug use? I 7
doubt it. Already the toll of drug use on American society—
measured in lost productivity, in rising health insurance
costs, in hospitals flooded with drug overdose emergencies,
in drug caused accidents, and in premature death—is surely
more than we would like to bear.

You seem to believe that by spending just a little more 8
money on treatment and rehabilitation, the costs of increased
addiction can be avoided. That hope betrays a basic misunderstanding of the problems facing drug treatment. Most addicts
don't suddenly decide to get help. They remain addicts either
because treatment isn't available or because they don't seek it
out. The National Drug Control Strategy announced by President Bush on Sept. 5 goes a long way in making sure that more
treatment slots are available. But the simple fact remains that
many drug users won't enter treatment until they are forced
to—often by the very criminal justice system you think is the
source of the problem.

As for the connection between drugs and crime, your un- 9
swerving commitment to a legalization solution prevents you
from appreciating the complexity of the drug market. Contrary to your claim, most addicts do not turn to crime to support their habit. Research shows that many of them were
involved in criminal activity before they turned to drugs.
Many former addicts who have received treatment continue to
commit crimes during their recovery. And even if drugs were
legal, what evidence do you have that the habitual drug user
wouldn't continue to rob and steal to get money for clothes,
food or shelter? Drug addicts always want more drugs than

they can afford, and no legalization scheme has yet come up with a way of satisfying that appetite.

10   The National Drug Control Strategy emphasizes the importance of reclaiming the streets and neighborhoods where drugs have wrought havoc because, I admit, the price of having drug laws is having criminals who will try to subvert them. Your proposal might conceivably reduce the amount of gang- and dealer-related crime, but it is fanciful to suggest that it would make crime vanish. Unless you are willing to distribute drugs freely and widely, there will always be a black market to undercut the regulated one. And as for the potential addicts, for the school children and for the pregnant mothers, all of whom would find drugs more accessible and legally condoned, your proposal would offer nothing at all.

11   So I advocate a larger criminal justice system to take drug users off the streets and deter new users from becoming more deeply involved in so hazardous an activity. You suggest that such policies would turn the country "into an armed camp." Try telling that to the public housing tenants who enthusiastically support plans to enhance security in their buildings, or to the residents who applaud police when a local crack house is razed. They recognize that drug use is a threat to the individual liberty and domestic tranquility guaranteed by the Constitution.

12   I remain an ardent defender of our nation's laws against illegal drug use and our attempts to enforce them because I believe drug use is wrong. A true friend of freedom understands that government has a responsibility to craft and uphold laws that help educate citizens about right and wrong. That, at any rate, was the Founders' view of our system of government.

Liberal Ridicule

13   Today this view is much ridiculed by liberal elites and entirely neglected by you. So while I cannot doubt the sincerity of your opinion on drug legalization, I find it difficult to respect. The moral cost of legalizing drugs is great, but it is a cost that apparently lies outside the narrow scope of libertarian policy prescriptions.

14   I do not have a simple solution to the drug problem. I doubt that one exists. But I am committed to fighting the problem on several fronts through imaginative policies and hard work over a long period of time. As in the past, some of these efforts will work and some won't. Your response, how-

ever, is to surrender and see what happens. To my mind that is irresponsible and reckless public policy. At a time when national intolerance for drug use is rapidly increasing, the legalization argument is a political anachronism. Its recent resurgence is, I trust, only a temporary distraction from the genuine debate on national drug policy.

Milton Friedman
A Response to William Bennett

William Bennett is entirely right (editorial page, Sept. 19) that "there was little, if anything, new in" my open letter to him—just as there is little, if anything, new in his proposed program to rid this nation of the scourge of drugs. That is why I am so disturbed by that program. It flies in the face of decades of experience. More police, more jails, more-stringent penalties, increased efforts at interception, increased publicity about the evils of drugs—all this has been accompanied by more, not fewer, drug addicts; more, not fewer, crimes and murders; more, not less, corruption; more, not fewer, innocent victims.   1

Like Mr. Bennett, his predecessors were "committed to fighting the problem on several fronts through imaginative policies and hard work over a long period of time." What evidence convinces him that the same policies on a larger scale will end the drug scourge? He offers none in his response to me, only assertion and the conjecture that legalizing drugs would produce "a public policy disaster"—as if that is not exactly what we already have.   2

Legalizing drugs is not equivalent to surrender in the fight against drug addiction. On the contrary, I believe that legalizing drugs is a precondition for an effective fight. We might then have a real chance to prevent sales to minors; get drugs out of the schools and playgrounds; save crack babies and reduce their number; launch an effective educational campaign on the personal costs of drug use—not necessarily conducted, I might add, by government; punish drug users guilty of harming others while "under the influence"; and encourage   3

large numbers of addicts to volunteer for treatment and rehabilitation when they could do so without confessing to criminal actions. Some habitual drug users would, as he says,
"continue to rob and steal to get money for clothes, food or
shelter." No doubt also there will be "a black market to undercut the regulated one"—as there now is bootleg liquor thanks
to high taxes on alcoholic beverages. But these would be on a
far smaller scale than at present. Perfection is not for this
world. Pursuing the unattainable best can prevent achievement of the attainable good.

4   As Mr. Bennett recognizes, the victims of drugs fall into
two classes: those who choose to use drugs and innocent victims—who in one way or another include almost all the rest
of us. Legalization would drastically reduce the number of innocent victims. That is a virtual certainty. The number of self-
chosen victims might increase, but it is pure conjecture that
the number would, as he asserts, skyrocket. In any event,
while both groups of victims are to be pitied, the innocent victims surely have a far greater claim on our sympathy than the
self-chosen victims—or else the concept of personal responsibility has been emptied of all content.

5   A particular class of innocent victims generally overlooked
is foreigners. By what right do we impose our values on the
residents of Colombia? Or, by our actions undermine the very
foundations of their society and condemn hundreds, perhaps
thousands, of Colombians to violent death? All because the
U.S. government is unable to enforce its own laws on its own
citizens. I regard such actions as indefensible, entirely aside
from the distortions they introduce into our foreign policy.

6   Finally, he and I interpret the "Founders' view of our system
of government" very differently. To him, they believed "that
government has a responsibility to...help educate citizens
about right and wrong." To me, that is a totalitarian view
opening the road to thought control and would have been utterly unacceptable to the Founders. I do not believe, and neither did they, that it is the responsibility of government to tell
free citizens what is right and wrong. That is something for
them to decide for themselves. Government is a means to enable each of us to pursue our own vision in our own way so
long as we do not interfere with the right of others to do the
same. In the words of the Declaration of Independence, "all
Men are...endowed by their Creator with certain unalienable
Rights, that among these are Life, Liberty, and the pursuit of
Happiness. That to secure these Rights Governments are instituted among Men, deriving their just powers from the consent

of the Governed." In my view, Justice Louis Brandeis was a "true friend of freedom" when he wrote, "Experience should teach us to be most on our guard to protect liberty when the government's purposes are beneficial. Men born to freedom are naturally alert to repel invasions of their liberty by evil-minded rulers. The greater dangers to liberty lurk in insidious encroachment by men of zeal, well meaning, but without understanding."

Milton Friedman
Hoover Institution
Stanford, California

VII.

SCIENCE AND SOCIETY

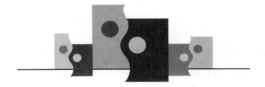

Introduction

No one doubts that science and technology have become central enterprises in our culture. Some scientists would like to have it otherwise, actually; they would like to insulate science as much as possible from social pressures. But that would be impossible: Not only is it impossible to keep scientific developments in medicine, genetic engineering, evolutionary biology, supercolliders, space exploration, and environmental science away from public scrutiny, it is also not in our interest to do so. For ultimately science and technology are themselves social creations, carried out through very human means for human purposes; that has already been made quite clear in the discussion of race in Part III of this book and in the controversies over abortion and censoring the Internet in Part V. To try to dehumanize science and technology is to diminish them. Nevertheless, as science and technology become more central to our society, it is inevitable that conflicts between science and technology (on the one hand) and society (on the other) will become more important and more complicated. The scientific enterprise will inevitably involve ethical and rhetorical dimensions.

The first readings in this part establish that very clearly. When in February 1997 the English scientist Ian Wilmut announced that he had successfully cloned a ewe called Dolly, people around the world began to debate the wisdom of permitting research that could lead to the cloning of human beings. With thoughts of Frankenstein no doubt in the back of their cultural memories, many people wondered whether cloning would lead to all sorts of monstrous developments—to the birth of all kinds of unimagined mutations. Others argued that cloning humans would be immoral on the grounds that it would be unfair and demeaning to cloned individuals, that it could change for the worse our fundamental notions of what it means to be human or motivate people to try to produce a master race, that it would amount to testing things on human beings, and that it would usurp the prerogative of God in creating human life. On the other hand, a number of people felt that cloning could have many good consequences—for example, it might offer a way for infertile couples to conceive a child, or permit the development of replacement body parts (such as skin that could benefit burn victims), or lead to improvements in the treatment of certain genetic diseases. Supporters tend to be less convinced that cloning would be immoral: wouldn't cloned human beings have the rights of any other human being?

Where do you stand on the issue? Is cloning moral? Would a ban on cloning be an unfortunate restriction on the human drive to know? Do the ethical concerns outweigh the possible benefits that might be derived from cloning technologies? Will the benign motives of those who would seek cloning be overwhelmed by those who would exploit the technology for personal gain? The first section of this part of *Conversations* takes up these and related questions in a way that will stimulate your own thinking.

The second section takes up the vexing question of AIDS: How should we fight this terrible, worldwide epidemic that has already claimed many millions of people throughout the world? (By 2000, as many as 20 million people are likely to have the disease.) First recognized in the United States in the early 1980s, AIDS (or acquired immune deficiency syndrome) seems to be caused by the human immunodeficiency virus—the HIV virus—that is spread through sexual contact, through the reuse of infected needles (especially by drug users), through childbirth (when the mother is infected), or through the transfusion of contaminated blood. Since the causes of the AIDS epidemic are well understood, the question arises: How should we fight it? Should citizens reconsider the sexual mores that have become conventional in the past few decades? Should health-care workers or other citizens have to undergo regular testing for the HIV virus? Should laws be passed requiring HIV carriers to inform their sexual partners that they carry the virus? Can health-care workers be required to treat AIDS patients? Will ingrained cultural practices need to be modified if AIDS is to be checked? This section mirrors a debate about a public health issue that is on everyone's mind these days.

The third section discusses one of the most controversial questions related to science and society today: the matter of euthanasia. Again, the question comes up because of advances in technology—because medical science has extended life expectancies and because medical technology can extend the life of the grievously ill and injured. But what are society's responsibilities to the very ill and incapacitated? Under what circumstances is it permissible to deny or remove medical treatment from a patient? And is it ever permissible to use medical technology actively to end a life—when someone is suffering, for example? Who should decide when euthanasia is permissible—family or physicians? Will an acceptance of euthanasia bring out our worst prejudices toward the aged, toward the mentally disadvantaged, toward the insane or deviant? Questions like these are taken up daily because of legal cases involving the "right to die" with dignity, because of highly publicized "right to die" organizations such as the Hemlock Society, and because some physicians have been quite public about assisting terminally ill patients to commit suicide.

This part and this book end appropriately with a look at one of the most important political and social developments of our times: the computer. Many people are convinced that computer technology has been an unqualified blessing for our society—that its use in speeding up routine operations and making information available with breathtaking ease is one of the great technological improvements of our day. They look forward to further applications of computer technology that we cannot begin to imagine, and they envision a more democratic society emerging from computer technology. But others aren't so sure, especially when it comes to Internet communications. What happens to our sense of community in the Computer Age? What happens to political institutions in the United States? Is the Internet making the fruits of technology available to more people, or is it simply offering even more advantages to the wealthy at the expense of the poor? And what of the other cultural effects of the computer: Will it smooth over differences? Will it fragment us into semiautonomous collections of special interest groups? How can we ensure that all Americans have access to the benefits of computers? What should the government's role be in promoting the "information highway"?

The advances brought by science and technology solve many human problems, but with these advances come a number of perplexing ethical dilemmas. This is the lesson of this final part of *Conversations,* and this is the challenge to all citizens, whether or not they are scientists, as we begin a new century.

SHOULD RESEARCH
ON CLONING BE PERMITTED?

Virginia Morell
A Clone of One's Own

Discover *magazine—a science-oriented publication owned by Disney that seeks a broad readership—published the following essay in May 1998.*

Last February, when Brigitte Boisselier, a French chemist, heard that Scottish scientists had produced Dolly, a sheep cloned from an adult cell, she was one of the few researchers whom the news did not surprise. A member of a fringe religious organization called the Raelian Movement, Boisselier had expected such a development: the group's leader, Rael, had predicted it 23 years before. It seems that Rael, a former French sports journalist, received the news of the impending discovery from extraterrestrials. They send him such announcements periodically, since he's half E.T. himself. According to a Raelian fact sheet (which could also serve as a script for The X-Files), his mother was transported aboard a UFO, where she was inseminated by one of these otherworldly beings. In 1946, Rael was born "from this union," and 27 years later he began receiving messages from the distant paternal side of his family. Most of these celebrate science and technology, predicting a future when we Earthlings will "rationally understand [our] origins" and begin making synthetic people. Cloning human beings, apparently, is one of the steps we must take on this path. 1

"Rael told us this would happen," says Boisselier, "so when we heard the news we weren't shocked; we were organized." Indeed, so organized that one month later—even as medical ethicists, politicians, and pundits debated whether the technique should ever be applied to humans, and President Clinton asked for a moratorium on such research—the Raelians launched a company called Valiant Venture Ltd., the world's 2 first human cloning firm. Advertised on the Web, Valiant Venture offers a service called Clonaid to help parents who want to have a child cloned from one of them. Boisselier signed on as the firm's scientific director and is now busy overseeing experiments that she believes will lead to the first cloned human in a mere two years.

3　　 "We need to do many experiments first with other species to be sure that it can be done without causing any damage," says Boisselier. "And we also need to raise more funds." Nevertheless, the company, now 14 months old, is making "good progress." As of late February, it had a list of more than 100 people (Raelians and nonbelievers) who would like to be cloned or to have someone they love cloned—for a minimum fee of $200,000. Boisselier claims that her firm's research is advancing, although she would not say where the studies are taking place or who is doing them, making it impossible to verify her claims. But because the procedure can be performed in a relatively simple, inexpensive laboratory, as other scientists have noted, there is also no reason to doubt that the Raelians are doing exactly what they say: taking the first experimental steps to produce a human clone. "We've subcontracted the work to labs where it's legal to do this," Boisselier explains, noting that human cloning is banned in France. "To say that human cloning is forbidden won't stop the science," she says. "It's important that society knows that this is possible, that it can be—and will be—done...In a few years, I expect there'll be a lot of cloned people, that it will be done everywhere in the world. This is what happens with technological advances."

4　　 Boisselier's outspoken enthusiasm for producing human clones is rare among scientists. Since Dolly's appearance, only one other researcher—Richard Seed, a Chicago physicist turned biologist—has jumped publicly into human cloning. He held a press conference in early January to say that he intends to open up shop as soon as he raises the funds. Like Boisselier, he has a list of people who want to be cloned (although his is shorter, only four candidates), and he also thinks human cloning can be a reality in a rather short time and with only a few million dollars for start-up costs. But most other researchers are far more cautious, especially since they have yet to clone an adult of any of our closest relatives, other primates. These researchers regard announcements like Seed's and Boisselier's as not only premature but off the wall. More than one referred to Seed as a kook, an oddball simply out to make a name for himself. Seed's announcement that human cloning was part of God's "plan for humankind [to] become one with God" did not help that image.

For all their faith in science and their apparently more rig- 5
orous approach to cloning, Boisselier and the Raelians are obviously far outside the mainstream. Their offer also plays on the fears of parents, says Mark Sauer, a reproductive endocrinologist at Columbia, since they propose to store the cells of living children. These cells could be used later to produce a clone of the child should the child die. "That's exploitation of the worst kind," says Sauer. "It plays on every parent's fears. And then what about a child who's produced that way? Will he or she be burdened by the memories of the first child?" Sauer adds that he suspects "in time, it will be possible to use adult cells to clone someone." But because of the many unanswered questions—both technical and ethical—human cloning "has not been endorsed by anyone, and certainly not by those of us working in reproductive medicine. It's premature to make these kinds of announcements and may lead to unwanted legislation." Indeed, as of late February, California had already banned human cloning, 24 other states were considering such laws, and eight bills were being weighed in Congress. Or cloning may be regulated by the Food and Drug Administration, which has asserted its right to do so.

Yet because cloning offers a way around certain repro- 6
ductive problems—primarily by giving an infertile or homosexual couple a chance to have a biological child—most researchers agree that one day it's likely to be an option at many fertility clinics. Human cloning, as horrific as the idea sounds to some, will happen, they say, perhaps not as soon as Boisselier and Seed estimate but far sooner than one would have guessed before Dolly trotted onto the world's stage. "It's no longer in the realm of science fiction," says Lee Silver, a Princeton geneticist and the author of *Remaking Eden*, a book about cloning and other reproductive technologies. "The technological breakthrough has already happened, although the details of how to do this with human cells still need to be worked out. Once they're refined, it'll be just a matter of time."

Those refinements are already taking place. In January, 7
scientists from a Massachusetts firm, Advanced Cell Technology, showed off three cloned calves, Charlie, George, and Albert, which were apparently produced via a more sophisticated (and patentable) technique than the one used to produce Dolly. At human fertility clinics, researchers are pursuing studies of human eggs that could lay the groundwork

for cloning, although that is not the purported intent. And the National Institutes of Health has funded two projects to clone rhesus monkeys, although only embryonic and fetal cells, not those from adults, will be used. Still, these types of studies bring human cloning closer to reality.

8   Good old-fashioned curiosity is pushing the field as well. "Ethics aside, I have to say as a scientist I find the technological problems fascinating," says David Ledbetter, a human geneticist at the University of Chicago, voicing a sentiment others in human reproductive biology share. "Why is this difficult to do? What will it take to make it work? How do you make a clone?" As Ledbetter's queries suggest, making a human clone is not simply a matter of following a recipe. The journal article announcing Dolly's birth didn't spell out a formula for cloning mammals; in fact, it didn't identify the actual cell that supplied Dolly's genetic material. Yet even without that key piece of information, Dolly's appearance was utterly astounding, since most biologists believed that it was impossible to produce a cloned mammal using any adult cell. "That's what everyone thought," says Don Wolf, a senior scientist at the Oregon Regional Primate Research Center in Beaverton, who's overseeing the rhesus monkey cloning project. "But Ian Wilmut [the Scottish scientist who led the Dolly project] came up with a clever innovation, a neat trick that proved us all wrong."

9   Before Dolly, researchers thought that adult cells could not be induced to produce a clone because they are already differentiated. As a fertilized egg develops into an adult, it divides into two, then four, then eight identical cells. Soon, however, the cells begin to specialize, becoming bone or skin, nerve or tissue. These differentiated cells all share the same DNA—the blueprint of the body—but they follow different parts of the instructions it contains. "In a sense, they're programmed," says Wolf, and as they age, it becomes more and more difficult to reprogram them, to make them switch functions. That's exactly what the Scottish team did when they produced Dolly: they took the genetic material from a differentiated adult cell and made it behave like the genetic material in a newly fertilized egg. Their success, however, does not mean that it is now easy to reprogram a human adult cell. If anything, notes Wolf, researchers suspect that every species is unique in its requirements for setting its cellular clock back to zero. Low-key and soft-spoken, Wolf stepped into the cloning spotlight last year, when the primate center announced that he had produced two monkeys, called Neti (an acronym

for "nuclear embryo transfer infant") and Ditto, using a technique similar to the one used to make Dolly. Despite Ditto's name and stories in the press, the monkeys are not identical copies of each other; they are only brother and sister. They were cloned using cells taken from two different embryos that shared an egg donor and a sperm donor. Still, their existence demonstrates that the formerly unthinkable is doable—and with primates.

Further, Wolf suspects he could produce clones from adult   10
monkey cells as well, although, he is quick to add, he's not attempting to do so. "I have no desire to compete with the Richard Seeds of this world," says Wolf. "Nor do I want to see a knee-jerk reaction from our legislators that bans everything we're trying to do, particularly with techniques that have such tremendous potential for biomedical research." Already Congress has made research on human embryos off-limits to anyone receiving federal grants. Those who do not comply will have their labs shut down. It's safer, Wolf and others say, simply to avoid the subject.

Wolf retired from the primate center in 1996; he came back   11
only after receiving the two NIH grants to produce a series of cloned monkeys for medical research and is now setting up his new lab. When complete, it will occupy three rooms in one of the center's squat beige buildings. In one, two researchers dressed in lab coats are peering through their microscopes at petri dishes filled with pinkish masses of monkey tissue. Somewhere in the gelatinous mix are the eggs, each about five-thousandths of an inch across. The researchers' task is to pluck out the good ones gently with a thin glass tube called a micropipette, then place these in a fresh dish for later use. Judging from the back and neck stretches the duo indulge in during a break, their efforts require almost as much concentration as trying to induce a spoon to bend. "This is going to be the main place of activity, Room 003," says Wolf, pausing briefly to check on his group's progress, then leading the way outside, where tall pines and firs tower overhead.

Wolf moves through the lushly landscaped grounds to a   12
nondescript conference room, where he pulls up a chair and begins explaining the enormous boon genetically identical monkeys will be to medical researchers trying, for example, to develop an AIDS vaccine. "They'd be an ideal model system," says Wolf, since they'd have identical immune systems, eliminating an important potential cause of confusion when scientists test such a vaccine or other treatment.

13   The center already raises rhesus monkeys for medical
research; most are used in experiments here and some are
sold to other medical research institutions. While awaiting
their fate, the monkeys live in grassy two-acre enclosures
where they pick at the grass, climb tree stumps, play, and
mate, keeping an eye out for their feeders. From a distance
and to the uninitiated, they all look so much alike they could
easily be clones. When mature, Neti and Ditto will join one of
these troops. For the time being, they're kept with other
young monkeys in a smaller yet roomy cage, although no one
seems sure which cage they're in or if they're even in the same
one. Since their brief moment of celebrity, they've been
treated like any other adolescent monkeys at the center, and
since they apparently look like the other adolescents, they are
no longer singled out for show.

14   To make Neti and Ditto, Wolf followed a procedure that
has frequently been used in the cattle industry for producing
prized breeds. It is not, however, easily done; even in cattle,
only 1 to 4 percent of such pregnancies yield offspring. In
light of that low percentage, Wolf's first efforts represented "a
tremendous success," says Dee Schramm, a reproductive
physiologist at the Wisconsin Regional Primate Research
Center in Madison. From 52 transplanted embryos, Wolf produced two healthy monkeys. "Yes, that's encouraging," Wolf
acknowledges, "but you really can't draw any conclusions or
expectations from what we did. After all, we've only done it
twice." Still, the success has encouraged Schramm and his
colleague David Watkins to attempt to clone rhesus monkeys
themselves. They, too, have a grant for work using fetal and
embryonic cells. They also plan to produce monkey embryos
from adult cells, to study the differences in embryonic development among clones produced from different sorts of cells.
However, they won't implant embryos produced from adults
into female monkeys; only clones made from fetal and embryonic cells will be carried to term. Schramm says he hopes to
have "several pairs of identical monkeys over the next two
years." The work is so slow and tedious, he adds, that "I don't
foresee any monkey cloning factories."

15   That's because it's tricky to reprogram any differentiated
cell, whether embryonic or adult. To turn a cell's clock back to
zero, researchers like Wolf and Schramm use a technique
called nuclear transfer technology. This is the basic method
that produced Dolly, Neti and Ditto, and the three identical
calves. In all three cases, the scientists removed an egg's
nucleus (that is, its DNA, the genetic material that makes

each individual unique) and replaced it with the nucleus from another cell. For Dolly, the nuclear material came from an adult cell; that of Neti and Ditto came from two separate embryos; and the calves' was derived from the cells of a single fetus. In all cases the cuckooed eggs were then persuaded to grow and divide normally.

That's the straightforward part of the formula. In between 16 lies a minefield of potential problems, many unique to whatever species is being cloned. "We're not following a recipe," says Wolf. The conditions under which the embryos grow vary widely: each animal has its own required temperature, for example. And an embryo's cells begin to differentiate at different moments for different species. Sheep, calves, monkeys, and humans all reach the eight-cell stage before they start differentiating, but mice begin when the embryo consists of only two cells, which is why no one is cloning them. "There's also a lot of variation among mammalian species just in the size and nature of the egg," Wolf adds. In some mammals, such as pigs, eggs are dark in color, making it hard to tell if they are viable. While that's not a problem for manipulating rhesus monkey or human eggs, where any discoloration means the egg is dead, simply getting the eggs is. "You can get buckets of eggs from slaughterhouses" for livestock species, explains Schramm. "But every egg you get from a monkey is worth its weight in gold."

In the case of Neti and Ditto, eggs were first harvested 17 from several rhesus females whose ovaries had been stimulated with hormones. "You give them hormone shots twice a day for eight days," says Schramm, and "then, if you're lucky, maybe you get 20 eggs. Out of these, 16 may be mature. And from these 16, perhaps 12 will be fertilized." The eggs are fertilized by placing them in a dish with the male monkeys' sperm, and the resulting cells are grown in a nutrient broth under what Wolf terms "well-defined conditions; this is something we know a lot about from human infertility studies and that can be applied to our monkeys." Each embryo is allowed to grow for three days, dividing into eight cells. At this stage, all the cells are still identical to one another and largely unprogrammed. "Theoretically, you could produce a complete individual from each of these cells," says Wolf, giving you eight identical monkeys. But only theoretically, because most do not survive the coming manipulations.

In the next step, the cells, called blastomeres, are carefully 18 teased apart; they constitute the donor nuclei. "Each one," explains Wolf, "is really one-eighth of an embryo," but that

one-eighth contains the key ingredient: the nuclear DNA, all
that's apparently needed to get the process ticking again.

19   You might expect that geneticists could divide each
embryo into eight blastomeres, wait for each blastomere to
grow into an eight-cell embryo, and repeat the process indefinitely. But that's not possible, says Wolf, because the embryo's
cells begin differentiating into limbs and organs after a certain amount of time has passed since its development began,
regardless of how many cells it has. An embryo grown from a
blastomere will have only an eighth as many cells to work
with as an entire embryo; if you divided it again, it would
have only a sixty-fourth as many cells. "As development proceeds, when time for it to differentiate arrives, it doesn't have
enough cells for the job," says Wolf, and even a blastomere
will be less viable than an entire embryo. Because the cues to
develop come from the cell's cytoplasm—the material that
fills the cell—rather than the nucleus, the blastomere's clock
can be reset by transferring its genetic material to a new egg
full of fresh cytoplasm.

20   Using micropipettes, the scientists remove and discard the
nuclear DNA from another batch of rhesus monkey eggs.
That leaves the cytoplast—that is, the egg's membrane and
the material that once surrounded its chromosomes. A donor
cell, one of the blastomeres, is then placed next to the chro-
mosome-free egg in a petri dish. "In normal fertilization, an
egg is in a quiescent state at the time it is ovulated," says
Wolf. "The sperm triggers the egg to be activated, and the
cytoplasm starts the program of events that will lead to development. But here, we aren't giving the cytoplast any sperm,
so we must artificially stimulate" the two cells with a chemical treatment. A pulse of electricity then causes the two cells
to fuse, and a "reconstituted" embryo is formed. The order of
these two steps, however, was reversed when the Massachusetts researchers at Advanced Cell Technology cloned their
calves; and the chemical treatment was apparently bypassed
altogether when Dolly was made. "It could be species differences, or it could be artifacts of the lab," says Wolf. "It's too
early to say.

21   "Once we have the embryo, we can treat it as we do any
other," he continues. "Most often we freeze them until we
have a monkey ready for an implant." That's the other big
hurdle—making sure that the recipient monkey is at the right
point in her cycle for the embryo to take. Prospective recipients are monitored for several weeks beforehand. To do the
actual transfer, a veterinarian surgically places the embryo

into the monkey's oviduct. "Women have short, straight cervixes," explains Wolf, "so surgery isn't required" when embryos are transplanted at fertility clinics. "But a monkey's cervix is tortuous, and the only way we can implant the embryos is surgically, although we're trying to come up with other methods."

At the end of all this labor, only eight twins can be produced, and that's assuming that every transfer succeeds, which is "pie in the sky," says Wolf. "It's not the optimal method, although we used it to make Neti and Ditto." But Wolf wants a series of clones, and for this, he says, "we need a lot of identical nuclei." He expects to retrieve these donor nuclei from the cells of fetal monkeys, such as their embryonic stem cells (undifferentiated precursors for other cell types) or fibroblasts (the cells that form the body's connective tissue, which are commonly grown in labs). Both kinds can be propagated in large numbers in test tubes, making it possible, he says, "to produce a clone size that is infinite in number." In other words, he expects to turn out identical monkeys, like a copying machine with a jammed "on" switch. "We don't know yet if we can do this; that's what we're working on now." 22

And in fact, this same technique—growing a line of fetal cells for subsequent nuclear transfer—enabled researchers at Advanced Cell Technology to produce the identical calves. "It's a very efficient method for us already," says Steven Stice, the firm's chief scientific officer. "We're producing more viable embryos than we have cows to put them in." (Oddly, the company has had no luck cloning a pig. "They are very different from cattle," says Stice. "Every step has to be reevaluated. We're not sure what we're doing wrong.") 23

Scientists first began trying to clone animals using adult cells in 1938, when the German embryologist Hans Spemann proposed making a clone by removing an egg's nucleus and replacing it with the nucleus from another cell. Those efforts failed until the 1970s, when frogs were finally cloned via the nuclear transfer method. None of the cloned frogs, however, made it past the tadpole stage. And that's where the idea of adult cloning stayed until Dolly arrived. 24

"It couldn't be done; that was what everyone said," explains Wolf, "which is why this was such a revolutionary discovery." The Scottish team "found a way to reprogram that adult cell." They did so by starving the adult cells, thus inactivating them. Wilmut began with a vial of frozen cells taken from the udder of a six-year-old sheep. His team thawed them and placed 25 them in a growth serum with only minimal nutrients for five days. "That's the trick that made all the difference," says Wolf. The adult cells were then fused with 277 different eggs. Out of all these attempts, only one lamb was born: Dolly. "That tells you that something was desperately wrong with the other 276," says Steen Willadsen, an embryologist at St. Barnabas Medical Center in Livingston, New Jersey.

26   Because of this low success rate, "we're a long ways off from getting adult cloning to work on a regular basis even in domestic animals," adds Lawrence Layman, a reproductive endocrinologist at the University of Chicago. "It'd be highly unethical at this stage to try it in humans," since the probability of miscarriages and birth defects is high. Stice agrees: "It'd be complete folly. We've used hundreds of thousands of eggs in cattle over the last ten years to achieve these results. To start at ground zero now with humans would be morally wrong and misguided."

27   Some researchers worry too that damage from aging DNA may be passed on to the cloned infant. "It's going to be very instructive, watching Dolly age," says Julian Leakey, a biochemist at the National Center for Toxicological Research in Jefferson, Arkansas. "If she goes through puberty, she may be okay." But she might also have acquired some random genetic mutation that could lead to problems early in life. "That's the potential danger of cloning adults," says Leakey, "which is why it would be useful to do controlled tests in short-lived mammals, such as rodents, first. Then you could work out the odds of using aged tissue versus young tissue for cloning."

28   There are other unanswered questions. It's not clear which cells were used to make Dolly. "They don't know which cell from the udder worked, or why it worked," says Ledbetter. "That's a big gap, and it means we don't have any idea if every cell type will work or only certain ones." Some researchers even question that it was an adult cell at all: the udder cells were taken from a pregnant sheep, and fetal cells are known to circulate in a mother's body. Nor do researchers know if the serum starvation trick will work with other species.

29   Despite the difficulties, says Willadsen, "the technique will be—is being—perfected"...somewhere. And once that happens, it's only a matter of time before we see the first cloned humans—individuals who are a physical copy, or twin, of their mother or father, but separated by at least a generation. "When that first cloned child is born, not only will no one know that he or she is different," says Lee Silver, "no one will

know that he or she is a clone. People will probably say things like, 'Oh, you look so much like your mother [if she was the nucleus donor],' and she'll smile. But no one will know, at least not until the kid is 16 and decides to sell her story to the tabloids for a million dollars."

From studying twins that were separated at birth and   30
raised in different families, researchers surmise that such clones will also be likely to share intellectual abilities and personality traits with their sole biological parent. Clones may thus follow in the footsteps of their parent but only in a very general way. "They will be separated by an entire generation," notes Sandra Scarr, a professor emerita of psychology at the University of Virginia in Charlottesville. "And as we all know, the cultural and social circumstances of the next generation are never the same as those of the preceding one. It's those social attitudes that shape a person's view of the world, including everything from how you view the stock market to the excesses of war. So the clones may be similar in intellect and personality, but their content will be different." Identical twins reared in the same house, she notes, listen to the same bedtime stories, eat at the family table together, attend the same schools, have the same friends and teachers. The clone and its parent, however, will share none of these experiences. "And these are the kinds of things that influence how one expresses one's genetic potential."

"People think it's going to be a robot or automaton," says   31
Thomas Bouchard, who's led the long-term twin studies at the University of Minnesota. "Nothing could be further from the truth. They'll be their own persons, and that's why the idea of cloning doesn't bother me in the least. It's nonsense to be afraid of it." Yet because of this culturally ingrained idea of what a clone is, some ethicists are concerned that the parent of a clone may try to exert excessive control over the child. "Parents already control their children to an extraordinary degree," says Lori Andrews, a professor at the Kent College of Law. "Will these clones be held in some kind of genetic bondage to their parent? They might put undue pressure on the child to grow up in a certain way, so that it really doesn't have its own identity."

Other researchers question how similar the clones will be,   32
even physically. "We already know from studying monkeys and children that there's considerable variation at birth," says Christopher Coe, a psychologist at the University of Wisconsin in Madison. Coe intends to explore this variation with the cloned rhesus monkeys that his colleagues Watkins and

Schramm are attempting to produce. Since the cloned embryos will be implanted in different mothers, they'll "give us the best opportunity we've ever had to clarify what we mean by nature versus nurture," says Coe. "It's the project I've dreamed about since graduate school, 20 years ago." For instance, how different will a cloned monkey that's implanted in an older mother be from one that's grown in a younger mother? "To what degree do in utero influences affect the development of the baby?" asks Coe. "And how much do the mother's actions, what she eats, and whether or not she's dominant or submissive, influence her baby's growth? The prenatal environment plays a far bigger role in shaping a baby than most people realize." The cloned monkeys, he believes, will probably look alike (although they could also differ in such things as their weight at birth) but will nevertheless "be quite different."

33   Other research on human twins also suggests that such things as how early the cells divide into twins and where the twins are placed in the uterus affect how "identical" they are after birth. "I think that's the real question: Just how different will these cloned babies be at birth, despite being genetically identical to their parent?" adds Coe. In an effort to establish the cloned monkeys' individuality, he will be measuring everything from their birth weight to how quickly they hold up their heads and how long they nurse.

34   Then too there's the question of the influence of the mitochondrial DNA. Not all of a cell's DNA is found in the nucleus; the mitochondria, tiny organs a cell uses to transform food into energy, have their own DNA. Although the donor egg will receive a new nucleus, it will retain its mitochondrial DNA, which may well be different from the donor's. "It's only a small amount of genetic variation, but it's there," says Silver, though, he adds, "there is nothing in the mitochondrial DNA that matters in making us different from each other."

35   In short, cloning yourself will not roll the clock back. It will not produce your soul mate and may not even give you your complete identical twin. What it will do is give you a baby that is more biologically related to you than anyone else. And that, says Silver, is why cloning will happen and few people will harshly judge those with infertility problems who choose it as a way to reproduce. "It's instinctive, I think, to want to have a biological child. That's what cloning offers—a chance for some people to have what they thought they never could have: a child of their own."

Charles Krauthammer
Of (Headless) Mice...and Men

*Charles Krauthammer is a cultural commentator whose views
appear in many magazines. He especially frequently contributes to the* Washington Post, *to* New Republic, *and to* Time
*magazine, where the following essay was published in January
1998.*

Last year Dolly the cloned sheep was received with wonder,   1
titters and some vague apprehension. Last week the
announcement by a Chicago physicist that he is assembling a
team to produce the first human clone occasioned yet
another wave of Brave New World anxiety. But the scariest
news of all—and largely overlooked—comes from two
obscure labs, at the University of Texas and at the University
of Bath. During the past four years, one group created headless mice; the other, headless tadpoles.

For sheer Frankenstein wattage, the purposeful creation of   2
these animal monsters has no equal. Take the mice. Researchers found the gene that tells the embryo to produce the head.
They deleted it. They did this in a thousand mice embryos,
four of which were born. I use the term loosely. Having no
way to breathe, the mice died instantly.

Why then create them? The Texas researchers want to   3
learn how genes determine embryo development. But you
don't have to be a genius to see the true utility of manufacturing headless creatures: for their organs—fully formed, perfectly useful, ripe for plundering.

Why should you be panicked? Because humans are next.   4
"It would almost certainly be possible to produce human bodies without a forebrain," Princeton biologist Lee Silver told
the *London Sunday Times.* "These human bodies without any
semblance of consciousness would not be considered persons, and thus it would be perfectly legal to keep them 'alive'
as a future source of organs."

"Alive." Never have a pair of quotation marks loomed so   5
ominously. Take the mouse-frog technology, apply it to
humans, combine it with cloning, and you are become a god:
with a single cell taken from, say, your finger, you produce a
headless replica of yourself, a mutant twin, arguably lifeless,
that becomes your own personal, precisely tissue-matched
organ farm.

6   There are, of course, technical hurdles along the way. Suppressing the equivalent "head" gene in man. Incubating tiny infant organs to grow into larger ones that adults could use. And creating artificial wombs (as per Aldous Huxley), given that it might be difficult to recruit sane women to carry headless fetuses to their birth/death.

7   It won't be long, however, before these technical barriers are breached. The ethical barriers are already cracking. Lewis Wolpert, professor of biology at University College, London, finds producing headless humans "personally distasteful" but, given the shortage of organs, does not think distaste is sufficient reason not to go ahead with something that would save lives. And Professor Silver not only sees "nothing wrong, philosophically or rationally," with producing headless humans for organ harvesting; he wants to convince a skeptical public that it is perfectly O.K.

8   When prominent scientists are prepared to acquiesce in— or indeed encourage—the deliberate creation of deformed and dying quasi-human life, you know we are facing a bioethical abyss. Human beings are ends, not means. There is no grosser corruption of biotechnology than creating a human mutant and disemboweling it at our pleasure for spare parts.

9   The prospect of headless human clones should put the whole debate about "normal" cloning in a new light. Normal cloning is less a treatment for infertility than a treatment for vanity. It is a way to produce an exact genetic replica of yourself that will walk the earth years after you're gone.

10   But there is a problem with a clone. It is not really you. It is but a twin, a perfect John Doe Jr., but still a junior. With its own independent consciousness, it is, alas, just a facsimile of you.

11   The headless clone solves the facsimile problem. It is a gateway to the ultimate vanity: immortality. If you create a real clone, you cannot transfer your consciousness into it to truly live on. But if you create a headless clone of just your body, you have created a ready source of replacement parts to keep you—your consciousness—going indefinitely.

12   Which is why one form of cloning will inevitably lead to the other. Cloning is the technology of narcissism, and nothing satisfies narcissism like immortality. Headlessness will be cloning's crowning achievement.

13   The time to put a stop to this is now. Dolly moved President Clinton to create a commission that recommended a temporary ban on human cloning. But with physicist Richard Seed threatening to clone humans, and with headless animals

already here, we are past the time for toothless commissions and meaningless bans.

Clinton banned federal funding of human-cloning re-   14
search, of which there is none anyway. He then proposed a
five-year ban on cloning. This is not enough. Congress should
ban human cloning now. Totally. And regarding one particular form, it should be draconian: the deliberate creation of
headless humans must be made a crime, indeed a capital
crime. If we flinch in the face of this high-tech barbarity, we'll
deserve to live in the hell it heralds.

Virginia Postrel
Fatalist Attraction

*In the summer of 1998, Virginia Postrel posted the following
essay on cloning to* Reason Online, *an Internet site that is dedicated to encouraging intelligent exchanges on important public issues. (Its motto is, "The best minds, the most important
issues.")*

Twenty years ago, the bookstore in which I was working   1
closed for a few hours while we all went to the funeral of one
of our colleagues. Herbie was a delightful guy, well liked by
everyone. He died in his 20s—a ripe old age back then for
someone with cystic fibrosis. In keeping with the family's
wishes, we all contributed money in his memory to support
research on the disease. In those days, the best hope was that
scientists would develop a prenatal test that would identify
fetuses likely to have C.F., allowing them to be aborted. The
thought made us uncomfortable. "Would you really want
Herbie never to be?" said my boss.

But science has a way of surprising us. Two decades later,   2
abortion is no longer the answer proposed for cystic fibrosis.
Gene therapy—the kind of audacious high-tech tool that generates countless references to *Brave New World* and *Frankenstein*—promises not to stamp out future Herbies but to cure
them.

This spring I thought of Herbie for the first time in years. It   3
was amid the brouhaha over cloning, as bioethicists galore

were popping up on TV to demand that scientists justify their unnatural activities and Pat Buchanan was declaring that "mankind's got to control science, not the other way around."

4   It wasn't the technophobic fulminations of the anti-cloning pundits that brought back Herbie's memory, however. It was a letter from my husband's college roommate and his wife. Their 16-month-old son had been diagnosed with cystic fibrosis. He was doing fine now, they wrote, and they were optimistic about the progress of research on the disease.

5   There are no Herbies on *Crossfire*, and no babies with deadly diseases. There are only nature and technology, science and society, "ethics" and ambition. Our public debate about biotechnology is loud and impassioned but, most of all, abstract. Cowed by an intellectual culture that treats progress as a myth, widespread choice as an indulgence, and science as the source of atom bombs, even biotech's defenders rarely state their case in stark, personal terms. Its opponents, meanwhile, act as though medical advances are an evil, thrust upon us by scheming scientists. Hence Buchanan talks of "science" as distinct from "mankind" and ubiquitous Boston University bioethicist George Annas declares, "I want to put the burden of proof on scientists to show us why society needs this before society permits them to go ahead and [do] it."

6   That isn't, however, how medical science works. True, there are research biologists studying life for its own sake. But the advances that get bioethicists exercised spring not from pure science but from consumer demand: "Society" may not ask for them, but individual people do.

7   Living in a center of medical research, I am always struck by the people who appear on the local news, having just undergone this or that unprecedented medical procedure. They are all so ordinary, so down-to-earth. They are almost always middle-class, traditional families, people with big medical problems that require unusual solutions. They are not the Faustian, hedonistic yuppies you'd imagine from the way the pundits talk.

8   And it is the ambitions of such ordinary people, with yearnings as old as humanity—for children, for health, for a long and healthy life for their loved ones—of which the experts so profoundly disapprove. As we race toward what Greg Benford aptly calls "the biological century," we will hear plenty of warnings that we should not play God or fool Mother Nature. We will hear the natural equated with the good, and fatalism lauded as maturity. That is a sentiment about which both green romantics and pious conservatives agree. And it deserves far more scrutiny than it usually gets.

Nobody wants to stand around and point a finger at this   9
woman [who had a baby at 63] and say, "You're immoral."
But generalize the practice and ask yourself, "What does it
really mean that we won't accept the life cycle or life course?"
Leon Kass, the neocons' favorite bioethicist, told *The New
York Times,* "That's one of the big problems of the contemporary scene. You've got all kinds of people who make a living
and support themselves but who psychologically are not
grown up. We have a culture of functional immaturity."

It sounds so profound, so wise, to denounce "functional   10
immaturity" and set oneself up as a grown-up in a society of
brats. But what exactly does it mean in this context? Kass can't
possibly think that 63-year-olds will start flocking to fertility
clinics—that was the quirky action of one determined woman.
He is worried about something far more fundamental: our
unwillingness to put up with whatever nature hands out, to
accept our fates, to act our ages. "The good news," says Annas
of human cloning, "is I think *finally we have a technology that
we can all agree shouldn't be used.*" (Emphasis added.) Lots of
biotech is bad, he implies, but it's so damned hard to get people
to admit it.

When confronted with such sentiments, we should remem-   11
ber just what Mother Nature looks like unmodified. Few bio-
technophobes are as honest as British philosopher John Gray,
who in a 1993 appeal for greens and conservatives to unite,
wrote of "macabre high-tech medicine involving organ trans-
plantation" and urged that we treat death as "a friend to be
welcomed." Suffering is the human condition, he suggested:
We should just lie back and accept it. "For millennia," he said,
"people have been born, have suffered pain and illness, and
have died, without those occurrences being understood as
treatable diseases."

Gray's historical perspective is quite correct. In the good   12
old days, rich men did not need divorce to dump their first
wives for trophies. Childbirth and disease did the trick. In traditional societies, divorce, abandonment, annulment, concu-
binage, and polygamy—not high-tech medicine—were the
cures for infertility. Until the 20th century, C.F. didn't need a
separate diagnosis, since it was just one cause of infant mortality among many. Insulin treatment for diabetes (highly
unnatural) didn't exist until the 1920s. My own grandmother
saw her father, brother, and youngest sister die before she was
in middle age. In 1964 a rubella epidemic left a cohort of
American newborns deaf.

These days, we in rich countries have the wonderful luxury   13
of rejecting even relatively minor ailments, from menstrual

cramps to migraines, as unnecessary and treatable. "People had always suffered from allergies.... But compared to the other health problems people faced before the middle of the twentieth century, the sneezing, itching, and skin eruptions had for the most part been looked at as a nuisance," writes biologist Edward Golub. "In the modern world, however, they became serious impediments to living a full life, and the discovery that a whole class of compounds called antihistamines could control the symptoms of allergy meant that allergic individuals could lead close to normal lives. The same story can be told for high blood pressure, depression, and a large number of chronic conditions."

14   Treating chronic conditions is, if anything, more nature-defiant than attacking infectious diseases. A woman doesn't have to have a baby when she's 63 to refuse to "accept the life cycle or life course." She can just take estrogen. And, sure enough, there is a steady drumbeat of criticism against such unnatural measures, as there is against such psychologically active drugs as Prozac. We should, say the critics, just take what nature gives us.

15   In large part, this attitude stems from a naive notion of health as the natural state of the body. In fact, disease and death are natural; the cures are artificial. And as we rocket toward the biological century, we will increasingly realize that a bodily state may not be a "disease," but just something we wish to change. Arceli Keh was not sick because her ovaries no longer generated eggs; she was simply past menopause. To say she should be able to defy her natural clock (while admitting that mid-60s parenthood may not be the world's greatest idea) doesn't mean declaring menopause a disease. Nor does taking estrogen, any more than taking birth control pills, mean fertility is a sickness.

16   "The cloned human would be an attack on the dignity and integrity of every single person on this earth," says German Research Minister Juergen Ruettgers, demanding a worldwide ban, lest such subhumans pollute the planet. (The Germans want to outlaw even the cloning of human cells for medical research.) Human cloning is an issue, but it is not *the* issue in these debates. They are really about whether centralized powers will wrest hold of scientists' freedom of inquiry and patients' freedom to choose—whether one set of experts will decide what is natural and proper for all of us—and whether, in fact, nature should be our standard of value.

17   Ruettgers is wildly overreacting and, in the process, attacking the humanity of people yet unborn. As Ron Bailey has

noted, human cloning is not that scary, unless you're afraid of identical twins, nor does it pose unprecedented ethical problems. No one has come up with a terribly plausible scenario of when human cloning might occur. Yet judging from the history of other medical technologies, the chances are good that if such a clone were created, the parents involved would be ordinary human beings with reasons both quite rare and extremely sympathetic. We should not let the arrogant likes of Ruettgers block their future hopes.

John Kilner

Stop Cloning Around

When the cloning controversy erupted in the spring of 1997, John Kilner was director of the Center for Bioethics and Human Dignity in Bannockburn, Illinois (near Chicago). He contributed the following article later that year to Christianity Today, *an evangelical Christian publication with a conservative editorial position. Kilner has written many articles and books on topics related to medical ethics. He later developed the argument presented here into a longer essay in a book he coedited called* The Reproductive Revolution *(1999).*

Cigar, the champion racehorse, is a dud as a stud. Attempts   1
to impregnate numerous mares have failed. But his handlers are not discouraged. They think they might try to have Cigar cloned.

If a sheep and a monkey can be cloned—and possibly a   2
racehorse—can human clones be far behind? The process is novel, though the concept is not.

We have long known that virtually every cell of the body   3
contains a person's complete genetic code. The exception is sperm or egg cells, each of which contains half the genetic material until the sperm fertilizes the egg and a new human being with a complete genetic code begins growing.

We have now learned that the partial genetic material in an   4
unfertilized egg cell may be replaced by the complete genetic material from a cell taken from an adult. With a full genetic

code, the egg cell behaves as if it has been fertilized. At least, that is how Dolly, the sheep cloned in Scotland, came to be. Hence, producing genetic copies of human beings now seems more likely.

5   We have been anticipating this possibility in humans for decades and have been playing with it in our imaginations. The movie *The Boys from Brazil* was about an attempt to clone Adolf Hitler. And in Aldous Huxley's novel *Brave New World,* clones were produced to fulfill undesirable social roles. More recently the movie *Multiplicity* portrayed a harried man who jumped at the chance to have himself copied— the better to tend to his office work, his home chores, and his family relationships. It all seems so attractive, at first glance, in our hectic, achievement-crazed society.

The Costs of Clones

6   But how do we achieve this technologically blissful state? *Multiplicity* is silent on this matter, implying that technique is best left to scientists, as if the rest of us are interested only in the outcome. But the experiments of Nazi Germany and the resulting Nuremberg Trials and Code taught us long ago that there is some knowledge that we must not pursue if it requires the use of immoral means.

7   The research necessary to develop human cloning will cause the deaths of human beings. Such deaths make the cost unacceptably high. In the process used to clone sheep, there were 277 failed attempts—including the deaths of several defective clones. In the monkey-cloning process, a living embryo was intentionally destroyed by taking the genetic material from the embryo's eight cells and inserting it into eight egg cells whose partial genetic material had been removed. Human embryos and human infants would likewise be lost as the technique is adapted to our own race.

Goal Rush

8   Yet, as we press toward this new mark, we must ask: Is the production of human clones even a worthwhile goal? As movies and novels suggest, and godly wisdom confirms, human cloning is something neither to fool around with nor to attempt.

Cloning typically involves genetically copying some living 9
thing for a particular purpose—a wheat plant that yields
much grain, a cow that provides excellent milk. Such utilitarian approaches may be fine for cows and corn, but human
beings, made in the image of God, have a God-given dignity
that prevents us from regarding other people merely as means
to fulfill our desires. We must not, for instance, produce
clones with low intelligence (or low ambition) to provide
menial labor, or produce clones to provide transplantable
organs (their identical genetic code would minimize organ
rejection). We should not even clone a child who dies tragically in order to remove the parents' grief, as if the clone could
actually be the child who died.

All people are special creations of God who should be loved 10
and respected as such. We must not demean them by fundamentally subordinating their interests to those of others.

There is a host of problems with human cloning that we 11
have yet to address. Who are the parents of a clone produced
in a laboratory? The donor of the genetic material? The donor
of the egg into which the material is transferred? The scientist who manipulates cells from anonymous donors? Who
will provide the necessary love and care for this embryo,
fetus, and then child especially when mistakes are made and
it would be easier simply to discard it?

The problems become legion when having children is 12
removed from the context of marriage and even from responsible parenthood. For instance, Hope College's Allen Verhey
asks whether parenting is properly considered making children to match a specific design, as is clearly the case with
cloning, or whether parenting is properly regarded as a disposition to be hospitable to children as given." Clearly, from a
biblical perspective, it is the latter.

Further, the Bible portrays children as the fruit of a one- 13
flesh love relationship, and for good reason. It is a context in
which children flourish—in which their full humanity, material and nonmaterial, is respected and nourished. Those who
provide them with physical (genetic) life also care for their
ongoing physical as well as nonphysical needs.

As Valparaiso University's Gilbert Meilaender told *Christian-* 14
ity Today, this further separation of procreating from marriage
is bad for children. "The child inevitably becomes a product,"
says ethicist Meilaender, someone who is made, not begotten.

"To beget a child is to give birth to one who is like us, equal 15
in dignity, for whom we care, but whose being we do not

simply control. To 'make' a child is to create a product whose destiny we may well think we can shape. Hence, the 'begotten, not made' language of the creed is relevant also to our understanding of the child and of the relation between the generations.

16   "If our purpose is to clone people as possible sources of perfectly matching organs," says Meilaender, "that clearly shows how we could come to regard the clone as a being we control—as simply an ensemble of parts or organs."

Xeroxing Michael

17   It is all too easy to lose sight of the fact that people are more than just physical beings, Meilaender's ensembles of organs. What most excites many people about cloning is the possibility of duplicate Michael Jordans, Mother Teresas, or Colin Powells. However, were clones of any of these heroes to begin growing today, those clones would not turn out to be our heroes, for our heroes are not who they are simply because of their DNA. They, like us, were shaped by genetics and environment alike, with the spiritual capacity to evaluate, disregard, and at times to overcome either or both. Each clone would be subject to a unique set of environmental influences, and our loving God would surely accord each a unique personal relationship with him.

18   The problem with cloning is not the mere fact that technology is involved. Technology can help us do better what God has for us to do. The problem arises when we use technology for purposes that conflict with God's. And, as C. S. Lewis argued, technology never merely represents human mastery over nature; it also involves the power of some people over other people. This is as true in the genetic revolution as it was in the Industrial Revolution. When human cloning becomes technically possible, who will control who clones whom and for what ends? Like nuclear weaponry, the power to clone in the "wrong hands" could have devastating consequences.

19   There is wisdom in President Clinton's immediate move to forestall human cloning research until public debate and expert testimony have been digested and policies formulated. But there is even greater wisdom in never setting foot on the path that leads from brave new sheep to made-to-order organ donors, industrial drones, and vanity children.

Ronald Lindsay

Taboos without a Clue

Ronald Lindsay is by training both a lawyer and a philosopher; his law degree is from the University of Virginia, and his Ph.D. in philosophy is from Georgetown. Not surprisingly, his work in philosophy focuses on bioethics; and also not surprisingly, he was very interested in the debates on cloning that have developed since Dolly was cloned in 1997. The following essay appeared in Free Inquiry, *a magazine featuring reasoned debates on public issues, in the summer of 1997.*

The furor following the announcement of recent experi- 1
ments in cloning, including the cloning of the sheep Dolly,
has prompted representatives of various religious groups to
inform us of God's views on cloning. Thus, the Reverend
Albert Moraczewski of the National Conference of Catholic
Bishops has announced that cloning is "intrinsically morally
wrong" as it is an attempt to "play God" and "exceed the limits of the delegated dominion given to the human race."
Moreover, according to Reverend Moraczewski, cloning
improperly robs people of their uniqueness. Dr. Abdulaziz
Sachedina, an Islamic scholar at the University of Virginia,
has declared that cloning would violate Islam's teachings
about family heritage and eliminate the traditional role of
fathers in creating children. Gilbert Meilander, a Protestant
scholar at Valparaiso University in Indiana, has stated that
cloning is wrong because the point of the clone's existence
"would be grounded in our will and desires" and cloning severs "the tie that united procreation with the sexual relations
of a man and woman." On the other hand, Moshe Tendler, a
professor of medical ethics at Yeshiva University, has concluded that there is religious authority for cloning, pointing
out that respect for "sanctity of life would encourage us to use
cloning if only for one individual...to prevent the loss of
genetic line."

This is what we have come to expect from religious author- 2
ities: dogmatic pronouncements without any support external to a particular religious tradition, self-justifying appeals
to a sect's teachings, and metaphor masquerading as reasoned argument. And, of course, the interpreters of God's will
invariably fail to agree among themselves as to precisely what
actions God would approve.

3   Given that these authorities have so little to offer by way of
impartial, rational counsel, it would seem remarkable if anyone paid any attention to them.... However, not only do these
authorities have an audience, but their advice is sought out
by the media and government representatives. Indeed, President Clinton's National Bioethics Advisory Commission
devoted an entire day to hearing testimony from various
theologians.

Questionable Ethics

4   The theologians' honored position reflects our culture's
continuing conviction that there is a necessary connection
between religion and morality. Most Americans receive
instruction in morality, if at all, in the context of religious
belief. As a result, they cannot imagine morality apart from
religion, and when confronted by doubts about the morality
of new developments in the sciences—such as cloning—they
invariably turn to their sacred writings or to their religious
leaders for guidance. Dr. Ebbie Smith, a professor at Southwestern Baptist Theological Seminary, spoke for many Americans when he insisted that the Bible was relevant to the
cloning debate because "the Bible contains God's revelation
about what we ought to be and do, if we can understand it."
5   But the attempt to extrapolate a coherent, rationally justifiable morality from religious dogma is a deeply misguided
project.... To begin, as a matter of logic, we must first determine what is moral before we decided what "God" is telling
us. As Plato pointed out, we cannot deduce ethics from
"divine" revelation until we first determine which of the many
competing revelations are authentic. To do that, we must
establish which revelations make moral sense.

Morality Is Logically Prior to Religion

6   Moreover, most religious traditions were developed millennia ago, in far different social and cultural circumstances.
While some religious precepts retain their validity because
they reflect perennial problems of the human condition (for
example, no human community can maintain itself unless
basic rules against murder and stealing are followed), others
lack contemporary relevance. The world of the biblical patri-
archs is not our world. Rules prohibiting the consumption of

certain foods or prescribing limited, subordinate roles for women might have some justification in societies lacking proper hygiene or requiring physical strength for survival. But they no longer have any utility and persist only as irrational taboos. In addition, given the limits of the world of the Bible and the Koran, their authors simply had no occasion to address some of the problems that confront us, such as the ethics of in vitro fertilization, genetic engineering, or cloning. To pretend otherwise, and to try to apply religious precepts by extension and analogy to these novel problems is an act of pernicious self-delusion.

To underscore these points, let us consider some of the more common objections to cloning that have been voiced by various religious leaders: 7

Cloning is playing god. This is the most common religious objection, and its appearance in the cloning debate was preceded by its appearance in the debate over birth control, the debate over organ transplants, the debate over assisted dying, etc. Any attempt by human beings to control and shape their lives in ways not countenanced by some religious tradition will encounter the objection that we are "playing God." To say that the objection is uninformative is to be charitable. The objection tells us nothing and obscures much. It cannot distinguish between interferences with biological process that are commonly regarded as permissible (for example, use of analgesics or antibiotics) and those that remain controversial. Why is cloning an impermissible usurpation of God's authority, but not the use of tetracycline?   8

Cloning is unnatural because it separates reproduction from human sexual activity. This is the flip side of the familiar religious objection to birth control. Birth control is immoral because it severs sex from reproduction. Cloning is immoral because it severs reproduction from sex. One would think that allowing reproduction to occur without all that nasty, sweaty carnal activity might appeal to some religious authorities, but apparently not. In any event, the "natural" argument is no less question-begging in the context of reproduction without sex than it is in the context of sex without reproduction. "Natural" most often functions as an approbative and indefinable adjective; it is a superficially impressive way of saying, "This is good, I approve." Without some argument as to why something is "natural" and "good" or "unnatural" or "bad," all we have is noise.   9

Cloning robs persons of their God-given uniqueness and dignity. Why? Persons are more than the product of their   10

genes. Persons also reflect their experiences and relationships. Furthermore, this argument actually demeans human
beings. It implies that we are like paintings or prints: the
more copies that are produced, the less each is worth. To the
contrary, each clone will presumably be valued as much by
their friends, lovers, and spouses as individuals who are produced and born in the traditional manner and not genetically
duplicated.

Beyond Theology

11   All the foregoing objections assume that cloning could successfully be applied to human beings. It is worth noting that this
issue is not entirely free from doubt since Dolly was produced
only after hundreds of attempts. And although in principle the
same techniques should work in humans, biological experiments cannot always be repeated across different species.

12   Of course, if some of the religious have their way, the general public may never know whether cloning would work in
humans, as research into applications of cloning human
beings could be outlawed or driven underground. This would
be an unfortunate development. Quite apart from the obvious, arguably beneficial, uses of cloning, such as asexual
reproduction for those incapable of having children through
sex, there are potential spinoffs from cloning research that
could prove extremely valuable. Doctors, for example, could
develop techniques to take skin cells from someone with liver
disease, reconfigure them to function as liver cells, clone
them, and then transplant them back into the patient. Such a
procedure would avoid the sometimes-fatal complications
that accompany genetically nonidentical transplants as well
as problems caused by the chronic shortage of available
organs for transplant.

13   This is not to discount the potential for harm and abuse
that would result from the development of cloning technology, especially if we also master techniques for manipulating
DNA. If we are able to modify a human being's genetic composition to achieve a predetermined end and can then create
clones from the modified genetic structure, we could, theoretically, create a humanlike order of animals that would be
more intelligent than other animals but less intelligent and
more docile than (other?) human beings. Sort of ready-made
slaves.

But religious precepts are neither necessary nor sufficient   14
for avoiding such dangers. What we require is a secular
morality based on our needs and interests and the needs and
interests of other sentient beings. In considering the example
just given, it is apparent that harmful consequences to normal human beings could result from the creation of these
humanoid slaves, as many could be deprived of a means of
earning their livelihood. It would also lead to an enormous
and dangerous concentration of power in the hands of those
who controlled these humanoids. And, although in the
abstract we cannot decide what rights these humanoids
would have, it is probable that, as sentient beings with at least
rudimentary intelligence, they would have a right to be protected from ruthless exploitation and, therefore, we could not
morally permit them to be treated as slaves. Even domesticated animals have a right to be protected from cruel and
capricious treatment.

Obviously, I have not listed all the factors that would have   15
to be considered in evaluating the moral implications of my
thought experiment. I have not even tried to list all the factors
that would have to be considered in assessing the many other
ways—some of them now unimaginable—in which cloning
technology might be applied. My point here is that we have a
capacity to address these moral problems as they arise in a
rational and deliberate manner if we rely on secular ethical
principles. The call by many of the religious for an absolute
ban on cloning experiments is a tacit admission that their
theological principles are not sufficiently powerful and adapt-
able to guide us through this challenging future.

I want to make clear that I am not saying we should turn a   16
deaf ear to those who offer us moral advice on cloning merely
because they are religious. Many bioethicists who happen to
have deep religious convictions have made significant, valuable contributions to this field of moral inquiry. They have
done so, however, by offering secular and objective grounds for
their arguments. Just as an ethicist's religious background does
not entitle her to a special deference, so too her religious background does not warrant her exclusion from the debate, provided she appeals to reason and not supernatural revelation.

HOW SHOULD WE FIGHT AIDS?

Hanna Rosin
The Homecoming

*Hanna Rosin published the following account of AIDS in the
African American community in the June 5, 1995, issue of* The
New Republic, *a middle-of-the-road magazine of political and
cultural affairs. (The essay reprinted after this one, by Ann
Louise Bardach, was in the same issue.)*

1   A middle-aged black man named Otis is about to reveal his
most intimate secret to a perfect stranger. He checks to make
sure nobody's lurking around the corner (lst and M, southeast
Washington, D.C., a block full of prostitutes and addicts). He
hears a dealer hawking "face" (heroin), and waits, tugging
anxiously at his faded blue sweatshirt, until the man skulks
away. Then he leans over to this stranger, an outreach worker
from the local AIDS clinic, and whispers that he has, "Well,
you know, the disease."

2   Otis says he found out he was HIV-positive in 1986,
during a wave of infections that alerted AIDS researchers
they had been wrong about the virus. At first, they predicted
it would shift away from white gay men to terrorize the broad
population, mutating into an equal-opportunity killer. Instead,
it found people like Otis—poor, addicted and black. Blacks,
12 percent of the population, account for one-third of all
AIDS cases. Three out of five new AIDS victims now are
black, up from one in five in 1986. Black women are now fifteen times more likely to have AIDS than white women, and
their children, eighteen times more likely. By now, AIDS
should be familiar, yet Otis can't bring himself to mention it
by name.

3   Otis's story helps explain how HIV has been able to make
such inroads in poor black America. He found out he was
positive by a fluke. When he was in prison on possession
charges, nurses from the National Institutes of Health offered
$15 to anyone who would agree to be tested, and Otis volun-

teered because he needed the money. (It took the nurse fifteen tries to find a live vein.) He's not sure where he got the virus—either from his girlfriend, whose husband was a junkie (now dead), or from his cousin, who once stole his works and lent them to a "small, skinny guy who had that look, you know, like he was a homo."

Each time Otis tells the truth, he becomes a pariah. He says   4
his wife left him when people found out he was positive and started calling her a "diseased bitch." His 14-year-old niece, visiting from Georgia with her son, "freaked when she found out, started screaming, 'He's been using the same bathroom, he touched my baby.'" When he confided in his minister, the man pointed at him the next day in church and preached about the sins of bad living. Otis won't go to an AIDS clinic, even for a prescription: "Nope. No way in hell. That's, you know... a homo place, and your mama or your cousin or anybody could see you go in and then you're branded for life." What about medicine? "Somebody told me it makes your hair fall out," he says defensively. Only once does Otis let down his defenses, when he talks about the night he went to a support group at a local church. Most of the people were in advanced stages, looked sickly and could barely move, and "it tore me down. I thought, 'This is my future.'"

Wayne Greaves has been chief of Howard University's   5
AIDS clinic since before it existed, when nine patients with a mystery disease were crammed into a corner of the hospital. A wiry, wound-up man, he is as apt to lash out at his no-show patients as at "bigots" at the NIH. Three years ago he co-authored a study that is perhaps the best clue to the virus's surge among blacks, although it remains buried in the *Journal of AIDS*. Greaves and two colleagues reviewed autopsy reports of seventy HIV-positive inner-city patients. What they found surprised even Greaves: about half had been diagnosed *after death*, even though most showed obvious symptoms of AIDS-related diseases. The shame around AIDS in black America makes prevention almost impossible and treatment widely refused, and it keeps infection on an increasingly upward curve. "There are some people who would rather not know," Greaves says angrily. "A lot, actually, would rather not know."

One reason they'd rather not know is the uneasiness in the   6
community about open homosexuality, still closely associated with the disease. "There's an enormous hidden population," says Frank Oldham, former director of Washington's Agency for HIV/AIDS, "a huge number of bisexual men who don't identify as gay. It's fascinating: they go to church, to the park

with their families, then at night you'll see them cruising the gay bars." Many see nothing wrong with this way of living. "Open homosexuality is viewed as something imposed on us by the gay white culture," explains Alonzo Fair, from a group called URBAN, which has widely polled Washington's blacks about AIDS. "The black community has always accepted homosexuality. There is always a gay person in church or who lives down the street or a cousin, and that's perfectly fine. It's only when that person defines himself as gay, you know, adopts the gay white culture, like doing the rainbow flag thing, that the community reacts negatively. For a black man, family comes first."

7   This devotion to family can end up destroying it. Men who do risky things but don't consider themselves at risk are the virus's welcome mat into the black home. Black men are twice as likely as white men to be bisexual, according to a recent study of 65,000 HIV-positive men published in *American Journal of Public Health*. Black drug users, who sometimes double as male prostitutes, are four times as likely. This makes black America vulnerable to the kind of heterosexual break-out that white America has so far avoided and that is the norm in other parts of the world. Half the black bisexual men in the study were married when they died. It's likely their wives didn't know: in a California AIDS study, only one-fifth of the black women responding were aware that their partners were bisexual. As a result, AIDS is now the leading killer of young black women.

8   Race itself does not affect one's chances of contracting HIV, as in, say, sickle-cell anemia. But inner-city ills do. For example, one-quarter of all black men in their 20s, and 15 percent of adult males, rotate through prison. Among inmates, unprotected anal sex is common. Prison is thus a place where the virus can spread to men who may have sex with men while in jail and with women when they get out. In 1990, doctors at Riker's Island conducted what is called a blind seroprevalence test. They took the name tags off blood samples used in mandatory syphilis tests and checked them for HIV. A quarter of both male and female samples tested positive, a result since replicated in other big city prisons. A study of long-term inmates in the Florida jail system found that 20 percent had contracted HIV while in prison. The confessionals in *Angoli*, the best of the prison magazines, tell all. One Louisiana inmate who tested positive in 1989 admitted that he and his cellmate did "every unsafe thing you could do." Another, who knew he was positive yet still had sex with other inmates,

mused, "Maybe I shouldn't do it no more...but if the guy is willing to go for it.... We all have to die sooner or later."

At the same time, suspicion and mistrust of mainstream 9 medical institutions make it harder to mount an effective, communal response. It's easy to see this phenomenon at work in east Washington, D.C., not far from Otis's block, at a place called Paradise Manor. Here, identical new swing sets perch on every trimmed lawn, and each tidy brick housing complex bears a name like Harmony, Freedom or Justice. Occupying four units of Miracle is the Abundant Life Clinic, a center for alternative therapies specializing in AIDS and run by Dr. Abdul Alim Muhammed, health minister for the Nation of Islam. Walk inside and the waiting room exudes none of the menacing air you find at Nation rallies; to the background accompaniment of a Whitney Houston tape, the staff chats flirtatiously, the women tossing back their brightly patterned veils. If not for the blown-up portrait of Louis Farrakhan and the Lyndon LaRouche pamphlets ("WHO OWNS HENRY KISS-INGER?"), you might mistake this for any other AIDS clinic.

Muhammed sweeps into the room, tall and striking in his 10 crisp white lab coat and mint-striped shirt, and greets me cheerfully. He has reason to be upbeat. Mayor Marion Barry has appointed him co-director of the AIDS transition team, elevating him to unofficial AIDS czar for the black community in Washington, D.C. Add that to an award in 1993 from then-Mayor Sharon Pratt Kelly and $500,000 in federal grants over the last two years, and he's the most prominent black anti-AIDS figure in the capital. We move into his office and he takes a seat behind his glass-topped desk. In this sterile, pleasant room, it's hard to picture him as he was a year ago, fulminating to a Baltimore crowd about AIDS being "the perfect genocidal weapon" manufactured by the white government against black people, issuing death threats to Baltimore Mayor Kurt Schmoke.

Muhammed's latest initiative is convincing Mayor Barry to 11 divert a $2 million grant from the city's largest AIDS clinic, run by, as he sees it, white homosexuals, to his own. With that money, he'll be closer to achieving his mission to "save the world." This mission includes widespread mandatory testing, followed by treatment with his miracle drug, Kemron. The drug was discovered by Joseph Cummins, a white veterinarian in Amarillo, Texas, the only white man whose photo will ever grace the walls of the Abundant Life

Clinic. In 1989, Cummins trekked to the Kenyan Medical Research Institute with his discovery, a protein-like drug called alpha interferon, which is used to treat a rare form of leukemia. There, doctors fed their patients wafers laced with low doses of the drug. After three months of a study with no control group, the doctors breathlessly announced a miracle. Ninety-nine of 101 patients bounded back to health, they claimed. "Fifty AIDS victims have already been cured!" cheered Kenyan President Daniel Arap Moi. On the other side of the world, his euphoria provided an occasion for New York's *Amsterdam News* to blast the "racist white press" for "cabalistically ignoring this amazing discovery."

12   It was hardly ignored. In 1991, the World Health Organization conducted a study of 150 patients in Zambia and concluded that Kemron produced no benefits. In an effort to settle the question, the National Institutes of Health in 1992 reviewed thirteen clinical trials from around the world. Their study concluded that alpha interferon "is not recommended for persons of HIV infection" and that patients using it should immediately switch to other drugs.

13   The news failed to squelch interest in Kemron. In March 1992, Farrakhan announced that the Abundant Life Clinic would market the drug aggressively in the United States. Ads ran every week in *The Final Call*, the group's paper, and the marketing campaign proved a smashing success. Thousands of patients, by the NIH's estimate, most of whom were poor and without insurance, shelled out money for the miracle drug. And at a premium: the Nation sells Kemron for $150 to $250 for a one-month supply, depending on the brand, and charges a $1,000 initiation fee. Other vendors price the drug at $65 for a thirty-day supply. It's clearly a profitable business.

14   At its worst, the story of Kemron is about the Nation's shameless manipulation of scared proselytes. There is also, however, a less scandalous, if ultimately more disturbing point here: so widespread are fears of government institutions and white doctors among African Americans, that they will take any alternative over conventional medical treatment.

15   One study attempted to quantify these fears. In 1990, researchers from the Southern Christian Leadership Conference (SCLC) handed out surveys to 1,000 black churchgoers in five cities: Atlanta, Charlotte, Detroit, Kansas City and Tuscaloosa. More than one-third agreed that AIDS was a form of genocide against blacks; another third were unsure. And more than a third believed HIV was produced in a germ-warfare

lab, a theory shared by 40 percent of black college students enrolled in Washington, D.C.

Consider these musings on the origin of the virus, solicited   16
from passersby in one random inner-city block in Albany one afternoon last December. They are set to a Public Enemy soundtrack in *HIV and Genocide: Responding to African American Community Concerns*, a New York State Health Department training video: "It came from Vietnam. It started with chemical warfare, and then the government put it out into the population." "It was an experiment, OK. It was an experiment and then someone spread it on one group of people, onto one nationality. I'm not saying I'm prejudiced because I'm not. But that's my opinion, and everyone has a right to an opinion." "I don't know if it was the government or some secret organization outside the government but I believe the government had a hand into it or the secret organization had a hand into it." "I think first it was some kind of laboratory experiment. Then they perpetrated it on people of color in Africa and Haiti and places that the powers that be think of as throwaway people. Now people like me—and I don't consider myself a throwaway person—now I have the virus."

"If it looks like a duck, and walks like a duck, well then?"   17
says Ron Simmons, director of Us Helping Us: People Into Living, the only group in Washington, D.C., founded by gay black men to support their own. Bundled in a black hooded sweatshirt, surrounded by photos of black men in zebra-print thongs and a stern portrait of Malcolm X, he puts his feet up on his desk and expounds on the origin of the HIV virus. "My thinking is they're killing black and brown folks, and the reason they gave it to white folks first is because it was too soon after the Atlanta child murders in '78, and there would have been riots."

Under the Centers for Disease Control and Prevention's   18
new community initiative, Simmons's group was recently awarded a $50,000 federal grant. It will use the money to expand an already-thriving network of support groups for black men through which group leaders promote a philosophy of holistic healing: herbs, vitamins, Chinese teas, breathing exercises and absolutely no AZT, or any other of the standard chemical drugs. Simmons says he never tells members not to take AZT; he just guides them toward an "informed decision": "One thing about corporate medicine is they find a way to make money off you until you're in your grave," he jeers, holding up a copy of his bible, *Poison by Prescription: The AZT*

Story. "Black folks have what I call a healthy paranoia. After all, they did it once, so they can do it again."

19   "They" is the U.S. government—specifically, the Public Health Service. What they did was the Tuskegee Syphilis Study, a forty-year experiment on untreated syphilis in 400 black sharecroppers in Alabama which followed them to "end point," or death. Researchers carried on with the experiment until 1972, twenty years after penicillin became the standard treatment for the disease, and could have been used to cure the men under study.

20   Long considered this country's worst large-scale violation of medical ethics, Tuskegee has become the parable by which many blacks understand their relationship to public health services. From Los Angeles to Atlanta, groups such as Us Helping Us preach the virtues of healthy paranoia. "Tuskegee has taken on a life of its own as a disaster myth," says Stephen Thomas, a professor at Emory University who conducted the SCLC conspiracy study and has since polled 6,000 blacks around the country. "It has transcended being a historical event and turned into an urban legend, a personification of medical abuses and racism."

21   The result has been a lot of refused treatment. Dr. Joe Timpone, director of D.C. General Hospital's AIDS Unit, estimates that about one-fifth of his 800 black patients will not take AZT. It's hard enough, he complains, to persuade people with no money for bus fare or a babysitter, who miss an average of half their appointments, to stick to a regimen of bimonthly visits and fifteen pills a day. Add in chronic suspicion and his job becomes "almost impossible." A study by the AIDS Research Consortium in Atlanta found that 80 percent of women who should have been taking AZT or other antiretroviral drugs weren't. "If an AIDS vaccine came out tomorrow," warns Thomas, "a significant number of blacks would not take it."

22   Not even if it were free. Wayne Greaves from Howard University spends his days convincing people to enroll in clinical trials, studies of experimental medicine, where patients receive free care and medication. Most of his efforts are fruitless. "Even here, where we are mostly black, they won't come near us. We go out and recruit, and they say, 'Yeah, yeah, the money's coming from the NIH, right, so who are you trying to kid?'" Mary Lynn, the outreach worker for the program, who hikes around Washington seeing hundreds of people a week, says that around 70 percent ask about Tuskegee. "They're

completely convinced they'll be used as guinea pigs for some
evil agenda."

In adults, AZT only slows HIV's progression; it doesn't cure   23
anyone. But in the case of babies born HIV-positive, the drug
actually can be a cure. In February 1994, a joint French-
American study found that giving AZT to a pregnant woman
and her infant child dramatically reduces the baby's chances
of contracting the virus from 25.5 percent to 8.3 percent—"by
far the most important and helpful news to come out of the
epidemic," says Elaine Abrams, director of Harlem Hospital's
AIDS Pediatric Clinic. But the news would be better if women
who heard it believed it. "They just say no," says Abrams, almost all of whose 200 patients are black. "Plenty of women
refuse to get tested, to have their infants tested or to take
medicine. Maybe they're afraid, or they see a healthy-looking
baby in their arms and it all doesn't make sense." In a recent
focus group on maternal transmission of HIV, conducted by
the New York State Health Department, two groups of pregnant women split evenly by race, with black mothers-to-be refusing to "take that poison," as one put it.

Black clergy, the community's natural leaders, only feed the   24
paranoia. When a clean-needles program was first proposed
in New York City in 1989, Calvin O. Butts of the Abyssinian
Baptist Church decreed he was "not in favor of cooperating
with the devil," meaning those who might perpetuate addiction. Leading the national charge was Reverend Graylan Ellis-
Hagler, who now presides over the Plymouth Congregational
Church in Washington. "First, the white establishment pushes
drugs in to the community," he told the *Atlantic* in 1993. "They
cripple the community politically and economically with the
drugs. They send the males to jail. Then someone hands us
needles to maintain the dependency."

Religious opposition killed needle-exchange programs in   25
every city except New York, which squeezed through a trial
program in 1991. The result is the only unqualified success
story in the prevention war. In a city where half of intravenous drug users test positive, the program cut infection rates
by 50 to 75 percent, according to a study of its 2,500 participants. Now, Ellis-Hagler is willing to relent, he says, "because
there aren't strong enough feelings from the community to
create a hysteria," although he still finds the program "a pitiful last resort, and racist." It may be too late. By now, momentum has died down. Washington, for example, has only

enough money for a tiny pilot program inconveniently located in a downtown federal building.

26   The vacuum has been filled by a kind of generic sermonizing, drained of any urgency. Ten years ago, ministers routinely refused to preside over funerals of people who died of AIDS, and funeral homes refused to bury them. That kind of disgust has mostly been replaced by evasive homilies, expressed by a scattered few, such as Washington's Reverend Pervis "Fireball" McKenna, who takes pride in insisting, "I preach against all sin and that's one of them. I'm with the Bible on sin, and all of it is against God, period, whether it be homosexuals or whatever." In milder forms, ministers presiding over funerals will say "this person was a sinner, but he renounced that world at the end of his life," or they won't mention how the person died.

27   A typical example is the Metropolitan Baptist Church, a favorite of Washington, D.C.'s, black gay community. On a recent Sunday, the pews were packed with men in crisp wool suits and women in white gloves with straightened hair, their well-behaved children in tow. The choir, 100 strong, seemed to be the refuge for many of the single, and some obviously gay men. The imposing Reverend H. Beecher Hicks Jr., draped in purple velvet vestments, presided. In his trembling baritone, he admonished his flock of "black bourgeoisie" to remember their roots, to exercise compassion outside the church walls.

28   The church has had an AIDS ministry for two years and its director has been instructed never to use the word "gay," says a former adviser. Mostly it educates congregation members that it's OK to shake hands with the HIV-positive, to "love the sinner but not the sin," says Hicks. Its mission is the same as the dozens of other help ministries run by the church. "I don't make a lot out of it," explains Hicks. "It's like Alcoholics Anonymous, Narcotics Anonymous, like people who are depressed or divorced. We find a way to meet everyone's personal needs, and don't lift one up over the other."

29   As of January, some 84,568 young African Americans had died of AIDS.

Ann Louise Bardach
The White Cloud

Ann Louise Bardach is a writer who contributes to Vanity Fair
*and other magazines that examine contemporary culture. The
following essay appeared in* The New Republic *in June 1995,
in the same issue as the previous item by Hanna Rosin.*

Freddie Rodriguez is discouraged. He has just come from   1
his afternoon's activity of trying to stop men from having unprotected sex in Miami's Alice Wainwright Park, a popular
gay cruising spot. Rodriguez, 29, is a slim, handsome Cuban-
American with a pale, worried face who works for Health Crisis Network. "I take a bag of condoms to the park with me
and I try talking to people before they duck in the bushes and
have sex," he explains. "I tell them how dangerous it is. Sometimes I beg them to use a condom. Sometimes they listen to
me. Today, no one was interested." Most of the men, he says,
are Latinos and range in age from 16 to 60. Many are married
and would never describe themselves as gay. "Discrimination
is not really the issue here. Most Latinos do not identify
themselves as gay, so they're not discriminated against," he
says, his voice drifting off. "Ours is a culture of denial."

To understand why the second wave of AIDS is hitting Lat-   2
inos particularly hard, one would do well to start in Miami.
Once a mecca for retirees, South Beach today is a frenzy of
dance and sex clubs, for hetero- and homosexual alike. "We
have the highest rate of heterosexual transmission in the
country, the second-highest number of babies born with AIDS
and we are number one nationwide for teen HIV cases," says
Randi Jenson, reeling off a litany that clearly exhausts him.
Jenson supervises the Miami Beach HIV/AIDS Project and sits
on the board of the Gay, Lesbian and Bisexual Community
Center. "And we have the highest rate of bisexuality in the
country." When I ask how he knows this, he says, "Trust me on
this one, *we know.* . . . The numbers to watch for in the future
will be Hispanic women—the wives and girlfriends."

Already, AIDS is the leading cause of death in Miami and   3
Fort Lauderdale for women ages 25 to 44, four times greater
than the national average. According to the Centers for Disease Control and Prevention (CDC), AIDS cases among Hispanics have been steadily rising. But any foray into the Latino

subculture shows that the numbers do not tell the whole story, and may not even tell half. CDC literature notes that "it is believed that AIDS-related cases and deaths for Latinos are understated by at least 30 percent. Many Hispanics do not and cannot access HIV testing and health care." Abetted by widespread shame about homosexuality, a fear of governmental and medical institutions (particularly among undocumented immigrants) and cultural denial as deep as Havana Harbor, AIDS is moving silently and insistently through Hispanic America. It is the stealth virus.

4　　"No one knows how many Latino HIV cases are out there," Damian Pardo, an affable Cuban-American, who is president of the board of Health Crisis Network, tells me over lunch in Coral Gables. "All we know is that the numbers are not accurate—that the actual cases are far higher. Everyone in the community lies about HIV." Everyone, according to Pardo, means the families, the lovers, the priests, the doctors and the patients. "The Hispanic community in South Florida is far more affluent than blacks. More often than not, people see their own family doctor who simply signs a falsified death certificate. It's a conspiracy of silence and everyone is complicitous."

5　　Freddie Rodriguez—smart, affluent, urbane—didn't learn that Luis, his Nicaraguan lover, was HIV-positive until it was too late to do anything about it. "He was my first boyfriend. He would get sick at times but he refused to take a blood test. He said that it was impossible for him to be HIV-positive. I believed him. One day, he disappeared. Didn't come home, didn't go to work—just disappeared." Frantic, Rodriguez called the police and started phoning hospitals. Finally, Luis turned up at Jackson Memorial Hospital. He had been discovered unconscious and rushed to intensive care. When Rodriguez arrived at the hospital, he learned that his lover was in the AIDS wing. Even then, Luis insisted it was a mistake. Two weeks later, he was dead. "I had to tell Luis's family that he was gay," Rodriguez says, "that I was his boyfriend and that he had died of AIDS. They knew nothing. He lived a completely secret life."

6　　Although Rodriguez was enraged by his lover's cowardice, he understood his dilemma all too well. He remembered how hard it was to tell his own family. "When I was 22, I finally told my parents that I was gay. My mother screamed and ran out of the room. My father raised his hands in front of his eyes and told me, 'Freddie do you see what's in front of me? It's a big, white cloud. I do not hear anything, see anything and I cannot remember anything because it is all in this big white cloud.' And then he left the room." One of Rodriguez's later boyfriends, this one Peruvian, was also HIV-positive, but far more duplicitous. "He flat out lied to me when I asked him. He knew, but he only told me after we broke up, *after* we had unsafe sex," says Rodriguez, who remains HIV-negative. "Part of the *machismo* ethic," Rodriguez explains, "is not wearing a condom."

Miami's Body Positive, which provides psychological and   7
non-clinical services to AIDS patients, is housed in a pink concrete bubble off Miami's Biscayne Boulevard. The building and much of its funding are provided by founder Doris Feinberg, who lost both her sons to AIDS during the late 1980s. The gay Cuban-American star of MTV's "The Real World," Pedro Zamora, worked here for the last five years of his life and started its P.O.P. program—Peer Outreach for Persons Who Are Positive. Ernie Lopez, a 26-year-old Nicaraguan who has been Body Positive's director for the last five years, estimates that 40 percent of the center's clients are Latino, in a Miami population that is 70 percent Hispanic. On the day I visit, I see mostly black men at the facility. Lopez warns me not to be fooled. "The Latino numbers are as high as the blacks, but they are not registered," he says. "Latinos want anonymity. They come in very late—when they are desperate and their disease is very progressed. Often it's too late to help them."   8

"Soy completo," is what they often say in Cuba, meaning, "I'm a total human being." It is the preferred euphemism for bisexuality and in the *machista* politics of Latino culture, bisexuality is a huge step up from being gay. It is this cultural construct that prevents many Latin men from acknowledging that they could be vulnerable to HIV, because it is this cultural construct that tells them they are not gay. Why worry about AIDS if only gay men get AIDS? "To be bisexual is a code," says Ernesto Pujol, a pioneer in Latino AIDS education. "It means, 'I sleep with men but I still have power.' I think there is a legitimate group of bisexuals, but for many bisexuality is a codified and covered homosexuality." Self-definitions can get even more complex. "I'm not gay," a well-known intellectual told me in Havana last year. "How could I be gay? My boyfriend is married and has a family."

Without putting too fine a point on it, what defines a gay   9
man in some segments of the Latino world is whether he's on the top or the bottom during intercourse. "The salient property of the *maricon*," my Cuban friend adds, "is his passivity.

If you're a 'top,'—*el bugaron*—you're not a faggot." Moreover, there are also many heterosexual Latino men who do not regard sex with another man as a homosexual act. "A lot of heterosexual Latinos—say, after a few drinks—will fuck a transvestite as a surrogate woman," says Pujol, "and that is culturally acceptable—absolutely acceptable." Hence the potential for HIV transmission is far greater than in the mainstream Anglo world.

10   According to Pujol, "only Latinos in the States are interested in other gay men. They have borrowed the American liberated gay model. In Latin America, the hunt is for 'straight' men. Look at the transvestites on Cristina's (the Spanish-language equivalent of "Oprah") talk show. Their boyfriends are always some macho hunk from the *bodega*." Chino, a Cuban gay now living in Montreal, typifies the cultural divide. "I don't understand it here," he says scornfully. "It's like girls going out with girls."

11   "If you come out," says Jorge B., a Cuban artist in Miami Beach, "you lose your sex appeal to 'straight' men" (straight in this context meaning married men who have sex with other men). The Hispanic preference for "straight men" is so popular that bathhouses such as Club Bodycenter in Coral Gables are said to cater to a clientele of older married men who often pick up young lovers after work before joining their families for dinner. Some men will not risk going to a gay bar, says Freddie Rodriguez. "They go to public restrooms where they can't be identified." While many gay Hispanics do eventually "come out," they do so at a huge price—a shattering loss of esteem within their family and community. "The priest who did Mass at my grandfather's funeral denied communion to me and my brother," recalls Pardo. "He knew from my mother's confession that we were gay."

12   Latino attitudes here are, of course, largely imported, their cultural fingerprints lifted straight out of Havana, Lima or Guatemala City. Consider Chiapas, Mexico, where gay men were routinely arrested throughout the 1980s; many of their bodies were later found dumped in a mass grave. Or Ecuador, where it is against the law to be a homosexual, and effeminate behavior or dress can be grounds for arrest. Or Peru, where the Shining Path has targeted gays for assassination. Or Colombia, where death squads do the same, characteristically mutilating their victims' genitals.

13   While Latino hostility to homosexuals in the United States tends to be less dramatic, it can also be virulent, particularly when cradled in reactionary politics. In Miami, right-wing

Spanish-language stations daily blast their enemies as "communists, traitors and Castro puppets." But the epithet reserved for the most despised is "homosexual" or "*maricon*." When Nelson Mandela visited Miami in 1990, he was denounced daily as a "*marijuanero maricon*"—a pot-smoking faggot—for having supported Fidel Castro.

On the other side of the country, AIDS Project Los Angeles   14
is the second-largest health provider for AIDS patients in the United States (after Gay Men's Health Crisis in New York). It's a sparkling facility with a food bank, a dental program and all manner of support services. Housed in the David Geffen Building at the corner of Fountain and Vine, it is well-provided for by a generous Hollywood community. Currently, AIDS Project Los Angeles attends to the needs of more than 4,500 clients, 60 percent of whom are gay men. Roughly one-fourth of the total are Latinos, and the majority of those are Mexican. Thirty-two-year-old Troy Fernandez is one of the project's senior aides on public policy. Born in Yonkers and of Puerto Rican descent, Fernandez is a caramel-colored black man with long dreadlocks streaming down his back. Dressed in crisp white jeans, he's as slim and elegant as a fountain pen. He's also HIV-positive—part of the second wave.

Although Fernandez "did the downtown dance scene and   15
Fire Island," in his 20s, he didn't go to the bathhouses, and he was never on the front line of the party scene. Even when the political equation of the gay revolution—"the more promiscuous, the more liberated"—still had currency, Fernandez was warier than his peers. By 1981, friends of his had started to die of the mysterious illness then known as the gay plague. Fernandez got himself checked out as soon as HIV testing became available, and came up negative year after year while he continued to practice safe sex. Then he moved to Los Angeles and met Rodrigo.

Rodrigo was a well-educated Mexican-American, a high-   16
level insurance executive, a Republican conservative and "completely closeted." Among Rodrigo's tightly knit family, only one of his brothers—also gay—knew his secret. When Fernandez asked his partner if he was HIV-positive, he said no. He'd never been tested, but he knew he wasn't. He also insisted he was monogamous. "It's all about what risks you are willing to take," says Fernandez slowly. "I understand why people stop practicing safe sex. One is always renegotiating the risk factors at some level. You see, you want to believe that your lover is telling you the truth."

17   In 1990, Rodrigo got sick. By then Fernandez had become
suspicious, and pressed his partner to be tested. "I told him
he had to do it for my sake," he says, "if nothing else." When
Rodrigo learned he was positive "it was a double whammy,"
says Fernandez. "He had to admit that he was sick and dying
and worse—he had to admit that he was gay." Within the year,
Fernandez learned that he, too, had the virus. Remembering,
he lets loose a long sigh. "I don't have an answer for why I
took a chance. I knew better, but it only takes one time."
Fernandez surmises on the basis of personal anecdotal experience that as many as "90 percent [of gay] Latinos are closeted. Many may have self-identified but tell no one else." He
bases his estimate on the number of married men who come
into AIDS Project Los Angeles. "They always say they need the
information for their brother or brother-in-law."

18   Rarely visible in the statistics are the wives and girlfriends
of these men—the group that experts predict will soar to the
top of the AIDS charts by the end of the decade. Currently,
blacks and Latinas make up 77 percent of all AIDS cases
among women; the number of Latina cases is seven times
higher than that of Anglo women. Researchers have long
known that the "receptive partner," is at greater risk of contracting not only HIV but all sexually transmitted diseases.
For reasons generally unknown, women tend to get sicker
sooner and die faster. Moreover, for many Latinas striving to
be good Catholic wives in a culture where church and family
are the co-pillars of the community, contracting HIV is an
unfathomable betrayal and an irredeemable disgrace.

19   Ernesto Pujol remembers a Salvadoran housewife in her
mid-50s, then living in Brooklyn. "She had just tested positive. She was crying. She was so bitter—so angry at her husband and the waste of her life. She had bought the whole
Latina martyrdom of being the faithful wife." The husband
was a drunk who had battered her, belittled her, and who
would finally kill her. Still, she maintained that her husband
had been infected by female prostitutes—and never looked at
the evidence that he had had sex with men. "None of the
women I worked with ever admitted that their spouses were
gay or bisexual," says Pujol. "They would say, 'He drinks, you
know.' They would rather blame prostitutes than consider the
culturally unacceptable possibility of other men."

20   Wanda Santiago, 36, has lived much of her life as a pariah.
A Puerto Rican lesbian, born and raised in Brooklyn, Santiago
learned in 1989 that she was HIV-positive. At 13, she started

doing drugs when her family moved to a rough neighborhood in Williamsburg. At 16, she was pregnant and married and drinking. After three years, her husband left. "I knew I was gay since I was 8," she says, "but I thought getting married would cure me." In 1978, Santiago came out and turned the care of her young son over to her mother.

Santiago suspects she contracted HIV during her romance 21 with an Ecuadoran woman who was stationed with the Navy in Virginia. "I was crazy about her," says Santiago, who lived with the woman for three years. "Every now and then, she would bring a man to our bed," says Santiago. "It could have been one of them, or maybe I got it from a needle." A few years after her relationship hit the skids, Santiago sobered up for good, but by then she was feeling tired all the time. "For a week after I tested positive, I refused to believe it," she says. "Total denial."

Until 1991, Santiago worked for the Health & Rehabilita- 22 tion Service screening Latinas with sexually transmitted diseases for HIV. "A lot of them refused to be tested," she says. "If they did test positive, they wouldn't believe it. The fear overwhelmed them. They would say, 'Don't talk about it,' 'I don't have it' and 'Don't tell my husband.' Many were in denial about their husbands screwing around. They thought they would get blamed for getting the disease. It's much worse in Hispanic culture than it is for whites or blacks because Hispanics won't even talk about it. A lot of the women were afraid to use condoms because they would get beat up by their husbands. See, if you're infected by a man, you're a whore. If you're infected by drugs, then you deserve it. But it's OK for a man to have HIV because it's OK for a man to whore around."

Mary Lou Duran has been working with the community in 23 East Los Angeles for twenty-one years, the last three and a half of them as a case manager for the HIV patients at Altamed Services. Her clients are women: primarily Mexican-American or Central American refugees, both legal and undocumented, ranging in age from 17 to 56, and including "several grandmothers." A few of the older women may have gotten the virus from blood transfusions during surgery in Mexico, before the availability of HIV testing. But the overwhelming majority were infected by spouses or lovers. "One woman, from Guatemala, died in October," Duran says. "She had a very aggressive virus and died in less than three and a half years. She got it from a boyfriend and left a child behind. I feel the majority of the women I see are innocent victims—

wives and girlfriends who have no idea what is going on."
Duran then relates a more personal experience: "In my own
family, there have been three deaths—three nephews who
were gay. But my family says, 'No one has died of AIDS.' They
call it cancer. We can't comfort each other because we can't
discuss it. 'They weren't gay,' they say, and 'They didn't have
AIDS.'"

24   By coincidence, one of Duran's ailing nephews ran into her
at a clinic where she was working. "He was shocked to see
me," she remembers. "He was sick—very progressed by the
time he came in for help." They chatted briefly, awkwardly. It
was her only personal contact with the tragedy in her family.
"I have always been a community worker and my family has
come to me when they have a need of sorts, but never while I
do this work. They have never asked for my help. They have
no interest or curiosity in my work. They never ask any questions. Nothing is ever said. The entire community is in denial.
They just don't believe it is happening. They think that AIDS
is about gay white males."

25   When not manning the AIDS project, Troy Fernandez
makes the rounds of Hollywood bathhouses, doing what
amounts to "interventions"—foisting condoms on men before
they have sex. "The culture of the bathhouses has changed,"
he says, his voice brightening. "Some people sit around and
talk. Sure, it's still mainly sex but there's some talk." Fernandez doesn't believe closing the bathhouses serves any purpose. "If you close the Hollywood Spa or the Compound,
people will simply go to Plummer Park or the restroom at the
Beverly Center. My friends in New York say the bathrooms at
Juilliard are very busy these days. Face it, we are not going to
stop people from having sex."

26   What then are the prospects of halting the second wave?
Fernandez is initially speechless, and it takes a few minutes
for him to get pumped up again. "We should get real that
what we're doing is not working." He sings the praises of another program he's involved in—*Saber es Poder* (Knowledge is
Power), which enables him and others to go into heavily Hispanic schools and talk to kids in grades seven through twelve.
"But I can't say 'dick' to a kid in a school program without losing funding," he complains. "The truth is, Joycelyn Elders
was right. We have to start talking to kids when they're young,
not when it's too late or the second wave will keep rolling
along and then the third wave and then the fourth wave."

As for Ernesto Pujol, he says he will never forget Carla, a 27 soft-spoken, graceful Puerto Rican he met during his days running the Brooklyn AIDS unit of New York's Crisis Intervention Services. Happily married to a Brazilian man, Carla was at work on her doctorate. "The entire family got sick about the same time," says Pujol. "Her husband, she and their 2-year-old daughter. He died first, then the baby. I remember the day in the hospital that she told her family that she had AIDS and of course they became hysterical. It was very sad. She was a devout Catholic and AIDS caused her a great crisis of faith—like a slap in the face. As a couple, they had everything going for them—white upper-middle-class Latinos who could pass, educated and charming. Her husband had told her that he got it from an old girlfriend who was an addict but I suspected that he had had prior bisexual behavior. She chose to believe what her husband told her and I wasn't about to take that away from her. He was a very terrific, wonderful guy who was also working on his doctorate. But he was haunted by his past—and HIV is a past that won't ever let go of you."

AIDS Public Education Ads

The ads on the following pages were developed as a part of AIDS-education campaigns. The first, from the United States Department of Health and Human Services, began appearing about 1990. The second, a product of the American Red Cross targeted at the Hispanic American community, began appearing in 1988.

Talk About AIDS

How About Dinner, A Movie, And A Talk About AIDS?

Marie: That's not exactly my idea of a great date.

Why?

Marie: Because it's kind of depressing.

When you think about AIDS and being single, what's the first thing that comes to mind?

Marie: Be careful!

AIDS scares you?

Marie: Sure. But, it's something I have to think about.

When you say you think about it, what do you mean?

Marie: I ask myself questions I never thought about before.

Do you ask guys?

Marie: I'm starting to.

How is that working out?

Marie: Actually, not so bad.

AMERICA
RESPONDS
TO AIDS
1-800-342-AIDS
1-800-AIDS-TTY

 U.S. DEPARTMENT OF HEALTH AND HUMAN SERVICES • PUBLIC HEALTH SERVICE • CENTERS FOR DISEASE CONTROL   CDC

¿Qué les espera en el futuro?

¡Protéjalos! Infórmese acerca del SIDA. Llame a la Cruz Roja en su comunidad.

Con nuestro agradecimiento a La Cruz Roja Colombiana, Seccional Caldas

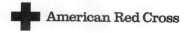

American Red Cross

Jesse Green
Flirting with Suicide

Jesse Green often contributes articles to the Sunday New York Times Magazine, *which carried the following item in September 1996.*

1   Mark Ebenhoch has on his "command" voice: the voice of fearless authority he learned during twelve years in the Marines. A fearless voice hardly seems appropriate now, in my hotel room, talking about sex; he wants to get rid of it but it keeps re-emerging. If he had the money, he'd also get rid of the tattoos: the one on the left arm that reads "U.S.M.C. and damn proud" and the one on his chest, the so-called meat patch with his social security number and blood type: B-positive. Which could be his catch phrase. Be positive.

2   So he talks about what has brought him to this state—he is H.I.V. negative but wonders how long he can hold on—as if he were announcing a baseball game. "Heck, I'd been such a good boy, followed my church upbringing, wouldn't cuss, even in the corps. I was celibate for 13 years instead of being gay! So then, last year when I finally came out, I came out flying like a bat out of hell. Wednesday, Friday, Saturday I'd go to this bar called Friends, which was outside a military base that was notorious for gay bashings. I'd walk in and it was a really friendly atmosphere, so I sat down and ordered a beer. Once, this guy, not even my type really, sat down next to me. He was military, which I could tell from his haircut, and it didn't take that long, a drink or two and a couple cigarettes, before he said, 'Do you want to go do something?' And it was like, O.K., let's go.

3   "He followed me home in the car and there was this incredible anticipation, with his headlights in the rearview mirror. *I wonder what he's like...I wonder what we're going to do.* And I'd show him the house and offer him something to drink but then the first time somebody swings that first kiss, you can just forget it. And by now, I've had four or five beers. I don't have any rubbers and stuff. In California the bars give you the condoms free; not in North Carolina, where I was living then. And no one brings it up. It's not thought about. Well, for a split second but I say to myself: I know this is a marine, I know he gets checked every six months and he's probably the safest bet in the world. And *this* one was married."

"It was like I was finally inside the candy store I'd been   4
looking at forever. I wasn't about to deny myself now. So during that time, those two or three months, I guess I had over 20
partners. A lot of the time I was drunk, though, so I can't say
for sure. Sometimes you'd go home with somebody you
might not really want because of loneliness, and in that position I sure wouldn't mention safe sex. I'd always wait for them
to say something about it." He nods his head sharply, as if dismissing an underling. "But no one did."

That no one mentioned safe sex to Mark Ebenhoch does   5
not mean no one knew what it was. Gay men have had more
than a decade to get the message—and for the most part,
have. In the years after AIDS was first reported, in 1981, the
gay community, largely on its own, masterminded what may
be the most intensive public health intervention ever. Armed
with explicit fliers and scary ads urging the use of condoms
for every sexual contact—and, later, with subtler messages
trying to promote this new behavior as fun—educators
undertook the complete reorganization of gay mating habits.
By some measures, the effort was amazingly successful: a
1994 New York City study showed that gay men's average
number of unsafe-sex contacts dropped from more than 11
per year in 1980 to 1 per year in 1991. But by other measures,
as Mark Ebenhoch's story and a thousand others like it demonstrate, the effort faded. Which leads to a question of perspective: Are the cemeteries half full or half empty?

Getting people to change their private behavior for the   6
public good, or even for their own well-being, has been a
chronic national problem. Recent reports—much politicized
this election season—show that drug use by teen-agers, after
a period of steady decline, more than doubled between 1992
and 1995. Highly visible efforts to combat the problem of
"children having children" haven't worked either: 4 out of 10
American women become pregnant by the time they reach
age 20—almost a million teenagers a year. Indeed, despite decades of effort, there is no clear consensus on what kinds of
interventions even make a difference. Prescriptive, authoritarian campaigns like Just Say No may be effective in certain
already-motivated populations, but they virtually repel those
who most need addressing. And even if successful interventions are found, they tend to stop working long before anyone
is willing to give them up.

An examination of AIDS prevention efforts in the gay com-   7
munity shows why. For a while, the safe-sex posters and fliers

worked well, at least while it was still believed that the disease
might disappear momentarily. The optimism engendered by
the early statistics led some AIDS organizations to conclude
that their educational mission was complete; San Francisco's
Stop AIDS Project disbanded in 1987. But when it became
clear that no cure was imminent, and that the changes
adopted for a finite emergency would have to be sustained
over a lifetime instead, the gay community was caught short.
By 1991, it was common knowledge that men who had been
safe for at least six years were slipping more and more often,
and that many men who had never been safe saw no point in
starting now.

8   The Stop AIDS Project reconstituted itself in 1990, but the
renewal of prevention efforts there and elsewhere took place
in a much grimmer context. It was by then evident that black
and Latino men (whose infection rates were much higher
than those of white men) had never been adequately reached,
and that young homosexuals especially were on the brink of
disaster. According to a 1991 study, more than half of the nation's 20-year-old gay men will contract H.I.V. during their
lifetime, if current trends continue. But even among the population of older, white gay men who most successfully absorbed the original prevention message, things began to look
less golden. Though the annual rate of new infections in San
Francisco had decreased from well over 10 percent in the
early 80's to 1.4 percent in 1990, that rate has nearly doubled
in just the last six years. Perversely, even the good news about
a new class of drugs called protease inhibitors—which have
reduced blood levels of H.I.V. in some patients to undetectable levels—has backfired: many gay men are now talking
about AIDS as a manageable disease, and using this premature hope as an excuse for returning to the unsafe practices of
the past.

9   Despite these reversals, the one-note educational strategy
of the prevention organizations has barely changed since
1985. That strategy basically boils down to normative, hand-
slapping variations on Just Say No, which are almost interchangeable with similar preachments about driving drunk,
smoking cigarettes and motorcycling without a helmet.
"These things can become jokes very quickly," says Lloyd
Johnston, who as program director at the University of Michigan's Institute for Social Research has studied adolescent
drug use for 25 years. "Remember the fried egg campaign?
This is your brain. This is your brain on drugs. It was only a

slogan, and the best you can say for a slogan is that it may work for a little while. This one did. It definitely spoke to kids, at least for a time; then it lost its persuasive power and maybe even became negative. In a way, the more successful these things are, the shorter their shelf life."

Aside from the paternalism of such campaigns, Johnston blames their eventual failure on a phenomenon he calls "generational forgetting." Improvement in one decade means that young people in the next see fewer examples, either first hand or in the media, of the consequences of risky behavior. At the same time, that improvement allows public health officials to let down their guard, and government agencies to cut back financing. With less negative and positive reinforcement, the cycle starts again. "Which is a strong parallel to AIDS," says Johnston. "At the beginning of the epidemic many young gay men knew about or cared for people who were dying; they felt that tragedy and pain personally. Now we have a new generation replacing them who haven't gone through it. The most convincing prevention message in any field is direct experience—but it's also the most costly."

How cost is measured is the crux of the problem. Our current notions of public health are based on old, even ancient, models. Developed to contain everything from the plague to polio, classical interventions targeted more cohesive and tractable societies, and made less intrusive demands. *Cover your mouth and nose when sneezing.* But how do you "do public health" (as public health people like to say) in a democracy? How do you weigh individual liberty against statistical risk? And what happens when the behavior in question isn't a sneeze but part of a person's deepest core of identity? What if it's something he profoundly enjoys and does not *want* to give up?

When a natural drive like sex gets tangled in unintended and even tragic results, public health is at its worst. "Moralistic slogans and intervention programs based unrealistically on no-sex vows do *not* reduce teen pregnancy or sexual activity," says Gloria Feldt, president of the Planned Parenthood Federation of America. "In fact, there have been studies that show they may actually *increase* the desire of teenagers to experiment: to find out what it is they've been told to say no to. And then because they haven't been given the tools with which to experiment safely—and because they've been told that they are bad people if they prepare—the likelihood of pregnancy only goes up. Basically such programs don't work," she concludes, "because ignorance is *not* bliss."

13   This is a phrase I've also heard from a Berkeley psychologist named Walt Odets, but Odets goes even further. Suggesting that coercive messages like "a condom every time" are unjustifiably broad, he has condemned AIDS prevention efforts as at best counterproductive and at worst dishonest—"not only withholding information from gay men but lying to them." In response to the huge stir such proclamations have caused in the AIDS community, Odets has dug in his heels; the question of whether prevention efforts have succeeded or failed is to him almost obscene. Indeed, though you can look at studies of gay men and make a credible case for either proposition, looking at gay men themselves, you cannot. Many of those who show up in the data as H.I.V.-negative are struggling in ways statistical analysis won't pick up until it's too late; some consider themselves *statistics to be.* Such men exist in an illogical limbo: they are not sick but don't feel safe and, despite years of posters and pamphlets, can barely tell the difference.

14   A living rebuke to the status quo in AIDS education, these men were largely ignored until Odets started asking a series of contrarian questions: *Have some prevention campaigns actually increased the likelihood of transmission? Are risk-elimination strategies for gay men actually homophobic?* For the last few years, Odets has insisted on a re-evaluation of the entire effort—a call to arms with implications for all public health campaigns. In a recent book, in impromptu jeremiads and in a series of withering articles (one of them called "The Fatal Mistakes of AIDS Education"), he has argued that prevention organizations have failed even the basic requirements of a sustainable initiative: to identify appropriate target audiences, provide them with accurate information and respect their right to weigh risk against benefit according to their own values. In doing so, he concludes, the groups have been guilty of ignoring the deepest root of gay men's unsafety: the psychological root, what they *feel.*

15   That Odets has been vilified for such conclusions is, in a way, just another sign of the brittleness of the gay community after 15 years of AIDS. But public health interventions are generally most necessary in exactly those communities most sensitive to criticism. In the gay community, that sensitivity has often resulted in the sacrifice of candor to political correctness. Until 1995, for instance, there was not a single AIDS prevention program for gay men in the country specifically targeted to those who were uninfected—the only logical audience—for fear of offending infected men *by suggesting their*

condition was something to avoid. And it is still taboo in AIDS circles to broach the subject of promiscuity. At one gay men's support group I attended, a 20-year-old who described himself as promiscuous was hissed into rewording his own experience: "All right, *slutty,*" he said, to applause.

Promiscuity is famously defined as any amount of sex 16 greater than what you are having. Admittedly, it's an unhelpful word. And yet, *promiscuous* is how many gay men describe at least a part of their life. Some of them mean a kind of innocent, adolescent freedom, but what others really mean is *compulsive* sex—sex that cannot be credibly taken as political liberation or personal ecstasy because it does not bring joy, cannot be controlled and is used, exactly like alcohol or drugs, to assuage a nonsexual need. Either way, these words are important in understanding AIDS, despite the inability of the AIDS establishment to utter them. Which is why, at a time when public health interventions of all kinds seemed to be failing, I set out to talk to H.I.V.-negative men who were having problems with unsafe sex: the ones who were floridly unsafe, the ones who slipped now and then, the ones who were so scared of being unsafe that they had no sex at all. I was hoping they would be able to answer the question that has bothered me since 1991: Why are gay men—ordinary gay men, who appear to function normally and enjoy the pleasures of life—systematically killing themselves?

"I do fit the bill and am interested," came the E-mail 17 response from Mark Ebenhoch—though at this point I still knew him only by his handle, Nailinch9. Sitting at my computer, I had posted messages on various electronic bulletin boards, explaining that I was looking for H.I.V.-negative gay men willing to talk about their unsafe sexual experiences. I did wonder what kind of person would respond to such an inquiry, but Nailinch9 addressed this problem at once. "My reasons are simple," he wrote. "If there is a way to prevent this type of behavior and share it maybe someone else would miss the selfish hell I've put myself through."

I had, through more traditional methods, spoken to many 18 men who also seemed to fit the bill, but most of them insisted on anonymity. Some said they were ashamed of the way they were endangering themselves and did not wish friends or family to know the difficult truths of their lives. Others—many others—were tormented about what even *constituted* unsafe sex. Over the last few years they had slowly come to accept the idea that unprotected anal sex was virtually the only way they might contract AIDS; Gay Men's Health Crisis, in New York, had reviewed dozens of scientific papers and found only four reports of "individuals presumed to have been infected by H.I.V. through oral sex" in the United States as of 1995. Then, in June, a report about oral transmission of an AIDS-like virus in six rhesus monkeys implied that the common wisdom was false. And though all of the major AIDS organizations dismissed that conclusion, the men I spoke to were left so confused that they could barely make rational de-·cisions about safety at all.

19   Mark Ebenhoch was not confused. Though he knew better, he had been unsafe at least several dozen times since his first adult sexual experience with a male, last year. He was forthcoming about the other things in his life that may have influenced him. Alarmingly, he seemed to match, point by point, each of the predictors of risk that AIDS educators have identified, combining in one short story the factors I had been hearing about singly from dozens of other men. For my purposes he was, in a way, *too* good. For his own purposes he was not good enough.

20   And goodness had much to do with it. Mark was born into a chaotic family that zigzagged between Ohio, Florida, Arizona and California; his mother, he says, was constantly getting married—"like Elizabeth Taylor without the money." His father left when Mark was 9, after which Mark shut down emotionally and devoted himself to fabricating a demeanor of perfect obedience and normalcy. If this was at the expense of real feelings, so be it; feelings tended to get in the way. At 10, his mother has told him, he was molested by a man assigned to be a big brother, Mark remembers nothing of the incident except being forced to wear a tiny blue-and-white swimsuit. "Which was agony," he says. "I was extremely bashful and had very low self-esteem. At 13 I still looked 9. Even now...."

21   Even now, at 36, only the slightly toughened skin of a marine and the weary cast of his gray blue eyes contradict the general impression of extreme youth. When I meet him in person, on a scorching April Los Angeles day, he's wearing a white mesh tank top, skimpy white corduroy shorts and strange, ill-fitting, orange-tinted sunglasses. He is thin—too thin—and pool-boy blond. Despite the gold hoop in his ear and the pink-triangle ring on his left pinky, he comes off a little blank: edging sometimes toward gruffness, sometimes toward warmth, but always watchful, as if on patrol.

22   What stability Mark has had in his life has come from the U.S.M.C.: "the most homophobic, macho service, which was

part of what attracted me to it." After joining directly from high school in 1977, he spent 12 of the next 18 years among "Uncle Sam's Misguided Children," either as a reservist or on active duty, including a stint as a Stinger antiaircraft gunner in the gulf war. Between enlistments he took various jobs—purchasing agent, mechanic, long-haul trucker—before ending up in Hollywood as an assistant military adviser on such films as "Platoon," "Forrest Gump" and, most recently, "Sergeant Bilko." Throughout it all he was celibate and lonely, though in his command voice there is no trace of sadness. "So when I finally decided to come out, it felt like a Niagra Falls of relief. It's not like I didn't know about AIDS. We had an AIDS-awareness class every six months in the corps. And, as a senior sergeant, when I knew the men were going out, I'd say, 'You know what's out there, you know what to do, just do it.' But when it came time for *me* to be safe, no one was there to say anything. Even if they had, I doubt I'd have listened. I was on a euphoric mission. 'I am going to experiment,' I said 'and see what it's all about.' *I want I want I want!*

"Maybe I'm an extreme case," he continues, "but I've met   23
plenty of people like me. Go down Santa Monica Boulevard and look in the bars: it's lost people. And people like us don't pay any attention to the posters and ads. Don't they get it? It's *hard* to be safe. Think of the situation if you're looking to meet someone. You have to put away a lot of alcohol in the first place, just to get up the nerve, and then your reasoning is off. Last time, I was so toasted, I remember the room spinning. Lucky I passed out so nothing happened. But you can't blame it all on alcohol either. It's something within you that makes you go on these binges. You remember what it feels like when somebody wants you: you're a god. And then it's over and you're a heel again. Alcohol is a tool to free yourself to destroy yourself if you already want to. And no poster is going to solve that."

If Mark Ebenhoch exemplifies many of the co-factors for   24
H.I.V. risk—recent emergence from the closet, lack of financial and domestic stability, alcohol use, depression, compulsiveness, a history of sexual abuse—he is not necessarily typical. Most of the men I spoke to fell into more definable single categories of risk. One group, consisting mainly of men over 40, seemed to be pushed toward unsafety by the accumulated grief of 15 years' devastation. Many suffer from survivor guilt, marked by depression, isolation and sometimes even a subconscious desire to seek communion with their lost

friends by courting the same fate. These men are often ridiculed as whiners, which reinforces their isolation. A letter last October to The Bay Area Reporter in San Francisco, responding to an article about the emergence of H.I.V.-negative support groups, sarcastically suggested the formation of similar groups for men who felt neglected because they didn't have *breast cancer.* Such men were invited to seek further information by writing "Victims-Are-Us" in the "PoorMe Building" at "4 Crybaby Lane."

25   Young men get more sympathy, if not more actual support. Several expressed to me the feeling that they would get AIDS no matter what they did; why even try to be safe? For them, ghoulish as it sounds, contracting the disease seemed almost like a rite of initiation into the gay community. Others were just too ecstatic about coming out of the closet to think about the consequences of their new-found freedoms. These young men, like young men of every stripe, felt themselves to be immortal or at any rate not subject to the biological facts that govern other lives. A 21-year-old named Danny O'Toole told me that "practically everyone" he knows has a lot of unsafe sex and that they justify it with all sorts of magical thoughts. "They seem to believe that just being in a relationship protects them from risk" he said, "even if the partner is H.I.V.-positive. And others don't even bother to ask, thinking: 'If he isn't concerned, why should I be?'"

26   Older men in "serodiscordant" couples, in which one partner is H.I.V.-positive and the other is not, sometimes don't want to face reality, either. They may already feel separated from one another by the difference in their status, and condoms seem to underline that. When *both* partners are uninfected, though there is of course no risk of transmission, fears about unsafety may arise anyway, in the form of questions about fidelity. One man I spoke to, who said he sometimes had sex outside of his long-term relationship, was afraid to tell his lover that they should consider using condoms. And another man, who was in a monogamous relationship, told me that, despite everything, he sometimes feared he was putting himself at risk. He had somehow acquired the belief that, whatever they might say and promise, gay men (like all men) were inherently untrustworthy.

27   It's not hard to see where he got that idea. The unwavering focus of safe-sex campaigns on external condom use—no matter what you think you know about your partner—has led Danny O'Toole, for instance, to a bleak conclusion: If you can't trust, you can't love, so why even bother having a rela-

tionship? And while celibacy is certainly a way of remaining uninfected, it isn't a very happy outcome of safe-sex education. Still for some, it's better than trusting the inconstant compass of self-preservation; a man need not be delusional, suicidal, alcoholic or self-loathing to slip once and make a fatal error. He need only be human.

"It's about love, finally, or what you think is love," Mark 28 says. Several days after our first meeting, he is telling me about the most unsafe of his unsafe encounters. Like all gay men I have spoken to, but unlike any prevention poster, he sees his behavior in an emotional context. "I'd made a decision to come out publicly. So the night before, New Year's Eve, I'm at this bar, and there's this one very good-looking individual about my age or so—preppy, brown hair and just cute, period. At 2 in the morning I make my attack, bum a cigarette. Alcohol wasn't a factor for me but *he* was sloshed. And he was into amyl nitrate, which I'd never been introduced to until I went home with him. So this went on for an entire weekend. Never thought about precautions. If we would have had to go through the whole nine yards of talking about it, you would have lost everything. This wild, instinctive, spontaneous, split-second fun would just...die. It's too much work. I mean, if you have to plan for three weeks to go on a camping trip for one day, that one day isn't worth it, right? Why even go?"

Mark isn't alone in his complaint. Most gay men (and 29 straight men, for that matter) agree that condoms interfere not only with physical sensation but with the spiritual sensation of union. They may also make sex more real than one's romantic illusions can tolerate; just tearing the foil package makes some people feel they are admitting the specter of death into their bedrooms.

"Thinking back on it, I should have definitely said some- 30 thing. But at the time I thought: it doesn't make any difference *now* whether I try to be safe or not. Especially because I was falling in love. And, of course, *that's* when I begin to find out that he was a very unhappy person, extremely promiscuous all over the world. And that's when I finally go, *Oh, my god*. I replayed the events over and over, looking to find out how many instances there could have been of transmission: were there any cuts or injuries? It stopped all of my sexual activity—for a while."

I ask Mark if he's heard of a strategy called "negotiated 31 safety," which is now a widely accepted approach to AIDS prevention for gay men in Australia, Canada and Great Britain. Instead of pushing "a condom every time," public health officials ask gay men to talk about risks with their partners and to tailor their condom use to the individual circumstances.

32   Mark responds acidly, as if I haven't understood his point. "Things are happening so fast you're just not thinking about that, I'm sorry. If the world was a perfect place, yeah, but not everybody is going to be perfect."

33   It is not the answer I wanted, and Mark knows it. He looks rather forlornly around my hotel room. "A teacher in North Carolina who just bought a brand new condo, yes, he's going to have negotiated safety or whatever. But where are the rest of us supposed to learn how to love right? Maybe I did it wrong, but I wanted to experience happiness. Isn't that what we all want? Someone who's there for you, even if just for a moment?"

34   Strangely, I'm reminded of the dilemma of poor, teen-age girls, for whom sex and even pregnancy may be a way of repairing, if only temporarily, a damaged sense of self-esteem. No wonder campaigns aimed at holding such girls to a vow of chastity, or that simply throw birth control at them, have so little chance of working; they are as misdirected as the safe-sex campaigns that have so far failed to reach Mark. Still, I make a little campaign of my own. "But don't you want to be safe," I ask, "so that you can try for that nice life you describe?"

35   "I can say that I would like to: that's the kind of answer you give yourself," Mark answers flatly. "But I don't know what I'm going to feel like next week after I get four or five rejections."

36   As the lilt of enthusiasm slowly fades, Mark's voice begins to resemble, in its sheer bewilderment, other voices I've been hearing. Listening to them individually, I had been able to think of unsafe sex as an individual problem; listening to them all combined in Mark's encompassing story, I begin to think of it as a problem of community. Not just the *AIDS* community, with its effective or ineffective messages, but the *gay* community, such as it is, which so fears the imposition of external values that it can barely promote any of its own.

37   "I regret a lot of things I did," he adds quietly. "But I regret that I have to be gay in a world that bashes you or gives you AIDS. I don't think I have it now, but I probably will eventually. And if I do, it'll be from hooking up with the wrong person, a lonely person, a person who doesn't feel he has any reason to care—someone like me."

A month earlier, Mark had rolled up his sleeve for an H.I.V.   38
test; to his surprise, he was still O.K. Still, it can take six
months for the antibodies to show up, so he was only slightly
relieved. "I'll get tested again in June," he says. "And then
we'll see."

"What the hell is this?" Walt Odets exclaims. A trim, hand-   39
some man with pale blue eyes and graying temples, Odets
reminds me of Warren Beatty—but on speed. Right now, he's
looking at an AIDS prevention poster that features photographs of various enthusiastic people with this legend: "Can't
be afraid...We have control." He almost blows up. "They
waste millions of dollars on this and they have no idea what
to say. 'We have control'? What does that mean? 'Can't be
afraid'? Why not? Men *are* afraid, they *don't* have control.
These messages are a complete denial of what is actually happening in men's lives!"

If Odets is a bit edgy, it's partly because he has never been   40
in a sex club before. Indeed, he has only come to this one, in
a bleak industrial San Francisco neighborhood on a Friday
night in February, to accompany his friend Ed Wolf, who
works for San Francisco's AIDS Health Project. Wolf spends
two evenings a month here, offering free, anonymous H.I.V.
testing and counseling to patrons; the club's owner has set
him up in an unused space on the second floor, formerly a
nursery school. Downstairs, though I am expecting a scene
that would shame a Bosch etching of hell, the club seems anything but decadent. Rather, there is a frank acceptance of the
mechanical nature of the enterprise. Explicit safe-sex warnings abound, and monitors, who strictly prohibit anal contact
of any kind, lend the place a kind of kindergarten propriety. I
guess it's true, as many people have said, that AIDS is happening more in bedrooms than in bathhouses: more for the hope
of love than for the always-reneged-upon promise of lust.
Still, for all the constant palaver about the joys of anonymous
sex, there is no joy here tonight. The customers—inside and
especially in the long line outside—look anything but liberated; they seem grim, determined, ground down by grief.

No one has yet come upstairs for testing, and while Wolf   41
sets out his fliers and forms, Odets paces the room, checking
the Mickey Mouse clock. Wolf, though he works for one of the
organizations whose efforts Odets once criticized, agrees
with much of what his friend says and has the equanimity to
tolerate the rest. "But the others," he whispers confidentially,

"they *hate* him. You don't know!" In fact, I do: Odets has made
such a pest of himself in San Francisco that none of the major
AIDS organizations there will work with him. Instead he has
consulted on projects for Gay Men's Health Crisis, 3,000 miles
away in New York.

42   It isn't hard to see why Walt Whitman Odets (named for
the poet) rankles. Raised in Manhattan, he is anything but the
laid-back Californian, and his habits, especially for a man
whose mission is risk reduction, seem immoderate. At 49, he
smokes, drinks, scarfs down eggs and bacon and rhapsodizes
about his days flying planes and driving motorcycles. He is a
daredevil, I come to realize, both physically and intellectually.
But that doesn't mean he's wrong.

43   "Most prevention efforts have been based on risk-elimination rather than risk reduction," he tells me during another of
our many talks over the course of a year. "But the question is
whether one *ever* eliminates risk for things that are valuable.
As a society, we do all kinds of things that may or may not be
in the interest of our long-term health because we consider
them important. We *weigh* the risks against the value. If you
say to a man, 'In order not to get H.I.V. you are never going to
have sex again without a condom,' his response would be that
that seemed impossible. But there's a difference between going out with a guy you've never met whose status you don't
ask about, and a friend you've known 10 years who tells you
he's negative. Education has refused to allow gay men even to
think about that difference. It's like telling people that if they
want to be safe drivers, they must always drive 35 miles per
hour without regard to when, where, or road conditions.
Which any sane person will instantly reject."

44   As it happens, this conversation is taking place in a cubicle
at a Mercedes dealership; Odets is waiting for his car to be
serviced while a $175,000 black convertible revolves on a
platform behind us. The lone sign on the wall seems to be a
relevant warning: *The State of California does not provide for a
cooling-off period. All contracts are final.*

45   But Odets is oblivious to his context. "We don't say to heterosexuals: 'A condom every time' for the rest of their lives.
We expect them to enter relationships and dispense with condoms when their H.I.V.-negative status is confirmed. It's a
very old story, telling gay men how to have sex; publicly
they're complying, privately they're doing something else.
We're the only country in the Western world that is continuing to even *discuss* the issue of oral sex in gay men. Oral sex

can transmit H.I.V., but the risk is comparable to everyday, ordinary risk in modern life, like driving a well-maintained car at moderate speeds on the superhighway with a lap belt and shoulder belt on. Not to acknowledge the low risk is to deny the value of sex between men. Of course, the educators don't mean any harm, and God knows they've been working longer than I have. They want to err conservatively, which is understandable. But if erring conservatively means giving instructions that we know will not be followed, is that the best approach to education?"

"How *would* you word the message?" I ask. 46

"'As a sexually active adult there are many occasions dur- 47
ing which you will probably have to use a condom to avoid transmission of H.I.V. and there are many others where you won't.' That sounds like something a person could conceive of doing for 60 years."

"So why have prevention agencies avoided saying just 48
that?"

"Partly, it's because education is still based on the feeling 49
that we need an absolutely reduced task for gay men," Odets says. "A single clear message—which is patronizing. And partly, it's because the campaigns are constructed from an advertising point of view, like soft drinks. They show a poster to a focus group and ask: 'Do you like this?' If no, they don't use it. Well, *why* don't they like it? Is it because it's addressing something difficult and true? You have to create anxiety; the anxiety is justly motivated. Instead we seem to produce comfy campaigns that leave people with a false sense of resolution and calm."

Like Odets, I have found some of these campaigns, partic- 50
ularly the ones that try to eroticize safer sex, coercive or coy. But I have to admit that I have been comforted by others. San Francisco's famous "Be Here for the Cure" series, which Odets has excoriated as dangerous, was beautiful and popular. Looking back on it now, though, I do wonder whom it was aimed at. Did it mean to tell men who were already infected that they should try not to die? Or uninfected men not to worry if they *did* contract AIDS? Odets has pointed out that the two groups need different kinds of support, and that you can't help protect H.I.V.-negative men unless you acknowledge that it is a disaster to become H.I.V.-positive. "You have to understand that we were working in an environment in which there was a real fear of offending H.I.V.-positive people," says Bill Hayes, who led the team that created the campaign. "But maybe we were overreacting. My own boyfriend,

who has AIDS, doesn't feel the need to have his self-esteem
supported by ad campaigns."

51   The unwillingness to distinguish between the two populations has produced what Odets calls a unique confusion in
the gay community between the normally distinct categories
of *carrier* and *public.* "H.I.V.-negative men should not be
thinking of themselves as carriers, or as destined to get H.I.V.
just because they're gay. By helping them think that way we
make it more likely that this will come true. But," he adds
darkly, "this confusion is part of a much larger mental health
problem. Partly it's a matter of the identification gay men already have with being dirty and defective."

52   Odets has often been criticized for drawing conclusions
from his experience with patients in his private practice: 25
privileged psychotics, they're sometimes called. (In reality,
there are only 20, none psychotic.) Be that as it may, the
H.I.V.-negative men I spoke to about their unsafe-sex adven-
tures all echoed at least some part of Odets's thesis. They feel
their dilemmas to be essentially psychological. Some of the
AIDS prevention organizations, on the other hand, suffer from
what has to be called an anti-psychological prejudice: a disbelief, almost, in the power of the subconscious. Understandably
eager to ingratiate themselves with the mainstream medical
establishment on which they depend for funds, they have
gravitated toward purely "medical" interventions. But what
this fails to acknowledge is that people are strange. They react
not only to rational thoughts but also to illogical feelings, and
do what appear to be insupportable, destructive things.

53   "The truth is that the community is rife with self-hatred,"
says Odets, displaying the genius for provocation that has got
him into so much trouble. "There is no question you can ask
that doesn't eventually go back to that. It's not necessarily
conscious; its a diffuse feeling about oneself. Which is why
gay men have the profound need to be liked and do good; if I
criticize the AIDS prevention programs they feel as if I'm saying that we *haven't* done good, that we've failed again. The
first failure, of course, is being homosexual. There's not a gay
man alive who doesn't feel he's failed his family. And then we
all got caught by a sexual epidemic, and we've beat a hasty retreat and been apologizing ever since."

54   Americans have difficulty discussing *any* kind of sex frankly,
which may be why our teen pregnancy rate is double the rate
of Canada, for instance. But anal sex, which for many gay men
is the defining act of gayness, is virtually unmentionable—
despite being common among heterosexuals too. Odets would

see this prudishness as another factor in gay men's self-loathing, another way they are "mangled" by a hateful society.

It's a strong word, and he uses it often; does Odets himself 55
feel *mangled?*

"My father"—the playwright Clifford Odets—"was open 56
and comfortable about homosexuality; but when he died...."
Odets pauses for perhaps the first time; he was 16 when his
father died, still yearning for public approval. "I felt unprotected from the rest of the world's disdain."

Only a few days after returning from Los Angeles, I receive 57
a series of breathless E-mails from Mark Ebenhoch. "I did
something now that I'm in seriously deep" the first one
begins. Feeling rather like the parent of an adolescent boy, I
brace myself for the rest of the message. As it turns out, my
fears are justified for what Mark has done is the most dangerous thing I can imagine. He has fallen in love.

"I left you on Tuesday and I went to Apache Territory, the 58
bar, to kinda think about what we discussed. As I was trying
to get picked up by this guy I had been getting to know, B. had
been watching me the whole time...until I couldn't take it
anymore and went over to say hi. That's where it all started.

"We did nothing sexually on Tuesday. And Wednesday we 59
went to the mountains...and the rest of the night was very
very sweet. We were safe but...." And here Mark goes on to
explain that his new friend has full-blown AIDS.

If any hardness lingered in my heart toward men who risk 60
their lives for sex, Mark has finally worn it down to a core of
helplessness. It would be easy to dismiss him as atypical;
most gay men do not appear to be as childlike, as impractical,
as self-destructive as he is. But of course Mark doesn't *appear*
that way either, thanks to the command voice and the other
forms of camouflage he has perfected over the years. It's only
when you get to know him that you see how far his life has
come from what he meant it to be. And then you wonder how
many other people are masking beneath a facade of daily
competence a willingness to flirt with disaster. In this main
trait, Mark is exactly like most gay men I spoke to about unsafe sex: he refuels himself over and over not so much from a
love of life itself as from an apparently bottomless reservoir of
hope for the companionship that makes life worth it.

"I hope I can hold on," one of the E-mails concludes. "I 61
don't know where to go from here. Someday maybe it all will
become clear. Thanks for the worry but I'll survive (always
have somehow) Mark."

62   The flier advertising the workshop was not like any I'd seen
before. In it, three men, average-looking and fully dressed, sit
around a table; one of them is thinking to himself: "If I tell my
friends that I've had unsafe sex, they don't know what to do."
Below the picture, the text describes a three-session workshop for H.I.V.-negative gay men or gay men who haven't
tested. Such men are invited to come talk about "testing, par-
tying, and the sex you are having, what it means to you and
what it may cost you."

63   It did not surprise me to learn that G.M.H.C. flier was, in
part, the result of a collaboration with Walt Odets. The tag
line, "Staying negative—it's not automatic," had the open-
ended quality I'd so often heard him endorse. What did surprise me was how effective it was. Some two dozen men
showed up at the sessions I attended, on Tuesday nights in
mid-July, visibly relieved to be talking to one another in a
noncommercial, nonsexual atmosphere. Usually safe, they
were worried about the times they'd slipped, or about slipping in the future. Most agreed that residual feelings of
shame over their homosexuality enhanced their risk, that
they were confused and anxious about the safety of oral sex;
that they wanted to be in long-term relationships, and that
the gay "community"—at least as it was most evident to them
in the form of bars and phone-sex ads—was not helping them
in their struggle to stay safe.

64   G.M.H.C., which began its programs for H.I.V.-negative
men in the spring of 1995, considers them highly successful,
as do I. Still, only a few other organizations have followed
their lead. For many in the prevention business, profound
questions remain about the validity of Odets's approach.

65   "It's a tricky issue," said David Nimmons, who with Richard Elovich helped develop the G.M.H.C. program. "Walt has
argued very persuasively against lumping H.I.V.-negative and
H.I.V.-positive men together, and I obviously agree. But that's
not to say there isn't a common interest in keeping as many
men uninfected as possible. Here's something uncanny: Men
who test positive are likely to be more consistently adherent,
as a group, to safe-sex practices than negative men. That's a
hard act to explain if you follow the model of self-interest
which is what most of AIDS prevention has been based on. On
the other hand, men who *should* have the motivation of self-
interest—H.I.V.-negative men—increasingly say that things
are getting in the way of their following out that self-interest.
It makes you want to look at other things, like altruism and
communal continuity, that cut across the serochasm."

It is something of a surprise to hear a discussion of spiri-   66
tual motivation from the head of the largest AIDS-prevention
education program in the world; Nimmons (who has recently
left G.M.H.C.) supervised a staff of 51 people and an annual
budget of about $3.9 million. But, unlike many others in the
field, Nimmons accepts the psychological nature of the epidemic. On the other hand, Nimmons would not go so far as
Odets in targeting gay men's low self-esteem. "Low compared
to what?" he asks. "Compared to women who are anorexic
and bulimic because they need to fit an externally determined
mold? Ours is a culture that instills self-loathing in *everyone*,
particularly in minority groups. It's part of what keeps the
power structure intact. I don't want to gainsay that it's there,
but are all *your* friends shriveled in self-doubt? We don't have
any more mental illness or psychopathology than anyone
else.

"Now I don't want to be a cheerleader either. Mental health   67
and community health are intrinsic to effective long-term
prevention. We've been looking obsessively at monads and
gonads: at people as individuals, not in communities, at sexual acts instead of sexual values. That's where we have to go
next. And we have to go there regardless of AIDS itself."

Regardless of AIDS itself. As I think about this phrase, I re-   68
alize that what Odets (if not Nimmons) has been suggesting
all along is that there is an epidemic beneath the epidemic we
know about. Beneath and beyond. It predates AIDS and will
probably outlast it and comes not from a virus but a vacancy.
Like most minorities in America, gay men grow up feeling
different, but uniquely they grow up both different and *alone*.
They are unlike, and often cannot speak to, the families that
raise them. Odets puts it plainly: "Gay adolescents are subjected to developmental abuses that make adult relationships
harder. Society has a lot of nerve subjecting them to this kind
of abuse and then, when they come out the other end of the
tube mangled at 25, to accuse them of depravity."

If, as Odets says, gay men feel inordinately bad about   69
themselves, many work doubly hard to make up for it by developing their capacities for empathy, decency and loyalty.
The epidemic has accelerated this process, or intensified its
substations: lo, we were actors, waiters, lawyers; now we're
lay epidemiologists and social workers. We were pansies and
perverts; now we're heroes on the 6 o'clock news. We are finally, if temporarily, accredited Americans, and part of the
reason AIDS organizations have so entrenched themselves
against the new realities is that hard-won halos are not easily

discarded. But halos cannot ameliorate the underlying problem, which stems from how homosexuals are hated. And while other groups are hated, too, the tragedy for gay men has been that the thing that makes them different (indeed, perhaps the *only* thing) is the thing that has bound them inextricably to the worst public health disaster of our era.

70   The problem, finally, isn't sex but love—and the 6 o'clock news doesn't want to talk about that. And while no one seriously argues that it is the job of public health to make gay men happy, ignoring the role that homophobia plays in the psychology of AIDS (or, for that matter, ignoring the role that joblessness plays in the psychology of drug addiction) means ignoring an element of disease at least as powerful as biology. If we care about public health, there is little choice but to care about people's feelings too. As Thomas Delbanco, a professor of medicine at Harvard Medical School, points out, you can find tons of papers analyzing the public health benefits of universal sigmoidoscopy to detect colon cancer—"but try to find one that tells you the best way to get a man or a woman to bare his or her bottom on a periodic basis to a large tube."

71   Delbanco, who was trained in an era when doctors were gods but now sees himself as a "hopefully expert adviser" to his patients, thinks it's time for prevention organizations to make the same kinds of attitude adjustment. It will not be easy. Public health has contented itself with maintaining *quantity* of life assuming that *quality* of life will (or ought to) take care of itself. If AIDS teaches us anything, it's that the formula works the other way around. At the same time, we seem to get the prevention we deserve. Politicians want quick fixes because they're cheaper and catchier than long-term solutions. (When prevention works, it's invisible of course: you can't see it because it *prevents* something.) And we abet those politicians by clamoring, albeit fitfully, for war instead of change. Democracy be damned—we want drug czars, AIDS czars—as if behavior driven by feelings could be corralled by an attack of the cavalry.

72   In a country that has outgrown its ability to promote strong norms, or finds the very idea of norms too normative, public health must find new methods of intervening in dangerous private behavior. What would that intervention look like? Instead of Just Say No, drug prevention might include nuanced discussions about the relative risks of marijuana and harder drugs, just as Odets wants gay men to distinguish between different kinds of sex. Instead of promoting vows of chastity, pregnancy prevention programs might ask a girl to

envision the kind of life she wants before weighing how a baby could enhance, or ruin it. What all such programs would rely on is candor: complete information, delivered in plain language, respectful of individual values—which seems obvious until you realize it's rarely done. And the bitterest pill in prevention today is that the programs already exist. Largely unfinanced or ignored, they sit even now in bookcases and file drawers, waiting for political winds to shift while the epidemics rage.

Mark Ebenhoch's command voice, which hasn't worked any better for him than it has for AIDS educators, is almost completely gone now. Even over the phone, when I speak to him in mid-July, I can hear the change. His affair with B. has ended unhappily and, he adds, almost as an afterthought, he has some news we have both been fearing: he is finally H.I.V.-positive himself. A psychiatrist has put him on antidepressants. "Sometimes I think that if I had gotten help three years ago—emotional help, psychiatric help—I most likely wouldn't be positive now. I'd have had a clearer head. But really, it was my own fault. There's no other way around it." 73

As a person with H.I.V., Mark is suddenly eligible for the whole range of benefits provided by AIDS organizations—including the free counseling that might have helped him earlier. And the Veterans Administration provides him with a handsome monthly disability check. In a way, becoming positive has been a windfall; could Mark be forgiven a bit of cynicism? In a world where financing for AIDS research keeps increasing but agencies that serve gay youths go begging for pennies, should we be surprised if gay men wonder whether the disease is more important than they are? For AIDS will someday end. And when the promise of the protease inhibitors is fulfilled, when the vaccine arrives in our elementary schools, will anyone turn as feverish a light on what *else* is destroying gay men? Will anyone see it as their responsibility to help assuage the damage inflicted, and replayed night after night, upon boys whose only real desire was to be liked, to be loved, to be good? 74

But somehow Mark *isn't* cynical. "I have an upbeat attitude," he says. "With the news about the new drug treatments, I'm cautiously optimistic. And I'm letting go of a lot of things. Because of the medication I'm on I cannot drink alcohol; and I quit smoking cigarettes. I've completely stopped the promiscuity, too. I want to live well. I'm eating better. Believe it or not, I have a date tonight, not a pickup but a real date. 75

With a guy I met through the Internet. I went into the Gay
and Lesbian Bulletin Board—where I met you—and looked in
the personals under H.I.V.-positive. And I found a guy that
was rather interesting. We're going to go out and have coffee
and something to eat, and talk. And that's it. I want to find
somebody who will"—he searches for the word he wants—
"*belong* to me. And that means somebody H.I.V.-positive now.

76   "In a way it's a relief," he says, echoing a sentiment I have
heard too frequently from newly infected men. "I don't have
to wonder anymore. That awful waiting is gone. So now, if I
do find someone, the relationship can be 100 percent real
with nothing in the way. That's what I want: 100 percent natural, wholesome and real. Maybe now that I'm H.I.V.-positive,
I can finally have my life."

EUTHANASIA

Anonymous

It's Over, Debbie

In 1988, the Journal of the American Medical Association *published the following anonymous contribution to its "A Piece of My Mind" opinion column. Nothing ever published there has been more controversial.*

The call came in the middle of the night. As a gynecology 1
resident rotating through a large, private hospital, I had come
to detest telephone calls, because invariably I would be up for
several hours and would not feel good the next day. However,
duty called, so I answered the phone. A nurse informed me that
a patient was having difficulty getting rest, could I please see
her. She was on 3 North. That was the gynecologic-oncology
unit, not my usual duty station. As I trudged along, bumping
sleepily against walls and corners and not believing I was up
again, I tried to imagine what I might find at the end of my
walk. Maybe an elderly woman with an anxiety reaction, or
perhaps something particularly horrible.

I grabbed the chart from the nurses station on my way to 2
the patient's room, and the nurse gave me some hurried details: a 20-year-old girl named Debbie was dying of ovarian
cancer. She was having unrelenting vomiting apparently as
the result of an alcohol drip administered for sedation. Hmm,
I thought. Very sad. As I approached the room I could hear
loud, labored breathing. I entered and saw an emaciated,
dark-haired woman who appeared much older than 20. She
was receiving nasal oxygen, had an IV, and was sitting in bed
suffering from what was obviously severe air hunger. The
chart noted her weight at 80 pounds. A second woman, also
dark-haired but of middle-age, stood at her right, holding her
hand. Both looked up as I entered. The room seemed filled
with the patient's desperate effort to survive. Her eyes were
hollow, and she had suprasternal and intercostal retractions
with her rapid inspirations. She had not eaten or slept in two

days. She had not responded to chemotherapy and was being given supportive care only. It was a gallows scene, a cruel mockery of her youth and unfulfilled potential. Her only words to me were, "Let's get this over with."

3   I retreated with my thoughts to the nurses station. The patient was tired and needed rest. I could not give her health, but I could give her rest. I asked the nurse to draw 20 mg of morphine sulfate into a syringe. Enough, I thought, to do the job. I took the syringe into the room and told the two women I was going to give Debbie something that would let her rest and to say good-bye. Debbie looked at the syringe, then laid her head on the pillow with her eyes open, watching what was left of the world. I injected the morphine intravenously and watched to see if my calculations on its effects would be correct. Within seconds her breathing slowed to a normal rate, her eyes closed, and her features softened as she seemed restful at last. The older woman stroked the hair of the now-sleeping patient. I waited for the inevitable next effect of depressing the respiratory drive. With clocklike certainty, within four minutes the breathing rate slowed even more, then became irregular, then ceased. The dark-haired woman stood erect and seemed relieved.

4   It's over, Debbie.

Name Withheld by Request

Charles Colson
It's Not Over, Debbie

Charles Colson (born 1931) was converted to Christianity while serving a prison term for his role in the Watergate scandal of the Nixon administration. He has written five books on Christian topics and contributes regularly to the evangelical publication Christianity Today, *where the following column appeared in 1988.*

1   The scene is a darkened hospital ward. An intern stands over Debbie, a young woman with terminal cancer. Her breathing is labored as she struggles for oxygen. She weighs 80 pounds. She is in horrible pain.

The doctor has never seen Debbie before, but a glance at 2
her chart confirms she is not responding to treatment. He
leans down to hear her whisper, "Let's get this over with."

Most doctors would have hurried to give relief against the 3
pain, or tried to offer some solace to the anguished relative
standing near the bed. But this intern measured out 20 milligrams of morphine into a syringe—enough, he wrote later, "to
do the job"—and injected it. Four minutes later, Debbie was
dead. The doctor's only comment: "It's over, Debbie."

Stories like this, publicized a few months back, are shock- 4
ing but should not surprise us. While no one likes to admit it,
active euthanasia is not uncommon. It has been closeted in
hospital ethics committees, cloaked in euphemisms spoken to
grieving relatives. It is the unnamed shadow on an unknown
number of death certificates—of handicapped newborns;
sickly, aged parents; the terminally ill in critical pain.

No, Debbie's case is something new only because of the pub- 5
lic nature of both its telling and the debate that has followed.

This story was first written, anonymously but without 6
apology, by the intern himself, and published in the *Journal of
the American Medical Association* (JAMA)—one of the most
respected medical journals in the world.

Following the article's publication, the commentary came 7
fast and furious. Some experts dismissed the incident as
fictional. Others believed it, but focused their criticism on
the young doctor's lack of familiarity with Debbie's medical
history.

But the article's greatest effect was to yank euthanasia out 8
of the closet and thrust it into the arena of national debate. On
the surface that might seem healthy, getting the whole ugly issue into the open. But there's a subtle danger here: The JAMA
article and the impassioned discussion it provoked offer a case
study of a recurring process in American life by which the unthinkable in short order becomes the unquestionable.

Usually it works like this: Some practice so offensive that it 9
could scarcely be discussed in public is suddenly advocated
by a respected expert in a respected forum. The public is
shocked, then outraged. The very fact that such a thing could
be publicly debated becomes the focus of the debate.

But in the process, the sheer repetition of the shocking grad- 10
ually dulls its shock effect. No longer outraged, people begin to
argue for positions to moderate the extreme; or they accept the
premise, challenging instead the means to achieve it. (Note
that in Debbie's debate, many challenged not the killing, but
the intern's failure to check more carefully into the case.)

11   And gradually, though no one remembers quite how it all happened, the once unspeakable becomes tolerable and, in time, acceptable.

12   An example of how this process works is the case of homosexuality. Not long ago it was widely regarded, even in secular society, as a perversion. The gay-rights movement's first pronouncements were received with shock; then, in the process of debate, the public gradually lost its sense of outrage. Homosexuality became a cause—and what was once deviant is today, in many jurisdictions, a legally protected right. All this in little more than a decade.

13   Debbie's story appears to have initiated this process for euthanasia. Columnist Ellen Goodman welcomed the case as "a debate that should be taking place."

14   So what was once a crime becomes a debate. And, if history holds true, that debate will usher the once unmentionable into common practice.

15   Already the stage is set. In a 1983 poll, 63 percent of Americans approved of mercy killing in certain cases. In a 1988 poll, more than 50 percent of lawyers favored legal euthanasia. The Hemlock Society is working to put the issue on the ballot in several states.

16   I don't intend to sound alarmist: legal euthanasia in this country is still more a threat than a reality. But 20 years ago, who would have thought abortion would one day be a constitutional right, or that infanticide would be given legal protection?

17   The path from the unmentionable to the commonplace is being traveled with increasing speed in medical ethics. Without some concerted resistance, euthanasia is likely to be the next to make the trip. As Ellen Goodman concluded her column, "The Debbie story is not over yet, not by a long shot."

18   Indeed.

19   Novelist Walker Percy, in *The Thanatos Syndrome*, offers one vision of where such compromising debates on the value of life might take us.

20   The time is the 1990s. Qualitarian Life Centers have sprung up across the country after the landmark case of *Doe* v. *Dade* "which decreed, with solid scientific evidence, that the human infant does not achieve personhood until 18 months." At these centers one can conveniently dispose of unwanted young and old alike.

21   An old priest, Father Smith, confronts the narrator, a psychiatrist, in this exchange:

"You are an able psychiatrist. On the whole a decent, gener-   22
ous humanitarian person in the abstract sense of the word.
You know what is going to happen to you."

"What?"   23

"You are a member of the first generation of doctors in   24
the history of medicine to turn their backs on the oath of
Hippocrates and kill millions of old, useless people, unborn
children, born malformed children, for the good of mankind—and to do so without a single murmur from one of
you. Not a single letter of protest in the august *New England
Journal of Medicine.* And do you know what you are going to
end up doing?"

"No," I say...   25

The priest aims his azimuth squarely at me and then   26
appears to lose his train of thought....

"What is going to happen to me, Father?" I ask before he   27
gets away altogether.

"Oh," he says absently, appearing to be thinking of some-   28
thing else, "you're going to end up killing Jews."

James Rachels
Active and Passive Euthanasia

*James Rachels (born 1941), a philosopher and teacher at New
York University, University of Miami, and the University of
Alabama at Birmingham (where he currently works), is particularly interested in ethics. He contributed the following essay
to the* New England Journal of Medicine *in 1975.*

The distinction between active and passive euthanasia is   1
thought to be crucial for medical ethics. The idea is that it is
permissible, at least in some cases, to withhold treatment and
allow a patient to die, but it is never permissible to take any
direct action designed to kill the patient. This doctrine seems
to be accepted by most doctors, and it is endorsed in a statement adopted by the House of Delegates of the American
Medical Association on December 4, 1973:

The intentional termination of the life of one human being by another—mercy killing—is contrary to that for which the medical profession stands and is contrary to the policy of the American Medical Association.

The cessation of the employment of extraordinary means to prolong the life of the body when there is irrefutable evidence that biological death is imminent is the decision of the patient and/or his family. The advice and judgment of the physician should be freely available to the patient and/or his immediate family.

However, a strong case can be made against this doctrine. In what follows I will set out some of the relevant arguments, and urge doctors to reconsider their views on this matter.

2　To begin with a familiar type of situation, a patient who is dying of incurable cancer of the throat is in terrible pain, which can no longer be satisfactorily alleviated. He is certain to die within a few days, even if present treatment is continued, but he does not want to go on living for those days since the pain is unbearable. So he asks the doctor for an end to it, and his family joins in the request.

3　Suppose the doctor agrees to withhold treatment, as the conventional doctrine says he may. The justification for his doing so is that the patient is in terrible agony, and since he is going to die anyway, it would be wrong to prolong his suffering needlessly. But now notice this. If one simply withholds treatment, it may take the patient longer to die, and so he may suffer more than he would if more direct action were taken and a lethal injection given. This fact provides strong reason for thinking that, once the initial decision not to prolong his agony has been made, active euthanasia is actually preferable to passive euthanasia, rather than the reverse. To say otherwise is to endorse the option that leads to more suffering rather than less, and is contrary to the humanitarian impulse that prompts the decision not to prolong his life in the first place.

4　Part of my point is that the process of being "allowed to die" can be relatively slow and painful, whereas being given a lethal injection is relatively quick and painless. Let me give a different sort of example. In the United States about one in 600 babies is born with Down's syndrome. Most of these babies are otherwise healthy—that is, with only the usual pediatric care, they will proceed to an otherwise normal infancy. Some, however, are born with congenital defects such as intestinal obstructions that require operations if they are to live. Sometimes, the parents and the doctor will decide not to operate, and let the infant die. Anthony Shaw describes what happens then:

> . . . When surgery is denied [the doctor] must try to keep the infant from suffering while natural forces sap the baby's life away. As a surgeon whose natural inclination is to use the scalpel to fight off death, standing by and watching a salvageable baby die is the most emotionally exhausting experience I know. It is easy at a conference, in a theoretical discussion, to decide that such infants should be allowed to die. It is altogether different to stand by in the nursery and watch as dehydration and infection wither a tiny being over hours and days. This is a terrible ordeal for me and the hospital staff—much more so than for the parents who never set foot in the nursery.

I can understand why some people are opposed to all euthanasia, and insist that such infants must be allowed to live. I think I can also understand why other people favor destroying these babies quickly and painlessly. But why should anyone favor letting "dehydration and infection wither a tiny being over hours and days"? The doctrine that says that a baby may be allowed to dehydrate and wither, but may not be given an injection that would end its life without suffering, seems so patently cruel as to require no further refutation. The strong language is not intended to offend, but only to put the point in the clearest possible way.

My second argument is that the conventional doctrine 5
leads to decisions concerning life and death made on irrelevant grounds.

Consider again the case of the infants with Down's syn- 6
drome who need operations for congenital defects unrelated to the syndrome to live. Sometimes, there is no operation, and the baby dies. But when there is no such defect, the baby lives on. Now, an operation such as that to remove an intestinal obstruction is not prohibitively difficult. The reason why such operations are not performed in these cases is, clearly, that the child has Down's syndrome and the parents and doctor judge that because of that fact it is better for the child to die.

But notice that this situation is absurd, no matter what 7
view one takes of the lives and potential of such babies. If the life of such an infant is worth preserving, what does it matter if it needs a simple operation? Or, if one thinks it better that

such a baby should not live on, what difference does it make that it happens to have an unobstructed intestinal tract? In either case, the matter of life and death is being decided on irrelevant grounds. It is the Down's syndrome, and not the intestines, that is the issue. The matter should be decided, if at all, on that basis, and not be allowed to depend on the essentially irrelevant question of whether the intestinal tract is blocked.

8   What makes this situation possible, of course, is the idea that when there is an intestinal blockage, one can "let the baby die," but when there is no such defect there is nothing that can be done, for one must not "kill" it. The fact that this idea leads to such results as deciding life or death on irrelevant grounds is another good reason why the doctrine should be rejected.

9   One reason why so many people think that there is an important moral difference between active and passive euthanasia is that they think killing someone is morally worse than letting someone die. But is it? Is killing in itself worse than letting die? To investigate this issue, two cases may be considered that are exactly alike except that one involves killing whereas the other involves letting someone die. Then it can be asked whether this difference makes any difference to the moral assessments. It is important that the cases be exactly alike, except for this one difference and not some other that accounts for any variation in the assessments of the two cases. So, let us consider this pair of cases:

10   In the first, Smith stands to gain a large inheritance if anything should happen to his six-year-old cousin. One evening while the child is taking his bath, Smith sneaks into the bathroom and drowns the child, and then arranges things so that it will look like an accident.

11   In the second, Jones also stands to gain if anything should happen to his six-year-old cousin. Like Smith, Jones sneaks in planning to drown the child in his bath. However, just as he enters the bathroom Jones sees the child slip and hit his head, and fall face down in the water. Jones is delighted; he stands by, ready to push the child's head back under if it is necessary. With only a little thrashing about, the child drowns all by himself, "accidentally," as Jones watches and does nothing.

12   Now Smith killed the child, whereas Jones "merely" let the child die. That is the only difference between them. Did either man behave better, from a moral point of view? If the difference between killing and letting die were in itself a morally important matter, one should say that Jones's behavior was

less reprehensible than Smith's. But does one really want to say that? I think not. In the first place, both men acted from the same motive, personal gain, and both had exactly the same end in view when they acted. It may be inferred from Smith's conduct that he is a bad man, although that judgment may be withdrawn or modified if certain further facts are learned about him—for example, that he is mentally deranged. But would not the very same thing be inferred about Jones from his conduct? And would not the same further considerations also be relevant to any modification of this judgment? Moreover, suppose Jones pleaded, in his own defense, "After all, I didn't do anything except just stand there and watch the child drown. I didn't kill him; I only let him die." Again, if letting die were in itself less bad than killing, this defense should have at least some weight. But it does not. Such a "defense" can only be regarded as a grotesque perversion of moral reasoning. Morally speaking, it is no defense at all.

Now, it may be pointed out, quite properly, that the cases   13 of euthanasia with which doctors are concerned are not like this at all. They do not involve personal gain or the destruction of normal healthy children. Doctors are concerned only with cases in which the patient's life is of no further use to him, or in which the patient's life has become or will soon become a terrible burden. However, the point is the same in these cases: the bare difference between killing and letting die does not, in itself, make a moral difference. If a doctor lets a patient die, for humane reasons, he is in the same moral position as if he had given the patient a lethal injection for humane reasons. If his decision was wrong—if, for example, the patient's illness was in fact curable—the decision would be equally regrettable no matter which method was used to carry it out. And if the doctor's decision was the right one, the method used is not in itself important.

The AMA policy statement isolates the crucial issue very   14 well; the crucial issue is "the intentional termination of the life of one human being by another." But after identifying this issue, and forbidding "mercy killing," the statement goes on to deny that the cessation of treatment is the intentional termination of a life. This is where the mistake comes in, for what is the cessation of treatment, in these circumstances, if it is not "the intentional termination of the life of one human being by another"? Of course it is exactly that, and if it were not, there would be no point to it.

Many people will find this judgment hard to accept. One   15 reason, I think, is that it is very easy to conflate the question of whether killing is, in itself, worse than letting die, with the very different question of whether most actual cases of killing are more reprehensible than most actual cases of letting die. Most actual cases of killing are clearly terrible (think, for example, of all the murders reported in the newspapers), and one hears of such cases every day. On the other hand, one hardly ever hears of a case of letting die, except for the actions of doctors who are motivated by humanitarian reasons. So one learns to think of killing in a much worse light than of letting die. For it is not the bare difference between killing and letting die that makes the difference in these cases. Rather, the other factors—the murderer's motive of personal gain, for example, contrasted with the doctor's humanitarian motivation—account for the different reactions to the different cases.

16   I have argued that killing is not in itself any worse than letting die; if my contention is right, it follows that active euthanasia is not any worse than passive euthanasia. What arguments can be given on the other side? The most common, I believe, is the following:

17   "The important difference between active and passive euthanasia is that in passive euthanasia, the doctor does not do anything to bring about the patient's death. The doctor does nothing, and the patient dies of whatever ills already afflict him. In active euthanasia, however, the doctor does something to bring about the patient's death: he kills him. The doctor who gives the patient with cancer a lethal injection has himself caused his patient's death; whereas if he merely ceases treatment, the cancer is the cause of the death."

18   A number of points need to be made here. The first is that it is not exactly correct to say that in passive euthanasia the doctor does nothing, for he does do one thing that is very important: he lets the patient die. "Letting someone die" is certainly different in some respects, from other types of action—mainly in that it is a kind of action that one may perform by way of not performing certain other actions. For example, one may let a patient die by way of not giving medication, just as one may insult someone by way of not shaking his hand. But for any purpose of moral assessment, it is a type of action nonetheless. The decision to let a patient die is subject to moral appraisal in the same way that a decision to kill him would be subject to moral appraisal: it may be assessed as wise or unwise, compassionate or sadistic, right or wrong. If a doctor deliberately let a patient die who was suffering from a routinely curable illness, the doctor would

certainly be to blame for what he had done, just as he would be to blame if he had needlessly killed the patient. Charges against him would then be appropriate. If so, it would be no defense at all for him to insist that he didn't "do anything." He would have done something very serious indeed, for he let his patient die.

Fixing the cause of death may be very important from a legal point of view, for it may determine whether criminal charges are brought against the doctor. But I do not think that this notion can be used to show a moral difference between active and passive euthanasia. The reason why it is considered bad to be the cause of someone's death is that death is regarded as a great evil—and so it is. However, if it had been decided that euthanasia—even passive euthanasia—is desirable in a given case, it has also been decided that in this instance death is no greater an evil than the patient's continued existence. And if this is true, the usual reason for not wanting to be the cause of someone's death simply does not apply. 19

Finally, doctors may think that all of this is only of academic interest—the sort of thing that philosophers may worry about but that has no practical bearing on their own work. After all, doctors must be concerned about the legal consequences of what they do, and active euthanasia is clearly forbidden by law. But even so, doctors should also be concerned with the fact that the law is forcing upon them a moral doctrine that may well be indefensible, and has a considerable effect on their practices. Of course, most doctors are not now in the position of being coerced in this matter, for they do not regard themselves as merely going along with what the law requires. Rather, in statements such as the AMA policy statement that I have quoted, they are endorsing this doctrine as a central point of medical ethics. In that statement, active euthanasia is condemned not merely as illegal but as "contrary to that for which the medical profession stands," whereas passive euthanasia is approved. However, the preceding considerations suggest that there is really no moral difference between the two, considered in themselves (there may be important moral differences in some cases in their consequences, but, as I pointed out, these differences may make active euthanasia, and not passive euthanasia, the morally preferable option). So whereas doctors may have to discriminate between active and passive euthanasia to satisfy the law, they should not do any more than that. In particular, they should not give the distinction any added authority and weight by writing it into official statements of medical ethics. 20

Sidney Hook
In Defense of
Voluntary Euthanasia

Sidney Hook (1902–1989) studied philosophy under John Dewey and became an outspoken, controversial, daring social thinker. A prolific essayist who also published some thirty books, a champion of Marx in the 1930s but of individual freedoms as well, Hook remained iconoclastic and independent throughout his career, which he chronicled in his 1987 autobiography, Out of Step: An Unquiet Life in the 20th Century. *He wrote the following essay for* The New York Times *in 1987.*

1   A few short years ago, I lay at the point of death. A congestive heart failure was treated for diagnostic purposes by an angiogram that triggered a stroke. Violent and painful hiccups, uninterrupted for several days and nights, prevented the digestion of food. My left side and one of my vocal cords became paralyzed. Some form of pleurisy set in, and I felt I was drowning in a sea of slime. At one point, my heart stopped beating; just as I lost consciousness, it was thumped back into action again. In one of my lucid intervals during those days of agony, I asked my physician to discontinue all life-supporting services or show me how to do it. He refused and told me that someday I would appreciate the unwisdom of my request.

2   A month later, I was discharged from the hospital. In six months, I regained the use of my limbs, and although my voice still lacks its old resonance and carrying power I no longer croak like a frog. There remain some minor disabilities and I am restricted to a rigorous, low sodium diet. I have resumed my writing and research.

3   My experience can be and has been cited as an argument against honoring requests of stricken patients to be gently eased out of their pain and life. I cannot agree. There are two main reasons. As an octogenarian, there is a reasonable likelihood that I may suffer another "cardiovascular accident" or worse. I may not even be in a position to ask for the surcease of pain. It seems to me that I have already paid my dues to death—indeed, although time has softened my memories they are vivid enough to justify my saying that I suffered enough to warrant dying several times over. Why run the risk of more?

Secondly, I dread imposing on my family and friends an- 4
other grim round of misery similar to the one my first attack
occasioned.

My wife and children endured enough for one lifetime. I 5
know that for them the long days and nights of waiting, the
disruption of their professional duties and their own familial
responsibilities counted for nothing in their anxiety for me.
In their joy at my recovery they have been forgotten. Nonetheless, to visit another prolonged spell of helpless suffering
on them as my life ebbs away, or even worse, if I linger on
into a comatose senility, seems altogether gratuitous.

But what, it may be asked, of the joy and satisfaction of liv- 6
ing, of basking in the sunlight, listening to music, watching
one's grandchildren growing into adolescence, following the
news about the fate of freedom in a troubled world, playing
with ideas, writing one's testament of wisdom and folly for
posterity? Is not all that one endured, together with the risk
of its recurrence, an acceptable price for the multiple satisfac-
tions that are still open even to a person of advanced years?

Apparently those who cling to life, no matter what, think 7
so. I do not.

The zest and intensity of these experiences are no longer 8
what they used to be. I am not vain enough to delude myself
that I can in the few remaining years make an important discovery useful for mankind or can lead a social movement or
do anything that will be historically eventful, no less event-
making. My autobiography, which describes a record of intellectual and political experiences of some historical value, already much too long, could be posthumously published. I
have had my fill of joys and sorrows and am not greedy for
more life. I have always thought that a test of whether one
had found happiness in one's life is whether one would be
willing to relive it—whether, if it were possible, one would accept the opportunity to be born again.

Having lived a full and relatively happy life, I would cheer- 9
fully accept the chance to be reborn, but certainly not to be
reborn again as an infirm octogenarian. To some extent, my
views reflect what I have seen happen to the aged and
stricken who have been so unfortunate as to survive crippling
paralysis. They suffer, and impose suffering on others, unable
even to make a request that their torment be ended.

I am mindful too of the burdens placed upon the commu- 10
nity, with its rapidly diminishing resources, to provide the adequate and costly services necessary to sustain the lives of
those whose days and nights are spent on mattress graves of

pain. A better use could be made of these resources to increase the opportunities and qualities of life for the young. I am not denying the moral obligation the community has to look after its disabled and aged. There are times, however, when an individual may find it pointless to insist on the fulfillment of a legal and moral right.

11 What is required is no great revolution in morals but an enlargement of imagination and an intelligent evaluation of alternative uses of community resources.

12 Long ago, Seneca observed that "the wise man will live as long as he ought, not as long as he can." One can envisage hypothetical circumstances in which one has a duty to prolong one's life despite its costs for the sake of others, but such circumstances are far removed from the ordinary prospects we are considering. If wisdom is rooted in the knowledge of the alternatives of choice, it must be reliably informed of the state one is in and its likely outcome. Scientific medicine is not infallible, but it is the best we have. Should a rational person be willing to endure acute suffering merely on the chance that a miraculous cure might presently be at hand? Each one should be permitted to make his own choice—especially when no one else is harmed by it.

13 The responsibility for the decision, whether deemed wise or foolish, must be with the chooser.

Leon R. Kass
Why Doctors Must Not Kill

A physician and professor at the University of Chicago, Leon R. Kass published the following in 1991 in a special issue of Commonweal *on euthanasia.* Commonweal *is a biweekly review of public affairs, religion, the arts, and literature (it publishes many book reviews). It has a generally liberal outlook and is associated with Catholicism.*

1 Do you want your doctor licensed to kill? Should he or she be permitted or encouraged to inject or prescribe poison? Shall the mantle of privacy that protects the doctor-patient relationship, in the service of life and wholeness, now also cloak

decisions for death? Do you want *your* doctor deciding, on the basis of his own private views, when you still deserve to live and when you now deserve to die? And what about the other fellow's doctor—that shallow technician, that insensitive boor who neither asks nor listens, that unprincipled money-grubber, that doctor you used to go to until you got up the nerve to switch: do you want *him* licensed to kill? Speaking generally, shall the healing profession become also the euthanizing profession?

Common sense has always answered, "No." For more than two millennia, the reigning medical ethic, mindful that the power to cure is also the power to kill, has held as an inviolable rule, "Doctors must not kill." Yet this venerable taboo is now under attack. Proponents of euthanasia and physician-assisted suicide would have us believe that it is but an irrational vestige of religious prejudice, alien to a true ethic of medicine, which stands in the way of a rational and humane approach to suffering at the end of life. Nothing could be further from the truth. The taboo against doctors killing patients (even on request) is the very embodiment of reason and wisdom. Without it, medicine will have trouble doing its proper work; without it, medicine will have lost its claim to be an ethical and trustworthy profession; without it, all of us will suffer—yes, more than we now suffer because some of us are not soon enough released from life.

Consider first the damaging consequences for the doctor-patient relationship. The patient's trust in the doctor's whole-hearted devotion to the patient's best interests will be hard to sustain once doctors are licensed to kill. Imagine the scene: you are old, poor, in failing health, and alone in the world; you are brought to the city hospital with fractured ribs and pneumonia. The nurse or intern enters late at night with a syringe full of yellow stuff for your intravenous drip. How soundly will you sleep? It will not matter that your doctor has never yet put anyone to death; that he is legally entitled to do so will make a world of difference.

And it will make a world of psychic difference too for conscientious physicians. How easily will they be able to care whole-heartedly for patients when it is always possible to think of killing them as a "therapeutic option"? Shall it be penicillin and a respirator one more time, or, perhaps, this time just an overdose of morphine? Physicians get tired of treating patients who are hard to cure, who resist their best efforts, who are on their way down—"gorks," "gomers," and "vegetables" are only some of the less than affectionate names they receive from the house officers. Won't it be tempting to think that death is the best "treatment" for the little old lady "dumped" again on the emergency room by the nearby nursing home?

5   It is naive and foolish to take comfort from the fact that the currently proposed change in the law provides "aid-in-dying" only to those who request it. For we know from long experience how difficult it is to discover what we truly want when we are suffering. Verbal "requests" made under duress rarely reveal the whole story. Often a demand for euthanasia is, in fact, an angry or anxious plea for help, born of fear of rejection or abandonment, or made in ignorance of available alternatives that could alleviate pain and suffering. Everyone knows how easy it is for those who control the information to engineer requests and to manipulate choices, especially in the vulnerable. Paint vividly a horrible prognosis, and contrast it with that "gentle, quick release": which will the depressed or frightened patient choose, especially in the face of a spiraling hospital bill or children who visit grudgingly? Yale Kamisar asks the right questions: "Is this the kind of choice, assuming that it can be made in a fixed and rational manner, that we want to offer a gravely ill person? Will we not sweep up, in the process, some who are not really tired of life, but think others are tired of them; some who do not really want to die, but who feel that they should not live on, because to do so when there looms the legal alternative of euthanasia is to do a selfish or cowardly act? Will not some feel an obligation to have themselves 'eliminated' in order that funds allocated for their terminal care might be better used by their families or, financial worries aside, in order to relieve their families of the emotional strain involved?"

6   Euthanasia, once legalized, will not remain confined to those who freely and knowingly elect it—and the most energetic backers of euthanasia do not really want it thus restricted. Why? Because the vast majority of candidates who merit mercy-killing cannot request it for themselves: adults with persistent vegetative state or severe depression or senility or aphasia or mental illness or Alzheimer's disease; infants who are deformed; and children who are retarded or dying. All incapable of requesting death, they will thus be denied our new humane "assistance-in-dying." But not to worry. The lawyers and the doctors (and the cost-containers) will soon rectify this injustice. The enactment of a law legalizing mercy killing (or assisted suicide) on voluntary

request will certainly be challenged in the courts under the equal-protection clause of the Fourteenth Amendment. Why, it will be argued, should the comatose or the demented be denied the right to such a "dignified death" or such a "treatment" just because they cannot claim it for themselves? With the aid of court-appointed proxy consenters, we will quickly erase the distinction between the right to choose one's own death and the right to request someone else's—as we have already done in the termination-of-treatment cases.

Clever doctors and relatives will not need to wait for such   7
changes in the law. Who will be around to notice when the elderly, poor, crippled, weak, powerless, retarded, uneducated, demented, or gullible are mercifully released from the lives their doctors, nurses, and next of kin deem no longer worth living? In Holland, for example, a recent survey of 300 physicians (conducted by an author who supports euthanasia) disclosed that over 40 percent had performed euthanasia *without the patient's request,* and over 10 percent had done so in more than five cases. Is there any reason to believe that the average American physician is, in his private heart, more committed than his Dutch counterpart to the equal worth and dignity of every life under his care? Do we really want to find out what he is like, once the taboo is broken?

Even the most humane and conscientious physician psy-   8
chologically needs protection against himself and his weaknesses, if he is to care fully for those who entrust themselves to him. A physician-friend who worked many years in a hospice caring for dying patients explained it to me most convincingly: "Only because I knew that I could not and would not kill my patients was I able to enter most fully and intimately into caring for them as they lay dying." The psychological burden of the license to kill (not to speak of the brutalization of the physician-killers) could very well be an intolerably high price to pay for the physician-assisted euthanasia.

The point, however, is not merely psychological: it is also   9
moral and essential. My friend's horror at the thought that he might be tempted to kill his patients, were he not enjoined from doing so, embodies a deep understanding of the medical ethic and its intrinsic limits. We move from assessing consequences to looking at medicine itself.

The beginning of ethics regarding the use of power gener-   10
ally lies in nay-saying. The wise setting of limits on the use of power is based on discerning the excesses to which the power, unrestrained, is prone. Applied to the professions,

this principle would establish strict outer boundaries—
indeed, inviolable taboos—against those "occupational hazards" to which each profession is especially prone. *Within*
these outer limits, no fixed rules of conduct apply; instead,
prudence—the wise judgment of the man-on-the-spot—finds
and adopts the best course of action in the light of the circumstances. But the outer limits themselves are fixed, firm,
and non-negotiable.

11   What are those limits for medicine? At least three are set
forth in the venerable Hippocratic Oath: no breach of confidentiality; no sexual relations with patients; no dispensing of
deadly drugs. These unqualified, self-imposed restrictions are
readily understood in terms of the temptations to which the
physician is most vulnerable, temptations in each case regarding an area of vulnerability and exposure that the practice of
medicine requires of patients. Patients necessarily divulge and
reveal private and intimate details of their personal lives; patients necessarily expose their naked bodies to the physician's
objectifying gaze and investigating hands; patients necessarily
expose and entrust the care of their very lives to the physician's skill, technique, and judgment. The exposure is, in all
cases, one-sided and asymmetric: the doctor does not reveal
his intimacies, display his nakedness, offer up his embodied
life to the patient. Mindful of the meaning of such nonmutual
exposure, the physician voluntarily sets limits on his own
conduct, pledging not to take advantage of or to violate the
patient's intimacies, naked sexuality, or life itself.

12   The prohibition against killing patients, the first negative
promise of self-restraint sworn to in the Hippocratic Oath,
stands as medicine's first and most abiding taboo: "I will neither give a deadly drug to anybody if asked for it, nor will I
make a suggestion to this effect.... In purity and holiness I
will guard my life and my art." In forswearing the giving of
poison, the physician recognizes and restrains a god-like
power he wields over patients, mindful that his drugs can
both cure and kill. But in forswearing the giving of poison,
when asked for it, the Hippocratic physician rejects the view
that the patient's choice for death can make killing him—or
assisting his suicide—right. For the physician, at least, human
life in living bodies commands respect and reverence—*by its
very nature.* As its respectability does not depend upon human agreement or patient consent, revocation of one's consent to live does not deprive one's living body of respectability.
The deepest ethical principle restraining the physician's
power is not the autonomy or freedom of the patient; neither

is it his own compassion or good intention. Rather, it is the dignity and mysterious power of human life itself, and, therefore, also what the oath calls the purity and holiness of the life and art to which he has sworn devotion. A person can choose to be a physician, but he cannot simply choose what physicianship means.

The central meaning of physicianship derives not from medicine's powers but from its goal, not from its means but from its end: to benefit the sick by the activity of healing. The physician as physician serves only the sick. He does not serve the relatives or the hospital or the national debt inflated due to Medicare costs. Thus he will never sacrifice the well-being of the sick to the convenience or pocketbook or feelings of the relatives or society. Moreover, the physician serves the sick not because they have rights or wants or claims, but because they are sick. The healer works with and for those who need to be healed, in order to help make them whole. Despite enormous changes in medical technique and institutional practice, despite enormous changes in nosology and therapeutics, the center of medicine has not changed: it is as true today as it was in the days of Hippocrates that the ill desire to be whole; that wholeness means a certain well-working of the enlivened body and its unimpaired powers to sense, think, feel, desire, move, and maintain itself; and that the relationship between the healer and the ill is constituted, essentially even if only tacitly, around the desire of both to promote the wholeness of the one who is ailing.

Can wholeness and healing ever be compatible with intentionally killing the patient? Can one benefit the patient as a whole by making him dead? There is, of course, a logical difficulty: how can any good exist for a being that is not? But the error is more than logical: to intend and to act for someone's good requires his continued existence to receive the benefit.

To be sure, certain attempts to benefit may in fact turn out, unintentionally, to be lethal. Giving adequate morphine to control pain might induce respiratory depression leading to death. But the intent to relieve the pain of the living presupposes that the living still live to be relieved. This must be the starting point in discussing all medical benefits: no benefit without a beneficiary.

Against this view, someone will surely bring forth the hard cases: patients so ill-served by their bodies that they can no longer bear to live, bodies riddled with cancer and racked with pain, against which their "owners" protest in horror and from which they insist on being released. Cannot the person "in the body" speak up against the rest, and request death for "personal" reasons?

17   However sympathetically we listen to such requests, we must see them as incoherent. Such person-body dualism cannot be sustained. "Personhood" is manifest on earth only in living bodies; our highest mental functions are held up by, and are inseparable from, lowly metabolism, respiration, circulation, excretion. There may be blood without consciousness, but there is never consciousness without blood. Thus one who calls for death in the service of personhood is like a tree seeking to cut its roots for the sake of growing its highest fruit. No physician, devoted to the benefit of the sick, can serve the patient as person by denying and thwarting his personal embodiment.

18   To say it plainly, to bring nothingness is incompatible with serving wholeness: one cannot heal—or comfort—by making nil. The healer cannot annihilate if he is truly to heal. The physician-euthanizer is a deadly self-contradiction.

19   But we must acknowledge a difficulty. The central goal of medicine—health—is, in each case, a perishable good: inevitably, patients get irreversibly sick, patients degenerate, patients die. Healing the sick is *in principle* a project that must at some point fail. And here is where all the trouble begins: How does one deal with "medical failure"? What does one seek when restoration of wholeness—or "much" wholeness—is by and large out of the question?

20   Contrary to the propaganda of the euthanasia movement, there is, in fact, much that can be done. Indeed, by recognizing finitude yet knowing that we will not kill, we are empowered to focus on easing and enhancing the *lives* of those who are dying. First of all, medicine can follow the lead of the hospice movement and—abandoning decades of shameful mismanagement—provide truly adequate (and now technically feasible) relief of pain and discomfort. Second, physicians (and patients and families) can continue to learn how to withhold or withdraw those technical interventions that are, in truth, merely burdensome or degrading medical additions to the unhappy end of a life—including, frequently, hospitalization itself. Ceasing treatment and allowing death to occur when (and if) it will seem to be quite compatible with the respect life itself commands for itself. Doctors may and must allow to die, even if they must not intentionally kill.

21   Ceasing medical intervention, allowing nature to take its course, differs fundamentally from mercy killing. For one

thing, death does not necessarily follow the discontinuance of treatment; Karen Ann Quinlan lived more than ten years after the court allowed the "life-sustaining" respirator to be removed. Not the physician, but the underlying fatal illness becomes the true cause of death. More important morally, in ceasing treatment the physician need not *intend* the death of the patient, even when the death follows as a result of his omission. His intention should be to avoid useless and degrading medical *additions* to the already sad end of a life. In contrast, in active, direct mercy killing the physician must, necessarily and indubitably, intend *primarily* that the patient be made dead. And he must knowingly and indubitably cast himself in the role of the agent of death. This remains true even if he is merely an assistant in suicide. A physician who provides the pills or lets the patient plunge the syringe after he leaves the room is *morally* no different from one who does the deed himself. "I will neither give a deadly drug to anybody if asked for it, nor will I make a suggestion to this effect."

Once we refuse the technical fix, physicians and the rest of   22
us can also rise to the occasion: we can learn to act humanly in the presence of finitude. Far more than adequate morphine and the removal of burdensome machinery, the dying need our presence and our encouragement. Dying people are all too easily reduced ahead of time to "thinghood" by those who cannot bear to deal with the suffering or disability of those they love. Withdrawal of contact, affection, and care is the greatest single cause of the dehumanization of dying. Not the alleged humaneness of an elixir of death, but the humanness of connected living-while-dying is what medicine—and the rest of us—most owe the dying. The treatment of choice is company and care.

The euthanasia movement would have us believe that the   23
physician's refusal to assist in suicide or perform euthanasia constitutes an affront to human dignity. Yet one of their favorite arguments seems to me rather to prove the reverse. Why, it is argued, do we put animals out of their misery but insist on compelling fellow human beings to suffer to the bitter end? Why, if it is not a contradiction for the veterinarian, does the medical ethic absolutely rule out mercy killing? Is this not simply inhumane?

Perhaps *inhumane*, but not thereby *inhuman*. On the con-   24
trary, it is precisely because animals are not human that we must treat them (merely) humanely. We put dumb animals to sleep because they do not know that they are dying, because

they can make nothing of their misery or mortality, and, therefore, because they cannot live deliberately—i.e., humanly—in
the face of their own suffering and dying. They cannot live
out a fitting end. Compassion for their weakness and dumb-
ness is our only appropriate emotion, and given our responsibility for their care and well-being, we do the only humane
thing we can. But when a conscious human being asks us for
death, by that very action he displays the presence of something that precludes our regarding him as a dumb animal.
Humanity is owed humanity, not humaneness. Humanity is
owed the bolstering of the human, even or especially in its dying moments, in resistance to the temptation to ignore its
presence in the sight of suffering.

25   What humanity needs most in the face of evils is courage,
the ability to stand against fear and pain and thoughts of
nothingness. The deaths we most admire are those of people
who, knowing that they are dying, face the fact frontally and
act accordingly: they set their affairs in order, they arrange
what could be final meetings with their loved ones, and yet,
with strength of soul and a small reservoir of hope, they continue to live and work and love as much as they can for as
long as they can. Because such conclusions of life require
courage, they call for our encouragement—and for the many
small speeches and deeds that shore up the human spirit
against despair and defeat.

26   Many doctors are in fact rather poor at this sort of encouragement. They tend to regard every dying or incurable patient
as a failure, as if an earlier diagnosis or a more vigorous intervention might have avoided what is, in truth, an inevitable
collapse. The enormous successes of medicine these past fifty
years have made both doctors and laymen less prepared than
ever to accept the fact of finitude. Doctors behave, not without some reason, as if they have godlike powers to revive the
moribund; laymen expect an endless string of medical miracles. Physicians today are not likely to be agents of encouragement once their technique begins to fail.

27   It is, of course, partly for these reasons that doctors will be
pressed to kill—and many of them will, alas, be willing. Having adopted a largely technical approach to healing, having
medicalized so much of the end of life, doctors are being
asked—often with thinly veiled anger—to provide a final
technical solution for the evil of human finitude and for their
own technical failure: If you cannot cure me, kill me. The last
gasp of autonomy or cry for dignity is asserted against a medicalization and institutionalization of the end of life that robs

the old and the incurable of most of their autonomy and dignity: intubated and electrified, with bizarre mechanical companions, once proud and independent people find themselves cast in the roles of passive, obedient, highly disciplined children. People who care for autonomy and dignity should try to reverse this dehumanization of the last stages of life, instead of giving dehumanization its final triumph by welcoming the desperate goodbye-to-all-that contained in one final plea for poison.

The present crisis that leads some to press for active eutha- 28
nasia is really an opportunity to learn the limits of the medicalization of life and death and to recover an appreciation of living with and against mortality. It is an opportunity for physicians to recover an understanding that there remains a residual human wholeness—however precarious—that can be cared for even in the face of incurable and terminal illness. Should doctors cave in, should doctors become technical dispensers of death, they will not only be abandoning their posts, their patients, and their duty to care; they will set the worst sort of example for the community at large—teaching technicism and so-called humaneness where encouragement and humanity are both required and sorely lacking. On the other hand, should physicians hold fast, should doctors learn that finitude is no disgrace and that human wholeness can be cared for to the very end, medicine may serve not only the good of its patients, but also, by example, the failing moral health of modern times.

Elizabeth Martinez

Is Rightful Death
a Feminist Issue?

Elizabeth Martinez is a Mexican American activist and a teacher of Women's Studies and Chicano Studies. She frequently writes on Latino issues and placed the following essay in Ms. *magazine in July/August 1993.*

1   A little after midnight the nurse called to say that my mother had just died. I had expected it to take much longer, and earlier in the day she seemed perhaps a little weaker but no more than that. When my daughter and I arrived at the nursing home in Oakland, the night nurse merely nodded as she unlocked the front door. Her lack of comment seemed unusual at the time, though not unwelcome.

2   It was hard to walk into my mother's room and I lingered in the doorway, feeling lost. Finally I walked to her bed. Her face was very beautiful. The puffiness of her cheeks had gone, perhaps because the feeding tube had been removed five days before; so, too, the lines of strain in her face. She looked handsome again for the first time in many months, a 92-year-old lady of grace and presence. Bending to kiss her forehead, I heard myself think: "It must have been the right thing to do."

3   We asked to talk to the nurse who had found her dead. From another patient's darkened room Virginia came striding out into the light of the corridor: tall, angular, strong. When I asked if she thought my mother had died in her sleep, her face became thoughtful and she said nothing. I persisted anxiously, "Do you think she died in a peaceful way?" Then Virginia understood and opened her long arms wide to wrap them around me, murmuring, yes yes, it was all right.

4   After the arrangements to have my mother's body removed to a mortuary had been completed, we could leave. The night nurse, Georgia, short and round-faced, walked us to the door. In a strong voice she called out across the moonless night: "Drive carefully. Drive carefully!"

5   That was her way: What else could Georgia have said? What does anyone say to a person whose mother has just died when it was that person who made it happen? Had I somehow wished Georgia would say the usual words, "I'm so sorry"?

This question was just one of many mysteries on a long   6
and wondrous journey.

Since 1987 my mother had been in "a persistent vegetative   7
state," as they say, kept alive by artificial means. In building
machines that can breathe, feed, and clean out wastes for
people, we have generated a host of anguishing, Faustian
questions: When should life-support measures be taken? If a
person's mind and spirit are gone, should these measures be
abandoned? If so, when, and who decides? Today we also
hear nationwide debate about doctor-induced death, largely
as a result of Dr. Jack Kevorkian's suicide devices.

Whether the issue is refusing to prolong life mechanically,   8
facilitating suicide, or more active euthanasia—in Greek, the
"easy death"—we eventually confront this society's attitude toward death itself. The dominant U.S. culture breeds fear (and
with it, dread of aging). To recognize a timely death as part of
planet life, as nature, and sometimes as a friend, does not
come easy for most of the Western world.

Defining medical care as a mystery only they can fathom,   9
many physicians disempower patients who might otherwise
decide their own life-or-death treatment. Health professionals
may also act out ageist attitudes toward the elderly. At the
same time patients and their relatives, conditioned by paternalism or perhaps fear of guilt, may *want* the physician to
make crucial decisions. Since U.S. doctors tend to be men,
who often regard female patients as "immature," "overemo-
tional," or even "hysterical," sexism can play a crucial role.
This is a major reason why the National Organization for
Women supports death with dignity as a feminist issue. NOW
notes that the courts have upheld 60 percent of the male requests to die and only 14 percent of the female requests.

Issues of class, race, and culture further complicate the   10
debate. If you live in a violence-ridden urban area, the right
to die must seem a ludicrous middle-class hang-up. When
you have no health insurance (up to 36 million Americans in
1992), you're not likely to worry about excessive use of life-
support technology. People of color, especially if they have
recently immigrated, may consider "the right to die" strange
or untrustworthy. There is a sinister side to the picture, too:
the right to die may be supported for very wrong reasons
by government cost-cutters who note the millions put out
for care of the indigent, and by hospital administrators worried about making money under Medicare's reimbursement
system.

11   I knew nothing of such debates when my mother suffered a
series of strokes in the early 1980s that left her almost comatose and requiring total care around the clock. Eventually her
house had to be sold to pay the nursing home bills. Packing
up her papers, I found a one-page typed living will written on
her birthday in 1967 and renewed 12 years later. In fact, copies surfaced all over the house. The paper said: "If a time
should come when my body can be kept alive only by artificial means which preserve the *breath* of life, but in no way
preserve life's *spirit*, I do not want artificial stimuli used. This
is my strict direction and my request."

12   It was no surprise: she had watched her own mother die
that way and hated it. The paper also signaled how she had
often been ahead of her time. She was an innovative high
school teacher of Spanish, a tennis champion without professional training, an astute social critic and supporter of liberal
causes, amateur pianist, world traveler, short story writer,
and bridge enthusiast. She took special pleasure in dancing
with my father until his death and later with a 78-year-old
boyfriend who wrote poetry at 3 A.M. and then called her to
read it over the telephone ("Do you think it's all right for me
to be seeing a younger man?" she asked at the age of 83). She
liked to be around hustle and bustle, young people, the unpredictable, anything that seized her imagination. Few people
love life more than she did.

13   This was the person we had seen over recent years grow
progressively incontinent and unable to walk, eat, talk, or see.
When she turned 90, still semialert, we celebrated in the nursing home with a big lunch on the sunny veranda, other relatives, and a mariachi band. On her next birthday she lay in
bed diapered and with a feeding tube, speechless and staring
open-eyed at the ceiling. Could she possibly want such an
existence?

14   Yet even after finding her living will, I snatched at the most
fragile sign of "life." If she uttered two words, as happened every few weeks, I was thrilled. The desire for her to "stay alive"
tugged at one end of my feelings; at the other stood the
knowledge of her desire to die with dignity. Visiting her became an encounter with reprimand, real or imagined; her
face seemed to ask me crossly, Why haven't you done what I
requested? Didn't you notice that it was my *strict* direction?
And I asked myself: Am I afraid of what people will think?

15   In recent years public opinion has been both liberal and
cautious about the right to die. A 1990 Gallup poll found that

84 percent of U.S. residents would want treatment withheld if they were on life-support systems with no hope of recovering. The poll also found that 66 percent believe someone in great and hopeless pain had a moral right to commit suicide. Another 1990 poll showed that 53 percent favor allowing a doctor's help in committing suicide.

At the same time voters rejected a 1991 Washington State   16
initiative that would have allowed doctors to end a person's life if two gave written opinions that death would naturally occur within six months. Last year a California "Death with Dignity" initiative would have given mentally competent, terminally ill adults the right to issue a directive requesting physician-aid-in-dying; it too was voted down, by a 54–46 margin. In both cases most voters apparently saw the act as lacking adequate safeguards against abuse or too vague on key requirements. On the other hand, many—like this writer—voted for the California initiative as being basically sound. Many "no" votes in that state must have stemmed from uninformed fear; the Catholic church and the medical establishment waged an almost $4 million opposition campaign against the initiative's $700,000. Future initiative-makers need to draw lessons from the weaknesses of these two.

Antiabortion forces have argued that *"Roe* v. *Wade* was a   17
precedent for killing people," and from there it's a "slippery slope" downhill to euthanasia. Thus they negate the right to control one's own body in matters of dying as in birthing. According to a 1990 *New York Times* report, antiabortion groups have blocked legislation in at least three states that would allow withholding of nutrients, which they see as "forced starvation" (they do not usually oppose disconnecting respirators).

Opposition has sometimes come from members of the dis-   18
abled community, who hear echoes of genocide in the idea that life may not be worth living for the so-called unfit. African Americans and Latinos have supported the right to die much less enthusiastically than other sectors of the population. History, of course, gives all people of color reason to suspect any law that grants power over their lives to mostly white strangers. Advocates of death with dignity as a right respond that the rich have usually been able to have it by virtue of their influence over doctors and their ability to travel if necessary. The poor—which includes so many people of color—should be guaranteed the same right to choose. Death with dignity is the final civil right.

19   In time it did become clear that I wasn't worried about disapproval from friends or relatives if I ended my mother's life. The battle lay within, between two kinds of love—one that wanted her still on this planet, for me, and one that affirmed respect for her personhood, from me. When she contracted pneumonia after a year of being inert, her doctor said: "It's the old folks' friend, a quick and easy way to go. If you want the antibiotics stopped, let me know." Three long days passed of articulating the decision as: "Today I have to decide whether to kill my mother or not." I finally gave the order, but she had already taken enough medication to recover.

20   More months passed and the living will would not go away. After another consultation the doctor reduced her fluids, as this might diminish her physical resistance. She showed no effects. The battle resumed in my head: perhaps she doesn't want to die, after all. Or, in better moments: Is she just laughing at me? The doctor refused to do any more. I assumed, based on reading newspaper stories about such cases, that the law gave him no choice.

21   Struggles for the legal right to die present a long, sad, and often surreal parade of cases like that of Karen Ann Quinlan, the young New Jersey woman in a coma whose parents finally got her respirator turned off by a historic court order. The parents of Nancy Cruzan, who existed on a feeding tube, went all the way to the U.S. Supreme Court. In 1990 the court issued a double-edged ruling. On one hand it upheld an individual's constitutional right to the discontinuance of life-support treatment. On the other hand the court maintained the right of a state—in this case, Missouri—to demand "clear and convincing evidence" of a patient's desire to avoid life-support measures. As a result the Cruzan family had to produce new witnesses before Nancy could finally die.

22   Galvanized into action by the court decision, Congress passed the Patient Self-Determination Act. It requires health care facilities that receive Medicare or Medicaid funds (95 percent of such centers) to inform new patients about their legal right to write a living will or choose a proxy to represent their wishes about medical treatment. The Supreme Court's decision also made thousands of people put their wishes in writing to evidence them.

23   Today all 50 states authorize some form of advance directive from a patient—either a living will or a durable power of attorney, which is the preferred method. (Doing both is best, some say: the first establishes your wishes, the second facili-

tates their implementation.) Legal uncertainty or conflict continues where the patient has given no directive and where the procedure contemplated—for instance, feeding tube removal—is not authorized. Only one state, Kentucky, specifically prohibits termination of tube-feeding. Others stand silent on the issue and therefore implicitly allow it. It's a legal crazy quilt.

Not knowing California was one of those states that implicitly allowed feeding tube removal at the time, I continued to do nothing about my mother. But the feeling became inescapable: it isn't right to be waiting for the easy or legal way out. 24

One Sunday, walking on the beach alongside the Pacific with a friend, we talked about my paralysis. She was a nurse, and over the afternoon hours she demystified the steps to be taken and their physical consequences. By sunset I could see the decision—huge and relentless, like waves rolling in. But also quieting. That evening I talked with a woman who had helped her own mother to die, and she told me what I might expect to feel along with the practical problems. Then she commented, "Perhaps you can think of this as an opportunity." 25

Until that moment I had thought of having accepted a painful necessity at last. But here was a chance to make my mother a gift: something worthy of the boundless devotion she had given me and my daughter for so many years, something I knew she wanted, something only I could give. Thinking this way, the weight of double guilt—for not carrying out my mother's will and then for wanting to carry it out—floated away. In its place rose an enormous and simple gratitude that she had endowed us with certainty about her wishes. 26

One large problem remained: no doctor to remove the feeding tube. 27

The American Hospital Association estimates that 70 percent of the deaths in the United States are somehow negotiated with patients, family, and doctors quietly agreeing not to use life-support technology. In 1986 the American Medical Association declared that all life-prolonging medical treatment could be ethically disconnected when a patient's coma is irreversible. Nevertheless, my mother's doctor had refused to do anything active. 28

In retrospect I imagine his position then was a matter of personal preference or morality. Health policy expert and practicing physician Dr. Thomas Bodenheimer of San Francisco 29 spoke to me about why doctors sometimes encourage life-support measures. "It is uncomfortable and time-consuming to talk to the family or patient about death. Also, docs may fear malpractice suits, if we don't 'do everything.' And we are trained to save life, not assist death—it's not easy to change our ways. A few unscrupulous doctors think about the fees they don't collect on a dead body, but mostly I think it is a matter of benign neglect. Docs will automatically put more time and thought into acutely ill patients."

30   An old friend, a doctor, agreed to remove the tube. "I agree with what you're doing," he said immediately. We wanted it done in the nursing home where my mother had received ex-ceptional care for five years. But the social worker there told me, "They think you are doing the right thing, they just couldn't handle it emotionally after taking care of her so long."

31   Without my asking, she quickly found another facility. The nursing director there, Jane—I have changed her name like others in this story—assured me that the staff would relieve any discomfort that lack of food caused my mother. They were required to offer nourishment and fluids by hand; if somehow my mother took them, this could prolong her life.

32   But that was the only legal issue that Jane mentioned; her time and heart went into other matters. "In cases like this," she explained, "I call a special meeting of the whole staff and explain the situation to them. I have to be sure that they feel clear about it and some will disagree with what you're doing. Then I ask for volunteers to take care of the person." Jane spoke without hesitation; it would never occur to her just to assign workers, as if they had no feelings. I nodded, wordless. "One more thing," Jane told me. "You should tell your mother what's going to happen. It doesn't matter if she seems not to hear you or understand. I think she will."

33   On the day of the transfer from the old nursing home to the new one, I sat down by her bed and said that the tube would be taken out in a few hours. That I was doing what she wished, at last. For all my belief in the rightness of this act, I couldn't make my words more direct than that. Nothing showed in her face and her eyes stared straight ahead.

34   At the new place, after she was settled, my daughter and I stood outside in the sun waiting for the doctor who would re-move the tube. Last-minute doubts and fears started to batter me: Was this really what she wanted? Why didn't she refer specifically to feeding tubes in her living will? Maybe she only meant to reject a respirator?

The doctor arrived, listened to my worries. "You know her, you know how she lived, what she wanted," he said. "In the end, what you are doing is right not just because of the living will but because you know what kind of person she is." Then he went in and, with Jane's help, removed the tube. When he came back, he smiled and just said, "This is an amazing nursing home." 35

The next day, returning to visit, I found my mother asleep in bed. On the pillow next to her head lay the miniature teddy bear that I had left on the bedside cabinet, and a fresh flower perched in her hair. The nurse walked in then, a woman named Frances, who looked at me and explained. "I always sleep with my teddy bear so I thought she might like it too, bless her heart." 36

Five days later my mother died. "Five days—so quick for such a strong person," friends and relatives commented. "She must have been ready." A few asked, "Why did it take you so long to do what she wanted?" I had no answer to that except it took both of us a long, long time—but then we did meet. 37

WHAT DO YOU MAKE
OF THE INTERNET?

John Perry Barlow
Is There a There in Cyberspace?

John Perry Barlow ran a cattle ranch in Wyoming for seventeen years while writing songs for The Grateful Dead. *Forced to sell his ranch in 1988, he began writing and speaking about computer-mediated communication. He is a cofounder of the Electronic Frontier Foundation and is on the board of directors of WELL (Whole Earth 'Lectronic Link). Barlow frequently discusses Internet issues in interviews and in his own writing. The essay below appeared in the March/April 1995 issue of the* Utne Reader, *a left-of-center magazine that publishes articles on issues of public interest, including several of the others in this section of* Conversations.

1   I am often asked how I went from pushing cows around a remote Wyoming ranch to my present occupation (which *The Wall Street Journal* recently described as "cyber-space cadet"). I haven't got a short answer, but I suppose I came to the virtual world looking for community.

2   Unlike most modern Americans, I grew up in an actual place, an entirely nonintentional community called Pinedale, Wyoming. As I struggled for nearly a generation to keep my ranch in the family, I was motivated by the belief that such places were the spiritual home of humanity. But I knew their future was not promising.

3   At the dawn of the 20th century, over 40 percent of the American workforce lived off the land. The majority of us lived in towns like Pinedale. Now fewer than 1 percent of us extract a living from the soil. We just became too productive for our own good.

4   Of course, the population followed the jobs. Farming and ranching communities are now home to a demographically insignificant percentage of Americans, the vast majority of whom live not in ranch houses but in more or less identical

split-level "ranch homes" in more or less identical suburban "communities." Generica.

In my view, these are neither communities nor homes. I   5
believe the combination of television and suburban population patterns is simply toxic to the soul. I see much evidence
in contemporary America to support this view.

Meanwhile, back at the ranch, doom impended. And, as I   6
watched community in Pinedale growing ill from the same
economic forces that were killing my family's ranch, the Bar
Cross, satellite dishes brought the cultural infection of television. I started looking around for evidence that community in
America would not perish altogether.

I took some heart in the mysterious nomadic City of the   7
Deadheads, the virtually physical town that follows the Grateful Dead around the country. The Deadheads lacked place,
touching down briefly wherever the band happened to be
playing, and they lacked continuity in time, since they had to
suffer a new diaspora every time the band moved on or went
home. But they had many of the other necessary elements of
community, including a culture, a religion of sorts (which,
though it lacked dogma, had most of the other, more nurturing aspects of spiritual practice), a sense of necessity, and,
most importantly, shared adversity.

I wanted to know more about the flavor of their interac-   8
tion, what they thought and felt, but since I wrote Dead songs
(including "Estimated Prophet" and "Cassidy"), I was a minor
icon to the Deadheads, and was thus inhibited, in some socially Heisenbergian way, from getting a clear view of what
really went on among them.

Then, in 1987, I heard about a "place" where Deadheads   9
gathered where I could move among them without distorting
too much the field of observation. Better, this was a place I
could visit without leaving Wyoming. It was a shared computer in Sausalito, California, called the Whole Earth 'Lectronic Link, or WELL. After a lot of struggling with modems,
serial cables, init strings, and other computer arcana that
seemed utterly out of phase with such notions as Deadheads
and small towns, I found myself looking at the glowing yellow
word "Login:" beyond which lay my future.

"Inside" the WELL were Deadheads in community. There   10
were thousands of them there, gossiping, complaining
(mostly about the Grateful Dead), comforting and harassing
each other, bartering, engaging in religion (or at least exchanging their totemic set lists), beginning and ending love
affairs, praying for one another's sick kids. There was, it

seemed, everything one might find going on in a small town, save dragging Main Street and making out on the back roads.

11   I was delighted. I felt I had found the new locale of human community—never mind that the whole thing was being conducted in mere words by minds from whom the bodies had been amputated. Never mind that all these people were deaf, dumb, and blind as paramecia or that their town had neither seasons nor sunsets nor smells.

12   Surely all these deficiencies would be remedied by richer, faster communications media. The featureless log-in handles would gradually acquire video faces (and thus expressions), shaded 3-D body puppets (and thus body language). This "space," which I recognized at once to be a primitive form of the cyberspace William Gibson predicted in his sci-fi novel *Neuromancer,* was still without apparent dimensions or vistas. But virtual reality would change all that in time.

13   Meanwhile, the commons, or something like it, had been rediscovered. Once again, people from the 'burbs had a place where they could encounter their friends as my fellow Pinedalians did at the post office and the Wrangler Cafe. They had a place where their hearts could remain as the companies they worked for shuffled their bodies around America. They could put down roots that could not be ripped out by forces of economic history. They had a collective stake. They had a community.

14   It is seven years now since I discovered the WELL. In that time, I cofounded an organization, the Electronic Frontier Foundation, dedicated to protecting its interests and those of other virtual communities like it from raids by physical government. I've spent countless hours typing away at its residents, and I've watched the larger context that contains it, the Internet, grow at such an explosive rate that, by 2004, every human on the planet will have an e-mail address unless the growth curve flattens (which it will).

15   My enthusiasm for virtuality has cooled. In fact, unless one counts interaction with the rather too large society of those with whom I exchange electronic mail, I don't spend much time engaging in virtual community at all. Many of the near-term benefits I anticipated from it seem to remain as far in the future as they did when I first logged in. Perhaps they always will.

16   Pinedale works, more or less, as it is, but a lot is still missing from the communities of cyberspace, whether they be places like the WELL, the fractious newsgroups of USENET,

the silent "auditoriums" of America Online, or even enclaves on the promising World Wide Web.

What is missing? Well, to quote Ranjit Makkuni of Xerox 17 Corporation's Palo Alto Research Center, "the *prāna* is missing," *prāna* being the Hindu term for both breath and spirit. I think he is right about this and that perhaps the central question of the virtual age is whether or not *prāna* can somehow be made to fit through any disembodied medium.

Prāna is, to my mind, the literally vital element in the holy 18 and unseen ecology of relationship, the dense mesh of invisible life, on whose surface carbon-based life floats like a thin film. It is at the heart of the fundamental and profound difference between information and experience. Jaron Lanier has said that "information is alienated experience," and, that being true, *prāna* is part of what is removed when you create such easily transmissible replicas of experience as, say, the evening news.

Obviously a great many other, less spiritual, things are also 19 missing entirely, like body language, sex, death, tone of voice, clothing, beauty (or homeliness), weather, violence, vegetation, wildlife, pets, architecture, music, smells, sunlight, and that ol' harvest moon. In short, most of the things that make my life real to me.

Present, but in far less abundance than in the physical 20 world, which I call "meat space," are women, children, old people, poor people, and the genuinely blind. Also mostly missing are the illiterate and the continent of Africa. There is not much human diversity in cyberspace, which is populated, as near as I can tell, by white males under 50 with plenty of computer terminal time, great typing skills, high math SATS, strongly held opinions on just about everything, and an excruciating face-to-face shyness, especially with the opposite sex.

But diversity is as essential to healthy community as it is to 21 healthy ecosystems (which are, in my view, different from communities only in unimportant aspects).

I believe that the principal reason for the almost universal 22 failure of the intentional communities of the '60s and '70s was a lack of diversity in their members. It was a rare commune with any old people in it, or people who were fundamentally out of philosophical agreement with the majority.

Indeed, it is the usual problem when we try to build some- 23 thing that can only be grown. Natural systems, such as human communities, are simply too complex to design by the engineering principles we insist on applying to them. Like Dr.

Frankenstein, Western civilization is now finding its rational skills inadequate to the task of creating and caring for life. We would do better to return to a kind of agricultural mind-set in which we humbly try to re-create the conditions from which life has sprung before. And leave the rest to God.

24   Given that it has been built so far almost entirely by people with engineering degrees, it is not so surprising that cyberspace has the kind of overdesigned quality that leaves out all kinds of elements nature would have provided invisibly.

25   Also missing from both the communes of the '60s and from cyberspace are a couple of elements that I believe are very important, if not essential, to the formation and preservation of real community: an absence of alternatives and a sense of genuine adversity, generally shared. What about these?

26   It is hard to argue that anyone would find losing a modem literally hard to survive, while many have remained in small towns, have tolerated their intolerances and created entertainment to enliven their culturally arid lives simply because it seemed there was no choice but to stay. There are many investments—spiritual, material, and temporal—one is willing to put into a home one cannot leave. Communities are often the beneficiaries of these involuntary investments.

27   But when the going gets rough in cyberspace, it is even easier to move than it is in the 'burbs, where, given the fact that the average American moves some 12 times in his or her life, moving appears to be pretty easy. You can not only find another bulletin board service (BBS) or newsgroup to hang out in, you can, with very little effort, start your own.

28   And then there is the bond of joint suffering. Most community is a cultural stockade erected against a common enemy that can take many forms. In Pinedale, we bore together, with an understanding needing little expression, the fact that Upper Green River Valley is the coldest spot, as measured by annual mean temperature, in the lower 48 states. We knew that if somebody was stopped on the road most winter nights, he would probably die there, so the fact that we might loathe him was not sufficient reason to drive on past his broken pickup.

29   By the same token, the Deadheads have the Drug Enforcement Administration, which strives to give them 20-year prison terms without parole for distributing the fairly harmless sacrament of their faith. They have an additional bond in the fact that when their Microbuses die, as they often do, no one but another Deadhead is likely to stop to help them.

But what are the shared adversities of cyberspace? Lousy   30
user interfaces? The flames of harsh invective? Dumb jokes?
Surely these can all be survived without the sanctuary provided by fellow sufferers.

One is always free to yank the jack, as I have mostly done.   31
For me, the physical world offers far more opportunity for
prāna-rich connections with my fellow creatures. Even for
someone whose body is in a state of perpetual motion, I feel I
can generally find more community among the still-embodied.

Finally, there is that shyness factor. Not only are we trying   32
to build community here among people who have never experienced any in my sense of the term, we are trying to build
community among people who, in their lives, have rarely
used the word *we* in a heartfelt way. It is a vast club, and
many of the members—following Groucho Marx—wouldn't
want to join a club that would have them.

And yet...   33

How quickly physical community continues to deteriorate.   34
Even Pinedale, which seems to have survived the plague of
ranch failures, feels increasingly cut off from itself. Many of
the ranches are now owned by corporate types who fly their
Gulfstreams in to fish and are rarely around during the many
months when the creeks are frozen over and neighbors are
needed. They have kept the ranches alive financially, but they
actively discourage their managers from the interdependence
my former colleagues and I require. They keep agriculture on
life support, still alive but lacking a functional heart.

And the town has been inundated with suburbanites who   35
flee here, bringing all their terrors and suspicions with them.
They spend their evenings as they did in Orange County,
watching television or socializing in hermetic little enclaves of
fundamentalist Christianity that seem to separate them from
us and even, given their sectarian animosities, from one another. The town remains. The community is largely a wraith
of nostalgia.

So where else can we look for the connection we need to   36
prevent our plunging further into the condition of separateness Nietzsche called sin? What is there to do but to dive further into the bramble bush of information that, in its
broadcast forms, has done so much to tear us apart?

Cyberspace, for all its current deficiencies and failed prom-   37
ises, is not without some very real solace already.

Some months ago, the great love of my life, a vivid young   38
woman with whom I intended to spend the rest of it, dropped

dead of undiagnosed viral cardiomyopathy two days short of her 30th birthday. I felt as if my own heart had been as shredded as hers.

39   We had lived together in New York City. Except for my daughters, no one from Pinedale had met her. I needed a community to wrap around myself against colder winds than fortune had ever blown at me before. And without looking, I found I had one in the virtual world.

40   On the WELL, there was a topic announcing her death in one of the conferences to which I posted the eulogy I had read over her before burying her in her own small town of Nanaimo, British Columbia. It seemed to strike a chord among the disembodied living on the Net. People copied it and sent it to one another. Over the next several months I received almost a megabyte of electronic mail from all over the planet, mostly from folks whose faces I have never seen and probably never will.

41   They told me of their own tragedies and what they had done to survive them. As humans have since words were first uttered, we shared the second most common human experience, death, with an openheartedness that would have caused grave uneasiness in physical America, where the whole topic is so cloaked in denial as to be considered obscene. Those strangers, who had no arms to put around my shoulders, no eyes to weep with mine, nevertheless saw me through. As neighbors do.

42   I have no idea how far we will plunge into this strange place. Unlike previous frontiers, this one has no end. It is so dissatisfying in so many ways that I suspect we will be more restless in our search for home here than in all our previous explorations. And that is one reason why I think we may find it after all. If home is where the heart is, then there is already some part of home to be found in cyberspace.

43   So . . . does virtual community work or not? Should we all go off to cyberspace or should we resist it as a demonic form of symbolic abstraction? Does it supplant the real or is there, in it, reality itself?

44   Like so many true things, this one doesn't resolve itself to a black or a white. Nor is it gray. It is, along with the rest of life, black/white. Both/neither. I'm not being equivocal or wishy-washy here. We have to get over our Manichean sense that everything is either good or bad, and the border of cyberspace seems to me a good place to leave that old set of filters.

But really it doesn't matter. We are going there whether we   45
want to or not. In five years, everyone who is reading these
words will have an e-mail address, other than the determined
Luddites who also eschew the telephone and electricity.

When we are all together in cyberspace we will see what   46
the human spirit, and the basic desire to connect, can create
there. I am convinced that the result will be more benign if
we go there open-minded, open-hearted, and excited with the
adventure than if we are dragged into exile.

And we must remember that going to cyberspace, unlike   47
previous great emigrations to the frontier, hardly requires us
to leave where we have been. Many will find, as I have, a
much richer appreciation of physical reality for having spent
so much time in virtuality.

Despite its current (and perhaps in some areas permanent)   48
insufficiencies, we should go to cyberspace with hope.
Groundless hope, like unconditional love, may be the only
kind that counts.

M. Kadi
Welcome to Cyberia

*M. Kadi is a pseudonym for the author, who works as a con-
sultant in the computer industry in the San Francisco Bay
Area of California but who wishes to write about computer
issues anonymously. She contributed this essay to the Winter/
Spring 1994–95 issue of* H2SO4, *which, as its name implies, is
an inexpensively produced, avant garde, irreverent, small-
circulation magazine based in San Francisco that publishes
literary and political commentaries, both serious and not-so-
serious, and tries to bring together both academic and nonacademic writers and readers. It publishes works from many political and cultural perspectives. The essay published here also
appeared in truncated form in the* Utne Reader *(which often
republishes items from the alternative press) along with several
other selections in this section of* Conversations, *by Barlow
and Rheingold.*

*Computer networking offers the soundest basis for world peace
that has yet been presented. Peace must be created on the bulwark of understanding. International computer networks will
knit together the peoples of the world in bonds of mutual
respect; its possibilities are vast, indeed.*
                                    —*Scientific American,* June 1994

*Cyberspace is a new medium. Every night on Prodigy, Com-
puServe, GEnie and thousands of smaller computer bulletin
boards, people by the hundreds of thousands are logging on to
a great computer-mediated gabfest, an interactive debate that
allows them to leap over barriers of time, place, sex and social
status.*
                                              —*Time* Magazine

*The Internet is really about the rise of not merely a new tech-
nology, but a new culture—a global culture where time, space,
borders and even personal identity are radically redefined.*
                                    —*OnLine Access* Magazine

1   Computer bulletin board services offer up the glories of
e-mail, the thought provocation of Newsgroups, the sharing
of ideas implicit in public posting, and the interaction of real-
time chats. The fabulous, wonderful limitless world of Communication is just waiting for you to log on. Sure. Yeah.
Right.

2   I confess, I am a dedicated cyber-junkie. It's fun. It's interesting. It takes me places where I've never been before. I sign
on once a day, twice a day, three times a day, more and more;
I read, I post, I live. Writing an article on the ever-expanding,
ever-entertaining, ever-present world of online existence
would have been easy for me. But it would have been familiar,
perhaps dull and it might have been a lie. The world does not
need another article on the miracle of online reality; what we
need, what I need, what this whole delirious, inter-connected,
global-community of a world needs, is a little reality check.

3   To some extent the following scenario will be misleading.
There *are* flat rate online services (Netcom for one) which offer significant connectivity for a measly 17 dollars a month.
But I'm interested in the activities and behavior of the private
service users who will soon comprise a vast majority of online
citizens. Furthermore, let's face facts. The U.S. government
by and large foots the bill for the Internet, through maintaining the structural (hardware) backbone, including, among
other things, funding to major universities. As surely as the

Department of Defense started this whole thing, AT&T or Ted Turner is going to end up running it, so I don't think it's too unrealistic to take a look at the Net as it exists in its commercial form in order to expose some of the realities lurking behind the regurgitated media rhetoric and the religious fanaticism of net junkies.

The average person, J. Individual, has an income. How much of J. Individual's income is going to be spent on computer connectivity? Does $120 a month sound reasonable? Well, you may find that a bit too steep for your pocketbook, but the brutal fact is that $120 is a "reasonable" monthly amount. The major on-line services have a monthly service charge of approximately $15. Fifteen dollars to join the global community, communicate with a diverse group of people, and access the world's largest repository of knowledge since the Alexandrian library doesn't seem unreasonable, does it? But don't overlook the average per-hour connection rate of $3 (which can skyrocket upwards of $10, depending on your modem speed and service). You might think that you are a crack whiz with your communications software—that you are rigorous and stringent and never, ever respond to e-mail or a forum while you're on-line—but let me tell you that no one is capable of logging on efficiently every time. Thirty hours per month is a realistic estimate. 4

In case you think 30 hours a month is an outrageous estimate, think of it in terms of television. (OK, so you don't own a television, well, goody-for-you—imagine that you do!) 30 hours, is, quite obviously, one hour a day. That's not so much. 30 hours a month in front of a television is simply the evening news plus a weekly Seinfeld/Frazier [sic] hour. 30 hours a month is less time than the average car-phone owner spends on the phone while commuting. Even a conscientious geek, logging on for e-mail and the up-to-the-minute news that only the net services can provide is probably going to spend 30 hours a month online. And, let's be truthful here, 30 hours a month ignores shareware downloads, computer illiteracy, real-time chatting, interactive game playing and any serious forum following, which by nature entail a significant amount of scrolling and/or downloading time. 5

If you are really and truly going to use the net services to connect with the global community, the hourly charges are going to add up pretty quickly. Take out a piece of paper, pretend you're writing a check, and print out "One hundred and twenty dollars—" and tell me again, how diverse is the on-line community? 6

7   That scenario aside, let's pretend that you're single, that you don't have children, that you rarely leave the house, that you don't have a TV and that money is not an issue. Meaning, pretend for a moment that you have as much time and as much money to spend online as you damn-well want. What do you actually do online?

8   Well, you download some cool shareware, you post technical questions in the computer user group forums, you check your stocks, you read the news and maybe some reviews—Hey, you've already passed that 30 hour limit! But, of course, since "computer networks make it easy to reach out and touch strangers who share a particular obsession or concern," you are participating in the online forums, discussion groups, and conferences.

9   Let's review the structure of forums. For the purposes of this essay, we will examine the smallest of the major user-friendly commercial services—America OnLine (AOL). There is no precise statistic available (at least none that the company will reveal—you have to do the research by HAND!!!) on exactly how many subject-specific discussion areas (folders) exist on AOL. Any online service is going to have zillions of posts pertaining to computer usage (e.g., the computer games area of AOL breaks into five hundred separate topics with over 100,000 individual posts), so let's look at a less popular area: the "Lifestyles and Interests" department.

10   For starters, there are 57 initial categories within the Lifestyles and Interests area. One of these categories is Ham Radio. Ham Radio? How can there possibly be 5,909 separate, individual posts about Ham Radio? 5,865 postings in the Biking (and that's just bicycles, not motorcycles) category. Genealogy—22,525 posts. The Gay and Lesbian category is slightly more substantial—36,333 posts. There are five separate categories for political and issue discussion. The big catch-all topic area, The Exchange, has over 100,000 posts. Basically, service wide (on the smallest service, remember) there are over a million posts.

11   So, you want to communicate with other people, join the online revolution, but obviously you can't wade through everything that's being discussed—you need to decide which topics interest you, which folders to browse. Within The Exchange alone (one of 57 subdivisions within one of another 50 higher divisions) there are 1,492 separate topic-specific folders—each containing a rough average of 50 posts, but with many containing close to 400 . . .

12   So there you are, J. Individual, ready to start interacting with folks, sharing stories and communicating. You have nar-

rowed yourself into a single folder, three tiers down in the AOL hierarchy, and now you must choose between nearly fifteen hundred folders. Of course, once you choose a few of these folders, you will then have to read all the posts in order to catch up, be current, and not merely repeat a previous post.

A polite post is no more than two paragraphs long (a 13 screenful of text which obviously has a number of intellectually negative implications). Let's say you choose ten folders (out of 1,500). Each folder contains an average of 50 posts. Five hundred posts, at, say, one paragraph each, and you're now looking at the equivalent of a two hundred page book.

Enough with the stats. Let me back up a minute and present 14 you with some very disturbing, but rational, assumptions. J. Individual wants to join the online revolution to connect and communicate. But, J. Individual is not going to read all one million posts on AOL. (After all, J. Individual has a second online service.) Exercising choice is J. Individual's god-given right as an American, and, by gosh, J. Individual is going to make some decisions. So J. is going to ignore all the support groups—after all, J. is a normal, well-adjusted person and all of J.'s friends are normal, well-adjusted people; what does J. need to know about alcoholism or incest victims? J. Individual is white. So J. Individual is going to ignore all the multicultural folders. J. couldn't give a hoot about gender issues and does not want to discuss religion or philosophy. Ultimately, J. Individual does not engage in topics that do not interest J. Individual. So who is J. meeting? Why, people who are *just like* J.

J. Individual has now joined the electronic community. 15 Surfed the Net. Found some friends. *Tuned in, turned on, and geeked out.* Traveled the Information Highway and, just a few miles down that great democratic expressway, J. Individual has settled into an electronic suburb.

Are any of us so very different? It's my time and my money 16 and I am not going to waste any of it reading posts by disgruntled Robert-Bly drum-beating men's-movement boys who think that they should have some say over, for instance, whether or not I choose to carry a child to term simply because a condom broke. I know where I stand. I'm an adult. I know what's up and I am not going to waste my money arguing with a bunch of neanderthals.

Oh yeah; I am so connected, so enlightened, so open to the 17 opposing viewpoint. I'm out there, meeting all kinds of people from different economic backgrounds (who have $120 a month to burn), from all religions (yeah, right, like anyone actually discusses religion anymore from a user standpoint), from all kinds of different ethnic backgrounds and with all kinds of sexual orientations (as if any of this ever comes up outside of the appropriate topic folder).

18   People are drawn to topics and folders that interest them and therefore people will only meet people who are interested in the same topics in the same folders. Rarely does anyone venture into a random folder just to see what others (the Other?) are talking about.

19   Basically, between the monetary constraints and the sheer number of topics and individual posts, the great Information Highway is not a place where you will enter an "amazing web of new people, places, and ideas." One does not encounter people from "all walks of life" because there are too many people and too many folders. Diversity might be out there (and personally I don't think it is), but the simple fact is that the average person will not encounter it because with one brain, one job, one partner, one family, and one life, no one has the time!

20   Just in case these arguments based on time and money aren't completely convincing, let me bring up a historical reference. Please take another look at the opening quote of this essay, from *Scientific American*. It was featured in their 50 Years Ago Today column. Where you read "computer networking," the quote originally contained the word *television*. Amusing, isn't it?

21   Finally, for me, there is a subtle and terrible irony lurking within the Net: the Net, despite its speed, its exchange, ultimately reeks of stasis. In negating physical distance, the immediacy of electronic transfers devalues movement and the journey. In one minute a thought is in my head, and the next minute it is typed out, sent, read, and in your head. The exchange may be present, but the journey is imperceptible. The Infobahn hype would have us believe that this phenomenon is a fast-paced dynamic exchange, but the feeling, when you've been at it long enough, is that this exchange of ideas lacks movement. Lacking movement and the journey, to me it loses all value.

22   Maybe this is prejudice. Words are not wine, they do not necessarily require age to improve them. Furthermore, I have always hated the concept that Art comes only out of struggle and suffering. So, to say that e-mail words are weaker somehow because of the nature, or lack, of their journey, is to romanticize the struggle. I suppose I am anthropomorphising text too much—but I somehow sense that one works harder to endow one's handwritten words with a certain strength, a

certain soul, simply because those things are necessary in order to survive a journey. The ease of the e-mail journey means that your words don't need to be as well-prepared, or as well-equipped.

Electronic missives lack time, space, embodiment and his-   23
tory (in the sense of a collection of experiences). Lacking all these things, an electronic missive is almost in complete opposition to my existence and I can't help but wonder what, if anything, I am communicating.

Howard Rheingold
The Virtual Community

This essay, excerpted from Rheingold's book The Virtual Community *(1993), first appeared in the* Utne Reader *with several other essays reprinted in this section of* Conversations.

In the summer of 1986, my then-2-year-old daughter   1
picked up a tick. There was this blood-bloated *thing* sucking on our baby's scalp, and we weren't quite sure how to go about getting it off. My wife, Judy, called the pediatrician. It was 11 o'clock in the evening. I logged onto the WELL, the big Bay Area infonet, and contacted the Parenting conference (a conference is an on-line conversation about a specific subject). I got my answer on-line within minutes from a fellow with the improbable but genuine name of Flash Gordon, M.D. I had removed the tick by the time Judy got the callback from the pediatrician's office.

What amazed me wasn't just the speed with which we ob-   2
tained precisely the information we needed to know, right when we needed to know it. It was also the immense inner sense of security that comes with discovering that real people—most of them parents, some of them nurses, doctors, and midwives—are available, around the clock, if you need them. There is a magic protective circle around the atmosphere of the Parenting conference. We're talking about our sons and daughters in this forum, not about our computers or our opinions about philosophy, and many of us feel that this tacit understanding sanctifies the virtual space.

3   The atmosphere of this particular conference—the attitudes people exhibit to each other in the tone of what they say in public—is part of what continues to attract me. People who never have much to contribute in political debate, technical argument, or intellectual gamesmanship turn out to have a lot to say about raising children. People you knew as fierce, even nasty, intellectual opponents in other contexts give you emotional support on a deeper level, parent to parent, within the boundaries of this small but warmly human corner of cyberspace.

4   In most cases, people who talk about a shared interest don't disclose enough about themselves as whole individuals on-line to inspire real trust in others. But in the case of the subcommunity called the Parenting conference, a few dozen of us, scattered across the country, few of whom rarely if ever saw the others face to face, have a few years of minor crises to knit us together and prepare us for serious business when it comes our way. Another several dozen read the conference regularly but contribute only when they have something important to add. Hundreds more read the conference every week without comment, except when something extraordinary happens.

5   Jay Allison and his family live in Massachusetts. He and his wife are public-radio producers. I've never met them face to face, although I feel I know something powerful and intimate about the Allisons and have strong emotional ties to them. What follows are some of Jay's postings on the WELL:

6   *"Woods Hole. Midnight. I am sitting in the dark of my daughter's room. Her monitor lights blink at me. The lights used to blink too brightly so I covered them with bits of bandage adhesive and now they flash faintly underneath, a persistent red and green, Lillie's heart and lungs.*

7   *"Above the monitor is her portable suction unit. In the glow of the flashlight I'm writing by, it looks like the plastic guts of a science-class human model, the tubes coiled around the power supply, the reservoir, the pump.*

8   *"Tina is upstairs trying to get some sleep. A baby monitor links our bedroom to Lillie's. It links our sleep to Lillie's too, and because our souls are linked to hers, we do not sleep well.*

9   *"I am naked. My stomach is full of beer. The flashlight rests on it, and the beam rises and falls with my breath. My daughter breathes through a white plastic tube inserted into a hole in her throat. She's 14 months old."*

10   Sitting in front of our computers with our hearts racing and tears in our eyes, in Tokyo and Sacramento and Austin, we

read about Lillie's croup, her tracheostomy, the days and nights at Massachusetts General Hospital, and now the vigil over Lillie's breathing and the watchful attention to the mechanical apparatus that kept her alive. It went on for days. Weeks. Lillie recovered, and relieved our anxieties about her vocal capabilities after all that time with a hole in her throat by saying the most extraordinary things, duly reported on-line by Jay.

Later, writing in *Whole Earth Review,* Jay described the experience: 11

"Before this time, my computer screen had never been a place   12
to go for solace. Far from it. But there it was. Those nights sitting up late with my daughter, I'd go to my computer, dial up the WELL, and ramble. I wrote about what was happening that night or that year. I didn't know anyone I was "talking" to. I had never laid eyes on them. At 3:00 a.m. my "real" friends were asleep, so I turned to this foreign, invisible community for support. The WELL was always awake.

"Any difficulty is harder to bear in isolation. There is nothing   13
to measure against, to lean against. Typing out my journal entries into the computer and over the phone lines, I found fellowship and comfort in this unlikely medium."

Many people are alarmed by the very idea of a virtual com-   14
munity, fearing that it is another step in the wrong direction, substituting more technological ersatz for yet another natural resource or human freedom. These critics often voice their sadness at what people have been reduced to doing in a civilization that worships technology, decrying the circumstances that lead some people into such pathetically disconnected lives that they prefer to find their companions on the other side of a computer screen. There is a seed of truth in this fear, for communities at some point require more than words on a screen if they are to be other than ersatz.

Yet some people—many people—who don't do well in spon-   15
taneous spoken interaction turn out to have valuable contributions to make in a conversation in which they have time to think about what to say. These people, who might constitute a significant proportion of the population, can find written communication more authentic than the face-to-face kind. Who is to say that this preference for informal written text is somehow less authentically human than opting for audible speech? Those who critique computer-mediated communication because some people use it obsessively hit an important target, but miss a great deal more when they don't take into consideration people who use the medium for genuine human

interaction. Those who find virtual communities cold places point at the limits of the technology, its most dangerous pitfalls, and we need to pay attention to those boundaries. But these critiques don't tell us how the Allisons, my own family, and many others could have found the community of support and information we found in the WELL when we needed it. And those of us who do find communion in cyberspace might do well to pay attention to the way the medium we love can be abused.

16   Although dramatic incidents are what bring people together and stick in their memories, most of what goes on in the Parenting conference and most virtual communities is informal conversation and downright chitchat. The model of the WELL and other social clusters in cyberspace as "places" emerges naturally whenever people who use this medium discuss its nature. In 1987, Stewart Brand quoted me in his book *The Media Lab* about what tempted me to log onto the WELL as often as I did: "There's always another mind there. It's like having the corner bar, complete with old buddies and delightful newcomers and new tools waiting to take home and fresh graffiti and letters, except instead of putting on my coat, shutting down the computer, and walking down to the corner, I just invoke my telecom program and there they are. It's a place."

17   I've changed my mind about a lot of aspects of the WELL over the years, but the sense of place is still as strong as ever. As Ray Oldenburg proposes in his 1989 book *The Great Good Place*, there are three essential places in people's lives: the place we live, the place we work, and the place we gather for conviviality. Although the casual conversation that takes place in cafés, beauty shops, pubs, and town squares is universally considered to be trivial, idle talk, Oldenburg makes the case that such places are where communities can come into being and continue to hold together. These are the unacknowledged agoras of modern life. When the automobilecentric, suburban, fast-food, shopping-mall way of life eliminated many of these "third places" from traditional towns and cities around the world, the social fabric of existing communities started shredding.

18   Oldenburg puts a name and a conceptual framework on a phenomenon that every virtual community member knows instinctively, the power of informal public life:

19   *"Third places exist on neutral ground and serve to level their guests to a condition of social equality. Within these places, conversation is the primary activity and the major vehicle for the display and appreciation of human personality and individ-*

uality. Third places are taken for granted and most have a low profile. Since the formal institutions of society make stronger claims on the individual, third places are normally open in the off hours, as well as at other times. The character of a third place is determined most of all by its regular clientele and is marked by a playful mood, which contrasts with people's more serious involvement in other spheres. Though a radically different kind of setting for a home, the third place is remarkably similar to a good home in the psychological comfort and support that it extends.

"Such are the characteristics of third places that appear to be universal and essential to a vital informal public life. . . .

"The problem of place in America manifests itself in a sorely deficient informal public life. The structure of shared experience beyond that offered by family, job, and passive consumerism is small and dwindling. The essential group experience is being replaced by the exaggerated self-consciousness of individuals. American lifestyles, for all the material acquisition and the seeking after comforts and pleasures, are plagued by boredom, loneliness, alienation, and a high price tag. . . .

"Unlike many frontiers, that of the informal public life does not remain benign as it awaits development. It does not become easier to tame as technology evolves, as governmental bureaus and agencies multiply, or as population grows. It does not yield to the mere passage of time and a policy of letting the chips fall where they may as development proceeds in other areas of urban life. To the contrary, neglect of the informal public life can make a jungle of what had been a garden while, at the same time, diminishing the ability of people to cultivate it."*

It might not be the same kind of place that Oldenburg had in mind, but many of his descriptions of third places could also describe the WELL. Perhaps cyberspace is one of the informal public places where people can rebuild the aspects of community that were lost when the malt shop became a mall. Or perhaps cyberspace is precisely the *wrong* place to look for the rebirth of community, offering not a tool for conviviality but a life-denying simulacrum of real passion and true commitment to one another. In either case, we need to find out soon.

Because we cannot see one another in cyberspace, gender, age, national origin, and physical appearance are not apparent unless a person wants to make such characteristics public. People whose physical handicaps make it difficult to form new friendships find that virtual communities treat them as they always wanted to be treated—as thinkers and transmitters of ideas and feeling beings, not carnal vessels with a certain appearance and way of walking and talking (or not walking and not talking).

25   One of the few things that enthusiastic members of virtual communities in places like Japan, England, France, and the United States all agree on is that expanding their circle of friends is one of the most important advantages of computer conferencing. It is a way to *meet* people, whether or not you feel the need to affiliate with them on a community level. It's a way of both making contact with and maintaining a distance from others. The way you meet people in cyberspace puts a different spin on affiliation: In traditional kinds of communities, we are accustomed to meeting people, then getting to know them; in virtual communities, you can get to know people and *then* choose to meet them. Affiliation also can be far more ephemeral in cyberspace because you can get to know people you might never meet on the physical plane.

26   How does anybody find friends? In the traditional community, we search through our pool of neighbors and professional colleagues, of acquaintances and acquaintances of acquaintances, in order to find people who share our values and interests. We then exchange information about one another, disclose and discuss our mutual interests, and sometimes we become friends. In a virtual community we can go directly to the place where our favorite subjects are being discussed, then get acquainted with people who share our passions or who use words in a way we find attractive. In this sense, the topic is the address: You can't simply pick up a phone and ask to be connected with someone who wants to talk about Islamic art or California wine, or someone with a 3-year-old daughter or a 40-year-old Hudson; you can, however, join a computer conference on any of those topics, then open a public or private correspondence with the previously unknown people you find there. Your chances of making friends are increased by several orders of magnitude over the old methods of finding a peer group.

27   You can be fooled about people in cyberspace, behind the cloak of words. But that can be said about telephones or face-to-face communication as well; computer-mediated communications provide new ways to fool people, and the most obvious identity swindles will die out only when enough people learn to use the medium critically. In some ways, the medium will, by its nature, be forever biased toward certain kinds of obfuscation. It will also be a place where people often end up

revealing themselves far more intimately than they would be inclined to do without the intermediation of screens and pseudonyms.

Point of view, along with identity, is one of the great vari-   28
ables in cyberspace. Different people in cyberspace look at their virtual communities through differently shaped key-holes. In traditional communities, people have a strongly shared mental model of the sense of place—the room or vil-lage or city where their interactions occur. In virtual commu-nities, the sense of place requires an individual act of imagination. The different mental models people have of the electronic agora complicate the question of why people seem to want to build societies mediated by computer screens. A question like that leads inexorably to the old fundamental questions of what forces hold any society together. The roots of these questions extend farther than the social upheavals triggered by modern communications technologies.

When we say "society," we usually mean citizens of cities in   29
entities known as nations. We take those categories for granted. But the mass-psychological transition we made to thinking of ourselves as part of modern society and nation-states is historically recent. Could people make the transition from the close collective social groups, the villages and small towns of premodern and precapitalist Europe, to a new form of social solidarity known as society that transcended and en-compassed all previous kinds of human association? Ferdi-nand Tönnies, one of the founders of sociology, called the premodern kind of social group *gemeinschaft*, which is closer to the English word *community*, and the new kind of social group he called *gesellschaft*, which can be translated roughly as *society*. All the questions about community in cyberspace point to a similar kind of transition, for which we have no technical names, that might be taking place now.

Sociology student Marc Smith, who has been using the   30
WELL and the Net as the laboratory for his fieldwork, pointed me to Benedict Anderson's *Imagined Communities*, a study of nation-building that focuses on the ideological labor involved. Anderson points out that nations and, by extension, communities are imagined in the sense that a given nation ex-ists by virtue of a common acceptance in the minds of the population that it exists. Nations must exist in the minds of their citizens in order to exist at all. "Virtual communities re-quire an act of imagination," Smith points out, extending Anderson's line of thinking to cyberspace, "and what must be imagined is the idea of the community itself."

Stephen Doheny-Farina

Immersive Virtualists and Wired Communitarians

Stephen Doheny-Farina teaches courses in technical writing, electronic communications, and the rhetoric of the Internet at Clarkson College in upstate New York. The following article is a chapter from his 1996 book (Yale University Press) entitled The Wired Neighborhood *which is an extended meditation on the meanings that the Internet holds for contemporary culture, especially for our notions of community.*

1   Many of the loudest voices of the net tell us that a revolution is going on, and that revolutions mean change, and that this change can be painful for some, but that overall the revolution is good. Notice the emphases, for example, in the following excerpt from National Public Radio's *All Things Considered*, a segment from February 3, 1994, entitled "Pile-Ups Could Be Problem for Information Highway." The real problem, this interview tells us, is the difficulty in getting everyone online. But once online, let the good times roll:

2   NOAH ADAMS, HOST: The traffic report for the information network, the Internet highway, is smooth going, but there's a pileup at the America Online ramp causing congestion. The computer on-line services offer bulletin boards and magazine articles, research, and shopping along with access to Internet, the vast grid of computer systems. The on-line services have become very popular, and America Online is the fastest growing. The membership more than doubled last year. But lately the service has often been slow, and sometimes subscribers simply aren't able to log on. Computer analyst Fred Davis joins us from KQED.

3   After some discussion:

4   ADAMS: Is it possible that this [electronic communication via Internet] is just a fad, just a fashionable thing to do, you're sort of browsing around and next year we'll be doing something else?

5   DAVIS: No, this is a major change in the way that humans communicate. And it's bringing people closer together all over the world. People are having international romances over

the Information Superhighway, Internet, fax machines, and so forth. It just brings us all closer together, and it's addictive. Once you get the feel of creating a community based on your interests rather than arbitrary geography, it's a really exciting and compelling thing for humans to do.

ADAMS: So we better figure out how to do it.   6

The net pulls you in—but (apparently) in a good way. It brings people closer together, enabling us to create vibrant communities while overcoming the caprice of geography. It entices us with the promise of romance, love, and (safe) sex. Everybody will get online and communicate with everyone else.

According to this view the old regime is crumbling. The   7
mass media as we know it is dead. Newspapers don't give us news, because in the time frame of the net what newspapers print is old news before ink meets paper. Book publishing is dead when anyone's words can reach millions of potential readers moments after the final draft is finished. The music industry withers away when any musician can make high-quality digital recordings at home and distribute them to the world via the net. Television networks are inconsequential when everyone has the power to produce programming for everyone else. Governments as we know them are increasingly powerless because nations become irrelevant when communication technologies make borders as porous as air. Power goes to those who can control the flow of information. But when all information, all music, all art, all words, all images, all ideas are digitized, then everyone can access, alter, create, and transmit anything, anywhere, anytime. Welcome to the spectacle. Enter the teeming, buzzing cacophony of cyberspace. The revolution is here. The kings are dead. Long live us all—all virtual citizens in the egalitarian, electronic democracy that is the net.

And we participate in this electronic parlor as children of the   8
convergence: that moment when the bandwidth widens, when all communication technologies blend seamlessly and transparently into a single, inevitable *pan*media—the melding of telecommunications, computers and computer networks, cellular, cable, and satellite data transmission, television, radio, and print media, and while we're at it, virtual reality technology, biotechnology, artificial intelligence, and nanotechnology, turning every one of us into the liberated, mind-expanded, and globally connected cyborgian citizens of the global community.

Says William Mitchell in *City of Bits:* "By this point in the evolution of miniature electronic products, you will have acquired a collection of interchangeable, snap-in organs connected by exonerves. Where these electronic organs interface to your sensory receptors and your muscles, there will be continuous bit-spits across the carbon/silicon gap. And where they bridge to the external digital world, your nervous system will plug into the worldwide digital net. You will have become a modular, reconfigurable, infinitely extensible cyborg."[1]

9   This vision represents the manifestation of our will to virtuality. If we are to achieve these dreams of the simulacrum, we must know that the virtual can sustain us—that the virtual is life and community. That is, as the virtualization of human relations continues, we come to see its product as life-giving and life-affirming. We recognize that we can live not only a life on the net but a rich and nurturing life on the net (this vision also incorporates the counter-position: we cannot live much of a life off the net). If we accept consciously or unconsciously that the net is life, we accept that it is natural and organic. It is the fertile ground on which we can grow a life with others in our virtual communities.

10   What is living and what is not is up for grabs in this electronic circus. First of all, you don't have to look hard to find tiny manifestations of the science fiction dreams of the human-like machine. If you start examining any number of magazines about science and technology, you can't swing a dead (computer) mouse without hitting an article about something new in biotechnology and artificial intelligence. Scientists at DuPont, for example, are creating silicon devices that simulate brain functions in increasingly complex ways. As these silicon-based machines evolve, they will work more like organic brains and less like standard digital computers. They will have different capabilities, just as digital machines have capabilities that organic brains don't have. "They will be less like the idiots that digital boxes are now," says Michael Gruber, "utterly dependent on flawless programming, and more like dogs: trainable, but with an inherent set of instincts and abilities, herding our processes and reactions and systems like a border collie runs a flock of sheep." At the Mobile Robot Lab at the Massachusetts Institute of Technology, Rodney Brooks and his team have developed a variety of robots that operate not by a preprogrammed plan but by adapting their capabilities to their surroundings. They read the environment and react accordingly. In short, they learn.[2]

But these machines with seemingly lifelike intelligences   11
pale in comparison to the sophisticated cyborgian organism,
the complex human-machine hybrid, already operating
within our midst. It has been given different names—I refer
to it as the net, while others call it the medianet (Kroker and
Weinstein), information (Barlow), the datasphere (Douglas
Rushkoff)—but these names refer to the same vast, amorphous, ever changing, immortal being with an unambiguous
social agenda: free the individual. Whereas the robotic devices I described may be able to perform tasks that empower
humans in a variety of ways, the net—according to many
technotopists—is an organic, political entity. It votes libertarian every time.

This libertarian life force can best be illustrated by first ex-   12
amining the Internet. In its current form the Internet is designed to operate as a decentralized network, with multiple
pathways along which information can flow. The genesis of
this system is described in Howard Rheingold's brief history
of the original core of the Internet, the U.S. Defense Department's ARPANET, which was designed so that if any part of the
network was disabled (in a nuclear attack), the rest of the network could function and all network traffic could simply be
rerouted. There would be no central command. This decentralized web appears organic to observers like Rheingold: "Information can take so many alternative routes when one of
the nodes of the network is removed that the Net is almost
immortally flexible. It is this flexibility that CMC telecom pioneer John Gilmore referred to when he said, 'The Net interprets censorship as damage and routes around it.'"[3] The
Internet thus appears immortal. If you choke off one tendril,
information can react and reach its destination via another
route.

The question here is one of agency: Who or what can ini-   13
tiate and carry out actions? I considered this question after
reading an article by John Perry Barlow in *Wired* magazine—a
lengthy piece that attempted to redefine intellectual property
in the digital age. I liked Barlow's argument because its
premise was that a unit of information is not an objective entity with a fixed meaning that can be transferred from one de-
coder to another; rather, meaning-making is a collaborative
process of negotiation in which participants interpret and
construct the meanings of the unit of information in a myriad
of ways. Information is a verb, not a noun.[4] What I did not like
was that Barlow, while arguing that information is an action

and not an entity, still spoke of information as an objective thing throughout the article.

14   I wrote him a note via e-mail (which he later forwarded to the magazine and which was printed in the June 1994 issue). I told him that I agreed with his overall position but thought that his piece suffered from a "debilitating metaphor":

> Throughout your argument you objectify information while you simultaneously try to undermine that objectification. That is, you argue effectively that information is not a thing but a process/relationship/verb; however, you cast information as a thing throughout the piece.
>
> I think the danger in how you characterize information is this: Many people are utterly convinced that information is a thing—a commodity that can be transferred—and they base their actions on this flimsy foundation.... While you argue against the concept of information transfer, you actually argue against yourself by continually casting information as an agent, not an action. Information doesn't want to be free, informers do. The meanings are rhetorical in nature: They are negotiated, they are constantly constructed and reconstructed during their interactions among participants in the communicative acts. By saying things like "information wants to change" etc., you give agency to the code—even though your purpose is just the opposite.[5]

My point is simply that the only agents in communication are humans. Things don't communicate; individuals interpret things and give them meaning.

15   Barlow's response reveals a very different position. He wrote:

> It's a problem of my personal semantics. I call a lot of nonthingish things things, like, to use a big one, this Thing Called Love. Language, or at least English, is limited in its ability to describe the nonspecific action or state of being.
>
> Actually, since I believe information is a life form, there are many cases where information may be seen to act upon...uh...things.[6]

Ah, so information does indeed want to be free. In Barlow's view, the "thing" has agency, and the net is an organic entity pulsating with information that seeks its own expression and cannot be censored.

But that's not all. According to Douglas Rushkoff, the net is   16
not only alive but has a variety of agendas. Rushkoff describes
the datasphere, an entity like Kroker and Weinstein's medianet, which encompasses all electronic communication networks from the vestiges of the traditional mass media to the
distributed connectivity of the Internet and of facsimile and
telephony technologies. You can recognize the datasphere as
the life force it is, according to Rushkoff, if you've grown up
after its ascendancy in the past two or three decades. Those
who have "don't just receive and digest media. They manipulate it. They play with it. The media is not a mirror—it is an
'other.' They are in a living relationship with it."[7] And this relationship makes possible a symbiotic effort to liberate people
and ideas in the face of the monolithic controls over public expression throughout the world.

While most people (those older than about age thirty) who   17
are critical of mass-communication technologies argue that
these technologies are used by centers of power to further the
status quo, younger people who share the life force with the
net, states Rushkoff, have appropriated its reach to unleash
"media viruses" to fight the power: "Those who grew up after
the development of the datasphere see the media very differently. More than a set of tools, the media is an entity unto itself that must be reckoned with on its own terms. The
initiators of media viruses depend on a very optimistic vision
of how the web of media nodes can serve to foster new cultural growth. Rather than stunting our natural development
by amputating our limbs and numbing our senses, the media
can accelerate evolution. The activists...believe the media
can extend the human, or even the planetary spirit."[8]

Citing the work of Noam Chomsky and others, Rushkoff ar-   18
gues that the datasphere is breaking the hold of the public relations era, the era of one-way mass communication. In the PR
era, a few messages came from a few sources, and those messages were geared to maintain the current power structure.
Now the datasphere enables interactivity; it fragments information providers. Viruses within the datasphere challenge authority and provide voice to individuals. And those in opposition,
those like myself, do not understand the symbiosis of humans
and the datasphere. As long as we don't look at the new communication technologies as part of our nature, we can never see
them as anything but the enemy of the natural. In Rushkoff's
view our relationship with the net is part of what makes us human; it is our natural world. Our place is in any number of virtual communities of interest. The new geography—unbound by

the nasty, dull, exclusionary necessities of physical space—is an unending and liberating virtual landscape where we can take social relations and collectives to a new level.[9]

19   Some technotopists who believe this argument will admit that virtuality alone cannot sustain a culture, society, or community. But what they do seem to argue is that the foundation for culture, society, or community is our symbiosis with virtualizing technologies. In *The Virtual Community*, for example, Howard Rheingold tells stories about people who develop emotional attachments by communicating electronically with each other in the parenting forum on the WELL, a computer conferencing system. Some of the most compelling stories involve people who became acquainted online and who go to great lengths to support each other in times of crisis—just as neighbors should in the ideal neighborhood. Rheingold uses these stories to anticipate his critics:

> Many people are alarmed by the very idea of a virtual community, fearing that it is another step in the wrong direction, substituting more technological ersatz for yet another natural resource or human freedom. These critics often voice their sadness at what people have been reduced to doing in a civilization that worships technology, decrying the circumstances that lead some people into such pathetically disconnected lives that they prefer to find their companions on the other side of a computer screen. There is a seed of truth in this fear, for virtual communities require more than words on a screen at some point if they intend to be other than ersatz.[10]

20   His tales of online relationships blossoming into offline human interaction and support apparently validate the foundation that is the online community. But if you read Rheingold's stories carefully, you begin to realize that nearly all the participants share a geographic place—a diverse place, undoubtedly, but a place nonetheless: the Bay Area around San Francisco. It is out of this foundation that so-called virtual relationships can grow into something that may not capture but may at least approach real community. It is out of the face-to-face WELL picnics at a public park that simple text on a screen begins to develop into something more than just the image of community.

21   Rheingold and Rushkoff see the net as a means for social empowerment. I share their goal but fear that both place

their faith in a shadow whose images are so lifelike that they appear real. I fear that the continual virtualization of community reveals that geophysical community is dying. As we invest ourselves in the simulation, the simulated phenomena disappear.[11]

The technotopists imbue the net, medianet, datasphere— whatever you want to call it—with agency. They believe that interacting with it is sustaining. They are convinced that it is possible to live within it. Humans lose agency, they say, and the medianet gains it.

I agree that the media virus enables a counterculture. The question is, counter to what? The culture is wholly maintained within the datasphere; nothing else exists. The counterculture that the media virus represents is thus not radical. To place your faith in the empowerment of the datasphere is a quintessentially conservative act: don't worry, be happy; surrender to the power of the datasphere. The most radical and most difficult act would be to resist that power.

But resistance is difficult, because social forces push us to lead virtualized lives. Many of the proponents of virtualization seem to fall into one of two camps. In one camp are those futurists and technotopian visionaries who argue that our destiny is to move from the material world to virtuality, that to examine our evolution is to see the movement away from the body and toward the intellect. To these people, being on-line is an end in itself; virtuality ultimately must become immersive, thereby making virtual community our goal.

Far less grandiose in vision are those of the other camp, who see the continuing virtualization of everyday life as a way to improve our material lives. Virtuality is a tool to help us solve social, psychological, economic, and environmental problems. To these people, our offline lives define our selves, and our goal is to participate in healthy geophysical communities.

If we speak of a healthy community, we cannot be speaking of a community that is merely human. We are talking about a neighborhood of humans in a place, plus the place itself: its soil, its water, its air, and all the families and tribes of the nonhuman creatures that belong to it. If the place is well preserved, if its entire membership, natural and human, is present in it, and if the human economy is in practical harmony with the nature of the place, then the community is healthy.... A healthy community is sustainable; it is, within

reasonable limits, self-sufficient and, within reasonable limits, self-determined—that is, free of tyranny.[12]

26   It is not unusual to read analyses of our post-industrial,
information-infused, media- and image-saturated, transition-
ary times telling us that traditional communities are irrelevant, endangered, or impotent in the face of sweeping
economic and social change.[13] One such vision, put forth by
Peter Drucker, represents a commonly held view of the
present and near future. In a broad analysis of what he
describes as the most pervasive cultural change in history—
the rise of the "knowledge society"—Drucker makes it clear
that the "old community" is dead. Unfortunately, the social
needs fulfilled by those old communities remain.[14]

27   The knowledge society is one in which the driving economic force is the development and application of new
knowledge. In such an economy—one fueled by education
and technology—the most important resource is not cheap labor, natural resources, or political will; it is the ability to develop and maintain a culture of learning. Unlike industrial
economies, a knowledge society will be able to survive global
competition only by providing its members with lifelong education so that they may create and use knowledge produc-
tively. "The acquisition and distribution of formal knowledge
may come to occupy the place in the politics of the knowledge
society which the acquisition and distribution of property
and income have occupied in our politics over the two or
three centuries that we have come to call the Age of Capital-
ism" (66). There will be less and less need for individuals to
obtain prescribed schooling during a set period (for example,
from ages seven to twenty-one). Instead, in order to succeed,
individuals will become lifelong students.

28   Such a scenario depicts communication technologies as
the response to a need for knowledge. New communication
technologies, remember, can deliver anything, anywhere,
anytime (or so we are told). Because knowledge will be widely
available, competition among knowledge creators, distributors, and users will increase dramatically. "The knowledge society will inevitably become far more competitive than any
society we have yet known—for the simple reason that with
knowledge being universally accessible, there will be no excuses for nonperformance. There will be no 'poor' countries.
There will only be ignorant countries" (68). And the same
applies for entities smaller than countries. Industries, corpo-

rations, and individuals will all succeed or fail based on their ability to manipulate knowledge.

At the same time, one of the prerequisites for success in   29
this hypercompetitive environment is constant change, the condition for continual social transience:

> People no longer stay where they were born, either in terms of geography or in terms of social position and status. By definition, a knowledge society is a society of mobility. And all of the social functions of the old communities, whether performed well or poorly (and most were performed very poorly indeed), presupposed that the individual and the family would stay put. But the essence of a knowledge society is mobility in terms of where one lives, mobility in terms of what one does, mobility in terms of one's affiliations. People no longer have roots. People no longer have a neighborhood that controls what their home is like, what they do, and, indeed, what their problems are allowed to be. (74)

The old community may be gone, but our need for the   30
kinds of protection and healing available in the old community has not disappeared. The problems that beset individuals and families—crime, domestic violence, substance abuse, divorce, and so on—will persist and, in an increasingly competitive society like the knowledge meritocracy Drucker describes, will probably intensify. The public sector will not be able to deal with those problems; witness the failures of the welfare state. Nor is the private sector appropriately equipped to handle the "social tasks" of the knowledge society: "In fact, practically all these tasks—whether education or health care; the anomies and diseases of a developed and, especially, a rich society, such as alcohol and drug abuse; or the problems of incompetence and irresponsibility such as those of the underclass in the American city—lie outside the employing institution" (72).

The answer, according to Drucker, lies in the middle   31
ground between the public and private sector. The services and opportunities of the "social sector" must fill the void. "The old communities—family, village, parish, and so on— have all but disappeared in the knowledge society," says Drucker. "Their place has largely been taken by the new unit of social integration, the organization. Where community was fate, organization is voluntary membership. Where community claimed the entire person, organization is a means to

a person's end, a tool" (76). The social sector consists primarily of volunteer-based, nonprofit enterprises, from churches
to charitable organizations. Through such organizations, individuals can both help and be helped, in a reciprocal spiral
that, in Drucker's view, can "create citizenship" and re-create
a sense of community. That is, only through the social sector—a salve to the socially dysfunctional—can individuals
take part in the process of maintaining a community. "Modern society and modern policy have become so big and complex that citizenship—that is, responsible participation—is
no longer possible. All we can do as citizens is to vote once every few years and to pay taxes all the time" (76). Unless, of
course, we become engaged in the work of the social sector.

32   I urge you to feel as sad about this vision as I do. Have we
devolved so far that the only way to participate in healing social wounds, creating social connections, and maintaining social bonds is by joining bureaucracies and institutions? No
matter how benevolent or socially and spiritually conscious,
they are still bureaucracies and institutions. Where is the future of interpersonal bonding unmediated by systems? Where
is the future of random, unexpected, unintended, but inevitable community-building of individuals of unlike mind and
appearances?

33   I'm afraid Drucker's social sector—even in its most efficient and grand state—is a paltry substitute for what is lost
when geophysical community disappears. The organizations
in a social sector unbound by community may serve as important nodes in a social service network, but they are like
nodes without the connecting strands. However closely
linked one organization is to another, they still float in the
ether, islands of service and good intentions. Factor into this
mix the pull of the net away from geographic ties and toward
the virtual, and you have at best a surrogate community atop
the spindly legs of procedural bureaucracies.

34   So while Drucker correctly recognizes the inadequacy of a
society built on the twin towers of the public and private sectors, I disagree that a third support can be constructed to fill
the void. Instead, the private and public sectors must be encompassed by the normal functionings of placed communities.

35   What we are left with is a politics of opposition between,
on one hand, proponents of individual freedom and, on the
other, bureaucracies that regulate individual actions. The
missing middle ground cannot arise without a collectivity of
individuals committed to inhabiting a place and to enduring

and working with each other to improve the condition of everyone in that place. "We have largely lost the sense that our capacity to live well in a place might depend upon our ability to relate to neighbors (especially neighbors with a different life-style) on the basis of shared habits of behavior" (79). We have come to accept that committing to a place is an expression of personal choice and personal taste. Or, quite often, it is forced on us either by our need to find work or by our need to live with or near another person.

I have a couple of friends who want to move away from   36
northern New York. Our north country is a vast stretch of farms, rolling hills, and rivers dropping out of the Adirondacks to the south and flowing into the great St. Lawrence River to the north. It is poor, cold, and, to many observers, desolate. My friends tell me that it can no longer sustain them. One is unhappy with her job and says, like many who talk about leaving, that she wants to live somewhere warmer. My other friend, however, loves the cold and the snow but wants to move east of the big lake, Champlain, and settle in Vermont. He believes that his business—often on the brink of bankruptcy here—has a better chance over there. But that is only part of the issue. Everything, he tells me, is better over there: the economy, the social life, the environment. People take better care of their homes and their businesses. They care more about their culture; they are less provincial; they aren't always suspicious of change and have achieved a balance between accepting the progressive and holding on to traditions. Vermont, he says, is more attuned to individual initiative. Simply put, there's just a different ethic over there.

I listen to these complaints and say, "Well, yeah, you're right.   37
Life in the north country can be difficult..." At this point I can't really think of much to say besides "but I want to stay." I'll admit I came here to take a job—but I also came here because I thought it might be a place to commit to. I'm willing to inhabit a place with faults, a place that is difficult to live in, a place where I cannot satisfy all my wants and needs. I am willing to do this for the sake of becoming part of a community.

My friend who wants to move to Vermont wants to commit   38
to that place. That is good. I have been in his position; I've given up on a place and moved away from people I was close to. Nonetheless, I am disheartened when I hear him talk about moving. It is such a long process to develop a friendship; I invest so much time and effort, and the older I get, the harder it is to stay in touch with remote friends and family

members. No amount of telephone conversations and e-mail can re-create the experience of sharing daily life. So when I hear people close to me talk of leaving, part of me wants to dispense with them immediately and go nurture other local relationships. Of course, I cannot do this; one doesn't eliminate emotional ties so coldly. No, I act as if I believe that after my friends or family members move, we can maintain our relationships by keeping in touch via technology. But we cannot really maintain those relationships, because over time the foundation for our relationship, the social and geographic ties of a common place, fades.

39   Sometimes I find myself assessing others on the basis of their interests in staying here. This is probably a foolish criterion. "The longing to become an inhabitant rather than a drifter," says Scott Russell Sanders, "sets me against the current of my culture, which nudges everyone into motion. Newton taught us that a body at rest tends to stay at rest, unless acted on by an outside force. We are acted on ceaselessly by outside forces—advertising, movies, magazines, speeches— and also by the inner force of biology."[15]

40   I find myself in the maddening position of recognizing the ever-increasing artificial mediation of the natural world while remaining committed to breaking down that mediation to regain a sense of the here and now. I'm seeking what Albert Borgmann describes in *Crossing the Postmodern Divide* as postmodern realism, the necessary response to our hypermediated condition: "Having left modernism behind us, we now have to decide whether to proceed on the endless and joyless plain of hypermodernism or to cross over to another and more real world. For this country in particular, the latter task comes to settling down in the land that has come to be ours, to give up the restless search for a hyperreal elsewhere, and to come to terms with nature and tradition in a patient and vigorous way." As we are on the brink of surrendering to the most powerful mediation engines of all, we must resist the lure of the hyperreal. And if we must become wired, we must turn that telepresence toward, as Borgmann describes it, the "focal realities" of the local places we inhabit.[16]

41   One day I received an e-mail message directed to all the members of an electronic forum—a "list"—devoted to discussing community computer networks. The writer described a murder that had occurred in her community: a child had been shot and killed by another child. She wondered what those of us interested in community networks had to say about that. Two responses follow.

From: MILTON LOPES <MLOPES@UGA.CC.UGA.EDU>

Subject: Re: A shooting in the community...or how do we stop the hemorrhage

X-To: "Communet: Community and Civic Network Discussion List" communet@elk.uvm.edu

Teenage violence is a subject that needs to be discussed on a   42
national forum. It involves no less than our future as a nation.
If this is not the place to discuss it, where is the place? I
recently facilitated a community meeting following the sense-
less shooting of two students by a fellow student who they
had earlier been harassing. The community was in an uproar.
Attending were school officials, police officers, community
leaders, parents, and youth. The youth made more sense than
any of the other groups. They simply called for teachers who
cared, parents who spent some time with them, complete
families, the teaching of and practice of morals, in the marketplace, at home, in school, in government. They looked at
us adults, and found us long on verbiage, but short on example. I have facilitated other meetings in which adult posturing
was simply no answer to the pleas of the children. We have
abandoned the basic principles which for most of us were
taught by our elders. We are too busy consuming, and selling,
and living for the moment. Listen to the children. I hope your
grief finds resonance with this entire list.

Milton E. Lopes

From: Tres English <tenglish@WEST.CSCWC.PIMA.EDU>

Subject: Making more time (Was: A shooting in the community...)

[After quoting from the preceding message, English added the following.]

I have concluded that the real reason for this accelerating   43
breakup of our society are those things which physically
break us up on a day-to-day, moment-to-moment basis. That
is the road system, TV, financial system, etc. that have the
effect of requiring us to spend more and more *time* separated from family and neighbors.
    It is not quality time that matters. It is simply time.
    I have a question for participants in this list.

How can we structure a community computer network so that we are able to recreate more stable geographic communities where people have more time to spend with each other, both as families and as neighborhoods?

I don't think there is a solution to kids killing each other, and all the rest, unless we can recreate the foundations of a stable society—the continuing, unplanned interactions between the same people for a long period of time.

Tres English.
Tenglish@west.cscwc.pima.edu

A community is bound by place, which always includes complex social and environmental necessities. It is not something you can easily join. You can't subscribe to a community as you subscribe to a discussion group on the net. It must be lived. It is entwined, contradictory, and involves all our senses. It involves the "continuing, unplanned interactions between the same people for a long period of time." Unfortunately, communities across the nation are being undermined and destroyed by a variety of forces. Global computer networks like the Internet, for example, represent a step in the continual virtualization of human relations. The hope that the incredible powers of global computer networks can create new virtual communities, more useful and healthier than the old geographic ones, is thus misplaced. The net seduces us and further removes us from our localities—unless we take charge of it with specific, community-based, local agendas. These agendas are currently under development in many communities through the community network movement. If we do not, as communities, as a society, support this movement, we risk the further disappearance of local communities within globalized virtual collectives of alienated and entertained individuals.

Notes

1. Mitchell, William J., *City of Bits: Space, Place, and the Infobahn* (Cambridge: MIT Press, 1995), 29–30. For another extensive discussion of our cyborgian destiny see Stone, Allucquere Rosanne, *The War of Desire and Technology at the Close of the Mechanical Age* (Cambridge: MIT Press, 1995).

2. Gruber, Michael, "Neurobotics," *Wired* 2.10 (October 1994): 111; on Brooks and his team see Freedman, David H., "Bringing Up RoboBaby," *Wired* 2.12 (December 1994): 74. (December 1994): 74.

3. Rheingold, Howard, *The Virtual Community: Homesteading on the Electronic Frontier* (Reading, Mass.: Addison-Wesley, 1993), 7.

4. Barlow, John Perry, "The Economy of Ideas," *Wired* 2.03 (March 1994): 84; Doheny-Farina, Stephen, letter to "Rants and Raves," *Wired* 2.06 (June 1994): 22.

5. I make this argument in detail in Doheny-Farina, Stephen, *Rhetoric, Innovation, Technology: Case Studies of Technical Communication in Technology Transfers* (Cambridge: MIT Press, 1992).

6. Barlow, John Perry, response to Stephen Doheny-Farina, "Rants and Raves," *Wired* 2.06 (June 1994): 22.

7. Rushkoff, Douglas, *Media Virus* (New York: Ballantine Books, 1994), 31.

8. Rushkoff, 21.

9. Rushkoff, 218. Rushkoff points out that critics like Kroker were born too early to understand the medianet. "Kroker's brilliant but misguided analysis is typical of his generation of philosophers who, growing up before the advent of mass media, have only the tools to observe media but not the language or translation skills to partake in it.... the inferences he draws totally ignore the nature of the new and growing relationship between our lives and our media. As long as we view media, or technology for that matter, as something separate from ourselves—something unnatural—we will always see it as the enemy to the natural unfolding of our culture."

10. Rheingold, 23.

11. Baudrillard, Jean, "Simulacra and Simulations," in *Selected Writings*, ed. Mark Poster (Stanford: Stanford University Press, 1988), 166–184. Virtual community is like Disneyland, and placed communities, like America: "Disneyland is there to conceal the fact that it is the 'real' country, all of 'real' America, which *is* Disneyland.... Disneyland is presented as imaginary in order to make us believe that the rest is real, when in fact all of Los Angeles and the America surrounding it are no longer real, but of the order of the hyperreal and of simulation. It is no longer a question of a false representation of reality…but of concealing the fact that the real is no longer real" (172).

12. Berry, Wendell, *Sex, Economy, Freedom, and Community* (New York: Pantheon Books, 1993), 14–15.

13. For example, the 150th anniversary issue of the *Economist* (January 1994).

14. Drucker, Peter, "The Age of Social Transformation," *Atlantic Monthly* 274, no. 5 (November 1994): 53–80. All quotations in the following discussion of Drucker's views are from this article.

15. Sanders, Scott Russell, *Staying Put: Making a Home in a Restless World* (Boston: Beacon Press, 1993), 117.

16. Borgmann, Albert, *Crossing the Postmodern Divide* (Chicago: University of Chicago Press, 1992), 126.

David Horsey
Broken Promises
of the Computer Age

David Horsey is an editorial cartoonist for the Seattle Post-Intelligencer. *He produced the cartoon below in November 1997; it was published not only in Seattle but also in many other newspapers across the country.*

Susan Herring

Gender Differences
on the Internet

Bringing Familiar Baggage
to the New Frontier

*Susan Herring teaches linguistics at the University of Texas at
Arlington. Her special interests are language and gender and
the study of computer-mediated communication, so the following presentation came naturally to her. She offered it first as a
talk at the annual meeting of the American Library Association, and then she made the talk available through the computer via the World Wide Web.*

1. Introduction

Although research on computer-mediated communication   1
(CMC) dates back to the early days of computer network
technology in the 1970s, researchers have only recently begun
to take the gender of users into account.[1] This is perhaps not
surprising considering that men have traditionally dominated
the technology and have comprised the majority of users of
computer networks since their inception, but the result is that
most of what has been written about CMC incorporates a
very one-sided perspective. However, recent research has
been uncovering some eye-opening differences in the ways
men and women interact "on-line," and it is these differences
that I will address in my talk today.

My basic claim has two parts: first, that women and men   2
have recognizably different styles in posting electronic messages to the Internet, contrary to claims that CMC neutralizes
distinctions of gender, and second, that women and men have
different communication ethics—that is, they value different
kinds of on-line interactions as appropriate and desirable. I illustrate these differences—and some of the problems that
arise because of them—with specific reference to the phenomenon of "flaming."

2. Background

Since 1991 I've been lurking (or what I prefer to call "carry-   3
ing out ethnographic observation") on various computer-

mediated discussion lists, downloading electronic conversations and analyzing the communicative behaviors of
participants. I became interested in gender shortly after sub-
scribing to my first discussion list, LINGUIST-L, an academic
forum for professional linguists. Within the first month after
I began receiving messages, a conflict arose on the list (what I
would later learn to call a "flame war") in which the two major theoretical camps within the field became polarized
around an issue of central interest. My curiosity was piqued
by the fact that very few women were contributing to this important professional event; they seemed to be sitting on the
sidelines while men were airing their opinions and getting all
the attention. In an attempt to understand the women's silence, I made up an anonymous survey which I sent to LIN-
GUIST-L asking subscribers what they thought of the
discussion and if they hadn't contributed, why not.

3. Initial Observations

4   The number one reason given by both men and women for
not contributing to the LINGUIST discussion was "intimidation"—as one respondent commented, participants were "ripping each other's lungs out." Interestingly, however, men and
women responded differently to feeling intimidated. Men
seemed to accept such behavior as a normal feature
of academic life, making comments to the effect that "Actually,
the barbs and arrows were entertaining, because of course
they weren't aimed at me." In contrast, many women responded with profound aversion. As one woman put it:

> That is precisely the kind of human interaction I committedly
> avoid. (...) I am dismayed that human beings treat each other
> this way. It makes the world a dangerous place to be. I dislike
> such people and I want to give them WIDE berth.

When I analyzed the messages in the thread itself, another
gender difference emerged, this time relating to the linguistic
structure and rhetoric of the messages. A daunting 68% of the
messages posted by men made use of an adversarial style in
which the poster distanced himself from, criticized, and/or
ridiculed other participants, often while promoting his own
importance. The few women who participated in the discussion, in contrast, displayed features of attenuation—hedging,
apologizing, asking questions rather than making assertions—

and a personal orientation, revealing thoughts and feelings and interacting with and supporting others.

It wasn't long before I was noticing a similar pattern in other discussions and on other lists. Wherever I went on mixed-sex lists, men seemed to be doing most of the talking and attracting most of the attention to themselves, although not all lists were as adversarial as LINGUIST. I started to hear stories about and witness men taking over and dominating discussions even of women-centered topics on women-centered lists.[2] In contrast, on the few occasions when I observed women attempting to gain an equal hearing on male-dominated lists, they were ignored, trivialized, or criticized by men for their tone or the inappropriateness of their topic.[3] It wasn't until I started looking at lists devoted to women's issues, and to traditionally "feminized" disciplines such as women's studies, teaching English as a second language, and librarianship, that I found women holding forth in an amount consistent with their numerical presence on the list. I also found different interactional norms: little or no flaming, and cooperative, polite exchanges.

4. Different Styles

As a result of these findings, I propose that women and men have different characteristic on-line styles. By characteristic styles, I do not mean that all or even the majority of users of each sex exhibit the behaviors of each style, but rather that the styles are recognizably—even stereotypically—gendered. The male style is characterized by adversariality: put-downs, strong, often contentious assertions, lengthy and/or frequent postings, self-promotion, and sarcasm. Below are two examples, one from an academic list (LINGUIST) and the other from a non-academic list (POLITICS).[4]

1) [Jean Linguiste's] proposals towards a more transparent morphology in French are exactly what he calls them: a farce. Nobody could ever take them seriously—unless we want to look as well at pairs such as *pe`re-me`re*, *coq-poule* and defigure the French language in the process.

[strong assertions ("exactly," "nobody"), put-downs ("JL's proposals...are a farce"; implied: "JL wants to defigure the French language")]

2) >yes, they did...This is why we must be allowed to remain
   >armed...who is going >to help us if our government
   >becomes a tyranny? no one will.

   oh yes we *must* remain armed. anyone see day one last
   night abt charlestown where everyone/s so scared of informing on murderers the cops have given up? where the reply to
   any offense is a public killing? knowing you/re not gonna be
   caught cause everyone/s to affraid to be a witness?

   yeah, right, twerp.

   >   —[Ron] "the Wise"—

   what a joke.

[sarcasm, name calling, personal insults]
The second example would be characterized as a "flame" by
most readers because of its personally offensive nature.

7   Less exclusively male-gendered but still characteristic of
male postings is an authoritative, self-confident stance
whereby men are more likely than women to represent themselves as experts, e.g., in answering queries for information.
The following example is from NOTIS-L.

3) The NUGM Planning meeting was canceled before all of this
   came up. It has nothing to do with it. The plans were simply
   proceeding along so well that there was no need to hold the
   meeting. That is my understanding from talking to NOTIS
   staff last week.

[authoritative tone, strong assertions ("nothing," "simply,"
"just")]

8   The female-gendered style, in contrast, has two aspects
which typically co-occur: supportiveness and attenuation.
"Supportiveness" is characterized by expressions of appreciation, thanking, and community-building activities that make
other participants feel accepted and welcome. "Attenuation"
includes hedging and expressing doubt, apologizing, asking
questions, and contributing ideas in the form of suggestions.
The following examples from a non-academic list (WOMEN)
and an academic list (TEST-L) illustrate each aspect:

4) >[Aileen],
   >
   >I just wanted to iet you know that I have really enjoyed all
   your posts about

>Women's herstory. They have been extremely informative and I've learned alot

>about the women's movement. Thank you!

>

>-[Erika]

DITTO!!!! They are wonderful!

Did anyone else catch the first part of a Century of Women? I really enjoyed it.

Of course, I didn't agree with everything they said . . . but it was really informative.

[Roberta]~~~~~~~~~~~~~~~~~~~~~~~~~~~~~

[appreciates, thanks, agrees, appeals to group]

5) [. . .] I hope this makes sense. This is kind of what I had in mind when I realized I couldn't give a real definitive answer. Of course, maybe I'm just getting into the nuances of the language when it would be easier to just give the simple answer.

Any response?

[hedges, expresses doubt, appeals to group]

The female style takes into consideration what the sociologist Erving Goffman called the "face" wants of the addressee—specifically, the desire of the addressee to feel ratified and liked (e.g., by expressions of appreciation) and her desire not to be imposed upon (e.g., by absolute assertions that don't allow for alternative views). The male style, in contrast, confronts and threatens the addressee's "face" in the process of engaging him in agonistic debate.   9

Although these styles represent in some sense the extremes of gendered behavior, they have symbolic significance above and beyond their frequency of use. For example, other users regularly infer the gender of message posters on the basis of features of these styles, especially when the self-identified gender of a poster is open to question. Consider the following cases, the first involving a male posting as a female, the second a suspected female posting as a male: 10

(i) A male subscriber on SWIP-L (Society for Women in Philosophy list) posted a message disagreeing with the general consensus that discourse on SWIP-L should be non-agonistic, commenting "there's nothing like a healthy denunciation by one's colleagues every once in a while to get one's blood flowing,   11

and spur one to greater subtlety and exactness of thought." He
signed his message with a female pseudonym, however, causing
another (female) subscriber to comment later, "I must confess
to looking for the name of the male who wrote the posting that
[Suzi] sent originally and was surprised to find a female name
at the end of it." The female subscriber had (accurately)
inferred that anyone actively advocating "denunciation by one's
colleagues" was probably male.

12   (ii) At a time when one male subscriber had been posting
frequent messages to the WOMEN list, another subscriber
professing to be a man posted a message inquiring what the
list's policy was towards men participating on the list, admitting "I sometimes feel guilty for taking up bandwidth." The
message, in addition to showing consideration for the concerns of others on the list, was very attenuated in style and
explicitly appreciative of the list: "I really enjoy this list (actually, it's the best one I'm on)." That prompted another
(female) subscriber to respond, "now that you've posed the
question ... how's one to know you're not a woman posing
this question as a man?" Her suspicion indicates that on
some level she recognized that anyone posting a message
expressing appreciation and consideration for the desires of
others was likely to be female.

13   The existence of gendered styles has important implications, needless to say, for popular claims that CMC is anonymous, "gender-blind," and hence inherently democratic. If
our on-line communicative style reveals our gender, then gender differences, along with their social consequences, are
likely to persist on computer-mediated networks.[5]

14   Entire lists can be generated in their style as well. It is tacitly expected that members of the non-dominated gender will
adapt their posting style in the direction of the style of the
dominant gender. Thus men on women's special interest lists
tend to attenuate their assertions and shorten their messages,
and women, especially on male-dominated lists such as LIN-
GUIST and PAGLIA-L, can be contentious and adversarial.
Arguably, they *must* adapt in order to participate appropriately in keeping with the norms of the local list culture. Most
members of the non-dominant gender on any given list, however, end up style-mixing, that is, taking on some attributes of
the dominant style while preserving features of their native
style, e.g., with men often preserving a critical stance and
women a supportive one at the macro-message level. This suggests that gender communication styles are deeply rooted—

not surprising, since they are learned early in life—and that some features are more resistant to conscious reflection and modification than others.

5. Different Communication Ethics

The second part of this talk concerns the value systems that underlie and are used to rationalize communicative behavior on the net. In particular, I focus on the phenomenon of flaming, which has been variously defined as "the expression of strong negative emotion," use of "derogatory, obscene, or inappropriate language," and "personal insults." A popular explanation advanced by CMC researchers[6] is that flaming is a by-product of the medium itself—the decontextualized and anonymous nature of CMC leads to "disinhibition" in users and a tendency to forget that there is an actual human being at the receiving end of one's emotional outbursts. However, until recently CMC research has largely overlooked gender as a possible influence on behavior, and the simple fact of the matter is that it is virtually only men who flame. If the medium makes men more likely to flame, it should have a similar effect on women, yet if anything the opposite appears to be the case. An adequate explanation of flaming must therefore take gender into account.

Why do men flame? The explanation, I suggest, is that women and men have different communication ethics, and flaming is compatible with male ethical ideals. I stumbled upon this realization recently as a result of a survey I conducted on politeness on the Internet. I originally hypothesized that the differences in the extremes of male and female behavior on-line—in particular, the tendency for women to be considerate of the "face" needs of others while men threaten others' "face"—could be explained if it turned out that women and men have different notions of what constitutes appropriate behavior. In other words, as a woman I might think adversarial behavior is rude, but men who behave adversarially might think otherwise. Conversely, men might be put off by the supportive and attenuated behaviors of women.

In the survey, I asked subscribers from eight Internet discussion lists to rank their like or dislike for 30 different online behaviors, including "flaming," "expressing thanks and appreciation," and "overly tentative messages," on a scale of 1 (like) to 5 (dislike). The survey also asked several open-ended questions, including most importantly: What behaviors bother you most on the net?

15

16

17

18   My initial hypothesis turned out to be both correct and incorrect. It was incorrect in that I found no support whatsoever
for the idea that men's and women's value systems are somehow
reversed. Both men and women said they liked expressions of
appreciation (avg. score of 2), were neutral about tentative messages (avg. about 3), and disliked flaming (although women expressed a stronger dislike than men, giving it a score of 4.3 as
compared with only 3.9 for men). This makes male flaming behavior all the more puzzling; should we conclude then that men
who flame are deliberately trying to be rude?

19   The answers to the open-ended questions suggest a different explanation. These answers reveal a gender contrast in
values that involves politeness but cannot be described in
terms of politeness alone. It seems women place a high value
on consideration for the wants and needs of others, as expressed in the following comment by a female net user:

> If we take responsibility for developing our own sensitivities
> to others and controlling our actions to minimize damage—
> we will each be doing [good deeds] for the whole world
> constantly.

Men, in contrast, assign greater value to freedom from censorship (many advocate absolute free speech), forthright and
open expression, and agonistic debate as a means to advance
the pursuit of knowledge. Historically, the value on absolute
freedom of speech reflects the civil libertarian leanings of the
computing professionals who originally designed the net and
have contributed much of the utopian discourse surrounding
it; the value on agonistic debate is rooted in the Western
(male) philosophical tradition.

20   These ideals are stirringly evoked in the following quote
from R. Hauben (1993) praising the virtues of the Usenet system, on which 95% of the contributors are estimated to be
male:

> The achievement of Usenet News demonstrates the impor-
> tance of facilitating the development of uncensored speech
> and communication—there is debate and discussion—one
> person influences another—people build on each other's
> strengths and interests, differences, etc.

One might think that uncensored speech if abused could
cause problems, but M. Hauben (1993) explains that there is
a democratic way of handling this eventuality:

When people feel someone is abusing the nature of Usenet News, they let the offender know through e-mail. In this manner. . . people fight to keep it a resource that is helpful to society as a whole.

In daily life on the Internet, however, the ideal of "people fight[ing] to keep [the net] a resource that is helpful to society as a whole" often translates into violent action. Consider, for example, the response of a male survey respondent to the question: "What behaviors bother you most on the net?" (typos are in the original):

> As much as I am irritated by [incompetent posters], I don't want imposed rules. I would prefer to "out" such a person and let some public minded citizen fire bomb his house to imposing rules on the net. Letter bombing an annoying individual's feed is usually preferable to building a formal hierarchy of net cops.

Another net vigilante responds graphically as follows:

> I'd have to say commercial shit. Whenever someone advertises some damn get-rich-quick scheme and plasters it all over the net by crossposting it to every newsgroup, I reach for my "gatling gun mailer crasher" and fire away at the source address.

These responses not only evoke an ideal of freedom from external authority, they provide an explicit justification for flaming—as a form of self-appointed regulation of the social order, a rough and ready form of justice on the virtual frontier. Thus a framework of values is constructed within which flaming and other aggressive behaviors can be interpreted in a favorable (even prosocial) light. This is not to say that all or even most men who flame have the good of net society at heart, but rather that the behavior is in principle justifiable for men (and hence tolerable) in ways that it is not for most women.

6. Netiquette

Further evidence that flaming is tolerated and justified   21
within a system of male values comes from the content of
written rules of network etiquette, or "netiquette," such as are

available on many public FTP sites and in introductory messages to new members of some discussion lists. I analyzed the content of netiquette rules from six lists, along with those found in the guidelines for Usenet and in the print publication *Towards an Ethics and Etiquette for Electronic Mail* by Shapiro and Anderson (1985). What do netiquette rules have to say about flaming?

22   The answer is: remarkably little, given that it is one of the most visible and frequently complained about "negatives" cited about the Internet. One might even say there is a striking lack of proscription against flaming, except on a few women-owned and women-oriented lists. And in the rare instances where flaming is mentioned, it is implicitly authorized. Thus the guidelines for new subscribers to the POLITICS list prohibit "flames of a personal nature," and Shapiro and Anderson advise "Do not insult or criticize third parties without giving them a chance to respond." While on the surface appearing to oppose flaming, these statements in fact implicitly authorize "flames other than of a personal nature" (for example, of someone's ideas or values) and "insulting or criticizing third parties" (provided you give them a chance to respond!). Normative statements such as these are compatible with male values and male adversarial style; the intimidating rhetoric on LINGUIST and many other lists is not a violation of net etiquette according to these rules.[7] Yet these are behaviors that female survey respondents say intimidate them and drive them away from lists and newsgroups. Can the Internet community afford to tolerate behaviors that intimidate and silence women? This is a question that urgently needs to be raised and discussed net-wide.

7. Conclusions

23   To sum up, I have argued that women and men constitute different discourse communities in cyberspace—different cultures, if you will—with differing communicative norms and practices. However, these cultures are not "separate but equal" as recent popular writing on gender differences in communication has claimed. Rather, the norms and practices of masculine net culture, codified in netiquette rules, conflict with those of the female culture in ways that render cyberspace—or at least many "neighborhoods" in cyberspace—inhospitable to women. The result is an imbalance whereby

men control a disproportionate share of the communication that takes place via computer networks.

This imbalance must be redressed if computer-mediated communication is ever to live up to its much-touted democratic potential. Fortunately, there are ways in which women can promote their concerns and influence the discourse of the net;[8] I will mention three here. First and foremost is to participate, for example, in women-centered lists. Such lists provide supportive fora for women on-line, and are frequently models of cooperative discourse whose norms can spread if subscribers participate in other lists as well. But separatism has its disadvantages, among them the risk of ghettoization. Women must not let themselves be driven by flame throwers away from mainstream, mixed-sex fora, but rather should also actively seek to gain influence there, individually and collectively, especially in fora where metadiscourse about the net itself takes place. 24

The second way to promote women's interests net-wide is to educate on-line communities about the rhetorical strategies used in intimidating others, and to call people on their behavior and its consequences when they use such strategies.[9] This is already happening on some women-centered lists such as WMST-L and SWIP-L—aware of the tendency for a single man or group of men to dominate discussions, female subscribers call attention to this behavior as soon as they realize it is happening; interestingly, it is happening less and less often on these lists. Group awareness is a powerful force for change, and it can be raised in mixed-sex fora as well. 25

Finally, women need to contribute in any way they can to the process that leads to the encoding of netiquette rules. They need to instigate and participate persuasively in discussions about what constitutes appropriate and inappropriate behavior on-line—seeking to define in concrete terms what constitutes "flaming," for instance, since women and men are likely to have different ideas about this. They must be alert to opportunities (or make their own opportunities) to write out guidelines for suggested list protocol (or modifications to list protocol if guidelines already exist) and post them for discussion. No greater power exists than the power to define values, and the structure of the Internet—especially now, while it is still evolving and seeking its ultimate definition—provides a unique opportunity for individual users to influence the normative process. 26

27   Indeed, it may be vital that we do so if women's on-line communication styles are to be valued along with those of men, and if we are to insure women the right to settle on the virtual frontier on their own—rather than on male-defined— terms.

Notes

1. A notable exception to this generalization is the work of Sherry Turkle in the 1980s on how women and men relate to computers.
2. For an extreme example of this phenomenon that took place on the soc.feminism Usenet newsgroup, see Sutton (1994).
3. Herring, Johnson, and DiBenedetto (1992, in press).
4. All names mentioned in the messages are pseudonyms.
5. This problem is discussed in Herring (1993a).
6. For example, Kiesler et al. (1984), Kim and Raja (1990), and Shapiro and Anderson (1985).
7. The discussion of politeness and communication ethics here is an abbreviated version of that presented in Herring (In press a, In press b).
8. For other practical suggestions on how to promote gender equality in networking, see Kramarae and Taylor (1993).
9. Cases where this was done, both successfully and unsuccessfully, are described in Herring, Johnson, & DiBenedetto (In press).

References

Hauben, Michael. 1993. "The social forces behind the development of Usenet News." Electronic document. (FTP weber.ucsd.edu, directory/pub/usenet.hist)

Hauben, Ronda. 1993. "The evolution of Usenet News: The poor man's ARPANET." Electronic document. (FTP weber.ucsd.edu, directory/pub/usenet.hist)

Herring, Susan. 1992. "Gender and participation in computer-mediated linguistic discourse." Washington, DC: ERIC Clearinghouse on Languages and Linguistics, document no. ED345552.

Herring, Susan. 1993a. "Gender and democracy in computer-mediated communication." *Electronic Journal of Communication* 3(2), special issue on Computer-Mediated Communication, T. Benson, ed. Reprinted in R. Kling (ed.), *Computerization and Controversy*, 2nd edition. New York: Academic (In press).

Herring, Susan. 1993b. "Men's language: A study of the discourse of the Linguist list." In A. Crochetière, J.-C. Boulanger, and C. Ouellon (eds.), *Les Langues Menacées: Actes du XVe Congrès International des Linguistes*, Vol. 3. Québec: Les Presses de l'Université Laval, 347–350.

Herring, Susan. In press a. "Politeness in computer culture: Why women thank and men flame." In M. Bucholtz, A. Liang and L.

Sutton (eds.), *Communicating In, Through, and Across Cultures: Proceedings of the Third Berkeley Women and Language Conference.* Berkeley Women and Language Group.

Herring, Susan. In press b. "Posting in a different voice: Gender and ethics in computer-mediated communication." In C. Ess (ed.), *Philosophical Perspectives on Computer-Mediated Communication.* Albany: SUNY Press.

Herring, Susan. Forthcoming. "Two variants of an electronic message schema." In S. Herring (ed.), *Computer-Mediated Communication: Linguistic, social, and cross-cultural perspectives.* Amsterdam/Philadelphia: John Benjamins.

Herring, Susan; Deborah Johnson; and Tamra DiBenedetto. 1992. "Participation in electronic discourse in a 'feminist' field." In M. Bucholtz, K. Hall, and B. Moonwomon, eds., *Locating Power: Proceedings of the Second Berkeley Women and Language Conference.* Berkeley Women and Language Group.

Herring, Susan; Deborah Johnson; and Tamra DiBenedetto. In press. "'This discussion is going too far!' Male resistance to female participation on the Internet." In M. Bucholtz and K. Hall (eds.), *Gender Articulated: Language and the Socially-Constructed Self.* New York: Routledge.

Kiesler, Sara; Jane Seigel; and Timothy W. McGuire. 1984. "Social psychological aspects of computer-mediated communication." *American Psychologist,* 39, 1123–1134.

Kim, Min-Sun and Narayan S. Raja. 1990. "Verbal aggression and self-disclosure on computer bulletin boards." ERIC document (ED334620).

Kramarae, Cheris and H. Heanie Taylor. 1993. "Women and men on electronic networks: A conversation or a monologue?" In Taylor, Kramarae and Ebben, eds., *Women, Information Technology and Scholarship,* 52–61. Urbana, IL: Center for Advanced Study.

Rheingold, Howard. 1993. *The Virtual Community: Homesteading on the Electronic Frontier.* Reading, MA: Addison-Wesley.

Seabrook, John. 1994. "My first flame." *The New Yorker,* June 6, 1994, 70–79.

Shapiro, Norman Z. and Robert H. Anderson. 1985. *Toward an Ethics and Etiquette for Electronic Mail.* The Rand Corporation.

Sutton, Laurel. 1994. "Using USENET: Gender, power, and silencing in electronic discourse." *Proceedings of the 20th Annual Meeting of the Berkeley Linguistics Society (BLS-20).* Berkeley: Berkeley Linguistics Society, Inc.

Turkle, Sherry, 1984. *The Second Self: Computers and the Human Spirit.* London: Granada.

Credits

Author/Title Index